An Anthology of

BEGINNINGS TO 1911

An Anthology of
Chinese Literature

BEGINNINGS TO 1911

Edited and Translated by

Stephen Owen

W. W. NORTON & COMPANY

NEW YORK • LONDON

The text of this book is composed in Sabon
with the display set in Optima
Composition by Com Com
Manufacturing by Haddon Craftsmen
Book design by Joan Greenfield

Library of Congress Cataloging-in-Publication Data

An anthology of Chinese literature : beginnings to 1911 / edited and
    translated by Stephen Owen.
        p.   cm.
    Translations from Chinese.
    Includes bibliographical references and index.
    ISBN 0-393-97106-6
        1. Chinese literature—Translations into English.   I. Owen,
    Stephen.
    P12658.E1A814   1996
    895.1'08—dc20   95-11409

W. W. Norton & Company, Inc., 500 Fifth Avenue, New York, N.Y. 10110
http://web.wwnorton.com
W. W. Norton & Company Ltd., 10 Coptic Street, London WC1A 1PU

Contents

Early China

EARLY CHINA: INTRODUCTION   3

The Chinese "Middle Ages"
THE CHINESE "MIDDLE AGES": INTRODUCTION 221

The Beginnings of Classical Poetry *(Shi)*   249

Anecdotes, Parables, and Profound Jokes   295

The Tang Dynasty

THE TANG DYNASTY: INTRODUCTION   365

Tang Literature of the Frontier

Mid- and Late Tang Poetry

The Song Dynasty

THE SONG DYNASTY: INTRODUCTION 553

Interlude: Li Qing-zhao's Epilogue to *Records on Metal and Stone*

Classical Prose

The Qing Dynasty

Pu Song-ling (1640–1715), *Liao-zhai's Record of Wonders*   1103

Qing Classical Poetry and Song Lyric   1128

Timeline

HISTORY

Founding of the Zhou Dynasty 1020 B.C. Western Zhou

Zhou capital moved east, beginning of the Eastern Zhou and the period of *The Springs and Autumns of Lu (Chun-qiu)* 770 B.C.

Confucius ca. 552–479 B.C.

Beginning of the Warring States period 403 B.C.

Period of the "Hundred Schools" of Chinese thought

Qin unification 221 B.C.

Fall of Qin 206 B.C.

Beginning of Western Han

Reign of Emperor Wu of Han 140–86 B.C.

Establishment of the Music Bureau *(yue-fu)* 120 B.C.

Chinese expansion into Central Asia

Usurpation of Wang Mang 8 B.C.

Restoration of Han and beginning of the Eastern Han A.D. 25

Buddhism introduced into China 1st century

Jian-an reign (196–220). Power in North China in the hands of Cao Cao

Formal end of the Han and beginning of the Three Kingdoms (220–265)

Jin Dynasty reunifies China 280

North China falls to non-Chinese invaders 316; the Jin court is reestablished south of the Yangzi. Beginning of the Southern Dynasties 317–589

LITERATURE

the "Temple Hymns" of the *Classic of Poetry (Shi-jing)* and the earliest sections of the *Classic of Documents (Shu-jing)*

Classic of Poetry reaches its final form ca. 600 B.C.

The Zuo Tradition

Zhuang Zhou and the early chapters of the *Zhuang-zi*

Qu Yuan (ca. 340–299 B.C.) and the traditional date of the "Lyrics of Chu" *(Chu-ci)*

Schemes of the Warring States (Zhan-guo ce)

"Mao Commentary" to the *Classic of Poetry*

Jia Yi (200–168 B.C.), poetic expositions and essays

Mei Sheng (d. 140 B.C.)

? poetic expositions attributed to Song Yu

poetic expositions *(fu)* of Si-ma Xian-ru (179–117 B.C.)

Historical Records of Si-ma Qian (ca. 154–87 B.C.)

final form of the "Great Preface" to the *Classic of Poetry*

Ban Gu (A.D. 32–92), *The Han History*

period of anonymous *yue-fu* and "old poems"?

Wang Can (177–217), poet

Cao Cao (155–220), ruler and poet

Cao Zhi (192–232), poet and Cao Cao's son

Ruan Ji (210–263), poet and recluse

Lu Ji (261–303). "The Poetic Exposition on Literature"

Wang Xi-zhi, Preface to the "Orchid Pavilion Poems" 353

Rise of the influence of Buddhism and major projects of sutra translation	Tao Qian (365–427), poet and recluse
	Xie Lingyun (385–433), landscape poet
	Bao Zhao (ca. 414–466), poet
	Liu Xie (ca. 465–522), critic and author of *Wen-xin diao-long*
	the poetry of the Southern courts
	Yu Xin (513–581), poet
Sui conquers Chen and reunifies China 589	
Tang Dynasty founded 618	
Reign of Xuan-zong (712–756), the "High Tang"	Meng Hao-ran (ca. 689–740), poet
Tang wars in Central Asia	Wang Wei (ca. 699–761), poet
	Li Bo (701–762), poet
An Lu-shan Rebellion 755	Du Fu (712–770), poet
	Tang tales *(chuan-qi)*
The "Mid-Tang"	Meng Jiao (751–814), poet
	Li He (791–817), poet
	Liu Zong-yuan (773–819), essayist
	Han Yu (768–824), poet and essayist
	Yuan Zhen (779–831), poet and author of *"Ying-ying's Story"*
	Bo Ju-yi (772–846) poet, "Song of Lasting Pain"
The "Late Tang"	Du Mu (803–852), poet
	Li Shang-yin (813–858), poet
	Yu Xuan-ji, poet
	Wen Ting-yun (d. 870), poet and early lyricist
	Wei Zhuang (ca. 836–910), poet and lyricist
Fall of the Tang 906; beginning of the "Five Dynasties"	
Song Dynasty reunifies China 960	Li Yu (937–978), last emperor of the Southern Tang, lyricist
	Liu Yong (987–1053), popular lyricist
	Yan Shu (991–1055), lyricist
	Mei Yao-chen (1002–1060), poet
Initial development of Neo-Confucianism	Ou-yang Xiu (1007–1072), poet, lyricist, and essayist
Enactment of Wang An-shi's "New Laws" policy 1069	Wang An-shi (1021–1086), poet and statesman
Commercial and state-sponsored printing	Su Shi (1037–1101), poet, lyricist, essayist, painter, calligrapher
	Yan Ji-dao, lyricist
	Huang Ting-jian (1045–1105), poet
	Zhou Bang-yan (1056–1121), lyricist
Jin invaders capture the two Song emperors and the Song is reestablished in the South 1127	Li Qing-zhao (1084–ca. 1151), lyricist, Epilogue to *Records on Metal and Stone*
Zhu Xi (1130–1200), Neo-Confucian philosopher and commentator on the Classics	Fan Cheng-da (1126–1191), poet
	Yang Wan-li (1127–1206), poet
	Xin Qi-ji (1140–1207), lyricist
Hang-zhou, the Southern Song capital, flourishes with major development of commercial printing	Lu You (1125–1210), poet and lyricist
	Jiang Kui (1155–1221), lyricist
	Wu Wen-ying (ca. 1200–ca. 1260), lyricist

Fall of the Southern Song; the Yuan reunifies China 1279	Wen Tian-xiang (1236–1282), *The Account of the Compass*
	Yuan vernacular song
	Guan Han-qing's variety play, *Rescuing One of the Girls*
Fall of the Yuan; founding of the Ming 1368	
Archaists, advocating imitation of earlier models, dominate classical literature, provoking reaction and growing interest in vernacular literature	Li Zhi (1527–1602), philosopher
	Yuan Hong-dao (1568–1610), poet and essayist
	Tang Xian-zu (1550–1617), *Peony Pavilion*
	The Romance of the Gods (16th century)
Fall of the Ming; founding of the Qing 1644	"Ten Days of Yang-zhou" (1645) by Wang Xiu-chu
	Feng Meng-long (1574–1646), story writer and collector of vernacular literature
	Lang-xian, story writer, "Censor Xue Finds Immortality in the Guise of a Fish"
	Wu Wei-ye (1609–1671), poet
	Zhang Dai (1597–1679), essayist
	Li Yu (1611–1680), "An Actress Scorns Wealth and Honor . . ."
	Gu Yan-wu (1613–1682), poet and scholar
	Wang Shi-zhen (1634–1711), poet
	Nara Singde (1655–1685), lyricist
	Pu Song-ling (1640–1715), *Liao-zhai's Record of Wonders*
	final version of *The Palace of Lasting Life* (1688) by Hong Sheng
	Peach Blossom Fan (1699) by Kong Shang-ren
Compilation of the *Complete Tang Poetry* 1705	Wu Jing-zi (1701–1754), novelist, author of *The Scholars* (published 1803)
	Cao Xue-qin (1715–1763), novelist, author of *Story of the Stone*
	Zhao Yi (1727–1814), poet
	Huang Jing-ren (1749–1783), poet
	Gong Zi-zhen (1792–1841), poet
	first publication of *Story of the Stone* (1791)
Opium War begins 1840	Huang Zun-xian (1848–1905), poet and diplomat
Tai-ping tian-guo Rebellion 1850–60s	
Boxer Rebellion begins 1899	Qiu Jin (1879–1907), poet and revolutionary
	Wang Guo-wei (1877–1927), poet, scholar, and Qing loyalist
Fall of the Qing; establishment of the Republic 1911	May 4 movement (1919) advocating the use of the vernacular in all writing

Introduction

The Chinese literary tradition extends continuously from early in the first millennium B.C. to the present. It was until very recently the basis of all Chinese reading, and a literate adolescent could read all but the earliest works in this tradition with little difficulty, if not always with perfect accuracy. The tradition's growing body of works—the classics, philosophy, history, and literature—unified Chinese civilization through its long history and across regional divisions of language.

As was true of ancient civilizations in general, what we now call literature was initially inseparable from history and thought. The stories of legendary heroes were neither history nor fiction in the modern sense, but the beginning of both: the "philosopher's" fantastic speculations admitted no clear differentiation between verbal invention and thought; and the lyric poem was considered the embodiment of moral and historical truths.

A sense of "literature" as a category of writing distinct from thought did eventually begin to take shape, although it was not always "literature" in the same way we use the term in the twentieth century. Like our own concept, the scope and definition of Chinese literature changed over the centuries. Poetry and non-fiction (including essays, letters, and even political documents) were considered serious literature; novels and prose fiction were not fully accepted as true literature until the last century in China—nor in England and Europe, for that matter. Drama, though immensely popular and sophisticated, acquired only marginal legitimacy in China. Yet these works, both "high literature" and the popular genres of fiction and drama, were perhaps the most beloved component of the textual unity of Chinese civilization. A nineteenth-century merchant, a Buddhist monk, and a Confucian official may have held profoundly different values; the nature and depth of their educations may have differed greatly; but all three would probably have known, loved, and memorized a few of the same poems by Li Bo. They would have memorized the poems as children and recited them throughout their lives when the occasion seemed appropriate.

Although the literary tradition was a unifying force, it was far from monolithic. Broadly defined, Chinese literature offered its people a wide range of human possibilities and responses. Literature could confirm social values, twist them, or subvert them altogether. The eighth-century poet Du Fu provided a Confucian voice of principled response to dynastic upheaval and social suffering. When Wen Tian-xiang, the captured hero of the Song resistance to the Mongol invasion, awaited his execution in Da-du, modern Beijing, he passed his time in prison composing poems made up of memorized lines of Du Fu rearranged. Later, when the Manchus conquered China in the mid-seventeenth century, Du Fu's poetry provided a model for how to give an account of the human suffering that was caused. Likewise, if a person felt expansive, there were the poems of Li Bo; if a person hungered for the simple life, there was the poetry of Tao Qian and Wang Wei; if a person was in love, there was the poetry of Li Shang-yin or Tang Xian-zu's play, *Peony Pavilion*. Popular literature in vernacular Chinese, especially prose fiction, also could represent the impulses that the civilization repressed. A person might believe that a son owed absolute obedience to his father, but that same person as a reader could enjoy reading in *The Romance of the Gods* how the divine child Ne-zha chased down his father with murderous intent.

Readers of another age and culture often have the impulse to identify some unitary "Chineseness" in this literature—perhaps isolating the image of an old fisherman in the misty mountains uttering words of Daoist wisdom. This imaginary China is constructed out of the motives and history of outside cultures; it is important to see this simplified image as such, and to recognize the immense diversity of traditional China throughout its long history.

One of the most distorting elements of the conventional Western image of traditional China is the belief in its changelessness. There were indeed continuities in the culture and no sense of profound alienation from the past until the twentieth century, but in both fact and self-image, traditional China was intensely "historical," each historical period characterized by its distinctive personality. Indeed, the reader's awareness of the period of which he or she was reading was an important part of the reading experience. Viewed from a large perspective, these works were part of a ongoing creation of a myth of Chinese cultural history.

There is a vast body of premodern Chinese literature, as befits a very large and old country that also had extensive commercial printing many centuries before Europe. Even an anthology such as the present one cannot hope to encompass its impressive size; but it can accomplish the critically important task of recreating the family of texts and voices that make up a "tradition" rather than simply collecting some of the more famous texts and arranging them in chronological order.

Vernacular and Classical

Written vernacular Chinese first appeared in Buddhist stories for performance before illiterate audiences who could not have understood classical Chinese. The real birth of vernacular literature, however, occurred in the thirteenth century, when commercial publishers sought to capitalize on the popularity of storytelling and theater in the great cities. Publications of drama and fiction tried to catch the lively cadences of the spoken language with linguistic usages that were strictly excluded from classical Chinese. Thereafter classical Chinese was used for poetry, essays, and some prose fiction, while vernacular was used for fiction, drama, and popular song.

The inevitable changes in language that occurred across millennia tended to enter Chinese written literature by accretion. The literary form of Chinese known as "classical" Chinese took its basic shape in the last three centuries B.C., and continued to evolve until the present century through new usages, syntax, and forms of argument. Although the influence of the evolving spoken language made itself felt in subtle ways, "classical" Chinese grew increasingly distant from it. As early as the eighth century A.D. there appeared a written "vernacular" literature, incorporating many elements of the spoken language.

The relation between "classical" and "vernacular" literature was roughly analogous to the way in which Americans use written English for essays and American for novels and plays. On the one hand, if an American, in writing an essay, uses "gotta" to express necessity, readers will unconsciously wince. If, on the other hand, a character says "must" in a play or a movie, the character is probably well educated and English. Americans subconsciously think of an immense linguistic range of literary and vernacular usage as one language, with different levels or "registers" appropriate to different genres and situations. This was roughly the sense of the Chinese language before the twentieth century.

The Present Selection

This anthology is organized to represent the literary tradition, not as a static arrangement of "monuments" in chronological order but as a family of texts that achieve their identity and distinctness in relation to one another. As in any interesting family, not all the voices sing in harmony. The anthology is neither a conservative notion of "canon" (though it contains a fairly comprehensive representation of that canon), nor an attempt to construct a counter-canon of texts suppressed and overlooked (though they are present as well). Texts have been chosen because they respond to one another, either addressing similar issues or responding to other particular texts. The tradition is a whole, and no anthology can be that whole; but an anthology can show how the tradition works. Commentary is included both to provide background information and to help non-Chinese readers notice what a premodern Chinese reader might have noticed instinctively.

The arrangement of the sections is primarily chronological, though these are interspersed with sections that cut across history to show differences and continuities from a larger perspective. Within the chronological sections I will sometimes offer a text from a thousand years in the future or from a thousand years in the past. Chronological history is the basis of a tradition; but literature, where there are no linguistic barriers, cuts across chronological history with ease. This is sometimes hard to recognize for the reader of English, in whose tradition texts quickly show their age. But in classical Chinese, a poem from a thousand years in the past might not be essentially different from a poem written yesterday; this is not to deny historical change, but, to return to the metaphor of a family, it is like having many generations living in the same house.

The anthologist who would create a version of a tradition faces one insurmountable limitation: long works. Chinese vernacular works are often very long indeed. Traditional novels frequently run to a hundred chapters, taking up four to five volumes in English translation. Forty or fifty acts are common in the huge plays called "dramatic romances," and they can fill a substantial volume in English. With numerous characters and intricate plots, these works do not easily lend themselves to excerpts. I have included a few acts from two of the most famous dramatic romances and a more extensive selection (about two fifths of the whole) from a third. To give the reader a sense of the vernacular novel, I have included three chapters which form a coherent episide in *The Romance of the Gods*. The major premodern novels have been translated, and they should be read outside of this anthology.

During the last fifty years there has been an immense amount of translation from the Chinese, with the inevitable result that any anthology which seeks to present many of the most famous works will inevitably repeat material translated elsewhere. I have tried to incorporate works that have long been considered important, together with some less well known ones. But my criterion of choice has been those texts which, working together, tell a story that embodies the concerns of the tradition and shows its coherence.

A Note on Translation

Translation is, for the scholar, a troubling art; it is literary history gone gambling. Knowledge and skill are essential, but only a small part of an enterprise where luck rules. Great fortunes are parlayed into nothing and small wagers become great. Important texts come out flat, whereas minor pieces succeed splendidly. Everything hangs on the moment, the translator's disposition, and the circumstantial sources and resources of the language.

If there is a single principle behind these translations, it is translating texts against one another: trying to create a complex family of differences that does not correspond to, but attempts to reinvent some of the differences perceived by a good reader of Chinese. Translators of Chinese often create their own vision of "Chinese" literature as a whole, either articulated against English literature or as a possibility within it. This elusive "Chineseness" was the one quality that was utterly beyond the grasp of the traditional Chinese reader. In their own literature, they perceived only differences in period, genre, style, and above all in the personalities of writers. As a translator, I have the conviction that the "Chineseness" of these works will show itself: my task is to find idioms that will catch the families of differences.

In his famous essay on translation, Friedrich Schleiermacher articulated the basic antithesis between adapting the material to the conventions of the host language and preserving the difference of the original, the antithesis that James J. Y. Liu was later to call "naturalization" and "barbarization." Both extremes are, of course, bad translation; and most translators work between them, choosing to "naturalize" some elements while respecting the difference of others. This translator is convinced that the differences of the Chinese literary tradition are profound enough that we do not need to exaggerate them. If I tend moderately to the "naturalization" camp, it is to offer an occasional insight into why these works were compelling in their own world, not why they have an exotic appeal to outsiders.

I have tried to avoid archaizing, but have at the same time endeavored to use the levels of English style to mark the strong differences in period and register in the Chinese. I translate classical Chinese into English and vernacular into American. The latter is a dangerous enterprise, and the discomfort that some American readers may feel on encountering Americanisms may echo in some small way the discomfort that some classically educated readers in the Ming and Qing felt on encountering the vernacular. As in the Ming and Qing, Americans permit their contemporary language in fiction and drama, but object when vernacular usage slips into our own formal genres.

Readers who are already familiar with the conventions used in translating classical Chinese literature may be surprised or puzzled, perhaps even annoyed, by some of the conventions adopted here. Rather than rejecting such unfamiliarity, the reader should reflect on the number of peculiar translation terms that the habit of recent translators has made seem natural. To solve the numerous problems of translation from the Chinese, Western scholars and translators have created their own special dialect of English. While some of the strangeness of this language is unavoidable, much of it is the deadwood of habit that contributes unnecessarily to the sense of the categorical strangeness of traditional Chinese literature.

I have tried, as they used to say, to "English" these texts; that is, to say something as one would say it in English. When precision is implicit in the Chinese, I have tried to be precise. For example, the Chinese *wan*, "ten thousand," is often used when the English speaker would say "thousands" or "millions," and that is the exact translation. In other cases, *wan* is used as a precise counter, and in those cases, "ten thousand" is the exact translation.

What follows are some of the conventions adopted in this volume, both in large matters of form and small matters of word choice.

Form

In translating poetry, I have generally tried to find very flexible English forms that do not seem too artificial: forms that can recreate a set of *differences* to echo the basic formal differences of Chinese poetry. I have been usually, but not universally, consistent in the following policies. Chinese lines of four and five syllables are translated as single English lines. Lines of *Chu-ci* and *fu*, in the original Chinese often broken into hemistiches by lightly accented syllables, are left as single lines in English with additional blank spaces in between the hemistiches. Lines of seven syllables are translated as a pair of lines with the second line indented, since the seven-syllable line began as a song line and was generally freer and looser than the five-syllable line.

In stanzaic poems, I have left an additional space between stanzas. In poems based on couplets, I have left additional space between couplets to set off the couplet as a unit. In poems before the fifth century, in quatrains, and in stanzaic poems, I have not left the additional space between couplets. In general, if the couplets in themselves seem to bear little formal weight, I have sometimes taken the liberty not to represent them with the extra space.

I have generally capitalized the first word in a rhyming unit and left the subsequent lines uncapitalized (however, in opening couplets where both lines rhyme, I have left the second line uncapitalized). This further sets off the couplet as the basic semantic unit in poetry, the equivalent of the sentence; and in song lyric this practice also sets off the semantic units articulated by rhyme, which serves as a punctuation. Here again, in poems that seem to overflow the couplet, I have sometimes taken the liberty to suggest this by punctuation and lower-case letters at the beginnings of couplets.

There is no way to be perfectly consistent without making the chosen English forms appear artificial. I have preferred inconsistency to obstrusiveness of form. There is also no way to echo the forms of Chinese poetry and still produce translations that are accurate and readable. Our purpose is rather to call attention to groupings such as stanzas, couplets, and the rhyme units of song lyric, and to create a recognizable structure of differences.

I have tried to keep footnotes to a minimum, though in some cases they were unavoidable. I have attempted to give as much of the essential background as possible in my own comments before and after the poems.

The calendar

Traditional China used a lunar calendar in which the months of thirty days were numbered from one to twelve, with discrepancies remedied by the addition of "intercalary months." The full moon was always to come mid-month, on the fifteenth. The first three months were spring, the second three were summer, and so on. The beginning of the year came at different times on the Western calendar, but it was generally some time in late January or in February. In the translations it is sometimes necessary to use the Chinese numbered months, but where possible I have followed the convention of translating the First Month as March, the Second Month as April, and so on. Although this is inexact, it corresponds roughly to our sense of the seasons. The reader who, for some reason, wants to know the exact Chinese date can convert immediately based on this system. I have not attempted to convert dates to their exact counterparts in European dating; thus December 22, 1076, is the twenty-second of the tenth month. The eleventh month, "January," would be given as 1077. I have converted reign dates and cyclical dates into their corresponding Western years.

Measures

I have kept a *cun* (varying through history from 2.25 to 3.2 centimeters) as an "inch"; a *chi* (10 *cun*) as a "foot"; and a *zhang* (10 *chi*) as a "yard." The *zhang,* from 2.25 to 3.3 meters, is the measure most seriously at odds with the English translation, and in cases where the measure jars with common sense (and with the poetic measure *ren*), I have sometimes converted into true English feet and yards.

Through history the Chinese *li* varied from 405 to 576 meters, or very roughly a third of a mile. I have used the translation "mile" and sometimes "league." In travel accounts this can sometimes give the impression that the travelers are making extraordinarily good time.

The standard large number is *wan,* "ten thousand." When some exactitude is called for, I translate it as "ten thousand" or "myriad"; however, when it is used loosely, as it often is, I use the natural English counterpart of "thousands" or "millions," depending on context.

Musical instruments

The *qin:* very few modern readers have heard a zither played; somewhat more may have seen one (but probably still more have seen a *qin* or *koto*). The *qin* is nothing like a lute, which has become the conventional translation. I have chosen to translate the *qin* as "harp" and the *se* as "great harp." The *kong-hou,* which in its vertical version is indeed a harp, will also have to be a harp. The choice of "harp" is an imperfect translation (especially if one thinks of a modern concert harp played by a woman in long white robes), but its antiquity and range of associations seem preferable. The problem with translating a *qin* as "harp" is that the *qin* has bridges.

The *pi-pa* in some ways more resembles a lute, but it was a popular instrument rather than one with the cachet of elegance that the lute possesses. The playing technique and timbre most closely approximate the Western mandolin, so I have translated it thus.

Hu

The word *Hu* was used as a general term for the peoples of Central Asia, including Indo-Iranian peoples as well as Turks, and the people of the city states as well as nomads. *Hu* refers to ethnicity, however imperfectly, rather than to a level of civilization, and "barbarian" is both inaccurate and often metrically offensive. Since in many periods the *Hu* were Turkic peoples, *Hu* will usually be translated as "Turks." I have great affection for the Turks; when they come out badly in a Chinese poem, it represents Chinese prejudices rather than my own.

Alcoholic beverages

Jiu is conventionally translated as "wine." Although true wine, once it was imported through Central Asia, was classified as *jiu,* most Chinese *jiu* was actually beer, made from grain rather than fruit. Sometimes I use "wine," but often I translate *jiu* as "beer." The choice of wine as the translation of *jiu* is pure snobbery, to project the image of the Mandarin as "cultivated." The process of making *jiu*—as well as Western wine and beer, though we do not see this in commercial production—involves lees and dregs. Thus the clarity or "thickness" of *jiu* is often referred to.

Buildings

There are several aspects of a traditional Chinese dwelling place that a reader needs to keep in mind. Upper-class dwellings were generally compounds surrounded by walls. The grander the family, the larger the compound and the more internal divisions it had. One entered a section of the compound through gates. Thus "layers" or "tiers" of gates suggested a wealthy household. The emperor's palace was spoken of as having a "thousand gates" and "nine tiers." Inside a gate was a "courtyard" or "yard." There were verandahs around the house and balconies on the upper stories. The term for a door to a chamber is different from the word for gate, but "to go out" is usually to go out the gate rather than to go out the door. Windows were covered with gauze or paper in the winter and often had elaborate grillwork. Since buildings were open, swallows would often fly in and make their nests in the rafters.

A "terrace," in the language of conventional translation from the Chinese, is not a patio. Chinese buildings were sometimes constructed on raised platforms of earth, faced with brick or stone. These are "terraces."

A *lou* is, roughly, a building of more than one story that is usually wider than it is tall. *Lou* were also built on top of city walls and over gates for defensive purposes. When positioned there, a *lou* is a "tower"; when on the ground, a *lou* is sometimes a "mansion," sometimes a "building," sometimes a "[room] upstairs," depending on context.

A *ge* gets translated as "tower," though it is generally (but not always) a building of more than one story that is more narrow than it is high.

Houses were supposed to face south, with the women's quarters in the back of the house on the north side.

Hair

Chinese women generally wore their hair in elaborate coiffures piled on the head. Such coiffures used long pins decorated with the shapes of insects or flowers, although sometimes the hair was decorated with real sprays of flowers. Brows were often shaved, then painted on high on the forehead.

Men also wore their hair long (the late imperial queue was a Manchu fashion imposed on Chinese by the Qing conquest). Informally, one might wear a headband or a turban, but officials wore caps, with their hair held in place by hatpins; thus, to "pull out one's hatpins" was to give up office. Letting one's hair down had approximately the same associations in Chinese as it has in English.

Flora and fauna

As the natural history of North America differs from that of Europe, so that of China differs from either. An American writing in English is in a rather bizarre situation. Much of our received *literary* language of flora and fauna is English and European—things and creatures with rich literary associations that the American has never or hardly ever seen. It is well known that nightingales, non-natives of North America, sing primarily in anthologies—"bird thou never wert." To take this already European-specific language to translate Chinese flora and fauna is a double hardship for American readers. In addition, we have become, by and large, city dwellers, and we know brand names with more precision than plant names, not having the variations of species and their signifiers available to us. I suspect that the majority of American readers can more readily distinguish a Coke from a Pepsi than a duckweed from a waterlily. Chinese literature is, not surprisingly, filled with the flora and fauna and minerals that writers encountered every day. It is ironic that some of the most exotic features of translation from the Chinese are the most everyday growing things. The reader of translation will never reach the rich associations of the language of flowers in Chinese; but let me quote a passage from the English literary tradition (Shakespeare's *The Winter's-Tale*) that might remind the English reader how effective the names of flowers can be:

> O Proserpina
>
> > For the flowers now that, frighted, thou let'st fall
> > From Dis's wagon; daffodils,
> > That come before the swallow dares, and take
> > The winds of March with beauty; violets dim,

But sweeter than the lids of Juno's eyes
Or Cytherea's breath; pale primroses
That die unmarried, ere they can behold
Bright Phoebus in his strength—a malady
Most incident to maids; bold oxlips and
The crown imperial; lilies of all kinds,
The flower-de-luce being one. O, these I lack
To make you garlands of, and my sweet friend,
To strew him o'er and o'er.

The translator cannot do that. I have, however, chosen the following synonyms to avoid some of the most painful moments of Chinese translation idiom—

Wu-tong: The *wu-tong* is a relatively common tree in China, but is not native to North America. It is slowly becoming naturalized as the "tung" tree. Perhaps I should have left it as such in the translations. The beech does not, so far as I know, grow in China. The two trees are rather different, but both are wide-spreading and beautiful. Admittedly, the *wu-tong* does its widespreading considerably higher up than the beech; but when you see a beech in these translations, it is a *wu-tong.*

Let:
   du-ruo be mint
   jie-ju be wintergreen
   hui be lavender or sage
   du-heng be asarum
   zhi trees be hawthorns
   zhi be white angelica
   quan be the iris
   bi-li be ivy
   lan be orchid

Early China

先秦西漢

EARLY CHINA: PERIOD INTRODUCTION Through most of the second millennium B.C., North China, along the Yellow River, was ruled by a dynasty known as the Shang or Yin. The Shang seems to have been a collection of city states under the nominal rule of a high king, who probably exerted very little direct authority over the farther reaches of the kingdom. The Shang had writing, which survives incised on tortoise shells and bones used for divination. If writing was used for other purposes, it was on softer materials that have long since disappeared. What Shang literature might have been like we can only guess: later ages invented songs and speeches that they attributed to the Shang, but such pieces belong to the historical imagination of those later ages rather than to the Shang itself.

The last century of the second millennium B.C. saw the rise of a new domain, the Zhou, to the west of the Shang heartland. In 1020 B.C. (though different dates have been proposed), the Zhou threw off its subordination to the Shang monarch and conquered the Shang. A small kingdom suddenly found itself in possession of large territories, and to administer those territories, members of the royal house were sent out to preside over feudal domains throughout North China. The Zhou feudal system, conceived as a family working together, was to have lasting consequences.

During the early centuries of Zhou rule, writing was used for divination, for commemorative inscriptions on bronze ritual vessels, and probably for basic recordkeeping. It is unlikely that writing was ever used for longer texts that we might recognize as "literature," even in the broadest definition of the term. As in Greece and India, the earliest extant literature of China was originally oral and passed down that way from one generation to the next.

There were two groups of works that were handed down orally and circulated through the Zhou feudal domains. Neither group was stable: while conserving very early material, both kinds of works were added to and varied over the centuries. The first of these consisted of sayings and speeches that supposedly came from the early kings, offering guidance in the principles on which the Zhou polity was founded; this became the *Classic of Documents (Shu-jing).* The second was a body of over three hundred poems that became the *Classic of Poetry (Shi-jing).* The *Classic of Poetry* contained ritual hymns and ballads that were supposed to date back to the beginning of the dynasty, along with more "recent" poems from the eighth and seventh centuries B.C. Because the *Classic of Poetry* grew and changed in the course of oral transmission over these centuries, it is impossible to date the oldest pieces with any certainty. Most of the works that can be dated by internal historical references come from before 600 B.C., the date that scholars often give for the collection becoming more or less fixed. But there are a few poems that seem to date from the late sixth century B.C., which suggests that the collection continued to grow and evolve.

During the long period in which the *Classic of Poetry* was taking shape, the Zhou monarchy was progressively losing power and authority. There was a brief period of restoration of the royal power under the reign of King Xuan (827–782 B.C.), but during the reign of his successor, non-Chinese invaders sacked the royal capital and forced the king to move east to a new capital near modern Luo-yang. Thus the first period of Zhou rule was known as the Western Zhou, and the second period as the Eastern Zhou. In the east, the area directly under royal control was very small, and the Zhou king, though he retained ritual importance, was politically at the mercy of the powerful feudal domains that surrounded him.

To the east of the new royal capital was the Duchy of Lu, a minor political power, but a domain of great cultural importance. The rulers of Lu traced their ancestry back to the Duke of Zhou, the virtuous younger brother of King Wu, who founded the Zhou. Lu was the domain that prided itself on the preservation and observation of proper Zhou customs. All the domains probably kept annals, but the court annals of Lu during this period survive; these are the *Chun-qiu, The Springs and Autumns [of Lu]*, sometimes translated as *The Spring and Autumn Annals*. These annals cover the years 720–481 B.C., and they give their name to the larger period of the eighth through the fifth centuries B.C. The annals are terse statements of what of importance happened during a given year; the second entry for 720 B.C. is characteristic: "The third month. The Duke [of Lu] and Yi-fu of Zhu took a blood oath at Mie." Since *The Springs and Autumns* were supposed to have been edited by Confucius (ca. 552–479 B.C.), Confucian scholars took their terseness as being replete with subtle moral judgments through the particular words chosen.

The period of *The Springs and Autumns* was a violent, yet aristocratic age. There was constant warfare throughout the domains as rulers of the larger domains struggled—through violence and diplomacy—to become *Ba*, Overlord, and compel the smaller domains to obey them. Yet warfare was still ceremonious and conducted on a relatively small scale. This same period saw the rise of new powers on the margins of the Zhou heartland. There was Qin in the West, the region from which the Zhou had originally come; Qin gradually drove back the non-Chinese tribes that had occupied the area and established itself as an important power. To the south, along the middle reaches of the Yangzi River, was the Kingdom of Chu, initially the most powerful of the peripheral domains. In the southeast, where the Yangzi joined the sea, were Wu and Yue. In varying degrees these new states felt little allegiance to the Zhou kings and Zhou traditions.

Confucius was born in the Duchy of Lu toward the end of this period. Confucius was intensely committed to his own vision of an idealized Zhou past, a world in which the old customs were followed, and through those customs, people treated one another with a natural grace. Confucius taught that the institution of those Zhou values within the present could restore harmony to society and the polity. From this particularly historical vision came Confucius' more profound legacy to the culture: the belief that the natural being and the social being in man could be reconciled.

As a teacher, Confucius was immensely persuasive and gathered a large following of disciples, who became the founders of the Confucian "school." In his desire to politically institute his principles, however, he had no success. He traveled from court to court, only to discover that the imperatives of practical politics outweighed all other values. After his death, the sayings attributed to him multiplied, but the Confucian school carried on his teachings and preserved a small corpus of authentic sayings, which were at last written down (? third century B.C.) in a work known as the *Lun-yu*, commonly translated in English as the *Analects*.

Not only did Confucius' teaching have no practical political consequences, but for almost three centuries after his death, warfare simply became more pervasive and efficient and residual Zhou customs more irrelevant. The period from 403 B.C. until the unification of China under the Qin in 221 B.C. is known as the Warring States. Earlier, during the *Springs and Autumns* period, the ministers and generals of the domains were largely drawn from aristocratic families, often tied by descent to the ruling house; far from tempering political behavior by family solidarity, this often led to internecine feuding that sometimes crippled domains for generations. As we move toward the Warring States, however, the rulers of the domains found that by professionalizing their military and bureaucracy they could achieve greater security and authority. In delegating authority to talented men from other domains or from the lower gentry, the ruler held their personal allegiance. But although such increasingly meritocratic governments gained in stability and efficiency, this new government elite felt none of the restraints of traditional custom, and its decisions were usually governed by expediency.

Rulers and ministers each seeking advantage for his own domain fostered a culture of expert advisers and contending political philosophies, the so-called hundred schools. This violent era of competition between the domains was one of the most intellectually creative in China's history. The philosopher Mo-zi, who probably lived in the late fifth century B.C., advocated a radical utilitarianism and the rejection of all traditions that did not serve the common good. His doctrine of "universal love" was nothing mystical; rather, it was an impartial benevolence which, when universally practiced, would work toward the general good. One unfortunately shortsighted doctrine of Mo-zi was that the improvement of techniques of defensive warfare would contribute to general peace and stability. After the master's death, the members of Mo-zi's well-organized school became technical experts in military fortification. What Mo-zi could not foresee was the stimulus this provided for the development of offensive warfare and siegecraft.

Certainly the most successful of these political experts was Shang Yang, who was made minister of the western domain of Qin in the middle of the fourth century B.C. Shang Yang was the parent of the political philosophy that would be known as Legalism, which became state policy in Qin. Shang Yang advocated a code of strict laws, applied universally and impartially. There was a system of consistent rewards and, above all, severe punishments. The resources of the state were mobilized to encourage agricultural production and to supply and train Qin's army. Whatever was useless or an impediment to the smooth functioning of the state mechanism was to be eliminated. Qin flourished under this system of total state control, and its armies were soon the dread of all the other domains.

Legalism found its most eloquent exponent in the writings of Han Fei (ca. 280–ca. 233 B.C.), who advised Qin as it grew toward empire. By Han Fei's time, Legalism had become intertwined with one strain of Daoism, represented by the *Lao-zi*, a rhymed philosophical text attributed to the shadowy philosopher Lao-zi advocating passivity and simplicity. The *Lao-zi* held that people were happiest when they were ignorant; the Legalists agreed and saw the state as a means to keep them so. The ruler at the center of the Legalist state apparatus was cast in the role of Daoist sage, governing through non-action, his power coming through the impersonal laws rather than the enforcement of royal will.

One Daoist thinker, however, took Daoist concerns in a very different direction. This was Zhuang Zhou, writing in the middle of the third century B.C. Unlike most of his contemporaries, Zhuang Zhou was a philosopher of the individual mind rather than society, and he stressed the relativity of perception and values. The historical Zhuang Zhou is believed to be the author of the early chapters of the book that bears his name, the *Zhuang-zi,* and those chapters contain some of the most daring and imaginative writing in early China.

The fourth and third centuries B.C. saw a proliferation of philosophical schools and types of expertise, all competing for the patronage of princes and the devotion of disciples. There were agrarian primitivists, philosophical solipsists, witty logicians, along with itinerant masters of pragmatic diplomacy and military science. Faced with this rich array of competitors, the Confucian school found someone in the late fourth century B.C. who could speak for Confucian values in a new way, adequate to the intellectually sophisticated climate of the times. This was Meng-zi, commonly referred to in English as Mencius. Fiercely anti-utilitarian, Mencius declared the essential goodness of human nature, a goodness that could be damaged or perverted by circumstance. Addressing rulers who sought success, Mencius told them that pragmatic success could come only from a moral perfection that was indifferent to such success. Mencius was followed in the next generation by another Confucian philosopher, Xun-zi, who took the contrary position that human nature was essentially bad, or more precisely, that it was driven by appetites that could be governed only by a Confucian moral education and the restraining force of ceremony.

In this age of new philosophies indifferent to the past, the Confucian school conserved older traditions such as the rituals of Zhou, the *Classic of Poetry,* the *Classic of Documents,* and *The Springs and Autumns.* Out of the Confucian school came *The Zuo Tradition,* the earliest historical work of China. The date of *The Zuo Tradition* has been much disputed; the late fourth century B.C. seems likely, though it may well have been earlier. *The Zuo Tradition* is given as a commentary on *The Springs and Autumns,* offering narrative accounts that flesh out the terse entries in the annals.

We cannot know exactly when writing came to be used in extended compositions such as the essays of the philosophers or *The Zuo Tradition.* It seems likely that there was a gradual expansion of written composition throughout the course of the Warring States. The tightly controlled Legalist state of Qin depended on writing for the dissemination of its laws and the accurate gathering of information. The Chinese characters used in this period were unlike those that came into use in the Han Dynasty, which can still be read by any reader of Chinese. Early script was cumbersome, unstandardized, and open to numerous ambiguities (though we may be sure that Qin found ways to avoid any ambiguity). Books were written on thin bamboo strips, bound together with string into bundles. A broken or rotten string could easily leave the book owner with a large, jumbled pile of bamboo strips, each containing a sentence or two. Some of the difficulties in reading early works are attributed to bungled attempts to reassemble such books. The sheer bulk and weight of these books presented practical difficulties with profound consequences. A work that now fills one modern printed volume could easily have required one or more wagons to transport. In the Warring States, relatively few people "read," though works might still be widely disseminated. Those who did read memorized and repeated what they had memorized—though human memory being what it is, variations and paraphrase crept in. In many of the early texts we now have, Han and later scholars have reconciled different versions; but in many other cases, we find retellings of the same story or passage, each different to a large or small degree, but including enough of the same wording that we can recognize them as variations of the same piece. Although the Warring States had written texts, it was still a world in which literature, broadly conceived, was primarily disseminated orally. The variations that accompany oral transmission might be included in a new written version, or more precisely, a version that was "written down."

Early writing often imitated the forms of speech. There were narrations and impersonal discursive treatises in early Chinese literature, but there was a particular pleasure in dialogue, and especially in oratory. Modern audiences have in large measure lost the taste for oratory, and its pleasures are diminished in writing (and further diminished in translation). But the written texts of early China were often crafted to recall the pleasures of a good speech, with the play of sounds and rhymes, rhythmic parallel phrases, and an intricate structure of analogies drawn to support an argument. Arising out of oratory came one of the most popular entertainment forms of the Han elite, the "poetic exposition" *(fu)*, long rhymed descriptions with rich vocabulary that were declaimed in courts.

Early in the third century B.C., the Kingdom of Chu extended from the borders of Sichuan down the full length of the Yangzi River. A major military and political power, Chu alone was a match for the growing power of Qin. Chu culture, particularly of its elite, had been influenced by long contact with the central Zhou domains, but Chu's ruling family was indigenous, and it remained a hybrid culture with distinct traits. During Chu's long political struggle with Qin, the aristocrat Qu Yuan (ca. 340–278 B.C.) represented the party opposed to any compromise with Qin. Eventually he was sent into exile by the king and, according to legend, drowned himself in despair in the Mi-luo River. To Qu Yuan was attributed a body of verse unlike anything else in ancient China. These works, along with later works in the same tradition, are known as the "Lyrics of Chu" *(Chu-ci)*. The earliest works in the collection were probably preserved orally in the lower Yangzi River region, where they came to the attention of the Han elite around the middle of the second century B.C.

The question of which, if any, of these pieces are actually by Qu Yuan remains a matter of scholarly debate, but some seem to represent authentic traditions of Chu shamanism. "The Nine Songs" are mostly hymns to the Chu gods. The collection also contains two "soul-callings," in which the shaman tries to persuade the wandering soul of someone dead or dying to return to its body. Most of the pieces mix shamanistic elements with moral and political motifs. The most famous work is the *Li Sao,* a long monologue in which the speaker is rejected by the king and rides with a cavalcade of deities through the heavens, protesting his virtue and seeking a mate.

The meters, the language, the images, and the fierce intensity of the "Lyrics of

Chu" are unlike anything from North China of the time, and they exerted a powerful influence on later writing. The shamanistic account of the flight through the heavens became the model for representing religious experience in Huang-Lao Daoism, prevalent in the Han Dynasty and concerned with techniques of spiritual mastery and attaining immorality. The impassioned poetry of longing for union with a goddess became the basis of a poetry of desire, whether erotic, spiritual, or allegorical. The ritual persuasion of the soul in the "soul-callings" became a model for moral persuasions, calling the errant spirit back to good behavior by threatening and alluring description.

The third century b.c. saw the steady rise of the well-disciplined and ambitious domain of Qin. The political alliances of other domains shifted back and forth, trying either to check Qin's expansion or placate it. Nothing, however, could stop the steady advance of Qin's armies eastward. In 249 b.c., Qin unseated the last Zhou king, Hui, who ruled as a petty local chieftain over his tiny domain, and put an end once and for all to the Zhou Dynasty. Finally, in 221 b.c., the unification of China was completed, and the Qin ruler assumed the new title of *huang-di,* "Emperor," calling himself the "First Emperor of Qin," Qin Shi-huang.

Qin took draconian measures to destroy not only all opposition but all diversity and regionalism as well. The script, weights and measures, and even the width of wheeled vehicles were standardized (regional differences in the distance between wheels created ruts of different widths, which were a major obstacle to travel through the country). These policies still seem reasonable for political unification, but others, such as the attempt to stamp out all political schools other than Legalism and to burn their books, are still remembered with horror. The Qin state apparatus was an efficient tool of imperial will, and without any checks, the imperial will passed from bold decisiveness to megalomania. Large-scale transfers of population and massive conscriptions of forced labor to build palaces and frontier fortifications helped create the social unrest that led to Qin's downfall after less than two decades of rule.

The death of the First Emperor in 210 b.c. and the weakness of his young heir led to widespread outbreaks of rebellion; the overextended Qin armies, previously invincible, fell apart in the attempt to put down uprisings on so many sides. The leaders of two rebel confederations, Xiang Yu and Liu Bang, competed for dominance. Although Xiang Yu long appeared the stronger of the two, in 202 b.c. he was surrounded by Liu Bang's forces and committed suicide.

The Han Dynasty is usually dated from 206 b.c. when Liu Bang took the title of "Prince of Han." On defeating Xiang Yu, Liu Bang found himself in the ruins of the Qin administrative structure with a fragile alliance of regional warlord armies. Politically astute, Liu Bang seems to have understood that no one could hold the empire as tightly as Qin had tried to in pursuit of its Legalist dreams of absolute state control. He kept part of his new empire under direct imperial control, appointing generals and family members as feudal lords of the farther regions. As conflicts between the central government and these feudal domains arose in subsequent reigns, the Han emperors conquered, divided, and whittled away at the feudal domains until the long reign of Emperor Wu (140–87 b.c.), when the Chinese heartland was securely centralized under imperial control and Chinese armies were off winning glory against the Xiong-nu Kingdom in Central Asia.

It was during the reign of Emperor Wu that Si-ma Qian (ca. 145–ca. 85 B.C.) set out to finish his father's task of compiling the history of China from the earliest times down to the present. His court office gave him access to the imperial library, which he supplemented by his own researches. Si-ma Qian's *Historical Records* preserve stories that we might best consider "historical romance." Such stories are driven by the pleasures of narrative and character rather than by verifiable facts. It is impossible to say whether this was in the character of Si-ma Qian's sources or was due to his own inclinations as a writer: probably it was a combination of the two. Si-ma Qian duly reports the legends of high antiquity and gives a detailed account of the political struggles closer to his own time, but he is at his most lively from the fifth century B.C. to the consolidation of the Han early in the second century B.C.

We have much writing that survives from ancient China, but probably nothing comes to us directly as an author wrote it. The earliest material passed through centuries of oral transmission before it was written down. The later material may have been composed in writing, but it passed through many centuries of recopying, with all the errors and misunderstandings that occurred in the process. Well into the Western Han there was little sense of the integrity of a text; sections could be added or deleted, and passages could be rephrased. The long process that occurred through the Han of reconciling the variant texts of the Confucian Classics led to the notion of a stable text that could not be altered; this, in turn, produced a notion of the stable literary text with which we are familiar.

In the Western Han, silk was used for writing, but it was a more expensive medium than bamboo strips. A form of paper was used in the first century A.D., but did not come into wide-scale use until several centuries later. The dates are uncertain, but between the first century B.C. and the end of the second century A.D. the scroll replaced the bundle of bamboo strips as the primary medium of writing. A scroll was easier to produce and use, and it was more durable. During the same period, script became increasingly standardized and easy to write. With the age of the scroll and the standardized script, we can begin to think of reading as the rule rather than the exception. It was still not the age of the printed book: scrolls were time-consuming to produce and treasured proportionately. But through the course of the Han, the written word became much more widely available and could be transported from one side of China to another with relative ease. A book in bundles of bamboo strips that would have required a wagon to carry it over rivers and bad roads could now be replaced by a light satchel of scrolls.

This small technological advance had immense consequences. Learning was no longer confined to centers where there were immovable masses of books and masters who controlled access to them. Stories could be conveniently written down and carefully copied rather than retold, with each retelling differing slightly from the last. Different versions of a text could be easily brought together, set side by side, and the versions compared. And this could be done by anyone who could purchase the scrolls or have them made. Though an oral literature of song and story continued in China, the scroll brings us into the age of the book and literature proper.

先秦西漢 The *Classic of Poetry:* Beginnings

The *Classic of Poetry (Shi-jing)* is a collection of just over three hundred poems from the Zhou Dynasty (1020–249 B.C.). Although the collection reached something like its present form around 600 B.C., the oldest pieces may date from as early as the tenth century B.C. Found in a section entitled the "Temple Hymns of Zhou," these early works are simple hymns used in dynastic rituals to address the deified spirits of the founders of the Zhou Dynasty, Kings Wen and Wu.

In these hymns, words can be a necessary part of ritual. As in modern rituals such as weddings or court proceedings, formally declaring something in words is necessary to make it so. Suppose a group of men lead cattle and sheep into a large hall. There they kill the animals, cook them over a fire, and eat the meat in silence. That is a meal. But if, as they lead the animals into the hall, they sing the following verse from the "Temple Hymns of Zhou," the same action becomes a ritual, and the spirit of King Wen eats the smoke that rises from the burning sacrifice.

Classic of Poetry CCLXXII "We Have in Hand"

> We have in hand our offerings:
> these are sheep, these the cattle,
> may Heaven favor them.
> This act is patterned on King Wen's rules,
> which daily bring peace to all the land.
> Exalted be King Wen!—
> he favors us by feeding on them.
> May we, early and by night,
>   stand in dread of Heaven's might,
> and in this way preserve it.

[handwritten note: Worshipping Rituals]

It is often necessary to name something in order for that thing to have its proper function in a system of ritual. This becomes a significant role of early poetry: To declare the names of things and actions, and to describe the orderly system of their relation, thus guaranteeing the continuity of ritual and social processes. The following is one of the agrarian hymns from the "Temple Hymns of Zhou."

Classic of Poetry CCXC "Mowing Grasses"

Mowing grasses, felling trees,
we till the churning soil.

A thousand pairs do weeding,
off to paddies, off to dikes.

Here the squire, here the firstborn,
here the nextborn, here the clan,
here the yeomen, here the hands,
hungry for their field-fare.
Comely are the wives,
sturdy are the men.
Sharp-tipped are the plowshares,
that turn the sod on southern tracts.

We scatter all the many grains,
the life is stored within the seed.
Then the bounty of the shoots,
and fullness in the single stalk.

Full indeed are all the sprouts,
row by row the weeders go.
In lines we come to harvest it,
and we have the grains in piles,
in myriads and millions.
Beer we make and the sweet ale,
to bestow on Foremothers and Forefathers,
and by this join the many rites.

Musky is the grain-smell,
the splendor of our homeland.
Pungent is its fragrance,
well-being for our elderly.

Not just this which is before us,
not just for now what is here now,
from early times it was as this.

The Zhou Founding

The *Classic of Poetry* has four large sections: the "Hymns" *(Song)*, the "Great Odes" *(Da-ya)*, the "Lesser Odes" *(Xiao-ya)*, and the "Airs" *(Feng)*. The next four poems are from the "Great Odes" and recount crucial episodes in the founding of the Zhou Dynasty. The first, "She Bore the Folk," tells the story of the miraculous birth of Lord Millet (Hou Ji), who created agriculture and whom the Zhou royal house revered as their ancestor. The legend as presented in "She Bore the Folk" is fragmentary, leaving later historians and commentators to fill in the missing details. An example of this is given in the later prose account of Hou Ji by the historian Si-ma Qian. "Liu the Duke" tells of the migration of the Zhou people into the land of Bin. In Bin, the Zhou people were eventually attacked by the Rong and Di tribes and migrated further to the territory around Mount Qi, where the people took the name of Zhou. The settlement of the "plain of Zhou" is told in "Spreading" Finally, in "The Greater Brightness," we have an account of how Zhou, gathering Power *(De)* by good works and advantageous marriages, at last received the Charge of Heaven to overthrow the Yin-Shang Dynasty and rule in its stead.

Although critics have often grouped these four and one other poem together as a set, they are essentially different poetic types. "Liu the Duke" and "Spreading" are narrative accounts of Zhou migration and settlement. "She Bore the Folk" is not so much a narrative as a ritual song that explains the origin of the harvest ceremony. "The Greater Brightness" is an unabashed piece of royal Zhou propaganda.

Despite millennia of scholarship and great progress in linguistics and philology during the past four centuries, much remains uncertain in the language of the *Classic of Poetry,* especially in the most archaic poems of the "Great Odes" and the "Temple Hymns of Zhou." There are many words in these poems that we understand only roughly, which leaves the translator to rely more heavily on the interpretation of the Zhou world from which the poems come. At one extreme are scholars, primarily Chinese, who see the Zhou as the model for later, imperial China, with Confucian values and a government consisting of a bureaucratic structure of offices. At the other extreme are those Western, Japanese, and some Chinese scholars who see the Zhou as a more "primitive" society, one held together by religion, heroic virtues, and family ties.

Classic of Poetry CCXLV "She Bore the Folk"

She who first bore the folk—
Jiang it was, First Parent.
How was it she bore the folk?—
she knew the rite and sacrifice.
To rid herself of sonlessness
she trod the god's toeprint
    and she was glad.
She was made great, on her luck settled,
the seed stirred, it was quick.
She gave birth, she gave suck,
and this was Lord Millet.

When her months had come to term,
her firstborn sprang up.
Not splitting, not rending,
working no hurt, no harm.
He showed his godhead glorious,
the high god was greatly soothed.
He took great joy in those rites
and easily she bore her son.

She set him in a narrow lane,
but sheep and cattle warded him
She set him in the wooded plain,
he met with those who logged the plain.
She set him on cold ice,
birds sheltered him with wings.
Then the birds left him
and Lord Millet wailed.
This was long and this was loud;
his voice was a mighty one.

And then he crept and crawled,
he stood upright, he stood straight.
He sought to feed his mouth,
and planted there the great beans.
The great beans' leaves were fluttering,
the rows of grain were bristling.
Hemp and barley dense and dark,
the melons, plump and round.

Lord Millet in his farming
had a way to help things grow:
He rid the land of thick grass,
he planted there a glorious growth.
It was in squares, it was leafy,
it was planted, it grew tall.
It came forth, it formed ears,
it was hard, it was good.
Its tassels bent, it was full,
he had his household there in Tai.

He passed us down these wondrous grains:
our black millets, of one and two kernels,
Millets whose leaves sprout red or white,
he spread the whole land with black millet,
And reaped it and counted the acres,
spread it with millet sprouting red or white,
hefted on shoulders, loaded on backs,
he took it home and began this rite.

And how goes this rite we have?—
at times we hull, at times we scoop,
at times we winnow, at times we stomp,
we hear it slosh as we wash it,
we hear it puff as we steam it.
Then we reckon, then we consider,
take artemisia, offer fat.

We take a ram for the flaying,
then we roast it, then we sear it,
to rouse up the following year.

We heap the wooden trenchers full,
wooden trenchers, earthenware platters.
And as the scent first rises
the high god is peaceful and glad.
This great odor is good indeed,
for Lord Millet began the rite,
and hopefully free from failing or fault,
it has lasted until now.

The following is the much later account of Lord Millet in the "Chronicles of Zhou," from the *Historical Records* of Si-ma Qian (ca. 145–ca. 85 B.C.). The *Historical Records* is the most important historical work treating ancient and early Han China. Si-ma Qian's version is essentially a prose summary providing answers to large questions left by the poem. Note how Si-ma Qian integrates Lord Millet into the legendary political structure of the times of the Sage-Kings; particularly significant is Lord Millet's transformation from demigod to political appointee. As the empire was to be brought to political unity in the Western Han, one of the functions of the Han historian was to bring the diverse fragments of myth, legend, and early history into a single unified story.

Historical Records, "Chronicles of Zhou"

Lord Millet (Hou Ji) of Zhou had the given name Qi, "the Castoff." His mother was the daughter of the ruler of Tai and was named Jiang "Yuan" ["first parent"]. Jiang was the principal consort of Emperor Gao. Jiang Yuan went forth into the wilderness and saw the print of a huge man. Her heart was filled with delight and she wanted to step in it. When she stepped in it, her body stirred like one pregnant. After her term, she bore a son. She thought of him as ill-omened and cast him away into a narrow lane, but the horses and cattle that passed by stood out of his way and did not step on him. She moved him and put him in the forest, but he encountered many people in the forest. She carried him elsewhere and cast him on the ice of a ditch, but birds in flight came to cover him with their wings. Then Jiang Yuan thought of him as a god, took him back, and raised him. Since she had first wished to cast him off, she named him Qi, the Castoff.

When Qi was still a boy, he had fully developed aims like those of an older person. In his games he was fond of planting hemp and beans, and his hemp and beans grew very well. When he grew up, he liked farming and working the soil; he could observe what crop the land was most suited to, and he planted and reaped the most suitable grains there. All the folk followed his example. Emperor Yao heard about him and raised Qi to be the

Master of Farming. He achieved much, and all the world had benefit from him.

Classic of Poetry CCL "Liu the Duke"

Duke Liu the Steadfast
neither bided nor enjoyed:
now marking plots and boundary lines,
now gathering, now storing;
now wrapping up the meal,
in pouches and in sacks;
and glorious by all amassed,
he brought forth bows and bolts,
shield and pike, ax and hatchet,
and then began the march.

Duke Liu the Steadfast
went and paused upon that plain:
teeming it was and bountiful,
yielding it was, word was spread,
nor were there long cries of woe;
he climbed and was upon the hill,
again came down upon the plain.
What was wrapped around him then?—
it was jade and jasper
studding the sheath of the Dirk.[1]

Duke Liu the Steadfast
went off to the hundred springs,
and scanned this vast plain.
Then he climbed the southern hill-spine,
beheld there the great citadel.
In the wilds around the citadel
there he stayed ever,
there he dwelt ever;
there he spoke ever,
there he talked with others ever.

Duke Liu the Steadfast
settled in the citadel;
with grave and reverent motion
proffered mat and proffered armrest;
he mounted the mat, he then reposed.
He had his bands next go
and seize a pig within the pen.

---

[1]The "Dirk" seems to have been one of the insignias of chieftainship.

He had wine poured in jugs of gourd,
they fed him, they gave him drink,
they made him lord, founder of the line.

Duke Liu the Steadfast
made his land vast and made it long,
he marked the shadows, then the hill lines,
he surveyed shadowed and sunlit slopes.
He observed where the springs flowed,
and his army went in three files.
He measured the bogs and plains,
he assessed the fields for his stores.
He measured slopes that stood to the evening sun,
his abode in Bin was verily grand.

Duke Liu the Steadfast
built the lodgings in Bin,
made a fording place to cross the Wei,
there took whetstones and hammerstones.
Foundations built, he marked off fields,
then we grew many, then we thrived.
On both sides of the Huang Creek,
and upstream to the Guo Creek.
We settled there and we grew teeming,
all the way to the bend of the Rui.

Insofar as these poems are narratives, it is worth noting what constitutes a satisfying conclusion. Rather than the completion of a conquest or the achievement of a deed, these poems often end with spreading, extension, and continuity. That is, the narratives avoid conclusion; they point instead to continuation.

Classic of Poetry CCXXXVII "Spreading"

Melons spreading, large and small,
when first the folk were born.
From Du he fared to Qi,
our duke of old, Dan-fu.
They fashioned dwellings in pits and cliffs;
they did not yet have houses.

Our duke of old, Dan-fu,
that morning sped his horse.
He followed the edge of the western river
and came to beneath Mount Qi.
Then he joined the woman Jiang,
they came and shared a roof.

The plain of Zhou was fat and fair,
where thistle and buttercup tasted like honey.
There he started, there he reckoned,
there he pierced our tortoise shells.
"Stop," it was, and "Stand,"
in this place they built houses.

Then he rested, then he stopped,
then he went left, then he went right,
then he marked borders, then he marked bounds,
then extended, set out fields.
From west he fared to east,
and everywhere he took charge.

He called to his Master Builder,
he called to his Master of Workmen.
He had them set up houses,
and the plumblines hung straight.
They lashed planks and raised it,
made the Ancestral Temple well aligned.

One after another they took earth in hods,
in countless loads they measured it.
With thud upon thud they rammed it hard,
and with scraping sounds they pared it flat.
A hundred wall segments rose together,
and drowned out the sounds of the drums.

Then they set up the outermost gate,
and the outermost gate loomed high.
Then they set up the central gate,
and the central gate was stately.
Then they set up the Altar to Earth,
where his war hosts set forth.

Yet he did not abate his ire,
nor did his repute subside.
The oaks were uprooted,
and roads were cleared through.
The Kun-yi tribes flew in panic,
how we harried them to gasping!

Yu and Rui gave warrants for peace,
King Wen laid their beasts on his altars.
He had all those both far and near,
he had those before and behind him,
He had those who would rush to his bidding,
he had those who would fend off slights.

The description of building the rammed-earth walls of the Zhou capital in "Spreading" is one of the more remarkable moments in early literature, distinguishing the Chinese tradition from others. The monumental labor that went into constructing the Pyramids, the walls of Babylon, the architectural monuments of Greece and Rome, or the castles of the Middle Ages were generally not subjects of the literature of those worlds, and the difficulties involved are only touched on fragmentarily in documents. But this poem, one of the most important public poetic texts of the Zhou Kingdom, is a celebration of collective endeavor.

Even though the final stanzas of "Spreading" are gleefully violent, Dan-fu was transformed into the exemplary pacifist. The following parable, telling of Dan-fu's migration from Bin, comes from some time between the fourth and second century B.C. It is taken from:

The *Zhuang-zi,* "Renouncing Kingship"

Dan-fu the great King was dwelling in Bin when the Di tribes attacked. He offered them tribute of skins and cloth, but they wouldn't accept it; then he offered tribute of dogs and horses, but they wouldn't accept it; he offered them pearls and jade, but they still wouldn't accept: for what they wanted was his land. Then Dan-fu the great king said: I could not bear to dwell among elder brothers whose younger brothers I had sent to death, or to dwell among fathers whose sons I had sent to death. You my people endeavor to continue living here—what's the difference between being my subject and being a subject of the Di? Besides, I have heard it said that one should not harm those one would nurture by the very means of their nurture. And then he left, leaning on his staff. His people all followed him in a long line, and a new state was established below Mount Qi.

"The Greater Brightness" begins with an account of the royal Zhou marriages that produced Kings Wen and Wu, who, following Heaven's plan, overthrew the Yin-Shang Dynasty. The word "Power" *(De)* is one of the most important terms in Zhou political thought and later in Confucian ethics. *De* literally means "attainment," a kind of charisma (and perhaps even sexual potency and fertility) amassed by doing good and proper works. With enough Power, the people stay loyal and enemies submit. In its later Confucian transformation, *De* became "virtue."

Classic of Poetry CCXXXVI "The Greater Brightness"

The brightness is below,
fierce splendor is on high.
Hard to trust in Heaven,
the kingship is not easy.
Yin's heir stood in Heaven's place,
yet it made him lose his lands around.

From Zhi the second daughter, Ren,
went from the land of Yin and Shang.

She came to marry into Zhou,
in its great city, foreign bride.
Together then with Ji the King
they did that work of Power.
And Great Ren became with child
and gave birth to our King Wen.

This King Wen of ours,
his prudent heart was well ordered.
He shone in serving the high god,
and thus enjoyed much fortune.
Unswerving in the Power he had,
he held all the domains around.

Heaven scanned the land below,
its charge was laid upon him.
In the first doing of King Wen
Heaven made a mate for him.
It was on the Xia's north shore,
there on the banks of the Wei,
King Wen found the woman fair,
daughter of a mighty land.

This daughter of a mighty land
was seen like Heaven's little sister.
He fixed by good custom a lucky time,
himself he welcomed her at the Wei.
He fashioned boats into a bridge,
with light great and glorious.

There was a charge from Heaven,
a charge for Wen the King,
In Zhou, in its great city,
this next queen, who was of Shen.
This eldest daughter did the work,
and steadfast, bore King Wu.
"I who preserve you, charge you
to join and smite the great Shang."

There, the hosts of Yin and Shang,
their standards like a forest.
An oath was made on the Pasture Ground,
"It is we who are in the ascendant.
The high god looks upon you,
be there no treachery in your hearts."

The Pasture Ground stretched on and on,
with sandalwood chariots glorious.
The teams of bays well muscled,

19

War Chief was our Shang-fu.
He was the falcon taking wing,
he showed the way for Wu the King.
They fell on great Shang and smote them,
the morning they gathered was clear and bright.

A number of the poems in the *Classic of Poetry* can best be described as the "propaganda of Zhou," celebrating the dynasty's foundation by right of receiving Heaven's Charge. The following poem, "Overbearing," is presented as the address of King Wen to the last ruler of the Yin-Shang Dynasty. Virtually all Chinese critics have taken this to be a covert denunciation of King Li of Zhou (ruled 878–842 B.C.), who is assumed to be the high god referred to in the poem. However, there is nothing in the poem to support such an interpretation, which would have first appeared more than six hundred years after the putative date of composition.

Classic of Poetry CCLV "Overbearing"

Overbearing is the high god,
he gives his rules to folk below.
Perilous, the high god's power,
many the rules within his Charge.
Heaven bore the teeming folk,
his Charge cannot be trusted.
All men begin well,
but few can keep it to the end.

King Wen said, Woe!
Woe upon you, Yin and Shang!
You have been the harsh oppressor,
you have been grasping and crushing.
You have been in the places of power,
you have held the functions.
Heaven sent recklessness down in you,
and you rise by acts of force.

King Wen said, Woe!
Woe upon you, Yin and Shang!
Cling to right and seemliness—
much hate comes back from harshness.
Loose words are given as answers,
plunder and pillage are in the center.
They rise up, they speak curses,
Without ceasing, without close.

King Wen said, Woe!
Woe upon you, Yin and Shang!
You have roared in the heartland,
you draw wrath as your Power.

You shed no light from your Power,
so none stand at your back or side.
Your Power sheds no light,
so none will stand with you and serve.

King Wen said, Woe!
Woe upon you, Yin and Shang!
Heaven does not swill you with wine,
you chase and choose things not right.
You have overstepped in your behavior,
unable to tell darkness from the light.
You howl and you shout,
and would have daylight be as night.

King Wen said, Woe!
Woe upon you, Yin and Shang!
You are like locusts, like grasshoppers,
like froth, like the soup that simmers.
Things great and small draw to destruction,
you men still follow this way.
You have domineered in the heartland,
and it spreads all the way to Gui-fang.

King Wen said, Woe!
Woe upon you, Yin and Shang!
Not the high god who is not good—
Yin does not act as it did of old.
And though it has no wise old men,
still it has its sanctions and codes.
Never have you heeded these,
and the Great Charge is overthrown.

King Wen said, Woe!
Woe upon you, Yin and Shang!
There is a saying among men:
When a tree falls and is torn from earth,
there is yet no harm to boughs and leaves—
the roots meet ruin first.
Yin's mirror lies not far away,
it is there in the reigns of the lords of Xia.

As with the ritual hymns, the poetry of royal Zhou often gave actions legitimacy and meaning by representing them in a way that reflected Zhou political ideology. Exultation in warfare and conquest was subordinated to a celebration of bringing order and peace to the land and to the king's heart. As Heaven delegated authority to the Zhou royal house, so the Zhou kings might delegate legitimate authority to their feudal lords, whose conquests were thus sanctioned. There is a group of narratives of military campaigns believed to date from the time of King Xuan (ruled 827–782 B.C.), whose reign saw a resurgence of Zhou royal power. The following ballad, telling of a campaign against the tribes of Huai River region, seems to have been written to celebrate the casting of a ceremonial vessel for the Duke of Shao, who is reminded of his ancestor and his family's historical allegiance to the house of Zhou.

Classic of Poetry CCLXII "Yangzi and Han"

Yangzi and Han go rolling on,
our warriors go flooding.
We do not rest, do not roam free,
we go to assail the Huai tribes.
We have brought our chariots forth,
we have lifted our falcon standards.
We do not rest, we take no ease,
we go to bring hurt to the Huai tribes.

Yangzi and Han sweep in torrents,
our warriors seethe and surge.
We bring order to the lands around
and declare the deed done to the king.
The lands all around are made peaceful,
the king's domain nigh settled.
Now there is no conflict,
and the king's heart may be at ease.

It was by the shores of Yangzi and Han,
the king gave a charge to Hu of Shao:
"Open the lands that lie around,
tax the lands within our bounds.
Neither injure nor oppress
to the farthest reach of the king's domain.
Go make boundaries, mark out fields
all the way to the southern seas."

The king gave a charge to Hu of Shao,
"Go everywhere, go make this known.
When Wen and Wu received the Charge,
a Duke of Shao was their support.
Say not: I am but a child—
you, Duke of Shao, are successor.
You persevered in these great works,
whereby I grant you blessings.

"On you I bestow the *gui* ladle,
one urn of black millet beer with spice.
With these inform your cultured Forebears
that I confer on you earth and field.
Here in Zhou you receive a charge
that derives from the charge to Ancestor Shao."

Hu bowed and touched his head to the ground:
"Live thousands of years, Heaven's Son!"

Hu bowed and touched his head to Earth,
he answered acclaiming the king's goodness.
He made the holy vessel of Shao's Duke—
thousands of years to Heaven's Son.
The Son of Heaven sheds shining light,
his fine renown will never end.
He spreads his Power gained by cultured works,
attunes the domains all around.

The preceding poems come from the section in the *Classic of Poetry* known as the "Great Odes" *(Da-ya)*, which by and large represents the public poetry of the dynasty. The section known as the "Lesser Odes" *(Xiao-ya)* also contains poems on military campaigns, but the way in which these poems treat such campaigns shows interesting differences from the highly political representation of military action in the "Great Odes." The speaker here is no longer focused on the king; he speaks for the officers and soldiers of the Zhou.

Among their adversaries, the non-Chinese Xian-yun were one of the Zhou's greatest threats. "Bringing Forth the Chariots" treats a royal expedition whose purpose is both to harry the Xian-yun and to build fortifications in the North, which would be the precursor of the Great Wall.

Classic of Poetry CLXVIII "Bringing Forth the Chariots"

We bring our chariots forth,
down upon the meadows.
From the Son of Heaven's place
we have been bidden to come.
The drivers have been summoned,
we have bidden them to load.
The king's work has great troubles,
they press upon us hard.

We bring our chariots forth,
upon the plain beyond the walls.
Raise high the Snake-and-Tortoise,
set the oxtail standards.
The Eagle and Snake-and-Tortoise—
see how they flap in the wind.
Our worried hearts are restless,
the drivers are harried and drawn.

The king commanded Nan-zhong,
"Go, build walls in Fang."
The chariots go surging forth,
the Snake-and-Tortoise and Dragon shine.

The Son of Heaven commanded us,
"Go, build walls in the northland."
Nan-zhong strikes terror,
slayer of the Xian-yun.

Long ago we marched away,
with millet in full flower.
Back we come today,
snow is falling in the mire.
The king's work has great troubles,
no chance to sprawl or sit.
Of course we long to go home,
but we dread what is written.[2]

Insects abuzz in the grasses,
katydids hopping about.
Before we saw our lord,
our worried hearts knew no ease.
Now that we have seen our lord,
our hearts begin to calm.
Nan-zhong strikes terror,
he who smites the Western Rong.

More slowly pass the days of spring,
heath and tree grow full and green.
Starlings sing in choruses,
tarragon is picked in throngs.
With some held for question and captured bands,
we now turn back and go home.
Nan-zhong strikes terror,
the Xian-yun are brought low.

Ancient Zhou warfare was a ceremonial activity, concluded in autumn (the seventh to ninth months). The Xian-yun raiders seem to have violated custom, striking in late summer, in the sixth month. The following poem, from the "Lesser Odes," celebrates another campaign.

Classic of Poetry CLXXVII "Sixth Month"

In the sixth month, all was in tumult,
war chariots were made ready.
The four-stallion teams were brawny,
our kits and outfits were loaded.
The Xian-yun came to raze widely,

[2]For all the soldiers' glee in Nan-zhong's military prowess, they are kept in the expedition by conscription lists that will result in punishment for deserters.

by this we were hardpressed.
The king sent forth his hosts,
to bring order to the king's domain.

Matched beasts, four black steeds,
well trained to the standard.
Now in this sixth month
our outfitting was done.
And when our outfitting was done,
we went our thirty leagues.
The king sent forth his hosts
to serve the Son of Heaven.

Four stallions, tall and broad,
stout and with great skulls.
They went to smite the Xian-yun
and show forth glorious deeds.
With strictness and with order,
we share this work of war.
We share this work of war
to settle the king's domain.

The Xian-yun did not reckon,
they stayed drawn up in Jiao and Hu.
They raided Hao and Fang
and reached the Jing's north shore.
Our woven designs, our bird devices,
our swallow-tail pennons gleaming.
Then ten of our great war wagons
went forth first to begin the advance.

Steady were the war chariots,
as if bearing down and looming high.
Four stallions moving in line,
moving in line well trained.
We went and smote the Xian-yun,
all the way to Great Plain.
Ji-fu, warlike and courteous,
was the model for all the lands.

Ji-fu feasts and makes merry,
much bounty he has received.
Back we came from Hao,
our journey far and long.
With drink he serves all the friends,
turtle roast and ground carp.
Who else was there present?
Nan-zhong, loyal to parent and friend.

Human Sacrifice: Making Exchanges

In the ceremonial and dynastic poems of the *Classic of Poetry,* naming a thing or action guaranteed its function within a structure of ritual exchange and order. The words for the rite stated what was received, what was given, the intentions or state of mind of those making the offering, and the correctness and continuity of the procedures. On the political level, poems work in a similar way, authorizing the delegation of power and asserting the correctness and continuity of the system.

Words can also declare more problematic exchanges and substitutions. This is not a world of obvious ritual and political order but one of mysterious series of correspondences revealed in words. In the following poem, every time the yellow bird perches on the branch of a different plant, a different member of the Zi-ju clan is named to accompany his lord in death. No causal relation is asserted, but some correspondence is implicit. In this poem, Heaven, who "slays our best men," is as dangerous as in the preceding poems, but it is less comprehensible. And the speaker in vain proposes a more open exchange, a ransom. The date is 620 B.C.

Classic of Poetry CXXXI "Yellow Bird"

> *Jiao* cries the yellow bird,
> it stops upon the briar.
> Who goes with Lord Mu?
> Yan-xi of the Zi-ju.
> And this man Yan-xi
> was the finest of a hundred,
> but standing by the pit
> he trembled in his dread.
> You Gray One, Heaven,
> you slay our best men.
> If this one could be ransomed,
> for his life, a hundred.
>
> *Jiao* cries the yellow bird,
> it stops upon the mulberry.
> Who goes with Lord Mu?
> Zhong-hang of the Zi-ju.
> And this man Zhong-hang
> could hold against a hundred,
> but standing by the pit
> he trembled in his dread.
> You Gray One, Heaven,
> you slay our best men.
> If this one could be ransomed,
> for his life, a hundred.
>
> *Jiao* cries the yellow bird,
> it stops upon the thorn.

Who goes with Lord Mu?
Qian-hu of the Zi-ju.
And this man Qian-hu
could ward against a hundred,
but standing by the pit
he trembled in his dread.
You Gray One, Heaven,
you slay our best men.
If this one could be ransomed,
for his life, a hundred.

Although the folk of Qin here lament the death of the three members of the Zi-ju clan, they accept it as a ritual necessity, something demanded by the "Gray One, Heaven." As such, this song is a remarkable document from an archaic world in which retainers were killed and buried with their lord.

The following account of the composition of "Yellow Bird" comes from *The Zuo Tradition,* the annalistic history composed in the late fifth or fourth century B.C. In this sightly later period it is not mysterious Heaven that is responsible, but human ethical decision.

The Zuo Tradition, an entry for the 6th year of Duke Wen (620 B.C.)

Qin's earl Ren-hao [Duke Mu] died. Three men of the Zi-ju clan—Yan-xi, Zhong-hang, and Qian-hu—were sent to die with their lord. All three were the best men of Qin. Men of the domain mourned for them and composed "Yellow Bird" on their behalf. A good man said, "It was most fitting that Mu of Qin did not become master of the covenant. When he died, he forsook his folk. When former kings passed from the world, they left a legacy of rules; they would hardly have stolen away its worthiest men."

Eventually substitutions could be made: clay figurines of men were exchanged for real liegemen accompanying their lord to the grave. Or a man bent on revenge, blocked from fulfilling his goal, could be satisfied by stabbing his victim's cloak, saying, "Thus I kill you and take revenge." Words become essential when such substitutions and exchanges take place; they may declare one thing as equivalent to another or protest improper exchanges.

The Zuo Tradition, an entry for the 19th year of Duke Xi (640 B.C.)

That summer the Duke of Song bade Duke Wen of Zhu to use the Lord of Zeng for sacrifice on the banks of the river Sui. He hoped in this way to win the adherence of the eastern tribesmen. His War Chief Zi-yu said, "In olden times the six domestic animals were not substituted for one another in sacrificial use; for small events they did not use large sacrificial animals—much less would they dare use a man! Sacrifices are made *for* men. The people are hosts for the god. And if you use a man in a sacrifice, who will eat it? Duke Huan of Qi preserved three domains from ruin and in that way won the adherence of the great nobility. Even so there are men of virtue who say that even his Power was slight. Now in one gathering you have treated brutally the lords of two domains; and beyond that, you have used one for sacrifice to a vile demon, the god of the river Sui. If you want to be overlord now, you will have a hard time of it. You will be lucky if you die!"

In the story above, the human being may be treated like an animal, a "thing" in the exchange system. Reversing the process, one might look on an animal with the sympathy usually reserved for fellow humans. The first case disqualified the man who conducted such sacrifice from becoming overlord of the domains; the second case would, we assume, ensure his qualifications.

Some three centuries after the date of *The Zuo Tradition's* account of the Duke of Song's human sacrifice, we have a famous transformation of this question of sacrificial exchange in the *Mencius,* the dialogues and sayings of the Confucian philosopher Meng-zi (latinized, "Mencius"). The great importance attached to sympathy in this dialogue is a measure of the changes in Confucian values from archaic ritualism to a humanistic ethics of moral feelings. Like the young men of the Zi-ju clan, standing beside the gravepit of Lord Mu, here the victim also trembles—and in this case is ransomed.

from *Mencius* I A, 7 (4th century B.C.)

King Xuan of Qi said, "May someone like myself really be the protector of the people?"

Mencius answered, "You may."

The king, "How do you know that I may?"

Mencius, "I heard from Hu He that once when Your Majesty was seated in the great hall, someone was pulling a bullock along across the other end of the hall. When Your Majesty saw it, you asked, 'Where is that bullock going?' And the answer was that it was being taken to be a blood sacrifice to anoint a newly cast bell. And Your Majesty said, 'Let it go free. I cannot bear the look of terror in it—like someone going innocent to the execution ground.' To this came the reply, 'Then shall we waive the blood sacrifice to anoint the bell?' And Your Majesty said, 'How can we waive the sacrifice? Use a sheep in its place.' I am not certain whether this happened."

The king, "It did."

Mencius, "A heart such as this is enough to bring the high kingship. All the common folk may have thought Your Majesty was being stingy, but I know quite well that it was because Your Majesty could not bear the sight."

The king, "This is so. And truly it was as you said with the common folk—but however small the realm of Qi be, I am not going to be stingy about one bullock.[3] It was because I could not bear the look of terror in it, like someone going innocent to the execution ground. It was for that reason I had a sheep used in its place."

Mencius, "Your Majesty should not think it strange that the common folk considered this as stinginess on your part. Since you used a small thing in place of a large one, how could they understand? If Your Majesty was touched by sadness at something going innocent to the execution ground, on what grounds could a distinction be made between a bullock and a sheep?"

The king laughed. "What really was in my mind then? It is not that I am stingy with possessions, and yet I did have a sheep used in its place. It's quite right that the common folk claim I was being stingy."

Mencius, "There is no cause to feel hurt. This was, in fact, the way of a man who feels sympathy. You saw the bullock—you did not see the sheep. A good man feels the following way about animals: when he has seen them alive, he cannot bear to see their death; when he has heard the sounds they make, he cannot bear to eat their flesh. This is the reason a good man stays far from the kitchen."

The king was delighted. "The *Classic of Poetry* (CXCVIII) has the lines:

The heart may be another's,
but I can take its measure.

This applies to you, sir. I was the one who did it, but when I turned to follow the process, I couldn't grasp what was in my own heart. But now that you have put it into words, there are the stirrings of such a feeling in my heart. . . ."

---

[3]"Stinginess" is the contextual translation of *ai,* to "begrudge," to "cling to something," a word for "love."

先
秦
西
漢

The *Classic of Poetry:* "Airs"

To different ages and different readers the *Classic of Poetry* has represented what they felt a "classic of poetry" should be. For some Confucian interpreters, the collection was the embodiment of the fate of the Zhou polity, manifested through the mouths of its people. In this view, the poems were judiciously chosen and arranged by Confucius to show ethical values at work in political and social history. To other Confucian interpreters, it represented the full range of natural human feeling and some permanent perfection of feeling's expression.

The poems in this section are drawn primarily from the first part of the *Classic of Poetry*, known as the "Airs" *(Feng)* or the "Airs of the Domains" *(Guo-feng)*. The "Airs" constitute more than half of the over three hundred poems that make up the *Classic of Poetry*, and they are probably among the latest poems to be added to the repertoire, which seems to have reached something like its present form around 600 B.C.

The "Airs" are grouped under fifteen regions, which represent many but not all of the feudal domains of the early Zhou monarchy. In some premodern and some modern interpretations influenced by anthropology, the "Airs" have been taken to represent folk poetry as the authentic voice of the common people, collected and transformed by musicians of the regional courts. More recently the argument has been made that the "Airs" do not and never did represent true folk poetry, but the poetry of the Zhou feudal courts. Both points of view are correct. Some of the "Airs" were clearly composed for court occasions, such as diplomatic weddings, while others make straightforward sense only when accepting their provenance in the peasantry. It is best then to see the "Airs" as representing regional song traditions, with lyrics drawn from diverse sources and transformed by the song traditions of the Zhou feudal courts.

Classic of Poetry I   "Fishhawk"

The fishhawks sing *gwan gwan*
on sandbars of the stream.
Gentle maiden, pure and fair,
fit pair for a prince.

Watercress grows here and there,
right and left we gather it.
Gentle maiden, pure and fair,
wanted waking and asleep.

Wanting, sought her, had her not,
waking, sleeping, thought of her,
on and on he thought of her,
he tossed from one side to another.

Watercress grows here and there,
right and left we pull it.
Gentle maiden, pure and fair,
with harps we bring her company.

Watercress grows here and there,
right and left we pick it out.
Gentle maiden, pure and fair,
with bells and drums do her delight.

Confucius (ca. 552–479 B.C.) made special comment on "Fishhawk" in his collected sayings, the *Analects* (III.20): "He said, 'Fishhawk' is delight without wantonness, sadness without hurtful pain."

Throughout most of the imperial period, Confucius was credited with having edited the *Classic of Poetry*. Since Confucius' arrangement of the anthology was supposed to have been purposeful, "Fishhawk," as the first poem in the collection, was made to bear a special interpretive weight. According to the traditional Confucian interpretation known as the "Mao commentary," the poem represented the "virtuous attainment" of the Queen Consort of King Wen of Zhou, who "delighted that pure and fair maidens had been found to be mated with the prince [i.e., King Wen]." Thus it has been read as a poem expressing an absence of jealousy, which in turn showed the perfect harmony of the royal household. In this way the poem was supposed to initiate King Wen's process of civilizing the land, beginning with the most intimate and close of relationships, then gradually extending his influence outward.

Classic of Poetry IX "The Han So Wide"

Tall are trees in the south country,
they give no shade to rest in.
By the Han the girls roam free,
but no man can pursue them.
So wide, the Han,
I can't wade over;
the river too long
to go by raft.

Heaps of kindling pile high;
cut away the gorse.
If only she would be my bride,
I'd offer fodder for her horse.
So wide, the Han,
I can't wade over;

the river too long
to go by raft.

Heaps of kindling pile high;
cut away the dodder.
If only she would be my bride,
her colts would not lack fodder.
So wide, the Han,
I can't wade over;
the river too long
to go by raft.

Often the association between disparate images—here the clearing of brush and the gathering of kindling—are linked by fortuitous rhymes with the man's wish to marry a certain woman.

Several early interpretations of this poem link the first stanza with the story of the two goddesses of the Han River who were encountered by one Zheng Jiao-fu. Fragments of this legend, in differing versions, appear in a variety of early sources. In some versions, the nymphs wore egg-sized pearls hanging from their sashes. Jiao-fu asked them for their pendants as a sign of promising their love for him. They untied the pendants and gave them to him. But after taking several steps to pick up the pendants, Jiao-fu found that they had disappeared; on turning around, he found that the goddesses too had disappeared. This is just one of many legends in which a mortal man encounters a goddess who, either with or without having sexual relations with him, finally proves elusive. If we take this poem as referring to the same river nymphs that Zheng Jiao-fu met, we should probably translate the third line as: "There are maidens swimming in the Han." The phrase *you-nü* can mean either "girls that swim" or "girls roaming free." "Girls roaming free" came to have strong associations of promiscuity, in contrast to *chu-nü,* "girls who stay home," later a term for virgins.

Through the course of the Eastern Han during the first and second centuries A.D., the so-called Mao commentary to the *Classic of Poetry* became dominant. The Mao commentary sought to explain all the Poems as part of the moral history of the Zhou Dynasty, and there was therefore no room in the commentary for recollections of sexual encounters with river nymphs, even though the poem makes the quest hopeless.

In the Mao explanation of this poem, the elusiveness of the maidens around the Han River is due to King Wen's ethical transformation of customs in the domains under his rule. The coy goddesses are transformed into prudent young ladies: "Thus far reached the breadth of Zhou's virtue. The true way of King Wen extended over the southern kingdoms, and such lovely civilizing force moved through the regions of the Yangzi and Han. No one thought of transgressing proper customs; if you sought such, you could not find them" (Mao, "Lesser Preface" to "The Han So Wide").[1]

---

[1]The Mao "Great Preface" treats the theory of poetry in general; the "Lesser Prefaces" offer interpretations of all the individual poems in the *Classic of Poetry.*

Other Voices in the Tradition

Jiao-fu's amorous nymphs of the Han River appeared often in later poetry, as in this very cryptic poem by the third-century poet Ruan Ji, in which the legend, shifting from Jiao-fu to a forsaken woman, suggests general betrayal and loss. The "dangerous beauty" mentioned in Ruan Ji's poem is literally "one to make a city fall," as in the verses Li Yan-nian sings (see p. 215) about his sister to Emperor Wu of the Han:

> She glances once, a city falls;
> a kingdom falls when she glances again.

The honey-tongued orator Song Yu ascribed to his lovely neighbor the ability to "beguile [the city of] Xia-cai."

Ruan Ji (A.D. 210–263), Songs of My Cares II

Two maidens roamed by river's shore,
they freely moved, borne by the breeze.
Jiao-fu put their pendants in his robes;
they were tender, young and sweet of scent.
By passion his heart was swept away—
he would never forget in a thousand years.
Such dangerous beauty beguiled Xia-cai;
fair features knotted his heart within.
Strong feelings, roused, brought troubled thoughts,
in orchid rooms were planted oblivion's blooms.
For whom now is her oiling and washing done?—
wish for rain reproaches the morning sun.
How can a bond strong as metal and stone
change in only a day to parting's pain?

Ruan Ji's strangely intense poem in turn makes a fine contrast with a famous poem by the Tang writer Meng Hao-ran, who, early in the eighth century, visited the supposed site of Jiao-fu's encounter.

Meng Hao-ran (ca. 690–ca. 740), Written at Wan Mountain Pool

I sat on a boulder, let my fishing line hang,
the water was clear, my mind also calm.

Fish swam along under trees by the pool,
and gibbons hung among vines on the isles.

Once roaming girls untied their pendants,
on this very mountain, so legend says.

He pursued them, he didn't get them—
moving in moonlight, I turn back with a rowing song.

Correspondences

Correspondences are an essential part of the *Classic of Poetry*. The most obvious correspondences are the connections between words created by rhyme, but the arbitrary linkages of sound often led to the assumption of deeper linkages. Many poems in the *Classic* are constructed of stanzas that have one set of alternations in the natural world in the first part of each stanza, with a parallel series of alternations in the human world occupying the last part of each stanza.

Traditional Chinese poetic theory made a clear distinction between cases in which there was an overt analogy between the natural image and the human condition, and those cases in which the natural image was more mysteriously associated with the human situation. The former was called "comparison" *(bi)*, and the latter was called a "stirring" or an "affective image" *(xing)*. In other poems, the alternations involve some human activity in the first part of the stanza and a feeling or thought in the second part of the stanza. But whether the first part of the stanza is a natural image or a human activity, the pattern always suggests a correspondence between seemingly unrelated things.

Classic of Poetry VI "Peach Tree Soft and Tender"

Peach tree soft and tender,
how your blossoms glow!
The bride is going to her home,
she well befits this house.

Peach tree soft and tender,
plump, the ripening fruit.
The bride is going to her home,
she well befits this house.

Peach tree soft and tender,
its leaves spread thick and full.
The bride is going to her home,
she well befits these folk.

Classic of Poetry X "Bluffs of the Ru"

All along the bluffs of the Ru
I hack the boughs and branches.
Until the time I see my prince,
I crave him like dawn hunger.

All along the bluffs of the Ru,
I hack the branches and boughs.
Once I have seen my prince,
he will not forsake me afar.

Tail of bream, flushed with red;
the royal house seems aflame;
but even though it seems aflame,
my father and mother are close by.

Sometimes, as in the poem above and in the one that follows, the last stanza shifts
to a more cryptic image, which has an uncertain relation to the theme established
in the opening stanzas.

Classic of Poetry XLI "North Wind"

Chilly is the north wind,
heavy falls the snow;
if you care and love me,
take my hand, we'll go.
Don't be shy, don't be slow—
we must leave now!

Icy is the north wind,
thickly falls the snow;
if you care and love me,
take my hand, come away.
Don't be shy, don't be slow—
we must leave now!

No red but the fox,
no black but the crow;
if you care and love me,
take my hand, share my cart.
Don't be shy, don't be slow—
we must leave now!

Classic of Poetry XII "Magpie's Nest"

O the magpie has its nest,
but the dove does take it as her own.
The bride is going to her home,
a hundred coaches greet her.

O the magpie has its nest,
but 'tis the dove that holds it.
The bride is going to her home,
the hundred coaches join her.

O the magpie has its nest,
but 'tis the dove that fills it.

The bride is going to her home,
a hundred coaches in her train.

The bird translated as a dove is a *jiu*, a term used for several distinct kinds of birds. Commentators believe that this *jiu* was a species that left its eggs in the nests of other birds, who unknowingly hatched and fostered them. This, however, is hard to reconcile with the dove itself occupying the magpie's nest, and the strange analogy to a bride going to her new home.

Classic of Poetry XX "Plums Are Falling"

Plums are falling,
seven are the fruits;
many men want me,
let me have a fine one.

Plums are falling,
three are the fruits;
many men want me,
let me have a steady one.

Plums are falling,
catch them in the basket;
many men want me,
let me be bride of one.

Classic of Poetry XXIII "Dead Roe Deer"

A roe deer dead in the meadow,
all wrapped in white rushes.
The maiden's heart was filled with spring;
a gentleman led her astray.

Undergrowth in forest,
dead deer in the meadow,
all wound with white rushes,
a maiden white as marble.

Softly now, and gently, gently,
do not touch my apron, sir,
and don't set the cur to barking.

Classic of Poetry XXX "First the Winds"

First the wind, then the storm,
you look on me and laugh,
Scorn and gibes and mockery,
till my heart aches inside.

First the wind, then blowing dust,
would you be kind and come?
For if you do not visit me,
longing lasts on and on.

First the wind, then dark skies,
dark skies come at any time.
I lie awake and cannot sleep,
I am frantic from yearning.

So dark now are the shadows,
and the thunder roars.
I lie awake and cannot sleep,
my heart is filled with yearning.

Classic of Poetry XXXV "Valley Winds"

Valley winds are howling;
bringing darkness, bringing rain.
I did my best to share your heart;
unfair—this rage of yours!
Pull up turnips, pull up radish,
not just for the bottom half.
In no way did I fail my good name—
I was with you until death.

Slowly then I walk my road,
I fault you in my heart.
You did not go so far with me,
just rushed me to the door.
Who says bitterroot is harsh?—
it tastes as sweet as cane.
But peace to you and your new bride,
be as kin, be as brothers.

The Jing is muddied by the Wei,
but then it settles, crystal clear.
Peace to you and your new bride,
you take me as a paltry thing.
But stay away from my fish-weir,
and don't upset my gill-net.
I am someone you cannot stand—
why should I care for what will come?

When you come to where it's deep,
cross by raft, cross by boat;
and when you come to the shallows,
wade across or swim.

What we had, what we lacked,
I did my best to get it.
When great ills came to others,
on hands and knees I helped them.

A man who could not care for me
but took me as his foe;
you spurned my honor
as goods that can't be sold.
Once it was fear I felt, and dread,
tumbling together with you;
but then I gave birth and suck,
and now you think of me like venom.

Fine dried foods I have
that still may last through winter.
But peace to you and your new bride:
you had me to last through the hard times.
Seething you were and storming,
you gave me the harshest tasks.
You gave no heed to earlier times,
when once you came and loved me.

In "North Wind" (XLI), given earlier (p. 35), we can see the image of the storm as a background of trouble, against which the lovers or friends should go off together. In the two preceding poems we can see the image of the storm as a counterpart of the troubles between lovers or spouses. But what can we do with the image as it appears in the following poem, "Wind and Rain"?

Classic of Poetry XC "Wind and Rain"

Chill and dreary, wind and rain,
the roosters crow together.
Now that I have seen my prince,
how else but heart's sweet ease?

Gust and spatter, wind and rain,
the roosters' cries are shrill.
Now that I have seen my prince,
how else but heart's relief?

Somber sky, wind and rain,
the roosters keep on crowing.
Now that I have seen my prince,
what else but heart's delight?

Classic of Poetry XLVI "Thorn-Vine on the Wall"

Thorn-vine on the wall
cannot be brushed aside.
What went on behind the screen
are words not to be told;
it might still be told,
but the words are ugly ones.

Thorn-vine on the wall
cannot be pulled away.
What went on behind the screen
are words not to be made full known;
it might be made full known,
but the words would last long.

Thorn-vine on the wall
cannot be cleared in sheaves.
What went on behind the screen
are words not to be repeated;
it might be repeated,
but the words defile.

Classic of Poetry LI "Rainbow"

There is a rainbow in the east,
but no one dares to notice.
A girl goes to be a bride,
far from brothers, mother, father.

There is dawn mist in the west,
it will rain the morning long.
A girl goes to be a bride,
far from brothers, mother, father.

Such a girl, behaving so!
the ruin of her wedding;
not to be trusted at all:
she defied what was bidden.

Classic of Poetry LXIII "Fox"

Fox on the prowl, on the prowl,
there on the weir of the Qi.
Troubled is this heart—
that person has no skirt.

Fox on the prowl, on the prowl,
there where the Qi runs shallow.
Troubled is this heart—
That person has no sash.

Fox on the prowl, on the prowl,
there by the edge of the Qi.
Troubled is this heart—
That person wears nothing at all.

Classic of Poetry XCIV "Creepers on the Moorland"

Creepers on the moorland,
dripping with the dew.
There was a lovely woman
with clear and sparkling eyes.
It was by chance we met,
I had what I desired.

Creepers on the moorland,
soaking in the dew.
There was a lovely woman
eyes sparkling and clear.
It was by chance we met,
together went for cover.

In the poem above and in the one that follows, the natural image may be as much the setting of the situation in the second part of the stanza as a counterpart of human feeling.

Classic of Poetry CXL "Willows by the Eastern Gate"

Willows by the Eastern Gate,
their leaves so thick and close.
Dusk had been the time set,
and now the morning star glows bright.

Willows by the Eastern Gate,
their leaves so dense and full.
Dusk had been the time set,
and now the morning star shines pale.

Classic of Poetry CLXXXIV "Crane Cries Out"

The crane cries out in deepest marsh,
its voice is heard upon the moor.
The fish dive down to depths of pools

or remain beside the isles.
How the garden brings delight!—
planted all with sandalwood,
whose leaves are shed beneath it.
The stones of other mountains
can be taken for our whetstones.

The crane cries out in deepest marsh,
its voice is heard in the skies.
The fish remain beside the isles
or dive to the depths of pools.
How the garden brings delight!—
planted all with sandalwood,
and scrub brush grows beneath it.
The stones of other mountains
we can use to work our jade.

Classic of Poetry V "Grasshoppers' Wings"

Grasshoppers' wings
are teeming, teeming;
fit that your offspring
be thus abounding.

Grasshoppers' wings,
are swarming, swarming;
fit that your offspring
go on never-ending.

Grasshoppers' wings,
are thronging, thronging;
fit that your offspring
be fruitful and grow rife.

Many of the *Classic of Poetry* poems tell of the military campaigns of the Zhou, particularly against the less settled peoples who raided Zhou territory. Among these nomadic invaders, the Xian-yun mentioned in this next poem were the most troublesome.

Classic of Poetry CLXVII "Gather the Fiddleheads"

Gather them, gather them, fiddlehead ferns,
fiddleheads now start to grow.
We want to go home, to go home
for the year soon comes to a close.
We have no house, we have no home

all because of the Xian-yun.
No chance to sprawl, no chance to sit,
all because of the Xian-yun.

Gather them, gather them, fiddlehead ferns,
fiddleheads now turn tender.
We want to go home, to go home,
our hearts are filled with care.
Careworn hearts are seething,
we hunger and we thirst.
Our expedition is not done,
and no one brings us word from home.

Gather them, gather them, fiddlehead ferns,
fiddleheads now are firm.
We want to go home, to go home,
the year is in winter's first month.
No man is slack in the king's work,
no chance to sprawl and rest.
Our careworn hearts are tormented,
off we went and came not back.

What is this that blooms so fair?—
it is the wild plum flowering.
What is the great rig there?
it is the chariot of our prince.
His war chariot now is hitched,
his four stallions are sturdy.
We dare not bide in one set place,
each month we have three clashes.

Hitched are the four stallions,
his four stallions stalwart.
This is ridden by our prince,
on both sides screened by common troops.
His four stallions move evenly,
ivory bow-tips, shark-skin quivers.
We must be watchful every day,
we are hardpressed by the Xian-yun.

Long ago we marched away
with willows budding in a haze.
Back we come today,
in falling snow, sifting down.
Slowly we walk the way,
we hunger and we thirst.
Our hearts are wounded with pain,
no man knows how much we mourn.

In many cases the connection between the opening image and the human sentiment seems arbitrary, perhaps an accident of rhyme or play on an image that may have been associated with a tune or tune type.

Classic of Poetry IV "Trees with Bending Boughs"

In the south are trees with bending boughs,
and ivy binds them all about.
Mirth and joy be to our prince,
and may fair fortune fall on him.

In the south are trees with bending boughs,
and ivy runs wild over them.
Mirth and joy be to our prince,
and may fair fortune prosper him.

In the south are trees with bending boughs,
and ivy twines around them.
Mirth and joy be to our prince,
and may fair fortune bide with him.

Classic of Poetry VII "Rabbit Snare"

The rabbit snare has mesh so fine,
with a thump we knock its pegs in.
A staunch and fearless warrior,
our lord duke's shield and bastion.

The rabbit snare has mesh so fine,
we stretch it in the wagon track.
A staunch and fearless warrior,
well paired with our lord the duke.

The rabbit snare has mesh so fine,
we set it in the forest.
A staunch and fearless warrior,
heart and gut of our lord duke.

Classic of Poetry LIX "Bamboo Pole"

There is flex and play in bamboo poles,
you can fish with them in the Qi.
How can I help longing for you?
You are far, I cannot reach you.

Quan fountainhead is on the left,
the river Qi lies to the right.
A girl goes off to be a bride,
far from brothers, mother, father.

The river Qi lies to the right,
Quan fountainhead is on the left.
The gleam of her beguiling smile,
her pendants in rich panoply.

The river Qi keeps flowing on,
oars of cypress, boat of pine.
I hitch my team, go roaming
to ease my troubled mind.

Understanding and Misunderstanding: The Need to Explain

By the sixth century B.C., passages from the *Classic of Poetry* were being cited, applied to contemporary situations, and given figurative explanations. Acts of interpretation accompanying the poems became a constant feature of the Chinese tradition; and when the *Classic of Poetry* changed from a primarily oral repertoire to a written text, the text rarely appeared without a commentary.

Rather than taking this need to explain what the poems "really" mean as mere Traditionalist (Confucian) scholasticism, we might note how often the question of possible misunderstanding arises within the *Classic of Poetry* itself and how often the poems incorporate acts of explanation. This often takes the form: "It is not X; it is Y."

Classic of Poetry XLII "Gentle Girl"

A gentle girl and fair
awaits by the crook of the wall;
in shadows I don't see her;
I pace and scratch my hair.

A gentle girl and comely
gave me a scarlet pipe;
scarlet pipe that gleams—
in your beauty I find delight.

Then she brought me a reed from the pastures,
it was truly beautiful and rare.
Reed—the beauty is not yours—
you are but beauty's gift.

Classic of Poetry LXI "The River Is Broad"

Who claims that the river is wide?—
A single reed can cross it.
Who claims that Song is far away?—
I rise on my toes and gaze at it.

Who claims that the river is wide?—
It won't hold even a dinghy.
Who claims that Song is far away?—
I can be there ere morning is done.

Classic of Poetry LXIV "Quince"

She cast a quince to me,
a costly garnet I returned;
it was no equal return,
but by this love will last.

She cast a peach to me,
costly opal I returned;
it was no equal return,
but by this love will last.

She cast a plum to me,
a costly ruby I returned;
it was no equal return,
but by this love will last.

Interpretation is the ability to know what things and gestures "really" mean beneath surface appearances. In the following poem, "Millet Lush," the speaker imagines himself being observed by others. Those who know him understand the feelings that lead him to pace back and forth, while others see only the surface, a man loitering, and question his motives.

Classic of Poetry LXV "Millet Lush"

There the millet is lush,
There the grain is sprouting.
I walk with slow, slow steps,
My heart is shaken within.
Those who know me
Would say my heart is grieved;
Those who know me not
Would ask what I seek here.
Gray and everlasting Heaven—
What man is this?

There the millet is lush,
There the grain comes to ear.
I walk with slow, slow steps,
My heart as if drunk within.
Those who know me

Would say my heart is grieved;
Those who know me not
Would ask what I seek here.
Gray and everlasting Heaven—
What man is this?

There the millet is lush,
There the grain forms its seed.
I walk with slow, slow steps,
My heart as if choked within.
Those who know me
Would say my heart is grieved;
Those who know me not
Would ask what I seek here.
Gray and everlasting Heaven—
What man is this?

The speaker in the next poem repeatedly forbids her lover to come any closer and then, afraid that he might misunderstand, has to explain herself.

Classic of Poetry LXXVI "Zhong-zi, Please"

Zhong-zi, please
don't cross my village wall,
don't break the willows planted there.
It's not that I care so much for them,
but I dread my father and mother;
Zhong-zi may be in my thoughts,
but what my father and mother said—
that too may be held in dread.

Zhong-zi, please
don't cross my fence,
don't break the mulberries planted there.
It's not that I care so much for them,
but I dread my brothers;
Zhong-zi may be in my thoughts,
but what my brothers said—
that too may be held in dread.

Zhong-zi, please
don't cross into my garden,
don't break the sandalwood planted there.
It's not that I care so much for them,
but I dread others will talk much;
Zhong-zi may be in my thoughts,
but when people talk too much—
that too may be held in dread.

Classic of Poetry XXVI "Boat of Cypress"

That boat of cypress drifts along,
it drifts upon the stream.
Restless am I, I cannot sleep,
as though in torment and troubled.
Nor am I lacking wine
to ease my mind and let me roam.

This heart of mine is no mirror,
it cannot take in all.
Yes, I do have brothers,
but brothers will not be my stay.
I went and told them of my grief
and met only with their rage.

This heart of mine is no stone;
you cannot turn it where you will.
This heart of mine is no mat;
I cannot roll it up within.
I have behaved with dignity,
in this no man can fault me.

My heart is uneasy and restless,
I am reproached by little men.
Many are the woes I've met,
and taken slights more than a few.
I think on it in the quiet,
and waking pound my breast.

Oh Sun! and you Moon!
Why do you each grow dim in turn?
These troubles of the heart
are like unwashed clothes.
I think on it in the quiet,
I cannot spread wings to fly away.

The version of "Boat of Cypress" below has the same title and the same opening image, but developed in a very different way.

Classic of Poetry XLV "Boat of Cypress"

That boat of cypress drifts along,
it drifts along midstream.
The boy with hanging locks of hair
is really right for me.
I swear I'll have no other till I die.
Oh mother! oh Sky!
Won't you put faith in me?

That boat of cypress drifts along,
it drifts by river's edge
The boy with hanging locks of hair
is really the mate for me.
I swear no switching till I die.
Oh mother! oh Sky!
Won't you put faith in me?

Other Poems

Among the poems in the *Classic of Poetry* we seem to have fragments of lyrics for old festivals. The following piece is from the *Poems* of the domain of Zheng, whose music and perhaps lyrics were associated with dangerous wantonness. As in other poems in the *Classic,* the gift of a flower or fruit is an essential part of the courtship exchange.

Classic of Poetry XCV "Zhen and Wei"

O Zhen and Wei together,
swollen now they flow.
Men and maids together,
chrysanthemums in hand.
The maid says, "Have you looked?"
The man says, "I have gone."
"Let's go then look across the Wei,
it is truly a place for our pleasure."
Man and maid together
each frolicked with the other
and gave as gift the peony.

O Zhen and Wei together,
flowing deep and clear.
Men and maids together,
teeming everywhere.
The maid says, "Have you looked?"
The man says "I have gone."
"Let's go then look across the Wei,
it is truly a place for our pleasure."
Man and maid together
each will frolic with the other
and give as gift the peony.

Among these poems we find hints of ancient rites: the daughter of Zi-zhong, chosen as the sacred dancer, is followed by crowds as she gives out handfuls of pepper plants, used to make offerings to the gods.

Classic of Poetry CXXXVII "Eastern Gate's White Elms"

Eastern Gate's white elms,
thorn-oaks of Wan Hill.
The daughter of Zi-zhong
goes dancing under them.

On a fine morning we choose her,
on the meadow to the south.
She does not spin her hemp today;
she dances in the marketplace.

On a fine morning we go our way,
we wend away in crowds.
We see you as the Lavender,
who gives us pepper in handfuls.

Short lyrics like "Within Ten Acres" below, which seems to have been a mulberry-picking song (mulberry leaves were used to feed silkworms), strongly suggest that at least some of the "Airs" were of peasant origin. Pieces with lyrics as simple as this may have been included only for the sake of their music, now long lost.

Classic of Poetry CXI "Within Ten Acres"

Within ten acres of groves,
slowly the mulberry pickers go,
shall you and I go back together?

Beyond ten acres of groves
merrily mulberry pickers go,
and why don't we go off together?

In some cases the basic situation of the poem is far from clear, as in "Dew on the Way," which seems to involve litigation of some sort.

Classic of Poetry XVII "Dew on the Way"

The dews are soaking the way;
of course I would go in the dark before dawn,
but I dread so much dew on the way.

Who will say that the wren lacks beak?—
how did it peck through my roof?
And who will say that you lack kin?—
how did you bring me so quickly to court?
But though you brought me quickly to court,
your house and kin are not enough.

Who will say that a rat lacks teeth?
how did it pierce my wall?
And who will say that you lack kin?
how did you charge me so quickly?
But though you charge me quickly,
you still will not have your way.

Classic of Poetry XXXIV "Dry Leaves on the Gourd"

Leaves are dry on the gourd now,
the crossing is deep on the Ji.
If deep, lash them to your waist,
if shallow, hang them at your back.

Floodwaters come, the Ji is full,
the hen pheasant sings *wei-wei*.
The Ji is full, it won't wet your axles,
the hen cries after the cock.

Wild geese cry out,
at dawn the sun grows bright.
If the well-born man would take a bride,
let him come before the banks ice up.

The boatman waves and waves;
others cross over, not I;
others cross over, not I;
I am waiting for my friend.

Classic of Poetry LVI "We Had Our Delight"

In the valley we had our delight,
a big man free and easy.
I sleep alone and waking speak,
vow never to forget him.

Upon the slopes we had our delight,
a big man winning and merry.
I sleep alone and waking sing,
vow never to betray him.

On the highlands we had our delight,
a big man and a shrewd one.
I sleep alone, then wake all night,
vow never to make it known.

The poem above is a fine example of the problems of interpretation in the *Classic of Poetry*. The phrase translated as "we had our delight" is *kao-pan*. The great Confucian philosopher and commentator Zhu Xi (1130–1200) took *kao-pan* to mean "ambling about," the behavior of a hermit. Other commentators think that the phrase means "to beat on an earthenware vessel"—supposedly as an expression of good cheer. I have followed the oldest interpretation of this phrase as "achieve perfect joy," although here the "joy" is supposed to be that of someone escaping the misgovernment of Duke Zhuang of Wei and finding happiness in a mountain valley. As the remainder of each stanza suggests that the situation is sexual rather than political, I have chosen the interpretation adopted by many modern commentators.

Classic of Poetry LXXXI "I Went Along the Broad Road"

I went along the broad road
and took you by the sleeve—
do not hate me,
never spurn old friends.

I went along the broad road
and took you by the hand—
do not scorn me,
never spurn a love.

Many of the "Airs" have a moving simplicity that is as clear now, even in translation, as it was two and a half millennia ago.

Classic of Poetry LXXXII "Rooster Crows"

The woman said, "The rooster crows."
The man said, "Still the dark before dawn."
"Get you up, man—look at the night!—
the morning star is sparkling;
go roving and go roaming,
shoot the wild goose and the teal.

When your arrows hit them,
I will dress them just for you;
when they're dressed, we'll drink the wine,
and I will grow old with you.
There will be harps to attend us,
and all will be easy and good.

If I know that you will come,
I'll make a gift of many jewels;
if I know you will accept,
I'll show my care with many jewels;
if I know you will love me,
I'll answer you with many jewels."

Classic of Poetry CXXXIII "No Clothes"

How can you say, "I have no clothes"?—
I will share my greatcoat with you.
The king is raising his army,
we will make ready pike and spear,
and I will share all foes with you.

How can you say, "I have no clothes"?—
I will share my shift with you.
The king is raising his army,
we will make ready halberd and pike,
and I will set out with you.

How can you say, "I have no clothes"?—
I will share my war-kilt with you.
The king is raising his army,
we will make ready buffcoat and dirk,
and I will march with you.

In addition to expressions of love and friendship, the "Airs" also contain satire, both personal and political. Misrule has always interested Chinese commentators far more than peace and prosperity. The Mao commentary forced many a love poem to serve as a veiled attack on rulers by those ruled. The political satire of "Huge Rat" is clear, and the poem has always been a favorite of those who wished to believe in the *Classic of Poetry* as a means to express social discontent.

Classic of Poetry CXIII "Huge Rat"

Huge rat, huge rat,
eat my millet no more,
for three years I've fed you,
yet you pay me no heed.

I swear that I will leave you
and go to a happier land.
A happy land, a happy land,
and there I will find my place.

Huge rat, huge rat,
eat my wheat no more,
for three years I've fed you
and you show no gratitude.

I swear that I will leave you
and go to a happier realm.
A happy realm, a happy realm,
there I will find what I deserve.

Huge rat, huge rat,
eat my sprouts no more,
for three years I have fed you,
and you won't reward my toil.

I swear that I will leave you
and go to happy meadows.
Happy meadows, happy meadows
where none need wail and cry.

Classic of Poetry CVII "Sandals of Straw"

So tightly wound, sandals of straw
can serve to walk through frost.
Slender and fine, the maiden's hands
can serve to stitch his clothes,
Can make the sash, can make the hem,
and a fine man will wear them.

And that fine man, so richly clad,
whirls around and leaves her,
hung with combs of ivory.
This is a man of ungenerous heart,
thus he gets the needle's barb.

Courtship, Marriage, and Love

Courtship, marriage, and the longings of separated lovers figure prominently in the "Airs," and these remain among the most appealing poems of the collection. The lyrics are put into the mouths of both common folk and the aristocracy, women as well as men.

Classic of Poetry CXXXVIII "Barred Gate"

Behind barred gates
a man may find peace.
And where a spring gushes,
hunger may be healed.

When eating fish, who needs
bream of the river?
When taking wife, who needs
a Jiang princess of Qi?

Eating fish, who needs
carp from the river?
Taking wife, who needs
the royal daughter of Song?

"Barred Gate" has the tone of folk wisdom. But the folk metaphor of fishing for courtship also appears in the following poem, which seems to be a celebration of a marriage between a Zhou princess, surnamed Ji, and a count of the ruling house of the domain Qi. "Barred Gate" could be read as a poor man's answer to "Ah, How Splendid."

Classic of Poetry XXIV "Ah, How Splendid"

Ah, how splendid—
the flowers of the cherry.
What but reverence and awe
for the coach of a royal Ji?

Ah, how splendid—
flowers of peach and plum.
King Ping's grandchild
and the son of the Count of Qi.

How then is fishing done?
the line is made of silk.
The son of the Count of Qi
and the grandchild of King Ping.

Classic of Poetry CLVIII "Cutting the Haft"

How do you cut a haft?—
you have to use the ax.
How do you get a wife?—
you have to use a go-between.

In cutting a haft, cutting a haft
the model is not far.
And now I see her face to face,
plates and tureens in rows.

Classic of Poetry XXII "The River Has Its Forkings"

The river has its forkings,
the bride goes to her home.
She will not take me with her,
she will not take me with her,
and later she will rue it.

The river has its holms,
the bride goes to her home.
She will not let me join her,
she will not let me join her,
and later she'll be sick with grief.

The river has its feeders,
the bride goes to her home.
She will not stop to visit me,
she will not stop to visit me,
and now I sing here wailing.

In the following piece, the singer boasts of illicit liaisons "in the mulberries" with the daughters of the greatest houses of North China.

Classic of Poetry XLVIII "In the Mulberries"

Where did I pick the sweet pear?—
it was right across the Mei.
Who was the woman I longed for?—
the noble Jiang's daughter fair.
In the mulberries she promised to meet,
she called me to her high bower,
and went off with me on the river Ji.

And where did I pick the wheat?
it was there, north of the Mei.
Who was the woman I longed for?—
fair daughter of the noble Yi.
In the mulberries she promised to meet,
she called me to her high bower,
and went off with me on the river Ji.

And where did I pick the radish?—
it was there, east of the Mei.
Who was the woman I longed for?—
the noble Yong's fair daughter.
In the mulberries she promised to meet,
she called me to her high bower,
and went off with me on the river Ji.

Classic of Poetry LXVI "My Prince Has Taken the Field"

My prince has taken the field,
he sets no time of return.
When at last will he come?
The chickens roost in hen-house,
and at the evening of the day,
cattle and sheep come down.
My prince has taken the field,
how can I not long for him?

My prince has taken the field,
no term of days, no term of months,
When at last will we meet?
The chickens roost in coops,
and the evening of the day,
sheep and cattle come down to the herd.
My prince has taken the field,
how can I not hunger for him?

Classic of Poetry LXXIII "Great Cart"

The great cart goes rumbling along,
a flannel coat as green as grass.
Well you know I long for you,
but fear you will not dare.

The great cart pitches and sways,
a flannel coat like rust red barleycorn.
Well you know I long for you,
but fear you won't run off.

Alive, we live in different rooms,
but dead, we'll share a single tomb.
If you say I can't keep faith,
it will shine as bright as the sun.

Classic of Poetry LXXVII "Shu Is on a Field Hunt"

Shu is on a field hunt,
no one is in the streets.
Is no one really in the streets?—
no one there is like Shu,
a gentle, handsome man.

Shu is on the winter chase,
no one drinks in the streets.
Does no one really drink in the streets?—
no one there is like Shu,
a good and handsome man.

Shu has gone to the wilds,
in the streets no one drives horses.
Does no one really drive horses?—
no one there is like Shu,
a soldierly, handsome man.

Classic of Poetry LXXXVII "Lift Your Kilts"

If you love me dearly,
lift your kilts and cross the Zhen.
And if you do not love me,
there are other men,
O rashest of all rash young men.

And if you love me dearly,
lift your kilts and cross the Wei.
And if you do not love me,
there are other squires,
O rashest of all rash young men.

Using the Poems and Early Interpretation

A literary tradition begins not only with important early literary texts but also with a system whereby those texts are received, understood, and used within the society. Early commentaries on language, writing, and most particularly the *Classic of Poetry* voiced concerns that would remain in poetry and other forms of writing throughout the Chinese tradition.

The *Classic of Poetry* was seen as an educational text, providing knowledge and models for speaking. In the *Analects,* comments on the *Classic of Poetry* attributed to Confucius were among the most influential and often quoted.

Analects XVII.9

The Master said, "My young ones, why not work at learning the *Poems*? By the *Poems* you can stir *(xing),* by them you can observe, by them you can have fellowship, by them you can express reproach. Close to home they let you serve your father; farther away, they let you serve your lord. And you recognize many names of birds, beasts, plants, and trees."

This passage suggests the importance of the poems from the *Classic* in public discourse. The term "stir" *(xing)* probably refers to using quotations from the *Poems* in political oratory to "stir" the listener's sympathies or to clinch an argument. "Observe" was taken by traditional commentators in the sense of "observe the flourishing and decline of customs"; i.e., finding in the *Poems* a mirror reflecting social and moral history.

Analects II.2

The Master said, "The *Poems* are three hundred, yet one phrase covers them: 'no straying.' "

"No straying" (or "In thought no straying") is itself a phrase from the *Poems,* describing the horses in a well-trained chariot team. In the Mao commentary on the *Classic of Poetry,* the meaningless particle *si* is interpreted as "thought," leading to the popular interpretation "in thought no straying." Confucius' application of the phrase to the *Classic of Poetry* as a whole was understood to mean that every poem was ethically correct. This, in turn, was taken as the basis for moral interpretations of all the poems in the *Classic.*

Analects I.15

Zi-gong said, "What do you think of someone who is poor but does not fawn or one who is wealthy but not haughty?" The Master said, "It's all right, but better still to be poor yet happy, or wealthy yet loving proper behavior." Zi-gong said, "When the *Poems* say,

> As if cut in bone or ivory,
> as if carved and polished,

is this what you mean?" Then the Master said, "Zi-gong, now at last I can speak of the *Poems* with you. I told you one thing, and you knew what followed from it."

The ability to "apply" the *Poems* to the situation at hand was an important part of the general education of the elite in the period of *The Springs and Autumns of Lu* (770–403 B.C.). *The Zuo Tradition,* an historical work running roughly parallel to *The Springs and Autumns of Lu,* contains many examples of the use of the *Poems* in oratory and judgment. Often, such use is quite straightforward; at other times, as in the following passage, figurative applications are made in much the same way as metaphors in folk rhymes. Usually the citation of the *Poems* is followed by a brief explanation.

The Zuo Tradition, an entry for the 31st year of Duke Xiang (542 B.C.)

It was the twelfth month. Bei-gong Wen-zi was serving as Adviser to Duke Xiang of Wei on a journey to Chu. It was in consequence of the oath at Song. As they passed the city of Zheng, Yin Duan lodged them in North Forest to offer consolation for the hardships of their journey. He treated them with the ceremonies for receiving foreign visitors and spoke gracious words to them. Then Bei-gong Wen-zi entered the city of Zheng as foreign ambassador, with Zi-yu serving as his herald. Feng Jian-zi and Zi-tai-shu met him as a guest. When matters were concluded, he went forth again and said to the Count of Wei, "Ceremony is preserved in Zheng, and it will bring them several generations of good fortune. I am sure that they will be free from assault by the great domains. As the *Poem* says:

> Who can take hold of something hot?—
> does he not first wet his hands?

The relation of ceremony to governing is that of water to something hot."

Wars were fought over small slights endured in the interaction between princes. The state of Zheng treated the Duke of Wei and his entourage with all courtesy and proper ceremony. The couplet from the *Poem* provides a metaphor of insulation that gives Bei-gong Wen-zi an intuition about the true nature of ceremony *(li)* as something that insulates from the conflicts that arise in human relations. In the violent world of the period of *The Springs and Autumns of Lu,* ceremony was indeed the only thing that could keep brutality and raw will under restraint. The *Classic of Poetry* was itself a complement to ceremony, sometimes part of it, but also a means to comment with authority on the quality of behavior, its adherence to ceremony or the failure to do so.

Yet it was early recognized that the *Poems* could also be quoted out of context to prove any point. In a wonderful passage in *The Zuo Tradition,* someone was criticized for marrying a wife of the same surname, which was taboo. He replied, "As in taking a passage out of context when reciting the *Poems,* I took only the part I wanted." This brings up the question: which is master, the poem or the interpreter?

The pious moralizing of the Traditionalists and their "application" of the *Poems* to ethical cases also did not escape parody by the Daoist writers who composed the later chapters of the *Zhuang-zi* from the third or second century B.C. The verses quoted in the following anecdote are not found in the current version of the *Classic of Poetry,* and it seems likely that they were invented for the situation.

The *Zhuang-zi,* "Outer Things"

Traditionalists break into tombs using the *Poems* and Ceremony.

The chief Traditionalist deigned to convey these words, "It beginneth to grow light in the east. How's it going?"

The subordinate Traditionalist responded, "I haven't got the skirt and jacket off yet, but there's a pearl in his mouth."

The high Traditionalist: "Verily it is even as the *Poems* say:

Green, green groweth grain
upon the slopes of the mound.
The man ungenerous alive,
in death his mouth will hold no pearl.

I'll grab the whiskers and pull down on the beard; you take a metal bar, break through his cheeks, and slowly part his jaws, but don't damage the pearl in his mouth."

The other side of "application" is interpretation, and traditional Chinese literary interpretation grew out of interpretation of the *Classic of Poetry,* which in turn grew out of a larger sense of how language worked. In the following passage, Mencius speaks as a moralist, but note the assumptions about how language is understood; it is not necessarily what a speaker or writer *intends* to say, but what he cannot help revealing through his words. Gong-sun Chou is questioning the great Traditionalist (Confucian) philosopher Mencius on what he considers to be his most important skills.

Mencius II A, 2.xi, xvii

GONG-SUN CHOU: What, sir, are your strongest points?
MENCIUS: I understand language and have mastered the fostering of that boundless and surging vital force.

. . .

GONG-SUN CHOU: What do you mean by "understanding language"?
MENCIUS: When someone's words are one-sided, I understand how his mind is clouded. When someone's words are loose and extravagant, I understand the pitfalls into which that person has fallen. When someone's words are warped, I understand wherein the person has strayed. When someone's words are evasive, I understand how the person has been pushed to his limit.

In Mencius, we also find the earliest examples of dispute over the interpretation of the *Poems*. In the following passage, a thorny ethical problem is posed: When Sage-King Yao abdicated the throne to Sage-King Shun, was Yao then Shun's subject? And furthermore, was Shun's own father then Shun's subject (an unthinkable situation in which the political and family hierarchies are at odds)? Hereditary monarchy ensured that such a situation would never arise; but among the Sage-Kings of earliest antiquity, a ruler would voluntarily cede the throne to a worthy younger man. Mencius has made an exception to the king's dominion in these cases, but Xian-qiu Meng cites the *Classic of Poetry* as an authority to prove that there are no exceptions. Mencius attacks Xian-qiu Meng's interpretation (but does not question the authority of the *Classic of Poetry* to decide such issues). The poem in question, Mencius says, arises from a particular situation in which an officer is caught between conflicting claims of duty to the king and duty to his parents. The "king's business" is the duty of all, but he feels as if he alone were charged with completing it. However questionable the particular interpretation may be, the way in which Mencius makes it is significant. The universal meaning of the *Classic of Poetry* can only be discovered through the particular circumstances of an individual poem.

Mencius V A, 4.ii

Xian-qiu Meng said, "I have accepted your declaration that the Sage-King Shun did not consider Yao [who abdicated the throne in favor of Shun] to be his subject. Yet there is a poem in the *Classic of Poetry:*

> Of all that is under Heaven,
> No place is not the king's land;
> And to the farthest shores of all the land,
> No man is not the king's subject.

I would like to ask how it could be, when Shun became Emperor, that his father, the Blind Old Man, would not be considered his subject?"

Mencius replied, "The poem is not talking about that. Rather, the poem concerns the inability to care for one's parents when laboring in the king's business. It says, 'Everything is the king's business [and should be a responsibility shared by all], yet I alone labor here virtuously.' In explaining the Poems of the *Classic of Poetry,* one must not permit the literary patterning to adversely affect the understanding of the statement; and one must not permit our understanding of the statement to adversely affect our understanding of what was on the writer's mind. We use our understanding to trace it back to what was in the writer's mind—this is how to grasp it."

Mencius' concept of understanding the *Poems* is not a grasp of the "meaning" in an abstract sense, but rather a knowledge of what was in the mind of the writer in a particular situation. Literary understanding was a form of personal understanding, which included ethical and conceptual issues, but went beyond them. Reading might thus offer a community of friends that could extend beyond one's local region and time. In the following passage, I have translated the term *shi* as "gentleman"; originally the *shi* were the knightly class who by Mencius' time had become the educated gentry of the Warring States.

Mencius V B, 8.ii

Mencius said to Wan-zhang, "A good gentleman in one small community will befriend the other good gentlemen of that community. The good gentleman of a single domain will befriend the other good gentlemen of that domain. The good gentleman of the whole world will befriend the other good gentlemen of the whole world. But if befriending the good gentleman of the whole world is not enough, then one may go on further to consider the ancients. Yet is it acceptable to recite their poems and read their books, yet not know what kind of persons they were? Therefore one considers the age in which they lived. This is 'going on further to make friends.' "

The following passage from the *Classic of Documents* is not from the oldest sections of that work, which date back to the early first millennium. The section of the *Classic of Documents* from which this statement is taken probably dates from the period of *The Springs and Autumns of Lu* or from the Warring States; but because, up until the modern period, it was believed to have been from the original *Classic,* it carried immense authority and was accepted as the canonical definition of poetry. This definition is pseudo-etymological, based on splitting the character for "poetry," *shi* 詩, into its two components. The first of these is *yan* 言, to "speak" or "articulate." The second element was erroneously interpreted as *zhi* 志, "what is on the mind intently," later often with the political sense of "aims" or "ambitions." The second definition takes the word *yong* 詠, a word for "song" or "singing," and divides it into *yan* 言, here translated as "language," and *yong* 永, to "prolong." Although this primarily refers to drawing out the syllables in singing, Confucian interpreters expanded the interpretation to a broader sense of extension, in which poetry, as repeatable words, could carry discourse to far places and future times.

Classic of Documents (Shu jing), "Canon of Shun"

The Poem articulates what is on the mind intently; song makes language last long.

There were many variations of this explanation, including the following passage from *The Zuo Tradition,* falsely attributed to Confucius, in which the idea of language's extension, "going far," is applied to the quality of *wen* 文, which means "patterning," "the well-written word," and later "literature."

The Zuo Tradition, an entry for the 25th year of Duke Xiang (548 B.C.)

Confucius said, "There is a record that says: the language is to be adequate to what is intently on the person's mind, and the patterning *(wen)* is to be adequate to the language. If a person does not use language, who will know what is on his mind? If the language lacks patterning, it will not go far."

The question of the adequacy of language to thought and of the adequacy of the written language to spoken language was a major concern in early thought, and one that came to play an important role in the theory of poetry. The following passage, from *"Appended Discourses,"* a philosophical treatise attached to the *Classic of Changes,* an ancient divination tract, became the most famous statement on this question. The attribution to Confucius is false.

Classic of Changes, "Appended Discourses"

Confucius said, "What is written does not give the fullness of what is said; what is said does not give the fullness of the concept in the mind."

"If this is so, then does it mean that the concepts in the minds of the Sages cannot be perceived?"

He said, "The Sages established the Images [of the *Classic of Changes*] to give the fullness of the concepts in their minds, and they set up the hexagrams to give the fullness of what is true and false in a situation; to these they appended statements to give the fullness of what was said. . . ."

The idea of "image" *(xiang)* became an important term mediating between concept and language. This is developed in a treatise on the "Images" of the *Classic of Changes* by the philosopher Wang Bi (A.D. 226–249).

Wang Bi, "Elucidation of the Images" *(Classic of Changes)*

The Image is what brings out concept; language is what clarifies the Image. Nothing can equal Image in giving the fullness of concept; nothing can equal language in giving the fullness of Image. Language was born of the Image, thus we seek in language in order to observe the Image. Image was born of concept, thus we seek in Image in order to observe the concept. Concept is fully given in image; Image is overt in language.

The claim that human thoughts and feelings could somehow be written in language, however problematic that process might be, was challenged in the *Zhuang-zi*, in the famous parable of Wheelwright Pian.

from the *Zhuang-zi*, "The Way of Heaven"

Duke Huan was reading in his hall. Wheelwright Pian, who was cutting a wheel just outside the hall, put aside his hammer and chisel and went in. There he asked Duke Huan, "What do those books you are reading say?" The duke answered, "These are the words of the Sages." The wheelwright said, "Are the Sages still around?" And the duke answered, "They're dead." Then the wheelwright said, "Well, what you're reading then is no more than the dregs of the ancients." The duke: "When I, a prince, read, how is it that a wheelwright dares come and dispute with me? If you have an explanation, fine. If you don't have an explanation, *you* die!" Then Wheelwright Pian said, "I tend to look at it in terms of my own work: when you cut a wheel, if you go too slowly, it slides and doesn't stick fast; if you go too quickly, it jumps and doesn't go in. Neither too slowly nor too quickly—you achieve it in your hands, and those respond to the mind. I can't put it into words, but there is some fixed principle there. I can't teach it to my son, and my son can't get instruction in it from me. I've gone on this way for seventy years and have grown old in cutting wheels. The ancients have died, and along with them, that which cannot be transmitted. Therefore what you are reading is nothing more than the dregs of the ancients."

The "Great Preface" to the *Classic of Poetry*

The "Great Preface" to the *Classic of Poetry* was the most authoritative statement on the nature and function of poetry in traditional China. Not only was it the beginning of every student's study of the *Classic of Poetry* from the Eastern Han through the Song, its concerns and terminology became an essential part of writing about poetry and learning about poetry. This was the one text on the nature of poetry known to everyone from the end of the Han on.

It is uncertain exactly when the "Great Preface" reached its present form, but we can be reasonably sure that it was no later than the first century A.D. Many readers accepted the "Great Preface" as the work of Confucius' disciple Zi-xia, and thus saw in it an unbroken tradition of teaching about the *Classic of Poetry* that could be traced back to Confucius himself. A more learned and skeptical tradition took the "Great Preface" as the work of one Wei Hong, a scholar of the first century A.D. It is probably anachronistic to apply the concept of "composition" (except in its root sense of "putting together") to the "Great Preface." Rather, the "Great Preface" is a loose synthesis of shared "truths" about the *Classic of Poetry*, truths that were the common possession of the Traditionalists (whom we now call "Confucians") in the Warring States and Western Han periods. In their oral transmission, these truths were continually being reformulated; we may consider the moment when they were written down as the "Great Preface" to be the stage in their transmission when reformulation changed into exegesis.

The "Great Preface" is given in its original context, joined to the first poem of the *Classic of Poetry*, "Fishhawk" (see p. 30), traditionally understood as celebrating the virtue of the Queen Consort of King Wen of the Zhou Dynasty.

"Fishhawk" is the virtue of the Queen Consort and the beginning of the "Airs" [*Feng*, the first large section of the *Classic of Poetry*]. It is the means by which the world is influenced *(feng)* and by which the relations between husband and wife are made correct. Thus it is used in smaller communities, and it is used in larger domains. "Airs" *(Feng)* are "Influence" *(feng)*; it is to teach. By influence it stirs them; by teaching it transforms them.

The text plays on the multiple meanings of the word *feng*, which primarily means "wind." It is a kind of poetry ("Airs"); it means "customs"; and it also means "to influence," often using the metaphor of the wind bending the grasses. For the Confucian tradition, the purpose of the "Airs" was to influence behavior.

The poem is that to which what is intently on the mind *(zhi)* goes. In the mind, it is "being intent" *(zhi)*; coming out in language, it is a "poem."

The affections are stirred within and take on form in words. If words alone are inadequate, we speak it out in sighs. If sighing is inadequate, we sing it. If singing is inadequate, unconsciously our hands dance it and our feet tap it.

This is the early psychological theory of poetry. It begins with an intense concern, understood as an accumulation of "vital breath" *(qi)*. A modest accumulation comes out as a sigh; a larger accumulation comes out in words as a song. And if the accumulation is too great to get out, it drives the body to dancing.

Feelings emerge in sounds; when those sounds have patterning, they are called "tones." The tones of a well-managed age are at rest and happy: its government is balanced. The tones of an age of turmoil are bitter and full of anger: its government is perverse. The tones of a ruined state are filled with lament and brooding: its people are in difficulty.

Personal concerns are understood in a social and political context, and that context can be seen in poetic expression. Since the poems of the *Classic of Poetry* were performed to music, the "tones" that reveal social and political context are contained in both the words and the music. When this was applied to poetry later in the tradition, "tone" was understood as the mood of the poem and its style.

Thus to correctly present achievements and failures, to move Heaven and Earth, to stir the gods and spirits, there is nothing more appropriate than poetry. By it the former kings managed the relations between husbands and wives, perfected the respect due to parents and superiors, gave depth to human relations, beautifully taught and transformed the people, and changed local customs.

Thus there are six principles in the poems: (1) Airs *(Feng)*; (2) "exposition" *(fu)*; (3) "comparison" *(bi)*; (4) "affective image" *(xing)*; (5) Odes *(Ya)*; (6) Hymns *(song)*.

The "six principles" include the three main divisions of the *Classic of Poetry* and three modes of expression. "Exposition" *(fu)* describes those poems that simply tell what happened. "Comparison" *(bi)* describes poems that use simile. "Affective image" *(xing)* has been discussed earlier; this is an image that is supposed to stir the emotions.

By *feng*, those above transform those below; also by *feng*, those below criticize those above. When an admonition is given that is governed by patterning, the one who speaks it has no culpability, yet it remains adequate to warn those who hear it. In this we have *feng*.

The poetry of the *Feng* is supposed to go in two directions within the social hierarchy. Superiors use it to make people instinctively feel the models of good behavior. But when the superiors are not governing well, those below them use poems to show their rulers the consequences of misrule. As long as the criticism is "patterned," that is, presented through poetry, the person who composes or uses such a poem cannot be punished. In part, this license to use poetry for political criticism is because poetry is supposed to emerge involuntarily from feeling.

When the Way of the Kings declined, rites and moral principles were abandoned; the power of government to teach failed; the government of the domains changed; the customs of the family were altered. And at this point the changed *Feng* ("Airs") and the changed *Ya* ("Odes") were written. The historians of the domains understood clearly the marks of success and failure; they were pained by the abandonment of proper human relations and lamented the severity of punishments and governance. They sang their feelings to criticize *(feng)* those above, understanding the changes that had taken place and thinking about former customs. Thus the changed *Feng* emerge from the affections, but they go no further than rites and moral principles. That they should emerge from the affections is human nature; that they go no further than rites and moral principles is the beneficent influence of the former kings.

The "changed" poems come from a period of general social decline. This passage attempts to resolve a serious problem: If poetry is supposed to express the social and political temper of the age, and if the social and political temper of the age is corrupt, how can such poems present good ethical models? The problem is resolved by assuming that the poems were composed by good people in bad times, people who were distressed about the conditions of their age.

> Thus the affairs of a single state, rooted in the experience of a single person, are called *Feng*. To speak of the affairs of the whole world and to describe customs *(feng)* common to all places is called *Ya*. *Ya* means "proper" *(zheng)*. These show the source of either flourishing or ruin in the royal government. Government has its greater and lesser aspects: thus we have a "Greater *Ya*" and a "Lesser *Ya*." The "Hymns" give the outward shapes of praising full virtue, and they inform the spirits about the accomplishment of great deeds. These are called the "Four Beginnings" and are the ultimate perfection of the Poems.

Here the Preface distinguishes the "Airs" *(Feng)* from the "Odes" *(Ya)*. The "Airs" are supposed to be the voice of a particular person in a particular place or situation. By contrast, the "Odes" are supposed to speak more generally and apply to the whole kingdom.

Selections from the "Record of Music" *(Yue ji)*

The *Classic of Rites (Li ji)* has only the most tenuous claim to the status of a Confucian Classic. It is a Western Han miscellany of largely Confucian texts from the Warring States and Han. Among its "chapters" is a treatise on the origin, function, and relation between music and rites: the *Yue ji* or "Record of Music." Much of the material in this work appears, only slightly recast, in the "Treatise on Music," *Yue shu*, in the *Historical Records (Shi ji)* of Si-ma Qian. In both of these texts we find again some of the material that went into the making of the "Great Preface," along with a fuller elaboration of the psychology on which the "Great Preface" is based.

The "Record of Music" and the "Great Preface" share a concern for reconciling the spontaneous expression of feeling and its normative regulation. As the "changed *feng*," composed by the "historians of the domains," are generated spontaneously, but stop at decent norms, so here "rites" are the natural expression of human feeling that finds a normative and limiting form. Out of this arises the beautiful distinction between the roles of music and rites in ceremony: rites assert the distinction of roles in human relations, while music overcomes these distinctions and unifies the participants.

> All tones that arise are generated from the human mind. When the human mind is moved, some external thing has caused it. Stirred by external things into movement, it takes on form in sound. When these sounds respond to one another, changes arise; and when these changes constitute a pattern, they are called "tones." When such tones are set side by side and

played on musical instruments, with shield and battleax for military dances or with feathered pennons for civil dances, it is called "music."

Music originates from tone. Its root lies in the human mind's being stirred by external things. Thus when a mind that is miserable is stirred, its sound is vexed and anxious. When a mind that is happy is stirred, its sound is relaxed and leisurely. When a mind that is delighted is stirred, its sound pours out and scatters. When a wrathful mind is stirred, its sound is crude and harsh. When a respectful mind is stirred, its sound is upright and pure. When a doting mind is stirred, its sound is agreeable and yielding. These six conditions are not innate: they are set in motion only after being stirred by external things. Thus the former kings exercised caution in what might cause stirring. For this reason we have rites to guide what is intently on the mind; we have music to bring those sounds into harmony; we have government to unify action; and we have punishment to prevent transgression. Rites, music, government, and punishment are ultimately one and the same— a means to unify the people's minds and correctly execute the Way.

All tones are generated from the human mind. The affections are moved within and take on form in sound. When these sounds have patterning, they are called "tones." The tones of a well-managed age are at rest and happy: its government is balanced. The tones of an age of turmoil are bitter and full of anger: its government is perverse. The tones of a ruined state are filled with lament and brooding: its people are in difficulty. The way of sounds and tones communicates with [the quality of] governance.

[This section omits elaborating the correspondences between the five notes and government offices, as well as the social problems implicit in musical disorder.]

All tones are generated from the human mind. Music is that which communicates [*tong,* "carries through"] human relations and natural principles. The birds and beasts understand sounds but do not understand tones. The common people understand tones but do not understand music. Only the superior person is capable of understanding music. Thus one examines sounds to understand tone; one examines tone to understand music; one examines music to understand government, and then the proper execution of the Way is complete. Thus one who does not understand sounds can share no discourse on tones; one who does not understand tones can share no discourse on music. When someone understands music, that person is almost at the point of understanding rites. And when rites and music are both attained *(de),* it is called *De* ["virtue"/"attainment"/"power"], for *De* is an "attaining" *(de).*

The true glory of music is not the extreme of tone; the rites of the Great Banquet are not the ultimate in flavor. The great harp used in performing "Pure Temple" [one of the Hymns in the *Classic of Poetry*] has red strings and few sounding holes. One sings, and three join in harmony: there are tones which are omitted. In the rite of the Great Banquet, one values water and platters of raw meat and fish; the great broth is not seasoned: there are flavors which are omitted. We can see from this that when the former kings set the prescriptions for music and rites, they did not take the desires of mouth, belly, ears, and eyes to their extremes, in order thereby to teach people to weigh likes and dislikes in the balance and lead the people back to what is proper.

Here the aesthetics of omission, so important in later Chinese literary thought, is given its earliest expression in an ethical context. The perfect music holds back from becoming an overwhelming force; the sense that something is omitted draws others in and brings response. The phrase "one sings, and three join in harmony" will come to be commonly used for precisely such aesthetic restraint that engages others. However, in its original context here in the "Record of Music," that restraint has an ethical rather than an aesthetic force: omission is the embodiment of the principle of proper limits in sensuous satisfaction.

A human being is born calm: this is his innate nature endowed by Heaven. To be stirred by external things and set in motion is desire occurring within that innate nature. Only after things encounter conscious knowledge do likes and dislikes take shape. When likes and dislikes have no proper measure within, and when knowing is enticed from without, the person becomes incapable of self-reflection, and the Heaven-granted principle of one's being perishes. When external things stir a person endlessly and when that person's likes and dislikes are without proper measure, then when external things come before a person, the person is transformed by those things. When a person is transformed by things, it destroys the Heaven-granted principle of one's being and lets a person follow all human desires to their limit. Out of this comes the refractory and deceitful mind; out of this come occurrences of wallowing excess and turmoil. Then the powerful coerce the weak; the many oppress the few; the smart deceive the stupid; the brave make the timid suffer; the sick are not cared for; old and young and orphans have no place—this is the Way of supreme turbulence.

For this reason the former kings set the prescriptions of rites and music and established proper measures for the people. By weeping in mourning clothes of hemp, they gave proper measure to funerals. By bell and drum, shield and battleax [for military dances], they gave harmony to expressions of happiness. By the cap and hairpin of the marriage ceremony, they distinguished male and female. By festive games and banquets, they formed the correct associations between men. Rites gave the proper measure to the people's minds; music made harmony in human sounds; government carried things out; punishments prevented transgression. When these four were fully achieved and not refractory, the royal Way was complete.

Music unifies; rites set things apart. In unifying there is a mutual drawing close; in setting things apart there is mutual respect. If music overwhelms, there is a dissolving; if rites overwhelm, there is division. To bring the affections into accord and to adorn their outward appearance is the function of music and rites. When rites and ceremonies are established, then noble and commoner find their own levels; when music unifies them, then those above and those below are joined in harmony. When likes and dislikes have this manifest form, then the good person and the unworthy person can be distinguished. By punishments one prevents oppression; by rewards one raises up the good; if these are the case, then government is balanced. By fellow feeling one shows love; by moral principles one corrects them, and in this way the management of the people proceeds.

Han Confucianism sought to hold opposing forces in balance. Rites define functions in social relations and thus are a system of distinctions (e.g., social superior and inferior is not a distinction of innate "quality" but a sanctioned social convention). As a system of role distinctions, however, rites always threaten to pull people apart and set them in opposition to one another. That dangerous centrifugal force in rites is countered by music, which is shared by all participants in a ceremony; it is music that makes them feel like a unified body, part of a single enterprise. However, that impulse to unity threatens to destroy distinctions, and thus it is counterbalanced by rites.

Music comes from within; rites are formed without. Since music comes from within, it belongs to genuine affections; since rites are formed without, they have patterning.

The supreme music must be easy; the supreme rites must be simple. When music is perfect, there is no rancor; when rites are perfect, there is no contention. To bow and yield yet govern the world is the true meaning of rites and music. There is no oppression of the people; the great nobility submit; armor is not worn; the five punishments are not used; no calamity befalls the masses; the Son of Heaven feels no wrath—when things are thus, music has been perfected. Within the four seas fathers and sons are joined in affection, the precedence between elder and younger is kept clear, and respect is shown to the Son of Heaven—when things are like this, rites are in practice.

The supreme music shares the harmony of Heaven and Earth. The supreme rites share the proper measure of Heaven and Earth. In the harmony of the former, none of the hundred things fail; in the proper measure of the latter, the sacrifices are offered to Heaven and Earth. In their manifest aspect they are rites and music; in their unseen aspect they are spiritual beings. When things are like this, then all within four seas are brought together in respect and love. Though acts differ in the performance of a rite, these acts share the quality of respect. Though music has different patterns, these are brought together in the quality of love. Since the affections involved in music and rites remain the same, wise kings have followed them. Thus, when act and occasion are matched, fame and accomplishment are joined.

This rapturous Confucian vision of society, functioning in harmony with human nature and universal nature through music and rites, is not directly related to literature. However, the vision provides an essential background for literature, recurring throughout the history of Chinese literary thought in the union of genuine feeling and form.

Other Voices in the Tradition

Tang Xian-zu, *Peony Pavilion* (1598)

The *Classic of Poetry* was continually reinterpreted throughout the imperial period. Such reinterpretations touched not only the explanation of individual poems but also the significance of the *Classic* as a whole. Despite the subtleties of such high scholarship, the *Classic of Poetry* also remained a school text with the Mao commentary or the twelfth-century Zhu Xi commentary, which laid even greater stress on the *Poems* as expressions of natural feeling, accepting many of the love lyrics as such rather than as political allegories. The painful contradiction between the Confucian teacher's imposition of external authority and the messages of this particular interpretation of the *Classic*, often involving love and natural feeling, made the *Classic of Poetry* a target for humorous treatment in vernacular literature.

Probably its most famous appearance in the vernacular is found in two scenes from Tang Xian-zu's play *Peony Pavilion (Mu-dan ting)* of 1598. The parents of Du Li-niang, the heroine, are thinking ahead to her marriage and have hired a tutor to instruct her in the *Classic of Poetry*. The results are unanticipated: Du Li-niang's study of the first poem, "Fishhawk," "stirs" (*xing*, a term that can also convey sexual arousal) her and leads her out of the schoolroom into the garden. A text that was intended as a lesson in obedient wifely virtue leads to rebellious erotic fantasy, initiating the action in the rest of the play. In these scenes the habits of Chinese scholasticism, embodied in tutor Chen, come into conflict with a more profound, though innocent desire to grasp the larger significance of canonical texts.

Like Shakespeare, Chinese dramatists love to exploit the comic possibilities of puns and quibbles. Except when accidents of language offer a lucky counterpart, the translator is helpless here. The maid Spring Scent's hilarious misreadings of "Fishhawk" depend on just such wordplay.

FROM SCENE VII: THE SCHOOLROOM FOR WOMEN

Enter the tutor CHEN ZUI-LIANG, *reciting a poem.*

CHEN:
> In recitation's aftermath I polish and change
>> lines I wrote last spring,
> breakfast over, my thoughts turn fondly
>> to noontime tea.
> An ant has climbed up on my desk
>> and skirts the inkstone's water,
> a bee comes through the window grate,
>> sipping nectar from blooms in the vase.

I've set up my school in Prefect Du's official residence; and since Miss Du's family has a tradition of studying the Mao tradition of the *Classic of Poetry*, I've been exceptionally favored by Madam Du's hospitality. Now that my morning meal is over, I can take a casual look over the Mao commentary again while I'm still alone.

[*Recites*]:

> The fishhawks sing *gwan gwan*
> on sandbars of the stream.
> Gentle maiden, pure and fair,
> fit pair for a prince.

The meaning of "Fit" is "fit." The meaning of "Pair" is "pair." [*Looks up*] The morning grows on, and I still don't see my pupil coming into the classroom. She's so dreadfully spoiled. I'll hit the gong a few times. [*Hits the gong*] Spring Scent, ask your young mistress to come to class.

Enter Du Li-niang, *carrying books.*

Du [*sings*]:
> Just now finished dressing in simple attire,
> slowly I walk to the classroom door,
> with serene indifference I come before
>   these clean desks and bright windows.

Spring Scent [*continuing the song*]:
> The plaque reads:
> "Virtuous Literary Grace,
> For Long Time Our Family's Place"—
> now that really puts a person off!
> But eventually
> I can successfully
> teach our parrot Polly
> to call for tea. [*Sees* Chen]

Du: Good morning, sir.

Spring Scent: Don't be mad at us, sir!

Chen: As soon as the rooster crows, all young ladies should wash up, rinse their mouths, comb their hair and do it up, then greet their parents. After the sun has risen, each should go about what she is supposed to be doing. As girl students, what you are supposed to be doing is study, so you absolutely must get up earlier.

Du: I won't do it again.

Spring Scent: I understand perfectly. Tonight we won't go to sleep, and at midnight we will come and ask you to give us our lesson.

Chen: Did you go over yesterday's poem from the *Classic of Poetry* thoroughly?

Du: I've been over it thoroughly, and now I wait for you to explain it.

Chen: Recite it.

Du [*reciting*]:
> The fishhawks sing *gwan gwan*
> on sandbars of the stream.
> Gentle maiden, pure and fair,
> fit pair for a prince.

Chen: Here is the explanation. "The fishhawks sing *gwan gwan*": the fishhawk is a bird, and *"gwan gwan"* is the sound it makes.

Spring Scent: What's that sound like?

CHEN *makes the sound of a pigeon,*[1] *and* SPRING SCENT *mockingly imitates him.*

CHEN: By its nature this bird delights in quiet and keeping away from strangers, hence it is "on sandbars of the stream."

SPRING SCENT: Now maybe it was yesterday, but if not, it must have been the day before—or maybe it was last year—but a mottled pigeon got shut up in the official residence. When Miss Du set it free, it flew off to the house of Assistant Magistrate He.[2]

CHEN: Utter nonsense! This is a *xing*, an "affective image," a "stirring."

SPRING SCENT: What is this *xing*, "stirring?"

CHEN: A *xing* or "stirring" means "to start up." It starts up what follows. Now this "gentle maiden pure and fair" is a good girl who is quiet and keeps away from strangers, waiting for her prince to come eagerly to form a couple with her.

SPRING SCENT: Why is he so eager to couple with her?

CHEN: You're getting far too sassy!

DU: Teacher, I can understand the poems line by line with the aid of the commentary, but I want you to expound on the broader significance of the *Classic of Poetry*.

CHEN [*sings*]:
> Of the Classics the *Poems* are the flower in full bloom,
> with much grace and refinement for women.
> It gives us proof
> > how Jiang the First Parent
> > birthed bawling babe,
> how the Consort's virtue perfected
> > kept her from jealousy.
> In addition there is:
> the poem that sings how "The Rooster Crows,"
> the poem that laments for the swallow's wings,
> the poem of weeping by the river's banks,
> the poem that broods "The Han So Wide"—
> poems washed clean of all powder and paint.
> It has "Airs" that influence,
> > it has the power to transform,
> it is suited for the chamber,
> > it is suited for the home.

DU: Is there that much in the *Classic?*

CHEN: "The *Poems* are three hundred, yet one phrase covers them." [*Continues singing*]
> Not so much—just
> two words: "No straying";
> and this, young people, I impart to you.
> Lesson over.

---

[1] The *ju-jiu* is the fishhawk. The second syllable alone, however, is the much more common word for "pigeon."

[2] Here is a series of untranslatable puns. *Gwan gwan,* the fishhawk's cry, can also mean "shut in, shut in," precisely the proper condition for a virtuous young lady who "delights in quiet and keeping away from strangers." "On sandbars of the stream," *zai he zhi zhou,* can be misunderstood as "at" *(zai)* He *(he)* "the assistant magistrate's *(zhi-zhou)* [house].

FROM SCENE IX: GETTING THE GARDEN IN ORDER

Enter SPRING SCENT.

SPRING SCENT [*sings*]:
> Little Spring Scent belongs
> to the highest sort of menial,
> leading a coddled life in painted chambers.
> I wait on my mistress' pleasure,
> dabble with powder and rouge,
> fastening kingfisher feathers,
>> holding flowers in fingers,
> ever beside her make-up stand.
> A companion to make her brocade bed,
> a companion to light the incense by night.
> Just a slip of a girl, the worst I must take
>> is a taste of Madam's cane.

[*Speaks in rhythmic doggerel*] I'm a serving maid, face like a flower, just in my early teens; springtime's here, I'm as cute as can be, and someone who knows what's what. And now at last I'm waiting for someone to stir my passions, to go with me everywhere, and at every footstep give me the eye.

I go with my young mistress day and night. Though she could be known as the fairest in the land, she watches out for the family reputation instead. Those cute and bashful tender cheeks assume a mature and grave look. Since her father engaged a tutor to give her lessons, she has been reading the *Classic of Poetry;* but when she got to the part of the first stanza that goes "gentle maiden pure and fair, fit pair for a prince," she grew pensive and put down the book, sighing, "In this the loving feelings of the Sage are fully revealed. How clear it is that those in the past had the same sentiments that we do today!" So then I suggested, "Miss, this studying is getting you down. What don't you take your mind off of it?" She pondered this a while, then rose hesitantly and asked me, "And just how do you suggest I take my mind off of it?" I answered, "I'm not thinking of anything particular—why don't we go for a walk in the garden at the rear of the house?" Then she said, "Stupid maid! What if my father hears about it!" So I replied, "Your father will be out in the countryside for several days."

She lowered her head and didn't say anything for the longest time. Then she got out the almanac and looked through it to choose a day. "Tomorrow is no good, and the next day won't do either, but two days from now would be a lucky time, one favored by the God of Short Outings. Go tell the garden boy to sweep the path clear under the flowering trees beforehand." I agreed at the moment, but now I'm afraid that Madam her mother will find out—but that's as it will be. So I might as well go give the garden boy his assignment. Hey! There's our teacher, Mr. Chen, coming around the corridor over there. As the lines go [*recites*]:
> Springtime's splendor is everywhere
>> calling to be enjoyed,
> but tell it to a silly old man
>> and he won't understand at all.

CHEN [*enters, singing*]:
> An old bookworm
> for a while has on loan

Ma Rong's crimson screen; that is,
> a teaching job;
and in the warmth of the sun
> the hooked-up curtains flutter.
Hey!
Around the corridor over there
is a little serving girl
who seems to be talking, but no words come—
I'll go closer to see who it is.
It's Spring Scent! Now tell me [*Continues singing*]
> where will I find the good Master,
> and where will I find his Lady,
> and why has my pupil not come with her books?

SPRING SCENT: Well, if it isn't our teacher, Mr. Chen! These past few days my young mistress has had no time to come to class.

CHEN: Why?

SPRING SCENT: Listen and I'll tell you.

[*Sings*]

The springtime in such glory is
just too much for our know-it-all princess,
and what she does now involves "a mood."

CHEN: And what is this "mood"?

SPRING SCENT: You still don't know, but her father is really going to put the blame on you.

CHEN: For what?

SPRING SCENT: I'm talking about that lecture you gave her on the Mao commentary to the *Classic of Poetry*. Well, you've gone and Mao'ed her up all too well. Ah, my poor young mistress!

[*Sings*]

All because of that poem
she was lectured into passion.

CHEN: All I did was lecture on "The fishhawks sing *gwan gwan*."

SPRING SCENT: And precisely because of this my mistress is saying, "The fishhawks may have been shut in but they still have their 'stirrings' on sandbars of the stream.[3] Is it possible a person can be less well off than a bird?"

[*Continues, singing*]

To read you must bury your head in a book,
but to taste the world around you,
> you lift your head and look.

And now I have instructions that the day after tomorrow we are to go on an outing in the flower garden behind the house.

---

[3]Again the pun on *gwan* and to be "shut in." The *xing* is not only the "stirring," the term of technical poetics from the Mao commentary, but also an "arousal" and a less sexual "excitement."

CHEN: Why are you going on an outing?
SPRING SCENT [*singing*]:

> She obviously feels stung by spring,
> and because spring is in such haste to go,
> she wants to lose her spring melancholy
> > in the flower garden.

CHEN: This really shouldn't be.

[*Sings*]

> If the young lady goes walking,
> people could watch her wherever she goes,
> so her steps should be shielded from sight.

Spring Scent, Heaven is my witness but in all my sixty years, I never have experienced the sting of spring, and I never have gone on an outing in a park in flower.
SPRING SCENT: Why?
CHEN: You may not know, but Mencius said it well: that the thousands of words of the Sage come down to recovering a heart that has been allowed to run free.[4]

[*Sings*]

> Just keep a normal heart—
> why should she feel the sting of spring?
> > why must she go on a spring outing?
> if she goes on an outing as spring goes away,
> > how will she set her heart at ease?[5]

Since the young mistress will not be coming to class, I might as well take a few days off myself. Now Spring Scent, [*sings*]

> go to the classroom regularly,
> and always go to the window,
> for I worry that swallow droppings will stain
> > the harp and books.

"Stirred" by the *Classic of Poetry*, Du Li-niang does indeed go on her spring outing into the garden, after which she has an erotic dream of the beloved she has not yet met, Liu Mengmei. Carried away by unfulfilled passion, she asks to be buried under a plum tree in the garden—then dies.

---

[4]There is a twist here in the use of a "heart allowed to run free" *(fang-xin)*. Mencius wanted people to recover the childlike innocence with which they were born and from which their hearts had "gone astray"; later the phrase came to have a stronger sense of wantonness, acting without restraint. And by Tang Xian-zu's time it had already acquired its conventional vernacular sense of "feeling relaxed," "not being anxious," "to set one's heart at ease."
[5]Again, the colloquial construction here calls to the fore the vernacular meaning of *fang-xin*, "set one's heart at ease"; however, in the background is the classical sense, "let one's heart run free," which in this context is opposed to the vernacular.

Early Narrative

秦
西
漢

Chinese historical writing began in the court annals of the various feudal domains of the Zhou Kingdom. The most famous of these court annals is *The Springs and Autumns [of Lu] (Chun-qiu),* kept by the domain
of Lu from 722 to 481 B.C. ("springs and autumns" was a generic term for
"annals"). These annals give terse entries on the most significant events
of the year and can scarcely be considered "narrative." Because Confucius himself
was believed to have been their author, Traditionalists of the late Warring States and
Han developed a doctrine of perfect expression, by which the precise phrasing of
the entries was a subtle reflection of Confucius' judgments on events. As an example we may take the famous entry from the sixteenth year of Duke Xi (644 B.C.):
"Spring, the king's first month, at the very beginning of the month there fell stones
[meteors] in Song, five of them; that month six albatrosses flew in reverse, passing
the capital of Song." *The Gong-yang Tradition,* a Western Han Traditionalist commentary on *The Springs and Autumns of Lu,* explains Confucius' positioning of the
numbers as follows: in the case of the meteors, the thing enumerated comes first because the meteors were seen first and their number discovered only later; in the case
of the albatrosses, first the number of birds was recognized, then the fact that they
were albatrosses.

Extended historical writing is first found in *The Zuo Tradition (Zuo zhuan)* and
the *Discourses of the Domains (Guo-yu),* both probably from the late fourth century
B.C., but based on earlier materials. *The Zuo Tradition* has been traditionally treated
as a commentary on *The Springs and Autumns of Lu,* providing a fuller account of
events recorded in the annals, along with other, unrecorded events. *The Zuo Tradition* was much admired in the Chinese prose tradition for its terse exposition of
events. Its narrative style is quirky and elliptical: rather than pure narrative, most of
the accounts in *The Zuo Tradition* are either frames for speeches in which ethical
values are expounded, or exemplary anecdotes in which the details of the story are
shaped by the ethical point to be made.

Two Sad Stories of Good Behavior

The first of the two following passages from *The Zuo Tradition* comes from a set of
anecdotes on the flight of the Jin army after its defeat by Chu at the Battle of Bi. Zhao
Zhan, a commander of the Jin army, is escaping on foot when his subordinate Feng
passes by, driving in a chariot together with his two sons. Four riders would slow
the chariot and leave them vulnerable to the enemy. Feng is presented with an ethical dilemma.

The Zuo Tradition, an entry for the 12th year of Duke Xuan (597 B.C.)

Zhao Zhan gave his two best horses to save his older brother and his uncle, and he was going back driving his other horses. He ran into enemy soldiers and could not get away, so he abandoned his chariot and ran off into the woods.

Feng, the Grand Master, was driving his chariot with his two sons. He told his sons not to turn and look back. But they did look back and said, "Zhao Zhan is there behind us." Feng was enraged with them. He made them get down from the chariot and, pointing to a tree, said, "I will find your bodies here." Feng then handed the mounting strap to Zhao Zhan and took him away from danger. The next day he went to where he had indicated his sons' bodies would be, and he found them both dead at the foot of the tree.

The Zuo Tradition, an entry for the 22nd year of Duke Xi (638 B.C.)

Chu was attacking Song to relieve Zheng. The Duke of Song was about to go into battle when Gu, his Grand War Chief, objected: "Heaven deserted the house of Shang long ago. My lord wants to raise it up again. This will not be forgiven." The Duke refused to pay him heed.

It was in winter, the eleventh month, on the day *ji-si,* which was the first day of the month. The men of Song had formed their battle lines, and the men of Chu had not yet crossed the river. The War Chief said: "They are many and we are few. Let me strike them now before they are done with the crossing." But the Duke said, No. When they had crossed but had not yet drawn up their battle lines, again the War Chief pleaded, and the Duke said, Not yet. He struck them only after they had fully drawn up their battle lines, and the hosts of Song were routed. The Duke was wounded in the thigh, and the palace guards were slain.

All the people of the land found fault with the Duke for this, but he said: "A nobleman does not wound someone twice, nor does he take captive someone with gray hair. When armies were used in olden days, they did not cut off the enemy in a narrow place. Though I may be only the remnant of a fallen dynasty, I will not smite an enemy who has not yet drawn up his battle line."

Zi-yu, the War Chief, said: "My Lord does not understand battle. If a more powerful foe is caught in a narrow place with his battle lines not drawn up, this is Heaven acting on our side. How is it wrong then to cut him off and smite him? Even if we did this, we would have cause for fear. This more powerful force we met today were all our foes. If we caught them, we should have taken them captive, even if they had been venerable and elderly men— what does it have to do with gray hair? 'Understanding shame' and training for battle is this: to try to kill our foes. If you wound someone but do not kill him, why not wound him again? If you spare him a second wound, it is as if you had not wounded him at all. If you spare those with gray hair, it is like surrendering to them. Our armies use the sharpest things; our metal drums raise the spirit by their sounds. Use it when and where it is sharpest; it is well done to cut foes off in a narrow place. The sounds swell to steady resolve; it is well to smite them in their disarray."

The domain of Song, where the descendants of the Shang royal house had been enfeoffed by the Zhou, had a reputation for folly and mad impracticality. Stories of the "man of Song" had something of the quality of an ancient Chinese ethnic joke. The most famous is the following parable from the *Mencius:* "There once was a man of Song who was upset that his sprouts were not growing tall, so he pulled on them. He went home in a weary daze and told his family, 'I'm really worn out today—I've been helping the sprouts grow.' His sons hurried to take a look, and the sprouts were all dried out."

An Exegetical Literature

One of the most striking characteristics of early Chinese literature is how often it comes back to acts of explanation and interpretation: people explaining their actions, attitudes, and decisions, or "experts" explaining such matters to princes. Early Chinese literature was, after all, composed by those who made their living by their ability to explain the causes and consequences of phenomena, especially in a political context. Thus Confucius enjoined his disciples to look behind appearances.

Analects II.10

The Master said, "Look to *how* it is. Consider from what it comes. Examine in what a person would be at rest. How can a person remain hidden?— how can someone remain hidden?"

In the following passage, the great domain of Chu has defeated the minor domain of Cai at Shen and taken its count into captivity. The Count of Cai bore a grudge against the Lord of Xi; in order to have revenge, he praises the beauty of Lady Gui of Xi to the ruler of Chu so that the ruler will seize her for his own.

The Zuo Tradition, an entry for the 14th year of Duke Zhuang (680 B.C.)

On account of what happened at Shen, Count Ai of Cai commended the Lady Gui of Xi in speech to the Master of Chu. The Master of Chu went to Xi; and bringing food for a feast, he entered that place and destroyed it. He brought back the Lady Gui of Xi with him and begat on her Du-ao and Cheng-wang. She never spoke. The Master of Chu asked her of this, and she answered, "I am but a single wife, yet I have served two husbands. Even though I have not been able to die, how can I continue to speak?"

Because the Count of Cai had brought destruction on Xi, the Master of Chu then attacked Cai. It was autumn, the seventh month, when Chu entered the city of Cai.

The Lady of Xi was much praised for her silence; yet she has to speak up in order to explain why she is keeping silent. Without words, the silence would not be understood.

Most of the entries in *The Zuo Tradition* are exemplary in that there is an ethical conclusion to be drawn from the event narrated. In the following example, there is something faintly comic in the lesson that the moralist is obliged to draw.

The Zuo Tradition, an entry for the 3rd year of Duke Ding (507 B.C.)

In spring, the second month, the third year, on the day *xin-mao,* the Master of Zhu was on the terrace over the gates, and he looked down into the courtyard. The gatekeeper was washing down the courtyard with a jug of water. The Master of Zhu saw him and was enraged. The gatekeeper said, "Yi Shi-gu pissed here." The Master of Zhu commanded that the man be seized; and when he was not taken, it fed his rage. He cast himself upon a bunk and fell into the embers of a brazier. He burned, then died. He was buried with five chariots, and five men went with him to the grave. Duke Zhuang of Zhu came to this on account of his hot temper and love of cleanliness.

The Zuo Tradition was much admired by the Chinese for its economy of style, a sharp terseness by which great things occur in a few words. In the following account, no one is sure who cut the orchids or why. That year in the entry in the annals of Lu, Duke Mu of Zheng, whose name was "Orchid," died. As he himself knew, his death corresponded with the cutting of the orchids. *The Zuo Tradition* tries to explain this occurrence; the explanation leads to an examination of how he received his name and how he eventually came to the throne of Zheng. The account begins with Orchid's birth to a lowborn concubine and how the other sons of Duke Wen, with better claim to the Zheng throne, were either killed or banished.

The Zuo Tradition, an entry for the 3rd year of Duke Xuan (606 B.C.)

In that winter Duke Mu of Zheng [Orchid] died.

At the beginning, Duke Wen of Zheng had a lowborn handmaiden, who was of the house of Ji from Yan. She dreamed that a messenger from Heaven gave her an orchid. He said, "I am Uncle Minnow; I am your forebear. This will be your son. And because [the] orchid has the sweetest smell in all the land, people will wear it in their sashes and be fond of it."

After that Duke Wen saw her. He gave her an orchid and bedded her. She sent him word, "I am not a person of high birth. I have been lucky to have a son, and it will not be believed that he is yours. May I take the orchid as proof?" And the Duke said, "Yes." She bore Duke Mu, and she named him "Orchid."

Duke Wen had committed incest with Gui of Chen, who had been the consort of the former Master of Zheng. She bore Zi-hua and Zi-zang. Zi-zang did a wrong and left the land. The Duke tricked Zi-hua and had him slain at South Hamlet. Then he set thugs to slay Zi-zang in the region between Chen and Song.

He then took a wife from the house of Jiang. She bore him Gong-zi Shi. Gong-zi Shi went to the court of Chu. Someone in Chu gave him poisoned wine, and he died when he reached Ye.

The Duke next took a wife from the Su. She bore him Zi-xia and Zi-yu-mi. Yu-mi died young. Xie Jia hated Zi-xia. Duke Wen also hated him, and therefore would not make him the heir. The Duke banished all his princes, and Prince Orchid fled to Jin. And Orchid later went with Duke Wen of Jin when he invaded Zheng.

Shi Gui said, "I have heard that when the house of Tsi [the Jin] and the Ji are mated, their offspring will always be teeming. The Ji are people of good luck. One of them was the foremost wife of Hou Ji. Prince Orchid is of the Ji on the distaff side. Heaven may well be opening the way for him; he will surely be the ruler, and his offspring will surely be teeming. If we are the first to bring him into the domain, we may keep his favor." With Kong Jiang-chu and Hou Xuan-duo he brought him into the domain and took an oath with him in the great palace and set him on the throne. By this peace was made with Jin.

Duke Mu became ill. He said, "When the orchid dies, will I not die? For by this was I born." They cut down the orchid and he died.

Heroes of the Will

Extended narrative for the most part developed around certain individuals who captured an interest that went beyond exemplary lessons to be learned from their behavior. We have accounts of spokesmen for ethical values or political expediency. Yet there were also stories of men embodying less approved values: heroes driven by fated misfortunes, irrational loyalties, or the hunger for revenge. In these stories, more than in others, we often note a fascination with balances and imbalances, acts of generosity repaid and hurts revenged.

The following story of Yu-rang is taken from the *Schemes of the Warring States (Zhan-guo ce)*, a compilation of historical anecdotes and framed political speeches from the early Western Han. The same story occurs also in the "Biographies of the Assassins" in the *Historical Records* of Si-ma Qian.

from the *Schemes of the Warring States (Zhan-guo ce)*

Yu-rang, grandson of Bi Yang of Jin, first entered the service of the houses of the Fan and the Zhong-hang, but he was unhappy there. He quit and went to the Earl of Zhi of Jin, who treated him with great favor. When the three branches of Jin divided up the realm of the house of the Earl of Zhi, it was Lord Xiang of Zhao who felt the greatest ill will toward the Earl of Zhi and took his skull as his drinking vessel. Yu-rang had fled into hiding in the hills and said, "A liegeman dies for the man who appreciates him; a woman makes herself beautiful for the man who is pleased with her. May I then take vengeance on this enemy of the house of the Earl of Zhi!" He changed his name and made himself a branded criminal. Thus he got into the palace as a plasterer of the latrines, with the purpose of assassinating Lord Xiang.

Lord Xiang was on his way to the latrine and had a trembling of the heart. He had the plasterer seized and questioned, and it turned out to be Yu-rang, who had put a sharp edge on his trowel. Yu-rang said, "I wanted to take revenge on the enemy of the Earl of Zhi." His entourage wanted to put Yu-rang to death, but Lord Xiang of Zhao said, "This is a liegeman of principle. I will merely keep him away from me. The Earl of Zhi is dead and has no offspring, yet one who served him will go so far as to seek revenge on his enemies. This is one of the most worthy men in the world." And in the end he had Yu-rang set free.

Yu-rang next put lacquer on his body to cover it with sores; he got rid of his whiskers and eyebrows and mutilated himself to alter his appearance. He then went begging. Even his wife did not recognize him. But she said, "Since this man doesn't look at all like my husband, why does his voice sound so much like that of my husband?" After this he swallowed ashes to make himself hoarse and changed the sound of his voice.

A friend said to him, "The course you are following is one of great hardship, yet one that does not do the deed. If you would be spoken of as a man of powerful will, then it will be so; but you will not be spoken of as a resourceful man. If you used your talents in the skillful service of Lord Xiang, he would certainly draw you close to him and make you his favorite. If you could get close to him, then you could do whatever you wanted. This would be very easy, and the deed could be done." Yu-rang then laughed and answered him, "This would be to take revenge on the second man who appreciated me for the sake of the first man who appreciated me. This would be to turn outlaw against a new lord for the sake of a former lord. Nothing could more violate the principle of the bond between a lord and one who serves him. What I intend in doing as I do is to make clear the bond between a lord and one who serves him—it is not to take the easy way. To give a pledge of fealty and serve a man while seeking to assassinate him is to serve one's lord with duplicity in the heart. This hard thing that I do now may even put to shame all those in the world who in later times serve their lords with duplicity in their hearts."

After some while, Lord Xiang was to go forth, and Yu-rang hid under a bridge across which he would have to pass. But when Lord Xiang reached the bridge, his horse reared, whereupon Lord Xiang said, "Yu-rang must be here." He ordered someone to question the man, and it was indeed Yu-rang. Thereupon Lord Xiang of Zhao faced Yu-rang and said, "Did you not once serve the houses of Fan and Zhong-hang? Yet when the Earl of Zhi destroyed those houses, you did not take revenge on him, but rather pledged him your fealty. The Earl of Zhi is dead now, so why only in this case are you so deeply determined to take revenge on his enemy?" Yu-rang said, "I served the houses of Fan and Zhong-hang, yet they treated me as an ordinary man. So in return I behaved toward them like an ordinary man. The Earl of Zhi treated me like one of the liegemen of the domain. So in return I behave like a liegeman of the domain."

Lord Xiang gave a great sigh and shed tears, saying, "Oh, Yu-rang! You have already become famous for what you have done on the Earl of Zhi's account. And I forgave you then—that too was enough. You make plans on your own behalf now, and I may not forgive you." And he ordered his men to form a ring around him.

Then Yu-rang said, "I have heard it said that a wise ruler does not force a man to conceal his principles and I have heard that one who serves with loyalty, to make his fame complete, does not cling to life. Before you were lenient and forgave me, and for this the whole world praises your virtue. I do indeed accept the punishment that must follow from what has happened today. Still, if I could ask for your coat and stab it, I would feel no resentment in my death. I cannot expect this, but I reveal what is within me."

Thereupon Lord Xiang saw that Yu-rang did indeed have principles, and he ordered one who served him to take his coat and give it to Yu-rang. Yu-rang drew out his sword, leapt around several times, shouted to Heaven, and stabbed the coat, saying, "By this I take vengeance for the Earl of Zhi." Then he fell on his sword and died. On the day he died the liegemen of Zhao heard of it, and they all wept.

Swindles and Bad Exchanges: The Problems Surrounding Bian He's Jade

There may be problems with exchanges. First of all, the worth of something offered must be recognized and the giver acknowledged. But beyond that, swindles are possible, particularly during the world of stratagem and deception of the Warring States, in which cleverness was the only match for raw power. Such exchanges are often matters of life and death, or body parts sacrificed.

The *Han Fei-zi* are the essays of the Legalist philosopher Han Fei (ca. 280–ca. 233 B.C.).

Jade" (or "Bian He's Jade"), from the *Han Fei-zi*

was a man of Chu, of the family He, who found a piece of jade in the
ut in the mountains of Chu. He presented it to King Li, who had his
ert examine it. The jade expert said, "This is ordinary stone." The
king thought that Bian He was trying to deceive him and had his left foot
cut off as a punishment. When King Li passed away and King Wu took the
throne, Bian He again took his jade and presented it to King Wu. King Wu
had his jade expert examine it, and again it was pronounced to be ordinary
stone. This king too thought Bian He was trying to deceive him and had his
right foot cut off. When King Wu passed away and King Wen ascended the
throne, Bian He took his jade in his arms and wept at the base of Chu Mountain. For three days and three nights he wept until he had no more tears left,
until blood fell from his eyes. The king heard of this and sent someone to
find out the cause. The envoy said, "There are many people in the world
whose feet have been cut off. Why are you weeping about it so sadly?" And
Bian He answered, "I'm not sad about having my feet cut off; I'm sad because this precious piece of jade has been judged a mere stone and because
a most honorable gentleman has been called a fraud—this is what makes
me sad." The king then had his own jade expert work on the stone, and he
found the gem within. Consequently the king commanded that it be called
"Bian He's Disk."

Bian He's jade is made into a disk, a *bi,* an object of power that was much prized
by the great nobility. As the disk made from Bian He's jade changes hands, we have
again problems of exchange value, fraud, and the threat of violence.

Historical Records (Shi-ji), from the "Biographies of Lian Bo and Lin Xiang-ru"

Lian Bo was Zhao's finest general. In the sixteenth year of King Hui-wen of
Zhao, Lian Bo served as Zhao's general in the attack on Qi, inflicting great
ruin upon them and taking Yang-jin. He was granted the post of high minister and was known for his boldness among the great nobility. Lin Xiang-
ru was also from Zhao and was the retainer of Miao Xian, commander of
the eunuchs.

It was in the days of King Hui-wen that Zhao got the jade disk of Bian
He of Chu. King Zhao of Qin heard of this and sent a man with a letter for
the King of Zhao, conveying his wish to exchange fifteen walled cities for
the jade disk. Upon hearing this, the King of Zhao took counsel with his
grand general Lian Bo and with his other great officers. When they considered presenting the jade to Qin, they feared that they would not get Qin's
cities in return, that they would be cheated and left empty-handed. And yet
when they considered refusing to present the jade, there was the danger that
Qin's troops would come upon them. Their course of action was not yet set-

tled, nor were they successful in finding someone who could be sent to Qin with their answer.

Miao Xian, the commander of the eunuchs, said, "My retainer, Lin Xiang-ru, could be sent."

The king asked, "Why do you think he could do it?"

And Miao Xian replied, "I was once held guilty for a misdeed and planned to flee to Yan, but my retainer Lin Xiang-ru stopped me, saying, 'Why do you think you can have confidence in the King of Yan?' I said to him that I had gone with Your Majesty to a meeting with the King of Yan at the frontier and that the King of Yan had clasped my hand and said, 'I wish to be your friend.' That was why I had confidence in him and thus intended to go there. But Lin Xiang-ru told me, 'Zhao is the stronger, Yan is the weaker, and you enjoyed the favor of the King of Zhao. That is why the King of Yan wanted a bond of friendship with you. If you now flee Zhao to Yan, Yan will be in fear of Zhao. The situation will be such that they will not dare let you stay; they will tie you up and send you back to Zhao. The best thing for you to do would be to bare the upper part of your body and bend down to the block and headsman's ax, asking for punishment for your misdeeds. If you do that, you might be lucky enough to be set free.' I followed that course of action he proposed, and Your Majesty was kind enough to pardon me. I think that this man is a bold fighter, and one with wise counsels. It would be fitting to let him be sent."

Thereupon the king summoned Lin Xiang-ru to an audience and asked him, "Qin wishes to exchange fifteen walled cities for my jade disk. Do I make him a present of it or not?"

Lin Xiang-ru said, "Qin is the stronger and Zhao the weaker—you have no choice but to agree."

The king said, "What can we do if they take my jade disk and don't present me with the cities in return?"

Lin Xiang-ru answered, "If Qin offers cities for the disk and Zhao does not agree, the fault lies with Zhao. If Zhao presents the jade and Qin does not present cities to Zhao in return, the fault lies with Qin. If we weigh these two stratagems in the balance, it is better to agree and make Qin bear the fault."

The king then said, "Whom can I send?"

And Lin Xiang-ru answered, "Your Majesty obviously has no one else. Let me take the disk and go as your envoy. If the cities come to Zhao, the disk will stay in Qin. If the cities don't come to us, then I would bring the disk whole back to Zhao." Thereupon the King of Zhao sent Lin Xiang-ru to bear the disk westward into Qin.

The King of Qin was sitting on Zhang Terrace when he received Lin Xiang-ru. Xiang-ru held the disk before him in his hands and proffered it to the King of Qin. The King of Qin was greatly pleased and handed it around to show to his beautiful women and courtiers, at which all his courtiers shouted their congratulations.

Observing that the King of Qin had no intention of compensating Zhao with the cities, Lin Xiang-ru then came forward and said, "There is a flaw in the jade disk, let me show Your Majesty." When the king handed him the disk, Lin Xiang-ru held it firmly and drew away, keeping his back to a column, the hair bristling against his cap in his rage. And he addressed the King of Qin, "When Your Majesty wanted to get the jade disk and sent an envoy with a letter to the King of Zhao, the King of Zhao summoned every one of his officers to discuss the matter. They all said, 'Qin is grasping. Because it is the stronger, it wants to get our jade disk with empty promises, and we fear we will not get those cities in compensation.' They had proposed not to present Qin with the jade disk. But it was my opinion that if commoners do not cheat one another in their dealings, the great domains are even less likely to do so. Moreover, it would not be fitting to oppose mighty Qin's power for a single disk of jade. Thereupon the King of Zhao fasted for five days, and sent me as the envoy to proffer the disk and to deliver his letter in your court. Why did he do this? To give due show of respect for the awe that we have for your great domain. Now I have arrived. Your Majesty receives me in an ordinary lodge and is extremely haughty in the forms of behavior with which you treat me. You get the jade disk and pass it around among your women to mock and insult me. Now that I see that Your Majesty has no intention of giving the cities in compensation to the King of Zhao, I have taken back the jade disk. I am sure that Your Majesty wants to have your people fall upon me now; but if you do, I will smash both my head and the jade disk on the column." Lin Xiang-ru held the disk firmly in hand, with his eyes on the column, ready to strike it.

The King of Qin, fearing that Lin Xiang-ru would break the disk, made excuses and entreated him. He summoned the man in charge to spread out a map, and with his fingers he pointed to the line beyond which the fifteen great cities would be Zhao's. But Lin Xiang-ru had the measure of the King of Qin, that he merely was pretending to present Zhao with the cities and that Zhao would never have them. He then addressed the King of Qin, "He's jade disk is a treasure known everywhere in the world. In his fear the King of Zhao did not dare to refuse to offer it. But when the King of Zhao sent it, he fasted for five days. It is fitting now that Your Majesty as well fast for five days and that you have a ceremony for officers of all ranks in your court. Then I will offer up the jade disk."

The King of Qin took the measure of the situation and knew that he would never be able to take the jade away by force. So he agreed to fast five days and gave Lin Xiang-ru apartments in the Guang-cheng Lodge. For his part Lin Xiang-ru had the measure of the King of Qin, that even though he was fasting, the king had determined to break the agreement and not to offer the cities in compensation. He then had one of the men who had come with him put on shabby clothes and conceal the jade disk in the folds. The man was to flee by the shortest route and bring the jade disk back to Zhao.

After the King of Qin had fasted for five days, he had the ceremony for officers of all ranks in his court, then had the envoy of Zhao, Lin Xiang-ru, led in. When Lin Xiang-ru arrived, he addressed the King of Qin: "Of the more than twenty lords of Qin from the time of Duke Miao there has never been one who has been steadfast in his oaths. Since I was truly afraid of being cheated by Your Majesty and thus failing Zhao, I ordered a man to take the jade disk back, and he should be in Zhao shortly. Qin is the stronger and Zhao the weaker. Your Majesty sent a single envoy to Zhao, and Zhao sent one back at once proffering the jade disk. Given Qin's superior strength, if it had first cut away fifteen of its cities and presented them to Zhao, Zhao could not possibly have kept the jade and, by its actions, shown itself guilty before Your Majesty. I understand that I must be executed for the crime of deceiving Your Majesty, so carry me off to the cauldron of boiling water. All I ask is that Your Majesty and his officers give this some discussion."

The King of Qin and his officers looked at one another in seething rage. Some among the courtiers wanted to drag Lin Xiang-ru away, when the king said, "If we kill Lin Xiang-ru now, we'll never be able to get the jade disk and we will break the goodwill that exists between Qin and Zhao. The best course is to treat him very well and send him back to Zhao. For how could the King of Zhao work a deception on Qin for the sake of a single jade disk?"

In the end he invited Lin Xiang-ru to a feast and sent him back after having treated him with all the courtesies.

Once Lin Xiang-ru had returned, the King of Zhao considered him a most worthy grand master who had kept him from humiliation before the great nobility. He appointed Lin Xiang-ru as High Grand Master. And Qin never presented Zhao with its cities, nor did Zhao ever present the jade disk to Qin.

The Story of Wu Zi-xu

There are basic differences between narrative in *The Zuo Tradition* and in the Western Han *Historical Records* of Si-ma Qian. *The Zuo Tradition* is an intricately structured total history of the domains, which remains true to its origins in the chronicle. Necessary pieces of information and related events appear in small pieces scattered over a span of years, each given under the year when it occurred. No single linear narrative can arise out of the totality of historical narrative, and thus the Wu Zi-xu narrative is submerged within the more intricate account of the rise of Wu and its defeat of Chu, then the rise of Yue and its ultimate conquest of Wu. These narratives are, in turn, bound by many threads to events in the other domains. In contrast, the narrative account of a particular person in the *Historical Records* is a relatively complete whole. Si-ma Qian usually worked with earlier historical materials, but he revised them and shaped them into a unity. The same information may be given in different parts of the *Historical Records,* but in each context Si-ma Qian refashioned the material according the needs of the story at hand. Before the *Historical Records,* the anecdote was the most fully developed narrative form; Si-ma Qian used biography, particularly the life of someone driven by a single purpose, to create a larger narrative unity.

The Wu Zi-xu story is a good example of how stories worked in early China. Stories were retold again and again, sometimes verbatim, sometimes differing in phrasing according to the idiom and period of the writer. Sometimes passages dropped out, but more often the process was one of elaboration, with old incidents expanded in greater detail and new incidents added. As can be seen in the comparison between the versions of the Wu Zi-xu story in the *Historical Records* and the earlier *Zuo Tradition*, the elaborations were often irresistibly "good stories," some of whose sources we can find in other early texts. The process was by no means completed with the version in the *Historical Records*. It was further elaborated in two Eastern Han works, *Springs and Autumns of Wu and Yue (Wu Yue Chun-qiu)* and the *Yue-jue shu*. The story found a vernacular version centuries later in the Tang, known as the *Wu Zi-xu Transformation Text (Wu Zi-xu bian-wen)*, and it continued to be reworked in plays and stories in the later imperial period.

For the sake of clarity we will give first the full version of the Wu Zi-xu story from the *Historical Records*, followed by the earlier accounts of incidents in Wu Zi-xu's life from *The Zuo Tradition*. Note how in the *Historical Records*, Si-ma Qian followed *The Zuo Tradition* very closely in some places and deviated in others. Since the narrative has many characters, a list of the major groups is given below:

Chu Royal Family
　　KING PING: who has Wu Zi-xu's father and brother killed
　　PRINCE JIAN: heir apparent, driven into exile by King Ping
　　KING ZHAO: another son of King Ping, and his successor
　　SHENG: son of Prince Jian, rescued by Wu Zi-xu

The Wu Family
　　WU SHE: the father, loyal adviser to King Ping
　　WU SHANG: Wu She's eldest son
　　WU ZI-XU (WU YUN): Wu She's younger son

Wu Royal Family
　　KING LIAO: ruler when Wu Zi-xu first came to Wu
　　KING HE-LÜ: formerly Prince Guang, conqueror of Chu, dead of a
　　　　wound in battle with Yue
　　KING FU-CHA: He-lü's son, defeated by Yue

Yue Royal Family
　　KING GOU-JIAN

Other Important Characters
　　FEI WU-JI: corrupt adviser to King Ping of Chu
　　BO PI: adviser to Kings He-lü and Fu-cha of Wu, bribed by Yue
　　BAO-XU OF SHEN: loyal minister of King Zhao of Chu, who
　　　　persuades Qin to come to the aid of Chu

Historical Records, "Biography of Wu Zi-xu"

Wu Zi-xu, or Wu Yun, was a native of Chu. His father was called Wu She; his elder brother was called Wu Shang. An ancestor, called Wu Ju, was famous for having served King Zhuang of Chu with his forthright counsels, and thus his descendants had a good name in Chu.

King Ping of Chu had a crown prince called Jian; the king commissioned Wu She as his chief tutor and Fei Wu-ji as his secondary tutor. Yet Fei Wu-ji was not faithful to Prince Jian. King Ping sent Fei Wu-ji on a mission to Qin to get a bride for the prince. The daughter of Qin was lovely, and Fei Wu-ji hurried back to tell King Ping: "This daughter of Qin is exceedingly beautiful—Your Majesty might take her himself and get another wife for the prince." Thereupon the king did indeed take the daughter of Qin for himself and doted on her exceedingly, from which union was born a son, Zhen. He got another wife for the crown prince.

Having used the daughter of Qin to win the favor of King Ping, Fei Wu-ji left the service of the crown prince to serve King Ping himself. But he feared the day when the king would die and the crown prince succeed to the throne; and he feared that then he would be killed. For this reason, he spoke ill of Prince Jian. Jian's mother was the daughter of the house of Cai and enjoyed no favor from King Ping. Bit by bit King Ping grew increasingly distant from Jian, and he sent Jian to hold Cheng-fu and watch over the troops on the frontier.

After a short while, Fei Wu-ji once again spoke of the crown prince's failings to the king day and night. "Because of the affair of the daughter of Qin, the prince cannot avoid bitterness. Your Majesty might want to take a few precautions for your own sake. Since the prince occupies Cheng-fu, has command of troops, and has dealings with the great nobility outside the kingdom, he may well want to move on the capital and create a rebellion." Then King Ping called his chief tutor, Wu She, to question him thoroughly about this. Wu She knew that Fei Wu-ji had spoken ill of the prince to King Ping, so he said: "How can Your Majesty become estranged from your own flesh and blood because of some maligning villain of a petty court official?" To which Fei Wu-ji said: "If Your Majesty doesn't stop it now, the matter will be accomplished, and Your Majesty will be seized." Thereupon the king flew into a rage, imprisoned Wu She, and sent the Commander of Cheng-fu, Fen Yang, on a mission to kill the prince. But before he reached the prince, Fen Yang sent someone ahead to tell him: "Your Highness should leave as quickly as possible; otherwise I will execute you." Prince Jian escaped and fled to Song.

Then Fei Wu-ji said to King Ping: "Wu She has two sons, both worthy men. If you don't execute them, they may bring troubles to Chu. With their father as a hostage, you may call them to court. Otherwise they may bring great evil upon Chu." The king sent an envoy to tell Wu She: "If you get your two sons to come, you will live; if you cannot, you will die." Wu She replied: "Wu Shang is kindly by nature; and if I call, he will certainly come. But Wu Zi-xu is by nature hard and untamed; he can put up with the shame, and he is capable of creating great problems. When he sees that he and his brother will both be seized if they come, his inclination will certainly be not to come." But the king would not listen, and sent someone to call the two brothers to court: "Come, and I will let your father live. Fail to come and I will kill Wu She immediately."

Wu Shang was ready to go, but Wu Zi-xu said: "When Chu calls both brothers to court, it is not because he intends to let our father live. He will fear that if we get free, we will work great harm in later times. That's why he is calling us to court with false assurances, using our father as a hostage. When we get there, we and our father will all die together. What will that do for our father's death? By going we will make it impossible to be revenged on our enemy. The best course would be to flee to some other domain and make use of their force to wipe away this shame that has been put on our father. It will do no good for all of us to be wiped out." Wu Shang answered: "I know that going will not save our father from his doom. But still I could not endure to have failed to go when our father has called us to save his life; if afterward I could not wipe away the shame done to him, I would end up being laughed at by the whole world." And he told Wu Zi-xu: "Get away yourself! You will be able to revenge us on our enemies. I am going to go die." When Wu Shang had gone to submit to arrest, the envoy tried to seize Wu Zi-xu. Wu Zi-xu bent his bow, notched an arrow, and pointed it at the envoy, who did not dare come any closer. Then Wu Zi-xu escaped. And hearing that Prince Jian was in Song, he went off to serve him.

Wu She heard that Wu Zi-xu had escaped, and he said, "The lord and court officials of the Kingdom of Chu now may well suffer war." When Wu Shang reached the capital, the king killed both Wu She and Wu Shang.

When Wu Zi-xu came to Song, the civil strife caused by the Hua clan broke out. Then together with Prince Jian he fled to Zheng. The people of Zheng were on very good terms with them. Prince Jian next went on to Jin. Lord Qing of Jin said: "Your Highness is on such good terms with Zheng that Zheng trusts Your Highness. If you would act for me from within the capital when I attack it from the outside, Zheng will surely be wiped out. When Zheng is wiped out, I will give Your Highness a fief." The prince then went back to Zheng. Before that action came to pass, it happened that the prince, for his own reasons, was going to kill one of his entourage. The man knew of the plot and told the Lord of Zheng. Lord Ding and his minister Zi-chan then executed Prince Jian. Jian had a son named Sheng. Wu Zi-xu was afraid, so he fled together with Sheng to Wu. When he reached the Zhao Barrier [between Chu and Wu], they were going to arrest him. Then Wu Zi-xu went running off on foot alone with Sheng, and they almost didn't get away. The pursuers were right behind them. They reached the river, on which there was a single fisherman in a boat. Understanding that Wu Zi-xu was hardpressed, the fisherman took him across. Once Wu Zi-xu was across, he took off his sword, saying: "This sword is worth a hundred in gold—I am giving it to you." The fisherman said: "There is a law in the Kingdom of Chu that whoever takes Wu Zi-xu will be rewarded with fifty thousand measures of rice and the jade badge of a court noble. What's a sword worth just a hundred in gold to that!" And he would not accept the sword. Before he reached the capital of Wu, Wu Zi-xu got sick and had to stop halfway along his journey to beg for food. When he reached the capital of Wu, King Liao was ruling, and Guang, a prince of the blood, was general. Then, through Guang, Wu Zi-xu sought a meeting with the King of Wu.

A long time later King Ping of Chu flew into a great rage because two women attacked one another in an argument over some mulberry trees, one from the Chu frontier town of Zhong-li, and the other from a Wu frontier town under the Bei-liang clan, both of which towns made silk. It reached the point where both kingdoms were raising troops to attack one another. Wu sent prince of the blood Guang to attack Chu, and he returned after taking possession Zhong-li and Ju-chao. Wu Zi-xu made an argument to King Liao of Wu: "Chu can be smashed. I would have you send Guang back again." But Guang told the king: "Wu Zi-xu's father and elder brother were slain by Chu, and his urging Your Majesty to attack Chu is only his desire to be revenged on his own foes. No attack on Chu can smash it yet." Wu Zi-xu understood that the prince Guang had aims that he was keeping to himself, that he wanted to kill the king and take the throne himself, and therefore could not be swayed to actions outside the kingdom. Wu then recommended Zhuan Zhu to the prince Guang, and withdrawing from court, went to farm in the wilderness with Prince Jian's son Sheng.

After five years King Ping of Chu passed away. Earlier, the daughter of Qin, whom King Ping had snatched away from Prince Jian, had given birth to Zhen; and when King Ping passed away, Zhen ultimately succeeded him as heir to the throne, known as King Zhao. King Liao of Wu took advantage of the mourning for the king and sent two princes of the blood with troops to make raids into Chu. Chu sent out troops to cut off the rear of the Wu troops, and the Wu troops were unable to get back. The Kingdom of Wu was left bare; then prince of the blood Guang ordered Zhuan Zhu to rush in and stab the king, after which he himself took the throne as He-lü, King of Wu. Once He-lü ascended the throne and his ambitions were fulfilled, he then called Wu Zi-xu to serve him in relations with other states; and he took counsel with him on matters of the domain.

Chu had executed two great officers of the court, Wan of Xi and Bo Zhou-li. Bo Zhou-li's grandson, Bo Pi, escaped and fled to Wu; and Wu went so far as to make him a Counselor. Previously the two princes and their troops, whom King Liao had sent to attack Chu, had their retreat cut off and could not get back. Hearing later that He-lü had killed King Liao and set himself on the throne, they surrendered with their troops to Chu, who gave them fiefs in Shu. Three years after He-lü took the throne, he raised an army and, together with Wu Zi-xu and Bo Pi, attacked Chu, took Shu, and seized the two former Wu generals who had changed sides. Thereafter he wanted to reach Ying, the Chu capital, but his general, Sun Wu, said: "Not yet—the men are worn out. Wait a while." Then he returned.

In the fourth year of his reign, Wu again attacked Chu, and took Lu and Qian. In the fifth year of his reign he attacked Yue and defeated it. In the sixth year, King Zhao of Chu sent the prince of the blood Nang Wa with troops to attack Wu. Wu sent Wu Zi-xu to meet him, and he smashed the Chu army at Yu-zhang and took Chu's city Ju-chao.

In the ninth year of his reign, He-lü, King of Wu, spoke to Wu Zi-xu and Sun Wu: "Before, you said I could not enter the Chu capital Ying. How is it now?" Both men answered: "Chu's general Nang Wa is a grasping man, and the domains of Tang and Cai both hold a grudge against him. If Your Majesty must make a major attack, it will work only if you first get Tang and Cai." He-lü listened to them. He raised his entire army and together with Tang and Cai attacked Chu, forming his ranks facing the Chu forces that were drawn up on the other side of the Han River. The king's younger brother Fu-gai asked to be sent after them, but the king would not agree. Then, with the five thousand men attached to him, Fu-gai struck the Chu general Nang Wa, who was defeated and ran away, fleeing to the state of Zheng. Thereupon Wu took advantage of its victory and advanced; and after five battles, it finally reached Ying. It was the day *ji-mao* when King Zhao of Chu fled the city; it was one day later, *geng-chen,* when the King of Wu entered Ying.

King Zhao escaped the city into the Yun-meng hunting preserve. There outlaws attacked the king, who was hurrying toward Yun. Huai, who was the younger brother of the lord of Yun, said: "Would it not be fair that since King Ping of Chu killed my father, I may kill his son?" The Lord of Yun was afraid that his brother would kill the king and joined the king in flight to Sui. Troops of Wu surrounded Sui and told the people of Sui: "It was Chu that wiped out all the heirs of the house of Zhou along the river Han." The people of Sui wanted to kill the king, but the prince-royal Qi sheltered him and was going to act the part of the king himself. The people of Sui made divination as to whether or not they should deliver the king to Wu. The result was unlucky. So they refused Wu and did not deliver the king.

In the beginning, Wu Zi-xu had been associated with Bao-xu of Shen. When Wu Zi-xu was escaping, he told Bao-xu: "I will be the ruin of Chu." To which Bao-xu replied: "And I will preserve it." When the troops of Wu entered Ying, Wu Zi-xu went looking for King Zhao; and since he couldn't find him, he dug up the tomb of King Ping of Chu, took out the corpse, and flogged it, stopping only after he had given it three hundred lashes. Bao-xu of Shen escaped into the mountains and sent someone to say to Wu Zi-xu: "Don't you think you have gone too far in your revenge? It is my understanding that masses of men may overcome Heaven, but that Heaven is certainly capable of smashing those men. You once were a liegeman of King Ping; you yourself served him, facing north to the throne; now you have reached the point of dishonoring a dead man. Don't you see that this is an extreme failure to follow Heaven's right way?" Wu Zi-xu replied: "Give my respects to Bao-xu of Shen. The day draws toward nightfall; my road is long. I go against the tide, yet I will do this in spite of all."

At this, Bao-xu of Shen hurried to Qin to tell them about the crisis, seeking succor from Qin. But Qin would not agree to help. Bao-xu stood in the courtyard of Qin and wept by day and by night. For seven days and seven nights the sound never ceased. Then Lord Ai of Qin took pity on him and said: "Even though Chu was wanting in the right way, it has liegemen like this! Can we do otherwise than save it?" Then he sent five hundred chariots to save Chu and strike Wu. In the sixth month of that year they defeated Wu's troops at Ji. It happened that He-lü had remained a long time in Chu seeking King Zhao; meanwhile He-lü's younger brother Fu-gai surreptitiously made his way back to Wu and set himself on the throne as king. When He-lü heard of it, he let go of Chu and made his way back to strike his brother Fu-gai. Fu-gai was defeated and ran, eventually fleeing to Chu. When King Zhao saw the internal strife in Wu, he reentered Ying. He gave Fu-gai a fief at Tang-xi, which became the Tang-xi clan. Chu again joined Wu in battle and defeated it, whereupon the King of Wu made his way home.

Two years afterwards, He-lü sent the Crown Prince Fu-cha with troops to attack Chu. They took Pan. Chu feared that Wu would come again in force and left Ying, shifting the capital to Ruo. It was in those days that Wu, using the counsels of Wu Zi-xu and Sun Wu, broke through its western borders with Chu, held Qi and Jin to make the north feel awe of their might, and to the south made the people of Yue yield.

Four years after that, Confucius was the minister in Lu.

Five years later they attacked Yue. The Yue king Gou-jian met them, defeating Wu at Gu-Su. They wounded He-lü's finger, and the army withdrew. He-lü, on the point of death from a sickness from that wound, told the Crown Prince Fu-cha: "Will you forget that Gou-jian killed your father?" Fu-cha replied: "I will never forget." That evening He-lü died. When Fu-cha ascended the throne, he made Bo Pi the Grand Steward, and had the troops practice archery. After two years he attacked Yue, and defeated Yue at Fu-jiao. Then Gou-jian, King of Yue, took temporary refuge on Kuai-ji with his remaining five thousand troops. He sent Counselor Zhong with rich gifts for Grand Steward Bo Pi, begging for an accommodation, and seeking to make his state a vassal of Wu. The King of Wu was about to agree, but Wu Zi-xu protested: "The King of Yue is the kind of man who is able to take suffering. If Your Majesty does not wipe him out now, you will certainly rue it later." But the King of Wu would not listen to him, and employed the Grand Steward Bo Pi to make peace with Yue.

Five years later, the King of Wu heard that Lord Jing of Qi had died and that the great officers of the state were struggling for the favor of the new lord, who was then young. He then raised his army to go north to attack Qi. Wu Zi-xu protested, saying: "When Gou-jian eats, he pays no attention to how the food tastes; he laments those who die and pays attention when people are sick; it would seem that he has plans to make use of them. So long as this man does not die, he will certainly bring affliction upon Wu. At present Yue's existence in relation to Wu is like a person having an illness in the heart or stomach. Can't Your Majesty see what a mistake it is to expend your efforts in Qi without first considering Yue?" The King of Wu did not listen to him. He attacked Qi and inflicted a great defeat on the Qi army at Ai-ling. Then he put the rulers of Zou and Lu in awe of his might and returned. And he paid increasingly less attention to Wu Zi-xu's counsels.

Four years after that, the King of Wu was about to go north to attack Qi, and King Gou-jian of Yue, following the counsels of Zi-gong, led his hosts to help Wu. Again he made presents of rich treasures to the Grand Steward Bo Pi. Bo Pi, having received the gifts of Yue, developed for Yue immense faith and fondness, and day and night spoke on its behalf to the King of Wu. The King of Wu had faith in Bo Pi's plans and followed them. Wu Zi-xu protested again: "Yue is an illness in the heart or stomach. In your present greed for Qi, you are giving faith to baseless statements and deceptions. If you smash Qi, it will be as a stony field—you will have no use from it. The Pan-geng Declaration in the [*Classic of*] *Documents* says: 'Whosoever overturns my will or transgresses or wants due reverence, his nose shall be hacked off and I will destroy him utterly, and I shall cause him to have no spawn remaining, neither shall I let him shift his sprouts to this my new city.' This was how the Shang rose. I would have Your Majesty let go of Qi and consider Yue first. If you do not do so, the regrets you will have later will do you no good." Yet the King of Wu did not heed him, but sent Wu Zi-xu as an envoy to Qi. When Wu Zi-xu was on the point of going, he told his son: "I have protested to the king on a number of occasions, but the king does not follow my advice. I now will see the destruction of Wu. It will do no good if you and Wu are destroyed together." Then he put his son under the protection of Bao Mu of Qi and returned to report to Wu.

Since the Grand Steward Bo Pi had a grudge against Wu Zi-xu, he spoke ill of him: "Wu Zi-xu is a hard and violent man, short on love, mistrustful, a spoiler; and I fear his resentments will bring deep troubles upon us. When before Your Majesty wanted to attack Qi, it was Wu Zi-xu's opinion that you should not; yet in the end Your Majesty did indeed attack Qi and won for yourself great glory. Wu Zi-xu feels humiliated that his counsels were not adopted; he feels a perverse resentment at your success. And now that Your Majesty will again attack Qi, Wu Zi-xu shows single-minded stubbornness in his unbending protests to wreck the undertaking. He will think Wu's defeat a happy outcome because it will show the triumph of his own counsels. Now Your Majesty is himself going, having brought together all the military force in the kingdom to attack Qi. Wu Zi-xu's counsels not being adopted, he withdraws, refusing to go on the pretext of illness. Your Majesty absolutely must take precautions, for in this situation it would not be difficult to cause troubles. Moreover, I sent a man to spy on him when he was on his mission to Qi; he even went so far as to put his son under the protection of the Bao clan. This is the sort of liegeman he is: failing to have his way within the kingdom, he will rely on foreign nobility; considering himself the counselor of the former king and finding his counsels not now adopted, he is always in a state of seething resentment. I would have Your Majesty do something about it as soon as possible."

   The King of Wu said: "Even apart from what you have told me, I would have doubted him." Then he sent an envoy to present Wu Zi-xu with the sword Zhu-lou, saying: "By this you die." Wu Zi-xu raised his head toward Heaven and sighed: "That malicious officer Bo Pi is creating havoc, and Your Majesty executes me instead. I made your father overlord. Before you took the throne, all the princes of the blood were contending for the succession; I was ready to support your cause to the death with the former king, and even so you came close to not succeeding to the throne. And when you did take the throne, you wanted to divide the Kingdom of Wu with me, but I refused it as not being something I expected. However, now you give heed to the words of a lying courtier and kill an honorable man." Then he informed his retainers: "Plant my tomb with catalpas, that they may be had for making coffins for Wu. Dig out my eyeballs and hang them above the eastern gate of the capital of Wu, so that I can watch Yue's thugs when they enter the great city and wipe out Wu." He then cut his throat and died. When the King of Wu heard this, he fell into a great rage; he got hold of Wu Zi-xu's corpse, and stuffing it into a leather wineskin, had it set afloat on the Yangzi River. But the people of Wu felt for him and erected a temple beside the river, which consequently was named Mount Xu.

   Having executed Wu Zi-xu, the King of Wu proceeded to attack Qi. The Bao clan of Qi killed their ruler Lord Dao and set Yang-sheng on the throne. The King of Wu wanted to chastise this crime, but had to withdraw without having achieved the victory. Two years later, the King of Wu called the rulers of Lu and Wei to meet with him at Tuo Meadow. The next year he followed this with a great meeting of the high nobility at Yellow Pool, where he claimed leadership over all the house of Zhou. But then the king of Yue, Gou-jian, made a surprise attack, killing the Crown Prince of Wu and smashing Wu's troops. As soon as the King of Wu heard this, he went back and sent an envoy with rich gifts to treat for peace with Yue. Nine years later, King Gou-jian of Yue wiped out Wu and killed Fu-cha, and further executed the Grand Steward Bo Pi for not having been loyal to his ruler and for taking rich presents from outside the domain, and for forming a faction for the King of Yue himself.

Sheng, the son of the Chu crown prince Jian, with whom Wu Zi-xu had first escaped, remained in Wu. During the time of King Fu-cha, King Hui of Chu wanted to call Sheng back to Chu, but Lord She protested: "Sheng loves daring and is secretly seeking knights who will die for him. Don't you imagine he has some private designs?" King Hui did not heed him and sent for Sheng, making him live in the frontier city of Yan, where he was called Lord Bo. Three years after Lord Bo's return to Chu, Wu executed Wu Zi-xu.

   Once Sheng, Lord Bo, had returned to Chu, he had a store of resentment against the domain of Zheng for having killed his father. And he secretly nourished knights willing to die for him in his quest to pay back Zheng. Five years after his return to Chu, he asked permission to attack Zheng; the Chu

Vizier Zi-xi allowed it. But before the troops set out, Jin attacked Zheng, and Zheng requested aid from Chu. Chu sent Zi-xi to go to their defense, and after taking a blood oath with them, he returned. Sheng, Lord Bo, was enraged and said: "I am not Zheng's foe; I am Zi-xi's!" Sheng was sharpening his sword, and someone asked him what he was doing. Sheng replied: "I am going to kill Zi-xi." When Zi-xi heard of this, he laughed and said, "Sheng is just a hatchling—what can he do?"

Four years later, Sheng, Lord Bo, and Shi Qi assassinated the Chu Vizier Zi-xi and Commander Zi-qi in the court. Shi Qi then said, "We have to kill the king too," whereupon they abducted the king and took him to the High Storehouse. Qu Gu, one of Shi Qi's followers, carried King Hui of Chu as they fled quickly to the palace of the Lady Zhao. On hearing that Lord Bo had rebelled, Lord She led people from his own fief to attack Lord Bo. Lord Bo's followers were defeated, and he escaped into the mountains, where he killed himself. Then, when they made Shi Qi a prisoner, they asked him where Lord Bo's corpse was, saying they would boil him if he didn't tell them. To this, Shi Qi replied: "Succeed and you are the Grand Minister; fail and you are boiled; each position has its own demands." He never was willing to tell where the corpse was. Then they boiled Shi Qi, and after searching for King Hui, they put him back on the throne.

The Lord Historian's comment:

The venom of rancor and resentment is a powerful thing in man. If even a king dare not incite it in his subjects, the case is even more serious among men of equal rank. Had Wu Zi-xu died together with Wu She, it would have been no different from the death of an ant. It is moving indeed that in renouncing that lesser act of virtue he wiped away a greater humiliation, and his name lasts on to later generations. When Wu Zi-xu was in desperate straits beside the river or begging for food on his journey, do you suppose that in his aims he forgot the capital Ying even for an instant? To endure quietly, to reach the deed and the glory of it—only a man of fierce will can achieve this. And if Lord Bo had not set himself up as the ruler, neither his deeds nor his designs would have been worth the telling.

The Zuo Tradition account of Wu Zi-xu's career follows. *The Zuo Tradition* takes for granted that its readers already know the characters and the general background. In the *Historical Records,* one of Si-ma Qian's tasks was to provide enough information for the narrative to stand on its own. In the first *Zuo Tradition* passage, we have Fei Wu-ji, the self-serving villain, who has sought to curry favor with the King of Chu by urging him to take the bride who had been brought from Qin for Crown Prince Jian. The king takes her for himself and has Crown Prince Jian sent off to the border fortress of Fang. Wu She, Wu Zi-xu's father, is the honest courtier, who raises objections to the king's high-handed behavior and thus wins the enmity of Fei Wu-ji.

The Zuo Tradition, an entry for the 20th year of Duke Zhao (522 B.C.)

Fei Wu-ji said to the Ruler of Chu: "Crown Prince Jian and Wu She are going to lead the area beyond Fang City to rise in rebellion, and they will set themselves on a par with Song and Zheng. Qi and Jin will make league to help them, whereby they will work harm on Chu. The deed draws to fullness now." The king believed him. He questioned Wu She. Wu She answered: "Your Majesty's first misdeed was great enough [referring to the king's having taken the crown prince's bride]; why believe maligning words?" The king arrested Wu She and ordered the Commander of Cheng-fu, Fen Yang, to kill the crown prince. Fen Yang ordered someone to precede him and send the crown prince away before he could arrive. The crown prince fled to Song. The king then summoned Fen Yang; and Fen Yang had himself arrested by men of Cheng-fu and taken to the king. The king said: "Words came forth from my mouth, they entered your ears. Who told Prince Jian?" Fen Yang answered: "I did. It was my lord's command: 'Serve Jian as you serve me.' I lack guile. I could not wrongly keep double faith. I have kept your first command throughout, and could not bear the later one. Therefore I sent him away. I have regretted this, still it avails nothing." The king said: "And how is it that you dare come to me?" He answered: "I was given an order and failed to carry out the command. To be summoned and not to come would have been a second treason. There would have been nowhere to escape." The king said: "Go back and continue to govern as before."

Fei Wu-ji said: "Wu She's sons have talents. If they were in Wu, they would surely bring grief to the Kingdom of Chu. Why not summon them by an offer to free their father? They have kindness and will surely come. Otherwise they will bring great evil upon Chu." The king sent someone to call them to court, saying: "Come and I will set your father free." Wu Shang, Lord of Tang, said to his younger brother Wu Zi-xu: "You go off to Wu. I will go back and die. My knowledge does not equal yours. I am able to die; you are able to take revenge. Hearing this command that would free our father, one cannot fail to hurry to answer it. Yet when kin are slain, one also cannot fail to take revenge. To hurry to one's death in order to free one's father is to act well as a son; to take the measure of the deed and carry it through is kindliness; to choose such a burden and leave is knowledge; to know one will die and not to flinch is courage. Our father must not be forsaken, yet our name must not perish. Do your utmost! It is best to let me go my way."

Wu Shang went back. When Wu She heard that Wu Zi-xu had not come with him, he said: "The Lord of Chu and his Grand Master will not be able to eat their dinners on time now."

Chu had them both killed.

Wu Zi-xu went to Wu and there spoke to Zhou-yu, King Liao, of the advantage of an attack on Chu. But the prince Guang [later King He-lü] said:

"This man's kin were slain, and he wants to pay back his foes. We may not follow his advice."

Wu Zi-xu said: "That man would seem to have aims all his own. For the while I will seek fighting men for him, and I myself will bide my time." It was then he had the prince meet Zhuan She-zhu, while he himself farmed in the wilderness.

The Zuo Tradition, an entry for the 4th year of Duke Ding (506 B.C.) (within the longer account of the defeat of Chu)

At first Wu Zi-xu had been a friend of Bao-xu of Shen. When he was escaping, he told Bao-xu of Shen: "I will be the ruin of Chu." To which Bao-xu of Shen replied: "Do your utmost! For if you are able to be its ruin, I will surely be able to make it rise up again." When King Zhao was in Sui [having fled the Wu army that had taken his capital], Bao-xu of Shen went to Qin to seek an army, saying: "Wu is a great boar, a long serpent that will devour the larger domains one by one. The evil has begun in Chu. My ruler has failed to guard his ancestral altars and is now at large in the wilderness. He has sent me to give you these words of his distress: 'The power of these savages knows no satiety; if they become your neighbors, it will be a great evil for your borders. Now, while Wu has not yet completed its conquest, come you and take your portion of us. If Chu then is to perish, it will be your land. But if, by your holy force, you show us grace, so will we serve you for generations.'"

The Duke of Qin commanded him to withdraw, saying: "I have heard the command. You go to the guest lodge for the while. I will make plans and inform you of them."

But Bao-xu of Shen answered: "My ruler is at large in the wilderness and has found no place of refuge. How can I, his liegeman, take my ease?" He stood there, resting against the courtyard wall and weeping. The sound did not cease by day or night. For seven days not a spoonful did he drink with his mouth. At last Duke Ai of Qin recited for him the *Poem* "No Clothes," at which he touched his head to the ground nine times and sat down. The armies of Qin then went forth.

By reciting "No Clothes," Duke Ai of Qin let Bao-xu know that he had agreed to take the field against Wu.

> How can you say, "I have no clothes"?—
> I will share my greatcoat with you.
> The king is raising his army,
> we will make ready pike and spear,
> and I will share all foes with you.

After Wu Zi-xu had completed his revenge against Chu, he remained as an adviser to Wu. When he protested against the policy of conciliating the neighboring kingdom of Yue and interfering in the intricate politics of the northern domains, he lost the favor of the new king, Fu-cha, and was ordered to commit suicide.

The Zuo Tradition, an entry for the 11th year of Duke Ai (484 B.C.)

Wu was about to attack Qi, and the Ruler of Yue led his hosts to pay his respects to the court of Wu. The king and his warriors all were given presents. The men of Wu were all delighted. Only Wu Zi-xu was afraid and said, "They fatten Wu up for the slaughter." And he presented his protest: "Yue's relation to us is that of an illness of the stomach or heart. Our lands would form a single whole, and they want to take ours from us. By such meekness and yielding they further their desire. If you achieve your aims in Qi, it is like getting a stony field—you will have no use from it. If you don't turn Yue into a lake, it is Wu that will be drowned. One never has a doctor get rid of a disease and tell him, 'You have to leave some of it.' The Pan-geng Declaration in the *Documents* says: 'Whosoever overturns my will or transgresses or wants due reverence, his nose shall be hacked off and I will destroy him utterly, and I shall cause him to have no spawn remaining, neither shall I let him shift his sprouts to this my new city.' In such a way the Shang rose. My lord now does otherwise, and in your search for greatness you will also find great troubles."

The king refused to heed Wu. He sent him as an envoy to Qi, where Wu entrusted his son to the Bao clan, and from that son came the house of Wang-sun. When he returned from his mission, the king heard of this and presented him with the sword Zhu-lou by which to die.

When he was ready to die, Wu Zi-xu said: "Plant my tomb with catalpa trees, that they may serve for coffin timbers. Wu is lost! In three years it will begin to weaken. What comes to fullness must go to ruin. It is Heaven's way."

Other Voices in the Tradition

The story of Wu Zi-xu is only one strand in the complicated saga of the struggle between southeastern domains of Wu and Yue. This saga continued to grow throughout the entire history of Chinese literature. After the account given in the *Historical Records,* two new figures rose to central importance. First there was Fan Li, the wise adviser of Gou-jian, King of Yue. In many ways, Fan Li is the successful double of Wu Zi-xu: as Fu-cha of Wu ignores Wu Zi-xu's warnings, King Gou-jian of Yue heeds Fan Li's advice and has his revenge on Wu. It was Fan Li who devised the famous stratagem of ruining Wu by sending to its king the most beautiful woman in the world—Xi Shi. The vision of the King of Wu's doomed carousing with Xi Shi, heedless of the forces of Yue gathering against him, was a favorite of Tang poets of the eighth and ninth centuries.

Among the many legends of Gou-jian's revenge, one story tells that he forced himself to suffer bitter hardships and deprived himself of sleep so as never to forget, even for a single moment, his hatred and his earlier humiliation by the army of Wu. In the heat of summer he would take hold of something burning hot, and in the cold of winter he would hold ice in his arms.

Yuan Zhen (779–831), A Winter "White Linen Song"

Night stretches on in the palace of Wu,
    the water-clock drips slowly,
curtains and draperies hang on all sides,
    the lanterns' flames shed warmth.
It is Xi Shi herself who is dancing,
    the king himself plays the pipes,
her snow white linens billow,
    plumes of cranes scattering,
the beat speeds up, strings strum swiftly,
    the dancer's waist grows weary.
The dancer's waist grows weary,
the king ceases drinking
and covers over Xi Shi
    with a phoenix flower brocade.
Her body is the bed where he rests,
    her arm will serve as his pillow;
jade pendants clink, men come to dawn court—
    but the king is sleeping late.

When he wakes at last, gatekeepers tell him
    "No problems here at all!"—
for after the death of Wu Zi-xu,
    speaking out is shunned.
The courtiers closest to the king
    divine the king's will well,
and they all laugh how the King of Yue
    must surely quake in fear,
who was holding ice in his arms each night,
    unable to sleep from the cold.

After encompassing the destruction of Wu, Fan Li, knowing that he would inevitably lose his own king's favor as Wu Zi-xu had lost the favor of Fu-cha, withdrew from his position as chief counselor and set off to sea (or onto the Five Lakes of the lower Yangzi). In making this decision he became, later in the tradition, a model for timely withdrawal from public office (a model of happy flight from public life made happier still by a romantic version of the story in which he sets off with the beautiful Xi Shi as his lover). When Fan Li, anticipating his ruler's disfavor, set off to sea, he took a rather unusual pseudonym—a reference to someone else who had lost his ruler's favor and also ended up in the river. Fan Li called himself "Master Leather Wineskin"—the very object King Fu-cha had used to dispose of the body of Wu Zi-xu. Thus, in the end, Wu Zi-xu and Fan Li, different types with different fates, become one.

When you visit the places where these events were supposed to have occurred, all that happened in the past can seem strangely unreal, as it seemed when the thirteenth-century lyricist Wu Wen-ying visited the Magic Cliff, which supposedly had once fallen as a meteor. This cliff was believed to have been the site of Fu-cha's palace. First there is empty space; into it a great stone falls, which becomes a cliff, and on that cliff trees and the palaces of Wu appear and then dissolve again, as the course of Wu's rise and fall is played out. It was all a drunken dream, a conjuror's illusion—which is the perspective of the too sober Fan Li, "weary wanderer on the Five Lakes." This too is the perspective of the later lyricist, who gazes on the site so long after the events for which it had become famous.

Wu Wen-ying (ca. 1200–1260), to "Eight-Note Gan-zhou," Visiting the Magic Cliff with Various Gentlemen of the Transport Office[1]

Empty skies recede far into mists all around—
and when was it
    that a streaming star came plummeting
    down from blue skies?
Then phantoms were conjured up:
    trees in clouds upon gray slopes,
    the gilded chambers of that famous maid,
    a broken overlord's walled palaces.
On Arrow Path a stinging wind shoots into the eyes,
and oily waters stained by the stench of flowers.
At times come afterechoes of her lovebird slippers—
autumn's sounds, leaves in the corridors.

In his palace the King of Wu lay in a drunken stupor,
all hangs on that weary wanderer on the Five Lakes
fishing alone, O so sober.
Ask the gray Heavens—they will not speak,
and my white-flecked hair cannot bear the green of hills.
The skies are drowned within these waters,
and from a high balcony,
I follow a chaos of crows in setting sunlight
    that descend on the beaches of fishermen.
Again and again I call for wine,
then go off up the Harper's Mound
where autumn is level with the clouds.

---

[1] In the song lyric the title of the melody is given first, indicated by "to." This is followed by the topic occasion on which the lyric is composed.

先秦西漢

Early Literary Prose: The Delight of Words

In early Chinese prose it is impossible to draw a clear division between thought, rhetoric, and literature. Exemplary anecdotes and parables, even stirring speeches, seem to have had great entertainment value; and the audience's appreciation of the pleasure of the telling seems to have been inseparable from their appreciation of the lesson. Many early prose texts are staged as scenes of instruction, dialogues in which one figure poses a question, and another, wiser figure responds with the main body of the discourse, leading to the general enlightenment of the questioner. In the discourses that are framed by such dialogues, we may distinguish three loosely constituted genres or types of writing: the argument or essay, the parable or exemplary story, and the description. The description was usually rhythmic and rhymed, either in whole or in part. When rhymed description predominates in such dialogues, we have a form that is close or identical to what were called "poetic expositions" *(fu)* from the Han on.

Such descriptions seem to have been an important form of literary entertainment during the late Warring States and early Western Han. Characteristically, the speaker will make a series of distinctions—sometimes a simple antithesis and sometimes a series of gradations—then he will amplify each component to make his point. The first piece below is an example of a descriptive mode that is close to pure entertainment, a poetic exposition on the wind. It is attributed to the legendary pre-Qin rhetorician Song Yu, who is the speaker in the frame, but it is probably a Western Han work. The second piece, set in a more intricate narrative, is one of the later chapters of the Daoist classic, the *Zhuang-zi,* in which a fictional Zhuang-zi appears in the guise of a Warring States orator to bring the King of Zhao to his senses. There the frame narrative is far more complex than the description of the allegorical swords embedded within it.

The Wind (Western Han?)

King Xiang of Chu was roaming through his palace compound at Orchid Terrace with Song Yu and Jing Zuo in attendance. A wind came along rustling, whereupon the king spread wide the folds of his gown, and said, "What a fine refreshing wind this is! Now here is something that I share equally with the common people, is it not?"

To this, Song Yu answered, "This wind belongs to the king alone—ordinary people could certainly never share it with Your Majesty!"

The king, "But wind is the breath of Heaven and Earth, which spreads evenly everywhere. It touches things without making distinctions between nobleman and commoner, between high estate and low. Do you have some explanation for your singular opinion that this wind is royally mine?"

And Song Yu answered, "I was told by my teacher that as crooks in a hawthorn bring nesting birds, so empty crevices will bring the wind. But the breath of a wind will differ according to where it lodges."

The king then asked, "And how is the wind first born?" To which Song Yu replied:

The wind is born in earth,
first rising in tips of green rushes.
It seeps oozing down into valleys,
it swells with rage in mouths of caverns.
It bends round the folds of Mount Tai
and dances beneath cypress and pines.
Blustering and whooshing,
it puffs in gales, flares in fury,
with booming sounds of thunder,
gusting and whirling, dashing together.
It kicks the stones, assails the trees,
flogs the forests and fields.

And when it is ready to subside,
it disperses flailing in all directions,
rams into holes, shakes doorbolts.
Then, glistening and sparkling,
it all dissipates, shifting on.

When you have such male wind, pure and cool,
it swirls aloft, rising then sinking,
and mounts up over the highest walls
and enters the palace's deepest parts.
Touching flowers and leaves, shaking loose scent,
it lingers about among pepper and cinnamon,
then soaring in flight over ruffled waters,
it is ready to strike the lotus blossoms.
It courses through clover,
runs upon rosemary,
flattens the rue,
and spreads sprouting willows.
Whirling, dashing, bounding up over,
its rustling strips all aromatics.

Thereafter it tarries in courtyards a while,
then northward climbs to the marble hall,
and striding through gauze draperies,
it passes into the women's chambers.
By this we recognize it as the king's wind.

And when this kind of wind strikes a person,
his manner shows shivers of apprehension,
and its chill will bring a sigh.
Icy and cool,
healing ills, dispelling grogginess—
it brings clarity to ear and eye,
calms the body and gives a man ease.
And this is what I mean by the king's male wind.

The king then said, "How well you explain things! And might I now hear of the wind of ordinary people?" Whereupon Song Yu said, "The wind of ordinary people:

rises rapidly within the back alleys,
in puffs of dust suddenly surging,
a troubled and turbulent whirling,
ramming holes and slipping through gates,
stirring grit grains,
blowing dead ashes,
kicking up refuse and filth,
lifting garbage and trash,
pushing through edges of jug-shard windows,
it gets into their rooms.

And when this kind of wind strikes a person,
his manner shows discomfort and revulsion,
driving in mugginess, bringing rheums.
People's hearts grow depressed,
it brings sickness, produces fevers;
it strikes the lips and makes them crack,
it gets into eyes which grow bleary and red,
coughing and sneezing,
with no relief in life or in death.
This is what I mean by the common folk's womanly wind."

"Of Swords" *(Zhuang-zi)*

A long time ago King Wen of Zhao took great pleasure in swordplay, and over three thousand men thronged his gates to receive his patronage as swordsmen. In his presence they would hack at each other day and night, and every year more than a hundred died of their wounds. But the king loved it dearly and never tired of it. It went on like this for three years, and as the kingdom's fortunes slid into decline, the nobility debated what to do about it.

Crown Prince Kui was appalled by the situation, and summoned his entourage: "I will offer a reward of a thousand pieces of gold to anyone who can dissuade the king from this mania of his and put a stop to these swordsmen."

Members of his entourage said, "Zhuang-zi can certainly do it."

The crown prince then sent a messenger with a thousand pieces of gold to offer to Zhuang-zi. But Zhuang-zi refused to accept the gold and went back with the messenger to see the crown prince. "What is it that the Crown Prince wants of me, presenting me a thousand pieces of gold?"

The crown prince said, "I have heard of your sagely understanding, and out of respect I offered you a thousand pieces of gold so that you could distribute it to your followers. Since you have refused to accept it, what more can I say?"

Zhuang-zi said, "I have heard of the purpose for which you want to employ me, which is to put an end to the king's amusements. Now let us suppose, on the one hand, that I try to persuade the king and in doing so, offend him, thus not satisfying you; in that case, I will be executed. What would I do with gold then? On the other hand, let us suppose that I persuade the king and do satisfy you. In that case, I could have anything I wanted in the Kingdom of Zhao."

The crown prince said, "True. However, our king will see only swordsmen."

Zhuang-zi: "Understood. But I am rather good with the sword."

The crown prince: "Be that as it may, the swordsmen that our king sees all have messy hair with bristling locks and slouched caps, plain, rough capstrings, robes hitched up in the back, bulging eyes, and stumbling speech. This is the sort the king prefers. Since you will no doubt visit the king wearing your scholar's clothes, the whole thing will inevitably be a complete failure."

Zhuang-zi: "Would you please have a swordsman's clothes prepared for me?"

Three days later, after the swordsman's clothes had been prepared, he met with the crown prince, and the crown prince presented him to the king, who waited for him with a bare blade drawn. Zhuang-zi entered the gate of the great hall without hurrying; and when he saw the king, he did not bow.

The king, "Now that you have had the Crown Prince put you forward, what do you expect to do for me?"

"I've heard that the king enjoys swordplay, so I've come to see the king by way of swordplay."

The king said, "How can that sword of yours defend you?"

"If I had an opponent every ten paces, I could go a thousand leagues without pausing."

The king liked that very much. "Then there's no match for you in the whole world."

Zhuang-zi said, "In swordplay one

displays himself as vacant,
initiates by advantage,

is the second to swing the blow,
is the first to strike home.

And I wish to have the chance to put this to the test."

The king said, "Stop now. Go to your lodgings and await my bidding. I'll invite you when I have arranged a contest to the death."

Then the king tried his swordsmen against one another for seven days, during which over sixty died of their wounds. Of these he got five or six men, whom he had bring their swords into the great hall. Then he summoned Zhuang-zi.

"Today I'm going to have my men match swords."

Zhuang-zi: "I've been looking forward to this for a long time."

The king: "Which would you use as your weapon, the long or the short?"

"For my own use, anything is fine. However, I have three swords that may be used only by a king. Let me tell you about these first, and then we will have the trial."

The king said, "Tell me about these three swords."

"There is an Emperor's sword, a sword of the great nobility, and the sword of an ordinary man."

The king said, "What is the Emperor's sword like?"

Zhuang-zi said, "The sword of an Emperor:

has as its point Yan Valley and Mount Stonewall,
has as its blade Tai Mountain in Qi,
has its blunt edge in the kingdoms of Jin and Wei,
has as its guard the kingdoms Zhou and Song,
has as its hilt the kingdoms Han and Wei;
its wrappings are the barbarians that surround us,
its sheath is the four seasons,
it is wound about by the Sea of Bo,
Mount Heng is the sash from which it hangs,
it is governed by the five phases,
it makes judgments of punishment or virtue;
it is brought forth through Dark and Light,
it is held through spring and summer,
and is used in autumn and winter.
This sword, when held straight, has nothing before it,
pointed up, has nothing above it,
pressed downward, has nothing below it,
and swung, has nothing around it.
It slashes the clouds that drift above,
it cuts to Earth's axis below.
Use this sword but once,
and the nobility will all be brought in line,
and the whole world will yield—
for this is the sword of an Emperor."

As if in a daze, King Wen was completely absorbed. He said, "What is the sword of the great nobility like?"

Zhuang-zi said, "The sword of the great nobility:

has as its point shrewd and valiant gentlemen,
has as its blade honest and unassuming gentlemen,
has its blunt edge in good and worthy gentlemen,
has as its guard loyal and wise gentlemen,
has as its hilt daring and outstanding gentlemen.
And this sword too, when held straight, has nothing before it,
pointed up, has nothing above it,
pressed downward, has nothing below it,
and swung, has nothing around it.
It takes model from the roundness of Heaven above,
whereby it moves with sun, moon, and stars.
It takes model from the squareness of Earth below,
whereby it moves with the four seasons.
From the center it knows the people's will,
by which it brings peace to lands all around.
Use this sword but once,
and it is like a rumbling quake of thunder.
Within the boundaries all around,
there is no man but yields to it
and obeys the bidding of their lord.
This is a sword of the great nobility."

The king then asked, "And what is the sword of the ordinary man like?"

Zhuang-zi said, "The sword of the ordinary man belongs to one with messy hair, with bristling locks and slouched cap, plain, rough cap-strings, robes hitched up in the back, bulging eyes, and stumbling speech, men who hack at each other in front of you. A high hack will chop off a neck, and a low one cuts liver or lungs. This is the sword of the ordinary man, and it is no different from cockfighting, with a life cut off in a single morning. It has no use at all in the workings of a kingdom. We have here a king, to whom belongs the position of an Emperor, and yet who is in love with the sword of the ordinary man. And for this king's sake I have taken the liberty of disparaging it."

The king then drew him up into the hall where the Master of the Kitchens was having food set out. The king kept circling the table, until Zhuang-zi said, "Sit calmly and settle your spirit. I have finished my expostulation on swords." Thereafter the king did not leave his palace for three months, and his swordsmen all perished on their own swordpoints in their places.

One of the favorite setpieces for rhymed description was the Way itself. The Way (*Dao*) was a general term used by many schools of philosophy in ancient China to describe the "course things do (or should) follow." One school, the Daoists, of whom Zhuang-zi was one, took their name from the Way. Their version of the Way was a radical sense of natural process, indifferent to human perspectives and distinctions. In the *Zhuang-zi* and elsewhere, the speaker will frequently lapse into rhapsodic depictions of the Way's transformations. Such passages, often in four-character lines, bear remarkable similarity to the Daoist work known as the *Lao-zi*. The following passage sets the description of the Way in a dialogue frame.

from "Heaven's Motions" *(Zhuang-zi)*

Cheng of Northgate once asked the Yellow Emperor, "My Lord, when you performed Heaven's Pool music in the wilderness on Mount Dong-ting, I was at first terrified by what I heard; then as I heard more, I felt a sense of apathy; finally, in the last part, I was all in confusion, swept along in a state of blankness, stupefied."

The Yellow Emperor answered: "That's just about how it was. First I played mankind in it, strummed it with Heaven, carried it forward with ceremony and right action, and gave it a basis in absolute clarity.[1]

> Four seasons alternated in rising,
> all things were born in their sequences:
> first a splendor and then a fading,
> peace and war, each in its place;
> something clear, then something murky,
> shadow and light in harmony blend.
> Insects first stir from hibernation—
> it was *I* who shook them with my thunders:
> its ending has no tail,
> no head to its beginning,
> only a dying and being born,
> a falling flat and rising up.
> The only constant is endlessness,
> but no single thing can one trust to endure.

And it was for this reason that you felt terror in it. Next I played it with the harmonies of Shadow and Light, and I set it ablaze with the shining of sun and moon, and the sounds:

> could be short or could be long,
> could be soft, could be strong,
> always changing but equal and one.
> If in a valley, they fill the valley;
> if in a pit, they fill the pit.
> Stuffing gaps they keep their spirit

---

[1]There is a section of thirty-seven characters here that most commentators suspect was an early commentary that got incorporated into the text. I have therefore omitted it.

and take their own measure from other things:
these sounds sweep everywhere and disperse
and their name is the High and Manifest.

"Because of this, demons and divinities keep to their hidden places, and sun, moon, and stars move in their courses. I made the sounds stop at the boundary of the limited, but set them rolling on without stopping. You tried to think about them, but you couldn't know them. You tried to look for them, but you weren't able to see them. You chased after them, but you weren't able to catch them. Then you found yourself standing in a daze, on a path with emptiness all around. You leaned against a dead tree and moaned, 'My eyes have been worn out by what I am trying to see. My strength flags in face of what I am trying to catch. I can't reach it and that's it.' Your form then became all empty within, to the point where it just slid along. And when you just slid along, you attained the condition of apathy.

"Then I played it again, this time with sounds in which there was no apathy, and I blended it with what is ordained by the way things are. As if:

chaotically chasing, clumps appearing,
a forest of music without form,
strewing, spreading and never bogged down,
hidden, dusky and lacking sound:
set into motion with no direction,
coming to lodge in sequestered blackness:
there were some who called it death,
and some who called it life,
some called it the fruit,
some called it the flowering:
it rolls on into dispersion,
dominated by no constant sound.

"The ordinary people of the age were uncertain about it and sought explanation of the Sage—for the Sage has achieved perfection in the dispositions of things and acts in accordance with what is ordained. When Heaven's initial motive impulses are not yet set in operation, yet all the internal organs are complete, this is called Heaven's music, in which the heart takes a wordless delight. Thus You-biao made an ode for it:

You listen to it but don't hear its sound,
you look at it but don't see its form;
it fills all Heaven and Earth,
and wraps around all six directions.

You were trying to listen to it, but you couldn't make contact. That's why you felt uncertain.

"That music began in terror, and from terror you felt dread. Then I followed it up with apathy, and from apathy you went along with it. I brought it to a close with confusion, and from confusion, you became foolish. In foolishness it was the Way. The Way can carry you and you can be together with it."

Works like the *Zhuang-zi* and Plato's *Dialogues* suggest that both philosophy and literature gain when the two are fused together. However, such exalted moments do not last. The sophisticated and elusive thought of *Zhuang-zi* was popularized and became a body of commonplaces on the flux of the world, the wheel of fortune, and the need for dispassion in face of life and death. What was lost in philosophical complexity was balanced by the way in which such values became intensely personal and applied to the circumstances of people's lives.

The writer Jia Yi (200–168 B.C.), having lost imperial favor and been exiled to the miasmal region of Chang-sha, transformed the complexities of Daoist thought into what might be called the "consolation of Daoism."

Jia Yi, The Poetic Exposition on the Owl

I, Jia Yi, was mentor to Chang-sha's prince. In the third year an owl flew into my lodgings and alighted on the edge of my seat. It was a Fu owl, like the common hoot owl, and a bird of ill omen. Since I have been banished to this low-lying and humid land of Chang-sha, I mourned my lot, taking this to mean that I did not have long to live. I then wrote a poetic exposition to make myself feel better.

> Chan-yan is the year,
> the fourth month, summer's first,
> The sun set on the day *geng-zi*
> when an owl perched in my lodging.
> It settled on my seat's edge,
> its visage unperturbed,
>
> When weird creature comes to roost,
> I wonder at the cause.
> I spread a book and read the signs,
> the omens told my fate:
> "A wild bird enters the house:
> the owner soon will leave."
>
> Of this owl I would ask,
> "On leaving, where will I go?
> Do you tell me words of luck,
> or ill words of my doom?
> Will my span end soon or late?—
> speak to me the time."
> A breath then passed the owl's beak,
> it raised its head, spread its wings.
> Its mouth incapable of words,
> let me give its heart's reply:

All things of this world move in change
with never a moment's pause or rest;

They flow past swirling and away,
sometimes forge forward and return,
Form and force in endless revolutions,
moving through change as if shedding husks.
Deep mystery is here that has no end—
how can I win the full telling?

Close on misfortune fair fortune presses,
under fair fortune misfortune lurks.
Worries and joys throng the gateway,
luck and mischance have common zones.

There once was Wu, great and strong,
whereby its king Fu-cha was ruined.
He drove Yue to refuge at Kuai-ji,
yet Gou-jian was overlord in his time.

Li Si roamed to Qin, fulfilled his aims,
he was put to death in the end.
Fu Yue was roped in a prison gang,
but then was adviser to Wu-ding, the king.

Misfortune stands with fair fortune
no different from strands that braid a cord.
What is ordained cannot be explained,
who can know how a thing will end?

Water, impelled, grows turbulent,
the arrow, impelled, goes far.
All things of the world bump and jostle
as they sweep along spinning around.

Cloud vapors steam, the rain descends,
teeming tendrils intertwining.
The Potter's Wheel is shaping things
in a boundless expanse with no margin.

None may outguess Heaven's plots,
none may outguess schemes of the Way.
Your end is ordained, either soon or delayed,
and its moment none can tell.[2]

For Heaven and Earth are the forge,
and the Fashioner is the smith;
Shadow and Light is his coal,
and the things of the world are his bronze.

---

[2]These two distiches do not rhyme, which indicates lines dropped out.

Merging and scattering, melting then solid—
where in this is enduring rule?
A thousand changes, mutations in myriads,
in which never has been an end.

All of a sudden it is a man—
why is that worth clinging to?
Then he is changed to some other thing—
and why is that an affliction?

Small wisdom favors the self,
demeaning others, honoring Me.
The Perfected Man has larger views,
that nothing there is that is not right.

Grasping men spend themselves for goods;
brash warriors spend themselves for glory.
The man overweening will die for power,
and the common man covets his life.

The sort who are thus lured and pushed
may go scampering east and scampering west.
But the Great Man does not bend,
a million changes he takes as the same.

The fool is tied to common custom,
hemmed like a prisoner in chains.
The Man Arrived leaves things behind,
is alone together with the Way.

The average man is filled with misgivings,
his loves and hates collect in millions.
The Genuine Man is indifferent and calm,
is alone in reposing with the Way.

He lets wisdom go, forsakes body's form,
rises above things, loses the self.
In the chaos of empty and boundless space
he soars around along with the Way.

If currents bear him, he passes on;
if he comes to an islet, he halts.
He lets his body free, accepts the ordained,
shows no special favor to self.

Such living is like drifting along,
such dying is like ceasing.
Serene like the stillness of deep waters,
afloat like an unmoored boat.

He does not treasure what pertains to himself,
he nurtures emptiness as he floats.
No cares bind the man who has it within,
he knows the ordained and does not worry.

Trivial problems, picayune troubles
are not worth bringing anxieties.

The *Zhuang-zi*

In its present form, the *Zhuang-zi* is a large miscellany of pre-Qin and Western Han texts from various sources. This is not at all unusual in the works that survive from the Western Han and earlier. What is remarkable about the *Zhuang-zi* is that it brings together such good texts. Even many of the pieces in the later chapters are superior to the best of their kind preserved elsewhere. And the later chapters pale in comparison with the first, so-called Inner Chapters, which contained prose writing unmatched by anything else in early China. The term *Zhuang-zi,* which means "Master Zhuang," can refer either to the Daoist philosopher Zhuang Zhou, or to this book that circulates under his name.

The "Discourse on Thinking of Things as Being on the Same Level" *(Qi-wu lun),* translated in its entirety below, is the second chapter of the *Zhuang-zi* and combines all three types of prose discourse set in a dialogue form (and in dialogues-within-dialogue). The untranslatable (somewhat incomprehensible) sections of argument draw on the mode of reasoning of Logicians such as Hui-zi and Gong-sun Long-zi, trying to prove paradoxes such as "A white horse is not a horse." The *Zhuang-zi* takes that mode of argument, treats it seriously to some degree, but carries it to the very edge of parody.

The *Zhuang-zi* can be very difficult. It is filled with fanciful characters, zany sages and allegorical interlocutors, who are sometimes passionately intense and sometimes joking. It often turns back on itself, making fun of an argument it has just developed. In many ways its philosophical message is as much in what it "does" as in what it says.

[handwritten marginal note: forget oneself in order to enter nature.]

"Discourse on Thinking of Things as Being on the Same Level" *(Qi-wu lun)*

Nan-guo Zi-qi was sitting propped up on an armrest. He looked up at the sky and heaved a small sigh, slumping over as if he had lost the other half of himself. Yan-cheng Zi-you, who was standing in waiting in front of him, said, "What's this! Can the outer form really be made like deadwood and can the mind really be made like cold ashes? Whatever this thing is propped up on the armrest, it is not what was propped there previously."

Then Zi-qi said, "Ah Zi-you—isn't it wonderful that you should ask this! Did you realize that just now I had lost the me? You have heard the flutes of men, but you have never heard of Earth's flutes. Or you have heard Earth's flutes, but you have never heard the flutes of Heaven."

Zi-you said, "Could I get to hear this lore?"

Zi-qi said, "When the greatest of clods, which is the Earth, exhales its breath, the name that we give it is 'wind.' But this is only when it is not in action. Once it acts, all the thousands of fissures bellow forth in their fury—haven't you heard them howling? In forests on rugged crags there are great trees whose trunks are a hundred armspans around; and they have holes and fissures like snouts and like mouths and like ears and like basins and like sockets and like mortars and like sinkholes and like oozes. There are splashings and whizzings and rantings and slurpings and screechings and wailings and dronings and keenings. The ones that get there first sing out, '*Heyyy* . . . ' and the ones that follow sing back, '. . . *yaaah.*' The little drafts blend in their small voices; the mighty blasts blend in their loud ones. And when the fierce gales have passed by, all the fissures are left emptied—haven't you seen them still swaying and creaking?"

Zi-you said, "Earth's flutes, then, are nothing more than the multitudes of fissures; the flutes of men are nothing more than bamboo pipes placed side by side. But if you would, I would like to hear of the flutes of Heaven."

And Zi-qi said, "They blow forth the thousands that are not the same and cause them to cease by themselves; each and every one chooses for itself, but who is it that excites them to do so?

> Great knowing is slow and capacious,
> small knowing is sly and capricious.
> Great words blaze with distinction,
> small words amaze making distinctions.

In their sleeping, souls cross; in their waking outer forms come apart.

> When we touch another, we set to contrive,
> every day minds struggle and strive.

Those curtained off, those stashed away, those closely hoarded.

> Small fears are anxious and skittish;
> great fears unfold sluggishly.[3]

They shoot forth as when a crossbow trigger pulls the pin—this is what is meant by close attention to claims of 'so' and 'not so.' They stay put as if oath-bound—this is what is meant by winning through holding fast. Their deadliness is like autumn and winter—this says that they dwindle day by day. They are drowned in the means of their own doing; one cannot make them return to the beginning. They are enclosed as if sealed up—this says that they grow senile in their aging. Hearts that draw nigh to dying, and none can make them return to the light.

---

[3]"Unfold sluggishly," *man-man,* something spreading like creepers or waters. This can be taken in a positive sense, suggesting the paradoxical calm of "great fears"; or it can be another negative condition, the beclouded mind swept helplessly along.

"Happiness and rage, sorrow and joy, worries, sighs, and changes, times of sluggishness, jitters, recklessness, moments of openness, posturings—these are the music that comes from *our* empty spaces, mushrooms forming of ground mist. By day and by night one follows after another here before us, and no one knows from where they sprout. That's all of it! From dawn to dusk these are what we get—but that from which they are born?

"Without these there is no me, and without me there is nothing for them to take hold of. Now we're really close, and yet we don't know what drives them on. It is as if there were someone truly in charge, but I cannot catch the least trace of him. I have faith that he can indeed act, yet I never see his outer form. He has a given nature but no outer form—just a hundred bones, nine bodily fissures, six organs within—I have a full set right here. Which of those am 'I' most akin to? Are you fond of them all equally, or is there some particular one you favor? And if it's this way, are they all able to act as loyal servants and handmaidens? Do such loyal servants and handmaidens have the capacity to govern themselves? Or perhaps they take turn acting as lord over the others? Or is there a true lord present there? Even if we try to grasp his given nature and fail, it adds nothing and takes nothing away from the truth of him. He is received once when we take on physical form, and we do not lose him until the end.

"Is it not a sad thing how we cut into things and grind against them, how we are cut and ground in return, going on to the end as if at a gallop that no one can stop? Can we help grief at toiling and toiling our whole lives through and never seeing anything achieved from it, how we labor so wearily to the point of exhaustion without ever knowing where we are going at last? A man claims that he will not die—what good does it do? His physical form undergoes change, and his mind goes along with it. Wouldn't you call that the saddest thing of all? The lives of men are blind in just this way. Am I the only blind man—are there others who are not blind? Each follows his own mind as it has reached its complete form and takes it as his guide. Is there a single person who lacks such a guide? Why must this guide belong only to the wise man, whose completely formed mind chooses for itself? A simpleton has one along with him too. To have a sense of 'so' and 'not so' before it has taken complete form within the mind is like Hui Shi's paradox of 'going off to Yue today and getting there some time ago.' This is to treat what-is-not as what is. And if you treat what-is-not as what is, even the holy Sage Yu cannot understand. What can I make of it all by myself?

"To say something is not just blowing forth breath. In saying there is something said, but what is said is never quite determined. So is there really something said or has there never been anything said? I hope we can take this as different from the sounds made by baby birds, but can we argue a distinction or not? How can the Way be hidden so that there is truth and falsity? How can something said be hidden so that it may be so or not so? How can the Way lead off and then not be here? How can words be here, but not be possible? The Way becomes hidden by being constituted on a small scale; something said is hidden by flowery flourishes. This is how we

115

come to have the 'so's' and 'not so's' of the Traditionalists and the Mohists,[4] each claiming that what others say is 'not so' is indeed 'so,' each claiming that what others say is 'so' is indeed 'not so.' If you want to claim that what others say is 'not so' is indeed 'so' and that what other say is 'so' is indeed 'not so,' the best thing to do is shed light on it.

"Every single thing is a 'that other'; every single thing is a 'this.' From the vantage point of the 'that other,' it does not appear; from the vantage point of knowing, it can be known. This is why we say that 'that other' grows out of 'this,' and 'this' is also contingent on 'that other'—which is the proposition that 'that other' and 'this' are born in tandem.

"However, no sooner is there a being born than there is a dying; and no sooner is there a dying than there is a being born. No sooner is there a 'possible' than there is a 'not possible'; no sooner is there a 'not possible' than there is a 'possible.' A contingent 'so' is a contingent 'not so'; a contingent 'not so' is a contingent 'so.' And this being so, the Sage does not go this way but instead reveals it in the light of Heaven—which is also a contingent 'so.' 'This' is also 'that other'; 'that other' is also 'this.' 'That other' is a unity comprehending 'so' and 'not so'; 'this here' is also a unity comprehending 'so' and 'not so.' Is there really a 'that other' and 'this,' or is there no 'that other' and 'this'? When 'that other' and 'this' can no longer find their complement, we call it the 'Pivot of the Way.'[5] And only when the pivot finds the very center of the ring can it respond and never be used up. The 'so's' are one of the things never used up; the 'not so's' are another of the things never used up. Which is why I said that the best thing is to shed light on it.

"To use a finger pointing out to convey the lesson that pointing out is not pointing out is not as good as using a non-pointing out to convey the lesson that a pointing out is not pointing out. Or to use a horse to convey the lesson that a horse is not a horse is not as good as using a non-horse to convey the lesson that a horse is not a horse.[6] Heaven-and-Earth are a single case of pointing out. And the thousands and thousands of things are a single horse.

"Is that possible!? It's possible. Is that not possible? It's not possible. It goes along the Way and achieves its completed form. As a thing is called,

---

[4]Followers of the utilitarian philosopher Mo-zi.

[5]This fiendish passage is accessible neither to philosophy nor philology. It is a parodic and playful twisting of the already playful style of the Logicians, willfully using the form of logical argument to tie the reader into knots. The Mohists and the Logicians had taken some care with using terms. Zhuang-zi purposely confuses two uses of the word *shi*. The first use is the antonym of *fei* and is usually translated as "so" against *fei* as "not so." The second usage, translated as "this," is the antonym of *bi*, "that." *Bi* has another antonym, *ci*, which is "this" or "this here." Zhuang-zi not only mixes the two pairs of usages together so that sentences are impossible to put together; he playfully drops in conventional phrases of prose argumentation, such as *shi yi*, translated as "This being so."

[6]These refer to the logical paradoxes set by Gong-sun Long. The play in this passage depends on the word *zhi*, which means both "finger" and "to point out." Contemporary philosophers had extended the meaning "point out" to a term for a single concept. Thus, in the following sentence, "Heaven-and-Earth" ("the world") are both "a single case of pointing out" (a concept) and "one finger."

that's how it is. How is it as it is? It is how it is in being how it is. How is it not as it is? It is not as it is in being not as it is. In a thing there is something by which it is really how it is; in a thing there is something which is really possible. No thing is not how it is; no thing is not possible.

"Then, taking as 'so' all straws and columns, pock-faced women and fair Xi Shi's, weird phantoms and eldritch apparitions—the Way makes them equivalent as one. Distinguishing them is their complete formation; the completion of their formation is their destruction. But any thing in which there is no completion of formation and destruction is again made equivalent as one. But only someone who has reached perfection knows that they are equivalent as one. 'Taking as so' is not practiced, but rather he gives them a place in the general. Such 'generality' is itself practiced, but its practice is making equivalent—and making equivalent is grasping it. And when you come to grasping it, you're almost there. Contingent 'so's are done. When they are done and you don't know how it is, it is called the Way. Even when you bring trouble to the spirit, it can be taken as one, but it doesn't know that it's all the same. And this is called 'three at daybreak.'

"What is meant by 'three at daybreak'? A monkey keeper was once distributing nuts and said, 'Three at daybreak; four at sunset.' The monkeys were all enraged. Then he said, 'All right—four at daybreak; three at sunset." And all the monkeys were delighted. There was no difference in either name or fact, yet joy and rage were put into practice, which is another contingent 'so.'

"This being so, the Sage brings harmony by his 'so's and 'not so's,' while he himself rests in the equipoise of Heaven. And this is called the Two Procedures.

"Among men of olden times knowledge got to something, but what did it get to? There were some who thought that there had not yet begun to be things—which did indeed get there, completely, able to go no further. The next thought that there were indeed things, but that there had not yet begun to be divisions among them. The next thought that there were divisions among them, but that there had not yet begun to be 'so's and 'not so's.' The appearance of 'so's and 'not so's' was how the Way attenuated. How the Way attenuated was clinging love completely taking form. But then were there really these events of completion of form and attenuation, or were there no completions of form and attenuation?

"There *is* something taking complete form and attenuating—Zhao Wen playing on his harp.

"There is *nothing* taking complete form and attenuating—Zhao Wen *not* playing on his harp.

"Zhao Wen playing on his harp, Music Master Kuang supported by his staff, the sophist Hui-zi leaning braced on his armrest of beechwood—three masters whose knowledge was so close! It swelled to fullness in all of them, and they carried it to the end of their years. Yet in their passion for it, they took it as different from what was other; in their passion for it, they wanted to shed light on it. What was other was not placed in the light when they shed light on something, and thus they ended up in obscurities of 'hard' and 'white.'[7]

"Zhao Wen's son also ended with his father's harp strings, yet to the end of his life he brought nothing to complete form. In a case like this, can we call it 'reaching complete form'? If so, even I have reached complete form. Or in a case like this, are we not able to call it 'reaching complete form' "— there is nothing that has reached complete form in things and myself? For this reason the Sage takes measures against the glare of slick bewilderments. He does not practice 'taking things as so' but gives them a place in the general. What this is called is 'shedding light.'

"I have something to say here, but do not know whether it belongs to the category of 'being so' or does not belong to the category of 'being so.' If belonging to a category and not belonging to a category can be joined together and taken as a category, then there is nothing at all to differentiate one from any other. But would you please let me get on with saying it:

There is what has begun.

There is what has not yet begun to be 'there is what has begun.'

There is what has not yet begun to be 'there is what has not yet begun to be "there is what has begun." '

There is a there is.

There is a there is not.

There is a not yet begun to be a 'there is not.'

There is a not yet begun to be a 'not yet begun to be a "there is not." '

All of a sudden there *is* a there is not! But I don't know whether 'there is a there is not' is actually a 'there is' or a 'there is not.'

"For my part now, there is something I meant. But I don't know whether in 'what I meant' I really meant 'something' or meant 'nothing.'

"In all the world there is nothing as large as the wisp of an autumn hair, yet Great Mountain is taken as small. No one lives to such old age as a child dead in infancy, yet Grandfather Peng passed away before his time. Heaven and Earth were born together with me, and the thousands of things are taken as one with me. Since we have been taken as one, can we further have the saying of it? But then I have already *claimed* oneness!—so can there not be the saying of it? The oneness and the saying of it are two. The two and their oneness are three. Going on from this point, even a person who is clever at arithmetic will not be able to grasp it, much less average persons!

"So if we proceed from 'there is not' to 'there is,' we reach three, and just imagine proceeding from one 'there is' to another! Or there is not the proceeding itself—contingent 'so's' cease.

"The Way had not yet begun to have boundaries. Saying things had not yet begun to have stable standards. Take this as 'so' and there are demarcations. Let me say something about these demarcations. Now there is left. There is right. There is consideration. There is taking a position. There is

---

[7]This refers to the discussion of attributives by Gong-sun Long.

making distinctions. There is showing by argument. There is contention. There is conflict. These are called the Eight Attained Powers.

"On the other side of the six bounds that enclose the cosmos, the Sage is simply there and makes no consideration. Within those six bounds the Sage may consider but takes no position. In the accounts of those former kings who through the ages managed their generations, the Sage took positions but did not show by argumentation. In making distinctions, there is what is not distinguished; in showing by argument, there is what is not shown by argument. 'What's this!' you say. What the Sage keeps within himself, ordinary men split up in argumentation to make a show to one another. This is why I say that in argumentation there is always something not revealed.

> The greatest Way is not affirmed;
> The greatest argument is not said;
> The greatest fellow feeling does not show fellow feeling;
> The greatest reserve shows no reserve;
> The greatest boldness is not hot-tempered.

> A Way is made visible, but not the Way;
> Things said make arguments, but do not get there;
> Fellow feeling becomes a standard, but not complete;
> Reserve becomes all pure, but wins no trust;
> Boldness grows hot-tempered, but not complete.

These five, in their rounded form, are almost at the method.

"Knowing to stop at what is not known is to have reached it. And who knows the argument that does not say or the Way that is not-Way [or "not spoken"]. If there were someone able to know it, such a person would be called Heaven's Storehouse. To pour into it but not fill it, to pour out from it but not empty it, and not to know from where it comes—such is called the Veiled Ray.

"Thus long ago Yao asked of Shun, 'I want to strike the chiefs of the Zong, the Kuai, and the Xu-ao. Why is it that I feel no contentment upon this throne?' Shun answered him, 'Those three chiefs are like creatures living in the sagebrush and prairie grass. How can such lack of contentment be? Long ago ten suns came out together and all the thousands of things were revealed in their light. Just think of Attained Power close to that of the sun!' "

Chomp-Gap asked Wang Ni, "Do you know what there is that all things would agree is so?"

And he replied, "How would I know?"

"Do you then know what you don't know?"

He replied, "How would I know?"

"Well then, is there nothing things know?"

He replied, "How would I know? Nevertheless, I will try to say something about it. How could I know that what I call knowing is not, in fact, not knowing? And how could I know that what I call not knowing is not, in fact, knowing?

"Or let me put some questions to you. When folk bed down where it is wet, their midsections ache and they lose feeling in half their bodies. But is the same thing true of a minnow? When folk stay in trees, they tremble and shake from terror. But is the same thing true of a monkey? Which of these three knows the 'right' place to dwell? Folk eat beasts that feed on hay and grains; the deer eat the wild grasses; the centipede has a taste for serpents; crows and owls hanker for rats. Which of the four knows the 'right' way things should taste?

"An ape will take a gibbon as mate; the roebuck mingles with the deer; minnows swim with the fish. The Furry Girl and Damsel Fair have been thought beautiful by men; but if a fish were to see them, it would dive deep under; if a bird were to see them, it would fly high away; if a deer were to see them, it would straightway bolt. Which of the four knows the 'right' version of the world's most desirable beauty? From where I look, the standards of fellow feeling and virtue, along with the paths of 'so' and 'not so,' are a hopelessly confused mess. How could I be able to know how to argue the case between them?"

Chomp-Gap answered, "If you know nothing of gain and loss, does the man who has achieved perfection truly also know nothing of gain and loss?"

Wang Ni said, "The man who has attained perfection is spirit! The great bogs may burn, but he can feel no heat. The Yellow River and the Han may ice over, but he can feel no cold. Claps of thunder rend the mountains and gales whip the seas, but he can feel no alarm. Someone like this rides upon vapors of cloud and has the sun and moon as his mounts. Facing life and death there is no change in him—still less are there questions of gain and loss!"

Master Mynah posed the question to Master Tallbeech, "From the Master I have heard that the Sage does not commit himself to common obligations, that he does not move to grasp gain, does not evade loss, does not seek joy, does not conform to the Way. In claiming nothing he claims something; in claiming something he claims nothing; and he roams out beyond the foul dust. The Master took these as preposterous words, yet I think of them as moving along the most subtle Way. What is your opinion, sir?"

Master Tallbeech replied, "This would baffle even the Yellow Emperor! As for Confucius, how could he have the capacity to understand it! As for yourself, you are forming your designs far too early—seeing an egg and looking for the rooster, seeing bird-shot and looking for roast squab. I will say it to you in an outlandish way, and you will listen to me outlandishly. How to stand by sun and moon, take the universe in arms,

> Do what fits perfectly as lips,
> Forsake all glib confusion,
> view those held in honor as slaves.

The throngs of men toil and toil,
The Sage is a simpleton,
He shares thousands of years that make one spring.
All the things of the world are thus,
And by this he garners them.

"How do I know that my joy in living is not befuddlement? How do I know that my hatred of dying is not as a child who has lost his home and does not know the way back? The Damsel Fair was the child of a borderer of Ai; and when she was taken by the house of Jin, she shed so many tears that she soaked her bodice. But then she came to the place of the king and shared the king's bed, ate livestock fed on hay and grain, and afterward felt embarrassed at her tears. How do I know that the dead do not feel embarrassed at how they used to pray so for life?

"One who drinks wine in dream may weep in the dawn. One who weeps in dream may go off on a hunt with the coming of dawn. But while they are still dreaming, they know not that they dream. In their dreams they may even read the meaning of dreams-within-dreams. But only after waking do they know it was a dream. So there may be a still greater awakening, after which we will know that this was the greatest dream. And yet simpletons take it that they are now awake—they know it with such cocksureness. Is he a lord? Is he a herdsman? Such bullheadedness! Yes, even Confucius and you are both dreaming. And when I claim that you are dreaming, that too is a dream.

"These things that have been said, their name is the Ultra-Outlandish. If in ten thousand generations we were to happen just once on a great Sage who knew how to explain them, we might take that as running into him all the time.

"Let us take the case that you and I argue a point. You best me; I don't best you; but does this really mean that what you said is so and what I said not so? Or I best you; you don't best me; but does this really mean that what I said is so and what you said not so? Is one position so and the other not so? Are they both so; are they both not so? If both you and I are unable to come to joint knowledge, others will be truly left in darkness. Who can I have decide what's right? Shall I have someone who agrees with you decide what's right? He already agrees with you, so how can he decide what's right? Shall I have someone who agrees with me decide what's right? He already agrees with me, so how can he decide what's right? Shall I have someone who has differences with both you and me decide what's right? He already has those differences with you and me, so how can he decide what's right? Shall I have someone who agrees with both you and me decide what's right? He already agrees with both you and me, so how can he decide what's right? And since this is the case, then none of us—you and I and others—are able to come to joint knowledge. But then do we depend on something else altogether?

"The interdependence of these voices, as they undergo change, is like their not being interdependent. Make them blend by using Heaven's Dividing Line, go along with them so that they spill over their bounds, and in this way you will live your years to their fullness. Forget the years, forget right, jolt into the Unceasing, and thus you will find a place for it in the Unceasing.

"What do I mean by 'make them blend by using Heaven's Dividing Line'? Answer: say 'so' to what is not so; take what is not the case as the case. For if so is really so, then there can be no argument about so being different from not so. And if the case is really the case, then there can be no argument about the case being different from not being the case."

Phantom asked Shadow, "You were moving before; now you've stopped. You were sitting before; now you're getting up. Can't you stick to anything?"

Shadow answered, "I wonder if this is the way it is because there is something I depend on? And I wonder if it is the way it is for what I depend on because there is something *it* depends on? I wonder if I depend on a snakeskin that has been shed or the husk of a cicada's wings? How can I tell why it is the way it is? And how can I tell why it is not another way?"

Once upon a time Zhuang Zhou was dreaming that he was a butterfly, a butterfly utterly absorbed and content in being what it was. But did he take this as a lesson about satisfaction? How could he? He didn't know he was Zhuang Zhou. All of a sudden he woke up. Then he was Zhuang Zhou, sprawled on his bed. But he didn't know whether he was Zhuang Zhou who had dreamed of being a butterfly, or a butterfly now dreaming of being Zhuang Zhou. And there surely must be some dividing line between a butterfly and a Zhuang Zhou! This is what we mean by things in change.

Coda

Li Bo (701–762), The Old Airs IX

Zhuang Zhou dreamed of a butterfly,
and that butterfly was Zhuang Zhou.

A single shape keeps changing,
a million things go on and on.

I know now the sea around Peng-lai
will again be clear and shallow streams.

The man who raised melons by Green Gate
was in olden days Count of Dong-ling.

> Since this is the way of honor and wealth,
> what do we seek in this scrambling?

Peng-lai was a mythical isle of the Undying far off in the Eastern Ocean (the Pacific Ocean). One common figure for the passage of eons was land and ocean changing place, so that the deep seas around Peng-lai dry up to trickling streams. The Qin Count of Dong-ling, who turned to raising melons after the fall of his dynasty, was a favorite example of drastic changes of fortune.

先秦西漢 Early Political Oratory

In early China, as in ancient Greece, persuasive oratory played an important role in political decisions. We know that Greek orators would write out their speeches and memorize them for delivery; afterwards such speeches would circulate in written form. We know far less about the practice of early Chinese oratory, and there was nothing like the institutionalization of Greek and Latin rhetoric, although some scholars have suspected that one text, the *Schemes of the Warring States,* was a manual of examples for rhetorical training. Most extant speeches from pre-Qin China are the speeches that might have been given or should have been given on a particular occasion, much like the invented speeches found in the works of the Greek and Latin historians.

The following examples are such political persuasions, either real or imaginary. Although the real persuasions served immediate political ends, their preservation (or their invention) satisfied a variety of interests quite independent of any documentary light they might shed on a particular political event. They served as the articulation of ethical positions and as models of how to present a political case. But beyond that, such writing had a certain value as entertainment. ("Entertainment" here should be taken in a large sense as a fascination with the way words were used and the beauty of an argument.)

The first case is a primitive argument, put in the mouth of Tang, the founder of the Shang Dynasty, publicly declaring his decision to overthrow Jie, the evil last ruler of the Xia Dynasty. The purported date is 1750 B.C. but the document is, in fact, a much later creation, perhaps from as late as the fifth century B.C. It is what Tang "should have said" on the occasion. "Tang's Vow" seems to consciously model itself on the archaic authority of the genuine Zhou declarations in the *Classic of Documents,* but it aims to add even greater terseness, as would befit a text supposed to be far older than those of the Zhou founding. Economically, Tang lays the responsibility for his revolt with Heaven, enumerates the charges against Xia, promises rewards, and at last threatens to kill the entire families of those who remain unpersuaded by his other arguments.

Classic of Documents, "Tang's Vow"

The king said:

Be this known to you, hosts of the folk, and heed ye all these my words. I am no young boy that dares stir up troubles. He who holds Xia has done many wrongs. Heaven has charged me to put him to death.

You, my hosts, now you say, "Our overlord shows no mercy on us, his hosts, He makes us to lay aside our tillage and march to smite Xia."

I hear your words, O my hosts. But the house of Xia has done wrongs.
I dread the high god and dare not fail to put them right.

You now may say, "What were these wrongs done by Xia?"

Xia's king has worn out the strength of his hosts; he worked harm on
the city of Xia; the hosts grow slack and there is discord among them. They
say, "When will this sun sink away? You and I will all perish." Such is what
Xia has attained for itself. I must now go against him.

I would have you stand by my side, I who am the one man, to bring upon
him Heaven's punishment. I will greatly reward you. Do not ye disbelieve
me. I do not eat my words. If you do not follow the words of this vow, I
will slay you and all your offspring and none will be forgiven.

In the following example from *The Zuo Tradition,* we have the dignity of appeal to
the Zhou tradition in a letter to the great nobility from Prince Zhao, the pretender
to the Zhou throne. The situation was as follows: There had been a struggle for the
succession to the Zhou throne, and one of the two pretenders, Zhao, had been driven from the capital by a claimant supported by Jin, then the most powerful of the
domains. Zhao fled to the Kingdom of Chu, which was frequently all too happy to
do Jin an ill turn. From Chu, Zhao sent this appeal to the nobility of the domains.
Zhao begins by a summary of Zhou history in which the remarkably violent history
of the royal house is described as a series of cases in which the brothers and uncles
(the great nobility) protected the Zhou throne.[1]

The Zuo Tradition, an entry for the 26th year of Duke Zhao (516 B.C.)

Of old King Wu conquered Yin,
  King Cheng brought peace to the four quarters,
  King Kang gave the people repose;
and all of them set their full brothers in fiefs
to be a hedge and a screen for Zhou.
This they said as well:
We do not keep the great accomplishments of Kings Wen and Wu for
  ourselves alone;
and should our descendants stray toward ruin
  or be overthrown and drowned in troubles,
then the nobility will bestir themselves and save them.

When it came to King Yi:
  the king had a disease in his person;
  not one among the nobility failed to rush to sacrifice in prayer for
    the king's person.

---

[1]The "prose" of this and some other selections in this section has been translated like verse to show
the rhythmical organization.

When it came to King Li:
    the king's heart was wayward and cruel;
    the myriads of the folk could not bear it.
    They then lodged the king in Zhe,
    and the nobility gave up their own places
    to attend to the king's government.
King Xuan possessed resolve,
    and they yielded back their offices.

When it came to King You:
    Heaven had no pity on Zhou,
    the king was blind and unfit,
    by misdeeds he lost his position.

King Hui usurped the Charge;[2]
    the nobility replaced him
    and set in his stead the king's true successor,
    whereby the capital was shifted to Ge-ru.

This, then, is how the brothers showed themselves able to exert
    themselves for the king's house.

When it came to King Hui:
    Heaven gave no peace to Zhou,
    it gave birth to Tui's destructive mind,
    which extended to Shu-dai.
    Kings Hui and Xiang fled the troubles
    and left the king's city.
    Then there were Jin and Zheng;
    both purged the unrighteous,
    thus soothing and settling the king's house.

This, then, is how the brothers showed themselves able to follow the
    Charge of the early kings.

It was in the sixth year of King Ding:
an apparition descended among the men of Qin;
it said:
    "Zhou will have a mustached king
    who will be able to carry out his office,
    and the nobility will submit to him.
    For two generations they will fulfill their offices.
    In the king's house there will be an intruder in the king's place,
    the nobility will make no plan against him,
    and they will suffer the blows of his misrule."

[2]The Heaven's Charge, the authority to rule granted by Heaven. Also the commands of early kings to their descendants.

126

When it came to King Ling:
   he was born with a mustache.
   The king was godlike and sagely;
   he was not hated by the nobility.
   King Ling and King Jing
   were thus able to finish their generations.

But now the king's house is in disarray:
   Qi of Shan and the Liu Di
   have thrown the world into turmoil;
   their despotic actions are unrighteous.
Of our former kings they say:
   "What constant principles are there?
   There is only what my own heart commands!"
Who dare reproach them?
They lead bands of merciless men
to wreak havoc on the king's house.
Their desires and encroachments are never sated,
there is no measure to what they seek.
Accustomed to outraging gods and demons,
wantonly casting aside punishments and laws,
betrayers of oaths taken with equals,
insolent in their behavior,
they have made a mockery of the early kings.
Jin has acted against the Way,
supported them, assisted them,
intending to give them free rein in their unrestrained designs.

I, unfortunate one,
have been shaken, driven afar,
hiding away in Jing-Man
with nowhere to go.
If a few of you, my brothers, my nephews, my uncles,
will acquiesce to the laws of Heaven
and give no aid to the wicked,
thereby following the Charge of the early kings
and avoiding hastening Heaven's retribution,
by pardoning and making provision for this unfortunate one,
then I will have my wish.

I will dare set forth fully what is in my mind,
which are the constant principles of the early kings;
and may the nobility seriously consider these in their plans.

The Charge of the olden kings states:
   Should the queen lack legitimate heir,
   then select the eldest for the throne.

If equal in years, choose by virtue;
if equal in virtue, choose by lots.
The king may not set a favorite on the throne,
the great lords may not have personal favorites.
This is the ancient rule.

Queen Mu and Crown Prince Shou died young.
Shan and Liu aided a favorite and put a younger on the throne,
thereby infringing on the early kings.

Would that my relations, both elder and younger, consider this in
  their provisions.

The passage that follows the letter in *The Zuo Tradition,* put in the mouth of a Jin
minister (the faction opposing Prince Zhao), is a chilling reminder of the realities of
political power and of the world in which the letter circulated. The "might of Jin,"
not long-dead feudal obligations, is what drives political actions.

Min Ma-fu heard these word of Zhao and said, "He is practicing ceremonies by the written word. Zhao has transgressed the mandate of King Jing
and has taken himself far from the might of Jin to accomplish his own personal ambitions, and this is want of ceremony in the extreme! What good
will these writings do?"

The following passage is one of the most famous examples of a fully developed ornamental persuasion from the pre-Qin period. The speech with its occasion is included in *Schemes of the Warring States (Zhan-guo ce).* One might note that, in spite
of both the hypnotic repetition of pattern that lends Zhuang Xin's speech its force
and the promise of the exordium, the speech is not a persuasion at all. Instead of
telling King Xiang of Chu how he can save the situation, Zhuang Xin offers an elaborate "I told you so."

from the *Schemes of the Warring States*

Zhuang Xin said to King Xiang of Chu, "You, my lord, keep the company
of the Count of Zhou on your right side and the Count of Xia on your left.
Your carriage is attended by the Lord of Yan-ling and the Lord of Shou-
ling. You do nothing but indulge yourself in wanton excess and vain amusements, paying no attention to governing the kingdom, and our great city of
Ying is surely in peril."

King Xiang replied, "Have you grown doddering in your old age? Do
you make baleful auguries for the Kingdom of Chu?"

Zhuang Xin said, "Truly it is that I see what must come. I would not
dare make baleful auguries for the kingdom. Yet the favor my Lord shows
these four men has never weakened, and the Kingdom of Chu must fall. I

ask your permission to take myself to safety in Zhao, where I will stay to observe it."

Zhuang Xin went away to Zhao; and after he had stayed there four months, Qin did indeed lay hold of the regions of Yan, Ying, Wu, Shang-cai, and Chen. King Xiang fled into hiding at Cheng-yang. He then sent someone with a mounted escort to Zhao with a summons for Zhuang Xin. Zhuang Xin agreed; and when he arrived, King Xiang said, "I did not do as you said, and now matters have come to this. What is to be done?"

Zhuang Xin replied: "The common folk have a saying: 'It is not too late to look for your dogs after seeing the hare nor too late to fix the pen after the sheep get away.' I have heard that long ago Kings Tang and Wu became glorious with territories of only a hundred leagues, while Kings Jie and Chow perished though they had the whole world. Though the Kingdom of Chu has become smaller, if you average out the larger and smaller parts, it is still several thousand leagues—far more than just a hundred leagues.

"Has the king ever seen a dragonfly? With its six legs and four wings, it flies hovering between earth and sky. It drops down to snatch gnats to eat and rises up to catch the sweet dew to drink. It believes that no harm will come to it and has no quarrel with man. Little does it know that a boy, just over three feet tall, is at that very moment taking a sticky line with sweet bait, which will catch it twenty feet up, and it will come down to be food for the ants.

"But the dragonfly is a small case; let us follow it with that of the brown sparrow. Bobbing down, it pecks the white grains; and turning up, it perches in leafy trees, whirring its small wings. It believes that no harm will come to it and has no quarrel with man. Little does it know that the young no-bleman, holding his slingshot under his left arm and in his right hand holding the pellets, will hit it fifty feet up, its neck as his target. By day it roamed through the leafy trees, and that evening it will be flavored with salt and vinegar. In the space of an instant it topples into the young nobleman's hand.

"But the sparrow is a small case; let us follow it with that of the golden swan. It roams about the rivers and lakes and lingers in the great ponds. Ducking its head down, it gobbles up eels and carp; then raising it up, it nibbles water chestnuts and cress. It spreads its great wings and rises on the clear wind, wheeling about as it soars on high. It believes that no harm will come to it and has no quarrel with man. Little does it know that at that very moment the fowler is preparing his bow and arrowheads and arranging the arrow's string to hit it hundreds of feet up. Those stone weights will drag on the thin line and bring it plummeting down, jerked out of the clear wind. By day it roamed over the rivers, and that evening it flavors the stewpot.

"But the golden swan is a small case; let us follow it with what happened to Count Ling of Cai. He roamed south to Highslope and to the north climbed Mount Wu. He drank of the current of Ru Creek and ate fish from the waves of the Xiang. He had his left arm around a tender young concubine and hugged a favorite with his right; he went galloping with them in Gao-cai and did not concern himself with the matters of his domain. Little did he know that at that very moment Zi-fa was receiving a charge from King Xuan to have him bound with red line and brought before the king.

"But what happened to Count Ling of Cai is a small case; let us follow it with what happened to Your Majesty. You kept the company of the Count of Zhou on your right side and the Count of Xia on your left. Your carriage was attended by the Lord of Yan-ling and the Lord of Shou-ling. Dining on the grain that was income of the fiefs and carrying gold of the treasury, you went galloping with them in Yun-meng preserve, not concerning yourself with the matters of the world and your kingdom. Little did you know that at that very moment the Count of Rang was receiving a charge from the King of Qin to bottle up all within Min Pass and cast yourself out beyond Min Pass."

When King Xiang heard this, the color drained from his face and his body shuddered. Thereupon he took the insignia that he carried and passed it to Zhuang Xin, making him the Lord of Yang-ling and giving him the territory north of the Huai.

Although written persuasions like Prince Zhao's letter are attributed to early periods, the Western Han saw the transformation of political oratory into a primarily written form. Such persuasions built upon the style of orations attributed to the Warring States period, but writing permitted far more allusiveness and intricacy of argumentation. With the written persuasions of the Han we leave the realm of the fictional or recreated speech and find texts that we can say with some confidence played a role in real political events.

In the following letter, much like a memorial to the throne, Mei Sheng (who died in 140 B.C.) plays the wise sage in a scene of instruction. But beneath the Daoist principles of royal Non-Action and homey metaphors such as the precariousness of a pile of eggs, there was much at stake in Mei Sheng's letter. Mei Sheng's patron, the Han prince of Wu, Liu Pi, led the rebellion of seven feudal domains against the Han emperor Jing, a rebellion that eventually cost Liu Pi his life. The position that Mei takes here is literally a matter of life and death, not simply for his patron but for himself as well. To side openly and loyally with the emperor would assure him of trouble from his patron; however, if the rebellion were to fail—as it did—any hint of support for the prince would be high treason.

The letter is an intricate piece of political rhetoric for an intricate political situation, with a complicated deployment of historical examples and nested analogies.

Mei Sheng (d. 140 B.C.), Letter of Protest to the Prince of Wu

I have heard that
> whosoever attains the perfection of a thing will flourish,
> whosoever falls short of perfection will perish.

Shun had not the land in which to set an awl,
> but came eventually to possess all the world.

Yu had not a cluster of ten households,
    but eventually became king of the great nobility.
The territories of Tang and Wu
    went no more than a hundred leagues.
He who
    causes no eclipse in the light of the Three Luminaries above,
    and harms not the hearts of the masses of people below—
such a person possesses the skills of kingship.

The Way of father and son is our nature endowed by Heaven:
If a faithful retainer remonstrates straightforwardly,
    not avoiding grave punishment,
    then no counsel will be overlooked in your affairs,
    and the deed will continue for thousands of generations.
I, Mei Sheng, wish to open my heart and demonstrate my simple faith,
and I wish only that my Prince pay some slight heed and attend to my
  words with a sympathetic heart.

Take a single thread as bearer of a burden;
    tie it to a weight of a hundred pounds;
    suspend it above from a limitless height;
    let it hang down below into an unfathomable abyss—
even a very foolish man
    knows enough to be anxious that it will break.
A horse will rear up, if you prod and alarm it;
what is tied will snap, if you weigh it down further.
And falling into the deep abyss,
    it will be hard to get it out again;
though between getting it out and not getting it out
    there may lie not even a hair's breadth.
If you can heed this faithful retainer's words,
    you will get out every time.
But if you must act as you wish, it will be:
    more precarious than a pile of eggs,
    harder than climbing to Heaven.
If you change what you wish, it will be:
    easier than turning over the hand,
    more secure than Tai Mountain.

You now wish:
    to reach the limit of the greatest old age ordained by Heaven,
    to fulfill the extremes of pleasures unending,
    to know an emperor's power, lord of ten thousand chariots.
Not
    taking a course of such ease as in turning over a hand, or
    residing in the security of Tai Mountain,

but instead wanting:
  to ride the precariousness of a pile of eggs, and
  rushing into the hardships of climbing to Heaven—
this is what so greatly bewilders your retainer.

In human nature there are some
  who fear their shadows and hate their footprints.
As they turn their backs and run,
    their footprints grow steadily more,
    their shadow becomes steadily swifter.
Best to go to some shady spot and stop:
  there shadow vanishes, footprints cease.
If you want others not to hear something,
  best not to speak;
If you want others not to know,
  best not to act.
If you want hot water to cool off,
    and one man fans the flames
    while a hundred men ladle it,
it would be better to stop the fuel and end the fire!
Not stopping one thing,
  while trying to fix it with another,
may be compared to taking an armload of kindling to put out a fire.

Yang Yi-ji was the expert archer of Chu.
He went a hundred paces from a willow leaf,
  in a hundred shots hit it a hundred times.
Considering the size of a willow leaf,
    to hit it a hundred times
    can be considered expert archery indeed.
Nevertheless, the point where he stopped
  was still but a hundred paces.
Compared to your retainer Sheng, he didn't know even how to hold a
  bow and arrows!

When fair fortune appears, it has some base;
when misfortune appears, it has some womb.
Preserve the base,
stop off the womb,
and how shall misfortune come?

The water that drips on Tai Mountain pierces stone;
the well-rope on a single stock breaks the roller.
Yet
    water is no drill for stone,
    rope is no saw for wood—
it is the gradual abrasion that makes it so.

If you weigh something grain by grain,
>you will always miss at the pound;
if you measure something inch by inch,
>you will always err at the yard.
If you weigh by the pound, gauge by the yard,
>you will go straight and seldom fail.

The tree of ten armspans in girth first grew as a shoot:
>your foot could scrape and break it,
>your hand could yank and pull it up—
this depended on its not being fully grown,
you acted before it took full form.

Grind and grate, rub and scrape—
>you see no harm from it,
>>but sometime it will get through;
seed and plant, nourish and tend—
>you see no gain from it,
>>but sometime it will be large.
Seed attainments, accumulate merits—
>you see no good from it,
>>but sometime it will be illustrious;
forsake Virtuous Attainment, reject the Pattern—
>you see no ill from it,
>>but sometime it will bring ruin.

I wish that my Prince would give mature consideration to his plans
>and practice this himself.
This is the Way that does not change in a hundred generations.

Political oratory begged for parody, yet there is remarkably little parody in the extant texts of early China. One of the rare cases is in the "Attaining Life" *(Da-sheng)* chapter of the *Zhuang-zi.*

Zhuang-zi, "Attaining Life" *(Da-sheng)*

The Master of the Sacrifice, in his black ceremonial hat, looked down into the pigsty and persuaded the pig as follows:

Why should you hate death?
I will
>fatten you for three months,
>make you abstain ten days,
>make you fast for three days,
>spread out white rushes, then
put your rump and shoulders on the finely carved platter—
you would go along with that, wouldn't you?

If I were making pig-plans, I would say,
    better to be fed with the dregs
    and be locked inside a pigsty.
If I were making plans for myself, then
    if in life I could have the honor of carriage and crown, and
    in death got to ride a fine hearse in a bunch of ornaments,
    then I would do it!

Making pig-plans, I would avoid it;
planning for myself, I would choose it—
what is this that distinguishes me from the pig?

Si-ma Qian
(ca. 145–ca. 85 B.C.)

Like the works of Greek and Latin historians, Si-ma Qian's *Historical Records (Shi-ji)* is read as much for the pleasure of the narrative as for historical information. The *Historical Records* (or, more properly, *Records of the Historian*) was begun by Si-ma Qian's father, Si-ma Tan, who held the post of *Tai-shi* under the great emperor Wu of the Han. Although we now translate this post as "Lord Historian," it was just as much "Lord Astronomer": the *Tai-shi* was charged with keeping account both of astronomical phenomena and the daily life of the court. As *Tai-shi,* Si-ma Tan had access to the documents in the imperial library and began to compile a history of China up to his own time. This enterprise was a personal project and had nothing to do with the duties of his office. Upon Si-ma Tan's death, Si-ma Qian inherited both his father's post and his project. When completed, the *Historical Records* not only set the model for later historical writing but changed the word *shi* from a post—something like "astronomer," "scribe," or "court diarist"—to the standard term for "history."

The form of the *Historical Records* is not continuous narrative. It includes annals of the imperial houses and of the royal houses of the feudal domains, chronological tables, and treatises on topics such as ceremony, the calendar, and music. But the greater part of the work is composed of biographies, some of single individuals and some in comparative pairings, as in Plutarch. At the end of each, Si-ma Qian offers his own comments as "Lord Historian."

The depth of Si-ma Qian's personal engagement with the historical figures about whom he writes has always been an important source of the work's appeal. Both the project of the history and the experiences of characters in history acquired a special significance to Si-ma Qian when, after enraging Emperor Wu by his defense of the failed frontier general Li Ling, he was sentenced to castration. The humiliation of this sentence was supposed to lead a person to honorable suicide or a request for execution in lieu of punishment. Si-ma Qian's decision to accept castration in order to finish his history made the work intensely personal to him. He gave an account of his experience and explained his decision in a famous letter to an acquaintance, Ren An, a letter that is not in the *Historical Records.* The version translated below is contained in Si-ma Qian's biography in Ban Gu's *Han History,* completed almost two centuries later: while varying Si-ma Qian's model, it essentially accepted his sense of how history should be written.

Letter in Reply to Ren An

The Lord Historian, your obedient servant Si-ma Qian to Ren An

Some time ago you were so kind as to grace me with a letter, instructing me to observe caution in my associations and to devote myself to recommending worthy gentlemen. Your manner then was earnest and forthright, as if anticipating that I would not do as you directed, but would rather be swayed by what ordinary people said. I would never dare to act in such a way. I may be an old horse that has outlived its usefulness, but I always harkened to the influences from my seniors. When I consider how my body has been mutilated, how fault has been found in whatever I have done, and how my desire to be of benefit has brought ruin to me instead, my heart bursts and I have no one to tell.

There is a saying: "For whom do you act, and who will pay attention to you?" When Zhong-zi Qi died, Bo Ya never played his harp again. Why was that? A man does something for the sake of someone who understands him, as a woman adorns herself for someone who is attracted to her. Some like me, whose flesh is now missing a part, can never be thought to flourish, even if I had qualities within me like Sui's pearl or Bian He's jade, or even if my actions were like those of Xu You or Bo Yi. In fact, all they could do is win me ridicule and humiliation.

I should have answered your letter immediately, but at the time I was coming back from the east with His Majesty and I was also beset by minor problems. Few were the days when we could meet, and I was always in such a hurry that there was never even a moment when I could tell you everything that was on my mind.

Now you yourself stand accused of the gravest crimes. As the weeks and months pass, the last month of winter draws near; and I am again constrained to accompany His Majesty to Yong. I fear that ultimately there will be no escaping your swift death. Were I never to have the opportunity to reveal all that torments me and make things clear to you, then in death your soul would harbor an unceasing resentment against me. Let me then tell you my thoughts, and please do not take it amiss that I have been negligent in replying.

I have learned that cultivating one's person is the treasurehouse of wisdom, that a love of offering things is the beginning of feeling for others, that taking and giving is the counterpart of a sense of right, that feeling shame determines courage, and that making one's name known is the ultimate end of action. Only after having all five of these may a man give himself to public life and be ranked among the best. There is no misfortune so miserable as desire for advantage, no grief so painful as a wound that festers within, no action more loathsome than one that brings dishonor upon one's ancestors, and no degradation greater than castration. Those who live on after castration are comparable to no one else. Nor is this true only of the present age—it has been this way from long ago in the past. In olden times when Duke Ling of Wei shared his carriage with the eunuch Yong-qu, Confucius left for Chen; Shang Yang arranged an audience through Eunuch Jing, and Zhao Lang's heart sank; when the eunuch Zhao Tan joined the Emperor in his coach, Yuan Si turned pale. This has been considered shameful ever since antiquity. When a man of even middling qualities has business to conduct with a eunuch, he always feels ill at ease—not to mention a gentleman of strong spirit! The court may need capable men these days, but would you have a person who has been gelded recommend the outstanding gentlemen of the world for service!

It has been more than twenty years since I took over my father's profession, and though unworthy, I have had the opportunity to serve the throne. When I think it over, on the most important level I have not been able to contribute my loyalty or show my good faith, winning esteem for remarkable plans and the power of my talents, thus forming a natural bond with my wise lord. On the next level I have not been able to catch matters that have been overlooked, summoning worthy men to court and recommending those with abilities, bringing to the public eye those who live hidden in caves in the cliffs. On a still lower level I have not been able to take a place in the ranks and in assaults on cities or in battles in the open, to win glory by beheading generals and seizing the enemy's colors. Finally, on the lowest level, I have not been able to accumulate a stock of merit through continuous service, getting high office and a good salary, thus bringing honor and favor to family and friends. Having been successful in none of these, it is obvious that I have merely followed expedience and tried to please others, achieving nothing that deserves either praise or blame.

Previously, among the ranks of minor grandees, I took part in lesser deliberations of the outer court. On those occasions I brought in no grand plans, nor did I give matters their fullest consideration. Now, as a castrated servant who sweeps up, as the lowest of the low, if I were to try to lift my head, arch my brows, and hold forth with judgments, wouldn't that be showing contempt for the court and offering insult to those gentlemen now in power? What more is there for somebody like me to say!

It is not easy to explain the sequence of events clearly. When I was young I had an ungovernable disposition, and as I grew older I won no esteem from the people of my locale. I was fortunate that, on account of my father, His Majesty allowed me to offer him my meager skills and to frequent the royal apartments. I felt that I could never gaze on Heaven with a bowl covering my head, so I cut off contact with my friends and gave up all thought of the family property; day and night I tried to exercise my miserable talents to their utmost, striving single-mindedly to carry out my office and thus to please His Majesty and win his affection. Yet one thing happened that was a great mistake and had a very different effect.

Li Ling and I had both been in residence in the palace, but we were never good friends. Our interests led us in different directions, so we never even shared a cup of beer or had a direct and earnest relation. Nevertheless, I observed that he was a remarkable person, showing a son's proper devotion to his parents, true to his word with other gentlemen, scrupulous in matters of property, possessed of a sense of right in matters of giving and taking; in questions of status he would yield place, and he behaved deferentially, demonstrating respect and temperance. Always he longed to put his life on the line in responding to some crisis of the empire. He had always harbored these virtues, and to my mind he possessed the qualities of one of the great men of the state. When a subject would brave death thousands of times without thinking to save his own life, going forth to meet threats to the commonwealth, it is remarkable indeed. It truly pained me personally that those courtiers who keep themselves and their families out of harm's way plotted to do him mischief when one thing went wrong out of all that he had done.

The foot soldiers that Li Ling took with him were less than five thousand, and they marched deep into the lands of the nomads; on foot they crossed the khan's own preserve to dangle bait in the tiger's mouth; they brazenly flaunted a stronger force of barbarians and stood face to face against an army of millions. For more than ten days they did continuous battle with the khan and killed more than their own number. When the tribesmen tried to rescue the dead and carry back the wounded, they couldn't take care of themselves, and their chieftains, dressed in wool and furs, were all quaking in terror. Then the Good Princes of the Right and Left were called up and anyone among the folk who could draw a bow; the whole nation surrounded them and attacked. They fought on the move across a thousand leagues, until their arrows were used up and they had nowhere to go. The relief column did not come; dead and wounded troops lay in heaps. Nevertheless, Li Ling gave a shout to cheer up his army, and not a soldier failed to rise; he was weeping, swallowing the tears running down his bloodied face. They drew their empty crossbows and faced down naked blades; facing north, they fought with the enemy to the death.

Before Li Ling was destroyed, a messenger brought word of him; and all the great lords, princes, and counts of Han lifted their goblets in a toast to his health. Several days afterward, the letter bearing news of Li Ling's defeat became known, and on this account His Majesty found no savor in his meals and took no pleasure in holding court. The great officers of the court were worried and fearful, not knowing what to do.

Without giving due consideration to my lowly position, I saw that His Majesty was despondent and distressed, and I truly wanted to offer him my sincere thoughts on the matter. I held that Li Ling always gave up fine food and shared meager fare with his attendant gentlemen, that he was able to get men to die for him to a degree that was unsurpassed even by the famous generals of antiquity. Though he was defeated, if one but considered his intentions, they should make up for it and repay what he owes the Han. Nothing could be done about what had happened, but those he had defeated were an accomplishment sufficient to make him famous in the empire. I had it in mind to make this case, but had not yet had the means. Then it happened that I was summoned and questioned; and I spoke highly of Li Ling's accomplishments in this way, wanting to set His Majesty's mind to rest and stop malicious comments.

I was not able to be entirely persuasive. Our wise ruler did not fully understand, thinking that I was trying to injure the Ni-shi general, Li Guang-li, and acting as a personal advocate of Li Ling. I was subsequently sent to prison. And never was I able to demonstrate the depth of my loyalty. In the end I was convicted of having tried to deceive the Emperor. My family was poor, and I didn't have the means to buy my way out. None of my friends came to my rescue. My colleagues, kin, and close friends did not say a single word on my behalf. The body is not a thing of wood or stone; and alone in the company of jailers, in the hidden depths of a dungeon, to whom could I complain? This you can see for yourself now, Ren An—was what happened to me any different? Since Li Ling surrendered alive, he ruined the good name of his family. Yet I too, in my turn, came to the silken chambers, where the knife is used, and I am the laughingstock of the world. Oh, the misery of it!

The matter is not easy to explain in a few words to ordinary people. My father's accomplishments were not such as would bring the imperial seal of investiture among the nobility; writers of history and astronomical calculations are close in status to diviners and soothsayers. His Majesty finds amusement in such, and we are kept by him on a par with singers and acrobats, thus held in contempt by the common opinion. Suppose that I had bowed to the law and accepted execution; it would have been like the loss of a single hair from a herd of cattle, a death no different from that of an ant or a cricket. And the world would never have granted that I might be compared to those who could die for principle. They would have considered it nothing more than a person finally accepting death because he could think of no way out of the gravity of his crime, someone with no other choice. Why is this? It would have been the consequence of the position in which I had so long established myself.

Human beings truly have but one death. There are deaths that seem heavier than Mount Tai, but to some death seems lighter than a piece of swansdown. The difference lies in what is done by dying. Uppermost is not to bring dishonor upon one's forebears; next is not to bring dishonor upon oneself; next is not to dishonor the right or appearances; next is not to dishonor one's own words; next is to bear the dishonor of bending in submission; next is to bear the dishonor of changing into the uniform of a prisoner; next is to bear the dishonor of being flogged, tied with a rope to the pillory; next is to bear the dishonor of having one's head shaved and bound in metal chains; next is to bear the dishonor of having one's flesh cut and one's limbs amputated; but the worst of all is castration—that is the ultimate.

Tradition says: "Physical punishments are not applied to grandees." This means that a gentleman has no choice but to be severe in guarding his honor. The fierce tiger dwells in the depths of the mountains, and all creatures there quake in fear of him; but when he falls into a pit, he wags his tail for food—this follows gradually from constraining his fearsome power.

Thus if you mark out the form of a prison cell on the ground, a gentleman will not enter it; and if you cut a piece of wood to represent the warden, he will not speak to it in his own defense; he has made of his mind to show who he is [by suicide]. But let him cross his hands and feet to receive the manacles and rope, let him expose his flesh to receive the blows of the rod, hide him away in an enclosed cell—and in a situation like this he will knock his head to the ground when he sees the warden and he will breathe hard in terror when he catches sight of the guards. Why is this? It is the natural outcome of constraining fearsome power. And brought to such a state, anyone who says that there is no dishonor is putting up a false front and deserves no esteem.

Yet King Wen, the Earl of the West, may have been an earl, but he was held in the prison at You-li; Li Si was a minister, yet he endured each of the five punishments; Han Xin of Huai-yin was a prince, yet he endured the stocks in Chen; of Peng Yue and Zhang Ao, who sat on the throne and called themselves rulers, one went bound to prison, and the other, to death; Jiang-hou Zhou-bo executed all the members of the Lu clan and his power was greater than that of the five earls, yet he was imprisoned in a dungeon awaiting death; Wei Qi was a great general, yet he wore the prisoner's uniform and was bound head, hands, and feet; Ji Bu became a slave of the Zhu clan; Guan-fu bore dishonor in the guest chambers.

All these men had reached the positions of prince, count, general, or minister, and their fame was known far and wide; but when they were accused and brought before the law, they could not summon the resolution to kill themselves. When one is lying in the dirt, it is the same thing, both in ancient times and in the present—how could one think they were not dishonored! Judging from these examples, courage and fearfulness depend on the situation; resolution and weakness are circumstantial. Reflect on it—there's nothing strange about it! For if a man cannot commit suicide before he is brought to the law, he is already slowly slipping down to the whips and rods. And if he wants to assert his honor then, it is already far out of reach. Certainly this is the reason why the ancients thought it a grave matter to apply physical punishments to grandees.

By their very nature all human beings are greedy for life and hate death, care about their parents, are concerned for their wives and children. But it is otherwise for those who are stirred up by their sense of right, and in fact they cannot help themselves. I had the misfortune to lose both my parents early in life; and not having brothers to be my close family, I was all alone. And you can see how much I took wife and children into consideration! Yet a man of courage does not necessarily die for honor; and when fearful man aspires to the right, he will strive in any way he can. I may have been fearful and weak in choosing life at any cost, but I also recognize quite well the proper measure in how to act. How then could I come to the dishonor of letting myself sink into prison bonds? If even a captive slave girl can take her own life, certainly someone like me could do the same when all was lost. The reason I bore through it in silence and chose to live at any cost, the reason I did not refuse to be covered in muck was because I could not stand to leave something of personal importance to me unfinished, because I despised perishing without letting the glory of my writings be shown to posterity.

The number of rich and noble men in ancient times whose names have been utterly wiped away is beyond reckoning; the only ones who are known are the exceptional, those outside the norm. King Wen of Zhou, when Earl of the West, was in captivity and elaborated the *Classic of Changes;* Confucius was in a desperate situation and wrote *The Springs and Autumns of Lu;* Qu Yuan was banished, and only then composed the *Li Sao;* Zuo Qiu-ming lost his sight, and he wrote *The Discourses of the Domains;* Sun-zi had his feet amputated, and then his *Techniques of War* was drawn up; Lu Bu-wei was demoted to Shu, from which has been preserved the *Synopticon of Lu;* Han Fei was imprisoned by Qin and wrote "Troubles of Persuasion" and "Solitary Outrage." The three hundred *Poems* were for the most part written as the expression of outrage by good men and sages. All of these men had something eating away at their hearts; they could not carry through their ideas of the Way, so they gave an account of what had happened before while thinking of those to come. In cases like Zuo Qiu-ming's sightlessness or Sun-zi's amputated feet, these men could never be employed; they withdrew and put their deliberations into writing in order to give full expression to their outrage, intending to reveal themselves purely through writing that would last into the future.

Being, perhaps, too bold, I have recently given myself over to writing that lacks ability. I have compiled neglected knowledge of former times from all over the world; I have examined these for veracity and have given an account of the principles behind success and defeat, rise and fall. In all there are one hundred and thirty chapters. In it I also wanted to fully explore the interaction between Heaven and Man, and to show the continuity of transformations of past and present. It will become an independent discourse that is entirely my own. The draft version was not yet completed when this misfortune happened to me; I could not bear that it not be completed, so I submitted to the most extreme punishment without showing my ire. When I have actually completed this book, I will have it stored away on some famous mountain, left for someone who will carry it through all the cities. Then I will have made up for the blame that I earlier incurred by submitting to dishonor. I could die thousands of deaths without feeling regret. This, however, may be said only to a wise man; you can't explain it to an ordinary person.

It is not easy to live enduring contempt, and the inferior sort of people usually put a malicious interpretation on things. It was by the spoken word that I met this misfortune; and if I am also exposed to the ridicule of the people of my native region, dishonoring my ancestors, how could I ever again face the tomb mound of my parents? The blot on our name would grow worse and worse, even after a hundred generations. Thus every day I feel a pang in the heart again and again. When I'm in the house, I am distracted, as though I am not there; when I'm outside, I don't know where I'm going.

My thoughts keep returning to this shame, and I always break into a sweat that soaks my clothes. I am fit to serve only in the women's quarters, and I would rather take myself off to hide deep away in the caves of the cliffs. But I keep on following the ordinary world, rising and sinking, moving with the times, keeping in communication with fools.

Now you, Ren An, instructed me to recommend worthy men—would not that be the wrong thing to do, considering my private aims? Even if I wanted to give myself refinement and explain myself with gracious words, it would do no good, because ordinary people would not credit me and I would only earn more humiliation. Only when I am dead will the final judgment be made.

Writing cannot say all that is in a person's mind, thus I give you only the rough account of my thoughts.

Even by the standards of earlier historical writings, Si-ma Qian was an idiosyncratic historian. Nowhere is this more clear than in the first of his "Biographies," on the ancient hermits Bo Yi and Shu Qi. These are the earliest figures treated in the biographies, and Si-ma Qian begins by trying to separate figures of history from figures of legend. Yet very quickly the issue turns to questions of yielding power, right, starvation, and the fairness of Heaven. In the background we can hear the resonance of Si-ma Qian's sense of his own wrongs. The historian opens by affirming his faith in the Confucian Classics, and closes with a flurry of quotations, trying to make sense of the suffering that good men have had to endure.

The Biography of Bo Yi and Shu Qi

Texts by men of learning range most widely in what they include, yet we look into the Six Classics for what is reliable. Although works were omitted from the *Poems* and *Documents*, still we can read writings from the times of Shun and Yu.

Sage-King Yao planned to cede the throne and yielded his place to Shun. Between Shun's accession and that of Yu, governors and prefects all recommended men. Shun tested them in posts and let them perform their offices over several decades; only after there was ample evidence of merit and ability did he hand over the reins of government. This testifies to the fact that the empire is a weighty vessel, and the kingship is the supreme office. Thus it is no easy thing to pass the empire from one person to another.

And yet tellers of tales say that Yao offered up the empire to Xu You, but Xu You would not take it and fled out of shame into hiding. Bian Sui and Wu Guang did the same in the time of Xia. But how did these men become widely known?

This is my opinion as Lord Historian: I personally climbed Mount Ji, on whose summit was reputed to be the grave of Xu You. When Confucius named the gentle, the good, and the sagely men of antiquity, he went into some detail in cases like Wu Tai-bo and Bo Yi. Now from what I have heard, Xu You and Wu Guang were supposed to have had the highest sense of right—why is it, then, that they are not even mentioned in passing in Confucius' writing?

Confucius said: "Bo Yi and Shu Qi did not brood on old hatreds, and thus they felt little bitterness of spirit." He also said: "They sought feeling for their fellow man and achieved it—so how could they have known bitterness of spirit?" I myself am moved by Bo Yi's sense of purpose, and when I look at his poem that has come down to us, I find it remarkable. This is the story about them.

Bo Yi and Shu Qi were two sons of the Lord of Gu-zhu. Their father wanted Shu Qi to take his place, but when their father died, Shu Qi yielded to Bo Yi. Bo Yi said: "Those were our father's orders," and he fled into hiding. But Shu Qi also refused to become Lord of Gu-zhu and fled into hiding. Then the people of the domain made the middle son lord.

Then Bo Yi and Shu Qi heard that the Earl of the West [King Wen of the Zhou] took good care of the elderly, and they considered going to put themselves under his protection. But when they arrived, the Earl of the West had died; and King Wu had taken his father's Spirit Tablet, given his father the title "King Wen," and gone east to attack King Zhow of the Shang. Bo Yi and Shu Qi stopped King Wu's horse and criticized him: "Can this be considered the right way for a son to behave, taking up arms even before your father's funeral rites have been completed? And can a subject murdering his ruler be considered feeling for one's fellow man?" The king's party wanted to put them to the sword, but his Counselor Tai-gong said: "These men have a sense of right." And he helped them up and sent them away.

When King Wu had settled the lawlessness of the Shang, all the world gave their allegiance to the Zhou; yet Bo Yi and Shu Qi thought that to be something shameful, and out of their sense of right they refused to eat the grain of Zhou. They lived as hermits on Shou-yang Mountain and picked bracken ferns to eat. As they were dying of hunger, they composed a song, whose words go:

> We climbed West Hill,
> we picked its bracken.
> Brute force for brute force—
> he knew not it was wrong.
> Shen-nong, Yu, and Xia
>   gone in a flash,
> where can we turn?
> Ah, let us depart now,
> our lifespans are done.

And then they died of hunger on Shou-yang Mountain.

Considered in this light, did they or did they not feel bitterness of spirit?

There are those who say: "The Way of Heaven shows no personal favorites and always provides for good men." Can we or can we not consider people like Bo Yi and Shu Qi good men? To have such a history of kindness to one's fellow men and to be so pure in actions, yet to die from hunger! Of his seventy disciples, Confucius singled out Yan Hui for praise for his love of learning. Yet Yan Hui lived in dire poverty and never ate his fill even of grain mash or bran. And he died before his time. How is it then that Heaven repays good men with its gifts?

Zhi the Outlaw killed innocent men every day and fed on their flesh. A brutal, savage man, he committed every kind of outrage and gathered a band of several thousand men who wreaked havoc all over the world. In the end he died at a ripe old age. From what virtue did this follow?

These are particularly clear and obvious cases. And if we come down to more recent times, conduct beyond the rules of morality and willful transgressions have brought lifetimes of carefree pleasures and great wealth passed on for endless generations. Others take care where they tread, speak up only when it is timely, take no dark byways, and are stirred only for justice and the common good; yet the number of such people who have met with disaster is beyond reckoning. I cannot understand this at all. Is this what is meant by the "Way of Heaven"?

Confucius said: "Men who follow different ways cannot make judgments for one another." Each person follows his own aims in life. He further said: "If wealth and noble station could be properly sought, I would seek them, even if it meant being the king's meanest servant; but since they cannot be sought, I will follow what I love." And: "Only in the cold of the year can you know that pine and cypress are the last to turn brown." When all the world is foul and corrupt, the pure man appears most clearly. Obviously what is considered so important by some is despised by others.

"The man of virtue is pained by the thought of dying without his name being known." [*Analects*]

Jia Yi wrote:

Grasping men spend themselves for goods;
brash warriors spend themselves for glory.
The man overweening will die for power,
and the common man covets his life.

"Things of equal light reveal one another; things of the same kind seek one another." [*Classic of Changes*]

"Clouds follow the dragon; winds follow the tiger; the Sage arises and all things are perspicuous." [*Classic of Changes*]

Although Bo Yi and Shu Qi were virtuous men, it was through Confucius that their names became more widely known. Though Yan Hui was devoted to learning, like the fly on the tail of a fine steed, his actions became more widely famed. It is most sad that men who live in caves in the cliffs may have an equal sense of appropriateness in their decisions, yet their good names are obliterated and never known. How can folk of the villages who wish to perfect their behavior and establish their names be known to later generations unless through some gentleman who rises high in the world?

In Si-ma Qian's accounts of the Han, we see fine judgments of character within a complex political world. But in many of the narratives of the Warring States and the founding of the Han, we find something that might best be called historical romance. This is a world of stratagems, heroism, and sometimes betrayal; the currency of honor is, more often than not, death. The Prince of Wei is the perfect Warring States lord, using his wealth and the power of deference to gather loyal retainers to employ in his own commitments of honor. Hidden among the common folk everywhere are worthy men, capable of deeds of strength or sage advice. The discerning lord knows how to find them and win them over. Such barely visible heroes are necessary to counter a great danger. The Kingdom of Qin is the rising military power of the day, threatening the smaller states of North China, such as Wei and Zhao.

The Prince of Wei

Wu-ji, the Prince of Wei, was the youngest son of King Zhao of Wei and the half brother of King An-li [r. 278–243 B.C.]. When King Zhao died, King An-li took the throne and enfeoffed the prince as Lord of Lin-ling.

That was the time when Fan Sui, out of his bitterness against Wei Qi, had fled Wei to become a royal adviser in Qin. Qin troops surrounded Da-liang and smashed Wei's army at the foot of Mount Hua-yang, sending Wei's general Mang Mao into flight. The King of Wei and the prince were deeply troubled because of this.

The prince was the sort of person who showed kindness to others and treated gentlemen with deference. No matter whether the person was virtuous or unworthy, he treated all with humility and received them with courtesy, taking care not to behave haughtily because of his wealth and noble rank. As a result gentlemen from several thousand leagues around flocked to his service, until he had three thousand retainers eating at his table. At this time, because of the prince's virtue and the number of his retainers, the high nobility of the domains did not dare use their troops in designs against Wei for more than ten years.

Once the prince was playing chess with the King of Wei when beacon fires were lit from the northern reaches of the kingdom. They were told that raiders had come from Zhao and crossed the border. The King of Wei quit the game and was going to summon his chief officers for consultation, but the prince stopped him, saying, "It's just the King of Zhao out on a hunt; he's not raiding us." They returned to their game of chess, but the king was apprehensive and his mind wasn't on the game. After a short while word was again brought from the north: "The King of Zhao is just hunting; he's not on a raid." The King of Wei was amazed and asked, "How did you know?" The prince replied, "One of my retainers has in-depth access to the King of Zhao's secrets. Whatever the King of Zhao does, my retainer reports it to me. This is how I knew." After that the King of Wei stood in awe of the prince's virtue and his abilities, and he dared not entrust the prince with political power in the kingdom.

In Wei there was a man named Hou Ying, who kept out of the public eye. Seventy years old, his household was poor, and he served as the gatekeeper of the Yi Gate in Da-liang. The prince heard of him and went to visit him, with the intention of giving him a generous gift. Hou Ying refused to accept it, saying, "For several decades now I have cultivated my virtue and acted blamelessly; I could never accept a present from you simply because of the hardships of my life as a gatekeeper."

The prince then held a great party with beer for his guests and retainers. When everyone was seated, the prince set off with his chariots and riders, leaving the place of honor at his left empty. He personally made an invitation to Hou Ying at Yi Gate. Hou Ying straightened his tattered cap and robes, then got right up on the prince's chariot and took the position of the social superior. He didn't defer to the prince because he wanted to observe him. The prince took the reins in his own hand and became increasingly respectful. Then Hou Ying said to the prince, "I have a retainer in the butcher shops of the marketplace—I would like you and your entourage to make a detour to visit him." The prince then turned his chariot into the marketplace, where Hou Ying got down and met with his retainer Zhu Hai. Watching out of the corner of his eye, he stood there a long time on purpose, talking to his retainer, and he secretly observed the prince. The prince's expression was even more calm. Meanwhile, Wei's generals, counselors, members of the royal family, and the prince's retainers filled his hall, waiting for the prince before beginning to drink. The people in the marketplace were all watching the prince holding the reins. And the attendant riders were all cursing Hou Ying under their breaths. Once Hou Ying saw that the prince's expression would never change, he took leave of his retainer and went back to the chariot.

When they reached his home, the prince led Hou Ying to the seat of honor, commending to him each of his guests in turn. The guests were all amazed. Then, growing merry from drink, the prince rose to offer a toast to Hou Ying. But then Hou Ying told the prince, "I've already done enough on your behalf today. I am but the person who bars Yi Gate, yet you came with chariots and horsemen to invite me personally into this great gathering of people. One should not overdo things, and today you have really overdone it. Nevertheless, I wanted to complete your reputation, so on purpose I made your chariots and riders stand there so long in the marketplace; I stopped by to visit my retainer in order to observe you, and you became even more respectful. The people of the marketplace all think of me as someone of no importance, and yet you found it within you to treat me with deference as an elder." At this the party ended, and thereafter Hou Ying became the most honored of the retainers.

Hou Ying told the prince, "The butcher I stopped by to visit is Zhu Hai. He is a worthy man, but no one has been able to recognize his worth, so he lives out of the public eye among the butchers." The prince went to pay his respects a number of times, but Zhu Hai purposefully did not return the greeting. And the prince thought it very strange.

In the twentieth year of King An-li's reign, King Zhaw of Qin had smashed the army of Zhao at Chang-ping and sent his troops on to surround the Zhao capital at Han-dan. The prince's sister was the wife of the Lord of Ping-yuan, who was the younger brother of King Hui-wen of Zhao. The Lord of Ping-yuan sent a number of letters to the King of Wei and the prince, asking that Wei save them. The King of Wei sent his general Jin Bi with a hundred thousand troops to save Zhao; but the King of Qin sent an envoy to tell the King of Wei, "I am attacking Zhao, and it will fall any day now; but if any of the great nobility dare to try to save it, I will move my troops to strike them first, once I have seized Zhao." The King of Wei grew frightened and sent someone to stop Jin Bi and hold his army in a fortified camp at Ye. He was to say publicly that he was going to save Zhao, but in fact he was to keep his options open while observing the situation.

One after another the caps and carriages of envoys from the Lord of Ping-yuan came through Wei and they reproved the prince: "The reason why I, Sheng, Lord of Ping-yuan, allied myself with you through marriage was because of your noble sense of right, which makes you rush to someone in dire need. Han-dan may fall to Qin any day now and no rescue has come from Wei—where now is your willingness to rush to help someone in dire need! But even if you care nothing about me and would abandon me to Qin, have you no pity at all for your sister?"

The prince was very upset by this and often pleaded with the King of Wei; and the political strategists among his retainers plied the king with thousands of persuasive reasons. But the King of Wei stood in dread of Qin and he never heeded the prince.

Taking the measure of the situation, the prince realized that he would never win over the king; and he decided that he could not stay alive himself while letting Zhao perish. He then called on his retainers, and gathered and mustered more than a hundred chariots and horsemen, intending to go against Qin's army with his retainers and to die together with Zhao.

He went past Yi Gate and met with Hou Ying, explaining to him the entire situation that led him to plan to die before Qin's army. As he said his farewell and went on his way, Hou Ying said, "Do the best you can! I'm old and can't go with you." After going several leagues, the prince felt uneasy and said to himself, "I have treated Hou Ying perfectly in every way! Everyone in the world knows about it. Now I'm going off to die, yet Hou Ying . never offered the least piece of advice to see me off. Could I have possibly failed him in some way?" He turned his chariot around and went back to ask Hou Ying, who laughed and said, "I knew quite well that you would be back." He continued, "You delight in gentlemen-retainers, and your reputation is known all over the world. Now there is a crisis, and having no other recourse, you plan to go against Qin's army. I would compare this to tossing meat to a ravenous tiger. What will you accomplish by that? How will you make use of your retainers? Still, you have treated me generously, so that when you left, I didn't see you off, knowing by this that you would feel wronged and come back."

The prince bowed to him several times and next asked him what to do. Hou Ying then made the others withdraw and spoke quietly to the prince: "I have heard that the tally authorizing Jin Bi to use his troops is always in the king's bedchamber. Lady Ru enjoys his favors most often; and since she passes in and out of the king's bedchamber, it is within her power to steal it. I have heard that Lady Ru's father was murdered, and this has occupied her thoughts for three years. She has sought to get revenge on her father's killer from the king on down, but she has never gotten satisfaction. When Lady Ru pleads weeping before you, send a retainer to cut off her enemy's head and respectfully present it to her. In her readiness to die for you Lady Ru would refuse you nothing, but she will not be able to think of any means. Indeed, all you have to do is open your mouth once and ask this of her, and Lady Ru will surely agree. Then you will get the tally to seize Jin Bi's army, go north to save Zhao, and make Qin retreat back to the west. This will be a campaign worthy of the Five Overlords."

The prince followed his plan and made the request of Lady Ru. And the outcome was that Lady Ru stole the tally for Jin Bi's troops and gave it to the prince.

When the prince set out, Hou Ying said, "When a general is away from the capital, there are cases when he will not accept his ruler's orders if it seems in the best interest of the kingdom. Once you match the tallies, if Jin Bi does not give you the troops and makes further inquiries, you will be in a very dangerous situation.[1] My retainer, the butcher Zhu Hai, should go together with you; he is a man of strength and force. If Jin Bi obeys, that would be best; but if he doesn't obey, have Zhu Hai strike him.

At this the prince began to weep, and Hou Ying said, "Are you dreading death—why are you weeping?" The prince replied, "Jin Bi is a stouthearted old general from way back. When I go there, I'm afraid he won't obey me and I'll have to kill him. That's the only reason I'm weeping. Of course I don't dread dying."

Next the prince went to make his request of Zhu Hai. Zhu Hai laughed and said, "I am just a butcher who wields a knife in the marketplace, yet you have personally paid your respects to me on a number of occasions. The reason why I didn't respond was that such a small courtesy would have been of no use. Now you are in a crisis, and this is the season for me to put my life at your disposal." He then went off together with the prince. The prince visited Hou Ying to take his leave, and Hou Ying said, "It would be right that I go with you, but I am too old. Reckon up the number of days you will be traveling, and on the day when you are to reach Jin Bi's army, I will face north and cut my throat as my farewell to you, my prince." Then the prince set off.

---

[1]Authority was delegated by means of a broken tally, of which the ruler kept half. By bringing the ruler's half of the tally and matching it up with the general's half, the bearer demonstrated that he was acting on the authority of the ruler.

When he reached Ye, he pretended that the King of Wei had ordered him to take Jin Bi's place. Jin Bi matched the tallies, but doubted him; raising his hand, he looked at the prince and said, "Here I am surrounded by a host of a hundred thousand, camped on the frontier, bearing a grave responsibility to the kingdom. How is it that you can come in a single chariot to take my place?" He was not going to obey. Zhu Hai drew an iron club weighing twenty-five pounds out of his sleeve and bludgeoned Jin Bi to death. The prince then took command of Jin Bi's army. He had his officers convey these commands to the army: "If a father and son are both in the army, let the father go home; if brothers are both in the army, let the elder go home; if there is an only son with no brothers, let him go home to take care of his parents." From this he got eighty thousand select troops and advanced to strike the army of Qin. The Qin army broke its siege and left. Thus he rescued Handan and saved Zhao.

The King of Zhao and the Lord of Ping-yuan personally welcomed the prince at the edge of the city. The Lord of Ping-yuan carried a quiver of arrows as a sign of respect, and he led the way for the prince. The King of Zhao bowed to him repeatedly, saying, "None of the virtuous and worthy men since ancient times is your equal." And at this time the Lord of Ping-yuan did not dare compare him with anyone.

The prince had said his farewell to Hou Ying; and when he had reached the army, Hou Ying at last faced north and cut his own throat.

The King of Wei was enraged that the prince had stolen his tally for the army, then bluffed Jin Bi and killed him. And for his own part the prince too knew this. Having forced Qin to withdraw and having saved Zhao, he had the generals take the army back to Wei, while he and his retainers stayed in Zhao.

King Xiao-cheng of Zhao was indebted to the prince for having seized Jin Bi's troops by a bluff and saved Zhao, so he planned with the Lord of Ping-yuan to give the prince five cities as a fief. When the prince heard of this, he felt very proud of himself and his face showed his sense of his own achievements. One of the prince's retainers counseled him, "There are some things that should not be forgotten and some things that you should always forget. If you are in debt to someone else, you should not forget it; but if someone else is in debt to you, I would encourage you to forget it. To have pretended to be acting under the King of Wei's order and seized Jin Bi's troops in order to save Zhao was indeed a great achievement to Zhao, but to Wei it was not being a loyal subject. You are in fact very proud of yourself and think it was a great achievement, but in my own opinion you shouldn't have taken this course."

At this the prince immediately rebuked himself, and it seemed as if he couldn't stand himself. The King of Zhao had the stairs swept and welcomed him personally; and carrying out the ceremony of a host, he led the prince to the western stairs. But the prince backed away and declined the honor, going up by the eastern stairs. He spoke of his own transgressions, having been disloyal to Wei and having accomplished nothing important for Zhao. The King of Zhao accompanied him drinking until sundown, but he couldn't bring himself to present the five cities because of the prince's modesty. In the end the prince stayed in Zhao. The King of Zhao gave him Hao as a tributary city, and even the King of Wei restored to him his fief of Xin-ling. But the prince stayed in Zhao.

The prince heard that in Zhao there was a recluse, one Master Mao, who hid himself among gamblers, and another, Master Xue, who hid himself among tavern keepers. The prince wanted to meet both of them, but they both concealed themselves and were unwilling to meet him. When the prince found out where they were, he went secretly on foot to keep them company, and he enjoyed it greatly. The Lord of Ping-yuan heard about this and told his wife, "I first heard of your brother the prince as someone without peer in all the world. Now I heard about him recklessly keeping company with gamblers and tavern keepers. The prince is a reckless man."

The lady informed the prince about this. The prince then took his leave of her, saying, "I first heard of the Lord of Ping-yuan as a worthy man, and for that reason I betrayed the King of Wei to save Zhao—to satisfy the Lord of Ping-yuan. Those with whom the Lord of Ping-yuan keeps company are only the arrogant and overbearing; he does not seek out gentlemen. When I, Wu-ji, was back in Da-liang, I heard constantly of the worthiness of these two men; and when I came to Zhao, I was afraid that I wouldn't get the chance to meet them. I was even afraid that they might not want me to keep them company. If now the Lord of Ping-yuan considers this a cause for embarrassment, then *he* is not worth keeping company." At this he started packing to depart.

The lady repeated everything that he had said to the Lord of Ping-yuan. And the Lord of Ping-yuan removed his cap and apologized, insisting that the prince stay. When the Lord of Ping-yuan's followers heard of this, half of them left the Lord of Ping-yuan for the prince; and again gentlemen from all the world over flocked to the prince, until the prince had taken all the Lord of Ping-yuan's retainers.

The prince stayed in Zhao for ten years without returning. When the Qin ruler heard that the prince was in Zhao, he constantly sent troops eastward to raid Wei. The King of Wei was deeply troubled by this and sent envoys to go ask help from the prince. But the prince was afraid that the king was angry with him, and he gave this warning to his followers: "Whoever dares come as an envoy of the King of Wei dies!" His retainers then all abandoned Wei and went to Zhao, and none of them dared urge the prince to return. Then both Masters Mao and Xue went to meet the prince and said, "The reason why you are treated with importance in Zhao and your fame is known among the great nobility is due only to the existence of Wei. Qin now attacks Wei. If you do not take pity on Wei in its hour of dire distress and then Qin should smash Da-liang and level the ancestral temples of its former kings, how will you have the face to stand up in the world?" Before they finished speaking, the expression on the prince's face suddenly changed; he told his drivers to prepare his train to go home and rescue Wei.

The King of Wei met the prince, and they came together in tears. And the king gave the prince the seal of the supreme general of his armies. The prince then took command. In the thirtieth year of King An-li of Wei, the prince sent envoys to all the high lords of the domains. When the high lords heard that the prince was the general, each sent generals with troops to rescue Wei. The prince led the troops of the Five Domains to crush the Qin army at He-wai, putting their general Meng Ao to flight and following up on their victory by pursuing the Qin army to Han-gu Pass, where they so subdued the troops of Qin that they did not dare come forth.

At this time the prince's power shook the whole world, and retainers of the high lords of the domains submitted their techniques of warfare to him. The prince put each down under its appropriate name, in what is commonly called today *The Military Techniques of the Prince of Wei*.

The King of Qin was greatly troubled by this and had ten thousand measures of silver transported to Wei to win over a retainer of Jin Bi. He ordered him to speak ill of the prince to the King of Wei, saying, "The prince fled the kingdom and lived for ten years in a foreign country. Now he is a general of Wei, and the generals of the high lords of the domains are all subordinate to him. The high lords have heard only of the Prince of Wei; they have not heard of the King of Wei. And if the prince should take advantage of the moment to establish himself as king and ruler, the high lords would stand in dread of the prince's power and would join to support his taking the throne."

On numerous occasions Qin made devious use of Wei's intelligence network by sending false congratulations to the prince regarding whether he had taken the throne as King of Wei. Hearing such slander every day, the King of Wei could not help believing it, and finally he sent someone to replace the prince as general.

Knowing that he had been removed from office because of repeated slander, the prince refused to go to court on the pretext of illness. He spent the whole night long drinking with his retainers, drinking strong brew, and consorting with many women. For four years he drank and made merry day and night, until at last he died of the effects of drinking. King An-li of Wei died that same year.

When Qin heard that the prince was dead, Meng Ao was sent to attack Wei. He took twenty cities and established them as the "Eastern Province." After that, Qin nibbled away at Wei, and eighteen years later took the King of Wei captive and sacked Da-liang.

When Gao-zu, the founder of our dynasty, first lived as a humble man, he frequently heard of the virtues of the prince. Later when he became Son of Heaven, he would always offer up prayers to the prince whenever he passed Da-liang. In his twelfth year [195 B.C.], returning from attacking against Jing Bu, he established five families to take charge of maintaining the prince's tomb so that offerings would be made to the prince in every season forevermore.

The Lord Historian: I have passed by the ruins of Da-liang and have looked for the place known as the Yi Gate. The Yi Gate was the eastern gate of the city. Among the princes of this world there were others who delighted in gentlemen-retainers. Still there was good reason why the Lord of Xin-ling made contact with those who lived, removed from the public eye, in the caves of cliffs, and felt no shame in forming relationships with those socially beneath him. It was not for nothing that his fame crowned the high lords of the domains. Whenever our Founder passed by there, he ordered that offerings be made without end.

When Duke Mu of Qin went to his grave in 620 B.C. (see "Yellow Bird," p. 26), the retainers who accompanied him in death were his subjects, men of good family. Warring States retainers of the fourth and third centuries were "bought"—by support, by outright gifts, and, as shown in the case of the Prince of Wei, by gestures of esteem. These men were often found in the lower strata of society—gatekeepers, butchers, or wandering men-at-arms. But once chosen, they were bound by a code of honor to die for their lords. Central here was the question of "name" or reputation that followed from their self-sacrifice. The story of Nie Zheng is a variation on this question, the story of the assassin-retainer who made his "name" by his determination to make his death anonymous.

from "Biographies of the Assassins": Nie Zheng

Nie Zheng came from the Deepwell section of the city of Zhi. He killed someone, and to escape his enemies' revenge, he went to Qi with his mother and sister. There he worked as a butcher.

Some time later Yan Zhong-zi of Pu-yang was in the service of Count Ai of Han, and he had a quarrel with Xia Lei, the Minister of Han. Fearing that he would be executed, Yan Zhong-zi fled and traveled about looking for someone who could get revenge on Xia Lei. When he reached Qi, some of the local people said that Nie Zheng was a man of courage and daring, who lived out of the public eye among butchers in order to escape his enemies.

Yan Zhong-zi went to his gate to pay his respects but was repeatedly turned away. After that he had beer prepared and went to offer a congratulatory toast to Nie Zheng's mother. When everyone was feeling the effects of the beer, Yan Zhong-zi presented a hundredweight of gold to Nie Zheng's mother to wish her a long life. Nie Zheng was alarmed at such generosity and was determined to refuse it. Yan Zhong-zi pressed it on him with just as much determination, but Nie Zheng refused, saying, "I am lucky to still have my aged mother. Our household may be poor, but I make my living here as a dog butcher so that I can provide her delicacies to eat every day. She is well provided for, and I dare not accept your gift."

Yan Zhong-zi had the others withdraw and then said to Nie Zheng, "I have an enemy and have roamed through many of the great domains. When I came to Qi, however, I heard of your high sense of right, sir, and this is why I presented the hundredweight of gold—to use for ordinary expenses in taking care of your aged mother and in that way to get on good terms with you. I wouldn't dare expect anything from you for it." Nie Zheng replied, "The only reason I have curtailed my ambitions and accepted the indignity of working as a butcher in the marketplace has been to take care of my aged mother. So long as my mother is alive, I do not dare commit myself to anyone." Yan Zhong-zi insisted that Nie Zheng give way, but in the end Nie Zheng refused to accept the gift. Nevertheless, Yan Zhong-zi played out his proper role as a guest and then left.

Some time later Nie Zheng's mother died. After she was buried and the period of mourning completed, Nie Zheng said, "To think that I am but a man of the marketplace, one who wields the knife as a butcher, while Yan Zhong-zi is an adviser of the high nobility, and yet he did not think it too much to turn his carriage and riders to meet me! The way I treated him was ungenerous in the extreme. I had done nothing important to deserve it, yet he offered a hundredweight in gold for my mother's sake. Even though I didn't accept it, in doing this he was simply showing how deeply he understood me. How can I just do nothing when a good and worthy man has been stirred to glaring rage and then personally shows his confidence in a poor and humble man? When he pressed me earlier, I acted as I did only because of my mother. Now that my mother has lived out her natural span, I will be of use to this man who so well understands me."

He next went west to Pu-yang, and meeting Yan Zhong-zi said, "The only reason that I could not commit myself to you earlier was because my mother was still alive. Now unfortunately her years are over. Who is it that you want me to take revenge on? Please let me carry this matter through." Yan Zhong-zi told him the whole story: "My enemy is Xia Lei, the Minister of Han. Xia Lei is also the uncle of the ruler of Han. His kindred are very numerous, and whenever he stays outside his compound, he is extremely well guarded. I tried to get people to assassinate him, but none was ever successful. Now I am lucky that you have not rejected me, so let me increase the number of carriages, mounts, and strong warriors to assist you." Nie Zheng replied, "The distance between Han and Wei is not very great. If you're going to kill a minister and that minister is also a relation of the ruler of a domain, the situation is such that you should not use many people. If you use many people, something will inevitably go wrong; if something goes wrong, word will inevitably leak out; and if word leaks out, the entire domain of Han will be your enemy. Then you really would be in danger!" Thus Nie Zheng refused carriages, horses, and men. He then said farewell and set out alone.

Sword in hand, he came to Han. Xia Lei, the Minister of Han, was seated in his office, and there was a great throng of men with weapons and pikes standing guard around him. Nie Zheng went directly in, climbed the stairs, and stabbed Xia Lei to death. His entourage was in great confusion. Nie Zheng gave a loud shout and killed several dozen men. Then he cut the skin off his face, gouged out his eyes, cut himself open and pulled out his entrails, and died.

The ruler of Han took Nie Zheng's corpse and had it exposed in the marketplace, trying to find out who the man was—but no one knew. He then offered a reward of a thousand silver pieces to anyone who could tell him who killed the minister Xia Lei. But after a long time no one came forward with this knowledge.

Nie Zheng's sister Rong heard that someone had assassinated the Minister of Han, but that the criminal could not be ascertained because no one in the kingdom knew his name; thus they had exposed his corpse and offered a reward of a thousand pieces of silver. At this she let out a moan. "Could this be my younger brother? Alas, Yan Zhong-zi understood my brother all too well!" She went to the capital of Han and to its marketplace, and the dead man was indeed Nie Zheng. She collapsed on the corpse, weeping with the utmost grief. And she said, "This man was known as Nie Zheng, from the Deepwell quarter of the city of Zhi." The crowds of people walking through the marketplace all said, "This man assaulted the minister of our domain, and the king has posted a reward of a thousand pieces of silver for his name—haven't you heard? How can you dare come here and recognize him?"

Rong answered them, "I have heard. Nevertheless, the reason why Nie Zheng endured disgrace and abandoned himself to the commerce of the marketplace was so that our aged mother would come to no harm and because I was not yet married. Once our mother had passed away and I had married, Yan Zhong-zi selected my brother to be his friend, even in his degraded position. He was so kind and generous that my brother had no choice. A gentleman will indeed die for someone who understands him. And now, because I was still alive, he has gone further, mutilating himself so there will be no traces to follow. How could I stand in dread of paying with my own life, and by doing so wipe away forever my worthy brother's name?" This amazed the people in the marketplace of Han. Then she called out to Heaven several times, until, with a piteous moan, she died at Nie Zheng's side.

When this story was heard in Jin, Chu, Qi, and Wei, everyone said, "It is not just that Nie Zheng showed ability—his sister too was a woman of fierce principles. Suppose that Nie Zheng had truly known that his sister lacked the determination to simply endure the situation and that she would surely cross a thousand leagues of perils, unmindful of the troubles that would come from recognizing the exposed corpse, just to proclaim his name. Had he known that, he would not necessarily have committed himself to Yan Zhong-zi."

But Yan Zhong-zi may indeed also be known as someone capable of acquiring gentlemen by his ability to understand a person's worth.

The *Chu-ci:* "Lyrics of Chu" 先秦西漢

The *Chu-ci* or "Lyrics of Chu" is, first of all, an anthology of rhymed, metrical works that represent a tradition of "poetry" quite distinct from that of the *Classic of Poetry*. This tradition originated in the pre-Qin Kingdom of Chu, a powerful state that grew up on the southern margins of the Zhou cultural region. As Chu collapsed in the third century B.C. before the eastward advance of Qin's armies, the capital of Chu and its cultural heritage moved east to the city of Shou-chun. It was Shou-chun and the surrounding area of Huai-nan and Wu that became the centers of *Chu-ci* learning early in the Western Han; from there it was taken to the Han capital and became a scholarly and literary enterprise. Thus the anthology called *Chu-ci* consists of late Warring States works from Chu, early Western Han works written in a living tradition of the "Lyrics of Chu," and scholarly continuations of that tradition later in both the Western and the Eastern Han.

No one fully understands the nature and provenance of the earliest and most important works in the "Lyrics of Chu." Traditionally, these earlier texts in the anthology have been interpreted as the compositions of one Qu Yuan (ca. 340–278 B.C.), an anti-Qin aristocrat who lost the favor of the Chu kings Huai and Qing-xiang, was sent into exile, and eventually committed suicide by drowning himself in the Mi-luo River. The early works in the *"Lyrics of Chu"* are taken to represent various stages in Qui Yuan's life and career, in which he allegorically laments his misfortunes, declares his virtue, attacks those who have defamed him, and goes on a cosmic quest for a worthy lord.

The debate about whether Qu Yuan wrote any or all of the works traditionally attributed to him continues and is not likely ever to be resolved. But most of the poetic phases in this bizarre political narrative correspond to stages in the relation of the shaman-lover to the goddess or god. The lover laments being spurned by the god or goddess, declares his beauty and worth, then goes through the heavens on a spirit quest. This shamanistic spirit quest, involving a circuit of the heavens with a vast cavalcade of gods and dragon-drawn chariots, early came to overlap with and serve as a representation of the Daoist adept's search for spiritual and physical "transcendence." Furthermore, this narrative of "transcendence" overlapped with Han Daoist notions of the emperor as god-king, ruling the world by non-action. In short, there is an intricate politico-religious structure of myth behind several of the most important works in the "Lyrics of Chu," and this same structure informs a large body of prose and poetic expositions *(fu)* from the late Warring States and Western Han. We can see parts of it, but we do not understand it fully.

The first two works translated below are from the early stratum of the "Lyrics of Chu." "The Nine Songs" are, in fact, eleven: nine are to deities from various parts

155

of China, one is for soldiers of the kingdom who have died in battle, and one is a short coda on the ritual itself. These are clearly liturgical works in a shamanistic tradition. Ten of the eleven are translated below. The *Li Sao,* which follows at p. 162, is a long first-person monologue (divided into ninety-two four-line stanzas and a coda) that has been traditionally read as the authentic voice of Qu Yuan. Whether it is indeed by Qu Yuan or not, we do know that in performance it would be the drama of Qu Yuan.[1]

Ling, usually translated as "the holy one[s]," sometimes refers to the deity in question and at other times to the sacred performers, who in some cases assume the role of the deity.

"The Nine Songs"

The Sovereign of the East: The One *(Dong-huang Tai-yi)*

On a day of good luck,   at the well-favored hour
with due awe we delight   the Sovereign on High.
Stroking our long swords,   jade are the hilt-guards,
with clinking of pendants,   onyx and agate.
On yao-fiber mats,   jades weight the corners,
we hold in their bunches   carnelian blooms,
joints wrapped in sage   on orchid-strewn cloths,
proffer cinnamon wine   and peppered beers.
Raise up the drumstick,   strike now the drums,
the beat sparse and slow,   steady the song,
play pipes and the zithers,   let the paean swell;
the holy ones sway,   gorgeous their gowns,
the scent spreads around us,   it fills the whole hall,
a tumult of all notes,   played swiftly together,
and our Lord is much pleased,   hale in his joy.

Lord in the Clouds *(Yun-zhong jun)*   *God of thunder*

In orchid baths bathed,   hair washed in blooms' scent,
our robes are resplendent,   with lavender flowers.
The holy one writhes,   he lingers within her,
she glows with a nimbus,   his light is unbounded.
He shall be here transfixed   in the Temple of Life,
He whose rays are the equal   of sun and the moon;
in his dragon-drawn cart,   the garb of the god,
he soars in his circles   around and around.

---

[1]Of the various verse forms in the "Lyrics of Chu," two of the most common break a line into hemistiches, divided by either the sound syllable *xi* or a lightly stressed syllable. In the translation I have represented this meter by leaving extra spaces at the break in the line. This roughly follows the long line of accentual verse in Old and Middle English, which was also divided sharply into hemistiches.

The holy one glistens,   for he has come down;
he lifts up in a gust,   afar into clouds.
He scans all the heartland   and far off beyond,
across seas on each side;   where does he end?
We yearn for our Lord   and heave a great sigh,
hearts greatly troubled,   and fretful within.

The Lady of the Xiang River *(Xiang jun)*

The Lady will not go,   still does she linger,
who is it stays her   on the isle midstream?
Lovely gaze, heavy-lidded,   her mouth shows a smile;
streaming swiftly I ride   my cassia boat,
and charge Yuan and Xiang   to be without waves,
and command River's waters   to steady their flow.

I gaze toward my Lady,   she will not come;
I blow on my panpipes,   for whom do I yearn?

I yoke flying dragons   and journey on north,
then bending my way   around Lake Dong-ting.
Hanging moss is my sail,   screens of sweet clover,
the oars are of iris,   orchids, my flags.
Gaze to Cen's sunlit banks,   to far northern shores,
and across the great river   I send my soul flying.

I send my soul flying,   still it can't reach her;
the woman so lovely   for me heaves a sigh;
my tears now flow freely,   trickling down,
and I long for the Lady,   I am tormented.

The paddles were cassia,   of magnolia, the sweeps,
I cut through the ice   and raised spray of snow.
It was picking hanging moss   in the middle of waters;
it was plucking the lotus   from tips of the trees.
When hearts are not one,   the go-between struggles;
her love was not strong,   it lightly was broken.

Over stone shallows   the current runs swift,
my dragons were flying,   beating their wings.
Her friendship was faithless,   reproach long remains;
untrue to her pledge,   she told me she had no time.

I galloped that dawn   on the plain by the river,
stayed my pace in the twilight   by northern isles,
where birds took their lodging   high on the roof
and the waters were circling   the base of the hall.
I threw a ring broken   down into the river,
my pendants I left   at the mouth of the Li.

I plucked lavender   on flowering isles
to give as gift   to the woman below.
This moment may never   be ours again,
let us wander off freely   and be at our ease.

The Senior Master of Lifespans *(Da si-ming)*

"Open them wide,   the gates of the heavens,
in a mass I come riding   dark purple clouds,
and charge the whirlwinds   to speed on ahead,
commanding a downpour   to moisten the dust."

My Lord sweeps in circles,   then He descends,
It is I who go with you   past Mount Kong-sang.
"Earth's nine domains   are teeming with men;
and their spans, long or short,   depend upon me."

High off we fly,   steadily soaring,
riding pure vapors,   He drives Shadow and Light;
then I and my Lord,   dashing swiftly ahead,
lead on the High God   down to Nine Hills.

Our robes are of cloud,   they flap in the wind,
our pendants of jade   sparkle and flash.
"Sometimes the Shadow,   sometimes the Light;
of the many, none know   that which I do."

I snapped off a hemp bud   and blossoms of yao-grass
to give as a gift   to Him Who Dwells Apart;
old age steals upon me   and now has arrived;
His affection withdraws,   He grows more remote.

He rides his dragon-car,   its wheels are rumbling,
and racing high off   He dashes to Sky,
I plait cassia twigs,   long stand fixed and gazing,
for increase of longing   thus troubles a man.

What is it then   that so troubles a man?—
I wish that now be forever,   and never wane.
Fixed is man's fate,   it is as it must be;
how may it happen   that the sundered rejoin?

The Junior Master of Lifespans *(Shao-si-ming)*, "Lord Iris"

Orchids of autumn,   the deer-weed,
they grow in their rows   at the foot of the hall,
green are their leaves,   pale their stalks,
their scent spreads around,   hanging upon us.
To men have been given   children so fair,
why should Lord Iris   be troubled so?

 good qualitity.

Orchids of autumn,   lushly they grow,
green are their leaves,   purple their stems.
The hall is filled   with fair women;
at once with me only   His eyes meet and fix.

He comes without speaking,   without farewell, goes;
He rides on the whirlwind,   bears banners of cloud.

No grief is so great   as parting while living;
no joy so strong   as love newly found.

His robe is of lotus,   sash wound with sweet clover,
He comes in a flash,   as suddenly leaves;
He lodges this night   in the fields of the god;
for whom waits our Lord   at the brink of clouds?

"With you I will roam   to the river's nine channels,
when blasts of wind rise,   heaving the waves;
I will wash my hair with you   in the Pools of Xian,
we will let your hair dry   in the Sun Gorge clefts.
I gaze for the Fairest,   she does not come;
I face the wind dazed,   loud I sing forth."

With peacock-plume canopies,   kingfisher streamers,
He mounts nine-banked Sky   and strokes comet's tail,
high he lifts long sword,   weak and young's bulwark—
Lord Iris alone is fit   to rule all the folk.

The Lord of the East *(Dong-jun)*

"I glow coming forth   in the eastlands,
I shine on my porch   by the tree Fu-sang,
then slapping my steeds   to a steady gallop,
the night is lit up,   and the day breaks.

My dragon team hitched,   I ride on the thunder,
bearing banners of cloud   streaming behind.
But I heave a great sigh   on the point of ascending;
there the heart falters,   I look back with care:
for the sounds and beauty   so give a man joy
those who watch are transfixed   and forget to go.

Harps tightly strung,   the drums alternating,
bells being rung,   chime frames shaking,
fifes sing out,   pipes are blown;
those who act holy ones,   wholesome and comely,
hover here winging,   suddenly mount,
reciting the lyrics   joining in dance.

Catching the pitch,   matching the rhythms,
the holy ones come,   they cover the sun.

imaginative animals.

east, spring, wood → metal

天狼星

In gown of green cloud   and white rainbow mantle,
I raise the long arrow,   I shoot Heaven's Wolf,
with yew-bow in hand   I now sink back under,
and seize the North Dipper   to pour cinnamon wine,
then clutching my reins,   I rush soaring high,
off far through darkness   voyaging east."

Things are cyclical

The Yellow River's Earl *(He-bo)*

With you I will roam   to the river's nine channels,
when blasts of wind rise   driving waves across stream,
we will ride my coach of waters,   its canopy, lotus,
hitched to paired dragons,   by basilisks flanked.

I climbed Mount Kun-lun,   I gazed all around,
the heart flew aloft,   it went sweeping off free.
Soon the sun was to set,   I, transfixed, forgot going,
and then to the far shore   I looked back with care.

My roofs are of fish scales,   halls of the dragon,
turrets of purple cowries,   palaces of carmine—
why is the holy one here,   down in the water?

We will ride on white turtles,   goldfish attend us,
with you I will roam   by the river's isles,
where the current is rushing,   there we'll go down.

You clasp your hands,   journeying eastward;
you go with the Fairest   to the southern shores
where the swell of the waves   is coming to meet us,
and the schools of fishes,   will send off my bride.

Spirit of the mountain

The Hill Wraith *(Shan gui)*

It seemed there was someone   in the cleft of the hills,
her mantle was hanging moss,   she was girded with ivy,
her eyes glanced upon me,   her mouth formed a smile:
"You who yearn for me,   who am so comely—

I ride the red leopard,   striped lynxes attend me,
with magnolia-wood wagon,   my flags, plaited cassia,
my cloak is stone-orchid,   my sash is asarum,
I snap the sweet fragrance,   gift for him that I love."

She dwells in bamboo's darkness,   she never sees sky;
the way was steep and hard,   late she came and alone.

Alone she stands forth,   high on the hill,
with clouds' rolling billows   there down below her;
it grows dim and blacker,   daylight turns dark,
and in gustings of east wind   the goddess rains.
I remain for the holy one,   transfixed, forget going,
the year has grown late,   who will clothe me in flowers?

I picked three-bloom asphodel   out in the hills,
on slopes rough and rocky,   through tangles of vines;
reproaching the Lady,   I in grief forget going,
for though she may love me,   she does not find time.

In the hills there is someone,   sweet smell of lavender,
she drinks from the stone-springs   in shadow of pines.

. . .

and though she may love me,   she holds back unsure.
The sky shakes in thunder,   with darkness comes rain,
the apes are all wailing,   in the night monkeys moan;
the whistling of winds   that howl through the trees;
I long for the Lady,   fruitless torment I find.

The Kingdom's Dead (Guo-shang)

Our great-shields we grasped,   donned jerkins of leather,
wheelhub scraped wheelhub,   short-swords met.

Banners blocked sunlight,   foemen like clouds,
bolts crossed and fell,   warriors pressed forward.

They break through our ranks,   they crush down our line,
the left horse has fallen,   the right horse takes wounds.

We dig in both wheels   and tie the team to them,
grasp the jade drumstick,   strike the great drum,
Fate is against us,   the spirits are angry,
all lie dead on the field,   left behind in the meadows.

We marched out but not back,   we went forth but not home,
the plains stretch on far,   the journey, a long one.

Long-swords at waists,   bows under arms,
heads cut from bodies,   hearts never yielding,
brave we were truly,   stout fighters too,
hard to the last,   not to be conquered,
our bodies are dead,   our souls are now gods,
among ghosts, the stalwart,   heroes among the wraiths.

Rites for Souls *(Li hun)*

The rites are done now,   drums beat together,
the wands are passed on,   new dancers take our place.
Fairest maidens' songs,   slowly sung and softly,
in spring the orchids come,   chrysanthemums in fall,
forever and unceasing from   the first and on forever.

The *Li Sao*

One of the most difficult aspects of the "Lyrics of Chu" is its use of flowers and aromatics, few of which have counterparts in English. These were clearly part of the ceremony and could stand for qualities of the deity, who is, on one occasion, addressed by a flower name. In the *Li Sao,* such sacred attributes merge with moral attributes. I have used English flowers and aromatics, which have their own associations, to substitute for some of the more exotic flora.

1
Of the god-king Gao-yang   I am the far offspring,[2]
my late honored sire   bore the name of Bo-yong.
The *she-ti* stars aimed   to the year's first month;[3]
geng-yin was the day   that I came down.

2
He scanned and he delved   into my first measure,
from the portents my sire   gave these noble names:
The name that he gave me   was Upright Standard;
and my title of honor   was Godly Poise.[4]

3
Such bounty I had   of beauty within,
and to this was added   fair countenance.
I wore mantles of river rush   and remote angelica,
strung autumn orchids   to hang from my sash.

4
They fled swiftly from me,   I could not catch them—
I feared the years passing   would keep me no company.
At dawn I would pluck   magnolia on bluffs,
in the twilight on isles   I culled undying herbs.

---

[2]Gao-yang was one of the mythic emperors of high antiquity, from whom the Chu royal house (and several other royal houses) claimed ancestry. Though not the ruling family, Qu Yuan's clan, the Qu, was one of the three royal clans of Chu and descended from Gao-yang.

[3]The *she-ti* stars were a constellation by whose position early astronomers determined the beginning of the year.

[4]To choose the name, the father reads his "measure": whether that comes from the astronomical conjunctions of his birth or his physiognomy is impossible to say. These "auspicious names" are not the names usually associated with Qu Yuan.

5

Days and months sped past,   they did not long linger,
springtimes and autumns   altered in turn.
I thought on things growing,   on the fall of their leaves,
and feared for the Fairest,   her drawing toward dark.[5]

6

Cling to your prime,   forsake what is rotting—
why not change   from this measure of yours?
Mount a fine steed,   go off at a gallop—
I will now take the lead,   ride ahead on the road.

7

The Three Kings of old   were pure and unblemished,[6]
all things of sweet scent   indeed were theirs.
Shen's pepper was there,   together with cassia,
white angelica, sweet clover   were not strung alone.

8

Such shining grandeur   had Kings Yao and Shun;[7]
they went the true way,   they held to the path.
But sloven and scruffy   were Kings Jie and Zhow;[8]
they walked at hazard   on twisted trails.

9

Those men of faction   had ill-gotten pleasures,
their paths went in shadow,   narrow, unsafe.
Not for myself   came this dread of doom—
I feared my king's chariot   soon would be tipped.

10

In haste I went dashing   in front and behind,
till I came to the tracks   of our kings before.
Lord Iris did not fathom   my nature within,[9]
he believed ill words,   he glowered in rage.

[handwritten margin note: King Not trusting Qu Yuan]

---

[5]The "fairest" is taken to be a figure for the Chu king as a beautiful woman. Thus his later quest for a mate is taken as a search for a prince who will appreciate his worth and employ him.

[6]The "Three Kings" are probably the early kings of Chu, though there is some disagreement on this point.

[7]Yao and Shun were the two Sage-Kings of antiquity revered in Traditionalist circles in North China. In Chu traditions, either by variant legend or by some strange syncretism, they play an important quasi-religious role. Shun, or Zhong-hua, supposedly buried at Cang-wu in southern Chu (stanza 47), will be the figure the speaker goes to visit to "state his case" about the moral consequences of princely behavior. Yao's two daughters married Shun; on Shun's death, they became the river goddesses of the Xiang.

[8]Jie was the last ruler of the Xia Dynasty and Zhow (actually Zhou, the spelling having been changed to differentiate him from the dynasty that supplanted him) was the last ruler of the Yin-Shang. Both are taken as exemplary bad rulers.

[9]"Lord Iris" is a kenning (compound) for the king, now figured as a male deity.

11

I knew well my bluntness   had brought me these woes,
yet I bore through them,   I could not forswear.
I pointed to Heaven   to serve as my warrant,
it was all for the cause   of the Holy One.

12

To me at first   firm word had been given,
she regretted it later,   felt otherwise.
I made no grievance   at this break between us,
but was hurt that the Holy One   so often changed.

the fairest
one

13

I watered my orchids   in all their nine tracts,
and planted sweet clover   in one hundred rods;
I made plots for peonies   and for the wintergreen,
mixed with asarum   and sweet angelica.

14

I wished stalks and leaves   would stand high and flourish,
I looked toward the season   when I might reap.
If they withered and dried,   it would cause me no hurt,
I would grieve if such sweetness   went rotting in weeds.

15

Throngs thrust themselves forward   in craving and want,
they never are sated   in things that they seek.
They show mercy to self,   by this measure others,
in them the heart stirs   to malice and spite.

16

Such a headlong horse race,   each hot in pursuit,
is not a thing   that thrills my own heart.
Old age comes on steadily,   soon will be here,
I fear my fair name   will not be fixed firmly.

17

At dawn I drank dew   that dropped on magnolia,
in twilight ate blooms   from chrysanthemums shed.
If my nature be truly comely,   washed utterly pure,
what hurt can I have   in long wanness from hunger?

18

I plucked tendrils of trees   to knot white angelica,
pierced fallen pistils   of flowering ivy.
I reached high to cassia   for stringing sweet clover,
and corded the coilings   of the rope-vine.

19

Yes, I took as my rule   those fair men before me,
it was not the garb worn   in the ways of our age.
Though it did not agree   with men of these days,
I would rest in the pattern   left by Peng and by Xian.[1]

20

Long did I sigh   and wipe away tears,
sad that men's lives   lay in such peril.
Though love of the fair   was the halter that guided me,
at dawn I was damned   and by twilight, undone.

21

Yes, I was undone   for sash hung with sweet clover,
then I added to it   the angelica and orchid.
Still my heart   will find goodness in these—
though I die many times,   I will never regret.

22

I reproach the Holy One's   unbridled rashness,
never discerning   what lies in men's hearts.
Women-throngs envied   my delicate brows,
they made scurrilous songs,   they said I loved lewdness.

23

Of these times the firm folkways: to be skillful in guile;
facing compass and square,   they would alter the borehole.
They forswear the straight line,   go chasing the crooked;
rivals for false faces,   such is their measure.

24

A woe wells within me,   to be so hapless,
alone at an impasse   in times such as these.
Best to die promptly,   to vanish away,
for I cannot bear   to show myself thus.

25

The great bird of prey   does not go in flocks,
so it has been   from times long ago.
The square and the circle   can never be matched,
what man can find peace   on a way not his own?

---

[1]Shaman Peng and Shaman Xian were two quasi-divine shaman ancestors. Traditional commentaries always took this as a single name, Peng Xian, both here and in The Ending Song (see p. 175). Peng Xian was supposed to have been a worthy adviser of a Shang king who committed suicide by drowning, hence Qu Yuan's decision to follow him in The Ending Song.

26
Bending one's heart,   quelling one's will,
abiding faults found,   submitting to shame,
embracing pure white,   death for the right—
these indeed were esteemed   by wise men before us.

27
I regretted my course   was not well discerned,
long I stood staring,   about to go back.
I turned my coach round   along the same path—
it was not yet too far   I had strayed in my going.

28
I let horses walk   through meadows of orchids,
to a hill of pepper trees I raced,   there rested the while.
I drew close, did not reach him,   I met with fault-finding,
I withdrew to restore   that garb I first wore.

29
Waterlilies I fashioned   to serve as my robe,
I gathered the lotus   to serve as my skirt.
Let it be over then,   no man knows me,
my nature in truth   has a scent sweet and steadfast.

30
High was my hat,   above me it loomed,
well strung, the pendants   that swung from my sash.
Sweet scent and stench   were all intermingled,
this gleaming flesh only   suffered no dwindling.

31
All at once I looked back,   and I let my eyes roam,
I would go off to view   the wild lands around.
Pendants in bunches,   I was richly adorned,
their sweet fragrance spread,   ever more striking.

32
Each man has a thing   in which he finds joy:
I alone love the fair,   in that I abide.
Though my limbs be cut from me,   I still will not change,
for how could my heart   be made to cower?

33
Then came the Sister,   tender and distressed,[2]
mild of manner   she upbraided me thus,

---

[2]"The Sister" is *nü-xu,* clearly a title rather than a proper name; however, the actual role or relationship implied by the phrase is uncertain. Early commentators took this as Qu Yuan's sister, and there is some evidence that *nü-xu* was a popular term for "sister"—though whether a literal or a figurative sister is again uncertain. It may also mean "wench."

she said: "Gun was unyielding,   he fled into hiding,
at last died untimely   on moors of Mount Yu.[3]

34
"Why such wide culling,   such love of the fair,
in you alone bounty   of beautiful raiment?
Haystacks of stinkweed   are heaped in their rooms;
you alone stand aloof   and refuse such attire.

Conversation between Characters.

35
"No swaying the throngs   person by person;
None says: 'Come, discern   this my nature within!'
Now men rise together,   each favors his friends,
why do you stand alone—   why not listen to me?"

36
I trust sages before us   for moderate judgment,
my heart swelled in torment,   it had come now to this.
I crossed Xiang and Yuan,   faring on southward,
reached Zhong-hua, King Shun,   to state him my case:

37
"King Qi had Nine Stanzas   and the Nine Songs—
extreme in wild pleasures,   he did as he pleased.
He was heedless of troubles,   made no plans for the morrow,
whereby the five sons   brought strife to his house.[4]

38
"Yi recklessly ventured,   he was lavish in hunts,
he also loved shooting   the great foxes.
Such turbulent wickedness   rarely ends well:
and Han Zhuo was lusting   to seize his bride.[5]

39
"Guo Ao garbed himself   in the stiffened leather;
he followed his wants,   he failed to forbear.
He lost himself daily   in wild pleasures.
whereby his own head   was toppled and fell.[6]

---

[3]Gun was a son of Gao Yang, who was charged by Sage-King Yao with controlling the great flood. When he failed, he was put to death and his body left on Mount Yu. According to one tradition, he was transformed into a bear.

[4]King Qi was the son of Great Yu, who was in turn the son of Gun and the founder of the Xia Dynasty. He brought back "The Nine Songs" from Heaven.

[5]Yi the Archer seized the kingship after King Qi's death, but was subsequently killed by his retainer Han Zhuo.

[6]Guo Ao was a son of Han Zhuo and Yi the Archer's stolen bride. He was killed by Shao Gang, who restored the Xia Dynasty.

40

"Xia's Jie was steadfast   in his misdeeds,
in pursuit of these   he met with his doom.
Shang's Zhow, the Lord Xin,   minced men to stew,
whereby Yin's great lineage   could not last long.[7]

41

"Yu the Mighty was stern,   respectful and godly;[8]
the right way was Zhou's norm,   it thus did not err.
They raised men of worth,   rewarded the able,
they kept the straight line,   they did not veer.

42

"Sovereign Heaven is slanted   in favor of none;
it discerns a man's virtues,   puts helpers beside him.
When wisdom and sense   do deeds that are splendid,
they may then act their will   in this land down below.

43

"I scanned times before us,   looked to times yet to come,
read the measures of men,   and the ends of their plans:
who found wanting in virtue   may be put to use?
who found wanting in good   may be still retained?

44

"By the brink stands my body,   I am in death's peril,
I discern my first nature   and still regret not.
Not judging the drillhole,   they squared the peg:
indeed, fair men of old   came to mince in a stew.

45

"Sighs come from me often,   the heart swells within,
sad that I and these times   never will be matched.
I plucked sage and lotus   to wipe away tears,
that soak my gown's folds   in their streaming."

46

I knelt with robes open,   thus stated my case,
having grasped so clearly   what is central and right.
I teamed jade white dragons,   rode the Bird that Hides Sky,
waiting on winds   to fleetly fare upward.

---

[7]Jie was the last ruler of the Xia and notorious for his misrule. Zhow was the bad last ruler of the Yin-Shang (see note to stanza 8).
[8]Great Yu, Gun's son, was the founder of the Xia.

168

47

At dawn I loosed wheel-block   there by Cang-wu,
and by twilight I reached   the Gardens of Air.[9]
I wished to bide a while   by the windows of gods,
but swift was the sun   and it soon would be dusk.

where sun god resides

48

I bade sun-driver Xi-he,   to pause in her pace,
to stand off from Yan-zi   and not to draw nigh.[1]
On and on stretched my road,   long it was and far,
I would go high and go low   in this search that I made.

don't want now older.

49

I watered my horses   in the Pools of Xian,
and twisted the reins   on the tree Fu-sang, — *free to heaven*
snapped a branch of the Ruo Tree   to block out the sun,
I roamed freely the while   and lingered there.[2]

driver of moon god

50

Ahead went Wang Shu   to speed on before me,
behind came Fei Lian,   he dashed in my train.[3]
Phoenix went first   and warned of my coming,
Thunder Master told me   that all was not set.

God of wind

51

I bade my phoenixes   mount up in flight,
to continue their going   both by day and by night.
Then the whirlwinds massed,   drawing together,
they marshaled cloud-rainbows,   came to withstand me.

52

A bewildering tumult,   first apart, then agreeing,
and they streamed flashing colors,   high and then low.
I bade the God's gatekeeper   open the bar;
he stood blocking gateway   and stared at me.

---

[9]Cang-wu was the mountain where Shun (Zhong-hua) lay buried. The "Gardens of Air," *Xuan-pu* or "Suspended Gardens," was a section of the Kun-lun Range and an abode of the Undying. The name is also rendered with a homophone as "The Gardens of Mystery."
[1]Xi-he is the goddess who drives the chariot of the sun across the sky. Mount Yan-zi was supposedly located in the farthest extreme of the West, the point where the sun goes down. Thus the poet is ordering the sun not to set.
[2]The sun rises from Sunrise Gorge, and in its rising is bathed in the Pools of Xian, coming out at last at the base of the Fu-sang Tree. The Ruo Tree is at the opposite extreme of the world, the point where the sun goes in.
[3]Wang Shu was the driver of the moon; Fei Lian the god of winds.

53

The moment grew dimmer,   light soon would be done,
I tied signs in orchids,   standing there long.
An age foul and murky   cannot tell things apart;
it loves to block beauty   from malice and spite.

54

At dawn I set to fare   across the White Waters,
I climbed Mount Lang-feng,   there tethered my horses.[4]
All at once I looked back,   my tears were streaming,
sad that the high hill   lacked any woman.

55

At once I went roaming   to the Palace of Spring,[5]
I broke sprays of garnet   to add to my pendants.
Before the blooms' glory   had fallen away,
I would seek a woman below   to whom I might give them.[6]

56

Feng Long I bade   to go riding the clouds,
to seek out Fu-fei   down where she dwells.[7]
I took pendant-sash,   I tied there a message,
and bade Lady Mumbler   act as my envoy.

57

A bewildering tumult,   first apart, then agreeing,
she suddenly balked,   she could not be swayed.
She went twilights to lodge   at Farthest-of-Rocks,
and at dawn bathed her hair   in Wei-ban Stream.[8]

58

She presumed on her beauty,   she was scornful and proud,
in wild pleasures daily   she wantonly strayed.
Though beautiful truly,   she lacked right behavior—
I let her go then,   I sought for another.

---

[4]Both White Waters and Mount Lang-feng are sections of the Kun-lun Range.

[5]The Palace of Spring belonged to the Emperor of the East, and thus was on the other side of the world from Kun-lun.

[6]"Woman below" may suggest a woman who dwells on Earth, as opposed to the woman of Heaven whom he could not reach. However, the phrase, as used in "The Nine Songs," suggests a water goddess, as Fu-fei indeed was.

[7]Feng Long was the god of the clouds, or perhaps of thunder. Fu-fei was the goddess of the river Luo.

[8]The goddess has apparently wandered to the Far West (in the river?). The Farthest Rock was supposed to be in the extreme West, the spot from which the Ruo waters had their source. Wei-ban Stream came off Mount Yan-zi, where the sun sets (see stanza 48).

59

I let my gaze sweep   over all the world's ends,
I roamed throughout Sky,   then I came down.
I viewed the surging crest   of a terrace of onyx,
there saw a rare woman,   the You-Song's daughter.[9]

60

I bade the venom-owl   make match between us,
and the venom-owl told me   she was not fair.
Early summer's dove-cock   went away singing,
and I still loathe   its petty wiles.

61

My heart then faltered,   doubts overcame me,
I wanted to go myself;   it was not allowed.
Already the phoenix   had given my troth gifts,
still I feared that Gao Xin   had come before me.[1]

62

I wanted to alight far away,   there was no place to halt,
so I drifted the while   and roamed at my ease.
If still not yet married   to Shao-kang the Prince,
there remained the two Yao girls   of the clan You-Yu.[2]

63

My envoy was feeble,   my matchmaker bumbling;
I feared words to charm them   would not hold fast.
An age foul and murky,   it spites a man's worth,
it loves to block beauty,   it acclaims what is ill.

64

Remote and far   are the chambers of women;
and the wise king also   is not yet aware.
I keep feelings within me,   do not bring them forth,
yet how can I bear   that it be thus forever?

65   a person who access the land.
I sought stalks of milfoil,   and slips to cast lots,
and bade Holy Fen   to divine the thing for me.
I said:
"Two lovely beings   must surely be matched;
whose fairness is steadfast   that I may adore her?

---

[9]The You-Song (the chieftain clan of the Song tribe) once provided a wife, Jian-di, for Di-gao, from which union came Jie, who was ancestor of the royal house of Shang.
[1]Gao Xin or Di-gao was the legendary emperor who married Jian-di, the "daughter of the You-Song."
[2]When Guo-ao still held the Xia throne, Shao-kang, the rightful prince, fled to the You-Yu, the chieftain clan of Yu, whose ruler gave him his two daughters in marriage.

66

"Consider the wide sweep   of these Nine Domains—
can it be only here   that a woman be found?"
He said:
"Undertake to fare far,   be not full of doubts;
none who seeks beauty   would let you slip by.

67

"Is there any place lacking   in plants of sweet fragrance?
why must you cherish   your former abode?
This age is a dark one,   eyes are dazzled and blinded,
no man can discern   our good or our bad.

68

"What men love and loathe   is never the same—
only these men of faction   alone stand apart.
Each person wears mugwort,   stuffed in their waists,
they declare that the orchid   may never be strung.

69

"If in judgment of plants   they still cannot grasp it,
can they ever be right   on the beauty of gems?
They seek shit and mire   to stuff their sachets,
and say that Shen's pepper   lacks any sweet smell."

70

I wished to follow Holy Fen's   lot of good fortune,
yet still my heart faltered,   doubts overcame me.
The Shaman Xian   would descend in the twilight,[3]
I clasped pepper and rice   to beseech him.

71

The gods blotted sky,   their full hosts descending,
spirit vassals of Many Doubts   joined to go greet them.[4]
In a light-burst the Sovereign   sent forth his spirit,
giving me word   of a lucky outcome.

72

He said:
"Undertake to fare high   and then to fare low,
find one who agrees   with the yardstick and square.
Yu the Mighty was stern,   he sought one who matched him,
he held to Gao Yao   as one able to suit him.[5]

---

[3]For Shaman Xian, see the note to stanza 19.
[4]Many Doubts (literally, "Nine Doubts," the number nine being used commonly for a vague "many")
was the range in the Far South where Shun was supposedly buried.
[5]For Yu, see the note to stanza 41. Gao Yao served as minister of Great Yu in the beginning of the
Xia.

73

"If one's nature within   loves what is fair,
what need to make use   of matchmaker or envoy?
Yue held an earth-ram   upon Fu's cliff;
Wu-ding employed him   and did not doubt.[6]

74

"Once there was Lü Wang   who swung a butcher's knife,
yet he met Zhou's King Wen   and he was raised up.[7]
And there was Ning Qi,   a singer of songs;
Huan of Qi heard him;   he served as the helper.[8]

75

"Yet act now before   the year grows too late,
now while the season   has not yet passed.
I fear only cries early   from summer's nightjar,
making all plants   lose their sweet scent."

76

My pendants of garnet,   how they dangle down from me—
yet the throngs would dim them,   cover them up.
These men of faction   are wanting in faith,
I fear their malice,   that they will break them.

77

The times are in tumult,   ever transforming—
how then may a man   linger here long?
Orchid, angelica change,   they become sweet no more;
iris, sweet clover alter,   they turn into straw.

78

These plants that smelled sweet   in days gone by
have now become nothing   but stinking weeds.
Can there be any reason   other than this?—
the harm that is worked   by no love for the fair.

79

I once thought that orchid   could be steadfast:
it bore me no fruit,   it was all show.
Forsaking its beauty,   it followed the common;
it wrongly is ranked   in the hosts of sweet scent.

---

[6]The Shang king Wu-Ding dreamed of someone suited to be his minister, and found him as a convict or corvee laborer named Yue, making rammed-earth ramparts on Fu Cliff, hence called Fu Yue.
[7]Lü Wang originally worked as a butcher, then became a fisherman; in his old age he was discovered by King Wen of the Zhou and made his minister.
[8]Ning Qi was originally a petty merchant who would sing as he rapped the horns of his buffalo. Duke Huan of Qi heard him and made him an aide.

80

Pepper is master of fawning,   it is swaggering, reckless,
only mock-pepper stuffs   sachets hung from waists.
It pressed hard to advance,   it struggled for favor,
what sweet scent remains   that is able to spread?

81

Truly, ways of these times   are willful and loose,
who now is able   to avoid being changed?
Look on orchid and pepper,   see them like this—
will less be true   of river rush and wintergreen?

82

Only these my own pendants   are still to be prized;
forsaken is loveliness,   and I come to this.
Yet their sweet scent spreads,   it is not diminished,
an aroma that even now   has still not abated.

83

In their blending's balance   I take my delight,
I will drift and will roam,   seeking the woman.
And while such adornment   is still in its glory,
I will range widely looking,   both high and low.

84

Since Holy Fen told me   my fortunate lot,
I will choose a luck-day,   and I will set out.
I snap sprays of garnet   to serve as my viands,
fine garnet meal   will serve as my fare.

85

For me have been hitched   those dragons that fly,
mixed onyx and ivory   serve as my coach.
How can a mind set apart   be ever like others?
I will go away far,   keep myself removed.

86

I bent my way round   at Kun-lun Mountain,
long and far was the road,   there I ranged widely.
I raised my cloud-rainbows,   dimming and darkening,
jade phoenix chimes rang   with a jingling voice.

87

At dawn I loosed the wheel-block   at Ford-of-the-Sky,[9]
by twilight I came   to the ends of the west.
Phoenix spread its wings,   and bore up my banners,
high aloft it soared,   its wingbeats were steady.

---

[9]The Ford of Sky is an asterism, the narrowest point in the Milky Way.

174

88

All at once I was faring   across Drifting Sands,[1]
I went down the Red Waters,   there took my ease.[2]
I signaled the dragons   to make me a bridge,
I called to West's Sovereign   to take me across.

a beginning of the world

89

Long and far was the road,   it was filled with perils,
I passed word to my hosts: drive straight and attend me.
I made way to Mount Bu-zhou,   there turned to the left,[3]
toward the Sea of the West,   my appointed goal.

90

Then I massed all my chariots,   a thousand strong,
jade hubs lined even,   we galloped together.
I hitched my eight dragons,   heaving and coiling,
and bore my cloud banners   streaming behind.

91

I then quelled my will   and paused in my pace;
the gods galloped high   far to the distance,
they were playing "Nine Songs"   and dancing "the Shao,"[4]
making use of this day   to take their delight.

92

I was mounting aloft   to such dazzling splendor—
all at once I glanced down   to my homeland of old.
My driver grew sad,   my horses felt care,
they flexed looking backward   and would not go on.

The Ending Song

It is done now forever!
in all the kingdom there is no man,   no man who knows me,
then why should I care   for that city, my home?
Since no one can join me   in making good rule,
I will go off to seek   where Peng and Xian dwell.

---

[1]The Drifting Sands is a general term for the imagined terrors of the northwestern deserts.
[2]The Red Waters were a river that flowed off the Kun-lun Range.
[3]Mount Bu-zhou is a mythical mountain in the Far West.
[4]Ancient ceremonial music and dance. These "Nine Songs" are legendary and not the shamanistic hymns given earlier.

先
秦
西
漢

The *Chu-ci* Tradition

Journeys Heavenly and Earthly

David Hawkes, a distinguished scholar of the "Lyrics of Chu," distinguishes two basic components in works following the tradition of "The Nine Songs" and *the Li Sao*. One of these he calls "tristia," in which the poet complains of his unhappiness, how he has been wronged or misjudged. The second component Hawkes calls "itineraria," the wanderings, in which the poet makes the circuit of the universe (though in "The Nine Songs," the circuit seems more restricted to the Xiao-Xiang River region). In many ways, all Chinese travel literature and landscape writing can be traced to the heavenly wanderings of the *Li Sao*. But the same model is no less true of spiritual journeys than of physical ones. The shaman's spirit journey through the heavens was closely related to the spirit journeys that attracted various kinds of Daoist adepts. "Far Roaming," included in the "Lyrics of Chu," is a Han Daoist transformation of the *Li Sao*'s heavenly journey.

"Far Roaming" includes many of the deities and fantastic locales of the *Li Sao*, but its poetic space is also populated by famous adepts who, by various techniques of breath control, diet, and alchemy, had undergone a metamorphosis and joined the Undying, also referred to as the Genuine Men and the feathered men. Such figures include the Master of Red Pine, the historical Han Zhong (who sought the Western Isles of the Undying for the First Emperor of Qin), and Qiao the Prince (Wang-zi Qiao). In addition to the adepts themselves, the poem makes extensive use of the jargon of Daoist Huang-Lao's techniques of metamorphosis.

Far Roaming

> I deplored the world's ways,   they hampered and hemmed me,
> I wished to rise lightly,   go roaming afar.
> Yet this flesh was crude stuff,   I had not the means,
> what carriage would bear me   floating up and away?
>
> I was drowning in filth,   soiled by things rotting,
> locked lonely in torment   with no one to tell.
> In the night I tossed restless,   I did not sleep,
> a fretfulness of soul   that lasted to dawn.
>
> Of Earth and Heaven   I thought on the endlessness,
> I mourned for man's life   and its lasting travail.

I never would reach to those who are gone,
I never would learn of those who will come.

With faltering pace,   thoughts turned to things far,
in anguish and woe   my cares long continued.
Turbulent fancies,   reckless and rash,
the heart in its gloom   enlarged sorrow's store.

Spirit fled in a flash,   it did not turn back;
outer form like dead wood   remained there alone.
I reflected within   upon the best conduct,
I sought out the source   from which comes Right Breath.

In a void that is still   there was placid delight,
then calm in not-acting,   I found myself there.
I had heard of Red Pine,   pure of all dirt,
I wished for the influence   of the model he left.

I prized fine Attainments   of the Genuine Men,
I esteemed the Undying   reached in ages gone by.
They went off with Change,   no longer were seen,
their names' glory is known,   each day spreading more.

A marvel, how Fu Yue   found his lodging in stars;[1]
and I envied Han Zhong,   who attained to the One.
Outer forms grew inert,   they receded still farther,
they departed men's throngs,   held aloof and withdrawn.

Through Breath's transformations   they rose to the heights,
fleet spirits racing,   wraithlike and eerie.
Now and then in a blur   we can see them afar,
incandescent essences   flitting to and fro.

They broke from dust billowing,   struck upon wonder,
never turned back   to those cities once home.
Shunning all ills,   they felt terror no more,
in their ages none knew   where they had gone.

I feared Heaven's seasons'   changing succession,
Holy Lights all ablaze   and voyaging west.
Faint frosts descend,   sinking down under,
alas, the sweet plants   leaf-stripped too soon.
I stroll carefree the while,   go rambling freely,
I had spent long years   with nothing achieved.
Who could share my delight   in the sweetness remaining?
I faced the dawn winds   and let feelings spread free.

---

[1]Fu Yue, who in the *Li Sao* was discovered in a labor gang by the Shang king Wu-ding and made his minister, was supposed to have mastered the Way and taken a place among the stars.

Remote was Gao-yang,   too faint in the distance,[2]
from whom would I take my model?

Reprise:
Springs and autumns are fleeting,   they do not abide,
how could I long linger   in the place I once dwelled?
I could not catch the Yellow Emperor and cling to him,
but Qiao the Prince I would follow   to frisk and be merry.

I dined on Six Breaths,   I drank magic dew,
in my mouth I swished sun-glow,   I chewed dawn's rosy clouds.
I preserved the pristineness   of the light of the soul,
essential Breaths entered,   the crude and foul fled.

I blew with the south wind   I roamed along with it,
I came to South Chao,   it was there that I rested.
I met Qiao the Prince   and greeted him gravely,
I queried him on balancing   Universal Breath.

He said,
The Way can be accepted;
it cannot be passed on.
So small, nothing within it;
so large, has no limit.
Spare your soul bewilderment—
it comes in its own course.
Universal Breath augments spirit,
at midnight keep it with you.
Be empty to attend on it,
prior to not-acting.
All categories thus complete,
this is Attainment's Gateway.

What I heard was much treasured,   I then set to go,
and all at once   I was on my way.
Nigh to the feathered men   on Cinnabar Hill,
I lingered in that olden land   of the Undying.

At dawn I washed my hair   in Sun Gorge's clefts
at twilight, dried my body   beneath its nine suns.
I sucked subtle distillates   from the cascades,
clasped to bosom the sparklings   of diamonds.

Jade complexion grew ruddy,   my face began to glow,
with essence strained pure,   I first felt my vigor.
All flesh-firmness melted,   I began to grow pliant,
the spirit grew slender,   moved with wanton abandon.

[2]Gao-yang was the mythical king to whom the speaker of the *Li Sao* traced his ancestry.

I admired the blazing Attainment   of southern lands,
found fair winter flowering   of cassia trees.
Hills bleak and barren   with no beasts there;
moors silent and gloomy,   without men.
I bore up my several souls,   I climbed to rose wisps,
and by floating clouds hidden,   I fared on above.

I charged Heaven's gatekeeper   to open the bar;
he pushed back the gates   and stared at me.
I called on Feng Long,   made him guide the way,[3]
I asked where was lodged   the god's palace of stars.

At Tiered Rays I alighted,   I went in the God's precincts,
pushed on to Xun-shi,[4]   viewed the Clear Citadel.
At dawn I loosed wheel-block   in the Sacred Yard;
and by twilight I hung above   Yu-wei-lü Hill.

Then I massed all my chariots,   a thousand strong,
in majestic tumult   we galloped together.
I hitched my eight dragons,   heaving and coiling,
and bore my cloud banners   streaming behind.

Upright bright pennons,   bearing cock-rainbows,
mixed of all colors,   dazzling, flashing.
Up sprung the yoke team,   low, then aloft,
the trace dragons coiled,   they burst headlong forward.

A jumble of riders,   mixed in confusion,
a motley surging cavalcade,   moving together.
I myself seized the reins,   I held the whip straight,
for we soon were to pass   the place of Gou Mang.[5]

We traversed Tai-hao   then bent to the right,[6]
Ahead went Fei Lian   to open the path.[7]
In glow of the sunlight   before the full rays,
we crossed Heaven's Pool   and forged straight ahead.

The Wind-Earl sped for me,   taking the van,
purged billowing dust,   it was clear and cool.
Phoenix spread wings   and bore up my banners,
I met with Ru-shou   where the West's Sovereign dwells.[8]

---

[3]Feng Long, the god of clouds or thunder, was employed by the speaker of the *Li Sao* to make a match with Fu-fei.
[4]Xun-shi was a star near the Dipper; it figures often in heavenly flights.
[5]Gou Mang was the tutelary god of the East.
[6]Tai-hao was the Emperor of the East.
[7]Fei Lian was a wind god, who also appears in the heavenly flight in the *Li Sao*.
[8]Ru-shou was one of the tutelary gods of the West.

I snatched up a comet   to serve as my standard,
I raised Dipper's handle   to serve as my sign.
Chaotic, pellmell,   we rose and dipped down,
we swam flowing waves   of fog-tendrils windstruck.

But the moment grew dimmer,   all darkened in shadow,
I called on Black Tortoise   to dash in my train.[9]
Behind went Wen Chang,   in charge of the columns,[1]
all the gods stood in order,   the wheelhubs were even.

The road kept on going,   it was long and far,
I slowed, pausing in pace,   and crossed up on high.
To my left the Rain Master   I made wait upon me,
to my right was Lord Thunder,   who served as my guard.

I wished to cross from the world   and forget to return,
my fancies ran wild,   were reckless and rash.
I felt merry within,   and I found myself fair,
I sought pleasure the while,   and wanton delight.

I fared through blue clouds,   I swam swirling currents,
all at once I glanced down   to my homeland of old.
My driver felt care,   my heart grew sad,
the outer horses looked back   and would not go on.

I longed for those I had known,   I imagined their forms,
I heaved a great sigh   and wiped away tears.
Adrift for amusement,   I rose to far places,
and then quelled my will   and gave myself ease.

Toward the Blazing God   I galloped straight forward,
ready to journey   to Southern Doubts Mountains.
I viewed seething blurs   beyond the world's bounds,
I streamed through the swirling   wending my way.

Zhu Rong gave the warning,   he cleared out my path,
I passed word to Phoenix,   encountered Fu-fei.
They performed "Pool of Xian,"
    played "Receiving Cloud,"
the two maidens attended,
    the "Nine Shao" were sung,
I had Xiang's Goddess strike the great harp,
I bade the Sea Lord to have Ping Yi dance.
Purple krakens and hydras came forward together,
forms wriggling, writhing,   they slithered along.

Iris Rainbow, fair and frail,   increasing her spirals,
phoenixes burst into flight,   flew soaring in circles.

---

[9]Black Tortoise, Xuan-wu, occupied the northern position in the Zodiac.
[1]Wen Chang was a constellation of six stars, later taken as being in charge of government offices.

A deluge of music   that spread without limit,
then I went on my way   and tarried a while.

Slow the pace, but together,   we galloped ahead
to the far and last limit,   to the Gateway of Cold.
I overtook fleet wind   at the Pure Source of Waters,
I had Zhuan Xu follow   across the tiered ice.[2]

By a bypath I passed   the Black God of Dark,
I rode Sky's Interstices,   turned to look back.
I called to the Demiurge,   had him appear,
and he took the lead for me   upon the flat road.

I went back and forth through the world's four bounds,
and flowed all around the Six Enclosures.
Rising I reached the Lightning Crack,
then plunging I gazed on the Great Chasm.

Vertiginous depths below me   where no land was,
a cavernous emptiness above   where was no sky.
It flashed and flared where I looked,   but I saw nothing,
a blurred rumble when I listened,   but I heard nothing.
I passed beyond non-acting,   I reached to the Clear,
the Very Beginning   became my neighbor.

The first-century writer Si-ma Xiang-ru's poetic exposition on "The Great One" represents the politicization of the heavenly journey, as Emperor Wu of Han is described as the shaman adept who flies through the cosmos and finally passes "beyond." Emperor Wu was a patron of elaborate shamanistic performances and had no doubt heard many trance reports of the upper universe. In the *Li Sao,* the speaker was gradually transformed from the concerned liegeman into a figure of domineering power who commands a turbulent cavalcade of divinities. It is that figure of power who becomes the point of departure for Si-ma Xiang-ru's panegyric.

The most interesting question raised is whether the figure described in "The Great One" is a figure of panegyric or of hyperbolic satire. Certainly within the tradition this vision of Emperor Wu has been interpreted as satire to warn the emperor against the evils of excessive interest in the cult of the Undying. Whether the poetic exposition is to be taken as panegyric or satire is a question of the putative intention of the author and of how one judges the values implicit in the text—values of kingship that are far removed from the Confucian vision of emperor as Chief Administrator and Liaison Officer with Heaven. The ruler in "The Great One" is a peculiar mixture of Chu shamanism, Huang-Lao Daoism, and Legalist absolutism. No doubt in the original performance of a poetic exposition like "The Great One," the emperor could beam with delight at the panegyric he heard, while the Confucian officers of the court could smile no less at what they heard as a savage satire on the excesses of the Huang-Lao Daoist quest for imperial transcendence.

---

[2]Zhuan Xu was the Emperor of the North.

Si-ma Xiang-ru (179–117 B.C.), The Great One

There was a Great One in this age,
he was here in the very heart of the land.
His dwelling filled thousands of miles,
but too paltry to hold him   even a while.
Oppressed by this age's ways,   crimping and curbing,
he rose lightly aloft   and traveled afar.
He bore crimson banners,   his device, the pale rainbow,
he carried cloud vapors   floating above him.
He raised a tall shaft   of golden vapors,
bound round with glowing   hung as bright bangles.
The star Xun-shi dangled,   strung as a tassle,[3]
behind comets trailed,   floating as streamers.
Pulsing and fluttering,   cascading upward,
throbbing and quivering,   those waving undulations.
He snatched the Sky's Pike-star   to serve as his pennant,
wound fractured rainbows   to serve as haft-wrappings.
The red grew remote,   all was murky and purple,
wind blasts gushed forth,   clouds went floating.

He drove an ivory car with winged dragons,
    heaving and slithering,
teamed scarlet serpents and blue basilisks,
    wriggling and writhing.
Upward and downward flexed straining straightened necks,
    they bounded flaunting,
sinuously spiralling humped bristling loping legs bent under,
    and arced away swaying.
Rearing and bucking head-tossing they balked,
    and faltered unbudging,
then broke loose unbridled amok they reared rampant
    in towering tangles.

Jerking forward and back, eyes rolling tongues lolling,
    slackening, they slithered,
then twined together cascading upward they boldly bolted
    gripping and grappling.

Wound coiling together, roaring and bellowing, they alighted
    and cleaved to the path,
then soared aloft buzzing and bounding burst upward
    dashing ahead in a frenzy.
With a whoosh and a sizzling crackle
    in flares they arrived, like lightning bolts passing,

---

³Cf. note 4, p. 179.

in a flash all fogs were gone,
bursting open, clouds dissolved.

Sheared obliquely past Shao-yang,   climbed to High Dark,
it was the Hallowed Man   that He was then seeking.
Bending round patches of dark,   He wheeled to the right,
fared straight across the Cascade   and directly on eastward.

He mustered all Spirits Assembled,   he selected among them,
He enlisted a god-band   at the star Quivering Rays.
He bade the Five Emperors   lead ahead on the way,
sent the Supreme One back,   had Ling-yang follow attending.
To his left, the Dark Spirit,   to his right, Qian-lei, Demiurge,
ahead was the sacred bird Chang-li,   behind, Summer-burgeoning.
Zheng Bo-qiao was his liegeman,   Xian-men served him,
and He summoned Qi-bo   to be his Lord Druggist.
The South's Lord, Zhu-rong,   warned to empty his path,
clearing murky miasmas,   only then He fared onward.

I have massed all my chariots   ten thousand strong,
I marshal cloud-canopies,   lift floriate banners.
I bid Gou Mang, East's Prince,   to lead the procession,
I am soon to set off   for the Mountain Nan-xi.
I fare past Sage-King Yao   on the Exalted Hill,
go on by Sage-King Shun   in the Many Doubts Range.
My hosts, a deep deluge,   all intermingled,
a bustling clamorous tumult,   we gallop side by side.
A frenzied turbulence tangled,   bumping and dragging,
a surging and boundless swill,   cascading spills forward.
Rallied ranks and rows swarming,   teeming the throngs,
then spewing strewn multitudes,   all scrambled about.

My path entered Thunder-house,   deepset its rumblings,
then out into Wraith Gorge,   of sheer looming crags.
I beheld the world's Eight Stays,   viewed all in the Encircling Seas,
I crossed back over Nine Channels,   I passed the Five Rivers.
I dealt with the Blazing Fires,   I floated on Ruo's waters,
I sailed past the Floating Isles,   I fared on Flowing Sands.

At Cong-ji I rested,   sported at the source of all waters,
bade Holy Crone play the harp,   had Ping-yi dance for me.
But the moment grew dim and shadowed,   dusky and turbulent,
I called Ping-yi to slay Wind-Earl,   and flog the Rain Master.
I gazed west to Kun-lun,   it was murky and vague,
and galloped straight thither   across San-wei Mountain.
I pushed Gates of Sky open,   I went in the God's palace,
I seized his Jade Maidens   and took them back with me.
We climbed Lang-feng Mountain,   gathered there afar,

then as birds soared aloft   and stopped all together.
We tarried sweeping around Shadow Mountain,   in spiralling curves,
for today I would behold   the West's Queen Mother.
Her hoary white head bears ornaments,   she dwells in a cave,
blessed to have the bird Three-Foot   to be her messenger.
As she does so I must live forever   and never die,
even ten thousand ages   would not be enough to give joy.

I turned my carriage and went back,
    my way went right over Mount Bu-zhou,
    and we joined for a feast in the Hidden City.
We sucked primal liquids,   we dined on dawn clouds,
we chewed caps of asphodel,   nibbled jasper blooms.
Facing up I fared forward,   I set forth on high,
my hosts through huge space   wended above.
We pierced through the flashes   of light down below,
we waded through Rain Master's   streaming downpour.
I sped the lead carriage   in a lengthy dive,
I left fogs behind me,   I raced off afar.
I was pressed by this realm,   by its narrow constraints,
drew away with slowing pace   from the margins of North.
I left my massed riders   at the Purple Towers,
I lurched ahead speeding   to Gates of the Cold.
Below were sheer heights,   all earth was gone,
above was huge hollowness   and no heavens.
Vision blurred and was dazzled,   sight was lost,
listening was indistinct,   hearing was lost.
And I rode on that Blankness   I passed far above,
beyond lack of others   I endured Alone.

The heavenly journey became important in the tradition of classical poetry *(shi)*, though as a shorter form it tended to treat the motif less fully, and eventually more formulaically.

Ruan Ji (A.D. 210–263), Songs of My Cares LXVIII

I looked out north on the Gorge of Dry Dark,
then westward I went to visit Shao-ren.
I peered round to Sky's Ford in the distance,
a rashness uncurbed was my heart's delight.
A shimmering wisp was Life and Death's gate,
roam there once and you will not seek it again.
Then I happened to meet with the dawn-wind hawk
and rode it in flight to the southern groves.
In the Pole-Star's incandescent floods

I sped instantly, indulging my most wanton will.
I repose at a feast in the Pure Citadel—
who now can stop me from leaving the world?

The heavenly journey is closely related to the development of Chinese landscape literature. Visits to the great mountains of China, with their Buddhist monasteries and Daoist covens, represented a process of physical struggle and spiritual attainment that found the most natural form of representation in the tradition of the heavenly journey. In the following poetic exposition by Sun Chuo, the archaic formulaic phrases and the litany of deities and fantastic places are gone, yet the spirit journey upward into light remains.

Sun Chuo (314–371), Wandering to the Tian-tai Mountains

The Tian-tai Mountains may well be the most divine and outstanding of the great mountains. What the isles Fang-zhang and Peng-lai are to those who fare upon the sea,[4] the Si-ming Cluster and Tian-tai are to those who move upon dry land. And all are places where the arcane sages wandered and were transformed, lair and lodging for holy beings and the Undying.

Their configurations that loom to high limits, their fine and fortunate loveliness, bear all the costly bounty of mountains and seas, include all the most breathtaking beauties of mortal men and gods.

The cause for such mountains not being ranked among the Five Great Peaks and for omission of their mention in surviving classics must surely be that they are situated in such a dark recess of the world, and that the road thither is so long and so hard to find. Some cast their reflections inverted into the dark deeps; others ensconce their peaks among a thousand other crests.

One begins by passing along goblin paths, until at last one strides through a realm without men. Not many men alive in an age can scale them; and no prince has a way to perform sacrifices there. Thus notice of them is absent in common texts, and their name is remarked only in accounts of things rare. Even so, should we think it for nothing that there is such an abundance of pictures and illustrations of them?

Unless a man gives up the world and practices the right Way, quitting common grains and feeding on asphodel, he cannot lift off in lightness and lodge there. Unless a man gives himself over to things remote and delves into dark mysteries, unless he is someone utterly sincere and in contact with the gods, he can never envision that remote place and hold it fast.

It was for this reason that I sent my spirit rushing and worked my thoughts, sang by day and stayed waking by night. And in the interval of a nod, it was as if I had gone up the mountain more than once. Now I will

---

[4] Fang-zhang and Peng-lai were two of the three isles of the Undying, said to be located in the Eastern Ocean.

untie these bands of an officer's cap to lodge forever on these crests. I cannot resist the full force of such visions and spontaneous chanting, so let me here make a show of fine phrases to disperse these concerns.

> Utter Void, hollow magnitudes,   lacking all limit,
> there worked elusive presence: What Is Naturally So.
> It liquefied and formed the streams and channels;
> it hardened and formed the mountains and knolls.
>
> Ah, crests of Tian-tai   are rare things upraised,
> in truth braced and bolstered   by light of the gods.
> It shadows the Herder star   with glowing peaks,
> lodged in Yue the Holy   for well-set foundation.
> Its roots knit more widely   than Mounts Hua or Dai,
> it points upward higher   than Many Doubts Range.
> It fulfills Tang's Canon's phrase: "Peer of the Heavens";
> it equals Zhou's Poem's words: "looming to limits."
>
> Remote are these tracts, far flung,
> secret recesses well sequestered.
> Stuck within senses, shortsighted wisdom goes not thither;
> since paths run out, those who would go never can know it.
> I scorn such summer bugs,   who doubt there is ice,
> I hold light wings straight,   I long to mount upward.
> No true pattern is hidden   or fails to be shown:
> two wonders divulged   show me the signs:
> there is Redwall, russet-cloud rising,   set as my marker;[5]
> there is the Cascade, stream in flight,   defining the way.
>
> Spying these witnesses of holy things,   I then fared ahead,
> and all of a sudden   I was off on my way.
> I sought men with feathers   on cinnabar hills,
> I searched the never dying   in the hallowed yards.
> If only I might climb   to Tian-tai's crest,
> what craving then would be left   for Tiered Walls Mountain.[6]
> Unbound from common yearnings   of earthly tracts,
> I set free noble passions   for passing beyond.
> I donned a wool tunic,   somber and dark,
> and brandished staff of metal,   clinking along.
> I pushed through thickets,   dense and concealing,
> I scaled sheer escarpments   looming above me.
> I waded the You Creek,   went straight on ahead,
> left five borders behind me   and fared swiftly forward.

---

[5]One of Tian-tai's peaks.
[6]Tiered Walls was the highest peak of the fabled Kun-lun Range in the Far West.

I strode over arch   of a Sky-Hung Walkway,[7]
looked down ten thousand yards   lost in its blackness;
I trod upon mosses   of slippery rock,
clung to the Azure Screen   that stands like a wall.
I clutched the long vines   from low-bending boughs
grasped stems hung in air   from the wild grape vines.
Though this one time I risk   the "rim of the hall,"[8]
I will be here forever   in life everlasting.
The heart's faith must match   the Mystery Hidden,
then one paces steep perils   and paths grow more smooth.

I succeeded surmounting   its nine sharp bends,
and the trail wound away,   long and on through.
I let eyes and ears roam   in those luminous magnitudes,
I let slow steps saunter   wherever they would.
I smoothed back frail grasses,   lush and so green,
took shade by tall pines   spread grandly above.
I viewed *luan* birds soaring,   bending their wings,
heard phoenixes sing   with melodious tones.
I crossed Holy Creek   and washed myself there,
drew far from the fancies   that troubled my heart.
The last dust was purged   in those swirling currents,[9]
I dispelled the Five Coverings   that move with us blinding.[1]
I pursued the lost tracks   of Fu Xi and Shen Nong,[2]
walked in the obscure footprints   of Lao-zi and Lao-lai-zi.[3]

I scaled heights and descended, spending two nights,
and at last reached the great citadel of the Undying.
Paired towers, thrust in clouds,   lined the road,
heaven-touching jasper terraces   hung there suspended.
Vermilion turrets appeared in fragments   through the forests,
halls of jade, revealed and blocked   in hills' lofty folds.
Involute bands of scarlet cloud   hovered in lattices,
shimmering beams of the brilliant sun   passed in the grillwork.
Eight cassias rise somber and dense,   last through the frost,
five-budded asphodels, bursting with spore,   spread open with dawn.
Gentle breeze hoarded scent   in sunlit forests,

---

[7]This is the famous stone bridge of Mount Tian-tai.
[8]A figure for peril.
[9]Although the dust here might be easily taken as merely worldly contamination, the Li Shan commentary identifies it as the "six forms of dust" that bring impurity to the soul: the five senses as well as the activities of mind.
[1]The "Five Coverings" are five vices—lust, wrath, sloth, levity, and uncertainty—that hinder Buddhist spiritual progress.
[2]Two sages of remote antiquity.
[3]Two of the early sages of Daoism.

sweet fountains spurted trickles   in shadowy channels.
The boughless Jian Tree lost its shadow   a thousand yards high,[4]
the tree of chalcedony twinkled and sparkled   dangling pearls.
Qiao the Prince harnessed his crane   and dashed to the heavens,[5]
A Buddhist arhat, with flying staff,   strutted through void.
Spirit-changes were racing,   with lightning swiftness,
all at once leaving Presence   and entering Absence.

Then when I finished my gaze all around,
my body grew tranquil, my heart was serene.
Whatever hurts horses had been left behind,[6]
all worldly problems here were forsaken.
Always the blade fell into empty spaces,
the ox in my eyes was never entire.[7]
I focused my thoughts on the hidden cliffs,
sang out clearly beside the long stream.
Now Xi-he brought the sun just overhead,
and drifting vapors lifted on high.
Dharma drums boomed,   their echoes resounded,
crowds of scents wafted,   their smoke ascending.
Then I encountered august Heaven,
and next there gathered the Undying Hosts.
Oils of purple-black jade were ladled out,
I imbibed the fountains of the Flower Pool.
Beyond-Image doctrines dissolved my ignorance,[8]
the texts on Non-Birth opened my heart.[9]
I realize that abandoning Presence   is not yet complete,
grasp that the journey to Absence   has its gaps.
I efface the emptiness of appearances,   merge all traces,
suddenly reach Presence   and grasp the mystery.
I expound how these two names   have a common source,
melt the Three Flags   in the unity of Absence.[1]
Indulging in the joys of talk   the whole day through
equals perfect silence   of not speaking.
I blur the thousands of images   by dark observation,
my body, insensate, identical with   What Is Naturally So.

---

[4]A mythical tree at the Earth's center on which the high gods rise and descend.
[5]Qiao the Prince was an adept who became one of the Undying.
[6]From a parable in the *Zhuang-zi* in which a boy herding horses was asked by the Yellow Emperor about ruling the world; he responded that one need only get rid of what hurts the horses.
[7]Echoing the parable of Butcher Ding in the *Zhuang-zi*. Butcher Ding never needed to sharpen his knife because his skill was such that the blade moved only through the "empty spaces."
[8]Neo-Daoist doctrine.
[9]The Buddhist principle of transcending the cycles of rebirth.
[1]The "Three Flags" was Buddhist jargon for three aspects of spiritual experience: appearance, emptiness, and contemplation. Their dissolution into Neo-Daoist Absence suggests not so much the victory of Neo-Daoism as the syncretism that pervades the entire poetic exposition.

The Encounter with the Goddess

Also out of the "Lyrics of Chu" grew poetic expositions on encounters with the goddess. The two earliest of these, "The Poetic Exposition on Gao-tang" and "The Goddess," are attributed to Song Yu, who was supposed to have been a follower of Qu Yuan (he appears elsewhere as an eloquent orator in the Northern manner). These two poetic expositions are certainly not by Song Yu; rather, they seem to be Han works attributed to Song Yu because he is the speaker in the frame. Song Yu was a very popular figure in the frame stories in which poetic expositions were set.

The prose frame of "The Poetic Exposition on Gao-tang" gives the most famous version of the encounter with the goddess, who comes as an apparition to the King of Chu and spends the night with him. On leaving, she claims to be the "clouds and rain," which gradually became a poetic term for sexual intercourse. The main body of the poetic exposition, a description of Gao-tang, is omitted below.

Song Yu (attributed), The Poetic Exposition on Gao-tang (opening)

Once upon a time King Xiang of Chu visited the high terrace at Yun-meng with Song Yu, when he gazed off toward the lodge of Gao-tang. Above it was a mass of cloudy vapors, first rising up towering, then suddenly changing its aspect, so that in a moment there were endless transformations.

And the king asked Song Yu, "What vapor is that?" Whereupon Song Yu replied, "That is what they call 'the clouds of dawn.' " And again the king: "What is meant by 'the clouds of dawn'?"

Song Yu: "Once upon a time one of the kings before you visited Gao-tang. He grew weary and lay down to rest during the daytime. He dreamed then of a woman, who said to him, 'I am the Maiden of Wu Mountain and am a sojourner here at Gao-tang. When I heard that my lord was visiting Gao-tang, I wanted to share a bed with you.' Then the king enjoyed her. And when she left, she said on parting, 'I am found on Wu Mountain's sun-lit slope, on the steeps of the high hill. In the early morning I am the clouds of dawn; in the evening I am the passing rain. So it is every morning and every evening beneath the Terrace of Light.' He watched for her in the early morning, and it was as she had said. And he then built her a temple and named it 'Clouds of Dawn.' "

The king then said, "When these clouds of dawn first come out, what do they look like?" And Song Yu replied:

> When they first come out,
>   they billow out like the perpendicular pine,
> when they come somewhat closer,
>   they glow like a comely maiden,
> who lifts her sleeves to screen away sun
>   and gazes off toward the one she loves.

Then suddenly their aspect changes,
    they are headlong as a four-horse team,
    with feathered pennons raised.
Nipping like the wind,
    chill like the rain,
    then the wind stops, the rain clears,
    and the clouds are nowhere to be found.
   . . .

Although the king's encounter with the goddess was fleeting and only in dream, it was at least consummated. "The Goddess" below represents a variation on the more common conclusion in which something blocks consummation.

The Goddess

King Xiang of Chu and Song Yu were roaming along the shores of Yun-meng Marsh, and the king ordered Song Yu to compose a poetic exposition about what had happened at Gao-tang. That night, while Song Yu was asleep, he dreamed that he himself met the goddess, whose appearance was very lovely. Song Yu marveled at her, and the next day he told the king, who then asked, "What was your dream like?" Song Yu answered:

The time was past twilight,
my spirit went into trance
and it seemed there was some cause for delight.
All excited I was and astir,
but I did not yet know what it meant.
Then colors appeared as a blur in my eyes,
at once I seemed to make something out.
I saw a single woman there,
a vision wondrous and rare.
As I slept she was in my dream,
but on waking I saw her not.
Dazed I was, I felt no joy,
I was wretched, thwarted in will.
Then I calmed my heart and steadied my breath,
and saw once again what I had dreamed.

The king said, "What did she look like?" And Song Yu replied:

She was in full bloom, she was beautiful,
all things good were there within her.
Splendid she was and lovely,
impossible to fathom it all.
She was such as never had been in the past,
and never yet seen in this present age.
Her gestures were jewels, her postures gems,
that far surpass all adequate praise.

When she first was coming—
there was a glow, like the sun just appearing
    and shining on roofs and beams.
And when she had drawn somewhat closer—
she glistened, like the bright moon
    unfurling its rays.
Then in an instant's interval
her fair, overwhelming visage appeared,
so glorious, like flowers in all their splendor,
so gentle, like jade's polished sheen.
From her sped all a rainbow's colors together,
I cannot completely describe them.
And if you stared at her too closely,
the eyes would be dazzled and blinded.
Such was her raiment's splendor:
meshes and lace and fabrics of every hue,
    and opulence of patterns,
superb garments with finely worked colors,
    shining in all directions.
She donned an embroidered gown,
wore vest and skirt,
whose thick cloth was not too short,
whose fine cloth was not too long.
With a stately grace she paced,
and the great hall was all aglow.
She suddenly changed her bearing,
stunning like the dragon that soars on cloud.
Sumptuous were the garments she wore,
her filmy attire was becoming.
Her hair was washed in orchid lotions,
she gave off the scent of pollia.
Pleasant and gentle of temper,
fitting to serve by one's side.
Meek and mild, her manner;
amiable in the heart.

The king said, "She was certainly magnificent. Why don't you compose a poetic exposition for me on the topic?" And Song Yu said:

Such beguiling beauty   has the Goddess:
she embodies rich adornments   of Darkness and Light.
Clothed in filagree finery   to be adored,
she resembles the kingfisher   wide-spreading its wings.
A semblance without peer,
a beauty without bound.
Mao Qiang would hide behind her sleeves,
unequal to such standards;

Xi Shi would cover her face,
by comparison lacking allure.
When close to her, so bewitching
that afar one is gazing ever.
The form of her frame is full of wonder,
she is fit to be mate for a lord.
When I stared at her, she filled my eyes—
who is there to surpass her?
She gave my heart singular pleasure
and my joy in her knew no measure.
Encounters are seldom, her grace rarely given—
I cannot recount it all.
No other man has beheld her,
but my king may survey her appearance.

Her appearance was so imposing,
how can I speak it thoroughly?
Her face plump and full,   firm it was and fair,
alabaster features   enfolding a kindly glow.
Her eye-pupils glinting,   sharp and radiant,
beaming and so beautiful,   fair to look upon.
The brows' delicate arching   were moths ascending,
red lips glistening   like cinnabar.
Her pale-fleshed torso   was thick and firm,
her will was easy and generous,   her body was relaxed.
Voluptuous charms achieved   in stillness and seclusion,
now she moved in undulations   within the human world.
A high hall was fitting   to give room to her intent,
there she let herself go winging,   open she was and free.
She stirred a fog of gauze   in her stately paces,
the sound as she brushed the pavements   was *swish, swish*.

She looked toward my curtains,   there let gaze linger,
like rolling of ripples   rising to waves.
She lifted long sleeves,   adjusted gown's folds,
and stood there wavering,   not at her ease.
Then rapt and still,   familiar and gentle,
her mind's state serene,   untroubled utterly.
Sometimes free and easy,   then she barely moved—
no full fathoming   of her intent.
Her mood seemed intimate,   but then was remote;
it seemed she was coming,   but then she turned round.
She lifted my bedcurtain,   entreated to serve me,
she wished to show fullness   of heart's steadfast love.
What she felt was bright and pure,   clear and unsullied,
but then in the end   she found fault with me.
I delivered fine phrases,   I tried to respond,

they had a sweet fragrance   as of orchids.
Our spirits intertwined,   passed back and forth,
our hearts were in bliss   with pleasure and joy.
My soul reached through to her,   but no tie was formed,
the psyche left lonely,   with no ground to rest.
The assent that was in her   was fated not to be;
a moan then rose from me,   I sighed out in sorrow.
Faintly angered she colored,   then mastered herself,
for never might any   trespass upon her.

Then
her pendants and ornaments swaying,
jade phoenixes ringing,
she straightened her clothes
and composed her face.
She looked round to her tutor,
to duenna gave orders;
and our passion unconsummated,
she took leave to go.
She drew body away,
I could not approach her.
Then as if withdrawing, but not yet gone,
midway it seemed that she turned her head,
and barely glancing from eye's corner,
a flash of spirit was conveyed;
and the will's bent broke through—
I cannot manage the full recollection.
Before our loves were sundered,
my heart and soul collapsed in dread.
There was no chance to say the proper goodbyes,
and my words were left incomplete.
I wished her to grant me but a moment,
but the Goddess pleaded haste.
The heart twisted, the spirit knew pain,
I fell and had no support.
Then suddenly all turned black,
and I knew not where I was.
What I feel in the secrecy of the heart—
to whom could I speak it?
I shed tears in my wretchedness
and kept seeking her until the dawn.

Cao Zhi's "The Goddess of the Luo" is the most famous of a number of poetic expositions on encounters with the goddess written early in the third century. The particular goddess is Fu-fei, rather than the goddess of Wu Mountain.

Cao Zhi (192–232), The Goddess of the Luo

In the third year of the Huang-chu Reign, A.D. 222, I had gone to the capital to attend court, and on my return I forded the Luo River. There is an ancient legend that the goddess of this river is named Fu-fei. Touched by Song Yu's response to what occurred between the King of Chu and the goddess, I myself composed the following poetic exposition.

> I was on my return from the capital
> back to my eastern domain,
> Yi Tower Peak lay behind me
> as I passed over Huan-yuan Hill,
> then made my way through Tong Valley,
> and crossed up over Mount Jing.
> The sun was bending down to the west,
> my carriage slowed, the horses balked.
> I unhitched my team by spikenard flats
> and set them to graze on asphodel fields.
> I rambled at ease in the Grove of Sunshine,
> and my gaze swept over the River Luo.

At that moment,

> my soul shuddered, my spirit was startled,
> in an instant all thoughts were dispersed:
> looking down I could make out nothing,
> but I raised my head and beheld a marvel.
> I spied a lovely woman there
> at the side of the steep slope.

I then seized my driver and asked him: "Did you catch sight of her? Who was she, to be so beguiling?" And my driver answered me: "They say that the goddess of the Luo goes by the name of Fu-fei. It must have been her that you saw. I would like to hear what she looked like." Whereupon I told him:

Her form:

> swept along lightly like startled swan,
> was sinuous as the swimming dragon,
> shimmering like sheen on fall's chrysanthemums,
> splendid like pines that swell in the spring.
> She was a blur   as when pale clouds form a film on the moon,
> she floated through air   as when winds send snow swirling.

When I gazed on her from afar,

> she shone like the sun through morning clouds mounting;

when nearer I viewed her,

she glowed like a lotus coming out of clear waves.

She achieved the mean between slender and stout,
between tall and short she met the right measure.
Her shoulders seemed hewn to perfection,
her waist was tight as if bound with white silk.
When she stretched her neck, the throat was fair,
and her radiant flesh was displayed,
unassisted by aromatic lotions
and with no powder lending it aid.
Her hair coiled high in lofty clouds,
and long brows formed delicate arches.
Scarlet lips on the outside luminous,
with shining teeth gleaming within.
Her bright eyes cast wondrous glances,
dimples stood close by her cheekbones.
A rare bearing, alluring, aloof,
her manner was poised, her body calm.
With tender feeling and lovely expression,
her speech was enthralling.

Her singular garb was unique in these times,
her figure well fitted what we find pictured.
She wore a gown of shimmering gauze,
in her ears were gems cut cunningly;
her head was adorned with feathers and jade,
and strung pearls made her body sparkle.
She wore patterned slippers for roaming far,
she trailed light sleeves of misty mesh.
Through a filmy aromatic haze of orchids
she paced, then paused on the fold of the hill.

All at once she broke loose, moving wild and free,
she skipped and cavorted here and there,
she leaned on bright streamers to her left,
to her right she was shadowed by cassia flags.
She bared bright wrists on those sacred shores,
and from seething shallows picked purple asphodel.

Thus my heart took delight in unblemished beauty;
the mind, swept away, could feel no cheer.
Lacking go-between to let our loves meet,
I trusted soft glance-waves to carry my words.
I wished my true feelings would be conveyed,
I untied my jade pendants to win her.
She possessed such beauty, she was truly fair,
familiar with custom, she knew the *Poems*:

she raised jasper bangles to answer me,
and made signs to the deeps where we should meet.
For her I felt a single-minded passion,
but feared that this spright might beguile me.
Troth to Jiao-fu broken touched on my heart,[2]
I paused, deeply troubled, and doubted.
I composed my face and calmed my will,
I pled custom's restraints and mastered myself.

Then the Luo Spirit too was much touched;
she lingered long in her hesitation.
The goddess' nimbus came and went,
sometimes in shadow, sometimes bright.
Like a crane her light body stood poised and tall,
as if ready for flight, not yet taking wing.
She walked in billowing scents of pepper tree paths,
stepped through swirling odors of spikenard clumps.
Then came a long moan of eternal desire,
a voice that was sharp, and pained, and lingering on.

The hosts of spirits massed in their multitudes,
calling and whistling each to companions.
Some went frisking in the clear currents,
and some soared off by the goddess' isles,
some went down to pick the bright pearls,
some went gathering kingfisher plumes
With the Xiang River Maidens they headed south,
or held hands with those girls who roam the Han's shores.

She sighed that the Pao-gua Star lacked a mate,
she sang how the Herder lived alone.
Her light blouse rose, it fluttered in breeze,
her long sleeves hid her, standing there long.
Her body, more fleet than ducks in their flight,
flitted past in a puff, like the goddess she was.
Her delicate footsteps swept over the waves,
and dust rose from her stockings of gauze.
To her motions there was no set pattern:
as if apprehensive, then as if at her ease.
And her movements were hard to predict:
she would seem to go off, then seem to turn back.
When she turned her gaze sidelong, the spirit flowed,
and light soaked those features so like jade.
She held back her words, she would not speak,
but her breath was like the aroma of orchids.

---

[2]Zheng Jiao-fu encountered two nymphs by the river Han, who gave him their pendants as tokens of their troth, then vanished along with their pendants, leaving Jiao-fu in despair.

There was in her glorious face such gentleness
that it made me forget all about eating.

Then Ping-yi gathered back his winds,
the Queen of the Waters stilled the waves.
Ping-I made the drums sound out,
while Nü Wa sang her clear, sharp song.
Goldfish vaulted, warned of carriages coming,
phoenix bells chimed as they all left together.
With six dragons matched, their heads held even,
cloud-coaches went off, swaying along.
Great whales surged up on each side of the wheels,
and the waterfowl soared around in escort.

They went off beyond by the northern shoals,
then passed down by the hills to the south.
It was there that she bent her pale neck round
and sent back flashing glances.
Her ruby lips stirred, and slowly she spoke,
explaining the laws for mating with gods,
and regretting how men and gods stood apart,
grieved that no match could be made in my prime.
Then she lifted gauze sleeves and wiped away tears
that flowed in streams on the folds of her gown.
"It is sad that our union is now lost forever,
once gone, we must dwell in realms set apart.
I have no way to show all the love in my heart,
but I give you bright earrings from southern lands.
Though I will dwell concealed in the shadow world,
my heart will forever be yours, my prince."
At once I could no longer grasp where she was;
I grieved that the goddess had vanished, her light hidden.

And I went back down the heights of the hill;
my feet left that place, but my spirit stayed.
My love remained with the vision of her form,
I looked back and gazed, my heart filled with pain.
I wished that the Holy One take form again;
I guided my skiff up against the current,
I sailed the long river, forgot to turn back,
my thoughts keeping on with growing yearning.

That night I was restless, I could not sleep,
the heavy frosts soaked me, and then dawn broke.
I ordered my driver to hitch up the carriage,
I set off to go back on that eastward road.
Then I pull up the reins and set by my whip,
I hung there in sorrow, I could not go on.

Other Voices in the Tradition

A popular story grew up around Cao Zhi's "The Goddess of the Luo," interpreting the piece as a figurative description of Cao Zhi's relation to a woman he loved, a woman who was married to his brother Cao Pi and became Empress Zhen. After her death, Cao Zhi was supposed to have encountered her spirit by the Luo. The story is, unfortunately, apocryphal. But in the Tang collection of classical stories entitled "Accounts of Marvels" *(Chuan-qi),* we have an authentication of the legend by none other than the spirit of Empress Zhen herself.

Pei Xing (825–880), "Accounts of Marvels" *(Chuan-qi):* Xiao Kuang (opening section)

During the Tai-he Reign (827–835), Xiao Kuang, a private citizen, was traveling east from Luo-yang and had reached Xiao-yi Lodge, where he rested for the night in the Double Beauty Pavilion. The moon was bright and the breeze was cool, when Xiao Kuang, who was a skilled harpist, took out his harp and was playing it. At around midnight the melody grew intensely plaintive; he suddenly heard someone heaving a great sigh over the waters of the Luo. The person gradually drew closer, and it turned out to be a beautiful woman. Xiao Kuang then put down his harp and bowed to her, asking, "Who might you be?" And she answered, "I am the goddess of the banks of the Luo. Don't you recall that Cao Zhi, the Prince of Chen, wrote a poetic exposition about me long ago?" Xiao Kuang replied, "I do indeed." Then Kuang went on to ask, "I have heard from some that the goddess of the Luo was in fact the Empress Zhen, who had passed away, and that Cao Zhi encountered her soul on the shores of the Luo. As a consequence he wrote 'Stirred by Lady Zhen.' Later he realized the impropriety of the matter and changed it to 'The Goddess of the Luo,' figuring his real intentions in the guise of Fu-fei. Is that what happened?"

She replied, "I am that very Empress Zhen. Because I was so taken by Cao Zhi's talent and manner, Cao Pi, the Emperor Wen, was enraged; I was locked away and died. Afterward my soul met the prince, Cao Zhi, by the River Luo and gave an account of the wrongs I had endured. He was touched and wrote about it. But he realized that the matter was indecorous and changed the title. What you said was not at all inaccurate."

All at once a serving girl appeared carrying a mat and prepared wine and hors d'oeuvres. Then the goddess said to Xiao Kuang, "When I recently married Mr. Yuan, I found I had a natural fondness for harp playing. Whenever someone played things like 'Sad Winds' or 'Streams Flowing in the Three Gorges,' I would always stay on through the whole evening. I happened to hear the clarity and grace of your harp playing and would like to listen to more." Xiao Kuang then played the toccata "The Parted Crane" and "Sad Winds." The Goddess heaved a long sigh. "You are truly the equal of Cai Yong." And she went on to ask Xiao Kuang about "The Goddess of the Luo." Xiao Kuang replied, "It had such genuine smoothness and clarity of description that the Liang prince Zhao-ming anthologized it with the most choice literary works." Then the goddess gave a faint smile. "Don't you think he went somewhat wide of the mark when he described my movements as 'swept along lightly like startled swan, sinuous as the swimming dragon'?"

After Fu-fei offers her critique of Cao Zhi's poetic license, the tale continues as Xiao Kuang takes the opportunity to ask the goddess all manner of questions regarding dragon lore and eventually consummates the sexual encounter that had eluded Cao Zhi six centuries previously.

The motifs and concerns of the "Lyrics of Chu" found their way into every aspect of Chinese literature. Even the ancient world of gods and goddesses, relegated largely to folk religion, did not disappear entirely from elite literature. The Tang poet Wang Wei, serving in a provincial post in the East (a post he could well have considered "exile" like that of Qu Yuan), wrote the following two poems for a shamanistic service on Fish Mountain.

Wang Wei (ca. 699–761), Songs for the Goddess' Shrine on Fish Mountain

Song Welcoming the Goddess

Beat the drums booming:
at the foot of Fish Mountain
blow the panpipes
and gaze to far shores.
Shaman girls enter
dancing in frenzy.
Onyx mats spread,
clear liquors infused.
A chill in the wind,   rain by night,
will the goddess come,   will she not?—
it makes my heart   suffer pang upon pang.

Song Sending the Goddess on Her Way

In a mass they come forward bowing,   before the hall,
eyes gaze with yearning   toward the alabaster mat.
She came but did not speak,   her will was not made known,
she was the twilight rain,   she made bare hills forlorn.
In the shrill pipes there is sadness,
and longing in swiftly strummed strings,
the holy one's carriage   is ready to turn.
At once the clouds draw back,   the rain ceases,
and the hills so green,   the waters splashing on.

In Wang Wei's poems, a trace of the ancient awe in face of divinity remains. By the ninth century, however, popular religion had been transformed into something like a "Gothic" taste for ruined temples, stormy nights, and dragons with gleaming eyes. Although his own interest in divinity is far more complex, the poet Li He was an important figure in creating this taste for the "poetic" shamanka (a woman shaman).

Li He (790–816), String Music for the Gods

The shaman woman pours wine,
    clouds fill the skies;
from jade brazier's burning coals
    scented smoke pulses.

Gods of the seas and hill wraiths
    come to their places to feast,

the paper money crackling
    sounds in the swirling gusts.

Passionwood mandolin inlaid
    with golden dancing phoenix;
she knits her brows and mutters,
    with each mutter, sweeps the strings.

She calls to stars and summons wraiths
    to taste from cup and plate,
when mountain goblins are feeding,
    men shudder and feel the cold.

Then over Zhong-nan the sun draws low
    into a level trough,
and the gods are hanging forever between
    being here and not.

With the god's rage or the god's delight
    the medium's face shifts,
then she sends the gods, riding in thousands,
    back to the green hills.

Wen Ting-yun (d. 866), Written on the Temple of Mount Xiao

An ancient path darkened by shadows of trees,
weed-grown shrine east of the hill's shadow.

Pines and firs, a whole courtyard of rain,
awnings and streamers, winds fill the hall.

Evening sands soaked from worshippers' libations,
a horse whinnies, the shrine empty in spring.

Thunder and lightning cease deep in night,
and the dragon goes into the ancient tarn.

Guan-xiu (832–912), Shrine by the River

The pines are dark and gloomy,
    the turbulent river churns,
an ancient shrine by the river,
    empty, its gates shut tight.
I am certain the holy being grew drunk
    on the village festival wine,
and the white tortoise gnawed apart
    the roots of the calamus.
Tattered blossoms cold and red,
    still drip with last night's rain;
the shell of the earthen dragon is soaked,
    demon eyes glint scarlet.
Sooner or later a sign from Heaven
    will come from the sapphire sky:

last night in the village up ahead
    the peals of thunder passed.

Later in the tradition, the goddess often disappears into the landscape and particularly into her own Wu (Shamanka) Mountain, by the Yangzi River gorges. The young Su Shi (Su Dongpo), traveling down the Yangzi for the first time from his native Sichuan, passed the place as a sightseer in the middle of the eleventh century. By now the goddess no longer appears. Divinity survives only as an eerie landscape, located on the other side of the river, reported by someone else who visited the spot many years ago.

Su Shi (1037–1101), Wu Mountain

Where the Ju-tang's winding course is done,
there the Wu Gorges rise looming.

Peak linked to peak, quite astonishing
how stone-hues change to blue-gray.

Heaven's workman used godly craft
to gradually make something grand and rare.

Its dips and sharp rises lead me in deeper,
and the mind cannot grasp this intricate frame.

When viewed sidelong passing, no pause to glance,
so I went on foot to those hidden clefts.

The gray slopes suddenly hemmed me in,
a sheer cliff wall where I shivered in awe.

Above I viewed its eight or nine crests,
in spry splendor mounting past flooding vapors.

Sky's vault stood high in a deluge of light,
the river seethed surging and leaping below.

Alone above others, standing fast, not yielding,
drawn up straight, an undaunted audacity.

Climbing along, I saw the goddess's lodge,
I took a place on the rock to sit and rest.

Across river's waves were craggy heights,
I asked the temple guide about each one.

In the distance I saw the Goddess Rock,
of such grace and charm, aptly named indeed.

Head lowered, she shows skewed coils of hair,
and sports a long shift of trailing red cloud.

A man's heart changes with what it meets,
from afar I was aware of deep meaning here.

An old rustic laughed out at my side:
"When young I made it there often.

"I would go up as the gibbons went
or sometimes try the ascent with ropes.

"Stone dolmens rest on that lonely peak,
jutting up, not of the usual kind.

"Men these days delight in marvels of gods,
and tell stories to amaze young children.

"Chu's poems too are groundless traditions—
how can there be gods or the Undying?"

I then asked of bamboo that swept her altar,
and he said, "It's still there today.

"Azure leaves hang down in a tangle,
the swaying dance of green phoenix tails.

"When a breeze comes they wave up and down,
as if driven on by some godlike thing.

"On the highest crest are three slabs of stone,
with the sworls and curves of old characters.

"This old man could, of course, not read them,
I saw them by chance, I can't recall.

"I went on in my search to the peak's other side
to gather and chop yellow poplars.

"Yellow poplars grow upon the rocks,
gaunt and hard, with patterns like lace.

"My greedy heart went without looking back,
through mountain gorges with thousand-yard drops.

"High on the hill wolves and tigers were gone,
deep in I went, untroubled and without dread.

"A dim murkiness, hidden plants and trees,
clouds moist and glossy, billowed around.

"Huge springs came from fissures within the rock,
they were slick and sweet like liquid marrow.

"All that morning through I bathed and rinsed,
a sharp chill cleared both skin and mind.

"I washed my clothes, hung them from branch tips,
found a beak of stone to sharpen my ax.

"I stayed still the sun grew late in the clouds,
and my thoughts turned with longing for the city.

"It's been ten years now since I went there,
frail and old, the strength of muscles spent.

"Of the trees I cut down at that time
the shoots from their stumps are already like arms."

I was dismayed by this old man's tale
and sighed about it the whole day through.

The gods and Undying do exist,
but it's hard to forget the promptings of gain.

Why did you love your poverty so?—
cast it away like shedding a slipper.

Too bad—for had you never returned,
forgoing food, you would surely never have died.

先秦西漢

Calling Back the Soul

The "Lyrics of Chu" have two formal soul-callings, "Calling Back the Soul" *(Zhao hun)* and "The Great Calling" *(Da-zhao)*. Both are literary versions of a religious ritual in which the shaman calls back the soul of someone dead, dying, or otherwise not in full possession of the senses (comatose, soul-wandering). The shaman first describes the terrors that lie in wait for the soul in all directions, then the pleasures that the soul can enjoy if only it comes back to the palace or great house at the center. Of the two soul-callings, "Calling Back the Soul" seems closer to the religious ceremony, making reference to particular aspects of the shamanistic rite.

As literary traditions develop, we often find a process of division into parts and elaboration of the separate parts. In the soul-calling, the major division is between the description of terrors, intended to frighten the soul into returning, and the description of delights, intended to lure the soul back. "Calling Back the Recluse" *(Zhao yin-shi)* (p. 211), a Han work included in the "Lyrics of Chu," is a transformation of the segment of soul-calling describing terrors, with the violent landscape taking the place of the demon-inhabited cosmos of "Calling Back the Soul."[1]

"Calling Back the Soul" *(Zhao hun)*

[The opening is apparently the fragment of a frame story.]

The god then gave word to Yang the Shaman, saying, "There is a man down below. I want to help him. His several souls are dispersing. Go cast the lots for him."

Yang the Shaman answered, " . . . Holder of Dreams . . . high god . . . hard to follow the traces. But if I must cast the lots, I fear that it is too late, for he is decaying and it will no longer be of any use."

Then Yang the Shaman went down and called:

---

[1]The description of delights has a far richer history. "Seven Stimuli," a work by the Western Han writer Mei Sheng, is a good example of how, very early, the ritual function of soul-calling intersected with the Northern orator's sense of mission in moral persuasion. Here an orator tries to rouse a sick and dissipated prince from his malaise by describing a series of delights. Calling the soul back to physical health merges with recalling the prince to moral and spiritual health, and thus bringing good government to the polity. The verbal display of sensual delights is set in contrast to the display of moral pleasures. This became part of the justification of the poetic exposition *(fu)*, but it was a problematic justification.

Soul! Turn back!
You have left your wonted frame—
why go to the four directions?
You forsake your places of delight
and will come upon cursed things.

Soul! Turn back!
No lodging for you in the east:
Giants a thousand cubits tall
seek only souls to eat.
Ten suns emerge in sequence,
melting metals, fusing stone.
All there find this usual,
but souls that go there soon dissolve.
Turn back! Turn back!
No lodging for you there.

Soul! Turn back!
No place to rest in the south.
Tattooed brows and blackened fangs
use meat of men in offerings,
and season their stew with the bones.
Cobras form jungle-tangles,
and giant foxes range a thousand miles.

Nine-headed stag-pythons
pass back and forth in a flash,
and swallow men to feed their minds.
Soul! Turn back!
No leisurely lingering there.

Soul! Turn back!
There is harm for you in the west,
where the sand flows for a thousand miles,
You whirl into the Thunder Pit,
you are ground to powder and may not rest.

If luck lets you escape,
beyond are boundless barrens.
With red ants like elephants
and black wasps like gourds.

Not one of the five grains grows,
clumps of straw-grass is the food.
The soil there grills a man,
he seeks water with none to be found.
He roams aimlessly with no shelter
in vast spaces that have no limit.

Soul! Turn back!
I fear you will bring yourself ruin.

Soul! Turn back!
No place to rest in the north.
Piling floes of ice loom high,
and the snows fly a thousand leagues.
Soul! Turn back!
You cannot stay there long.

Soul! Turn back!
Do not climb to the heavens.
By its nine-fold gates, leopards and tigers
rend men from Earth below.
Each one has nine heads
and tears up nine thousand trees.
And wolves turn their eyes upon you,
prowling around you in packs.
They string men up for sport,
then cast them into the deepest pit.
And only when the god ordains
can he close eyes in darkness at last.
Soul! Turn back!
Should you go, I fear your peril.

Soul! Turn back!
Go not down to the Unseen City.
The Ground-Earl has nine tails,
and his horns are razor-sharp.
His back is humped, his talons bloody,
he goes bounding after men.
Three are his eyes, a tiger's head,
and his body like a bull.
All of these find men savory,
Turn back! Turn back!
I fear you bring upon yourself doom.

Soul! Turn back!
Enter in through these soul-gates.
The Spell Master summons you,
goes before you walking backwards.

A basket from Qin, thread from Qi
laced over with Zheng's satins.
All summoning implements are on hand;
and now I keen and wail:
Soul! Turn back!
Come home where you used to dwell.

In Heaven, Earth, and the four directions
many are the evils and perils.
I will set forth semblances of your chambers,
secure, peaceful, and calm.
A high hall, closets deepset within,
rimmed with high-tiered balconies.
Banked terraces dense with belvederes
look down from the high hill.
Grillwork entries, interlaced vermilion,
with continuous angular friezes carved.
For winter here are deepset salons,
in summer the chambers are chill.
Gullies with streams run straight and bend back,
their currents babbling.
Sunlit breezes bend sweet clover
and send waves through the clumps of orchid.
Through the great hall into the back rooms
go vermilion awnings and mats.

Rooms faced with stone, kingfisher wings
hung from hooks of carnelian.
Quilts of kingfisher feathers and pearls,
each glowing with equal light.
Wall covers made of rush and crêpe,
gauze canopies extended.
Red and motley plaits, silks patterned and plain,
knotted to agate half-rings.

To be seen within the chambers
are many cherished marvels.
Bright candles, tallow scented with orchid,
of sparkling faces a full array.
In two rows of eight they wait at your bed,
taking turns for your evenings.

Chaste daughters of the nobility
much surpassing the commoners.
Piled hair and hanging tresses, styles not alike
fill full your grounds.

Well matched in figure and features,
they are truly the best of this age.
Gentle of face, firm of intent,
and, ah, they possess desire.

Comely features and tall statures
are found all through the harem.

Mothlike brows and liquid eyes
from which dark pupils flash.

Smooth faces, skin's glossy tracery,
from which glances of love are given.
Behind tall drapes in pavilions apart
they await upon my lord's leisure.

Kingfisher curtains and draperies
adorn the high halls.
Red walls and ochre boards
and beams faced with black jade.

Above you see the graven timbers,
with paintings of dragons and serpents.
Sitting in hall or leaning on rail
you look over curving basins.
There the lotuses begin to come out
mingled with waterlilies.
Watermallows with purple stalks
make patterns along with the waves.
Guards dressed in rare-patterned leopard skins
attend on the sloping shore.
When the great coach at last arrives,
both foot and horse stand in their ranks.
At the entry are planted orchid clumps,
trees like jewels form your hedge.
Soul! Turn back!
Why do you keep so far?

The household comes to show you reverence
with foods of many kinds.
Rice, millet, wheat, barley
combined with yellow millet.
The very bitter, the salty, the sour,
the hot and the sweet are used,
The leg tendons of the fat ox
cooked tender and smelling sweet.
Mixing the bitter and the sour,
they serve the broth of Wu.
Braised terrapin, lambs roasted whole,
there is sauce of sweet potato.
Sour-boiled goose, braised duck,
simmered swan and fishhawk.
Seared fowl, chowdered turtle
fiery, but not mouth-burning.
Doughballs and honey buns,
sweetcakes as well.

Precious brews, quaffed like mead,
brim feather-patterned flagons,
the pressed mash drunk chilled as ice,
and the clarified wine, cool.
Well-wrought ladles have been set
and there is the precious brew.
Turn back to your old chambers
where you are honored and free from offense.

Before those morsels make the rounds,
girl musicians move to their lines.
They ring the bells and roll the drums,
performing the recent songs:
"Wading the River," "Pick Caltrops,"
then breaking into "O Brightness."
And as the beauties grow more drunk,
their rosy faces flush.
Eye's teasing gleam, the half-lidded gaze,
glances come wave upon wave.
Patterned cloaks, fine-woven gowns,
flashy but yet not garish.
Long tresses and trailing locks,
sensual, bright, and alluring.

In two rows of eight, in unison,
they begin the dances of Zheng.
Then, sleeves crossed like staves before them,
slowing the beat they withdraw.
With pipes' and psalteries' wild concert,
they hammer booming drums
Till the whole court of the great house shakes
and the "Frenzied Chu" begins.[2]
The lays of Wu, lyrics of Cai,
and they play the Great Lü.

Men and women are sitting together,
mixed and not kept apart.
Sashes and ribbons are cast down,
the places all in confusion.
Seductive diversions of Zheng and Wei
are performed mixed in among them.
But the coda of the "Frenzied Chu"
is the finest of them all.

Smoky-jade markers and ivory pieces
they play the game of Six Whites.

---

[2]The "Frenzied Chu" is a dance.

Dividing in teams, they attack together,
and press one another hard.
The throw succeeds, the score is doubled,
one shouts: "Five white!"

Horn buckles of Jin-craft,
aglow like bright suns.
Bells are rung, chime frames shake,
they sweep the catalpa-wood harps.

Joys of the wine are not set aside
as they pass through days and nights.
When bright lamps burning orchid oil
are set in their splendid frames.
Verses are made to speak longing,
with phrases finely wrought.
And in the heights of their passion,
joined hearts recite.
Drinking we reach the crest of pleasure
to give the ancestors joy.
Soul, turn back!
Return here where you once dwelled.

The Ending Song

The entering year, the onset of spring,
it was then that we made our way south.
The green leaves of duckweed lay even,
and the white iris grew.

Our course cut across the Lu River,
tall jungles lay to the left.
By the pools edging the floodplain,
our gaze swept wide and far.

Jet black steeds were yoked in teams,
a thousand chariots held the line.
The hunters' torches stretched off,
and the black smoke rose.

Those on foot reached to where we charged,
and the hunt leader galloped ahead.
We curbed their stampede to an easy gait,
then bent the chariots round to the right.
With the king I dashed through the fens,
we raced to see who would be the first.
The king himself made the shot,
the black buffalo was slain.

Red dawnlight follows the night,
the time does not let us linger.

Marsh orchids blanket the trail,
the path here fades away.

The river rolls in swollen floods,
above there are maples.
The eyes reach a full thousand leagues
wounding the heart in spring.
O soul! Turn back!
Have pity on the Southland.

"Calling Back the Recluse" *(Zhao yin-shi)* is attributed to a courtier of the Han prince of Huai-nan. Huai-nan was well to the east of the original Chu homeland, but it was the site of the last Chu capital at Shou-chun. The Han principality of Huai-nan included much of the region of Wu as well. It was in this large region that the "Lyrics of Chu" seem to have been preserved, and other works of the area show strong traces of old Chu learning, such as the essay collection compiled in the Huai-nan court, the *Huai-nan-zi.*

"Calling Back the Recluse" *(Zhao yin-shi)*

Dense groves of cassia   in hills' hidden places,
writhing shapes rising,   boughs locked together,
where hill vapors loom   with rocks jutting high,
where chasms drop deep   and waters raise waves.
Packs of apes shriek,   leopards and tigers roar,
there he snapped cassia branches   and lingered a while.

A royal prince wandered,   he did not come home:
in spring the plants grew,   thick and so green;
and then with year's ending,   he grew dejected,
the cicadas were singing   their mournful cries.

Jagged and craggy,   clefts of the hills,
there the heart lingered,   dazed with dread,
its murky recesses   sent shivers of fright,
caves of leopards and tigers,
in deep forest thickets   a man climbs from fear.

Steep is its sheerness, rocky and rugged,
looming and lofty, strewn with great stones,
tree limbs locked together,
woods dense with leaves and twigs;
green sedge grows between the trees,
and high grass rattles, whipped by winds.
The white deer and the hart,
sometimes bounding, sometimes still,
there poised on the heights,   on the towering cliff,
in the gloomy chill   and the soggy air.

211

Apes and baboons,   black bears and brown,
each yearns for its own   and feels the grief.

He snaps cassia branches   and lingers a while,
leopards and tigers battle,   bears bellow,
then beasts and birds shudder,   they do forget kin.
Come home now my prince—
in the hills one may not linger so long.

As the shaman sets out to summon the soul, the orator uses words to rouse the prince to Good Behavior, to call him home to do his duty. In "Calling Back the Soul," the shaman speaker concluded the main portion of his verse with a description of a feast and orgy, whose express purpose was to give pleasure to the spirits of the ancestors. Offerings of meat and wine were an important component of rituals for the dead (though not orgies as in "Calling Back the Soul"). Yet the dead rarely gave their opinion of the practice. During the third and fourth centuries, however, poets were able to imagine the soul trying to make its way back. The soul may survive the body's dissolution, but it needs the body to eat and drink in the usual way.

Other Voices in the Tradition

Ruan Yu (d. 212), Seven Sorrows

Hard to meet youth a second time,
honor and riches will not come again.
Life's best moments are suddenly past,
and body is nothing but soil and ash.
The Deep Springs' chambers are somber and dark,
forever in mansions of endless night.
Body is gone, the breath's force spent,
and the soul has nothing to which to return.
Fine foods are served, yet you cannot dine,
and the best wines fill the flagons.
Come forth from the tomb, gaze on your home,
and see nothing but weeds and brambles.

Tao Qian (365–427), Pall Bearer's Song II

I used to have no wine to drink,
today it spills uselessly over the cup.
A spring brew with its floating lees—
when can I ever taste it again?
Before me a table is filled with fine foods,
kin and old friends weep by my side.
I try to speak, but my mouth makes no sound,
I try to see, there's no light in my eyes.
I used to bed in a high-roofed hall,
now I spend nights in a land of wild grass.

One morning at dawn I went out my gate,
and I truly have not yet made it back.

The negative half of the soul-calling—the warning about the perils of going far—does reappear occasionally in later literature, though with a hyperbole that may be tongue-in-cheek. The following is perhaps the most famous negative summons in the tradition, in which Li Bo, a native of Shu, part of modern Sichuan, warns an imaginary traveler from Chang-an not to undertake the hardships of the journey through the mountains.

Li Bo (701–762), Hard Ways to Shu

Aiyaiyai!! High!! My, my!! Steep?!! Yep. Yipes!!
The way to Shu is hard,
    harder than climbing blue sky.
Dzhom-dzhung and Ngiu-bhio
in the far, murky past founded this land;[3]
for forty-eight thousand years after them
hearth smoke of men did not stretch through
    the passes into Qin.
Over Mount Tai-bo directly west
    there is a way for birds
whereby they can cut straight across
    Mount E-mei's crest.
There once was a landslide, an avalanche,
    and warriors died in their prime,[4]
and only after that time
    did ladders to sky and plankways on stone
    link it through, one to the other.
Above there is the high ensign
    where the team of six dragons bends the sun,
and below is the stream
    that winds around
        with dashing waves surging back crashing.
Even in flight the brown crane
    cannot pass,
apes and monkeys want to cross
    and sadly strain,
        dragging themselves along.
At Blue Silt it looped and twisted,
each hundred steps had nine sharp turns
    that curved around ridges and peaks.
You will pat the Plow-Star, pass by the Well,
    look up and gasp,

[3]The legendary founders of the Kingdom of Shu are here given in their Tang pronunciation.
[4]This refers to a story of how King Hui of Qin once offered his five daughters in marriage to an ancient King of Shu. The Shu king sent five stalwart men to get them. On their return, one of the men saw a huge snake whose tail was sticking out of its hole. He grabbed the tail and was joined by his four companions; together they pulled so hard that the mountain collapsed, killing both them and the five daughters of Qin.

with your hand stroke your breast,
    sit and sigh in pain.
I ask: from your westbound wanderings
    when you will return?—
for I am dismayed by paths so craggy
    they can't be scaled.
You will hear and see only sorrowing birds
    that wail in leafless trees,
the cock flies on, and the hen follows,
    winding their way through woods.
You will also hear the nightjar
    crying to the night moon
and casting a gloom in deserted hills.[5]
The way to Shu is hard,
    harder than climbing blue sky,
causing wrinkles to form in youthful features
    of any who hear this song.

Peak joined to peak, short of Heaven
    just less than a foot,
barren pines hang upside down,
    clinging to sheer cliff face.
Torrents burst over bluffs in cascades
    in bellowing duels,
boulders roll smashing down slopes
    thunder in thousands of canyons.

Since here there is such peril
you who have come so far on this way, why
    have you come at all?
Sword Tower looms high, juts into sky,
one man holds the gate
and thousands cannot break through.
And the one who holds it may prove no friend,
may change into wolf or jackal.

At dawn we dodge fierce tigers,
at dusk we dodge long snakes.
They sharpen fangs to suck out blood
and kill men like scything down hemp.
Men may speak of the joys in Brocade Town,[6]
but best to turn home as soon as you can.

The way to Shu is hard,
    harder than climbing blue sky,
I sway gazing off toward the west
    and give a mighty sigh.

---

[5]The nightjar was supposed to have been a metamorphosis of the ancient Shu ruler Wang-di.
[6]Brocade Town is Cheng-du, the capital of Shu.

Interlude Between the "Lyrics of Chu" and *Yue-fu:* "The Biography of Lady Li"

先
秦
西
漢

The following short biography, an excellent example of the historian's art, focuses on the question of desire, seeing, and illusion. The Confucian historian Ban Gu distrusts surface appearances and here purports to show us the truth beneath them, although one need only consider how unlikely it would be for the historian to have knowledge of the dialogue between the dying Lady Li and her sister to realize that the imaginative construction of an ethical example is at work here rather than reporting known facts. The relation between appearances, desire, and political power particularly troubles the moralist. It is also a situation in which poetry of varying sorts plays an essential role, with each form of poetry involving the question of illusion. We have here one of the earliest examples of the five-syllable poetic line in its characteristic form, in the lyrics of the court singer Li Yan-nian; we have the irregular extempore verse of Emperor Wu, which is later set to music by the Music Office *(Yue-fu);* and we have the emperor's elegy, a composite piece joining the *Chu-ci* tradition of the lost goddess and a more personal lament.

Ban Gu (A.D. 32–92), *The Han History,* from "The Biographies of the Imperial In-Laws"

Emperor Wu's Lady Li originally entered the court as a singing girl. In the beginning the Lady's brother Li Yan-nian had an innate understanding of music and was skilled in both singing and dance. Emperor Wu was quite fond of him. Whenever he did his variations on popular songs, the audience never failed to be stirred. Once, when attending on the Emperor, Li Yan-nian rose to dance and sang:

> In the north country is a lady fair,
> she stands alone beyond compare.
> She glances once, a city falls;
> a kingdom falls when she glances again.
> Surely you know that a lady so fair,
> she for whom cities and kingdoms fall,
> will never be found again.

The Emperor heaved a great sigh: "Wonderful! But could there really be such a woman in our own time?" Princess Ping-yang thereupon said that Li Yan-nian had a younger sister; and when the Emperor summoned her to an audience, she was indeed a remarkable beauty who was skilled in the dance. From that encounter she received the Emperor's favors and bore him a son,

215

who became Prince Ai of Cheng-yi. Lady Li died an untimely death while still in her youth. The Emperor was deeply saddened and had her likeness painted in Sweet Springs Palace. Four years after the Empress Wei-si was removed, Emperor Wu himself passed on. The Grand Marshal Huo Guang then acted in accord with the Emperor's long-standing wishes and made sacrificial offerings to Lady Li jointly with those to the Emperor, giving her the title "Emperor Wu's Empress."

Earlier, when Lady Li's sickness had become grave, the Emperor himself had come to see how she was. The Lady covered herself with her blanket and refused to let him see her, saying, "I have been lying sick for a long time, and my looks have been marred; I can't see you this way. But I ask to that you take care of the prince, my son, and my brothers." The Emperor replied, "My Lady, you are seriously ill, and it may be that you never get up again. Wouldn't it ease your mind to let me see you this one time and charge me with the care of the prince and your brothers?" The Lady said, "A woman does not let her ruler see her when she is not properly adorned. I would not dare see Your Majesty as disheveled as I am now." The Emperor replied, "If you will just let me see you once, I will grant you a thousand pieces of gold and give your brothers high posts." The Lady said, "High posts depend on the Emperor; they do not depend on letting you see me once." The Emperor again said that he absolutely must see her, but the Lady turned away from him, sobbing, and said no more. At this the Emperor was put out of countenance and rose to leave.

Then the Lady's sister reproached her, saying, "Weren't you willing to let him see you just once in order to charge him with the care of your brothers? Why did you so anger the Emperor like this?" The Lady replied, "The reason that I was unwilling to let the Emperor see me was precisely because I wanted him to feel a stronger responsibility to take care of my brothers. From a lowly position I won the Emperor's love and favor because of the beauty of my appearance. If one serves another through physical attraction, then love slackens when those attractions fade. The reason why the Emperor pays me such regard and feels such attachment to me is because of the way I used to look. If he now were to see the ruin of my beauty, that my face is not as it was before, he would inevitably recoil from such ugliness and reject me. Would he then still have been willing to give future thought to my brothers and show pity on them?"

When the Lady died, the Emperor had her interred with rites befitting an Empress. Afterwards the Emperor made the Lady's elder brother, Li Guang-li, the Er-shi general and enfeoffed him as the Duke of Hai-xi. Li Yan-nian was made Director of Imperial Music.

The Emperor could not stop longing for Lady Li. A wizard of Qi, known as the Young Old Man, said that he would be able to bring back her spirit. When it was night, he hung up lamps and candles and erected a curtained enclosure, where he set out meat and wine. Then he made the Emperor take his place within another curtained enclosure. Gazing from the distance he saw a lovely woman, whose appearance was like that of Lady Li, walking around the place set for her within the curtains. But he could not go to take a closer look. The Emperor then felt longing and sadness even more strongly, and wrote this poem:

> Is it her
> or is it not?
> I stand and gaze at her,
> yet she glides along, so slow
>   in her coming.

He ordered the musicians of the Music Bureau to make a song of it, set to the accompaniment of strings. His Majesty also wrote a poetic exposition to lament the Lady Li. These are its words:

> Lithe and lovely,   of features fair,
> lifespan sundered,   it did not last.
> A spirit-lodge well fitted,   long did I wait;
> she vanished, not returning   to her home of before.
> Despair wells within me,   she rots with the weeds,
> she dwells in dark places,   and I feel the pain.
> I untied coach and horse   from the hill's pepper tree,
> all at once, long night,   no light of the sun.
> Bleak air of autumn,   somber and chill,
> cassia boughs shed   and then waste away.
> My soul, forsaken,   yearns for one far,
> the spirit roams drifting   beyond all the bounds.
> Long time and forever   she stays sunk in shadow,
> I regret her full flowering   reached not its zenith.
> I brood that forever   she will not return;
> I conceive a faint presence   roaming afar.
> Enclosed stamens unfurl,   awaiting the wind,
> then fragrances hoarded   grow ever more clear.
> Bright being in motion,   graceful and yielding,
> wind-whirled swirling,   it grew overpowering.
> Festive and wanton,   brushing the columns,
> her gaze swept around,   she lifted her brows.
> Stirred and aroused,   my heart did pursue her,
> she hid her flushed face,   it does not appear.
> We shared intimate pleasures,   now we are parted;
> I wake up from dreams,   I am lost in a daze.
> All at once she was Changed   and does not turn back,
> her soul was set free,   her breath rose away.
> Such a baffling blur   is her hallowed spirit,
> I linger lamenting,   I falter in distress.
> Her course carries her   each day further from me,
> and I was bewildered   as she took her leave.
> Going beyond in a journey westward,

moving swiftly, now unseen.
At last I am left forlorn
in a stillness without sound.
My longing is like the rolling waves,
and sorrow is here in my heart.

The Closing Piece

From splendid beauty full of light,
the crimson petals fall.
How can those paltry and envious women
weigh in the balance with you?
In the very height of your season
you were stricken before your years.
Your child and brothers sob,
tears bubble in their despair.
Overcome with sorrow
wailing cannot be stopped.
Echoes left unanswered—
it is all over now!
Gaunt from grief I moan
and sigh for your young son.
So wretched I cannot speak—
trust him on whom you relied.
Kind hearts need make no vows,
still less are pacts made with kin.
Since you have gone and will not come,
I add to this my troth.
You have gone from the world of light,
you have entered into dark.
You did descend to the spirit-lodge
but will not come back to your former grounds.
O the sadness of it!
I envision your soul.

Afterwards, Li Yan-nian's younger brother Li Ji was implicated in licentious acts in the imperial harem. Li Guang-li surrendered to the Xiong-nu. The entire family was exterminated.

The Chinese "Middle Ages"

東漢魏晉南北朝

THE CHINESE "MIDDLE AGES": PERIOD INTRODUCTION

The great Chinese empire of late antiquity, the Han, reached its height during the long reign of Emperor Wu (140–87 B.C.). The central government had effectively broken the power of the Han feudal lords, and Han armies were waging successful campaigns in Central Asia against the Xiong-nu kingdom. In the reigns that followed Emperor Wu, however, imperial power gradually weakened, leading finally to the usurpation of the throne by Wang Mang, who ruled over the brief Xin ("New") Dynasty (A.D. 9–23). Wang Mang tried to push through an ambitious program of political and cultural reforms, but in doing so, he stirred opposition from powerful interests all over the empire. The most serious problem for Wang Mang, however, arose from the shift of the course of the Yellow River. The ensuing floods and agricultural dislocation in what was then China's major population center led to large-scale famine. The government was unable to cope with the extent of the disaster, and a huge peasant revolt was initiated by the Red Eyebrows, so-called because the rebels painted red on their foreheads to distinguish themselves from imperial troops. Several of Wang Mang's armies were defeated, and as the Red Eyebrows spread, regional armies were raised to oppose Wang Mang's armies and the government. From one such army came Liu Xiu, a minor descendant of the Han imperial house, who, after Wang Mang's armies were defeated, was declared the emperor Guang-wu of the restored Han Dynasty in A.D. 25. Liu Xiu was far from the only claimant to the throne, and the next decade saw a series of civil wars from which Liu Xiu emerged victorious.

In the course of Emperor Guang-wu's rise, the Red Eyebrows had occupied and devastated the capital, Chang-an. The new emperor subsequently moved the capital east to Luo-yang, and thus the restored dynasty came to be known as the Eastern Han. Although the Eastern Han survived for almost two centuries, it never recovered the power of the first half of the dynasty, subsequently known as the Western Han. In the capital, powerful families formed factions that competed for central government positions, and in the provinces regional autonomy grew.

Aware of the greater military and political power of their Western Han predecessors, Eastern Han rulers and intellectuals sought to distinguish their own period by its observance of Confucian values. During the course of the Western Han, Confucianism had come to play an increasingly important role as the ideological basis of the state; by the Wang Mang regime and the Eastern Han, Confucianism and the imperial system had become inseparable. For reasons of state or personal belief, later emperors might offer lavish patronage to

Daoism or Buddhism, but the state itself could not be conceived apart from Confucianism (although in the thirteenth century the Mongols briefly attempted to do so).

Although there was nothing in the Han like a true Confucian orthodoxy, the increasing importance of the Confucian Classics to political life intensified the need to reconcile variant texts and interpretations. Schools of classical scholarship were roughly divided between "New Text" and "Old Text." The "New Text" schools were so called because they supposedly represented oral transmission of texts and commentaries on the Confucian Classics, which, after the burning of the books in the Qin, were written down in the reformed script after the establishment of the Han. The "Old Text" school primarily represented written texts recovered after the Han. The difference between the "New Text" and "Old Text" schools was, however, more profound than simply textual lineages of the Confucian Classics. The "New Text" schools represented an older style of Confucian learning, based on personal transmission of texts and interpretation by a master whose authority would be traced in unbroken succession back to the disciples of Confucius. Though the "New Text" classics and their interpretations were written down, they remained very much schools in which students studied one particular classic under the master and simply repeated the authoritative interpretation of the master.

The "Old Text" schools included scholastic lineages such as that of the Mao *Classic of Poetry,* yet the very idea of the "Old Text" classics was based on a break in the personal transmission of the Confucian Classics and the ability of later scholars to offer interpretations from written texts. Wang Mang was a strong supporter of the "Old Text," and although "New Text" scholarship enjoyed a brief revival in the early Eastern Han, the "Old Text" schools gradually emerged triumphant. Their success was due in no small part to their dissemination among private scholars, who felt confident in working with written texts and drawing their own conclusions rather than relying on the authority of a master. Out of this tradition, comparison and determination of authoritative versions of the texts of the Confucian Classics continued through the Eastern Han; and in A.D. 175, under state sponsorship, texts of the so-called Five Classics were carved in stone and set up outside the Imperial Academy in Luo-yang so that students would have authoritative versions of the classics from which to study.[1]

In the Western Han, poetic expositions *(fu)* had been one of the primary forms of court literary entertainment. These poetic expositions were long, rhymed descriptions that made use of a rich vocabulary; those declaimed in court were usually direct or indirect panegyrics of imperial power, though often including encouragement to restraint. Emperor Wu's court poet Si-ma Xiang-ru (179–117 B.C.) praised the emperor as "The Great One" (see p. 182), an adept Daoist who marshaled the forces of the cosmos and rode to transcendence. Si-ma Xiang-ru also wrote a famous poetic exposition describing the imperial hunting park, naming the flora and fauna from all over the empire that had been gathered there. In his younger days, the writer and intellectual Yang Xiong (53 B.C.–A.D. 18) had similarly praised the hunts and ceremonies of Emperor Wu's successors, but in the writing of his later years,

---

[1]These were the *Classic of Poetry,* the *Classic of Documents,* the *Classic of Changes,* the *Yili* (one of the ritual books), and *The Springs and Autumns [of Lu].*

readers witness some of the changes in public values that were occurring as the Eastern Han approached. Yang Xiong renounced the poetic expositions of his youth on the grounds that they encouraged imperial extravagance and failed in what he saw as their primary purpose, which was to offer moral guidance to the emperor. Following in the tradition of Yang Xiong, the public literature of the Eastern Han often tended to Confucian moralizing.

As a genre, poetic exposition continued to be important throughout the Eastern Han, and it came to be used informally as a demonstration of education and talent by young men seeking appointment in the central government. Such use of literary composition in the appointment process outlasted the Eastern Han; eventually, it became fully institutionalized in the examination system of the seventh century.

State Confucianism was only a thin layer of elite ideology, beneath which lay a complex world of popular religion and cults of esoteric knowledge. Confucianism itself came to be permeated by such beliefs from the Western Han on. Han rulers placed particular faith in prognostication by omens, and though the Confucian Classics themselves offered little support for such practices, there was an extensive body of Confucian apocrypha promising the esoteric knowledge for which many Han intellectuals hungered. Huang-Lao Daoism went much further than esoteric Confucianism, offering techniques of yoga and alchemy by which the adept could refine his physical being and attain immortality. Huang-Lao Daoism gradually developed a large following among the populace, and it was spread in cults headed by charismatic leaders with messianic pretensions. In A.D. 184, the weakened Han state was shaken by two almost simultaneous cult uprisings in different parts of the country: the Yellow Turbans and the "Five Pecks of Rice." These military-religious communities defeated imperial armies and established local kingdoms in the disintegrating empire.

In addition to the uprisings of the Daoist cults, the last decades of the second century saw local generals with independent armies establishing themselves as regional powers. One general, Dong Zhuo, took advantage of factional fighting in the capital in 189 and seized the emperor Xian; he then plundered and burned Luo-yang, driving its inhabitants west to reestablish the capital in Chang-an. A year later, Dong Zhuo was himself killed by his officers, Chang-an was sacked, and the empire collapsed into total anarchy. Emperor Xian, providing the weak aura of Han legitimacy, passed from one warlord to another until he came into the hands of Cao Cao (155–220), who was gradually establishing his position as the preeminent military leader in North China.

By the early third century, the weaker warlords had fallen by the wayside and the former empire was divided into the "Three Kingdoms" that give their name to the period. In the West was the Shu-Han Kingdom, ruled by a remote descendant of the Han imperial house; in the South along the Yangzi River was the Kingdom of Wu, whose river fleet protected it against invasion; and in the North was Cao Cao, proclaimed "King of Wei," but not emperor. In holding Emperor Xian as his puppet, Cao Cao kept alive the fiction of the Han Dynasty; but on Cao Cao's death in 220, his son, Cao Pi, deposed the emperor and proclaimed himself emperor of the new Wei Dynasty.

The heirs of Cao Pi proved to be far less able than either Cao Cao or Cao Pi, and the Wei soon came under the domination of the powerful Si-ma family. The Wei was still nominally in existence when Northern armies incorporated the Shu-Han Kingdom in 263, but in 265 the Si-ma family deposed the Caos, just as the Caos had deposed the Han emperor less than half a century earlier. With this began the Jin Dynasty, which in 280 at last conquered the Kingdom of Wu and briefly reunified China.

The gradual dissolution of Han power in the second half of the second century and the constant warfare of the Three Kingdoms proved to be one of the most fertile and transformative periods in Chinese literature. The long reign of the ill-fated Emperor Xian, from 196 to 220, was known as the Jian-an, and it gave its name to the literature of the period. Older forms such as poetic exposition continued to be written, but their range expanded to include topics from everyday life. At the same time, popular song and a new form of classical poetry in the five-syllable line were adopted by well-known literary men. Unlike the poetic exposition, classical poetry was a genre that invited accounts of personal experience and expression of private feeling: the poetry of the Jian-an gave voice to the instability and uncertainty of life during the period. Cao Cao, himself an accomplished poet, was the great patron of contemporary writers, who gathered to the relative security of his court. His son and heir, Cao Pi, was not only a distinguished writer but also composed the first treatise on literature. A younger son of Cao Cao, Cao Zhi, became the most famous writer of his day, provoking the jealousy of his older brother.

The intellectual temper of the times had changed profoundly from the public seriousness of the first part of the Eastern Han; there was a strong reaction against the commitment to public life demanded by Confucian ethics. Thinkers such as Wang Bi (226–249) wrote commentaries on Confucian and Daoist Classics, focusing on metaphysical issues without regard to their social, ethical, or political implications. Writers and intellectuals were increasingly drawn to the values of private life and did their best to avoid serving in the government. Those who did serve were often caught in the constant factional struggles and many were executed. Already in the mid-third century we see a fascination with eccentricity, accompanied by extravagant gestures rejecting the norms of social behavior. Many such intellectuals were drawn to alchemy and the Daoist quest for physical immortality.

The messianic Daoists of the late second century were finally defeated militarily, but in their place a Daoist "church" took shape with an organized religious hierarchy, a body of esoteric scriptures, and a large popular following to support it. In contrast to the atheistic philosophical Daoism of the pre-Qin period, the Daoist church worshipped a large pantheon of deities organized in celestial bureaucracies not unlike the imperial government.

Buddhism made its initial appearance in China in the first century A.D., and by the third century a growing number of missionaries from Central Asia were winning converts everywhere. In the turmoil of the times, Buddhist doctrines of personal salvation and release from the inevitable suffering of life held great appeal. Sutras, the Buddhist scriptures, offered a taste of the complexities of Indian philosophy, and large-scale translation projects demanded a new kind of reflection on the Chinese language. With Buddhism came a highly developed church and monastic structure that provided a model for religious Daoism, Buddhism's chief religious competitor.

After only thirty-seven years of ruling over a unified China, the Jin capital in Luo-yang fell in 316 to non-Chinese invaders from the North. As "barbarian" armies established their hold over North China, many great families fled with their retainers and possessions south of the Yangzi River, where, in 317, a Jin prince, Si-ma Rui, proclaimed himself the Jin emperor. Following the model of the Zhou and Han when the capital moved east rather than south after dynastic crisis, this came to be known as the "Eastern Jin." For more than two and a half centuries, a succession of Chinese dynasties ruled the Yangzi River region in a period known as the "Southern Dynasties." During this same period, North China was under the sway of various non-Chinese kingdoms. Thus the period from 317 until the reunification of China under the Sui in 589 is known as the "Northern and Southern Dynasties."

When viewed by most objective standards, the Southern Dynasties were small, regional regimes. By far the greater part of the Chinese population still lived in the North. The Northern Dynasties patronized Buddhism and Confucian scholarship, and their legacy in religious art can still be seen. But in literature they were proportionally insignificant, and the role of literature in defining Chinese cultural continuity was such that subsequent ages thought of the Southern Dynasties as the main lineage linking the Western Jin with the great medieval empires of Sui and Tang.

The intellectual concerns of the Wei and Western Jin continued to grow during the Southern Dynasties. Although the state was still understood in Confucian terms, personal happiness and the experience of the individual or a group of like-minded friends were considered of greater importance than service to the state. Tao Qian (365–427) voluntarily renounced his administrative post because he felt that its demands violated his nature, and his poetry celebrated his decision to return to work his own fields in the farming community that was his home. For others, a stylish eccentricity marked the individual's refusal to conform to social customs. Buddhism spread and flourished in both the North and South, and its monastic communities provided the means to renounce the secular world altogether. In the South, temples and monasteries were established deep in the mountains, and among monks and laity alike there developed a new appreciation of landscape and natural beauty. When earlier poets had traveled, it was a means to get from one place to another. In the fifth century, we begin to find poets undertaking travel for its own sake, wandering through the mountains to appreciate the beauty of nature.

Not only was the overall population of the South much smaller than that of the North, the émigré ruling house and great families constituted only a small minority of the Southern population. These émigré families comprised an aristocracy. Edicts to preserve the purity of Northern bloodlines were soon ignored, but the culture of the South had become aristocratic. By the late fifth century aristocratic society drew inward, with literary composition increasingly restricted to the courts of the emperor and imperial princes in the capital, Jian-kang (modern Nanjing). Poems were written on the occasion of imperial and princely outings, and topics for composition would often be set as a pastime. Literary issues were debated, in which literary and political factionalism were closely intertwined. Old song lyrics were carefully conserved, anthologies of older and contemporary literature compiled, and literary history undertaken.

Such a fragile world could not last long, and in 549 the rebel Hou Jing took Jian-kang and sacked it. The ruling Liang Dynasty eventually put down the rebellion and recovered the city, but it never fully recovered its political or military power. In the decades that followed, a new dynasty was installed, the Chen, but the Southern rulers became puppets of the militarily powerful North. The 580s saw the rise of a powerful new Northern state, the Sui, which first unified the divided kingdoms of the North and then, in 589, conquered the Chen and reunified the empire.

The Sui instituted a number of institutional and economic reforms that would be the basis of government for the following centuries, but the Sui itself did not endure long. The astute first Sui ruler built a sound political structure that was badly mismanaged and overextended by his successor, Emperor Yang. Indeed, Emperor Yang moved the Sui capital from Chang-an to one of the great Southern cities, Yang-zhou, and fell under the spell of the pleasure-loving court culture of the South. Outbreaks of rebellion occurred all over the country. After less than thirty years, the Sui was replaced by a new dynasty, the Tang, which would rule China for the next three centuries.

Yue-fu[1] 東漢魏晉南北朝

In 120 B.C., a special bureau was established in the Han government to provide music and songs for state rituals and imperial entertainments. This bureau was known as the *Yue-fu,* or "Music Office," and the same term came to be applied to the lyrics of the songs themselves. The bureau used not only music and lyrics composed at court and in the office itself but also lyrics that seemed to have been folk poems. Such use of popular songs in the court was reminiscent of the "Airs" of the *Classic of Poetry,* in which lyrics that originated among the common people found currency in the regional courts of the Zhou princes. A handful of Western Han lyrics still survive that probably came from the original institution, the Han "Music Bureau." Among these are pieces that seem to have originated in folk poetry, including the two following pieces: a lover's oath of eternal fidelity and a poem breaking off with an unfaithful lover.

Heaven Above (Western Han *yue-fu*)

By Heaven above,
I will be your true love,
let it be forever and never wane.
When hills no longer rise,
when the river's water dries,
when winter thunder rolls,
and snow in summer falls,
when sky and earth fuse,
I'll stop loving you.

The One I Love (Western Han *yue-fu*)

The one I love
is south of the sea.
What gift can I send him?—

---

[1]The category of *yue-fu,* as it has been used for the past millennium, represents a complex historical aggregation of types of poems. What makes a poem a *yue-fu* is its title. Although it often suggests the theme of the poem, the title is essentially considered the title of a melody, even if the melody is long lost. The term *yue-fu* includes all anonymous poems from before the seventh century written to *yue-fu* titles. Many of these are folk poems. The category also includes all poems by known writers which use that body of *yue-fu* titles, as well as poems by known writers to titles that can be recognized as variations on the original set of pre-seventh-century titles.

a hair-clasp of tortoise shell,
    set with paired pearls,
and wound all about with jade.

Then I heard that his heart had changed,
I broke it and burned it in a pile,
broke and burned it,
threw the ash to the wind.
From this day on,
no more longing, no more love,
my love for him is done.

When roosters crow and the dogs all bark,
my brother, his wife will know,
tra-la-la,
the autumn winds howl, the pheasants shrill,
soon the east will grow bright
    and all will be known.

Some of these Western Han *yue-fu* recall earlier ritual songs, such as the following lyric speaking for soldiers who died for an unknown cause in an unknown battle. This Han song should be compared with the Chu ritual song, "The Kingdom's Dead" (see p. 161), which also allows those dead in distant battle to speak. Although it does not echo or derive from "The Kingdom's Dead," "South of the Walls We Fought" serves the same function of allowing the community to acknowledge the bravery and loyalty of the dead.

South of the Walls We Fought (Western Han *yue-fu*)

"South of the walls we fought,
north of the ramparts we fell,
fell in the meadows, left unburied,
    food for the ravens.
Speak to the ravens for us, say:
we were brave men, far from home,
we fell in the meadows, left unburied,
how can our carrion flee you?"

Where the waters run deep and clear,
the reeds and the rushes are dark:
the horsemen all died in battle,
their tired mounts linger and neigh.

"On the bridge a guardhouse is built—
how can we cross south?

228

how can we cross north?
If the grain is not taken in harvest,
    how shall our lord eat?
we want to be loyal liegemen,
    but how can this be done?"

"We think on you, good liegemen,
good liegemen should be in our thoughts:
at dawn you went forth to battle,
and at evening did not return."

The original "Music Office" was closed in 6 B.C., but the term *yue-fu* continued to be applied to anonymous poems that seem initially to have been folksongs. We have a considerable body of such poems, probably dating from the Eastern Han in the first and second centuries A.D. Some such songs, like "East of Ping-ling" below, deal with the kinds of situations in the lives of the common people that almost never appear in "high" literature.

East of Ping-ling (Eastern Han?)

East of Ping-ling, the royal tomb,
beech tree, cypress, and pine,
there is someone—I can't say who—
    has kidnapped our good lord,
they kidnapped our good lord
    right from his own great hall,
the ransom is set at a million coins
    and a pair of the swiftest steeds.
A pair of the swiftest steeds
is going to be hard indeed:
I look back and see the wardens coming,
    my heart quails and grows cold,
my heart grows cold within,
the blood drains dry,
I go home and tell the kin
    that the brown calf must be sold.

In later Chinese song traditions, songs were often performed in sets, with the different sections thematically playing off one another. In a few of these Eastern Han *yue-fu,* such as "Prelude: White Swans in Pairs," we have an indication of how such song sets might have been structured. The opening segment often deals with an animal, bird, or plant; then a central segment deals with a human situation that is parallel with or contrasts to the opening segment; finally, there is a conventional coda in which the singer wishes his audience long life and blessings.

Prelude: White Swans in Pairs (Eastern Han?)

In pairs white swans came flying,
came flying from the northwest,
five by five and ten by ten,
all in lines uneven.
Suddenly one was struck sick
and could not fly with the rest.
Every five leagues he looked back once,
every six leagues he lingered.
"I would take you in my beak,
but my beak is shut and won't open;
I would bear you on my back,
but my feathers are broken and fallen."
Great joy comes with first meeting,
then grief, when parted in life.
He faltered and looked round to the flock,
and unawares tears were falling.

As my thoughts fix on parting with you,
the breath in me chokes, I cannot speak.
Let each take care for himself, herself,
the road is far, return will be hard.
And I will stay in my chamber alone,
our gates kept closed and doubly barred.
If you live, we will meet again;
if you die, we will join down below.

Live this day with delight on delight,
Long life to you, ten thousand years.

Many of the anonymous Han *yue-fu* were probably composed by professional singers, and they show characteristics of oral composition, such as formulae and shared lines. In their original form, these anonymous *yue-fu* were probably not fixed "texts," but were instead continually changed in each performance until at last someone wrote one version down and the words became fixed. By a remarkable accident of preservation, we have the following three versions of the same song from the Eastern Han. As is often the case in English or Scottish ballads, these songs leave much unsaid. Each version hints at something not stated directly: one brother wronging another; the young wife not attending to domestic tasks but instead entertaining someone.

Cocks Crow (Eastern Han?)

Cocks crow in the treetops,
dogs bark deep behind walls,
where is the wanderer heading,

now that the world is at peace?
Nothing slips past the law,
the wicked meet justice, the helpless get care.

Golden is your gate,
and emerald is your hall,
where flasks of wine are set in pairs,
and Han-dan singers there perform.
Roof tiles of lapis lazuli
appear on roofs of lesser clans.

Behind the rooms a square pool lies,
and in that pool are ducks in pairs,
seventy ducks and two,
all in order, formed in lines,
and when they sing, their sad cries
are heard on the eastern porch of our hall.

Brothers there are, four or five,
all are attendants on the king,
when they come home one day in five,
the roadsides fill with onlookers.
Gold winds round their horses' heads,
gleaming and sparkling fine.

A peach tree grew by an open well,
a pear tree grew by its side:
worms chewed away the peach's roots,
but the pear tree fell in its stead.
A tree will offer itself for another,
but brother forgets brother.

Meeting (Eastern Han?)

We met upon the narrow lanes,
on roads so narrow no coach could pass,
I knew not what young man it was,
wheel to wheel, asked of your home.
Easy is your home to know,
easy to know, hard to forget.
Golden is your gate,
white jade is the hall,
and in the hall are flasks of wine,
and Han-dan singers there perform,
with cinnamon trees in the courtyard
where sparkling lanterns brightly shine.

Brothers there are, two or three,
the second, attendant to the king,

when he comes home one day in five,
the whole roadway fills with light,
gold winds round his horse's head,
and roadsides fill with onlookers.

He enters his gates, he looks around
and sees only ducks in pairs,
seventy ducks and two,
all in order, formed in lines.
and he hears the sound of melodious cries,
cranes sing on porches east and west.

The eldest wife weaves the silken mesh,
the middle wife weaves the yellow floss,
the youngest wife does nothing at all,
harp in her arm, she mounts the hall.
"Sit calmly, my lord, and listen a while,
for the play of the strings is not yet done."

Chang-an Has Narrow Alleys (Eastern Han?)

Chang-an has narrow alleys,
alleys so narrow no coach can pass.
I chanced on two young men,
wheel to wheel, I asked of your home.
Your home is beside New Market,
easy to know, hard to forget.

The eldest son brings in two thousand pecks,
the middle son, constable of the king.
The youngest son has no post at all,
in cap and gown he serves in Luo-yang.
When the three sons together enter the room,
all through the room a light appears.

The eldest wife weaves silks and linens,
the middle wife weaves the yellow floss,
the youngest wife does nothing at all,
harp in her arm, she mounts the hall.
"Be still, my lord, and listen a while,
for the play of the strings is not quite done."

Other Voices in the Tradition

Later poets often took some striking line or passage from earlier poetry and elaborated
it in a separate poem. In the closing passage of the preceding two versions, we do not
know the full situation, but we do know that there are three brothers and three wives.
Two of the wives are doing what wives should do: they are weaving. The third is doing

something else—entertaining someone she addresses with respect (in the final version we are told that the youngest brother, her husband, is off in Luo-yang). Poets of the fifth and sixth centuries could not resist the erotic implications, and they often composed short poems to two new *yue-fu* titles, "The Sensual Charms of the Three Wives" and "The Middle Wife Weaves the Yellow Floss," echoing the endings of the songs above.

Shen Yue (441–513), The Sensual Charms of the Three Wives

The eldest wife wipes off boxes of jade,
the middle wife knots beaded curtains,
but the youngest wife does nothing at all,
she fixes her brows in the mirror.
"Lie quietly, love, just for a while—
later tonight we'll do private things."

When enthusiasts began to collect folksongs and ballads in England and Europe in the eighteenth and nineteenth centuries, they would often "improve" them, revising passages and leaving out segments that seemed "garbled" or "corrupt." In more recent times, scholars have recognized that such incongruous elements are a natural part of folksong traditions, which do not follow the same rules as the literature of the elite. We have a fine example of this in two versions of the Eastern Han(?) "Song of White Hair." One version is included in the "Treatise on Music," part of an official history compiled in the late fifth century; this treatise preserves many of the best Han *yue-fu* and seems to represent the transcription of singers' repertoires. The second version comes from roughly the same period and is found in an early sixth-century anthology, *Recent Songs from a Terrace of Jade (Yu-tai xin-yong)*, which included many *yue-fu*. Like the European folksong collectors of the eighteenth and early nineteenth centuries, the editor of *Recent Songs from a Terrace of Jade* seems to have "fixed" some of the *yue-fu*. In his version of "Song of White Hair," the editor regularizes the stanzas and omits passages that seem incongruous, creating a coherent lyric of a woman breaking off with a faithless man. The sections in the original version that are omitted in the "literary" version are given in italics below.

Song of White Hair (Eastern Han?)

As bright as the snow on mountaintop,
as clear as the moon between clouds,
I have heard that you love another,
I have made up my mind to break it off.

We have both lived our lives in this city,
but when have we met with a flask of wine?
We meet today with a flask of wine,
then tomorrow at dawn, by the royal moat,
we'll linger there by the royal moat,
where the water flows off east and west.

There's a woodcutter east of the city,
there's a woodcutter west of the city too;
both woodcutters heave together—
with no friends for whom can I show off?

Sad and dreary, sad and dreary,
when a woman marries, she should not cry,
I wanted a man with a faithful heart,
till white hair came, never to part.

The bamboo pole bends with the strike,
The fish's tail flips violently.
In a man value true feeling;
money is no use at all.

A horse is chomping at the hay,
and on the river great gentry play.
Live this day with delight on delight,
Long life to you, ten thousand years.

The following two songs treat roughly the same theme—a man approaches a beautiful young woman and his advances are rebuffed—in very different ways. The second of these songs is attributed to an otherwise unknown figure, Xin Yan-nian, probably a professional singer of the Eastern Han. The motif bears interesting comparison to the poetic exposition "The Goddess" (see p. 190), in which the poet meets the goddess and is rejected just before they consummate their love.

Mulberries by the Path (Eastern Han?)

Sunrise in southeast
shines on the halls of our house of Qin,
and the house of Qin has a lovely girl
whose name, they say, is Luo-fu.
Luo-fu is skilled with silkworms
she picks mulberry leaves south of the wall.
The straps of her basket are of blue silk,
its handle, a branch of cinnamon;
Her hair has a trailing ponytail,
in her ears are bright moon pearls.
Her skirt below is saffron damask,
of purple damask, her vest above.
When passers-by see Luo-fu, they
drop their loads and stroke their beards;
when young men see Luo-fu,
their hats fall off and their headbands show.
Men at the plow forget the share;
men with the hoe forget the hoe,

when they go home there's always a fight,
all because of seeing Luo-fu.

From the south the lord governor came,
and he halted his five-horse team;
the lord governor's sent a runner
to find out who that maiden is:
"The house of Qin has a lovely girl
whose name, we shall say, is Luo-fu."
"And just how old is this Luo-fu?"
"Not yet up to twenty,
and just beyond fifteen."
The governor invites Luo-fu:
"Now will you ride with me?"
Luo-fu came forward and said these words:
"The lord governor's a foolish man:
the lord governor has his own wife;
I, Luo-fu, have my man.
In the east are a thousand riders and more,
and my husband is head of them all.
How can you tell who my husband is?—
he rides a white horse, a black colt behind,
the horse's tail is wound in blue silk,
and gold is the halter on its head,
at his waist is a wound-pommel sword,
worth perhaps a million or more.
At fifteen he was a county runner,
by twenty, a great lord at court,
by thirty, in the Emperor's entourage,
by forty, the master of a city.
His skin is smooth, his skin is white,
his beard is wispy and long,
he walks with slow pace through the courts,
with stately steps he goes through the hall.
There are thousands that dine at his board,
and all of them say how grand he is!"

Xin Yan-nian, Officer of the Guard (Eastern Han)

A bondsman of the house of Huo,
Feng by name, Feng Zi-du,
hid behind the Lord General's power
and trifled with the Turkish tavern girl.
Fifteen was the Turkish maid,
alone at the bar one day in spring,
a long-hung skirt, twined-ribbon sash,

billowing sleeves, acacia vest.
On her head she wore Lan-tian jade,
in her ears she wore pearls from Rome,
her hair in two buns was so lovely
there was nothing like them in the world:
one bun was worth five million in gold,
and the two together, more than ten.
"I never expected this dashing guard
to stop by our tavern so gallantly,
his silver saddle sparkling,
his blue-covered coach waiting empty."
And he comes to me wanting clear wine:
I brought him a rope-handled jug.
And he comes to me wanting fine things to eat;
a golden plate with carp fillet.
And he gives me a green bronze mirror
and grabs hold of my skirts of red gauze.
"I don't care if my red gauze gets torn,
such cheap treatment is what I expect:
a man always wants a new woman,
but a woman values the man she has;
in human life there are new things and old,
the highborn do not mix with the low.
No thank you, officer of the guard,
private love isn't worth it."

By the end of the Eastern Han, in the last part of the second century A.D., literary men began to write poems in the spirit of the anonymous *yue-fu,* and these too came to be known as *yue-fu. Yue-fu* became important as a kind of poetry in which a poet could speak not in his own voice but as a character type: the abandoned woman, the frontier soldier, the young nobleman. The settings of literary *yue-fu* are imaginary scenes, such as Chen Lin imagining the following exchange between a conscript laborer on the frontier and his wife.

Chen Lin (d. 217), I Watered My Horse at a Spring by the Wall

I watered my horse at a spring by the Wall
with water so cold my horse hurt in its bones.

They went to the boss-man beside the Great Wall,
saying,
    "Don't keep us Tai-yuan lads long past our time."

"Let's keep the state work on schedule, boys,
so lift your mallets to the rhythm of the sound."

"Better for a man to die fighting
than bear pounding earth to build the Great Wall."

And the Great Wall keeps stretching on and on,
on and on three thousand miles.
There's many a stout lad on the frontier,
and many a wife alone at home.
I wrote a letter to my wife:
"Better find another man,
    don't you wait for me;
be good to your new man's family,
just now and then remember me."

A letter came back to the frontier land,
said, "What's this foolishness you're telling me?"

"Since I've got troubles, why should I
try to hold down a woman no blood-kin of mine?
If you have a boy, don't raise him,
if you have a girl, feed her well.
If you could only see how it is by the Wall,
with the bones of dead men stacked in a pile . . . "

"They dressed my hair as a woman
    and I went to be your wife,
now my heart knots with misery;
I see well how you suffer on the frontier,
and I don't think I'll be long for life."

After the Han, *yue-fu* became a very broad category of poetry, encompassing all anonymous popular songs as well as literary works done in what different ages saw as the "spirit" of the original *yue-fu*.

Yue-fu of the South

A type of anonymous popular song very different from the old Han *yue-fu* flourished south of the Yangzi River from the third through the fifth centuries. These were mostly quatrains, with many different lyrics made to a single title that probably represented a song or melody type. Some of the song types seem to have been sung only by women, while others allowed either a male or a female voice. These short lyrics are mostly love songs, some movingly direct in their simplicity and others witty and mischievous. They make heavy use of a small group of puns, including: *lian,* "lotus" or "passion"; *si,* "silk," "thread," or "longing"; *ou,* "lotus root" and "mate"; and *pi,* "bolt" [of cloth] and "match." These popular songs came to have a great influence on the formation of the literary quatrain.

Such songs became very popular with the aristocrats of the Southern court, and in the early sixth century, choruses of women were imported into the palace and trained to perform them. The largest and most famous group of these quatrains are known as the "Zi-ye Songs," *Zi-ye* being a term for "midnight," and supposedly the name of a famous courtesan of the mid-fourth century. Most of the Zi-ye Songs are in a woman's voice, but the first two seem to form a dialogue between a man and a woman.

Zi-ye Songs

I–II

"I went out the gates at sunset,
and glimpsed you passing by.
Enchanting features, tresses fetching,
a sweet scent filled all the road."

"The sweet scent was made by perfume,
enchanting features I cannot claim.
But Heaven won't thwart a person's desire,
and on purpose it let me see you."

XII

At dawn I long to go out the gates,
at dusk I long to go back to the isles.
I'll laugh and chat with anyone,
but my heart in secret thinks of you.

XVI

My love was taken by another,
he betrayed me more than one time.
I opened the door, didn't set the bar,
which is to say: "Close no more."

No. XVI is a punning quatrain. The open door ("Close no more") is *wu fu xiang guan,* both "not locked any more" and "I'll have nothing to do with you any more." Of course, the open door also suggests the woman's availability for a new lover.

XIX

When my love is sad, I'm also down;
when my man laughs, I'm happy too.
Have you never seen two trees entwined:
from different roots shared branches rise?

XX

I was moved by how loving you were at first,
now I sigh how distant and cold you've grown.
Pound out gold leaf on a tortoise shell—
all glitter outside, nothing deep within.

XXIII

Who can feel longing and not sing out?
Who can be starving and not eat?
The sun grows dark, I lean by the door,
so upset that I can't help thinking of you.

XXIV
I held my dress, not tying the sash,
I painted my brows and went to the window.
My gauze skirt is easily whirled by the breeze—
if it opens a bit, just blame the spring wind.

XXXIII
The night lasted on, I could not sleep,
and the moonlight shone so bright.
I thought I heard my true love call,
and I wasted an answering "Yes!" to the sky.

XXXVI
I am that star at the Dipper's end
that never shifts in a thousand years.
My lover's heart is like the sun,
in the east at dawn, at dusk turning west.

The Zi-ye Songs of the Four Seasons

Spring Songs

VI
The cuckoo is singing in the bamboo,
plum blossoms fall, filling the road.
Girls seeking pleasure roam in spring moonlight.
their gauze skirts trail through fragrant grass.

IX
Skirt of gauze, tight red sleeves,
hairpin of jade and full-moon earrings.
Roaming for pleasure, I walk the spring dew,
wanton and seeking a like-hearted man.

X
Flowers so lovely in the spring groves,
the mood so sad of birds in spring.
Then the spring breeze, so full of desire,
blows open wide my skirts of gauze.

Winter Songs

XIII
Where will we tie our true-love-knot?—
under the cypress of Western Mound.
Windswept and bare, no shelter there,
and the hard frosts will freeze me to death.

There seems to have already been a culture of romance in which extempore quatrains were exchanged, using simple rhymes, stock images, and repeated lines. Lines from this strange, dark quatrain reappear in another quatrain from the same period, dubiously attributed to the famous courtesan "Little Su."

> I ride the coach with polished sides,
> my love rides a dark mottled horse.
> Where will we tie our true-love-knot?—
> under pine and cypress of Western Mound.

Such anonymous quatrain lyrics often show an erotic directness that is rare in early Chinese poetry. No one knows what the tune title *Yan Pan-er* means; the same lyric is also included with a group of lyrics to another melody, *Du-qu*, which may mean "solo song."

Yang Pan-er (also *Du-qu* Song)

> I happened to go out before White Gate
> where the willows can hide the crows.
> My love is the aloeswood incense,
> and I am the brazier where it burns.

"White Gate" was one of the gates of the Southern capital Jian-kang. Crows are not the only things that can be hidden by the dense and low-hanging fronds of willow trees. Judging by the smoking metaphor in the second couplet, the singer here had better luck than the lover who waited by the willows in the *Classic of Poetry* CXL (see p. 40).

Yue-fu of the Northern Dynasties

From the same period as the Southern *yue-fu* we also have a small gathering of very different songs, from the non-Chinese regimes in North China of the fourth to sixth centuries. These have a stylized masculinity that ever afterward became associated with "Northern" modes. In contrast to the soft world of the South, the Northern songs are haunted by death and violence. While it seems probable that many of these songs were indeed originally from the North, they were for the most part preserved in Southern sources and collections, and represented, either by selection or modification, a southerner's idea of what typical "Northern" poetry should sound like.

Qi-yu Songs (Northern Dynasties *yue-fu*)

> I
> A man should act with daring,
> many friends he does not need.
> The hawk goes flying through the sky,
> wrens surge away on either side.

IV

A man is a pathetic bug:
once out his gate, he fears his death:
a corpse that rots in a narrow ravine,
white bones that none will gather and bury.

Song of the Prince of Lang-ya (Northern Dynasties *yue-fu*)

I just bought a five-foot sword,
from the central pillar I hang it.
I stroke it three times a day—
better by far than a maid of fifteen.

In the fourth to sixth centuries, the long anonymous *yue-fu* narrative ballads of the Eastern Han were no longer written in the Southern Dynasties, but they did survive in the North. Below is the famous Northern ballad of a girl, Hua Mu-lan, taking the place of her father in military service. The rulers of the Northern Dynasties were non-Chinese. Note that the ruler is not only referred to by the Chinese title of Emperor but by the non-Chinese title of Khan.

The Ballad of Mu-lan (Northern Dynasties *yue-fu*, 4th–6th century)

Tsk, tsk, and *tsk, tsk,*
Mu-lan weaves by her window.
We cannot hear the shuttle's sound,
we only hear the girl's sighs.
"Now tell me, girl, who's on your mind,
and tell me, girl, who's in your heart?"
"There's no one on my mind at all,
and no one in my heart.

"Last night I saw conscription lists,
the Khan is calling troops everywhere.
The army's rolls were in twelve scrolls,
and every scroll had Father's name.

"My father has no older son,
Mu-lan has no big brother.
I wish to go buy horse and gear
and march to the wars for Father."

In the east mart she bought a fine steed,
in the west mart bought blanket and saddle.

In the north mart she bought a long whip,
in the south mart bought bit and bridle.

At dawn she took her parents' leave,
by the Yellow River she camped at dusk.
She did not hear her parents' calls,
she heard only the sounds of the waters
    of the Yellow River rolling.

In the morning she left the river,
she came to Black Mountain at dusk.
She did not hear her parents' calls,
she heard only the sad whinnying
    from Turkish horsemen on Mount Yan.

She went thousands of miles to battle,
she flew across fortified passes.
The north wind carried the sounds of the watch,
and cold light shone on her armor.
After many a battle the general died,
after ten years the stout troops went home.

She came back and saw the Emperor,
the Emperor sat in his Hall of Light.
Her deeds raised her rank by twelve degrees,
and he gave her a hundred thousand and more.
The Khan then asked her what she wished;
"I've no use to be Grand Secretary.
Just loan me a camel with far-running feet
to carry this lad on its back to home."
When her parents heard that their daughter had come,
they came out of town, leaning each on the other.
When her sister heard that big sister had come,
at the window she made herself up with rouge.
When young brother heard that his sister had come,
he sharpened his knife and got pigs and sheep.
Then she opened the door to her room in the east,
and she sat on her bed in her room in the west.
She took off her buffcoat for battle,
and put on the skirt she used to wear.
At the window she combed her wispy locks,
in the mirror she put on rouge.
Then she went out the gate to see her companions,
and all her companions were struck with surprise.
"We marched together for twelve long years,
and you never knew that Mu-lan was a girl.

The male hare's legs have a nervous spring,
the eyes of the girl hare wander;
but when two hares run side by side,
who can tell if I'm boy or girl?"

As in many other song traditions, lines and segments reappear in different places, often in very different contexts. The opening of "The Ballad of Mu-lan" returns in a group of Northern Dynasties quatrains, in the voice of a more conventional *yue-fu* heroine who is thinking about getting married.

Breaking the Branches of Willows (Northern Dynasties *yue-fu*)

I
A date tree grows before my gate,
year after year it never gets old.
If Mother does not have me married,
how will she get a grandson to hold?

II
Tsk, tsk, and woe is me,
the girl weaves at the window.
We cannot hear the shuttle's sound,
we only hear the girl's sighs.

III
"Now tell me, girl, what's on your mind,
and tell me, girl, what's in your heart?"
"Mother promised to have me married,
and this year again there's no good news."

Other Voices in the Tradition: The Later Lineages of Yue-fu

Once a *yue-fu* such as "South of the Walls We Fought" (p. 228) was established, later poets might compose their own versions under the same title. Such poets frequently thought of themselves as continuing or recreating the mood of the original version, but more often than not, these later versions only remind us of the profound differences separating later imperial China from the more stark and simple world of the anonymous Han *yue-fu*.

Of the great Tang poets, Li Bo (701–762) was the most fascinated by the world of the old *yue-fu*, yet the contrast between his version of "South of the Walls We Fought" and the Han ballad is striking: naming the trouble spots on the Tang frontier and beyond replaces the nameless battleground of the old ballad; and a political message against war takes the place of the ritual acknowledgment of the service of the dead soldiers. Note, however, that the Tang's Central Asian enemies are anachronistically called the Xiong-nu, the great Central Asian kingdom that fought the Han.

Li Bo, South of the Walls We Fought

We fought last year at the Sang-gan's source,
this year we fight on the Cong River road.
We washed weapons in the surf of Tiao-zhi,
grazed horses on grass in Sky Mountain's snow.[2]
Thousands of miles ever marching and fighting:
until all the Grand Army grows frail and old.

The Xiong-nu treat slaughter as farmers treat plowing;
since bygone days only white bones are seen
    in their fields of yellow sand.
The House of Qin built the wall
    to guard against the Turk;
for the House of Han the beacon fires
    were blazing still.

Beacon fires blaze without ceasing,
the marching and battle never end.
They died in fighting on the steppes,
their vanquished horses neigh,
    mourning to the sky.
Kites and ravens peck men's guts,
fly with them dangling from their beaks
    and hang them high
        on boughs of barren trees.
The troops lie mud-smeared in grasses,
and the general acted all in vain.
Now I truly see that weapons
    are evil's tools:
the Sage will use them only
    when he cannot do otherwise.

During the Song Dynasty (960–1279), poetry became increasingly rarefied or reflective, characteristic of the sophisticated self-conscious world that was the Song. But in the fourteenth century, many poets began to look back to the Tang and earlier ages as offering poetic models of directness and simplicity of feeling that seemed to have answers to the various dissatisfactions poets felt with their own "modern" world. In the Archaist movement of the Ming, during the late fifteenth and sixteenth centuries, we can particularly see a longing for the roughness and direct force of Han poetry. Ming Archaist poets often imitated the Han ballads, their imitations much admired in their own time but reviled by critics and poets from the seventeenth century on for being too derivative. The following version of "South of the Walls We Fought" shows something of the Ming desire to recapture the original vitality of the Han song. In place of the austerity of the Han ballad, however, a "Gothic" excess is now evident.

---

[2]The Sang-gan was a river in northern He-bei where the Tang fought the Khitan. The Cong River was in the Pamirs, where the Tang fought the Tibetans. Tiao-zhi was off in Afghanistan, while Sky Mountain was in Xin-jiang. Together, these locations suggest the campaigns in the North and Northwest.

Wang Shi-zhen (1526–1590), South of the Wall We Fought

South of the wall we fought,
by the ramparts south of the wall,
north of the wall black clouds pressed low.
Troops lay in ambush to our east,
while to the west
    scattered horsemen harried us.
They gave us no rest.
The brown dust circled us all around.

The sun turned blue-black,
the sky was a blur.
Gongs and drums sounded,
shouting and clamor.
Turkish riders drew back,
then charged swift as a gale.
The trees seemed like weeds,
the grass was sere.
Who is that crying out?—
a father gathering up his son.
A wife asks of her husband,
pikes and armor in piles,
blood covers skulls.
Every household calls back a soul,
every company mourns its own.

Go tell the Lord General,
if the Lord General does not know.
In our lives we were troops of the borders;
why should we grieve to have graves on the steppes?
The food in the pot,
was not cooked at noon.
Too bad!—the hasty alarm came,
    then we parted for good,
and never were able to finish our meals.
Over the steppes wind whistles
    and with it run our souls.

Can't they glimpse our Lord General,
who sits in the fort with an ivory staff
    beneath a great banner?
In his lifetime he'll surely be made a great noble;
and when dead, in his ancestral temple
    he will eat his fill.

In these versions, we can see something of the operation of the poetic tradition, how earlier poetry was continually reworked for new circumstances. During the sixteenth century, when Wang Shi-zhen wrote the version of "South of the Walls We Fought" above, the Ming had been having major frontier wars with the Mongols. Similarly, the following version by Li Ye-si offers a grotesque vision of violence and ravaged cities that would be hard to dissociate from the horrors of the Qing invasion, through which Li Ye-si lived. The utter collapse of the Ming armies before the invading Manchus (Qing) and the subsequent destruction of poorly defended cities could easily be seen as the inversion of the heroic Han ballad, where soldiers fought to the death and the community acknowledged their service. Far more than Wang Shi-zhen's version, Li Ye-si's version is meant to be read ironically against the original Han ballad: the troops flee rather than die, and the speaker addresses "carrion wrens" rather than ravens.

Li Ye-si (1622–1680), South of the Walls We Fought

South of the walls we fought,
east of the walls we fled;
and though grain grows ripe in the wild,
    it will not save our lord.
Whose skeletons are those
strewn scattered in the streets?
Yellow maggots gorge by day,
lairs of foxes appear by night,
    right by mattress and pillow.
Yellow maggots are teeming,
blood red rivers streaming;
the old woman shuts the gate and cries,
a young child leans on the door and dies.
I went back home,
all the neighbors were gone,
the kitchen was destroyed.
I took a basket, went out the gate,
    arrows were shot at me—
I had wanted to die of starvation,
    it seems I won't get my wish.
I turn my head and see wrens,
and say to the wrens—don't fly away!
Dawn's gaunt flesh will be evening's carrion,
and that will appease your hunger.

The *yue-fu* romantic quatrains of the South also captured the imagination of later writers. While the original anonymous *Yang Pan-er* went as follows:

I happened to go out before White Gate
where the willows can hide the crows.
My love is the aloeswood incense,
and I am the brazier where it burns

the following transformation by the Tang writer Li Bo makes the effective simplicity of the earlier anonymous *yue-fu* elaborate. As was characteristic of Tang myths, Li Bo renders the scene of singing the song itself as part of the song.

Li Bo, *Yang Pan-er*

> You were singing *Yang Pan-er*,
> I urged you to drink more Xin-feng beer.
>
> What is it matters most to me?—
> the crows that cry in White Gate's willows.
>
> The crows cry hidden in willow flowers,
> you grow drunk and stay at my home.
>
> In a mountain-shaped brazier
>   the aloeswood incense burns,
> two columns of smoke form a single vapor
>   passing the purple wisps of cloud.

As literary men wrote their own versions of the old Han and Southern folk poems, many of the basic motifs of those poems also took on a different kind of continuity, reappearing in later lyrics of anonymous singers.

We often find remarkable continuities in the Chinese song tradition, with motifs appearing first in the *Classic of Poetry,* then in *yue-fu,* and again in later song up to the twentieth century. Rather than seeing such continuities as the direct influence of earlier lyrics on later ones, it is best to think of some of these enduring motifs as recurrent expressions of constant social functions. For example, given the general fickleness of the human heart, lovers must swear oaths, as in "Heaven Above," the Western Han song quoted at the beginning of this section:

> By Heaven above,
> I will be your true love,
> let it be forever and never wane.
> When hills no longer rise,
> when the river's water dries,
> when winter thunder rolls,
> and snow in summer falls,
> when sky and earth fuse,
> I'll stop loving you.

Such lovers' vows appear in later popular songs declaring conditions for separation remarkably similar to those in the old Han *yue-fu.* One of the anonymous song lyrics found in the Tang manuscripts recovered in the Dun-huang caves early in the twentieth century follows.

Anonymous Song Lyric to "Boddhisattva Barbarian" (9th–10th century)

> On our pillows we made a thousand vows:
> if you want to end things,
>   you'll have to wait—
>   till the green hills fall;

till steel weights float on the water,
you'll have to wait
    till the Yellow River
    dries to its bed;

 till the stars Shen and Chen
    in broad daylight appear,
till the Northern Dipper moves round to the south.
If you want to end things, it won't be all right
till the sun shines brightly
    at midnight.

The Beginnings of Classical Poetry (Shi)

東
漢
魏
晉
南
北
朝

Sad songs can take the place of tears, far gazing can take the place
of return.   —"Sad Song" (Eastern Han *yue-fu*)

Although traditional critics have always traced the Chinese poetic tradition back to the *Classic of Poetry* and the "Lyrics of Chu," the real beginning of the classical tradition, unbroken for two millennia, is best understood as beginning in the Eastern Han, when a new personal lyric poetry grew up alongside the *yue-fu*. This new "classical poetry" *(shi)* was written in lines of five syllables, the most popular meter for *yue-fu*, and was very different in tone from the stiff, archaic poetry in four-syllable lines that was still written in the Han, in imitation of the *Classic of Poetry*.

The earliest classical poems are anonymous, the so-called Old Poems (*gu-shi*). The most famous of these anonymous lyrics, probably dating from the second century A.D., are the "Nineteen Old Poems." Another group of anonymous parting poems was circulated as the works of Li Ling and Su Wu, two famous figures of the Western Han (though the poems actually date from the second and third century A.D.). In addition to these two groups, there are various other early anonymous "old poems" scattered through early sources.

Although we find a few clumsy attempts at classical poetry in the five-syllable line earlier, it was at the end of the second century A.D. that well-known literary men adopted the new form of classical poetry, just as they began to write *yue-fu* in the same period.

Yue-fu and classical poetry came to be seen as quite distinct in later centuries, but during this early period they are very close and sometimes indistinguishable. The two forms shared a set of common themes and situations which, taken together, embodied the basic concerns of the period, as the Han Dynasty collapsed and warring armies tore the country apart. In *yue-fu*, the speaker often assumed the voice of another person in an imagined situation; classical poetry, by contrast, developed into a first-person lyric, with the poet speaking for himself or herself in the historical present. Although this distinction is by no means consistent in the early period, it guided the evolution of the two forms in separate directions. *Yue-fu* may have been performed by professional singers, probably illiterate; early classical poetry, even in the anonymous "Old Poems," shows at least a rudimentary education; and while both forms were no doubt enjoyed by the educated elite, classical poetry came from them.

In the following selection we first treat *yue-fu*, the anonymous "Old Poems," and early classical poetry by known writers together, showing how they share and make

249

different use of a body of common themes. Then we look at some of the known poets writing in the third century.

The thematic headings are arranged to tell a simple hypothetical story: parting, longing on the road (either on the part of the traveler or the person who remained behind), coming to the city, being alone at night, the message or gift sent to the beloved, the stranger encountering a woman, feasting, impermanence and disillusion, and finally the return. Beneath the story that these themes tell, we can see the overriding concerns of the poets of the period: separation, relationships torn apart and new relationships formed. This is very much a poetry of dislocation, a poetry about outsiders who have left their communities and gone to the city, into service, or into the army.

As we look at some of the phases of this "story," we should also keep in mind the literary historical changes that were occurring. For example, in the first section, on "Parting and Going Off," we see a *yue-fu* version in which the man leaves his family to perform some unnamed act of violent desperation. There are "old poems" on the parting of friends, with consolation offered. On a more sophisticated level, there is the "application" of the conventions of parting to a specific historical experience: in A.D. 192, after rebel factions devastated the capital Chang-an, Wang Can takes leave of friends and kin, and on the road he sees another, terrible example of abandonment and breaking of the bonds of kinship. Finally, from the middle of the third century, Ruan Ji invokes the motif as a general principle—perhaps as part of a decision to quit the social world for the private life of a recluse.

Parting and Going Off

East Gate (Eastern Han? *yue-fu*)

He went out East Gate,
no hope to return;
he came in the gate,
he was shaken with grief.

No food in the kettle;
no clothes on the rack.
He drew his sword,
    he went out the gate,
his children wept and wife pulled at his clothes.

"Other wives want wealth and honor,
I gladly share gruel with you,
share gruel with you:
By broad Heaven above,
by our babies here below,
this is wrong!"

"Get out of my way! I go!
I've waited far too long!

Already my hair hangs white,
    I cannot stay here forever!"

The following two parting poems are preserved in the corpus spuriously attributed to Li Ling and Su Wu. The first is spoken in a woman's voice, saying goodbye to a man leaving for the wars.

Anonymous Old Poem (attributed to Su Wu)

When I bound my hair and became your wife,
there were no doubts in the love we shared.
Our pleasure is just for this evening now,
joy must be had while the time is here.
A traveler thinks on the long road ahead:
you rise and check the time of night.
The stars Shen and Chen have already set,
and you go, taking leave from this moment on.
You are marching off to the battlefield,
we do not know when we'll meet again.
Holding your hand, I give a great sigh,
wet with tears for this parting in life.
Try hard to take care of your years of youth,
and forget not the times of our pleasure.
If you live, you will come back again,
if you die, I will think of you forever.

Anonymous Old Poem (attributed to Su Wu)

Flesh and blood join as branch to leaf;
companions as well depend on each other.
And if on this earth all men are brothers,
no man is a traveler alone on the road.
We two were trees linked limb to limb,
you and I were like one body;
we were once those ducks that mate for life,
now split like the stars Shen and Chen;
once always found at each other's side,
now far as Qin from Turkestan.
When we thought how each must go his way,
our love was renewed with each passing day.
The deer cry out, they think on wild grasses:
which may serve as a figure for honored guests,
and here I have a flask of wine
to offer you, soon to be far away.

251

> I want you to stay and pour it out,
> solace for a lifetime's closeness.

"The deer cry out, they think on wild grasses" is a slightly altered quotation from one of the most famous poems in the *Classic of Poetry,* "Deer Cry" (CLXI) (see p. 275). This piece continued to be performed at banquets to welcome guests. The level of literary education in the poem is suggested less by the act of citing the *Classic of Poetry* than by the stock exegetical response in the following line. This line is the "right answer," the standard interpretation, as if "Deer Cry" had been an identification question on an elementary quiz on the *Classic of Poetry.* Such naïve use of the *Classic of Poetry* may be contrasted with the more sophisticated reference in Wang Can's poem below.

"Seven Sorrows" can be dated with some precision to the year 192 or soon thereafter. In 190, Dong Zhuo had sacked Luo-yang, the "Eastern Capital," abducted the Han emperor Xian, and carried him to Chang-an, the "Western Capital." In 192, fighting broke out between Dong Zhuo's subordinate generals in Chang-an. Wang Can decided to seek refuge with Liu Biao, the governor of Jing-zhou (Jing-man), who had been a student of Wang Can's grandfather.

Wang Can (177–217), Seven Sorrows I

> In Chang-an the fighting was out of control,
> jackals and tigers contrived our doom.
> I abandoned the heartland, I went away,
> to take myself far to the land of Jing-man.
> In sorrow my kinsmen stood facing me,
> my friends came after me, clinging.
> I went out the gates, no one was seen,
> only white bones hiding the meadows.
> On the road was a starving woman
> who abandoned her baby in the grass.
> She heard it wail, she looked around,
> she wiped away tears but did not turn back.
> "I know not where I myself will die,
> I cannot keep us both alive."
> I whipped on my horse and left her there,
> such words I could not bear to hear.
> To the south I climbed the slope of Ba Mound
> and turned my head to gaze on Chang-an.
> And I understood why someone wrote "Falling Stream"—
> I gasped and felt that pain within.

Ba Mound was the tomb of the Western Han emperor Wen, who presided over an age of prosperity and good government that stood in sharp contrast to the war-torn Chang-an of A.D. 192. "Falling Stream" was the title of a poem in the *Classic of Poetry* (153) recalling another capital. It begins:

Biting chill, that falling stream
that soaks the clumps of asphodel.
O how I lie awake and sigh,
thinking of Zhou's capital.

Poets of the end of the second century and the first decades of the third century gave accounts of the collapse of Han civilization—its cities in ruins, human relationships torn apart, unburied bones throughout the countryside. The reason that these large historical upheavals were represented in Chinese literature was perhaps the expectation, articulated in the "Great Preface," that the poet would be the voice of the age.

In the following somewhat later poem by Ruan Ji, the parting is not from anyone in particular, but from the entire social world and the very possibility of having a family. Yet the next-to-last couplet recalls the words of the mother to her abandoned baby in Wang Can's "Seven Sorrows."

Ruan Ji (210–263), Songs of My Cares III

A path will form beneath fair trees,
in eastern gardens, peach and plum.
Autumn winds blow bean leaves flying,
from now begins wasting and the fall.
The glory of flowers comes to tatters,
briar and brush grow in the hall.
I forsook it all, I galloped away,
went off up the foot of Western Hill.
I cannot protect myself alone,
much less take care of wife and child.
Frost blankets the grass of the meadows,
and the year too has reached its end.

Longing on the Road

Nineteen Old Poems I

Keep on going, on and on,
parted from you while alive.
Ten thousand miles apart and more,
each of us at a corner of sky.
The road between is blocked and long,
will we ever meet face to face again?
A Turkish horse leans to the north wind,
a Yue bird nests in the southernmost bough.[1]
Every day we grow farther apart,

---

[1] Yue was the southeastern part of China.

every day my sash hangs looser.
Drifting clouds block the bright sun,
and the traveler does not look to return.
To think of you makes a person old,
and the time of year is suddenly late.
Let it go now, say no more!
just eat well and take care.

The point of the fourth couplet is that each creature longs to be where it belongs: the horse from the North faces north, while the Yue bird chooses to nest on the southernmost bough of a tree. The poem does not indicate the genders of those people parted from, nor is it clear whether the poem is spoken from the viewpoint of the traveler or of the person left behind. In one common alternative interpretation, the last line is understood as the speaker rejecting longing: he or she declares, "I will eat well and take care of myself."

The following poem is early, but more literary than the "Nineteen Old Poems." It uses the conventional images and phrases of the "old poems," but it is also much more specific in the situation it describes.

Qin Jia (2nd century), To His Wife (first of three) (attributed)

Liken man's life to morning dew,
our time in the world is much trouble and pain:
worries and hardships come always too soon,
joyous reunions are always so late.

I brood on my present mission,
each day I go still farther from you.
I sent a carriage to take you home:
alone you went and alone will return.

When I read your letter, I was sad,
at meals, unable to eat.
I sit alone in the empty room,
with no one there to cheer me,
and through long nights unable to sleep,
I toss and turn on the pillow.
Sorrow comes like tracing a ring—
the heart is no mat to be rolled away.

The poem ends with a recollection of *Classic of Poetry* XXVI "Boat of Cypress" (see p. 47):

... This heart of mine is no stone;
you cannot turn it where you will.

This heart of mine is no mat;
I cannot roll it up within . . .

Coming to the City

Coming to the city is less a phase in its own right than the condition of the feast, in which new relationships of closeness are briefly formed in face of danger and death. These relationships are collective rather than individual, and the voice is quite different from the voice that spoke of well-established individual relationships in parting. For a fuller treatment of this theme, see the section on "Feast" (pp. 274–294)

Nineteen Old Poems III

Cypress on grave mound, green so green,
and in the ravine, rocks heaped in piles.
Man is born between earth and sky;
he goes swift as a wayfarer traveling far.
So take your joy in beakers of ale,
pour it full, not stingily;
Drive the cart harder, lash on the nag,
in Luo-yang and Wan good times are had.
Luo-yang is a city teeming full,
where fine hats and sashes seek out their own.
Narrow lanes line the thoroughfares
with many great houses of princes and earls.
Two palaces face each other afar,
paired towers, a hundred feet high and more.
So feast to the end, give the heart glee,
why let grim woes beset you?

Nineteen Old Poems IV

A good feast brings us together today,
of such revels and mirth it is hard to tell all.
The harp is struck, the notes rise free,
new tunes so fine they touch the gods.
Those with virtue sing high words,
those skilled in song will hear what's true.
All of one heart, we share the same wish,
but the thought is withheld, not fully shown.
Man is born into only one time,
a sudden thing, dust whirled in the wind.
So why not whip your fine steed on,
seize a stronghold before some other?
Don't stay a common man and poor,
ever in hardship, always beaten down.

Alone at Night

Nineteen Old Poems XIX

Moonlight glowing so bright
shines on my bed curtains of lace.
From worry and sadness I cannot sleep,
I pull on my clothes, rise and pace.
Though travels are said to have their joys,
better by far to turn home soon.
I go out the door and walk alone,
to whom can I tell these dark thoughts?
I crane my neck, go back in the room,
and tears that fall are soaking my gown.

We may recall that Wang Can was the poet who, in the first of his "Seven Sorrows," was fleeing Chang-an in 192. The following poem was written after he escaped south to refuge in Jing-man; but even there he was unhappy, unable to sleep, "alone at night."

Wang Can, Seven Sorrows II

Jing-man is not my home,
so why do I linger here so long?
In a double boat I went upriver
until sunset saddened my heart.
The last light hung on the ridges of hills,
in the folds of cliffs the shadows increased.
Foxes went scurrying to their lairs,
birds flew circling native groves.
Rolling waves stirred clear echoes,
and monkeys howled from high on shore.
A sudden breeze ruffled my skirt and sleeves,
and silver dew soaked the folds of my gown.
Alone that night I could not sleep,
then lifting my robe, I stroked the harp.
Its silk and beechwood stir passions
and make me bring forth sad melody.
This wayfaring will never end,
the sting of care is hard to endure.

Ruan Ji, Songs of My Cares I

In the night I could not sleep,
restless I rose and plucked the harp.
Thin curtains mirrored the bright moon,
cool breeze blew into gown-folds.
A lone swan screeched out on the moors,

in the north woods birds flew singing.
I wavered then, what would I see?—
troubled thoughts injure a heart all alone.

The motif of longing at night appears also in the following piece from the "Nineteen Old Poems" on the Oxherd and Weaver stars, doomed by the gods to be lodged apart in the heavens because of their love affair. They are allowed to meet only once a year, on the seventh eve of the seventh month, when they cross the River of Stars—the Milky Way—on a bridge formed by magpies.

Nineteen Old Poems X

Faraway lies that star, the Oxherd;
she sparkles, the Maid in the River of Stars.
She stretches her pale and delicate hand,
clacking, she whiles away time with the shuttle.
A day is spent and her weaving not done,
as her tears fall down like the rain.
The River of Stars is shallow and clear,
nor are they so very far apart.
But across that bright and brimming stream,
she gazes with longing and cannot speak.

The story of the Oxherd and the Weaver and their meeting on the Seventh Eve, crossing a bridge of magpies, was a favorite theme of poets over the ages. It was usually treated in terms of frustrated longing (as in the tenth of the "Nineteen Old Poems") or the brevity of the lovers' meeting. The eleventh-century Song lyricist Qin Guan, however, later writing lyrics to the melody "Gods on the Magpie Bridge," gave the theme a memorable twist.

Qin Guan, (1049–1100), to "Gods on the Magpie Bridge"

Fine wisps of cloud sport their craft,
shooting stars bear word of the lovers' pain,
and now far off in the River of Stars
    they are making the crossing unseen.
To meet just once in fall's metal wind
    and in the jade white dew
turns out to be better by far
    than the countless meetings of mortals.

Their tender feelings seem like water,
this sweet moment is as in dream—
how can they bear to turn their heads
    to the path leading back over Magpie Bridge?
But so long as both of them love
    and so long as their love lasts on,

it does not need to be done
every night and every morning at dawn.

The Message and Gift

Watering My Horse by the Great Wall (Eastern Han? *yue-fu*)

Green, green the grass by the river,
thoughts on far travels go on and on;
I can't bear to think on his travels,
I saw him last night in my dreams,
in dream I saw him right by my side,
when I woke he was off in another land,
in another land and a different place,
I tossed and turned and saw him no more.
The mulberry, bare, knows Heaven's wind,
the ocean's waters know Heaven's cold.
Whoever comes shows love for his own,
and no one wants to comfort me.

A stranger came from a far-off land,
and gave me a paired-carp letter case;
I called for the boy to cook the carp
and in it I found the letter.
I read the letter on my knees,
and what did the letter say?—

It began, "Take care of yourself,"
and ended, "I love you forever."

Nineteen Old Poems IX

There is a rare tree in my yard,
green are its leaves, rich in flowers.
I pulled its boughs to pluck a bloom
to send to the one I love.
Sweet scent filled my gown and sleeves,
the way is too far to send it.
What value has the thing itself?—
it only recalls how long since he left.

The Stranger and the Woman

This phase of our hypothetical narrative may be seen as related to "Mulberries by the Path" (p. 234) and "Officer of the Guard" (p. 235), both translated in the *yue-fu* section. The difference is that in these versions the perspective is, at least in part, the man's. The *yue-fu* "Prelude" is a typically fragmentary narrative of a woman showing kindness to the stranger and her husband coming in and viewing them with suspicion.

Prelude (Eastern Han? *yue-fu*)

Swallows go winging before the hall,
gone with the winter, in summer back.
Once there were brothers, two or three,
who were drifters in faraway lands.

"There was no one to patch my worn-out clothes,
there was no one to sew me new ones,
but then I found this good lady,
who took them and sewed them for me."

And her husband comes in through the gate,
he looks at them sideways and glares northwest.
"My husband, do not glare so:
when the water's clear, stones can be seen."

"Stones jut up all along the stream;
it is best to go home and not travel afar."

Nineteen Old Poems II

Green, green is the grass by the river,
in garden the willows are all dense and full.
High in the tower a woman so lovely,
she glows in the window, white and so pure.
Rouge on her cheeks, bright in her beauty,
and she puts out a pale and delicate hand.

Once long ago I sang in the bar room,
now I'm the wife of a traveling man.
He travels for pleasure and never comes home now,
A lonely bed can't be kept empty for long.

Nineteen Old Poems V

To the northwest stands a tower high
whose top is level with drifting clouds,
its windows are meshed with latticework,
with eaves all around, three flights of stairs.
From above came song and the sound of a harp
whose echoes were sad as they could be.
And who could sing a song like that?—
it must be someone like Qi Liang's bride.[2]
The minor tones came out clear with the wind,

---

[2]After her husband was killed in battle, Qi Liang's wife wept for ten days, then committed suicide. The association here is primarily musical: "Qi Liang's Wife's Lament," fancifully attributed to her, was a standard piece in the harp repertoire.

and then they faltered, mid-melody;
once she strummed, then sighed again,
impassioned and filled with melancholy.
I don't care that the singer feels pain,
what hurts is that few understand the sound.
I wish we could be two golden swans
to fly with great wingbeats high and away.

Impermanence and Disillusion

The speaker rides out the city gates, looks at the tombs outside the city, and reflects on the brevity of life. He may decide that the best thing to do is enjoy himself in the present, or he may be left in despair.

Nineteen Old Poems XIII

I drove my wagon out Upper East Gate
and gazed at far tombs north of the walls.
Winds whistled in silver poplars,
cypress and pine lined the wide lanes.
Beneath them lay men long dead,
fading far off into endless night.
They sleep under Yellow Springs sunken from sight,
and never will wake in a thousand years.
Shadow and Light move in endless floods,
our destined years are like morning's dew.
Man's life is as brief as a sojourner,
old age lacks the firmness of metal or stone.
They have brought men here for thousands of years,
a span unmatched by good man or Sage.
With pills and diets men seek the Undying,
and are usually duped by elixirs.
The better way is to drink fine ale
and dress yourself in satin and silk.

Nineteen Old Poems XIV

Each day those gone are farther withdrawn,
each day newcomers grow more like kin.
I went out the gate, stared straight ahead,
and all I saw were barrows and tombs.
The ancient graves have been plowed to fields,
their cypress and pines smashed to kindling.
Mournful winds fill silver poplars,

in their moaning a woe that destroys a man.
I long to turn back to my native town,
I wish to return, but there is no way.

Nineteen Old Poems XV

Life's years do not reach a hundred,
but we always have cares for a thousand.
The daylight so short, the night so long—
why not go roaming, candle in hand?
Joy must be seized at its moment—
why should you wait for times to come?
The fool who cannot bear to spend
wins only mocking in later days.
Qiao the Prince, a man Undying—
it is hard to match his term of years.

The Return

Anonymous Old Poem

At fifteen I went with the armies,
now at eighty at last I come home.
On the road I met one from my village,
"Who remains of my family now?"
"You can see your house far over there,
in the cypress and pines and rolling tombs."
Hares come in through the dog-holes,
and pheasants fly up from the beams.
Wild grains grow in the courtyard,
greens take root by the well.
I boiled the grain for my gruel,
and picked the greens for a soup.
When soup and gruel were both ready,
there was no one to give them to.
Then I went out the gate and gazed east,
and the tears fell, soaking my robes.

One of the most durable openings of *yue-fu* and the "old poems" was going out the gates of Luo-yang, the Eastern Han capital, as in "Nineteen Old Poems" XIII. From the eastern gates could be seen the great cemetery in the Bei-mang Hills. In what seems to be a poem on returning to the city, an ironic reversal occurs: Cao Zhi (or Mr. Ying, as referred to in the title) climbs Bei-mang and looks back on Luo-yang itself, in ruins, sacked by Dong Zhuo in 190 and now virtually deserted.

Cao Zhi (192–232), Sending Off Mr. Ying (first of two)

On foot I climbed up Bei-mang's slopes
and gazed afar on Luo-yang's hills.
Luo-yang, so silent and forlorn,
its halls and palaces all burned away.
Each wall has collapsed and crumbled,
briars and brambles stretch to sky.
I saw no old folks from times before,
in my eyes were only new young men.
I walked at an angle, there was no path,
fields had run wild, tilled no more.
Long had the traveler not returned,
he can no longer tell the boundary paths.
And the moors, so barren and bleak,
no hearthfires seen for a thousand miles.
When I think on this place I used to live,
breath chokes within, I cannot speak.

Coda: Reencounter

Old Poem

I climbed the hill to pick deerweed,
going down I met my husband of old.
I knelt down and asked my husband,
"And how do you find your new bride?"
"Though good do I find my new bride,
she's not so fine as my wife of old.
In fairness of feature both are alike,
but in skill of hands you are not the same.
When the new bride entered the gate in front,
the old wife left by the door at the side.
The new bride weaves the golden silk,
the old wife wove the plain.
Of golden silk, four yards a day,
to more than five yards of the plain.
Then put the plain silk by the gold,
the new bride cannot match the old."

The Poets

Although we do have poems and songs by literary men from earlier in the Eastern Han, the period when we begin to find *yue-fu* and "old poems" written extensively by known authors was during the Jian-an (196–219), the last, and purely nominal

Han reign period, when both the emperor and North China were in the hands of the warlord Cao Cao (155–220), the "Lord Protector."

Cao Cao gathered to himself many of the itinerant intellectuals and writers of the day. The most famous of these intellectuals constituted the so-called Seven Masters of the Jian-an. Cao Cao himself left a small but remarkable collection of *yue-fu*. Cao Cao's son and heir, Cao Pi (187–226), who declared the establishment of the Wei Dynasty, left a somewhat larger collection of both poetry and *yue-fu*. The most distinguished poet and writer of the period, however, was one of Cao Cao's younger sons, Cao Zhi (192–232).

The poets of this period tended to take the forms of treatment of the *yue-fu* and "old poems" and apply them more specifically to their present circumstances. Thus, in the following *yue-fu*, Cao Cao applies the poem on the hardships of travel to a military campaign in which he was engaged.

Cao Cao (155–220), The Bitter Cold

Northward we climbed the Tai-hang Range,
the way was hard-going and steep,
the slopes wound round like sheepguts
and on them our wagon wheels broke.
Trees were bare and bleak,
where the voice of the north wind moaned.
Bears crouched right before us,
tigers roared on both sides of the road.
Few folk dwell in these valleys,
where the snow comes down so thick.
I craned my neck and heaved a sigh,
many the cares on far campaigns.
My heart was then so full of woe
I wished at once to turn back east.
But the rivers were deep, the bridges broken,
mid-journey I faltered, unsure.
In confusion I lost my former path,
and at sundown had no place to rest.
On and on, going farther each day,
men and horses both starving.
With sacks on our backs we gather kindling,
and chop at ice to make our gruel.
Sad is that poem "Eastern Mountains":
it makes my heart always grieve.

When Cao Cao shows his learning, there is often political propaganda involved. "Eastern Mountains" was a poem in the *Classic of Poetry*, attributed to the Duke of Zhou, on a campaign in the East. The Duke of Zhou had been the uncle and "Protector" of the Zhou king; the potential historical analogy, wrapping himself in the respectable mantle of the Duke of Zhou, must have been irresistible for Cao Cao, who held the young Han emperor a virtual captive. The first stanza of "Eastern Mountains" (CLVI) follows:

> We marched to those eastern mountains,
> streaming on and never turning.
> And now we come back from the east,
> in the pall of driving rain.
> We are returning from the east,
> our hearts are grieving for the west.
> Prepare those wraps and gowns,
> make us serve no more with the soldier's gag.
> Now caterpillars are creeping and crawling,
> teeming in mulberry fields.
> I sleep alone all curled up
> right here under the chariot.

We can also see such political use of the *Classic of Poetry* in the following poem by Wang Can, describing his journey to Cao Cao's domain ("the borders of Qiao") as leaving a land in ruins and coming to the "happy land" described in "Huge Rat" (CXIII; see p. 52). Wang Can wrote this poem after leaving Jing-man (see "Seven Sorrows" II, p. 256).

Wang Can (177–217), With the Army V

> I kept faring down roads choked with weeds,
> with a trudging pace, my heart in sorrow.
> When I looked around, no hearth fires seen,
> all that I saw were forests and mounds.
> City walls grew with brush and briars,
> footpaths were lost, no way to get through.
> Canes and cattails to the broad bog's end,
> reeds and rushes lined the long stream.
> A cool breeze blew up at sundown
> and swept my boat gliding swiftly along.
> Wintry cicadas sang out in the trees,
> and the swan ranged, brushing the sky.
> The traveler's sorrows were many;
> I could not stop my falling tears.
> Then at dawn I crossed the borders to Qiao,
> where cares melted, I felt easy and free.
> Roosters were crowing on every side,
> millet swelled the level fields.
> Inns and lodgings filled the hamlets,
> men and women thronged the crossroads.
> Unless in domains ruled by a Sage,

who could enjoy such blessings?
The Poet once praised a "happy land"—
though a stranger here, I still wish to stay.

One of the most common motifs in *yue-fu* and old poems was to see a bird and long to fly away with it, or if a woman were involved, to become a bird and fly away to her or with her (see "Nineteen Old Poems" V). Again, one might recall the last stanza of "Boat of Cypress" (XXVI) in the *Classic of Poetry*:

O Sun! and you Moon!
Why do you each grow dim in turn?
These troubles of the heart
are like unwashed clothes.
I think on it in the quiet,
I cannot spread wings to fly away.

In the Jian-an, this visionary desire to escape can be attached to so mundane a misery as too much work in the office. Like Wang Can, Liu Zhen was one of the "Seven Masters of the Jian-an."

Liu Zhen (d. 217), Unclassified Poem

The work in my office keeps piling up,
with documents scattered everywhere.
My writing brush speeds, no chance to eat,
into late afternoon I have no rest.
I am lost among records and registers,
my head whirling in confusion.
I get away, go west of the walls,
climb the heights and let my gaze roam.
There, a square pool with silvery water,
and in it are ducks and wild geese.
O to have such fleet feathers
and to bob in the waves along with you.

In Cao Zhi's famous "Unclassified Poem," the passing bird is not the means of visionary escape but a potential message bearer, albeit a failed one.

Cao Zhi, Unclassified Poem I

High on the terrace are sad strong winds,
the dawn sun shines on northern woods.
The man is thousands of miles away,
past lakes and rivers, deep and far.
How can my double boat reach him?—
this separation is hard to bear.

A lone goose came flying on its way south
and passing my yard, gave a long sad call.
My thoughts took wing, I yearned for him far,
and wished by this bird to send him word.
But its shape and shadow were suddenly gone,
its swift wingbeats wound my heart.

Things that fly—wild geese or clouds—might serve as messengers to carry word to those far away. In the poem below, note that Chinese bronze mirrors required constant polishing to keep giving a reflection. Xu Gan was another of the "Seven Masters of the Jian-an."

Xu Gan (171–218), Chamber Thoughts III

Clouds go drifting in billowing floods,
and by them I wished to send these words.
They tossed in the wind, wouldn't take my words,
and I faltered here helpless in longing.
All others who part will meet again;
you alone give no date for return.
Since you have gone away,
my bright mirror darkens, unpolished.
Like flowing waters I long for you—
there is never a time that they end.

The closing simile of Xu Gan's poem, with its memorable simplicity, offers a good illustration of how the poetic tradition worked. "Since You Have Gone Away" became a *yue-fu* title in the fifth and sixth centuries, with dozens of attempts to rewrite the last four lines of Xu Gan's poem as a quatrain. The first line is always "Since you have gone away"; the second line speaks of something neglected; the third and fourth lines offer a simile of longing:

Yan Shi-bo (5th century)

Since you have gone away,
the scented curtains hang unraised.
Like whirling snow I long for you,
turbulent sifting, no edge or end.

Wang Rong (467–493)

Since you have gone away,
in the golden brazier no incense burns.
Like the bright candle I long for you,
at midnight burning down uselessly.

Chen Shu-bao (553–604)

Since you have gone away,
cobwebs darken my curtains of lace.
Like the setting sun I long for you
that even a moment does not turn back.

Cao Zhi (192–232)

The turn of the third century was a remarkably violent and dangerous period in Chinese history. Power was not secure. Cao Cao's son and successor, Cao Pi, Emperor Wen of the Wei Dynasty, was naturally uneasy about collusion between the other Cao princes, among whom was his half brother Cao Zhi, considered then and now to be the greatest literary talent of the age. After summoning the princes to his capital in 223, Cao Pi is believed to have arranged the murder of one of his brothers, the Prince of Ren-cheng. Fearful of plots, Cao Pi objected to his brothers' spending time together outside the watchful eyes of the palace. As a result, when his brothers Cao Zhi and Cao Biao planned to journey back to their domains together, Cao Pi forbade them to lodge in the same place overnight. The prohibition enraged Cao Zhi and stirred him to muster his considerable poetic talent in one of the finest sets of poems of the period. Here Cao Zhi portrays himself in a role with great cultural resonance, as the wronged liegeman like Qu Yuan, faring on an endless journey, tormented by the malice of ill-wishers.

Presented to Cao Biao, Prince of Bai-ma

In July of 223, the fourth year of the Huang-chu Reign, the Prince of Bai-ma, the Prince of Ren-cheng, and myself all went to court in the capital for the seasonal gathering of the great nobility. After we reached Luo-yang, the Prince of Ren-cheng departed this life. When it came to September, I was planning to go back to my own domain in the company of the Prince of Bai-ma; but subsequently an official in charge of such matters thought that it would be best if we two princes, returning to our fiefs, should spend our nights at separate locations. The thought continues to provoke resentment in me. Since our final parting will be in a few days, I wanted to show how I feel in these poems, to take my leave of the prince. I completed them in a state of outrage.

I

We greeted the Emperor in Cheng-ming Lodge,
and were soon to turn back to our old frontiers.
We set forth in dawn's cool from the royal city,
and by sundown had passed Mount Shou-yang.
The Yi and the Luo were deep and broad,
we wished to ford, but there was no bridge.
Then sailing by boat we traversed huge waves,

resenting how long was our road to the east.
I looked back with longing to palace towers;
stretching to see them, my heart ached within.

II
Great Valley, so barren and vast,
the trees on the hills, dense and gray.
Torrents of rain turned the road to mud,
the runoff was flooding all around.
Where the roads joined, the tracks broke off;
I changed my course and climbed a high hill.
A long slope stretched to the cloud-covered sun,
my horses were black and smeared brown.

III
Though black and smeared brown, they could still go on,
but my thoughts were a knotted tangle within.
A knotted tangle from what concern?—
that dear kin and I must lodge apart.
At first we had planned to go side by side,
midway it changed, we could not be together.
Owls were hooting on my carriage yoke,
wolves and wild dogs stood in the road.
Blue flies mar both black and white,
those who speak ill estrange kin.
I want to turn back, but there is no path;
I pull back on the reins and stand wavering.

IV
I waver, yet why do I linger here?—
this longing I feel knows no bounds.
Autumn winds bring a faint chill,
cold-weather cicadas cry out by my side.
The moors, so bleak and gloomy,
as the sun is abruptly hid in the west.
Returning birds head to tall trees,
their wingbeats are urgent and swift.
A lone beast goes running, seeking the herd,
plants in its mouth, no chance to eat.
Being touched by these things wounds my cares,
I touch my chest and heave a long sigh.

V
I heave a long sigh, but what can I do?—
Heaven's charge runs afoul of me.
Can I help longing for my full brother,

now gone for good, body never to return?
His lonely soul hovers about his old realm,
his sarcophagus rests in the capital.
Those who survive will go suddenly too,
perish utterly, their bodies decay.
Man's life finds lodging in but one age,
and he goes as the morning dew that dries.
My years sink westward among the stars,
shadow and echo cannot be pursued.
I look on myself, neither metal nor stone,
and I gasp at the sorrow this brings to the heart.

VI

Sorrow in heart shakes my spirit,
let it go then, describe it no more!
A true man's aims include all the world,
a thousand miles is as a near neighbor.
If only this love neither fail nor flag,
though far away, fate brings us closer.
Why need we share bed curtains and quilt,
and only then state the strength of our care?
If troubled thoughts become a fever,
it is naught but the passions of boys and girls.
But such turmoil of love for my flesh and blood—
can I help harboring bitterness?

VII

What broodings come in my bitterness?—
that Heaven's charge truly wins distrust.
It is vain to go seek the Undying,
Red Pine the Undying misled me long.
The last change can come in an instant,
who can seize for himself a century's span?
Now as we part, so long ere we meet,
when again will we thus clasp hands?
Prince, take fond care of your precious self,
may we both enjoy times of frail white hair.
I cease my tears and take the long road,
grasping my brush, I say farewell here.

As earlier in Han poetry, the situation that brought forth poetry more quickly than any other was a threatened relationship: being kept apart from one's kin and friends, being unable to return to one's roots, or, as in the poem that follows, lacking the power to act to help another. Worried that he has the actual power to protect his friends, Cao Zhi invents a parable of protection and gratitude.

Song of a Brown Wren in Wild Fields (*yue-fu*)

High in the trees are sad strong winds,
the ocean's waters lift up their waves.
If you have no sharp sword in hand,
what point in making many friends?

Didn't you see the wren in the fields
that saw the hawk and flew in the net?
The fowler rejoiced in catching a wren,
but a young man saw it and felt sad.
He drew his sword and cut the net,
and the brown wren was able to fly away.
It flew and flew till it touched the sky,
then came again down to thank the young man.

Unclassified Poem II

Tumbleweed rolling, severed from root,
tossed tumbling along with the steady wind.
"I did not expect to rise in whirling gusts,
that blew me off high into the clouds.
Going higher and higher, reaching no bound,
Heaven's roads never run out."
Of such kind too is the traveler
who risks his life on the far campaign.
His woolen tunic leaves limbs exposed,
greens and beans never fill him.
Keep going then, say no more!
brooding troubles make a man old.

Ruan Ji (210–263)

Ruan Ji was an important intellectual figure of the third century and one of the "Seven Sages of the Bamboo Grove." Like many other intellectuals of the period, he was deeply involved in politics; and like most of them, he tried his best to avoid its dangerous entanglements. His poems, all entitled "Songs of My Cares," are often read as containing veiled protests against the Si-ma clan's usurpation of power from the Caos, the ruling house of the Wei, followed by the eventual overthrow of the Wei and the establishment of the Jin Dynasty.

In the first poem, the earlier Warring States Kingdom of Wei, whose capital was Da-liang, seems to be a figure for the Wei Dynasty of the third century. The reference to the Fire of the Quail (a constellation) facing south refers to a prophecy in *The Zuo Tradition* foretelling Jin's overthrow of the state of Guo. Again the pre-Qin domain of Jin may be used as a figure for the Jin Dynasty of the Si-ma clan that supplanted the Wei.

Songs of My Cares XVI

> I was walking about beside Peng Pond
> when I turned my head and gazed on Da-liang.
> The green waters raised their mighty waves,
> the broad moor stretched off boundless.
> In every direction beasts swiftly ran,
> birds soared in flight each following others.
> 'Twas the season when Fire of the Quail faced south,
> when sun and moon stood straight apart.
> North winds were harsh, bitter and cold,
> and the shadowy air shed faint frost.
> I, on a journey and lacking companion,
> in an instant felt pain within.
> Lesser men reckon the due for their deeds,
> the better man stays ever with the Way.
> No regrets that he ends up wasted and gaunt,
> and this is the burden of my song.

From this period we begin to find an increasing number of poems celebrating the exemplary figures of the simple life, such as the Qin Count of Dong-ling, who after the fall of the Qin lived happily as a well-known melon farmer.

Songs of My Cares VI

> I have heard of Count Dong-ling's melons
> close outside Chang-an's Green Gate.
> Patch by patch, they stretch to the paths,
> baby melons and mothers, all joined together.
> Their many hues glow in the morning sun,
> drawing fine visitors from all around.
> An oil-fed fire burns itself out,
> much property brings its owner harm.
> One may spend a life in commoner's clothes,
> put no trust in stipends and popularity.

Songs of My Cares XXXIII

> One more day, then one more evening,
> one more evening, one more dawn.
> Complexion changed from what it was,
> by itself the spirit wastes away.
> I hold fire and boiling water in my breast,
> all things in change are calling to me.
> Thousands of problems that have no end,

more than deftest schemes can comprehend.
I fear only that in an instant
my soul will be whirled away by wind.
All my life I have walked upon thin ice,
and none understand how this heart seethes.

Turning Away

The poets of the generation after Ruan Ji, the poets of the Western Jin (265–316),
continued to use the same themes as the preceding century, polishing them and re-
casting them in ever more elegant diction until the last vestiges of the popular origins of *yue-fu* and classical poetry had disappeared. But already in the poetry of Ruan
Ji a group of new concerns had become increasingly prominent: the desire to sever
relationships rather than to rebuild them, the rejection of the social life, and a turning away from the city to the safety of unpopulated landscapes whose beauties could
take the place of the trappings of wealth and honor. This new poetry of the private
life and the natural landscape was the beginning of interests that would come to dominate literature over the next few centuries. In the following Western Jin poems, nature explicitly replaces a rich mansion, with its fine decorations and entertainments,
which had been the site of sensual delights in "Calling Back the Soul" (p. 204).

Lu Ji (261–303), Calling to the Recluse

At daybreak I felt uneasy at heart,
I dusted my clothes and paused a while;
and pausing there, wondered where to go—
to the recluse who lives in his deep ravine.
At dawn he picks cress in the southern stream,
at twilight he rests by the foot of West Hill.
Light branches like structures stretching to clouds,
dense foliage forms his green feather screens.
The "Frenzied Chu" halts in orchid-filled groves,[3]
and swirling fragrance meets stately trees.
Such tinkling comes from mountain rills,
falls scour jade stones and make them ring.
Magic waves bear away tones of lament,[4]
through layered bends toppling echoes depart.
There is nothing false in this perfect joy,
why strive to mar the simple and pure?
If honor and wealth are hard to devise,
let me unhitch my team and do what I will.

---

[3]The "Frenzied Chu" was the dance performed in "Calling Back the Soul."
[4]The "tones of lament" are those of a fallen state in the "Great Preface" to the *Classic of Poetry*.

Zuo Si (ca. 253–ca. 307), Calling to the Recluse I

I leaned on my staff and called to the recluse
whose weed-grown path is blocked now as ever.
No structures are built in the caves on cliffs,
yet a harp is playing among the hills.
A white cloud halts on the shadowed ridge,
red petals gleam in sunlit groves.
Stony streams scour their agates and jades,
fine fins rise to the surface and sink.
There is no need here for harps or flutes,
hills and streams make their own clear notes.
And why depend on whistling or song,
when tree clumps hum so movingly?
Dried grains are mixed with fall's chrysanthemums,
hidden orchids inserted in folds of gowns.
As I pace here, pausing, my feet grow weary—
I would cast down the pins of my officer's cap.

東漢魏晉南北朝 # Feast

The feast played an important and ever-changing role in traditional Chinese culture, as it does in other cultures; poems and songs, in turn, played an essential role in the feast. The feast and its songs were part of the harvest ritual, as in "She Bore the Folk" from the *Classic of Poetry* (p. 12). In the harvest feast, the community comes together to consume what has been accumulated and to share it with ancestors. The time of the feast is one of relaxation: community restraints are eased, and it is therefore a dangerous moment. The words of a feast song are intended to help the participants into the world of the feast and through its perils. Judging by the content of feast songs in traditional China and elsewhere, pleasure is surprisingly difficult: human beings have to be prodded to it, taunted, cajoled. Once they are persuaded to indulge, there is the danger of dissolution and excess, and the poem must play the opposite role of urging restraint. Side by side in the *Classic of Poetry* we have those two contrasting voices, one mocking restraint, the other urging it.

Classic of Poetry CXV "Hawthorn on the Mountain"

Hawthorn on the mountain,
elm tree in the marsh:
Gown and robe have you,
but never donned, never worn;
cart and horses have you,
never driven, never ridden;
when you wither up and die,
they will delight another man.

Gao tree on the mountain,
niu tree in the marsh:
court and chamber have you,
but never swept or sprinkled down;
bell and drum have you,
never beaten, never struck;
when you wither up and die,
another man will hold them.

Lacquer tree on mountain,
chestnut tree in marsh:
food and drink have you,

so why not have the zither played
to take your joy,
draw out your days,
for when you wither up and die,
another man will take your home.

Classic of Poetry CXIV "Cricket"

Cricket in the hall,
the year draws to its end.
If we don't take our joy now,
the days and months will pass us by.
Yet let not pleasure go too far,
just think upon your stations;
delight should not get out of hand,
the well-born man is circumspect.

Cricket in the hall,
the year is on its way.
If we don't take our joy now,
the days and months will leave us.
Yet let not pleasure go too far,
just think what lies beyond this moment;
delight should not get out of hand,
the well-born man is prudent.

Cricket in the hall,
the chariot lies idle.
If we don't take our joy now,
the days and months will flee us.
Yet let not pleasure go too far,
just think upon your cares;
delight should not get out of hand,
the well-born man is steady.

"Deer Cry" became the representative feast poem, celebrating the ceremonial welcome of one's guests.

Classic of Poetry CLXI "Deer Cry"

Yoo, yoo cry the deer,
eating shoots in the meadow:
Worthy guests are here with me,
play the harp and blow the pipes.
Blow the pipes, trill their reeds,
baskets offered are received.

Men who like me well
show me the ways of Zhou.

Yoo, yoo cry the deer,
eating the cress in the meadow:
Worthy guests are here with me,
their virtue's fame is bright.
They do not look on men with spite,
they are the model for a prince.
And thus I have this fine wine,
for worthy guests to feast and revel.

Yoo, yoo cry the deer,
eating the greens in the meadow:
Worthy guests are here with me
play the harp and psaltery.
Play the harp and psaltery,
bathed in common pleasure.
Thus I have this fine wine,
to feast and delight my worthy guests' hearts.

Death is often not far from the poetry of the feast. The *Classic of Poetry* taunts the listener to feast now, otherwise another man will enjoy what he has gathered after he is dead. But perhaps, even dead, he can still enjoy a party. In "Calling Back the Soul," one of the great feasts of Chinese literature is described—it is an orgy, whose explicitly stated purpose is to give pleasure to the ancestors or the soul of the dead.

from "Calling Back the Soul"

Before those morsels make the rounds,
girl musicians move to their lines.
They ring the bells and roll the drums,
performing the recent songs:
"Wading the River," "Pick Caltrops,"
then breaking into "O Brightness."
And as the beauties grow more drunk,
their rosy faces flush.
Eye's teasing gleam, the half-lidded gaze,
glances come wave upon wave.
Patterned cloaks, fine-woven gowns,
flashy but yet not garish.
Long tresses and trailing locks,
sensual, bright, and alluring.

In two rows of eight, in unison,
they begin the dances of Zheng.
Then, sleeves crossed like staves before them,
slowing the beat they withdraw.

With pipes' and psalteries' wild concert,
they hammer booming drums
Till the whole court of the great house shakes
and the "Frenzied Chu" begins.
The lays of Wu, lyrics of Cai,
and they play the Great Lü.

Men and women are sitting together,
mixed and not kept apart.
Sashes and ribbons are cast down,
the places all in confusion.
Seductive diversions of Zheng and Wei
are performed mixed in among them.
But the coda of the "Frenzied Chu"
is the finest of them all.
. . .
Horn buckles of Jin-craft,
aglow like bright suns.
Bells are rung, chime frames shake,
they sweep the catalpa-wood harps.

Joys of the wine are not set aside
as they pass through days and nights.
When bright lamps burning orchid oil
are set in their splendid frames.
Verses are made to speak longing,
with phrases finely wrought.
And in the heights of their passion,
joined hearts recite.
Drinking we reach the crest of pleasure
to give the ancestors joy.
Soul, turn back!
Return here where you once dwelled. . . .

As the ceremony for the dead turns at last to pleasure, even to ecstasy, so a moment of celebration may turn suddenly somber. The sudden motion from one extreme feeling to another became a commonplace in the tradition, as in the line: "at pleasure's height, many a sad thought comes." The source of the line is a feast song attributed to Emperor Wu of the Han.

Song of the Autumn Wind

Autumn winds rise,   white clouds fly,
plants turn brown and fall,   wild geese go south,
the orchid has its bloom,   chrysanthemum its scent,
my thoughts are on the fairest,   her I can't forget.
I sail in a great galley   across the River Fen,

we breast the midstream current,   raising white waves;
drums and fifes sing out,   a rowing song begins,
at pleasure's height,   many a sad thought comes:
how long does youth's prime last?—   no hope against old age.

In the middle of the feast, dark thoughts come. The feaster may rise, leave the party in the great house, and like the wandering soul to be called back, go wandering off through the darkness. Chen Lin was another of the "Seven Masters of the Jian-an."

Chen Lin (d. 217), [no title]

It was a fine feast, joy suddenly left,
and I, a stranger, could not keep my cheer;
dark thoughts came from deep within,
a sadness stirred by song's clear notes.
I set down my cup and left the happy board,
went aimlessly walking among tall trees,
where the wind whistled down mountain valleys,
and tracks through sky darkened with cloud.
Lost in sad thought I forgot to turn home,
and tears fell with sighs and soaked my robes.

The two following lyrics were originally Han funeral songs. It is said that in the Eastern Han, they came to be commonly performed at feasts.

Dew on the Onion Grass (Han funeral song)

On onion grass the dew
dries quickly in the sun,
dries in the sun but tomorrow
    it will settle again at dawn;
when a person dies he is gone,
    never to return.

The Graveyard (Han funeral song)

Whose yard is it, the graveyard?
where they muster souls of good men and fools,
and the Wraith Master drives them without respite,
man's doom doesn't waver a moment.

The feast song often takes the voice of persuasion; it rejects sadness as waste and calls the listener to pleasure, bidding him light a candle and continue merriment through the night:

West Gate (anonymous *yue-fu*, Eastern Han?)

Out West Gate
I walked in thought:
if we don't take pleasure today,
what day are we waiting for?—
the taking of our pleasure
must come at its due time:
why should we stay in dark brooding
awaiting the moment to come again?

Drink the strong wine,
broil the fat ox,
call to the one your heart loves—
and in this way be sorrow-free.
Man's life does not reach a hundred,
but we always have cares for a thousand:
the daylight so short, the night so long—
why not go roaming, candle in hand?

I am not the undying Qiao the Prince
nor can I match his count of years.
I am not the undying Qiao the Prince
nor can I match his count of years.
A man's life is not of metal or stone,
how can one expect to live a full span?
The miser who cannot bear to spend
wins only mocking in later days.

The feast had another essential function. During the Warring States period, the princes of the domains would gather retainers and maintain them. These were called *si-shi*—"knights ready to die." As they were feasted by the prince, so they were supposed to be ready to sacrifice themselves for him. The dissolution of Han society in the second century A.D. and the rise of warlordism has left us lyrics that seem to represent the return of such a world, in which a lord welcomes retainers as if to say, Drink, take your pleasure now, dark days lie ahead.

Grand (anonymous *yue-fu*, Eastern Han?)

Hard times wait in days to come,
mouth will be parched, lips will be dry,
today we should take our pleasure,
And everyone should be merry.

I passed through all those fabled hills,
and roamed through fields of asphodel,
there the undying Qiao the Prince
gave me a philter in a pill.

I'm sorry these sleeves are so short—
that hands drawn in still feel the cold;
and shamed that there is no Ling-che
to pay his debt to Xuan of Zhao.[1]

The moon is setting, Orion rises,
the Northern Dipper hangs aslant:
kin and comrades at my gate,
hungry, but never getting to eat.

Days of pleasure left are few,
days of pain are many:
how can we forget our sorrow?—
with zithers and drinking songs.

Eight lords came to Huai-nan's Prince:[2]
the true Way brings no bother,
just hitch six dragons to your coach
and frolic at the edge of clouds.

Cao Cao was the greatest of the warlords, and "Short Song" is one of the most famous feast songs in the tradition. Cao Cao takes the conventions of a banquet song like "Grand," and bends it to his political purposes. The second stanza is built on two quotations from the *Classic of Poetry*, the first (according to the standard interpretation) expressing admiration for students (perhaps the itinerant intellectuals of the period), and the second, "Deer Cry," being the standard *Poem* for welcoming guests.

Cao Cao (155–220), Short Song

The wine before me as I sing:
how long can a man's life last?
I liken it to morning's dew,
and the days now past are too many.
The feeling is strong in me,
brooding thoughts I can't ignore.
How can I banish melancholy?—
by Du Kang's gift of wine.

"Blue, blue are your gown's folds,
ever you are in my heart,"
and only because of you,
my concerns keep on till now.

---

[1]The third stanza refers to a story in *The Zuo Tradition* in which Lord Xuan of Zhao fed the starving Ling-che. While serving as a guard, Ling-che later thwarted an assassination attempt against Lord Xuan.

[2]The Han prince of Huai-nan, Liu An, was said to have taken a drug of immortality and ascended to Heaven in broad daylight, along with his eight chief retainers.

"Yoo, yoo cry the deer,
eating the shoots in the meadow:
Worthy guests are here with me
so play the harp and blow the pipes."

Bright and full is the moon—
when will its passage cease?
cares come from deep within,
nor can they be halted.
You crossed the paths and lanes,
taking the trouble to visit me,
now feasting and chatting after hard times,
your hearts consider old kindness done.

The moon is bright, the stars are few,
and magpies come flying south,
three times around they circle the tree,
where is the branch on which to roost?
The mountain does not mind its height,
the ocean does not mind its depth.
The Duke of Zhou broke off his meals,
and all the world turned to him in their hearts.

[Handwritten annotations in margins:]
Shi Jing (learned person).
friends. strong pronoun I.
feel the pressure of being alone.
high expectation of himself.
Theme on drinking

The Duke of Zhou, who served as regent for the Zhou king, was so zealous in taking care of the business of the kingdom that he would spit out his food in the middle of a meal to attend to a problem. Cao Cao, perhaps comparing his own possession of the puppet Han emperor to the Duke of Zhou's regency, also claims the Duke of Zhou's zeal in welcoming his guests, or potential retainers.

Since the height of pleasure often seems to be also the edge of death and destruction, the voice in the feast poem may turn suddenly to caution a wary restraint: "Hold it at fullness, without spilling over." Cao Pi was Cao Cao's son and successor.

Cao Pi (187–226), Grand (*yue-fu*)

This morning let there be joy upon joy,
drink till we're tipsy, never feel drunk,
from passionate strings stir recent tunes,
and from long flutes a clear breath comes,
songs sung to strings can touch man's heart,
all at the party may feel the delight.

All is hushed in the high halls,
and cool winds enter my chamber.
Hold it at fullness, without spilling over,
one with virtue can bring things to happy ends;
yet a good man's heart is full of worries,

his cares are not just one alone;
he comes decently down from his plain rooms,
bolting his food so as to miss naught.
The guests are full now and go home,
yet the host's cares never are done.

Two birds, wing to wing, soar through upper air,
no fowler can take them in his toils:
calm and indifferent, they find Nature's state,
what are glory and splendor to them?

The sudden shifts of mood and topic in Cao Pi's song are the last of the old ballad tradition. During the same period, a new and more formal banquet poetry was coming into being. The "prince" in the first line of the following poem is probably Cao Zhi's half brother, Cao Pi himself.

Cao Zhi (192–232), Public Banquet

The prince honors dearly loved guests,
and he tires not to the party's end.
We roam West Park on clear, cool nights,
canopied coaches one after another.
With clear rays the bright moon washes all pure,
the constellations lie scattered.
Fall's orchids blanket the long slopes,
red blooming covers green pools.
The sunken fish leaps in limpid waves,
and in high boughs the fine birds sing.
Numinous gusts catch our russet hubs,
light carriages move along with wind.
Whirled along, our spirits are free—
may it stay this way forever!

Poetry continued to be composed for state banquets throughout the imperial period, but these excited no more enthusiasm than public banquets anywhere. During the third century, the intellectual and literary interests of the elite increasingly turned to private life and the free associations of friends. In May 353 was held what was perhaps the most famous of all parties: the gathering at the Orchid Pavilion. Wang Xi-zhi, the greatest calligrapher of the day, wrote the preface to a collection of poems written by those present at the party. The poems are no longer frequently read, but the Preface remains the classic statement on parties. The pleasure of the moment, and the impermanence of both the pleasure and those who enjoyed it, remained the dominant themes. But in Wang Xi-zhi's hands these motifs were utterly transformed:

the pleasures enjoyed were tranquil ones and the recognition of their impermanence stirred melancholy reflection rather than despair.

Wang Xi-zhi (321–379), Preface to the "Orchid Pavilion Poems"

In the year 353, the ninth year of the Yong-he Reign, early in the last month of spring, there was a gathering at the Orchid Pavilion on the northern slopes of the Kuai-ji Mountains; our purpose, to carry out the spring ceremonies of purification. Many a good man came, the young and old alike. The place was one of mighty mountains and towering ridges covered with lush forests and tall bamboo, where a clear stream with swirling eddies cast back a sparkling light upon both shores. From this we cut a winding channel in which to float our winecups, and around this everyone took their appointed seats. True, we did not have the harps and flutes of a great feast, but a cup of wine and a song served well enough to free our most hidden feelings.

The sky that day was luminous, and the air was clear; gentle breezes blew softly around us. Above us we looked on the immensity of the universe; then, lowering our eyes, we saw nature's infinite variety. And as we let our eyes roam and our hearts speed from thought to thought, we could experience the greatest delights of ear and eye—this was true happiness.

The times that human beings may be together occur within the fleeting glance of a lifetime: some find them in emotions spoken openly, face to face, in a single room; others invest their feelings in something external as they roam free, beyond the body's world. Our inclinations and aversions have a million different forms; the active man and the contemplative man are unlike; but still, when joy comes with a chance encounter, there is a brief moment of satisfaction, a cheerful self-containment with never a thought of old age coming on. Then, as we weary of the direction in which we are going, our mood shifts with life's events, and depression inevitably follows. In the blink of an eye the joy that has been becomes an experience past—yet still we cannot help having our feelings stirred by it. Even more there are our lives, whether long or short, changing and transforming, but ultimately bound to an end. As was said long ago, "Life and death are the greatest concerns." No escaping the pain in this.

Each time I examine the causes that brought emotion to men in the past, it is as though I have found there the mirror image of my own feelings. Never have I looked upon such writings without a brooding sigh, nor can I find words adequate to explain to myself why. But this I have learned: the belief that life and death are the same is a grand deception; to say that Ancestor Peng's centuries are no more than the lifespan of an infant who died untimely—this is delusion, a forced conceit. Those in later times will look on today as we today look on the past—there is the sadness! For this reason I have written out the list of those present at that time and copied their com-

.ions. Though ages change and experiences differ, all may share what
s deep feelings. And those who read this in later times will also be moved
/ what is in this writing.

More than any other Tang poet, Li Bo was fascinated by the world of the old *yue-fu,* and he recreated the tone of the *yue-fu* feast poem in his own characteristically extravagant way. (The "Prince of Chen" is Cao Zhi.)

Li Bo, Bring In the Wine

Look there!
    The waters of the Yellow River
    coming down from Heaven,
    rush in their flow to the sea,
    never turn back again.
Look there!
    Bright in the mirrors of mighty halls
    a grieving for white hair,
    this morning blue-black strands of silk,
    and now with evening turned to snow.
For satisfaction in this life
    taste pleasure to the limit,
And never let a goblet of gold
    face the bright moon empty.
Heaven bred in me talents,
    and they must be put to use.
I toss away a thousand in gold,
    it comes right back to me.
So boil a sheep,
    butcher an ox,
        make merry for a while,
And when you sit yourselves to drink, always
    down three hundred cups.
    Hey, Master Cen,
    He, Dan-qiu,
    Bring in the wine!
    Keep the cups coming!
And I, I'll sing you a song,
Lend me your ears and take heed—
The bells and drums, the tasty morsels,
    these are not what I love—
All I want is to stay dead drunk
    and never sober up.
Sages and worthies of ancient days
    lie silent now forever,

And only the greatest drinkers
    have a fame that lingers on!
Once long ago
    the Prince of Chen
        held a party in Ping-le Lodge.
A gallon of wine cost ten thousand cash,
    all the joy and laughter they pleased.
        So you, my host,
How can you tell me you're short on cash?
Go right out!
    Buy us some wine!
        And I'll do the pouring for you!
Then take my dappled horse,
    take my furs worth a fortune,
Just call for the boy to get them,
    and trade them for lovely wine,
And here together we'll melt the sorrows
    of all eternity!

The paradox of the poetry of feasting and drinking is the "decision to act sponta-neously," a self-conscious anticipation of unself-consciousness. The drinker con-templates his own unruly behavior and is proud of it; he not only drinks but also contemplates himself drinking. To some degree this lies beneath the tongue-in-cheek hyperbole of Li Bo's "Bring In the Wine." The interplay between forgetting oneself and knowing better attains a characteristic depth in the work of the famous eighth-century poet Du Fu. Du Fu has gone with some friends to White Emperor Cas-tle on a hill east of Kui-zhou on the Yangzi River, where Du Fu was staying at the time. There he gets drunk and decides to show off his horsemanship.

Du Fu (712–770), Having Fallen Off my Horse Drunk, Various Gentlemen Come to Visit Me Bringing Wine

I, Du Fu, have all my life
    been a guest of men of rank;
I set down my wine, sang drunkenly,
    and brandished a gilded spear.

I went off riding, at once recalling
    how I used to be when young;
those hooves set free kicked stones falling
    down into Ju-tang Gorge.

White Emperor Castle's gates lie high,
    up beyond river and cloud,
I hunkered over, sped straight downslope,
    some eight thousand feet.

Lightning bolts arced past white battlements—
    my purple reins trailing;
then to the east I reached the plateau,
    that came from the Heaven-formed cliff.

River villages, wilderness lodges
    all showed themselves to my eyes,
riding whip dangling and bit hanging loose,
    I sped over purple lanes.

In an instant this white-haired old man
    shocked people in the thousands,
but I trusted in my youthful skills
    to ride a horse and shoot.

How could I know of such spirit set free
    in those hooves that chased the wind?—
its bloody sweat and headlong gallop
    like spurting flecks of jade.

Unexpectedly it stumbled at last,
    and I ended up hurt—
when you do what you want in human life,
    humiliation follows.

Then I was utterly miserable,
    confined to pillow and sheets;
and worse still, age's frailties
    added to my vexation.

When friends came by to ask of me,
    I hid the chagrin in my face;
I forced myself up on my cane,
    leaning upon my servant.

As soon as we spoke, we broke at once
    into open-mouthed laughter,
and hand in hand cleared a new spot
    by the bend of the clear creek.

Meat and wine came heaped like mountains
    yet another time,
the plaintive strings at the start of the feast
    stirred the brash music of flutes.

We gestured all to the sun in the west,
    it is unforgiving to man,
we shouted and hooted, tipped upside down
    the green wine in the cup.

What need you come express concern
    for my galloping on my horse?—
have you not seen
    how Xi Kang took such care of his life
    and at last was executed?[3]

Han Yu's poetry sometimes shows a prosaic garrulousness, evident in the following poem; his verse ramblings do give the sense of someone who is, as the title informs us, "drunk." Among a group of friends, Han Yu's interpretation of the feast serves to create a small elite society. In this case, drinking is not to banish sorrow but to free poetic inspiration. The style of each of the poets present at the party is described with an impressionistic image.

Han Yu (768–824), Drunk, to Zhang Shu of the Imperial Library

Others always insist that I drink;
I act like I do not hear;
yet coming to your house today,
I call for wine and urge it on *you*.
The reason—these guests at your table,
and I as well, can write with skill.

Your own poetry is filled with charms:
clouds billowing through spring skies.
Meng Jiao always shocks the common:
Heaven's bloom emitting outlandish bouquet.
Zhang Ji works at antique clarity:
crane on a coach, shunning common flocks.
A-mai doesn't know his characters,[4]
but has outstanding grasp of archaic script:
we let him copy each poem we make,
and he too serves to augment my troops.
These are the reasons I wished to get wine,
awaiting its glow in order to write.

The wine's flavor is biting,
the wine's force swells in the blood.
Our mood grows gradually loose and free,
banter and laughter abounding.

---

[3]Xi Kang (223–262) was a third-century recluse interested in various techniques for prolonging life. The most elementary precaution was to stay out of the troubled politics of the era. He unfortunately failed in this, running afoul of the powerful Si-ma family, and was finally executed.
[4]A-mai is a child's name, and the passage on A-mai's calligraphic skill is probably a joke on a child's handwriting.

Herein the true sense of wine is fulfilled—
all else but this is mere muddle.
All wealthy young men of Chang-an
have rich-smelling meat and garlic served;
but they don't grasp literate drinking,
skilled only in getting red-skirted courtesans drunk.
Although they may find a moment's pleasure,
they're a bit like a crowd of mosquitoes.

I and these various others today
have nothing rank in our sweetness.
Our daring diction daunts demons' courage;
magnificent phrases consort with Canons.
These most perfect jewels are not engraved;
they are spirit-work, spurning all tending.
We are entering now an age of great peace,
men of talent aid a ruler like Shun or Yao.
Our sort are lucky to have no concerns—
may we go on like this from dawn to dusk!

Han Yu's friend and contemporary Meng Jiao offers a more desperate vision of poets drinking. Destruction hangs over them, and their fate is to lose themselves in the celebration of the moment.

Meng Jiao (751–814), Inviting Writers to Drink

Cao Zhi and Liu Zhen could not shun death—
none dare turn their backs on spring's glory.
So let no poet turn down the wine,
for a poet's fate belongs to the flowers.
Han Yu was sent into exile;
Li Bo was prideful by nature.
All time seems suddenly much the same:
in a brief span everyone comes to sighs.
Who says that Heaven's Way is straight?—
it alone skews the shapes of Earth.
The Southerner grieves, being always ill;
the Northerner, joyless at leaving home.
Plum blossom songs pour already through flutes,
and the willows' colors cannot yet hide crows.
So I urge you to cease your songs of the snow,
and in turn drink sadly the rose-cloud wine.
When we sober up, we cannot pass over
this ocean of sorrow, vast without shore.

Li He much admired the work of Li Bo, but carried that poet's extravagance to a level of strangeness Li Bo would never have imagined. Here, as elsewhere in Li He's poetry, the feast becomes almost demonic.

Li He (790–816), Bring In the Wine

In goblets of lapis lazuli,
an amber dark and strong,
from small casks the wine dribbles down
    in pearls of red.
Stew a dragon, roast a phoenix,
    let tears of marble fat be shed;
mesh curtains and broidered arras
    enfold an aromatic breeze.

Blow dragon fifes,
strike lizard-skin drums,
gleaming teeth sing,
frail waists dance.
Now most of all in the green of spring
    with the sun about to set,
and a tumult of peach blossoms falling,
    rainstorms of red.
I urge you to spend this whole day through
    reeling drunk,
for wine will never reach the soil
    of the grave of Liu Ling.[5]

At another extreme, this quiet quatrain by Bo Ju-yi sets up a warm world of light and color inside, contrasted with the cold darkness outside. The scene "invites" even before the explicit invitation is given.

Bo Ju-yi (772–846), An Invitation for Mr. Liu

Green lees of beer newly brewed,
red coals, a brazier's small fire.
Late in the day the sky looks like snow—
would you come drink a cup with me or not?

The tradition of the feast poem continued in the short song lyrics of the tenth and eleventh centuries. These songs were written for professional singing girls to sing at

---

[5]Liu Ling was a third-century eccentric known as a great drinker.

parties. The song title in the following lyric has nothing to do with the theme of the lyric.

Feng Yan-si (903–960), to "The Pleasures of Kicking the Football"

The wine was gone, and the songs
    were ending, but we
    still weren't ready to go, strolling together
    beside the small bridge and clear waters.
You could see the plum blossoms swaying
    in ripples, white
    in the heart of the water;
and the wind blew her dress
    clinging cold against her body—
"But let's not go back just yet, we have to
    stay with the songs to the end,
    and the pleasures of the evening."

Yan Shu (991–1055), to "Washing Creek Sands" (*Huan xi sha*)

Only a moment, this season's splendor,
    this body, a bounded thing;
to part now as if it didn't matter
    easily breaks the heart;
so don't be hasty, refusing
    the party's wine, the banquet's song.

Mountains and rivers fill our eyes, but care
    is wasted on things too far;
besides which, this grief at spring passing,
    at wind and the rain bringing down flowers;
it is better by far to take as your love
    the person before your eyes.

to "Reaching Golden Gates" (*Ye jin-men*)

The autumn dew descends,
dripping away all the red tears
    of orchids from the South.
Experiences past and bygone loves
    bring a mood that has no bounds—
when I think on it, it seems a dream.

The face is older than last year,
but the wind and moon are no different at all.

At my table are welcome guests,
    spiced wine is in the cups,
so don't refuse to spend the evening drunk.

From earliest times, poets realized that utter abandonment to the pleasures of the party was hard to achieve. Eventually a note of retrospective melancholy appears in the poetry of the feast. The poet is too old and has been through it all before. He sets his cushion and pillow beside the mats laid out for the performance of the singing girls, anticipating that he will drink a little and then fall asleep—but still he goes.

Zhou Bang-yan (1056–1121), to "Fragrance Fills the Yard" (*Man ting fang*). Written on a summer day at Wu-xiang Mountain in Li-shui

Breezes age oriole nestlings,
rains fatten the plums,
at noon the fine trees' shade grows cool and round.
The land lies low, hills are near,
brazier's smoke spent on mildewed clothes.
The person calm, hawks exult,
and past the small bridge
    a fresh green trickles on.
Long I lean on the balustrade—
yellow reeds and bitter bamboo
make me think to set sail on that boat of Jiu-jiang.

Every year like the swallows
    on the springtime festival,
drifting wind-tossed over deserts,
come to lodge in these long rafters.
Do not long for what is beyond you—
have a cup of wine always brought.
Weary traveler in the Southland,
    looking battered and worn,
who cannot bear to listen
    to shrill flutes and strings swiftly played.
Beside the mats for the singers
I first set cushions and pillows,
a space to sleep when I get drunk.

We come at last to a small party that equals in fame the gathering at Orchid Pavilion described by Wang Xi-zhi. A group of friends are eating and drinking in a boat on the Yangzi River. They are carried beneath Red Cliff, from which the great Cao

291

Cao had planned to launch a fleet to invade the Southern Kingdom of Wu. The admiral of the Wu fleet, Zhou Yu, launched an attack with fireboats and burned Cao Cao's entire fleet. It was before this great battle that Cao Cao was supposed to have composed his "Short Song," quoted earlier (p. 280):

> The wine before me as I sing:
> how long can a man's life last?
> I liken it to morning's dew,
> and the days now past are too many.
> The feeling is strong in me,
> brooding thoughts I can't ignore.
> How can I banish melancholy?—
> by Du Kang's gift of wine. . . .

Su Shi (1037–1101), The Poetic Exposition on Red Cliff

It was the autumn of 1082, the night after the full moon in September, when I, Su Shi, together with some companions, let our boat drift, and we were carried beneath Red Cliff. A cool breeze came gently along, but it raised no waves in the water. I lifted my wine and toasted my companions, reciting the piece from the *Classic of Poetry* on the bright moon and singing the stanza on the woman's grace:

> The moon comes forth, glowing bright,
> comely woman, full of light,
> Her motions slow, of gentle grace—
> heart's torment, heart's pain.

After a while the moon did indeed come forth over the mountains to the east and hung there in between the Dipper and constellation of the Ox. A silver dew stretched across the river until the light on the water reached off to the very sky. We let this tiny boat, like a single reed, go where it would; and it made its way across thousands of acres of bewildering radiance. We were swept along in a powerful surge, as if riding the winds through empty air. And not knowing where we would come to rest, we were whirled on as if we stood utterly apart and had left the world far behind, growing wings and rising up to join those immortal beings.

By then I had been drinking to the point of sheer delight. I tapped out a rhythm on the side of the boat and sang about it. The song went:

> Oars made of cassia,   magnolia sweeps,
> beat formless brightness,   glide through flowing light,
> far off and faint,   she for whom I care,
> I am gazing toward a lady fair   there at the edge of sky.

One of my companions played the flute, accompanying me as I sang. The notes were resonant and low, as if expressing some deep wound, as if yearning, as if sobbing, as if declaring some discontent. The afterechoes trailed away, attenuating like a thread but not breaking off. Such notes made the dragons dance as they lay sunken in their dark lairs, and caused women who had lost their husbands to weep in their lonely boats.

I too grew melancholy. I straightened my clothes and sat upright. And I asked my companion, "Why did you play it like that?" My companion answered:

> "The moon is bright, the stars are few,
> and magpies come flying south.

Isn't that Cao Cao's poem? Here facing Xia-kou to the west and Wu-chang to the east, where the mountains and the river wind around each other with the dense green of the forests—isn't this the place where Cao Cao was set upon by young Zhou Yu? Once Cao Cao had smashed Jing-zhou, he came down to Jiang-ling, going east with the current. The prows and sterns of his galleys stretched a thousand leagues, his flags and banners blotted out the very sky; he poured himself some wine and stood over the river, hefted his spear and composed that poem—he was indeed the boldest spirit of that whole age, and yet where is he now? Consider yourself and I by comparison, fisherman and woodsman on the great river and its islands, consorting with fish and friends of the deer. We go riding a boat as small as a leaf and raise goblets of wine to toast one another. We are but mayflies lodging between Heaven and Earth, single grains adrift, far out on the dark blue sea. We grieve that our lives last only a moment, and we covet the endlessness of the great river. We would throw an arm around those immortal beings in their flight and go off to roam with them; we would embrace the bright moonlight and have it done with forever. And since I knew that I could not have these things immediately, I gave the lingering echoes of that desire a place in my sad melody."

I replied, "And do you, my friend, indeed understand the water and the moonlight? As Confucius said as he stood by the river, 'It passes on just like this,' and yet it has never gone away. There is in all things a fullness and a waning to nothing, just as with that other thing, the moon; and yet it has never increased and never vanished altogether. If you think of it from the point of view of changing, then Heaven and Earth have never been able to stay as they are even for the blink of an eye. But if you think of it from the point of view of not changing, then neither the self nor other things ever come to an end. So then what is there to covet? Between Heaven and Earth each thing has its own master. If something is not mine, then I cannot take it as mine, even if it is only a hair. There is only the cool breeze along with the bright moon among the mountains. The ears catch one of these, and it is sound; the eyes encounter the other, and it forms colors. Nothing prevents us from taking these as our own. We can do whatever we want with them and they will never be used up. This is the inexhaustible treasure trove of the Fashioner-of-Things, and it serves the needs of both you and I alike."

My companion laughed in amusement, and washing out his cup, he poured himself another. The snacks and fruits had been finished, with plates and cups scattered all around. We all leaned against one another in that boat, unaware that the east was brightening with day.

Anecdotes, Parables, and Profound Jokes

東
漢
魏
晉
南
北
朝

The strength of early Chinese narrative lay not in epic scope and long, intricate plots, but in short narrative forms: the anecdote, the parable, and even the profound joke. There is a wealth of such stories, and they remain, even today, the most widely known legacy of the literary past. Although we cite here "original" sources (many of the stories appear in various early sources and in several variations), such stories were always retold. Some are still being retold and used in modern proverbs.

The philosophers of the Warring States commonly used anecdotes and parables to illustrate their points, and two of the Daoist Classics, the *Zhuang-zi* and the *Lie-zi,* are made up largely of such parables. From one point of view, the anecdote or parable is merely the means to illustrate a philosophical point and make it memorable; but frequently the story becomes greater than any simple lesson that can be summarized from it. In modern Chinese writing and speech, an immediate situation often will be explained by a reference to some particular story from the vast repertoire that has grown up over the millennia.

In the Western Han, current stories and those from antiquity began to be gathered into anecdote books. These were not considered "fiction" in anything like the modern Western sense of the term. Later in the Han we begin to find specialized types of anecdote books, such as ghost stories and joke collections. Though many of the earlier collections have been lost, the best anecdotes were reprinted time and again in later collections. The selection in this section contains works up to the sixth century, but the tradition of anecdote and joke collections continued to the twentieth century.

from the *Zhuang-zi*

The third-century B.C. writer Zhuang Zhou (or Zhuang-zi) was the master of the allegorical parable, familiar in Western literature but relatively rare in Chinese after the *Zhuang-zi.* The following is an allegory of the origin of the universe, which began out of utter undifferentiation ("All-Mixed-Together"). In an instant ("All-of-a-Sudden" suddenly divided) there were the apertures of the senses for seeing, smelling, hearing, and tasting. The senses recognized difference, which was the symbolic death of the primordial state of undifferentiation.

The Emperor of the Southern Ocean was "All-of-a"; the Emperor of the Northern Ocean was "Sudden." The Emperor in the middle was "All-

295

Mixed-Together." All-of-a and Sudden got together in the territory of All-Mixed-Together, who treated them very well. All-of-a and Sudden took counsel together on how they might repay All-Mixed-Together for his generosity: "Every person has seven openings by which they see, listen, eat, and breathe. Only All-Mixed-Together doesn't have any. Let's drill some." Every day they drilled a new opening, and on the seventh day All-Mixed-Together died. . . .

The first seven of the *Zhuang-zi*'s thirty-three chapters are believed to have been composed by Zhuang-zi himself. The remaining twenty-six chapters loosely represent what might be called the "school of Zhuang-zi" (though there is some material from other philosophical schools). The anecdotes in these chapters, probably dating from the late Warring States and Western Han, often make Zhuang-zi himself the central figure.

The parable can say more than a simple statement. In the following anecdote, Zhuang-zi's old friend and rival Hui-zi is afraid that Zhuang-zi wants to take his position. If Zhuang-zi had simply said, "I don't want your position," the claim might be suspect. Through the parable of the mythical *yuan-ju* bird and the owl, Zhuang-zi can successfully evoke a perspective that credibly embodies his contempt for the mundane honor whose value Hui-zi takes for granted.

> When Hui-zi was Minister of Liang, Zhuang-zi set out to go see him. Someone told Hui-zi, "Zhuang-zi is coming to replace you as minister." At that Hui-zi grew frightened and searched for him throughout the kingdom for three days and nights.
>
> When Zhuang-zi saw him, he said, "In the South is a bird name the *yuan-ju*—have you heard of it? Now the *yuan-ju* set out from the Southern Ocean and was flying to the Northern Ocean. It would roost only on the great beech tree; it would eat only the choicest of foods; and it would drink only from springs of sweet water. It happened that an owl had gotten a rotting mouse; and as the *yuan-ju* passed it overhead, the owl looked up, kept an eye on it, and said, 'Beat it!'
>
> "Now that you have the kingdom of Liang, are you telling me to 'Beat it'?" . . .

Hui-zi belonged to a philosophical school that is properly known as the "School of Names" and is sometimes translated as "Logicians." Through witty dialectic, the Logicians addressed elementary questions of logic and epistemology, much as the pre-Socratics did in Greece. The pre-Socratics, however, did not have to contend with the anarchic relativism of a Zhuang-zi, who, for his own philosophical reasons, was willing to make every argument absurd and expose the linguistic basis of questions. In the following anecdote, Zhuang-zi takes the interrogative of Hui-zi's question, "on what grounds" ("how"), and mischievously interprets it as a literal "where," bringing him to his own, no less profound epistemological answer to the question of his knowledge—he knows in "being here."

Zhuang-zi and Hui-zi were strolling on a bridge over the Hao River. Zhuang-zi said, "The minnows are out swimming around. This is a fish's delight."

Hui-zi replied, "You're no fish—on what grounds do you know what a fish's delight is?"

Zhuang-zi answered, "You're not me, so how do you know that I don't know what a fish's delight is?"

Hui-zi: "I'm not you, so I clearly don't know what you know. By the same token you're clearly no fish, so the case is made that you don't know what a fish's delight is!"

Zhuang-zi, "Let's go back to the beginning. What you said was: '*On what grounds* do you know what a fish's delight is?' You already knew that I knew it in asking the question. It know it right here by the Hao River." . . .

We can never precisely define the boundary where a parable or philosophical anecdote passes over into the profound joke, but as in the Jewish tradition, China valued the profound joke as an insight into the limits and motives of human understanding. When Duke Huan of Qi does not respond to his medical mumbo-jumbo, Huang-zi Gao-ao tries another way to cure the duke of his anxiety.

Duke Huan was hunting in the marshes with Guan Zhong, driving his chariot. There he saw a demon. The Duke clasped Guan Zhong's hand: "Zhong, what did you see?" Guan Zhong answered, "I saw nothing." When the Duke returned, he grew sick and fell into a coma. For several days he didn't come out of it.

One of the Qi gentry, Huang-zi Gao-ao, said, "My Lord Duke, you are causing this harm to yourself. How could a demon hurt you? In the concatenation of vital humors, an unrecovered dispersal thereof leads to an inadequacy thereof; when they ascend without a consequent descent, they make a person prone to wrathfulness; when they descend without a consequent ascent, they make a person prone to forgetfulness; and when they neither ascend nor descend, but occupy the heart in the middle, they produce illness."

Duke Huan said, "All right, but do demons exist?" Gao-ao replied, "They do. The hearth has the Li, and the stove has the Ji. And in the shit-pile just inside the door lives the Lei-ting. At the foot of the northeast corner hop the Pei-a and the Hua-long. At the foot of the northwest corner live the Yi-yang. Waters have the Wang-xiang; the hills have the Shen; the mountains have the Kui; the prairie has the Fang-huang; and the marshes have the Wei-tuo."

The Duke said, "Pray tell, what is the appearance of the Wei-tuo?"

Huang-zi Gao-ao replied, "The Wei-tuo, now, is as big around as a wheelhub and as tall as a chariot shaft is long; it wear purple clothes and has a crimson hat. As a creature, it's hideous. When it hears the sound of thunder or a chariot, it lifts its head and stands upright. And whoever sees one is about to become the Overlord of the Domains."

Duke Huan broke into a broad grin. "This was what I saw."

Thereupon he straightened his clothes and set his cap on straight, took his seat, and before the day was over his sickness had gone away without him even noticing. . . .

Warring States orators delighted in the use of serial analogies for a human situation. The *Zhuang-zi* could twist such serial analogies to its own purposes: if we humans can see a hierarchy of awareness below us, each level unaware of what lies above it, then might not we also be unaware of what lies above us? The motif of predation lends an immediacy to the question.

Zhuang Zhou was roaming through the hunting part of Diao-ling when he spied a strange magpie coming from the south, with a wingspan of seven feet and eyes a full inch in diameter. It touched Zhuang Zhou's forehead and then alighted in a chestnut grove. Zhuang Zhou said, "What bird is this? Its wings are huge, but it doesn't go very far; and its eyes are large, but it doesn't notice things." He hitched up his gown, scampered over, took his crossbow in hand, and aimed at it.

Then he caught sight of a cicada that had just found some welcome shade and had completely forgotten itself. A mantis was hanging on to a concealing leaf ready to pounce on it; and seeing the prey it had found, it had forgotten its own person. The strange magpie had come up behind it and was taking advantage of the opportunity; seeing this opportunity, it had forgotten its true situation.

At this Zhuang Zhou shivered in fear. "Oh, how creatures do enmesh each other in troubles, and each calls upon itself something of its own kind." He threw down his crossbow and ran away, and the gamekeeper came chasing after him, yelling.

When Zhuang Zhou got back home, he was disspirited for several days. Lin Ju came and asked, "Why have you been so dispirited recently, Master?" Zhuang Zhou replied, "I take care of my person yet forgot myself. I looked upon muddy water and mistook it for a clear, deep pool. From my master I learned, 'Follow the customs of the country.' Recently I was roaming in Diao-ling and forgot myself. A strange magpie touched my forehead, then roamed into a cypress grove and forgot its true situation. The keeper of the cypress grove thought I was violating it. This is the reason I am disspirited." . . .

Ultimately, in the *Zhuang-zi,* wisdom is not to be found either in the social hierarchy or in the contentious claims of knowledge by contemporary philosophers. Wisdom often comes from simple people who are sages without knowing it. Such anecdotes stage the simple yet profound answer to a difficult question.

The Yellow Emperor was going to meet the Supreme Lump on Ju-ci Mountain. Square-Bright drove the chariot. Chang Yu rode by his side. Zhang Ruo and Xu Peng preceded the horses, while Kun-hun and the Trickster followed the chariot. These seven sages all became lost and there was no one from who to ask the road. Then they came upon a boy herding horses and asked him where the road was.

"Do you know where Ju-ci Mountain is?"

"Sure."

"Do you know where the Supreme Lump can be found?"

"Sure."

And the Yellow Emperor said, "Remarkable young fellow, aren't you! Not only do you know where Ju-ci Mountain is, you even know where the Supreme Lump is to be found! Pray tell me about running the world."

The boy said, "Running the world is nothing more than doing this right here—there's no work to it! When I was younger, I myself went roaming within the Six Ends of the Earth, but it happened that my eyes started to go bad. An elder told me to go ride the chariot of the sun and roam the moors of Xiang-cheng. Now my disease has gotten a little better, and I will again roam out beyond the Six Ends of the Earth. But running the world—that's nothing more than doing this right here—there's no work to it for me."

Then the Yellow Emperor said, "Running the world is indeed no work for you, my boy. Nevertheless, pray tell me about running the world."

The boy tried to refuse, but the Yellow Emperor kept asking. Then the boy said, "How is running the world any different from herding horses? That too is nothing more than getting rid of anything that hurts the horses."

The Yellow Emperor bowed again and again, then touched his head to the ground. And calling the boy Heavenly Teacher, he withdrew.

from the *Han Fei-zi* (3rd century B.C.)

The *Zhuang-zi* may have staged profundity in simple statements, but the philosophers of ancient China were not unaware of the difference between the level of awareness behind a statement and the depths that an interpreter could find in the statement. The *Han Fei-zi* here offers us another profound joke.

Someone in Ying [the capital of Chu] was sending a letter to the minister of the state of Yan. He was writing at night, and there was not enough light, so he said to the person holding the candle for him, "Raise the candle!" And by mistake he wrote down in the letter, "Raise the candle." Now "Raise the candle" was not something he had intended to write in the letter.

The minister of the state of Yan received the letter and was pleased by it: " 'Raise the candle.' This means to honor brilliance. And honoring brilliance means to promote good and worthy men and employ them." The Minister of Yan told this to the king, and the king was greatly pleased. Thus the domain came to be well governed.

Good government is good government, but that was not the intent of the letter. Scholars of recent times much resemble this example.

The right to speak was itself an important motif in the tradition. The "Great Preface" to the *Classic of Poetry* insisted that those who protested in verse could not be held culpable. "Free speech" was an issue in ancient China, and the short paragraph at the end of the following anecdote tersely sums up the consequences of its suppression.

from *Discourses of the Domains (Guo-yu)* (3rd century B.C.)

King Li of Zhou was a tyrant, and the people of the land spoke ill of the king. The Duke of Shao told this to the king, "The folk cannot endure your rule." The king flew into a rage and got a shaman of Wei to go observe who was speaking ill of him. When he informed on someone, the king had that person killed. The people of the land dared say nothing, and on the road, they merely looked at one another with their eyes.

The king was delighted and informed the Duke of Shao, "I have been able to get rid of criticism—indeed, they dare not even speak!"

The Duke of Shao said, "You have only blocked it. Stopping up the mouths of the folk is worse than stopping up a river. A river, dammed, breaks through and always causes great harm to people. So it is too with the folk. This is why those who control rivers make breaches to direct the flow, and those who would govern the folk give them latitude to speak. Thus when the Son of Heaven attends to business of state, he has his dukes, ministers, and everyone down to his gentlemen bring him poems that they have heard:

> blind music master brings him songs;
> chroniclers bring documents;
> the music tutors, conduct rules;
> the sightless singers, expositions;
> dim-eyed chanters, recitations;
> the common players, remonstrations;
> peasants' words come indirectly;
> the "king's friends" offer action's norms;
> the royal kin amend and watch.
> Music master and chronicler instruct him;
> elders and wise old men correct him.

And only then does the king deliberate a matter. This is how the king's business is carried through without going awry.

"The mouths of the folk are like the mountains and rivers of the land, from which goods and useful things come forth. They are like the plain and marsh and bottomland and floodplain, from which our food and clothing is produced. The words spread by the mouth are where our virtues and failings are revealed. By practicing the virtues and guarding against failings we amass goods and useful things, food and clothing. When the folk worry about something in their minds, they express it in their mouths; what takes shape comes out—how can it be right to dam that up! If you dam up their mouths, how many of them will be with you?"

The king refused to listen to him. Thus none of the people in the land dared say anything. After three years the king was driven into exile in Zhi.

In the following anecdote, the Daoist principles of the relativity of values and the alterations of fortune reemerge in something that seems like folk wisdom.

from the *Huai-nan-zi* (2nd century B.C.)

There was a man who lived near the frontier who was well versed in the workings of fate. For no reason his horse ran away into the land of the nomads. Everyone else commiserated with him, but his father said, "How do you know this won't unexpectedly turn out to be good luck?"

After several months his horse returned with fine nomad horses. Everyone else congratulated him, but his father said, "How do you know this won't unexpectedly turn out to be bad luck?" The family was rich in fine horses, and the man's son liked to ride. He fell and broke his hipbone; and everyone commiserated with him; but his father said, "How do you know this won't unexpectedly turn out to be good luck?"

After a year, the nomads made a great raid into the border. The young men in their prime took their bows and went to do battle. Of those who lived near the frontier, nine out of ten died. But this father kept his son only because he was lame.

Thus good fortune turning into misfortune and misfortune turning into good fortune is a transformation without end, and the depths of it cannot be penetrated.

The story of the King of Chu losing his bow appears in several variations. Here it is linked to the large body of apocryphal sayings attributed to Confucius.

from *The Park of Stories (Shuo-yuan)* (1st century B.C.)

The King Gong of Chu was out hunting and lost his bow. His entourage wanted to go look for it, but King Gong said, "Stop. Someone of Chu lost a bow; someone of Chu will find it. Why should we look for it further?"

When Confucius heard of this, he said, "It's too bad he didn't think in broader terms. He might have simply said, 'A person lost a bow; a person will find it.' Why did it have to be only Chu?" This is what Confucius meant by the larger community.

The *Lie-zi* is a collection of Daoist and other texts that may have reached its present form as late as A.D. 300. Most of its stories, however, probably come from the late Warring States and Western Han. One of the most famous of these is the parable of the gulls, making a distinction between unself-conscious action and acting with a "motive" or purpose.

from the *Lie-zi* (?–A.D. 300)

Among those who live by the seashore there was once a man who loved seagulls. Every morning by the shore he would roam around with the gulls, and the gulls that would come to him were never less than hundreds.

His father said, "I've heard tell that the gulls always go roaming with you. Bring some to you so that I can enjoy it."

The next day the man went to the seashore, but the gulls danced above him and would not come down.

Thus they say that the perfection of language is getting rid of language and the perfection of action is action's absence. What is known to average cunning is shallow indeed. . . .

The following parable tells of a hoax that reveals much about the nature of human feeling.

There was a native of Yan who grew up in Chu; and when he reached old age, he returned to his native land. As he was passing the capital of Jin, his traveling companions put one over on him and, pointing to the city, they said, "These are the city walls of the capital of of Yan."[1]

The man's expression changed and the emotion showed on his face.

Then the traveling companions pointed out a shrine and said, "This is the local shrine of your own neighborhood." And the man gave a deep sigh.

Then they pointed out a house and said, "And this was the dwelling place of your ancestors." At this tears began to well up in the man's eyes.

They next pointed out a mound and said, "Here are the graves of your ancestors." And the man could not stop himself from weeping out loud.

His companions doubled over with laughter and said, "We were fooling you before—this is just the capital of Jin!"

The old man was terribly embarrassed. But when he reached Yan and saw the real city walls and shrine, and when he saw the real home and tombs of his ancestors, his feeling of sadness was much diminished. . . .

The story of Venerable Slow-Wit, sometimes called "the foolish old man who moved mountains," was a favorite of Mao Ze-dong's.

---

[1] Yan was a state in far Northeast China; Chu was in South-Central China along the Yangzi River. The state of Jin lay in between.

The two ranges known as Tai-hang and the King's Roof cover seven hundred square leagues and stand hundreds of thousands of yards high. Originally they were located between the southern part of Ji-zhou and the north of He-yang.

The Venerable Slow-Wit of North Mountain was nearly ninety and his dwelling faced these ranges. He was offended at how they blocked the way north and made comings and goings tortuous, so he assembled his household and discussed the matter with them: "Why don't you and I try our best to level those steep slopes so that we could go straight through to southern Yu-zhou and all the way to Han-yin." The various people assembled all promised to do so.

His wife, confessing her doubts, said, "With your strength you could never remove even Kui-fu Hill; how are you going to handle Tai-hang and the King's Roof? And where will you put the earth and rocks?"

Everyone said, "We'll throw them at the edge of the Bo Sea, north of the Shadowland."

Then he led his son and grandson—together, three men to do the carrying—and they broke rock and laid open the soil, transporting it in baskets to the edge of the Bo Sea. A neighbor, the widow Jing-cheng, had an orphan son; and no sooner had he lost his baby teeth than he leapt up to go off and help them. After the seasons had changed several times they came back for the first time.

Old Mr. Know-It-All of the River Bend laughed and wanted him to stop: "You're really not very clever at all! The strength left to you in these final years of your life cannot destroy even a sprout on the mountains. How are you going to manage the dirt and rock?"

The Venerable Slow-Wit of North Mountain gave a long sigh. "Your mind is so rigid and obtuse, there's no getting through to it. You're worse off than the widow and her young child. Though I will die, I have a son who will live on after me. My son has borne me a grandson, and my grandson will also have a son; his sons will have sons, and their sons will bear them grandsons, until there are sons and grandsons without end. Yet the mountains are not going to get any bigger. Why worry that we won't level them?"

Old Mr. Know-It-All of the River Bend could find nothing to say.

The Spirit called the Serpent-Handler heard of this and was frightened that that Slow-Wit would never give up. He reported it to the high god; and the high god, touched by Slow-Wit's sincerity of purpose, charged the two sons of Kua-e to take the mountain ranges on their backs. One they set down in Shu-dong, and the other they set down in Yong-nan. And from that day on there have been no obstacles blocking the way between the southern part of Ji-zhou and Han-yin. . . .

Both the *Zhuang-zi* and the *Lie-zi* contain stories about the perfect mastery of some art. Although there is nothing specifically Daoist about these particular arts, mastery itself and its utter absorption in action seemed close to the condition of the Daoist sage. The following anecdote from the *Lie-zi* gave the tradition its most famous images of the power of music.

Xue Tan studied singing from Qin Qing; but before he had fully mastered Qin Qing's art, he convinced himself that he had learned it all and thus took leave of his master.

Qin Qing would not stop him. He held a parting feast at the road outside the city and sang a sad song, beating out the rhythm. His voice shook the trees in the wood, and the echoes halted the clouds in their motion. Xue Tan then apologized and asked to come back. And for the rest of his life he did not dare speak of going away.

Qin Qing looked around and said to a friend, "Once upon a time the Fair Maid of Han was going east to Qi when she ran short of food. Passing the Yong Gate of Qi, she sold a song for a meal. Once she left, the afterechoes drifted around the beams and rafters for three days without ceasing, and those around thought that she had not gone.

"She passed an inn, and the innkeeper abused her. Thereupon the Fair Maid of Han sang mourning and weeping in long-drawn-out notes. Throughout the whole neighborhood everyone, from the young children to the old people, felt miserable; they faced one another with tears streaming down their faces, and for three days they did not eat. Then immediately they went to find her. The Fair Maid returned, and this second time she sang a lengthy song with drawn-out notes. Throughout the neighborhood everyone, from the young children to the old people, leapt for joy and danced to the clapping of hands, unable to restrain themselves and forgetful of their previous sorrows. Then they sent her off with generous gifts. It is for this reason that to this day the people of Yong Gate are skilled at song and lament, imitating the lingering notes of the Fair Maid." . . .

The story below is found in various sources and is not specifically Daoist.

Duke Jing of Qi paid a visit to Ox Mountain. To the north he looked out over his capital city and tears streamed from his eyes. "Isn't this city lovely—so rich and full of life! How can I bear to be swept away from this city by death? If one never had to die, could I ever leave this place and go elsewhere?"

Shi Kong and Liang-qiu Ju followed his example, and their eyes filled with tears. "We depend on what our lord grants us. We have coarse grain and poor meat to eat; we have old nags and rickety wagons to ride. And if even we don't want to die, imagine how our lord must feel!"

Yan-zi was laughing by himself over at the side.

The Duke rubbed away his tears and looked over to Yan-zi: "I'm feeling melancholy on my outing today. Kong and Ju are both joining me in weeping. Why are you laughing by yourself over there?"

Yan-zi replied, "If a good and worthy man could keep this land forever, then the former Dukes Tai and Huan would have kept it forever. If a brave man could keep this land forever, then the former Dukes Zhuang and Ling would have kept it forever. And had these various lords kept the land forever, you, my lord, would be wearing a straw coat and a bamboo hat, standing in the grainfield. You would be concerned only about your work, with no time to brood on dying. Moreover, my lord, how did you reach your present position? Each in his turn occupied the place you hold by another's departure, until it came to you. Yet you are the only one weeping about it—this shows a lack of feeling for others. I saw a prince who lacked feeling for others; I saw fawning, ingratiating courtiers. And seeing the both of these was the reason I was laughing to myself."

Duke Jing was embarrassed and drank down a goblet as a sign that he had been bested. Then he made his two courtiers drink down two goblets each for the same reason.

from *The Forest of Jokes (Xiao-lin)* (3rd century)

The original *Forest of Jokes* (*Xiao-lin*) was compiled by Han-dan Chun early in the third century and began a lengthy tradition of joke books. Although *The Forest of Jokes* itself has been long lost, a few of its anecdotes have survived in later collections. The following "joke," with its play on value and illusion, is directly in the tradition of Daoist parables.

A man of Chu was carrying a mountain stork when a traveler on the road asked him, "What bird is that?" The man carrying the bird fooled him and said, "It's a phoenix!" The traveler said, "I've long heard of the existence of phoenixes, and now I can see a real one. Will you sell it?"

"Of course."

Then he offered a thousand taels of silver, but the man wouldn't accept it. He doubled the price, and the man gave him the bird. He was going to present the bird to the King of Chu, but during the course of the night the bird died. The traveler didn't give a thought to the loss of his silver, but only regretted not being able to present the bird to the king.

When people in the kingdom told the story, they all thought that it had been a real phoenix and valuable, thus appropriate to present to the king. The king, moved by how the man had wanted to present the bird to him, called him to court and rewarded him richly, ten times what it had cost him to buy the phoenix.

from *The Forest of Tales (Yi-lin)* (362)

The Forest of Tales was a compilation of anecdotes made by Pei Qi in A.D. 362. As is often the case in the early anecdote collections, the original book has been lost, but many of the stories survive by having been copied into other works.

The "profound joke" below belongs to a family of stories about the fabulously wealthy Shi Chong (249–300). The humor is sustained by an interest in the "natural," which was shared by serious writers of the fourth century. The fact that Liu Shi cannot finally "go" reveals the existence of an inner sense of what "feels natural," a sense that proves stronger than the body's urgings and the mind's conscious intentions.

Liu Shi went to see Shi Chong and had to go to the toilet. He saw a large framed enclosure surrounded by crimson gauze hangings, with exquisite mats and pillows, and two servant girls holding holding brocade sachet bags.

Liu Shi immediately turned around and ran back, telling Shi Chong, "I just went into your bedroom by mistake." Shi Chong replied, "That's just the toilet!"

When Liu Shi went back again, the brocade bags that the toilet attendants had been previously holding were in fact to be used to wipe oneself.

After the longest time he couldn't go. He then said to Shi Chong, "A poor gentleman like myself can't use a toilet like this."

He then went to someone else's toilet.

from *Sundry Accounts of the Western Capital (Xi-jing za-ji)* (3rd century)

The following anecdote is the earliest version of the story of Lady Wang, more commonly known as Wang Zhao-jun, sent off by mistake to become the bride of the Khan of the Xiong-nu. Wang Zhao-jun was a favorite topic of later poets and her story was the subject of a famous fourteenth-century Yuan variety play, *Autumn in the Palace of Han.*

Since there were many women in the harem of Emperor Yuan [r. 48–33 B.C.], he didn't have a chance to see them regularly. So he had painters do their portraits, and on consulting the portraits he would summon women to his bed. The court ladies all bribed the painters, some giving as much as a hundred thousand taels, and at the very least offering no less than fifty thousand. Lady Wang alone refused to pay a bribe, and as a result she did not get to see the Emperor.

The Xiong-nu came to court seeking a beautiful woman to be the Khan's bride. Thereupon His Majesty consulted the portraits and chose Wang Zhao-jun to go. When she was leaving, he summoned her to an audience. Her features were the loveliest in all the harem; she was quick in her replies and graceful in her bearing. The Emperor regretted it, but her name had already been decided on. The Emperor had repeatedly commended her to the foreigners, so he couldn't make an exchange.

He then made a thorough investigation of what had happened, and the painters were all beheaded in the marketplace, and the vast fortunes of their households were all confiscated.

Among the painters was Mao Yan-shou of Du-ling; in drawing the human form, he always captured the true image of beauty, ugliness, youth, and age. Chen Chang of An-ling and Liu Bai and Gong Kuan of Xin-feng were all skilled in catching the moving forms of cattle, horses, and birds in flight, but in the beauty of the human form they were not equal to Mao Yan-shou. Yang Wang of Xia-du was a skilled painter, particularly in the use of color; Fan Yu was also good at using colors. On the same day they were all beheaded in the marketplace. Thereafter, painters were rather scarce in the capital.

Of all the collections of anecdotes in the tradition, none had the enduring popularity of Liu Yi-qing's *New Stories and Tales of the Times.* This contained a gallery of wits, fools, eccentrics, and sages primarily from the third and fourth centuries.

Liu Yi-qing (403–444), from *New Stories and Tales of the Times (Shi-shuo xin-yu)*

Cao Pi, Emperor Wen, once commanded Cao Zhi, the Prince of Dong-a, to compose a poem as he took seven steps; if he failed to complete it, he would be executed. Immediately he composed the following poem:

> Beans boiled to make a soup,
> peas puréed to make the base.
> Beanstalks blaze beneath the pot,
> while in the pot the bean sheds tears:
> "We both were born from the same roots—
> how quick you are to burn me!"

The Emperor flushed deeply with embarrassment. . . . (IV.66)

Emperor Wu of the Wei [Cao Cao] was about meet the envoy from the Xiong-nu. Thinking that his own stature was unimposing and incapable of overawing visitors from faraway lands, he had Cui Jigui take his seat, while he himself stood, sword in hand, at the head of the dais.

When the interview was completed, he had someone ask, "What did you think of the King of Wei?" The envoy answered, "The King of Wei really does have an extrardinarily polished appearance, but the man holding the sword by the dais—now that was a warrior-hero!"

When the King of Wei heard this, he speedily dispatched someone to kill the envoy. . . . (XIV.1)

The Reverend Zhi-dun loved cranes. He was living on Mount Yang in eastern Shan when someone sent him a pair of cranes as a gift. After a short time their wings had grown and they were ready to fly away. Zhi-dun didn't want this to happen, so he clipped their wing feathers. The cranes leapt up beating their wings, but they were no longer able to fly. Then they looked around at their wings and hung their heads, looking as though they were in despair.

Zhi-dun said, "Since they are built to cross above the highest clouds, how can they be willing to serve as familiar playthings for men's senses?" He cared for them so that their wing feathers were full grown, then he let them fly away. . . . (II.76)

Huan Chong, the Horse and Chariot General, did not like to wear new clothes. After he had bathed, his wife brought new clothes for him on purpose. The general flew into a great rage and had them taken away quickly. His wife had them taken back to him with the message: "How can clothes ever get to be old if they've never already been new?" Lord Huan laughed heartily and put them on. . . . (XIX.24)

Liu Ling felt awful after drinking too much and was very thirsty, so he told his wife to find him some beer. His wife got rid of the beer and broke the vessels, then, tears streaming down her face, tried to reason with him: "You're drinking too much. This is no way to guard your health. You really should stop!"

Liu Ling replied, "Fine! But I can't restrain myself on my own. The only thing I can do is pray to the gods and spirits and make a vow to stop. So prepare meat and beer for the ceremony." His wife said, "I'll do as you say."

She brought meat and beer before the god's image and asked Liu Ling to make his vow. Liu Ling knelt down and prayed:

> Liu Ling did Heaven bear
> to have a name for drinking beer,
> he downs a gallon at a time,
> then five pints his head to clear—
> anything my wife might say
> be careful not to hear!

Then he took the beer, had the meat brought to him, and ended up collapsed in a stupor. . . . (XXIII.3)

Liu Ling would constantly go on binges and act any way he pleased. Sometimes he would take off his clothes and be naked in the middle of the room. People who saw him criticized him. Liu Ling said, "I think of Heaven and Earth as roof and rafters; I think of my house and rooms as my gown and underdrawers. What are you all doing, getting into my underdrawers?" . . . (XXIII.6)

Bi Zhuo said, "A crab claw in one hand and a cup of beer in the other— to dogpaddle in a pool of beer is enough for me in this life!" . . . (XXIII.21)

Wang Hui-zhi was living in Shan-yang. There was a great snow, and he woke from his sleep at night; he opened up the doors of the rooms, poured himself beer, and everwhere he looked around him was glistening white. Then he stood and hung a mment in thought, reciting "Calling to the

Recluse." Suddenly Dai Kui came to mind. At the time, Dai was at Shan Creek.

Right then and there he got in a small boat and set off for Dai's house in the darkness. He reached it after traveling throughout the night, but once he reached the gate, he went no further, but turned back.

Someone asked him why, and he said, "I set out originally riding my whim; the whim was gone and I turned back. There was no need to see Dai." ... (XXIII.47)

Xi Xi, also known as Xi Gong-mu, served as governor of Yang-zhou. He was Xi Kang's elder brother. When Ruan Ji was in mourning, Xi Xi went to offer his condolences. Ruan Ji was able to show the whites of his eyes as well as the pupils; and when he met a conventional, run-of-the-mill gentleman, he would look at him with the whites of his eyes. When Xi Xi came, Ruan Ji did not lament but showed the whites of his eyes. Xi Xi felt uneasy and withdrew. When Xi Kang heard of this, he went to Ruan Ji with his harp and some beer, and they subsequently became good friends. . . . (XXIV.4—Commentary)

Tao Qian's "Account of Peach Blossom Spring" remains one of the most beloved stories in the Chinese tradition. By Tao Qian's time, the tension between the state and the individual had developed fully. The "Account" offered the image of a third and idyllic possibility, that of a small farming community cut off from history and the larger state.

Tao Qian (365–427), An Account of Peach Blossom Spring

During the Tai-yuan Reign of the Jin (376–396), there was a native of Wu-ling who made his living catching fish. Following a creek, he lost track of the distance he had traveled when all of a sudden he came upon forests of blossoming peach trees on both shores. For several hundred paces there were no other trees mixed in. The flowers were fresh and lovely, and the falling petals drifted everywhere in profusion. The fisherman found this quite remarkable and proceeded on ahead to find the end of this forest. The forest ended at a spring, and here he found a mountain. There was a small opening in the mountain, and it vaguely seemed as if there were light in it. He then left his boat and went in through the opening. At first it was very narrow, just wide enough for a person to get through. Going on further a few dozen paces, it spread out into a clear, open space.

The land was broad and level, and there were cottages neatly arranged. There were good fields and lovely pools, with mulberry, bamboo, and other such things. Field paths crisscrossed, and dogs and chickens could be heard. There, going back and forth to their work planting, were men and women whose clothes were in every way just like people elsewhere. Graybeards and children with their hair hanging free all looked contented and perfectly happy.

When they saw the fisherman, they were shocked. They asked where he had come from, and he answered all their questions. Then they invited him to return with them to their homes, where they served him beer and killed chickens for a meal. When it was known in the village that such a person was there, everyone came to ask him questions.

Of themselves they said that their ancestors had fled the upheavals during the Qin and had come to this region bringing their wives, children, and fellow townsmen. They had never left it since that time and thus had been cut off from people outside. When asked what age it was, they didn't know of even the existence of the Han, much less the Wei or Jin. The fisherman told them what he had learned item by item, and they all sighed, shaking their heads in dismay. Each person invited him to their homes, and they all offered beer and food.

After staying there several days, he took his leave. At this people said to him, "There's no point in telling people outside about us."

Once he left, he found his boat; and then as he retraced the route by which he had come, he took note of each spot. On reaching the regional capital, he went to the governor and told him the story as I have reported. The governor immediately sent people to follow the way he had gone and to look for the spots he had noticed. But they lost their way and could no longer find the route.

Liu Zi-ji of Nan-yang was a gentleman of high ideals. When he heard of this, he was delighted and planned to go there. Before he could realize it, he grew sick and passed away. After that no one tried to find the way there.

The Poetry of the Southern Dynasties

東漢魏晉南北朝

In 317, after the reigning Jin emperor was seized by non-Chinese invaders from the North, the Prince of Lang-ya, Si-ma Rui, declared the reestablishment of the Jin Dynasty in the South and in the following year took the throne as Emperor Yuan. This period is known as the Eastern Jin; it was followed by a succession of other short-lived dynasties—the Song (or Liu-Song, to distinguish it from the more famous Song), the Qi, the Liang, and the Chen. The new capital was established at Jian-ye, later called Jian-kang, in still later times Jin-ling (finally becoming modern Nan-jing). This period, which lasted until 589, when the Sui finally extinguished the puppet Chen regime, is known collectively as the Southern Dynasties.

To this region, often called Jiang-nan, "South of the Yangzi" or the Southland, came many refugees from the North, transferring their own version of Northern culture into the South. They spoke a different dialect from the local inhabitants, a dialect referred to with some pride as "the idiom of Jin." The great émigré families constituted an aristocracy; and even though, with the passage of centuries, this Northern elite mixed with local families, they still prided themselves on their distinction and their role as the true inheritors of Chinese culture. Safe behind their river defenses, they looked with politic disdain on the Northern Dynasties and their non-Chinese overlords.

The old *yue-fu* and virtually all the extant literature of the Han and Wei were preserved in the South. To a large degree, our own view of earlier literature has been shaped by their anthologies and their view of literary history. If earlier Chinese literature had as its highest values the perfect integration of the individual, society, and the polity, the literature of the Southern Dynasties touches on fragmentation and isolation in many forms. China was divided; Southern society was divided, between northerner and indigenous southerner; and despite the claims of the Northern aristocracy, the continuity of cultural history was suspect. We have two great poets of isolation, Tao Qian and Xie Ling-yun, both of whom celebrate solitude and in different ways show a longing for reconstituting bonds with others—Tao Qian praising the anonymous community of farmers, and Xie Ling-yun seeking the true friend who could share his appreciation of the magnificent landscapes of the South.

Toward the end of the fifth century, a new version of fragmentation occurs: the literary coterie or salon, whose members took pride in being a literary elite. These "small societies" were miniature versions of the aristocratic society of the South. Each under the patronage of imperial princes, literary salons were often linked to the political factions that surrounded the princes.

311

Tao Qian (Tao Yuan-ming, 365–427) Jin 265-420

Tao Qian, now the most famous poet of China before the Tang, was the child of a minor gentry family that may possibly have had ties to a more illustrious branch of the Tao clan. Tao Qian himself held and resigned several minor posts before his final decision to give up public life and "return to his gardens and fields." More than anything else, that act of decision was the topic of Tao Qian's poetry—retelling the decision, justifying the decision, proclaiming his contentment with his decision, praising exemplary figures in the past who were models for such a decision. Although the work of some earlier poets had pointed in similar directions, Tao Qian created a poetry of the individual and glorified the individual's claims against the claims of public life. Within the Chinese tradition, however, public life held such authority over the individual that Tao Qian's poetry has often been read as an implicit condemnation of the failure of the Eastern Jin government (i.e., his choice of the private life was a sign of his political disillusionment, and he would have served had the political situation been better). Yet Tao Qian rarely speaks about good government or bad; his target is the oppression inherent in living a public life. Tao Qian asked, as few had before him, what it meant to be happy, and how a person could choose the happy life.

In contrast to the artfully allusive poetry of his contemporaries, Tao's poetry seems unadorned; the impression of simplicity, however, can be misleading. Beneath the surface, Tao Qian took serious early works that others treated as mere ornaments of erudition. We start with a famous passage from the *Analects* (the first part of XI.26), which talks of what it means to be happy and to satisfy one's aims in life. Commentators differ as to why, by the end of the passage, Confucius is "with Zeng Xi," but it has something to do with Zeng Xi's capacity to envisage his own happiness.

Confucius, *Analects* XI.26

> Zi-lu, Ran You, Gong-xi Hua, and Zeng Xi were sitting in attendance on the Master. The Master said, "Don't take into account that I am a few days older than you. Each of you is always saying, 'I am not understood.' If it happened that you were understood, how would you have things be?"
>
> Without giving it a second thought, Zi-lu answered, "Take a domain that could muster only a thousand chariots, a domain wedged in between the great domains, and further a domain that had suffered the passage of armies so that it was reduced to starvation. If I had such a domain in my charge, in about three years I could make them have courage, and moreover understand proper behavior."
>
> The Master grinned at him.
>
> "Ran You, how would you have it be?"
>
> Ran You answered, "Take an area sixty or seventy miles square— perhaps fifty or sixty—if I had charge of it, in about three years I could make it have enough people in it. But when it comes to music and rites, I would have to await a superior man."

"Gong-xi Hua, how would it be for you?"

He answered, "I am not saying that I am capable of this, but I would
like to try to learn it—I would like to be a minor assistant in a black
gown and ceremonial hat in the ceremonies at the ancestral temple
and in the great meeting of lords."

"Zeng Xi, how would it be for you?"

Zeng Xi, who had been playing his harp, let the lingering notes trail
away, then put his harp aside and rose, saying, "It would be
different from the preferences of these other three."

The Master said, "No matter. Each person has told us his life's aims."

Zeng Xi then said, "It would be the end of spring when the spring
clothes had been readied: with five or six young men and six or
seven young boys I would bathe in the River Yi and feel the breeze
on the Rain Altars, and then we would go home singing."

The Master let out a sigh. "I am with Zeng Xi."

In the following poem, Tao Qian does not simply allude to the *Analects* passage;
the entire poem is built around it, as Tao rediscovers the perfect happiness it describes, and then realizes his own isolation and distance from the past.

Seasons Shift

"Seasons Shift" is about roaming at the end of spring. When my spring
clothes had been readied and there was a gentle look to the scenery, I roamed
alone, joined only by my shadow. Distress and delight met in my heart.

I

Ever onward seasons shift,
now gentle grace of this fine dawn.
Attired in my springtime clothes,
I come to the eastern meadows.
From hills is washed a lingering haze,
and Sky's vault veiled by faint wisps.
A breeze is here from the south
and sits brooding over new shoots.

II

Broad waters of the level marsh,
there I rinse, there I bathe.
A scene remote, muted and faint,
I feel delight and peer about.
There's something people often say:
to content the heart is enough.
I toss the dregs from my cup
and cheerfully tipsy, find joy.

III
My eyes run out to midstream,
I remotely fancy the clear river Yi.
Young men and boys, alike in study,
calmly chanting along the way home.
I wish such serenity as my own,
waking and sleeping I beckon to them.
Yet troubled that ours are different times,
so remote I cannot reach them.

IV
On this morning and this eve,
I rest here in my cottage.
Flowers and herbs divided by rows,
trees and bamboo giving shade.
The clear-toned harp across my couch,
a half-full jug of thick wine.
No reaching Yao or Yellow Emperor,
distressing solitude lies in me.

Measuring himself against Zeng Xi, Tao cannot quite reach such satisfaction. But describing himself as a fictive other, he can attain the perfection of anonymous joy. "Master Five Willows" is Tao Qian's image of himself.

Biography of Master Five Willows

We don't know what age the master lived in, and we aren't certain of his real name. Beside his cottage were five willow trees, so he took his name from them. He lived in perfect peace, a man of few words, with no desire for glory or gain. He liked to read but didn't try too hard to understand. Yet whenever there was something that caught his fancy, he would be so happy he would forget to eat. He had a wine-loving nature, but his household was so poor he couldn't always get hold of wine. His friends, knowing how he was, would invite him to drink. And whenever he drank, he finished what he had right away, hoping to get very drunk. When drunk, he would withdraw, not really caring whether he went or stayed. His dwelling was a shambles, providing no protection against wind or sun. His coarse clothes were full of holes and patches; his plate and pitcher always empty; he was at peace. He often composed literary works for his own amusement, and these gave a good indication of his aims. He forgot all about gain or loss, and in this way lived out his life.

The summation: Qian-lou's wife once said, "Feel no anxiety about loss or low station; don't be too eager for wealth and honor." When we reflect on her words, we suspect that Five Willows may have been such a man—swigging wine and writing poems to satisfy his inclinations. Was he a person of the age of Lord No-Cares? Was he a person of the age of Ge-tian?[1]

The following poem requires some knowledge of the double ninth festival (the ninth day of the ninth month). "Nine" *(jiu)* was homophonous with "long time," the "long" of the second line, which is why everyone "loves its name." To promote longevity, chrysanthemums were taken in an infusion with wine; but Tao, lacking wine, eats his chrysanthemums dry.

Dwelling in Peace on the Double Ninth

I was dwelling in peace and loved the name "double ninth." Fall's chrysanthemums filled the garden, yet I had no means to take strong brew in hand. So I swallowed the flowers of the ninth by themselves, and expressed what I felt in words.

Our span is short, desires are many,
so mankind delights in living long.

With star signs the day and month arrive,
and all, by custom, love today's name.

The dews are cool, sultry winds cease,
the air is crisp, the heavens' bodies bright.

No shadows remain from departed swallows,
but sounds aplenty from wild geese coming.

Wine has the power to drive off cares,
chrysanthemums curb declining years.

How can a man in a cottage of thatch
do nothing but watch seasons sink toward an end?

My dusty cup shames the empty jar,
these cold-weather flowers blossom in vain.

I pull my gown close, sing calmly alone,
then, lost in my musings, deep feelings rise.

The quiet life has indeed many joys,
there is something achieved in just lingering on.

---

[1]"No-Cares" and Ge-tian were mythical rulers from the dawn of antiquity—a time when all the world had peace and plenty.

Drinking Wine V

I built a cottage right in the realm of men,
yet there was no noise from wagon and horse.

I ask you, how can that be so?—
when mind is far, its place becomes remote.

I picked a chrysanthemum by the eastern hedge,
off in the distance gazed on south mountain.

Mountain vapors glow lovely in twilight sun,
where birds in flight join in return.

There is some true significance here:
I want to expound it but have lost the words.

Returning to Dwell in Gardens and Fields I

My youth felt no comfort in common things,
by my nature I clung to the mountains and hills.

I erred and fell in the snares of dust
and was away thirteen years in all.

The caged bird yearns for its former woods,
fish in a pool yearns for long-ago deeps.

Clearing scrub at the edge of the southern moors,
I stay plain by returning to gardens and fields.

My holdings are just more than ten acres,
a thatched cottage of eight or nine rooms.

Elms and willows shade eaves at the back,
peach and plum spread in front of the hall.

The far towns of men are hidden from sight,
a faint blur of smoke comes from village hearths.

A dog is barking deep in the lanes,
a rooster cries out atop a mulberry.

No dust pollutes my doors or yard,
empty space offering ample peace.

For long time I was kept inside a coop,
now again I return to the natural way.

Moving My Dwelling I

Long I've wanted to dwell in south village,
and not just because it's a lucky site.

I heard there were many simple-hearted men,
and would enjoy passing mornings and evenings with them.

I had this in mind for many a year,
and this is the task I follow today.

No need that my ramshackle cottage be grand,
I find it enough that it cover my bed.

Neighbors will come from time to time,
we'll have spirited talks of days gone by.

In rare writings we'll find a shared delight,
between us we'll work out problems of meaning.

The Sixth Month of 408: We Had a Fire

My thatch cottage was set in a narrow lane,
that willingly kept splendid coaches away.

It was high summer, steady winds blew hard,
in a moment my grove and house burned down.

Not a building was left on my property,
so we sheltered in a boat before the gate.

Far and wide, this eve of new autumn,
spreading high above, the moon almost full.

Vegetables and melons again begin to grow,
the birds, frightened off, have not yet returned.

In night's midst I stand, I brood on far things,
one glance covers the nine-tiered skies.

Since youth I have clung to lone steadfastness,
all at once it has been more than forty years.

My body and deeds pass on with Change,
yet the seat of my spirit is ever at peace.

In its own right my being is pure and firm—
indeed there is no jade so hard.

I envision those times of Dong-hu[2]
when spare grain was left overnight in the field.

They patted full bellies and longed for nothing,
got up at dawn and at dusk went to sleep.

But since I wasn't born in those times,
I'll just go on watering my garden.

Begging

Famine came, it drove me off,
I did not know where to go.

I finally came to this village,
knocked at a gate, fumbled with words,

The owner guessed what I had in mind;
he gave—I had not come for nothing.

We joked and chatted through evening;
when a pitcher came, we emptied our cups.

Heart's ease in joys of newfound friends,
as we sang and recited poems.

I was touched by such kindness the washerwoman showed,
and am shamed that I lack the gifts of Han Xin.[3]

So much within me, I know not how to thank you,
I must pay you back from the world beyond.

Reading the *Classic of Mountains and Seas* I

Summer's first month, all plants grow tall;
around my cottage, trees dense and full.

There flocks of birds rejoice to find lodging,
and I too cling with love to my cottage.

With the plowing done and the sowing,
now and then I can read my books.

These narrow lanes keep out deep ruts,
and tend to turn away old friends' carts.

In pleasure I pour out the wine of spring
and pick from the garden's vegetables.

---

[2]Like "No-cares" and Ge-tian earlier, Dong-hu was a ruler of mythical antiquity in a world of plenty, free of conflict.

[3]Han Xin was one of the great generals in the founding of the Han. Once he was in desperate straits and a washerwoman fed him, refusing reward. Tao is saying that, unlike Han Xin, he will not rise to high position.

A light rain is moving in from the east,
a nice breeze comes along with it.

I browse in the tales of the King of Zhou
look through the charts of the *Mountains and Seas*.[4]

In an instant I have covered the universe—
if this is not joy, what is?

Xie Ling-yun (385–433)

The beauty of mountains and streams has been commented on by all since ancient times. High peaks that enter into the clouds; clear currents that reveal their
beds; stone cliffs on both shores glinting with all the colors of the rainbow. They
are furnished with green forests and azure bamboo all the year long. As the early
morning fog is about to lift, a tumult of birds and gibbons cry out; and as the
evening sun is about to sink away, sunken fins seem to vie with one another in
vaulting from the waters. This is, in truth, the great city of the Undying within
this World of Earthly Desires. And yet since the time of Xie Ling-yun there has
never again been anyone able fully to be a part of these wonders.
  —Tao Hong-jing (452–536), "Letter in Answer to Xie of the Secretariat"

Xie Ling-yun is perhaps the least read major poet of traditional China. He was an
aristocrat, born into one of the greatest families of the period, and had a tempestu-
ous political career that culminated in his execution. Xie Ling-yin is remembered,
however, as the first great landscape poet of China. His densely crafted couplets and
difficult diction were greatly admired in his age and throughout the following century. Unlike most earlier poets, who used elements of landscape as figures for human
concerns, Xie Ling-yun saw in the landscape the wondrous embodiment of nature's
forms, the experience of which would lead the contemplative viewer to a kind of
enlightenment.

Fu-chun Isle

By night we passed over Fisherman's Deeps,
and by dawn reached the outskirts of Fu-chun.

Steady Mountain far and faint in clouds and fog;
at Crimson Pavilion there was no tarrying.

Countering currents, I bashed through swift dashings;
close by the bank I was blocked by what was strewn.

In truth I was lacking Bo-hun's endowments;
and in peril I passed through Lü-liang's canyon.

---

[4]The *Tales of King Mu* (the "King of Zhou") recount his wanderings through the fabled lands beyond the Chinese heartland. The *Classic of Mountains and Seas* is a fantastic geography.

"To pooling it cometh": best to be inured;
"mountains joined": value halting and lodging.

Lifelong affinity with designs for withdrawal,
floundering, fumbling, burdened by weaknesses.

Long evincing appeals for preferment,
but now fulfilling a pledge for far wandering.

The perennial heart progressively unfolds,
of a million problems each falls away.

Now my concerns are unfurled in the light,
all things beyond me pointlessly stretch and shrink back.

As a poet, Xie Ling-yun was immensely erudite and a dense stylist, which makes his work difficult to appreciate in translation. The fourth couplet above alludes to two Daoist parables of remaining calm in a dangerous situation. In the first, to instruct Lie Yu-kou to keep a steady mind while shooting a bow, Bo-hun Mao-ren walked backward to the edge of a high cliff until his heels were over the edge. In the second, Lü-liang Canyon was a violent stretch of water where Confucius once saw a man floundering: thinking the man was in danger, Confucius sent one of his disciples to rescue him. It turned out, however, that the man was a swimmer who had learned to be at home in such violent flux. After alluding to these two stories of the mind's conquest of fear, Xie looks into the landscape and sees forms that seem to be the very embodiments of phrases in the *Classic of Changes:* "to pooling it cometh" and "mountains joined." In both cases he quotes the advice offered in the *Classic of Changes* and applies it to his own case.

Written on the Lake, Returning from the Chapel at Stone Cliff

Dawnlight to dusk transmuted the atmosphere,
streams and hills infused with a luminous glow:

Such luminous glow can so beguile a man
that the traveler, rapt, neglects to go.

The sun was still low when I left the valley,
its light now grows faint as I board my boat.

These wooded canyons gather hues of the dark,
as white clouds and red draw back twilight haze.

Caltrop and lotus alternate shining verdure,
cattails and reeds rest each on the other.

Pushing back brush, I rush down the southbound trail,
and cheerfully lie by my eastern portal.

When man's cares calm, the world's things grow light,
with the will content, the patterns don't go amiss.

These words I send to those nurturing life:
just try using this Way to search for it.

Climbing an Upper Story by the Pool

A dragon, submerged, enhances sequestered charms,
the swan in flight sends its voice echoing far.

Chagrined by one reaching the drifting cloud-wisps,
shamed by the other, settled in stream's deepest chasm.

My wisdom too awkward to rise by virtue;
my strength that cannot bear retiring to plow.

Now to sea's very edge in pursuit of income,
I lie here ailing, facing barren woods.

Quilt and pillow have blinded me to seasons,
now lifting the curtain, I briefly peer out.

I turn my ear to hearken to waves,
lift eyes to catch sight of towering cliffs.

In this new scene are altered the lingering winds,
fresh sunlight transfigures the shadows that were.

Pond and pool grow with grasses of spring,
garden willows vary the birds that there sing.

Such bounty brings pain at the songs of Bin,
lush growth touches thoughts of Chu's lays.

Dwelling solitary easily comes to last long,
apart from others, hard to steady the heart.

Holding fast to standards is not only of old—
"Being free from distress" is confirmed right now.

Appearing in the middle of a stylistically very elaborate poem, the line "Pond and pool grow with grasses of spring" (in the eighth couplet above) caught the imagination of many traditional critics as being particularly beautiful. In an early anecdote, Xie Ling-yun claimed to have received the couplet in a dream and that it was not truly his own. Whatever its provenance, this couplet became a touchstone of poetic perfection. Immediately following such a "natural" couplet, the very words Xie finds to describe the natural scene recall to him the earlier poems in which the same words were used.

Visiting the Southern Pavilion

Season's close, evening skies clear to translucence,
clouds go their ways as the sun hurries west.

Dense woodlands, infused with a lingering cool,
while a far summit shadows half of Sol's disk.

Long unwell and deluged by sufferings,
from the lodge I stare to where meadow paths fork.

Marsh orchids gradually blanket the trails,
lotuses start to come forth in the pools.

Green springtime was sweet—not wearisome yet;
crimson brightness moved in—this already observed.

Cheerless, I sigh, stirred by all things around;
Star-flecked they hang, these whitened hairs.

Medications and nourishment, desires stop there;
ailments and frailties are suddenly upon me.

To pass away I'll wait for the autumn floods,
let my shadow pause, reclining on former bluffs.

For whom can I clarify hopes and dreams?—
a mind that appreciates will know on its own.

More than any poet before him, Xie Ling-yun used phrases from the classics and older literature to give depth to his work, a depth that is impossible to catch in translation. In the poem above, images and phrases from "Calling Back the Soul" give a ghostly resonance to the scene described. The poet, long sick, rises and looks out the window:

Long unwell and deluged by sufferings,
from the lodge I stare to where meadow paths fork . . .

What he claims to see echoes the strange scene at the end of "Calling Back the Soul" (see p. 210), where the speaker is riding in the dark marshes on a hunt with the king, and they lose the trail:

With the king I dashed through the fens,
racing to see who would be first.
The king himself made the shot,
the black buffalo was slain.
Red dawnlight follows the night,
the time does not let us linger.

Marsh orchids blanket the trail,
the path here fades away.

Bao Zhao (ca. 414–466)

Bao Zhao was a somewhat younger poet than Xie Ling-yun, and in his own land-scape poetry he could not escape Xie's immense influence. Bao Zhao, however, was fascinated by *yue-fu* and song—by its images of passion, heroism, and powerful feeling in an age in which poetry was becoming increasingly controlled and restrained. Bao Zhao's most famous work is a series of verses set to a song, "Hard Traveling"; in place of the dense description and philosophical description of landscape poetry, these pieces utilize dramatic intensity.

Hard Traveling IV

Spill water out on level ground—
it flows off east
or west or north or south.
A man's life too has its destiny—
how can I walk and sigh,
then sit here in despair?
So pour the ale and take your ease,
lift your cup and cease to sing
"Hard Traveling."
My heart is not of wood or stone,
how can I help being moved?—
I waver, swallow back my voice,
and dare not speak a sound.

Hard Traveling II

A Luo-yang craftsman of renown
cast an incense burner of gold,
with thousands of cuts and incisions,
on top he carved Qin's royal daughter
whose hand the immortal lover held.
To sustain your pleasures on cool nights
it was set within bedcurtains
next to bright candles.
On the outside it showed russet glitter,
the scales of a dragon;
inside was held the lavender smoke,
fragrance of musk.
But now your heart has changed overnight,

long I'll sigh facing this
all the years of my life.

Hard Traveling VI

I face the table, I cannot eat,
I draw my sword, I strike the post
and heave a long sigh.
How long can man's life last in this world?—
can I hobble around with drooping wings?
I gave it up, quit office, left,
returned to my home, rested in ease.
At dawn I went forth taking leave of kin,
at twilight turned back to be by kin's side.
I enjoy my son who plays by the bed
and watch my wife as she weaves at the loom.
Good men and sages since ancient times
have all been humble and poor,
which is even more for those like me
upright and alone.

Singing and the scene of singing had always been an important topic in early poetry, but Bao Zhao was particularly interested in dramatizing the occasion of song,
as in the following piece in which the "Song of the Bright Moon" appears within the
poem of the same name. Lady Wei and Zhao Fei-yan are mentioned as types of beautiful women.

Song of the Bright Moon

The bright moon comes forth from eastern hills,
outside the grillwork windows it shines.

Inside the windows, many lovely women,
dressed all in lace, entrancing and fair.

Seeing to make-up, they sit within curtains,
or in the doorways they play clear strings.

Their tresses more beguile us than Lady Wei,
their bodies surpass Zhao Fei-yan by far.

"Now let me sing a song for you,
the song I'll make is called 'Bright Moon.' "

As the wine takes effect, the face relaxes;
the voice is gentle, the heart made known.

A thousand gold pieces don't matter—
what counts is the strength of feeling.

The Southern Courts

Although Tao Qian and Xie Ling-yun were greater poets than any in the late fifth and sixth centuries, the changes that took place in poetry during that time were to have an impact on the development of Chinese poetry far deeper than that of the major poets. This is the period that saw the perfection of the poetic language inherited by the Tang. There was the gradual development of tonal balancing within the couplet, which shifted finally into regulated verse in the seventh century. This was accompanied by a fascination with poetry as a craft, with the style and art of the couplet. Poets judged each other's works, and errors of many kinds might open a poet to criticism. There was also a greater sense of the history of poetry than ever before. Lines of earlier poets or themes from the old *yue-fu* provided topics for endless variation. Moreover, the quatrain folksongs of the South became popular in the Southern courts and provided the inspiration for a new literary quatrain. Poets would send quatrains to one another and answer ones they had received. Taken together, such quatrain sets became an early version of a form of group composition that would mature in the Tang as "linked verse." Quatrains that had no response were called, among other things, "cut-off lines" *(jue-ju),* which later became the term for the quatrain as a distinct verse form.

Many poets of this period were connected with the literary salons presided over by imperial princes of the Xiao family, which ruled both the Qi and the Liang dynasties. There was much composition to set topics: a prince might demand a poem on the occasion of an outing or party, or might test a poet's ingenuity by proposing some object as the topic of a poem.

The theme of the following poem became a favorite *yue-fu* topic in this period and later. The great warlord Cao Cao (155–220) decreed that after his death, his palace ladies should be lodged in the palace known as "The Terrace of the Bronze Sparrow": "My consorts and concubines are all to remain on the Terrace of the Bronze Sparrow, and on that terrace set a six-foot couch surrounded by lace hangings. In the morning and late afternoon let them set out wine, meat, and grain and such things. At dawn on the fifteenth of every month they are to perform before the screen, and then from time to time climb the terrace and gaze toward my tomb in Western Mound" ("Tales of Old Ye"). The curtained enclosure (the "soul-screen") around the couch was the space where Cao Cao's spirit might reenter the world of the living.

The play of sounds in He Xun's version of the "Terrace of the Bronze Sparrow" shows a controlled mastery of presentation that few earlier poets could have achieved. The poem opens with the sound of the wind in the trees, in which begins the music of instruments, then song, and it ends with the sound of the wind in the cypress and pine trees planted on the tomb. He Xun also enjoyed the rich irony of the performers offering wine to the empty spirit enclosure while singing Cao Cao's own banquet song:

> The wine before me as I sing:
> how long can a man's life last?
> I liken it to morning's dew,

and the days now past are too many.
The feeling is strong in me,
brooding thoughts I can't ignore.
How can I banish melancholy?—
by Du Kang's gift of wine.

He Xun (d. ca. 518), Performers on the Terrace of the Bronze Sparrow

Leaves fall from trees in the autumn wind,
through its rustling, clear notes of flutes and harps.

They gaze toward his tomb and sing "Facing the Wine,"
in an empty city they dance at the soul-screen.

In the lonely stillness beneath the broad roof,
the curtains are light and flap in the wind.

Song done, they look at each other and rise:
the sun sets with the sounds of cypress and pine.

Another poet of the same period, Xie Tiao, gives a different treatment of the theme, with Cao Cao's palace women expressing a more decorous grief.

Xie Tiao (464–499), A Companion Piece for Xie Jing's "Terrace of the Bronze Sparrow"

Lace curtains flap on the open frame,
the goblet of wine as it used to be.

The trees grow so thick on Western Mound,
how can he hear the songs sung to flutes?

Tearmarks stain the gowns' sweet folds;
their tender feelings return in vain.

Desolate still is his throne of jade,
even more, our bodies of such small worth.

One of the most interesting poets of this period was the imperial prince Xiao Gang, who later became Emperor Jian-wen of the Liang. Xiao Gang was not a very good ruler, a mere figurehead in the collapsing Southern state, but he was a fine poet and an influential patron. His was a poetry of beautiful, enigmatic patterns, often drawing the eye closely to some detail. Sadly, his attention to sensuous surfaces, to distorting perspectives and illusions in reflection, made his work seem to later Confucian judges of literary value both trivial and morally suspect.

Xiao Gang (503–551), Song of Yong-zhou: II North Isle

Shores shaded by hanging willow fronds,
smooth stream with white parapets within.

Glad to meet others beside these walls,
girls often encountered in boats rushing by.

Sapphire waters splash their long sleeves,
and drifting mosses dye the light paddles.

Source of Pain II

In lonely stillness, echoes from twilight eaves,
dark and somber, the colors with curtains drawn.
There is only the moss on the drain tiles,
like seeing the lacework of spiders.

Song: Every Night

The Dipper stretches across the sky,
the heart every night feels its pain alone.
From the side on my pillow fall moonbeams;
in lamplight half of the bed is in shadow.

Roaming in the North Park by Night

Star sparkles break through trees on the ridge,
moonglow is shadowed by wall tower.
When blooms open in darkness, we cannot tell,
but the bright waves stir, showing currents.

Sending a Palace Lady Back by Night to the Rear Boat

Rows of brocade curtains shelter her barge,
magnolia oars drift, brushing the waves.
Her departing candle still patterns the waters,
her lingering scent still fills my boat.

On a Lone Duck

It dives in shallows for beakfuls of moss,
heads to sandy isles to preen its feathers.
It was ready to fly off all by itself,
then found its reflection and lingered.

New Swallows

In response to the season new birds return,
all fly to the chambers where music plays.
Into the curtains, ringing bangles alarm them,
through windows they're blocked by the dancers' gowns.

The Reflection of a High Building in the Water

At the water's bottom a tracery screen appears,
among the duckweed an inverted vault afloat.
When breezes comes, the colors are unruined;
the waves pass on, the reflection remains.

The courtly quatrain, particularly treating motifs of women and love, became a popular form in the early sixth century. The poet would quickly sketch a scene of desire, longing in absence, or charm, with feeling revealed by some gesture or piece of evidence.

Liu Yan (Emperor Wu of the Liang, 464–549), Zi-ye Song

In her yearning it seems she wants to come closer,
but she's bashful and will not advance.
From lips' red emerges a song of passion,
white fingers stroke the charming strings.

Shen Yue (441–513), Going Out Early and Meeting an Old Love, I Give This to Her in Her Carriage

Traces of rouge yet darken your skin,
and a dusting of powder remains there still.
Where was it you stayed last night
that this morning you make your way home in the dew?

Madam Shen (early 6th century), Song on Reflections in Water

Her light tresses mimic the drifting clouds,
her twin brows copy the crescent moon.
Where waters clear, she straightens skewed hairpins;
where duckweed opens, she smooths tousled hair.

Wu Jun (469–520), Quatrains on Various Topics I

Day's cicadas had already brought yearning's pain,
then night's dew once again soaked her robes.
Before, of course, there was parting's heartache,
and now this evening, the fireflies.

Wang Seng-ru (465–522), Spring Longings

The snows are over, branches turn green,
ice opens, the water is blue.
And again I hear the oriole's longing,
that leads me to write these songs of love.

Liu Xiao-chuo (481–539), On a Woman Unwilling to Come Forth

Where the curtain opens, I see hairpin's shadow,
when the hangings stir, I hear bracelets' sound.
She hesitates and will not come forth,
always shy of the candle's light.

Southern poets of the sixth century developed a sense of poetic craftsmanship that remained at the heart of later Tang poetry, though Tang poets tended to be less heavy-handed with the craft of the parallel couplet. Poets of the Southern courts would often go on excursions with princes or emperors and would be asked to write poems on the same topics or using the same rhymes as imperial poems. The first of the following poems by Yu Xin is written as he accompanies a Liang prince, Xiao Yi, on an excursion on the Yangzi River.

Yu Xin (513–581), Respectfully Answering "Drifting on the River"

The spring river comes down past White Emperor Castle,
and our painted barges head toward Brown Ox Gorge.

Brocade rigging bends around shoals of gravel,
magnolia oars avoid sandbars of reeds.

Drenched petals drift along with the waters,
empty nests go with currents, chasing their trees.

Boat-building scaffolds came down to Jian-ping,
then war galleys came floating to Jing-men.

Many tall trees by shrines on the shore,
enough far towers on castles in hills.

As the sun goes down, winds calm on the river,
the dragon sings out and turns back upstream.

When the Jin set out to conquer the Three Kingdoms' state of Wu, the general Wang Jun had a river fleet constructed upstream in Sichuan. The Wu governor of Jian-ping found pieces of the scaffolding for boat construction floating downstream and knew that an attack was impending. Although Yu Xin celebrates the excursion with poetic grace, these historical echoes recall the serious threat that the Liang Dynasty faced from the North.

Study in the Hills

I sought in vast stillness calm chambers,
I went through dense foliage to my study in the hills.

Oozing and trickling, waters moistened the road,
arching in domes, stones reclined on the stairs.

A log in the shallows, not budging at all,
roots coiling round, only half buried.

Round beads plummet from evening chrysanthemums,
slender fires fall from the hollow ash tree.

yet only the gloom of the wind-blown clouds
makes me feel still more how heart's cares have erred.

A Companion Piece for Grand Master Yan's "Newly Cleared Skies"

Vapors over water consume evening's light,
rays thrown back shine on the river's high banks.

Sopping petals blow away, but not far,
shadowy clouds draw in and still lower.

Swallows dry up and again turn to stone,
the dragon falls apart and once more is mud.[5]

A sweet-smelling spring pours a chilly torrent,
a small skiff fishes in a brook of lotuses.

If only the mind could take all things as equal—
why feel distress that things are not equal at all?

The Image of the Southern Dynasties

As important as the Southern Dynasties were in their own right in the history of Chinese literature, they were no less important as a world evoked in the poetic imagination of later centuries: witty recluses, zany aristocrats, pleasure-loving and decadent emperors. This image of the Southern Dynasties was by and large a creation of ninth-century poets, who perhaps found in the South of the third to sixth centuries an alluring counterpart to the Tang's own slow dissolution.

The following rather straightforward ballad recounts the beginning of the Southern Dynasties with the Jin Dynasty's loss of the North in the Yong-jia reign (307–312).

---

[5]There is a legend of stone swallows that turned into birds when it rained, then became stone again when they dried out. Dragons were formed of mud and clay in sacrifices for rain.

Zhang Ji (ca. 767–ca. 830), A Ballad of the Yong-jia

Then the blond-headed Xian-pi
    entered Luo-yang,
and Turks with pikes in hand
    climbed the Hall of Light.

The house of Jin's Son of Heaven
    surrendered as a prisoner,
as his lords and nobles fled swiftly
    just like cattle and sheep.

On the purple lanes pennons and banners
    bumped one another in darkness,
chickens and dogs of every household
    climbed to the roofs in alarm.

Married women went out their gates
    along with rebel soldiers;
when their husbands died before their eyes,
    they did not dare to weep.

Great nobles of the nine domains
    each looked to his own lands,
and not a one led soldiers
    to go protect their prince.

Of Northerners who fled the Turks
    most were found in the South;
and to this day the Southerners
    speak the idiom of Jin.

Zhang Ji's rather plain narrative may be contrasted with the following dramatic scene by Wen Ting-yun, written perhaps half a century later. The poem is set five centuries earlier, in the year 383; the scene is the villa of Xie An, the great statesman of the Eastern Jin, who has sent off his nephew Xie Xuan and his younger brother Xie Shi to meet the invasion of the Northern warlord Fu Jian, who was making a bid to reunify China. As if unconcerned, Xie An is playing a game of "chess," or *go*, with the great courtiers of the Eastern Jin all gathered around him waiting for him to make his move. The chess game is the microcosm in which Xie An is mysteriously encompassing the defeat of Fu Jian at the Battle of the Fei River (by the river Huai). The poem builds on the anecdote given in Liu Yi-qing's *New Stories and Tales of the Times (Shi-shuo xin-yu)*, VI.35:

Lord Xie was playing *go* with someone when all at once a messenger came from Xie Xuan, who was at the river Huai. After he finished reading the letter, he kept perfectly silent and slowly turned back to the gameboard. One of his visitors asked him whether the event on the Huai had gone well or ill, and he an-

swered: "The young people have completely smashed that thug." His countenance and behavior were no different from usual.

Wen Ting-yun (ca. 812–866), A Song of Lord Xie's Villa

To the south of Redbird Pontoon Bridge
    there winds a fragrant path,
to Master Xie's eastern villa
    stretching to spring's green sky.
Doves sleep high in the willows,
    sunlight suffused everywhere,
breeze gusts through grillwork kiosks
    where are guests from the Royal Court.

On the squares of grained catalpa wood
    petals are randomly strewn;
before his plans have fully formed,
    stars are filling the pool.
None of the guests made the least noise,
    beech and bamboo were hushed,
lords of golden cicadas and scepters of jade
    all rested their chins on hands.
He faces the board, he knits his brows,
    he sees a thousand miles,
and the capital has already seized
    the long serpent's tail.
The Southland's royal aura
    twines through his open lapels—
and he never let Fu Jian
    cross the river Huai.

The poetic expositions of the Han included monumental works on the great Han
imperial hunts. The following song begins with a stylish and diminutive imperial hunt
in the Southern Dynasties, going out before the dawn, riding horses decked with jewels. The song gradually turns into a vision of the Southland's decadence, showing
the Last Ruler of the last of Southern Dynasties, the Chen, hiding with his empresses
in the palace well to escape the conquering troops of the Sui. In the tradition of sensuous love songs of the Southern Dynasties such as those given above, the Last Ruler
of the Chen composed a song entitled "In the Rear Court Flowers on Trees of Jade."
The "Great Preface" to the *Classic of Poetry* asserted that one could tell the condition of a government by the quality of the poetry and music of the period. It is said
that when his courtiers heard this song by the Last Ruler, they wept, knowing that
the dynasty would not last long. At the end of Wen Ting-yun's poem, we find that
the white flowers celebrated in the song endure, but on wild trees that grow over
the remains of the Southern Dynasties' parks and palaces.

Song for the Bank Where the Cock Crowed

When the Southern Dynasties Emperor
    went off to shoot pheasants,
the silvery sky-river sparkled
    with scatterings of stars.
In bronze water-clocks the dripping ceased,
    as first they woke from dreams;
dust rose high from the jeweled horses,
    no one knew at all.

Fish leapt east of the lotuses,
    rippling palace pools,
a drizzling haze in royal willows
    where roosting birds hung suspended.
Red rouge through thousands of doors,
    there was spring within the mirrors,
a single sound from sapphire trees
    and all the world turned dawn.

Their coiling, crouching power wore out
    after three hundred years,
the Southland's warlike aura
    turned to melancholy mist.
Comet tails brushed the Earth,
    waves rolled over the sea;
battle drums crossed the river,
    dust flooded the skies.

Embroidered dragon and painted pheasant
    stuffed the palace well,
and winds were driving the wildfires
    that burned the nine royal tripods.
Their great halls made nests for swallows,
    the pavements grew with weeds,
on the twelve statues of metal
    frost was glittering.
A continuous carpet of green grows over
    foundations of Palace City,
the warm colors of springtime sky,
    ancient slopes where plants run wild.
Who would have thought that the melody,
    "In the Rear Court Flowers on Trees of Jade,"
would linger on in the crabapples
    and their branches like the snow.

The Southern Dynasties capital at Jian-kang, also referred to as Jin-ling, later became
Nanjing, the "Southern Capital" of the Ming. In 1644, when Qing armies took the

North, Ming loyalists tried to establish a successor Ming reign in the South, in Nan-jing. This last short "Southern Dynasty" remembered its predecessors in the old city. Qian Qian-yi, one of the most famous writers of the day, served and betrayed the Southern Ming; watching a game of chess, he could probably not help recalling Xie An's famous chess game thirteen centuries before.

Qian Qian-yi (1582–1664), In Jin-ling: A Second Series on Watching a Chess Game (one of six) (1647)

Still and somber, a bare chessboard,
    echoes in vast silence,
autumn grows old by the Qin-Huai,
    whose cold high waters moan.
White-haired in the candlelight
    and sensing the chill of night,
in the last pieces of the game
    I see the Southern Dynasties.

Traditional Literary Theory 東漢魏晉南北朝

In traditional China, as in many civilizations, various kinds of critical and theoretical writing about literature developed side by side with the actual texts. These writings are valuable to us because they give some indication of how literature was conceived and how it was read. They tell us what both readers and writers thought was important in their literature and some of the assumptions they shared.

Comments on literature in the pre-Qin period and in the Han concerned primarily the ethical force of literature and its consequences for social and political behavior. As in other civilizations, there was a strong sense of literature's power to shape values and hence to influence behavior, either for the better or the worse. On the one hand, the Confucian Classics and literary works that followed in the tradition of the classics were seen as the only way to preserve and teach basic cultural values. On the other hand, we often find a sense of danger about certain works of literature, an anxiety that they somehow might stir immoderate desires and threaten the social order. Thus the earliest critics often served as apologists for literature, defending its potential usefulness and encouraging forms of writing that supported political and social values.

After the fall of the Han Dynasty, a wide variety of new concerns began to appear in writing about literature. Literature was not yet conceived as an autonomous art, entirely separate from social and political life; nevertheless, these new concerns broadened the sense of literature. The earliest extant essay devoted exclusively to the discussion of literature was written by Cao Pi (187–226), emperor of the Wei Dynasty, son of the great warlord Cao Cao, and elder half brother of Cao Zhi, the most admired writer of the period. In this work, the "Discourse on Literature" *(Lun wen),* we find rudimentary formulations of many of the perennial interests of later critics: the relation between personality and style, literary talent as a unique gift that cannot be passed on like a skill or craft, and literary achievement as a means to attain cultural immortality.

In literary theory, as in literature itself, we sometimes encounter a work of such originality that it could not have been anticipated from what preceded it. "The Poetic Exposition on Literature" *(Wen fu)* by Lu Ji (261–303) is just such a work. Not only had nothing like it ever been written about literature, Lu Ji himself never wrote anything else quite like it. Cao Pi's "Discourse on Literature" was a personal, even idiosyncratic organization of literary issues; unique as it was, however, it was still comprehensible as a transformation of certain old questions about writing. Lu Ji addressed a whole new range of questions about the act of writing, and he strained the language of his day to find words to describe the process. Modern critics have often observed that "The Poetic Exposition on Literature" does what it describes: that it is a poetic treatment of poetry. This aspect of the work contributes to both its difficulty and its appeal.

Lu Ji largely ignores earlier concerns about literature—its ethical purpose, its reflection of the social and political circumstances of its time, and its embodiment of the author's personality. Instead, "The Poetic Exposition on Literature" is based on the Neo-Daoist theory of mind and a "spirit-wandering" that is the rough counterpart of a Western theory of the imagination. After a prose preface in which he speaks of the problem of representing in words a process as elusive as writing, Lu Ji gives an orderly description of how composition takes place. First, the writer prepares himself by nurturing the imaginative capacity and by internalizing the works of past writers; the mind then wanders through the microcosm of the self, encountering things that will be the "material" of the literary work. Lu Ji next turns to the problems of expressing interior experience in words, giving it order and controlling its turbulent complexity. Finally, the "Poetic Exposition" treats various problems of writing, concluding with a description of imaginative "dryness," when inspiration fails.

Lu Ji (261–303), The Poetic Exposition on Literature *(Wen fu)*

Whenever I consider what has been written by persons of talent, I find that I can somehow grasp their strenuous efforts, how they used their minds. Many indeed are the variations in the ways they brought forth their words and phrases, yet we can still understand and explain what is beautiful and valuable in them.

Whenever I myself compose a literary work, I can see quite well their states of mind. Yet I constantly fear failure because my own conceptions are unequal to the things of the world, or because my writing is unequal to my conceptions. I suppose it is not that understanding is difficult, but rather that the difficulty lies in being able to do it well.

For this reason I have written "The Poetic Exposition on Literature": first to pass on the splendid complexity of craft that we find in earlier writers, and second, to consider how success and failure come about in writing. I hope that someday this will be recognized as having treated all the fine points of the subject in detail.

When it comes to taking an ax in hand to chop an ax handle, the model is not far from you; however, it is hard indeed for language to follow the variations of motion in that hand. What can be put into words is all here.

> He stands in the very center and scans the darkness,
> Fosters feelings and aims in classics of old.
> He moves with four seasons and sighs at their passing,
> Views all the world's things, broods on their fullness;
> He grieves for leaves falling in harsh autumn,
> He delights in sweet spring's supple branches;
> His mind shivers as he takes frost to heart;
> His aims are remote, they look down upon clouds.
> He sings glorious achievements, inherited by our age,

Chants of pure fragrance, left from those before;
He roams in the groves and treasuries of literary works,
And admires the perfect balance in their well-wrought craft.
With strong feeling he puts book aside and takes his writing brush
To make it appear in literature.

This is how it begins:
    retraction of vision, inversion of listening,
    absorbed in thought and seeking all around,
    essence galloping to the world's eight ends,
    the mind roaming thousands of yards, high and low.
And when it is attained:
    light gathers about moods and they grow in brightness,
    things become luminous and draw each other forward;
He then quaffs the word-hoard's spray of droplets,
And rolls in his mouth the sweet moisture of classics;
He drifts between Heaven and the abyss, at rest in the current,
He bathes in falling streams, immersed in their waters.
Then, phrases from depths emerge struggling
    as when swimming fish, hooks in their mouths,
        emerge from the bottom of deepest pools;
and drifting intricacies of craft flutter down,
    as when winging birds, caught by stringed shafts,
        plummet from the high-tiered clouds.
He reaps what was unwritten by a hundred generations,
And picks rhymes neglected for a thousand years;
For it falls away—dawn's glorious bloom, unfurled already;
There opens instead the unblown bud of evening.
He sees past and present in a single instant,
Touches all this world in the blink of an eye.

Only then
    he selects ideas, sets out their kinds,
    tests his phrases, puts them in ranks,
    he strikes open all that contains the light,
    he plucks everything that holds sound within.
He may trust to branches to shake the leaves,
    Or trace waves upstream to find their source;
He may track what is hidden and reach the apparent,
    Or seek the simple and obtain the difficult.
The tiger shows its stripes, beasts are thrown to confusion,
    The dragon appears, birds fly off in waves.
It may be steady and sure, and simply enacted,
    Or tortuously hard, no ease in it.
He empties his unblurred mind, he concentrates thought,
Unites all concerns and brings forth words.
Earth and Heaven he cages within fixed shape;

All things he crushes beneath brush tip.
At first it hesitates upon his dry lips,
But finally flows freely through the moist pen.
Nature's laws bear the substance, they are a tree's trunk;
Patterns hang as the branches, a lavish lacework.
Truly mood and manner never fail to match:
Each variation is there upon the face.
When thought moves in joy, there will surely be laughter;
When we tell of lament, sighs have already come.
He may have grasped the tablet and dashed it off lightly,
Or held brush in lips, mind far in the distance.

Yet in this event there is truly a joy,
Held in firm honor by good man and Sage:
This trial of void and nothing to demand of it being,
A knock upon silence, seeking its sound.
He contains far expanses on writing's silk sheet,
He emits boundless torrents from the speck that is mind.
Language gives breadth, it is ever-expanding;
Thought pursues, growing deeper and deeper.
It spreads the rich scent of drooping blossoms,
Brings the dense darkness of green twigs:
Sparkling breeze flies, whirling gusts start;
Swelling clouds rise from writing brush groves.

There are tens of thousands of different forms,
The things of the world have no single measure:
Jumbled and jostling, they go fleeting past,
And shapes they have are hard to describe.
Diction shows talents in contests of craft;
Concept controls, it serves as the craftsman.
And there he strives between being and nothing,
In the deep or the shallows, not giving up.
Though he strays from the ruled circle and square,
He hopes to reach limits of features and shape.
Thus to make a brave display for eyes, prize extravagance;
But for the mind's content, honor the apposite.
That the words run out is no impediment:
Discourse attains its ends only in broadening.

Poems follow from feeling, they are sensuous, fine;
Poetic expositions give forms of things, clear and bright;
Stele inscriptions unfurl patterns to match substance;
Lamentations swell with pent-up sorrow;
Inscriptions are broad and concise, warm and gentle;
Admonitions repress, being forceful and sharp;
Odes move with grand ease, being opulent;

Essays treat essence, expansive and lucid;
Statements to the throne are even, incisive, dignified, calm;
Persuasions are flashy, deluding, entrancing.
Though fine distinctions are made in these,
They forbid deviation, restrain rash impulse.
Ask that words attain their ends, that principle come forth;
Have nothing to do with long-winded excess.

In things there are many stances,
In forms there are frequent shiftings.
When shaping conceptions, value deft craft,
In delivering words, honor allure.
When it comes to the alternation of sounds,
They are like the five colors, each sets off the other:
Though there is no law in their passing or halting—
A rocky path, one that we cannot make easy—
Still, if one grasps variation and knows succession,
It is like opening channels to draw in a stream.
If you miss your chance, draw together too slowly,
Your beginnings will always be following ends.
Errors in orientation of Earth and of Heaven
Bring mere muddiness and no vividness.

Sometimes you may transgress against previous sections,
Or trespass ahead to some later part.
Sometimes diction is faulty, yet principle right,
Or language is smooth, but the idea is blocked.
Avoid both failings and beauty is doubled;
If the two occur jointly, twice then the harm.
Judge relative merit by tiniest measures;
Choose to keep or discard by the breadth of a hair:
If what has been trimmed to most accurate measures
Follows truly straight lines, then it must be just right.

Perhaps pattern is lush and the principle rich,
But in terms of concept, it has no point.
It reaches its limit, no further significance;
It is used up entirely, it cannot increase.
Set a pregnant phrase in some essential spot,
And it will be a riding crop for the whole piece:
Though the word-hoard may follow the rules,
One must have this to strive for great merit.
The achievement large, the obstacles few,
Choose what is enough and do not change it.

Perhaps complex thoughts cohere, patterned finely,
They have lucid loveliness, splendidly bright,
They shimmer like brocades of many colors,

Move deeply, like a concert of strings.
But suppose you find what you aimed at lacks distinction—
Your work matches unwittingly some piece long ago.
Though the shuttle and loom were in my own feelings,
I must dread lest others have gone here before;
If it injures integrity, transgresses right,
Though I begrudge the doing, I must cast it away.

Perhaps blossom comes forth, a grain spike stands straight,
Removed from the crowd, detached from the sense:
A shape is here that no shadow can follow,
A sound to which no echo can join.
It stands there looming, inert and alone,
Not woven together with constant tones.
Mind in desolate zones where nothing answers;
Ideas circle aimlessly, unable to leave.
The mountains shimmer when jade lies in stone,
Streams have charm when their waters bear pearls;
Thornbush and underbrush need not be cut—
They too can have splendor when kingfishers roost.
If we link the art song to a popular tune,
We may enhance what made it rare.

Suppose words are put in rhymes too short;
They come to dead ends, the heart stirred all alone.
They look down to bleak stillness, lacking companion;
They look up to vast spaces and continue nothing.
Compare this to a string of limited range, strung alone—
Within it lies clear song, but nothing responds.

Suppose you trust your lines to dreary tones:
Words with aimless languor and wanting in splendor;
Forms compounded of lovely and ugly mixed,
Good substance encumbered by blemishes.
Like pipes in the hall too shrilly played—
Though there is response, it lacks harmony.

Suppose you neglect nature's laws, keep what is strange,
Pointless quest for the empty, pursuit of the subtle:
The words will want feeling, be short on love,
Your lines will drift randomly to no end.
As when strings are too thin and the bridges too tight,
There may be harmony, but no strong feeling.

But suppose you let yourself rush into choral unisons,
Lost in beauty bewitching, an orgy of sound:
You please the eye pointlessly, match common tastes,

The sound may be loud, but the tune will be low.
Be aware of songs like *Fang-lu* and *Sang-jian*—
Though strong feeling is there, it may lack dignity.

Suppose chaste indifference and graceful restraint,
Always pruning complexities, excising excess:
It will lack that "flavor withheld" of ritual broth,
Like the too pristine tones of a temple harp.
Though several join in with the one who sings,
Dignity you may have, but still lack allure.

In the degree it is cut, terse or elaborate,
In its forms, either sinking or ascending:
One enters variations by what then seems proper,
Fine turns will convey the most subtle moods.
Sometimes language is artless, but the lesson is artful;
Sometimes principle is plain, and the diction light;
Sometimes pursuit of the old yields something new;
Sometimes moving with murkiness restores clarity;
Sometimes glancing overviews give requisite insight;
Sometimes essence comes after toilsome honing.
Like the dancer who flings her sleeves to the rhythm,
Or a singer, sending voice in response to the strings.
This Wheelwright Pian could not put into words,
Nor can glittering discourse catch the quintessence.

The overall laws of phrasing and writing's rules
Are things to which my heart has submitted:
I have a fine sense of this age's consistent flaws,
And recognize what is pure in good men before:
Though something comes from deep in the craftsman's mind,
It may still be mocked in the eyes of fools.
Such agate flourishes and filigree of jade
Are as common as wild beans on the central plain,
Never exhausted, like the Great Bellows,[1]
All nurtured together with Heaven and Earth.
Yet however abundant they are in these times,
I sigh that they do not fill my own open hands.
I am cursed by small capacity, too often empty,
It is hard to continue the past's apt words.
So I limp along in rhymes too short,
Bring forth commonplace tones to conclude my songs,
And some regret always remains at the end—
Never is my heart full, never am I satisfied.

---

[1] The "Great Bellows" is a Daoist figure for the generative processes of the universe.

I fear this vessel will be tested, lying in dust,
It will surely be mocked by the ringing jade.

At the conjunction of stirring and response,
At the boundary between blockage and passage,
What comes there can never be halted,
What goes off cannot be stopped.
When it hides, it resembles the shadow vanishing,
When it moves, it resembles the echoes that rise.
When Heaven's impulses move swiftly along the best course,
What confusion exists that cannot reach order?
Then winds of thought rise within the breast,
Word-streams go flowing through lips and teeth,
Bubbling forth in tumultuous succession,
Something only silk and writing brush can catch.
The writing gleams and overflows eyes;
The tones splash on, filling the ears.

But when the emotions are stalled and hampered,
Mind strains toward something, but spirit is unmoved,
I am left as inert as a bare, leafless tree,
Or a gaping void like a dried-up stream.
I draw the soul to search secret recesses,
Gather vital forces to seek from myself;
Nature's laws are hidden and sink away farther,
Thought strives to emerge, as if tugged along.
Sometimes I wear out my heart, and much is regretted;
Sometimes I follow thoughts' bent with few failings.
Although this thing does lie in the self,
It is not in the scope of my concentrated force.
I may ponder heart's void and turn against self,
That I do not know how to open this blockage.

Coda

The functioning of literature lies in its being
The means for all principles of nature.
It spreads thousands of miles and nothing can bar it;
It passes millions of years, is a ford across.
Ahead it grants models to ages coming,
Retrospectively contemplates images of old.
It succors the old kings' Way, on the verge of collapse;
It makes reputation known, does not let it be lost.
No path lies so far it cannot be included;
No principle so subtle it cannot be woven in.
Peer of clouds and rain with its nurturing moisture,
Divinity's semblance in its transformations.

When it covers metal and stone, virtue is spread;
Through strings and flutes flowing, it is daily made new.

Liu Xie (ca. 465–522), *Wen-xin diao-long* ("The Literary Mind Carves Dragons")

The courts and princely salons of the Southern Dynasties around the turn of the sixth century saw what was probably the most glorious age of Chinese literary theory and criticism. In those courts and salons, writers and courtiers debated fine points of style and basic principles of literature, compiled anthologies, defined genres, and reached the judgments on earlier writers that would become the basis of later accounts of the literary history. Here Zhong Rong (ca. 468–518) wrote his *Grades of the Poets (Shi pin),* offering terse evaluations of major poets and tracing lineages of influence. In the conservative court of the Liang crown prince Zhao-ming (501–531), *The Anthology (Wen xuan)* was compiled, which was to be the core of Tang and later understanding of literature before the turn of the sixth century. Soon afterward, in the court of Xiao Gang (503–551), the Liang emperor Jian-wen, Xu Ling (507–ca. 582) compiled an anthology of love poetry and the witty poetry of the court, *New Songs of the Jade Terrace (Yu-tai xin-yong),* whose preface defended a literature of sentiment and play.

In this world of literary discussion and debate appeared a remarkable and anomalous work, written by Liu Xie (ca. 465–522), a lay scholar who had left the Buddhist monastery school to enter the salons of the princely courts. This was the *Wen-xin diao-long,* which may roughly be translated as "The Literary Mind Carves Dragons," a systematic treatise on how literature was conceived around the turn of the sixth century.

The *Wen-xin diao-long* consists of forty-nine regular chapters, and a concluding Afterword in which Liu Xie gives his motives for the composition of the book and its structure. After four opening chapters on the Way, the Sage, the Classics, and the Confucian Apocrypha, Liu treats the major genres. The second half of the work, beginning with Chapter 26, contains a remarkable series of chapters on basic concepts of literary theory.

The *Wen-xin diao-long* is a difficult work to read in translation (as it is in the original). It makes frequent reference to writers and works with which the English reader is not familiar, and it is written in the florid, elliptical style that was popular in the period. In choosing the following excerpts, I have omitted sections of chapters that would require heavy annotation or would for other reasons be of less interest to most English readers. At the end of each chapter is a "supporting verse" *(zan),* which summarizes the points made. I have omitted some of these.

The first chapter sets out to establish the range of the concept of *wen. Wen* has a wide range of meanings and associations: it is "literature," "prose" as opposed to poetry (though not used in this way in *Wen-xin diao-long*), "rhymed writing" as opposed to unrhymed writing, "cultivation," the "civil" aspect of the government as opposed to the military, "decoration," the "written word," and often when applied to literary style, "ornamentation." Finally, in the context of this chapter, *wen* is used in the broadest sense of all, as "pattern." Liu Xie sets out to show that *wen* (pattern) came into being in the very beginning of the universe once there was a distinction, and hence a relation, between Heaven and Earth. From that primordial "pattern," all other patterns followed: the "pattern of Heaven" (*Tian-wen*, "astronomy") and the "pattern of Earth" (*Di-wen*, "topography"). The *wen* of human beings is pattern revealed in their nature, which is to be the vessel of mind. This human version of *wen* is literature—writing that has pattern and that embodies the patterned world contemplated by mind.

Its Source in the Way: Chapter 1

As an inner power in things, pattern *(wen)* is very great indeed, and it was born together with Heaven and Earth. How is this? All colors are combined from two primary colors, the purple that is Heaven and the brown that is Earth. All forms are distinguished through two primary forms, Earth's squareness and Heaven's circularity. The sun and moon are disks of jade that follow one another in succession, showing to those below images that cleave to Heaven. Rivers and mountains are a glittering finery, unfolding shapes that show the order of the Earth. These are the pattern of the Way.

In considering the radiance given off above and reflecting on the loveliness that inheres below, the positions of high and low were determined, and the Two Standards were generated [*Yang* and *Yin*, Heaven and Earth]. Only human beings, who are endowed with the divine spark of consciousness, rank as a third with this pair. Together they are called the Triad [Heaven, Earth, and human beings].

Human beings are the flower of the elements: in fact, they are the mind of Heaven and Earth. When mind came into being, language was established; and with the establishment of language, pattern became manifest. This is the natural course of things, the Way.

If we then go on to consider things in all their myriad kinds, we find that each plant and animal has its own pattern. Dragon and phoenix portend good fortune by their intricate and colorful designs; the visual appearance of a tiger is determined by its stripes, and that of a leopard in its spots. The sculpted forms and colors of the clouds possess a subtlety that goes beyond the painter's craft; the involute splendor of trees and plants does not need the marvels of any embroiderer. These are in no way merely external adornments: they come from Nature. And when we consider the echoes that form in the fissures of the forest, these are tuned together like harps and organs; the tones stirred by streams running over stones make a harmony like chimes and bells. When shape is established, a coherent unit stands out as complete; when sound emerges, a pattern is generated. Since these things that lack the power of comprehension may still possess such splendid colors, how can this human vessel of mind lack a pattern appropriate to it?

In the following paragraph, *wen,* as the "written word," is traced back to the *Classic of Changes,* a divination manual of great antiquity whose layers of commentary gradually transformed it into a Confucian Classic with important philosophical significance. At the heart of the *Classic of Changes* are sixty-four hexagrams, each made up of a set of six broken and unbroken lines (the number of possibilities of variations being 2^6; that is, sixty-four). Each hexagram was believed to embody a distinct phase of change and was produced by the interaction of two constituent trigrams, sets of three broken and unbroken lines (of which there were eight, 2^3). These patterns of broken and unbroken lines are seen as the primordial "writing," *wen*.

From the mythical sage Fu Xi, who first drew the trigrams, down to Confucius, who was credited with the composition of the cosmological tracts known as the "Wings," the evolution of the *Classic of Changes* is given here as the earliest history of *wen*, the markings of pattern. As Liu Xie notes, one of the "Wings" is even titled *Wen-yan*, "Patterned Words."

The origins of human pattern began in the Primordial *(Tai-ji)*. The Images of the *Classic of Changes* were first to bring to light hidden spiritual presences. Fu Xi marked out the initial stages, and Confucius added the "Wings" to bring the work to a conclusion. Only for the two positions of Qian and Kun did Confucius make the "Patterned Words." For is not pattern in words "the mind of Heaven and Earth"? And then it came to pass that the "Yellow River Diagram" became marked with the eight trigrams;[2] and the "Luo River Writing" contained the Nine Divisions.[3] No human being was responsible for these, which are the fruit of jade tablets inlaid with gold, the flower of green strips with red writing: they came from the basic principle of spirit.

When the "tracks of birds" took the place of knotted cords, the written word first appeared in its glory. . . .[4]

[In an omitted section that follows, Liu Xie treats the legendary evolution of writing from primordial simplicity to its full development in the classics, noting the moment at which basic genres first appeared.]

Thus we know that the Way bequeathed its pattern through the Sages, and that by their writing [or "patterns"] the Sages made the Way manifest. It extends everywhere with no obstruction, and it is put to use every day and never found wanting. The *Classic of Changes* says, "That which stirs all the world into motion is preserved in these statements." That by which a statement can stir all the world into motion is the pattern of the Way.

---

[2]There was a legend that the trigrams, the core elements of the hexagrams of the *Classic of Changes*, first appeared in a diagram carried by a dragon that emerged from the Yellow River.

[3]Another legend had it that when Yu was controlling the great flood, a sacred tortoise appeared in the Luo River, which carried the "Nine Divisions"—nine sets of enumerated categories that comprehended the operations of nature and the state. They appear in the "Great Plan" *(Hong-fan)* chapter of the *Classic of Documents*.

[4]Cang Jie, the "recorder" of the Yellow Emperor, came up with the idea for written characters by observing the tracks of birds; earlier, knotted cords had been used for keeping records.

Supporting Verse

The mind of the Way is subtle,
Spirit's principle gives the teaching.
Glorious is that Primal Sage,
In whom fellow feeling and filial piety shine.
The diagram on the Yellow River dragon offered a form;
The writing on the tortoise showed its features.
Here the pattern of Heaven can be observed,
For all the people to emulate.

"Spirit Thought" is the first of the chapters on concepts of literary theory that make up the second half of *Wen-xin diao-long*. "Spirit Thought" is the capacity and state of mind that Lu Ji treated in the opening of "The Poetic Exposition on Literature," the counterpart of the Western theory of imagination. Liu Xie treats the nurturing of this capacity in terms of meditation practices.

Spirit Thought: Chapter 26

Long ago someone said that a person's body might be on the rivers and lakes, yet his mind could remain by the palace towers of Wei. This is what is meant by spirit thought. And spirit does indeed go far in the thought that occurs in writing. When we silently concentrate, thought may reach a thousand years into the past; and when the face stirs quietly, the eyes can see thousands of miles. When we sing, the sounds of pearls and jade come forth; right before our eyelashes the colors of clouds in the wind unfurl. This is something achieved by the basic principle of thought.

When that basic principle of thought is at its keenest, the spirit wanders together with things. Spirit resides within the breast. Our aims and our vital forces control the gate to let it out. The things of the world come in through our ears and eyes, and language has charge of the hinge. When that hinge permits passage, nothing can hide its face; but when the bolt to that gate is closed, spirit is concealed within.

In the shaping of literary thought, the most important thing is emptiness and stillness within. Cleanse your inner organs and wash the spirit pure. Accumulate learning in order to build a treasury; consider the principles of things in order to enrich your talent; explore and experience things to know all that appears; then guide it along to spin your words out. Only when you do this can the butcher, who cuts things apart mysteriously, set a pattern that follows the rules of sound, and the uniquely discerning carpenter wield his ax with his eye to the conceptual image.[5] This is the most important technique in guiding the course of *wen* and the foundation of planning a work.

---

[5]This sentence refers to two parables in the *Zhuang-zi* of craftsmen who work by intuition. The first of these, the story of Butcher Ding, is found in the chapter *Yang-sheng*, "Nurturing Life." Butcher Ding explains to Lord Wen-hui, who has expressed admiration of Ding's skills in cutting up an ox, that he does it by the unconscious operations of spirit, by moving through the empty interstices in the body of the ox. Other cooks, who actually cut with their knives, have to change knives often;

Once spirit thought is set into motion, thousands of courses that might be taken compete for attention; at this point the rules and regulations are still unrealized structures, and the cutting and carving as yet are unformed. If you climb a mountain, your feelings are filled by the mountain; if you gaze at the sea, your ideas are swelled to overflowing by the sea. According to the degree of talent that resides within, you may speed along with the wind and clouds.

Whenever someone takes his writing brush in hand, his vital force is twice what it is when the words have come. When a work is completed, we find that it went no farther than half of that with which the mind began. Why is this? Marvels come easily when our ideas soar through the empty sky; but it is hard to attain the mastery of the craft that can give them realized expression in words. The idea is received from the process of thought, and language in turn is received from the idea. These may be so close that there is no boundary between them, or they may be so far apart that they seem a thousand leagues from one another. Sometimes the principle is to be found within the mind itself, and yet one seeks it far beyond this world; sometimes a truth is close by, but thought goes off beyond mountains and rivers in pursuit of it. Therefore, if you can master your own mind and foster its skills, you will not need to meditate laboriously. If you can retain the design within and keep control, you need not strain your emotions. . . .

[A section is omitted in which Liu Xie contrasts examples of those who composed quickly and those who composed laboriously.]

When the mind of a person with agile wits combines all the essential techniques, his very quickness preempts reflection, making instant decisions in response to the demands of the moment. The state of mind of someone who broods deeply is filled with forking paths: he sees clearly only after uncertainties and makes his decisions only after thoughtful reflection. When one is quick of mind in response to the demands of the moment, the accomplishment is brought about swiftly; when reflection is full of uncertainties, it takes a much longer time to achieve one's goals.

Although ease and difficulty in composition differ, both depend on a broad perfection of one's capacities. If learning is shallow, the person who is slow to compose is slow to no purpose. If talents are diffuse, quickness will do no good. As far as I know, neither of these types has ever achieved much. As you prepare to write and compose your thoughts, there are two dangers: if the principle is blocked from appearing, you have poverty of content; and if the language gets bogged down, you have confusion. In cases like this wide experience is the provision that can feed poverty of content,

---

but Ding has used his knife for nineteen years without ever needing to sharpen it. The "uniquely discerning carpenter" is Carpenter Shi, referred to in the *Zhuang-zi.* Carpenter Shi was famous for being able to swing his ax and remove a speck of plaster from his friend's nose.

while continuity is the remedy for confusion. Wide experience together with continuity aids the force of mind.

The varieties of states of mind are remarkable and various; the variations of form shift just as often. Plain and simple diction may be made pregnant by some clever idea; fresh concepts can make commonplace matters spring to life. Compare hempen cloth to threads of hemp—though some might say the threads themselves are of little value, when the shuttle and loom put their accomplishments before us, the cloth is prized for its shimmering splendor.

But when it comes to those tenuous implications beyond the reach of thought, the fine variations in sentiment beyond the text, these are things that language cannot pursue and the point where my writing brush knows well to halt. That subtlety can be brought to light only by reaching ultimate essence; that order can be comprehended only by reaching the ultimate in variation. Yi Yin could not tell of the art of cooking;[6] Wheelwright Pian could not speak of the ax. These are the real fine points.

Supporting Verse

> Spirit gets through by images,
> Engendering variations of feeling.
> Things are sought by outer appearance,
> But mind's response is to basic principle.
> Craftsmanship is given to the rules of sound,
> Coming to life in comparisons and affective images:
> Drawing one's thoughts together, take charge,
> And behind hanging tent-flaps ensure victory.[7]

The chapter on "Nature and Form" begins by taking up an issue that has no near counterpart in Western literary criticism: how the particular internal "nature" of some type of thing becomes manifest in a normative form; for example, the predatory nature of a hawk might be said to be physically realized in the hawk's form. (Such an interpretation, moving from the inside out, sharply contrasts with modern Western thought, which would rather see the "nature" of a thing taking shape as a consequence of some physical limitation or capability.) The terms Liu Xie uses are broad ones, and by using such terms he subsumes literary phenomena under more general principles. The most important literary applications of the word *ti*, translated as "form," are genres and styles, and each genre has some inherent nature that gives it its form. In the same way, a particular literary style follows from the individual nature of the writer. The argument is important for Liu Xie because he wants to show that the norms of literature are not arbitrary or merely historical, but rather have their basis in nature. The chapter concludes by addressing the potential conflict between

---

[6]Yi Yin, who was to become the minister of King Tang of the Shang Dynasty, was originally a cook, and by legend is said to have been unable to explain the secrets of his art.

[7]The reference here is to General Zhang Liang, who won great victories by staying in his tent and planning.

following one's particular nature and the study of all normative styles, recommending that a novice writer first master all the normative styles.

Nature and Form: Chapter 27

When feelings are stirred, language gives them an outer shape; and when the inherent principle emerges, pattern is clear. By following a course from what is hidden, we reach something manifest. What appears on the outside corresponds to what lies within.

But the degree of talent ranges from brilliance to mediocrity; the degree of vital force, from the firm to the yielding; the degree of learning, from the profound to the shallow; and the degree of practiced skill, from deftness to awkwardness. All of these are melted together in the crucible by a person's nature and his disposition; and they are fused together according to how that person has himself been shaped and influenced. For this reason there is a marvelous variety of shapes in the realm of the writing brush and a diverse spectrum of waves in the garden of letters.

No one can go beyond the measure of talent that is displayed in the brilliance or mediocrity of his grasp of principles or in his use of language. No one can alter the quality of vital force, whether firm or yielding, in his manner. It is unheard of that someone goes contrary to the extent of learning shown in the depth or shallowness of his knowledge of facts and truths. Few can reverse the habits that yield deftness or awkwardness in form. Each person takes as his master the way his own mind has been formed, and these are as different as faces.

If we may generalize about the different courses that may be followed, we find that the full range consists of eight styles [normative forms]: *dian-ya*, the authoritative and dignified; *yuan-ao*, the abstruse; *jing-yue*, the terse; *xian-fu*, the perspicuous; *fan-ru*, the fulsome; *zhuang-li*, the vigorous and lovely; *xin-qi*, the novel and unusual; *qing-mi*, the light and delicate.

The authoritative and dignified style takes its model from the Classics and keeps the company of the Confucian school. The abstruse style hides all sensuous flashiness, has its own decorum, and is concerned with occult doctrines. The terse style weighs each word and line, making judgments by the finest measures. In the perspicuous style, the ideas are spread out before us and satisfy us by their adherence to natural principle. The fulsome style is dazzling, yet has broad implications, and the ramifications are brilliant and scintillating. The vigorous and lovely style offers noble arguments and grand judgments with a rare splendor. The novel and unusual style rejects the old and apes the modern; it shows a skewed delight in the bizarre. The light and delicate style uses flimsy embellishments that lack solid basis; it has an airy vagueness that appeals to the common taste. We can see that the dignified style is set in opposition to the unusual; the arcane style differs from the perspicuous; the fulsome and terse are at odds; the vigorous and light styles contrast. These are the roots and leaves of literature, and the garden of letters contains them all.

349

These eight forms often vary from one to the other, but success in each is accomplished by learning. The power of talent resides within and begins as vital force in the blood. Vital force makes a person's aims concrete, and those aims determine the language. The glory that emerges from this process is always that of the writer's nature and his feelings. . . .

[Here is omitted a list of famous writers, with comments on how the particular personality of each was revealed in his style.]

If we investigate each of these writers according to his kind, we see that inside and outside always correspond. This can only be their permanent endowment from Nature, the general case of the workings of vital force and talent.

Talent may be endowed by Heaven, but in learning we must pay particular heed to early training: as in carving hardwood or dyeing silk, success depends on the first transformation. When the shape of a vessel has already been formed or the color has been set, it is impossible to alter or undo it. Therefore, when a child learns to carve, he should learn the dignified, normative patterns first. Beginning from the roots, we reach the leaves, and the cycles of thought achieve a perfect circle. Although the eight styles differ, there is a way of joining them that encompasses all. Once you attain the center of the ring, all the spokes will meet there to make a wheel. Therefore it is fitting that a person study the normative styles in order to fix his habits; then, according to his individual nature, he may refine his talents. The compass of writing points along this path.

Supporting Verse

> Talents with individual natures have distinct realms,
> The forms of literature are wondrously rich.
> The words used are skin and sinew,
> Aims are the solid bone and marrow.
> Patterned ritual robes have dignity and beauty;
> Vermilion and purple are a corrupting artfulness;[8]
> Yet practice may firmly set what is genuine,
> And from that true accomplishment gradually follows.

If "Nature and Form" addressed the way in which a particular internal nature corresponded to some normative external form, "Continuity and Variation" addresses the question of literary norms and the particular. Were literature constituted only of normative forms, it would be dull and unchanging. Liu Xie draws the terms "continuity" and "variation" from the *Classic of Changes* in order to explain how a single form can admit infinite variation. Note that in the preceding chapter, "form" *(ti)* was

---

[8]*Analects* XVII.18: "He said, 'I hate how the color purple robs the vermilion [of its beauty]; I hate how the music of Zheng confuses the Ya music; I hate how a facile tongue topples states and families.' "

used in the sense of a type of style; in the beginning of this chapter, "form" is used in its other meaning as "genre."

Continuity and Variation: Chapter 29

Although there are unchanging norms in the forms in which literature appears, there is no limit to their variation. What do I mean by this? In poems, poetic expositions, letters, and memoirs, the name depends on the basic principle of the form. These are examples of unchanging norms in literary forms. But the particular phrasing and the vital force can last only by continuities and variations, and these are limitless.

Since there are unchanging norms in the name and basic principle involved, each form is necessarily endowed with some prior content. But since the continuities and variations are limitless, they must always be infused with fresh articulation. In this way we can hurry along an endless road, yet drink from an inexhaustible source. In seeking to drink from the inexhaustible source, the person whose well-rope is too short will suffer thirst; in hurrying along an endless road, the person whose feet tire will have to halt. In cases such as this it is not that the possibilities in literature have been used up, but rather that the technique of continuity and variation is weak. Literature may be considered by analogy to plants and trees. Trunk and root cleave to the soil and share a common nature, yet the qualities of fragrance and flavor will differ according to the exposure to sunlight. . . .

A section follows on how works of literature have developed from the plain to the ornamental, while keeping in mind earlier works and the norms they represent. Liu Xie contrasts this with recent literary works, which seem to him to have lost sight of the authoritative first texts and thus have gone beyond the bounds of legitimate variation. Liu goes on to contrast a notion of variation that always returns to the source with variation that forgets the source and builds only upon the immediately preceding variation. This is expressed through the metaphor of dyeing, in which a shade can be produced by the secondary dyeing of a primary color, but any further dyeing will simply yield muddiness. The Han writers Yang Xiong and Liu Xin are cited as examples of those whose work was based on the Confucian Classics; the writers who follow them fail because they build on Yang and Liu rather than returning to the source.

The color blue comes from the indigo; maroon comes from madder red: though these colors have gone beyond their original color, they cannot be further transformed. Huan Tan once said, "I have seen beautiful works brought forth recently; but no matter how lovely they are, I get nothing from them. But whenever I read the words of Yang Xiong and Liu Xin, I always find something immediately." This exemplifies what I mean. To get a refined blue and a purified maroon, one must return to the indigo and madder red. We must come back to a reverence for the Classics in order to correct what is false and confound shallowness. We can discuss continuity and variation only with someone who has given careful thought to the relation between substance and patterning and who can apply the proper standard when considering questions of dignified elevation and colloquial ease.

Grand description of the sounds and visual appearances of things reached its height early in the Han. Afterwards, writers followed them as if on a ring. Although they sometimes soared high above the tracks of their predecessors, they ultimately remained within the same scope. In the "Seven Stimuli," Mei Sheng wrote:

> My gaze passes far to the Eastern Sea,
> Stretching on continuously to the gray heavens.

In his poetic exposition on Shang-lin Park, Si-ma Xiang-ru wrote:

> I look on limitlessness,
> Examiner of the unbounded,
> Where the sun emerges from its pool in the east,
> And the moon appears over slopes in the west.

Ma Rong, in his panegyric on Guang-cheng Palace, wrote:

> Heaven and Earth, a continuous expanse,
> No limit, no boundary at all:
> A mighty gleaming emerges in the east,
> And the moon appears over slopes in the west.

Yang Xiong, in his poetic exposition on the Stockade Hunt, wrote:

> Emerging, sinking—sun and the moon,
> And Heaven, remote from the Earth.

Finally, in the poetic exposition on the Western Capital, Zhang Heng wrote:

> Then sun and moon emerge and sink back in—
> Images of the Fu-sang Tree [in the Far East] and Meng-si Pool [in the farthest West].

Yet all five of these writers are the same in describing an immensity. There are many similar examples, for writers always follow one another. Sometimes following, sometimes breaking with precedent—in the intricate combination of the two lies the law of continuity and variation.

To grasp the general unity of the literary tradition, one should give broad consideration to overall form: first by wide reading to study its essentials, then by a synthesis of general principles in order to integrate the work. Only then can the writer blaze trails and have the bolt to his gates firmly fixed. He will achieve continuity by trusting to his feelings and will move through variations by depending on vital force. The work thus produced will be brightly colored like the upraised arch of the rainbow and will shake its wings like the redbird. This will be writing that breaks free of confinement. But if the writer is cramped by some merely partial comprehension and is overproud of some single achievement, then he will be galloping in circles within a small yard—it will not be the unfettered paces that go on for thousands of miles.

Supporting Verse

> The rule of literature is to move in full cycle,
> Its legacy is found in daily renewal:
> By variation it can last long;
> By continuity nothing is wanting.
> To seize the right time brings fruition,
> To take the occasion means no anxiety.
> Looking to the present, construct the marvelous;
> Keep the past in mind to make its laws secure.

The term translated as "momentum" in the following chapter is *shi*, whose primary meaning is "power." The meaning is, however, much broader than English "power": events have *shi*, a directed momentum in their unfolding that is related to, but more vigorous than, the English "tendency." As a force that can be directed, *shi* was an important concept in military theory. Later, the term was adapted to describe a sense of direction and kinetic force in calligraphic brushstrokes. Related to this use of the term in aesthetic vocabulary is its application to visual forms of nature: the way in which a mountain may seem to "thrust upward" or "loom" would be an example of *shi*. Liu Xie adapts the term to literature in a peculiar way: "momentum" is the quality of the text's unfolding, following from the nature of the writer and the normative style that suits that writer.

Determination of Momentum: Chapter 30 (selection)

The moods of the heart are different, and there are distinct techniques for variation in literature; but the form is always determined by the writer's state of mind; then, according to that form, a momentum is given. Momentum develops by following the path of least resistance. It is the tendency of Nature, like the straight path of a crossbow bolt released by the trigger or the circling movement of swift eddies at the bend of a mountain stream. What is round [as Heaven is round] gives the pattern of a form, and, accordingly, its momentum is to rotate. What is square [as Earth is square] takes that shape as its basis, and its momentum is to be at rest. This is exactly how form and momentum function in a literary work.

"Hidden and Out-standing" describes two antithetical virtues of a literary work: the quality of "hidden" carries a sense of concealed significance, while the "out-standing" is an immediately striking quality in the text. "Out-standing" is *xiu*, originally a tall ear of grain, and it was early extended to a particular kind of excellence; thus it is like English "outstanding," though recalling the root sense that it "stands out" and catches the reader's attention immediately. Modern aesthetic values inevitably favor a sense of depth and concealed significance, and we are apt to dismiss the "out-standing" as merely showy. Nevertheless, in Liu Xie's scheme these are given as equal and different values, though it becomes apparent that Liu too favors the hidden.

Hidden and Out-standing: Chapter 40

When mind stirs into motion, its ways reach very far; and the variations of feeling in literature go deep. When the source is profound, streams grow and branch out from it; and when the root thrives, the ears of grain stand tall. Thus in the splendor of literature there are hidden aspects and aspects that stand out. The hidden is comprised of layers of significance that lie beyond the text; the out-standing is that which comes out as singular within the work. The hidden achieves perfection by complex, multiple concepts. The out-standing displays its art in preeminent superiority. These are the finest achievements in old literary works, the ideal conjunction of talent and feeling.

When the hidden is a form in its own right, the most important significance lies beyond the text; elusive echoes come through from every direction, and concealed flashes of allure emerge from deep below. This may be compared to the way in which the lines and images of a hexagram in the *Classic of Changes* transform into another hexagram, or to the way in which rivers may contain pearls and jade. Thus when the individual lines are transformed in the body of a hexagram, they change into the Four Images [the four component digrams]. In the same way pearls or jade under the water will form round or square ripples.

The finest pieces constitute less than a tenth of a writer's collected works; and within a work lines that stand out are scarcely two in a hundred. A writer happens on both fine works and out-standing lines by a peculiar conjunction of thought; they cannot be sought by studious endeavor.

Sometimes mere obscurity is mistaken for depth; although it may have some quality of mystery, it is not the hidden. Or intricate craftsmanship may aspire to some particular grace of art; though it is lovely, it is not the out-standing. Only Nature can compound such subtlety, like the glory of plants and trees in their flowering. A beauty obtained by added colors is like plain silk dyed red or green. Silk dyed red or green may be deeply colored, rich and fresh; the flowers that glow on the trees have soft colors, but splendid ones. This is the way an out-standing line shines in the garden of letters.

["Hidden and Out-standing" is a fragmentary chapter that breaks off soon after this (although a "Supporting Verse" is preserved).]

"The Sensuous Colors of Physical Things" treats one of the most important concerns in Chinese literary thought: the relation between the writer and the natural world. The chapter begins with a beautiful evocation of seasonal change and how human beings are part of nature rather than being merely observers of nature. The chapter then moves to a more active relation to nature, in which the writer "moves with" things in his imagination (much as in Lu Ji's "Poetic Exposition on Literature"). Finally, the chapter turns to questions of representation, using the *Classic of Poetry* as the model. The descriptive compounds of the *Classic of Poetry* seemed to possess a perfection that captured the true "quality" of a thing. Liu Xie goes on to trace the evolution of literary descriptions of nature, in the *Chu-ci* and poetic expositions, coming at last to more recent poetry, in which the craft of the descriptive couplet played a particularly important role.

The Sensuous Colors of Physical Things: Chapter 46

Springs and autumns follow in succession, with the gloom of dark Yin and the cheering brightness of Yang. And as the sensuous colors of physical things are stirred into movement, so the mind too is shaken. When the Yang force sprouts in the twelfth month, black ants scurry to their holes; and when the Yin begins to coalesce in the eighth month, the mantis feasts. Touching the responses of even the humblest insects, the four seasons stir things into movement deeply. Tablets of jade suggest things to the kindly mind, and the splendor of flowers draws clear vital force to its peak. All the sensuous colors of physical things call to one another; and how amid all this may man find stillness?

When spring appears with the incoming year, feelings of delight and ease infuse us; in the billowing lushness of early summer, the mind too becomes burdened. And when autumn skies are high and the air is clear, our minds, sunken in the darkness of Yin, become intent upon far things; then frost and snow spread over limitless space, and our concerns deepen, serious and stern. The year has its physical things, and these things have their appearances; by these things our feelings are changed, and from our feelings comes language. The fall of a single leaf may correspond to something we know [that autumn is coming];[9] in the voices of insects we find something capable of stirring our thoughts. We are even more strongly affected by cool breezes and a bright moon together on the same night, or by radiant sunlight and spring groves in the same morning.

When poets [of the *Classic of Poetry*] were stirred by physical things, the associations were endless.[1] They remained drifting through all the images of the world, as far as they could go, and brooded thoughtfully on each small aspect of what they saw and heard. They sketched vital force and delineated outward appearance, as they themselves were rolled round and round in the course of things; they applied bright colors and matched sounds, lingering on about things with their minds.

Thus the phrase "glowing" catches the quality of freshness in peach blossoms; "waving lightly" gives the fullness of the manner of willows; "shimmering" is the way the sun looks when it just comes out; "billowing" imitates the quality of snow falling; *jie-jie* catches the voice of the oriole; *yao-yao*

---

[9]This echoes a famous line from the *Huai-nan-zi:* "We see one leaf fall and know that the year is coming toward its end."

[1]Because Liu Xie goes on to cite descriptive phrases from the *Classic of Poetry,* the primary reference here is probably to those poets; however, the statement is meant to apply to all who write poetry.

emulates the tones of insects in the grasses. A "gleaming sun" or "faint stars" each gives, in a single phrase, the natural principle in its entirety. "Of varying lengths" and "lush and moist" say in two characters everything that can be said about shape. All of these use little to comprehend much, with nothing omitted of circumstance or appearance. Even if one gave these lines a thousand more years of consideration, one could not change or alter anything in them.

When the *Li Sao* appeared in its turn, a more extensive treatment was given to things encountered. It is hard to fully represent the appearances of things, and thus different descriptions were piled one on top of another. At that point, descriptive phrases for qualities such as "towering heights" and "vegetative lushness" were gathered in great numbers. By the time we get to Si-ma Xiang-ru and those around him, the scope of mountains and waters was displayed with bizarre momentum and outlandish sounds, and characters were strung together like fish. This is what Yang Xiong meant when he said that the poets of the *Classic of Poetry* were terse in their language, using beauty to give a normative standard, while the rhetoricians were lush in their lines, using beauty to seduce us.

When they wrote on the wild plum blossoms in the Odes [of the *Classic of Poetry*], it was "some yellow, some white." When the *Chu-ci* tells of the autumn orchid, it's "dark green leaves" and "purple stalks." Whenever describing colors, it is important to note what is seen in season: if green and yellow appear too often, then it is an excess not worth prizing.

More recently value has been placed on resemblance to the external shapes of things. Writers look to the circumstantial quality in scene and atmosphere, and they sculpt the appearances of the vegetation. The depth and extent of their aims are revealed when they recite the work. They consider describing the forms of things to be the fine point of writing, and close adherence to the original to be the greatest accomplishment. Their artful language catches the manner of things like a seal impressed in paste, minutely delineating even the finest details, with no need of further embellishment. Thus by looking at the language, we see the appearance; and through words, we know the moment.

Things have constant appearances, but thought has no predetermined rule. Sometimes we reach the heights spontaneously and quite by chance; sometimes the more intensely we think, the more it eludes us. Moreover, the standard established by the *Classic of Poetry* and *Li Sao* has occupied all the essential ground, so that even the most gifted writers of these later ages tremble to compete with them. All our modern writers follow their methods to borrow their artfulness, and we meet their momentum to achieve something remarkable. If a writer has mastered the skill of responding to what is essential, the work will become completely fresh, though old.

The four seasons move on in their lush cycles; but stillness of heart is important for them to enter into a writer's meditations. However opulent and dense the sensuous colors of physical things may be, their expression in language demands succinctness. This will produce a flavor in the writing that floats above the world; it will make the circumstance glow and be always new. Since ancient times writers have followed in each other's footsteps from age to age; but all have produced variation, each in different ways. The greatest achievement lies in the capacity both to follow and to change radically. The ability to leave something of the mood lingering on after having finished presenting the sensuous colors of physical things is an attribute that shows the attainment of perfect understanding.

Mountain forests and the marshy banks of rivers are indeed the mysterious treasuries of literary thought. Yet if the words are too brief, the description will lack something; and if too detailed, it will be too lush. Yet the reason Qu Yuan was able to run the full gamut of a poet's moods was, I am sure, the assistance of those rivers and mountains.

Supporting Verse

> The mountains in folds with rivers winding,
> Mixed trees where the clouds merge:
> When the eyes have roamed over them,
> The mind expresses them.
> The days of spring pass slowly,
> The winds of autumn howl.
> Our affections go out as a gift,
> And stirring comes back like an answer.

"The One Who Knows the Tone" is Liu Xie's treatment of the good critic and reader. It begins by raising the distinction between those who can judge a work on its own merits and those who are attracted merely by the aura of antiquity. It goes on to address the very difficult question of immediate appreciation, which follows from the critic's particular disposition as opposed to a more educated and catholic taste. The title is based on a famous anecdote told in the Daoist work *Lie-zi:*

Bo-ya was a master of playing the harp, and Zhong Zi-qi was a master of listening. When Bo-ya played his harp, his mind might be intent upon climbing a high mountain, and Zhong Zi-qi would say, "Masterful! Uprearing, towering like Mount Tai." Then Bo-ya's mind might be intent upon the flowing water, and Zhong Zi-qi would say, "Masterful! Onrushing and roiling like the Yangzi and Yellow River." Whatever was in Bo-ya's mind, Zhong Zi-qi knew it. Bo-ya wandered to the dark north slope of Mount Tai and suddenly encountered a terrible rainstorm. Stopping beneath the cliff, his heart full of melancholy, he took up his harp and played it, first a melody of the downpour, then the tone of the mountain itself collapsing. And at every melody he played, Zhong Zi-qi followed the excitement to the utmost. Then Bo-ya put down his harp and said with a sigh of admiration, "Masterful, masterful indeed—the way you listen. The images you see in your mind are just the same as the ones in mine. How can I keep any sound concealed from you?"

The One Who Knows the Tone: Chapter 48 (Selection)

Hard it is to know the tone, for the tone is truly hard to know; and such knowledge is truly hard to come upon—to come upon someone who knows the tone may occur once, perhaps, in a thousand years. Since ancient times those who have known the tone have often held their contemporaries in contempt and cared most for those of the past. This is what is meant by "not driving the horses that are brought to you every day, but instead longing for those whose reputation is known from afar." Long ago when the "Discourses" of Han Fei first appeared, the First Emperor of Qin expressed regret that he was not a contemporary; Han Wu-di did the same when the "Master Emptiness" of Si-ma Xiang-ru was just completed. When the writers were discovered to be, in fact, contemporaries, Han Fei was imprisoned and Si-ma Xiang-ru treated with contempt. This is a clear example of how contemporaries are treated with disdain. . . .

Works of literature are diverse; their content and patterning combine in many ways. What we recognize usually involves bias; in no one is judgment as perfect and comprehensive as it should be. When they hear a voice sing out, impulsive people will tap out the rhythm. Those who feel more strongly than they outwardly show will be transported when they perceive a confidential manner. The hearts of frivolously clever people will leap in delight when they see some intricate fine point. Those who love strangeness will listen in amazement when they hear something bizarre. People recite admiringly whatever corresponds to the way they themselves are, and in the same way they will reject whatever differs from themselves. Each sticks to his own biased understanding, but would use it to judge the thousands of forms of variation. This is what is meant by the saying, "not seeing the western wall because you are looking east."

You can understand sound only after playing thousands of tunes; you can recognize the quality of a sword only after examining a thousand. To achieve the sense that comes from comprehensive understanding, first endeavor to observe widely. Look at the highest mountain to understand the proportions of a little knoll; consider the waves of the sea to know the meaning of a ditch. Only after freeing oneself from a purely private sense of what is and what is not valuable, only after escaping prejudice in one's likes and dislikes, can one have a balanced view of the principles involved. Only then can one see the words clearly, as in a mirror.

To judge the presentation of emotions in a literary work, put these six points before you for consideration: (1) the form; (2) the arrangement of words; (3) continuity and variation; (4) the degree to which it is normative or unusual; (5) the events and principles contained in it; and (6) the euphonic aspect. By this technique the relative values will be obvious.

In composing a literary work, the emotions are stirred and then words emerge; but in reading, we open the text and then move into the emotions of the writer, we go against the current to find the source. Although this may be hidden at first, it will eventually become apparent. No one can see the actual faces of those who lived in remote ages, but by viewing their writing, one may immediately see their hearts.

A fully realized literary work is never too deep; rather, we should worry that our own capacity to grasp it is too shallow. Someone's mind was once fixed intently upon the mountains and rivers, and a harp was able to express those feelings. This is even more true when things are given shape by the tip of a writing brush; then it is impossible that the basic principles of things remain hidden. The way in which the mind apprehends basic principles is like the way in which our eyes apprehend shapes. If the eyes are undimmed, then we can make out every shape. And if the mind is alert, every principle reaches it. . . .

Only those who can grasp what lies deep and who can see into the profound will feel the thrill of inner joy in reading. This is much like the way ordinary people will bask in the warmth of a terrace in spring, or the way in which music and food will stay a passing traveler. I have heard that the scent of the marsh orchid, the most fragrant plant in the land, becomes even sweeter when it is worn. Writing also is a glory of the land, and it becomes most beautiful when appreciated. I hope that a superior person who knows the tone will consider this.

Supporting Verse

> A great bell of thousands of pounds
> Must be tuned by music masters.
> When excellent works fill a bookchest,
> Only subtle discernment can correct them.
> The drifting music of Zheng seduces,
> Don't be misled by listening to it.
> Only by these regulations
> Can one avoid erring on the path.

Cao Pi (187–226), A Discourse on Literature *(Lun-wen)*

"A Discourse on Literature" by Cao Pi is usually considered the first essay devoted exclusively to the discussion of literature. Although it may seem somewhat disorganized and simplistic, it raises important questions—about literature and reputation, about talent or skill as a unique attainment, and about literature as a means for cultural immortality.

One of the difficulties of reading Chinese literary criticism in translation is that it assumes the reader is familiar with a range of authors and works. Cao Pi's "Discourse" makes fewer demands than many later critical texts: Fu Yi, Ban Gu, Zhang Heng, and Cai Yong were the giants of the Eastern Han, the major writers of the two centuries preceding Cao Pi. Cao's main concern, however, is those writers of a generation older than himself, the "Seven Masters of the Jian-an." All had been friends of Cao Pi, and all were dead. Cao Pi tries to assume the role of critic and even-handed judge, beginning by addressing the question of vanity and envy.

Literary men have always insulted one another. Fu Yi [d. 90] and Ban Gu [32–92] were virtually brothers, but Ban Gu made fun of Fu Yi in a letter to his elder brother Ban Zhao, "Fu Yi got to be Imperial Librarian because he had a 'facility' in writing—that is, whenever he put his writing brush to paper, he couldn't stop himself."

Everyone is good at putting himself forward; but since literature is not restricted to one particular norm, few people can be good at everything. Therefore each person makes light of those things in which he is weakest by the criteria of his strengths. As the saying in the villages has it, "A worn-out broom is worth a thousand pieces of gold, so long as it belongs to me." This is a failure due to lack of self-awareness.

The great literary men of the day are Kong Rong, Chen Lin, Wang Can, Xu Gan, Ruan Yu, Ying Chang, and Liu Zhen. These seven masters have a full store of learning and their language does not simply borrow the colors of their predecessors. Yet they have found it hard to gallop head to head on their mighty steeds a thousand leagues, thus to pay one another the respect due.

A superior person looks to himself when taking the measure of others and in this way avoids such entanglements of envy. Thus I have written this discourse on literature.

Wang Can excels in poetic expositions. Even though Xu Gan sometimes shows a certain languor of energy, he remains Wang Can's match. Even the great Han writers such as Zhang Heng and Cai Yong have not done better than works like Wang Can's "Beginning of the Journey," "Climbing High in a Building," "The Locust Tree," or "Thoughts on Travel," or works like Xu Gan's "The Black Gibbon," "The Syphon," "The Circular Fan," or "The Orange Tree." Their other writings are not on a par with these. In memorials, letters, and records, Chen Lin and Ruan Yu are preeminent.

Ying Chang's style is agreeable but lacks vigor. Liu Zhen's style is vigorous, but entirely on the surface with nothing held in reserve. Kong Rong's mastery of form and the quality of energy in his work is lofty and subtle, with something about it that surpasses everyone else. But he cannot sustain an argument, and the presentation of natural principle in his work is weaker than his command of diction—to the point that he sometimes includes playful spoofing. But at his best he rivals the Han writers Yang Xiong and Ban Gu.

Most people value what is far from them and treat what is close at hand with contempt. They respect reputation but disregard real substance. They also suffer all the hazards of a failure of self-awareness in claiming to be men of great worth.

On a basic level all literature is the same, but it acquires differences as it unfolds in its various branches. Generally speaking, memorials to the throne and disquisitions should have dignity; letters and discourses should be based on natural principles; inscriptions and eulogies should respect the facts; poems and poetic expositions should be beautiful. Each of these four categories is different, and a writer's abilities will lead him to favor some over others. Only a comprehensive talent can master all these forms.

Qi, "vital force" or "breath," is the most important factor in literature. *Qi* has its own norms, either clear or murky. And it is not something that can be brought about by force. As "breath," we may compare it to flute music. Two performers may be equal in knowing the melody and following the rules of the rhythm; but when there is an inequality in drawing on a reserve of *qi* or breath, we can tell a skillful player from a clumsy one. A father cannot pass this on to his son, and an elder brother cannot pass it on to his younger brother.

Literary works are the greatest accomplishment in the workings of a state, a splendor that never decays. Glory and pleasure go no further than this mortal body. To extend both of these to all time, nothing can compare with the unending permanence of a work of literature.

It was for this reason that writers of ancient times gave their lives to the ink and the brush and revealed what they thought in their writings. Without recourse to a good historian or dependence on a powerful patron, their reputations have been passed on to posterity on their own force.

When King Wen of Zhou was in prison, he wrote additions to the *Classic of Changes;* even in his glory the Duke of Zhou made the prescriptions that are the *Rites.* The former did not forsake writing even in hardship; the latter was not distracted by health and pleasure. We can see from this that the ancients cared nothing for those great jade disks that were marks of wealth, but instead treasured the moment, fearful lest time pass them by.

Yet people tend not to exert themselves in this way. In poverty and low position, they fear hunger and cold; when they are rich and honored, they let themselves drift in the distractions of pleasure. They occupy themselves with immediate demands and neglect an accomplishment that will last a thousand years. The days and months pass overhead; here below the face and body waste away. We will pass suddenly into change with all the things of this world—and this causes great pain to a man with high aspirations. Kong Rong and the others have all passed away, and only the discourses composed by Xu Gan represent a truly individual accomplishment.

The Tang Dynasty

李唐

THE TANG DYNASTY: PERIOD INTRODUCTION   When the Tang came to power in 618 by defeating the Sui Dynasty, no one would have guessed that this was not simply another short-lived, bloodthirsty Northern dynasty. We now know that the real political credit for the founding of the dynasty must go to Li Yuan, posthumously known by his imperial title Gao-zu. In 626, Li Yuan's son Li Shi-min, later known by his imperial title Tai-zong, seized power in a palace coup, killing his brother, the heir apparent, and forcing the abdication of his father. Historical truth is, however, often less important than images, and Tai-zong was a master of political and cultural images. Tai-zong had the historical record rewritten, portraying himself as a fil-

ial son and the central figure in the founding of the dynasty. Tai-zong then set out to play the role of the perfect Confucian ruler—responsible, self-critical, and attentive to the counsel of his Confucian advisers. This image outlived Tai-zong's long reign and played its role in stabilizing the dynasty with an aura of virtuous legitimacy. Rather than the victor in a risky palace coup, Tai-zong appeared as the true recipient of the Mandate of Heaven.

After Tai-zong's death in 649, his successor Gao-zong soon fell under the spell of the beautiful Wu Zhao, who had previously been a minor concubine in Tai-zong's harem. Victorious in a series of court and harem intrigues, Wu Zhao had Gao-zong's reigning empress deposed and in 655 succeeded to her place. For the next half century, Empress Wu effectively ruled China, first as the power behind the throne and then as sole ruler after Gao-zong's death. Politically astute and ruthless when necessary, Empress Wu was Tai-zong's true successor. After Gao-zong's death, one of Empress Wu's sons took the throne as Zhong-zong; like his father before him, Zhong-zong was under the sway of his own wife, whose family represented a powerful political force and were opponents of Empress Wu. After reigning only six weeks, Zhong-zong was taken physically from his throne by the imperial guard and deposed by his mother, who then put another of her sons on the throne in his place. Six years later, in 690, she deposed this second son and declared her own dynasty. As one might expect, Confucian moralists in later times did not at all approve of Empress Wu, yet she was a remarkably able ruler, who consolidated the Tang's military and political power.

The success of the Tang was in no small measure due to the institutional and military structures inherited from the Sui. One particular Sui institution that was to become of great importance to the Tang and subsequent dynasties was the civil service examination. This began with lower degrees and led ultimately to the metropolitan examination for the *jin-shi* ("presented scholars"). The first half of the Tang was aristocratic, with great families wielding considerable power and maintaining that power by placing their members in the bureaucratic structure. Rulers like Tai-zong and even Empress Wu could not govern autocratically: the influence of the great families permeated the political structure. The examination system, meritocratic in spirit if not always in practice, brought outsiders, usually members of lower gentry families, into the government. No doubt to counter the influence of the great families, Empress Wu saw to it that some remarkably talented men of undistinguished backgrounds rose to high positions in the government. After her reign, the metropolitan examination remained the most prestigious and legitimate route for upward social mobility throughout the dynasty.

The examination for the *jin-shi* was conceived as a "literary" examination, based on the composition of essays and poetic expositions to set topics. The form of such composition was highly stylized—it should not be thought of as testing a capacity to write imaginative literature—but it differed from a competing and less prestigious examination based on memorizing the Confucian Classics. The requirements for the metropolitan *jin-shi* examination changed throughout the course of the dynasty, but it is said that it was in Empress Wu's reign that the composition of classical poetry was first included. Many scholars have linked the flourishing of classical poetry in the eighth century to the introduction of poetry as a required part of the *jin-shi* examination. Examination poems themselves were stilted and have little literary merit, yet it may be true that a required mastery of the form contributed to the spreading interest and competence in poetry during the eighth century.

In 705, Empress Wu was overthrown in a palace coup, and she died later the same year. The two sons she had deposed each ruled briefly in turn in a court still dominated by women, but the new empresses and princesses were not the political equals of Empress Wu. In 712, a new Tang prince established himself firmly on the throne: this was Xuan-zong, who was to hold the throne for more than forty years. The reign of Xuan-zong has long been considered the high point of Tang culture and political and military power; in literature, this period is known as the "High Tang."

The Tang expansion into Central Asia had actually occurred in the seventh century, but Xuan-zong continued the activist policies of his predecessors, expanding the frontier and warding off threats from surrounding states. The Tang capital at Chang-an was the terminus of the legendary Silk Road, along which goods and learning passed between China and the "West" (including India, the newly Islamic Middle East, and Byzantium). Chinese garrisons occupied many of the great oasis cities of Central Asia, and Chang-an hosted a community of Central Asian merchants, artisans, and scholars. Tang literature and the visual arts show a fascination with the exotic West. Ceramics depict westerners with exaggeratedly large noses and beards. The poet Cen Shen, while on garrison duty in Central Asia, watched a whirling, ecstatic Central Asian or Middle Eastern dancing girl and concluded that Chinese dances simply could not compare. Imperfect attempts have been made to reconstruct Tang music, but of one thing we can be certain: the titles of popular melodies suggest a widespread fascination with non-Chinese music. It is probably a mistake to call Tang China a truly cosmopolitan culture; except for Buddhism, all cultural imports remained exotic. But more than any other period in China until the late nineteenth century, Tang China was eager to experience foreign culture.

Though trade flowed over the Silk Road, the Tang frontiers were by no means quiet. In the Northeast, there was constant skirmishing and small-scale warfare with changing tribal configurations. Holding the Southern frontier swallowed several Chinese armies in the jungles of Southeast Asia. Maintaining the Central Asian corridor required repeated campaigns against recalcitrant city states and the Turkish kingdoms. In 751, the Tang general Gao Xian-zhi (a Korean) met an Arab force at the Talas River in the western part of the corridor and was defeated. Although the battle was a minor one, it paved the way for the Islamicization of the region once Tang troops were withdrawn to fight in China proper less than a decade later.

The major military power that Tang China faced was Tibet in the west. Not yet fully converted to Buddhism, much less to Lamaism, Tibet was a fierce and canny political opponent. In Central Asia, Tang expansionist policies came into conflict with Tibetan expansionist policies, far more than with the Arabs. Treaties were made and broken, and Chinese princesses were sent off to the rude capital of Lhasa following the standard Chinese policy of peace by marriage. In the period of China's greatest weakness after the An Lu-shan Rebellion, Tibetan armies briefly occupied Chang-an, and the border with Tibet was drawn only a short distance from the capital, deep within what is now considered Chinese territory.

The Tang royal house bore the surname Li, and Tang rulers fancifully traced their lineage back to the supposed founder of Daoism, Lao-zi, also surnamed Li. Daoism had a fully developed religious apparatus as early as the fifth century, but apart from imperial patronage of individual Daoist adepts, it had not been a state religion. During the seventh century, the Tang established Daoist temples in all the prefectural capitals and sponsored the compilation of the Daoist scriptures. The state also sponsored the foundation of Buddhist temples and monasteries and new translation projects for the Buddhist sutras. Whatever personal devotion emperors and empresses may have felt toward Buddhism and Daoism, the state establishment of these two religions was primarily a political attempt to exercise some control over them.

In the two centuries preceding Xuan-zong's reign, the composition of classical poetry had become in large measure centered on the court and court occasions. Perhaps spurred on by the requirement to compose poems in the *jin-shi* examination, in the first half of the eighth century the range of poetic practice spread widely. More people were writing poems on a wider range of topics and social occasions than ever before. Composing poetry seems to have become an expected activity at banquets and partings, or when visiting friends and famous sites. Members of the bureaucracy traveled a good deal—on missions or to serve in provincial offices. When traveling, officials would often write poems on the whitewashed walls of the government post stations where they spent the night; other official travelers, staying at the same post station later, might write their own poems on the walls answering the work of earlier travelers. The bare walls of public and private places seem to have invited literary decoration. Scrolls were, of course, the primary means by which texts were disseminated, but popular poems also spread quickly by word of mouth and were often sung by entertainers.

Quite apart from the formal composition required on the *jin-shi* examination, poetic skill became a means for social advancement. Poems were presented to influential patrons and could win a provincial invitations to join social circles from which he might otherwise be excluded. The bolder and more unconventional talents were often ill-suited to the kinds of formal composition required on the *jin-shi* examination, and some of the best known poets of the High Tang either never attempted the examination or attempted it and failed; their reputation, however, could often secure them lesser posts through the patronage of powerful officials.

Late in his life, Xuan-zong became enamored of Yang Yu-huan, originally a minor concubine of one of his sons. Like Empress Wu before her, Yang Yu-huan rose quickly through the ranks of the harem and was eventually given the title "Prized Consort," *gui-fei,* which is how she came to be known in later ages, as Yang Gui-fei. Unlike Empress Wu, who held on to power personally, Yang Yu-huan used the emperor's favor to win positions for members of her family, including a distant uncle, the unscrupulous Yang Guo-zhong, who rose to the position of Chief Minister. Yang Guo-zhong became embroiled in a personal feud with a frontier officer who had also risen rapidly by the whims of imperial favor: this was An Lu-shan, made commander of all the Tang armies in the Northeast. Afraid that Yang Guo-zhong would eventually succeed in persuading Xuan-zong to strip him of his powers, in 755, An Lu-shan led the northeastern armies in a rebellion, at first under the pretext of punishing Yang Guo-zhong, and then as a rebellion against the dynasty itself.

The eastern capital, Luo-yang, fell quickly, and a hastily organized imperial army was routed. Ge-shu Han, commander of the Tang northwestern armies, assembled another force behind the impregnable fortifications of Tong Pass, which blocked the road between Luo-yang and Chang-an. Yang Guo-zhong grew fearful of Ge-shu Han's power and instigated a political campaign to get the general to confront An Lu-shan's army in open battle. Forced at last by court orders to leave his fortifications with his ill-prepared army, Ge-shu Han was disastrously defeated and the rebel armies advanced on Chang-an. Xuan-zong was compelled to flee the capital in haste. At Ma-wei post station, the imperial guard refused to go on unless Yang Guo-zhong and Yang Yu-huan were executed. Reluctantly complying with the army's demands, Xuan-zong proceeded on to Cheng-du, the major city in the West. His son, the heir apparent, remained behind to organize the resistance and soon proclaimed himself emperor. Xuan-zong abdicated. Gathering together the remains of the defeated Tang armies, stripping the Central Asian garrisons, and calling in Uighur allies, the new emperor and loyalist forces retook the capitals. An Lu-shan himself was assassinated in 757, but his son and lieutenants carried on active warfare with imperial forces for many years to follow.

The aftermath of the An Lu-shan Rebellion left the Tang weakened and exhausted. Central Asia was lost and the northeastern provinces remained in the hands first of rebels and later of independent warlords who had made an uneasy peace with the dynasty. Many provinces had been militarized during the rebellion, and their commanders were unwilling to give up power. When such commanders died, the local armies would force the helpless court to appoint successors of their own choosing, often the former commander's son, thus creating hereditary local regimes. The loss of tax revenues and unreliability of supposedly loyalist armies made it very difficult for the court to reassert central control. Only once again in the dynasty's history was central government control reasserted; this was during the reign of Xian-zong, who took the throne in 805.

Xian-zong's reign and the decades leading up to it are known as the "Mid-Tang." The Mid-Tang was one of the most intellectually lively in Chinese history. Out of the sense of cultural crisis that followed in the wake of the An Lu-shan Rebellion, there came many calls to return to Confucian values. The most important figure in this movement to "restore antiquity" was Han Yu (768–824). Tang Confucian learning had previously been primarily scholastic, requiring the rote memorization of the Confucian Classics and learning their authorized commentaries. Han Yu advocated the personal assimilation of Confucian values through the classics, making them part of one's life. He also championed what came to be called "old style prose," breaking free of the stylized formality of much Tang prose to a kind of writing more suited to argumentation and the expression of ideas. In these and other principles, Han Yu was later seen as the precursor to the Neo-Confucianism of the Song Dynasty.

The new popularity of "old style prose" in the Mid-Tang is believed to have encouraged the development of longer and more complex prose narrative. Still short by Western standards, the classical language tales of the Mid-Tang built on the motifs of earlier short fiction with tales of encounters with ghosts, amorous fox-women, and other supernatural beings. In the Mid-Tang, however, we also find stories of purely human romances set in the demimonde, the world of courtesans and kept women. In this gray area between prostitution and legally binding marriage, women often enjoyed relative financial independence and a liberty in choice of partners. The existence of mutual choice in relations between the sexes made possible a true culture of romance, for which we begin to find evidence in the late eighth and ninth centuries.

Although many women of the Tang elite were literate, a fully developed women's literary culture did not take shape in China until the sixteenth and seventeenth centuries. Tang women, however, enjoyed far greater autonomy than did women in the dynasties that followed. During the reign of Empress Wu and the short reigns that followed before Xuan-zong took the throne, the women of the court played an important role in cultural life. Although very little of her work survives today, Shang-guan Wan-er was probably the most influential literary figure of the first decade of the eighth century—something possible in the Tang as it could not have been for the rest of the history of imperial China. After her entire family was executed in a palace purge, Shang-guan Wan-er, her face tattooed with the mark of a criminal, was taken into Empress Wu's service, where she rose to become the empress's private secretary. When the empress was deposed, Shang-guan Wan-er in middle age was made a consort of the empress's restored son Zhong-zong. In that role she became the arbitrix of court taste, presiding over poetry competitions and the mixed-sex outings of the court.

The role of women in this period was unique, but even in Xuan-zong's court the favored Yang Yu-huan and the women of the harem enjoyed a degree of liberty unheard of in later dynasties. As a true culture of romance developed toward the end of the eighth century and into the ninth, poetry played as much of a role as stories. Courtesans such as Xue Tao (768–831) developed reputations as poets, and their acquaintance was sought by famous male poets. For the first time, women became heroines in stories rather than simply exemplars of virtue. As often happens in a culture of romance, such stories of suffering or daring in love and boldness in action seem to have escaped fiction and entered the realm of social behavior. In the ninth century, we have anecdotes of young Chang-an women of merchant families falling in love with poets simply by hearing their poems recited. The historical truth of such anecdotes is hard to determine, and, if true, such behavior was certainly the exception rather than the rule. What is significant, however, is the general belief, on the part of both men and women, that such things could happen. And once a culture of romantic love and free choice came into being as an imaginative possibility, it never disappeared—even though the social realities were arranged marriages and sexual availability gained by financial and social power.

The Tang did not fall in a single dramatic event but attenuated through the course of the ninth century. Local rebellions in the middle of the century deprived the central government of important sources of tax revenue; and in 880 one such rebellion, led by Huang Chao, took Chang-an and sacked the city. From then until the end of the dynasty in 906, the Tang exercised direct control over only a small area around the capital. The last boy emperor of the Tang ended up the puppet of a local warlord, who finally deposed him. The period of regional regimes that followed until the founding of the Song Dynasty in 960 is known as the "Five Dynasties."

Tang Poetry: General Introduction 李 唐

Occasions: "Sorry to Have Missed You"

A large proportion of extant Tang poetry is "occasional," consisting of poems once used in a particular social exchange. During the Tang, a poem was often as much a social act as a literary work of art, and the capacity to compose verse with reasonable grace in a wide variety of social situations was an important accomplishment for an educated person. Some of the best of these acts were preserved and passed on, becoming "literature" in the more conventional sense. Yet even as literary texts, such poems always recall the everyday world from which they came, and remind us that although a poem may have been read by a million readers over the course of a millennium, it was originally written for one person.

To offer an example: If someone visited a friend and found that the friend was not home, or if a friend had paid a visit while the poet was away, a poem might be written to say, "Sorry to have missed you." Such was the case one day toward the middle of the eighth century, when a certain Mr. Su, who held an honorary post in the Bureau of Forestry, stopped by the villa of the poet Wang Wei. Wang Wei was not at home, so Su left a poem noting his visit. In such a circumstance, it was only polite that Wang Wei write back—an answering poem—thanking Su for his visit. Mr. Su, dead now for over a thousand years, survives as a flicker in the collective memory of mankind because he once wrote a poem, now lost, to which the famous Wang Wei wrote an answer. The poem's opening, setting the scene for Mr. Su's approach to Wang Wei's villa, is, at the most generous, uninspired. But the moment Wang Wei imagines Mr. Su's discovery of his absence, Wang Wei's genius for evoking a scene in a few images becomes apparent. Su turns his attention outward toward the empty landscape around the house, following the evidence of human presence ever further into the distance, until, hidden behind far clouds, sounds penetrate the silence.

Wang Wei (ca. 699–761), Answering the Poem Left by Mr. Su, Nominally of the Bureau of Forestry, When He Stopped by My Villa at Lan-tian

> Humbly I dwell by the valley's mouth,
> where tall trees ring an unkempt village.
>
> In kindness you turned down my stony path;
> no one answered the gate of my home in the hills.

A fishing boat, stuck to the frozen shore,
hunters' fires burned on the cold moor.

All there was, out beyond the white clouds:
a bell's infrequent tolling that broke
    through gibbons' night cries.

Wang Wei was probably responding to a poem much like the one written some decades later by Wei Ying-wu (737–ca. 792). Tang officials were usually given one day off in ten.

Wei Ying-wu, Going to Visit Censor Wang on My Day Off and Not Finding Him Home

Nine days of hustle and bustle,
    now one day of ease,
I looked for you, I found you not
    and turned back home in vain.
Yet I was amazed how thoughts for poems
    so chilled a man to the bone,
where your gate stood facing cold torrents
    and snow was filling the hills.

When the visitor found his host not home, he looked to the scene around the dwelling, his attention heightened by the absence of the other person. In "looking for" the other person in the scene, the poet sees the landscape or dwelling more perfectly. He may find that the surroundings embody the way of life and the character of the absent person, and thus he may even be said to have "met" the person through the scene. This is the message of the following famous poem by Qiu Wei, composed around the middle of the eighth century.

Qiu Wei (fl. 743), Walking in the Hills and Looking for the Recluse, But Finding Him Not In

On the very summit his thatched-roof hut
led me uphill for thirty leagues.

I knocked at his gate, no servant there;
I peered in the window, just a table.

If he's not off covering his rickety cart,
he is surely fishing in autumn waters.

My timing was off, we did not meet,
but I paused in undemonstrated esteem.

Plants whose colors show recent rains,
through your windows pines heard late in day.

Utter privacy here agrees with me,
the place, by itself, cleanses ear and eye.

Though we did not play the guest and host,
I have grasped well the meaning of purity.

The mood departed, I went downhill;
there was no longer need to wait for you.

Sometimes such a scene of absence around the dwelling can be dramatized, as in the following famous quatrain by Jia Dao:

Jia Dao (779–845), Looking for the Recluse and Not Finding Him Home

I asked his servant under the pines,
he said: "The master has gone to pick herbs.
He is somewhere out there in the hills,
but the clouds are so deep I know not where."

The situation could also be turned around. If a visitor was expected and did not come, the disappointed host might send him a poem, telling him what a lovely evening scene he missed:

Meng Hao-ran (ca. 689–740), Spending the Night in Reverend Ye's Mountain Chamber. I was expecting the senior Mr. Ding, but he did not come

When evening sun passed over western peaks,
all the valleys grew suddenly dark.

The moon through pines brought in night's cool,
and a breeze on the stream filled listening ears.

The woodsmen have almost all gone home,
and birds now settle on misty roosts.

The man made a promise to come for the night,
my harp waits alone on the vine-hung path.

Much of the poetry we have from the Tang is only a fragment of a world full of human exchanges both grand and simple. When sets of exchange poems survive, we can see how much the weight of the words in a poem can depend on knowing what the poet is responding to. Wang Wei's poem below is often read in isolation, but it becomes richer when read in conjunction with Pei Di's initial work.

Pei Di (fl. 720–750), I Chanced on Rain at Wang-kou and Recalled Mount Zhong-nan: Thus I Offered the Following Quatrain

Rains dense and steady darken deserted bends,
from level sands drifting glitter is gone.
Wang River's waters keep going on,
but where now is Mount Zhong-nan?

Wang Wei, Answering Pei Di

Murky and flooding, cold currents broaden,
a vague gray, darkened by autumn rains.
You ask me of Zhong-nan Mountain—
I know in my heart it's beyond the white clouds.

This pair of quatrains between Wang Wei and his friend Pei Di plays on how the clouds and mist of a rainstorm hide Mount Zhong-nan, whose towering presence would otherwise dominate the scene. Wang Wei looks to where the mountain should be, imagines it there, perhaps even believes—because be knows it must be there—that he can vaguely make out its outline. Yet behind the simple exchange lies the Buddhist conviction of the illusion of the senses and the insubstantiality of the perceptible world.

Parting

Poems were also composed at parties, on group excursions, and when visiting friends. The whitewashed walls of pavilions, government post stations, and the cells of monks provided adequate surfaces on which to leave poems as graffiti; and finding a poem on a wall left by an acquaintance would often occasion a companion piece. On journeys, travelers would frequently compose poems to record places visited, and such poems were then sent back as letters to friends at home. The various stages and events of a journey were fixed poetic types: setting out early, meeting someone on the road, lodging for the night. A popular poetic occasion was the "meditation on the past" *(huai-gu)*, composed when visiting some ancient site. The most common social use of poetry was as a letter, the level of formality differing according to the social status of the recipient. Verse letters could range from simple quatrains to long formal poems of hundreds of lines. Such poems were often answered by the recipient, sometimes using the same rhymes. By the ninth century, we find entire collections of these exchange poems.

　　Parting was one of the most important social situations for which poetry was composed. Although partings often occurred under less formal conditions, in one standard pattern, the traveler's friends accompanied him on the first stage of a journey, then held a banquet (sometimes staying overnight), after which came the parting proper. Each of these phases—the send-off *(song)*, the parting banquet *(jian)*, and the parting *(bie)*—might be accompanied by the composition of poems. Parting was an occasion that encompassed true private distress at separation from friends and a public ritual (originally associated with the religious ritual of the sacrifice to the god of the roads). A large number of Tang parting poems have survived, many of them graceful but uninspired verses produced on demand by using the wide range of poetic clichés available to every poetaster. This corpus of Tang parting poems also contains some of the most famous poems in the language.

The following quatrain by Wang Wei was set to music (often called "The Song of Yang Pass") and became a standard lyric to be sung at any parting—a popular ritual much like the singing of "Auld Lang Syne" on New Year's Eve. The speaker urges the traveler, setting off on a mission far into Central Asia (where the An-xi Military District and Yang Pass were located), to drink now and take his pleasure in the present moment, strengthening the persuasion with an ominous vision of the future.

Wang Wei, Sending Mr. Yuan on His Way on a Mission to An-xi

By the walls of Wei City the rain at dawn
    dampens the light dust,
all green around the guest lodge
    the colors of willows revive.
I urge you now to finish
    just one more cup of wine:
once you go west out Yang Pass
    there will be no old friends.

Parting

I get off my horse, offer you wine
and ask you where you are going.

You say that nothing turned out as you wished,
you go home to rest by South Mountain.

Go off then, I will ask nothing more—
white clouds there that never end.

Meng Hao-ran, Parting from Mr. Xue at Guang-ling

There are some men, their aims unfulfilled,
roaming restless through lands of Wu and Chu.

Our chance meeting in Guang-ling done now,
you return by boat on Lake Peng-li.

A mast appears among river trees,
waves rise to mountains over the sea.

Tomorrow your wind-blown sail will be far—
where again shall I share your company?

Li Bo (701–762), Sending a Friend on His Way   *classical poetry*

Green hills stretch past the north ramparts,
white waters circle the eastern wall.

Once we have parted in this spot
the tumbleweed goes on thousands of miles.

Drifting clouds: the traveler's thoughts;
sinking sun: an old friend's mood.

We wave, going off from here,
and our horses whinny on parting.

Most parting occasions could be treated in a variety of styles and forms. One can scarcely imagine a greater contrast than the dignified austerity of Wang Wei's "Parting" above (p. 375) and Li Bo's extravagant parting song below, to one Mr. Cen, about to return to his home at Ming-gao. A rather ordinary place in He-nan is transformed into a fantastic, even demonic landscape, calling to mind the setting of "The Hill Wraith" in "The Nine Songs" (see p. 160).

A Song of Ming-gao: Sending Off Mr. Cen, a Gentleman in Retirement Who Was Summoned to Court

It seems there is someone,   he longs for Ming-gao,
his way blocked by snowdrifts,   heart harried, distraught.
The huge river is frigid and may not be directly crossed,
this ice-dragon's scales   leave no room for his scull.
Remote lie those towering crests
    on the hills of the Undying,
where you hear the raucous din
    of Heaven's flutes.
Their frosty slopes are satin white in rising tiers,
as if steady winds were fanning the sea
and heaving huge waves from the dark deeps.
Jet black gibbons, dark green bears,
wait on sheer summits with lolling tongues,
roaring boughs, shuddering rocks,
make the gall flinch and tremble the soul,
the packs cry out, to each other howl.
Perilous precipices where paths end,
snagging the stars on the high cliff's crags.

We send you homeward along your way,
which stirs this new work on Ming-gao.
The drums mix with pipes, strings are plucked,
as we drink to you in the Qing-ling Pool pavilion.
Yet you do not go—why do you wait,

like a yellow crane turning with backward gaze?
You outshone all talents in the gardens of Liang,
and you raised the "Great Odes" to the east in Luo.
Your wagon is readied,   you cross rough roads,
seeking lodging sequestered   upon lofty bluffs.
Sprawled on white stones,   in pale moonlight seated,
on your harp, "Wind in Pines,"   thousands of valleys hushed.

I will gaze and not see you,   my heart swells in turmoil,
in vines' murky darkness,   the sleet pelting down.
Waters cut through caves and are clear down below,
the waves sound faintly, are heard up above.
Tigers wail in valleys, they bring on the wind,
streams conceal dragons, exhaling clouds.
Cranes in the darkness give forth their shrill cries,
and starveling squirrels chitter and screech.
In the still isolation you dwell there apart,
empty hills grow forlorn, and it saddens a man.

historical references
imagination

Chickens gather in flocks, they fight over food,
alone flies the phoenix, none by its side.
The lizard taunts the dragon, — *(chaos in the world.*
fish-eyes are confused with jewels,
Mo-mu the Crone wears brocade,
the lovely Xi Shi bears kindling.
Were one to force Chao-fu and Xu You
    to be fettered by coach and crown,
would it be any different from Kui and Long
    limping in dusty wind?
For what pain did one man weep and rescue Chu?
For what pride did another brag, making Qin withdraw?
I truly cannot ape those two,
    buying fame, showing off honor,
    to win glory in their age;
I resolve to forsake Earth and Heaven,
    to leave this body behind:
when a white gull comes to you flying,
I will join you forever as friend.

After having conjured up Ming-gao as a Gothic landscape where Cen will live as a
recluse, Li Bo turns in the final section of his poem to heap scorn on the public world
where values are upside down ("The lizard taunts the dragon"). Mo-mu the Crone
was the notoriously ugly wife of the Yellow Emperor, while Xi Shi was the legendary
beauty whom Gou-jian, the King of Yue, sent to infatuate the King of Wu and bring
about his ruin. In this world of inverted values, the ugly woman finds favor while
the beauty is neglected. Chao-fu and Xu You were two ancient recluses who refused

the offer of rule or high position; Kui and Long were both wise advisers. To force Chao-fu and Xu You to serve the state would be counter to their nature, just as to leave Kui and Long in obscurity would be to waste their abilities.

When the army of Wu sacked the capital of Chu, Bao-xu of Shen went to Qin and wept in the courtyard until the Duke of Qin sent armies to rescue Chu. With immense self-confidence in his abilities as an orator, Lu Zhong-lian persuaded the armies of Qin to withdraw from the state of Zhao, even after they had utterly crushed Zhao's army. Li Bo, while tacitly claiming the same abilities as these two famous figures of antiquity, claims that he, like Mr. Cen, has no inclination for such fame and would rather go join Cen at Ming-gao.

Other Poem Types

Not all Tang poetry was tied to social occasion. There was a pure lyric form based simply on writing one's feelings, often called *yong-huai* ("singing of what is on my mind"). These were sometimes associated with a type of poem popular in the late second and third centuries that made use of emotional directness and presumed political engagement, and went under several generic names, the most common of which was the "old manner" *(gu-feng)*.

The various cults of religious Daoism also occupied a very important place in the Tang, and were patronized both by the court and by a wide range of intellectuals. The cult of the Undying *(xian,* sometimes translated as "immortals"), and the colorful Daoist pantheon, attracted many poets, whether as a matter of faith or for the sheer delight in the fantastic. Daoist motifs appear throughout Tang poetry, both for their own sake and as conventional metaphors for the imperial court (Heaven) and erotic intrigues (described in terms of encountering a goddess). More purely Daoist-inspired poetry delighted in endless descriptions of flights through the heavens and accounts of the wonders seen there. One such lyric type associated with Daoist ritual was called "Lyrics for Walking the Sky" *(Bu-xu ci);* these lyrics are found in large numbers.

In a more seriously Confucian vein, a poet might write "poems on history" *(yong-shi shi),* evoking some moment in the past, often making moral judgment. There were narrative ballads treating themes of history or legend, and terse, epigrammatic quatrains summing up large events in a few words. In the ninth century we even have large sets of such quatrains, chronologically arranged, covering the famous events of history in the Tang.

Finally, there were "poems on things" *(yong-wu).* By the Tang, each animal and plant had developed a complex body of literary lore that was collected in large reference works called *lei-shu* (commonly translated as "encyclopedias"). Man-made subjects and a wide variety of other natural "things" and relationships were also included. The encyclopedias would often give something of the natural history of the chosen subject; its appearance in accounts of human history; famous anecdotes in which it appeared; and related poems, poetic exposition, and prose pieces about it. These served as models for treatment by later poets, who might be called on to write on a particular subject in an examination, at a party, or simply for pleasure.

The following poem is an example of a standard treatment of the wild goose, the kind of verse that a well-trained literary person was expected to produce as a social skill. Geng Wei is writing to an assigned topic (probably given him at a party), and he carefully brings in some of the expected motifs such as the bows of nomad hunters in the North, and Heng-yang, the Southern terminus of the goose migration. He must also bring in the further restriction of the topic, "on the sands," which he does in the sixth and seventh lines.

Geng Wei (latter part of 8th century), On the Set Topic: "Wild Goose on the Sands"

Still a long road to travel to Heng-yang,
wings weakened, distress in its voice.

I wonder when it will return to the borders—
the bowstring's twang has so troubled its heart.

Night's shadows, companions are far ahead;
fall's chill, the lake behind it is deep.

What thoughts as it stands alone on the beach?—
only worries that frost and sleet will come.

Du Fu's version is, by contrast, strange and very personal, implicitly identifying his own isolation with that of the wild goose. The second and third couplets are both highly ambiguous: one may read the subject as the lone goose and the object sought as the lost flock, or the subject as the poet and the lost object of vision as the lone goose that has flown on its way.

Du Fu (712–770), Lone Wild Goose

Lone goose, not drinking or pecking for food,
it cries out in flight, voice yearns for the flock.

Who pities that single silhouette,
lost in ten thousand folds of cloud?

Gaze as far as possible, as if still seen,
sad cries many, as though heard once more.

The crows on the moors pay it no heed,
cawing and squawking in chaotic multitudes.

Du Fu and Geng Wei picture a particular situation. Du Mu, the ninth-century poet, envisions scenes in places and times he cannot see: the frontier (Golden River), the Han palace, and the lush landscape of plenty in the South by the Xiao and Xiang rivers.

Du Mu (803–852), Early Migrating Geese

Mid-autumn by Golden River,
    a nomad's bowstring stretched full,
they fly up alarmed among the clouds,
    strewing sad cries all around.

On the palms of immortals the moon is bright,
    a lonely shadow crosses;
at Chang-men Palace the lamps grow dark
    as a few sounds arrive.

They surely realize Turkish horsemen
    are still up north in droves;
must they follow the wind of spring,
    each single one returning?

Weary not of the Xiao and Xiang
    because so few men dwell there:
sesame seeds fill the waters,
    and the shores are rich in moss.

Du Mu uses many of the standard elements appropriate for writing on wild geese, but he transforms them by his imagination. As in Geng Wei's poem, he mentions the birds beginning their migration by fleeing the nomad archers north of China. Du Mu, however, begins with a bow stretched full, and the sudden upward flight of the geese that follows parallels the bowshot that is left unmentioned. Once in flight, these geese become insubstantial, only shadows and sounds. The second couplet, which takes place as the wild geese fly over Chang-an by night, refers first to the statue of a bronze immortal, erected by Emperor Wu of the Han, whose open hands held a pan to catch the autumn dew from which an elixir of immortality might be made. Over the solid figure of permanence a shadow briefly passes in the moonlight, the shadow of a lone goose separated from the flock. The parallel line refers to the palace to which Empress Chen was banished after she lost Emperor Wu's favor. There in the growing darkness she hears the cries of the passing geese, which remind her of the coming autumn (aging) and her isolation. Turning away from these motifs of mortality, in the second half Du Mu seems to invite the geese to break the seasonal cycle and stay forever in the warm and bountiful South.

Character Types and Vignettes

Tang poetry was by no means all social verse or first-person lyric; there was also a large body of poetry describing popular character types. The best of such poems give a quickly drawn scene that embodies a character type or catches some action or gesture that reveals emotion, such as the frontier soldier looking at the moon and thinking of home. These conventional character types were often linked with regions, and so although Tang soldiers served on all the Tang's frontiers, the poetic soldier is usually in the North or Northwest. The swaggering young nobleman and the "knight errant" (an imperfect translation for *you-xia,* a violence-prone righter of wrongs) tend to be associated with the capital. The court lady who has lost the emperor's favor is linked not so much to the capital as to the inner court compounds of the palace. The lower reaches of the Yangzi River had their beautiful young peasant girls and carefree fishermen, while the full length of the great river belonged to the merchants. Other figures, such as the woman in isolation (her husband being away either on military campaign or because he was a heartless rogue) and the immortal, were tied to no particular geographical location. All these are only the most common character types; numerous other figures appear with less frequency, as well as many variations on the more standard types.

Often these figures turn up in briskly staged incidents that can best be called vignettes, which are perhaps the beginnings of the sense of scene found later in Chinese drama. The following are two unrelated cases of coin tossing, the first by a bored palace lady and the second by a peasant girl.

Wang Jian (751–ca. 830), Palace Lyrics XCV

> Her sleep has been fitful since spring began,
>   she does not comb her hair,
> too lazy to go with her lord and ruler
>   on trips to the northern parks.
> For a while she goes and sits on the stairs
>   patterned with flowers of jade,
> and flipping a coin, manages to win
>   two or three tosses.

Yu Hu (early 9th century), Song of the Southland

> She had happened to go by the river
>   to gather white duckweed,
> then went along with her girlfriends
>   to pray to the river god.
> In the crowd she did not dare
>   to speak out openly,
> but furtively tossed a silver coin
>   to find the fortune of someone far.

A favorite figure of male fantasy was the beautiful peasant girl of Wu or Yue picking lotuses. The following are characteristic versions of the type by Li Bo.

Li Bo, Lotus-Picking Song

> By the side of Ruo-ye Creek
>   a girl picking lotus,
> her laughter screened by lotus flowers,
>   she is talking with someone.

The sunlight shines on fresh make-up,
  bright beneath the water,
and breeze billows her scented sleeves,
  lifted into the air.

Who are the young men on the shore
  out looking for pleasure?—
in groups of three or five
  through hanging willows seen.

A dark-maned roan whinnies and goes
  off into falling flowers;
catching sight of this, someone falters,
  a heart breaking for naught.

Lyrics for the Girls of Yue

I
A young Wu girl from Chang-an,
brows fair as the moon and eyes like stars.
Her feet seem like frost in her sandals,
for she does not wear the crow-black hose.

II
Wu youths all have light complexions,
and they love to play at boating games.
They give someone the eye, throw their hearts away,
snap sprays of blooms to tease travelers.

III
A girl picking lotus on Ruo-ye Creek
sees the traveler return with a boating song.
She goes laughing off into lotus flowers
and feigning shyness, she won't come out.

IV
A Dong-yang girl with pale white feet;
a Kuai-ji lad in a pale white barge.
They see each other ere the moon goes down—
it just happens that hearts get broken.

V
Mirror Lake's waters are like the moon,
on Ruo-ye Creek the girls like snow.
Fresh make-up bobs in fresh waves,
two scenes of brightness, both marvels.

Bo Ju-yi (772–846), Lotus-Picking Song

Leaves of water chestnuts curl in waves,
    the lotus tossed by a breeze,
to a spot deep in the lotus blooms
    the small skiff makes its way.
Meeting her love, she is ready to speak,
    then lowers her head with a smile,
and her hair-pick of dark green jade
    falls right into the water.

An Example of Verse Form

Chinese poetic meter was primarily "syllabic," based on the number of syllables in a line. Lines of five or seven syllables were the most common, with lines of three, four, and six syllables appearing less frequently. Neither quantitative meters (based on variations in syllable length) nor qualitative meters (based on variation in syllable stress) were possible in classical Chinese, in which words have only one or two syllables.

In addition to the number of syllables, the patterning of tones in the language came to form an important part of metrics during the Tang. Recent scholarship has suggested that an awareness of the possibility of tonal patterning came from the attempt to translate Buddhist religious verse and the elaborate quantitative meters of Sanskrit during the Southern Dynasties. Somewhat less than half of the syllables in medieval Chinese were in the "level tone" *(ping-sheng),* with the other three tones grouped together as "deflected tones" *(ze-sheng).* In the late fifth century, poets began the practice of alternating level and deflected tones between key positions within a line and between corresponding positions in the two lines of a couplet. This metrical practice gradually led to verse forms that were called, in the Tang, the "recent style" *(jin-ti).*

Tang poems were divided between those in the "recent style" and those in the "old style." "Recent style" poems required tonal balancing, the use of parallel couplets in all but the first and final couplets of the verse, and a rhyme in a level tone. "Old style" poems did not require tonal balancing or parallel couplets and could rhyme in a deflected tone. Quatrains *(jue-ju)* might be in the "recent style" or in the "old style." The following is a regulated verse *(lü-shi)* in five-syllable lines by Wang Wei, entitled "Stopping By the Temple of Incense Massed." First we will give an English translation, then a word-for-word gloss of the Chinese. Note that the Chinese poetic language rarely uses tense markers, pronouns, or prepositions. There is, moreover, no distinction between singular and plural. The translator supplies these by context.

Stopping By the Temple of Incense Massed

I knew not of the Temple of Incense Massed,
I went several miles into cloudy peaks.

Ancient trees, trails with no one there,
deep in hills, a bell from I knew not where.

A stream's sounds choked on steep-pitched stones,
and hues of sunlight were chilled by green pines.

Towards dusk at the bend of a deserted pool,
in meditation's calm I mastered passion's dragon.

不	知	香	積	寺
not	know	Incense	Heap-Up	Temple
數	里	入	雲	峰
several	*li* (miles)	enter	cloud(y)	peak(s)

I knew not of the Temple of Incense Massed,
I went several miles into cloudy peaks.

古	樹	無	人	徑
ancient	tree(s)	is-no	person	path
深	山	何	處	鐘
deep	mountain	what	place	bell?

Ancient trees, trails with no one there,
deep in hills, a bell from I knew not where.

泉	聲	咽	危	石
stream	sound	choke	sheer	stone(s)
日	色	冷	青	松
sun	color	cold (by)	green	pine(s)

A stream's sounds choked on steep-pitched stones,
and hues of sunlight were chilled by green pines.

薄	暮	空	潭	曲
towards-dusk		empty/deserted	pool	bend
安	禪	制	毒	龍
stillness	Chan	control	poison	dragon

Towards dusk at the bend of a deserted pool,
in meditation's calm I mastered passion's dragon.

High Tang Poetry

The forty-odd years from the Tang emperor Xuan-zong's enthronement (712) to his abdication after fleeing the capital ahead of An Lu-shan's rebel army (755) is known as the "High Tang." This period has been, correctly or incorrectly, considered the apogee of Tang culture and military power. In the popular imagination it came to be regarded as the high point of classical poetry *(shi),* before which all was anticipation, and after which all was falling off or distant echo.

A period such as the High Tang becomes interesting not by a single characteristic but by a variety of very different concerns occurring together. The poets of the High Tang present us with remarkable variety, becoming much like characters in a novel, setting each other off. Here we will concentrate on the three most famous: Wang Wei, Meng Hao-ran, and Li Bo. Du Fu deserves separate consideration.

Wang Wei (ca. 699–761)

Many people have tried to define the genius of Wang Wei's poetry. He was a poet who often used the simplest language for a vision of the world that was uniquely his own. Consider a single line from "Written on Climbing the Small Terrace of Pei Di":

> The setting sun goes down beside a bird.

It is a line that could not have been written before Wang Wei: no earlier poet would have defined the motion of a large, regular, and slow thing like the sun in relation to so small and volatile a creature as a bird. Wang Wei is, moreover, concerned with perspective and the illusions of the senses, related to his Buddhist convictions that the world of human experience is only sensuous illusion. We know that the sun is not "beside" the bird, but only seems so from a particular distant perspective, a "point of view" that can shift as quickly as the bird. Yet in the line the only thing that moves is the sun.

Wang Wei came from one of the most distinguished families of the period, and from early in his life he moved with ease in the highest circles of Tang society. The simplicity and restraint of his voice as a poet should be understood against that background, as a personal choice. Although he could write the highly stylized social poetry that was common in upper-class gatherings, Wang Wei was profoundly drawn to various forms of a private, contemplative life: Buddhism, landscape, and the poetry of Tao Qian.

PERSPECTIVE, MOTION, AND ATTENTION

In addition to being a poet, Wang Wei was an important Tang landscape painter (though all the original versions of his paintings have been long lost). In an often-quoted couplet, Wang wrote:

> Born in this age, I mistakenly turned out a writer;
> in a past life I was surely a painter.

Critics have often remarked that Wang's poetry shows something of the painter's attention to space, shapes, and the pattern of relationships formed by objects in space. To this gift may be added the Buddhist devotee's sense that the world of the senses is illusion, as are the emotions we feel through attachment to this world of the senses. Wang Wei's visual patterns often imply both motion and attention, with a play between engagement and detachment from those patterns. Through a series of scenes he can show how, on a journey, the eyes can be fixed on a destination; but once the destination is discerned, the traveler's attention suddenly turns to places left and lost.

Written Crossing the Yellow River to Qing-he

> The boat set sail upon the great river
> whose swollen waters stretched to sky's edge.
>
> Sky and waves split apart suddenly—
> the district capital's thousands of homes.
>
> Moving on, I can see the town market
> and vaguely make out mulberry and hemp.
>
> I turn to gaze back toward my homeland—
> only vast floods that stretch to the clouds.

Watching a Hunt

> The wind blows hard, the hornbow sings,
> the general hunts by Wei's old walls.
>
> The plants stripped bare, the hawk's eye keen,
> where the snow is gone, horse hooves move light.
>
> All at once they are past Xin-feng Market,
> then back once more to Thin-Willow Camp.
>
> I turn to look where the eagle was shot:
> a thousand miles of twilight clouds hang flat.

When Wang Wei treats scenes of violent force, as in the poem above, he transforms them into a tightly controlled pattern. In the poem that follows, Wang Wei comes upon a village festival near Liang-zhou, a northwestern border region where a few

Chinese farming families were trying to eke out a living. The "straw dogs" he mentions were part of the ritual to the field gods; they were treated with great reverence during the ceremony, but after the rites were finished, they were thrown on the ground and trampled. As the ancient Daoist classic, the *Lao-zi,* observed:

> Heaven and Earth are not kind:
> for them all things are straw dogs.

Sight-Seeing in the Moors Outside of Liang-zhou

> Old men of the prairie, two or three homes,
> a frontier village, few neighbors around.
>
> A swaying dance for the local festival,
> pipes and drums worship the god of fields.
>
> Ale is sprinkled, wetting straw dogs,
> they burn incense, bow to the wooden idol.
>
> The shamanka dances in frenzy,[1]
> dust shows on her stockings of gauze.

THE IMAGE OF THE FARMER

The observer may be fascinated by what he sees, but so long as he remains an observer, he can never fully enter the world on which he looks. This is evident in some of the poems in which Wang treats the life of farming—an idyllic world to which he was greatly drawn.

Farming Homes by Wei River

> The setting light falls on a hamlet,
> through narrow lanes cattle and sheep return.
>
> An old man, concerned for the herdboy,
> leans on his staff and waits by the door of a shack.
>
> A pheasant cries out, wheat sprouts rise high,
> the silkworms sleep, the mulberry leaves now few.
>
> Fieldhands come, hoes over shoulders;
> when they meet, their talk is friendly and warm.
>
> At this moment I yearn for freedom and ease,
> and, downcast, I sing "Hard Straits!"

---

[1] A woman shaman.

Other Voices in the Tradition

The last line in the poem above alludes to the *Classic of Poetry XXXVI*. According to the Mao interpretation, this was written when the Count of Li was in Wei and his liegemen were trying to encourage him to return home.

Classic of Poetry XXXVI "Hard Straits"

Hard straits, hard straits,
why not now go back?
Only on our lord's behalf
are we here upon the road.

Hard straits, hard straits,
why not now go back?
Only for a man, our lord,
are we here within the muck.

The reason Wang Wei sings "Hard Straits" is not for the full context given in the orthodox Mao interpretation, but only for the line, "Why not now go back?" This line had been used three centuries earlier by Tao Qian in his famous rhapsody, "Return," in which he declared his decision to give up service to the government and return to his farm. The "Farming Homes" that Wang Wei describes from the viewpoint of an outsider make up the world to which Tao Qian actually returned to dwell. Thus, in the second of Tao's "Returning to Dwell in Gardens and Fields," we can find several of the images later developed in Wang Wei's poem.

Tao Qian, Returning to Dwell in Gardens and Fields III

In the outlands few things trouble a man,
and narrow lanes do lessen coach wheels.

In daylight I close the door of my shack,
a bare room from worldly fancies removed.

Now and then in the village bends,
men come and go, pushing back brush.

When they see each other, their talk is pure
of all but how tall hemp and mulberry grow.

Each day the mulberry and hemp grow taller,
each day my land extends more widely.

Yet I always fear that the frost will come
and they will fall to ruin with common weeds.

There cannot be very much to say about the state of the mulberry and hemp, but the *idea* of talking about the mulberry and hemp—the idea of a world whose only concerns were simple, practical, and immediate—was a topic of endless interest and appeal to poets of rural life. We find it also in Wang Wei's older contemporary, Meng Hao-ran. Although Meng Hao-

ran was not of the same social status as Wang Wei, Meng's friend was probably a gentleman farmer rather than a poor peasant.

Meng Hao-ran, Stopping by the Manor of an Old Friend

My old friend cooked chicken and millet,
and invited me to his farm.

Green trees converge on the village's edge,
blue hills slant outside the stockades.

He lays out our feast facing his garden,
we chat, wine in hand, of mulberry and hemp.

Let's wait till the Double Ninth comes
and I'll come back for chrysanthemums.

Gazing into the Wilds Under Newly Cleared Skies

Newly cleared skies, the meadows vast,
no speck of dust as far as eyes can see.

Town gates stand by the crossing,
village trees reach to a stream valley's mouth.

Beyond the fields, silver waters bright,
behind hills a sapphire peak appears.

No one's at ease in the farming months—
all the household is working the southern acres.

To Pei Di

The scene is lovely at the evening of day,
as here with you I write new poems.

Serene we gaze into distant skies,
our chins resting upon our canes.

Spring breeze is stirring all the plants,
and the orchids grow in my hedge.

A hazy sun warms the chambers,
as a field hand comes to give word:

"Joyously spring returns to the marsh,
the waters rise churning up the banks.

Though peach and plum have not yet bloomed,
buds and sprouts now fill their boughs."

Ready your staff, sir, to turn home—
be advised that the time for farmwork is soon.

THE QUIET LIFE

Wang Wei is best known for celebrating the joys of private life, removed from the struggles and responsibilities of the government office.

When Living Quietly at Wang-chuan I Gave This to Pei Di

Cold mountains grow ever more azure-gray,
fall's floods churn more loudly each passing day.

And I rest on my staff outside this rough gate;
breeze on my face, I listen to twilight cicadas.

The ford holds the remnants of setting sun;
from a hamlet rises a lone column of smoke.

Now once again I meet Jie Yu, the drunk,
that reckless singer before the five willows.[1]

Villa on Zhong-nan Mountain

In my middle years I came to much love the Way
and late made my home by South Mountain's edge.

When the mood comes upon me, I go off alone,
and have glorious moments all to myself.

I walk to the point where a stream ends,
and sitting, watch when the clouds rise.

By chance I meet old men in the woods;
we laugh and chat, no fixed time to turn home.

Answering Magistrate Zhang

Now late in life I love only stillness,
the world's concerns touch not my heart.

I look within and find no great plans,
know only to return to the woods of my home.

There wind through pines blows my sash untied,
moon of the hills shines on playing a harp.

---

[1]Jie Yu was the ancient "madman of Chu," who once sang to Confucius of the phoenix and the decline of virtue. The "five willows" refers to "Master Five Willows," Tao Qian's nameless recluse who was a figure for himself.

You ask the pattern of failure and success?—
the fisherman's song reaches deep past the shore.

Other Voices in the Tradition

The fisherman was an important figure in the tradition, a figure of rustic freedom and someone who both rides with the times and bides his time. The "fisherman's song" mentioned in
the last line above recalls the famous song sung by the legendary fisherman who met the
distraught exile Qu Yuan and offered him wise advice. The work is from the "Lyrics of Chu"
and the *Historical Records:*

The Fisherman (*Chu-ci,* author unknown, 3rd century B.C.?)

Qu Yuan had been cast out, and he roamed by the river's deep pools, reciting
verses as he went by the marshy banks. His countenance looked wretched and
drawn; his shape was shriveled and gaunt. A fisherman saw him and asked, "Are
you not the Thane of the Three Clans?—for what cause have you been brought to
this?"

Qu Yuan then said,

> "The whole of this age is filthy,
> and I alone am clean.
> The crowds of men are all drunk,
> and I alone am sober.
> For this I have been cast out."

Then the fisherman said,

> "A Sage does not get bogged down in things,
> he is able to shift and get by with his age.
> If all the men in this age are filthy,
> why not stir their mud and ride the wave?
> If the crowds of men are all drunk,
> why not feed on the mash and sip the foam?
> What purpose in somber broodings to rise above them
> that you caused yourself to be cast out?"

Qu Yuan answered, "This I have heard: whoever has recently washed his hair must
dust off his cap, and whoever has just bathed must shake out his clothes. How can
I permit such untainted purity as mine to receive defilement from worldly things?
Far better to journey to the currents of the Xiang and there to be interred in the bellies of the fish. How can I permit such radiant whiteness to endure being covered by
the foul dust of the ways of this age?"

The fisherman smirked and went his way, rhythmically dipping his paddle. And
as he went, he sang:

> "When Cang-lang's water is clean,
> I can use it to wash a sheet;
> when Cang-lang's water is dirty,

I can use it to wash my feet."

Then he was gone and said nothing more.

Note that what the fisherman actually would wash when Cang-lang's waters were clean were the strings that held his hat on. Like a "sheet," these would come up dirtier than they went in if the water were less than perfectly clean. I have substituted the sheet both to carry the point and to catch the sense of a jingle.

THE "WANG STREAM COLLECTION"

Perhaps Wang Wei's most famous single work is the "Wang Stream Collection," twenty quatrains on various spots on his Wang Stream estate. Wang Wei's close friend Pei Di wrote another twenty quatrains on the same sites. Wang's quatrains are difficult to translate, not because they present linguistic problems, but because they are so flat and plain. Even in their extreme simplicity, Wang Wei's endless fascination with seeing and the relativity of perception is evident.

This set of poems is associated with a painting Wang Wei did of his estate that contained the sites mentioned. The painting now survives only in many dubious copies.

The Hollow by Meng's Walls

New home in a breach in Meng's walls,
where of ancient trees remain dying willows.
Who will be those who are yet to come?—
pointless grief at the holding by men before.

Hua-zi Hill

The birds in flight go off without ceasing,
once again autumn's hues come to joined hills.
I go up and go down Hua-zi Hill,
when will this downcast mood reach its end?

Fine-Grained Apricot Wood Lodge

I cut fine-grained apricot for its beams,
and sweet-smelling rushes were tied for the roof.
I did not expect that the rafters' clouds
would go off to make rain in the mortal world.[2]

---

[2]The clouds and rain here recall, enigmatically, the goddess of Wu Mountain, who had a sexual encounter with the King of Chu in a dream.

Jin Bamboo Ridge

Lissome stalks shine in deserted bends
and roll, green and sapphire, in the ripples.
Enter unseen on the Shang Mountain road,
and even the woodsmen do not know.

Deer Fence

No one is seen in deserted hills,
only the echoes of speech are heard.
Sunlight cast back comes deep in the woods
and shines once again upon the green moss.[3]

Magnolia Fence

Autumn hills draw in the last sunlight,
birds in flight follow companions ahead.
The glittering azure is often quite clear,
and nowhere is evening's haze to be found.

Dogwood Strand

When they form their berries red and green,
it seems like the flowers blooming again.
If we have a guest linger here in the hills,
I will set before him this dogwood cup.

The Lane of Palace Ash Trees

A slanting path, shaded by palace ash,
in hidden shadows is much green moss.
The gatekeeper sweeps only for visitors,
wary a mountain monk may come.

Pavilion Overlooking the Lake

A light scull greets my worthy guest
who comes from afar across the lake.
We will sit facing wine by the balcony
with lotuses blooming on every side.

---

[3] "Sunlight cast back" refers to the late afternoon sunlight which, being low in the skies, comes in under overhead obstructions and seems to cast its rays back toward the east.

South Cottage

A light boat goes off to south cottage;
north cottage, hard to reach over vast floods.
On the far bank look at men's houses—
we can't tell them apart so far away.

Lake Qi

Playing the pipes we pass to far shores,
I bid you a twilight farewell.
Upon the lake turn your head just once—
hills' green is rolling the white clouds up.

Willow Waves[4]

Lacy trees, touching in separate rows,
reflect in clear ripples upside down.
Do not copy those by the royal moat
that suffer from parting in the spring breeze.

Rapids by the Luan Trees

The moaning of wind in autumn rain,
swift waters trickling over the stones.
Leaping waves strike one another—
a white egret flies up in alarm, then comes down.

Gold Dust Spring

You drink each day from Gold Dust Spring,
with a little you'll live a thousand years.
A blue phoenix coach soars with striped dragons,
feathered ensigns go to Jade Emperor's court.

White Stone Rapids

White Stone Rapids are shallow and clear,
green reeds almost ready to gather in hand.
There are homes on both sides of the water
and gossamer washed in bright moonlight.

---

[4]Willow branches were commonly snapped when parting from a friend, "willow" *(liu)* being homophonous with "stay" *(liu)*. Since officers in Chang-an were constantly being sent off in military service or to civil posts in the provinces, the willows by the royal moat tended to have more snapped branches than most.

North Cottage

North cottage, north of lake waters,
mixed trees half hide its red railings.
South river's waters wind far away,
appear and vanish at green forest's edge.

Lodge in the Bamboo

I sit alone in bamboo that hides me,
plucking the harp and whistling long.
It is deep in the woods and no one knows—
the bright moon comes to shine on me.

Magnolia Dell

On the tips of trees are lotus blossoms,
red calyces come out in the mountains.
Silent gate by a torrent, no one there:
in tangled masses they blossom and fall.

Lacquer Tree Garden

That man of old was no disdainful clerk,[5]
he just lacked the mission to run the world.
He happened to lodge in a minor post—
several trees swayed there dancing.

Pepper Tree Garden

A cinnamon beaker greets the god's child,
the asarum, a gift for the fairest of all.
On onyx mats peppered libations of beer
to bring down the Lord in the Clouds.[6]

Meng Hao-ran (ca. 689–740)

Display of scorn for the compromises that must be made in public life was one of
the most attractive poetic gestures for eighth-century poets and readers alike. The
Tang elite admired free spirits, and Meng Hao-ran made a name for himself as a free
spirit. Meng was a provincial who went to the capital of Chang-an in hopes of gaining a post in the central government; although he did eventually serve briefly on the

---

[5]The "disdainful clerk" was Zhuang-zi, who once held the post of clerk of "Lacquer Tree Garden."
[6]The "Lord in the Clouds" and other images in this quatrain are drawn from "The Nine Songs" of
the "Lyrics of Chu."

staff of a provincial governor, he did not succeed in his political ambitions. Nevertheless, he won the admiration of a wide range of writers and intellectuals.

Going from Luo-yang to Yue

Restless and troubled for thirty years now,
with nothing achieved by book or by sword.

I go looking for landscapes in Wu and Yue,
dusty winds in the capitals weary me.

This small boat will sail the lakes and seas,
with long bows I leave both lords and grandees.

I will find brief joy in that thing in the cup,[7]
and think no more of my name in the world.

Gazing from a Boat in the Early Morning

We set our sails and gazed southeast
to the blue hills and river lands far.

Prows push ahead in the struggle for gain,
back and forth, meeting winds and high water.

Then ask me where am I headed now?—
to visit Tian-tai and its Bridge of Stone.

I look now on morning's colored clouds
and they seem the crest of Redwall Mountain.

Early Cold on the River: Something on My Mind

Trees shed their leaves, the geese cross south,
and the north winds bring cold to the river.

My home is where the Xiang's waters bend,
I am blocked from it far by Chu's clouds' edge.

Tears for home have been spent in travels,
I watch a lone sail at the margin of sky.

Having missed the ford, if you should ask—
level lake and vast floods in the evening.

---

[7]"That thing in the cup" is a kenning for ale.

Other Voices in the Tradition

The visual image given in the final couplet of the preceding poem has a special resonance, echoing one of the most famous passages in the *Analects* (XVIII.6). Confucius, on his way back to his native state of Lu, seems to have been looking for nothing more than a way across the local river. He did not anticipate that the question would be posed to a pair of zany Daoist plowmen, who tended to understand things figuratively rather than literally.

Confucius, *Analects* XVIII.6

> Chang-ju and Jie-ni were plowing as a team. Confucius passed by and sent Zi-lu to ask about the ford from them.
> Chang-ju said, "Who is that holding the wagon?"
> Zi-lu replied, "That is Confucius."
> "The Confucius of Lu?"
> "The very one."
> "He already knows of the ford!"
> Then Zi-lu asked Jie-ni, and Jie-ni said, "Who are you?"
> He answered, "I am Zhong You, called Zi-lu."
> "Are you the follower of Confucius?"
> He replied, "That is so."
> "A vast, surging flood—the whole world is thus. And who can change it thereby? It would be better for you to follow those who flee the world altogether than to follow someone who flees this person and that." And he continued plowing without pause.
> Zi-lu went and told the Master, who sighed and said, "We cannot join the flocks of birds or the packs of beasts. What can I be a part of except to be a man among other men? If the Way were already in the world, I would not seek to change things."

Li Bo (701–762)

Li Bo was a native of Sichuan, a region renowned for its swashbuckling knights er-rant, its writers, and its eccentrics. His family background was uncertain: some have suggested that he was of Turkish descent. As a young man he became involved with Daoist adepts, and through the patronage of the Daoist Wu Yun, he was introduced to the court of Xuan-zong, where he enjoyed a brief period of imperial favor, serv-ing as an imperially appointed Han-lin Academician. His unconventional (by some accounts, rude) behavior provoked hostility and eventually led to his dismissal, after which he wandered through the East and Southeast, living off his reputation and com-plaining about his loss of court favor. After the outbreak of the An Lu-shan Rebel-lion, he joined the Prince of Yun, who was attempting to establish an independent regime in the Southeast. When the An Lu-shan Rebellion was put down and the cen-tral government reasserted its authority, Li Bo was arrested for treason. Eventually he was pardoned and died a few years later, without ever regaining the imperial favor he both sought and scorned.

LEGENDS AND CHARACTERS OF THE YUE-FU

Li Bo was, above all, a poet of fantasy. An attractive image from the world of the *Chu-ci* or from the *yue-fu*, the noblest recluse or the bravest soldier—Li Bo could imagine all these and himself living in such roles. In the following *yue-fu*, an essentially "poetic" recreation of the world of ancient myth has replaced the religious vision of the Xiang River goddesses that we have in "The Nine Songs."

This song is based on the legends that grew up around the Xiang goddesses, who were supposed to have been the daughters of the Sage-King Yao and wives of his successor Shun. Shun, who was said to have had double pupils in each eye, died roaming in the Far South and was buried at Cang-wu in the Nine Doubts mountain range. Upon hearing of his death, his two wives drowned themselves and became goddesses of the Xiang River. The tears they shed when they learned of Shun's death fell on bamboo and stained them, producing the spotted bamboo of the Xiang region.

Parted by Great Distances

Parted by great distances:
so it was long ago with two women,
    Yao's daughters, E-huang and Nü-ying.
It happened south of Lake Dong-ting,
on the shores of the rivers Xiao and Xiang.
The great lake's waters are deep,
    a thousand miles straight down;
could anyone say this separation
    was anything but pain?

The sun was veiled and somber,
    clouds hung shadowy black,
apes were screeching in the mists,
    wraiths wailed through rain.
Even were I to tell you all,
    there's nothing I could mend.
I fear the god's heavens will never shine
    and show my steadfast honor;
thunder booms,
    roaring in fury.

Yao and Shun held it,
    yet abdicated to Yu:
ruler lost subject,
    dragon turned to fish;
power went to subject,
    the rat became a tiger.

Others say:
Yao was kept close in prison,

Shun died out in the wilds,
Yet the Nine Doubts Range
    is an unbroken line of peaks
    and each looks much alike—
we will never know where to find the lonely tomb
    of the king with two pupils in each eye.

The regal daughters are weeping
    off within green clouds;
they went along with the wind and waves
    and never returned.

It moves me to tears,
    I gaze afar
and see deepset hills
    at Cang-wu.
The mountain at Cang-wu may fall,
    and the Xiang may stop its flow,
only then will the stains disappear
    of their tears upon bamboo.

Li Bo was often drawn to the stock figures of *yue-fu*, and would elaborate scenes out of the old *yue-fu* titles, as in the poem below.

The Crows Cry by Night

Beside the walls in yellow clouds
    the crows are ready to roost,
back they fly with a *Caw, caw, caw*
    and cry out on the boughs.

Weaving brocade upon her loom,
    a girl from the rivers of Qin
speaks beyond a window of gauze
    green like sapphire mist.

Then, downcast, she stops her shuttle,
    recalling the man far away,
and stays in her chamber all alone
    where her tears fall like the rain.

Other Voices in the Tradition

We may compare one of the Southern Dynasties *yue-fu* quatrains on this subject to get a sense of the difference between the lively folk version and the more sentimental Tang literary treatment.

/mous, "Songs of the West," The Crows Cry by Night IV

ateful old crow!
neer ballyhoo that it tells the dawn.
t sang out for nothing at midnight,
and my love went off in the dark.

Reproach

The fair woman raises the beaded drapes,
then sits far back and knits her brows.
You see only damp traces of her tears,
cannot know the man who bears her reproach.

THE UNDYING

Li Bo was very much part of an eighth-century "counterculture," consorting with wizards like Si-ma Cheng-zhen and experimenting with various elixirs and drugs. He became a Daoist initiate, and one cannot separate his belief from his poetic image of the world beyond ours. Stories of encounters with immortals and flights through the heavens appear again and again in his poetry.

The Old Airs V

How gray and green stands Mount Tai-bo,
with stars lined in dark ranks above.

Short of heaven but three hundred miles,
remote and disjoined from the world of men.

Up there an old man with blue-black hair,
mantled in cloud, lies in snow of pines.

He does not laugh, he does not speak,
in darkness he roosts in cave on cliff.

I have come to meet this Genuine One,
long I kneel to ask for a spell.

He then shows teeth sparkling like jade
and gives the prescription for refining herbs.

It is written on bone to pass on his words,
his body shoots up, flares out like lightning.

I look after him but cannot reach him,
my passions, swelling in me, burn.

I will work on the nugget of cinnabar
and leave forever the men of this world.

The Old Airs VII

There was once one Undying on a crane
who flew and flew up over Purest Ether.

He raised his voice within sapphire clouds
and said that his name was An-qi.

Then couple by couple, came lads like white jade
blowing lavender phoenix pipes in pairs.

Fleeting outlines at once no longer seen,
whirling gusts send their sounds back from sky.

I look up, from afar gaze after them,
tossed through the air like shooting stars.

I would dine on that herb called Goldenray,
and live a long life, matching Heaven's span.

A Song on Visiting Heaven's Crone Mountain in a Dream: On Parting

Seafarers speak of that isle of Ying—
but in blurred expanses of breakers and mist
    it is hard indeed to find.

Yue men tell of Heaven's Crone,
appearing, then gone, it may be seen
    in the clouds and colored wisps.

Heaven's Crone reaches to sky
    and sideways runs to the sky,
its force stands over the Five Great Peaks,
    it casts Redwall in the shade.
Mount Tian-tai is forty and eight
    thousand yards high,
yet facing this it seems to tip,
    sagging southeastwardly.

And I, wishing to reach that place,
    once dreamed of Wu and Yue,
I spent a whole night flying across
    the moon in Mirror Lake.

The lake moon caught my reflection,
and went with me on to Shan Creek.
The place where Lord Xie spent the night
    is still to be found there now,
where green waters are ruffled in ripples,
    and the gibbon's wail is clear.

I put on the clogs of Lord Xie,[8]
and scaled that ladder into blue clouds.
Halfway up cliffside I saw sun in sea,
and heard in the air the Heaven-Cock crow.

A thousand peaks and ten thousand turns,
    my path was uncertain;
I was lost among flowers and rested on rock,
    when suddenly all grew black.

Bears roared and dragons groaned,
    making the cliff-streams quake,
the deep forests were shivering,   tiered ridges shook,
clouds hung blue,   portending rain,
troubled waters rolled,   giving off mists.

Thunder-rumbling in Lightning Cracks,
hill ridges split and fell;
then the stone doors of Caves to Heaven
swung open with a crash.
A billowing vast blue blackness
    whose bottom could not be seen,
where sun and moon were gleaming
    on terraces silver and gold.

Their coats were of rainbow,   winds were their steeds,
the lords of the clouds   came down in their hosts.
Tigers struck harps,   phoenixes drew coaches in circles,
those who are the Undying   stood in ranks like hemp.
All at once my soul was struck,   and my spirit shuddered,
I leapt up in dazed alarm,   and gave a long sigh.
I was aware only   of this moment's pillow and mat,
I had lost those mists and bright wisps   that had been here just
  before.

All pleasures in our mortal world
    are also just like this,
whatever has happened since ancient times
    is the water flowing east.

When I leave you now, you go,   when will you ever return?
just set a white deer out to graze
    upon green mountainsides,
and when I must go, I'll ride it
    to visit mountains of fame.

---

[8]The "clogs of Lord Xie" are the mountain-climbing shoes that Xie Ling-yun supposedly invented.

How can I pucker my brows and break my waist
    serving power and prestige?—
it makes me incapable
    of relaxing heart or face.

[handwritten margin notes: Not interest power. in imperial power / Escape from the world / other world.]

Dialogue in the Mountains

You ask me why it is
    I lodge in sapphire hills;
I laugh and do not answer—
    the heart is at peace.
Peach blossoms and flowing water
    go off, fading away afar,
and there is another world
    that is not of mortal men.

POEMS ALMOST OF THIS WORLD

Even when speaking from the world "of mortal men," there is often a strong element of imaginative transformation in Li Bo's poetry. He was a performer, whose gestures and claims were larger than life. Great civilizations are built on the immense restraint of individuals, and individuals consequently tend to be drawn to artistic figures of unrestraint, able to break free of convention. The great popularity of Li Bo's poetry was in no small measure due to such an image of himself displayed in his poems.

[handwritten margin note: Alcohol important image.]

Drinking Alone by Moonlight

Here among flowers one flask of wine,
with no close friends, I pour it alone.

I lift cup to bright moon, beg its company,
then facing my shadow, we become three.

The moon has never known how to drink;
my shadow does nothing but follow me.

But with moon and shadow as companions the while,
this joy I find must catch spring while it's here.

I sing, and the moon just lingers on;
I dance, and my shadow flails wildly.

When still sober we share friendship and pleasure,
then, utterly drunk, each goes his own way—

Let us join to roam beyond human cares
and plan to meet far in the river of stars.

[handwritten: Qi - bigger than self / Carefree 春情天]

Summer Day in the Mountains

Lazily waving a white feather fan,
stripped naked here in the greenwood,
I take off my headband, hang it on rockface,
my bare head ruffled by wind through pines.

Rising Drunk on a Spring Day, Telling My Intent

We are lodged in this world as in a great dream, — *[handwritten: Daoist]*
then why cause our lives so much stress?

This is my reason to spend the day drunk
and collapse, sprawled against the front pillar.

When I wake, I peer out in the yard
where a bird is singing among the flowers.

Now tell me, what season is this?—
the spring breeze speaks with orioles warbling.

I am so touched that I almost sigh,
I turn to the wine, pour myself more, *[handwritten: Qi - inspiration.]*

Then sing wildly, waiting for the moon,
when the tune is done, I no longer care.

Getting Out What I Feel

I face my wine, unaware of darkness growing,
the falling flowers cover my clothes.
Drunk, I rise, tread moonlight in creek—
the birds turn back, men too grow fewer.

A Lament for Old Mr. Ji, the Finest Brewer in Xuan-cheng

Old Mr. Ji in the Yellow Springs[9]
again must be brewing his "ripe spring" beer.
Day never breaks on the Terrace of Night,
and who will buy his beer down there?

Han-shan: The Master of Cold Mountain

The Tang poets included a large number of Buddhist monks. Most poet-monks worked entirely within the secular poetic tradition, though sometimes making reference to Buddhist terms or adopting a mode of reclusive or landscape poetry that vaguely suggested Buddhist values. In addition to these works, there is also a large

---

[9]The Yellow Springs is a term for the underworld.

body of doctrinal versification of little literary merit that is conserved in the corpus of Buddhist religious writing.

The closest thing to true "religious poetry" in the Tang was a corpus of poems attributed to one Han-shan ("Cold Mountain"), and a smaller group of poems attributed to his companion, Shi-de. Tradition once placed Han-shan in the seventh century, but modern scholarship has shown that the poems in this corpus were written in at least two different centuries, and it is quite possible that a series of monks were composing "Han-shan" poems through the entire course of the Tang. Whoever is responsible for them, the best poems in this corpus give a vision of "Cold Mountain" as a place that is also a state of mind, unlike anything in the secular poetic tradition. The word for "road" *(dao)* in the first line of the poem below is also the term for the "Way" *(Dao),* thus the line also refers to "Cold Mountain's Way," a spiritual route that is more than physical.

III
It's fun to be on Cold Mountain Road,
yet it has no tracks of horses and carts.

Valley joins valley, bends past recall,
bluff upon bluff, too many to count.

A thousand different plants with tears of dew,
but pines all the same, moaning in wind.

When you lose the path at a moment like this,
shape asks shadow: "Which way to go?"

XVI
Someone asked me the way to Cold Mountain—
to Cold Mountain no road goes through.

The ice does not melt on summer's days,
when sun comes out, the fog there glows.

How did someone like me get there?—
my heart is not at all like yours.

If your heart were just like mine,
then you could get there right away.

XXXII
I go climbing up the Cold Mountain road,
and Cold Mountain's paths do not end.

Boulders lie heaped in the long ravines,
broad torrents, and plants in the misty spray.

Moss, wet and slippery, not due to rain;
the pines make sounds without using wind.

Whoever is able to pass the world's toils
may sit here with me inside the white clouds.

CCXXXII
Man's life in this dust-clouded world
is just like a bug in a bowl.

He spends all day going round and round,
but he doesn't leave that bowl.

The gods and Undying he cannot reach,
unnumbered illusions afflict him.

Years and months are like water that flows,
and then, in an instant, he's old.

CCXXXIII
When Han-shan utters these words,
he may also seem like a crazy man.

When I've something to say, I say it right out,
which is plenty to make others hate me.

If the heart is straight, the words are straight,
a straight heart has no other side.

When we die and cross the river Nai,[1]
who will be still spouting drivel?

So dark it will be on those paths down below,
trapped in the toils of our karma.

The High Tang Quatrain

The quatrain or *jue-ju* was one of the most popular forms of verse; well over ten thousand survive from the Tang. Quatrains could be dense and finely wrought, or they could be freely composed, extempore. Quatrains, particularly those in the seven-syllable line, were often sung by professional singing girls and performers. The brevity of the form placed particular weight on the last line, which might be a beautifully suggestive image, subtle understatement, or a witty punch line.

The High Tang was one of those periods, like the Elizabethan era in England, when the language and a shared poetic practice permitted otherwise unknown or undistinguished writers to produce great poems, poems that are still widely known. In the High Tang such poems were often quatrains, the swift and perfect gift of a moment's inspiration.

Zhang Xu, Peach Blossom Creek

Half-hidden, a bridge soars up
    beyond the mists of the moors,
on the west edge of the stone jetty
    I ask the fishing boat.

---

[1]The river Nai, which must be crossed by the souls of the dead, flows with blood out of Hell.

Blossoms of peach all day long
        follow the flowing water,
but at what spot is found that cave
        upon the blue creek?

The cave would lead to "Peach Blossom Spring," the idyllic farming community deep in the mountains that was described by Tao Qian. The Tang imagination had transformed it into a true otherworldly realm, whose inhabitants had been made immortal.

Wang Han, Song of Liang-zhou

Sweet wine of the grape,
        cup of phosphorescent jade,
at the point of drinking, mandolins play
        on horseback, urging us on.
If I lie down drunk in the desert,
        do not laugh at me!—
men marched to battle since times long ago,
        and how many ever returned?

The tone or mood of a poem was of great interest to traditional critics. In this case, the bravado of the drinking is a foil for the soldier's sense of desperation. The Qing critic Shen De-qian (1673–1769) comments, "Though he [Wang Han] uses the terms of reckless drinking, the sadness is at its extreme." "Song of Liang-zhou" was a popular song evoking moments of a soldier's life on the frontier, and various poets wrote lyrics for it.

Wang Zhi-huan (688–742), Song of Liang-zhou

The yellow sands stretch off and up,
        up into white clouds,
the walls of a lonely fortress
        on a mountain ten thousand feet high.
Why is that Tibetan flute
        playing "Willows" with such bitter pain?—
the winds of spring have never passed
        Jade Gate Barrier.

"Breaking Willows" was another popular song, one that often spoke of the pain of parting and separation. The reason why a soldier in an isolated Chinese garrison would be playing it so mournfully is obvious; but the speaker feigns ignorance, reminding the listener that since there are no willows here, there should be no cause for pain at the sight of spring willows, whose branches were customarily snapped by people saying goodbye to one another.

Parting

> The willows, trees of the eastern gate,
> stand green as they line the royal moat.
> They have recently suffered branches snapped—
> I suppose because partings were many.

Climbing Stork Tower

> The bright sun rests on the hills and is gone,
> the Yellow River flows into the sea.
> If you want to see a full thousand miles,
> climb just one more story of this tower.

Other Voices in the Tradition

Later ages would remember only Wang Zhi-huan's famous quatrain above, and not the quatrain by the Southern Dynasties poet Zhang Rong (444–497) that set the model for it.

Parting

> The bright clouds on the hills are gone,
> the cool breeze ceases beneath the pines.
> If you want to recognize parting's sorrow,
> see the bright moon over the lonely terrace.

Tang poets often took images and patterns from poems of their predecessors and reworked them time and again. Sometimes, as was the case with Wang Zhi-huan's quatrain, a Tang poet would produce a version so perfect that it would become a classic and the earlier versions would be largely forgotten.

Quatrains sometimes celebrated specific cities and regions, each with its own reputation. The simple "Song of Xiang-yang" that follows is presented as a courtesan's song.

Cui Guo-fu, Song of Xiang-yang

> Xiang-yang is a young man's place,
> they come and go through the city.
> All the fun-loving men of the town
> know my skill on the harp of Qin.

Midcurrent Song

When I came back, the sun still was high,
I wished to go on to the flowering isles.
But at the crossing the current was hard,
and my boat whirled around, out of control.

A Little Chang-gan Song

The moon grew dark in the wind
    that came with the rising waters,
and I was out looking for you,
    but couldn't find my way—
then a song of picking water chestnuts
    was sung again and again,
and I knew you were here,
    somewhere on the pond.

Wang Chang-ling (ca. 690–ca. 756), Army Song

A dust storm over the Gobi,
    darkening the sunlight,
red banners half-furled
    come forth from the general's gate.
The forward columns fought by night
    north of the river Tiao—
word has come that they've captured
    the Tu-yu-hun alive.[2]

In the song below, the Han emperor Wu is meeting his future empress Wei for the first time. She was originally a singer and dancer in the palace of Princess Ping-yang.

Song of the Spring Palace

Last night the breeze brought to bloom
    the peach by the open well,
in front of Wei-yang Palace
    the moon's orb stands high.
A dancer of Princess Ping-yang
    has recently found favor—

---

[2]The Tang loved the exotic names of Central Asia as people everywhere have loved sonorously exotic names. The Tu-yu-hun was actually the name of a Central Asian people, but here it clearly stands for the chief.

against spring's chill beyond the drapes
    he gives her a coat of brocade.

Reproach in the Women's Chambers

The young wife in her chambers
    had never known of sorrow,
on a spring day with her make-up on
    she climbed the blue upper story.
She suddenly saw beside the lane
    the colors of the willow,
and regretted having sent her husband
    to seek glory in the army.

Chu Guang-xi (707–760), The Roads of Luo-yang: Presented to the Director Lü Xiang (one of five)

The spring ice melts on the river Luo,
in Luo-yang's walls spring trees turn green.
Just look on the great roads at daybreak,
how around horses' hooves the fallen flowers swirl.

Song of the Southland (one of four)

When on the long river the sun goes down,
he invites her to come to the crossing.
Fallen flowers, as if with a will of their own,
go back and forth chasing the wakes of boats.

The following is an excellent example of an extempore, epigrammatic style—a profound joke in verse that is close to doggerel. Jing-yun carries the conventional praise of a painting's verisimilitude a step too far.

Jing-yun (monk), Painting of a Pine

That painted pine looks exactly
    like a real pine tree—
now wait a moment and let me think
    whether I can recall—
It was up upon Mount Tian-tai
    that I saw it once before,
to the south side of the Stone Bridge,
    the third trunk over.

Cang Jie was the legendary inventor of Chinese characters. The idea for the characters supposedly came to Cang Jie's mind after seeing the tracks of birds.

Cen Shen (715–770), On the Terrace of Cang Jie's Invention of Characters at the San-hui Temple

A wilderness temple, its grass-grown terrace at dusk,
the weather cold, its ancient trees groan.
On deserted stairs there are tracks of birds—
still like that time when he first invented writing.

AN OUTING ON LAKE DONG-TING

In the autumn of 759, a group of old friends, then exiles, who had known one another in the capital in better days, met in the South by Lake Dong-ting. One of these friends was the poet Li Bo; another was Jia Zhi. They all went out on a boating excursion onto Lake Dong-ting in the evening, and there Li Bo wrote a series of five of his most famous quatrains celebrating the beauty of moment. Three quatrains by Jia Zhi on the occasion also survive and show how the power of a shared style could enable a minor literary talent to write almost as the equal of one of the two greatest poets of the dynasty. Li Bo's poems show his inclination to transform earthly scenes into scenes of fantasy; Jia Zhi's poems are written in the more characteristic quatrain style of the age but are every bit as memorable. Both poets called to mind echoes of exile and death beyond the edges of the vast lake, places like Chang-sha, where the Han intellectual Jia Yi was banished, and the Xiang River region, where the Lady of the Xiang and her sister must still be weeping for their husband, the Sage-King Shun.

Li Bo, Accompanied by My Kinsman Li Ye, Formerly Vice Director of the Ministry of Justice, and by Jia Zhi, Formerly Drafter in the Secretariat, I Go on an Excursion on Lake Dong-ting (four of five poems)

I

West I gaze from Lake Dong-ting
    where the river divides in Chu,
waters stretch southward to the sky,
    with not a cloud to be seen.
The sun is setting in Chang-sha,
    autumn's colors are far,
and I, unaware of the place where she weeps—
    the Lady of the Xiang.

II

South on the lake the autumn waters
    are without mist this night—
would that we could ride these currents
    straight up into sky!
Come for the while to Lake Dong-ting,
    stock up on moonbeams,

411

then take your boat and buy some wine
    beside the white clouds.

IV

To the west of Lake Dong-ting
    is the glow of the autumn moon,
north of the rivers Xiao and Xiang
    the swans are flying early.
Drunken travelers fill the boat
    all singing "White Linen,"
unaware that the frost and dew
    gets into their autumn clothes.

V

To Xiao and Xiang the royal daughters
    went and did not return,
all that remains are the autumn grasses
    edging Lake Dong-ting.
The bright lake, swept calm and clear,
    opens its mirror of jade,
and there in bright colors painted
    is the Mountain of the Lady.[3]

Jia Zhi (718–772), On First Arriving in Ba-ling, Joining Li Bo and Pei, We Go Boating on Lake Dong-ting (two of three)

I

These men that I've met on the river
    are all companions of old,
ever gazing on the hills of the Xiang
    brings unbearable melancholy.
The bright moon, the autumn wind,
    the waters of Lake Dong-ting,
a lone swan, the falling leaves, a tiny skiff.

II

A chaotic tumult of maple tree shores,
    the falling leaves so many,
the autumn floods on Lake Dong-ting
    late in the day bring waves.
In a light boat we go with our whim,
    no care whether near or far,
among white clouds in bright moonlight
    weep the Maidens of the Xiang.

---

[3]The Mountain of the Lady, Jun-shan, is in the middle of the lake, so named because it was supposedly visited by the goddesses, the wives of Shun.

Du Fu (712–770) 李唐

Ever since the importance of Du Fu's poetry first came to be recognized early in the ninth century, readers of many different periods and types have considered Du Fu to be the greatest poet of the Chinese tradition. Such general (though not universal) consensus can partially be explained by the immense variety of Du Fu's work, which sustained quite different tastes and historical changes in fashion. In part, that consensus was also a consequence of the inertia of "canon"; like Shakespeare in the English tradition, Du Fu's poetry came to be so deeply bound up with the constitution of literary value that generation after generation of poets and critics rediscovered themselves and their interests in some aspect of the poet's work. Consequently, when challenges were posed to the tradition of classical poetry as a whole—as occurred in the late Ming—Du Fu bore the brunt of the critique.

Chinese critics from the Song Dynasty on often referred to Du Fu as the "poet-historian"; and indeed, if a reader is interested in the particular details of the period of the An Lu-shan Rebellion, he or she will find in Du Fu comments on current events and powerful images of the historical moment eliciting an immediacy that always eluded the historian proper. The Confucian interpretation of the *Classic of Poetry* as bearing witness to the history of the Zhou Dynasty lent authority to such a use of poetry; Du Fu saw himself in the role of the engaged witness of a general political and social situation that reveals itself in particulars. In a larger sense, Du Fu was the historian of himself, creating in his responses to particular situations a coherent life story.

It was perhaps this sense of the poet's life that made Du Fu one of the first to have his poems arranged chronologically in early editions, a practice that continued in most later editions of his work. For this reason, Du Fu's poems have been traditionally read in the context of the stages of his life. Though much in his poetry transcends a purely biographical reading, this remains a convenient way to first approach it.

Early Du Fu

Du Fu's earliest extant poems date from his maturity as an aspirant for office in Chang-an. He was already someone more than merely competent in the various kinds of writing that were popular in the 740s and early 750s, though his work did not yet give evidence of the depth and complexity that was to come. Some of his early occasional poems show him to be one of the most remarkable stylists of the period. Du Fu was the grandson of Du Shen-yan, a major figure in the court poetry of the turn of the eighth century, and it seems that Du Fu took particular pride in his mastery of that densely descriptive style.

Another Poem on Mr. Zheng's Eastern Pavilion

> This splendid pavilion enters azure mists,
> where comes autumn sun's clear glow in disarray.
>
> Fallen boulders slant upon mountain trees,
> and clear ripples trail sheets of algae.
>
> Lavender scales vault, colliding with shore,
> a blue-gray hawk returns to guard the nest.
>
> Towards evening I seek the road I must take,
> with tattered clouds flying past horse's flank.

Du Fu's early poems are not all as stylishly elegant as "Another Poem on Mr. Zheng's Eastern Pavilion." In the same period, he also wrote in the bolder and freer style of the 740s, with an extravagance reminiscent of Li Bo. Mei-pi Lake, at the edge of South Mountains southwest of the capital, was a popular place for excursions.

A Mei-pi Lake Song

> The brothers Cen have a passion for wonders
> and took me to visit Mei-pi far away.
> Earth and sky grew ashen and somber—
>   their color suddenly changed,
> then thousands of acres of mighty waves,
>   a hoard of amethyst.
>
> And into amethyst vistas spread
>   our boat set sail:
> the experience strange, elation crested,
>   anxious thoughts then came,
> of Behemoth rising and Leviathan,
>   ship-swallower—these are known no more,
> but, alas, who will be by my side
>   in cruel winds and white water?
>
> My host's brocaded sails
>   unfurl on my behalf,
> and the boatman's joy is great
>   that murky fog is gone.
> Ducks scatter in confusion,
>   a rowing song begins,

while murmurings of far music come
    through the formless azure air.

Depths unmeasured
    by plumbline or pole,
leaves of water chestnut, blossoms of lotus
    drift as if freshly scrubbed.
And now in the very midst of the waters,
    clear as some arm of the sea,
sinking infinite beneath us,
    the black form of South Mountain.

South of midslope all the hill
    lies here submerged,
a shimmering reflection stirred
    in a plain of vast waters.
Upon its darkness our skiff rams
    the cliff temple, Edge of Clouds,
till the moon comes out on the face of the waters
    through the pass at Indigo Fields.

It is at this moment a jet black dragon
    puffs a pearl from its jaws;
the god of waters strikes his drum,
    the herds of dragons scurry.
Dancing and singing the spirits come forth,
    the Han's Maidens, the Ladies of Xiang,
tasseled poles golden, kingfisher banners,
    a radiance hovering in the half-real.

They are close by me—yet I worry only
    that their thunder and rain will come:
and through the vast space the god's intent
    is not understood.

Youth and your prime do not endure,
    no escape from old age,
yet still there has ever been
    much sorrow, great joy too.

"Mei-pi Lake Song" was written in a song style using a seven-syllable line. Each of the main formal genres of poetry had its own distinct personality. The following poem from about the same period also treats an excursion on Lake Mei-pi, but this poem is a regulated verse in the seven-syllable line. In the Gothic excess of the preceding poem, visions of gods and goddesses appear dancing as wisps of dark cloud stream past the moon; the images of the regulated verse are, in contrast, almost precious, as the reflections of dancers' fans appear in the bubbles made by fish.

Boating on the Reservoir West of the City

Dark blue brows and gleaming teeth
    are on this towered barge,
the transverse flutes and short fifes
    lend sadness to far-off skies.

In the breeze of spring we let ivory masts
    move along where they will;
through the drawn-out day we calmly watch
    the brocade cables pulled.

Fish puff tiny waves
    rippling the dancers' fans,
swallows strut through windborne petals
    falling on mats for dancing.

Had we not these smaller boats,
    so skillful in plying their oars,
how could we have brought these hundred jugs
    of ale that flows like a fountain?

Giving Account of Oneself

If one meaning of "lyric" is that the poet writes about himself, Chinese poetry had, by the Tang, become a distinctly lyric poetry. Nevertheless, no poet before Du Fu, with the possible exception of Tao Qian, had ever made such elaborate efforts to give an account of himself. "A Song of My Cares . . ." is the long poem Du Fu wrote on leaving the capital to visit his family just before the rebellion of the frontier general An Lu-shan. There was a general sense of foreboding and unease about the political situation at the time. Du Fu successfully weaves together self-analysis, political comment, and an account of public and private tragedy.

    One reason for the appeal of Du Fu's poetry, and a reason his work often fails in translation, is his mastery of the full range of the literary language, its nuances and registers. Du Fu can be the most colloquial of High Tang poets, and also the most erudite. Much of his work is studded with allusions and phrases with a cultural resonance that eludes translation. The most obvious references require notes, and translation must sacrifice the more subtle choices of words. To mention just two cases here: when, in the fourth line, Du Fu says that he "secretly likened himself" to Hou Ji and Xie, he deliberately echoes Confucius' comparison of himself to an ancient sage in the *Analects,* and Du Fu's assumption of the authoritative voice of Confucius remains an undercurrent throughout the poem. Furthermore, not only were Hou Ji and Xie good ministers of their respective rulers, each was the ancestor of a dynasty. (This is ironically echoed later in the poem in the death of Du Fu's son from hunger.) The second case occurs in the following couplet, when Du Fu says that he has become "too large to be useful." Every contemporary reader would recognize this phrase as the attribute of Hui-zi's gourd in the *Zhuang-zi.* The philosopher Hui-zi once complained to Zhuang-zi that he had grown a gourd that was "too large to be useful," too heavy to carry liquid and too clumsy to handle, so that he finally smashed it. Zhuang-zi chided him, saying that he simply did not know how to put things to their proper use, that he could have made it into a boat and sailed away in it (a possibility that Du Fu picks up on later when he speaks of his "goal to live on the rivers and lakes"). Thus Du Fu mocks himself as being of little practical use to the state, but at the same time quietly asserts the magnitude of his capacities, if only their use were known.

A Song of My Cares When Going from the Capital to Feng-xian

A man of Du-ling in commoner's clothes,
the older he grows, the more foolish his fancies.

So naïve in all that he swore to become!—
he secretly likened himself to Hou Ji and Xie.[1]

He proved at last too large to be useful,
white-haired now, and willing to bear privation.

When the coffin closes, all will be settled;
yet these goals ever look for fulfillment.

I worry for our folk to the end of my years,
I sigh, and my guts are in turmoil within.

I earn sneers from old men, once fellow students,
yet I sing out loudly, and with fierce intensity.

I do have aims to live on rivers and lakes,
there to see off my days, aloof and serene.

But I've lived in an age of a Yao or a Shun[2]
and could not bear to withdraw forever.

Yet now the Halls of State are fully complete,
in the building's structure, no gaps at all.[3]

Like sunflower and pulse, I bend to the sun—
truly hard to rob a thing of its nature.

Then I look around on this ant-breed of men,
who can only go seeking their own little holes.

---

[1]The significance of the particular two ancient sages to whom Du Fu compares himself is ambiguous. On the one hand, Hou Ji and Xie were important ministers, Hou Ji serving the Sage-King Yao as Master of Farming, and Xie serving Yu as the supervisor of education. But Hou Ji was also the ancestor of the Zhou royal house, while Xie was the ancestor of the Shang.

[2]It was conventional politeness to speak of the reigning emperor, in this case Xuan-zong, as a sage-king, like Yao or Shun in high antiquity.

[3]That is, there are enough talented men to fill the necessary posts in the government and he, Du Fu, is not needed.

Why should they aspire to be Leviathan
planning rashly to sprawl in the deeps of the sea?[4]

Hereby I am aware of the pattern of life,
and am ashamed to alone strive for favor.

I have gone on thus stubbornly until now—
I could not bear to just sink to the dust.

But at last I'm chagrined before Chao-fu, Xu You,[5]
men unable to alter their firm resolve.

I drink deeply to banish these thoughts for the while,
then burst into such an unhappy song.

It was year's end, all plants were dying,
and the high hills had cracked in sharp winds.

The royal avenues lay sunken in shadow
as the traveler set forth at midnight.

The frosts were harsh, my coat's belt snapped,
my fingers were stiff, I could not tie it back.

At the break of dawn I passed Mount Li,
the imperial couch on its towering crest.[6]

Ill-omened auroras stuffed a cold sky,
and I tramped along slippery valley slopes.

Vapors surged swelling from Jasper Pool,
where the royal guardsmen rub and clack.

There lord and courtiers linger in pleasures,
music stirs, thunders through empty space.

All granted baths there have long hat ribbons,[7]
no short tunics join in their feasts.

Yet silk bolts apportioned in the royal court
came first from the homes of poor women.

Whips were used on their menfolk,
and taxes were gathered to present to the palace.

His Majesty's kindness in baskets for courtiers
is, in fact, to bring life to the principalities.

---

[4]In this context, Leviathan, the monstrously large sea creature, seems to be a figure for grand vision and high ambitions.
[5]Chao-fu ("Nest-father") and Xu You were exemplary recluses who refused the reins of government when they were offered.
[6]This was Hua-qing Palace, the pleasure resort of Xuan-zong and Yang the Prized Consort.
[7]The primary attraction of Hua-qing Palace was its hot springs. Those with "long hat ribbons" are, of course, the great officers of the court.

If the courtiers scorn this ultimate rule,
it is not that Our Lord throws these things away.

Many officers now are filling the court,
it is fitting that kindly men tremble in fear.

Moreover, I've heard golden plate of the Household
is now all in the homes of the Marriage Kin.[8]

In the midst of great halls goddesses dance,
diaphanous film flares from marble flesh.

There are cloaks of sable to warm the guests,
as sad notes of flutes follow harps' clear tones.

Guests are urged to taste camel-hoof soup,
frosty oranges weigh on the sweet tangerines.

Crimson gates reek with meat and wine,
while on the streets, bones of the frozen dead.

Grimness and grandeur, a mere foot apart,
so upsetting I cannot continue to tell.

My northbound cart came where the Jing meets the Wei,
at the official crossing I again changed my track.

Masses of waters came down from the west,
looming high as far as the eye could see.

It seemed as if Kong-tong Mountain had come,
I feared it would knock and break pillars of sky.

We were lucky the bridge had not yet collapsed,
yet the sounds of its crossbeams creaked and groaned.

Travelers reached hands to help each other over,
if the river grew broader, we could not cross.

I had lodged my wife off in a different county,
ten mouths to protect from the winds and snow.

Who could go long without looking to them?
I hoped now to share their hunger and thirst.

When I came in the gate I heard crying out:
my young son had just died of hunger.

I could not suppress a wail of my own
when the whole lane was sobbing.

---

[8]The reference here is to the Yangs, the kin of the Prized Consort, who took every opportunity to enrich themselves while the consort enjoyed Xuan-zong's favor.

What troubles me is in being a father
my not getting food caused this infant's death.

 I could not have known that before the harvest
such calamity would come to our poverty.

All my life I have been exempt from taxes,
and my name is not registered for conscription.

Considering what bitter things happened to me,
ordinary people must be truly in dire straits.

I brood silent on those who lost livelihoods,
then think of our troops on far campaigns.

Reasons to be troubled are as great as South Mountain,
a chaos that no one can gasp.

The Poetry of the Rebellion

In 755, the northeastern frontier command under An Lu-shan rebelled against the central government and moved into the interior, first taking the Eastern capital, Luo-yang, and then, after crushing the imperial army sent against them, occupying Chang-an itself. Du Fu found himself behind enemy lines in the capital, commenting on the battles that loyalist troops were losing to An Lu-shan's armies and reminiscing about the splendors of the capital during Xuan-zong's reign—splendors that seem to have vanished so quickly.

The View in Spring

A kingdom smashed, its hills and rivers still here,
spring in the city, plants and trees grow deep.

Moved by the moment, flowers splash with tears,
alarmed at parting, birds startle the heart.

War's beacon fires have gone on three months,
letters from home are worth thousands in gold.

Fingers run through white hair until it thins,
cap-pins will almost no longer hold.[9]

While Du Fu was behind rebel lines in Chang-an, the well-meaning but militarily naïve minister Fang Guan was given charge of a large loyalist force sent against the rebels. This army was divided into three divisions, and the central division first met An Lu-shan's troops at Chen-tao Marsh. Fang Guan, a Confucian with great faith in early texts, followed an ancient Zhou practice of putting the troops in oxcarts flanked by horses. The rebels used fire to panic the oxen, and the imperial troops were slaugh-

---

[9]The cap that Du Fu would have pinned in his thinning hair was that of an official.

tered. Soon afterward, a similarly disastrous defeat was inflicted on the southern division of the army at Greenslope.

Lament for Chen-tao

In winter's first month, from ten provinces
    sons of good families—
their blood became the water that stood
    in the marshes of Chen-tao.

The moors were wide, the sky was clear,
    of battle there was no sound:
forty thousand imperial troops
    had died on the very same day.

Bands of Turks were coming back
    wiping their arrows clean,
still singing their nomad songs
    they drank in the capital market.

Citizens of the capital turned
    to face the north and weep,
day and night they keep looking
    for loyalist armies to come.

Lament for Greenslope

Our army was at Greenslope
    right by the eastern gate,
weather was cold, they watered their horses
    in pits of Mount Tai-bo.

The blond-haired tribes of Xi folk
    move farther west each day,
several horsemen bent their bows
    and dared to dash forth to attack.

Mountains snowy, the river frozen,
    bleak winds of evening howl;
the blue is smoke from the beacon fires,
    the white is their bones.

If only I could send a letter
    and let it reach our troops—
hold on and wait until next year,
    don't act rashly!

Du Fu did not hesitate to offer strategic advice to the imperial armies (which were much in need of good advice). About the same time, he visited the desolate Bending River Park and its pleasure palaces in the southeastern corner of Chang-an, and there he recalled the splendid outings of Xuan-zong and Yang the Prized Consort. At the time, Yang the Prized Consort, bearing popular blame for the rebellion, had already been killed by the emperor's guard at Ma-wei Post Station, while Xuan-zong continued his flight to the west, passing Sword-Tower Pass. Once safe in Cheng-du, the capital of the Western region of Shu, Xuan-zong acquiesced in his abdication in favor of his son, who became the new emperor Su-zong.

Lament by the River

An old man, a countryman from Shao-ling,
    sobs swallowing back the sound,
he walks hidden on a day in spring
    by a bend of the Bending River.

By the river the palace galleries
    locked in by a thousand gates,
thin willow branches and fresh reeds—
    for whom do they show their green?

I think back when rainbow banners
    came down to this Southern Park,
and the thousands of things within the park
    all took on a bright complexion.

That woman, who was first of all
    in the Zhao-yang Galleries,
went with her lord in the same palanquin
    and attended by his side.

The handmaidens who rode in front
    all bore arrows and bows
on white horses that chomped and foamed
    on bits of yellow gold.

They bent back and, facing sky,
    shot arrows into clouds;
a single shaft brought plummeting
    a pair of wings in flight.

Those bright eyes and sparkling teeth—
    where are they today?
Blood has stained her roaming soul,
    she cannot make it home.

From here where the clear Wei flows on east,
    to the depths of Sword-Tower Pass;
between those who went and those who stayed,
    there is no exchange of news.

If any man has feelings,
    tears will soak his breast,
the river waters and river flowers
    will never come to an end.

Turkish horsemen in gathering dusk,
    dust is filling the city,
I am on my way to south of the city
    but turn and gaze to the north.

Du Fu escaped the rebel-held capital and made his way to the temporary capital at Feng-xiang, where the new emperor Su-zong fulfilled Du Fu's lifelong ambition by giving him a post close to the throne. After a short period of service, Su-zong granted the poet permission to visit his family, whom he had earlier removed to a place of safety in the North. The following poems give an account of Du Fu's arrival at Jiang Village where his family was lodged.

Jiang Village (two of three)

I
From west of the towering ochre clouds
the sun's rays descend to the plain.

In the brushwood gate birds raise a racket:
from a thousand miles the traveler comes home.

Wife and children are amazed I survived,
when surprise settles, they wipe away tears.

I was swept along in the turmoil of the times,
by chance I managed to get back alive.

Our neighbors are filling the wall,
deeply moved, they're sobbing too.

Toward night's end I take another candle,
and face you, as if still in a dream.

III
The flock of chickens squawked frantically:
when guests arrive, the chickens fight.

I drove the chickens up in the trees,
then heard the knock on my brushwood gate.

There were four or five elders
come to ask of my long travels far.

Each had brought something in hand,
from jugs we poured brew thick and clear.

423

"Please don't refuse our weak beer—
there's no one to plow the millet fields.

Since armed struggle has not yet ended,
our boys are all on campaign in the east."

"Old gentlemen, let me sing for you;
in such hardship your kindness shames me."

The song ended, I looked to Heaven and sighed,
and everyone present shed streaming tears.

Shortly thereafter imperial forces retook Chang-an, and Du Fu returned to the capital to resume a post at court. The following poem, suggesting something of the poet's later style, is usually ascribed to the period shortly after the recapture of Chang-an.

Bending River (first of two)

When a single petal falls away,
    it is spring's diminishment,
a breeze that tosses thousands of flecks
    quite makes a man dejected.

I watch them the while, till almost gone,
    blossoms passing my eyes,
weary not, though the harm be great,
    of ale that enters lips.

At river's side small manors
    are roosts for kingfishers,
high tomb barrows by the park
    give unicorns' repose.

Careful research on the pattern of things
    sends men to seek delight—
what use to let hopes of tenuous glory
    fetter this body of mine?

When An Lu-shan's rebel armies were advancing quickly from the Eastern capital Luo-yang westward toward Chang-an, the experienced frontier general Ge-shu Han was given the charge to block their advance. He initially deployed his troops behind the well-fortified defenses at Tong Pass; but later, succumbing to pressure from the court for more decisive military action, he abandoned the pass to meet An Lu-shan's armies in the open. Loyalist forces were crushed in the Battle of Peach Grove and the way was opened for the rebel advance on Chang-an. In the following poem, Du Fu is making his way through the pass after An Lu-shan's forces have been driven back to the east. Du Fu meets an officer in charge of rebuilding the fortifications: the ensuing dialogue is a fine example of Confucian judgment regarding the relative merits of technology and personnel.

These straightforward narrative poems dramatizing contemporary social, political, and military issues were considered the finest embodiments of the Confucian sense of poetry's true function. Early in the ninth century, such poems by Du Fu inspired Bo Ju-yi and others in creating the "New *Yue-fu*," treating political issues of their own day. Later, when the Ming was falling to advancing Manchu armies in the 1640s, many hundreds of such poems were written, leaving us accounts of small but telling incidents of the time.

The Officer at Tong Pass

Such bustling hubbub, as our troops
pound earthen walls on Tong Pass Road.

No iron can match the main wall,
with lesser walls rising thousands of yards.

I ask the Tong Pass officer,
"When repaired, can it then repel the Turk?"

He invites me to get off my horse and walk
as he points out the mountain's folds to me.

"Ramparts stretch all the way to the clouds,
a bird in flight could not pass through.

If the Turks come, just hold this fast,
the Western Capital need worry no more.

Just look, sir, at those strategic points!—
so narrow they let just one cart through.

In danger just snatch a long pike,
one man could hold it forever."

How sad, though, the Peach Grove battle,
when a million men were fed to the fish.

"Do instruct the general guarding the pass
not to follow the model of Ge-shu Han."

Qin-zhou and Cheng-du

Despite his immense confidence in his own political judgment, Du Fu was not a skilled survivor in court politics. His spirited defense of the good but incompetent minister Fang Guan led to his dismissal from court in the form of a transfer to the post of personnel administrator in Hua-zhou. Du Fu soon gave up this minor post in disgust and set off with his family to Qin-zhou in the Northwest, where he had relatives. After a short stay he moved on again, crossing the mountains to take up residence in Cheng-du, the greatest city in Western China.

Connoisseurs of Du Fu's poetry have developed a strong sense of the changes in style and voice in the various periods of his life. There is a grim simplicity to the

Qin-zhou poems that matches the bleakness of the northwestern landscape. In earlier poetry, Du Fu had touched on moments of his domestic life, something rarely seen in earlier Tang poetry. In the poems from Qin-zhou, for the first time, we see Du Fu beginning to treat the small matters of everyday life, and finding in those small things deep significance. Thus, in the following poem, China's greatest poet cleans up the debris of his vegetable garden.

Taking Down a Trellis

> These sticks, tied together, are falling apart,
> the gourd leaves grow fewer and shriveled.
>
> I enjoyed good luck that its white flowers formed,
> it can hardly refuse to shed its green vines.
>
> Autumn insects' voices do not leave it,
> and what will the birds think at twilight?
>
> But the cold is coming, all now grows bleak—
> man's life too always begins well.

The last line of the preceding poem not only links the fate of the trellis with human fate, it does so in the grandest terms, the fate of dynasties, echoing the denunciation of the Shang in the poem "Overbearing" from the *Classic of Poetry* (CCLV) (see p. 20):

> Overbearing is the high god,
> he gives his rules to folk below.
> Perilous, the high god's power,
> many the rules within his Charge.
> Heaven bore the teeming folk,
> his Charge cannot be trusted.
> All men begin well,
> but few can keep it to the end. . . .

The unstated conclusion of Du Fu's poem is an inglorious end for the rickety trellis—and the course of human affairs.

I Stand Alone

> A single bird of prey beyond the sky,
> a pair of white gulls between riverbanks.
>
> Hovering wind-tossed, ready to strike;
> the pair, at their ease, roaming to and fro.
>
> And the dew is also full on the grasses,
> spiders' filaments still not drawn in.
>
> Instigations in nature approach men's affairs—
> I stand alone in thousands of sources of worry.

Readers of Du Fu's poetry have often shown particular fondness for the work he wrote while living in Cheng-du, the capital of Sichuan, also known as "Brocade City," where the site of his thatched hut early became a major tourist attraction. Du Fu's poetry gives the impression that he was happier in Cheng-du than at any other time in his life. The poetry of this period is light, often finely observed, often with a rare whimsy just beneath the surface.

The River Flooded

The river flooded outside my scrapwood gate,
my boy brought the news, how fast the current was.

As I got out of bed, it rose a few feet,
I leaned on my cane as it sank isles midstream.

Gently shaken, swallows fly into the wind,
and gulls, lightly rocking, go following waves.

The fisherman twirls his small paddle,
and turns the prow round so easily.

River Village

A bend in the clear river flows
    embracing the village,
in the river village all summer long
    everything is still.

Coming and going as they please,
    swallows in the rafters,
getting friendly, coming closer,
    gulls upon the water.

My aging wife marks lines on paper
    to serve as our chessboard,
my young son hammers a needle
    to be his fishing hook.

Often ill, my requirements
    are merely medicines,
for myself beyond things like that
    what more have I to seek?

Enjoying Rain on a Spring Night

A good rain knows its season,
it brings things to life right in spring.

It enters the night, unseen with the breeze;
it moistens things gently and without sound.

Over paths through moors are clouds all black,
a boat on the river, a single fire bright.

At daybreak look where the red is soaked,
the blossoms are heavy in Brocade City.

On Painting

Although earlier poets had sometimes written on painting, Du Fu was the first poet to do so extensively. These poems include some of Du Fu's finest work and often served as a means for the poet to reflect on the nature of art in a larger sense. In sharp contrast to writers on painting in later dynasties, Tang connoisseurs often delighted in the trompe d'oeil in a particular mode. The best paintings seemed ready to come alive, yet in that illusion there arose an immense tension between the living world of movement or change and the stasis of the painting. To the extent that the poet "captured" the object painted, that object was imprisoned in the flat surface of the work of art. Du Fu was fascinated by this paradox, especially in paintings of birds of prey. In the finest of such paintings the painted bird will strain to break free.

Painted Hawk

Wind-blown frost rises from plain white silk,
a gray falcon—paintwork's wonder.

Body strains, its thoughts on the cunning hare,
its eyes turn sidelong like a Turk in despair.

You could pinch the rays glinting on tie-ring,
its stance, to be called to the column's rail.

When will it strike the common birds?—
bloody feathers strewing the weed-covered plain.

Ballad of the Painted Eagle

High in the hall I saw a live bird,
vibrant, its bones of autumn stirred,

and at first I marveled how without the jesses
they got it to stand there looming.

Then I understood, it was a painter's marvel,
a skill that scraped a hole in Creation,

and drew this stance of godlike grandeur
to serve as a creature in your eyes.

Magpies and crows fill the low-bending boughs,
they soar aloft, fearing its coming forth.

It tilts its skull and looks at blue clouds,
never to hide from the common bird.

Its long wings are like knives or swords
that might carry it over the realm of men.

Between Earth and Sky is a vast, empty height,
and a moment of gloom in the powder and ink.

It yearns for far places, cloudy sands' edge,
it has the flesh of haze and fog.

Why now do my thoughts feel such pain,
as I walk, looking back, feelings twisted within?

"Song of a Painting" is perhaps Du Fu's most famous poem on art. It was written on meeting Cao Ba, who had earlier been one of Xuan-zong's favorite court painters and bore the title of "General" for a largely honorary post he held in one of the imperial guard units. When the poem was written, Du Fu had encountered Cao Ba wandering in the West after the rebellion. Cao Ba was the descendant of the great warlord and sometime poet of the end of the Han, Cao Cao. Du Fu traces Cao Ba's beginnings, his moments of glory in the court, and his present fate. Everywhere the poem is concerned with transmission and lineage—lineage from ancestor to descendant or from teacher to disciple, and transmission of likeness from living person or creature to painting.

Song of a Painting

Descended from Wei's Warrior King, you, General,
now belong to the common folk,
    to a house pure in its poverty.[1]
Then heroes wrested the land apart, held fast—
    all that now is gone;
but the brilliance of his arts and his grand manner
    survive in you still.
You studied calligraphy, beginning your studies
    with Lady Wei of the Jin;
your only regret was never surpassing
    the master Wang Xi-zhi.[2]
In painting you took no note
    of old age coming on;

---

[1]"Wei's Warrior King" is Cao Cao. When his son, Cao Pi, abolished the Han and declared the establishment of the Wei Dynasty, he declared his father posthumously as its first emperor. As both a poet and a general, Cao Cao combined the virtues of *wen* (civil or literary and artistic talents) and *wu* (martial talents).
[2]Both Lady Wei and Wang Xi-zhi were great calligraphers of the Jin Dynasty. Wang Xi-zhi was generally considered the greatest of all calligraphers.

wealth and rank seemed to you
    no more than drifting clouds.

In the Kai-yuan Reign you were always
    summoned to audience;
and in royal favor often you mounted
    the Hall of Southern Scents.
In "Over-the-Mists" the portraits of founders
    had little color left;[3]
but where you, General, touched with your brush,
    their living faces appeared—
There on the good minister's head
    was the cap called "Promote the Best";
and there at the waists of fierce generals
    were the arrows called "Great Fletch."
The hairs bristled on Lord Bao and Lord E,
and swaggering forms of heroes came,
    drunk from the battle.

Of his Late Majesty's horses-of-Heaven
    there was Flowers of Jade, a dapple;
painters massed like hills around it;
    no likeness was its match.
On that day they led it forth
    to the foot of the Crimson Stairs;
it circled and stood by the palace gates;
    steady winds blew from it.
Royal command bade you, General,
    spread the white silk—
brooding art-thoughts struggled there,
    between plan and execution.
It emerged in an instant—true dragon horse
    from Heaven's nine tiers,
wiping aside once and for all,
    common horses of all time.

This Flowers of Jade was hung there,
    above the royal dais—
the one by the dais, the one in the yard
    each loftily faced the other.
His Majesty smiled: he gave you gold,
as grooms and stableboys
    all stood there in despair.

---

[3]In the gallery entitled "Over-the-Mists" were the portraits of those generals and political advisers who had achieved outstanding merit in the service of the dynasty.

Among your disciples Han Gan
    was early the worthy follower,[4]
good also at painting horses,
    catching their strangest forms;
but Han Gan paints only the flesh;
    he does not paint the bone,
and will let the fire of the boldest steed
    melt away and be lost.

In your mastery of painting, General,
    some divinity lies;
whenever you met a fine scholar,
    you would paint his portrait true.
Yet now you drift along
    on the edge of a war-torn land,
often sketching the faces of ordinary
    travelers on the road;
At journey's end you often meet
    contempt from the common eye—[5]
in all the world there has never been
    one fallen so low as you.

Just look from ancient times till now
    at the greatest names of all,
how all their days hardships and troubles
    entangled them.

Kui-zhou and Du Fu's Final Years

In 765, Du Fu left Cheng-du and began a journey down the Yangzi River, lodging briefly in various places. In late spring of 766 he settled in Kui-zhou, at the head of the Wu Gorges, where he stayed until early in 768.

Du Fu had many heroes, but none captured his imagination so strongly as Zhu-ge Liang (181–234). Zhu-ge Liang was the minister of Liu Bei, who tried to found a Han revival state in the West when the Eastern Han collapsed. Zhu-ge Liang had been the architect of that kingdom. He was a politician of immense talent and energy, but the political situation was such that no matter how great his talents, all he could do was keep the Shu-Han Kingdom on an equal footing with Cao Cao in the North and Sun Quan's Kingdom of Wu in the South. For Du Fu, Zhu-ge Liang became the very embodiment of *bu yu shi*, "being born at the wrong time." Near Kui-zhou, where Du Fu was living, there was a formation of dolmens which appeared as the Yangzi River sank. This was supposed to have been Zhu-ge Liang's symbolic

---

[4]Despite Du Fu's praise of Cao Ba over Han Gan, Han Gan is generally considered the greatest of the Tang painters of horses.
[5]Literally, "showing the whites of the eye." There is a story about Ruan Ji that when he encountered someone for whom he had contempt, he would show only the whites of his eyes.

representation of the military formations his army should assume in the conquest of Wu. Du Fu's dense quatrain in the "Eight Formations" embodies the elliptical best of the Chinese historical poem.

The Diagram of Eight Formations

His deeds overshadowed a land split in three;
his fame was achieved in these Eight Formations.
The river flows on, the rocks do not budge,
pain surviving from failure to swallow Wu.

Du Fu's "Ballad of an Old Cypress" is the most famous poetic treatment of an old metaphor of timber as talent or capacity (in fact the two words, both *cai,* are essentially the same word written with two different graphs: a person's potential for service to society is the quality of his "timber"). In this case, the metaphor cannot be separated from the commemorative trees planted in front of the shrines to Zhu-ge Liang in both Kui-zhou and Cheng-du (where the shrine was dedicated both to Zhu-ge Liang, the "Warrior Count," and to his prince, Liu Bei). The real commemorative tree before Du Fu's eyes (in Kui-zhou), the remembered tree in Cheng-du, and the allegorical tree that signifies talent all are fused together in this poem.

Ballad of an Old Cypress

In front of the shrine of Zhu-ge Liang
    there was an aging cypress,
it boughs were like green bronze,
    its roots were like the stone.
Its frosted bark was streaked by rains
    forty armspans round,
dark arch of mascara touching sky
    two thousand feet above.
Already the minister and his lord
    have met their moment,
yet still is this tree
    cherished by men.
When clouds come, its vapors touch
    the full length of Wu Gorges;
as the moon appears, its chill reaches
    the white of the Mountains of Snow.

I think back now where the road wound
    east of Brocade Pavilion,[6]

---

[6]In Cheng-du.

where the Ruler of Shu and his Warrior Count
    share a common shrine.
Trunk and branches loomed high there,
    ancient upon the meadows,
with paintings dark and hidden away
    through the empty doors and windows.
Spreading wide, roots coiled and clasped—
    but though it found firm place,
high and alone in the black of sky
    there are many violent storms.
Surely that which holds it up
    is the might of some bright god;
its upright straightness is finally due
    to the deed of the Fashioner.
If some great mansion should collapse
    and they needed rafters and beams,
ten thousand oxen would turn their heads
    at its weight, which is a mountain's.
Even before it shows its grain,
    all the world is amazed;
it would not object to being cut,
    but who would be able to send it?
Its bitter core cannot keep out
    intrusions of termites,
yet its fragrant leaves have ever given
    night's lodging to the phoenix.
Let neither sigh—not the man of grand aims
    nor the man who lives hidden away—
it has always been true that the greatest timber
    is hardest to put to use.

Du Fu's years in Kui-zhou were poetically his most productive. Few of the Kui-zhou poems have the lightness of the Cheng-du ones, but they have a density and power of vision that sets them apart. The following sequence from the Kui-zhou years has as good a claim as any to being the most famous group of poems in the Chinese language. The modern scholar Ye Jia-ying gathered together all the best-known premodern commentaries on them and added her own judgments to produce a Chinese book of 449 pages on the 64 lines of these eight poems.

    A few points of geography are helpful in reading the sequence. The poems move back and forth between a "here" and a "there": Kui-zhou and a Chang-an of the past and of Du Fu's imagination. Kui-zhou was on the north bank of the Yangzi River, about halfway between Cheng-du and Lake Dong-ting. On a hill to the east of Kui-zhou stood White Emperor Castle, built in the Han by the Sichuanese separatist Gong-sun Shu and named after the god of the West, who is also the god of autumn. Kui-zhou stands at the head of the Three Gorges to the east, the first of which is Ju-tang Gorge and the second Wu Gorge, flanked to the north by Wu Mountain.

Du Fu's Chang-an of memory consists primarily of its palace compound and the places for excursions in and around the city. The world of the court was conventionally described in terms of the palaces of the gods in Heaven, so that the heavenly world above and the earthly world of the past to the north blur together through the course of the sequence. To heighten this effect, Tang Chang-an also is described in terms of Chang-an during the reign of the Han emperor Wu. To the south of Chang-an is the range known as South Mountains (or *Zhong-nan*), a landmark that lasts through the change of dynasties. In the southeastern part of the city is Bending River Park. Near the city was also Kun-ming Pool, built by the Han emperor Wu for a naval display. On one side of the pool was a statue of the Weaving Maid, normally seen from Earth as a star, and a stone sea monster with mechanical fins that moved in the wind. Moving further out from the city toward the southwest, one follows Yu-su Brook past Purple Tower, one of the peaks of South Mountain, to Lake Mei-pi.

Autumn Stirrings (eight poems)

I

Jade white dew scars and harms
    forests of maple trees,
on Wu Mountain and in the Wu Gorges,
    the atmosphere bleak and dreary.

Between river's margins the waves
    churn level with sky,
wind-driven clouds over passes
    cast shadows touching earth.

Chrysanthemum clumps twice bring forth
    tears of another day,
and a lonely boat once fastened
    a heart of its homeland.

Everywhere clothes for cold weather
    hasten ruler and blade,
walls of White Emperor Castle high,
    pounding blocks urgent in dusk.

II

On Kui-zhou's lonely walls
    setting sunlight slants,
then always I trust the North Dipper
    to lead my gaze to the capital.

Listening to gibbons I really shed
    tears at their third cry,[7]
accepting my mission I pointlessly follow
    the October raft.[8]

The muraled ministry's censer evades[9]
    the pillow where I lie,
hill towers' white-plastered battlements
    mute the sad fifes.

Just look there on the stones,
    in wisteria the moon
in front of sandbars has cast its light
    on flowers of the reeds.

III
A thousand homes of the mountain town
    are serene in the glow of dawn;
day by day in my river tower
    I sit in an azure haze.

Out two nights, the fishermen
    once again drift along;
in clear fall skies the swallows
    keep flying on as ever.

Kuang Heng's advice on policy—
    deed and name both slight.

---

[7] An old rhyme said that a traveler in the gorges would shed tears when the gibbons cried out three times.

[8] "There is an old story that the Milky Way, 'Heaven's River,' connects with the ocean. In recent times there was a man who lived on a small island in the ocean, and every year in October, without fail, a raft would float past. The man conceived an unusual intention: he set up a high tower on the raft in which he laid up a large store of provisions, and then he went off riding the raft. For more than ten days he could still see the sun, moon, stars, and planets; but after that everything became murky and hazy, so much so that he could not even tell day from night. After over ten more days he suddenly came to a place that had the form of a city, whose buildings were constructed very regularly. From afar he could look into the palace, in which there were many weaving girls. Then he saw a man leading oxen to the bank to water them. The oxherd was startled and asked, 'How did you get here?' The man told how he had planned the trip, and also asked what place this was. He was told in reply, 'When you get around to Shu, if you go seek out Yan Jun Ping, you will find out.' He never disembarked onto the shore, but went on back as he had been told. Later he got to Shu and asked Jun Ping about it, who said that in such-and-such a year, in such-and-such a month, on such-and-such a day there had been a wandering star that had trespassed into the constellation of the Oxherd. When they reckoned the year and month, it had been precisely when this man had reached Heaven's River."—(Zhang Hua, *Bo-wu zhi*).

[9] The "muraled ministry" is where the commemorative portraits of officers, civil and military, who had done exceptional service to the dynasty were located.

Liu Xiang passing on Classics—
    heart's goal gone awry.[1]

Those young men, once friends in student days,
    are most not of low degree;
by Five Barrows their horses are plump
    and the mantles they wear are light.[2]

IV
I have been told that Chang-an
    looks like a chessboard,
a hundred years, a lifetime's troubles,
    grief beyond enduring.

Mansions of counts and princes
    all have new masters,
the civil and army uniforms
    differ from olden times.

Straight north past fortified mountains
    kettledrums are thundering
from wagon and horse on western campaign
    winged dispatches rush.

Fish and dragons grow silent now,
    autumn rivers grow cold,
the life I used to have at home
    is the longing in my heart.

V
Palace towers of Peng-lai[3]
    stand facing South Mountain,
a golden stalk that catches dew[4]
    is high in the Milky Way.

---

[1]Du Fu is here comparing his aims and contrasting his fate with two eminent Han intellectuals. Kuang Heng was a famous Han statesman who rose to high position precisely because of the policy positions he presented to the throne. In the same way, Liu Xiang was an important and successful scholar of the classics.

[2]Five Barrows, named for the tumuli of five Han emperors, had become in the Tang a fashionable residential area just outside Chang-an. The rest of the stanza alludes pointedly to a famous passage in the *Analects* (V.25) in which Zi-lu, responding to a request from Confucius that he state his wishes, said: "I wish for horse and carriage, and to be mantled in light furs, then to share them with my friends; and even if they were to ruin them, I would not be distressed."

[3]Peng-lai Palace, named after the island in the Western Ocean inhabited by the gods, was part of the Han palace compound. Tang palaces were commonly referred to by Han names.

[4]The "stalk" is the bronze column erected by the Han emperor Wu, on which a statue of an immortal held a pan to catch dew from which an elixir of immortality could be made.

Gazing west to Onyx Pool
    the Queen Mother is descending,[5]
from the east come purple vapors
    and fill Han Pass.[6]

Pheasant tails shift in clouds,
    palace fans reveal
sunlight circling dragon scales,
    I see the Emperor's face.

By the gray river I lay once and woke,
    alarmed that the year had grown late—
how often did I, by the gates' blue rings,
    take my place in dawn court's ranks?[7]

VI
From the mouth of the Ju-tang Gorge
    to the Bending River's side,
thousands of miles of wind-blown fog
    touch pale autumn.[8]

Through the walled passage to Calyx Manor
    the royal aura passed,
and into tiny Lotus Park
    the frontier's sorrows entered.[9]

Beaded hangings and sculpted pillars
    surrounded brown swans,
from brocade cables and ivory mast
    rose a white gull.

The head turns with pity and love
    for those places of song and the dance:

---

[5]Emperor Wu of the Han was once visited by the goddess known as the Queen Mother of the West. During her visit she gave him various magic herbs and told him all about the world of the gods. "That night, when the water-clock had reached the third mark, there were no clouds in the sky, but there was a rumbling like thunder, and at last the sky turned lavender. In a short while the Queen Mother arrived, riding a lavender coach, with Jade Maidens attending on either side; she wore seven kinds of hair ornaments and black obsidian, phoenix-patterned boots, green vapors like clouds, and there were two bluebirds, as large as ravens, attending at the Queen Mother's side. When she descended from her coach, His Majesty greeted her bowing, and invited the Queen Mother to sit, asking for the herbs that conferred immortality."—*The Tales of Emperor Wu.*
[6]Lao-zi, the Daoist sage and supposed ancestor of the Tang royal house, went through Han Pass off westward to become immortal. The attendant of the pass, seeing a purple vapor coming from the east, knew it was the sage coming and hurried out to greet him.
[7]The reference here is to the palace gates, which were painted with a pattern of blue chainlinks. Beneath these gates the court officials assembled for the dawn audience with the emperor.
[8]I.e., the distance from Kui-zhou to Chang-an.
[9]Calyx Manor was part of the Xing-qing Palace complex in the eastern part of the city. Between there and Lotus Park by Bending River directly to the south was a walled passageway through which the emperor could pass privately.

Qin since ancient times has been
    land of emperors.

VII

The waters of Kun-ming Pool
    are a deed of the days of Han,
pennons and banners of Emperor Wu
    are right before my eyes.

Loom threads of the Weaving Girl
    lie empty in night's moon,
stone Leviathan's fins and scales
    stir the autumn wind.

Waves toss a kumi seed
    sunk in black of cloud,
dew is chill on the lotus pod
    from which tumbles powdery red.

Fortified passes stretch to the skies,
    a way only for birds,
lakes and rivers fill the earth,
    and one old man, fishing.

VIII

At Kun-wu Hill the Yu-su Brook
    winds around and away,
where the shadow of Purple Tower's crest
    falls into Lake Mei-pi.

Sweet-smelling rice, pecked the last,
    for parrots, the grains;
sapphire beech trees, perch of old,
    the phoenix's branches.

Fair maidens gathered kingfisher plumes,
    paying their calls in spring,
sharing a boat, Undying companions
    moved further on that evening.

My colored brush in times gone by
    ventured against the atmosphere,[1]
now white-haired, I sing and stare,
    head hanging in bitterness.

---

[1]Once the poet Jiang Yan dreamed that the earlier poet Guo Pu appeared to him and asked for the return of his colored brush, which he claimed to have left with Jiang for many years. When Jiang Yan woke up, he found that his poetic talent had completely left him.

Quatrain

Birds are still whiter against river's sapphire,
blooms in hills' green seem about to catch flame.
And as I watch, this spring too is passing,
and when will be the time that I turn home?

Where Yangzi Meets the Han

Wanderer, homesick, where Yangzi meets Han,
Confucian hack, between Earth and Sky.

Wisp of cloud, the sky shares such distance,
endless night, the moon same as I in solitude.

Setting sun, the mind still has vigor;
autumn wind, sickness almost cured.

From ancient times they have kept old horses;
they need not take to the distant road.

End of Spring: On My Newly Rented Thatched Cottage at Rang-xi III

Clouds brightly colored, now shadowed, now white,
trees of brocade, green with the dawn.

Myself and this age: a pair of tangled tresses;
Earth and Heaven: a single thatched pavilion.

With sad songs, sometimes self-pity;
drunken dancer—for whom should I care to be sober?

In fine rain I stand with my hoe on my shoulder
as river gibbons hum on the azure cliffs.

Night's Midpoint

West tower, more than a hundred yards high,
in night's midpoint I pace light's tracery.

Shooting stars white as they pass the waters,
setting moonlight, a shapeless stirring on sand.

In the well-chosen tree I know is the hidden bird,
and beneath the waves I imagine the mighty fish.

Friends and kin fill all Earth and Heaven,
yet in war's violence word rarely comes.

Sunlight Cast Back

To the north of the Chu king's palace
    just now is twilight's dusk,[2]
west of White Emperor City
    streaks of raindrops pass.

The sunlight cast back enters the river,
    rolls over cliffs of stone,
returning clouds engulf the trees,
    hill villages disappear.

Asthmatic in my years of decline,
    I can only rest aloof,
at remote frontiers mourning the times,
    I long ago shut tight my gate.

I cannot linger long
    in the troubles of jackals and wolves—
truly there is in the Southland
    a soul never called back.

---

[2]This refers to the ancient palace built by the King of Chu in honor of his meeting with the goddess of Wu Mountain.

Interlude: Xuan-zong and Yang the Prized Consort

In the Chinese literary tradition, as in the European, the conflict between love and duty has been a favorite motif. The conflict seems to have been best represented in a ruler who has both the greatest obligations and the greatest power to follow his private desires. In Virgil's epic the *Aeneid,* the hero Aeneas, in love with the Carthaginian queen Dido, dutifully follows the command of the gods to abandon her and set off to Italy; more commonly, however, both in European and Chinese literature, love proves a stronger force than duty. Chinese readers were fascinated with emperors who were so infatuated with one woman that she came to matter more than all the empire, although such infatuation inevitably brought ruin to the empire and to the lovers. Of all imperial passions none was so famous as that of the Tang emperor Xuan-zong for Yang Yu-huan, the "Prized Consort."

The true extent of the historical responsibility of Lady Yang, the Prized Consort, and her kin in preparing the way for the An Lu-shan Rebellion in 755 is unclear; what is certain is that she and her family were held responsible for Xuan-zong's downfall in the popular imagination. She was the subject of gossip during her lifetime and the stuff of legend after her death.

In "Lament by the River," written after the fall of Chang-an to the forces of An Lu-sang, the poet Du Fu recalls Lady Yang visiting the Bending River Park in her glory, then contrasts that with her death:

> That woman, who was first of all
> in the Zhao-yang Galleries,
> went with her lord in the same palanquin
> and attended by his side.
>
> The Handmaidens who rode in front
> all bore bows and arrows,
> on white horses that chomped and foamed
> on bits of yellow gold.
>
> They bent back and faced the sky,
> shot arrows into clouds,
> A single shaft brought plummeting
> a pair of wings in flight.
>
> Those bright eyes and sparkling teeth—
> where are they today?
> blood had stained her roaming soul,
> and she cannot get to return.

441

During the half century following the An Lu-shan Rebellion and the execution of Yang the Prized Consort, her legend took shape, embellished time and again in prose anecdotes and in poems. Such accounts sometimes drew stern lessons about the consequences of failure to pay attention to business, and sometimes lamented the sadness of broken love. The story reached its first full expression in Bo Ju-yi's (772–846) long ballad "Song of Lasting Pain," and in Chen Hong's prose account written to accompany it. Comparison between these two versions of the story gives a good sense of the very different forces at work in shaping poetic narrative and prose narrative.

Bo Ju-yi (772–846), Song of Lasting Pain

Han's sovereign prized the beauty of flesh,
    he longed for such as ruins domains;
for many years he ruled the Earth
    and sought for one in vain.
A daughter there was of the house of Yang,
    just grown to maturity,
raised deep in the women's quarters
    where no man knew of her.
When Heaven begets beauteous things,
    it is loath to let them be wasted,
so one morning this maiden was chosen
    to be by the ruler's side.
When she turned around with smiling glance,
    she exuded every charm;
in the harem all who wore powder and paint
    of beauty then seemed barren.

In springtime's chill he let her bathe
    in Hua-qing Palace's pools
whose warm springs' glistening waters
    washed flecks of dried lotions away.
Those in attendance helped her rise,
    in helplessness so charming—
this was the moment when first she enjoyed
    the flood of royal favor.

Tresses like cloud, face like a flower,
    gold pins that swayed to her steps;
it was warm in the lotus-embroidered tents
    where they passed the nights of spring.
And the nights of spring seemed all too short,
    the sun would too soon rise,
from this point on our lord and king
    avoided daybreak court.

She waited his pleasure at banquets,
    with never a moment's peace,
their springs were spent in outings of spring,
    he was sole lord of her nights.
In the harems there were beauties,
    three thousand there were in all,
but the love that was due to three thousand
    was spent on one body alone.
Her make-up completed in chambers of gold,
    she attended upon his nights,
when in marble mansions feasts were done,
    their drunkenness matched the spring.

Her sisters and her brothers all
    were ennobled and granted great fiefs;
a glory that any would envy
    rose from her house.
This caused the hearts of parents
    all the world through
to care no longer for having sons,
    but to care to have a daughter.

The high places of Mount Li's palace
    rose up into blue clouds,
where the music of gods was whirled in winds
    and everywhere was heard.

Songs so slow and stately dances,
    notes sustained on flutes and harps,
and all day long our lord and king
    could never look his fill.
Then kettledrums from Yu-yang came
    making the whole earth tremble
and shook apart those melodies,
    "Coats of Feathers, Rainbow Skirts."[1]

From nine tiers of palace towers
    dust and smoke were rising:
a thousand coaches, ten thousand riders
    moving away southwest.

Swaying plumes of the royal banners
    were moving ahead, then stopped
west of the gates of the capital,
    just over a hundred miles.

---

[1]A famous musical suite and dance associated with Yang the Prized Consort.

The six-fold army would not set forth,
    nothing could be done,
and the fragile arch of her lovely brows
    there perished before the horses.

Her flowered hairpins fell to earth,
    and no one picked them up,
the kingfisher wing, the sparrow of gold,
    the jade pick for the hair.
Our lord and ruler covered his face,
    unable to protect her;
he looked around, and blood and tears
    were flowing there together.

Brown dust spread in billows,
    howling was the wind,
plank walkways wound into the clouds
    as he climbed by Sword Tower Peak.
And at the foot of Mount E-mei
    travelers were few,
the royal banners shed no light,
    the beams of sun were pale.

Shu's rivers' sapphire waters,
    the green of hills in Shu—
the state of His Royal Majesty's heart
    every morning, every night.
From an exile's palace he saw the moon,
    hues that give heart pain;
in the rain of night he heard the bells,
    sounds that broke him within.

Heaven revolved, the days spun round,
    the dragon-carriage turned home,
but reaching that spot he faltered
    and could not leave it behind.
Beneath the slopes of Ma-wei,
    there in the mud and mire,
he could not see where those features,
    white as marble, died for naught.

Ruler and ministers looked at each other,
    all soaked their clothes with tears,
then facing east toward the capital gates,
    he let his horse take him home.

When he was home, his pools and parks
    were all as they had been before,

there were lotuses in Tai-ye Pool,
    and willows at Wei-ang.

But the lotuses looked like her face,
    and the willows seemed like her brows,
before such scenes how could he stop
    his tears from streaming down?—
On days when plums and peaches
    opened in breeze of spring;
and in the season of autumn rain
    when beeches shed their leaves.

In the western palace and southern compound
    were many autumn plants
whose fallen leaves filled pavements,
    red, not swept away.
Performers of the Pear Garden,
    their hair newly touched with white;
eunuch attendants of pepper-walled harems,
    their blue-black brows showed age.

As glowworms flew through twilight courts,
    he would sink into silent thought,
the wick of his lonely lamp burned low
    and still he could not sleep.
In the slow, slow beat of bells and drums
    his long nights would begin,
till the stream of stars was sparkling
    in skies approaching dawn.

The lovebird tiles were chill,
    heavy with flakes of frost,
the kingfisher quilts were cold
    without someone to share.
On forever, living and dead
    were parted through the years,
and never once did her wandering soul
    find way into his dreams.

In Lin-qiong there was a wizard,
    guest in the gods' great citadel,
who by the perfection of essence
    could bring the souls of the dead.
He was touched by our ruler's
    restless, tossing love,
and thus he gave the magician a task
    of making an earnest quest.

He rode on vapors through the void,
    he sped like lightning along,
up into Heaven, down into Earth,
    seeking her everywhere.
But from the sapphire star-web above
    to the yellow springs below,
both were infinitely vast,
    in neither did he find her.

He came to learn that on the seas
    were mountains of the Undying,
those mountains lie in Emptiness
    remote and ethereal.

Sparkling grillwork of halls and towers
    where rainbow-clouds arose,
and in them the Undying were teeming,
    beings lovely and lissome.
Among there was a certain one
    who had the name Tai-zhen,
whose snowy flesh and flowerlike face
    seemed much like her he sought.

At the western cloister of golden tower
    he knocked at a door of jade,
and had the servant Little Jade
    take word to the Maid Shuang-cheng.
When she heard the news of a messenger
    from the Son of Heaven of Han,
within the nine-flower hangings
    her dreaming soul woke with alarm.

She threw on robes, pushed pillow away,
    rose and paced about;
pearled dividers and silver screens
    opened down winding halls.
Her cloudlike tresses were half askew,
    she had freshly woken from sleep,
and her hat of flowers was not set straight
    as she came into the room.

Wind blew upon the goddess's sleeves,
    billowing as they rose,
and it still resembled her dancing
    "Coats of Feathers, Rainbow Skirts."
Her marble features were sad and still,
    her tears were streaming down,

446

she was a branchful of blooming pear,
    bearing the rain of spring.

Biting back feeling, she fixed her gaze,
    sent thanks to the ruler and lord:
once voice and visage are torn apart,
    vast emptiness lies between.
Broken forever, the love that was shared
    in the Court of Shining Light,
now days and the months pass but slowly
    in the Palace of Peng-lai.

When she turned her head to gaze back down
    to the realm of mortal men,
Chang-an she did not see,
    she saw only dust and fog.
She could only use things once shared
    to convey her depth of love—
an inlaid box and hairpin of gold
    he should carry back with him.

"Of the hairpin I will keep a leg,
    of the box I keep a panel;
the gold of the hairpin is sundered,
    the box's inlay divided.
If only your heart can be as firm
    as the inlay or the gold,
in Heaven or among mortal men
    we will someday meet again."

Time came to go, and with passionate care,
    she sent a few more words,
and in those words there was a vow
    known to their hearts alone.
On the seventh day of the seventh month
    in the Palace of Lasting Life,
it was midnight, no one else was there,
    as they whispered privately:
if in Heaven, may we become
    those birds that fly on shared wing;
or on Earth, then may we become
    branches that twine together.
Heaven lasts, the Earth endures
    yet a time will come when they're gone,
yet this pain of ours will continue
    and never finally end.

Chen Hong (early 9th century), An Account to Go with the "Song of Lasting Pain"

During the Kai-yuan Reign, the omens of the Stair Stars showed a world at peace, and there were no problems throughout all the land within the four circling seas. Xuan-zong, having been long on the throne, grew weary of having to dine late and dress while it was still dark for the dawn audience; and he began to turn over all questions of government, both large and small, to the Assistant Director of the Right, Li Lin-fu, while the Emperor himself tended either to stay deep in the palace or go out to banquets, finding his pleasure in all the sensual delights of ear and eye. Previously the Empress Yuan-xian and the Consort Wu-hui had both enjoyed His Majesty's favor, but each in turn had departed this world; and even though there were in the palace over a thousand daughters of good families, none of them really caught his fancy. His Majesty was fretful and displeased.

In those days every year in December the imperial entourage would journey to Hua-qing Palace. The titled women, both from the inner palace and from without, would follow him like luminous shadows. And he would grant them baths in the warm waters there, in the very waves that had bathed the imperial sun. Holy fluids in a springlike breeze went rippling through those places. It was then that His Majesty's heart was smitten: for he had truly come upon the one woman, and all the fair flesh that surrounded him seemed to him like dirt. He summoned Gao Li-shi to make a secret search for this woman in the palaces of the princes; and there, in the establishment of the Prince of Shou, he found the daughter of Yang Xuan-yan. She had already become a mature woman. Her hair and tresses were glossy and well arranged; neither slender nor plump, she was exactly of the middle measure; and there was a sensuous allure in her every motion, just like the Lady Li of Emperor Wu of the Han. He ordered a special channel of the warm springs cut for her and commanded that it be offered to her gleaming fineness. When she came out of the water, her body seemed frail and her force spent, as if she could not even bear the weight of lace and gauze; yet she shed such radiance that it shone on all around her. His Majesty was most pleased. On the day he had her brought to meet him, he ordered the melody "Coats of Feathers, Rainbow Skirts" played to precede her. And on the eve when their love was consummated, he gave her, as proofs of his love, a golden hairpin and an inlaid box. He also commanded that she wear golden earrings and a hair-pick that swayed to her pace. The following year he had her officially listed as Gui-fei, Prized Consort, entitled to half the provision as an empress. From this point on she assumed a seductively coy manner and spoke wittily, suiting herself to His Majesty's wishes by thousands of fetching ways. And His Majesty came to dote on her ever more deeply.

At this time the Emperor made a tour of his nine domains and offered the gold-sealed tablets in ceremonies on the Five Sacred Peaks. On Mount Li during snowy nights and in Shang-yang Palace on spring mornings she would ride in the same palanquin as the Emperor and spend the night in the same apartments; she was the main figure of feasts and had his bedchambers all to herself when he retired. There were three Great Ladies, nine Royal Spouses, twenty-seven Brides of the Age, eighty-one Imperial Wives, Handmaidens of the Rear Palace, Women Performers of the Music Bureau—and on none of these was the Son of Heaven the least inclined to look. And from that time on, no one from the Six Palaces was ever again brought forward to the royal bed. This was not only because of her sensual allure and great physical charms, but also because she was clever and smart, artful at flattery and making herself agreeable, anticipating His Majesty's wishes—so much so that it cannot be described. Her father, her uncle, and her brothers were all given high honorary offices and were raised to ranks of Nobility Equal to the Royal House. Her sisters were enfeoffed as Ladies of Domains. Their wealth matched that of the royal house; and their carriages, clothes, and mansions were on a par with the Emperor's aunt, Princess Tai-chang. Yet in power and the benefits of imperial favor, they surpassed her. They went in and out of the royal palace unquestioned, and the senior officers of the capital would turn their eyes away from them. There were doggerel rhymes in those days that went:

> If you have a girl, don't feel sad;
> if you have a boy, don't feel glad.

and:

> The boy won't be a noble,
>   but the daughter may be queen;
> so look on your daughters now
>   as the glory of the clan.

To such a degree were they envied by people.

At the end of the Tian-bao Reign, her uncle Yang Guo-zhong stole the position of Chancellor and abused the power he held. When An Lu-shan led his troops in an attack on the imperial palace, he used punishing Yang Guo-zhong as his pretext. Tong Pass was left undefended, and the Kingfisher Paraphernalia of the imperial entourage had to set out southward. After leaving Xian-yang, their path came to Ma-wei Pavilion. There the Grand Army hesitated, holding their pikes in battle positions and refusing to go forward. Attendant officers, gentlemen of the court, and underlings bowed down before His Majesty's horse and asked that this current Chao Cuo be executed to appease the world.[2] Yang Guo-zhong then received the yak-hair hat ribbons and the pan of water, by which a great officer of the court presents himself to the Emperor for punishment, and he died there by the edge of the road. Yet the will of those who were with the Emperor was still not satis-

---

[2]Yang Guo-zhong is referred to as Chao Cuo, a Western Han censor who advised the emperor Jing to reduce the territories of the imperial princes, which was the excuse for the Rebellion of the Seven Domains. Yang Guo-zhong is similarly being accused of having provoked An Lu-shan to rebellion.

fied. When His Majesty asked what the problem was, those who dared speak out asked that the Prized Consort also be sacrificed to allay the wrath of the world. His Majesty knew that it could not be avoided, and yet he could not bear to see her die, so he turned his sleeve to cover his face as the envoys dragged her off. She struggled and threw herself back and forth in panic, but at last she came to death under the strangling cord.

Afterward, Xuan-zong came to Cheng-du on his Imperial Tour, and Su-zong accepted the succession at Ling-wu. In the following year the Monster himself [An Lu-shan] forfeited his head, and the imperial carriage returned to the capital. Xuan-zong was honored as His Former Majesty and given a separate establishment in the Southern Palace, then transferred to the western sector of the Imperial Compound. As time and events passed, all joy had gone from him and only sadness came. Every day of spring or night of winter, when the lotuses in the ponds opened in summer or when the palace ash trees shed their leaves in autumn, the performers of the Pear Garden Academy would produce notes on their jade flageolets; and if he heard one note of "Coats of Feathers, Rainbow Skirts," His Majesty's face would lose its cheer, and all those around him would sob and sigh. For three years there was this one thing on his mind, and his longing never subsided. His soul sought her out in dream, but she was so far away he could not reach her.

It happened then that a wizard came from Shu; and knowing that His Majesty was brooding so much on Yang the Prized Consort, he said that he possessed the skills of Li the Young Lord, the wizard who had summoned the soul of Lady Li for Emperor Wu of the Han. Xuan-zong was very pleased, and ordered him to bring her spirit. The wizard then used all his skills to find her, but could not. He was also able to send his spirit on journeys by riding vapors; he went up into the precincts of Heaven and sank down into the vaults of the Earth looking for her; but he did not meet her. And then again he went to the margins and the encircling wastelands, high and low, to the easternmost extreme of Heaven and the Ocean, where he strode across Fang-hu.

He saw there the highest of the mountains of the Undying, with many mansions and towers; at the end of the western verandah there was a deepest doorway facing east; the gate was shut, and there was written "The Garden of Tai-zhen, Jade Consort." The wizard pulled out a hatpin and rapped on the door, at which a young maiden with her hair done up in a double coil came out to answer the door. The wizard was so flustered he couldn't manage to get a word out, so the maiden went back in. In a moment another servant girl in a green dress came out and asked where he was from. The wizard then identified himself as an envoy of the Tang Son of Heaven and conveyed the command he had been given. The servant said, "The Jade Consort has just gone to bed; please wait a while for her." Thereupon he was swallowed up in a sea of clouds with the dawn sun breaking through them as down a tunnel to the heavens; then the jasper door closed again and all was still and without a sound.

The wizard held his breath and did not move his feet, waiting at the gate with folded hands. After a long time, the servant invited him to come in and said, "The Jade Consort is coming out." Then he saw a person with a bonnet of golden lotuses, wearing lavender chiffon, with pendants of red jade hanging from her sash and phoenix slippers, and seven or eight persons in attendance on her. She greeted the wizard and asked, "Is the Emperor well?" Then she asked what had happened since the fourteenth year of the Tian-bao Reign. When he finished speaking, she grew wistful and gestured to her servant to get a golden hairpin and inlaid box, each of which she broke in parts. She gave one part of each to the envoy, saying, "Express my gratitude to the Emperor and present him these objects as mementos of our former love."

The wizard received her words and these objects of surety; he was ready to go, but one could see in his face that something was troubling him. The Jade Consort insisted that he tell her what was the matter. Then he knelt down before her and said, "Please tell me something that happened back then, something of which no one else knew, so that I can offer to His Majesty as proof. Otherwise I am afraid that with the inlaid box and the golden hairpin I will be accused of the same kind of trickery that Xin Yuan-ping practiced on Emperor Wen of the Han." The Jade Consort drew back lost in thought, as if there were something she were recalling with fondness. Then very slowly she said, "Back in the tenth year of the Tian-bao Reign, I was attending on His Majesty, who had gone to the palace on Mount Li to escape the heat. It was autumn, in the seventh month, the evening when the Oxherd and the Weaver Star meet. It was the custom of the people of Qin on that night to spread out embroidery and brocade, to put out food and drink, to set up flowers and melons, and to burn incense in the yard—they call this 'begging for deftness.' Those of the inner palace hold this custom in particularly high regard. It was almost midnight; and the guards and attendants in the eastern and western cloisters had been dismissed. I was waiting on His Majesty alone. His Majesty stood there, leaning on his shoulder, then looked up at the heavens and was touched by the legend of the Oxherd and Weaver Star. We then made a secret vow to one another, a wish that we could be husband and wife in every lifetime. When we stopped speaking, we held hands, and each of us was sobbing. Only the Emperor knows of this."

Then she said sadly, "Because of this one thought so much in my mind, I will be able to live on here no longer. I will descend again to the world below and our future destiny will take shape. Whether in Heaven or in the world of mortal men, it is certain that we will meet again and form our bond of love as before." Then she said, "His Former Majesty will not be long in the world of men. I hope that he will find some peace of mind and not cause himself suffering."

The envoy returned and presented this to His Former Majesty, and the Emperor's heart was shaken and much afflicted with grief. For days on end he could find no cheer. In the summer of that year, in the fourth month, His Majesty passed on.

In winter of the first year of the Yuan-he Reign, the twelfth month (February 807), Bo Ju-yi of Tai-yuan left his position as Diarist in the Imperial Library to be the sheriff of Chou County. I, Chen Hong, and Wang Zhi-fu of Lang-ya had our homes in this town; and on our days off we would go together visiting sites of the Undying and Buddhist temples. Our discussion touched on this story, and we were all moved to sighs. Zhi-fu lifted his winecup to Bo Ju-yi and said, "Unless such an event finds an extraordinary talent who can adorn it with colors, even something so rare will fade away with time and no longer be known in the world. Bo Ju-yi is deeply familiar with poetry and has strong sentiments. Why doesn't he write a song on the topic." At this Bo Ju-yi made the "Song of Lasting Pain." It is my supposition that he was not only moved by the event, but he also wanted to offer warning about such creatures that can so enthrall a man, to block the phases by which troubles come, and to leave this for the future. When the song was finished, he had me write a prose account for it. Of those things not known to the general public, I, not being a survivor of the Kai-yuan, have no way to know. For those things known to the general public, the "Annals of the Reign of Xuan-zong" are extant. This is merely an account for the "Song of Lasting Pain."

One of the most popular ways to treat the story of Xuan-zong and Lady Yang in the Tang was in poetry about Hua-qing Palace, the imperial pleasure palace built beside the thermal springs on Mount Li, east of Chang-an. Since Mount Li was within sight of one of the most traveled roads in the empire, poets often had occasion to "pass by Hua-qing Palace" and there recall Xuan-zong's wild revels with Lady Yang, the Prized Consort. In the following famous set of quatrains by Du Mu, the first poem alludes to another of the favorite stories of Lady Yang, that when she longed for the lychees of her native region, Xuan-zong had post riders bring them to her by relays so that they would arrive fresh. This was considered a gross abuse of imperial prerogatives to suit a woman's private whim.

The second poem refers to investigators sent by Xuan-zong to An Lu-shan's Northeastern Command at Yu-yang to discover if, as rumors suggested, An Lu-shan was plotting rebellion. The investigators were bribed by An Lu-shan and reported back that all was well. The third alludes to the story that An Lu-shan, who was immensely fat, was skilled at the popular Central Asian dance the Whirl *(hu-xuan),* probably something like a dervish dance. He used to dance the Whirl to entertain the emperor and Lady Yang, and when he did so, all the palace maidens would clap their hands to the rhythm.

Du Mu, On Passing by Hua-qing Palace (three quatrains)

I
Turn and look back from Chang-an
    to embroideries heaped in piles;
on the hill's high crest are a thousand gates
    standing open in rows.

Through red dust a man goes riding;
    the Consort smiles;
and no one else there knows
    that her lychees are on the way.

II
Through the green trees of Xin-feng
    the brown dust is rising—
several men riding from Yu-yang,
    the investigators return.
That one melody, "Rainbow Skirts,"
    up over a thousand peaks—
she danced the heartland to pieces,
    and only then came down.

III
Piping and singing from thousands of lands,
    they were drunk on an age of peace,
great halls resting by Heaven,
    where moonlight shone so clear.
Wild rhythms struck in the clouds—
    An Lu-shan was dancing—
and the wind crossed ridge after ridge,
    bringing down the sounds of laughter.

Wang Jian (ca. 767–ca. 830), Gazing on Hua-qing Palace at Daybreak

At daybreak those mansions and towers
    are yet more fresh and bright,
when the sun comes forth over balconies
    see deer go moving by.
Our Warrior Emperor knows himself
    that his body will never die;
he watches them build a jade palace
    and names it "Lasting Life."

The following poem describes an imperial banquet at Dragon Pool in which the ladies of the court and the imperial princes are being feasted by Xuan-zong. Screens were used to separate court ladies from men. The mention of drums in the second line alludes to Xuan-zong's well-known predilection for percussion instruments.

He summoned Gao Li-shi to make a secret search for this woman in the palaces of the princes; and there, in the establishment of the Prince of Shou, he found the daughter of Yang Xuan-yan.
        —Chen Hong, An Account to Go with the "Song of Lasting Pain"

Li Shang-yin (ca. 813–ca. 858), Dragon Pool

At Dragon Pool he offers wine,
　　and mica screens are spread,
the rams-hide drums play loudly,
　　all other musicians cease.
At midnight they come back from feasting,
　　the water-clock drips on—
the Prince of Xue is reeling drunk,
　　the Prince of Shou is sober.

The quatrain above is an excellent example of the epigrammatic historical poem, of which Li Shang-yin was a master. Without knowing the full context, one can scarcely imagine a more dull piece of poetry. If one knows the context, however, the last line is chilling—the Prince of Shou is compelled to attend a party at which his father is accompanied by Lady Yang, the prince's own former concubine. The following poem is also by Li Shang-yin.

Stirred by Something at Mount Li

Cascades fly from Mount Li's cliffs,
　　warm scent flows in the stream,
nine dragons here stand guard
　　on jade calyx of the lotus.
Always at daybreak His Majesty goes
　　to the Palace of Lasting Life—
refusing to join the golden coach
　　there is only the Prince of Shou.

But the favorite poetic image of Hua-qing Palace was as a site of absence, empty now of the glory and exciting events that once occurred there.

Wang Jian (ca. 767–ca. 830), Ballad of the Former Palace

Silent and empty, former palace of pleasure,
palace flowers in stillness turn to red.
White-haired now, the palace maids still there
sit peacefully telling tales of Xuan-zong.

The connection of the abandoned palace in Luo-yang with Xuan-zong is uncertain, but it remains a wonderful example (again by Wang Jian) of the topic.

Passing by Lace-Crest Palace

> Its jade mansions lean at a tilt,
>   the plaster walls are bare,
> green hills in layer on layer
>   surround the palace of old.
> The Warrior Emperor went away,
>   the gossamer sleeves are gone,
> the wildflowers and butterflies
>   hold sway over winds of spring.

The story of Xuan-zong and Lady Yang, the Prized Consort, went on to enter the standard repertory of Chinese literature in both classical poetry and vernacular literature, including drama and fiction. It was in drama that the most famous later versions of the story appeared: in the variety play *(za-ju) Rain on the Beech Tree (Wu-tong yu)*, by Bai Pu (1227–1306), and in the long dramatic romance entitled *The Palace of Lasting Life (Chang-sheng dian)*, by Hong Sheng (1605–1704).

Addendum: "The Whirl"

During the Tang, music imported from Central Asia became extremely popular. With the music came whirling Central Asian dances that must have resembled something like the dances of the Turkish dervishes. An Lu-shan (as we have just seen) was adept at the Whirl, and in the hands of moralizing poets of the early ninth century, its dizzying fascination became a figure for dangerous beguilement.

The topical occasion behind the following song was a dancer presented as part of the tribute from the Central Asian kingdom of Sogdiana toward the end of the Tian-bao. The term *Hu*, which is by convention here translated as "Turks," was loosely applied to the peoples of the Northern and northwestern frontiers, usually nomadic people, but sometimes, as below, to the city states of Central Asia. Some of these peoples were Turkish, but the Sogdians—and An Lu-shan was of Sogdian descent—were an Indo-Iranian people.

Yuan Zhen (779–831), The Girl Who Danced the Whirl

> The Tian-bao was in its final years,
>   the Turks were planning strife,
> the Turks on purpose sent a girl
>   skilled in dancing the Whirl.
> She so whirled our enlightened prince
>   that he did not know he was lost,
> when a beguiling Turk came suddenly
>   to the Palace of Lasting Life.

455

The real truth of the Whirl
    was grasped by none in that age,
but what the Whirl looked like
    I can here pass on.
A tumbleweed snapped from frosty roots
    swift round in the gusting wind,
or a red plate swung from a pole,
    the dazzling fire-orb.
Paired pearls of outflung earrings,
    aping the dragon stars,
light scarves of rainbow glow,
    commanding lightning bolts.
The sunken Behemoth unseen sucks
    sea's waves backward,
the turning winds dance wildly
    sleeting in the sky.
Of ten thousand transitions, who
    can tell beginnings and ends?
who of the seated audience is able
    to tell the front from the back?
Those who watched among palace ladies
    to one another said:
the way to receive our ruler's love
    lies in the changing circles.
Right and wrong, good and ill
    hung on the ruler's word;
east and west, south and north
    depended on his glance.
Lithe and soft body of the senses,
    wearing pendants and sash,
circling around the finger,
    the same as bracelet or ring.
When fawning courtiers heard this,
    their own hearts first were turned,
befuddling the ruler's heart,
    and the ruler's eyes were dazzled.
If my ruler says that it's crooked,
    then it's bent as a fishhook;
if my ruler says that it's direct,
    it's as straight as an arrow.
An artfulness went with the clear shadow,
    going everywhere,
for finesse they mimicked spring orioles,
    a hundred kinds of warbling.
They toppled Heaven and upturned Earth
    using the ruler's force;

yet blocked it from sight and covered all,
    fearing the lord would see.
When the Kingfisher Coach journeyed southward
    to the Myriad League Bridge,[3]
then Xuan-zong first realized
    how Heaven and Earth had turned round.
I send these words to those who bewhirl the eyes
    and those who bewhirl the heart,
whoever hold household or realm
    should join in reproof.

Bo Ju-yi, The Girl Who Danced the Whirl

Whirling girl,
whirling girl,
heart answers strings,
hands answer drum,
when strings and drums sound together,
    both of her sleeves lift high,
and she drifts in twirls like circling snow,
    and dances the spinning tumbleweed.

She whirls to the left, spins to the right,
    never growing weary,
thousands of rings and revolutions
    seeming never to end.
No class of thing in this mortal world
    can be compared to her:
sluggish, the wheels of a speeding coach,
    and hurricanes are slow.
When the tune is done, she makes her bows,
    thanking the emperor,
and for her sake the emperor
    faintly shows his teeth.

Whirling girl
from Sogdiana—
for nothing you've had to come east
    these ten thousand leagues and more.
For the Central Plain has its own
    people who know the Whirl;
and contesting finesse and skill,
    you are no match for them.

---

[3]Myriad League Bridge was in Cheng-du, the major city of Sichuan, to which Xuan-zong fled after the fall of Chang-an.

In the final years of the Tian-bao Reign,
    when the times were about to change,
everyone, lady and courtier alike,
    was learning to turn in circles.
Within the court was Lady Tai-zhen,
    outside was An Lu-shan,
and these two were known most of all
    for ability to whirl.

In the Garden of Pear Blossoms
    one gained a Consort's rank;
and beneath the Screen of the Golden Cock
    the other was raised as a son.

When An Lu-shan did the Whirl,
    he bewildered the ruler's eyes;
even when troops crossed the Yellow River,
    it was doubted that he had rebelled.

When Yang the Prized Consort did the Whirl,
    she befuddled the ruler's heart;
when she was left dead at Ma-wei Station,
    he yearned for her ever more.
From that time on the Axis of Earth
    and the Stays of Heaven revolved,
and for the past fifty years
    they have not been brought in control.

So whirling girl,
don't dance in vain,
but sing this song again and again
    that our lord may see the light.

Tang Literature of the Frontier

In the seventh century, and particularly in the first half of the eighth century, Tang armies operated deep in Central Asia. The frontier poetry of the first half of the eighth century, the "High Tang," is often taken as the direct response of intellectuals to those Central Asian wars and was sometimes proudly expansionist and sometimes strongly anti-war in sentiment. The conventional use of the figures and images of the great Central Asian wars of the Han Dynasty might be seen as either glorifying Tang achievements or criticizing them.

Although High Tang frontier poetry must, to some degree, be understood in light of contemporary military history, it also offers an excellent example of the complex relation between literary tradition and the historical world. The stock images of frontier poetry were formed in the *yue-fu* of the Southern Dynasties and were the creation of poets who never had and never would come anywhere close to the imaginary world they described: the bleak landscapes of the steppes, the sufferings and glory of soldiers on campaign. If such poetry touched the historical circumstance of those poets, it would have been in a more subtle way, as nostalgic gestures of their tenuous claim to be the legitimate heirs of the Han and its successful wars against the Central Asian peoples who were the ancestors of those presently occupying North China. These well-established conventions of frontier poetry were received by the Tang poets of the seventh century as one component of the larger tradition of court poetry inherited from the Southern Dynasties.

In the seventh century, however, Tang armies were moving through the very regions that were part of the literary landscape of frontier poetry, and it may be that seventh-century poets wrote their own frontier poems conscious of contemporary military realities. Then, with the emperor Xuan-zong's expansionist policies in the first half of the eighth century, the Central Asian wars increased in distance and intensity, with a few poets actually serving in the frontier armies on the civilian staffs of generals. Many more poets ventured to the safe territories on the margins of the frontier. While there are some differences in High Tang frontier poetry, the frontier world such poets found was remarkably similar to the poetic images of the region that they had learned of from their reading.

As in the relationship between images of war given in cinema and the realities of war in modern times, there is a complicated interplay between the experience of art and experience in the world outside of art. The images of art are assimilated long before one experiences the "real thing," and they shape the understanding of "real" experience. Not only do such representations in art shape our understanding, they often influence behavior itself. It is said that Alexander crossed into Asia Minor under the spell of the *Iliad,* and we may wonder how much Xuan-zong's expansionist dreams were shaped by powerful literary images of Han military glory.

459

Frontier poetry finally proved more lasting than imperial control of Central Asia, and as it had been written before the Tang Central Asian conquests, so it also continued to be written long after Tang armies had fallen back into China proper. As a poetic theme, frontier poetry can serve as a common ground to show the differences in Tang poetry—both the differences between individual poets and the literary historical changes that took place during the three hundred years of the dynasty.

Although frontier poetry was created by poets of the Southern Dynasties, their works are generally very poor when compared to Tang frontier poems. The following example by the mid-sixth-century poet Zhang Zheng-jian has the stiff mechanical parallelism that often characterizes the poetry of the period. "Crossing the Barrier Mountains" was a *yue-fu* title.

Zhang Zheng-jian (mid-6th century), Crossing the Barrier Mountains

Barrier mountains, crossed in dawn's moon,
these swordsmen are going on far campaign.

From Yun-zhong go forth the turning columns,
past horizon deployed are daring formations.

Wheels smashed halt the departing standards,
trees upturned block hanging banners.

Sands rise, darkening Zigzag Slope,
clouds gather, shedding light on Elm Creek.

Horses weary, they sometimes graze on grass,
men exhausted, often looking for the fort.

On cold steppes the Turkish pipe sounds harsh,
in empty forests the Han drums resound.

And when they hear the sobbing waters,
all are stricken by the heartbreaking sound.

Poets of the Early Tang (seventh century) improved on their Southern Dynasties predecessors, but still their individually brilliant couplets rarely come together to form a coherent whole. The original version of the following ballad, on p. 236, shows how different is Yu Shi-nan's "imitation." The Lou-lan was another Central Asian kingdom and people.

Yu Shi-nan (early 7th century), I Watered My Horse at a Spring by the Wall: Imitating the Old Ballad

We galloped our horses across river's edge,
the current was deep, the crossing was hard.

We met the Envoy ahead in his silk-hung rig:
"The Lord Protector is now in Lou-lan!"

The light horse keep their mounts bridled,
while decoy troops uncinch their saddles.

Hot springs send down steep mountain streams,
plank walkways connect the sheer ridges.

They have taken land, deeds still unrewarded;
if they lose a fort, the law shows no mercy.

There is moonlight, but the passes still are dark;
all through spring the Long region stays cold.

The sky overcast, there are no more shadows;
ice covers the river, hard currents unheard.

In my thoughts is my Lord; I cannot meet him,
yet by this I may repay him for a single meal.[1]

Lu Zhao-lin (ca. 635–689), Falling Snow: A Song

At autumn's end nomad horsemen break through,
flat clouds over passes for thousands of leagues.

Snows darken like the sands of Turkistan,
and the ice is as bright as the moon of Han.

At Tall Turret Pass the turrets are silver,
on the Great Wall walls are formed of jade.

Their standards and banners have all fallen,
and the Son of Heaven does not know their names.

Luo Bin-wang (b. ca. 640), With the Army: A Ballad

What matters in their lives: to be seen with respect;
from the Grand Army a bold aura surges.

Sunlight on steppes divides the pikes' glint;
Heaven's stars match with sword patterns.[2]

Bows drawn full embrace the moon of Han;
horses' hooves trample the Turkish sand.

They do not seek to reenter the passes alive;
it is right that they die to repay their lord.

---

[1] The "single meal" is an allusion to the Han Xin, one of the important generals in the founding of the Han. When still young and obscure, he was fleeing for his life, and an old washerwoman sheltered and fed him. The story became a common allusion for owing a debt of gratitude. In poetry and prose, Tang soldiers always seek to repay the emperor for the favor he has shown them.
[2] Brave soldiers produced a spirit-aura, *qi,* that was said to be visible over a valiant army. Swords were often forged with star patterns in the metal.

The High Tang Frontier Poem

The memory of the great Han generals appears frequently in High Tang frontier poetry, either as flattering comparison with Tang generals or, by contrast, as wishes
that the Tang had such generals. The most famous of the Han commanders was Li
Guang, the "Flying General," though "Light Horse" Huo Qu-bing and "Light Wagon"
Li Cai are also commonly invoked. While boundaries of all kinds did not usually
play a major role in the traditional Chinese cultural imagination, the major exception was on the Northern and northwestern frontier, where there was the awareness
of a clear division between "us" and "them." Frontier poetry often speaks of the crossings and incursions such divisions create.

Wang Chang-ling (ca. 690–ca. 756), Out the Passes

> Bright moon of the days of Qin,
>   passes of the Han,
> on they marched for thousands of miles,
>   the men did not return.
> If only that Flying General
>   of Dragon Fort were here,
> he would not let the Turkish horses
>   make the crossing of Shadow Mountain.

Many frontier poems often seem to consist of strings of sensuous images, concluding with a gesture either of loyalty to the emperor or of complaint about the hardships and futility of military campaigns. In the best of such poems, however, the images work together to build a world or tell an implicit story.

In the following poem by Wang Wei, notice the way in which images are
arranged in sequence to create a day of battle: first the single sound of the bugle
rousing the sleeping troops, followed by the hubbub of the army rising and breaking camp. The second couplet mixes the sound of fifes played during the march with
the neighing of horses as the column squeezes together crossing a river into nomad
country (you may also imagine splashing, the noise of the movement). Up to this
point the poem is dominated by sounds. Then, in the third couplet, a visual scene
is presented—and the visual scene becomes dominant as the poet draws away from
being among the troops to the position of a remote observer. There is the darkening
scene of twilight, and in the desertscape a great cloud of dust that hides the Chinese
and nomads in combat. The fact is known by sounds; the visual scene, with its illusory calm, is given only to conceal the more violent events that are presented in
sound. The final couplet is a declaration of victory and promise of return.

Wang Wei, With the Army: A Ballad

> A bugle blown sets marchers in motion,
> with a loud din the marchers rise.

Fifes wail, a tumult of neighing horses,
as they struggle to cross Golden River.

At sundown on the great desert's edge,
the sounds of battle within haze and dust.

We have bound the necks of their foremost chiefs
and go back to present them to the Emperor.

Armies usually received news of nomad raids by a system of beacon fires on watch-towers. In the following poem, also by Wang Wei, the full reason for the courier's urgency is withheld until the last line, in a beautiful image of snow whirling in the passes so that those watching for a signal could not tell whether they were seeing smoke or snow.

Long-xi: A Ballad

Every ten miles a horse is set galloping,
every five miles the whip is raised.

A dispatch has reached the Lord Protector:
the Xiong-nu are besieging Wine-Spring![3]

Snow now blows in the barrier mountains—
beacon fires are cut off, no smoke.

Li Bo (701–762), The Old Airs XIV

Sandstorms fill Turkish passes,
where bleak winds forever howl.

When trees shed leaves and plants turn brown,
they climb heights to watch for raiders.

Weed-grown forts lie abandoned in deserts,
of frontier towns no wall remains.

White bones last through a thousand frosts,
jumbled heaps covered by clumps of brush.

Who was it, then, worked such brutality?—
"Heaven's darlings" show venom of violence.

---

[3]The Xiong-nu were the great Central Asian nation that warred with the Western Han, and the siege of the garrison at Wine-Spring refers to events that occurred in the Han. The aesthetic distance of Han settings was preferred by many poets, even when they were intended to refer to military events in the Tang.

His Majesty stirs to a terrible wrath,
he makes trial of his troops to serve war's drums.

Spring's gentle light turns to deadly weather,
soldiers are mustered, heartland's turmoil.

Three hundred and sixty thousand men
all weeping tears that fall like rain.

And they worry that going to serve on campaign
they will not be able to care for their farms.

If you never have seen the lads on the march
you can't grasp the harshness of barrier mountains.

Li Mu, the general, is with us no more—
on the frontier men feed jackals and tigers.

Rather than one of the famous Han generals, Li Bo here invokes the example of Li Mu, the great general of the old Warring States Kingdom of Zhao, who defeated the Xiong-nu so thoroughly that they did not dare raid China for more than a decade thereafter. The Xiong-nu were famous for claiming to be "Heaven's darlings."

Moon Over the Mountain Passes

The bright moon comes out from Sky Mountain
in a vast spreading ocean of clouds.

A steady wind stretches for thousands of miles
and blows straight through the Jade Gate Pass.

Han troops moved down the Bo-deng Road,
the Turks kept watch by Kokonor's bays.

Places always of marching and battle
from which no one is ever seen to return.

Garrisons gaze on the frontier's features,
many faces show suffering, longing for home.

And in high chambers on this same night
the sighs, I am sure, are not yet still.

Regret for the suffering and death caused by the Central Asian wars was not the only response of poets. Li Bo could just as easily compose the following bloodthirsty and jingoistic *yue-fu*. The last line is a quotation from a short song by the founder of the Han Dynasty.

The Turks Are Gone!

Harsh winds blow the frost,
    grass shrivels by Kokonor,
now compound bows are strong and hard,
    the Turkish horses exult.
Warriors of the House of Han
    three hundred thousand strong,
whose general also commands
    Light Horse Huo Qu-bing.

The blade Shooting Star and white-fletched shafts
    are hanging at his waist,
sword's pattern of autumn lotus shoots
    beams of light from within the sheath.
Imperial soldiers shine in snow
    descending from Jade Gate Pass,
nomad arrows come like the sands
    and stick in coats of mail.

"Cloud" and "dragon," "tiger" and "wind"—
    our formations interchange;
the Morning Star lies in moon's halo:
    a sign that the foe can be crushed.

The foe can be crushed,
the Nomad Star put out:
we tread on Turkish entrails,
    we wade through Turkish blood.

We hang up Turks in the blue sky,
we bury Turks by Purple Pass.
The Turks are gone!
The Han is glorious!
May His Majesty live three thousand years
and sing how the great wind
    sweeps the clouds along:
"How will I find fierce warriors to guard my land all around?"

Wang Chang-ling, Variation on "Hard Traveling"

Towards evening the piping grew mournful,
windborne it blended with neighing steeds.

The vanguard takes banners and standards,
battle clouds circle a thousand miles.

The Khan comes down from the Mountain of Shadow;
winds howl over empty gravel and sand.

465

"In one battle you can get made a nobleman—
no more yearning now for the women's rooms!"

By the Passes: A Song (second of a set)

I let my horse drink, then crossed autumn waters;
the waters were cold, the wind like a knife.

A horizon of sand where the sun had not set,
in the growing darkness I could see Lin-tao.

Battles fought by the Wall in olden days—
they always say how their spirits were high.

But brown dust fills both present and past,
and white bones lie scattered in sagebrush.

Unlike any of the preceding poets, Cen Shen actually served with the Tang armies in Central Asia. But rather than "realism," we find in his frontier songs the "Gothic" extravagance fashionable in poetry of the 740s and early 750s.

Cen Shen (ca. 715–770), Song of White Snow: Sending Off Assistant Wu on His Return to the Capital

The north wind rolls up the earth,
    white grasses snap,
In the Turkish skies of October
    the snow is flying.

All at once it seems in a single night
    that breeze of spring has come:
On thousands of trees, on millions of trees
    blossoms of pear appear.

They come scattering through beaded curtains,
    melt soaking the lacework drapes,
Our fox furs give us no warmth,
    our quilts of brocade are too thin.
The general finds he cannot pull
    his compound bow of horn,
the Lord Protector's coat of mail
    grows too cold to put on.

Over the Gobi's vast reaches
    a hundred yard thickness of ice,
And somber masses of solid cloud
    cast gloom across thousands of leagues.

In the central divisions we set out wine
    to toast our homebound friend,
With the Turkish fiddle and mandolin
    and the nomad flute.

A whirling blizzard of evening snow
    descends on the headquarters' gate,
And winds clutch the red banners,
    which freeze and no longer flap.

At the eastern gate of Bugur
    we send you on your way,
And as you go the snow will fill
    the Heaven Mountain Road.
As the mountain bends, so the road turns,
    and we will no longer see you,
leaving only the marks in the snow
    to show where your horse has passed.

The Ballad of Running Horse River: Sending Off the Army on a Western Campaign

Have you not seen
    Running Horse River
        beside a sea of snow,
a vast expanse of level sands
    stretching yellow to the sky?

At Bugur in November
    the winds are roaring by night,
with a whole river of shattered stones
    as large as dippers,
and along with the wind that fills the earth
    the stones run tumultuously.

When the Xiong-nu grasses turn brown,
    the horses are at their sleekest,
west of Golden Mountain we see
    smoke and dust flying:
the House of Han's Grand General
    is taking the army west.

The general's coat of mail
    is not removed by night,
as the army moves on at midnight,
    pikes bump each other,
the edge of the wind is like a knife,
    faces are as if sliced.

The coats of horses are streaked with snow,
    steam rises from their sweat,
dappled spots like linked coins
    instantly turn to ice,
drafting indictments back in camp,
    the inkstone's water freezes.

When nomad horsemen hear of him,
    their hearts will surely quail,
my opinion is they will never dare
    cross their swords with ours:
at the western gate of Ju-shi we
    await news of the victory.

Cen Shen stands waiting for news of a glorious Tang victory; but back in Chang-an, Du Fu had a very different perspective on the massive conscriptions necessary to keep the frontier armies at full strength.

Du Fu, The Army Wagons: A Ballad

The wagons went by rumbling,
horses snorted and neighed,
men on the move, bows and arrows
    on each man hung at the waist.
Poppas and mammas, children and wives
    ran along saying goodbyes,
and the dust was such you could not see
    the bridge at Xian-yang.
Tugging their coats, stamping their feet,
    weeping and blocking the road,
the sound of weeping rose up straight
    and beset high wisps of cloud.

Someone passing by that road
    asked of the men on the move,
and one of them just said,
    "They're calling men up often.
Some from the age of fifteen
    are up north guarding the river,
then on until age forty
    they serve west on army farms.
When I left, the village headman
    gave a turban for my head;
when I get home, my hair will be white,
    then back to patrol the frontier again.

"The blood that has flowed at frontier posts
     would make waters of a sea,
yet our Warlike Sovereign's will to expand
     is not yet satisfied.
Haven't you heard:
in two hundred districts east of the hills
     that belong to the House of Han,
thousands and thousands of hamlets and towns
     grow with thorns and briars.

"Even with a sturdy wife
     who can hold the hoe and plow,
grain grows over the field banks,
     you can't tell east from west.
But then it is worse for troops of Qin,
     they have suffered the cruelest battles,
driven to it, treated no different
     from dogs or barnyard fowl.

"You, sir, well may ask;
does a conscript dare complain?

"Now take the winter this year—
they won't stop taking troops from Guan-xi,
The county officials will press for tax,
but from where will the grain tax come?

"I have learned that bearing males is bad,
but bearing girls is good.
If you bear a girl you can still manage
     to marry her to a neighbor;
if you bear a male he'll end up buried
     out in the prairie grass.

"Haven't you seen
on Kokonor's shores
white bones from ancient days
     that no one gathers?
The new ghosts there are tormented with rage,
     the older ghosts just weep;
when the sky grows shadowed and rains pour down,
     you hear their voices wailing."

Mid- and Late Tang Frontier Poetry

The withdrawal of Tang armies from most of Central Asia after the middle of the eighth century did not prevent the composition of vivid frontier quatrains.

Lu Lun (ca. 748–ca. 798), By the Passes

5-Character per line

The moon was black, the geese flew high,
the Khan was fleeing by night.
We wanted to send light horse in pursuit:
a blizzard covered our bows and swords.

Wang Jian (ca. 767–ca. 830), With the Army: A Ballad

The House of Han pursues the Khan,
the sun sets by bends of Cross Rivers.

Drifting clouds rise beside the road,
the troopers spend nights under wagons.

A stockade surrounded by bugles and drums,
tents follow the contours of hill valleys.

Horses' backs hung with wine jugs;
knifepoints portion out jowl meat.

When they first set out from the high halls,
fathers and mothers prepared their baggage.

They turn their heads and see not their homes,
the blowing winds have shredded their clothes.

Blade scars appear on limbs and joints,
they help each other pull arrowheads.

I have heard tell that in western Liang-zhou
in every household the women weep.

There are a few pieces that give a more direct representation of the historical situation on the Tang frontier. Wang Jian has the folk of Liang-zhou lamenting constant warfare; below, Zhang Ji acknowledges the loss of the major frontier prefecture of Liang-zhou to the Tibetans, represented here as *Hu* (conventionally translated as "Turks").

Zhang Ji (776–ca. 829), Long-tou Ballad

5-Chara

The road to Long-tou is cut off,
    and no man travels there,
by night the Turkish horsemen
    entered Liang-zhou's walls.

Everywhere the Chinese troops
    died fighting hand to hand,
in one morning we lost the whole
    region of Long-xi.

They drove us, folk of the borders,
    off among the Turks,
and let their sheep and cattle graze
    upon our millet and grain.

Children who only last year
    were raised to be Chinese
now dress themselves in cloaks of felt
    and learn the speech of Turks.

Who can employ another Li Cai,
    the Light Wagon General,
to once again take Liang-zhou
    into the House of Han?

For the Mid-Tang poet Li He, the conventions of frontier poetry were purely material on which his unique poetic imagination could work.

Li He (790–816), Song for the Governor of Wild Goose Barrier

Black clouds weigh down on the walls,
    the walls seem about to collapse;
light glinting from armor faces the sun,
    golden scales appear.

Trumpet sounds fill the heavens
    within the colors of fall,
borderland soil is tinted rouge
    that hardens to night's purple.

Our crimson banners stand half-furled
    beside the river Yi;
the frost is heavy, drums are cold,
    their sounds do not rally.

We will pay back the honor shown by our lord
    upon the Terrace of Gold
and we take in hand the jade dragon-swords
    and die now for our lord.

By the Passes: A Song

The Turkish horn draws the north wind,
Ji Gate is whiter than water.

Sky swallows the road to Kokonor,
a thousand miles of moon on the Wall.

Dewfall, banners in misty drizzle,
cold metal sings the hours of the night.

Tibetan armor, interlocked snake-scales,
horses neigh in the white of Green Tomb.[4]

In autumn's stillness see the Nomad Star,
the sagebrush somber, the sands stretch far.

North of the tents the sky must end,
flowing out from the passes the river's sound comes.

By the time of Guan Xiu, not only were all the frontier conquests lost, but the central government (if the Tang still survived when the following poem was written) no longer controlled much of China. Yet the tradition of frontier poetry remained, here as a Gothic fantasy of pulverized bones of dead soldiers blowing into the eyes of the next wave of Chinese armies.

Guan Xiu (late 9th–early 10th century), By the Passes: Songs (second of four)

Bones from battles are trampled to dust
that flies into eyes of men on the march.

Brown clouds suddenly turn to black
as the ghosts of battle form weeping ranks.

Shadowy winds roar over the desert
and the fire signals do not show forth.

Who will stand before the Son of Heaven
and sing out this song of the border forts?

Du Fu: The Formation of a Soldier

The frontier soldier of the *yue-fu* tradition was a conventional literary type with a limited range of expected responses to the hardships of frontier warfare. In the following series, Du Fu uses and complicates those conventional responses to create something like the psychological formation of a soldier, beginning as a youthful civilian who weeps at leaving home and then passing through various phases of bravado, disillusionment, and professional determination until at last he speaks as a mature, self-assured man, who understands the necessity of guarding the frontiers and will willingly sacrifice himself in the service of the empire.

---

[4]The Green Tomb was the burial place of Wang Zhao-jun, the Chinese court lady married off to a Khan. Her tomb was supposed to stay green throughout the year.

Out to the Frontier (first series)

I
Cheerless, they leave their hometowns
and go far, far away to Cross Rivers.

The officers have their strict schedules;
deserters are meshed in trouble.

Our lord is already rich in lands,
yet how wide he extends the frontiers!

Forsaking forever their parents' love,
voices choked back, they march, shouldering pikes.

II
Farther each day from the gates they left,
they won't take the gibes of their comrades.

Their love for kin is of course unbroken,
but a man can die here at any time.

They gallop their horses, bridles removed,
in their hands they twirl blue silk reins.

Headlong down hills of a thousand yards,
they crouch low and try to lift banners high.

III
In the waters that flow on Long-tou
the sounds of unseen sobbing.
I gaze far away to the streams of Qin
and my heart is ready to break.

> —*Song of Long-tou* (*anonymous* yue-fu)

I sharpened my sword in those sobbing waters,
the water turned red, the blade cut my hand.

I had tried to ignore those heartbreaking sounds,
but the heart's thoughts have long been in turmoil.

When a true man swears to serve the realm,
what place is left for anguish or rage?

Deeds of fame are pictured in the Royal Gallery—
and bones left from battle turn swiftly to dust.

IV
To take troops to the front there is someone in charge,
for holding far forts there are only ourselves.

To life or to death we go forward,
sergeants need not take the trouble to shout.

On the road I once met a person I knew,
I sent a letter with him home to my kin.

It's a sad thing that we are kept apart
and will never share our hardships again.

V
Into the distance, more than ten thousand leagues
we were led till we reached the Grand Army.

In the army some suffer and others delight—
I'm sure the Commander has not heard all.

Past the river I saw Turkish riders,
in an instant, a band of hundreds.

For the first time now I've become a slave—
when will I do those deeds of glory?

VI
When you pull a bow, make sure it's a strong one,
make sure that the arrows you use are long ones.

To shoot a man, first shoot the horse,
to capture the foe, first capture their chief.

Yet there are limits to killing men,
and a realm is secured by natural bounds.

If only we can check their raids—
it is not how many we wound and kill.

VII
We galloped on, the sky looked like snow,
the army marched off into high mountains.

The paths were steep, we clung to cold rock,
fingers fell off into piles of ice.

Already gone far from China's moon,
when shall we return from building the Wall?

Drifting clouds journey on southward at dusk;
we watch them, we cannot go along.

VIII
The Khan has sacked one of our forts,
wind-blown dust darkens a hundred miles.

Manly swords swing just a few times,
and their army flees before us.

We return, taking captive their best-known chiefs,
necks bound, presented to the Commander's gate.

And I hide, just one of the company—
by itself one victory doesn't matter.

IX
I have been with the army more than ten years,
you may guess that I've done some small deeds.

Most men prize any chance for advantage;
I might speak, but feel shame to be like them.

There is fighting now in the heartland,
and worse still, with the frontier tribes.

A true man's concerned with all the world—
how can I refuse to hold fast in hardship?

Aftermath

The following is a piece of lyric prose that evokes the gloom of an ancient battle-field to argue against further Tang military expansion in Central Asia.

Li Hua (ca. 715–ca. 774), A Lamentation at an Ancient Battlefield

In the vast sweep of boundless and level sands there was no one visible far into the distance. Here the Yellow River winds around, and ranges of mountains form tangled clusters. It is indeed somber and cheerless scenery, with the winds whistling and the skies overcast. Tumbleweeds break from their roots, and the grasses are sere in the shivering chill of a frosty dawn. Birds in their flight will not come down, and beasts, lost from their packs, dash through.

The man in charge of the government way station here told me, "This is an ancient battlefield, where a Grand Army lies covered forever. Ghosts of the dead weep everywhere—when the skies darken you can hear them."

What a heartrending sight! Was it Qin? Was it Han? Or was it some more recent age? I have heard how the ancient domains of Qi and Wei sent out garrisons and how mercenaries were hired from Jing and Han. Forced marches across thousands of miles, years on end spent exposed to the dew. In the sandy grasses they pastured their horses in the early morning; and when the river iced over, they crossed by night. The land is immense, its skies stretch on and on, and they did not know the road home. They sacrificed

475

their lives on the point and the sharp blade, with no one to whom they could protest what they felt within them.

Since the times of the Qin and Han, many have been our troubles with the nomads all around us. The heartland has squandered its strength here, with no generation free of it. It is claimed that in olden days neither Chinese nor barbarian defied the king's armies. But the peaceful influence of culture has failed to spread, and instead military officials applied their own irregular solutions. The irregularity of military solutions is distinct from fellow feeling and right. And in this the Royal Way went wide of the mark and no longer worked.

I can imagine how it was back then, when the north wind blasted the sands and the Turkish soldiers watched closely for the advantage. The Grand Marshal scorned the foe and took the assault at the headquarters gate. On the steppes the flags and banners stood upright; the river turned back buffcoat and armor. The orders were heavy; hearts were skittish; authority was honored; life was held cheap. Sharp arrowheads pierced bone; winds blasted sand into faces. Defender and attacker grappled; the rumbling shook mountains and streams. The uproar split the great rivers; the onslaught bore down like lightning and thunder.

But then all became locked in darkest shadow, and it was biting cold at the corner of the sea. Their calves sank into the drifts of snow and hard ice formed on their beards. Even birds of prey kept to their nests, and warhorses faltered. Cotton and silk provided no warmth; fingers fell off and skin cracked.

At a time of such bitter cold, Heaven lent strength to the Turk. Their murderous spirit was overwhelming, whereby they struck and slaughtered. Coming in a straight column, they cut the baggage train in half; then ranged in a line, they fell upon the troops. The Commandant has just surrendered; the general has perished, buried under a heap. Corpses pack the slopes of great gulches; blood fills the watering holes of the Great Wall. One cannot bear to tell of it, how they all became bleached skeletons, with no distinction of rank or degree.

> The drumbeats dwindled,   their strength was gone,
> the shafts gave out,   bowstrings broke.
> Silver blades crossed,   jeweled dirks snapped,
> two armies crushed together,   life or death decided.
> Will it be surrender?—
>   to end one's days among nomads?
> Will it be to fight on?—
>   and leave bare bones in the gravel and sand?
> The birds make no sound,   the mountains are still,
> the night stretches on,   the winds howl.
> Souls coalesce   in skies dark and murky,
> wraiths and spirits cluster,   clouds hang as shrouds.
> Sunbeams are cold,   the grass grows as stubble,
> the moon's color bitter,   the frost is white.

It pains the heart and grieves the eye that it is like this.

I have heard that Li Mu took troops of Zhao and utterly smashed the Turks of the forest, opening a thousand miles of territory, sending the Xiong-nu into flight. But Han conquered all the world, expending its wealth and injuring its strength—it was a question of the men employed and not a question of numbers. The Zhou pursued the Xian-yun northward all the way to Tai-yuan. Then, having fortified the northlands, they returned with their army intact. They drank to their victories in the ancestral temple and judged rewards in a gentle peace and ease; then all was dignified and gracious in the relation between prince and officers. Qin raised the Great Wall, closing the land off all the way to the sea. They were poisonous to living things, and the color of clotted blood stretched ten thousand miles. The Han struck the Xiong-nu; and though they took the Mountain of Shadow, skeletons lay in piles all over the steppes—and the great deeds done did not make up for the harm.

Of the teeming folk bred by the Gray One, Heaven, none lacks a father and mother to provide for and support, fearing lest they not live to great old age. No one lacks brothers, who are like hands and feet. No one lacks wife or husband, who are like guest and like friend. Yet living, what kind of love did these men enjoy; and for what grave charge were they slain? And their families never knew whether they perished or survived. Or perhaps someone gave them word, but they did not know whether to doubt it or believe; their hearts were left deeply troubled, and, both sleeping and waking, they saw their loved ones. They would pour a libation and gaze weeping off toward the horizon. Heaven and Earth were sad on their account, and the plants and trees were forlorn. For if the lament and sacrifices could not reach them, on what could the dead rely? There had to be years of misfortune in consequence, with the people sundered and in flight.

Alas! Was it the times or was it ordained? Yet from earliest times it has been like this. What can be done? Imperial virtue must spread to the barbarians all around.

Coda

Lu Lun, Encountering a Wounded Soldier

When he travels he often suffers from wounds,
    when he stops he has no provisions.
he makes his way home over thousands of miles
    and has not reached there yet.
With unkempt hair he groans in pain
    beneath an ancient fort:
he cannot bear when autumn's air
    touches the scars of the blade.

Mid- and Late Tang Poetry

Readers and critics after the Tang reserved their highest praise for the poetry of the High Tang during the first half and middle of the eighth century. In making this judgment they were, in fact, following the opinion of poets and critics of the Mid- and Late Tang, from the last decade of the eighth century through the ninth century. Some critics called this entire period the "Late Tang," but the obvious differences between the poetry of the first part of the period and later has led most critics to divide the period into Mid-Tang and Late.

Though many Mid- and Late Tang poets felt that they had fallen from the glory of the age of Li Bo and Du Fu, theirs was an age of immense energy and variety, an age of unusual poetic personalities and self-conscious poetic experiment. Both they themselves and their readers in later periods may have felt that Mid- and Late Tang poetry did not equal that of Du Fu, but the canonical stature of Du Fu was, in no small part, the product of their own literary judgment: they recognized the value of his work as none of his contemporaries could.

The most salient characteristic of the Mid-Tang is its self-consciousness. Unlike their High Tang predecessors, Mid-Tang writers asked large questions about poetry's value, its cultural role, and its craft. We begin to find literary groups with explicitly articulated principles. In the High Tang, poetry was largely accepted as part of social life; Mid-Tang writers asked what poetry "should be" and shaped their writing to fulfill the answers they found to that question. There is no simple unity among Mid-Tang poets: they are "more" everything—more relaxed and genial, more angry, more daring in their images, more didactic and ethically engaged. No small part of the attraction of High Tang poetry had been a basic confidence that they understood how the world worked and that they could represent that world in words. That confidence is gone in the Mid-Tang; poets continually invent interpretations and explanations for phenomena, and their words no longer seem so securely tied to the things of the world.

During the Song Dynasty and afterward, a deep hostility developed toward Mid- and Late Tang poetry. From allusions and imitations we know it continued to be widely read, but critics would either declare its inferiority to the High Tang or say that it should not be read at all, lest it corrupt the judgment. Perhaps one reason for such hostility was that in their self-consciousness, their experimentation, and their intellectual restlessness, Mid-Tang writers anticipated the elite literary culture of the next millennium, a culture that would always aspire, unsuccessfully, to return to the High Tang.

Meng Jiao (751–814)

The oldest poet of the Mid-Tang was Meng Jiao, a troubled southeastern intellectual who was already approaching middle age when he went to Chang-an in the early 790s to take the *jin-shi* examination and won the admiration of the younger Han Yu, around whom a group of marginal intellectuals was already forming. Meng Jiao's poetry has a forcefulness and harshness that was generally uncharacteristic of the Chinese poetic tradition. The fierce intensity of his best work also limited his scope.

Tormented

The bad poets all win public office,
good poets uselessly cling to the hills.

Cling to the hills, shivering cold,
their faces grieve the whole day through.

Good poets, moreover, spite one another,
swords and pikes grow out of their teeth.

Good men of the past are long dead,
yet we still are chewing over them.[1]

With this last tip of my life
pure and austere, I cultivated peace.

I sought peace but found no peace—
the packs mock me, glaring, roaring.

Lying Sick

Sickness in poverty, true disgrace,
on an old bed with no fresh cloak.

Spring's beauty burns the flesh,
the throat hurts with the season's dishes.

Sick of lying in bed, mind in a blur,
I force out words, but the voice is feeble.

Polite to my guests, I manage to cope:
there are tears within, but they dare not flow.

But in the utter hush of the heart
dawn's sorrows last to twilight's sorrows.

---

[1]"Chewing over" was the standard term for studious rumination, but in this context the dead metaphor comes grotesquely to life.

What Was in My Heart on a Spring Day

The rains drip the sprouts out,
growing taller day by day,

and the breezes blow willow strands hanging,
whose each branch is twined with another,

only the face of a joyless man
passes spring as if not caring;

for the while he may take a cupful of wine—
then frenzied songs and frenzied laughter come.

Informal Composition

Come not too close to the sharp sword,
to a lovely woman come not too near.

Too near, the sharp sword wounds a hand;
too near, the woman will wound a life.

Road's perils are not in its distance:
just ten paces can crack a wheel.

Love's troubles are not in numbers:
just one evening scars the soul.

What Came to Me in a Mood

The plant does not die if you pull up the stalk;
remove its roots, and the willow still prospers;

Only the man who has failed in his hopes
walks without strength, as if in a daze.

Before, we were branch twined with branch;
now I am notes from a broken string.

As a branch twined with others, I mattered;
but as broken string now, only sneers.

I would go on ahead in my lonely boat,
but the Gorges' waters are unsteady;

I would drive my wagon and horse along,
but the Tai-hang's trails loom perilous.

All things have their root in a single force—
then why do they tear one another down?

Plagiarizing Poems

A starving hound gnaws a dry bone
and gulps down only his ravenous drool.

Recent writing and ancient writing—
he finds each one his favorite.

Or it's like a toddler eating,
mouth slobbering over a candied peach:

there is only that tiny spot of taste;
unnoticed, the daylight's fleet passage.

An old man sits alone on a cot,
he silently looks over something passed down.

But at last he should give up writing,
compose yet another "Roaming Free."[2]

Formerly writing was something chaste;
even then it did not make a good man worthy.

Old Man's Bitterness

I have no child to take down my writings—
what an old man chants mostly falls away lost.

Sometimes I blurt them into my bed,
but my pillow and mat don't understand.

Battles of ants on the tiniest scale,
yet in sickness I hear them so clearly.

To tell no difference between large and small
is the true nature of things, Heaven's gift.

Something Touched Me One Night and I Try to Get It Out

I studied at night, by dawn was not done,
droned words so bitter that gods and ghosts grieved.

Why is it then that I have no peace?—
my heart and my body are enemies.

Shame in death is a moment's pain;
shame in living is long humiliation.

On the pure cassia, no straight boughs—
I think on past travels upon the green rivers.

---

[2]"Roaming Free" *(Xiao-yao you)* is the title of the first chapter of the *Zhuang-zi.*

Autumn Cares II

The autumn moon's complexion is ice,
aged wanderer, will's energy thinned.

Chill dews drip his dreams to pieces,
biting winds comb the bones cold.

On his mat the seal-print of sickness,
while in his gut turn sorrow's coils.

Suspicions, though based on nothing;
listening to emptiness, things without source.

A beech tree looming and bare,
sound and echo like sad notes plucked.[3]

A Visit to the South Mountains

The South Mountains block up earth and sky,
on its rocks are born sun and moon.

The high crests keep sunlight into the night,
deep valleys don't brighten in daytime.

In mountains men are by nature straight,
though paths are steep, the mind is even.

Steady winds drive through cypress and pine,
their sounds brush pure thousands of ravines.

Reaching this place I repent my learning,
each dawn drawn nearer to groundless renown.

A Ballad of Mount Jing

Swarms of flies cluster around my sick horse,
its blood flows so freely it cannot move.

On the road behind night's hues are rising,
in the mountains ahead I hear tigers roar.

At a moment like this the traveler's heart
is a flag in the wind a hundred feet high.

Seeing Off Reverend Dan XII

A poet suffers making poems—
better go flying away in the sky.

A lifetime's breath of pointless clucking—
not making protests or lampooning wrong.

---

[3]The "beech" *(wu-tong)* provided resonant wood for harps. Here the real tree sounds like music.

Broken loose and sere, cold twigs dangle,
cast aside, no more than a drop of spit.

Pace after pace, always begging
for patch after patch of clothes.

All who relied on poems for livelihood
from ancient times have rarely been fat.

Starving from poems, old without rancor,
I have troubled the monk to shed streaming tears.

Answering a Friend's Gift of Charcoal

In a plain cottage among green hills
    there is a kindly man,
he gave me charcoal, its value greater
    than two black silver rings.

By the place I sat it drove away
    a thousand layers of cold,
and in my stove it burned forth
    a whole scene of spring.

The sun played on red clouds blows,
    the light unsteady,
warmed a body bent and twisted
    into a straight body.

I tried to climb Zhao-cheng tower, but wasn't able to make it all the way up. I expressed my disappointment in the garden of my nephew, the monk Wu-kong

I wanted to climb that thousand-step tower
to ask Heaven a couple of things;

I hadn't gone more than twenty steps
when heart and eyes reeled like waves in the wind.

Each handhold clutched my panicked soul,
each footstep tread my spirit plummeting;

then the flow reversed back into former hands
as I clung to the sides, ready still to slip swiftly away.

Old now and sick, I feel only self-pity:
wood with thousands of scars from ancient worms.

I can hardly flaunt an old man's strength:
one duckweed stalk on an autumn sea.

Alone and aged, where can I turn?—
in daylight my eyes see a world of dusk.

Now always afraid I will lose my footing
and descend into the marketplace.

For my kin I form my ties with a monk;
this bamboo cane is a child's helping hand.

My frankness, a fruitless intensity;
and my aspirations abide to no end.

Words from the earth and this speck of man's heart—
how could high Heaven even hear them?

Han Yu (768–824)

Han Yu is generally considered the greatest master of classical prose in the Tang. He was an important Confucian intellectual and served as the sponsor of many literary figures of the turn of the ninth century. Although he was Meng Jiao's strongest supporter, Han Yu was himself a very different poet. Han Yu wrote in many modes, often with a discursiveness and experimental daring. The following selection does not represent the full range of his work, but demonstrates several of his distinct styles: the enigmatically simple domestic scene of "Autumn Thoughts"; the tongue-in-cheek encounter with a local divinity in "Visiting the Temple of Mount Heng . . ."; and an imaginative myth of Li Bo and Du Fu in "Written Playfully to Zhang Ji."

Autumn Thoughts (eighth of eleven)

Blown tumbling, leaves that fall to the ground,
before my porch they run with the wind.

There seems some intent in the sounds they make,
toppling over, chasing swiftly each other.

Then twilight came to my empty hall,
I sat there silent, not speaking.

The boy came in from the outside
and lit the lamp in front of me.

He asked how I was, I did not reply;
he brought me food, I would not eat.

He drew back and sat by the western wall,
read out poems, completing a few.

Their writers were not men of today,
already a thousand years have gone by.

But something touched me in their words,
that made me again feel discouraged.

I looked around, saying, "You, boy,
put the books down and go to bed.

There's something on my mind just now,
a task to be done that never ends."

Mount Heng was the southernmost of the "Five Great Peaks." Han Yu was passing it on the way to a new provincial posting, after exile in the Far South.

Visiting the Temple of Mount Heng, Then Spending the Night at the Buddhist Monastery: I Wrote This on the Gate Tower

The ritual ranks of the Five Great Peaks
 are all as the Lords of State,
they ring and ward the four directions,
 Mount Song stands in the center.

Toward fiery points the land runs wild,
 there demons and phantoms abound,
so Heaven lent this peak the might of a god
 and made its manliness dominant.

Surges of cloud and oozing fogs
 hid its waist halfway up;
and though a summit it must have had,
 none could get all the way through.

I came here just at the time
 of the season of autumn rains,
it was shut up in shadowy vapors,
 there was no clear breeze.

If to silent prayers from my secret heart
 an answer is here given,
it must be because one upright and true
 is able to touch and sway.

In an instant all was swept clear,
 the throngs of peaks emerged!
I looked up and saw them towering there,
 buttresses of blue sky.

Purple Awning fanning out
 till it touched Pillar-of-Heaven,
and Stone Granary in hurtling vaults
 piling on Firegod Peak.

My soul was darkly stirred,
 I got down from my horse and bowed,
and along a path of cypress and pine
 I rushed to the house of the god.

Its white plaster walls and crimson posts
    cast flashes of color,
paintings depicting demons
    filled it with reds and greens.

I climbed those stairs hunched over
    to offer dried meats and wine,
I wished by such trifling things
    to show what I felt inside.

The priest in charge was an old man
    who knew the will of the god,
with bulging eyes he scanned the signs,
    his body bent in a ball.

He took the talismans in his hand
    and showed me how to toss them,
said, "This is most lucky of all,
    no other cast can compare!"

Banished from sight in barbarian jungles,
    lucky not to be dead,
my food and clothing just barely enough,
    willing to meet my end.

To be prince, lord, minister, general,
    all hope has long ago fled—
though the god might wish my good fortune,
    it is something not easily done.

I lodged in a Buddhist temple that night
    and climbed its high tower,
the light of stars and moon was veiled,
    pale glow behind the clouds.

When gibbons shrieked and the bell stirred
    I did not know it was dawn,
till, gradually growing, the wintry sun
    appeared off in the east.

In the following poem, "the marks of their chisel and ax" refers to the literary works fashioned by Li Bo and Du Fu, but in this metaphor (which later became a cliché) their literary creation is compared to the legendary deeds of the Sage-King Yu, who drained away the great flood by cutting the waterways of China. Han Yu's Sage-King Yu is not the usual, very human character of the Confucian tradition, but a figure of titanic proportions.

Written Playfully to Zhang Ji

Li Bo's and Du Fu's writings endure,
a blazing halo ten thousand yards high.

I don't understand that pack of fools—
why did they malign them so willfully?

Such are ants that would shake a mighty tree,
absurdly blind to their own capacity.

While I, who was born thus after them,
only crane my neck and gaze from afar.

I often see them by night in dreams,
in daylight they fade when I think of them.

We see only the marks of their chisel and ax,
can't view the voyage that tamed the flood.

I imagine the moment such hands were used:
a huge blade raised, scraping sky.

Cliff and bank sheared, crashing open,
Earth and Sky shuddered with thundering roar.

And yet always these same two men
were in private life distressed and in need.

The god wished them to keep on chanting poems,
on purpose he made them stand, then fall flat.

He clipped their wings, put them into a cage,
forced them to see all the common birds soar.

Through their lifetimes millions of poems were left
in golden script on carnelian slabs.

Then the god in charge bade the Six Angels
come down in lightning to gather them;

some slipped and fell to our human world—
but a wisp of hair compared to Mount Tai.

My wish is to grow a pair of wings
to hunt them down past the world's confines.

This honest soul suddenly contacts them
and a hundred marvels enter my chest.

With a flip of the hand I snatch the whale's tooth,
pour Heaven's nectars, lifting a gourd.

My body mounts, striding space unbounded,
not stuck in the course of the Weaver's star.

I look back and say to my friend on the Earth:
"Don't work so hard at planning things out!

I will lend you a sash of flying red cloud;
you can join me up here, winging high and low."

Mountain Stones

Mountain stones ragged and broken,
    tiny the trail I walked,
it was dusk when I reached the temple,
    the bats were flying forth.

I mounted the hall, then sat on the stairs
    in droplets of recent rain,
the banana leaves had grown large,
    the gardenias had grown plump.

The monk said that old walls here
    had fine paintings of Buddha;
he took a torch to show them to me,
    but what I saw was scant.

He spread my pallet and brushed the mat,
    served me rice and broth,
yet this rough fare was plenty
    to satisfy my hunger.

I lay in stillness deep that night,
    the insects' sounds all ceased;
a clear moon came up over the ridge,
    its light came in my door.

I went off alone at daybreak
    through places without a trail,
in and out, high then low,
    all through the drizzling mists.

The hills were red, streams sapphire,
    swarming with sparkling color,
at times I caught sight of oaks and pines,
    each one ten armspans around.

In the current I went barefoot,
    stepping on stones of streams,
with sounds of the rushing waters,
    and the winds blowing my clothes.

Moments like this in our lives
　　bring a joy in themselves—
why must we stay fettered and tied,
　　put in the harness by others?

But then with a sigh I think of those lads,
　　the two or three of my circle—
how could I manage to stay till old age
　　and never return again?

Li He (791–817)

In his brief life, Li He produced some of the most remarkable poetry in the Chinese tradition. A remote member of the Tang royal house, Li He was sponsored by Han Yu in the district examinations, but was prevented from taking the metropolitan examination, which opened the way to a career in the Tang government. An enemy objected that if he were accepted as a candidate *jin-shi* ("presented scholar"), the title would violate the taboo against a son having the same name as his father (Li He's father's name had a homophonous character). He later gained a minor post by hereditary privilege, but had an undistinguished and short career. He died in his mid-twenties of unknown causes.

Li He's work is best known for its brilliant images, morbidity, and fascination with the supernatural, so much so that in later times he was known as the "demonic talent" *(gui-cai)*. The Mid-Tang in general showed an interest in "otherness," but for Li He, it was a preoccupation, as it had been for his great precursor Li Bo. Li He was most drawn to what was beyond the immediate and everyday world: to the world of wraiths and the Undying, to dramatic moments in history and legend, and to the sensuous world of the women's chamber.

When he does treat his own experience, he transforms it poetically into something rare and strange, as when he picks up an arrowhead on an ancient battlefield.

Song of an Arrowhead from the Battlefield of Chang-ping

Char of lacquer, powder of bone,
　　pebble of cinnabar:
in the chill gloom the ancient blood
　　blooms flowers in the bronze.
The white feathers and gilt shaft
　　have gone in the rains,
and all that remains is this
　　three-spined, broken wolf's fang.

I went searching over that level plain,
　　driving my two-horse team,
through the stony fields east of the station
　　by the foot of a weed-grown slope;

Daylight shortened, the wind was steady,
    stars hung in its moaning,
black banners of cloud were draped soaking
    in empty night sky.

To my right and left their wraiths
    cried out, starving, lean:
I poured a jug of cream in libation,
    took a lamb to roast.
Insects settled, the geese flew sick,
    the sprouts of reeds turned red,
and spiraling gusts sent the traveler on his way,
    blowing their shadowy fires.

Seeker of the past, tears streaming,
    I reaped this snapped barb,
whose broken point and red-brown cracks
    once cut through flesh.
On a southern lane in the capital's eastern ward
    a boy on horseback
tried to get me to trade the metal
    for an offering basket.

The following poem, whose title suggests an ordinary "meditation on the past," turns out to be a ghostly apparition, an act of imagination by a poet who, so far as we know, had never been near the southern tomb of the Southern Dynasties courtesan "Little Su," Su Xiao-xiao. This act of imagination was inspired by a short, enigmatic quatrain attributed to Little Su herself:

I ride the coach with polished sides,
my love rides a dark mottled horse.
Where will we tie our true-love-knot?—
under pine and cypress of Western Mound.

It was the last line, suggesting union only in death, that caught Li He's imagination.

Little Su's Tomb

Dew on the hidden orchid
is like an eye with tears.
Nothing that ties a true-love-knot,
flowers in mist, can't bear to cut.

The grass like the riding cushion,
the pines like the carriage roof.
The wind is her skirt,
the waters her pendants.
The coach with polished sides
awaits in the twilight.

Cold azure candlelight
struggling to shine.
Beneath Western Mound
wind blows the rain.

As he envisages the return of spirits, Li He can also evoke the world of the gods.

Dream of Heaven

Aged Hare, the wintry Toad[4]
    weep colors of the sky,
its mansions of cloud half revealed,
    their walls a slanting white.
Wheels of jade crush the dew,
    moist globes of light,
phoenix pendants meet
    on paths of cassia scent.

Brown dust or clear waters
    beneath the Three Mountains,[5]
a thousand years change in succession
    like horses at a gallop.
They gaze afar to this heartland,
    nine specks of mist,[6]
the clear depth of the ocean
    spilled from a cup.

Song of a Young Nobleman at the End of Night

Coiling smoke of sandalwood,
crows cry out, scene of night's end.
A winding basin, lotus waves,
encircling his waist, white jade cold.

Release from Melancholy: Song (written under the flowers)

Autumn winds blow over the earth,
    all the plants grow dry,
in blossoming faces and sapphire shadows
    there rises evening's chill.

---

[4]The Toad and Hare are inhabitants of the moon, from which the dew was supposed to fall (perhaps explaining the "weeping" in the second hemstich of the first line).
[5]The Three Mountains are the isles of the Undying in the Western Ocean, which, once eons have made land and sea change places, will be surrounded by dust.
[6]"Nine specks of mist" may refer to the nine regions into which China was once divided, or perhaps to the nine continents said to be found in the world's ocean.

And I, now at twenty years,
 frustrated in my aims,
all my heart drops away in melancholy
 like an orchid brown and sere.

My clothes are knotted like quails in flight,
 my horse is like a dog;
where the road divides, I strike my sword,
 it gives a roar of bronze.
By the tavern sign I dismount from my horse
 and take off my autumn jacket,
trying to pawn it for a jug
 of the finest Yi-yang wine.

I shout at Heaven in my jug,
 but clouds don't roll away,
thousands of miles of daylight, idle
 and chill, where eyes lose their way.
The tavern keeper urges me
 to care for mind and bones,
and not let the world's petty things
 weigh down and stifle me.

Other Voices in the Tradition

The reference in the preceding poem to "Heaven in my jug" probably refers to one of the favorite stories of the exiled gods and Undying who walk among us. The story occurs in the fifth-century *History of the Eastern Han:*

Fei Chang-fang of Ru-nan was once the officer in charge of the market; and in the market there was an old man who sold herbs. He had one jug hung up in front of his shop, and when it was time for the market to close up, he suddenly jumped into the jug. No one else at the market saw him, but Fei Chang-fang, watching from high in a building, caught sight of him. He thought this very strange, and consequently went to pay respects to the old man, offering him wine and dried meat. The old man realized that Fei Chang-fang had divined that he was a god, and so he said to him, "You can come again tomorrow." The next morning Chang-fang went again to see the old man, and the old man took him into the jug together with him. There he saw jade halls well framed and lovely, with fine wines and delicacies overflowing within. When they both had finished drinking, they came out. The old man made him agree not to tell anyone else. Afterward he waited for Chang-fang high in a building and said to him, "I am a god, one of the Undying. I am being punished for a fault. Today the sentence is completed and I must go—do you think you are able to go along? At the foot of the building there is a little wine which I give to you for our parting." When Chang-fang sent someone to get it, the person was not able to lift it. Then he ordered ten men to try to lift it with a pole, but they still couldn't get it off the ground. When the old man heard of this, he laughed and went down from the building, picked it up with one finger and went back up. If you looked at the vessel, it seemed a bit over a quart, yet the two men drank from it for the entire day without finishing it.

Long Songs Following Short Songs

> Long songs wrecked my clothes,
> short songs snapped white hair.
> The King of Qin may not be seen,
> dawn to dusk fevers rage within.
>
> When thirsty, drink wine in the jug,
> when hungry, pull up grain on the slope.
> A dreary chill at the close of June,
> a thousand miles at the same time green.
>
> How clear they stand, the peaks by night,
> bright moon falls to the base of stones.
> It lingers, I chase it along the rocks,
> then it shines forth beyond the lofty peak.
> I can't get to roam along with it,
> my locks turn white ere the song is done.

In the end of this slightly mad poem, Li He goes chasing after the moon to be his companion, but the moon escapes him and leaves him in solitude. The lines play off Li Bo in "Drinking Alone by Moonlight," where the poet succeeds in gaining the moon as a companion.

> I sing, and the moon just lingers on;
> I dance, and my shadow flails wildly.
> When still sober we share friendship and pleasure,
> then utterly drunk, each goes his own way—
> Let us join to roam beyond human cares
> and plan to meet far in the river of stars.

Some interpreters take the King of Qin who "may not be seen" as an expression of the poet's frustration at not receiving recognition from the emperor. But there is another "King of Qin," the First Emperor, whose megalomaniacal ambition and hunger for immortality made him a fascinating exemplar of excess—or perhaps only a drunken dream of excess.

The King of Qin Drinking

> The King of Qin rode his tiger
>   and roamed to the ends of Earth,
> the skies were lit by rays from his sword,
>   Heaven turned sapphire.

In her chariot Xi-he rapped the sun,[7]
    there was the sound of glass.
Ashes of kalpas had all blown away,[8]
    past and present were even.
Dragon-head ewers streamed with wine,
    he invited the Wine-Star to come.
Mandolins with gilt bridges
    twanged away in the night,
The raindrops of Lake Dong-ting
    came as the reed organs played.
Feeling the wine, he yelled at the moon,
    made it run back in its course.
Through streaks of silvery clouds
    his marble halls grew bright.
The herald at the palace gate
    called out the first hour of night.
In the flowered high rooms Jade Phoenix
    had a voice both feral and sweet.
Mermen's gossamer, striped in red,
    with a faint and delicate scent.
Yellow maidens stumbled in dancing,
    the goblet's thousand-year health.
Candelabra in shapes of immortals,
    where the waxy smoke rose light.
The clear harp's notes, his drunken eyes,
    tears like a deep, clear spring.

The idea of cruel gods was exceedingly rare in the Chinese tradition. The Daoist philosopher Lao-zi spoke of Heaven and Earth's ruthless indifference, but active cruelty was something altogether different. In the Mid-Tang, however, we find the possibility raised by several members of the Han Yu circle. As Han Yu himself speculated about the hard lives of Li Bo and Du Fun in "Written Playfully to Zhang Ji" (p. 487):

> The god wished them to keep on chanting poems,
> on purpose he made them stand, then fall flat.
>
> He clipped their wings, put them into a cage,
> forced them to see all the common birds soar.

In "Don't Go Out the Gate!", one of Li He's most bizarre works, the poet ostensibly seeks to exonerate the god of intentional malice. Li He describes here the demonic world of "Calling Back the Soul," filled with monstrous beasts hungry to eat the speaker. Of the several traditional interpretations of "Calling Back the Soul," one imagines it writ-

---

[7]Xi-he was the goddess who drove the sun chariot.
[8]Kalpas were Buddhist eons of something over 4 million years, after which the Earth was burned clear and a new world begun.

494

ten to call back the distraught soul of Qu Yuan, wandering in exile. Qu Yuan (or the poet as a Qu Yuan figure) is the one "who wears orchids strung from sash."

The final line refers to the traditional story about Qu Yuan's composition of a work called the "Heaven-Questions" *(Tian-wen),* a collection of rhymed questions on figures of ancient myth and legend. Qu Yuan was supposed to have composed these when he saw paintings illustrating the legends on a wall. The second-century commentator Wang Yi adds that the work was entitled "Heaven-Questions" rather than the more natural "Questions to Heaven" because Heaven is too exalted to be questioned.

Don't Go Out the Gate!

Heaven beclouds and bewilders,
Earth keeps its secrets close.
Bear-ogres eat men's souls,
snow and frost snap men's bones.

Dogs are unleashed, their mouths loll open,
    sniffing after prey,
those who lick palms find him just right,[9]
    the one who wears orchids strung from sash.

The god sends a carriage to ride,
    afflictions then vanish,
stars of Heaven fleck his sword,
    the carriage-yoke is gold.

Though I set my horse cantering,
    I cannot make it back,
waves on Lake Li-yang
    are large as mountains.
Venomous dragons stare at me,
    shaking metal coils,
griffin and chimera spit
    ravenous drool.

Bao Jiao spent a whole lifetime
    sleeping in the grass;
Yan Hui at twenty-nine
    had locks streaked with white.
It was not that Yan Hui had grown infirm,
nor did Bao Jiao disobey Heaven.[1]

---

[9] Figures of eating and being eaten run throughout this poem. "Palm-licking" refers to a legend that bears, hungry in their winter hibernation, sustain themselves by licking their own palms (bear's paws were considered a delicacy in ancient China).

[1] Bao Jiao was a hermit who refused to eat anything but what he himself had grown; on discovering that he had eaten dates that he himself had not planted, he spat them out and died. Yan Hui was Confucius' favorite disciple, famous for his grace in great poverty. His hair turned white while he was still in his twenties and he died at an unusually young age.

Heaven dreaded lest they be chewed and gnawed,
and for that reason made it so.
It's so perfectly clear, but still I fear
    you don't believe—
just look at him yelling at the wall,
    writing out "Questions to Heaven."

Don't Plant Trees

Don't plant trees in the garden,
trees are four seasons of sorrow.
I sleep alone, moon in south window,
this autumn like autumns past.

Bo Ju-yi (772–846)

The diverse group of writers around Han Yu represent only one aspect of Mid-Tang poetry. Another face of the period appears in the works of Bo Ju-yi and his circle of literary friends. Like Han Yu himself, and unlike the more limited range of Meng Jiao and Li He, Bo Ju-yi wrote in a variety of styles. He always considered his most "serious" works to be his "New *Yue-fu*," narrative poems dramatizing what he saw as social and political abuses. Here Bo felt that he was fulfilling the true vocation of the Confucian poet, which was to reflect how government functioned in the lives of the people. Bo Ju-yi's most famous poems, however, were two long narrative ballads, "The Mandolin Ballad" *(Pi-pa xing)* and the "Song of Lasting Pain" *(Chang-hen ge)*, the latter treating the love between Xuan-zong and Yang the Prized Consort with a sympathy inconsistent with the stern reproof that a Confucian standpoint would have demanded of such a disastrous affection.

It was not Bo Ju-yi's narrative poems but his occasional poetry that exerted the deepest influence on the poets of the Song and later dynasties. Bo was a prolific and often very witty writer, who celebrated the details of his daily life in poetry and continually exchanged verses with his numerous friends. He assumed a carefully studied pose of casualness and an easygoing disposition, yet at the same time repeatedly insisted that he was indifferent to how he appeared to others. Bo was nevertheless an intensely self-conscious poet, ever watching himself, as in the following poem, in which he views his own portrait.

On My Portrait

I didn't even know my own face,
then Li Fang painted my portrait true.

Observe with dispassion the spirit and frame—
this has to be some mountain man!

Wood of willow and cane soon decay;
the heart of a deer is hard to tame;

Why then in the palace's red plazas
have I waited five years on His Majesty?

And worse, my too stiff and inflexible nature,
cannot join the world and wallow in its dirt.

These features not only foretell no honors,
I fear in them cause that will bring my ruin.

Best resign and depart, the sooner the better,
withdraw this body fit for clouds and streams.

What Came to Mind When Chanting My Poems

Lazy and sickly, with much free time;
when free time comes, what is it I do?

I can't put away my inkstone or brush,
and sometimes write a poem or two.

Poems finished are bland, lacking tang,
and often much mocked by the public.

They first complain that my rhymes are off,
they then deplore maladroit phrasing.

I sometimes read them out to myself;
when I finish, I feel a longing:

The poets Tao Qian and Wei Ying-wu[2]
were born in ages other than mine;

Except for them, whom do I love?—
there is only Yuan Wei-zhi;[3]

He has gone off to Jiang-ling in exile,
for three years to serve as subaltern.

Two thousand leagues apart we are—
so far off he knows not when a poem is done.

Bumbling naïveté, spontaneity, and a zany disregard for polite self-control, both in verse and in behavior, were part of a self-image that attracted many Tang intellectuals. Public life (and Bo had a successful official career) required great self-restraint to conform to the norms of polite behavior; but for his private life, Bo could invent quite a different persona.

---

[2]Wei Ying-wu (737–ca. 792) was the most famous poet of the generation immediately preceding Bo's own.
[3]Yuan Wei-zhi is better known as Yuan Zhen (779–831). He was Bo's best friend, an important poet in his own right, and the author of the prose tale "Ying-ying's Story."

Reciting Aloud, Alone in the Mountains

Each person has some one addiction,
my addiction is to writing:

All worldly attachments have melted away,
I am left with this sole affliction.

Whenever I chance on a lovely scene,
or face some dear friend or family,

I sing out a poem in a loud voice,
in a daze as if touched by some god.

Since I sojourned here by the river,
I spend half my time in the hills.

There are times when a new poem is finished,
and I go up along the east cliff road,

I lean against scarps of white stone,
bend and snap twigs of green cassia.

Mad chanting alarms the wooded ravines,
birds and gibbons turn all eyes on me.

I'm afraid I'll be mocked by the times,
so I come to this place where no man is.

On My Laziness

I have a post but
    I'm too lazy to take the appointment;
I have fields, I'm too lazy to farm them.

Holes in the roof—I'm too lazy to patch them;
rips in my gown—too lazy to mend them.

Wine I have, but I'm too lazy to pour it,
so it's just like having my cup ever empty.

I'm too lazy to pluck the strings of my harp,
the same as that famous "Harp Without Strings."

My family tells me the rice is all gone—
I'd like a bowl, but am too lazy to hull some.

I do get letters from friends and kin,
want to read them, but
    I'm too lazy to break the seals.

Some people say that old Xi Kang
spent his whole life in laziness:

But he *did* play the harp and work the forge—[4]
next to me, he
    scarcely counts as lazy at all.

Choosing a Dwelling Place in Luo-yang

Back from three years in charge of a province,
what I gained was not silk and not gold:

Two rocks from India Mountain there,
and a single crane from Hua-ting:

The one I feed with rice and grain;
the others I wrap in fine mats.

I know quite well it's a waste of trouble,
I can't help that I care for them.

I brought them from Hang-zhou's outskirts afar,
we arrived together in Luo-yang's streets.

The burden set down, I brushed roots-of-cloud;
I opened the cage and it spread frosty wings.

Things pure of feature may not mix with others,
high natures deserve what suits them.

So I went to a ward that was free of dust
and sought lodgings that had some waters.

To the southeast I found a quiet place,
its trees were aged, its cold spring green.

Beside a pool, much shade from bamboo,
few tracks of men in front of the gates.

I don't ask the pay of a palace cadet,
I unhitched my two horses and sold them.

I'm not watching out for myself alone—
my rocks and crane must have a haven.

When serving in a provincial post, instead of bewailing his lot as an exile, Bo celebrated the small advantages offered by the locale. Not only did the Mid-Tang poet
notice the small details of life, he could also be so crass as to take the price of goods
into consideration. The Mid-Tang poet often played with levels of language and with
allusions, as in the fifth couplet of the poem below, in which there is a luridly "poetic" description of bamboo shoots. The couplet that follows is a tongue-in-cheek

---

[4]Xi Kang (223–262) was an eccentric writer and thinker. A famous harpist, it was said that he played
the instrument on the way to his execution, trapped at last by the political intrigues he had tried so
hard to avoid. "Working the forge" refers to his alchemical experiments.

reference to the *Analects* (VII.13), which tell us that when Confucius heard a performance of the ancient ceremonial Shao music, "for three months [a whole season] he did not experience the taste of meat." The vegetarian gourmet inserts himself in the place of the Sage's lingering sense of awe.

Eating Bamboo Shoots

This province is truly a land of bamboo,
in spring the sprouts fill hills and valleys.

Men of the hills snap them in armfuls,
and bring them to market as soon as they can.

Things are cheapest when plentiful,
for a pair of coppers a whole bunch can be had.

Just put them into the cooking pot,
and they will be done along with the rice

Their purple sheaths, shreds of ancient brocade,
their pale flesh, broken chunks of newfound jade.

Every day I eat them more than I need,
through their whole season I yearn not for meat.

I was long resident in Chang-an and Luo-yang,
and never had my fill of the taste of these.

Eat while you can, don't hesitate,
soon south winds will blow them into bamboo.

There are, however, moments when Bo's geniality breaks down, as in the powerful "Winter Night" that follows.

Winter Night

I dwell in poverty, kin and friends scattered,
my body unwell, contacts and roaming ceased.

Not a single person before my eyes,
I lie alone, closed in this forest cottage.

Sinking and cold, the lamp fire darkens,
tattered and flapping, my torn curtains.

Then there's a rustling before my windows,
and I hear once again the new snow fall.

As my years increase, I sleep gradually less,
at midnight I rise and sit up straight.

Had my heart not learned meditation's oblivion,
how could I endure such silent gloom?

Insensate, this body is lodged in the world;
the heart rides the flood, yielding to Change.

It has been like this four years now,
one thousand and three hundred nights.

In his "New *Yue-fu*," Bo Ju-yi addressed questions of political and social policy as
well as imperial behavior. Such verse invoked the ancient principle in the interpretation of the *Classic of Poetry* that poetry should be a means to make popular grievances known to the ruler. In these poems, of course, "popular opinion" is defined
as Bo's own political opinions and those common to his class. The following poem
is less interesting as poetry than as an example of "New *Yue-fu*" and of the hostility
of Confucian officialdom, of which Bo was a representative, to signs of wealth in a
nascent bourgeoisie.

The imperial monopoly on salt and iron required an intermediary merchant
class which lived by its profits rather than by the salary that a government official
received. Unlike the peasantry, these merchants were not registered in the population of their local districts and thus were not under the control of local officials; they
were "attached" instead to the emperor himself. Sang Hong-yang (152–80 B.C.), mentioned in the closing of the poem, was a Western Han manager of the salt and iron
monopoly who curbed the merchants and ensured that the profits went into the imperial treasury. In Bo Ju-yi's time the imperial government had serious problems collecting enough taxes to keep it on a sound fiscal footing; thus he sees the loss of potential revenue to the state as an outrage. It is interesting to note that Bo Ju-yi's ire
is directed not at the salt merchant himself but at the salt merchant's wife.

Salt Merchant's Wife (in hatred of profiteers)

The salt merchant's wife
has silk and gold aplenty,
but she does not work at farming,
    nor does she spin the silk.
From north to south to east to west
    she never leaves her home,
wind and waters, her native land,
    her lodging is the boat.
Once she came from Yang-zhou,
    a humble family's child,
she married herself a merchant,
    a great one from Jiang-xi.
Her glinting hair-coils have grown rich,
    there golden pins abound,
her gleaming wrists have gotten plump,
    her silver bracelets tight.

On one side she shouts to her servants,
    on the other, yells at her maids,

501

and I ask you, how does it happen
    that you come to live like this?
Her husband has been a salt merchant
    for fifteen years now,
attached to no county or province,
    attached to the Emperor.
Every year when salt profits
    are to enter official hands,
the lesser part goes to officials,
    the greater part goes to himself.
Official profits are meager,
    private profits are rich,
the Secretary of Iron and Salt
    is far and does not know.

Better still, here on the river,
    where fish and rice are cheap,
with pink fillets and oranges
    and meals of fragrant rice.
Having eaten her fill, in thick make-up
    she leans by the cabin aft,
both of her rosy cheeks
    are buds about to bloom.
This salt merchant's wife
was lucky to marry a merchant:
All day long fine food to eat,
all year long good clothes.
But good clothes and fine food
    have to come from somewhere,
and she would be struck with shame
    before some Sang Hong-yang.
But Sang Hong-yang
died many years ago:
this happened not in the Han alone,
    it happens also now.

Du Mu (803–852)

Although he lived less than a decade beyond Bo Ju-yi, Du Mu is considered a Late Tang rather than a Mid-Tang poet. His work has a wide range, but he is best known as a master of the quatrain. He had a moderately successful public career, yet also created an image of himself as a sensualist, enjoying the pleasures of wine, women, and misty landscapes.

    The beautiful scenes of poetry were indeed seductive and could seem somehow more true than the increasingly hopeless political world that touched the lives of all who served in the government; therefore, ninth-century poets often granted poetry an importance and an independence as an art far beyond what we find in eighth-century poetry. As Du Mu once wrote (alluding to the *Lao-zi*):

> In this world adrift, except in poems
> all names are forced on things.

Poetic language becomes the only true language in a world of conventional lies.

Late Tang poets sometimes came close to their Western counterparts in making poetry an autonomous realm of words that obeyed different rules from the things of the world. When the High Tang poet Wang Wei wrote, "The setting sun goes down beside a bird," he took a scene that could be seen, and recast it in words that called attention to human perspective. When Du Mu writes in the poem below, "for all time a single bird in flight," it is a scene that can exist only in words, not in the world. Such a quality of permanence may seem appropriate to that single point of the bird moving in the empty sky and focusing attention, but it is an image created of words rather than an empirical possibility.

Pouring Wine Alone

> A long stretch of sky, vast sapphire,
> for all time a single bird in flight.
>
> All my life, ease with drinking companions,
> but how much ease is there, drunk and sad?
>
> Deep lies the mist round Sui's temples,
> where blood red leaves darkly shine.
>
> Jug hanging from waist, I go roaming alone—
> to an autumn hair Mount Tai is small.

The ability to see great Mount Tai as small in comparison with a hair or filament in the autumn air was a proverbial expression of the relativity of value.

Du Mu loved traveling through the misty landscapes of the Southeast with their memories of the Southern Dynasties, "the fallen kingdom, like wild swan gone." One of his favorite places was Xuan-zhou, associated with the poet Xie Tiao (464–499).

Written on the Kai-yuan Temple at Xuan-zhou

> Xie Tiao's mansion from Southern Dynasties,
> most deepset of places in eastern Wu.
>
> The fallen kingdom, like wild swan gone,
> left this temple in misty hollow concealed.
>
> The great hall soars up ninety feet,
> by a porch of four hundred pillars ringed.
>
> Between the highest heights and lowest depths,
> winds turn through the pines and cassia.

Green mosses shine by its crimson towers,
white birds talk to each other in pairs.

The brook's sound enters the dreams of monks,
And the moonlight glows on its stucco walls.

The scene surveyed, whether dawn or dusk,
lean on its railings, past and present too.

I linger here with my flagon of wine,
and watch spring rain in the hills ahead.

I Wrote This on the Tower by the Water at the Kai-yuan Temple in Xuan-zhou; on the lower side of the temple compound was Wan Creek, which had people living on both sides of it

Fine artifacts of the Six Dynasties—
    the grasses stretch to the sky;
in Heaven's translucence, in calm of clouds
    present and past the same.

Birds go off and birds come back
    in colors of the mountain;
people sing and people weep
    within the sound of waters.

Deep autumn now, all curtains down,
    rain on a thousand homes;
setting sun, a great house on a terrace
    and a single flute in the wind.

Disheartened that there is no way
    to see Fan Li now—[5]
misty trees here and there
    to the east of Five Lakes.

Spring in the Southland

For a thousand miles orioles sing,
    the green sets off the red;
river hamlets and mountain towns
    with wind on tavern signs.
The Southern Dynasties' temples,
    four hundred and eighty in all,

---

[5]Fan Li was the adviser of King Gou-jian of Yue, who, after helping the king in the conquest of Wu, retired to spend the rest of his life sailing the Five Lakes.

are how many high halls and terraces
    in the misty rain?

Three Poems Thinking on Past Travels

I

For ten years I was a drifter,
    outside the norms and rules,
I presented myself my own winecup,
    then toasted myself in return.
On autumn's hills, in rain of spring,
    I recited there serenely,
and all across the South I leaned
    from every temple's balcony.

II

It was outside Cloud Gate Temple
    I chanced on a terrible storm,
the woods were black, the mountains high,
    and the raindrops strangely long.
I served once at Meadow Altar,
    close attendant of the throne,
and clearly recall the clustered ranks
    of the pikes of the royal guard.

III

Here Li Bo wrote a poem
    on the temple West-of-the-Water,
with ancient trees and winding cliffs
    and the wind in hall and tower.
I was half sober, half drunk too
    as I wandered there three days,
among flowers, red ones and the white,
    that bloomed in the mountain rain.

Other Voices in the Tradition

An uninteresting and unremembered quatrain by Liu Yu-xi (772–842) is probably where Du Mu "got" the last line of the first quatrain in the set above. Even through the haze of translation, the comparison shows the difference between poetry and verse.

Liu Yu-xi, Quitting My Post at He-zhou and Visiting Jian-kang

Autumn's waters, clear and lacking force,
cold mountains bring many thoughts at dusk.
No demands to my post, I don't estimate itineraries,
I climb all the temples of the Southern Dynasties.

It was perhaps Du Mu's capacity to evoke a poetic scene that gave unusual force to his remembrance of the human history that lies behind the natural world, as in the following famous poem on the Han tombs near Chang-an.

Going Out on the Le-you Plain

Under vast skies, limpid and clear,
    a single bird vanishes;
decay and downfall since time began
    all have occurred right here.
Look at the case of the House of Han,
    achievements beyond compare—
its five great tomb mounds, bare of trees,
    where rise the autumn winds.

Late Autumn in the Qi-an District

When winds came to willow-lined shores,
    holes grew in the reflections;
the home of the lord governor
    resembles a rustic's dwelling.

Features of clouds and poise of water
    are still to be enjoyed,
I chant my hopes, sing my moods,
    I am content with myself.

Rain sheds dark round the dying lamp,
    soon put the chessboard away;
I sober from wine on my lonely pillow
    as the wild geese first come past.

What moves me most, how at Red Cliff,[6]
    where heroes fought to cross,
there's only an old man in a raincoat,
    sitting there and fishing.

Above all, Du Mu was a master of the quatrain of many moods: playful, sensuous, celebratory. There are several addenda to his collected poems, in which most of the poems are quatrains; some are surely by the poet, but many were apparently works found by his later admirers, quatrains so fine it seemed to someone the poet must

---

[6]Red Cliff was the site of a famous river battle during the Three Kingdoms, when the forces of Wu burned the flotilla that Cao Cao had assembled.

have been by Du Mu. The following half dozen examples are, however, reliably Du Mu's.

A Quatrain on the Pool Behind the District Office in Qi-an

Water chestnuts pierce floating algae,
    a pool of green brocade,
a thousand trills from summer warblers
    playing among the roses.
All the day with no one here,
    I am watching the light rain,
and two ducks, mated, face to face
    bathing their clothes of red.

Egrets

Garments of snow, tresses of snow,
    beaks of green jade,
the flock snatches at fish
    in a brook's reflections.
Then startled they fly off afar,
    and shine against sapphire hills:
an entire tree of pear blossoms
    shed in the evening breeze.

At the Yangzi and Han

They roll on and on, rippling and surging,
    where white gulls fly,
deep in the spring, they are clear and green,
    so green they could dye my clothes.
Going off south, then coming back north,
    a man simply grows old;
but here the evening sun always sends
    the fishing boat on its way home.

Sent to Judge Han Chuo in Yang-zhou

Its green hills lie in shadows,
    and its waters stretch afar,
in the Southland autumn is ending,
    the plants and trees grow sere.
Yang-zhou has twenty-four bridges,
    and on nights when the moon is bright,

507

at what spot is a girl, white as marble,
    being bidden to play on the flute?

The Yellow River at Bian-zhou Blocked by Ice

When a thousand miles of long river
    first freeze over,
from jade chimes and agate pendants come
    the irregular echoes.
Our life adrift resembles exactly
    the waters beneath this ice:
flowing on eastward by night and day
    and no one can tell.

A Quatrain Written on the Road

White strands of hair in my mirror—
    I'm used to their troubling me;
and the stains of filth on my garments
    get harder to wipe away.
It saddens me that this hand that held
    a fishing pole on the lakes
now instead shades my eyes from sun in the west
    as I head on toward Chang-an.

Other Voices in the Tradition

When Tang poets particularly admired a poem or passage, they would often rewrite it in their own way. Du Mu's hand, which served him both as recluse and as officeseeker, returns some decades later in a poem by Si-kong Tu (837–908) to serve both the hunter, who takes life, and the Buddha, who abhors it.

Si-kong Tu, The Pavilion of Revising History

Above my turban of black silk
    there is blue Heaven,
constrained to keep writing back to friends
    now for forty years.
Who would have thought that this hand
    that a lifetime held the hawk,
would turn up the lamp and itself deliver
    coins before the Buddha?

Yu Xuan-ji (mid-9th century)

Yu Xuan-ji was the most distinctive woman poet of the Tang. After having been the concubine of one Li Yi, she became a Daoist nun, a social role that allowed a woman a certain amount of independence. Yu Xuan-ji maintained extensive literary friendships with male writers in Chang-an, but in her early twenties she was accused of murdering her maid and executed.

During the Tang, a woman was considered to be in the prime of her beauty in her mid-teens. Following the conventional identification of a woman with a flower, someone in her early twenties was already fading. In her most famous poem, "Selling Tattered Peonies," Yu Xuan-ji figuratively "sells herself."

Selling Tattered Peonies

Facing the wind, my sighs are stirred
    at the flurry of falling flowers,
unnoticed, their sweetness melts away,
    one more spring goes by.

I'm sure it's because the price is high
    that no one wants them,
and due to their overpowering scent
    butterflies won't draw nigh.

Blooms of red that are fit to grow
    in the palace compound alone—
how can those azure leaves endure
    to be stained by dust of the road?

A day will come when their roots are moved
    to the park of the Emperor,
and then my prince will have bitter regret
    that he has no way to buy.

In premodern China, women writers usually wrote in a voice unmarked by gender, or they assumed the conventional "woman's" voice constructed by the male tradition. Only rarely do we find someone speaking as a woman against the limitations of gender roles.

After passing the government examination to qualify for public office, the new graduates would hold a party at one of the Buddhist or Daoist temples in the capital. In the following poem, Yu Xuan-ji sees the evidence of such a gathering in the names written out in fine calligraphy ("silver hooks"). The composition of poems was part of the examination, but no matter how poetically talented, women were excluded.

Visiting the Southern Tower of Chong-zhen Temple: Seeing Where the Recent Graduates of the Examination Have Written Their Names

Cloud-covered hilltops fill my eyes,
    I revel in springtime light,
here clearly ranged are the silver hooks
    that grew at their fingertips.
I have bitter regret that skirts of lace
    hide the lines of my poems,
and lifting my head in vain I covet
    the publicly posted name.

On Yin-wu Pavilion

Flowers of springtime, autumn's moon
    find their way into my poems,
in broad daylight and clear, cool nights
    an immortal with no duties.
I merely roll up the beaded curtains,
    I never pull them down,
and there I always move a couch,
    where I lie, facing the hills.

Li Shang-yin (813–858)

Li Shang-yin, now considered the greatest of the Late Tang poets, was very much caught up in the factional politics of the mid-ninth century, and his political career was complicated by close relations with both of the feuding factions.

Li Shang-yin's poetry has a wide range, but he is best known today for his poetry on historical moments and for his hermetics, which often uses language so dense and allusive that we can only guess at the putative referents. In the Chinese poetic tradition such a cryptic style, while suggesting the poet's talent and erudition, usually implied some secret "message." Whether there really was some historical or biographical circumstance behind these poems, we will never know; but we do know that in writing them and circulating them, Li Shang-yin was aware readers would suspect as much.

These hermetic poems employ the imagery of passion and the immortals. Such images were appropriate for three quite distinct kinds of "hidden message": biting political satire, sincere petitions for political favor, and illicit love affairs. Different interpreters of Li Shang-yin's poetry have appealed to each of these in turn; those who would have the poems refer to an illicit love affair have suggested one involving connections to the imperial household and/or the Daoist religious establishment. In addition to being more appealing to most modern readers, the interpretation of at least some of these poems as treating illicit love is probably correct (while some other hermetic poems must be interpreted politically). At the very least, we can say that these poems contributed phrases and lines to the standard repertoire of the Chinese love lyric in later centuries.

There were two women named Mourn-No-More *(Mo-chou),* and Li Shang-yin seems to have fused them. One Mourn-No-More was an unhappy wife in the Lu household in Luo-yang, while the other was a Southern Dynasties singer of Stone City, a romantic character of *yue-fu* quatrains. Poets were, of course, delighted with the possibilities of her name, and Li Shang-yin referred to her many times. The Small Damosel of Blue Creek was a minor local goddess, who, as goddesses often did, chose mortal lovers. Li Shang-yin has in mind a cult song about her, surviving from the Southern Dynasties:

> Her gate opens on silver water
> at the side, near the bridge.
> There dwells the Small Damosel
> all alone without a lover.

Left Untitled (second of two)

> Layers of draperies hang into depths
>   of the hall of Mourn-No-More;
> once she lies down, the clear night
>   stretches on moment by moment.
>
> The goddess's life as a mortal
>   was essentially but a dream;
> where the Small Damosel is dwelling
>   no lover ever was.
>
> To wind and waves one does not entrust
>   the water chestnut's frail stalks,
> in moonlight and dew who was it caused
>   cinnamon leaf to smell so sweet?
>
> Well you may say that love's passion
>   does us no good at all—
> it does not keep us from despair
>   at this clarity in madness.

Titles of Tang poems always alert the reader to the topic or the occasion. A poem "Left Untitled" tells the reader that the poet is purposely withholding that information (there is a different term for a poem whose title has been lost).

Left Untitled (one of four)

> That she would come was empty words;
>   gone, no trace at all;

the moon bends past the upstairs room,
    a bell tolls night's last hour.

In dreams we are parting far away,
    weeping won't call you back;
a letter rushed to completion,
    the ink not yet ground dark.[7]

Candlelight half envelops
    kingfishers of gold;
odor of musk faintly crosses
    embroidered lotuses.

Young Liu already frets
    that Peng Mountain lies far,
but further beyond Peng Mountain
    are ten thousand slopes more.[8]

In the following poem, E-lü-hua was a goddess who visited the home of one Yang Quan six times in November of the year 359. Only Li Shang-yin knows why he chose this relatively insignificant divinity, whose limited span of infatuation with a mortal is noted with such detail in the source text. Du Lan-xiang was discovered as an abandoned baby and raised by a fisherman. When she was in her teens, Blue Lads from Heaven came down to take her away. On leaving, she explained to her adopted father, the fisherman, that she was a goddess who had been banished to Earth for some transgression and that she was now to return. These obscure references suggest little more than a short affair with a mortal man, a few unexpected visits, followed by a return to a place where the woman will be out of reach.

Again Passing the Shrine of the Goddess

Her doorway set in white stone cliff
    with sapphire mosses moist;
banished below from the high pure realms,
    chance to return delayed.

All spring long the dream-rains
    blow constantly over the tiles,
entire days when no god-breeze
    fills her banners.

---

[7]Chinese ink came in the form of a stick, which was ground with water on an inkstone to reach the proper thickness.

[8]Young Liu is a playful reference to Emperor Wu of the Han (surnamed Liu) and his role as the lover of the goddess Queen Mother of the West. Peng Mountain was one of the three islands in the Eastern Ocean inhabited by the Undying. The figure here suggests that the beloved is out of reach.

In the comings of E-lü-hua
    there is never a certain place;
Du Lan-xiang goes away,
    not staying very long.

Here she may meet the Jade Gentleman
    and be listed among the Undying,[9]
recalling when on Heaven's Stairs[1]
    you asked of purple asphodel.

As with many of Li Shang-yin's poems, commentators speculate on what situation in the mortal world the following poem might refer to—if any. The scene seems to be set in a city in Heaven, echoing a legend of a city fashioned of sapphire-colored clouds in the sky. Lang-feng Park and Maiden's Bed Hill, both mentioned in the second couplet, are places where the gods live. The third couplet seems to describe the whole world below, seen from the perspective of Heaven, watching the stars as they set and pass below the bottom of the Western Sea. The setting of the stars leads to daybreak in the last couplet, whose "pearl" is the sun, perhaps reduced in dimensions by the distance from which it is supposedly seen. The final line probably refers to a story about Zhao "Flying Swallow," the favorite of the Han emperor Cheng. "Flying Swallow's" body was supposed to have been so light that she flew when she danced and was in danger of being caught by the wind. The emperor was afraid she might be blown away, so he had a huge bowl of crystal made, to be held over her by palace ladies, and in this she performed her flying dance.

Citadel of Sapphire Walls (first of three)

Citadel of sapphire walls, twelve turns
    of its balustrades,
horn of narwhal wards off dust,
    fire opal wards off cold.

When letters come from Lang-feng Park,
    they are mostly sent by crane;
not a tree grows on Maiden's Bed Hill
    that has no phoenix perching.

When stars sink to the ocean's floor,
    at these windows they may be seen,
and as rain passes the river's source,
    you can watch it over the table.

---

[9] The Jade Gentleman *(Yu-lang)* was the deity entrusted with keeping the registry of those included among the inhabitants of Heaven.

[1] "Heaven's Stairs" was a constellation, and the purple asphodel was a plant that granted the eater immortality.

> If only that pearl of daybreak
>> could stay both bright and still,
> I would spend my whole life facing
>> a bowl of crystal.

Even in less cryptic poems, Li Shang-yin often manages to evoke a mood of strangeness:

Midnight

> It is night's third hour, its third division,
>> thousands of households asleep,
> the dew is about to turn to frost,
>> and the moon plummets in mist.
> Squabbling mice emerge in the hall,
>> bats come flying forth,
> as now and then the jade harp stirs
>> strings resting by the window.

Sunbeams Shoot

> Sunbeams shoot through a gauze window screen,
>> wind gusts rattle the door,
> sweet-smelling silks cover her hands,
>> spring's work gone awry.
> An encircling porch joins on all sides,
>> wistful stillness enclosed,
> where a sapphire green parrot faces
>> the red roses.

In the two following quatrains, the Blue Woman is the goddess of frost, while the Pale Maid is Chang E, the goddess of the moon. In the first, these goddesses are simply personifications of frost and moonlight. The second quatrain, with its ghostly play of light and the implication of a lonely woman staying awake at night, refers to the myth that Yi had requested the elixir of immortality from the Queen Mother of the West, but before he could swallow it, his wife Chang E stole it and fled to the moon, where she became an immortal spirit.

Frost and Moon

> When first I heard the migrating geese,
>> cicadas were already gone,
> south of the hundred-foot tower
>> the waters stretched to the sky.
> The Blue Woman, the Pale Maid
>> both put up with the cold,

in moonlight and in the frost they hold
    a contest of beauty and grace.

Chang E

Upon the screen of mica
    a candle's reflection deep,
the long star-river steadily sets,
    the dawn stars sink away.
Chang E must surely repent
    the theft of that magic herb—
in the sapphire sea, the blue heavens,
    her heart night after night.

Li Shang-yin also wrote well in more conventional modes.

Written During the Rain One Night and Sent Back North

You asked when I was coming back:
    no date fixed yet;
in Ba's hills the rain by night
    spills over autumn ponds.
When will we trim the candle's wick
    together beside west window,
and speak back about this moment
    of night rain in hills of Ba?

The pleasure of Li Shang-yin's poems on history will inevitably be a difficult one for Western readers, since these poems depend upon the immense store of historical lore and stories that were shared by all educated Tang readers. Like other Late Tang poets, Li Shang-yin was fascinated by those pleasure-loving emperors whose extravagant self-indulgence seemed to have resulted in the destruction of their dynasties. Two such emperors appear in "The Sui Palace." The earlier is the "last ruler of Chen," whose sensual song "In the Rear Court Flowers on Trees of Jade" revealed that he was unfit for serious responsibility, and when his courtiers heard it, they wept, knowing that the state would not last long. Indeed, in 589, the Chen Dynasty was overthrown by the Sui, which reunified China. The Sui, however, proved to be itself a very short-lived dynasty. After a vigorous reign by the dynasty's founder, his son, Emperor Yang, became intoxicated by the allure of the same sensual life of the South that had ruined the Chen. Against the vigorous protests of his advisers, he abandoned Chang-an with its palace at Lavender Springs, and moved his primary residence to Yang-zhou, which he renamed Jiang-du, the "River Capital." It was believed that Yang-zhou, earlier in ruins, had been the site on which Bao Zhao composed his famous poetic exposition "The City of

Weeds" *(Wu-cheng fu),* tracing the course of the city's early passage from splendor to ruin.

Stories of Emperor Yang's extravagant projects in Yang-zhou soon became legendary. One was the construction of a great canal to the north, which Emperor Yang had lined with willows, a project that remained one of the most visible legacies of the Sui Dynasty—the "willows of the Sui embankments." To travel up on the canal to Da-liang, Emperor Yang ordered the construction of five hundred boats, the imperial boat fitted with sails of palace brocade. Another story tells how he ordered all the fireflies (believed to be born of rotting plants) in the region to be gathered, then one evening he went out on an excursion and set them all loose, and their light lit up the mountains and valleys. Yet another story tells how Emperor Yang once dreamed that he encountered the last ruler of the Chen with his palace ladies. One among them was exceptionally beautiful, and she turned out to be Li-hua, the last ruler's favorite. Emperor Yang requested that she dance for him the famous "In the Rear Court Flowers on Trees of Jade."

Emperor Yang, paying no heed to the troubles of governing in his various amusements, was eventually overthrown by the Tang. Li Shang-yin was fascinated by Emperor Yang and wrote a number of poems about that ruler and his ill-fated dynasty.

The Sui Palace

The halls of the palace at Lavender Springs
    shut in mists and rose clouds,
but he wished to occupy City of Weeds
    to serve as the Emperor's home.

Had the jade scepter not, by consequence,
    gone to him with the sun-knobs,[2]
I am sure that those brocade sails
    would have made it to the horizon.

Even today the rotting plants
    are bare of fireflies,
yet for all time the hanging willows
    will have their twilight crows.

If under the Earth he happens to meet
    the last ruler of Chen,
it would not be right again to ask
    for "In the Rear Court Flowers."

---

[2]Before the Tang founder rose in rebellion against Emperor Yang, he was observed to have "sun-knobs" on his forehead, protuberances that were a sign in his physiognomy that he was destined to become emperor.

The Sui Palace

He roamed off to the south on a whim,
    no precautions for the journey,
who in the palace reflected on
    those boxes filled with protests?
In spring breeze the entire land
    was cutting up palace brocade—
half to be mudguards for his saddles,
    half to be for his sails.

李唐 Tang Tales *(chuan-qi)*

During the Tang, an old tradition of prose anecdotes was transformed into a fully developed fictional form, later known as *chuan-qi*—"transmitting accounts of remarkable things." Although the majority of such stories treated some form of the supernatural, there were also purely human love stories and tales of heroism. One of the most common types combined the supernatural with the love story or erotic encounter.

A common concern in tales of love was faith kept and faith broken. By keeping faith with another, a creature of the spirit world could rise to the level of a human being, and by breaking faith a human being could sink to the bestial. The model of such relationships is pragmatic and economic: each party gives something essential, and so long as accounts are balanced, no mechanism of retribution is set into motion. If, however, one party fails to pay back what is given, the consequences are dire.

Many of these stories take place in Chang-an and give us a vivid picture of life in the city in the eighth and ninth century. One important narrative device for putting young heroes in the beds of young heroines was Chang-an's ward system, by which the city was divided in various "quarters," each separated from the others by walls that would be locked at sunset and opened only at daybreak. Anyone who found himself in a quarter other than his own at dusk would have to stay the night.

Two Tales of Keeping Faith

Shen Ji-ji (fl. ca. 800), "Ren's Story"

Ren was a woman of the werefolk.

And there was Wei Yin, now a lord governor, ninth in seniority in his branch of the family, maternal grandson of Li Hui, the Prince of Xin-an. Wei Yin was an undisciplined and wild young man, who loved to drink.

And there was his uncle's sister's husband, surnamed Zheng, though I don't recall his given name. In his early years Zheng had practiced the martial arts, and he too loved wine and pretty women. Being poor and without family of his own, he lived as a dependent of his wife's family. Once he and Wei Yin found one another, they were inseparable wherever they went.

In August of the summer of 750, Wei Yin and Zheng were riding together on the lanes of Chang-an on their way to a drinking party in the Xin-chang Quarter. When they reached the southern part of the Xuan-ping Quarter, Zheng excused himself for some reason or other and asked Wei Yin to go on ahead by himself, saying that he, Zheng, would be along shortly. Wei

Yin then went off east riding his white horse, while Zheng rode his donkey south into the north gate of the Sheng-ping Quarter. There he came upon three women walking along the street, of whom the middle one, dressed in white, was a rare beauty. No sooner did he see her than Zheng was infatuated. He whipped his donkey now in front of her, now behind, always on the point of bantering with her flirtatiously, but not daring. From time to time the woman in white cast a sidelong glance at him, having understood what was on his mind. Then Zheng joked with her, "And how is it that such a beautiful woman as yourself is going on foot?" The woman in white laughed, "What can I do but go on foot if someone doesn't loan me his mount?" Zhang replied, "This miserable mount is hardly an adequate alternative to such a lovely person walking, but I will offer it to you at once. I would be quite content to follow you on foot."

They looked at each other and laughed out. As they went along together, he fell increasingly under her spell, and they gradually began to behave quite familiarly with one another. Zheng followed the women; and by the time they reached the Le-you Gardens in the east, it was already getting dark. Here they came to a compound with earthen walls and a carriage gate. The buildings inside were quite well built and properly proportioned. As the woman in white was about to go in, she looked around and said, "Wait here for a little while." Then she went inside, leaving one of her female bondservants in the open gate. The bondservant asked his name and family; and after Zheng had told her, he asked of the woman in white. The servant answered, "Her name is Ren, and she is the twentieth in seniority."

After a short while he was invited in. Zheng tied his donkey at the gate and left his cap on the saddle. He first met a woman in her thirties, who welcomed him. This was Ren's elder sister. Rows of candles were lit, various dishes set out, and cups of wine were raised in frequent toasts. Having changed her attire, Ren came out. They drank until they were tipsy and very merry. As the night drew on, they finally went to bed. Her features were captivating and her body was beautiful. In the way she looked when singing and laughing and in all her movements there was a sensual loveliness that was virtually not of this mortal world.

When it was almost dawn, Ren said, "You had best go now. My brothers are attached to the Music Academy, which is under the jurisdiction of the Southern Guard Command. Early in the morning they will rise and go out, so you cannot linger here." They agreed on a future meeting, and he left.

Having set out, he came to the ward gates, which had not yet been unbarred. There was the shop of a Turkish pastryseller beside the gate, whose owner was just then hanging up his lanterns and firing his ovens. Zheng went in through the curtains to rest and sat down to wait for the drums that would announce the opening of the gates. As a consequence he got to talking with the shopowner, and pointing to where he had spent the night, Zheng asked him, "When you turn east from here, there's a gate. Whose compound is that?" The shopowner replied, "That's just wasteland surrounded by a broken-down wall—there are no buildings there." Zheng said, "But I just passed by the place—how can you say that there's nothing there?" and he argued with the man stubbornly. Then the shopowner realized, "Ah! now I understand. There is a fox there that often seduces men to spend the night with her. I've already seen this happen a few times now. Are you another one who has met her?" Zheng's face flushed and he didn't tell the truth: "No, no."

In full daylight he went back to look at the spot and did see the earthen wall and carriage gate just as before; but when he peered inside, it was all overgrown with scrub, with abandoned garden plots. After he got home, he saw Wei Yin, who berated him for missing the party. Zheng didn't let on what had happened and excused himself with some other story. Nevertheless, he kept imagining Ren's sensual beauty, and the desire to see her again remained unforgotten in his heart.

A dozen or so days passed. Zheng was out and going into a clothing store in the Western Market when all at once he saw her, accompanied by her servants as before. Zheng instantly shouted to her. Ren turned to the side and tried to lose herself in a crowd to avoid him. But Zheng kept shouting to her and pushed his way forward. Finally she stood with her back to him, screening her face from his sight with a fan that she held around behind her. "You know, so why do you come near me?" He answered, "I do know, but I don't care." She replied, "The situation makes me very embarrassed. It's hard to look you in the face." Zheng then said, "Since I think on you so intently, how can you bear to reject me?" She replied, "How could I dare reject you? It's just that I am afraid of being despised by you."

Zheng then swore an oath, and the import of what he said was very moving. At this Ren turned her eyes to him and removed the fan, revealing the same dazzling sensual beauty that she had before. To Zheng, she said, "I'm not the only one of my kind in the human world. You just don't recognize them. Don't think of me as a singular freak." When Zheng entreated her, telling her of his joy in her, she replied, "The only reason my kind is despised and loathed by human beings is because we are thought to harm people. I'm not like that. If you don't despise me, I would want to serve you all my days as your wife." Zheng agreed and began to make plans where she could live. Ren said, "To the east of this spot, where a large tree comes out from among the roof beams, there is a quiet, secluded lane; you could rent a place there for me to live. That man who went riding a white horse east from the southern part of the Xuan-ping Quarter earlier—wasn't he your legal wife's brother? His house has ample furniture and household goods that you could borrow."

At the time Wei Yin's uncle was serving in posts out in the provinces, and three apartments' worth of his household goods were kept in storage. Following her suggestion, Zheng first went to inquire about the lodgings, then went to see Wei Yin to borrow the household goods. When Wei asked what he wanted them for, Zheng said, "I have just gotten myself a beautiful woman and have rented lodgings for her; now I need to borrow household goods to fix the place up." Wei Yin laughed. "Considering your looks, you must surely have gotten yourself a spectacularly ugly woman. How could you possibly get a perfect beauty?"

After loaning him things like curtains, beds, and mats, Wei had a quick-witted servant boy follow Zheng and spy out where he was going. In a short time the lad rushed back to make his report, panting and streaming with sweat. Wei Yin met him and asked, "Was she there?" and further, "What did she look like?" The lad said, "She is a wonder—the world has never seen her like." Wei Yin's family and kin were widely spread and numerous; moreover, having gone on escapades since his early years, he had come to have extensive grounds to make judgments of beauty. He then asked, "Is she as beautiful as so-and-so?" The lad answered, "That person is not of her caliber." Wei Yin brought up four or five beautiful women for comparison, and in each case the boy said, "Not of her caliber." At that time Wei Yin's sister-in-law, the sixth daughter of the Prince of Wu, had a full and sensual beauty like that of a goddess, and both sides of the family had always acclaimed her the foremost in beauty. So Wei Yin said, "Is she as beautiful as the sixth daughter of the Prince of Wu?" And again the boy said, "Not of her caliber." Wei Yin slapped his hand down in amazement. "How could there be such a person in the world?" He instantly ordered water to be drawn so that he could wash his neck, put his turban on, applied lip balm, and set off.

Zheng happened to be out when he arrived. On entering the gate, Wei Yin saw a young servant boy holding a broom sweeping; there was a bond-servant at the gate, but he saw no one else. He then asked information of the servant boy, who laughed and said, "There's no such person here." Wei Yin was looking all around the inside of the rooms, when he caught sight of a red skirt showing beneath a door panel. He forced his way in to check it out and saw Ren, who had curled up to hide behind the door panel. Wei Yin dragged her out, bringing her over into the light so he could take a look at her. She virtually exceeded what he had been told. Wei Yin wanted her so much that he behaved like a madman. He threw his arms around her and forced himself on her, but she would not submit. Wei Yin used his strength to hold her fast, and when the situation became desperate, she said, "I submit, but please loosen your grip a little."

When he did as she asked, she fought back as she had before. This happened several more times, until Wei Yin exerted all his strength to hold her fast. Ren's own strength was exhausted, and she was sweating as if she had been soaked by rain. Realizing that she couldn't escape, she let her body relax and didn't resist any more, yet her expression changed to one of heartfelt sadness. Wei Yin asked why, saying, "How unhappy you look!" Ren gave a long sigh. "It's just that I feel sorry for Zheng." Wei Yin said, "What do you mean?" She replied, "Zheng is six feet tall yet is unable to protect one woman—how can he be a real man! You, sir, have led a life of wild excess since your youth and have had many beautiful women—a multitude of those you have encountered have been comparable in beauty to me. Yet Zheng, who is poor and of humble background, has only myself to suit his fancy. Can a heart that has had something in abundance be so hardened as to plunder the same from someone who does not have enough? I feel sorry for his poverty and want, that he is unable to stand on his own. He wears your clothes and eats your food, and thus he is bound by you. If he could provide even simple food for himself, he should not be brought to this." In Wei Yin's domineering arrogance there was some sense of justice. Hearing what she had said, he immediately set her down, and straightening his clothes, he apologized, saying, "I can't do this."

A short time later Zheng arrived, and looking at Wei Yin, he beamed with joy. From that point on, Wei Yin provided Ren with all her firewood, grain, and meat. Now and then Ren would stop by. In her comings and go-ings she would sometimes go by carriage, sometimes ride a horse, sometimes travel in a sedan chair, and sometimes walk—her choice was not uniform. Wei Yin would go about with her every day, and be extremely happy to do so; the two grew very familiar and intimate with one another, and there were no barriers between them, except for sexual intimacy. Wei Yin came to love her and honor her. He begrudged her nothing, and at every meal and every time he drank, she never left his thoughts. Ren knew that he loved her, so she apologized to him. "I am ashamed to be loved by you so much, but this poor body is inadequate to answer your generous feeling. I cannot betray Zheng, thus I cannot accommodate myself to your pleasure. I am from this region of Qin, and I grew up in this, Qin's greatest city. My family is one of entertainers, and many of my relations on both sides have been kept as con-cubines. For this reason I am well acquainted with all the winding lanes of Chang-an's pleasure quarters. There may be some beautiful and pleasing young girl who has not yet been taken—let me bring one for you. For I want by this to repay your goodness." Wei Yin said, "What good luck!" In the bazaar there was a woman who sold clothes called Miss Zhang, with smooth and bright skin. Wei Yin had always been attracted to her, so he asked Ren if she knew her. Ren replied, "That is my cousin. It will be an easy matter to bring her to you." And after about two weeks she finally brought her.

A few months later, Wei Yin grew tired of her and dismissed her. Ren then said, "The women of the marketplace are easy to procure and not worth much effort. If there is someone absolutely out of reach, someone hard to devise a plot to get hold of, just tell me—for I want to be able to use all my strength and wit in this." Wei Yin then said, "During this most recent Cold Food Festival I was visiting Thousand Blessings Temple along with a few other companions.[1] There I saw a musical performance arranged by Gen-eral Diao Mian in the great hall. There was a skilled flageolet player of about sixteen years of age, her hair done in a pair of coils that hung down to her ears. She had an air of sweetness about her and was utterly desirable. Do

---

[1]The Cold Food Festival was a spring festival in which the use of fire was forbidden.

you know her, by chance?" Ren replied, "That is Chong-nu. Her mother is, in fact, a cousin of mine. It's possible to go after her." Wei bowed to her with respect, and Ren promised him.

Ren then began to pay frequent visits to the Diao household. After somewhat more than a month, Ren wanted two bolts of the highest grade silk to use as a bribe. Wei Yin provided these. Two days later, Ren was dining with Wei when Diao Mian sent a servant leading a black steed to bring Ren to see him. On hearing this summons, she said to Wei Yin with a smile, "It's worked." Earlier Ren had given Chong-nu something that made her grow sick, an illness that neither acupuncture nor medicines could relieve. Her mother and Diao Mian were extremely worried about her and were going to summon a soothsayer. Ren secretly bribed the soothsayer, and pointing out where she lived, she ordered him to say that it would be lucky to transfer her there. After examining the illness, the soothsayer said, "It is not advantageous for her to be in this house; she should go reside at such-and-such a place to the southeast where she will obtain quickening life forces." When Diao Mian and the girl's mother made a thorough survey of the location, it turned out that Ren's residence was in the area. Diao Mian consequently asked that Chong-nu be allowed to stay there. Ren made a pretense of objecting on the grounds that her house was small and cramped, and agreed only after they entreated her earnestly. Then Chong-nu, with all her clothes and ornaments carried in litters and accompanied by her mother, was sent to Ren's. When she got there, her sickness got better. Just a few days later Ren secretly led Wei Yin to her, and he had intercourse with her. After a month she was pregnant. Her mother was frightened and immediately took her back to Diao Mian's, from which point the affair was over.

On another occasion Ren said to Zheng, "Would you be able to get five or six thousand cash? I have a scheme to make you a profit." Zheng said, "All right"; and by going to borrow money from people, he got six thousand cash. Ren then said, "In the market there is someone selling a horse with something wrong with one of its legs. Buy it, take it home, and take care of it." Zheng went to the market and at last saw a man leading a horse and looking for a buyer. There was a flaw on one of its left legs. Zheng bought it and took it back home with him. His wife's brothers all ridiculed him, saying, "That creature was just something someone was trying to get rid of. Why did you buy it?" Not long afterward Ren said, "Sell the horse now. You should get thirty thousand cash for it." Zheng then went to offer the horse for sale. When someone offered him twenty thousand cash, Zheng refused to part with it. The whole market was saying, "What problem does the first man have that he is willing to spend so much, and why does the other man love the horse so much that he won't sell?" Zheng rode the horse back home, and the man who had wanted to buy it followed after him, repeatedly raising his offer until it reached twenty-five thousand. Zheng, however, would not part with it, saying, "I won't sell it for less than thirty thousand." His wife's brothers all crowded around and berated him; unable to maintain himself against them, he sold it, never getting the full thirty thousand.

Afterward he secretly confronted the buyer and asked him why he had been willing to pay so much. It turned out that one of the imperial horses kept in Zhao-ying County had something wrong with one of its legs. This horse had died three years ago, and the functionary in charge had not promptly taken it off the official records. The government office had sent an allowance for its upkeep totaling sixty thousand cash, and he speculated that if he were to buy another for half that amount, he would still be reaping a handsome profit. If there were a horse to make the full complement, then the functionary would get its entire allowance for fodder and grain. And since what he would have to pay would be less than he made, he bought it.

Since her own clothes were old and frayed, Ren also asked Wei Yin for clothes. Wei was going to buy whole bolts of cloth to give her, but she didn't want that: "I want to get clothes that are ready-made." Wei Yin then called someone from the market, Old Zhang, to make the purchases for her, and he had Zhang meet Ren to find out what she wanted. When he saw her, Zhang was alarmed and said to Wei Yin, "This woman has to be a goddess or someone related to the imperial house whom you have secretly carried off. She is not someone who should be kept in the mortal world. I urge you to send her back as quickly as possible before some disaster befalls you." That was how much her beauty could stir people. In the end he found ready-made clothes for her, and she did not sew them herself. He did not, however, understand why.

More than a year later, Zheng was selected for a military post and was appointed assistant director for military affairs of the Huai-li district, which was in Jin-cheng County. Since Zheng had a legal wife and household, he might go out for the day, but he always slept home at night. It always upset him that he could not have Ren with him every night. When he was about to leave to take up his post, he invited Ren to go along with him. Ren did not want to go: "Traveling together for weeks on end cannot be considered a pleasure. Please just estimate how much will keep me provided with meat and grain, and I will stay here as always, awaiting your return." Zheng entreated her earnestly, but she grew only less willing. Zheng then sought out Wei Yin to provide help in persuading her, and together they urged her once again and questioned her on her reasons for refusing. After a long time Ren said, "A soothsayer said that it would be unlucky for me to travel west this year, and that's why I don't want to go." Zheng was completely infatuated with her and could think of nothing else. Together with Wei Yin he laughed, saying, "How can you be so intelligent, yet be led astray by such mumbo-jumbo?" They stuck to their request, and Ren said, "If by chance the soothsayer's words prove true, what good will it do if I die for you for nothing?" And both of them said, "How could this happen?"—and they pleaded as earnestly as before. Unable to have her own way in this, Ren went. Wei Yin loaned her a horse and held a parting banquet for them at Lin-gao, waving his arms to them as they went off on their way.

After two days of travel, they reached Ma-wei. Ren was riding her horse in front, and Zheng was riding his donkey behind. Further behind, the two women servants were riding apart. At that time the Imperial Groom of the West Gate had been hunting with his dogs for ten days in Luo River County, and he happened to meet them on the road. One of his dark gray dogs leaped out from among the grasses, and Zheng saw Ren fall to the ground in a flash, reverting to her original shape and running south. The gray dog chased her. Zheng ran after it shouting, but he couldn't stop it. After a little more than a league the dog caught her.

With tears in his eyes, Zheng took money from his purse and paid to have her buried. And he had a piece of wood carved as the grave marker. When he went back, he saw her horse grazing on the grasses beside the road. Her clothes were left draped on the saddle, and her shoes and stockings were still hanging in the stirrups, as if a cicada had metamorphosed from its shell. Nothing else was to be seen but her hair ornaments, which had fallen to the ground. The two women servants were also gone.

After a little more than ten days, Zheng returned to the city. Wei Yin was delighted to see him and greeted him, asking, "No harm has come to Ren, has there?" Zheng's eyes streamed with tears as he replied, "She's dead." Hearing this, Wei Yin was stricken with grief, and the two men clasped one another there in the room, giving full expression to their sorrow. Softly Wei asked the cause of her death, and Zheng replied, "She was killed by a dog." Wei Yin then said, "However fierce a dog may be, how could it kill a human being?" Zheng answered, "It was not a human being." Wei Yin was shocked. "What do you mean, 'not a human being'?" Then Zheng told him the whole story from beginning to end. Wei Yin was amazed and could not stop sighing. On the next day, he ordered a carriage to be made ready and went off with Zheng to Ma-wei. He opened her tomb, looked at her, and went back feeling a lingering unhappiness. When he thought back on all that had happened, only the fact that she did not make her own clothes was rather strange in comparison to human beings.

Afterward Zheng served as a supervisor-general, and his household became very wealthy, with over ten horses in his stables. He died at the age of sixty-five.

During the Da-li Reign, I, Shen Ji-ji, was living in Zhong-ling and used to go about with Wei Yin. Wei told this story often, with the result that I learned many of the details. Later Wei Yin became Palace Censor, as well as Prefect of Long-zhou, where he died without returning to the capital.

I am struck that such humanity could be found in the feelings of a creature so alien. When someone used violent force on her, she did not abandon her principles, and she met her death by sacrificing herself for someone else. Among women today there are those who are not her equal. It is unfortunate that Zheng was not a perceptive man, merely attracted by her beauty and not seeing the evidence of her nature. Supposing there had been some scholar of profound discernment, he would surely have been able to investigate the principles in such a transformation, to discern the lines of distinction between human beings and spirits, to write it out in a beautiful style, and thus to transmit such subtle feelings to posterity—he would not limit himself to just savoring her good looks and a love story. It is a pity!

In 781, I left my post as Reminder of the Left and was going to Wu. General Pei Ji, the Vice Governor of Chang-an Sun Cheng, the Director of the Ministry of Revenue Cui Xu, and the Reminder of the Right Lu Chun all happened to be going to live in the Southeast. In the journey from Qin to Wu we all followed the same route, both land and water. At the time, the former Reminder Zhu Fang was also traveling, and he went along with us. We floated down the Ying River and then the Huai, our double boat carried along by the current. By day we would feast and at night tell stories, with each of us presenting strange tales. When these gentlemen heard of the events surrounding Ren, all were deeply touched and amazed. As a consequence, they asked me to transmit it as an account of strange things.

—Written by Shen Ji-ji

True self-sacrifice is most often found in women, but answering devotion in men is also acknowledged. From "Ren's Story," it may seem that a love affair with a creature from beyond the human world was a safe undertaking; but Ren's surprise on finding that Zheng still wanted her, in spite of the fact that she was a were-fox, was more in keeping with conventional wisdom that miscegenation with supernatural beings or ghosts was bad for one's health and fortune. Nevertheless, a willingness to brave such a prohibition might be as much a proof of love and reciprocating faith as of overwhelming lust, as seems to have been the case with Zheng.

Li Jing-liang (fl. 794), "Li Zhang-wu's Story"

The ancestry of Li Zhang-wu, otherwise known as Li Fei, was traced to the Zhong-shan region. From his earliest years he was intelligent and well informed, and whatever happened he knew what to do. He was, moreover, a skilled stylist, and his writings always reached the height of perfection. Although he had a high opinion of his own achievements in improving himself, he abhorred putting on airs. He was of a refined and handsome appearance and was genial to those who approached him. He was a good friend of one Cui Xin of Qing-he, another cultured gentleman and a collector of antiquities. Because of Zhang-wu's astute intelligence, Cui Xin would often seek him out for discussions; together they penetrated the most subtle mysteries and thoroughly investigated questions. Contemporaries compared Zhang-wu to Zhang Hua of the Jin Dynasty.

In the year 787, Cui Xin had taken the post of administrative aide to the prefect of Hua-zhou, and Zhang-wu came from Chang-an to visit him. Several days later he was out walking, and saw a very beautiful woman on the northern avenue of the market. He then concocted a story, telling Cui Xin that he had to have some dealings with an old friend outside the city. He next rented lodgings in the beautiful woman's home. The master of the house was named Wang, and the woman was his daughter-in-law. Zhang-wu was greatly attracted to her and took up intimate relations with her. Staying there somewhat over a month, the experience cost him more than thirty thousand cash, which was doubled by the expenses of providing things for the daughter-in-law. Yet their two hearts were in perfect accord, and their love for one another grew steadily stronger.

Eventually Zhang-wu had to attend to his own matters; and when he told her that he would be returning to Chang-an, he spoke of their parting with great feeling. Zhang-wu left her a piece of silk, patterned with a mated pair of ducks, their necks entwined. He also gave her a poem:

> This silk patterned with mated ducks—
> ties knotted for a thousand years.
> After parting recall their necks entwined—
> you will surely feel sad for these times before.

The daughter-in-law answered him with a white jade finger ring and a poem:

> Pick up this finger ring of longing,
> when you see this ring, remember me.
> I want you to wear it always,
> going round in rings that have no end.

Zhang-wu had a servant, Yang Guo, to whom the daughter-in-law furnished a thousand cash as reward for his zealous services.

Eight or nine years passed after they parted. Zhang-wu's home was in Chang-an and he had no way to keep in contact with her. Then in 791, because his friend Zhang Yuan-zong had taken up lodging in Xia-gui County near Hua-zhou, Zhang-wu once again left the capital and went to join Zhang Yuan-zong. All of a sudden he thought of that past love and turned his course across the Wei River to visit her. It was getting dark when he reached Hua-zhou, and he planned to stay over at the Wangs' house. But when he reached the gate, the place was silent and deserted, with no trace of anyone there. There was only a bench for guests placed outside. Zhang-wu thought that they had either passed away, or that they had given up their profession and returned to farming, staying for a while in rural areas, or that they had simply been invited to a gathering and had not returned.

He was standing there at the gate, ready to go find lodging elsewhere, when he saw a woman who lived next door to the east. He went up to her and inquired about them, and she told him that the elder Wangs had indeed given up their profession and gone off somewhere, but that the daughter-in-law had died two years previously. He continued to chat with her to get more of the details, and she said, "My name is Yang, and I am the wife of their neighbor to the east. May I inquire what your name is, young sir?" Zhang-wu told her. Then she added, "Did you once some time ago have a menial by the name of Yang Guo?" Zhang-wu replied, "I did." Hearing this, she wept and told him, "I have lived in this quarter of the city for five years and was on very good terms with the young Mrs. Wang. She once told me,

'My husband's house is like a hotel, and I have caught the eye of many men. Some made advances to me as they came and went, and they all used up their fortunes, said pretty words, and swore great vows. But none of them ever stirred my heart. Then some years ago a man named Li Zhang-wu took up lodging at our house. When I first saw him, I was lost before I knew it. Afterward I shared a bed with him and received real love and joy from him. It has now been many years since I parted from him, yet my heart still yearns for him, so much so that I sometimes go the whole day without eating and cannot sleep the whole night through. Of course I can't confide this to anyone in the family. Furthermore, I get taken one place and another by that husband of mine, so there is little chance that I would meet with him even if he were to come. If he should, by chance, come here, you could recognize him by his attractive looks and his name. Try to see if it is him, and if there is no mistake, confide my devotion to him and also tell him how deeply I feel. If the man has a servant named Yang Guo, it's him.'

"Not two or three years after that she grew sick and bedridden. When she was close to death, she again confided in me. 'I am only a poor person of humble birth. I have had the undeserved good fortune to receive the kind attention of a man of the best sort, and my heart is always stirred by thoughts of him. This has gone on so long now that I have become sick, and I do not expect to recover. Giving him my heart long ago has unexpectedly led to this. Yet I want to express to him the unhappiness I will have to endure in the underworld and my sighs that we must be separated now forever. If it does happen that he asks again to stay here, I hope for a spirit meeting in the phantom realm.' "

Zhang-wu then asked the neighbor's wife to open the gate, and he ordered his attendants to go buy fodder, firewood, and food in the market. As he was about to prepare his bedding, a woman suddenly appeared, broom in hand, coming out of the chamber sweeping the ground. The neighbor's wife did not recognize her, so Zhang-wu inquired of her from whence she had come, and she said that she was a person of the household. When he pressed her with further questions, she said softly, "The deceased wife of the Wang family has been touched by the depth of your feeling for her and will meet you. But she is worried that you might be frightened, so she sent me to communicate with you." Zhang-wu then swore an oath, saying, "It was for this that I came here. Although the world of light and the dark world below differ, and though mortal men all look on the dark world with dread and loathing, because of the intensity of the love I bear her, I truly have no hesitations." When he finished saying these words, the woman holding the broom appeared much gladdened and withdrew, pausing for a moment half-hidden behind the gate, then no longer to be seen.

Zhang-wu had food and drink prepared, and he called for the spirit to come and taste his offerings. After he finished eating and drinking, he lay down to go to bed. A little after ten o'clock the oil lamp to the southeastern side of his bed suddenly dimmed. When this happened repeatedly, Zhang-wu knew in his heart that a transformation was occurring, and he had the lamp moved up against the wall in the southeastern corner of the room. All at once he heard a rustling sound at the northern edge of the room, and it seemed as if there were a human form gradually drawing closer. After five or six steps he could make out her features. When he looked at her attire, it was indeed the daughter-in-law of his former host. She appeared no different from before, but her movements had an airy suddenness and the tone of her voice was lighter and more clear. Zhang-wu got out of bed, embraced her, and took her hand, and their joy in each other was just as openhearted as it once was. Then she said, "Since I have been entered in the register of the dead, I have forgotten all my kin and dear ones. Only my heart's longing for you is still as it used to be." Zhang redoubled his intimacies, and nothing was different from before—except that she asked someone to check for the morning star several times, for when it appeared, she would have to soon go back, not being permitted to stay there long. And always, when resting from their lovemaking, she would express the sincere gratitude she felt for her neighbor, Madam Yang, saying, "Were it not for her, who would have communicated my silent suffering to you?"

When the last hour of night arrived, someone was there to tell her she should go back now. She got out of bed weeping and went out the gate, arm in arm with Zhang-wu. She looked up and gazed on the Milky Way and gave a long, sad moan, then went back into the room. She untied a brocade bag that hung from the sash at her waist and took something from it to give to him. Its color was sky blue, and the material was dense and hard. It was like jade but colder, and its shape was like that of a small leaf. Zhang-wu did not recognize it, and she said, "This is called a Mo-he jewel from the Dark Garden on Mount Kun-lun. It is not something you could ever find. I was playing with the Lady of the Jade Capital near the Western Peak, and I saw this among all her jewels and earrings. I was quite taken with it and spoke to her about it, whereupon the Lady took it and gave it to me, saying, 'Whenever one of the immortal hosts in the Caverns to Heaven gets one of these jewels, he considers it a glorious event.' Since you serve the occult way of Daoism and are a sincere person, I will make a present of it to you. Treasure it always, for it is not something that exists in the mortal world." Then she gave him a poem:

> The River of Stars sinks downward now,
> this soul is ready to pass beyond.
> I want you to hold me one more time,
> for after this moment forever farewell.

In return, Zhang-wu gave her a precious white hairpin. He also answered her with a poem:

> World of darkness, world of light divide our fate,
> who would have thought this meeting could occur?
> Who could refuse to part once again,
> yet I sigh for where you will go from here.

Thereupon he took hold of her, weeping, and held her a long time in his arms. She then gave him another poem:

With our last farewell I longed to meet again,
this parting now is forever.
A new grief joins with former pain
locked for all time in the world below.

To this, Zhang-wu answered:

Future meeting so far no date can be set,
and the pain felt before comes again.
On our separate paths no letters pass,
so how can I send you my love?

When they finished telling each other all that they felt so deeply on part-ing, she went back toward the northwest corner. After taking several steps, she looked around and wiped away her tears, saying, "Li Zhang-wu, don't put me out of your heart—think of me when I am down in the world below." Again she stood there a long time, choked with tears; then, seeing that the sky was growing bright, she rushed over to the corner of the room and dis-appeared. There was only a murky darkness left in the room and the cold lamp flame, half extinguished.

Zhang-wu hastily packed his belongings, ready to leave Xia-gui and re-turn to the Wu-ding Fortress in Chang-an. The magistrate of Xia-gui and Zhang Yuan-zong had a drinking party to see him off. When he grew some-what tipsy, Zhang-wu thought of her and referred to what had happened in a poem:

Waters do not turn back west,
    the moon, but briefly full:
this brings heartache to the man
    beside these ancient walls.
Early tomorrow, in dismal gloom,
    our paths will split apart—
I wonder what year will ever come
    when we will meet again.

After he finished reciting that, he took his leave of the magistrate. He went on alone for several leagues and again recited the verse. All of a sud-den, out of nowhere, he heard a sigh of appreciation. When he listened again carefully, it was in fact Wang's daughter-in-law. And she said, "In the dark world, places are strictly divided. When I leave you now, we will never be joined together again. Knowing how you yearn for me, I have braved the chastisement by the Overseers of Shades and have come to see you on your way. Take care of yourself!" And Zhang-wu was even more enthralled by her.

When he reached Chang-an, he told the story to a Daoist companion, Li Zhu of Long-xi. He too was touched by Zhang-wu's true love and composed a poem:

Stones sink in Liao's vast sea,
mated swords parted by Chu's long sky.
He knows they will never meet again,
sundered from her, heart filled with setting sun.

Zhang-wu served in the Chief Minister's bureau at Dong-ping; and once when unoccupied, he called a jade carver to come look at the Mo-he jewel that he had acquired. Not recognizing what it was, the jade carver did not dare work on it. Later, Zhang-wu was sent on a mission to Da-liang and called in another jade carver, who had a rough notion of what it was. Keeping close to its original form, he carved it to resemble hemlock needles. Later again Zhang-wu was sent on a mission to the capital, and he always kept this object inside the folds of his coat. When he reached the eastern avenue of the market, he chanced to see a Central Asian monk, who immediately approached his horse, kowtowed, and said, "You have a jewel inside your coat. I beg you to let me see it." Zhang-wu led the monk to a quiet place, took it out, and showed it to the monk, who spent a long time rolling it over and over in his hand. Then he said, "This is one of the rarest objects from Heaven and it is not found in this mortal world."

Later, whenever Zhang-wu passed through Hua-zhou, he would visit Madam Yang and give her gifts, which he continues to do to this day.

Two Tales of Faith Broken

The lover who keeps his faith is finally rewarded, receiving an object that is solid and precious evidence of a moment when the supernatural realm crossed over into the human realm. Precarious moments are balanced out by equal exchanges of love, poems, and objects. A failure to give equal exchange, however, can be like a bad debt that never goes away.

Jiang Fang (fl. early 9th century), "Huo Xiao-yu's Story"

During the Da-li Reign (766–779), one Mr. Li of Long-xi, with the given name Yi, passed the *jin-shi* examination. In the following year he was to take the higher examination, "Picking Out the Finest," and waited to be put to the test by the Ministry of Personnel. He reached Chang-an in August of that summer and took a lodging in the Xin-chang Quarter of the city. He was from an illustrious family and had shown real talent since his childhood. At the time people said that his elegant phrases and splendid lines were unequaled, and well-established men who were his seniors were unanimous in acclaiming him. Whenever he thought with pride about his superior qualities, he longed to find a fair companion. He sought widely among the famous courtesans, but after a long time he still could discover no one suitable.

There was in Chang-an at the time one Miss Bao, a procuress, who had formerly been a maid of Commander-escort Xue. It had been more than a decade since she bought back her indenture contract and made a respectable marriage. With her ingratiating nature and clever tongue, she had contacts with all the powerful families and kinsmen of the imperial consorts, and she was commended as the best person around for quickness and savvy. Having constantly received good-faith commissions and rich presents from Li Yi, she was particularly well disposed toward him.

It happened that several months later, Li Yi was idling away the time in the southern pavilion of his house. In the course of the midafternoon he suddenly heard an urgent knocking at his gate, which turned out to signal the arrival of Miss Bao. He hurriedly straightened his clothes to go greet her: "My dear Miss Bao, what brings you here so unexpectedly today?" Bao replied: "And has my young bookworm been having a pleasant dream? I have for you a fairy princess who has been banished to this lower world. She asks no money—she yearns only for a man of gallantry and feeling. Someone of this caliber is a perfect match for you."

When Li Yi heard this, he leapt for joy and wonder. Drawing Bao by the hand, he bowed and expressed his gratitude, "I'll be your slave my whole life; I would die for you without flinching." Then he asked the girl's name and where she lived. Bao told him all the details. "She is the youngest daughter of the former Prince Huo, Xiao-yu by name. The prince was extremely fond of her. Her mother's name is Jing-chi, a maidservant who enjoyed the prince's favor. Soon after the prince passed away, Xiao-yu's brothers were not inclined to keep her in the household because she came from such a humble background, so they gave her a share of the wealth and sent her off to live elsewhere. She has changed her name to Zheng, and no one knows that she is the prince's daughter. In all my life I've never seen such a voluptuous figure. Yet she has noble sentiments and an independent manner. She surpasses others in every way. She understands everything from music to poetry and calligraphy. Recently she sent me to find her a good young man who is her equal in quality. I told her everything about you, and since she already knew of your name, she was exceptionally pleased and satisfied. She lives in Old Temple Lane in the Sheng-ye Quarter, in the house just beyond the carriage gate. I've already set a date for you to meet—tomorrow at noon. Just go to the end of the lane and look for her maid Cinnamon, and you're there."

After Bao had left, Li Yi made all his plans for the visit. He ordered his houseboy Qiu-hong to go to his cousin, Lord Shang, the Capital Administrator, to borrow his fine black yearling and a golden bridle. He had his clothes laundered, and he bathed, taking special care to be well groomed. The combination of joy and excitement prevented him from sleeping the entire night. As daylight broke, he put on his turban and looked at himself in the mirror, afraid that she wouldn't find him to her liking. Then he paced back and forth until it was noon, at which point he rode with great haste directly to the Sheng-ye Quarter. When at last he reached the place agreed upon, he saw a maid standing there waiting. She greeted him and asked, "Aren't you Li Yi?" He got down from his horse, and she led it next to the house, locking the gate securely behind her. He then saw Miss Bao coming out from inside. Still at a distance, she laughed and said, "Now what brings you barging in here?" Li Yi continued joking with her as she led him in through a central gate. In the courtyard there were four cherry trees, and from the one in the northwest corner there was hung a cage with a parrot in it. When it saw Li Yi come in, it spoke: "A man is coming—quick, pull down the curtains!" By nature Li Yi was proper and reserved, and his heart was still apprehensive and beset by doubts. When he heard the bird speak out so suddenly, he was overcome with panic and didn't dare go on further.

While he was still hesitating there, Miss Bao led Jing-chi down the stairs to greet him. She invited him in, and they sat down across from one another. Jing-chi was perhaps somewhat over forty, delicate and still very attractive. She laughed and chatted and made herself agreeable. Then she said to Li Yi, "I had heard before that you were a man of both talent and feeling. Now I can see for myself the elegance of your appearance and bearing. This is clearly not a case when there's nothing behind a reputation. I have one daughter, and though she has been but poorly educated, her looks are not altogether ugly. It would be most fitting if she could make a match with a true gentleman. Miss Bao has discussed this idea with me often, so I will now order her to serve you respectfully as a wife." Li Yi thanked her. "I am a very ordinary and awkward person, of no particular distinction. I had not expected to receive such kind regard. If only you would condescend to choose me for this, it would be a glory for me, alive or dead."

Then she ordered that wine and food be served and had Xiao-yu come out from her chamber on the eastern side of the hall. Li Yi went to greet her, but all he was aware of was something like an alabaster forest and jade trees throughout the whole room, casting their dazzling radiance back and forth, and as he turned his gaze, the crystalline rays struck him. Xiao-yu then went and sat by her mother, who said to her, "You are always fond of reciting:

When I opened the curtains, wind stirred the bamboo,
and I thought it was my old friend coming.

Those lines are from a poem by this very Li Yi. Better to see him in person than to spend the whole day imagining him as you recite." Xiao-yu lowered her head, giggling, and whispered softly, "But better still to hear of his reputation than to see him in person, for how could a man of talent be wanting in looks to match?" At once Li Yi rose and bowed, saying, "The young lady loves talent; I value beauty. These two preferences here illuminate one another in a conjunction between talent and good looks." Mother and daughter looked around at one another smiling. Then they raised their winecups in several rounds. Li Yi stood up and asked Xiao-yu to sing. At first she was unwilling, but her mother insisted. Her voice was bright and clear, and the handling of the melody was precise and wondrous.

When the drinking was finished, Miss Bao led Li Yi to the western wing to rest for the night. The courtyard was peaceful and the chamber was a spacious one, with splendidly worked curtains. Miss Bao ordered the servants Cinnamon and Washed Gauze to help Li Yi take off his boots and undo his sash. A moment later, Xiao-yu arrived. What she said to him was loving and tender, and the manner of her words was winsome. The instant she took off her gauze robes, he saw that her body was gorgeous. They lowered the bed curtains and drew close to one another on the pillows, experiencing the transports of pleasure. To Li Yi's mind, even what happened on Wu Mountain and by the banks of the Luo could not have been better.

In the middle of the night, Xiao-yu suddenly began to weep as she gazed on Li Yi: "I come from a courtesan background and know that I am not a proper match for you. Now, because of your love of beauty, I have been given to someone as kind and worthy as yourself. But I worry that one morning my beauty will be gone, and your love will leave and go elsewhere. Then the clinging vine will have nothing to cling to, and summer's fan will be cast away in the growing cool of the autumn. In the instant we were at pleasure's height, without realizing it sadness came." When Li Yi heard this, he could not help being stirred to sighs. Then he pillowed her head on his arm and said softly, "Today I have gained everything that I hoped for in this life. I swear never to abandon you, or may my body be torn to pieces and my bones ground to powder. My lady, how can you say such a thing? Please bring me a piece of white silk so I can write a vow on it."

Xiao-yu then stopped weeping and ordered her servant Cherry to lift up the bed curtains and hold a candle, after which she gave Li Yi a brush and ink. Whenever she had spare moments from practicing music, Xiao-yu had always liked poetry and calligraphy. The brush and inkstone brought from her chests had previously been from the prince's household. She then got out an embroidered bag from which she took three feet of white silk ruled with fine black lines, a type known as "Yue maiden." This she gave to Li Yi. Li Yi had always been quite talented, and no sooner did he take brush in hand than he had completed it, drawing metaphors of mountains and rivers, pointing to sun and moon as witnesses to his faith. Every line showed the utmost sincerity, and whoever heard it was much moved. When he finished writing, he ordered that it be put in a jeweled box. From then on, they clung to one another like kingfishers in the paths through the clouds. They were together day and night like this for two years.

In the spring of the following year, Li Yi passed the higher examination, "Picking Out the Finest," by his skills at calligraphy and composition; and he was given the post of Recorder of Zheng County. In June he had to go to take up his office, and he was supposed to also go to Luo-yang to pay his respects to his parents. Most of his kinsmen and close friends in Chang-an went to the parting banquet. At the time there were still some remaining traces of spring, and the scenes of summer were first coming into their glory. When the drinking was done and the guests went their separate ways, thoughts of the coming separation were twisting through their thoughts. Xiao-yu said to him, "Because of your reputation due to your talent and your family status, many people admire you. I am sure that quite a few will want to form a marriage connection with you. Moreover, you are in the position when, as they say, 'there are strict parents at home and no legitimate wife in your chamber.' Once you leave, it is inevitable that you are going to an advantageous marriage. The words of the vow that you wrote were nothing more than empty talk. Nevertheless, I do have one small wish that I want to put before you right now. Carry it forever in your heart. Will you hear me out?"

Li Yi was shocked and amazed, "What have I done wrong to have you say something like this? Say what you have to say and I will have to accept it." Xiao-yu then said, "I am eighteen now and you are twenty-two. There are still eight more years until you reach that season of your prime when a man should establish a household. During this period, I want to experience a lifetime of love and pleasure. After that it will still not be too late for you to make a fine choice from a noble family and conclude a marriage alliance. I will then cast the affairs of mortal men behind me, shave off my hair and put on the black habit of a nun, and in doing so a long-standing wish will be fulfilled."

Li Yi was both touched and ashamed, and without realizing it his eyes were streaming with tears. He then said to Xiao-yu, "What I swore by the shining sun will be so until death. Even growing old together with you does not fully satisfy my intentions, so how could I have such a recklessly fickle heart? I beg you not to doubt me. Just live as usual and wait for me. By October I will surely have made it back to Hua-zhou. Then I will find someone to send to bring you to me. Our meeting is not that far away." In a few more days Li Yi said his final goodbyes and went east.

Ten days after he reached his post, he asked for leave to go to Luo-yang to see his parents. Even before he reached home, his mother had already worked out the arrangements to have him marry Miss Lu, and the agreement had been settled. His mother had always been strict and unbending, so that Li Yi wavered in indecision and did not dare refuse. In consequence he had to go to the bride's family to thank them according to custom, after which a close date was set for the wedding. The Lus were, moreover, a family of the highest rank; and when they married off one of their daughters, the value of the wedding gifts offered had to be set at a million cash. If there were anything less than this sum, propriety would demand that they not proceed. Li Yi's family had always been poor, and the wedding required that he go looking for money. Using various pretexts, he went far off to visit friends and relations, spending the period from autumn to summer traveling in the Yangzi and Huai River region. He had, of course, betrayed his vow and had gone long past the date set for his return. By silence and having her hear nothing from him, he wanted to put an end to Xiao-yu's hopes; and he charged his friends and relations in Chang-an not to let word leak out to her.

Ever since Li Yi had missed the appointed time for him to send for her, Xiao-yu had often sought news of him, but the various wild rumors and speculations were never the same from one day to the next. She went to consult soothsayers and tried all the various means by which fortunes could be told. For more than a year she kept her anxiety and her sense of outrage to herself. She lay wasting away in her empty chamber until she became seriously ill.

Despite the fact that Li Yi's letters had stopped altogether, Xiao-yu's hopes and fantasies did not leave her. She sent gifts off to friends and acquaintances in order to get them to pass on any news to her. In her desperation to get some word of him, the savings on which she lived were all used up. She would often give private instructions to the maids to secretly sell some ornament or piece of clothing from her trunks. Usually she would entrust these to Hou Jing-xian's pawnshop in the Western Market to be put on sale. Once she instructed her maidservant Washed Gauze to take a hairpin of purple jade to have it sold at Hou Jing-xian's establishment. On the street, Washed Gauze met an old jade carver from the Imperial Craftshops. When he saw what she was carrying, he came up and identified it. "That hairpin is a piece I myself made. When in years gone by the Prince of Huo's youngest daughter was going to have her hair put up into coils for her coming of age, he had me make this and gave me ten thousand cash in return. I have never forgotten it. Who are you and how did you come by this?" Washed Gauze said, "My young mistress is that very daughter of the Prince of Huo. The household was dispersed and she has fallen on hard times, having given herself to a man. A while ago her husband went off to Luo-yang, and she has heard no news of him. It has been almost two years now, and she has become ill through her misery. She ordered me to sell this so that she could offer gifts to people and try to get some word of him."

The jade carver was moved to tears: "To think that the sons and daughters of the nobility could fall into such misfortune and end up like this! The years left to me will soon be done, and to see such reversals from splendor to decline is a pain not to be borne." He then led Washed Gauze to the mansion of the Princess Yan-xian, where he recounted the whole story in detail. The princess too was deeply moved and gave her one hundred and twenty thousand copper pieces.

At this time the daughter of the Lu family, to whom Li Yi was betrothed, was in Chang-an. Having completed his task of gathering together sums adequate for the marriage gifts, Li Yi returned to Zheng County. In the final month of that year, he once again asked for leave to go into the city. In secret he chose out-of-the-way lodgings and didn't let anyone know where he was. Li Yi had a cousin, one Cui Yun-ming, a graduate of the examination in the Confucian Classics. Cui had an extremely generous nature, and in years gone by he had always accompanied Li Yi to drinking parties at Xiao-yu's house. As they laughed and chatted over food and drink, he had never been treated with the least formal reserve. Whenever he had gotten a letter from Li Yi, he would always report it faithfully to Xiao-yu. And Xiao-yu for her part would always provide firewood, fodder, and clothing to help Cui out, so that Cui was especially grateful to her. When Li Yi arrived in Chang-an, Cui went and told Xiao-yu the entire truth. Xiao-yu sighed in indignation, "How can such things happen in the world?" She then asked all her friends to use any means possible to get him to come to her.

Li Yi was aware that he had not kept the date he set with Xiao-yu and had betrayed his vow. He further knew of Xiao-yu's condition, that her sickness had made her an invalid. In his shame, he hardened his heart against her and absolutely refused to go. He would go out in the morning and come home at night, trying in this way to avoid her. Xiao-yu meanwhile wept day and night and entirely forgot about eating and sleeping. She had hoped to see him at least once more, but finally there seemed to be no way. Her rage at the wrong he had done her deepened, and she lay sprawled helplessly on her bed. There were, of course, those in Chang-an who knew of her. Men of delicate feeling were uniformly moved by the strength of Xiao-yu's passion, while men of the more bold-hearted and impetuous sort were all enraged at Li Yi's casual heartlessness.

The season was May, and everyone was going on spring outings. Li Yi and five or six of his friends had gone to Chong-jing Temple to enjoy the peonies. They were walking along the western gallery, taking turns reciting lines of poetry. Wei Xia-qing, a native of the capital and intimate friend of Li Yi, was walking along with him in that company, and he said to Li Yi, "Today the weather and the scenery are splendid. All the trees and plants are in full flower. But think of poor Xiao-yu in her empty chamber, having to swallow the wrong done to her. The fact that you have been able to abandon her so absolutely shows that you are truly a hard-hearted person. A man's heart shouldn't be like this. You really ought to think about it!"

At the very moment he was criticizing Li Yi with such feeling, there suddenly appeared one of those bold-hearted and impetuous fellows, wearing light robes with a yellow satin shirt, carrying a bow under his arm. He was a handsome, dashing fellow, splendidly attired, with only one shaved-head Turkish servant in attendance on him. He had come up unseen and had listened to the conversation. All of a sudden he came forward and greeted him, saying, "Aren't you Li Yi? My family comes originally from Shan-dong, and we are related by marriage to the kinsmen of the imperial consorts. Although I myself am lacking in the literary graces, I enjoy the company of worthy men. Having so admired your illustrious reputation, I have always longed to encounter you. What a fortunate meeting this is today that gives me the opportunity to cast eyes on your exquisite features! My own poor lodgings are not far from here, and I have there such musical entertainments as can provide pleasure to the heart. There are also eight or nine beguiling wenches and ten or so fine steeds, as you prefer. I would like you to stop by for a visit."

Li Yi's companions all listened to these words, and each in turn was moved by such eloquence. Thereupon they all went riding off in the company of this bold-hearted gentleman. They wound their way swiftly through several quarters of the city until they came at last to the Sheng-ye Quarter. Because they were getting closer to where Xiao-yu was staying, Li Yi lost his inclination to stop by for a visit, and inventing some excuse, he tried to turn his horse back. But the bold-hearted gentleman said, "My place is just a little further. You're not going to back out on me, are you?" And with this he took hold of the reins of Li Yi's horse and led him along. Delaying in this fashion, they came at last to Xiao-yu's lane. Li Yi's spirit was in a daze; he whipped his horse, trying to turn back. But the bold-hearted gentleman abruptly ordered several servants to hold him and make him continue on. Moving swiftly, he pushed Li Yi in through the carriage gate and had it locked fast. He then announced, "Li Yi has arrived." The whole household was so startled with delight that their voices could be heard outside.

The night before, Xiao-yu dreamed that a man in a yellow shirt had brought Li Yi to her; and when he reached the place to sit down, he had Xiao-yu take off her shoes. Xiao-yu woke with a start and told the dream to her mother, who explained, "Shoes come in pairs, like the pair formed when a man and wife are rejoined. To take off is to come apart. Coming apart after being rejoined must mean the final farewell. From this I can tell that you will surely see him again, but after seeing him you will die."

At the break of dawn, Xiao-yu asked her mother to comb her hair and do her make-up. Because Xiao-yu had been sick so long, her mother secretly thought that she was delirious and didn't believe her. Reluctantly she forced herself to comb Xiao-yu's hair and put on her make-up. But no sooner had she finished than Li Yi arrived. Xiao-yu had been bedridden for quite some time and needed another person's help even to turn over. But when she heard that Li Yi had come, she rose in a flash, changed her clothes, and went out, as if some divine force were moving her.

When she saw Li Yi, she held back her anger and gazed at him fixedly, saying nothing. Her wasted flesh and lovely features gave the impression that she could endure it no longer. For a moment she hid her face behind her sleeve, then looked back at Li Yi. Such things touch people painfully, and everyone present was sobbing. In a little while a few dozen dishes of food and jugs of wine were brought in from the outside. Everyone present was startled to see this, and they immediately asked where the food had come from. All of it had been sent by the bold-hearted gentleman in the yellow shirt. When the food and drink were laid out, they went to sit down.

Xiao-yu leaned to the side and turned her face, gazing sidelong on Li Yi for a very long time. Then she raised a cup of wine and poured it out on the ground, saying, "I am a woman; my unhappy fate is like this. You are a man; your faithless heart may be compared to this. Fair of face and in the flower of my youth, I perish swallowing my resentment. I have a loving mother at home, yet I will not be able to care for her. My fine silken clothes and the music of pipes and strings will from this point on be forever ended. I must carry my suffering to the underworld, and all of it was brought on by you. Li Yi, Li Yi! We must now say farewell for good. But after I die, I will become a vengeful ghost and allow you no peace with your wives and concubines for the rest of your days." With that, she grasped Li Yi's arm with her left hand and threw the cup to the ground. With several long and mournful cries, she died. Her mother lifted the corpse and rested it in Li Yi's arms, telling him to call back her soul. But she did not revive.

Li Yi dressed himself in white mourning robes on her account and wept for her day and night with the deepest sorrow. Then, on the evening before she was to be buried, all of a sudden he saw her within the white-curtained spirit enclosure, her appearance as lovely and desirable as she used to be. She was wearing a pomegranate-colored skirt with a purple tunic and a red and green cape. She leaned against the curtain, took her embroidered sash in hand, and looking around at Li Yi, said, "I am embarrassed to see that there is still such feeling in you that you have come like this to see me on my way. Even in the dark realms below, I could not help being moved to sigh." Once she finished speaking, she was no longer to be seen. On the next day she was buried in the Yu-su Plain near Chang-an. Li Yi came to her graveside and mourned until he could mourn no more, then turned back.

Somewhat more than a month later, he carried out the wedding ceremonies with Miss Lu. Feelings of sadness and sympathy filled his heart, and he had no joy in it. In July that summer he went back to Zheng County together with his wife Lu. Ten days after he arrived, he was sleeping together with Lu when all of a sudden he heard the sound of someone calling outside the curtains. Li Yi woke with a start and looked: there was a man who seemed somewhat over twenty, with a graceful and handsome appearance, hiding behind the curtains and repeatedly calling to Lu. Li Yi rose frantically and went around the curtains several times, but all of a sudden the man was nowhere to be seen. From that point on, he began to harbor evil suspicions in his heart and was jealous of everything. There were none of the easy pleasures of life between husband and wife. He had a close friend who reassured him, going over the affair in detail, and his mind gradually eased. But then again ten days later he was coming in from the outside as Lu was playing the harp on the couch. Suddenly he saw, tossed in from the gate, a box of variously colored ivory and gold filigree, a bit larger than an inch in diameter. This fell in Lu's lap. Around it was a piece of light silk tied in a love-knot. When Li Yi opened it and looked inside, there were two love beans, a scarab, a passion pill, and some aphrodisiac made from a foaling donkey. At that point Li Yi bellowed in rage, his voice like a tiger. He took the harp and beat his wife with it, questioning her to make her tell him the truth. But Lu could not explain any of it. After that he would often whip her violently and practiced every manner of cruelty on her, until at last he accused her publicly in open court and sent her away.

Once he had divorced Lu, Li Yi would sometimes share a bed with women of the lower classes, serving girls and concubines; but always he would grow jealous and suspicious. Sometimes he would find some reason and kill them. Li Yi once visited Guang-ling and there obtained a well-known young woman known as Miss Ying. Her appearance was sleek and seductive, and Li Yi was very pleased with her. Whenever they sat together, he would tell her, "In such-and-such a place I got such-and-such a girl, who committed such-and-such an offense, and I killed her in such-and-such a way." He would tell such stories daily, hoping in this way to make her frightened of him and keep his women's quarters free of sexual misconduct. When he went out, he would take a washing tub and put it over Ying on the bed; then he would set seals all around it. When he got back, he would check the seals all around, and only when he was satisfied would he break the seals and let her out. He also kept a very sharp sword and would say to his serving girls, "This is Ge Creek steel from Xin-zhou, to be used especially for cutting off the heads of those who commit transgressions." Whatever woman Li Yi met, he would instantly become jealous. He married three times, and each of the others went like it did the first time.

It is very hard to read "Ying-ying's Story," below, without taking sides, or without at least deciding which side the story really takes. Some, accepting that this is an autobiographical work by Yuan Zhen, argue that, in the context of the public Confucian values of the period, Zhang's behavior is justified. However, such an interpretation ignores the values of the Tang love story, which were as powerful or more powerful than the Confucian pieties by which Zhang excuses his actions at the end of "Ying-ying's Story." "Huo Xiao-yu's Story" bears witness to such values. The most chilling possibility is that "Ying-ying's Story" is indeed an autobiographical work, an attempt by the author to exculpate himself, and that some peculiar blindness on the part of the author, having convinced himself by his own rationalizations, prevents him from seeing the shabbiness of his actions.

In the end, nothing survives unsullied in this story: neither Zhang nor Ying-ying, neither Tang images of love nor Confucian virtues. Poetry seems false; formal prose is ludicrous; and the articulation of social virtues seems something too conveniently deployed for private motives. Some modern Chinese critics, looking for a pleasant love story, are appalled by the tale. But even though its numerous retellings smoothed over everything that makes the story uncomfortable, it remains one of the most compelling and influential narratives in the Chinese tradition.

Ying-ying's letter, quoted in full (though the author purports to give only the gist of it), is a remarkable piece of prose, with the most complicated twists and turns of the heart working at cross purposes with the Tang delight in formal eloquence. Ying-ying the stylist sits uncomfortably beside Ying-ying the woman driven to distraction. In the same way, the Ying-ying who wants to show the self-effacing concern of a model wife is in conflict with another Ying-ying who is both desperate and enraged. If this is not a real document, it is a recreation with a psychological verisimilitude unparalleled in the period. We should note that Zhang's letter to Ying-ying was not included. From Ying-ying's reply, it is clear that this letter again declared his love for her, which makes his behavior on receiving her letter all the more questionable.

Yuan Zhen (779–831), "Ying-ying's Story"

In the Zhen-yuan Reign (785–804) there was a certain man named Zhang, of a gentle nature and handsome appearance. He held steadfastly to his personal principles and refused to become involved in anything improper.

Sometimes a group of friends would go off to a party and behave riotously. While the others tried to outdo one another in wanton and unbridled recklessness, Zhang would remain utterly composed, and they could never get him to act in an intemperate manner. At this time he was twenty-three and had never been intimate with a woman. When a close friend questioned him about this, Zhang excused himself, saying, "The famous lecher of antiquity, Deng Tu-zi, was not a man of passionate desire; his were the actions of a brute. I am someone who is truly capable of passionate desire, but simply have not encountered it. How can I say this? Things of the most bewitching beauty never fail to leave a lasting impression on my heart, and this tells me that I am not one of those free of passion." And the one who had questioned him acknowledged this in him.

Not long afterward, Zhang visited Pu-zhou. About a dozen leagues east of the city there was a residence for monks known as the Temple of Universal Salvation, where Zhang took up lodgings. It happened that a widow, one Madam Cui, was on her way to Chang-an; and since her journey took her through Pu-zhou, she too stopped over at this temple. Madam Cui had been born a Zheng, and Zhang's mother had also been a Zheng. When they traced the family connection, it turned out that she was his maternal aunt at several removes.

That year Hun Zhen, the Military Governor, passed away in Pu-zhou, and Ding Wen-ya, the court officer left in charge, was not liked by the troops. After the funeral, they rioted and pillaged widely in Pu-zhou. Madam Cui had a great wealth of household goods as well as many servants. The hostel was frantic with alarm, and they did not know where to turn for help. Zhang had earlier developed friendly relations with the circle around the commandant of Pu-zhou, and he asked for guards to protect Madam Cui. As a result, no harm came to her. About a dozen days later, the Investigator Du Que arrived with an imperial commission to take charge of the troops, and he issued commands to the army, after which the disturbance ceased.

Madam Cui was exceedingly grateful for Zhang's kindness, so she had a feast prepared in his honor. As they dined in the central hall, she said to Zhang, "Your widowed aunt lives on, carrying her young children with her. I have had the misfortune of a close call with a major outbreak of violence among the troops, and I truly could not have protected these children's lives. Thus it is as if my young son and daughter owe their lives to you. What you have done for us cannot be compared to an ordinary kindness. I would now insist that they greet you with all the courtesies due to an elder brother, in the hope that this might be a way to repay your kindness." Then she gave this order to her son. His name was Huan-lang, a gentle and handsome boy somewhat over ten years old. Next she gave the order to her daughter: "Come out and pay your respects to your elder brother; you are alive because of him." A long time passed, and then the girl declined on the excuse that she wasn't feeling well. Madam Cui said angrily, "Mr. Zhang protected your life. Otherwise you would have been taken captive. How can you still keep such a wary distance from him!" After another long wait, the daughter came in. She wore everyday clothes and had a disheveled appearance, without having dressed up specially for the occasion. Tresses from the coils of her hair hung down to her eyebrows and her two cheeks were suffused with rosy color. Her complexion was rare and alluring, with a glow that stirred a man. Zhang was startled as she paid him the proper courtesies. Then she sat down beside her mother. Since her mother had forced her to meet Zhang, she stared fixedly away in intense resentment, as if she couldn't bear it. When he asked her age, Madam Cui said, "From September 784, the first year of the emperor's reign, until the present year, 800, makes her seventeen years old." Zhang tried to draw her into conversation, but she wouldn't answer him.

Finally the party ended. Zhang was, of course, infatuated with her, and he wanted to express his feelings but had no way. The Cuis had a maidservant named Hong-niang. Zhang greeted her courteously a number of times and then seized an opportunity to tell her what he felt. The maid was scandalized and fled in embarrassment, at which Zhang regretted what he had said. When the maid came the next day, Zhang was abashed and apologized, saying nothing more about what he wanted. But then the maid said to Zhang, "What you said is something you should not have dared to say and something you should not dare allow to get out. However, you know the kinship ties of the Cuis in some detail. Given the gratitude Madam Cui feels toward you, why don't you ask for her hand in marriage?"

Zhang replied, "Ever since I was a child I have by nature avoided unseemly associations. When I have been around women, I would never even give them suggestive glances. I never would have thought that a time would come when I found myself so overwhelmed by desire. The other day at the party, I could scarcely control myself. For the past few days I walk without knowing where I am going and eat without thinking of whether I am full or not. I'm afraid I won't last another day. If I had to employ a matchmaker to ask for her hand marriage, with the sending of betrothal tokens and formal inquiries about names, it would be another three months, and I would be a fish so long out of the water that you would have to look for me in a dried fish store. What do you think I should do?" The maid replied, "Miss Cui is virtuous and guards herself scrupulously. Even someone she held in the highest regard could not lead her into misconduct by improper words; plans laid by lesser folk will be even harder to carry through. She does, however, like to compose poems and is always mulling over passages, spending a long time on pieces of wronged love and admiration. You should try to seduce her by composing poems that express your love indirectly. Otherwise there will be no way."

Zhang was overjoyed and immediately composed two "Spring Verses" to give to her. That evening Hong-niang came again and handed over a piece of colored notepaper to Zhang, saying, "Miss Cui has instructed me to give

you this." The piece was entitled "The Bright Moon of the Fifteenth." It
went:

> I await the moon on the western porch,
> my door half ajar, facing the breeze.
> Flower shadows stir, brushing the wall—
> I wonder if this is my lover coming.

Zhang understood the subtle message implied. That night was April 14.
There was an apricot tree on the eastern side of her apartments, and by
climbing it, he could get into her quarters. On the following evening, the fifteenth, when the moon was full, Zhang climbed the tree and got into her
quarters. When he reached the western porch, the door was indeed half ajar.
Hong-niang was lying there asleep in her bed, and Zhang roused her. Hong-
niang was startled: "How did you get in here?" Zhang lied to her, "Ying-
ying's note summoned me. Now go tell her that I'm here." Soon afterward
Hong-niang returned, saying over and over again, "She's here! She's here!"
Zhang was overjoyed and surprised, certain that he would succeed in this
enterprise. But when Ying-ying did arrive, she was in proper attire with a
stern expression on her face. She proceeded to take Zhang to task item by
item: "By your kindness you saved our family, and that was indeed generous. For this reason my sweet mother entrusted you with the care of her
young son and daughter. But how could you use this wicked maid to deliver
such wanton verses to me? I first understood your saving us from molestation as virtue, but now you have taken advantage of that to make your own
demands. How much difference is there between one form of molestation
and the other? I had truly wanted to simply ignore your verses, but it would
not have been right to condone such lecherousness in a person. I would have
revealed them to my mother, but it would have been unlucky to so turn one's
back on a person's kindness. I was going to have my maid give you a message, but I was afraid she would not correctly convey how I truly feel. Then
I planned to use a short letter to set this out before you, but I was afraid you
would take it ill. So I used those frivolous and coy verses to make you come
here. Can you avoid feeling shame at such improper actions? I want most
of all that you conduct yourself properly and not sink to the point where
you molest people!" When she finished her speech, she whirled about and
went off. Zhang stood there in a daze for a long time. Then he went back
out the way he had come in, by that point having lost all hope.

A few nights later, Zhang was sleeping alone by the balcony when all of
a sudden someone woke him up. He rose in a flash, startled, and found that
it was Hong-niang, who had come carrying bedding and a pillow. She patted Zhang, saying, "She's here! She's here! What are you doing sleeping!"
Then she put the pillow and bedding beside his and left. Zhang rubbed his
eyes and sat up straight for a long time, wondering whether he might not
still be dreaming. Nevertheless, he assumed a respectful manner and waited
for her. In a little while Hong-niang reappeared, helping Ying-ying along.

When she came in, she was charming in her shyness and melting with desire, not strong enough even to move her limbs. There was no more of the prim severity she had shown previously. The evening was the eighteenth of the month, and the crystalline rays of the moon slanting past his chamber cast a pale glow over half the bed. Zhang's head was spinning, and he wondered if she might not be one of those goddesses or fairy princesses, for he could not believe that she came from this mortal world. After a while the temple bell rang and day was about to break. Hong-niang urged her to leave, but Ying-ying wept sweetly and clung to him until Hong-niang again helped her away. She had not said a word the entire night.

Zhang got up as the daylight first brought colors to the scene, and he wondered to himself, "Could that have been a dream?" In the light there was nothing left but the sight of some make-up on his arm, her scent on his clothes, and the sparkles of her teardrops still glistening on the bedding. A dozen or so days later it seemed so remote that he was no longer sure. Zhang was composing a poem called "Meeting the Holy One" in sixty lines. He had not quite finished when Hong-niang happened to come by. He then handed it to her to present to Ying-ying.

From that point on, she allowed him to come to her. He would go out secretly at dawn and enter secretly in the evening. For almost a month they shared happiness in what had earlier been referred to as the "western porch." Zhang constantly asked about how Madame Zheng felt, and she would say, "I can't do anything about it." And she wanted him to proceed to regularize the relationship. Not long afterward Zhang was to go off to Chang-an, and before he went he consoled her by telling her of his love. Ying-ying seemed to raise no complaints, but the sad expression of reproach on her face was very moving. Two evenings before he was to travel, she refused to see him again.

Zhang subsequently went west to Chang-an. After several months he again visited Pu-zhou, and this time his meetings with Ying-ying lasted a series of months. Ying-ying was quite skilled at letterwriting and a fine stylist. He repeatedly asked to see things she had written, but she would never show him anything. Even when Zhang repeatedly tried to prompt her by giving her things he himself had written, he still hardly ever got to look over anything of hers. In general, whenever Ying-ying did show something to someone else, it was always the height of grace and polish; but she appeared unaware of it. Her speech was intelligent and well reasoned, yet she seldom wrote answering pieces in response to what he sent her. Although she treated Zhang with the greatest kindness, she still never picked up his verses in a poetic exchange. There were times when her melancholy voluptuousness took on a remoteness and abstraction, yet she continually seemed not to recognize this. At such times, expressions of either joy or misery seldom showed on her face. On another occasion she was alone at night playing the harp, a melancholy and despairing melody. Zhang listened to her surreptitiously, for had he asked her to play, she would not have played any more. With this Zhang became even more infatuated with her.

Soon afterward Zhang had to again go west to Chang-an, to be there in time for the literary examination. This time, on the evening before he was to leave, he said nothing of his feelings, but instead sighed sadly by Ying-ying's side. Ying-ying had already guessed that this was to be farewell. With a dignified expression and a calm voice, she said gently to Zhang, "It is quite proper that when a man seduces a woman, he finally abandons her. I don't dare protest. It was inevitable that having seduced me, you would end it—all this is by your grace. And with this, our lifelong vows are indeed ended. Why be deeply troubled by this journey? Nevertheless, you have become unhappy, and there is no way I can ease your heart. You have always claimed that I am good at playing the harp, but I have always been so shy that I couldn't bring myself to play for you. Now that you are going to leave, I will fulfill this heartfelt wish of yours." Thereupon she brushed her fingers over the harp, playing the prelude to "Coats of Feathers, Rainbow Skirts." But after only a few notes, the sad notes became so unsettled by bitter pain that the melody could no longer be recognized. All present were sobbing, and Ying-ying abruptly stopped and threw down the harp, tears streaming down her face. She hurried back to her mother's house and did not come back.

The next morning at dawn, Zhang set out. The following year, not having been successful in the literary competition, Zhang stayed in the capital. He then sent a letter to Ying-ying to set her mind to rest. The lines Ying-ying sent in reply are roughly recorded here:

I received what you sent, asking after me. The comforting love you show is all too deep. In the feelings between man and woman, joys and sorrows mingle. You were also kind to send the box of flower cutouts and the five-inch stick of liprouge—ornaments that will make my hair resplendent and my lips shine. But though I receive such exceptional fondness from you, for whom will I now make myself beautiful? Catching sight of these things increases my cares, and nothing but sad sighs well within me. From your letter I am given to understand that you are occupied by the pursuit of your studies in the capital. The path to progress in studies does indeed depend on not being disturbed. Yet I feel some resentment that I, a person of so small account, have been left behind forever in a far place. Such is fate. What more is there to say?

Since last autumn I have been in a daze as though I did not know where I was. In the chatter of merry gatherings I sometimes make myself laugh and join in the conversation, but when I am alone in the still of night, tears never fail to fall. And when I come to dream, my thoughts usually are of the misery of separation, which stirs me until I am choked with sobbing. When we are twined together, absorbed in our passion, for a brief while it is as it once used to be; but then, before our secret encounter comes to its culmination, the soul is startled awake and finds itself sundered from you. Although half of the covers seem warm, yet my thoughts are on someone far, far away.

Just yesterday you said goodbye, and now in but an instant the old year has been left behind. Chang-an is a place of many amusements, which can catch a man's fancy and draw his feelings. How fortunate I am that you have not forgotten me, negligible and secluded as I am, and that you were not too weary of me to let me occupy your thoughts for at least a moment. My humble intentions have no means to repay this. But when it comes to my vow to love you forever, that is steadfast and unwavering.

Long ago, connected to you as a cousin, I happened to be together with you at a banquet. Having inveigled my maidservant, you consequently expressed your private feelings. Young people are unable to maintain a firmness of heart. You, sir, stirred me as Si-ma Xiang-ru stirred Zhuo Wen-jun, by playing the harp. Yet I did not resist, as did Xie Kun's neighbor by throwing her shuttle when he approached her. When I brought my bedding to your side, your love and honor were deep. In the folly of my passion I thought that I would remain in your care forever. How could I have foreseen that, "once having seen my lord," it would be impossible to plight our troth? Since I suffer the shame of having offered myself to you, I may no longer serve you openly as a wife. This will be a source of bitter regret that will last until my dying day. I repress my sighs, for what more can be said? If by chance in the goodness of your heart you would condescend to fulfill my secret hope, then even if it were on the day of my death, it would be for me like being reborn. But, perchance, the successful scholar holds love to be but of little account and sets it aside as a lesser thing in order to pursue things of greater importance, considering his previous mating to have been a vile action, his having taken enforced vows as something one may well betray. If this be so, then my form will melt away and my bones will dissolve, yet my glowing faith with not perish. My petals, borne by the wind and trailing in the dew, will still entrust themselves to the pure dust beneath your feet. Of my sincerity unto death, what words can say is all said here. I sob over this paper and cannot fully express my love. Please, please take care of yourself.

This jade ring is a thing that I had about me since I was an infant. I send it to you to wear among the ornaments that hang at your waist. From the jade is to be drawn the lesson of what is firm and lustrous, thus unsullied. From the ring is to be drawn the lesson of what continues on forever, never breaking. Also I send a single strand of tangled silken floss and a tea grinder of speckled bamboo. These several things are not valuable in themselves. My message is that I would have you, sir, be as pure as the jade, that my own poor aspirations are as unbroken as the ring, that my tearstains are on the bamboo, and that my melancholy sentiments are like this twisting and tangled thread. Through these things I convey what I feel, and will love you always. The heart is close, though our bodies are far. There is no time set for us to meet. Yet when secret ardor accumulates, spirits can join even across a thousand leagues. Please take care of yourself. The spring breeze is often sharp, and it would be a good idea to force yourself to eat more. Be careful of what you say and guard yourself. And do not long for me too intensely.

Zhang showed her letter to his friends, and as a result many people at the time heard of the affair. One good friend, Yang Ju-yuan, was fond of composing verses and wrote a quatrain entitled "Miss Cui":

Pure luster of this young Pan Yue—
    even the jade cannot compare;
sweet clover grows in courtyard
    as snows first melt away.
The amorous young talent
    is filled with spring desires—
poor Miss Xiao, her broken heart
    in a letter of just one page.

I, Yuan Zhen of He-nan, completed Zhang's "Meeting the Holy One"
in sixty lines.

Pale moonlight breaks in above curtains,
fireflies flash through the sapphire air.
The distant skies begin to grow dim,
and below, trees have grown leafy and full.
Past the yard's bamboo come notes of dragon flutes,
the well-side beech is brushed by phoenix song.

Her filmy gauze hangs like a thin haze,
soft breezes resound with her waist-hung rings.
Crimson standards follow the Goddess of the West,
the heart of clouds proffers the Lad of Jade.
As night's hours deepen, people grow still,
or meeting at dawn in the drizzling rain.
Pearl-glow lights up her patterned shoes,
blooms' brilliance hidden by embroidered dragon.
Jade hairpin, its colored phoenix in motion,
gauze cape that covers red rainbows.
He says that from this Jasper Flower Beach
he must go to dawn court at Green Jade Palace.

By his roaming north of the city of Luo
he chanced on Song Yu's eastern neighbor.
When he flirted, at first she gently refused,
but in secret soft passions already conveyed.
From her lowered coils the tresses' shadows stirred,
her circling steps obscured in jade white dust.
Face turned, glances flowed like flowers and snow,
she mounted the bed, bunched satins born in arms.
Mated ducks, their necks twined in dance,
kingfishers encaged in passion's embrace.
Her black brows knit in modesty,
her carmine lips, warming, grew softer.
Breath pure as the fragrance of orchids,
her skin glossy, her marble flesh full.

Worn out, too tired to move her wrist,
so charming, she loved to curl up.
Her sweat flowed in beads, drop by drop,
her tangled tresses thick and black.

No sooner made glad by this millennial meeting,
she suddenly heard night's hours end.
At that moment resentful, she lingered on,
clinging with passion, desire unspent.
A sad expression on languid cheeks,
in sweet lines she vowed the depths of love.
Her ring-gift revealed a union fated,
a love-knot left showed hearts were the same.
Cheeks' powder in tears flowed on night's mirror,
lamp's last flickering, insects far in the dark.
As the sparkling rays still dwindled away,
the sun at dawn grew gradually bright.

She rode her cygnet back to the Luo;
he played his pipes as he climbed Mount Song.
Her musk still imbued the scent of his clothes,
his pillow oily, still flecked with her rouge.

Thick grow the grasses beside the pool,
wind-tossed, the tumbleweed longs for the isle.
Her pale harp rings with the crane's lament,
she looks toward the stars for the swan's return.

The sea is so vast, truly hard to cross;
and the sky is high, not easy to reach.
Goddess moving in cloud, nowhere now to be found;
and Xiao-shi is there in his high chamber.

Every one of Zhang's friends who heard of the affair was stirred to amazement. Nevertheless, Zhang had already made up his mind. I was on particularly good terms with Zhang and asked him to explain. Zhang then said, "All such creatures ordained by Heaven to possess bewitching beauty will inevitably cast a curse on others if they don't do the same to themselves. Had Cui Ying-ying made a match with someone of wealth and power, she would have taken advantage of those charms that win favor from a man; and if she were not the clouds and the rain of sexual pleasure, then she would have been a serpent or a fierce dragon—I do not know what she would have transformed into. Long ago King Shou-xin of Yin and King You of Zhou controlled domains that mustered a million chariots, and their power was very great. Nevertheless, in both cases a woman destroyed them. Their hosts were scattered, they themselves were slain, and even today their ignominy has made them laughingstocks for all the world. My own virtue is inadequate to triumph over such cursed wickedness, and for this reason I hardened my heart against her." At the time all those present were deeply moved.

Somewhat more than a year later, Ying-ying married another, and Zhang too took a wife. He happened to pass through the place where she was living and asked her husband to speak to her, wanting to see her as a maternal cousin. Her husband did speak to her, but Ying-ying refused to come out. The fact of Zhang's pain at such a rebuff showed on his face. Ying-ying found out about this and secretly composed a piece whose verses went:

> Ever since I have wasted to gauntness
> > and the glow of my face has gone,
> I toss and turn thousands of times,
> > too weary to get out of bed.
> Not because of him at my side
> > that I am ashamed to rise—
> grown haggard on your account, I'd be
> > ashamed in front of you.

And she never did see him. A few days later, Zhang was ready to go and she composed another poem to say a final farewell.

> Rejected, what more can be said?—
> yet you were my love back then.
> Take what you felt in times gone by
> and love well the person before your eyes.

From that point on, he knew nothing further of her.

People at the time generally accepted that Zhang was someone who knew how to amend his errors. At parties, I have often brought up this notion. One would have those who know not do such things, but those that have done such things should not become carried away by them.

In a November in the Zhen-yuan Reign, my good friend Li Shen was staying over with me in the Jing-an Quarter. Our conversations touched on this affair, and Li Shen made particular comment on how remarkable it was. He consequently composed "Ying-ying's Song" to make it more widely known. Cui's childhood name was Ying-ying, and he used this in the title.

The Song Dynasty

趙宋

THE SONG DYNASTY: PERIOD INTRODUCTION   In 960, just over half a century after the last puppet Tang emperor was deposed, Zhao Kuang-yin overthrew the "Later Zhou," the large regional regime that dominated North China, and declared the establishment of his own Song Dynasty. Unlike its predecessor state, the Song proved equal to its imperial pretensions, and over the next two decades it conquered the five or so remaining regional states and reunified the country. A new capital was chosen at the economically strategic city of Kai-feng (Bianjing), located at the head of the Grand Canal, on which tax grain was shipped from the rich farmlands of the lower Yangzi River region.

In premodern Chinese political theory, the imperial government was based on two complementary principles: *wu,* the military aspect of government, and *wen,* a term that encompassed civil government, cultural values, and "literature." Having built his dynasty out of the constant and immensely destructive warfare of the first half of the tenth century, the first Song emperor made a conscious decision that his would be a dynasty guided by the principle of *wen.* In addition to his own experience, the lesson of history seemed to clearly demonstrate the consequences of militarization for the Tang, whose central government never fully recovered from the widespread formation of regional military commands after the An Lu-shan Rebellion. The Song thus never sought the conquests in Central Asia, Korea, or Vietnam that the Han, Sui, and Tang had. After only a hundred and fifty years of peace, however, the Song's remarkable military ineptitude would lead to the loss of North China.

The first Song emperor was a strong supporter of scholarly projects. He commissioned large compilations of Tang institutions, classical literature, and tales; these works survive and preserve much Tang material that would have been otherwise lost. The government also sponsored a new manuscript edition of the Daoist Canon (the collected scriptures of Daoism) and, more important, printed versions of the Confucian Classics. Printing had existed in the Tang, but its use was strictly limited; early in the Song, however, the imperial printing shops provided uniform (if not always carefully edited) editions to be used throughout the empire. Also in the late tenth century, a version of the Buddhist Canon (the collected Buddhist scriptures) was printed. Commercial printing flourished in the Northern Song and even more in the Southern Song. People continued to use manuscripts alongside printed books throughout the Northern Song and afterward, but as in Europe four and a half centuries later, the advent of printing brought about a profound change in the availability of earlier works and the dissemination of new ones. Not only were books more available, their form changed from the Tang scroll and folding book to the Chinese bound book of light paper. Not only could a literate person afford to own more books, they presented less of a problem of storage and were easier to consult.

The social basis of power had changed so dramatically from the Tang that an entirely new style of officeholder was recruited by the Song civil service examination. The Tang had been, at its very core, an aristocratic society. Although the examination system did bring in outsiders, appointment to positions still depended heavily on family and patronage. The grand old families of the first half of the Tang gave way to military clans and other newly powerful families, but the role of patronage did not change. The continual violence during the last decades of the Tang and throughout the Five Dynasties effectively eliminated all such powerbrokers, and the examination system of the Song was far more perfectly meritocratic than its Tang antecedents. Patronage and a strong bond between an examiner and the candidates he graduated continued, but the primary loyalty of the new bureaucracy was to the state and its institutions.

In the fundamental reconstitution of the Chinese cultural and political order that occurred early in the Northern Song, a new kind of writer and intellectual emerged. This new intellectual was generally more learned, possessed broader interests, and cultivated a sensibility very different from his Tang predecessors. One of the best examples is Ou-yang Xiu (1007–1072). Before the Song, the most famous writers had almost always been on the margins of real political power, and only in the Mid-Tang had they been important in a major intellectual movement. Ou-yang Xiu stood at the center of his age. He was an important political figure and an excellent judge of talent in younger men, promoting some of the most important political and literary figures of the dynasty. One of the most symbolically important projects undertaken by any new dynasty was to write the "official history" of the preceding dynasty; Ou-yang Xiu was given charge of the rewriting of the existing history of the Tang. While some modern critics have faulted his historiographical principles, Ou-yang Xiu gave serious thought to how history should be written, in contrast to many of his Tang predecessors who simply recompiled earlier materials. He was an antiquarian scholar whose collection of inscriptions, with attached colophons, was a foundational text in Chinese epigraphy, and he was a literary writer whose poetry and prose helped establish the lucid, balanced, and genial manner that has become the hallmark of the Northern Song style.

Ou-yang Xiu also pioneered a new style of informal writing: random notes of thoughts, experiences, and current affairs whose casual grace gave the impression of the "gentleman at home." Among his informal writings was a small booklet entitled *Remarks on Poetry (Shi-hua),* consisting of reminiscences and judgments on earlier and contemporary poetry. This work set the model for and gave its name to an important genre of literary criticism in which fragmentary observations carried more authority than the elaborate arguments of formal literary theory. Informality of a very different kind can be seen in Ou-yang Xiu's lyrics for popular songs composed for parties. These celebrate the pleasures of flirtation, the agonies of longing, and the charms of typical beauties; indeed, some of Ou-yang Xiu's lyrics are much more erotic than those of his contemporaries. In all these areas, Ou-yang Xiu contributed to the formation of a new literature of private life.

In yet another area, Ou-yang Xiu proved to be a figure of great significance. The imperially sponsored printed edition of the Confucian Classics had been printed with the commentaries mostly authorized during the early seventh century. These commentaries represented a cumulative tradition of scholastic interpretation stretching from the Han to the seventh century. Relatively little significant scholarship on the classics had been done in the Tang itself. Song intellectuals began to reexamine the texts and measure them against the received commentaries. No longer content simply to accept the authority of the written tradition of interpretation, they began to question both the interpretation of specific parts of the Confucian Classics and their deeper meaning. Ou-yang Xiu's commentary on the *Classic of Poetry* was a seminal work in this process, rejecting many of the scholastic interpretations of the *Poems* for more natural readings. This movement became "Neo-Confucianism," or, in the Chinese phrase *Dao-xue,* "the study of the [Confucian] Way."

The Confucianism of the Tang elite in many ways resembled pre-Reformation Catholicism: the truth of its principles was accepted without question, certain practices were scrupulously observed, and it was intertwined with social and political authority. But Confucianism was not a creed that one generally "took to heart" in every aspect of one's life, measuring one's own attitudes and behavior against the values embodied in the Confucian Classics. In the early ninth century, Han Yu had called for a more personal commitment to Confucian values, and the depth of Han Yu's convictions, conjoined with the fierce eloquence of his prose, made him a cultural hero to many Northern Song intellectuals. Tang Confucians were committed to the texts of the classics; Song Neo-Confucians were concerned with the values in the texts, which developed into an elaborated philosophy and personal religion. The old scholastic interpretations of the classics had addressed disagreements, but they represented a consensus, a single authoritative interpretation; Song Neo-Confucianism soon produced multiple and divergent interpretations. It is, perhaps, no accident that both Neo-Confucianism and the European Reformation accompanied the wide dissemination of texts in a new culture of the printed book.

The Song soon had a lesson in the hazards of taking even the most admirable values too seriously in the complex realities of the political world. Between 1069 and the early 1070s, the Confucian reformer Wang An-shi persuaded the new emperor Shen-zong to enact sweeping cultural and political reforms. Wang's proposed reforms were directed toward solving the empire's increasing fiscal crises and improving the morals of the populace, but they were justified through Wang's own independent interpretations of the Confucian Classics (Wang himself wrote several commentaries). Wang An-shi's policies were enacted as the "New Laws." The success of the New Laws has been much debated: they clearly achieved some of their fiscal objectives, but at the price of suffering and some popular unrest. On a more profound level, they represented the attempt of the central government to exercise direct social and economic control over the provinces to an unprecedented degree. They constituted a new kind of government power, fortified by a grim sense of moral conviction, and they marked the end of the relatively tolerant gentility and free political discussion that had characterized the Song government earlier. Convinced that all the failures of the New Laws were due to the interference of the opposition, Wang An-shi and his followers forced into retirement or exiled everyone who disagreed with them. Among Wang's opponents was the most famous writer of the day, Su Shi (1037–1101), whose poems were scrutinized for insults to the government; real and imagined slights were discovered, and Su was thrown into prison and put on trial, a trial from which he barely escaped with his life. Such experiences contributed to the growing separation between political life and a new set of private values, known as "literati" culture, which separated itself from engagement in public affairs.

The problems that the policies of Wang An-shi and his party sought to address involved foreign relations as well as the budget. Having resisted the dangerous and expensive course of expansion on its Northern frontiers, the Song found itself facing small but militarily powerful states that grew up between the steppe and China: these were Xi-Xia in the Northwest and the Liao in the Northeast. In 1125, the Liao was overthrown by a Jurchen people, who named their new dynasty the Jin. The following year, Jin armies moved easily through Song defenses and took Kai-feng. Then, in 1127, the emperor Hui-zong and his son were carried north to the Jin capital, and the conquest of the North was completed. That same year a Song prince declared himself emperor south of the Yangzi River, whose cities were filling with a stream of refugees from the North. The Yangzi, with its large warfleets, proved an impassable barrier to the Jin armies, and the period known as the Southern Song began, with its capital in the great commercial center of Hang-zhou.

Tang Chang-an had been a great city, but it was a city constructed for the maintenance of imperial control. Each of its wards had walls and gates that were closed in curfew every night; trade was limited to the capital markets. In contrast, the two Song capitals, first Kai-feng and then Hang-zhou, were open inside the city wall and had a lively night life. These cities represented a true early modern urban culture. With their markets, entertainment districts, artisan quarters, booksellers, and parks, the Song capitals were enjoyed as cities in ways that Chang-an never was. The Song did not discourage trade, and both capitals thronged with merchants. Kai-feng was said to have supported fifty theaters, the largest of which could admit a thousand viewers. Writers took a special delight in the lore of the city—its scenic spots, good restaurants, skilled entertainers, and festivals. Copies of a long handscroll painting of a spring festival in Kai-feng survive, depicting the bustle of the city in loving detail.

Painting reached new heights of development in the Song, and numerous paintings from the dynasty still exist. The motifs are various: monumental landscapes and pastoral scenes, ink paintings of bamboo the quality of whose brushwork recalls calligraphy, paintings of birds and flowers done in meticulous detail, swift cartoonlike sketches associated with the "sudden enlightenment" of Chan (Zen) Buddhism. Paintings might be done on commission or, in the Southern Song, for sale, but painting also became a part of "literati" culture, a leisurely pastime for amateurs, done for amusement or to be given to friends. Literati painting represented a reaction against the growing skill in representation and the professionalism it demanded; an expressive clumsiness or naïveté in ink paintings done on the spur of the moment was prized. Painting became one among a range of artistic activities including the composition of poetry, calligraphy, and musical performance.

Any image of Chinese literature as static is fundamentally wrong; nevertheless, the nature of change in Chinese literature was profoundly different from the modern Western notion of change in which new fashions and interests supersede their predecessors. Cultural change in premodern China was essentially accretive, with new styles and forms added to older ones that themselves changed but were rarely abandoned. Thus the Song inherited the forms of classical poetry *(shi)* established in the Tang; no new forms were added, but Song poets handled those forms and many traditional topics in a way that was quite distinctive and recognized by all subsequent readers of poetry as being characteristically "Song." Though begun in the

Tang, the song lyric *(ci)* was the poetic genre that later readers associated with the Song. In this case, Song writers did expand the genre formally and thematically and put their own stamp on it. "Old style prose"—prose that did not use strict parallelism and rhyme—had been advocated by the Tang writer Han Yu. This was taken up in the Song and used as the medium for lucid and complex argumentation. And new kinds of informal prose were explored, seeking to convey something of the naturalness and ease of speech in classical Chinese.

No written language ever exactly reproduces a spoken language, but when the written and spoken languages have diverged to such a degree that it is no longer possible to ignore the difference, we often find the attempt to create a new written language to approximate speech. As a non-alphabetic script, some aspects of written Chinese could effectively conceal historical and dialectical phonological variation. A Chinese character in the *Classic of Poetry* would have been pronounced very differently in 600 B.C. than it is in the present; yet the modern reader pronounces that character without needing to take into account the vast phonological changes. Linguistic change, however, goes far beyond the pronunciation of individual words: there were new compounds, new usages of old words, new grammatical particles, and new syntactic patterns. To write the spoken Chinese of the Song, even imperfectly, required the invention of new characters or using old ones in new ways to represent the sounds of the spoken language. Chan Buddhism had always stressed the immediacy of the spoken word over the "dead letter" of Buddhist scripture; and, perhaps ironically, when the sayings of the Chan masters were transformed to written texts, there was an attempt to reproduce in writing the immediacy of their vernacular speech. The Neo-Confucians learned many lessons from Buddhism, and when the sayings of the greatest master of Southern Song Neo-Confucianism, Zhu Xi (1130–1200), were written down, these too were written in the vernacular. But the most important use of the written vernacular was in first producing written versions of the oral literature that flourished in the urban culture of the Song.

In the entertainment quarters of the great urban centers there was a rich world of performance literature that was enjoyed by commoners and elite alike. Professional storytellers were divided by specialty: among these specialties were the elaboration of Buddhist sutras, chivalric romances, and men who popularized history, elaborating the standard histories in vernacular Chinese with a wealth of invented incidents and narrative devices to hold the interest of the audience. Another category of storyteller specialized in *xiao-shuo,* the term now translated as "fiction." *Xiao-shuo* included love stories, stories of heroic bandits, and crime stories with the Confucian magistrate as detective. There were also musical narratives mixing verse and prose—the verse serving either to advance the narrative or to create a pause and express the sentiments evoked by the situation. The Tang tale "Ying-ying's Story" appears recast and elaborated in several such performance genres. Out of this tradition of popular retelling, the story finally emerged in the theater, in the fourteenth-century play *Account of the Western Verandah (Xi-xiang ji,* also translated as *The Moon and the Zither).* Such performance literature was never intended for writing, but the commercial publishers of the Southern Song, always searching for new markets, discovered its appeal. Thus in this period we have the beginnings of a continuous tradition of written vernacular literature in print.

The dominant intellectual figure of the Southern Song was Zhu Xi. Zhu consolidated the philosophical speculations of his predecessors and produced his own commentaries on many of the Confucian Classics. But perhaps Zhu Xi's greatest influence came from his interest in Confucian pedagogy. From the classics he selected the "Four Books"—the *Analects,* the *Mencius,* and two chapters from the *Classic of Rites*—which, together with his commentary, were to serve as the basis of a Confucian education. In the following dynasty, the Yuan, Zhu Xi's commentaries on the classics were made state orthodoxy, and the "Four Books" became the core of a streamlined Confucianism.

Safe behind the Yangzi River, the Southern Song flourished. Frontier conflicts with the Jin Dynasty continued sporadically, but generally the two dynasties settled down to more or less regular diplomatic relations. To the north, however, a new and far greater threat was growing. In 1206, a young Mongol leader declared himself Genghiz Khan, uniting the Mongol tribes and some of the eastern Turks. Mongol armies spread through Central Asia and attacked the Jin to the east. In 1234, they conquered North China and put an end to the Jin. Mongol energies in the following years were largely occupied by their campaigns in the West; however, when Khubilai became Khan in 1260, the Mongols were ready to turn their attentions to the prosperous Song. In 1271, Khubilai set himself up as emperor in the Chinese style and proclaimed his new dynasty as the Yuan. By 1276, Mongol armies entered Hangzhou and accepted the surrender, and in 1279 the final Song resistance was crushed in a naval battle off the coast of Guang-dong.

Traditions of Song Lyric (Tang and Song Dynasties) 趙宋

The forms of classical poetry *(shi)* reached their full complement in the Tang Dynasty and they continue to be used, unchanged, to the present day; these were verses of predominantly regular line lengths with the rhyme falling on the last syllable of each couplet. Through the Tang, but not afterward, classical poetry was often sung; in the eighth century, however, a new kind of song lyric appeared, which by the tenth century had completely supplanted classical poetry for the lyrics of popular music.

The primary formal trait of this new song lyric was the use of lines of uneven length, with the rhyme falling after one, two, three, or more lines. Thus the couplet—the formal building block of the classical poem—was replaced by a more fluid and irregular movement between lines; and that fluidity seemed to listeners and lyricists alike to provide a better medium for the expression of mood and feeling. Many scholars believe that the rise of the new song lyric came alongside new melodies and performance traditions, some from Central Asia, whose irregular musical phrases required lyrics to match. Each new melody had its own character and requirements. These new song lyrics were often called simply *qu-zi ci,* the "lyrics of songs." From this latter term came what is now the most common term for such song lyrics: *ci.*

Ci have "tune patterns," a matrix containing a set number of lines of given length, rhymes in fixed positions, and tonal requirements at certain positions in each line. In Chinese, one does not speak of "writing" *ci* but of "filling in" *ci;* that is, "filling in lyrics" to a known melody. Thus lyrics are identified by the title of the tune, prefaced with "to." Especially from the tenth century on, there is usually no relation between the theme of the lyric and the tune title. By the eleventh century, it became common practice to add, after the tune title, a note on the occasion when the lyrics were composed or on their topic.

The social situation of song deserves some comment. Before the late eleventh century, when the song lyric became a more personal form composed and performed by both genders, such songs were often performed by hired women singers at parties, women whose services might be sexual as well as artistic. The themes are primarily the pleasures of the party, love, and images of desire. At the same time, in this earlier period of the song lyric, all the known lyricists are men. Thus we have the peculiar situation of men writing words, often explicitly, in the voices of women, to be sung back to them.

Although it was revived as a purely literary form in the seventeenth century, the great age of the song lyric spans the second half of the Tang, the Five Dynasties, and the Song—from the middle of the eighth through the thirteenth century. In this section, we will treat that entire period. Before the twentieth century, our knowledge of the origins of the song lyric depended on a small corpus of short songs by known

Tang poets. Early in the twentieth century, however, a large library of manuscripts was discovered in the caves of Dun-huang, a trading center and garrison town of the bleak Northwest. The Dun-huang manuscripts, which had been sealed into the caves early in the eleventh century, contained a rich store of texts on religion, thought, and popular literature. Among them were a large number of anonymous song lyrics from the eighth through the tenth centuries. In language and sensibility, these works represent a picture of the early song lyric that is very different from what we find from elite lyricists of the period.

The following pair of poems should give some indication of the difference between "high" literary style and the popular style found in the lyrics preserved in the Dun-huang manuscripts. The first is a quatrain attributed to the second half of the eighth century; the author is variously given as Li Duan or Geng Wei. The title, "Bowing to the New Moon," is the theme: a young woman comes out in the evening, bows to the moon, and makes vows or prayers concerning her beloved. Although the lyric may have been intended to be sung, it represents elite poetic values that contrast sharply with the second piece, an anonymous Dun-huang lyric to the same tune title and on the same theme. The quatrain is visual—we cannot see into the woman's heart or hear her words, and therefore everything must be inferred from surfaces described. In the popular lyric, however, the woman speaks her feelings directly. The more literary quatrain depends upon the aesthetics of indirectness: a suggestion of deep feeling that is never made explicit, revealed in words spoken but unheard. In the more vernacular anonymous song, delivered in the voice of the woman herself, nothing is withheld. Such extensive explicitness is the virtue, the pleasure, and sometimes the limitation of popular literature in the vernacular.

Bowing to the New Moon (late 8th century, attributed to Li Duan or Geng Wei)

Opening drapes, she sees the new moon,
at once she goes down the stairs and bows.
No one hears her whispered words,
on her skirt's sash the north wind blows.

Anonymous (Dun-huang), to "Bowing to the New Moon" *(Bai xin yue)* (before 850)

My traveling man's off in another land,
already now it's the new year, and
 he still has not returned.
I am galled by his loves, so like water:
wherever he roams he strays recklessly
and takes no thought of his home.
Beneath the flowers I point far away,
 and to gods of Heaven and Earth I pray—

up to this very day
he has left me alone to stay in my empty room.

Above me Heaven's blue arch remains,
there sun, moon, and stars surely know,
    though far away.
I sit against the curtain screen,
in drops my tears stream
on my gauze gown with golden beads.
I sigh at my unlucky destiny;
bad karma has brought me to this.
But still I wish to see his face
and swear never to betray him.

The following anonymous lyric is a song comprised of two stanzas in which each stanza represents a voice in an imaginary dialogue between a woman and a magpie. The call of a magpie was supposed to indicate the imminent arrival of a visitor from far away. The woman hopes it will be her absent beloved returning.

Anonymous (Dun-huang), to "The Magpie Steps on the Branch" *(Que ta zhi)*

"I can't stand that 'lucky' magpie—
    its words are full of lies;
it brings good news, but never
    news of something true.
Several times it's flown here,
    now I've captured it alive
and locked it in a cage of gold
    to stop it talking to me."

"I simply wanted to be nice
    and bring her some good news,
I never thought she'd lock me up
    inside this cage of gold.
I really hope her soldier man
    comes home very soon—
she'll set me free to fly away
    off into blue clouds."

Like popular songs everywhere, the Dun-huang songs often evoke scenes of fantasy rather than the singer's immediate world. Below is a fisherman's song, set in the far-away lush lakes region of the Southeast.

Anonymous (Dun-huang), to "Washing Creek Sands" *(Huan xi sha)*

I roll away my books and poems,
    climb in a fishing boat,
wearing rainhat and raincoat,
    my fishing rod in hand.
I row away to the deepest spot
    within those sapphire waves,
past rapids after rapids.

I'm not like those who fished before,
for me it is because this age
    hates good and worthy men.
And that is why I take myself
    down to the swamps and cliffs,
and will not go to Emperor's court.

Treatment of a Motif: The Drunken Husband's Return

As in earlier classical poetry, song lyrics often elaborate and play upon a body of conventional poetic situations. One of the most common of such situations in "love" poetry was the wife lying awake at night waiting for her absent man to return. The genius of the popular tradition was to not quite parody such a languidly erotic situation, but to add enough irony to make it human. Thus the question arose: What happens if the man comes home drunk? There are a number of popular treatments of this motif in song lyrics from the eighth to tenth centuries. In the late ninth or early tenth century, the theme made its way into elite literary song lyrics, and the way it was transformed offers an excellent example of what happens to popular themes when they enter the "high" tradition. The first few popular lyrics that follow are filled with events; not only does the woman speak, in the first lyric we even see her lugging the drunken man to bed. As the motif becomes increasingly elevated, static descriptions of the boudoir replace action, and the woman's response becomes increasingly subdued, until she is at last reduced to poignant silence.

Anonymous (8th century?), to "The Drunken Lord" *(Zui gong-zi)*

The hound is barking at the gate,
I know that my man has come.
I go down scented stairs in stocking feet—
my darling's drunk tonight.

I lift him through the bed's gauze curtains;
he won't take off these robes of gauze.
If he's drunk, well let him be drunk then—
it's still better than sleeping alone.

Tang and Song lyricists enjoyed playing with different levels of language. One of their favorite devices was moving suddenly from artificially "poetic" language to something earthier and more direct. Here the wife's response is quite different from that in the preceding lyric.

Anonymous (Dun-huang), to "Fisherman's Lyrics" *(Yu ge ci)*

Behind the embroidered curtains
a lovely woman lies asleep,
when the hound in the yard barks frantically.
And the maidservant says:
"The master's back."
He's helped off his splendid steed,
    dead drunk.

She comes from behind the screen,
straightening hair like piles of cloud,
and sheds tears of love as orioles sing.
"You've been messing around with someone else!"
He says, "I have not!"
"It's obvious you have betrayed me."

Wei Zhuang (834?–910), to "Immortal in Heaven" *(Tian xian zi)*

He comes home late always staggering drunk
to be hoisted through tassels onto the bed,
    still not sober.
The smell of alcohol on his breath
    blends with musk and orchid scent.[1]
He wakes from his stupor with a start,
laughs out loud and always says,
"How long does a man's life last?"

Xue Zhao-yun (early 10th century), to "The Drunken Lord" *(Zui gong-zi)*

Languidly binding her dark strands of hair,
her Wu mesh stockings are ironed smooth.
On the bed a small hamper for scenting clothes,
with a new piece of fabric,
    Shao-zhou's "faded red."

---

[1]The "musk and orchid scent" suggests that he has been with courtesans. "How long does a man's life last?" was a venerable cliché in drinking songs.

Oh no!
    Out of nowhere
he comes sneaking in,
      stained with wine from head to toe.
He pesters me until
    I groggily open my eyes
and asks me all sorts of silly things.

In the following "high" version (much preferred by later critics), notice how the wife's silent response to evidence of infidelity has taken the place of an exchange of words. As in the earlier pair of poems on "Bowing to the New Moon" (pp. 560–561), the repressed suggestion of feeling was felt to have greater intensity than its direct expression.

Yin E (early 10th century), to "The Drunken Lord" (*Zui gong-zi*)

Evening mist veils the mossy pavements,
the gate of the mansion, still not shut tight.
All the day long he's been drunk,
    off seeking springtime pleasures,
and as he returns,
    his body is swathed in the moonlight.

He left his saddle with arms around
    some girl with embroidered sleeves,
and on his kerchief that fell to the ground
    a tangle of petals stuck.
But what thing in particular
    upsets the lovely lady most?—
it is the marks of lipstick,
    fresh upon his clothes.

Although popular motifs were transformed when they were assimilated into elite poetry, their livelier, more vernacular forms did not necessarily disappear. The accidental survival of the Dun-huang manuscripts gives us a fortunate glimpse of popular song of the Tang and Five Dynasties. A craze to collect popular songs some six centuries later bears witness to the remarkable continuity of the popular song tradition. The following song, in seventeenth-century slang, is included in Feng Meng-long's (1574–1646) collection of the *Gua-zhi-er*, "Hanging Branch Songs."

Anonymous (collected early 17th century), "Hanging Branch Song"

Late at night my lover comes home,
he's gotten himself smashed—
crashed flat on his face,
    asleep in his clothes. A disgrace!—

I would have preferred
    if he hadn't come back at all.
I waited past midnight,
    wasted my time,
    me and my lonely light.
But,
    on second thought,
    he's not drunk all that often.
Even
    a drunk lover in my arms
beats lying in bed alone.

Tang and Five Dynasties Lyrics

Song lyrics were not really considered a separate genre by elite literary writers late in the eighth and early in the ninth centuries. Poets would try their hand at writing lyrics for popular melodies. The short song "Dream of the Southland" *(Meng Jiang-nan)*, composed in this manner, was popular in the early ninth century.

Huang-fu Song (early 9th century), to "Dream of the Southland" *(Meng Jiang-nan)*

Oil, scented with orchid, burns down in the lamp,
and on my folding screen the red
    banana flowers grow dark:
I peacefully dream of the Southland,
    of the day when plums are ripe,
of a flute played in a boat by night,
    as the rain pelts down,
of someone speaking on the bridge
    by the way station.

Wen Ting-yun is generally considered the first truly distinctive literary writer of song lyric. His lyrics belong very much in the tradition of "the poetry of the women's chambers"—scenes of opulently furnished bedrooms and extensive gardens, in which the woman's gestures or the objects of her attention become signs of her inner state. This was the highly stylized imagery of love poetry used for romantic communication between the sexes in the entertainment quarters of the Tang capital Chang-an.

Wen Ting-yun (d. 870), to "Boddhisattva Barbarian" *(Pu-sa man)*

Inside a curtain of crystal,
    on a pillow of lapis lazuli,

warm incense coaxes a dream,
    bedspread embroidered with lovebirds:
beside the river, willows like mist,
wild geese flying and a sky
    of dying moonlight.

Threads of lotus root, fall colors pale,
cloth figures cut in various forms,
two long tresses blocked by scented red,
and the jade hairpin: wind on her head.

Vignettes of the bedroom, of musical performance, and of the complex interactions
between men and women became a favorite topic for song lyric.

He Ning (898–955), to "Mountain Flower" *(Shan-hua-zi)*

Cold notes from silver-inlay pipes,
    a melody held long.
Chill is the ripple-patterned mat,
    cool the painted screen.
Her alabaster wrist weighed down
    with bracelets of gold,
hair combed, and lightly made up.

Again and again she adds incense,
    her slender hand grows warm,
and once trying the wine,
    her ruby lips gleam.
Feigning to play with the red strands
    of the fly-whisk,
she swats her true love.

Songs such as the following lyrics to "Boddhisattva Barbarian" were popular homages
on the joys of the Southland. Wei Zhuang has other lyrics to the same tune on the
same topic, developed in phases.

Wei Zhuang (ca. 836–910), to "Boddhisattva Barbarian" *(Pu-sa man)*

I
Everyone says that the Southland's fine,
in the South the traveler should remain
    till old and gray.
Springtime waters are bluer than sky,
in a painted boat lie,
    listening to the rain.

Beside the bar, a woman like moon,
her gleaming wrists both of compacted snow.
Never go home until you are old,
for if you go home, it will break your heart.

II
And now I think back on the Southland's joys,
a youth in those days, my spring clothes thin,
I rode my horse by the slanting bridge,
and the upper rooms were filled
    with red sleeves beckoning.

An azure screen with hinges of gold,
drunk, I spent nights in clumps of flowers.
When I now catch sight of branches in bloom,
I vow not to go home till my hair is white.

Ou-yang Jiong (896–971), to "The South Country" (Nan xiang zi)

In his bright-colored skiff he rests his oars.
Beyond the hedge of rose of Sharon blooms
    bamboo screens a bridge.
Traveler on the waters,
    maiden on the sands:
she turns her head, she looks around
and smiling points to where she lives,
    in the grove of plantain.

to "Washing Creek Sands" (Huan xi sha)

Speak no more when we meet
    of tears that filled your eyes,
when the wine is done we can again
    speak our pleasure and delight,
behind phoenix screens on lovebird pillows
    a night spent in golden bedding.

A delicate scent of orchid and musk,
    I hear her breathing hard,
and the fine threads of lace she wears
    reveal flesh—
at such a time does she still resent
    that her lover was untrue?

Li Yu (937–978) was the best known and most loved of all the early lyricists. Li Yu was the last emperor of the Southern Tang, one of the several regional states into which China was divided after the breakup of the Tang. This short dynasty, founded by Li Yu's father, owed its name to the fictitious claim that the family was descended from the Tang royal house and was the legitimate successor to the Tang. When Li Yu took the throne in 961, the Southern Tang was a client state of the new Northern military power, the Song, which was successively eliminating the regional states and consolidating its rule. In 975, the Song formally ended the Southern Tang and sent Li Yu off to its new capital at Kai-feng to live under house arrest.

The pathos of the pleasure-loving Southern emperor who loses his domain and thinks back on vanished glories was a powerful image in the tradition. The first of the following lyrics shows Li Yu writing in the tradition of the erotic vignette.

Li Yu (937–978), to "Boddhisattva Barbarian" *(Pu-sa man)*

> The flowers are bright, the moon is dark,
>   veiled beneath light fog:
> tonight would be the perfect time
>   to go and see her love.
> She treads the stairs in stocking feet,
> holding in hand
>   slippers with golden threads.
>
> To the south of the painted hall they meet,
> she trembles a moment in his arms.
> "It's so hard to get out now—
> let's grab all the pleasure we can."

to "Pleasure in the Lovely Woman" *(Yu mei-ren)*

> Flowers in spring, moonlight in fall,
>   when will they ever end?
> and how much can we know
>   of what is past and gone?
> Upstairs in my room last night
>   the east wind came again;
> I cannot bear to turn and look home
>   in the light of the moon.
>
> Its carved railings and marble pavements
>   are, I'm sure, still there—
> all that changes is the flush
>   on the face of youth.
> Tell me then of sorrow—how much can there be?
> It is exactly like:
>   a whole river of springtime waters
>   flowing off to the east.

(attributed), to "The Pleasures of Meeting" *(Xiang-jian huan)*

> Without a word I climbed the western tower—
> the moon was like a hook.
> The silent yard stretched deep
>   through chestnut trees,
> enclosing autumn, cool and clear.
>
> You can cut it, but never cut it through,
> get it set,
>   then it's a mess again—
> that's the sadness of being apart.
> It has a flavor all its own
>   in the human heart.

The Party Songs of the Eleventh Century

The short song lyrics of the first part of the Song Dynasty continued traditions of the preceding centuries, though in a new context of political and social stability. Many such lyrics were party songs, performed at gathering by hired entertainers. Often they celebrated the joys of the moment, urging the guests to drink, to be mindful of life's brevity, and to take note of the flashing glances of paid flirtation.

The two most prolific of such lyricists were Yan Shu (991–1055) and Ou-yang Xiu (1007–1072). Although the lyrics themselves might conjure up images of young wastrels spending their lives in wine, women, and song, both Yan Shu and Ou-yang Xiu were, in fact, distinguished senior statesmen and literary figures. At the same time, we can be certain that they enjoyed a good party.

Yan Shu (991–1055), to "Breaking Through the Ranks" *(Po zhen-zi)*

> That time of year when swallows are set to go,
> and in high rooms last night, west wind.
> I sought a small party in
>   this mortal world,
> we held our golden cups beside
>   clumps of chrysanthemums.
> The songs lasted long, and faces
>   powdered white flushed red.
>
> Then sinking sunlight again
>   pierced the curtains,
> light chill progressively touched the beech.
> So much in the heart I could not say—
> on slips of fine paper
>   I wrote into melody
> these feelings, in thousands, one after another.

The following, also by Yan Shu, is one of the most famous of all song lyrics, in which the woman singer urges the listener to take his joy in the moment.

to "Washing Creek Sands" *(Huan xi sha)*

Only a moment, this season's splendor,
    this body, a bounded thing;
to part now as if it didn't matter
    easily breaks the heart;
so don't be hasty, refusing
    the party's wine, the banquet's song.

Mountains and rivers fill our eyes, but care
    is wasted on things too far;
besides which, this grief at spring passing,
    at wind and rain that bring down flowers;
it is better by far to take as your love
    the person before your eyes.

Ou-yang Xiu (1007–1072) (or Feng Yan-si), to "Butterflies Love Flowers" *(Die lian hua)*

Deep, so deep within the yard,
    how deep I cannot say,
piles of mist among willows,
veil behind veil beyond number.
His jade-studded bridle and well-wrought saddle
    are there where he takes his pleasures;
from the upper chamber she cannot see
    the Zhang Terrace road.

The rain is violent, winds blow wild,
    it is the end of May;
the gate stands shut in twilight,
no clever plan to make spring stay.
With tears in eyes, then ask the flowers—
    but the flowers have nothing to say:
a tumult of red flies away
    past the swing.

to "Immortal by the River" *(Lin-jiang xian)*

Beyond the willows soft thunder,
    rain upon the pond,
and the sound of rain as it splatters
    lotuses to shreds.
By the small tower's west corner
    a broken rainbow bright,

where we lean upon the railing
waiting for moonlight.

The swallows come in flying,
    peer from rafters and beams,
from a jade hook dangles the curtain sash.
Motionless ripples of coolness,
    the bedmat's patterns flat.
There a pair of crystal pillows
and beside them, a fallen hairpin.

The Songs of Romance

Nowhere is the boundary between fantasy and reality more blurred than in romance. Cultural images of romance take shape somewhere in the space between the impulse of desire and the stability of the social institution of marriage. On the one hand, romance has to be something more than mere desire; it aspires to duration (in contrast to a party song's invitation to joy in the moment). On the other hand, in the premodern world, both in China and the West, romance is generally located outside marriage—either in courtship or in extramarital relationships. The reason for this may simply be that romance depends on a liberty of choice on the part of both parties (or the illusion thereof). In premodern China, where marriages were arranged by families, the site of romance was the "entertainment quarters," somewhat like the "demimonde" of nineteenth-century Paris. In the Tang capital of Chang-an and the Song capital of Kai-feng, these quarters were special sections of the city.

Like the singers, dancers, and actresses of nineteenth-century Paris, the women of the entertainment quarters were performers, usually singers, and romance was the predominant theme of their songs. As in the French demimonde, the boundary between a singer taking lovers and simple prostitution was a gray area. In the Chinese case, some evidence suggests that a singer might continue to have sex with many clients, but consider one to be her lover. Such singers generally belonged to establishments to which they were indebted for their upbringing and training. If she found sufficient favor with a man of means, a singer might hope to be bought out and established as a concubine.

The images of romance in songs and stories hide the social inequalities and the economic necessities that were the reality of liaisons in the entertainment quarter. But images of romance, rather than simple sex, were what these singers sold. And romance, with its possibility of freely choosing and being freely chosen, had a way of beguiling both those who listened and those who sang. Although many surely enjoyed or used the images as a polite fiction, people did fall in love.

Traditional China had an elaborate repertoire of images of romance. While some form of separation between lover and beloved may be essential to all love poetry— the preferred form of separation in the West was that of the beloved not yet attained— in China the emphasis was on the separation of those who were already lovers. Before the eleventh century, love poetry was most commonly a male fantasy of a woman in love, enduring exquisite tortures of the heart while awaiting the return of

571

her beloved (who was away either because he was a heartless rake or because he was in the army). In the eleventh century, however, the male lover also became a central figure in the repertoire of love images, and his sensibility was closely modeled on that of the woman in love. The new prominence of this figure of male longing marks a significant change in the culture of romance in China.

Yan Ji-dao, the last of the Northern Song masters of the short lyric, wrote songs that served in several ways as an afterecho of the tradition of party song: not only are they the last, they often evoke memories and scenes of love and pleasure lost.

Yan Ji-dao (mid-11th–early 12th century), to "Butterflies Love Flowers" *(Die lian hua)*

I was drunk as I left the western hall;
    then sober, I couldn't recall.
A springtime dream, clouds of fall,
join and scatter all too easily.
My window half-filled with the moon descending—
    small sleep again.
Peacefully spread on a painted screen
    are the green hills of the South.

On my clothes the stains of wine
    and in my poems the words—
a lot of dots and lines which mean,
taken on the whole, despondency.
My red candle is moved
    but sees no resolution;
and wastes its tears on my behalf
    in night's cold.

to "Partridge Weather" *(Zhe-gu tian)*

With such feeling your brightly colored sleeves
    held up the goblet of jade to me,
    but in those days we didn't care
    if faces flushed red with the wine,
when you danced the moon low in the willows
    and sang out the breeze in the peach blossom fan.

Then,
    after we each went our way,
    I thought back on when we first met
    and have joined you so often in dreams,
that perhaps tonight I overdo it,
    taking the silver lamp in hand

to shine on you, still afraid
that this meeting too is a dream.

to "Partridge Weather" *(Zhe-gu tian)*

A short lyric while drinking,
    it was there I met Yu-xiao,
between silver lamps and the melody,
    gorgeous beyond compare.
If during the song I fell down drunk,
    no one would care—
then, the singing done, I made my way back,
    the wine not gone from my blood.

The springtime is so quiet,
the night lasts on and on.
And the sky with its sapphire clouds
    is as far as the Palace of Chu.
In dream my soul has the habit
    of breaking free of its bonds,
and again I strode over willow flowers,
    across the Xie Bridge.

to "Springtime in the Mansion of Jade" *(Yu-lou chun)*

The east wind did it again, unsentimental
    in its designs; it blew the land full of petals,
    passionate red and fetching white.
High in green mansions curtain shadows won't block away
    melancholy—same mood as last year
    on the same day.

You'd never know how I've always botched
    spring's last moments so badly, with wasted tears
    climbing high places everywhere.
But this time I'll have my golden flagon
    filled to the rim. How often drunk hereafter
    will I watch the blossoms all fall away?

to "Young Ruan Returns" *(Ruan lang gui)*

Here at the world's edge dew turns to frost
    on the statues' golden palms, while clouds pursue
    long lines in the sky, geese-drawn.
I make the most
    of the Double Ninth—red sleeves

and glasses of green wine. The human heart
works here much as it does at home:
purple orchids in sashes
and yellow chrysanthemums stuck in hair.
I really try to govern that old wildness.
And I want to make a trade: deep drunkenness
    for this dreariness, so stop that clear singing
    which tears at the heart.

The preceding lyrics belong to the category of "short songs" *(xiao-ling)*. There was
another song form known as "long lyrics" or *man-ci.* Anonymous "long lyrics" can
be found among the Dun-huang songs. Many early literary lyricists tended to avoid
the form, but it seems nevertheless to have been popular in the demimonde. The
early eleventh-century lyricist Liu Yong, however, not only composed lyrics for the
"long song" melodies, he also made extensive use of the vernacular and a range of
romantic situations far greater than those found in "short songs." As a result, he was
the most truly "popular" lyricist of his day, the darling of the demimonde, while despised by many of the more old-fashioned lyricists. It was Liu Yong who began the
fashion of writing songs about male longing, a motif picked up by the younger Yan
Ji-dao.

Liu Yong (987–1053), to "Turning Back After Seeing the Flowers" *(Kan-hua hui)*

When I reckon up these hundred years
    burdened with life,
high times and wretchedness follow each other.
The tug of advantage, the lure of renown—
    both go by in a flash,
and nothing stops the two orbs,
    a jade moon rushing,
        a golden sun in flight.
The bloom on your cheeks becomes white hair,
and what good does having the highest rank?

Worldly troubles are always too many,
    fine parties are always too rare.
So how can you help breaking into a smile?
In the deepest spot of the painted hall
    songs are sung to flutes,
and never forget the cup of wine
    and the woman, a spray of flowers.
The scenes are sweet in the land of drunkenness—
take my hand and we'll go there together.

It is ironic that Liu Yong, the poet of the demimonde, was also the first poet to use the lyric to describe landscapes—though usually, as in "Joy at Midnight," he reserves the last stanza to declare his longing for his beloved back in the capital.

to "Joy at Midnight" *(Ye-ban le)*

> A solid mass of cloud,
>   dark and gloomy weather,
> in a tiny boat
> riding my whim
>   I left the river isles;
> and passed through thousands of canyons and cliffs
> to the deepest spots in the creeks of Yue.
> There raging waves gradually calmed,
> and a breeze of woodsmen suddenly rose,
> when I heard merchant travelers
>   shouting back and forth.
> With sails raised high
> painted prows glided,
>   they bent swiftly past the southern shores.
>
> Tavern signs flashed in my gaze,
> a village lay clumped in the fog,
> and several lines of frosty trees.
> As the fading sun set, the fishermen
>   made their way home, knocking clappers.
> Broken lotus shed petal shreds,
> dying willows appeared in bits;
> by the bank in twos and threes
> girls washing gauze
> fled the traveler,
>   bashful and giggling to one another.
>
> Coming here, my thoughts turn
> to splendid chambers too lightly left,
> and myself, wave-borne duckweed that cannot rest.
> Too bad that our pact to meet, made earnestly,
>   will finally be hard to keep.
> Depressed at being apart, helplessly upset
>   that I can't make the date
>   to return to you late in the year.
> Tears well in my eyes,
>   the road to the capital stretches faint and far.
> Far off the voice of a wild goose,
>   lost from the flock,
>   in the long skies of evening.

By the late eleventh century, the song lyric was on its way to becoming a truly literary art rather than popular song. In some cases, as in Su Shi's lyrics, this meant expanding the genre by drawing on diction and motifs previously reserved for classical poetry. Another larger group of writers made the song lyric a specialized art for the connoisseur, with carefully crafted phrases and subtle turns of mood—a poetry of fine sensibility. Lyricists such as Zhou Bang-yan utilized the repertoire of love images, as in the following song, in which the lover stands outside the house of his beloved.

Zhou Bang-yan (1056–1121), to "Gallant" *(Feng-liu-zi)*

A new green in the tiny pond,
breeze stirs curtains, dancing
    shattered shadows in setting sun.
How I envy their passage
    in and out of her gilded rooms—swallows, the same
    that nested there before—
    and the flowering vines that twine
    on mossy walls
    as in a previous time.
From within her splendid chambers
    deep behind figured veils
    I hear the harps and oboes play.
There is something she would say, then refrains,
    and her troubled thoughts fail
    their sweet communication.
Before she can sing, her voice chokes in sobs
    and, dejected, she has someone bring
    a cup of clear wine.

Though far from her, I know
    her make-up has just been done,
and opening her vermilion door,
    I am sure she waits alone for the moon
    in the western corridor.
Most bitter of all for the dreaming soul
    that tonight I will not reach her side.
And I wonder when she will tell to me
    sweet words and secrets of her heart.
She sends me Qin Jia's mirror,
and Han Shou's perfume in furtive exchange.[2]
What's to keep Heaven
    from letting us meet just a little while!

---

[2]Qin Jia's mirror (received from his wife) and the incense given to Han Shou by the daughter of a superior official (who fell in love with Han at first sight) are both figures for love tokens.

Peach Creek was the place where two young scholars met goddesses and remained with them a while before returning to the mortal world. Such brief encounters with divine women were favorite figures for romantic liaisons.

to "Spring in the Mansion of Jade" *(Yu-lou chun)*

> At Peach Creek I did not stay
>   enjoying myself at leisure;
> once lotus roots break in fall,
>   they never can be rejoined.
> I waited for her back then
>   on the bridge with red rails,
> and today I follow all alone
>   a path of yellowed leaves.
>
> Lines of hilltops in the mist
>   green beyond counting,
> geese turn their backs to evening sun
>   toward dusk growing redder.
> The person, like clouds coming after the wind
>   and moving onto the river;
> the passion, like floss that sticks to the ground
>   in the aftermath of rain.

Su Shi (1037–1101)

Su Shi (Su Dong-po), greatest of all the Song writers, also tried his hand at song lyrics. Su largely abandoned the themes of parties and lost love, turning instead to the more reflective themes of classical poetry. The following famous lyric is based on a poem by Li Bo, but the old motif is soon transformed by Su Shi's characteristic panache.

to "Song for the River Tune" *(Shui-diao ge-fou)*

1076, mid-autumn, drinking till dawn I wrote this. Also thinking of my brother Su Che.

> How long has the moon been up there?—
> I ask blue Heaven, wine in hand.
> And I wonder
>   in those palaces of sky
> what year this evening is?
> I would ride the wind up there,
> but fear
>   those marble domes and onyx galleries
> are up so high I couldn't bear the cold.
> I rise and dance, clear shadow capering—

what can compare
    to this world of mortal men!

Curving past crimson towers,
then lower past grillwork doors,
it shines upon the sleepless.
It should not trouble me,
but why, when people part,
    is it always full and whole?
For mortals there is grief and joy,
    coming together and going apart;
the moon has bright and shadowed phases,
    wholeness and then something gone—
things never stay at perfection.
So I wish that we continue long
to share across a thousand miles
    its lovely graces.

to "Immortal by the River" *(Lin-jiang xian)*

I was drinking that night on Eastern Slope,
    I sobered and got drunk again,
and when I went back it seemed about midnight.
My servant boy was snoring,
    it sounded like the thunder,
When I knocked at the gate, no one answered,
then I leaned on my staff
    and listened to the river.

I've always resented how this body
    has never been my own,
will the time ever come when I can forget
    being always busy?
The night ended, the winds calmed,
    the wrinkled waves grew flat,
I'll set off from here in my small boat,
on river and lakes lodge the rest of my days.

to "Settling Wind and Waves" *(Ding feng-bo)*

On May 7 I ran into a rainstorm on the Sand Lake Road. The raincoats had
all been sent on ahead, and the people traveling with me were all thrown
into confusion. I didn't even notice. Soon it cleared up, and I wrote this.

Pay no heed to those sounds,
    piercing the woods, hitting leaves—
why should it stop me from whistling or chanting
    and walking slowly along?

With my bamboo cane and sandals of straw
    I move more free than on horse.
Who's afraid?
Let my life be spent with a raincoat
    in the misty rain.

A biting chill in the spring breeze
    blows me sober from wine.
A bit cold,
but the sunshine that sinks on the hilltop
    comes back to welcome me.
Turn your head to where you just were,
    where the winds were howling,
go back—
on the one hand, it's not a storm;
    on the other, not clear skies.

To "The Charms of Nian-nu" is probably Su Shi's most famous lyric, written on a visit to what he thought was the site of the great battle at Red Cliff during the Three Kingdoms. Cao Cao had brought his army to the northern shore of the Yangzi River and was preparing a fleet to cross over and invade the southern kingdom of Wu. For protection, he had his warships chained together. Zhou Yu, the admiral of the Wu river fleet and brother-in-law of the King of Wu, sent fire ships disguised as a grain convoy. By the time the ruse was discovered, it was too late and Cao Cao's fleet was sunk. Su had made an historical error: it was the wrong Red Cliff. But it scarcely matters.

to "The Charms of Nian-nu" *(Nian-nü jiao):* Meditation on the Past at Red Cliff

Eastward goes the great river,
its waves have swept away
a thousand years of gallant men.
And they say
    that west of the ancient castle here
is that Red Cliff
    of Zhou Yu and the Three Kingdoms.
A rocky tangle pierces sky,
leaping waves smash the shore,
surging snow in a thousand drifts.
Like a painting, these rivers and hills
where once so many bold men were.

I envision Zhou Yu back then,
just wedded to the younger Qiao,
his manly manner striking.
With black turban and feather fan
    laughing in conversation

as embers flew from mast and prow
and the smoke was sinking away.
The spirit roams that long-ago land—
you will laugh at this sentimental me,
hair streaked with white before my time.
Yet this human world is like a dream
and I pour out my winecup as offering
into the river's moonbeams.

Li Qing-zhao (1084–ca. 1151)

Although the surviving corpus of lyrics that can confidently be attributed to her is rather small, Li Qing-zhao's work has a distinct quality all its own. Song lyric often aspired to join technical mastery and an ease that gives the impression of natural speech. Some of Li Qing-zhao's longer songs achieve precisely this quality. Li Qing-zhao was also one of the earliest theorists of the song lyric, and her "Discourse on Lyric" *(Ci-lun)* asserts the difference of the genre from classical poetry *(shi)*.

Like a Dream *(Ru meng ling)*

when she was younger.

I will always recall that day at dusk,
    the pavilion by the creek,
and I was so drunk I couldn't tell
    the way home. My mood left me,
it was late when I turned back in my boat
and I strayed deep among lotuses—
how to get through?
how to get through?
and I startled to flight a whole shoal
    of egrets and gulls.

imagery.

Poets inevitably became concerned with the ability of language to adequately represent the world and convey the quality of human experience. Their hope was that poetic language could somehow get beyond ordinary language. In the ninth century, the poet Du Mu had written:

In this world adrift, except in poems
    all words are forced on things.

The following song lyric, Li Qing-zhao's most famous, begins with an untranslatable series of two-syllable compounds evoking the "atmosphere" in the human heart and in the outer world. The lyric tries to capture the mood of the moment, measuring it, finally, against the common word "sorrow" to remind us of the difference between the particularity of a state of mind and the imprecise, strangely impersonal words that we normally use to categorize experience—words "forced on things."

to "Note After Note" *(Sheng-sheng màn)*

Searching and searching, seeking and seeking,
so chill, so clear,
dreary,
    and dismal,
        and forlorn.
That time of year
    when it's suddenly warm,
        then cold again,
now it's hardest of all to take care.
Two or three cups of weak wine—
how can they resist the biting wind
    that comes with evening?
The wild geese pass by—
that's what hurts the most—
and yet they're old acquaintances.

In piles chrysanthemums fill the ground,
looking all wasted, damaged—
who could pick them, as they are now?
I stay by the window,
how can I wait alone until blackness comes?
The beech tree,
    on top of that
        the fine rain,
on until dusk,
the dripping drop after drop.
In a situation like this
how can that one word "sorrow" grasp it?

[handwritten annotations: Combination of sounds & words / Its compound. Contrast between earlier and later age. / later after death of husband. / autumn-season of loneliness. on art. / Before marriage after Biograph., husband dies.]

In "Southern Song," there is a confusion between the scene of a real lotus pond in autumn, with its withering and broken vegetation, and the scene of a lotus pond decorating an old dress, whose flaking gilt imitates the autumnal scene of real lotuses.

to "Southern Song" *(Nan-ge-zi)*

Up in heaven the star-river turns,
in man's world below
    curtains are drawn.

A chill comes to pallet and pillow,
    damp with tracks of tears.
I rise to take off my gossamer dress
and just happen to ask, "How late is it now?"

The tiny lotus pods,
    kingfisher feathers sewn on;
as the gilt flecks away
    the lotus leaves grow few.
Same weather as in times before,
    the same old dress—
only the feelings in the heart
are not as they were before.

[handwritten annotations: "→ outside.", "autumn.", "possibly shoes", "later."]

Originally composed for women singers, the early song lyric often represented a stylized "feminine" voice—although a feminine voice constructed by male writers. It was felt to be a language of sensibility, with the capacity to express feeling more perfectly than the symmetrical regularity of classical poetry. In lyricists such as Li Yu, and later in the lover's discourse of Yan Ji-dao and Liu Yong, that "feminine" language of sensibility was appropriated (or reappropriated) by male writers to speak in the first person in ways impossible in classical poetry. Partially in reaction to Liu Yong, Su Shi created a new kind of song lyric that seemed, to premodern readers, to represent a "masculine" style; and thereafter the styles of song lyrics conveyed a strong sense of gender difference.

    The "masculine" style was called *hao-fang,* loosely translated as "bold and extravagant"; the "feminine" style was called *wan-yue,* something like "having a delicate sensibility." Although male lyricists might write in either or both styles, women lyricists like Li Qing-zhao generally adopted the "feminine" style, as in the lyrics above. To the surprise and general approval of traditional critics, the following lyric shows Li Qing-zhao writing in the masculine style.

to "Free-Spirited Fisherman" *(Yu-jia ao)*

Billowing clouds touch sky and reach
    the early morning fog,
the river of stars is ready to set,
    a thousand sails dance.
My dreaming soul moves in a daze
    to where the high god dwells—
I hear Heaven speak,
asking me with urgent concern
    where I am going now.

And I reply that my road is long,
    and, alas, twilight draws on;

I worked at my poems and for nothing have
    bold lines that cause surprise.[3]
Into strong winds ninety thousand miles
    upward the Peng now flies.[4]
Let that wind never stop,
let it blow this tiny boat away
    to the Three Immortal Isles.

The Early Southern Song

By the later part of the twelfth century, the song lyric had become a highly "literary" form, sometimes still sung but no longer a popular song. Lu You is considered the greatest classical poet of the Southern Song. His song lyrics differ from his poetry in tone and treatment; but unlike earlier song lyrics, they treat the same kinds of topics as classical poetry.

Lu You (1125–1210), to "Partridge Weather" *(Zhe-gu tian)*

My home is set in blue-gray mists,
    within the waning light;
the world's concerns concern me not
    a whit, nor a hair.
Misty fluids, marble white, poured to the last drop,
    I walk my way through bamboo;
tracts on extending my life rolled away,
    I lie here and look at the hills.

I yearn for carefree independence,
yet accept that my body grows frail—
but it won't stop me from cracking a smile
    no matter where I go.
At last I grasp the Creator's mind,
    so different from mortal man's:
he lets his heroes age away
    with utter unconcern.

The following three short songs by Xin Qi-ji are not the kind of lyric for which he was best known; those were the long lyrics in which he expressed his despair over

---

[3]The first line of the second stanza recalls Wu Zi-xu's response after flogging the corpse of the King of Chu, declaring his indomitable will. The line that follows echoes Du Fu, speaking with pride of his own poetry.

[4]The Peng was a huge mythical bird described in the *Zhuang-zi*. Li Qing-zhao uses it as a figure of such greatness that smaller creatures cannot comprehend its magnitude.

the loss of the North to the non-Chinese Jin Dynasty and his frustration at the Song government's inability to recapture it.

Xin Qi-ji (1140–1207), to "Clear and Even Music" *(Qing-ping yue).* An account on the Censer Mountain Road

A harness goes flying beside the willows,
the weight of a travel coat soaked with dew.
A sleeping egret peers at the sand
    its lonely reflection stirs;
and I am sure that its dreams
    are filled with fish and shrimp.

Bright moonlight and the scattered stars
    lie all along the stream,
the gorgeous outline of a woman
    washing filmy gauze.
She laughs and turns from the traveler,
    goes off back to her home
at the sound of a child crying in front of her gate.

to "West River Moon" *(Xi jiang yue).* Expressing what was on my mind

I was drunk and craved some pleasure and fun—
no time for sorrow even had I wished.
Just lately I've grasped that in books of the past
there are really some points that are not at all true.

Last night I fell over drunk by a pine,
and asked that pine, "Just how drunk am I?"
It seemed the pine moved to give me a hand,
I shoved the pine and said to it, "Scram!"

to "Ugly Slave" *(Chou nu-er)*

When I was young, I didn't know
    how sorrow tastes.
    I loved to climb up high in a tower,
    I loved to climb up high in a tower,
And writing new songs, I forced myself
    to speak of sorrow.

But now I know the taste of sorrow all too well.
    I'm ready to speak of it, then stop,
    I'm ready to speak of it, then stop,
And say instead, "Cool weather—a nice autumn."

The Master Craftsmen

Jiang Kui represents a new type of literary figure that appeared in the Southern Song: the more or less professional writer-musician who lived as a client of the rich and powerful. Jiang Kui never served in public office, nor did it seem that he had any inclination to do so. He was, above all, a craftsman who sought the perfect union of word and melody. The following song, with its lengthy preface, combines the artist's fascination with the technical details of his craft, an act of devotion to a local cult deity, and praise of the Southern Song's security against aggression from the Jin Dynasty in North China. In the last part of the Preface, Jiang refers to one of Cao Cao's attempts to invade the southern kingdom of Wu, whose king was Sun Quan.

Jiang Kui (ca. 1155–1221), to "Red Filling the River" (*Man jiang hong*)

The old pattern for lyrics to the song "Red Filling the River" rhymed in an oblique tone and often failed to match the requirements of the music. Consider, for example, the closing lines in Zhou Bang-yan's version:

> Most bitter to her were the butterflies
> filling the garden in flight—
> to whisk them away she had no heart.

Only when a singer modulates the word "heart" *(xīn)* into the falling tone *(xìn)* will it go along with the requirements of the music. For a long time I had wanted to do a version using the level tone but had not been able to get it just right. It happened that I was sailing on Nest Lake and heard the sounds of pipes and drums on the far shore. I asked the boatman what the music was, and he explained: "It is the local inhabitants offering their good wishes to the Old Lady of the Lake." I then made a prayer: "If I can get a steady wind that will carry me straight across to Ju-chao, I will compose lyrics for 'Red Filing the River' rhyming in the level tone to serve as a song to welcome the goddess and send her on her way." No sooner were my words finished than both the wind and my writing brush sped swiftly along, and in an instant the lyrics were completed. As a closing line I had "and the rings on her sash were heard," in which the rhyme did indeed answer the requirements of the music. I copied it out on a piece of green notepaper and let it sink under the white-capped waves. That was on the last day of March, 1191. In August of that year I again passed by the shrine and had the lyrics carved between the pillars. A traveler later came from Ju-chao who told me that the locals would always sing these lyrics in their prayers to the Old Lady.

I would add that when Cao Cao reached the mouth of the Ru-xu River, Sun Quan sent him a letter, saying, "When the spring floods rise, your lordship had best be swiftly gone." To which Cao Cao replied, "Sun Quan does not bluff"; whereupon he decamped his army and turned back. The mouth of the Ru-xu is close to East Pass, through which flows the waters of the river and the lakes. I hold the notion that there must have been someone overseeing that moment when the spring floods rose. And I gave credit for the deed to the Old Lady of the Lake.

When the Old Lady came, the goddess undying,
her gaze took in these thousand acres
    of azure rippling.
Her pennons and banners descended together
    with seething clouds
that blurred the view of the mountains ahead.
She bade her dragon herds be hitched,
    golden were their yokes,
and all the handmaidens in her train
    wore crowns of jade.
As the night grew deep, the winds died down
    in the unpeopled stillness,
and the rings on her sash were heard.

This spot where the goddess worked wonders—
come have a look!—
She holds secure the Huai's right bank,
bulwark of the Southland;
She sent six stout angels in lightning and thunder
specially to hold East Pass.
And I laugh at those warrior heroes,
    that none were any good:
a boat-pole's depth of springtime floods
    sent little Cao Cao running—
but then how could he have known
    that She who did it all
    was in this small red chamber
in the shadows of the blinds?

The following is Jiang Kui's most famous lyric, on the topic of plum blossoms. The melodies that Jiang composed for this lyric and others still survive.

to "Fragrance from Somewhere Unseen" *(An xiang)*

In the winter of 1191, I went off in the snow to visit Fan Cheng-da at Stone Lake. When I had stayed with him a month, he handed me some paper and asked for some lines to appear in a new style song. I composed these two melodies. Fan Cheng-da couldn't get over his pleasure in them, and had a pair of singing girls practice them until the tones and the rhythms were sweet and smooth. Then I gave them the name "Fragrance from Somewhere Unseen" and "Broken Shadows."

The moon's hue of days gone by—
I wonder how often it shone on me
playing my flute beside the plums?
It called awake that woman, white marble,
and heedless of cold,
    together we snapped off sprays.
But now this poet grows old,
and the pen that once wrote songs
    of the breeze in spring
    is utterly forgotten;
I'm just intrigued by those sparse blooms
    over beyond the bamboo,
how their chill scent
    seeps into party mats.

These river lands now
lie somber and still.
And I sigh
    to send them to someone traveling far,
as tonight their snow begins to heap high.
With kingfisher cups
    and easily brought to tears,
restive, I recall
    pink petals that never speak.
I always think back where we once held hands:
where the freight of a thousand trees weighed
    on West Lake's cold sapphire.
Now petal by petal once more
    they all blow away,
never again to be seen.

Shi Da-zu (fl. 1200), to "Scent of Lace" *(Ji luo xiang)*. On spring rain

A deed of chill betrays blossoms,
its mist-work beleaguers the willows,
it furtively hastens spring's finale
    for thousands of miles around.
Murky and overcast all the day through,
in the gloom it seems just ready to fall,
    then desists.
Dismayed by pollen's weight, the butterflies
    wait the night in the western parks;
and swallows, finding delight in the sticky mire,
    bring it home to the southern shore.

Worst, how it frustrates lovers:
>they cannot meet,
for her inlaid coach will never make it
>down Du-ling Street.

I gaze as far as I can
>through the river's murky fog,
which then at dusk is borne swiftly away
>by springtime floods;
and I can't discern the post road ford.
Hazy and vague, peaks faraway
are Miss Xie's brows in a charming pout,
>appearing with tears.
I look down the steep bluff
>as green foliage grows anew,
and see there fallen specks of red
>in the current, conveying melancholy.
I recall that day
>when our gates closed in the blooms of the pear,
we kept trimming the wick of the lamp
>and talking till deep in the night.

Wu Wen-ying achieved the height of sophistication in the art of the song lyric, sometimes pressing the Chinese poetic language to extremes never before reached. To his opponents, his lyrics were fragments that "dazzled the eyes." To weave those fragments together required deep familiarity with the traditions of the song lyric in order to catch the subtle shifts in mood and time. His was a highly ornamented poetry of carefully chosen words, strange figures, and sometimes precious images, as in the following lyric in which the bees dash themselves against the swing rope, drawn helplessly by the lingering fragrance of the now-absent beloved.

Wu Wen-ying (ca. 1200–ca. 1260), to "Wind Enters Pines" (*Feng ru song*)

I listened to wind and listened to rain
>passing the Festival of Light,
too sad to draft a eulogy
>for funerals of flowers.
The green before my hall darkens
>the path where clasped hands parted,
every inch of those willow fronds
>is an inch of tender passion.
Then shivering at spring's chill,
>the wine hits me,
and warbling through my morning dream,
>orioles sing.

Day after day in the western park I sweep
    the pavilion in the grove
and enjoy as ever the newly cleared skies.
Orange bees often go batting against
    the rope of the swing
where is printed the scent of her tiny hand
    from days gone by.
Despair that those paired duck slippers do not come,
and moss on the secret stairs grows all night long.

to "Night-Closing Flowers" *(Ye he hua)*. Going along the Crane River on my way to the capital, I moored at Feng Gate and was moved to write this

Where willows darken the river bridge
and orioles stay sunlit in terraced parks,
there my short walking cane is often lured
    by scents of spring.
Once before we moored here by night
when we voyaged deep into passion's land.
Hard rhymes were set for the lyrics,
wine-filled cups kept coming.
We trimmed waxen sparks of the candle
    as the water-clock's arrow sped on.
Those spots where together we roamed:
wave-walking footsteps on azure paths,
    lines of oars at Heng-tang.

Ten years spent in one long dream, now dreary.
And it seems that West Lake's swallows have gone
to nest in an unkempt inn in Wu.
Coming again I am moved in so many ways,
and shout, as before, for a pitcher of wine.
On the creek the rain drives hard,
flowers toss wildly on the shore.
I enjoy the last crows flying past
    in this gray magnitude.
On this upper story once shared with my friend
for whom can I now point out
plants blooming here in the setting sun?

to "Treading the Sedge" *(Ta suo xing)*

Glossy marble swathed in lace,
lips' cherry rests upon a fan,
braided bracelet still bearing

lotion scent faint.
Pomegranate hearts in empty folds,
    the red of her dancing skirt;
tarragon twigs surely must weigh
    her sad hair-coils to tangles.

Noon dreams, thousands of hills,
through the window, an arrow of light,
wrist's scented ringmark, removed just recently,
    the red threads.
She is there across the river
    inside the sound of the rain,
the evening wind in the kumi leaves
    stirs sadness and reproach.

Interlude: 趙 宋
Li Qing-zhao's Epilogue to
Records on Metal and Stone

Li Qing-zhao (1084–ca. 1151) was not only one of the finest lyricists of the Song Dynasty, she also left one of the most remarkable accounts of domestic life, the fall of the Northern Song, and the Song passion for collecting books and antiquities. The account was appended to her late husband's monumental collection of old inscriptions, *Records on Metal and Stone.* Her "Epilogue" is a work that unites both love and deep resentment; it commemorates her husband, Zhao De-fu's scholarly labors while at the same time warning her readers of the folly and danger of too great an attachment to mere things.

Literary Chinese generally omits pronouns, which are usually clear from context. In Li Qing-zhao's "Epilogue," however, this omission creates a significant problem: we cannot tell the first-person plural ("our collection") from the third-person singular ("his collection). We can see how the couple's antiquarian interests gradually passed from a shared pleasure to the husband's personal obsession, an obsession from which Li Qing-zhao felt increasingly excluded; at a certain point in the translation, it thus seems appropriate to shift from "we" to "he."

What are the preceding chapters of *Records on Metal and Stone?*—the work of the governor Zhao De-fu. In it he took inscriptions on bells, tripods, steamers, kettles, washbasins, ladles, goblets, and bowls from the Three Dynasties of high antiquity all the way to the Five Dynasties (immediately preceding our Song); here also he took the surviving traces of acts by eminent men and obscure scholars inscribed on large steles and stone disks. In all there were two thousand sections of what appeared on metal and stone. Through all these inscriptions one might be able to correct historical errors, make historical judgments, and mete out praise and blame. It contains things which, on the highest level, correspond to the Way of the Sages, and on a lower level, supplement the omissions of historians. It is, indeed, a great amount of material. Yet catastrophe fell on Wang Ya and Yuan Zai alike: what did it matter that the one hoarded books and paintings while the other merely hoarded pepper? Chang-you and Yuan-kai both had a disease—it made no difference that the disease of one was a passion for money, and of the other, a passion for the transmission of knowledge and commentary. Although their reputations differed, they were the same in being deluded.

In 1101, in the first year of the Jian-zhong Reign, I came as a bride to the Zhao household. At that time my father was a division head in the Ministry of Rites, and my father-in-law, later a Grand Councilor, was an executive in the Ministry of Personnel. My husband was then twenty-one and a

591

student in the Imperial Academy. In those days our two families, the Zhaos and the Lis, were not well-to-do and we were always frugal. On the first and fifteenth day of every month, my husband would get a short vacation from the Academy; he would "pawn some clothes" for five hundred cash and go to the market at Xiang-guo Temple, where he would buy fruit and rubbings of inscriptions. When he brought these home, we would sit facing one another, rolling them out before us, examining and munching. And we thought ourselves persons of the age of Ge-tian.[1]

When, two years later, he went to take up a post, we lived on rice and vegetables and dressed in common cloth; but he would search out the most remote spots and out-of-the-way places to fulfill his interest in the world's most ancient writings and unusual script. When his father, the Grand Councilor, was in office, various friends and relations held positions in the Imperial Libraries; there one might find many ancient poems omitted from the *Classic of Poetry,* unofficial histories, and writings never before seen, works hidden in walls and recovered from tombs. My husband would work hard at copying such things, drawing ever more pleasure from the activity, until he was unable to stop himself. Later, if he happened to see a work of painting or calligraphy by some person of ancient or modern times, or unusual vessels of the Three Dynasties of high antiquity, he would still pawn our clothes to buy them. I recall that in the Chong-ning Reign, a man came with a painting of peonies by Xu Xi and asked twenty thousand cash for it. In those days twenty thousand was a hard sum to raise, even for children of the nobility. We kept the painting with us a few days, and having thought of no plan by which we could purchase it, we returned it. For several days afterward my husband and I faced one another in deep depression.

Later we lived privately at home for ten years, gathering what we could here and there to have enough food and clothing. Afterward, my husband governed two prefectures in succession, and he used up all his salary on "lead and wooden tablets" for scholarly work. Whenever he got a book, we would collate it with other editions and make corrections together, repair it, and label it with the correct title. When he got hold of a piece of calligraphy, a painting, a goblet, or a tripod, we would go over it at our leisure, pointing out faults and flaws, setting for our nightly limit the time it took one candle to burn down. Thus our collection came to surpass all others in fineness of paper and the perfection of the characters.

I happen to have an excellent memory, and every evening after we finished eating, we would sit in the hall called "Return Home" and make tea. Pointing to the heaps of books and histories, we would guess on which line of which page in which chapter of which book a certain passage could be found. Success in guessing determined who got to drink his or her tea first. Whenever I got it right, I would raise the teacup, laughing so hard that the tea would spill in my lap, and I would get up, not having to been able to

---

[1]Ge-tian was a mythical ruler of high antiquity, when everyone lived in a state of perfect contentment.

drink any of it at all. I would have been glad to grow old in such a world. Thus, even though we were living in anxiety, hardships, and poverty, our wills were not broken.

When the book collection was complete, we set up a library in "Return Home" Hall, with huge bookcases where the books were catalogued in order. There we put the books. Whenever I wanted to read, I would ask for the key, make a note in the ledger, then take out the books. If one of them was a bit damaged or soiled, it would be my responsibility to repair the spot and copy it out in a neat hand. There was no longer the same ease and casualness as before. This attempt to make things convenient led instead to nervousness and anxiety. I couldn't bear it. I began to plan how to make do with only one meat dish in our meals and how to do away with all the finery in my dress. For my hair there were no ornaments of bright pearls or kingfisher feathers; the household had no implements for gilding or embroidery. Whenever he came upon a history or the work of a major writer, if there was nothing wrong with the printing and no errors in the edition, he would buy it on the spot to have as a second copy. His family always specialized in the *Classic of Changes* and *The Zuo Tradition,* so the collection of works in those two traditions was the most perfect and complete. Books lay ranged on tables and desks, scattered on top of one another on pillows and bedding. This was what took his fancy and what occupied his mind, what drew his eyes and what his spirit inclined to; and his joy was greater than the pleasures others had in dancing girls, dogs, or horses.

In 1126, the first year of the Jing-kang Reign, my husband was governing Ze-chuan when we heard that the Jin Tartars were moving against the capital. He was in a daze, realizing that all those full trunks and overflowing chests, which he contemplated so lovingly and mournfully, would surely soon be his possessions no longer. In the third month of spring in 1127, the first year of the Jian-yan Reign, we hurried south for the funeral of his mother. Since we could not take the overabundance of our possessions with us, we first gave up the bulky printed volumes, the albums of paintings, and the most cumbersome of the vessels. Thus we reduced the size of the collection several times, and still we had fifteen cartloads of books. When we reached Dong-hai, it took a string of boats to ferry them all across the Huai, and again across the Yangzi to Jian-kang. In our old mansion in Qing-zhou we still had more than ten rooms of books and various items locked away, and we planned to have them all brought by boat the next year. But in the twelfth month Jin forces sacked Qing-zhou, and those ten or so rooms I spoke of were all reduced to ashes.

The next autumn, the ninth month of 1128, my husband took charge of Jian-kang Prefecture but relinquished the position in the spring of the following year. Again we put everything in boats and went up to Wu-hu and Gu-shu, intending to take up lodging on the river Gan. That summer in the fifth month we reached Chi-yang. At that point an imperial decree arrived, ordering my husband to take charge of Hu-zhou and to proceed to an audience with the Emperor before he took up the office. Therefore he had the household stop at Chi-yang, from which he went off alone to answer the summons.

On August 13, he set off to carry out his duty. He had the boats pulled up onto the shore, and he sat there on the bank, in summer clothes with his headband high on his forehead, his spirit like a tiger's, his eyes gleaming as though they would shoot into a person, while he gazed toward the boats and took his leave. I was terribly upset. I shouted to him, "If I hear the city is in danger, what should I do?" He answered from afar, hands on his hips: "Follow the crowd. If you can't do otherwise, abandon the household goods first, then the clothes, then the books and scrolls, then the old bronzes—but carry the sacrificial vessels for the ancestral temple yourself. Live or die with them; don't give *them* up!" With this he galloped off on his horse.

As he was hurrying on his journey, he suffered sunstroke from the intense heat, and by the time he reached imperial headquarters, he had contracted a malarial fever. At the end of September, I received a letter that he was sick in bed. I was very alarmed, considering my husband's excitable nature and how nothing had been able to prevent the illness from deteriorating into fever; his temperature might rise even higher, and in that case he would have to take chilled medicines; then the sickness would really be something to worry about. Thereupon I set out by boat and traveled three hundred leagues in one day and one night. At the point when I arrived he was taking large doses of *chai-hu* and yellow *qin;* he had a recurring fever with dysentery, and the illness appeared mortal. I was weeping and in such a desperate state I could not bring myself to ask him what was to be done after his death. On October 18 he could no longer get up; he took a brush and wrote a poem. When he finished it, he passed away, with no thought at all for the future provision of his family.

After the funeral was over, I had nowhere to go. His Majesty had already sent the palace ladies elsewhere, and I heard that future crossings of the Yangzi were to be prohibited. At the time I still had twenty thousand *juan* of books, two thousand copies of inscriptions on metal and stone with colophons, table services and mats enough to entertain a hundred guests, along with other possessions equaling those already mentioned.[2] I also became very sick, to the point where my only vital sign was a rasping breath. The situation was getting more serious by the day. I thought of my husband's brother-in-law, an executive in the Ministry of War on garrison duty in Hong-zhou, and I dispatched two former employees of my husband to go ahead to my brother-in-law, taking the baggage. In February that winter, the Jin invaders sacked Hong-zhou and all was lost. Those books which, as I said, it took a string of boats to ferry across the Yangzi were scattered into clouds of smoke. What remained were a few light scrolls and calligraphy pieces; manuscript copies of the collections of Li Bo, Du Fu, Han Yu, and Liu Zong-yuan; a copy of *Current Tales and Recent Bon-mots;* a copy of

---

[2]A *juan,* originally a "scroll," came to be something like a chapter. The size of a library was measured not in volumes but in *juan.*

Discourses on Salt and Iron; a few dozen rubbings of stone inscriptions from the Han and Tang; ten or so ancient tripods and cauldrons; and a few boxes of Southern Tang manuscript editions—all of which I happened to have had removed to my chambers to pass the time during my illness, now a solitary pile of leftovers.

Since I could no longer go upriver, and since the movements of the invaders were unpredictable, I was going to stay with my younger brother Li Hang, a reviser of edicts. By the time I reached Tai-zhou, the governor of the place had already fled. Proceeding on to Shan through Mu-zhou, we left the clothing and linen behind. Hurrying to Yellow Cliff, we hired a boat to take us toward the sea, following the fleeing court. The court halted a while in Zhang-an, then we followed the imperial barge on the sea route to Wen-zhou and Yue-zhou. In February, during the fourth year of the Jian-yan Reign, early in 1131, all the officials of the government were released from their posts. We went to Qu-zhou, and then that May, now the first year of the Shao-xing Reign, we returned to Yue-zhou, and in 1132 back again to Hang-zhou.

When my husband had been gravely ill, a certain academician, Zhang Fei-qing, had visited him with a jade pot—actually it wasn't really jade but alabaster. I have no idea who started the story, but there was a false rumor that they had been discussing presenting it to the Jin as a tribute gift. I also learned that someone had made formal charges in the matter. I was terrified and dared say nothing, but I took all the bronze vessels and such things in the household and was ready to turn them over to the imperial court. But by the time I reached Yue-zhou, the court had already gone on to Si-ming. I didn't dare keep these things in the household any longer, so I sent them along with the manuscript books to Shan. Later when the imperial army was rounding up defeated enemy troops, I heard that these had all been taken into the household of General Li. That "solitary pile of leftovers," of which I spoke, had now been reduced by about fifty or sixty percent. All that remained were six or so baskets of books, paintings, ink and inkstones that I hadn't been able to part with. I always kept these under my bed and opened them only with my own hands.

At Kuai-ji, I chose lodging in a cottage belonging to a local named Zhong. Suddenly one night someone made off with five of the baskets through a hole in the wall. I was terribly upset and offered a substantial reward to get them back. Two days later, Zhong Fu-hao next door produced eighteen of the scrolls and asked for a reward. By that I knew that the thief was not far away. I tried every means I could, but I still couldn't get hold of the rest. I have now learned that they were all purchased by the Circuit Fiscal Supervisor Wu Ye. Now seventy or eighty percent of that "solitary pile of leftovers" is gone. I still have a few volumes from three or four sets, none complete, and some very ordinary pieces of calligraphy, yet I treasure them as if I were protecting my own head—foolish person that I am!

Nowadays when I chance to look over these books, it's like meeting old friends. And I recall when my husband was in the hall called "Calm Governance" in Lai-zhou: he had first finished binding the volumes, making title slips of rue leaves to keep out insects and tie ribbons of blue silk, binding ten *juan* into one volume. Every day in the evening when the office clerks had gone home, he would do editorial collations on two *juan* and write a colophon for one inscription. Of those two thousand inscriptions, colophons were written on five hundred and two. It is so sad—today the ink of his writing seems still fresh, but the trees on his grave have grown to an armspan in girth.

Long ago when the city of Jiang-ling fell, Xiao Yi, Emperor Yuan of the Liang, did not regret the fall of his kingdom, yet destroyed his books and paintings [unwilling to see them fall into the hands of his conquerors]. When his capital at Jiang-du was sacked, Yang Guang, Emperor Yang of the Sui, wasn't concerned with his own death, only with recovering his books [demonstrated when his spirit overturned the boat in which they were being transported so that he could have his library in the land of the dead]. It must be that the passions of human nature cannot be forgotten, even standing between life and death. Or perhaps it is Heaven's will that beings as insignificant as ourselves are not fit to enjoy such superb creatures.[3] Or perhaps the dead too have consciousness, and they still treasure such things and give them their devoted attention, unwilling to leave them in the world of the living. How hard they are to obtain and how easy to lose!

From the time I was eighteen [two years younger than Lu Ji was supposed to have been when he wrote "The Poetic Exposition on Literature"] until now at the age of fifty-two [two years after the age at which Chu Bo-you realized the error of his earlier life]—a span of more than thirty years— how much calamity, how much gain and loss have I witnessed! When there is possession, there must be loss of possession; when there is a gathering together, there must be a scattering—this is the constant principle in things. Someone loses a bow; another person finds a bow; what's so special in that? The reason why I have recorded this story from beginning to end in such detail is to let it serve as a warning for scholars and collectors in later generations.

—Written this second year of the Shao-xing Reign (1132), the first of October.

Li Qing-zhao

---

[3]"Superb creatures," *you-wu,* here figuratively applied to books and antiques, usually refers to dangerously beautiful women, who inspire destructive passion in those attracted to them.

Classical Prose 趙宋

In the modern West, the category of "literature" tends be confined to poetry, drama, and narrative fiction. Other prose forms, such as essays and speeches, may be considered marginally "literary," but by and large non-fictional prose has come to be excluded from the domain of literature. In classical Chinese literature, as in Greek, Latin, and earlier European literatures, non-fictional prose was considered an essential part of the domain of literature; fictional narrative (in verse or prose) and drama, however, were not considered fully legitimate literary forms until very late in the tradition.

Prose was one of the primary means by which a member of the educated elite participated in political and social life. The examination essay was essential to becoming an accredited member of the imperial civil service (and all sense of noble duty aside, this involved very attractive privileges, e.g., exemption from military service and taxes). Letters, "policy discussions" *(yi)*, and memorials to the throne were the only means by which those outside the decision-making inner circle of government could comment on and participate in the formulation of public policy. In social life, one would be called upon to produce "accounts" *(ji)* describing places or buildings, prefaces, inscriptions, and commemorative funerary forms, as well as letters. The writing of prose was not merely functional, however: a great prose writer might hope to be remembered for his public writing. The standard histories had special sections devoted to men of letters, usually prose writers, and in other biographies the histories would often incorporate complete essays, memorials, letters, and other forms.

Classical Chinese prose must be approached through its genres. Each genre served a distinct function and each had its own history. The most public and political genre (apart from drafting government decrees) was the memorial to the throne, by which a political opinion could be formally presented to the emperor and his inner circle of advisers.

Memorial

Although memorials to the throne (which have survived in the tens of thousands) are often important documents for the study of history, memorials that have become famous in the classical prose tradition tend to be those that reflect on the character of the writer. Han Yu's "Memorial Discussing the Buddha's Bone" has perhaps some historical significance as representing the resentment of certain Confucian intellectuals against the influence of Buddhism (though we may wonder whether this social phenomenon makes Han Yu's famous memorial historically significant or whether

Han Yu's famous memorial makes the social phenomenon worthy of attention). This memorial was, however, a singularly ineffective political act, resulting only in Han Yu's banishment (although brief suppressions of Buddhism later in the ninth century followed in part from advisers who took the same line as Han). What made the memorial one of the most famous examples of Han Yu's prose were the same qualities that made it politically ineffective: it is belligerently uncompromising and, as a memorial to the throne, disrespectful to the edge of personally insulting the emperor. Not only is the writing too blunt, the scarcely concealed message in Han Yu's litany of imperial lifespans is that an emperor who reveres Buddha will not live long.

Longevity was ever a touchy point in the imperial presence, and promises of longevity had been among the chief theological commodities of the Daoists, with competition from the Buddhists. Han Yu here begins as a Confucian purveyor of moderate life extension: to live out a full span of years His Majesty need only be like the Sage-Kings, governing over an empire no longer infested by Buddhists.

Han Yu (768–824), Memorial Discussing the Buddha's Bone

One of Your Majesty's officers speaks.

I am of the opinion that Buddhism is nothing more than a religion of the outlying tribes. Since the Eastern Han it has made inroads into the heartland, but such a thing never existed in high antiquity. In days of yore the Yellow Emperor sat on the throne for a hundred years and the years of his life reached one hundred and ten. Shao-hao sat on the throne for eighty years and the years of his life reached a hundred. Zhuan-xu sat on the throne for seventy-nine years and the years of his life reached ninety-eight. Emperor Gu sat on the throne for seventy years and the years of his life reached one hundred and five. Emperor Yao sat on the throne for ninety-eight years and the years of his life reached one hundred and eighteen. The emperors Shun and Yu both lived to be a hundred. And in those days the world enjoyed perfect peace; the common people were secure in their happiness and lived to ripe old age. Yet at this time there was no Buddhism in the heartland.

Afterward Tang of the Yin also lived to a hundred years. Of Tang's descendants, Tai-mou sat on the throne seventy-five years, and Wu-ding sat on the throne fifty-nine years. The histories do not say to what ages they lived; but taking into account recorded spans of years, it seems probable that both lived no less than a hundred years. King Wen of the Zhou lived to ninety-seven; King Wu, to ninety-three; King Mu sat on the throne a hundred years. And at this time too the Buddhist religion had not yet made inroads into the heartland—so they did not achieve such spans because they served the Buddha.

The Buddhist religion appeared only in the reign of Emperor Ming of the Han, and Emperor Ming sat on the throne for only eighteen years. After him, turmoil and destruction were continuous, and fate gave no long reigns. From the Song, Qi, Liang, Chen, and Toba Wei on, devotion to the Buddha became increasingly intense; and reign spans were exceedingly short. There was, of course, the case of Emperor Wu of the Liang, who sat on the throne for forty-eight years. Three times at different periods in his life he offered up his own body as a gift to the Buddha: no red meat was used in the sacrifices in the ancestral temple, and during the day he ate only one meal, which was restricted to vegetables and fruit. But afterwards he was beset by the rebel Hou Jing. He starved to death in his palace compound of Jin-ling, and his dynasty also subsequently perished. He sought good fortune through devotion to the Buddha, but reaped only his own downfall. Consideration of these cases leads us to understand that the Buddha does not merit devotion.

When Gao-zu, the Tang founder, first took the sacred authority of rule from the Sui, proposals were made to get rid of it. But court officials in those times lacked far-seeing judgment. They were incapable of any deep understanding of the Way of the early kings, or of what is fitting in both ancient and modern times, or of how to expound the matter fully for His Majesty's enlightened grasp and thereby to preserve us from this scourge. The issue was subsequently set aside, which is something I have always deplored.

In the past several millennia and centuries, there has never been the like of Your Wise and August Imperial Majesty, holy in sageliness, spirited in war. When you first took the throne, Your Majesty did not permit people to take vows to become monks, nuns, or Daoist priests; you further did not permit the foundation of new monasteries and Daoist temples. I had always thought that the intention of the founder Gao-zu would surely be carried out at last by Your Majesty's hand. Even though this has not yet been accomplished, how can you give them free rein and make them prosper even more than before!

I recently heard that Your Majesty has commanded a group of monks to welcome the Buddha's bone in Feng-xiang; then, as you watch from an upper chamber, it will be carried with ceremony into the palace precincts. You have also ordered that all the temples take turns welcoming it and paying it reverence. Although I am very foolish, I suspect that Your Majesty has not, in fact, been actually so deluded by the Buddha as to carry out such august devotions in search of blessings and good fortune; rather, at a time when the harvest is abundant and the people are happy, I suspect that you are simply accommodating the hearts of the people by putting on a display of illusory marvels and the stuff of a stage show for the inhabitants of the capital. How could such a sagely and enlightened ruler as yourself bring himself to have faith in this sort of thing?

Nevertheless, the common people are foolish and ignorant, easy to lead into error and hard to enlighten. If Your Majesty behaves like this, they will assume that you serve the Buddha from genuine feeling. All will say, "The Son of Heaven is a great Sage, yet still he gives Buddha his wholehearted respect and faith. What are we common folk that we should begrudge even our lives?" They will set their heads on fire and burn their fingers. In tens and hundreds they will undo their clothes and distribute coins; and from dawn to dusk they will try harder and harder to outdo one another, worrying only that they are not acting swiftly enough. We will see old and young in a desperate scramble, abandoning their places of business. If one does not immediately strengthen the prohibitions against this, they will pass from one temple to another, cutting off arms and slicing off flesh as devotional offerings. This is no trifling matter, for they will be the ruin of our good customs, and when the word gets out, we will be laughed at by all the world around.

The Buddha was originally a tribesman from outlying regions. His language is incomprehensible to those who inhabit the heartland, and his clothes were of a strange fashion. He did not speak the exemplary words of the early kings, and he did not wear the exemplary garb of the early kings. He did not understand the sense of right that exists between a ruler and his officers, nor the feelings between father and son. If he were still alive today and, on the orders of his own kingdom, were to come to an audience with Your Majesty in the capital, Your Majesty would tolerantly receive him, but with nothing more than a single meeting in Xuan-zheng Palace, the single feast to show politeness to a guest, and a single present of clothing. Then he would be escorted to the border under guard in order to keep him from leading the people astray.

But now he has been dead for a very long time. Is it fitting that you order his dried and crumbling bone, this disgusting and baleful relic, to be brought into the imperial palace? Confucius said, "Respect gods and spirits, but keep far away from them." In ancient times when a member of the great nobility made a visit to a state to offer condolences, he would command a shaman to precede him with a peach branch and a broom of reeds to ward off malignant influences. Only under these conditions would he offer his condolences. Now for no good reason you are receiving this disgusting and decaying object, and you will personally inspect it—but without a shaman preceding you and without using the peach branch and reed broom. Not one of your many officials has told you how wrong this is, nor have your censors brought up the error of it. Of this I am truly ashamed.

I beg you to hand this bone over to the charge of someone who will throw it into fire or water and finish it forever, thus putting an end to the confusions of the world and stopping this delusion in generations to come. This will result in having all the people of the world understand that what a great Sage does infinitely surpasses the ordinary. Wouldn't it be splendid! Wouldn't it feel good!

If there is any divine power in the Buddha that can bring down curses, whatever calamity should befall, let it fall on me. Heaven will observe me from above, and I will feel no ill will or regret. Deeply stirred and filled with the utmost loyalty, I respectfully offer this memorial for Your Majesty's ears.

Your Majesty's officer trembles with awe.

Although the memorial here is a serious one and has been treated all too seriously by the tradition, it is memorable because of its humor. Such humor is closely allied to Han Yu's revulsion at pollution—pollution from contact with death and with things foreign. Han Yu has taken a relic that usually commanded great devotion and has placed it in a new context, deflating its religious aura and making the devotion showed to the relic ludicrous: "Ugh, the crumbling bone of a long-dead barbarian." One imagines a courtyard full of monks all chanting and the emperor Xian-zong standing on a balcony watching piously. In the center is a raised reliquary. Into this scene walks Han Yu in his severe Confucian garb. He steps through the chanting crowd, opens the reliquary, and, with a look of evident disgust, gingerly picks up the bone in two fingers and carries it to the nearby river, where he tosses it away.

Beneath the Confucian values here lies the *Zhuang-zi,* with its technique of radically shifting perspective in order to show the relativity of value. The tacit claim made by Han Yu in using such a technique is that it will reveal the inherent quality of things as opposed to the false honor accorded them by custom. In the *Zhuang-zi,* Confucian ceremony is often the butt of the act of devaluation; in Han Yu, the butt is Buddhist relic-worship.

Essay

The essay *(lun* or *shuo)* was a genre much like its Western counterpart, ranging from formal exposition to quirkier and more personal explanations of a question. In the following piece, Liu Zong-yuan gives an account of a thesis advanced by Han Yu and twists it with his own conclusion. Han's proposition is so unlike the positions he takes elsewhere that we do not know whether to read this as tongue-in-cheek, as a dark mood, or as a tour de force done for the sheer pleasure of working out a shocking hypothesis.

Liu Zong-yuan (773–819), A Theory of Heaven

Han Yu addressed Master Liu, "Do you know my theory about Heaven? Well, I will tell you my theory. These days whenever someone suffers from the torment of disease or is worn down by humiliation or endures hunger and cold, he looks up and cries out to Heaven: 'Those who harm folk flourish; those who help folk perish!' Or they look up and cry out to Heaven: 'Why have you caused things to go so utterly wrong?' No one who behaves like this truly understands Heaven.

"When a piece of fruit or a melon has become too rotten to eat, insects grow in it. When the vitality of a man's blood fails and becomes sluggish, abscesses, swelling pustules, and hemorrhoids form; insects grow in these too. When wood rots, there are grubs within; when plants putrefy, fireflies come forth from them. These are obviously things that appear only after decay sets in. When something decays, insects are born out of it; and when the Primordial Force or Yin and Yang decayed, out of that human beings were born.

"When insects grow in that thing, it decays even further. Chewing at it, boring holes in it, the harm that the insects inflict on the thing increases greatly. If someone were able to get rid of them, such a person would have done a good deed on behalf of the thing; but whoever lets them multiply and gives comfort to them is the enemy of the thing. The incremental decay that human beings cause to the Primordial Force and to Yin and Yang has also increased greatly. Men plow meadows and fields; they cut down the mountain forests; they dig down to underground springs to find wells that provide them with drink; they excavate graves in which to put their dead. Moreover, they dig latrines; they pound hard earthen walls to surround their homes and their cities; they raise platforms of pounded earth on which to build pavilions and lodges for their excursions; they dig channels for rivers and canals, irrigation ditches, and ponds; they kindle wood for fires; they alter metals by smelting them; they mold pottery and grind and polish stone. Everything in the world looks the worse for wear and nothing can follow its own nature—human beings are responsible for this. Seething in their fury, constantly battering, they assault, destroy, ruin, and wreck; nor have they ever desisted. Is not the harm they inflict on the Primordial Force and upon Yin and Yang even worse than what insects do?

"In my opinion if one were able to cut away at humanity and make them dwindle over the days and years, then the harm inflicted on the Primordial Force and Yin and Yang would steadily diminish. Whoever could accomplish this would have done a good deed for Heaven and Earth. But whoever lets them multiply and gives comfort to them is the enemy of Heaven and Earth. These days no one understands Heaven, so they cry out to it in reproach. In my opinion, when Heaven hears their cries of reproach, then those who have done it a good deed will inevitably receive a rich reward; but those who have inflicted harm on it will inevitable receive grave punishment. What do you think of what I have said?"

Master Liu then said, "Was there something that got you truly worked up that you propose this? It is well argued indeed and beautifully put. But let me carry this theory to its conclusion. Human beings refer to what is dark, mysterious, and above us as Heaven; they refer to what is brown and beneath us as Earth. They refer to that vast, undifferentiated murkiness in between as the Primordial Force; and they refer to the cold and heat as Yin and Yang. However large these are, they are no different from fruits and melons, abscesses and pustules, or plants and trees.

"Let us suppose there were someone or something able to get rid of what bores holes in them—would there be any reward for such a creature? Or one that let them multiply and gave them comfort—would there be any anger against such? Heaven and Earth are a large fruit. The Primordial Force is a large pustule. Yin and Yang are a large tree. How could such things reward a good deed or punish harms inflicted? Those who do such good deeds, do so on their own; those who inflict harm, inflict it on their own. To expect either reward or punishment is great folly. Those who cry out in reproach, expecting Heaven will feel sorry for them and be kind to them, show even greater folly. As for you, you trust in your own sense of kindness and right and move freely within that, during your life and on until your death. Why attribute your preservation or destruction, your gains and your losses, to a piece of fruit, a pustule, or a tree?"

Letters

The epistolary tradition is a very old one in China. *The Zuo Tradition* contains what purport to be diplomatic letters from the period of the "Springs and Autumns of Lu," and by Western Han we have personal letters whose attribution we can accept with confidence. Like the essay, the letter is an open genre whose topic is not circumscribed by occasion. Furthermore, the level of formality can vary greatly according to the circumstances to which the letter speaks and the social relation between writer and addressee. What one does not find in the early period is the engagement in the details of everyday life that make Latin letters by Cicero and Pliny the Younger so attractive. The following letter by Bo Ju-yi is an early example of the Chinese informal letter.

Bo Ju-yi (772–846), Letter to Yuan Zhen (Yuan Wei-zhi)

The night of June 10. Bo Ju-yi writes:

Wei-zhi, Wei-zhi, it's been three years since I have seen your face and almost two years now since I have received a letter from you. How long does life last that we can be separated so distantly as this? This is something we feel all the more strongly when two hearts are bonded together, yet in bodies set far apart, as if one were in Turkistan and the other in Yue. Whatever we do, we can neither be together nor can we forget one other. We are both joined together and kept apart, until our hair turns white. How can this be, Wei-zhi? It is our destiny, and nothing can be done about it!

When I first reached Xun-yang, Xiong Wan-deng came and brought me a note that you had written the preceding year when you were gravely ill. In the first part you told me about the symptoms of your illness, then you gave an account of what was in your mind while you were sick, and finally you talked about this friendship that we have shared over a lifetime. And you wrote then, "At this moment of crisis I have no time for anything else except gathering together a few packets of my writings to be sealed with the note: 'To be sent to Bo Ju-yi at some future time, hoping that they will serve in place of a letter.' " I was very deeply moved by the feeling you showed for me in this. At the same time I cast eyes on the poem that you sent when you heard of my demotion.

No flame in the dying lamp,
    rays blurred and quivering;
this is the evening I heard that you
    were exiled to Nine Rivers.
In sickness and drawing close to death,
    I sat straight up in alarm—

in the dark the wind was blowing rain
into my cold window.

Even a stranger could scarcely bear to read lines like these—imagine how much they touched my own heart! Even now every time I recite them, it still makes me throb. But let me leave these matters aside and give you a rough account of what has been on my mind of late.

It has already been three years since I came to Nine Rivers. My body is strong, and my mind is very much at ease. Both I and the members of my household have been fortunate not to have any illnesses. Last summer my elder brother arrived from Xu-zhou, bringing with him six or seven young boys and girls of the extended family who had lost their parents. Everyone about whom I had previously been worried was here with me, and we can share good times and bad, feast and famine—and this is the first reason I feel such peace of mind.

The weather tends to be cool here in Jiang-zhou, and the region has little unhealthy miasma. Although there are poisonous snakes, mosquitoes, and gnats, they are rather uncommon. The fish from the river Pen are quite plump, and the river wines here are excellent; the other things eaten here are much the same as we have in the North. Even though the number of mouths to feed in the household is far from few and a vice-prefect's salary is not great, we are able to provide for ourselves by frugal management of what I bring in, so that we can avoid having to ask others for help in food and clothing. This is the second reason I feel such peace of mind.

Last autumn I visited Mount Lu for the first time. When I reached the foot of Incense Burner Peak in between Westgrove and Eastgrove Temples, I saw cloudy streams and springs flowing over the rocks—it was the most marvelous sight in the whole world. I was so fond of it I couldn't let it go, so I built a thatched cottage there. In front of the cottage there are a dozen or so tall pines and more than a thousand long stalks of bamboo. Green hanging moss serves as the fence, and white stones serve as a bridge; flowing waters wind in a circle down below the building, and a waterfall comes down beside the eaves. Red pomegranates and white lotuses grow ranged along the ponds and pavements. This is just the general picture; I can't give a full account. Every time I go there by myself, I end up spending ten days. Everything I most enjoy in life is right there. Not only do I "forget to return," I could well stay there throughout my old age. And this is the third reason I feel such peace of mind.

When I reckon up how long it has been since you received a letter from me, I'm sure you must be expecting one with increasing anxiety. I have set down these three reasons for my peace of mind on purpose, to let you know how things are and forestall any worry you may feel. As for other matters, I will describe them item by item as follows.

Wei-zhi, on the night I am writing this letter I am right here in my thatched cottage, by my window in the mountains, letting my pen run freely, scribbling randomly as my thoughts carry me; and now that I am about to seal it up, I find that, unbeknownst to me, it is almost dawn. When I lift my head I see only one or two mountain monks, sitting or sleeping. And I also hear the gibbons wailing on the mountain and the birds chirping sadly in the valley. The friends of my life are thousands of miles away. At this moment thoughts on the foul world suddenly creep upon me; and drawn on by old habits, I write these couplets:

> I recall sealing a letter to you
>> on a night long ago,
> behind Golden Phoenix Palace
>> as the sky was growing bright.

> When I seal this letter to you tonight
>> where do I find myself?—
> inside a lodge upon Mount Lu
>> in front of a candle at dawn.

> Bird in a cage, monkey behind bars—
>> but neither are yet dead;
> meeting again in this mortal world
>> will happen in what year?

Wei-zhi! Can you understand how I feel this night?

Prefaces

Prefaces come in a great variety of forms, from the scholarly to the lyrical and descriptive. The more lyrical and descriptive prefaces tend to be those for banquet collections in which a group of people compose poems for a party and one of the number is delegated to write the preface. The following preface is an early example of such, composed in A.D. 400 by an anonymous member of the Buddhist circle around the famous monk Hui-yuan, on an excursion to Stonegate Mountain in the Lu Mountain Range. Notes on geography, a stylized appreciative description of the landscape, and a meditation on the significance of the experience come together in the high style of Southern Dynasties prose.

Anonymous (member of Hui-yuan's circle), A Preface for the Poems Written on an Excursion to Stonegate

Stonegate lies somewhat over ten leagues south of the temple chapel and is also known as Screen Mountain. Its base connects with the main peak of Lu Mountain, but its form is disjoined from all the other hills. It opens the way for the confluence of those three streams, which together begin their flow upon it. Sheer crags shine in dark mystery above, their noteworthy shape received from What is Naturally So. It was from this shape that the mountain got its name. Although this is but one corner of the Lu Mountain Range, it is truly the most remarkable vista in the region. This judgment is always handed down as received wisdom, but many are those who have never laid eyes on the place. Those who have been there are rare, because of its cascading rapids and perilous pinnacles where the tracks of men and beasts disappear, and because of paths turning through the twisting hills where the road is full of obstructions and hard going.

In April of the fourth year of the Long-an Reign (400), our abbot Hui-yuan made an excursion there, leaning on his meditation staff, in order to compose verses on these mountains and waters. More than thirty companions who shared the same inclination joined him, brushing off their robes and setting off in the morning, their discontent at not having previously gone there augmenting their elation. Though the forested ravines were remote and out of the way, still we opened a path and eagerly pushed forward; though we mounted precarious places and found our footing over rocks, we were content because of the delight we were experiencing. When we reached Stonegate, we pulled our way along by taking hold of trees and clinging to vines, crossing the full stretch of the perilous slope. Dangling arms like apes, we pulled one another along until at last we attained the summit.

Thereupon, as we rested on those crags, we embraced the splendid scenery and surveyed in detail what lay below. Then did we realize that of all the beauties of Lu Mountain's seven peaks, the most wondrous were all contained in this place. Twin turrets towered before us, and behind us craggy cliffs stretched off in tiers, each setting off the others. Ridges of hills encircled us as a screen, with prominent cliffs arranged on all sides to serve as our frontier domains. In the middle were formations that resembled stone platforms and stone pools and lodges within a palace compound. Such shapes, each according to its kind, touched us with delight. Clear streams flowed apart, then poured together in a confluence, with pellucid deeps that cast mirroring reflections purer than those of Pool-of-Heaven. Patterned stones gave off bright colors, beaming like relaxed faces. Red-willows, pines, and aromatic plants lit up our eyes with their leafy richness. This is the full measure of its divine beauty.

That day the feelings of all present sped with pleasure, and we viewed all that lay around us without tiring. Not long after we had been letting our gaze drift, the atmosphere began a series of frequent changes. Where fog and wisps of cloud accumulated, the shapes of the thousands of images were hidden; where sunbeams on the water cast back light, reflections of all the mountains hung upside down. And in the manner of such moments of revelation and concealment, there seemed some divine spirit that could not be fathomed. When it was as if this spirit would mount up to us, the soaring birds beat their wings and the shrill cries of the gibbons resounded. The clouds turned their coaches round to return home, and one could imagine therein the forms of the Undying, the feathered folk; in the harmonious mingling of melancholy sounds there seemed lodged the notes of their mysterious melodies. Though only in the vaguest way could we still hear them, our spirits were elated by this; though finding delight in unanticipated pleasures, the good cheer this brought us lasted throughout the day. There was truly a unique flavor to such serene contentment, yet it is not easy to put into words, something to think back upon after we had withdrawn from the place.

Here among the slopes and valleys there was nothing to govern our grasp of these phenomena; the way in which our feelings gave rise to elation should not have occurred, affecting a person as profoundly as this. It must have been that our capacity for unbiased perception lent clarity to their appearances, and that our calm indifference and distance guaranteed the genuineness of such feelings. We talked about this over and over again, yet it still remained something obscure that we could not fully understand. Soon afterward the sun announced the impending evening, and this scene we had kept before us was gone. At this point we were enlightened to the mysterious reflections of the recluse and achieved understanding of the larger conditions that are constant within phenomena. The appeal was one of spirit, and not merely a landscape of mountains and waters.

Thereupon we paused on the lofty summit and let our gaze roam all around. Nine Rivers was like a sash, and the mountains and hills became but bumps. Investigating the question from this perspective, as the shapes of things may be huge or tiny, so human wisdom too should be the same. Then we heaved great sighs, that even though the universe lasts on into remote spans, past and present fit together as one. Vulture Peak [in India, where the Buddha Sakyamuni received a sutra] lies far from sight; and paths to it, grown over with vegetation, make it more inaccessible with each passing day. Had there not been the wise Sakyamuni, who would have preserved any trace of its quality? In consequence of these deep places here we have become enlightened regarding something far away; and, strongly moved, such thoughts continue within us. We were each individually joyful at the shared pleasures of this single encounter, and we were moved that such a fine moment will be unlikely to recur. Feelings came forth from within, whereupon we all wrote poems about it.

During the Tang, when someone was setting out on a journey and all his friends gathered for a formal leavetaking, they would often compile the poems composed on the occasion in a small collection, for which one member of the group would write the preface. From this practice developed the genre of the "presentation preface" or "parting preface," which came to be written to stand alone without poems. In the following presentation preface, Han Yu puts the defense of the private life into the mouth of his friend Li Yuan, though the defense begins as a praise of public success.

Han Yu, A Preface on Sending Li Yuan Back to Winding Valley

On the south slopes of the Tai-hang Range is found Winding Valley. The springs are sweet in Winding Valley and the soil is rich, so that trees and plants there grow in leafy abundance. Few men dwell there. Some say, "The valley is called 'Winding' because it circles around between two mountains." Others say, "This valley is set in a remote place, and its shape is shut off from the outside; it is a place where recluses go 'Wending' their way." My friend Li Yuan dwells there.

Yuan has said, "I understand quite well what people call 'a man of substance.' He is of use to others and extends his generosity to them; in his own time his name is prominent. He sits in the imperial councils of state; he moves ahead through the official ranks or down; he helps the Son of Heaven issue commands. When he is outside the central government, he raises the battle flag, lines up his men with their bows and arrows; he is the warrior who shouts as he takes the lead, and those who follow him fill the road. Each of the men for whom he provides attends to what he should, and they hurry back and forth on both sides of the road. When he is pleased, he gives rewards; when he is angered, he metes out punishments. When a group of talented men crowd before him, he draws examples from past and present and commends abundance of virtue; he listens without becoming irritated. His brows arch finely and his cheeks are plump; he has a pleasing voice and a relaxed body; he is splendid on the outside and astute within. Women with their light gowns billowing, hiding behind long sleeves, faces powdered white and brows painted blue-black, live peacefully in rows of chambers, envious of favor shown to others, confidently trusting to their own charms. They compete in sensuality and win his affection. These are the things that happen when a man of substance meets the appreciative understanding of the Son of Heaven, and exerts his energy in his own times.

"It is not that I despise these things and run away from them; rather fate is involved. You can't get such things just by chance. I live in the humblest way and remain in the wilderness; I climb up to the heights and gaze into the distance or spend the whole day through sitting under a leafy tree; I bathe in clear springs and keep myself clean. In the mountains I pick wild plants that are delicious to the palate; I fish in the streams for a catch that is fresh to eat. There are no set times to restrict my daily doings—only what I am easy with. It is better to avoid the assault that must follow than to enjoy the commendation that comes before. It is better not to have one's heart troubled than to enjoy bodily pleasures. I am not bound to follow regulations in regard to carriage and uniform; the headsman's ax will not fall on me; order and turmoil are unknown; dismissals and promotions are unheard of. My life here is what a man of substance does when he does *not* meet with his proper time, and this is what I do. Others serve at the gates of great lords; they go scurrying along the paths of power; their feet are about to carry them forward, but they falter in uncertainty; their mouths are about to speak, but they swallow their words; they stay amid filth and foulness and feel no shame; they meet with punishments and are executed; and if they are lucky beyond all measure, they can finally quit by dying of old age. How would you make the decision whether this is a worthy course or one unbefitting?"

I, Han Yu of Chang-li, heard what he said and found it resolute. I gave him some wine and made a song for him that went:

In Winding Valley
you have your mansion.
The soil of Winding Valley
can serve for planting.
The streams of Winding Valley,
can bathe a man and be followed.
The fastness of Winding Valley
means none strive for your place.
It is deep and sequestered,
providing vast space.
It twists and turns,
when you seem to go, you return.
Ah, for the joys of wending about,
joys that have no end.
Tigers and leopards stay far from your steps,
dragons hide themselves away.
Gods and goblins protect you,
and ward away all baleful things.
Drink there and eat, live long and be hale,
here is enough, what more should you hope for?
Grease my carriage, feed my horse,
I will follow you in wending around,
end my days roaming free.

Ou-yang Xiu (1007–1072), Preface on Sending Xu Wu-tang Off on His Way Home South

The living things of the world, its birds and beasts and plants and trees, as well as the masses of men may differ in the way they live; but in their dying all are the same. All come at last to putrefaction, dissolution, and oblivion. Yet among the masses of men there are sages and men of worthiness. It is certainly true that they too live and die among the others, yet they have a single difference that sets them apart from birds and beasts and plants and trees and the masses of men: though they die, they do not perish, and the longer the span of time that passes, the more perfectly they endure. What makes them sages or men of worth is something cultivated in their persons, put into practice in their actions, or revealed in their words. It is by these three things that they are able to endure and not perish.

There is nothing that cannot be attained when cultivating it in one's person. Putting it into practice in actions, however, sometimes succeeds and sometimes does not. And when it comes to revealing it in words, there is an additional question of skill. It is all right to put it into practice in actions but not to reveal it in words. The men who have come down to us in the *Classic of Poetry*, the *Classic of Documents*, and the *Historical Records* were certainly not all skilled at words.

It is also all right to cultivate it in one's person, yet not put it into practice in actions or reveal it in words. Among the disciples of Confucius there were indeed some skilled in political action and there were some skilled in words. But there was also someone like Yan Hui, who stayed in a narrow alley, pillowed his head on his elbow, and went to bed hungry. When he was in a crowd, he would spend the entire day in silence, as if he were a simpleton. Yet all the disciples at that time held him in the highest honor and felt that they could never hope to be his equal. Even hundreds and thousands of years after him, there has never been anyone who could equal him. The fact that he has endured and not perished obviously did not depend on his putting it into practice in his actions, much less in his words.

I have read the "Bibliographical Treatise" of Ban Gu and the catalogue of the Tang Imperial Library, and I have seen the entries listed there. From the times since the three ancient dynasties and Qin and Han, those who have written extensively have had more than a hundred works credited to their name, and those who had written less still have had thirty or forty. The number of such men is beyond reckoning. But through scattering, destruction, and loss, less than one or two out of a hundred there listed survive. I have felt saddened by such men—the essays they wrote were beautiful and they were skilled in the handling of words; but at last they were no different from the blossoms of plants and trees being whirled away by the wind, no different from the fine sounds of birds and beasts passing the ear. The great efforts that they expended in the employment of mind and energy—how does that differ from the scrambling and hustling of the masses of men? All of a sudden they were dead. And though it sometimes came sooner and sometimes later, they finally joined the other three—plants and trees, birds and beasts, and the masses of men—in returning to oblivion. Such is the untrustworthiness of words. Those who study today all aspire not to perish, just as the ancient sages and men of worth did not perish. And they strive earnestly their whole lives through, spending their hearts in writing—such sadness I feel for them all!

In his youth Xu Wu-tang of Dong-yang studied literary writing with me, and gradually he came to be well spoken of by others. He has gone off and joined other scholars in taking the examinations at the Board of Rites. He ranked high in the examination and from this his name became well known. His writing makes steady progress, like surging waters and mountains emerging. But I wished to curb his overweening enthusiasm and urge him to reflection. For this reason I have addressed these words to him on his return.

But it is true that I also delight in writing, and in this I am admonishing myself as well.

Accounts of Visits *(you-ji)*

Chinese landscape prose cannot be separated from geographical and topographical traditions. The most important early work in this genre is the *Commentary* to the *Classic of Rivers (Shui-jing zhu)* by Li Dao-yuan (d. 527), which goes far beyond the original work and draws on a variety of sources to detail the geography of China. Although sometimes used privately, through the eighth century the "account" was primarily a public genre to commemorate a building in its landscape setting. Liu Zong-yuan's (773–819) "accounts of visits" written during his exile, the most famous of which was the "Eight Accounts of Yong-zhou," helped to transform the genre into a private and meditative form. Visiting a place, the writer of the account would both describe it and reflect on the experience, discovering large questions in everyday circumstances.

The two pieces by Liu Zong-yuan that follow are both from the "Eight Accounts of Yong-zhou." The first account plays on the motif of acquisition and the transformation of the acquired piece of land both through landscaping and the imagination. The second piece describes finding a small mountain that resembles a city wall, leading to a half-serious, half-tongue-in-cheek meditation on a creator of the world.

Liu Zong-yuan, An Account of the Small Hill West of Gu-mu Pond (from the "Eight Accounts of Yong-zhou")

Eight days after I reached West Mountain, I was exploring about two hundred paces along the road that leads northwest from the mouth of the valley, and I found Gu-mu Pond. Twenty-five paces west of the pond, where the water flowed swift and deep, a fish-weir had been made. Above the fish-weir was a hill growing with trees and bamboo. Almost beyond counting were its rocks, which jutted out menacingly, rearing themselves aloft, spurning the earth in their emergence and rivaling one another in rare shapes. The ones that descended, interlocking downward from sharp clefts, seemed like cattle and horses watering at the creek. The ones that rose, thrusting their rows of horns upward, seemed like bears climbing on a mountain.

The hill was so small it did not even cover an acre; one might have kept it packed in a basket. I asked the person in charge, who said, "This is land of the Tang family for which they have no use. They put it on the market, but couldn't sell it." I asked how much they wanted for it, and he said, "Only four hundred pieces." I couldn't let go of it, so I bought it. At the time Li Shen-yuan and Yuan Ke-ji had come along with me, and they were both overjoyed at such an unexpected turn of events. We each in turn went to get tools, scything away the undesirable plants and cutting down the bad trees, which we set fire to and burned. Then the fine trees stood out, the lovely bamboo were exposed, and the unusual rocks were revealed. When we gazed out from upon it, the heights of the mountains, the drifting of clouds, the currents of streams, and the cavorting of birds and beasts all cheerfully demonstrated their art and skill in performance for us below the hill. When we spread out our mats and lay down there, the clear and sharply defined shapes were in rapport with our eyes; the sounds of babbling waters were in rapport with our ears; all those things that went on forever in emptiness were in rapport with our spirits; and what was as deep and still as an abyss was in rapport with our hearts. In less than ten full days I had obtained two rare places. Even those who loved scenic spots in olden times may well never have been able to equal this.

I must say that if I were to transport this splendid scenery to Feng, Hao, Hu, or Du-ling, the nobility who are fond of excursions would rival one another to purchase it. Every day its price would increase by another thousand pieces, and it would grow ever harder to afford. But now it is left forsaken in this province; as they pass by, farmers and fishermen think it worth nothing, and even with a price of only four hundred pieces it has not been purchased for years on end. Yet I, together with Li Shen-yuan and Yuan Ke-ji, have been singularly delighted to get it. Isn't this a case of having a lucky encounter at last? I wrote this on stone to celebrate this hill's lucky encounter.

An Account of Little Rock Rampart Mountain (from the "Eight Accounts of Yong-zhou")

From the point where West Mountain Road comes out, I went straight north, crossing over Yellow Rush Ridge and coming down the other side. There I found two roads. One went off to the west; I followed it, but found nothing. The other went north a bit and then turned to the east, where, after no more than a hundred and twenty-five yards, the dry land stopped at the fork of a river. There a mass of rock lay stretched across the margin. Along the top were the shapes of battlements and timbers, while to the side were palisades and a keep, which had something like a gateway in it. When I peered inside, it was completely black. I tossed a stone in, and there was a splash of water in a cavernous space. The echoes continued to resound for a long time. By circling around I could climb to the summit, where I gazed far into the distance. There was no soil, yet fine trees and lovely shafts of bamboo grew there, sturdy and quite unusual. The way they were spread out in clumps and open spaces, together with the angles at which they were set, made it seem like they had been placed there by some intelligence.

For a long time now I have wondered whether there was a Creator or not. When I came to this spot, I became even more convinced of his existence. But then I thought it peculiar that he did not make this in the heartland, but instead set it out here in an uncivilized wilderness where, in the passage of centuries and millennia, he could not even once advertise his skill. Thus all his hard labor was to no purpose. Given that a deity should not be like this, perhaps he does not exist after all. Someone said, "It is to provide solace for virtuous men who come to this place in disgrace." Someone else said, "Here the divine forces produce no outstanding men, but instead produce only these things, so that south of Chu there are few people and many rocks." I do not believe either claim.

Chinese writers from the Song Dynasty on often chose pseudonyms, and such pseudonyms often described their self-image as a private person. Ou-yang Xiu, a distinguished intellectual and political figure, styled himself the "Drunken Old Man." Then he had a pavilion constructed, to which he also gave his pseudonym. There he could play this role he had chosen, display it to others, and celebrate it in prose.

Ou-yang Xiu, An Account of the Pavilion of the Drunken Old Man

Encircling Chu-zhou all around are mountains. The wooded gorges of the various peaks to the southwest are overwhelmingly lovely. The one that stands out in the view, rising thick with dense growth, is Lang-ya Mountain. Going six or seven miles into the mountain, you gradually begin to hear the sound of flowing water; and the watercourse that spills out from between the two peaks is Brewer's Stream. As the path turns with the bend of the cliff, there is a pavilion, its wings outspread, standing beside the stream; and this is the Pavilion of the Drunken Old Man.

Who was it who built the pavilion? It was the mountain monk Zhi-xian. Who was it gave the pavilion its name? This was the governor himself. The governor would come with his guests to drink here; and when he had gotten a little drunk, he, being the eldest of the company, gave himself the nickname "Drunken Old Man." The Drunken Old Man's interest was not in the wine itself but in being here amid the mountains and waters. The delight in mountains and waters was first found in the heart and then lodged temporarily in the wine.

When the sun comes out and the forest haze lifts, or when the clouds come back to the hills and the caves in the cliffs grow dark, all the transformations of light and shadow are the passages from dawn to dusk in the mountains. Wildflowers spring up and give off secret fragrances; then the cassia trees rise high and form dense shade; then winds blow high up and the frost gleams in purity; then the waters sink and stones appear: these are the four seasons in the mountains. At dawn we go there and at dusk return; and as the scenery of the four seasons is never the same, so our delight too is limitless.

And as for those who carry burdens along the paths and travelers who rest under the trees, the ones in front shout and those behind answer; hunched over with age or with children in tow, they go back and forth without ceasing. These are the travels of the people of Chu-zhou. By the creek, we fish: the creek is deep and the fish are plump. We use the stream's water in brewing wine; and since the water smells sweet, the wine is sharp and clear. Pieces of fish and game from the mountains and vegetables from the wilds are served to us in varying dishes; and these are the banquets of the governor. Our delight when tipsy at these banquets does not come from the music of harps and flutes. Someone playing toss-pot makes his throw; someone playing chess wins; horn-cups and wine tallies are all jumbled together amid the noisy chatter of people getting up and sitting down; and these are the pleasures of the assembled guests. And the person with his face darkened by age and white-haired, lying passed out in the middle, is the governor, drunk.

613

Then the evening sun is in the mountains and the shadows of people scatter in disarray; this is the governor going home and his guests following. As the woods become veiled in shadow, there is a singing above and down below, and this is the delight of the birds at the departure of the human visitors.

And yet the birds may experience the delight of the mountain forests, but they do not experience the delight of the people. The other people may experience the delight of coming to visit this place with the governor, but they do not experience the governor's delight in their delight. The person who in drunkenness can share their delight and who, sobering up, can give an account of it in writing is the governor. And who is the governor? Ou-yang Xiu of Lu-ling.

Funerary Genres

In *The Zuo Tradition,* Confucius is credited with the saying: "If the language lacks patterning, it will not go far." This has been given grand implications in the tradition of Chinese literary thought, but on one level at least, *wen,* "patterning," simply means "writing." Writing enables words to be carried distances in space and last through time: it is in some essential way commemorative. In China, as in many cultures, early traditions of writing served an important role in honoring and commemorating the dead. There were several prose genres that played various roles in helping the living place themselves in relation to the dead. These genres included laments, inscriptions, and prayers or ceremonial addresses. Although such prose genres were often intended to serve normative purposes, it is usually the most personal, the most individual, and the least normative works that are still appreciated today.

Cao Zhi (192–232), A Lament for Golden Gourd, Jin-hu

Jin-hu was my firstborn daughter, and though she had not yet learned to speak, she could already recognize expressions on a person's face and knew what was in our hearts. She died an untimely death, after a life of only one hundred and ninety days. I wrote these lines for her:

> Caressed and nursed   in swaddling clothes,
> already child's laughter,   though not yet speaking.
> In less than a year   untimely gone—
> why was she punished   by sovereign Sky?
> It was surely brought on   by my misdeeds,
> I grieve for this infant,   she had no fault.
> She has left the embrace   of father and mother,
> her small bones dissolve   in the filth of soil.
>
> Sky is forever, Earth endures,
> how long does a man's life last?
> Whether sooner or later we do not know,
> but a time will come when I go with you.

Tao Qian, one of the most unconventional figures in the Chinese tradition, has left perhaps the most unconventional use of a highly formal funerary genre, the "sacrificial prayer for the dead."

Tao Qian, A Sacrificial Prayer for the Dead on My Own Behalf

The year is 427,
the pitch-pipe's note signals November.
The weather is cold, the nights grow long,
there is a gloom in the atmosphere.
Wild geese and swans are on their migrations,
all growing things yellow and shed their leaves.
And Master Tao is taking his leave
    of this inn where he lodged on his journey
to return forever to his earliest dwelling.
Old friends are upset and grieve for him,
having come together this evening
    to feast him before he sets off.
They have laid a table with fine vegetables
and offered him a round of clear wine.
But when he looks at their faces, they are already dim;
when he listens to voices, they seem ever more blurred.
Such a sad moment!

This earth, this huge clod of soil, is so vast,
and the high welkin stretches on and on.
These give birth to the thousands of things,
and I happened to become a man.
And ever since I became a man,
it was my fortune to be poor.
Gourd and foodbasket were ever bare,
summer's thin clothing laid out in winter.
Yet happy inside, I drew water from vales
and sang as I carried my firewood along.
Hidden behind my brushwood gate
I did my work both night and day.

Springs and autumns passed in succession,
there were tasks to be done in my garden.
I did my hoeing, I did my weeding,
then it was nurtured, then grew lush.
I found delight in my books,
I accompanied them with my seven-string harp.
In wintertime I sunned myself,
in summer I bathed in streams.
No energy remained in me after my labors,
yet my heart was ever at peace.

I rejoiced in Heaven, accepted my lot,
and reached my full span of years.

And this full span of years—
everyone clings to them so.
Men fear they will accomplish nothing,
greedy for days and begrudging their seasons.
When alive they are treasured by the age;
even when gone men think of them.
But I, alas, go my singular way,
I have ever been different from men like these.
To find favor gave me no sense of glory,
nor could any soiling stain me.
I lived aloof in my bare cottage,
drinking till tipsy, composing poems.

Though I recognize fortune and understand fate,
who can help turning to look back fondly?
Yet in this change I will now undergo
I can be without resentment.
I have passed a full span to ripe old age
seeking comfortable privacy for myself.
And aged now, I meet my end—
what more is there to yearn for?
Cold and warm seasons move on,
those gone differ from those alive.
Kin of mother and wife come in the morning,
good friends rush to my side by night.

Bury him in the midst of the meadow
to give peace to his soul.
I will move on, blind in the darkness,
grim is the door to the grave.
The excess of Song's liegeman would shame me,
I laugh at the thrift of Yang Wang-sun.[1]

I have vanished into vast darkness,
I have gone far from all agony.
Raise no mound and plant no trees,
let sun and moon pass overhead.
I did not value praise when alive,
who cares for songs of me afterward?
Life was truly difficult,
I wonder how death will be?
Alas.

---

[1]"Song's liegeman" was Huan Tui, who had a lavish stone casket made that took more than three years to complete. Yang Wang-sun, on the other hand, commanded his children to bury him naked.

Parables

Although they were an important part of Chinese prose writing since antiquity, "parables" were not considered a distinct genre in the repertoire of Chinese prose genres. Nevertheless, such short works remain among the best known and loved of classical prose writings. The lessons of these later parables, sometimes made explicit as in the second of the two by Liu Zong-yuan that follow, are more often than not political.

Liu Zong-yuan, "Three Cautionary Tales": The Fawn of Lin-jiang

A man of Lin-jiang once caught a fawn while hunting and wanted to raise it. When he entered his gate, his pack of dogs began to drool, and they all began to advance on it, their tails wagging. The man was furious and made them cower to him; then every day he would carry the fawn in his arms over to the dogs until they got used to seeing it. He forced them not to misbehave and gradually got them to play with it.

After a long time the dogs all behaved as the man wanted; and as the fawn gradually grew larger, it forgot that it was a deer. It believed that the dogs were its true friends, and became increasingly familiar with them, butting them and knocking them over. In fear of their master, the dogs would romp with the deer in a very friendly manner—although every once in a while one would bite on his own tongue.

Three years later the deer wandered out the gate and saw another pack of dogs on the road. There was a large number of them, and the deer went running toward them, wanting to play. These other dogs were at once delighted and stirred to fury. Together they killed the deer, ate it, and left bits of the carcass strewn all over the road. Until the very moment it died, the deer didn't understand.

The Story of the Fuban, or Pack Beetle

The fuban is a small insect that excels at carrying loads on its back. When it chances on something as it walks along, it immediately takes hold of it, and then, raising it up with its head, it loads the thing onto its back. The weight on its back gets increasingly heavy, but it will not stop what it does, even in dire straits. Its back is quite rough, so that the things it has accumulated do not slip off. It eventually collapses and just lies there, unable to get up. Sometimes a person will feel pity for it and get rid of its load. But no sooner is it able to walk again than it takes hold of things just as it did before. It also likes to climb high places; and when it does so, it will continue to use every bit of its strength until it falls to the ground and dies.

Those in our own times who lust to lay hold of things will never back away when they chance on possessions by which to enrich their household. They don't understand that it encumbers them; rather, they fear only that they won't accumulate enough. When they become weary and stumble, they are dismissed from office or sent into banishment. They even think that an ill has befallen them in this. If they can get up again, they will not forbear. Every day they think about how they can get a higher position and increase their income, and their greed for acquisition intensifies. As they draw near to falling from their perilous perch, they may consider those who have similarly perished before, yet they never take warning from the example. Though their bodies are immense by comparison, and they are named "human beings," yet their wisdom is that of a small insect, and also worthy of pity.

Informal Prose

In addition to the older prose genres, new and relatively informal genres of classical prose grew in popularity from the Song Dynasty on. The language in these works ranged from an easy classical style to a mixed style in which elements and constructions from the vernacular appear within the classical. These new genres included informal letters, travel and personal diaries, collections of "random jottings" *(bi-ji)*, memoirs, and colophons (short prose pieces written in comment on books, paintings, and pieces of calligraphy).

Su Shi (1037–1101), Written After Seeing the Paintings of Wu Dao-zi

Those with knowledge first fashion a thing; those with ability carry it through. It is not accomplished by one person alone. The superior man in his study and all the various artisans in their skills reached a state of completion in the passage from the Three Dynasties of antiquity through the Han down to the Tang. When poetry reached Du Fu, when prose reached Han Yu, when calligraphy reached Yan Zhen-qing, and when painting reached Wu Dao-zi, then all the variations of past and present and all the possibilities in the world were over. Wu Dao-zi's paintings of people and things are like casting a reflection with a lamp; in anticipating what is to come and recalling where they were, seen from side or angle, slanting or level, each is perfect in degree, and he achieves the proportions of nature, without erring in the smallest detail. He displays fresh thoughts within strict rules and leaves the most subtle sense of pattern beyond swaggering self-expression. This is what Zhuang-zi meant by plenty of space for the blade to move or a wind rising from plying the ax. He is absolutely unique in ancient and modern times. As for other paintings, I may not necessarily be able to tell the painter's name. But when it comes to Wu Dao-zi, no sooner do I look at one than I can tell if it is genuine or a fake. Few indeed are the genuine ones in our age, yet the one Shi Quan-shu has in his collection is such as I have seen only once or twice in my life.
 —Written October 7, 1085.

The following is a colophon attached to a prose account *(ji)* written by Fu's friend Dai Ting-shi (the Feng-zhong referred to in the colophon) about a tower that Dai himself had constructed, the inspiration for which was a dream Dai had had.

Fu Shan (1609–1684), Colophon on the "Account of the Scarlet Maple Tower"

Because of Feng-zhong's dream, there was a tower; because of the tower, there was an account of the tower. The tower resembles how it was in his dream, and the account resembles his tower. But then who can say that these really correspond? In any case, dream and account both having been completed, he further enjoined me, old fellow that I am, to write on the topic. Now it happens that I am someone quite able in telling dreams. I once maintained that the most remarkable men in the world, the most remarkable events, the most remarkable creatures, the most remarkable scenes, and the most remarkable transformations were none so remarkable as a dream. When it comes to dream's elusive presences and spectral fleetings, the literary man's writing brush cannot describe one thing in a million.

Nonetheless, insofar as the elusive scenes in literary works themselves resemble dreams, they lie beyond our common expectations. Feng-zhong truly has a great love of literature. For my own part, I cannot write—but I can dream. Now and then I'll be reading some piece out loud for Feng-zhong, and all at once I'll find myself in a scene of dream. Both of us will be all groggy and confused; and then as we come to our senses again, we will forget it. I can still recall one or two things, but Feng-zhong immediately forgets everything and retains nothing. This is why I am the one who tells dreams and Feng-zhong is the one who listens to dreams. Now telling dreams and listening to dreams are poles apart. It is most fortunate that Feng-zhong forgets them. For if the least of them lingered in his mind, I would lead Feng-zhong into a land of engulfing blackness, and he would never awaken.

趙宋 Place

China has an immense literature of "place," which includes descriptive geography, "accounts" *(ji)* of scenic landscapes and buildings, travel diaries, poems, and numerous local gazetteers that compiled a wealth of information on the natural, political, cultural, and literary history of each region.

China was the largest territory of the premodern world whose inhabitants had a sense that it was "one place." Other cultural regions were divided by language and rival ethnic groups or were unified as a single people (such as the Arabs). However vague its boundaries, China was seen (perhaps erroneously) as a unified territory, polity, people, and culture. Chinese religious, diplomatic, and commercial travels, along with continuous emigration outward, especially into Southeast Asia, show that the Chinese were no less venturesome than their European counterparts. In Europe, however, accounts of marvels seen on distant voyages were the norm of travel literature and no small force behind the European age of exploration. Although accounts of distant journeys do play a role in Chinese literature, that role is much smaller than the role played by the literature of internal travel. China had the first tourist industry, and its huge territory was gradually mapped by writing—poems, prose accounts, inscriptions, travel diaries—until the pleasure of travel became in no small part the physical experience of a place already known from texts.

Cold Mountain's sense of "place" as purely a state of mind was relatively rare in classical Chinese literature, its most famous expression being Tao Qian's "the mind far away, its place becomes remote." Most "places," however, are made by configurations of nature or by accidents of history: places have a physical form and historical lore that the writer encounters and to which he responds. The lore of a place and even ways to observe a place's physical forms are transmitted in such texts.

The Master of Cold Mountain (Tang)

> Someone asked me the way to Cold Mountain—
> to Cold Mountain no road goes through.
>
> The ice does not melt on summer days,
> when the sun comes out, the fog there glows.
>
> How did someone like me get there?—
> my heart is not at all like yours.
>
> If only your heart were just like mine,
> you could get right there right away.

When Su Shi, the most famous of all Song writers, visited Lu Mountain, he resolved at first to be an "innocent" traveler, wanting to experience the mountains without writing poems (as a modern tourist might resolve to travel without taking photographs). This initial resolution quickly fell prey to demands arising from his fame as a poet. Then a friend sent him a guide to the mountain, which told him where to go and what to look for, quoting famous poems by previous visitors, and Su Shi could not stop himself from responding to earlier poems about the mountains. Indeed, the final quatrain in the account below, which is taken from Su's collection of informal accounts, *The Forest of Records,* became one of the most famous of all Lu Mountain poems.

Su Shi, Account of a Visit to Lu Mountain (from *The Forest of Records*)

When I first entered the Lu Mountain Range, I found its mountains and valleys extraordinary. Never before in my life had I seen their like, and I had hardly any time to come up with the expected responses. At this point I had the notion that I didn't want to write any poems. But afterward, whenever I met monks or laymen in the mountains, they always said, "Su Shi is here!" Before I knew it, I had written a quatrain that went:

> Straw sandals, cane of green bamboo,
> I roam, leaving strings of a hundred cash.[2]
> But I marvel how deep in the mountains
> everyone knows the old count.[3]

Having finished this, I scoffed at myself for the folly of my earlier decision. Then I wrote two more quatrains that went:

> Green hills feel no cause to act familiar;
> haughty they rise and refuse to be amiable.
> If I want to recognize Lu Mountain's face,
> in some future year it will be an old friend.

And another:

> I recall long ago admiring this place,
> and then first roamed in its distant haze.
> But this time it isn't in a dream—
> this really is Lu Mountain.

On that day someone sent me a copy of Chen Ling-ju's "Account of Lu Mountain." I read it as I went along, and saw that he mentioned poems by

[2]This refers to a story of the monk Zha-dao who, when he ate some dates by the roadside, left a string of cash hanging from the tree to pay for his meal.
[3]The "old count" is the Count of Dong-ling, who took up planting melons after the fall of the Qin Dynasty. Su Shi uses the reference playfully here to term himself someone who formerly held high office and now acts the role of the commoner.

Xu Ning and Li Bo. Before I knew it, I couldn't help laughing. In a short while I entered the Kai-yuan Temple, and the abbot there asked for a poem, whereupon I wrote a quatrain [on the Cascade] that went:

> The god sent this silvery river
>   that hangs in a single stream,
> for all time its only lines of verse
>   were written by Li Bo.
> The splashing spray of its flying current—
>   I wonder how much there is—
> not enough to wash away
>   one bad poem by Xu Ning.

I went back and forth in the northern and southern parts of the range for over ten days, finding it to be the most splendid scenery, finer than one can adequately describe. If I were to select the two most entrancing spots, Scoured Jade Pavilion and the Three Gorges Bridge are beyond comparison. Thus I wrote two poems for them. Last of all, I went with old Chang-zong to visit West Forest Temple and wrote another quatrain:

> See it stretched before you in a ridge;
>   from the side it becomes a peak,
> no matter from where I look at the mountain
>   it is never exactly the same.
> I cannot tell the true face
>   of Lu Mountain,
> which is simply because I myself
>   am here within the mountain.

My Lu Mountain poems are summed up in this.

Those who wrote landscape "accounts" *(ji)* often gave the history of a place, telling of its previous visitors and explaining the origin of its name. In the following famous "Account of Stone Bell Mountain," Su Shi speaks as the venturesome empiricist, correcting the failures of his predecessors and demonstrating the link between the place and its name.

Account of Stone Bell Mountain

It is written in the *Classic of Waters:* "By the mouth of Lake Peng-li we find Stone Bell Mountain." Li Dao-yuan [d. 527, the commentator on the *Classic of Waters*] gave the opinion: "If you stand over the deep pools and a faint breeze agitates the waves, then water and stone will smack against one another, giving the sound of a huge bell." Such is the story—though people have always been dubious about it. If you place a bell or chimes in water, they won't ring no matter how strong the winds and waves are—much less stone.

In the Tang, Li Bo was the first to go seek out the place where this was supposed to occur, and he found two stones by those pools.[4] He struck them and listened: the sound of the one on the southern side was muffled and deep, while the tone of the one on the northern side was clear and carried far. When he stopped using the drumstick, the aftertones kept rising, until the last resonances slowly came to an end. And here he thought he had found the source of the story. I find, however, that I have even more doubts about this version than I have about Li Dao-yuan's. Stones with ringing tones are much the same anywhere, so why was this place singled out with the name "Bell"?

In 1084, the seventh year of the Yuan-feng Reign, on July 14, I was on my way by boat from Qi-an to Lin-ru. My eldest son, Mai, was going to take up his post as commandant in De-xing County in Rao-zhou. I went along with him to the mouth of the lake to see him off, and this gave me a chance to visit the so-called Stone Bell. One of the monks at the temple had his young servant boy take a hatchet to strike one or two rocks chosen from a jumble of rocks there. The little *clink clink* they made was truly ludicrous, and I found it utterly incredible.

As the night came on and the moon grew bright, Mai and I got in a small boat and went off all by ourselves to a spot beneath the sheer cliff. The huge rock stood leaning a thousand feet above us, like some fierce beast or strange demon ready to seize human beings in that brooding darkness. And then, high on the mountain, a roosting falcon, hearing human voices, flew up suddenly with a screeching cry among the clouds. Then also there was something like the sound of an old man's giggling laughter among the mountain valleys. Someone said that this was the stork.

At that point my heart was shaken and I was ready to turn back, when a huge sound came out over the waters, booming like a bell being struck continuously. The boatman was quite frightened. But when I took the time to examine the phenomenon closely, I found that there were crevices in the rocks at the foot of the mountain, whose depth I couldn't tell. When a small wave entered them, it heaved and sloshed about, producing this sound.

The boat turned back and passed between two mountains at the entrance to the mouth of the bay. There in midcurrent stood a large rock, with room enough for a hundred persons to sit on it. It had hollow spaces inside and many cavities that either sucked in or spurted out wind and water, producing sounds like *ding-dong* and *ding-a-ling*. These answered the earlier booming sounds as if music were being played. I laughed and said to Mai, "Do you recognize it? The one that goes *boom* is the famous *wu-yi* bell of King Jing of the Zhou; the ones that go *ding-dong* and *ding-a-ling* are the song bells once given to Wei Jiang [by Lord Dao of Jin]. The ancients weren't deceiving us."

Can a person make a decision regarding the existence of something purely on the basis of his own fancy, without having seen it with his own

[4]This Li Bo is not the poet, but a prose writer who composed an essay on the site in 798.

623

eyes or heard it with his own ears? What Li Dao-yuan saw and heard was pretty much the same as what I had just experienced, yet he didn't speak of it in enough detail. If a grand gentleman weren't willing to moor a small boat at the foot of the sheer cliff in the night, he couldn't know about it. Though the fishermen and navigators on the lake know about it, they can't express it. This is the reason the explanation was not passed down to the present times. And some fool tries to find the source of the story by striking rocks with an ax and thinks he has gotten the truth. This is my record of the matter, deploring the brevity of Li Dao-yuan's account, and laughing at the folly of Li Bo.

Thrills

Su Shi's investigation of the empirical basis of the mysterious sound of bells plays counterpoint to the eerie boating scene that precedes it. Many landscape accounts are soberly philosophical and descriptive, but there are also those that deliberately seek to evoke the thrills of travel, to recapture some of the excitement of the unknown in a genre whose primary function is to make the place known and familiar.

Chao Bu-zhi (1053–1110), An Account of a Visit to North Mountain at Xin-cheng

Thirty miles north of Xin-cheng we went ever deeper into the mountains, where the plants, trees, streams, and rocks became increasingly isolated. At first we could still ride among the teeth of the stones. On every side were huge pines, some bent over like the awnings of carriages and others straight like parasols; those that stood upright were like human beings, and those that lay down were like great serpents. Among the grasses beneath the pines were streams bubbling up, then disappearing until they fell into wells of stone with a ringing sound. Among the pines were vines some twenty or so feet long, twisting around like great eels. On the top there were birds, as black as mynah birds, with red crests and long beaks, bobbing their heads up and down and pecking with a rapping sound.

A little farther west a single peak rose abruptly to a prominence, and there was a path marking a division on it, a path that could be traveled only on foot. We tied our horses to outcroppings of stone and went up, helping each other along. When we looked up through the bamboo, we could not see the daylight. We went on like this for four or five leagues until we heard the sounds of barnyard fowl. Monks in cassocks of plain cloth and slippers came out to greet us. As we talked with them, they stared at us in wide-eyed amazement, like deer that could not be touched. At the summit there was a building with twenty or so rooms, its balconied outer hallway curving along the course of the cliff wall, twisting like the course of a snail or a rat, after which we came out into the open again. There doors and windows faced one another. As we sat down, a howling gust of mountain wind came, and all the chimes and clappers in the halls were set ringing. We few looked around at one another in surprise, not knowing into what kind of realm we had come. And when it was evening, we all went to bed.

It was then November; the heavens were high and the dew clear, the mountains deserted and the moon bright. We looked up at the stars, which together shed a great light, as if they were right over us. Through the window twenty or so stalks of bamboo began tapping against one another with an endless clacking. Among the bamboo, palm and plum trees stood dark and ominous, looking like disheveled demons holding themselves apart. And we few again looked around at one another, our spirits so shaken that we couldn't get to sleep. As it gradually grew light outside, we all left.

Several days after I returned home, I was still in a daze as if I had encountered something, so I wrote this account from memory. I never went there again, but I always see what occurred in my mind's eye.

The following popular anthology piece is an even more sophisticated attempt to evoke the mood of a trip and the alternation between terror and exhilaration on the part of the travelers. The writer's obvious pleasure in the thrill of danger (even though the danger proves imaginary rather than real) is counterbalanced by the conclusion, in which he solemnly chastises himself for his lack of caution—reminding the reader that in the Confucian tradition the thrill of danger is illicit.

Cheng Min-zheng (ca. 1446–ca. 1500), Night Passage Over Two Passes

I asked for leave to return to my home in the South. In winter, on December 16, 1478, I crossed Great Spear Ridge and reached Great Willow Station. It was only a little after noon, and I didn't want to stop just there. When I asked the attendant of the way station, he deceived me, saying, "You can still make it to Chu-zhou by evening." I got on my horse and had gone thirty miles, when I dimly heard one of my party saying, "Clear Current Pass lies ahead—it's terribly dangerous—many tigers." That stuck in my mind.

When we reached the pass, it was already getting black, and there was no place to which we could turn back. At that point I sent someone to have the official couriers hurry ahead at the foot of the mountain, holding gongs and carrying torches as we proceeded. At the opening of the pass, two peaks rose up several thousand feet high on either side of us; and when I looked up, I couldn't see all the way to their summits. The stone walkway being steep and rough, everyone dismounted, and we went up at such an incline that we seemed to be climbing on each other's shoulders. We further agreed that if there were some cause for alarm, those in front and behind would respond by shouting and making loud noises. At that moment it happened that there was a large shooting star, flaring brightly as it coursed from east to west. Then a cold wind came up violently, and the torches all went out. The plants and trees on the mountains all around us were making howling sounds in the wind. From all of this everyone felt in grave danger, and we shouted and made noise without letup. The gongs were rung, and the mountain valleys shook with their echoes. We went on about six or seven miles and reached the summit, where we suddenly saw the moon come out like a gleaming plate of silver, casting its glow everywhere. At this point we raised our hands and congratulated one another. But even so, as we went down the mountain my heart was still apprehensive, and I couldn't calm down for quite a long time. I surmise that this pass was the very place where the Palace General Zhao Kuang-yin smashed the Southern Tang and captured its two generals. Although this trip was dangerous and full of strangeness, it was, I'm sure, the crowning moment of my entire life. At about ten o'clock that night we reached Chu-yang.

At noon on the seventeenth, we passed Quan-jiao and were hastening to He-zhou. Having luckily gotten out of one dangerous situation, I had become blasé and had no further anxieties. We went on forty miles and crossed Back River, when I saw the shadowy form of a mountain directly facing us. I asked someone in my party and was told that we would have to climb this before we could reach the Xiang-lin Temple in He-zhou. In a little while the sun gradually passed behind the peak, and the horses moved into a spur of the mountains. The ridges and peaks bent around and merged, with carefully laid out mulberry fields and several villages just like Wu-ling or Mate Pool Mountain, and I found it delightful.

Then evening came on, and as we went further in, it became increasingly mountainous. Plants and trees blocked the road, which seemed to go on so far that we did not know where it would end. We passed a temple in the wilds where I met an old man, whom I asked, "What mountain is this?" He said, "This is the old Zhao Pass. It's still more than thirty miles to Xiang-lin Temple. You had better hurry because there are people setting fires on the mountain ahead of you, burning the plateaus to drive off the tigers."

That time we had prepared neither gongs nor torches. At the side of a mountain we waded through a swift torrent, and there were eerie rocks like a forest. The horses shied away from these. The whole party thought the rocks were tigers crouching to pounce, and people turned to run in the opposite direction, falling over on top of one another. The sounds of our shouts was very weak, but even when we forced ourselves to yell loudly, we couldn't drive them away. After quite a long time we got up again. As we went on along the ridge, I peered intently down the slopes and into the crevices, but they were so deep I couldn't see the bottom. There were the splashing waters of a torrent that seemed fast or slow according to how strongly the wind was blowing. I looked up and saw the stars and constellations filling the sky. And I predicted that I would probably not escape this time. Then I thought how once long ago Wu Zi-xu found himself in great difficulty in this very pass. I wonder if this sort of thing is inevitable for anyone who comes to this terrible place. It was after ten o'clock when we reached Xiang-lin Temple. In the lamplight I was lost in a daze, as if I had been reborn.

Since I had been away from my parents for such a long time, I showed no foresight in anything. Challenging danger and traveling by night, I had crossed two passes and braved the lairs of tigers. Though I stood on the brink of peril, I had the good fortune to escape. And this may well be called lack of caution. I have dutifully noted it down as a warning to posterity.

People and Places

In Chinese popular religion, as in Greco-Roman antiquity in the West, there were spirits of place—gods or demigods who had a claim to certain natural objects or territories. Writers in an elite culture did not often directly acknowledge such spirits (Han Yu was one of the exceptions), but in their place we often find a personified landscape. Like people, landscapes come to public notice or hide themselves away like recluses; and also like people, landscapes depend on human beings for recognition.

Wen Zheng-ming (1470–1559), Preface to the "Joint Collection of Poems on Seeking Plums on Xuan-mu Mountain"

Xuan-mu Mountain is in the southwestern part of Wu Prefecture, overlooking the Great Lake. Western Summit and Copper Pit shine beside it on either side. There can be found thousands of sprays of alabaster plums, growing mixed together with pine and bamboo. At the juncture between winter and spring there is a rich profusion of fragrance and color from the blossoms. And on the sheer cliffs, among the melting patches of snow, they give off a glow, both above and down below in the rippling vastness of light upon the waters, thousands of acres within a single sweep of the eye. All the mountains of Lake Dong-ting are as if tightly stacked on a bookcase. It is the supreme realm, the region of those pure beings who live forever.

Yet the place is remote and out of the way, with few people living there, and unreachable by horse and carriage. Even though it has ancient monasteries and famous abbeys, these have become rundown through the long years; and their eminent monks and their lively and spirited gentlemen have gradually disappeared into the past. No one can truly grasp the quality of the place unless they have genuine perceptiveness and their sentiments are inclined to such isolated places. Nor can one ramble through such a realm without feeling a full measure of that excitement that comes with high spirits and a willingness to go off on one's own. Furthermore, to express the place in poetry, to celebrate in verse each variety of thing viewed, requires a deep insight into its splendors. In this regard I find something worthwhile in the compositions on seeking plums by Messrs. Fang and Wu.

In ancient times, notable mountains were made glorious by particular persons; yet the reason they were so valued was not merely for roaming around sight-seeing. Those people had some notable worthiness whereby they honored such places, and found some insight into those mountains through their own elevated sentiments and the grace of their temperaments. Nevertheless, without the robust brilliance of literary works to bring out what was remarkable and otherwise hidden, these places still would have ended up dim and unknown. So it matters not whether a mountain is low or high, near or far: if it happens to encounter some notable person, that is always enough to have its splendors celebrated all the world over.

This homeland of mine, Wu, is called the prefecture of mountains and waters. Yet the most famous places nowadays are Tiger Hill and Spirit Ridge, which became important because of the prose of Gu Ye-wang and poems by the Daoist Qing-yuan, by Li Bo, by Wei Ying-wu, and by Bo Ju-yi. The splendors of Xuan-mu Mountain are really in no way inferior to those other two, but at the moment there have been few who were capable of expressing what makes the place noteworthy. I can only conclude that the mountain had not yet found the right people for it, and that its own literary works had not yet been written and accepted.

It has been said that the various mountains of Yong-zhou and Liu-zhou became widely known through the writings of Liu Zong-yuan. Yet the exceptional qualities of Liu Zong-yuan's prose could only have been brought out by those very mountains of Yong-zhou and Liu-zhou. Other poems by Messrs. Fang and Wu do indeed have great clarity and beauty, but critics say that the pieces on Xuan-mu Mountain are particularly fine. Might we not then say that the exceptional qualities of that particular landscape had something about it that brought out the best in them as well? And their own genuine perceptiveness and their sentiments inclined to isolated places, together with that excitement that comes with high spirits and a willingness to go off on one's own—these truly made it possible for them to have insight into the place. Moreover, both of these men have refinement and have established themselves; they have been eminent in public service, and known for their principles when withdrawing into private life, unwilling to assume commonplace obsequiousness toward others. The sum of what they have achieved will surely make them eminent. And in time to come someone will surely read their poems and imagine seeing the persons, all through their enjoyment of the splendors of this mountain. Thus I wrote this preface for posterity.

One of the earliest and best-known discussions of the principle whereby a place becomes known through a particular person is the following account by Ou-yang Xiu. On Mount Xian near the city of Xiang-yang was the famous "stele for shedding tears," dedicated to the third-century governor Yang Hu. On this mountain, Yang Hu wept when he considered how many worthy people had died, their names now forgotten. For Ou-yang Xiu, the account is an occasion to consider the significance of *ming,* which means both "name" and "fame."

Ou-yang Xiu (1007–1072), An Account of the Pavilion on Mount Xian

Mount Xian looks down on the river Han; when I gaze at it, I can barely make it out. It is surely the smallest of the major mountains, yet its name is particularly well known in Jing-zhou. This is, of course, because of the persons associated with it. And who are those persons? None other than Yang Hu and Du Yu.

The Jin was engaged in a military struggle with the state of Wu, and it was considered of great importance to hold Jing-zhou. These two men, Yang Hu and Du Yu, were governors here in succession; and thus in the conquest of Wu and in the fulfillment of Jin's destiny, their glorious deeds crowned that age. Some lingering echo of their valiant and dashing manner still suffuses the whole region, where the Yangzi meets the river Han; and people today still think on them. But it is on Yang Hu that they think most deeply.

Du Yu is, perhaps, the more famous for his deeds, while Yang Hu is famous for his kindness. Although these two men differed in their actions, in both cases what they did was sufficient to bring them immortality. But I do wonder why it was that they were both so anxious about their fame in later ages. The story goes that Yang Hu once climbed this mountain and in depression said to his entourage that the mountain would be here forever, while men of ages past had perished utterly and no more was heard of them. Then he considered his own case and fell into deep sorrow. Little did he realize that the mountain would become famous because of him. Du Yu, on the other hand, had his achievements inscribed on two stones; one of these he set up on the mountain, and the other he threw in the deepest part of the river. He understood quite well that valleys and hills would someday change their places. What he did not understand was that the stone would someday wear away. Was it that they both went too far in their concern for immortality out of too much pleasure in fame? Or did they long for such remote goals because they paid themselves too much honor?

The mountain has had a pavilion from early times. Tradition has it that this is the place Yang Hu visited. It has often fallen into ruin and just as often has been rebuilt; the reason for this is that there have been so many in later ages who admired Yang Hu's name and thought about the kind of person he was. In 1068, my friend Shi Zhong-hui left his post as ceremonial director and came here to Xiang-yang as governor. Because the pavilion was getting old, the following year he enlarged it and renovated it, surrounding it with a magnificent balcony and extending its rear porch, making these as popular as the pavilion itself.

Shi Zhong-hui's name is well known in our times, and his excellent reputation follows him wherever he goes. Xiang-yang's people are peaceful under his government, and they delight in going with him on excursions. Thus it was that they came to give his former office title to the name of the new porch—"The Porch of the Ceremonial Director." They wanted, moreover, to record the occasion on stone so that it would be transmitted far into the future along with the names of Yang Hu and Du Yu. Shi Zhong-hui was unable to prevent them in either matter, so he came to me to write the account.

I am of the opinion that since Shi Zhong-hui understands so well the proper admiration for Yang Hu's manner and how to follow in his footsteps, we can know the kind of person he is and his aspirations. Because the people of Xiang-yang love him and are contented with him, we can know the way he has governed Xiang-yang. This is written because of the desires of the people of Xiang-yang.

When it comes to the splendid forms of the mountains and rivers around the pavilion, the blurring haze of plants, trees, clouds, and mist coming into view and disappearing in the broad and empty expanse, hanging between presence and absence, which can fully satisfy the gaze of a poet as he climbs these heights and writes his own *Li Sao*—it is best that each viewer find such things for himself. As for the frequent ruin and repair of the pavilion, either accounts already exist or the details do not merit close examination. I will say nothing more.

—An account written by Ou-yang Xiu
on the twenty-second day of December, 1070

A City: Yang-zhou

Take all this world's bright moonlit nights,
    divide them in three parts,
and the two most breathtaking
    are the city of Yang-zhou. . . .

—from Xu Ning, "Recalling Yang-zhou"

Like all the great cities of China, Yang-zhou was very much a "place," with a complex history and personality. Yang-zhou was once Guang-ling, popularly believed to have been the "Weed-Covered City" on whose ruins Bao Zhao (ca. 414–466) wrote a famous poetic exposition. The city described there was a great commercial center whose inhabitants showed their arrogance and heedless extravagance until suddenly fortune reversed itself and the city was reduced to a wasteland. Yang-zhou's reputation as a city of pleasure lured Emperor Yang of the Sui to leave Chang-an and establish his "River Capital" there (sound political reasons for making Yang-zhou a capital weigh little beside the force of its legendary sensuous attractions). Here Emperor Yang built his fabled Labyrinth *(Mi-lou)*, in which he housed his palace ladies.

Emperor Yang's notorious extravagance in the "River Capital" was held to have been one of the factors responsible for his fall and the destruction of the Sui Dynasty by the Tang. Emperor Yang was buried in his beloved city, at a spot called Thunder

Basin. By the Tang, the city had acquired a reputation for its moonlight and melancholy sensuality. As Du Mu wrote to his friend Judge Han Chuo in Yang-zhou:

> Yang-zhou has twenty-four bridges,
>   and on nights when the moon is bright,
> at what spot is a girl, white as marble,
>   being bidden to play on the flute?

Du Mu was Yang-zhou's poet, and lines of his poetry were always associated with the city. Du Mu's most famous poem—and the most famous poem of the city—speaks of a decade spent by the poet in love affairs with the courtesans of Yang-zhou's entertainment quarters, the "blue mansions."

Du Mu, Getting Something Off My Mind

> Footloose and lost on the rivers and lakes
>   I went my way carrying wine,
> Chu women's waists, slender and fine,
>   danced lightly on my palm.
> After ten long years I woke at last
>   from a Yang-zhou dream—
> I had won only fame for careless love
>   in its blue mansions.

[handwritten margin note: Yang Chou - many entertainment like Gisha women not prostitutes.]

Presented to Someone on Parting

> She is graceful, lithe, and winsome—
>   just somewhat past thirteen,
> a cardamom bud on branchtip
>   early in April.
> There were ten miles of springtime breeze
>   along the streets of Yang-zhou;
> the beaded curtains were all rolled up,
>   and none could compare with you.

Yang-zhou (first of three)

> The soil of Yang-di's Thunder Basin Tomb,
> his former Labyrinth for losing one's way.
>
> At whose home do they sing his River Song
> as the bright moon fills Yang-zhou?
>
> Fitting that splendid horses go idly forth;
> well done—a thousand in gold tossed away.
>
> In all the din a drunken young man
> half removes his cloak of purple fur.

The serenity of one of Yang-zhou's most famous Buddhist temples exists in counterpoint to that city of pleasure.

Written on Chan-zhi Temple in Yang-zhou

Rain passes, a cicada's piercing cry,
wind whistles, an autumn of cassia and pines.

Green moss fills its pavements and stairs,
where white birds linger willingly.

Twilight haze appears deep in the trees
as the sun goes down by a small tower.

Who would have known down the Bamboo West Road
the singing and piping that is Yang-zhou?

Du Mu's contemporary Zhang Hu thinks of Chan-zhi Temple in a very different way.

Zhang Hu (9th century), Roaming Free in Huai-nan

For ten miles long avenues
    join markets and neighborhood wells,
and on the Bridge of Bright Moonlight
    I watch the goddesses go.
The best thing in human life would be
    to die in Yang-zhou:
Chan-zhi and Shan-guang Temples
    have good fields for tombs.

As a rich and low-lying city north of the Yangzi, Yang-zhou was beyond the protection of the river fleets that guarded the great cities on the southern shore. Thus, Yang-zhou often came to be sacked and destroyed during invasions from the North. When the Jin Dynasty wrested North China away from the Song, Yang-zhou remained generally under Southern Song control, but was several times devastated by Jin attacks. In 1176, the young Southern Song lyricist Jiang Kui passed by the ruins and recalled Du Mu's city.

Jiang Kui (1155–1221), to "Yang-zhou Andante"

On the first day of winter in 1176, I passed by Wei-Yang. The night snow was just clearing from the sky, and shepherd's purse and millet filled my gaze. When I entered the city walls, a desolation lay all around me. The cold waters grew sapphire as the colors of twilight gathered, and the garrison bugles moaned sadly. My heart was stricken with grief, and I was stirred to sorrowful thoughts on the city's past and present. Therefore I composed this melody. The Old Man of a Thousand Cliffs thought that it had the kind of sadness that we find in "Millet Lush" in the *Classic of Poetry*.

Famed metropolis East of the Huai,
splendid spots at West of Bamboo,
where I uncinched my saddle pausing a while
    on my journey's first stage.
Through "ten miles of springtime breeze" I passed
and everywhere was millet so green.
Ever since the Turkish horses
    spied across the river, then left,
its ruined pools and towering trees
seem weary of telling of war.
Dusk comes on gradually
with clear bugles blowing the cold
all here in this deserted city.

Young Du Mu supremely admired it;
yet I would guess
    that were he to come again today,
        he would be shocked.
Even though
    his lines on the cardamom bud were skilled
    and his dream of blue mansions was fine,
it is hard to write these stronger feelings.
The twenty-four bridges are still here,
and swept along in the heart of the waves
is the cold and soundless moon.
I think on the red peonies by the bridge—for whom
do they come again year after year?

As Ou-yang Xiu recalled the site on Mount Xian where Yang Hu once shed tears thinking of human mortality, many of the places associated with Ou-yang Xiu himself became "famous because of the person." One of the best known of such sites was Level Mountain Hall, just outside Yang-zhou. Su Shi wrote the following song lyric on revisiting the hall after Ou-yang Xiu's death.

Su Shi, to "Moon Over West River": on Level Mountain Hall

Thrice I've passed by Level Mountain Hall—
in half the sound of a finger's snap.
Ten years since I saw that old man, the immortal,
whose written words are dragons still
    flying upon these walls.

I will grieve for him, stylist and governor,
singing "willows and spring wind" still.
Just tell me no more how all things vanish
    in the turning of a head—

even before my head could turn,
they were all already a dream.

There is the truth understood by Ou-yang Xiu that a place becomes recognized on account of a person. Ou-yang Xiu's own Level Mountain Hall was often destroyed and just as often rebuilt because the building was supposed to be there. Literate inhabitants of Yang-zhou, officials serving a tour of duty in the area, and visitors all expected its presence. Modern Western sensibilities prefer ruins or an empty space with a plaque marking the site; the Chinese have preferred imaginative reconstruction. Just as literary accounts were written on behalf of buildings, buildings came to be erected on behalf of literary accounts, thereby producing new literary accounts.

Level Mountain Hall was rebuilt in honor of Ou-yang Xiu's literary genius and his status as a Confucian culture hero. Yet there was an incongruity that such a site should be so close to Yang-zhou, the city of wealth and sensual pleasure; all this comes together in the seventeenth century when the hall is rebuilt yet again.

Wei Xi (1624–1680), An Account of the Reconstruction of Level Mountain Hall

Level Mountain Hall is some five miles northwest of the walls of Yang-zhou. It was constructed by Ou-yang Xiu in the Song. Ou-yang Xiu was governor of this prefecture toward the end of the Qing-li Reign in the late 1040s when all the world enjoyed universal peace. Preferring easygoing simplicity in governing, he was able to initiate this undertaking, and he would drink and compose poems here with guests and colleagues.

Now after more than six hundred years, it has fallen into ruin and been rebuilt more than once. It even came to the point where it was completely swept away, leaving nothing but underbrush and weeds; it was illegally seized and made into a Buddhist temple. And yet this place, because of Ou-yang Xiu, has become increasingly well known throughout the world. Those who climb up here and gaze out are deeply touched by the very same sort of thoughts one has on Mount Xian.

Yang-zhou has been acclaimed as a scenic spot since ancient times, yet the place itself has very little of the beauties of mountain forests or hills and ravines. Within the city itself there is only one little mound called "Kang's Mountain," from which the waters of the Han Canal can be seen on three sides. But outside the city there is Level Mountain Hall, giving the most extensive view of all the mountains of the Southland. There was a building on "Kang's Mountain," yet at the same time Level Mountain Hall long lay in ruins. Since this hall was first constructed, Yang-zhou has suffered the horrors of war on several occasions. In 1230, early in the Shao-ding Reign, one hundred and eighty-two years after Level Mountain Hall was built, Li Quan was in rebellion; but he still could hold a grand drinking party there. I wonder if this hall might not have had the good fortune to be spared burning during the wars; or perhaps it was destroyed by fire and some worthy person restored it.

In our own time the surveillance commissioner Jin Zhen used to govern this prefecture. Once he had his administration running smoothly, he was distressed that no offerings were being made to his worthy precursor Ou-yang Xiu and that the prefecture's most scenic spot had been left so long abandoned. Together with Wang Mao-lin, who is from a prominent local family, he planned an extensive rebuilding; the hall was completed in fifty days, without collecting a single copper from the common people.

There was a terrace and the hall, behind which was a building of several stories, with two wings outspread, where offerings could be made to the spirit of Ou-yang Xiu. It was airy and spacious, with a splendid beauty, giving access to thousands of scenic views. I don't know how it compares to Ou-yang Xiu's building back then, but from it we can infer His Excellency Jin Zhen's intentions regarding the moral education of the people and the promotion of virtuous customs.

The customs of Yang-zhou are, in fact, a melting pot for people from every corner of the land. It is a concourse for the fish trade, for the salt trade, and for money. Those who have served in office and powerful families move here. Therefore its people have a great lust for gain, love parties and excursions, procure singers and pursue courtesans, wear fine clothes, and live for the pleasure of the moment in order to show off their splendor to others. Only the most worthy among them still has any interest in things of culture.

Once His Excellency had restored the ruin, he often drank and composed poetry here with members of prominent local families and those who came to visit him. This practice had the following result: what these people heard and cast their eyes on here gave them a joyous admiration for both the landscape and things of culture. Soon every family and household was reciting poems, until the way of literature and of the *Classic of Poetry* gradually changed the atmosphere of money and horse-trading. Moreover, the land of Yang-zhou is flat and soggy; only this mountain is somewhat higher and thus fit to be a place for fighting. By building the hall here and making it a place for the regular use of ceremonial vessels, His Excellency may well have intended to mollify its bellicose atmosphere by the presence of cultural activities.

His Excellency's given name is Zhen, and his courtesy name is Chang-zhen. He is a native of Shan-yin in Zhe-jiang. In mid-autumn 1677, I was staying in Yang-zhou, and His Excellency happened to come up from the Southland to take care of the regulations of the salt monopoly. He halted his coach and entourage and walked on foot down my winding lane; and then with great courtesy asked me to compose this account. And I considered how Kang Mountain received its name only from the Ming writer Kang Hai, while Level Mountain Hall's name is known all over the world because of Ou-yang Xiu. Since a place is valued because of a person, what you have done here will go far indeed.

The Ornaments of 趙
"Literati" Culture 宋

The Master said: "Set your ultimate aims on the Way. Cleave to
virtue. Keep close to gentleness. At your ease roam in the arts."
—*Analects* VII.6

The literature of the Tang showed an immense cultural confidence that can be seen
in other aspects of the dynasty. Literature still seemed to be, in Lu Ji's remarkable
phrase, "the means for all principles of nature"—the external pattern through which
the workings of the world and of human beings could be made manifest. Whether in
consequence of changes in society, in thought, or in the internal momentum of literary traditions themselves, Song classical literature as a whole presents a very different
face from that of the Tang.

With commercial printing and a significantly larger educated class, the actual
practice of classical literature was far more widespread in the Song than in the Tang.
The surviving corpus of Song poetry and literary prose is many times larger that what
survives from the Tang. At the same time, literature in the Song Dynasty seems to
have lost something of its grandeur and sense of importance. During this dynasty,
classical literature took on the role it would retain until the twentieth century: as a
leisurely pastime, one art among many. Despite some famous memorials to the
throne written in the Song, official prose works increasingly came to be seen as mere
documents rather than works of literature. Other literary genres, which served in people's private lives, became central to one of the Song Dynasty's most important cultural achievements: the creation of a realm of private life and leisure that could be
kept to some degree separate both from the demands of state service and from the
unremitting moral seriousness of Neo-Confucian self-examination and self-cultivation. This kind of literature—along with its attendant arts of painting, calligraphy,
and approved forms of music—became the heart of "literati" culture, a space of freedom and sanctioned pleasure within an increasingly intrusive public world. To
these arts were added a wide range of other elite pastimes, such as collecting, anti-
quarianism, and the creation of gardens. Literature was the matrix that unified this
set of cultural activities, commenting on and interpreting them, giving meaning to
their display and exchange.

Connoisseurship

The arts, including poetry itself, became an important topic within Song writing. A
poem often served as an act of appreciation—to praise a friend, to offer thanks for
a gift, or to take pride in a new "find." Connoisseurship, collecting, and antiquari-

anism went hand in hand with composition. The following poem by Ou-yang Xiu tells of his discovery in 1045 of a short inscription by the famous eighth-century calligrapher Li Yang-bing, a master of seal script, an archaic style of writing Chinese characters (the English translation "seal script" is because this style of writing was used in making seals). The style of the poem, derived ultimately from the Tang poet Han Yu, is one the characteristic poetic "types" for commenting on works of art and antiquities: a section of imaginative description is embedded in a rambling, discursive verse style.

Ou-yang Xiu begins with a letter to his friends, explaining the situation and telling them what they are supposed to do:

Ou-yang Xiu, Seal Script in Stone (1045)

Dear friends,
Recently, by the grace of the court, I was made governor of this prefecture. In the southwestern part of the prefecture is Lang-ya Mountain, with the stream made famous by Li Yao-qing, onetime Mentor of the Heir Apparent. Earlier when I was in the Academy, the Royal House sent an order to seek out texts on old steles all over the world, which were to be collected in the Academy. It was there that I had a chance to see Li Yang-bing's seal script "Inscription for the Mentor's Stream." Those who make a study of seal script say that even though there are many extant examples of Li Yang-bing's work, none of them can compare to this particular inscription. For the past ten years I have constantly wanted to get hold of a copy, but with no success. When I came here, I obtained one. But in addition, at the side of the stone that bears the inscription, there is another group of more than ten characters by Li Yang-bing. These are even more marvelous than the text of the inscription itself, even though they are rarely seen in circulation. A mountain monk, one Hui-jue, pointed them out for me, and I lingered for a long time beneath them, unable to tear myself away. Accounts, both recent ones and older ones, have thoroughly documented remarkable sites in these mountains, and I felt especially distressed that this inscription alone had escaped their mention. I wanted to describe it, but feared lest my own writing prove inadequate for my thoughts. The men whose writing I cherish yet cannot equal are you two, Mei Yao-chen and Su Shun-qin. For this reason I am sending you both this poem together with an ink rubbing of the inscription, asking of you poems about the calligraphy carved in that stone.

> From cold cliff a cascade flies,
>   it falls upon green moss,
> Here a wonder!—script in stone
>   set by cascade's side.
>
> The man who wrote it now is dead,
>   his bones have rotted away,
> but these his words do not perish,
>   in the mountain's folds they stay.

An aging monk of the mountains
  feared erosion of the stone
and made a print upon paper,
  rubbed with the charcoal of pine.

He wished a copy to be shared
  by people of our times,
and took one to give to me,
  a match for finest jade.

It seemed to me these characters
  were made by no stroke of the brush,
it seemed in fact things not to be done
  by human powers at all.

When first the Earth and Heavens
  in embryo split apart,
the Primal Force congealed to this
  high and looming thing.

In those days birds of the wilderness
  stepped on this mountain stone,
they left their tracks forever here
  upon these slate gray slopes.

The god of the mountain did not want
  men to see it often:
he gave off constant clouds and fog
  to bury it deep away.

When bands of immortals fly through sky
  and wish to come down to read,
they always employ the moon's clear light
  as it rises over the sea.

Poor me, who lacks ability
  to judge the calligrapher's skill—
when I see this, I am only aware
  that it opens both heart and eyes.

Good phrases stint me, my words are dull
  and not worth writing down,
so I wrap them and mail them far away
  to Su Shun-qin and Mei Yao-chen.

Ou-yang Xiu's playful myth that the inscription was actually bird tracks made at the beginning of the universe echoes the legend of the invention of Chinese characters by Cang-jie, who drew his inspiration from observing the tracks of birds. Ou-yang Xiu had asked for answering poems from his friends Mei Yao-chen and Su Shun-qin. Those poems survive and show neither Mei nor Su at his best. From Mei Yao-chen's verse we may quote a couplet that only a Song poet could have written:

> You, sir, understand this stone,
>   the stone does not understand you;
> but you, sir, and that man before [Li Yang-bing]
>   are certainly true friends.

Su Shun-qin, whose poetry often shows strained hyperbole in imperfect emulation of his Tang predecessors, has one brilliant image of the script as the horns and talons of dragons buried within the stone:

> And then it seems like dragons and basilisks
>   sprouting talons and horns,
> hiding away in the azure rockface,
>   coiled up and not stretching out.

Su Shi's writings on the arts are among the most remarkable in the Song. His poems have all the virtues of Song poetry and at times they raise its very weaknesses to the status of high art. Su Shi is chatty, humorous, sometimes perverse. The following poem is to an acquaintance who was adept in "draft cursive" *(cao-shu)*, a free, often unreadable script in which a man of culture was supposed to be able to give expression to an otherwise suppressed extravagance of spirit.

Su Shi, Shi Cang-shu's "Hall of Drunken Ink" (1068)

> All worry and woe in life begins
>   from learning to read and write—
> be able to roughly mark your name
>   and then you should call it quits.
>
> What point is there in cursive draft
>   that flaunts the spirit's speed?—
> the blur in my eyes when I open a scroll
>   makes me ill at ease.
>
> Yes, I too have been fond of it,
>   but always I laugh at myself;
> how can we cure this affliction
>   as it shows itself in you?
>
> You tell me that in doing this
>   you find a perfect joy,
> mind's satisfaction, not distinct
>   from spirit's roaming free.
>
> Just recently you built a hall
>   and named it "Drunken Ink,"

comparing this art to drinking wine
    that melts anxieties.

I see now that Liu Zong-yuan
    wrote something not untrue:
such affliction may crave dirt and ash
    as if it were haute cuisine.

Still we may say that in this art
    you have achieved the heights:
worn-out brushes pile by your walls
    like little hills and knolls.

When the whim strikes, one swish of the hand
    and a hundred sheets are gone:
in a fleeting moment a splendid steed
    bestrides the entire land.

My own script takes shape to my mood,
    I have no special technique:
the dots and lines just follow my hand,
    it's a bother to try too hard.

Then tell me why in your critiques
    I am singled out for praise,
isolated words and scraps of paper
    all find themselves collected.

Your script may be properly judged
    no lower than Zhong or Zhang;
on a lower level my own is still better
    than that of Luo or Zhao.

You should no longer sit by the pool
    and practice so ardently,
in the end just take all that writing silk
    and use it to stuff a quilt.[1]

The artist's passion and his utter absorption in his art are treated humorously in the poem above. Yet Shi Cang-shu's half-foolish obsession is related to one of the highest values in painting: a loss of self in the thing depicted, as in the following famous poem by Su Shi on a painting of bamboo by his close friend Wen Tong.

---

[1]The penultimate couplet, echoing old traditions of evaluative comparisons, refers to the great calligraphers Zhong Yao and Zhang Zhi, and to the good but less distinguished calligraphers Luo Shu-jing and Zhao Yuan-si, all from the beginning of the calligraphic tradition in the first three centuries A.D. The last line refers to an anecdote about Zhang Zhi, whose own specialty was draft cursive: he would practice his calligraphy by a pool so often that it became black with his ink.

On the Paintings of Bamboo by Wen Tong in the Collection of Chao Bu-zhi (first of three)

At the moment Wen Tong was painting bamboo,
he saw the bamboo and no person—

Not just that he saw no person,
he was emptied, let go of the self;

His person was transformed with bamboo
in an endless production of freshness.

There is no Zhuang Zhou alive in this world—
who now grasps such fusion of spirit?

A somewhat different and more subtle development of this notion of art can be seen in the famous opening of Su Shi's account of bamboo paintings, again by Wen Tong.

from "An Account of Wen Tong's Paintings of the Slanted Bamboo of Yun-dang Valley"

When bamboo first grow, they are sprouts only an inch long, yet all their joints and leaves are already complete. They pass from shedding their sheaths, like cicada husks and snakeskins, and reach a point when they thrust up like swords ten yards high: this occurs as something innate within them. Nowadays painters do them joint by joint and accumulate their foliage leaf by leaf—and there is nothing left of a bamboo in it! The reason is that in order to paint bamboo, the painter must get the bamboo beforehand in his breast; then, when he takes hold of the brush and looks fully, he actually sees what he wants to paint and quickly sets out in its pursuit, and it is completed with a flourish of the brush, in which he goes after what he has seen like a falcon swooping down on a bounding hare—if you go off just a little, it gets away. This is what Wen Tong taught me. I could not do this, yet I recognized that it was true. When the mind has recognized how something is true, yet is unable to do it, the internal and the external are not the same; mind and hand do not respond to one another, which is an error of inadequate learning.

Whenever there is someone who sees it within himself yet has not reached the mature stage to take hold of it, he may normally consider himself to be fully developed: yet on the point of doing something, he loses it. This goes beyond the question of bamboo. . . .

"On the Painting of Tiered Bluffs . . . " is one of Su Shi's finest poems on painting, first "reading" the scene, then linking the experience of art to fantasy and memory.

On the Painting of Tiered Bluffs and the Misty River in the Collection of Wang Ding-guo (1088)

A sad heart upon the river,
    hills in a thousand tiers,
azure masses adrift in sky
    as if they were clouds and mist.

Whether a mountain or whether a cloud
    from afar no one can tell,
then in misty skies clouds scatter,
    the mountain remains as it was.

I see only two slopes, slate gray,
    that darken sheer valley below,
and into it go a hundred courses
    of streams cascading down;

They wind through forests, encircle stones,
    now hidden, now seen again,
wending on down to the valley's mouth
    forming a rushing river.

The river grows level, the mountains divide,
    the forested foothills end:
there a small bridge and a wilderness inn
    rest before the mountain.

Someone walking has passed just a bit
    beyond the towering trees;
there's a fishing boat, like single leaf,
    where river swallows the sky.

From where did the governor
    get hold of a work like this?
adorned by the finest brushwork,
    so clearly fresh and fine.

I know not where in this mortal world
    one might find such scenery,
but I would want to go there at once
    and buy a two-acre field.

Have you ever seen that spot so remote
    at Fan-kou in Wu-chang
where I, the Master of Eastern Slope,
    remained for five long years?

There spring breezes shook the river,
 the sky spread opening wide;
and when twilight clouds rolled away rain,
 hills showed their winsome charms.

Crows beat their wings through red maples,
 companions of nights spent afloat,
and snow-loads falling from tall pines
 woke me sharply from drunken sleep.

Peach blossoms and flowing water
 do exist in the world of men;
Wu-ling's dwellers need not be all
 gods and the undying.

The rivers and hills are empty and pure,
 but I belong to the dust;
though there may be a path to reach them,
 it is not my fate to follow.

So I give you back this painting
 and I sigh repeatedly,
yet I'm sure
 old friends in the hills will write
 poems calling me to come home.

The reference to peach blossoms and Wu-ling echoes Tao Qian's famous story of "Peach Blossom Spring," a community secluded from human history. Tang writers began to treat this place as if it were inhabited by immortals (an unwarranted elaboration of Tao's story to which Su Shi strenuously objected elsewhere).

The act of appreciation is closely related to the act of evaluation and judgment. The praise of one painter often requires the dispraise of another; and when the artist dispraised is highly regarded by most people, the act of appreciation can become the assertion of "true taste" against conventional opinion. In the following poem by the eleventh-century poet Wang An-shi, the famous painter Ju-ran is lightly dismissed in favor of two painters preferred by Wang, who rarely lacked self-confidence in his judgments. As in Su Shi's poem above, the experience of the painting is given as a personal fantasy stirred by the painting. In both cases, the initial fantasy jogs the viewer's memory—in Su Shi's case, a memory of his years of exile in Huang-zhou, and in Wang An-shi's case, the memory of another painting he liked.

Wang An-shi (1021–1086), My Brother Wang Chun-fu Brings Out a Painting by the Monk Hui-chong and Engages Me to Write a Poem on It

Painters there are in droves,
 and hardly worth the listing;

but of the more recent, Hui-chong
    is the one I most esteem.

It is August; clouds of a heatwave
    come welling up from woods;
yet this transports me, wild and free,
    and drops me down on an isle.

In broken stubble of yellow reeds
    snow blankets the ground,
ducks and geese stand serenely,
    each with a companion.

Scenes witnessed in times gone by
    stand now before my eyes:
level sands and unruffled waters,
    the beach of West River.

Twilight haze engulfs a boat,
    it hides the fishing net;
a man is sleeping, slumped in sounds
    like the creaking of the oars.

I strongly suspect this painter-monk
    has powers of Perfection Achieved—
the skill to detach and carry away
    landscapes of elsewhere.

He filled a basin with water,
    mixed herbs of fantasy,
then splashed them over raw silk
    and changed this heat to chill.

Ju-ran's few panels of mountains
    in the Han-lin Academy
show needless excess of pigment and ink,
    haphazard in execution.

But Cui Bai of Hao-liang
    is a good painter as well;
once I saw his blossoms of peach,
    serene in their first bloom.

Tipsy with wine, his carefree brush
    brought up a springtime breeze,
and I feared they would be whirled away
    in a rain of pink petals.

The gliding oriole sought a branch,
    winsome and ready to speak,

645

> honeybees were collecting pollen
> > in a train of wings and legs.
>
> A single age with two masters, both
> > the apogees of art,
> with tattered clothes and worn-out horses
> > longtime wayfarers.
>
> In splendid halls the price was deemed high—
> > ten thousand pieces of gold—
> as they stressed the point that painters today
> > could not equal those of old.

During the Northern Song, there appeared many new forms of writing on the arts. In contrast to the rare but grand comments by Tang writers, Song intellectuals took pride in creating a casual, almost offhand discourse in both poetry and prose. A new critical genre, "Remarks on Poetry" *(Shi-hua)*, took its name from a work by Ou-yang Xiu consisting of random comments and reminiscences on poetry.

Song writers were intensely aware of the differences that separated them from their Tang predecessors. Sometimes they spoke with pride of their own accomplishments, but often we can see something like an awe of the Tang. As collectors and scholars, they were also keenly aware of texts and artifacts lost, and the loss of past greatness was strangely linked to the physical loss of such texts and artifacts, as well as to the deterioration of what has survived, as in the following entry.

from Ou-yang Xiu, *Remarks on Poetry (Shi-hua)*

In these days when literature is at the height of its glory, Secretary Chen Cong-yi has received singular praise for his old style learning. His poems are very much like those of Bo Ju-yi. After Yang Yi and Liu Yun wrote their series of group compositions and the "Xi-kun Collection" became current, aspiring writers did their best to imitate that style. Poetry underwent a complete change, and the new fashion was called the "Xi-kun style." Because of this, the poetry collections of the great Tang masters were virtually abandoned and were not found in general circulation. At one point Chen chanced to obtain an old edition of Du Fu's poetry, whose text was full of errors and lacunae. In Du Fu's poem sending off Waterworks Commissioner Cai, there was the line:

> His body light: a single bird . . .

One word had been lost. Thereupon Chen and several of his friends tried to fill in the missing space. One tried:

> [His body light: a single bird] goes swiftly.

Another tried:

[His body light: a single bird] sinks.

And another:

[His body light: a single bird] rises.

And another:

[His body light: a single bird] descends.

No one could get it just right. Later Chen got hold of a good edition, and found that the line was in fact:

His body light: a single bird in passage.

Chen accepted his defeat with a sigh: as he saw it, even though it was a question of only one word, neither he nor any of his friends could equal Du Fu's choice.

The preceding anecdote reappears in the following poem by Su Shi, written to a friend to thank him for the gift of the tattered remains of a painting by Wu Dao-zi, the greatest Tang painter of Buddhist subjects. It is an urbane, rambling poem, filled with references, yet it touches on many of the essential questions of connoisseurship: the ability to recognize true art, the destruction of art, and the relation between art's value as art and as commodity.

Su Shi, "Some Time Ago in Chen Han-qing's House in Chang-an I Saw a Painting of the Buddha by Wu Dao-zi. It was unfortunately tattered and falling to pieces. When I saw it again over ten years later in Xian-yu Zi-jun's house, it had been mounted and restored. It was given to me by Zi-jun and I wrote this poem to thank him" (1078)

> Noblemen whose wealth is great,
>   whose lives are spent in ease,
> are rivals to purchase painting and script
>   and never reckon the cost.
>
> They have taken the script of Yin Tie-shi
>   to serve as their Wang Xi-zhi's,[2]
> and have further introduced Zhu Yao's work
>   in the place of Wu Dao-zi.[3]

---

[2]Su Shi's note: "Yin Tie-shi lived in the time of Emperor Wu of the Liang (r. 502–549). Nowadays, among the model calligraphy sheets attributed to the elder Wang, there are some with the name 'Tie-shi.'" Wang Xi-zhi was generally considered the greatest calligrapher of all time.
[3]Su Shi's note: "Many of the paintings currently collected as Wu Dao-zi's are actually the brushwork of Zhu Yao."

Reeking of smoke and water-stained,
　　these are mounted on rollers of jade;
who understands which valued more—
　　gray disk or its deerskin pouch?[4]

Wu Dao-zi's paintings of Buddha,
　　were gifts of divine spirit;
in the metamorphosis of dream he became
　　an immortal flying the skies.

Then waking, he would start to paint,
　　heedless of painstaking thought;
matchless marvels divine would come
　　out through his brush's hairs.

I saw this painting long ago
　　when staying in Chang-an,
and I sighed for this perfect treasure,
　　my eyes were streaming with tears:

I could not bear to look upon
　　its shredded silken threads,
they had become like butterflies
　　fluttering in air.

Yet you were able to have it mended,
　　to patch and repair its gaps;
though the whole remains dismembered,
　　its spirit is still complete.

By Bao-zhi, the monk, I vaguely see
　　the ruler and the knife;
its ashuras are still dauntless;
　　its heavenly maids still fair.

Just as when thinking of Du Fu's
　　line on the bird in flight:
though you want to add the missing word,
　　you know there is no way.

I wonder, receiving this from you,
　　if you truly had this intent:
to act for the sake of the common eye,
　　by this to wash them clear.

---

[4]In a story in *The Han History,* the jade disks presented to the throne were worth less than the deerskin pouches in which they were presented. Here the reference may suggest the inability of aristocratic collectors, concerned only with fine mountings, to appreciate the paintings themselves. In the context of the preceding lines, however, it may well suggest that the mountings are, in fact, worth more than the examples of painting and calligraphy they have collected.

Once those noblemen see this,
    they will surely blush with shame;
the thousand sheets in their brocade bags
    won't be worth tossing away.

No need to find for them further use
    to trade for threads of hemp—
just put a single torch to them
    and let them fly off in smoke.

Ordinary Things

If they had lost something of the magic of Tang poetry, many Song writers embraced the unmagical everyday world and sought to celebrate it in their poems. We often find a delight in the trivial and its imaginative transformation into poetry. Song poets made it their business to notice things previously left unnoticed. Ou-yang Xiu's older contemporary Mei Yao-chen often embedded these details in verse that was willfully unpoetic. His ideal of "mellow blandness" *(ping-dan)* had an admixture of the unpoetically harsh, as in the following lines in which he describes his poetry:

> I write poems that suit my nature and mood,
> and come quite close to mellow blandness.
> Rough phrases are left unfinished,
> they jab the mouth worse than burrs.
> I would have poured forth a great dark sea,
> but my vessel is small, and already brimming over.

If Tang poets were the ocean (great talent), the Song poet would accept his smaller vessel and make a virtue of it. The last line of the following poem is not simply bad, it is willfully bad, breaking the grand Tang poetic ending just as the trivial topic mocks Tang poetic sleeplessness.

Mei Yao-chen (1002–1060), A Companion Piece to Xie Jing-chu's "Spending the Night in My Wife's Study, Hearing Mice, and Being Greatly Troubled"

> Blue burned the lamp flame, the man was asleep,
> hungry mice came gradually forth from their holes.
>
> With the ringing of basins and bowls overturned,
> he wakes startled and listens, dreaming ceased.
>
> He worries they'll thump table's inkwell,
> then fears lest they gnaw the shelves' books.
>
> His son, naïve, mocks a cat's meow—
> that was really a childish idea.

In the Rain, Spending the Night in the Library of Messrs. Xie, Xu, and Pei

The hard rain rang as it dashed on the window,
I was just going to sleep by the dying lamp.

Insects' voices kept up terribly long,
the echoes were carried to my lonely pillow.

The rest were all drunk, seemed not to hear,
I was forced to listen, and it was awful.

The night was short, I never slept—
my eye was irritated by a dust speck.

Mei Yao-chen became famous for the following poem on the blowfish, a seasonal delicacy relished in spite of (or because of) its deadly poison, which, when errors are made in the preparation, has been the final meal of many a daring gourmet.

At a Party Given by Fan Zhong-yan the Guests Spoke of Eating "River-Hog," or the Blowfish

Spring isles grow with shoots of reeds,
spring shores fly with willow flowers.

At such times "river-hog" is prized
beyond the common run of fish.

Its form may make one marvel,
there is also no worse poison.

Its raging belly is like a great hog,
its furious eyes like a southeastern frog.

When fried in the kitchen, if things go amiss,
it will enter the throat like the sword Mo-ya.

Why give sustenance to tooth and palate
with something that wrecks the body like this?

If one dare question the Southerners thus,
they band to defend it and boast its merit.

They all say it's tasty beyond any measure,
none think of how many folk die from the pleasure.

And since to my views they will make no concession,
I helplessly sigh and give no more expression.

When Han Yu came to Chao-yang at last,
at a dinner of snakes he was left aghast.

When Liu-zhou was Liu Zong-yuan's abode,
he learned to grow fond of the taste of toad.

Although both creatures may be abhorrent,
one's life is not risked by an accident.

Such flavor may truly be like nothing else,
but within is mayhem that's limitless.

"Great beauty has some evil as pair"—
I really think that saying is fair.[5]

Though the small things of life find their way into the work of many Song writers, the poet closest to Mei Yao-chen in the poetic celebration of the quotidian was Yang Wan-li. In contrast to Mei Yao-chen's sometimes willful clumsiness and plainness, Yang Wan-li found in such topics inviting occasions for wit and small wonders of daily life. Yang Wan-li's poetry often involves playful transformations and metaphors: a sheet of ice becomes a fragile gong, or a line of ants carrying food becomes the return from a royal hunt laden with spoils.

Yang Wan-li (1127–1206), A Child Playing with Ice

From the metal bowl a child
    took early morning ice,
he pierced it with colored thread
    to serve as silver gong.
Struck, it echoed like a jade chime
    piercing through the woods,
then all at once the sound of glass
    shattering on the ground.

Watching Ants

When one of them chances to meet another,
    he whispers, asking the way,
I can't understand the reason
    they're so often moving house.
How much provision is necessary
    to feed bodies so small?—
returning home from the hunt,
    their wagon train is filled.

[5]Here Mei Yao-chen paraphrases a passage from *The Zuo Tradition,* humorously but aptly applied to the situation.

651

Both of Yang Wan'li-s quatrains above are pure play. In other cases, the poetic attention to small things hints at something deeper.

Su Shi, Thirteen Companion Pieces for Wen Tong's "Garden Pool in Yang-zhou": Bridge Over the Lake

Its red railings and painted posts
    brightly reflect in the lake,
in white linen and black gauze cap,
    you go, dragging your feet.
Beneath the bridge turtles and fish
    are teeming late in the day:
for they recognize the sound of your staff
    crossing over the bridge.

Yang Wan-li, June 10, 1177, Traveling by Boat to Take Up My Post at Pi-ling. Held up by adverse winds, we stayed the night at the mouth of the Zhou-pi River

I can't stand hearing the cries
    of insects from both shores
and take a candle to melt melancholy,
    along with a cup of wine.
I wonder who stayed the night on this boat
    as melancholy as I?—
the roof of the boat still bears
    the streaks of candle soot.

The act of poetic imagination that makes the small thing the focus of attention is often given as a minor triumph over some harsher reality:

Su Shi, East Slope

Rains have bathed Eastern Slope,
    the moonlight's colors are clear,
the passage of market folk is done,
    only wilderness folk walk now.
Let no one hate that the path on the ridge
    is rocky and too rough—
I myself am fond of the clatter
    of my staff as it drags along.

Particularly in the Southern Song, the use of poetry to create in miniature a world of the imagination became commonplace. In the face of many kinds of restriction, acts of poetic imagination might restore freedom and power. The next two poems are by Lu You, the most famous of Southern Song poets.

Lu You (1125–1210), Snowy Night

I

My books lie scattered all around,
    boxes of pills among them;
huddled in blankets, from time to time
    I burn incense from Hai-nan.
Growing old and slow, I laugh at myself,
    that a young man's heart survives,
that still loves to listen to northern winds
    blow snow across my bed.

II

On village lanes the snow turns slush,
    and people cease their goings;
the dot of a Buddhist temple lantern
    is a bright grain of red sand.
How late now the falcon returns
    to his mountain home to roost—
the winds bear the whir
    of mighty wings.

It is one thing to possess a childish fascination with the small things of the world; it is something else to claim to possess such naïveté, to hold that as the highest value, and to celebrate one's own innocence:

Drawing Water from the Well and Making Tea

I get up sick, done looking at my books,
pull hands into sleeves, clear night stretching on.

All the neighborhood's silent, nowhere a sound,
and the lamp fire now burns chill and low.

My servant boy too is sleeping soundly,
so I go draw water and make my own tea.

There's the sound of the well pulley creaking:
a hundred feet down the ancient well sings.

Inside, my organs shiver from the cold,
then from bone to hair, I'm revived, aware.

I go back; moonlight fills the corridors
and I can't bear to step on sparse shadows of plums.

653

As Lu You, Yang Wan-li, and other writers imaginatively transformed the world around them by acts of words, they also actively staged such experiences in the physical world. The leisure life, from the agenda of a planned excursion to the construction of gardens, was shaped by images given in poetry; and those activities and constructions in turn gave rise to poems.

The Song saw the appearance of new forms of casual prose consisting of random jottings on various topics. Sometimes these books of jottings treated political matters, sometimes they treated literary matters, and sometimes, as in the piece that follows, they addressed such basic questions as sunning oneself in winter. This passage from a miscellany entitled *Rustic Chat from the East of Chi (Qi-dong ye-yu),* by the thirteenth-century Southern Song writer Zhou Mi, gives a good illustration of the interplay between art and private life, with its odd mixture of playfully displayed erudition, bodily comfort, "home improvement," and the writing of poems. He begins with examples of sunning oneself in earlier anecdotes and poems.

Zhou Mi (1232–1298), "Sunning Oneself" (from *Qi-dong ye-yu*)

Yuan An would lie with his back to the sun and have his boy scratch his back, saying, "Now that really feels good!" Zhao Sheng would bare his back to the sun on an open patio, waiting for woodsmen and herdsmen to return. From this we have the lines in Du Fu's poetry:

> My back to the light, I wait for woodsmen and herdsmen.

and:

> My back to the light, I am near a high wall.[6]

and from "Sunning Oneself in West Tower":

> When, shivering with chills, I weary of black winter,
> I revel in this soaring tower, my back to the light.

and later there is:

> In a while my hair feels gently warmed,
> gaunt flesh grows imperceptibly more plump and glossy.

> The sun truly shows its deep kindliness,
> waning energies suddenly have a recourse.

> Teetering, I must bother to pay close attention,
> but effortless now, I draw my sick feet.

Bo Ju-yi's "Sunning" goes:

---

[6]This seems to be the second line of a poem entitled "Evening," which Zhou Mi has either misremembered or had access to a variant reading no longer extant. Present editions read: "To toast my back, I draw near to the sunlight on the wall."

With a glow the winter sun comes forth
and shines on my room's south corner.

My back to the light, I sit with eyes closed,
gentle breath courses through starving flesh.

At first it's like drinking a heady wine,
and then like one reviving from hibernation.

Thawing outside, all my bones stretch,
content within, I have not a single care.

I feel expansive, I forget where I am,
my mind joins together with the void.

All of these are examples of a deep understanding of the quality of sunning one's back.

Winter days merit such fondness that they truly seem like things to be offered as presents. Chao Duan-ren once had a case of the chills that no medicine could cure. It got better only when he toasted his back in the winter sunlight. Zhou Bang-yan once wrote a poem that went:

Winter sunshine is like village beer—
its strange warmth lasts but a moment.
One insists that it go on and on,
but however we yearn, it is suddenly gone.

I once built a small tower for sunning myself in Nan-rong and named it "Porch for Offering Sunlight." I hung it all around with white, oiled cheesecloth so that the open brightness of sunlight was plentiful throughout the whole day, and the comfortable relaxation of my limbs was not limited to a mere moment. It happened that a visitor joked with me, "This is what is meant by the cotton-padded jacket of the world," and we had a laugh about it. Then later I saw He Si-ju's "Song of the Yellow Cotton-Padded Jacket," whose preface went:

In March there was a great snowfall that did not stop for ten days. When the sun came out, in the house next door they called to one another to go lie in the sun, saying, "The yellow cotton-padded jacket is out."

On reading this, I realized that the expression had already been used before. But then Wang Li-zhi had also named his window for taking the sun "the Overcoat Porch."

[Zhou Mi then goes on to quote the poem written for Wang Li-zhi's porch and other examples of sunning oneself in the past.]

Perhaps the finest poetry on the small experiences of life occurs not when those experiences are staged or transformed by a witty interpretation, but when they are presented as accidental discoveries, in which something is noted that has interest but no obvious meaning.

Chao Duan-you (11th century), Spending the Night at an Inn Outside the West Gate of Ji-zhou

> Winter woods in the last sunlight,
>   crows about to roost;
> blue lamp flames flicker on the wall,
>   at once there, at once gone.
> In the stillness of a gentle rain
>   I pretend to be asleep,
> I lie listening to a tired horse
>   munch on the last of the hay.

In Chao Duan-you's poem above and Huang Ting-jian's below, we have two roughly contemporary quatrains—we don't know which is the earlier—that make the same "discovery." Either in dream or lying with his eyes closed, the poet seems to hear the "poetic" sound of rain, but in reality it is a horse munching on hay. As in so many poems of the period, the comparison calls attention to the imagination's transformation of everyday experience. In that process, the usually unpoetic image—a horse munching on hay—acquires a nearly magical dignity. But almost certainly one of these two poets was writing not from a fresh, imaginative experience of everyday life, but from having read the other poem. It might be mere literary imitation, or perhaps the second poet actually did experience the similitude in real life, but noticed it only because he had read the other poem. Even more than in earlier periods, in the Song the relation between poetry and experience became reciprocal: poems grew out of experience, but the experience of poetry also shaped experience in the world outside poetry.

Huang Ting-jian (1045–1105), August 17, Sleeping in Daytime

> In this world's red dust, wearing hat of straw
>   and raven black hose,
> I imagine seeing a pair of white birds
>   upon the gray-green isles.
> A horse is munching on dry straw,
>   a sound by my pillow at noon,
> as the dream forms, it is wind-blown rain
>   rolling the waves on the river.

Pastoral Scenes

Song Dynasty writers were not so much interested in everyday experience in its own right as in staging or discovering the extraordinary within the ordinary. They romanticized the details of the simple life to create an essentially pastoral vision of satisfied domesticity. The poetic worlds they described in their own lives were closely related to a more traditional pastoral poetry—"snapshots" of rural scenes and the timeless contentments of village life. Like modern photographers, they would carefully frame such scenes and try to catch their subject at a significant moment. At the same time, when they themselves are the subjects of the "snapshot," there is a strong sense that they are posing but trying hard to appear to have been caught unawares.

He Zhu (1063–1120), A Walk in the Wilds

From the ford a tiny path
    slants off toward the city;
where waters sink, a single village
    lies across soft sands.
In a hut of yellow thatch
    soaked by sporadic rain
a white-haired old lady sits,
    watching over her melons.

Kong Ping-zhong (d. after 1101), The Grain Is Ripe

The millet smells sweet in the west wind
    across a hundred miles,
streams draw back to underground channels,
    the harvest is brought in.
The old ox has pretty much done with
    obligations of the plow:
chewing grass at the top of a bank,
    it rests in the setting sun.

Ou-yang Xiu, Ox

As the sun comes over the eastern hedge,
    brown sparrows fly up in alarm;
the snows melt and springtime stirs
    the sprouts of plants to growth.
Earthen embankments stretch level,
    the paddy fields are vast;
bearing a young boy stretched on its back
    and leading a calf, it walks.

Fan Cheng-da (1126–1191), A Description of Walking in the Meadows on Cold Food Festival (first of two)

A wilderness inn by a dock with weeping willows,
a rundown temple in clumps of bitter bamboo.

Waters where egrets peer through reed-weirs,
winds where crows peck ashes of paper cash.

657

An old woman leads a girl with thick make-up,
a boy helps an old man, reeling drunk.

In this remote village the festival was good—
I'm sure because last year's harvest was rich.

Lu You, Visiting West-of-the-Mountain Village

Don't laugh at the old farmers
    all muddled with winter beer,
in years of plenty they entertain guests
    with chicken and suckling pig.

Hills in layers, stream after stream,
    it seems there's no way through;
willows conceal, the flowers are bright,
    then here is another village.

Flutes and drums in succession,
    Spring Festival draws near;
their clothes and caps are simple,
    the old ways linger here.

From this day on, if you permit,
    I'll come idly in moonlight,
and unexpectedly, propped on my staff,
    knock at your gate one night.

Walking in the Wilds

Afternoon butterflies dance in the vegetable plot;
under clear skies doves sing in wheat fields.

Sometimes I go to the shade and briefly rest,
then walk privately along the path.

Village women peer at me through the hedge,
old men of the hills brush off mats in welcome.

Can things like this be found in court and market?—
a good laugh is solace for life's last days.

Fan Cheng-da was the master of the rural vignette. His most famous and much imitated work was a series of sixty "Various Occasions of Interest in the Fields and Gardens Through the Four Seasons." Each is a brief moment in the imagined lives of a farming household.

Fan Cheng-da, Various Occasions of Interest in the Fields and Gardens Through the Four Seasons

XV

Butterflies go in pairs
    culling pollen from the flowers;
through long days no visitors come
    to the farmer's home.
Then chickens fly over the hedge,
    a dog barks in his lair,
and you know a traveling peddler
    is here to sell his tea.

XXXI

At daybreak, out to weed the fields,
    in evening hemp is spun,
boys and girls of the village
    each has a role in the home.
The younger children don't yet know
    how to help with tilling or weaving,
they too, in the shade of a mulberry,
    are learning to plant melons.

XXXIII

A traveler in the brown dust,
    his sweat flowing like broth,
stops a while at a farmhouse
    to drink from the sweet-smelling well.
They offer him a flat stone
    to sit before the gate:
noon in the shade of willows
    is where the breeze is most cool.

XL

He calmly watches a spider weave
    its web hanging low from the eaves,
it somehow or other obstructs
    small insects from flying through.
A dragonfly hangs upside down,
    a wasp is also trapped—
they frantically call to the mountain boy
    to help them break the siege.

XLIV

A newly constructed threshing floor,
    clay surface as flat as a mirror,
where every family beating the grain
    make the best of the frosty weather.

In the sounds of singing and laughter
    the rumble of light thunder:
the flails echo all night long
    until the day grows light.

LII
The burning sap of a pine brand
    serves them as a lamp;
its thick smoke resembles ink
    and darkens all the room.
Towards evening they wipe clean
    the paper on southern windows,
taking note that the setting sun
    is twice as red as before.

Wit

Tang poets occasionally composed clever epigrams, but the numerous shades of wit
and humor played a much larger role in Song poetry, which often prided itself on a
lightness of touch. Such poems usually aimed for the hint of a smile rather than a
laugh. Sometimes we barely notice.

Yang Wan-li, Strolling Along a Juniper Path in the Morning (second of two)

The rain stopped and in the groves
    a chill arose,
when wind pierced through into the path,
    the morning seemed still more fresh.
I walked where I pleased and chanced to come
    to a spot where no one was—
I startled the mountain birds to flight,
    and I also was startled.

Lu You, On the Three Peaks of Magic Stone Mountain

Wondrous peaks welcome my horse
    and startled a weak old man:
the summits of Shu and mountains of Wu
    are all washed away to nothing.
Green and gray they poke from the Earth
    to a height of five thousand yards:
and I troubled them to coil themselves up
    into this tiny poem.

In the following poem, Lu You refers to himself by his pseudonym, the "Old Man Set Free."

Plum Blossoms III (1202)

They tell me that the plums
    bloomed in the morning breeze,
their snowy piles are everywhere
    all around in the hills.
Is there some method to transform
    one body into billions?—
for each tree of blossoming plums,
    one Old Man Set Free.

Yang Wan-li, For Play

Wild chrysanthemums and moss
    mint coins of their own:
yellow of gold, green of bronze,
    rivals both in charm.
Heaven's Lord disburses these
    to poor poets—
but they purchase only melancholy
    and purchase him no fields.

Coda: Self-Consciousness

The ancient definition of classical poetry was to "speak what the mind is intent on" ("Great Preface") or to "sing one's feelings and nature." Song poets continued to write poems about interior experience, but when doing so they often located the point of view outside themselves: they set up the camera and then hurried to take their place in the snapshot. Their wit and irony, and sometimes a capacity for self-mockery, followed from such self-consciousness. They not only know what a poet's sensibility should be, they also know what he is supposed to look like.

Lu You, Meeting a Gentle Rain on the Sword-Gate Pass Road (1172)

The dust of travel on my clothes
    mixes with stains of wine,
nowhere I go in these distant travels
    fails to melt the heart.
I wonder—should this body of mine
    have been a poet or not?—

riding a donkey in gentle rain
    I enter Sword-Gate Pass.

In Moonlight

The moonlight white, the yard is bare,
    the shadows of trees are spare,
magpies, unsettled on their roosts,
    go flying around the boughs.
This old man is imitating
    childish girls and boys,
batting the passing fireflies
    and letting dew soak his clothes.

Su Shi (1037–1101) 趙宋

Su Shi, also commonly known by his pen name Su Dong-po, was the most out-standing literary figure of the Song. Unlike most Tang and writers of earlier periods, Su Shi enjoyed the full measure of adulation as a cultural hero in his own lifetime—his role strengthened by his political difficulties during the regimes of Wang An-shi and his followers.

A native of Mei-shan in Sichuan, Su Shi, with his father Su Xun and his brother Su Che, set out for the capital in the middle of the eleventh century to seek office. Ou-yang Xiu was their patron, and the examiner who passed both brothers in 1057. After taking the *jin-shi* examination, Su Shi began a promising political career, serv-ing first in a provincial post, then in the capital. In 1069, Wang An-shi began to put his political reform policies into practice and came into conflict with many of the leading intellectuals of the day; these he either forced into retirement or sent out to provincial posts. Late in 1071, Su Shi himself was sent off to govern Hang-zhou; thereafter, except for a few brief periods in the capital, Su spent the remaining thirty years of his life in one provincial post after another.

Su Shi's political difficulties enhanced rather than harmed his role as a cultural hero. As a young man, he was generously promoted by figures such as Ou-yang Xiu, and as he grew older he was eagerly sought by young men seeking his support in turn. Su Shi was the master of all literary forms: classical prose, classical poetry, song lyric, and informal prose (friendly letters, colophons, and notes). He was also a painter and calligrapher of distinction.

Su Shi was the spokesman for one powerful current in Song intellectual culture: a casual engagement with experience that was equally distinct from Buddhist de-tachment and from the rigid ideological engagement of Wang An-shi and some of the Neo-Confucians. Such casual engagement offered a relaxed pleasure that was quite different from the intensity of passion and was a value that Su Shi held and es-poused. It was, however, not a value that Su, with his immensely turbulent person-ality, could comfortably live up to.

Account of the Hall of Precious Artworks

The superior person may let his interests find temporary lodging in exter-nal things, yet he may not let those interests remain caught up in things. When our interests find temporary lodging in external things, even the hum-blest things can bring delight and even the most beguiling things can bring no harm upon us. But if our interests do remain caught up in things, even the humblest things can do us damage and even the most beguiling things bring no delight. It was Lao-zi who said, "All the colors together blind the

663

eyes. All the musical notes deafen the ears. All flavors ruin the palate. And galloping on field hunts brings out a madness in the mind of man." But the Sage never gives these four things up—he simply lets his interests lodge in them only temporarily. Liu Bei, the founder of the Shu-Han Kingdom, had the gift of bold action, yet he loved to plait animal hair. Xi Kang, the Daoist eccentric, achieved the spirit's perfection, yet he loved the labors of a smith. Ruan Fu was a free spirit, yet he loved waxed clogs. These are hardly the sensual pleasures of sound, physical beauty, smell, or taste; yet throughout their lives these men found an unflagging delight in such things.

Among all the things that bring us joy and have the capacity to please a person without swaying him, nothing can compare to books and paintings. But when our interests remain caught up in them and cannot get loose, the evil they can wreak is beyond the telling. By these Zhong Yao was brought to vomit blood and dig up a tomb.[1] Emperor Xiao-wu of the Liu-Song, who wanted to be the dominant calligrapher of the time, came to feel spite for Wang Seng-qian. Huan Xuan's speeding boat, in which he carried his collection of books and paintings in order to have them with him always, and Wang Ya's multiple walls, by which he protected his collection, were both childish amusements that harmed the nation and brought ruin on the men themselves. Such is the evil of having one's interest caught up in things.

When first I was young, I loved both books and paintings. I feared only losing what I already had and that others would not give me what they themselves had. But then I laughed at myself and said: "I care so little for wealth and honor, yet I treat books with the highest regard. I care little about my life or death, but my paintings are important to me. Doesn't it seem that I've gotten things upside down and lost what is basic in the heart?" From that point on, I didn't dote on them any more. Even though, when I came upon something that gave me pleasure, I would sometimes keep it, I no longer cared when such things were taken by someone else. Compare them to clouds and mist shapes passing before the eyes or to all the different birds that stir the listening ear—of course we rejoice when we encounter them; but when they are gone, our thoughts do not hang on them. Thus books and paintings always give me delight, yet they can do me no damage.

Although Commander Escort Wang Shen hails from the quarter of the imperial in-laws, in his clothing, in his sense of ceremony and right, in his learning, and in his literary accomplishments, he is of equal stature to poor scholars. His style of living eschews rich foods and fancy fare; he keeps apart from the sensual pleasures of ear and eye and devotes himself to books and paintings. To the east of his mansion he has built a Hall of Precious Artworks where he keeps what he has acquired; and he has asked me to write an account for it. Worried lest he have the misfortune to be as I was in my youth, too much loving these things, I have made a point of telling him this,

---

[1] Zhong Yao, the third-century calligrapher, saw a specimen of Cai Yong's calligraphy and beat himself for three days until he was black and blue. When Wei Dan died and had the piece of Cai Yong's calligraphy buried with him, Zhong Yao dug up the tomb to get hold of it.

in hopes that he can enjoy the fullness of their delights and keep far from the potential damage.

> —An account written this twenty-second day of September, 1077

to "Fragrance Fills the Yard" *(Man-ting fang)*

Hollow glories won on a snail's horn,
on a fly's head some small advantage gained:
when I think about it, why
    do we go to such pointless trouble?
Everything that happens
    has been settled long before—
no one comes out short,
    no one comes out ahead.
So I'll make the most of my leisure,
    and the fact I'm not yet too old,
and indulge myself to my limit
    in a little wildness.
In life's possible hundred years
you should let yourself get drunk in total
thirty-six thousand times.

I have considered it,
and how much longer do we have—
with gloomy winds and rain
keeping us from half?
Also why should we
spend the rest of our lives arguing
    over what's better, what's worse?
We are lucky to have cool breeze
    and also the silvery moon,
a cushion of moss spread for us,
    a tent of cloud stretched high.
The Southland is fine,
a thousand cups of sweet wine,
and a song: "Fragrance Fills the Yard."

Account of the Terrace "Passing Beyond"

In all things, however ordinary, there is something that deserves reflection. And insofar as there is something that deserves reflection, there is in all such things something in which we can find delight, and it need not be unusual or peculiarly beautiful. You can still get drunk chewing the dregs or guzzling weak beer. Fruit and vegetables and other growing things can all provide plenty to eat. Extending this by analogy, I will find delight no matter where I go.

What we mean by seeking good fortune and avoiding adversity is that good fortune brings happiness, while adversity brings sadness. But human desires are endless, while the things that can satisfy our desires are limited. So long as distinctions of attraction and aversion battle within me and so long as decisions on which course to choose converge before me, few things bring delight, while the things that bring sorrow remain ever numerous. This may, in fact, be thought of as looking for adversity and turning down good fortune.

To look for adversity and turn down good fortune is hardly human instinct. If someone does so, there is something in external things that clouds his instinct. Such people move within external things and not beyond them. Things have no real distinctions of magnitude in their own right; and yet when someone reflects on them from within, every single one of them looms large. Should things loom large over me, my eyes are always dazzled and confused. As if watching a struggle through a crack, how can one tell who is the victor and who the loser? In this way attractions and aversions spring up out of control, and anxieties and delights emerge from them. Can we help feeling sorry for someone in such a situation?

When I left Qian-tang [Hang-zhou] to take up the administration of Jiao-xi [Mi-zhou], I forsook the steadiness of the boat and submitted to the difficulties of going by horse and coach. I left behind the attractions of carved walls and took shelter in a dwelling with plain beams. I turned my back on vistas of lakes and mountains to walk through a wilderness of mulberry and hemp. On the day I arrived, I found the harvest had been bad for several years running. There were bandits everywhere in the outlands, and complaints clogged the courts. I kept to a plain diet, each day eating only medlar and chrysanthemums. Obviously people suspected I was unhappy. But when I had been there for a full year, my features looked increasingly healthy; and the white in my hair every day progressively reverted to its former black. For I found delight in the purity of their customs, while office workers and populace alike were comfortable with my ineptness.

At that point I had work done in the park, and had the buildings and grounds cleaned up; I ordered the tall, dense trees on An Hill cut down to repair what had been broken; and I made plans to complete the work whatever way I could.

In the northern part of the park there was an old terrace built into the contours of the city wall. I had the building there thatched and renovated a little. And from time to time I go up there with others and look around, giving my mood free rein. To the south there is a view of Horse-Ear Mountain, while Chang Mountain is sometimes hidden and sometimes dimly appears, seeming both close at hand, yet far away—perhaps there are good men living in seclusion there? Then to the east you have Lu Mountain, into which Lu Ao went into retreat during the Qin Dynasty. To the west there is a view of Mu-ling, shadowing like ramparts, where the lingering glories of Lü Shang and Duke Huan of Qi still survive. To the north I look down over the river Wei, where strong feeling overwhelms me when I think on the deeds of Han Xin, Count Huai-yin, and lament how his story did not come to a good end. The terrace is high and stable, deepset and bright, cool in summer and warm in winter. In dawns when the snow is falling or on evening of wind and moonlight I never miss a chance to be there, and my guests never miss a chance to go along with me. We pick vegetables in the garden, take fish from the ponds, brew sorghum beer, boil and eat unpolished rice. And we say, what a delight to visit the place!

At this time my brother Zi-you happened to be in Ji-nan, heard about this place, and wrote a poem about it in which he gave the terrace the name "Passing Beyond." In this he saw that my ability to find delight wherever I go comes from the fact that I roam beyond things.

Occasions of delight, whether staged or accidentally encountered, are a recurrent motif in Su Shi's writing. Literary works, particularly poems, celebrate such moments, reflect on their significance, and reaffirm Su's conviction that joy is possible only when we do not cling to it. The moment's magic is, by its very nature, transitory.

Getting Up at Night in a Boat (1079)

It was the rustling of a faint breeze
  blowing through rushes and reeds:
I opened the door to watch the rain,
  but moonlight filled the lake.

The boatmen and the waterbirds
  were both in the same dream,
a large fish leapt, then dived deep down,
  like a frightened fox fleeing away.

In night's depths both creatures and men
  lie outside each other's concerns,
and I was alone, a body and shadow
  for our mutual amusement.

In the dark, rivertides rose on the isles
  with the sad sounds of winter worms,
the sinking moon hung in the willows
  which I saw as a spider's web.

This life goes by me in a flash
  with anxiety and troubles,
clear scenes like this pass my eyes
  and last but for a moment.

Roosters crow, the bell tolls,
  the birds all go scattering;

>they beat the drum at the front of the boat
>again shouting each to the other.

Although Su Shi warns against the dangers of clinging to things and to experience, writing often serves as the means to catch the moment before it gets away from him. The following are entries from one of Su's collections of informal prose, *The Forest of Notes (Zhi-lin)*. The Song pleasure in informal prose is closely related to the fascination with the moment—its accidents, its random details and unexpected pleasures.

Visiting White Waters. Written for my son Su Mai (from *The Forest of Notes*)

December 12, 1094. I visited the Monastery of the Buddha's Footprints with my young son Mai. We bathed in the pool formed by the hot springs there, which were very hot indeed, being virtually able to cook something. We went east following the contours of the mountain, and a little to the north there was a waterfall a hundred yards high. This flowed off around the mountain in a number of sharp turns, then at one bend formed a pool whose deepest parts were plumbed to a depth of forty-five feet without reaching the bottom. The waters splashed with snowy froth and roared like thunder, both delightful and awe-inspiring. On the water's bank there were some twenty or thirty huge human footprints, which are known as the "Buddha's Footprints." At twilight we went home, and retracing our steps, we watched while they burned away the vegetation on the mountain—quite a fire. In no time at all we passed several valleys and reached the river. When the moon came out over the mountains, the highlands were awash in midcurrent, and we scooped watery handfuls of pearls and jade rings. We got home about ten o'clock, and again I drank with Mai as we ate the remaining sweets and boiled vegetables. I looked at my woozy shadow but wasn't very sleepy, so I wrote this out for Mai:

>—The Old Man of East Slope

Account of a Visit One Night to Cheng-tian Temple (from *The Forest of Notes*)

December 12, 1083, nighttime. I had taken my clothes off and was about to go to sleep when the moonlight came in through the window. Delighted, I got up and went for a walk. I kept thinking how there was no one to enjoy this with me, so I went off to Cheng-tian Temple looking for Zhang Huai-min. Huai-min also hadn't gone to sleep, and we walked together in the courtyard. At one end of the courtyard there was an elusive radiance, as if from a body of water, and in that water there seemed to be the intricate pattern of waterplants. These were, in fact, shadows of cypress and bamboo. Will there ever be a time without moonlit nights, or is there any place that has no cypress and bamboo? It is only that there are few easygoing people like the two of us.

The "Record of Music" in the *Classic of Rites* observed that temple music should not be too loud and extravagant, giving a sense of restraint by omission. In the same way, ceremonial dishes served in the temple should be bland, leaving out some possibilities of flavor. Any kind of experience, carried to the limits of intensity, reverts quickly to its opposite, as in the famous line of a song attributed to Emperor Wu of the Han: "when pleasure crests, grim thoughts are many." A certain reserve seemed to make the continuity of pleasure possible. The very lack of excitement in the following poem ensures the perfection of the poet's pleasure, which lingers on into the composition of the poem, looking back to catch the memory of the fleeting moment.

On the Winter Festival I Visited Lone Mountain and the Two Monks Hui-jin and Hui-si (1071)

The sky looked like snow,
clouds were filling the lake,
terrace and tower appeared and vanished,
    the hills seemed there, then gone.

Waters so clear that stones were revealed,
    and I could count the fish;
deep in the woods there was no one,
    birds called each to the other.

On this winter festival I didn't go home
    to be with children and wife,
I sought these holy men, known by repute,
    which was really to please myself.

Where was the holy men's lodging found?—
in front of Jewel Cloud Mountain
    where the road twists and turns.

There was Lone Mountain, so completely alone
    who would build his hut here?—
yet if holy men have the holy Way
    then the mountain cannot be lonely.

Paper windows and bamboo roof,
    deep within it was warm,
wrapped in cassocks they sat asleep
    on mats for meditation.

The cold weather and journey's distance
    made my servant worried;
the carriage was readied, I hurried back,
    before it was late afternoon.

When we left the mountain I turned to gaze—
    it was covered by clouds and trees,
and all I could see was a wild hawk
    circling the pagoda.

The very blandness of this trip
    left its residue of pleasure:
when I reached home I was in a daze,
    still shaking myself from dream.

I wrote this poem as swift as fire
    to catch what was fleeting away,
for once a clear scene escapes us
    it cannot be grasped again.

Account of a Visit to Pine River (from *The Forest of Notes*)

Some time ago I was transferred from Hang-zhou to Gao-mi, and I went in a boat with Yang Yuan-su. Chen Ling-ju and Zhang Zi-ye both followed us, and we visited Li Gong-ze in Hu-zhou. Next we were joined by Liu Xiao-shu, and we all went to Pine River. At midnight the moon came out, and we had a drinking party at Hanging Rainbow Pavilion. Zhang Zi-ye was eighty-five years old and was known all over the world for his song lyrics. There he composed a version of "Settling Wind and Waves," whose summation went:

It is said that worthy men have gathered
    under the astral lines of Wu,
and should you ask—
I'm sure at their side you'll find
    the Old Man's Star.

Everyone at the party was having a great time, and some of us were so drunk we passed out. I have never forgotten that joy. Now seven years have passed. Zhang Zi-ye, Liu Xiao-shu, and Chen Ling-ju have all joined the world of shades. On September 9 this year, an ocean storm brought a tidal wave that left over nine feet of water on level land; the pavilion and bridge over Pine River were swept away and not a trace was left. When I think on that bygone moment, it was truly a dream.
    —February 12, 1072, written at night in Lin-gao Pavilion in Huang-zhou

"The Ocean Mirage at Deng-zhou," about a mirage at sea, is one of Su Shi's finest poems, characteristically balancing engagement and disengagement, visionary intensity and play, and turning at last to measure Su's poetic experience with a similar experience by Han Yu. The central term that begins the poem is "emptiness"—*kong*—a technical term in Buddhist thought referring to the illusoriness and insubstantiality of sensory perception. Both the mirage created by the sea god and the poet's imaginative representation are "empty" things, "airy" visions.

After the sea god performs his conjurer's trick in producing empty illusions for Su Shi's amusement, Su recalls one of Han Yu's most famous poems, "Visiting the Temple of Mount Heng, Then Spending the Night at the Buddhist Monastery: I Wrote This on the Gate Tower," composed when Han was returning from a term of exile in the far south where he served as governor of Chao-yang (see p. 485). Han had hoped to get a good view of Mount Heng, but

> . . .
> Surges of cloud and oozing fogs
>   hid its waist halfway up;
> and though a summit it must have had,
>   none could get all the way through.
>
> I came here just at the time
>   of the season of autumn rains,
> it was shut up in shadowy vapors,
>   there was no clear breeze.
>
> If to silent prayers from my secret heart
>   an answer is here given,
> it must be because one upright and true
>   is able to touch and sway.
>
> In an instant all was swept clear,
>   the throngs of peaks emerged!
> I looked up and saw them towering there,
>   buttresses of blue sky.
>
> Purple Awning fanning out
>   until it touched Pillar-of-Heaven,
> and Stone Granary in hurtling vaults
>   piling on Firegod Peak.

Assuming that the god of the mountain had answered his silent prayer, Han Yu reverently goes off to the temple of the god, overseen by a scruffy priest who tells his fortune.

> . . .
> He took the talismans in his hand
>   and showed me how to toss them,
> said, "This is most lucky of all,
>   no other cast can compare."
>
> Banished from sight in barbarian jungles,
>   lucky not to be dead,
> my food and clothing just barely enough,
>   willing to meet my end.
>
> To be prince, lord, minister, general,
>   all hope has fled long ago—

> though the god might wish my good fortune,
>   it is something not easily done.

In contrast to Han Yu's painful irony, the Song poet offers an altogether different answer:

The Ocean Mirage at Deng-zhou (1085)

I had long heard about the ocean mirage at Deng-zhou. Old men told me that it usually appeared in spring and summer and, since it was now later in the year, it wouldn't be appearing again. I went there five days after reaching my post; and thinking it would be too bad if I didn't get to see it, I made a prayer in the temple of the sea god Prince of Extensive Virtue. On the following day the mirage appeared, and I wrote this poem.

> In the cloudy sea off to the east,
>   there is emptiness on emptiness,
> where immortal hosts appear and vanish
>   in an empty radiance.
>
> As this drifting world is swept along
>   there are thousands of images born,
> but how could there really be cowry gates
>   hiding palaces of pearls?
>
> This mind knows well that what it sees
>   are all but conjured forms,
> yet to please my ears and eyes I dared
>   bother the craftsman-god.
>
> In the cold of the year the water is chill,
>   Heaven and Earth are closed tight,
> but on my behalf He roused from sleep
>   and whipped on dragons and fish.
>
> Its tiers of mansions, its azure hills
>   came forth in frosty dawn—
> an event so rare it thoroughly shocked
>   even centegenarians.
>
> Whatever we get in this mortal world
>   permits being taken by force,
> but beyond this world there are no "things,"
>   and who can intimidate there?
>
> What I made was but a casual plea;
>   the god did not refuse:
> truly this monstrosity was wrought by man,
>   not troubles Heaven-sent.

When the governor of Chao-yang
    returned from his southern exile,
he was cheered to see "Stone Granary
    piling on Firegod Peak."

He thought that someone upright and true
    had touched the wraith of the hill;
how could he know that the Shaper of Things
    just felt pity for his frailty?

The face relaxes, a moment's laughter
    is not a thing easily had:
indeed the god did answer you,
    and generously as well.

In thousands of miles of dying sunlight
    a lone bird sinks away,
then all I see is the sapphire sea
    polishing its green bronze.

This new poem of mine and its fancy words,
    have they any more point than this?—
they will join it, change and vanish away
    along with the eastern wind.

Poetry may be as insubstantial and pointless as the ocean mirage at Deng-zhou, a mere construct of "fancy words" and wit, like the following poem on peonies that bloomed in winter. But the poem still can have serious consequences.

Companion Pieces to Chen Xiang's "Peonies on a Winter Day" (1073) (first of four)

A single bloom of beguiling red,
    an azure almost dissolving,
shining back the glory of spring,
    shaming the frost and snow.
The Artist of Change wants only to show
    a novelty of craft
and will not allow these idle flowers
    even the briefest respite.

Chinese poets would sometimes write political commentary into the most innocuous poems. Readers might often discover such political messages, even when they were not intended.

    Su Shi was strongly opposed to the "New Laws" policies of Wang An-shi and his followers, and in 1079, the poet was thrown into prison on the charge of slandering the regime in his poetry. A record of his trial has survived, known as "The

Poetry Trial on Wu Terrace," and it is one of the most remarkable documents of Chinese poetic interpretation and misinterpretation. Poems are brought up by the prosecution and the "slanderous intent" is explained. Some of these poems clearly do make unkind references to the current government, but lyrics like the one above, an apparently harmles and witty comment on the unseasonable blooming of some peonies, were also included in the indictment. In regard to the set from which the poem above is taken, the charge against Su was: "These four poems were ridiculing the senior officials then overseeing government policy by comparing them to the Artist of Change, seeking only to come up with novel schemes and preventing the common people from enjoying even a brief respite."

Escaping the serious charges against him, Su Shi was sent off to a low post in Huang-zhou, where he wrote some of his most famous poetry. The "Eight Poems on Eastern Slope"—"*Dong-po,*" from which he took the name by which he is often known—take Su back to basics, to farming, and to the theme of hardship overcome by effort and imagination. The Preface and the first two poems of the set follow.

from "Eight Poems on Eastern Slope" (1081)

Two years after arriving at Huang-zhou, I found myself in ever greater want with each passing day. An old friend, Ma Zheng-qing, felt sorry that I had so little food, and from the government office he requested a few dozen acres for me on the site of an old military camp so that I could grow things for myself there. This land, long left to run wild, was a field of thorns, shards, and stones. In addition, there was a major drought this year. All my energy was virtually exhausted in the effort to reclaim the land. I set aside my plow with a sigh and wrote these poems, both to console myself for my labors and in hopes that I would forget these efforts with the onset of the coming year.

I
An abandoned fort for which no one cared,
its fallen walls filled with scrub.

Who would spend willingly muscles' strength
in efforts unrewarded later in the year?—

Only the solitary wayfarer,
left with nothing by Heaven, with nowhere to flee.

At last he comes here, picks up shards and stones,
the year has been dry, no moisture in soil.

From this rugged place among the thorns
he wants to scrape an inch of growth.

Then he sets his plow aside with a sigh—
when will my granary be piled high?

II
Though these weed-filled fields have run wild,
there are crops that suit its high and low spots.

In the damp bottoms I will plant my rice,
set dates and chestnuts on flats to the east.

This scholar of Shu in the Southland
has already been offered mulberries.

And good bamboo are not hard to grow—
I just worry the shoots will spread uncontrolled.

I still have to choose a fine spot
and measure it out to site my house.

When my servant boy burned the dry grass,
he ran to tell me a well was uncovered:

I don't yet dare expect full meals,
but of a bucket of water I am assured.

Also from Su Shi's period in Huang-zhou came the two famous "Poetic Expositions on Red Cliff." The following passage is the second (for the first, see pp. 292–294).

The Second Poetic Exposition on Red Cliff

It was the night of the full moon in December of the same year. I was walking back from my Snow-Viewing Lodge on my way to Lin-gao. Two companions were with me as we passed Brown Mud Slope. A frost had fallen and the trees had all lost their leaves; our shadows were there on the ground, and I looked up and saw the bright moon. Then I looked around and saw that it had delighted the others. We went our way singing songs in response to one another.

Eventually I sighed, saying, "I have companions but no wine, or wine but nothing to eat along with it. The moonlight is silvery and the breeze is cool. What can we do on a wonderful night like this?" One companion said, "Today as it was getting dark, I pulled up my nets and had caught a fish with a very large mouth and tiny, delicate scales, which looked like a Pine River bass. But then where will we get some wine?" When we got back, we consulted with our wives, and my wife said, "I have a gallon of wine which I've kept put away for a very long time in anticipation of just such an unforeseen need."

Thereupon we took the wine and the fish and again went to visit the base of Red Cliff. You could hear the sound of the river's current, and the shore rose up sharply for a thousand feet. The mountains were high and the moon small; the water level had fallen, and rocks had emerged from the surface.

It had not been all that many months and days since the first time we came here, yet the mountains and the river had become unrecognizable. Then I gathered up my robes and stepped onto the bank, finding my footing up the steep slope and pushing back the undergrowth. I crouched on a tigerlike boulder and climbed a dragon-twisting tree. I pulled my way up to the precariously perched nest of the roosting hawk and looked down into the hidden palaces of Ping-yi, the river god. My two companions were not able to follow me there.

Then there came a long, piercing screech. The trees shuddered; the mountains resounded and the valleys echoed; the wind came up and the waters were seething. I too was struck dumb and distressed, shivering and afraid, and I felt such a chill that I could not stay there long. I went back and got in the boat, and we pushed off to midstream, to come to rest wherever the boat might take us. It was then about midnight and all around us was a forsaken gloom. It happened then that a solitary crane was coming over the river from the east. Its wings seemed like wagon wheels, and it had a black lower garment with a pure white jacket. It gave a long, shrill cry, and, making a close pass over our boat, it went off to the west.

Soon afterward my companions left, and I too went to go to sleep. I dreamed of a Daoist wizard, soaring lightly in his feathered robes, and as he was passing by Lin-gao, he descended. He bowed to me and said, "Did you enjoy your visit to Red Cliff?" When I asked him his name, he bowed his head and would not answer me. But ah!—then I understood. "Wasn't that you this last night who flew past us and cried out?" The Daoist looked around smiling, and I woke up with a start. When I opened the door and looked for him, I couldn't see him anywhere.

The experience of more or less continual administrative exile, being transferred from one post to another, imparted a sense of unreality to all past experience, along with intense attention to the details of the present moment.

to "Down and Out Drunk" *(Zui luo-po)*, Written on Leaving Jing-kou

> The clouds were thin, the moon was faint—
> I sobered up around ten o'clock
>   just as the boat was shoving off.
> As I turned to gaze on the lonely city,
>   gray mists closed around it.
> I recall the time she was singing,
> but I don't recall coming back.
>
> My turban askew, fan fallen from hand,
>   the hammock slick,
> when I woke there was no one there
>   to tell my secret dreams.

Throughout this life I am swept along,
    when will it ever cease?
My home is in the southwest,
but I am always setting off
    to go farther on southeast.

Su Shi continued to be transferred from post to post, and in his last years was sent as far south as possible—to Hai-nan Island. In 1100 he was recalled, but died in 1101 before making it back to the North. The second of the two following poems was written while making the crossing from Hai-nan back to the mainland.

Tong-chao Tower at Zheng-mai Station (1100)

For the rest of my days I would grow old
    in a village of Hai-nan,
and the god will send down Shaman Yang
    to summon back my soul.
Dim in the distance, at the base of sky,
    where a hawk is sinking away,
is a hair's breadth line of green mountains,
    and that is the heartland.

Crossing the Sea, June 20, 1100

Orion lies flat, the Dipper bends down,
    it is almost midnight now,
after harsh rains and daylong wind
    skies also know how to clear.

When clouds scatter, the moon shines bright,
    who needs add decoration?—
for Heaven's complexion and colors of sea
    are basically clear and pure.

All that remains is that old man of Lu's[2]
    wish to sail off on a raft;
and I roughly discern the melody
    of the Yellow Emperor's music.[3]

In southern jungles I died nine times
    yet I feel no cause for complaint—
this present trip's utter wonder
    crowns my entire life.

---

[2]The "old man of Lu" is Confucius, who, in despair that the Way was not in practice in the world, once expressed a wish to sail off to sea on a raft.
[3]The *Zhuang-zi* tells of the Yellow Emperor performing his cosmic music in the wilderness by Lake Dong-ting.

Relationships

Even more than their Tang precursors, Song poets wrote within a web of literary and personal relationships. Poems were to be read in relation to other poems, both present and past, and they invoked knowledge and memories shared with friends and kin. Su Shi's most frequent poetic correspondent was his brother Su Che. Su Che's "Thoughts of Former Times at Mian-chi," to which the following was a companion piece, survives, but it is poor. Su Shi's poem, however, stands on its own, speaking of the vanishing traces of things that survive only in shared memories.

A Companion Piece to Su Che's "Thoughts of Former Times at Mian-chi"

Human life no matter where—
    do you know what it is like?
It must be like the swan in flight
    that treads in slushy snow.

By chance it leaves within the slush
    the marks of its feet;
the swan flies on—thereafter who
    can reckon its direction?

The old monk there has died,
    a new pagoda is made;
there is no way on his crumbling wall now
    to see poems we wrote there before.

But those rocky roads of days gone by—
    do you recall them still?—
how the way was long and we were worn out
    and my limping donkey brayed.[4]

In the following poem, Su Shi's patron, the great Ou-yang Xiu, was indulging in one of his favorite poetic modes: hyperbolic description in the manner of the Tang poet Han Yu. This style was considered particularly appropriate for praising works of art. The poem by Su Shi that follows at p. 680 seems to be on the same stone screen, now in the possession of Ou-yang Xiu himself—or perhaps on another screen very much like the first, in which the patterns in the stone were developed by ink brushwork. Not only does he adopt the style of Ou-yang Xiu's poem; Su Shi playfully responds to the earlier work and refutes Ou-yang Xiu's myth that the patterns in the stone were made by "gods and demons" at the beginning of creation or perhaps made purposely to humiliate mortal men and their limited talents. In Su Shi's version, the spirits of two famous former painters, frustrated by their incorporeality, have been working at their craft in the afterlife.

---

[4]Su Shi's original note says: In that past year my horse had died at Er-ling, and I rode a donkey to Mian-chi.

[Ou-yang Xiu], On the Carved Stone Screen of Wu Kui,
the Han-lin Academician (1056)

When dawn's rays enter the woods,
    all birds awake with a start;
and flying in flocks with a whir of wings,
    the crows cry out raucously.

They wind through the woods in all directions,
    then cast themselves into sky,
for yellow-beaked fledglings in the nest
    wait famished to be fed.

The female comes down to peck the ground,
    the male wheels high overhead,
then female and male to each other call
    and go flying back again.

The woods are empty of people,
    the voices of birds rejoice,
an ancient tree touches Heaven
    with gnarled, twisting boughs.

Beneath it is an eerie stone
    stretched among the trees,
buried in mists and grasses,
    streaked with lichens and moss.

Tell me now, who could depict
    a scene such as I have described?—
it is, in fact, in Wu Kui's house
    on his screen of stone.

A Guo-zhou craftsman hewed the hills
    and took the mountain's bones,
he carved by dawn and hacked at dusk—
    no task of a single day—
then thousands of images all came forth
    from there within the stone.

I sigh at man's folly in failing to see
    how hard it was at first
        for He Who fashioned Heaven and Earth;
they claim, instead, existing things
    arose spontaneously,
        mere processes of Nature.

Don't men know how they chiseled and carved,
    cutting out representations
        of loathsome things and things that please,
all the thousands of poses and postures

that can never be exhausted,
how gods suffered and demons wept
  by day and night never
    finding any ease?

Were it otherwise, how could we have in this screen
  what perfected skill and fullest forethought
    of finest craftsmen could not achieve?—
half present and half unseen
  in a filmy blur
    of rising clouds and haze.

When gods and demons worked this deed,
  Earth and Heaven begrudged the possession;
it was hidden in Guo-zhou's mountains,
  in the most remote of their stones.

If man but have the will,
  there is nothing he cannot obtain;
though Earth and Heaven are godlike,
  they could not hide it away.

Or it also seems that demons and gods
  love always to prevail
    and show their spite for our kind,
wishing here to show ultimate strangeness
  past the point our talents fail,
and did, in fact, have Zhang Jing-shan
  bring it from the west.

Wu the Academician
  saw it and merrily chortled,
he drunkenly dipped his lavender brush,
  streaming with charcoal ink.

Your talent, sir, may well compete
  to rival demons and gods,
but unfortunately I have grown very old
  and can't keep you company.

Ou-yang Xiu Asks Me to Write a Poem on a Stone Screen That He Owns (1071)

Who sent you that stone screen
on which there are of ink
  the very faintest traces?

No tall forests are depicted there
  nor mighty growths,
just a lone pine

unaging after thousand of years,
    on a snowy ridge west of E-mei.

Cliffs have collapsed, streams are cut off,
    you can gaze but never
        reach that spot
where lonely mists and setting sun
    join in a dimming haze.

It rises writhing, shaped by winds,
    its true appearance achieved—
I believe at last in this carved depiction
    there is Heaven's skill indeed.

But then I suspect that Bi Hong and Wei Yan
    lie buried beneath Guo-zhou's hills,
and though their bones may rot away,
    their hearts last on forever.

The promptings of spirit and clever ideas
    could find no outlet there;
these were transformed to blankets of mist
    that sank within the stone.

The great painters since ancient days
    have been no common men:
in describing the likenesses of things
    they are much the same as poets.

I would have you write a poem, sir,
    to console their untimely fates,
do not let those two men,
    biting back their fury, weep
        in secret mansions of the tomb.

Many of Su Shi's prose accounts are also part of his large network of friends and acquaintances. In an account of a friend's pavilion and his pet cranes, we can hear echoes of his belief in not letting one's feelings "remain caught up in things." One keeps what one loves by always letting go of it; thus the cranes always return to the man who "sets them free" every day.

An Account of the Pavilion for Setting the Cranes Free

In the autumn of 1077 there was a great flood at Peng-cheng, whose waters reached halfway up the door of the thatched cottage of Zhang Tian-ji of Cloud Dragon Mountain. In the spring of the following year the waters receded, and Zhang moved to the east of his former dwelling, up to the foothills of the eastern mountains. When he climbed to the heights and looked out, he found a rare vista and built a pavilion on the summit. The ridges and crests of Peng-cheng's mountains join around the city on all sides, as if protecting it by a great ring, the only gap being about twenty percent of the western edge. Our mountain man's pavilion happened to be situated exactly facing that gap. During the passage from spring into summer, the trees and vegetation stretch to the sky. During the snowy months of autumn and winter, a thousand leagues around are all the same color. In the shifting from darkness to sunlight during rainstorms there are a hundred variations both above and below.

Our man of the mountains had two cranes, which were well trained and fine fliers. At dawn he would set them free toward the gap in the mountains to the west, letting them go wherever they pleased. Sometimes they would stand on some field on the slopes; at other times they would soar above the clouds. Then at twilight they would head for the eastern mountains and return. For this reason he named it "The Pavilion for Setting the Cranes Free."

Together with some companions and subordinates, I, Su Shi, the governor, once went to see this man of the mountains. We drank wine in his pavilion and enjoyed ourselves. Then I bowed to him and declared, "Do you know how enjoyable such a private life is, living here in seclusion? One would not exchange it for anything, even to be the ruler of the realm. In the *Classic of Changes* it says: 'A crane cries out in the shade; its young ones join in.' And the *Classic of Poetry* says:

> The crane cries out in deepest marsh,
> its voice is heard in the skies.

"For the crane is indeed a pure and aloof creature, at ease and free, passing beyond all the world's filth. For this reason the writers of the *Changes* and the *Poems* used it as a figure for worthy men, good men, and men of private virtue. To be the familiar of cranes and to amuse oneself with them seems something that should have benefit and do no harm. Nevertheless, Duke Yi of Wei destroyed his domain because of his love of cranes. The Duke of Zhou composed the 'Declaration Against Wine' and Duke Wu of Wei gave admonition in the *Poem* 'Dignified'; both considered wine as the very worst thing, making people besotted and bringing ruin. Yet Liu Ling, Ruan Ji, and their sort used wine to keep themselves entirely genuine and established a reputation in later ages. Think of it! The ruler of the realm cannot be permitted to love even so pure, aloof, easy, and free a creature as a crane—for if he loves it, he will destroy his domain. Yet someone who withdraws from the world to the mountain forests cannot be harmed even by so besotting and ruinous a thing as wine—much less by cranes! Considering the matter from this point of view, the delights of the recluse and the ruler cannot even be spoken of in the same breath."

Our man of the mountains was amused and laughed. "That's right!" Then I composed songs for setting the cranes free and calling them back.

> The cranes go off in flight
> to the gap in the western hills,
> soaring high and scanning below,

they choose where they will go.
Drawing in wings in a whir,
it seems they will alight—
but what do they suddenly see
again beating their wings aloft?
They spend whole days among valleys and streams,
pecking sapphire mosses and treading white stones.

The cranes are coming back
to the shadows of eastern hills.
Below them is a man,
yellow cap, straw slippers,
homespun coat, playing the harp.
He eats what he grows himself;
you cranes have your fill on what's left.
Turn back, turn back!
In the western hills you cannot linger long.
—An account written this eighth day of January, 1078

趙宋 Song Classical Poetry

The classical poetry of the Song Dynasty presents a very different face from that of Tang poetry; it offers its own, quite distinct pleasures. Still, despite the great diversity of Song poetry, there remains in it some direct identity when compared to the poetry of the Tang. Critics have remarked on the Song classical poets' geniality and reserve, in contrast to the intensity of the Tang poets, and on Song poetry's self-consciousness. One of the oldest critiques, offered in the Song itself, was of Song poetry's explicit philosophizing, in contrast to what seemed the more authentic expression of emotion in Tang poetry. "Philosophizing" (suggesting a diminutive and popularized form of philosophical reflection) may adequately describe the Song classical poets' discursiveness and their constant tendency to offer rationalizations or witty explanations for phenomena and experience. Though generally valid, all of these characterizations of Song poetry and contrasts with the Tang are inadequate attempts to explain what was a basic shift in sensibility.

As with every generalization, there are many exceptions to broad characterization, and many refinements that should be made. Song poets loved a fine couplet no less than a Tang poet, but to later readers, the Song couplet would often show the "traces of the hatchet"—a sense of conscious, careful craft that seemed to contrast with the ease of the best High Tang couplets. The finest Song couplet seemed like something made; the finest High Tang couplet seemed like something found.

Song poets retained the forms of Tang classical poetry, but something deep had changed. To their own taste and to the taste of later poets and readers, Tang poetry was often preferable (though there were groups who modeled themselves on Song poets in the Qing). Tang poetry may have been preferred, but the world that had produced such a poetry was gone; in its place was a new, and in many ways more modern age.

Ou-yang Xiu (1007–1072)

Ou-yang Xiu was the dominant cultural figure of his day and the first representative Song literary figure. He was an historian, politician, antiquarian, epigrapher, literary critic, writer of prose, poetry, and song lyric, as well as the patron of most of the important figures in classical literature of the eleventh century. His achievements in classical poetry should probably be ranked last among his many accomplishments.

Although Tang poets often imitated their predecessors, in the Song, modeling poems on earlier poets became a pervasive phenomenon. The poetic tradition had evolved into a repertoire of styles and voices, each associated with a particular poetic genre and type of situation, and available to the Song poet when he sought to

684

assume a role. The first poem below, in which Ou-yang Xiu declares his chosen persona as the "Drunken Old Man," is modeled on several poems by the Mid-Tang poet Bo Ju-yi. Here the weighty act of self-naming, of choosing a pseudonym, is figured as an accident and chance whim.

On the Pavilion of the Drunken Old Man in Chu-zhou

Forty is not yet old, and I
just chance to sign poems "Drunken Old Man."

When drunk I leave everything behind,
so why would I still need to note my age?

I love simply how this pavilion's brook
makes its way here through tangles of peaks,

Sounding as though it were falling from sky,
spilling straight down toward these two eaves.

Then off it flows to the stream by the cliff,
where hidden springs add to its gurgling;

Its sound never drowns out conversation,
its clarity, unlike that of flutes and harps.

Of course I find flutes and harps lovely,
but their music is much too fast and loud;

Therefore I often take wine in hand
and walk far away to this purling stream.

Wild birds peer at me when I'm drunk,
and creek's clouds keep me here asleep.

Hill flowers waste their practiced smiles,
not knowing how to speak with me.

Only the breeze that comes from the cliff
will blow me back sober again.

The famous calligraphy paper known as "Clear Heart" paper, properly "Clear Heart Hall" paper, was made for Li Yu, the last emperor of the so-called Southern Tang, one of the Five Dynasties ("a century of warfare when pike and shield/streamed with battle's blood"). A Song collection of literary anecdotes remarks that this particular paper was not considered very valuable at the very beginning of the dynasty, but once Ou-yang Xiu wrote the following poem, its price rose dramatically, to the point where it became virtually unattainable. The judgment of the connoisseur can never be fully disentangled from commercial value.

The poem is characteristic of some of Ou-yang Xiu's best-known poetic work: a chatty exposition, occasionally dropping in a fine metaphor, with many lines that are flabby verse rather than poetry. In such poems, Ou-yang Xiu unfailingly promotes his friends, just as, in this case, he also promotes the value of "Clear Heart" paper. Yet such garrulous verse seemed to fulfill the Song interest in a casual and natural poetic form to express a genial, generous personality.

A Companion Piece to Liu Chang's "Clear Heart Paper"

Have you not seen how those truly rare talents,
　　Shi Man-qing and Su Shun-qin,
were long cast down into hardship
　　and buried at last in brown dust?

Though Su Shun-qing lived a pauper's life,
　　in death he grew in esteem:
scraps of writing and incomplete drafts
　　are now like precious gems.

Shi Man-qing in drunkenness wrote
　　a poem on a red plaster wall;
patches of plaster have crumbled away,
　　dusky from charcoal smoke.

Like the river spilling from Mount Kun-lun,
　　its momentum twisting round bends;
or snows weighing down on Great Mount Hua,
　　looming high above.

Ever since these two young men
　　perished, one after the other,
the atmosphere of our rivers and hills
　　stands everywhere subdued.

Though your household came to possess
　　the paper called "Clear Heart,"
I wonder who there is left alive
　　who would dare set brush to it?

Mei Yao-chen, Xuan-zhou's old poet,
　　is starving and near to death;
when the golden swan breaks its wings,
　　sad are the sounds of its cries.

From time to time he eats his fill,
　　and then he can speak fair,
like listening to loud singing
　　as golden flagons are quaffed.

Though both the younger men are dead,
　　this older man survives;

aging craftsman, capable still
    of skillfully trimming to size.

Why did you not send the paper to him?—
    why set it instead before me?—
it's like spurning honest discourse,
    preferring banter and wit.

Sad to say, I am in my decline,
    no more what I used to be,
and all I can do is take this bundle
    to open, then roll up again.

A century of warfare when pike and shield
    streamed with battle's blood;
now all that kingdom's songs and dance
    are terraces grown with weeds.

Yet the artifacts of those bygone days
    are all good and finely made,
they lie abandoned everywhere
    buried in brush and scrub.

From where did you get hold of
    paper such as this?—
pure and tough and glossy,
    a roll of a hundred sheets.

The duties of my office
    happily leave me leisure;
poems exchanged with the Secretariat
    continue and redouble.

From ancient days the world was never
    lacking in literature—
how do we know that in times to come,
    such writers won't show up again?

Though Ou-yang Xiu is best known for longer monologues in which he assumes the role of the "Drunken Old Man" or the generous patron, some of his most attractive poems are virtually anonymous pieces such as "Boating on West Lake" and "White Egret," close in style and sensibility to his song lyrics.

Boating on West Lake: to Zhang Shan, Academician and Fiscal Commissioner

Light on the waves, colors of willows,
    veils of sapphire haze,
to winding isles and arching bridges
    our painted skiff makes its way.

The farther we go, the more lovely,
  we fear only that it will end;
but on deeper within, the more secret,
  and it seems a space without bounds.

In the fragrance of figured satins
  fine guests are brought to stay,
and the sound of harps and piping
  sweeps in with evening's wind.

Half-drunk then, we turned the boat,
  uncertain of our direction,
there were mansions and terraces high and low
  in the light of the evening sun.

White Egret

Splashing on stones, the rapids' sounds
  are like the drums of battle,
a surface of waves that toss the sky
  seems like silver hills.
When rapids leap and waves smash,
  in wind as well as rain,
it stands there alone with dignity,
  thoughts even more serene.

Mei Yao-chen (1002–1060)

Ou-yang Xiu saw himself as a patron on the model of Han Yu, and one of the functions of a patron was to gather a circle of writers and champion them. Anyone who assumed the role of Han Yu needed someone to correspond to Meng Jiao, the impoverished older poet whose unappreciated genius was to be promoted. Ou-yang Xiu found his Meng Jiao in Mei Yao-chen, a politically unsuccessful older man who had turned his attention fully to poetry. At this point the resemblance between Meng Jiao and Mei Yao-chen stops (although Mei, so often explicitly compared to Meng Jiao, occasionally attempted to imitate the Tang poet in more substantial ways). The violence of the following poem, one of Mei's most famous, is similar in some superficial ways to Meng Jiao's work.

A Lone Hawk Over the Buddha Tower of the Monastery of Universal Purity

From my newly rented lodgings
  I saw the temple's tower,
its green and gold stood shining
  before my ramshackle rooms.

Over the tower with my own eyes I saw
    pigeons in their flocks,
nesting, perching, drinking, feeding,
    heedless of passing time.

Carved rafters, muraled walls were stained
    by droppings everywhere;
they soiled even the shoulders and head
    of the statue of the Buddha.

Monks of the temple did not dare
    make use of slings and arrows,
then all at once a gray hawk appeared
    spreading its deadly talons.

Crows cawed, the magpies squawked,
    mynah birds were screeching,
for thither the savage hawk had come
    to seek out the smell of flesh.

The hawk's fierce and fiery heart
    stood in no awe of their numbers;
in a flash it shattered a single skull,
    the others around were alarmed.

The dead bird came plummeting down,
    and before it hit the ground,
with turning wing the hawk took it
    like a whirling gust of wind,

Then perched alone on the roof's ridge,
    freely shredding its prey,
ripping flesh in beak, laying liver open,
    flinging the guts away.

An old owl, lacking the skill,
    cruel yet cowardly,
wheeled in circles, ready to close,
    and pierced it with famished eyes.

Soon afterwards the hawk was full
    and flew away on its own;
fighting for scraps one could not tell
    vultures from common birds.

Groups of children were pointing,
    passers-by all laughed,
I now recall this and make it a poem
    beside this autumn river.

Mei Yao-chen's large collection of poetry (close to three thousand poems) contains a great variety of work. He is best known for the topics he took up, often close observations of details of everyday life that had not previously been treated in poetry. His work sometimes extended to criticism of social abuses. Mei's simplicity shows itself to advantage in the moving poems on the death of his first wife and of several of his children. Mei Yao-chen's poetic ideal was the difficult term *ping-dan,* something like "mellow blandness," an aesthetic flatness whose beauty was supposed to grow on the reader rather than striking him or her immediately.

Writing of My Sorrow

Heaven took my wife from me,
then also took my child.

And though my eyes are never dry,
this heart is ready to die.

Rain falls and enters the ground,
a pearl sinks to the floor of sea.

If you go to the sea, you may see the pearl,
or dig in the ground, you may see the water.

But men, when they go to the streams below,
we know they are gone forever more.

I stroke my chest, who can tell me why?—
this gaunt and worn ghost in the mirror.

Listening to a Neighbor Singing at Night

I couldn't get to sleep one night,
a neighbor sang—I heard something rare.

I envisaged her red lips in motion,
and fancied dust flying from beams.

A beat missed—surely she smiled to herself;
I rose and dressed to listen unobserved.

But when I had dressed, her song was done,
I was left with glow of the moon in my window.

On March 26, 1048, I Had a Dream

Since the time that I remarried,
two years she stayed out of my dreams.

But then last night I saw her face,
and mid-evening was struck by pain.

The darkening lamp showed its faint light,
it somberly shone on the rafters and beams.

Out of nowhere snow beat on my window,
borne along, as well, by a furious wind.

Crescent Moon

When the crescent moon comes shining
    on the corner of my roof,
the dog on the west side barks,
    the eastern neighbor is troubled.
Deep in the night bright spirits
    and wraith-things are astir,
on the ancient plain there's a rustling
    and there is no wind.

Wang An-shi (1021–1086)

Wang An-shi was a scruffy Confucian political theorist, of totalitarian inclinations, firmly convinced of the correctness of his own views and of the urgency of their implementation for the redemption of the Song state. He had the misfortune to have his reform program taken seriously by the new emperor Shen-zong, and his political agenda was put into practice in the "New Laws" policy of 1069, which gained him the immediate opposition of conservative and pragmatist alike. Although he has a few poems on social issues, Wang An-shi is best known—somewhat incongruously—as a fastidious stylist of quatrains and regulated verses and as an ardent admirer of Du Fu.

The Temple of Shooting Stars

Into jutting clouds terrace and hall
    rise looming upward;
long river that reaches thousands of miles,
    a single cup of wine.

From here I see streams and mountains
    swallow down sun and moon,
while far in the distance no wagon or horse
    brings along dust and dirt.

Wild geese fly on paths through cloud,
    their voices pass down low,
the visitor draws near Heaven's Gates,
    and quickly comes back from dream.

The scope of such splendor only a poem
    could tidily display;
but I, lacking talent, am put to shame,
    having come here so casually.

Jin-ling, the ancient seat of the Southern Dynasties, had long been a favorite topic for poets. Although Wang An-shi carefully keeps the historical moment undefined in the following poem, he is probably referring to Jin-ling primarily as the capital of the Five Dynasties Kingdom of the Southern Tang and to its surrender to the Song. To Ou-yang Xiu, the artifacts of the Southern Tang were simply lying around for the taking, as he says in "A Companion Piece to Liu Chang's 'Clear Heart Paper' ":

> Yet the artifacts of those bygone days
>   are all good and finely made,
> they lie abandoned everywhere
>   buried in brush and scrub.

Note that Wang An-shi more correctly recognizes tomb robbery as the source of so many antiquarian treasures.

Meditation on the Past at Jin-ling III

> The lay of the land bends eastward here
>   on the river's thousands of miles,
> among the clouds, "Heaven's Turrets,"
>   paired peaks for eternity.
>
> In those days troops moved over the earth,
>   a manly hero took it;
> when a Sage came forth in the heartland,
>   each place surrendered in turn.
>
> In a vast silence of river and hills
>   the royal aura lies buried,
> a gloomy bleakness of mist in the wind
>   fills the windows of monks.
>
> Ruined barrows and rifled tombs
>   stripped of their caps and swords—
> who again will weep on his sash
>   and pour out a cup in libation?

Climbing Bao-gong Pagoda

> My tired servant and worn-out horse
>   I left at the gate of pine,
> while I myself took my long bamboo cane
>   to lean on these roots of stone.
>
> The river moon wheeled through sky,
>   making its own daylight,
> as clouds over ridges split darkness
>   and cast a shadowy dusk.
>
> A rat shook the stillness of summits,
>   along its passage sounds rose,

in the desolate chill a crow mounted swiftly,
    its shadow's wingbeats faced it.

In a place like this we do not know
    who is guest and who is host—
this holy man forgets the self,
    while I myself forget words.[1]

Wu-zhen Monastery

Stream in the wilds running zigzag,
    scouring stairs to the rooms,
noontime window, a fading dream
    as birds call one to the other.
Day after day the breeze of spring
    blows on the fragrant plants
until north of the hill and south of the hill
    the path is almost gone.

One Day Coming Home: Ballad (on the death of his wife)

When we were poor I rushed here and there
    to provide us clothing and food;
a hundred days spent rushing here and there,
    and I could come home only one.

It pains me that we will not live out
    a lifetime's worth of pleasure,
My wish was that when we were old
    we could stay together.

It is gloomy in the empty room
    where the coffin curtains hang,
the blue lamp flame at midnight,
    the sound of weeping faint.

I can envisage face and voice,
    but where now are you yourself?—
and if we meet in the world below,
    will it be you or not?

Huang Ting-jian (1045–1105)

For all his importance in the history of Chinese poetry, Huang Ting-jian's poetry is difficult for modern Chinese readers to appreciate and even harder to appreciate in translation. Song poets were already intimidated by the achievements of their Tang

---

[1]"Forgets the self" also has the sense of "forgets about me."

predecessors, and Huang Ting-jian's generation had Song literary giants such as Ou-yang Xiu and Su Shi before them. Huang Ting-jian's response was to use the work of his predecessors and transform it. His poems are studded with allusions and phrases drawn from earlier poetry, cleverly reworked. Even more significant is the play of registers, mixing vernacular expressions with recognizably "poetic" phrases. Out of all this comes a playfully urbane delight in language and poetic tradition. This was apparent to well-educated Song readers who shared Huang Ting-jian's own background, and his work was so much admired it was taken as the beginning of a whole school of poets, the "Jiang-xi School," which remained active through the rest of the dynasty. For modern Chinese readers, however, such sophistication is reduced to copious footnotes; and for readers of translation, it is altogether invisible.

Following the Rhymes of Huang Da-lin's "Sent to Su Che"

Half a lifetime's fellows and friends
    are gone with the passing water,
for how many men will portraits of honor
    enter the Royal Gallery.

In springtime wind and springtime rain
    the flowers pass my eyes,
north of the river and south of the river
    water strikes the skies.

I am ready to take off my badges of bronze,
    I am soon to seek the Way,
knowing full well that friendship like stone
    is in different to unequal years.

For each wagtail there is the frustration[2]
    of longing to go home,
with days and months hastening
    a forehead filled with snow.

To Huang Ji-fu

I am lodged by the northern sea,
    you, by the sea in the south,
I would send a letter by wild goose,
    but forbear, being unable.

Peach and plum in springtime breeze,
    a single cup of wine;
night rain on the rivers and lakes,
    a lamp ten years before.

---

[2]The "wagtail" refers to the third stanza of *Classic of Poetry* CLXIV: "Wagtails in the meadows,/brothers pressed by troubles." It suggests the unchanging love of brothers for one another (Huang Da-lin was Huang Ting-jian's elder brother).

To keep a household all I have
    are four bare walls,
in healing ills I do not hope
    to three times break my arm.[3]

I imagine you there studying,
    your head already white,
with gibbons wailing across the creek
    among miasmal vines.

Asking for a Cat

Since autumn the rodents have taken
    a gross advantage of cat-death:
they eye my crocks, upset my plates,
    disturb my sleep by night.
I've heard tell that your pussikins
    has littered several young,
I purchased a fish strung on willow twig
    to beseech you for a kitty.

Lu You (1125–1210)

Lu You was the most famous of the Southern Song poets and the most prolific poet before the Ming, with approximately ten thousand poems to his credit. Such productivity is all the more remarkable because Lu You destroyed virtually all the poems he wrote before middle age. Modern Chinese critics lay special weight on his poems expressing the frustrated desire to conquer the North and reunify China. Even though this "patriotic" impulse was important to Lu You, such poems form only a very tiny portion of his work as a whole, most of which celebrates the moments of his daily life with genial wit. Poetry in such volume, chronically arranged, approaches diary: although there is almost nothing in his collection that rises to the heights of the best Tang poets, Lu You is rarely clumsy and boring. The easygoing pleasures provided by his work are different from those we normally expect of poetry.

Small Garden

Misty plants of my small garden
    reach to my neighbor's home,
and through the shade of mulberries
    a single path slants.
I lay here reading Tao Qian's poems,
    but before I finished the book,

---

[3]The phrase "three times break my arm" echoes a proverb in *The Zuo Tradition* that after thrice breaking an arm one can become a good doctor. Huang Ting-jian is probably referring to his capacity to "doctor" the ills of the folk he governs.

I took advantage of gentle rain
    to go and weed my melons.

Gazing in the Evening North of My Cottage

I
Red trees and green forests
    streaked with twilight mist,
ever beside the bridge there is
    a boat where fish are sold.
The lines of Du Mu's poetry,
    the paintings of Li Cheng,
all can be found right here beside
    the master's walking stick.

II
Every day by the crossing
    my tiny boat stays tied,
an old man grown too lazy
    to travel beyond his gates.
A single bamboo walking cane
    passing beyond my sparse hedge
gives full command of a thousand cliffs
    and Fall in ten thousand valleys.

End of Spring (1197)

A thatched cottage of several rooms
    on the shores of Mirror Lake,
a thousand-volume library
    doesn't help my poverty.

Swallows come and swallows go,
    I pass another day,
flowers blossom, flowers fall,
    the course of spring is run.

I open a book with joy to see
    the friends I've known in life,
and I'm shocked by the mirroring water—
    not the man I used to be.

I laugh at myself, how this heart remains
    that wants to destroy the Turk;

when I stand on the heights, I am carried away
    and I almost forget where I am.

Lonely Cloud

I've lived on this very mountain
    for the past forty years,
I served at court and did no good,
    and so came home again.
Don't think me strange if, standing long,
    I lean on this balcony—
it's because I love that lonely cloud
    so calm the whole day long.

Lu You took as his pseudonym the "Old Man Set Free." In addition to celebrating mild domestic pleasures, he also enjoyed assuming a role of extravagant excess in the manner of Li Bo. This was the proper frame of mind for writing in the wild calligraphic style of draft cursive.

Song of Draft Cursive

To brew three thousand gallons of beer
    I bankrupt my family,
yet for thousands of gallons of wistfulness
    this beer will be no match.

Early this morning my drunken eyes
    saw lightning flashing on cliffs,
I seized my brush, looked all around—
    hemmed in by Earth and Heaven.

All of a sudden the brush went sweeping,
    I was utterly unaware:
wind-blown clouds had entered my breast,
    Heaven had lent me its force.

Dragon gods battled on wild plains
    shrouded in reeking fog;
strange wraiths shattered the mountains
    blackening the moonlight.

At this moment I drove away
    the sorrow lodged in my chest:
I slammed the bench with a loud shout,
    in frenzy my turban fell.

The paper of Wu and Shu's white silk
    did not suit my mood:
I consigned it all to the great hall
    whose walls were nine feet high.

The following famous poem is supposed to have been written by Lu You on his deathbed.

For My Sons

Dying now, I know full well
    that nothing truly matters,
and yet I'm sad I did not see
    China united once more.
The day the royal armies quell
    our heartland in the North,
forget not in our family rites
    to let this old man know.

Yang Wan-li (1127–1206)

By the Southern Song, the standard themes and forms of expression of classical poetry had been fully explored. It was always possible to give a new twist to an old image, but the language of poetry had come to seem increasingly commonplace and flat. The poet Yang Wan-li addressed this problem by a militant vitalism—an intention to make all that was habitual and moribund alive and lively. Yang Wan-li borrowed the term "vitalism" *(huo-fa)* from Chan Buddhist discourse, where it referred to the way in which Chan teaching might make the truths of Buddhist scriptures immediately apparent. In Yang Wan-li's poetic use, "vitalism" appeared as the impulse to shock and surprise, by wit and humor, by reference to the gritty details of life, by daring metaphors, by taking note of what poets commonly overlooked, and by an aggressive use of vernacular, even slang, terms in classical poetry.

Yan Ji-sheng, Chancellor of Education, Invited His Junior Colleagues to Visit the Pei Garden. In our boat we sailed around Lone Mountain enjoying the lotus blossoms. Then late in the day we moored at the imperial park at Yu-hu. I wrote ten quatrains (one of ten)

As soon as the boat shoved off
    we were far from the world's dirt,
and swept along, we rode the winds
    crossing the Great Void.
One of the party, by accident,
    dropped some pastry crumbs:

fish and turtles in countless numbers
    came out within the waves.

During an Intercalary August After the "Arrival of Autumn" It Was Hot in the Evening and I Went to Be Cool in the Prefectural Garden (first of two)

When I made it to the top of the wall,
    at once my eyes saw clearly:
twilight hills were rivals to offer me
    several sharp points of green.
Then weeping willows ceased their dance
    of leaves within west wind—
for the longest time one leaf alone
    did not stop.

One Day Before New Year's Eve, While Returning by Boat, We Moored at Qu-wo Market, and I Spent the Night in Zhi-ping Temple

The river was broad, the winds were strong,
    cold cut through my thick coat,
there were more rocky rapids than shore
    as the boat made its way upstream.

The market was not so far away,
    but the boat could not put in,
yet my fancies had already rushed ahead
    to a spot beside bright lanterns.

That night I stayed in an old temple,
    which I entered slogging through mud,
the soggy kindling when set ablaze
    crackled like insects' cries.

Cold windows and freezing walls
    combined to keep me from sleep—
but better by far than the flimsy boat roof
    where I looked up and saw the sky.

In the market the people shouted and sang,
    keeping the holiday,
while a huddled poet's pair of knees
    rose higher than his cheeks.

When I make it home, my children
    will ask me how things were—
but tomorrow I won't be able to bear
    telling this mood tonight.

Just Before the Mid-March 1164 Festival, I Heard That My Father Was Not Feeling Well. Going back west I saw plum blossoms and had these thoughts (first of two)

Along the highway at Tong-jiang
    I keep on heading west,
a thousand trees of wild plums
    hang over the sparse hedge.
Just yesterday in the capital
    borne in a bamboo tray
for three hundred copper coins
    you could buy a single spray.

Besides allusiveness, Yang Wan-li's poetry delighted in jargon and slang terms, which he embedded in classical verse as some modern American poets mix vernacular and literary English. The following poem uses Chan Buddhist jargon and the cryptically magisterial tone of Chan. The third line reminds the reader that the cassock and begging bowl are mere customs and not an essential part of Buddhism; the analogy is that poetic traditions, which seem so necessary and constricting, are not an essential part of poetry. The fifth line refers to the famous couplet of Xie Ling-yun's "Climbing an Upper Story by the Pool" (see p. 321):

Pond and pool grow with grasses of spring,
    garden willows vary the birds that there sing.

Yang Wan-li's couplet suggests that not only should the line of poetry be beautifully crafted as something to be envisaged, it should also have an elusive attraction "beyond the words." The final image of food suggests something of a unique, indefinable flavor.

Two Companion Pieces for Li Tian-lin (first of two)

You've got to cut loose to learn poetry,
trust your own hand to bring unique heights.

Cassock and begging bowl are no old tradition,
a hill's weight is just like a hair's.

Within the line there are "grasses in pond,"
yet beyond the words, both eyes are dazzled.

So tasty!—what can I liken it to?—
a frosty crab pickled in dregs of beer.

Ten Stanzas on the Autumn Rain (one of ten)

I was sick of hearing the rain drip
    from the beech beside the well,
I got up to see the drizzling sky
    everywhere in my gaze.

The eastern hills lay stretched out
>for thirty miles:
beyond a curtain of pearls
>an azure-colored screen.

March 5, 1180. In early morning crossing on the Great Marsh ferry (first of two)

The river and hills beyond the fog
>I cannot clearly see,
only by dogs and roosters
>can I tell there's a village ahead.
All over the planks of the ferryboat
>the frost is thick as snow,
printed by my straw sandals
>is the very first mark.

The play of contrived metaphors in the following poem might seem more characteristic of the baroque poetry of Marino or Gongora than of Chinese poetry. The crescent moon becomes a bowl, presumably of silver foil over lacquer, from which the silver has worn away except around part of the rim. Then it becomes the eye of the moon-maiden herself, blank to show her contempt for the poet; or, lit around the edge, it becomes a sidelong glance, showing suppressed love. Finally, the orb becomes the wheel of her coach, led away in the dawn by the morning star (a plum of jade) and followed by a host of lesser stars.

Going to the Palace Library Early in the Morning with the Crescent Moon Just Rising

I rushed toward my office, lantern in hand,
gates were still shut on both sides of the street.

Alone the pale moon-maiden had risen early
to wash her jet bowl in a sapphire pond.

Its costly rim peeling and showing its lacquer,
around half the rim remained silver light.

All at once she gave me contempt's blank eye,
rebuke's round stare, directed at me.

Through her pupil black vapors threaded,
glancing sidelong, not daring to show what she feels.

There was one gleaming plum of jade
that went ahead leading her voyaging wheel.

And several flickering grains of gold
served as her train in the coach's dust.

Dawn's roosters announced their message thrice,
and the capital's riders went galloping.

Star-rays were gradually almost gone,
and moonbeams grew pale, with vanishing streaks.

Then the Golden Crow flew up into the sky
and spewed forth a red dragon's scales.

A Child Crying for Food

Warm and well fed, could I fail to know
    my lord's kindness to me?—
but that small child, used to poverty,
    is always hungry.
The moment I hear the child crying
    every morning at dawn
is exactly the time when the millet
    is almost fully cooked.

The reference to cooking millet in the last two lines recalls the Tang tale in which a dreamer lives a lifetime filled with successes and sufferings, only to wake and find that all had occurred in the time it took a pot of millet to be fully cooked.

Coda

For all their wit and fine sensibility, the Southern Song poets were also writing their poems while the millet was still cooking. Having ruthlessly crushed Southern Song's rival, the Jin Dynasty, in 1276 Mongol armies under the command of Bayan, the rough Mongol general ironically referred to as "Grand Minister," descended into the South and put an end to the Song. Wang Yuan-liang, whose exact dates are unknown, was a court musician who ultimately accompanied the Song imperial harem north to captivity in the Mongol capital of Beijing. The scene in the following poem is the surrender of the Southern Song.

Wang Yuan-liang, Songs of Hu-zhou (third of ninety-eight)

In the palace halls crowds of officials
    are dumbstruck and say nothing,
Grand Minister Bayan demands we be quick
    with the document of surrender.
The women of the harem all
    stand behind the beaded curtains,
while thousands of horsemen with wild hair ride
    in circles before the hall.

The following anonymous Northern song lyric comes from a century or so later. The peaks referred to are on either side of West Lake in Hang-zhou, the Southern Song capital. Like the Southern Dynasties before it, the Southern Song has become a faded dream in a land of pleasure.

to "Leaves of a Thousand Lotuses" *(Qian-he ye)*

Tall peak to the south,
tall peak to the north,
with caves in mist and pale cloud.
Founder of the Southern Song,
the whole stage now left bare,
As always in the hills of Wu
    breeze blows the tavern streamers—
twice dreamt now,
    that dream of the Southland.

趙宋 Interlude: Wen Tian-xiang (1236–1282) and the Fall of the Song

The Mongol conquest of China proceeded by stages over the course of a half century, from their first battle with the Northern Jin Dynasty in 1227 until the naval battle off the coast of Guang-dong in 1279, which saw the death of the last claimant to the Song throne. Not only were the Mongols ruthless in battle, theirs was a cosmopolitan savagery that for a while inoculated them against the blandishments of Chinese civilization. Content to enrich themselves from the Confucian tax machine, the Mongols initially felt contempt for Confucian civil virtues. That double experience of the Mongols' ruthlessness and their cultural contempt helped produce a remarkable group of Chinese writers in the thirteenth century, the so-called loyalists *(yi-min)*. The Chinese term *yi-min* means literally "the people left behind," those who, after the establishment of a new dynasty, retain their loyalty to the former dynasty either by active resistance or by a passive refusal to take public office. Although the Mongol dynasty, under its Chinese name the Yuan, soon mellowed to something closer to the familiar Chinese dynastic routine, the initial shock of Mongol hostility helped to create a sense of national identity in the conquered elite.

Wen Tian-xiang's achievements as a writer are inextricable from the dramatic experiences of his life and death in the Yuan subjugation of the Southern Song. The top graduate of the palace examination of 1256, Wen began a promising political career as the Southern Song was beginning to face a Mongol threat in the North. With the Mongol invasion of the South, he played a role in the unsuccessful military defense of the dynasty. When at last in 1276 the Mongol commander Bayan camped his army on Gao-ting Mountain near the Southern Song capital of Hangzhou, Wen Tian-xiang was made Grand Councilor and sent to Bayan's camp to negotiate. Bayan placed him under house arrest and had him accompany the Yuan armies; en route Wen Tian-xiang escaped. He was eventually recaptured and witnessed the final stand of Song forces in the great naval battle of 1279. At last Wen was sent to Da-du, modern Beijing, where he was kept in prison, refusing repeated offers from Khubilai to serve in the Yuan government. Enfeebled and almost blind, Wen Tian-xiang requested death, which was finally granted to him in 1282 when he was executed in the marketplace.

Wen Tian-xiang's early writings show him an able but not especially gifted writer in the Southern Song mode. The story of his initial detention, his escape, and recapture is told in two collections, the first and second series of *The Account of the Compass* (Chinese compasses took the southern end of the compass needle as the primary indicator, thus the compass could serve as a figure for Wen's loyalty to the South). These two collections are essentially of poetry, but there is so much connecting prose between the poems in the first account that the work becomes, in effect, a poetic diary.

In the following selection from *The Account of the Compass (Zhi-nan lu)*, Wen and a group of other Song officials are being taken north. When they reach Zhen-jiang on the Yangzi, they escape from their Northern guards and, after many difficulties, reach Zhen-zhou somewhat upriver on the opposite bank. Zhen-zhou is under the command of Miao Zai-cheng, whose superior, Li Ting-zhi, the Military Commissioner of the Huai-dong Region stationed in Yang-zhou, suspects Wen of being a spy for the northerners. Li Ting-zhi orders Miao Zai-cheng to put Wen to death. Miao cannot bring himself to carry out these orders and instead puts Wen Tian-xiang outside the city walls and bars the gates against him. From there, Wen sets off toward Yang-zhou and beyond, through a countryside infested with Northern troops.

Wen's simple prose, with its sense of excitement and detail, is often superior to his flaccid verse that usually merely summarizes the situation described in the prose. To give a sense of the structure of the poetic diary, some of the verses have been translated; others have been omitted.

from "The Escape from Jing-kou" *(The Account of the Compass)*

At night on April 29 we got out of the city of Jing-kou, and taking a short-cut across the floodplain to the river, we embarked by boat. We went upstream past Gold Mountain and hurried toward Zhen-zhou. We ran into hardships and difficulties in every imaginable form. I have given an account of each of these with a poem.

The Difficulty of Deciding on a Plan

Ever since I was taken captive outside the capital, I had plotted to escape but with no success. At Xie Village on the way here, I almost got away. At Ping-jiang I had again wanted to flee my captors, but it hadn't worked out. When we reached Zhen-jiang, making some kind of plan seemed even more urgent. We discussed making a dash to Zhen-zhou. Du Hu, the Archivist, and the Lecturer Yu Yuan-qing plotted with me in earnest. Du said to me, "If this succeeds, we'll be incredibly lucky. If we're not lucky and the plot gets out, we'll all die. Do you resent the prospect of dying?" I put my hand on my heart and swore, "No regrets, even to the death." And I kept a dagger on me to be ready to kill myself if the enterprise did not succeed. Du also asked to die to show his loyalty. The plan was decided.

> To go north or south—every man
>   suffers torment at a crossroads,
> but bold hearts, whatever the cost,
>   vowed to go southeast.
> Had we not then hacked the table[1]

---

[1]During the Three Kingdoms period, when the Northern warlord Cao Cao invaded the Southern kingdom of Wu, many of the King of Wu's advisers wanted to surrender to him. The king drew his sword and hacked apart the table in front of him, saying that anyone who again suggested surrendering to Cao Cao would end up like the table.

and willingly risked our lives,
which man of us that midnight
would have dared break free from our guard?

The Difficulty of Going on the Streets

Jing-kou had no walls, but there were barricades on all the major streets. The city was about ten leagues away from the river. We chanced to find an old army drover, who led us on a shortcut through a number of back alleys, and then we found ourselves all at once in the open moors. We hurried to the bank of the river, which turned out to be quite close. If we hadn't found out about that shortcut and had just gone down the main streets of the market district, we never would have made it.

Chimney smoke linked all the rooftiles,
    enclosed as though in an iron jug,
and we had to find a shortcut
    to reach the river shore.
Who was that man, willing to be
    last recourse for the general?—
an old soldier of the garrison
    who longed for officials of Han.

The Difficulty of Finding a Boat

The Northerners' boats were everywhere on the river, and the common folk didn't have a single boat left that we could ask to use. Du Hu tried to arrange something, but because there were no boats we all sighed and gave up. After that, Yu Yuan-jing met an old acquaintance who was in charge of the boats for the Northerners. He made him a secret proposal, promising him two thousand taels of the Pacification Commissioner's silver. But the man said, "What's money got to do with it? I will have saved the Grand Councilor for the sake of the dynasty and accomplished a great deed. All I want is a note to prove at some future date that I came to your aid." Afterward we gave him the note testifying to his service, and we gave the Pacification Commissioner the responsibility of making him take a hundred taels. He was a good man. It would have been all over if we hadn't had this single encounter.

We planned and plotted for ten days,
    but alas there was no boat;
in misery I beat my breast,
    my tears flowed with blood.
It seemed to me that fisherman
    was sent to us by a god,

we met him on the Yangzi,
    on the great river's bank.[2]

The Difficulty of Getting Past the Barricades

Everywhere in the villages and markets the Northerners had set up barriers, using a dozen or so horses to block the roads. We were coming to one of the barricades when the horses shied. We were terrified, but fortunately the Northern soldiers were all sound asleep, so we got away.

> Daggers in our sleeves,
>   learning to go gagged,[3]
> we were crossing by the barrier gate
>   when the horses grew suspicious.
> The night was still, the sky was dark,
>   our shadows scattered away,
> and the snoring of the Northern troops
>   was just then like thunder.

The Difficulty of Going Upriver

Once we had embarked in the boat, I thought we would go directly upriver and that nothing else would come up, I hadn't known that, in fact, boats of the Northerners lay all along the riverbank for twenty or thirty leagues. There was a frenzy of activity everywhere, with the sounds of the watchmen's rattles and crying out the hours of the night. Our boat had no alternative but to pass right beside every one of the boats of the Northerners. Luckily no one questioned us; but when we had gone seven leagues, a river patrol suddenly appeared, and they shouted over, "What boat are you?" We yelled back that we were a fishing vessel out to catch blowfish. Then the patrol called out in a loud voice, "Snoopship!" ("Snoop" was what the Northerners called spies.) The patrol boat was going to cut in front of our boat, but it just so happened at that moment that the river tide was ebbing, and their boat stuck in the shallow waters, unable to reach us. At that point everyone in our boat was sweating. It was just sheer luck that they didn't catch us.

> War galleons along both banks
>   lined the long stream;
> like mice we hid in our lone skiff
>   and rowed on forward.
> After seven leagues on the riverside
>   we were startled by a shout,

---

[2]Wen is comparing the man who got them a boat with the fisherman who rescued Wu Zi-xu on his flight to Wu.
[3]In wartime, soldiers were required to wear wooden gags in their mouths to keep them from talking.

    but Heaven caused the tide to ebb
        and the patrol boat ran aground.

The Difficulties in Gazing Toward the City

As soon as we caught a favorable breeze, I thought we could reach the outskirts of Zhen-zhou by the final hour of night. But after a long time the wind calmed, and when the sky brightened, we were still more than twenty leagues from Zhen-zhou. We were quite afraid that boats of the Northerners were chasing us, and we were also frightened that mounted patrols would be on the Huai shore. The anxiety and pressure of that moment was more than I can express. The men in our boat pulled the oars and pushed the poles with all their might. Where the boat could be pulled along, we went onshore and hauled the tow rope. But even though we felt the urgency in our hearts, our strength wasn't up to it. And to see the city in the distance and yet be unable to make any further headway was terrible—the difficulty of escaping from the mouth of a tiger.

The Difficulty of Going Onshore

The moat around Zhen-zhou is linked to the river; but only when the tide is high can one reach the city by boat. That day we moored at Five-League Village and went onshore. It was desolate outside the city walls; all was still, with no one in sight. The land all around us was flat as the palm of a hand, with no barriers anywhere; and our only concern was to be lucky enough to reach the walls. As we went along the road, we kept turning our heads apprehensively, afraid that pursuing cavalry would burst down upon us. When we made it to into the city gates, we heard that the morning of the day before Northern mounted scouts had reached Five-League Village. It was the first of May.

    Five leagues we went along the bank
        and entered Zhen-zhou,
    outside the walls it was desolate,
        even ghosts grieved there.
    We suddenly heard folk on the road
        saying with a sigh
    that the morning before mounted scouts
        had reached the riverside.

The Difficulty of Getting into the City

Once we reached the foot of the walls of Zhen-zhou, people who heard about us gazed at us in crowds. We told them that the Grand Councilor Wen Tianxiang had escaped at Zhen-jiang and had fled directly here for refuge. The various officers in command of the city came forward and immediately invited us inside the walls. Miao Zai-cheng, the governor of the city, met me and welcomed me. We talked for some time about the situation in the country, and I was stirred to such rage that I wept. He immediately urged me to stay in the official residence, and I was lodged in Qing-bian Hall. After that, my companions arrived. We were led to an officer, who searched our persons for weapons. Only when it was found that we had none were we trusted. The precautions they took were so strict! If it had happened that fears and suspicions had run rampant in people's hearts and they had closed their gates and refused to take me in, then where would I have gone in the vastness of this world? It was a precarious situation indeed.

> My body light and tossed about
>   into Luan-jiang,
> the governor greeted me with joy
>   and gave me a refuge.
> But had they closed their walls,
>   not answering my cries,
> through this world 'twixt life and death
>   my road would have kept going on.

After the party made it safely to Zhen-zhou, the governor Miao Zai-cheng received orders from his superior, Li Ting-zhi, to have Wen Tian-xiang killed as a Northern spy. Wen's dramatic escape seemed implausible without the connivance of the Northerners. Unable to bring himself to carry out the order of execution, Miao Zai-cheng had Wen evicted from the city.

Some geography is helpful here. Wen is in the Huai region north of the Yangzi, divided into two military districts, Huai-dong (East-of-the-Huai) and Huai-xi (West-of-the-Huai). Miao urges Wen to go to Huai-xi, whose Military Commissioner is not hostile to Wen. Wen wants instead to go north to Yang-zhou, the center of the Huai-dong district, to meet Li Ting-zhi and clear his name. After his courage fails him at Yang-zhou, Wen continues north to Gao-you (or Gao-sha), then turns southeast toward the coast. The Song armies are spread everywhere in garrisons, permitting the Yuan forces to defeat them piecemeal. It was Wen's hope to unite the various regional commands and thereby offer more effective resistance.

from "Leaving Zhen-zhou" *(The Account of the Compass)*

On the third day after I reached Zhen-zhou, Governor Miao said, "After breakfast, take a look at the walls." I was pleased and agreed to do so. A little while later Commander Lu came and took me to Lesser West Gate, where I could get a good view from atop the wall. Soon after that Commander Wang arrived, and we strolled outside of the wall. All at once Commander Wang said, "There is a man in Yang-zhou who has given information against you." He then took out a dispatch from the Military Commissioner Li Ting-zhi. I examined it, and it turned out that someone who had escaped from the Northerners had given testimony regarding what he had witnessed. He had said, "There is a certain Grand Councilor who has been sent to Zhen-zhou to betray the city." Wang was not supposed to have let me see it. As I stood there, upset and shaken, the two commanders suddenly whipped their horses and rode back into the city. Lesser West Gate was shut on me and I couldn't get back in. I stood there outside the walls in complete confusion, not knowing where I would die.

> That morning I agreed to wear armor
> and go off to look at the walls,
> we rode in a group beside the moat,
> and I sighed at the dust of war.
> I never expected to be thrown out,
> locked beyond Western Gate,
> worn down by troubles in these times,
> with no one to tell my case.

Suspecting that I was in the employ of the Northerners and that Governor Miao's loyalty had been subverted by me, the Military Commissioner, Li Ting-zhi, had sent a supervisor to Zhen-zhou. He said, "It is simply not reasonable that a Grand Councilor could have been able to escape. And even if he had been able to escape, it is not reasonable that he could have brought a dozen men with him. Why didn't you have them shot down with arrows? Instead you opened the city gates and let them inside!" His intention was to make Governor Miao kill me in order to show his own loyalty. It was terrible!

> Last night from Yang-zhou
> a courier came riding,
> wrongly suspecting and ready to kill,
> a man who was loyal and good.
> "No wonder, Governor Miao,
> that you seem to lack shrewdness—
> the other day you never should
> have let the gates be opened."

The Military Commissioner wanted me killed; Governor Miao couldn't shield me. Miao was torn between doubting me and trusting me, but his compassion for me was the stronger.

As soon as I was lucky enough to escape and reach Zhen-zhou, I had begun discussions on uniting the armies of the two Huai regions to work for the restoration of the dynasty. But Li Ting-zhi, the Military Commissioner, suspected me of being in the employ of the Northerners and wanted me killed. Everyone in the Southland and in the North knows that I am loyal; only in the Huai region am I not trusted. My reputation and my works during a lifetime of public service have reached nowhere in this area. In the vastness of this world, to whom can I speak?

I remained outside the gate a long time. Suddenly two men came out. These were Captains Zhang and Xu of the militia. I charged them to give me an explanation, and the two men said, "Miao Zai-cheng sends you this message: that he has sent the two of us to accompany you and find where Your Excellency plans to go." I replied that I had no choice but to go to Yang-zhou and see Li Ting-zhi. One of the captains said, "Governor Miao says that you can't stay in Huai-dong." I said, "I don't know Xia in Huai-xi and I have no way to get there. I'll trust my life to Heaven and go to Yang-zhou." Then the two captains said, "Let's get going, then." After a long time a company of fifty men with bows and swords came along to join us. The two captains rode ahead, with Du Hu and I side by side on two horses following behind. And thus we set out.

While I was outside of Lesser West Gate, beside myself with anxiety and with nowhere to turn, my traveling companion Du Hu cried out to the heavens and almost threw himself into the moat to die right there. Those who had followed me were all drained of color and didn't look like living men; no one knew what to do. I couldn't get back in the city walls, and outside the city there might be unforeseen encounters with soldiers. We stood there on the wild moor with nothing to eat or drink, and I brooded to myself, "How can I die here?" I paced about, feeling as though I had been stabbed in the heart. Later we got the two captains to go along with us, and Governor Miao also sent bundles of clothing and supplies. It was the third day of the month.

> My fortune spent, perils braved,
>   I escaped the felt-cloaked Mongols,
> I never thought that a Southern official
>   would be treated like a foe!
> I will remember all that happened
>   outside Lesser West Gate,
> and every year on the third of the month
>   I will weep by the riverside.

The captains led us on for several leagues, to a point from which we could still look back and see the walls of Zhen-zhou. All of a sudden, right there in the wilderness, the fifty soldiers suddenly took hold of their swords, halted, and went no further. I came up from behind, and the two captains asked me to dismount, saying there was a matter we had to discuss. The situation looked very alarming. I dismounted and asked them what it was they wanted to discuss. They said that we should walk on a ways. When we had walked some distance, they then said, "Let's sit while." I thought they were going to kill me right there. I began talking with them. The two captains said, "What happened today was not Governor Miao's idea. In fact, the Military Commissioner Li Ting-zhi sent someone to have Your Excellency killed. Governor Miao couldn't bear to see you harmed, so he sent us to accompany you. But now where do you want to go?" I said, "I'm going to Yang-zhou—where else is there for me to go?" They said, "What if they have Your Excellency killed in Yang-zhou?" I told them, "No matter—I'll go there trusting in fate." The two captains then said, "Governor Miao has sent us to accompany you to Huai-xi." I replied, "Huai-xi is right across from Jian-kang, Tai-ping, Chi-zhou, and Jiang-zhou, all of which have been occupied by the Northerners, and there is no way to get there. I just want to meet Military Commissioner Li; and if I can get him to trust me, then I still want to combine the troops to work for the restoration. Otherwise I'll take the road to Tong-zhou and go by sea to the imperial headquarters."

The two captains then said that the Military Commissioner had already refused my plan, and that the best thing for me to do would be to hide out in some stockade in the mountains. I replied, "What good would that do? If I really am meant to live, then I'll live; if I'm to die, then I'll die. It will be decided by the walls of Yang-zhou." Then the two captains said, "Governor Miao has made a boat ready for you on the shore. Your Excellency should travel by river, and then you can go to either the Southern side or the Northern side." I was shocked and said, "What's this you're saying? This means that Governor Miao also suspects me!" The two captains saw how sincerely I rejected their suggestion and said, "Governor Miao didn't know whether to believe you or not, so he ordered us to act on our own discretion. We can see what kind of person you are, a loyal servant of the throne in everything you say. We wouldn't dare kill you. Since Your Excellency is really going to Yang-zhou, our company will escort you there." It was then that I realized that Governor Miao had not made up his mind and had actually sent the two captains to keep an eye on the direction of my speech and then to act on their own discretion. If at any point my answers had not been on the mark, I would have been killed right there in the wilderness and no one would have known anything more about it. It was very upsetting.

I took out one hundred and fifty taels of silver I had brought with me and gave it to them for the fifty troops, promising them another ten taels when we reached Yang-zhou. As for the captains, I promised to give them a hundred taels to divide between them. Then we set forth.

> Out in the moors I dismounted,
>   they asked me where I would go,
> my life or death actually hung
>   on their personal discretion.
> Had not those local militiamen
>   been clearsighted in judgment,
> none would have known of the puddle of blood
>   unjustly shed.

On the road the two captains turn back, leaving Wen and his party with an escort of twenty men to accompany them to Yang-zhou; a little farther along the way, those men too desert and tell Wen to follow a peddler, who will lead the party to Yang-zhou. Once he reaches Yang-zhou, Wen Tian-xiang has second thoughts about giving himself up to the judgment of the Military Commissioner who has ordered his death. He and his party turn instead to a roundabout route that will bring him to the camp of the fleeing Song government.

from "Reaching Yang-zhou" *(The Account of the Compass)*

We traveled by night in complete silence, and when we reached the western gate of Yang-zhou, it was locked up tight. Nearby was a temple to the god San-shi-lang, with only the walls remaining—it had no roof at all. Our whole party spread out, lying against one another on the ground. The time was already midnight; the wind was cold and the dew was soaking us. Our distress was beyond description.

When I had left Zhen-zhou, I really had no place to go and had no choice but to proceed with all haste to Yang-zhou, hoping that I might be cleared of suspicion by the Military Commissioner. But now that we had reached the walls, in the dismal cold of wind and dew, I could hear a deathly, murderous sound in the drums and bugles. I was left in confusion, not knowing what to do.

> Depressed that in all Earth and Heaven
>   I have nary a place to go,
> in wind and dew from Level Mountain,
>   what time of night is it now?
> How can I let old Li Ting-zhi
>   have his way with me?
> from the high tower come bugles and drums—
>   why do they sound so sad?

The Military Commissioner had sent orders to Zhen-zhou to have me killed. If I knocked at the gates of Yang-zhou now, I was afraid that he might have me shot. This spot outside the wall was quite close to the Yang-zi Bridge. But it was dangerous, and there were also patrols. I could neither go on or withdraw.

> The helmets on the city wall
>   watch me, swords in hands;
> on the plain all around Turkish horsemen
>   ride circling the town.
> All my life I never knew
>   the tears that Yang Zhu shed,[4]
> but coming here I understand
>   that either course is hard.

Du Hu thought that since Li Ting-zhi wanted me killed, the best course would be to find some spot as soon as possible where we could avoid the

---

[4]The ancient philosopher Yang Zhu was supposed have wept at a crossroads, not knowing which way to go.

patrols for a day, then to make a dash for Gao-you by night and try to reach Tong-zhou. Then we could go by sea back to the Southland, where I might get an audience with the two princes and show my determination to serve the dynasty.[5] It would accomplish nothing just to die by the walls.

Captain Jin Ying maintained that since there were patrols outside the walls and it was five or six hundred leagues before we got to Tong-zhou, there was no way we could get there. It would be better to die by the walls of Yang-zhou than to die after undergoing such hardship. We would still be dying in the South. But he still thought that Li Ting-zhi might not kill us.

> The ocean clouds are faint and far
>   at the end of the skies of Chu,
> the dust from Turks fills all the roads,
>   we cannot go as we please.
> Supposing that some morning we
>   are carried off, captives of war—
> better to throw our lives away
>   and die in Yang-zhou.

I couldn't decide whether to go on or stay, and then Yu Yuan-qing brought out a man who sold firewood, saying, "Your Excellency is in luck!" I asked him, "Can you guide us to Gao-sha?" And he replied that he could. Then I asked him, "Where can we hide away for a day?" He said that his own house would do; and when I asked how far away it was, he said it was twenty leagues or so. I next asked him whether they had patrols or not, and he answered that there hadn't been a single one in the past few days. I asked, "What if the patrol comes today?" And he answered, "It depends on whether your luck holds."

> Beside the road by chance we met
>   a man who sold kindling;
> he said to us he could find the way
>   to take us to Gao-sha.
> "My own home lies thirty leagues
>   away from here:
> a nook in the hills where for a while
>   you can shun the dust of war."

While Wen was trying to decide whether to risk entering Yang-zhou or to head to Gao-you (Gao-sha), the day was gradually breaking. Fearing discovery, four of his friends left him in indecision and set off on their own. Wen panicked and went off after them, away from Yang-zhou.

---

[5]These were the Prince of Yi and the Prince of Guang, who were in Wen-zhou, directing the Song resistance.

I had no choice but to leave the outskirts of Yang-zhou and make haste toward the home of the firewood seller. But the sky was gradually getting brighter, and we couldn't go on any further. When we had gone fifteen leagues, there was an earthen-walled enclosure halfway up the hillside, which had once been a peasant's dwelling. It had been thoroughly gutted and had no roof beams or tiles left. In the middle were heaps of horse dung. At the time we were afraid that the Northerners would have lookouts on the heights, and as soon as they saw a band of travelers, they would come in pursuit. All we could do was hide out for a while inside the earthen-walled enclosure. We had bungled very badly in our planning, and our lives were at the mercy of Heaven's will.

> By starlight we were on our way
>   to the home of that rustic man,
> then light of dawn spread everywhere,
>   the journey seemed too far.
> In our panic all we found to do
>   was stop halfway up the hill,
> in crumbling walls, above which lay
>   just a cover of white cloud.

When we entered the earthen-walled enclosure, the hills all around us were utterly silent and there wasn't even the distant form of a person anywhere. At the time we had no rice to eat; and even if we had rice, we had no fire where we could cook it. Our money did us no good.

> On our way we came on a broken hut
>   good only as chicken coop,
> a plain hut out in the wilderness
>   where even ghosts wept in sorrow.
> In our sleeves we carried money
>   but had no rice to buy,
> and even had we plenty of rice,
>   we still had no fire to cook.

There was no way to avoid the dung and filth inside the earthen walls. We just cleaned out space for a few people. I spread some of the clothing I brought to be between me and the bare ground. I would sleep, get up, then sit back down, get up again, and then lie down to sleep. The day seem to drag on unbearably, and my spirits were beginning to flag. It was a terrible situation.

As a rule the Northerners send out their patrols only before noon, and then these return separately in the afternoon. We held out from sunrise to the afternoon, at which point we were exhilarated and said, "Our lives have been given to us this day!" All of a sudden we heard the loud noise of human voices. When we peered out from the wall, it turned out to be several thousand Northern cavalry heading to the west. At this point I blamed myself for not dying by the walls of Yang-zhou, but instead letting myself be captured here. It was a bitter thing indeed! At that very moment a strong wind suddenly rose, and black clouds came rolling up over us. Then several drops of light rain fell, and the hills grew all murky and black, as if some god were working to rescue us.

> Tossed here and there, dispirited,
>   I had reached the end of my road,
> I scratched my head and paced about
>   as the sun drew overhead.
> Then from nowhere the sounds of men's voices
>   came like a boiling tide,
> and black clouds burst upon us,
>   and winds were filling the hills.

Those several thousand cavalry kept on going, following the curve of the hill, and passed right behind our earthen enclosure. Everyone in our party went white and no one looked like a living person any more. We sat hunched down right against the wall, afraid they might see us through the doorway. If one of those horsemen had ridden in, we would have ceased to be members of the human race then and there. At the time the sounds of the horses' hooves and their quivers were clearly in our ears, with only a single wall between. Fortunately it began to rain hard, and the horsemen just passed right on. It was terrifying.

> As midday ended thousands of riders
>   suddenly came from the east;
> we hid away in that broken-down farm,
>   our fate was feather-light.
> When beyond the wall we heard only
>   the rainstorm in its passage,
> each of us looked at his shadow
>   congratulating rebirth.

There were eight of us in that earthen-walled enclosure: myself, Du Hu, Jin Ying, Zhang Qing, Xia Zhong, Lü Wu, Wang Qing, and Zou Jie. It was already past noon and we thought that no more patrols would come. At the bottom of the hill a league away there was an old temple with a beggar woman living in it. There was a well in front of the temple, so I sent Lü Wu and Zou Jie down the hill to draw some water for us. I thought they also might be able to get some rice or vegetables to ward off our hunger a little. A patrol came by unexpectedly, and both men were captured. They took out the nearly three hundred taels of silver they were carrying and gave it all to the patrol. The Northerners took the silver, and they managed to avoid getting killed. They came back only after the patrol passed. They wept facing us, but once again we had been lucky enough to get away with our lives.

Earlier, when we had not been able to go on further with the firewood seller and had consequently gone into the earthen-walled enclosure, I had given the firewood seller the task of going into the city to buy some rice to save our lives. I said, "We can't endure going the entire day without eating. The officials in the city will open the gates in the late afternoon, so when the rice arrives, it will be dusk." That day, several hundred Northern cavalry made a sortie against the western side of the city. Thus they didn't open the gates and the firewood seller couldn't get out. We were starving and utterly at a loss as to what to do. Furthermore, we were exposed to the sky in the earthen-walled enclosure and couldn't sleep. Therefore we went down the hill and put up in the temple, to stay there with the beggar woman.

Once we reached the temple and before we had settled in, a man carrying a club suddenly arrived. After some time, three or four others came in one after another. I thought we were not going to get away this time for sure. But then I learned that in fact these men had come from the city to look for firewood by night and then take it back into the city early in the morning to sell it. They had no bad intentions toward us. Several of them cooked up some rice soup and gave what was left to us. That evening one of them, a young lad still in his teens, lit a fire in the courtyard, which shone very brightly. None of the woodcutters went to sleep. I and my friends were worn out and went to sleep. It was beyond description.

> We stopped that night in an old temple
>   seeking a soup of boiled greens,
> there were a few woodsmen
>   whose names I didn't know.
> But the young lad seemed to know
>   that I had troubled dreams—
> he lit a fire of green wood
>   that burned until the dawn.

After talking with the woodcutters, the men agree to take Wen and his party to their village, from which they set out to Gao-you.

from "On the Gao-sha Road" *(The Account of the Compass)*

We had hired mounts and were making swift progress toward Gao-sha by night. After having gone more than forty leagues, we came to a plank bridge and lost the road. All evening long we went through the level fields, unable to tell east from west. Our bodies were soaked all over by droplets of mist in the air, and both we and our horses were worn out and hungry. We simply went on through the fog, unable to make anything out.

Then in a moment the hills around us gradually brightened, and all at once I saw the shadowy forms of Northern horsemen. There was a bamboo thicket by the road, and we hurriedly went into it to get away from them. A moment later there were twenty or so horsemen surrounding the thicket and shouting. The Military Inspector Zhang Qing was hit in the left eye by an arrow; he took two blade wounds in the neck; then they cut off his hair and left him naked on the ground. Wang Qing, an officer in the Ministry of War, was tied up and taken off. When Du Hu and Jin Ying were captured in the thicket, they took out the gold they were carrying, bribed the patrol, and managed to escape. I lay hidden in a spot not far from Du. When the Northern horsemen entered the thicket, they passed right by me three or four times and never saw me. I didn't think I would get out of this alive. Zou Jie, a groom in the Royal Stud, was lying under a clump of small bamboo; a horse had stepped on his foot when passing and he was bleeding. Lü Wu, of the Office of Military Administration, and his personal attendant Xia Zhong, fled to a different spot. I expected that I was surely going to die in this enterprise.

When things became most desperate, the wind began howling through all the cracks and crevices of the earth, confusing men's voices. The Northerners were in a state of alarm that they hadn't caught everyone and suspected some god must be aiding us. The horses left. Then I heard them making plans to burn the bamboo, and I hurriedly scrambled toward the hill in front of me, looking for another clump of bamboo in which to conceal myself. Not knowing which road to take and on top of that having nothing to eat, no situation in a person's life could be more desperate than this. A little while later when Lü Wu brought me the news that the Northern horsemen had gone back to the Bay, and also let me know that Yu-nian Levee was by the road, I didn't entirely believe what he was telling me.[6] Nevertheless, we had no alternative if we wanted to stay alive, so we did our best to get there as quickly as possible, this being one chance in a million. We were in a panic, scrambling ahead on our hands and knees, unable to walk.

When we had made our way out from Yang-zhou previously, there had been three men leading the way and three men bringing along the horses. Now there were only two left, the others having fled or been captured. When those two came out of their daze, each grasped his cudgel and followed after us, with intent to do us harm. We walked on, not sure what to do, but we had no choice. As it grew later, we suddenly came upon several woodsmen, who seemed to have descended upon us like Buddhas. We happened to find a large basket that a person could sit in, and we fastened it with cords. Then we hired six fellows and took turns being carried; in this way we rapidly came out west of the walls of Gao-you. We couldn't cross the river until dawn had come, and we were in constant fear that at any moment horsemen would appear, chasing us. We stayed over at Chen's inn, lying on its straw-covered floor and enduring our hunger. In the full light of dawn, we crossed the river and our hearts calmed at last. When a hurt is over, a person thinks about it, and then tears fall like rain.

---

[6]The bay was just north of Yang-zhou, where the Mongol army attacking Yang-zhou was encamped.

This long story is followed by a still longer poem of 172 lines, one of Wen Tian-xiang's best, in which he retells the whole story in poetic fashion. There the account continues.

The Northerners thought that Gao-you had been sending rice to relieve the siege of Yang-zhou, so that night they had sent cavalry from the Bay to cut off all the river crossings, of which Yu-nian Levee was one. If we had-n't lost our way that night, we might have reached the levee by two or three in the morning, and then we would have all been caught in their net with no one escaping. I then realized that our panic all evening long and losing our way was also as if the gods and spirits were operating in our midst, stir-ring things up. In the aftermath of such chaos, though I felt lucky to still be alive, I wondered what I had done to deserve to be brought to such extreme straits.

from "Reaching Gao-sha" *(The Account of the Compass)*

When we got to Gao-sha, there were very strict precautions against enemy spies. At the time we were using the basket as a sedan chair, and those who saw us felt sorry for us. Moreover, blood was oozing all over Zhang Qing's face, and his clothes were all stained. Everyone knew this was because we had run into the Northerners, and they no longer suspected us of being spies. I heard, however, that Li Ting-zhi had sent documents to all the various com-mands informing them that the Grand Councilor might try to come and be-tray their city, and ordering them to be on guard to keep him out. There-fore we didn't dare go into the city itself, but quickly bought a boat and left.

Setting Out from Gao-sha

At dawn I set out from Gao-sha
    lying in a barge,
a vast extent of level sands,
    a spreading stretch of waters.
The boatman points out for me
    the shore with roiling mist—
this very year, North against South,
    so many battlefields.

For a thousand leagues around the level Huai the dune grasses formed into hummocks, rising out of the high sands, bleak and desiccated every-where I looked. The waters at Gao-you connected with those of the Bay, going down to Hai-ling and up into Shi-yang, passing Lian-shui County, all belonging to this district. On April 6, there had been a battle at the Cheng-zi River in which our army won a great victory. People had pointed out a certain place as being the site of that battle.

Beside the Cheng-zi River
    tangled corpses lie,

the bloody flesh on the south shore
    is fainter and hard to make out.
North and south of the Tai-hang Range,
    out beyond Yan Mountain,
how many are the wandering souls
    that go chasing the horses' hooves?[7]

When we reached the Cheng-zi River, heaps of corpses covered the moors and there were countless corpses carried along in the current of the river. The stench of rotting was unbearable, and continued up and down the river for almost twenty leagues without interruption. On April 6, Commissioner Liu Yue and Hong Lei-zhen caught the baggage train accompanying the Northerners; from Ji Family Village they struck its vanguard, and from Gao-you they struck its center. It was a major defeat for the Northerners. Liu Yue died in the battle, and Hong Lei-zhen is now in Gao-you. I've heard it said that since the Northerns entered the Yangzi and Huai area, this is the only battle in which our troops had a major victory.

All day long we passed on through
    piles of white bones,
losing a rudder in the current
    can break a person's heart.
Our oarsmen from Hai-ling
    always look around dread—
when boats approach on the water
    or horses approach on land.

As we passed through the battlefield that day, there was an utter stillness in every direction. The oarsmen were edgy, constantly afraid that someone would come forth from the Bay, and also afraid that horses would come after us on land. In the midst of our fear and sense of desperation, the rudder happened to snap, and it took a long time to get it fixed. It was a dangerous moment indeed.

Eventually, Wen made his way to the seashore at Tong-zhou, then took an ocean-going vessel down the coast to the Song court at Wen-zhou. His loyalty proven, he was involved in a series of unsuccessful defenses against the advancing Yuan armies until early in 1279, when he was recaptured by Yuan forces in Guang-dong.

---

[7]The Tai-hang Range and Yan Mountain were in North China; Wen is imagining the souls of the Northern battle dead trying to get back to their homeland.

720

The Yuan and Ming Dynasties

THE YUAN AND MING DYNASTIES: PERIOD INTRODUCTION

Over the centuries, North China had passed through long periods of war, devastation, and conquest by non-Chinese peoples, but the Mongol conquest of the North in 1234 was in many ways unique, chiefly in the indifference of the Mongols to the benefits of Chinese civilization—except as those benefits served the Mongol war machine. Legend has it that Genghiz Khan considered turning his newly conquered territory into a large pastureland for Mongol ponies, and judging from the history of his conquests, he probably had the will, the means, and the ruthlessness to effect such a decision. He was dissuaded, the story goes, on being shown that the Chinese tax system would prove to be a more profitable use of the land. The Mongol conquest of North China was, like early Mongol conquests everywhere, of stunning ferocity, depopulating entire regions. But for the Confucian intellectuals who had ruled China and wrote its history, such mere physical violence was hardly a greater affront than the change in their own status in the new Mongol hierarchy of professions—close to the bottom of a list graded by usefulness. Slightly better than beggars and inferior to artisans and Buddhist monks, the Chinese intellectuals who had comfortably served the Jurchen Jin Dynasty saw what had seemed an immutable social order turned upside down. When, in a milder mood, the Mongols conquered the Southern Song some forty years later, an ethnic hierarchy placed the Mongols on top, followed by foreigners from the Mongol conquests in the West, then Northern Chinese, followed by "Southerners" at the very bottom.

Despite the profound cultural affront, in South China the Mongols and their foreign henchmen (such as Marco Polo) were a mere irritant. The Mongols, in their new Chinese guise as the Yuan Dynasty, recognized that the region was a profitable enterprise, so they disrupted neither commerce nor patterns of landholding. Despite heartfelt regrets about the end of the Song, carefully buried in elaborate metaphors, the old Southern Song elite essentially remained in place and continued Southern urban culture largely unchanged.

The Mongols' Chinese capital at Da-du (modern Beijing) was, however, a truly cosmopolitan city and very different from the Chinese cities of the South. Chinese elite culture was represented there, yet at the same time a truly popular urban culture flourished with unprecedented confidence and vitality. The vernacular songs of Da-du delighted in boasting, caustic satire, buffoonery, and direct eroticism, all treated in the lively argot of the city. Voices that had been rigorously excluded from the decorum of elite literature here found expression, and these voices gained much of their energy precisely because they violated such rules of decorum. This was a counterculture, and we have indications that such a counterculture already existed in the Song, though its texts were rarely preserved; from the Yuan, however, printed songbooks have been preserved, attesting not only to the existence of such a literature but that it had become a commodity that could be sold in print to a literate readership.

Closely related to vernacular songs were the "variety plays," *za-ju,* each of whose four acts was built around a song suite interspersed with dialogue. The topics of these plays were largely shared with storytelling: stories from history, particularly the Three Kingdoms; romances elaborated from Tang and Song classical tales; stories of Wu Song and his righteous bandits from the end of the Northern Song; and court cases, in which a mystery is resolved by a wise magistrate. The variety plays were associated with Da-du; the Southern cities had their own local drama, differing from variety plays in music and structure. In contrast to the variety play's four acts, the Southern plays were long, sprawling affairs with many acts and many singers.

The earliest Southern plays, dating from the Yuan, were preserved in manuscript. Variety plays, however, like the songbooks, were first printed in the Yuan. From the Yuan also comes the earliest printed edition of vernacular stories. Both storytelling and drama predated the Yuan, but the Yuan stands out as a moment when vernacular literature entered print culture and became available in the privacy of one's home as well as in the street.

Although it left its mark on the Chinese cultural imagination, Mongol rule of all China lasted less than a century. By the second quarter of the fourteenth century, regional rebellions were already breaking out everywhere in response to the ineptitude and corruption of the Yuan government. A scheme to issue paper money, for example, led to runaway inflation and economic disaster. In 1356, Zhu Yuan-zhang, at the head of a regional army, conquered the old Southern Dynasties capital of Jin-ling and used it as a base to defeat other warlords and the Yuan armies sent against him. In 1368, the last Yuan emperor abandoned Da-du and fled back to Mongolia. In the same year a new dynasty, the Ming, was proclaimed, with its capital at Jin-ling, now renamed Nanjing. In a subsequent reign at the turn of the fifteenth century, the primary capital was moved to Da-du, which was renamed Beijing.

Zhu Yuan-zhang, the founder of the Ming, was not an attractive ruler: he was autocratic, bloodthirsty, and narrow-minded. His son Zhu Di, who usurped the succession, was a match for his father. He executed not only the individuals who opposed his usurpation but their families and associates. It is said that in response to Fang Xiao-ru's opposition to his taking the throne, Zhu Di put to death almost a thousand people—all Fang's extended family members, friends, and neighbors. In contrast to the relatively tolerant emperors of the Tang and Song, who expressed displeasure by sending offending officials into exile, the Ming represented a new style of imperial rule and a degree of intimidation that changed forever the relation between the emperor and officialdom.

Despite some disastrous wars with the Mongols in the frontier region and the depredations of Japanese pirates along the coast, the Ming was, by and large, a period of peace and unprecedented prosperity. Particular acts of imperial tyranny, and later of the tyranny of the imperial eunuchs, had relatively little impact on the cultural, social, and economic history of the dynasty.

One sign of the confidence of the new dynasty was a series of six imperially sponsored voyages undertaken between 1405 and 1422, commanded by the eunuch Zheng He. These voyages took him to Southeast Asia, the Indian subcontinent, and ultimately down to Zanzibar on the east coast of Africa. The voyages were carried out on an immense scale: the first included almost 28,000 men, and 62 large and 255 smaller ships. The largest of these ships measured 440 feet in length and were

186 feet wide, many times bigger than the largest ships in the subsequent European age of discovery. Despite encounters with pirates and battles with local rulers, the voyages of Zheng He were a combination of trading expeditions and diplomatic missions. Ultimately it was the sheer magnitude of these expeditions and the enormous costs they incurred that led to their end. Unlike the later European voyages, they were not profitable on such a scale. Moreover, the European powers' control of their newly established colonies took a very different turn in the Chinese case, where the spread of traders and colonists throughout Southeast Asia was a private undertaking that carried the émigrés away from the control of the Chinese polity.

Education spread rapidly in the Ming, with the "Four Books"—Zhu Xi's compact selection of the essence of the Confucian Classics—as the imperially sanctioned core of the curriculum. The unprecedented number of aspirants to public office, all of whom knew the "Four Books" by heart, required an examination system that could exclude the majority. Out of the older requirement for the composition of formal prose developed a new kind of examination essay called the "eight-legged essay," *ba-gu wen,* requiring a highly formalized argument in eight balanced parts, developing some Neo-Confucian theme. It was a form that invited error and awkwardness, thus offering some common criteria for grading. The genre, however, tested skills that were of no practical use for the bureaucracy, either in matters of statecraft or in the documentary eloquence essential to the smooth functioning of the bureaucracy.

Classical poetry and "old style" prose continued to be written, but contemporary critics felt strongly that these forms had become weak and awkward in comparison to the Tang and earlier periods. Toward the end of the fifteenth century a new movement arose among intellectuals, seeking the renewed vitality of classical literature by the strict imitation of earlier writers. Several generations of these intellectuals are grouped together as the "Archaists." The Archaists believed that each of the major genres of classical literature had achieved a degree of formal perfection at a certain historical moment, and that the compositions of that brief period of flourishing should set the immutable norms for all subsequent writers. Prose was supposed to have reached its moment of perfection in the Qin and Han; poetry in the "old style" reached perfection in the Eastern Han and Wei; and regulated poetry reached perfection in the High Tang. If the aspiring writer confined himself to these formal models, he would be able to infuse them with his own spirit and concerns.

The Archaists' own literary works were uninspiring in the realization of their agenda for literary reform. Their open advocacy of imitation produced a strong countermovement in the last part of the sixteenth century, and an enduring hostility that remains enshrined in Chinese textbooks on the history of literature. Despite being almost universally reviled in later times, their more subtle influence was enormous. In a society that had developed an immense appetite for the forms of elite culture, they offered a version of literary composition that could be taught. Their anthologies, pedagogic in intent, had a wide circulation; and the poems and prose pieces that they selected as exemplary models have remained part of the literary canon to the present day.

The Ming also saw the large, amorphous cycles of popular storytelling emerge as novels. Although such novels are conventionally assigned authors, the authors named are historically very suspect. These novels are essentially anonymous, the commercial compilation of story cycles that had evolved over centuries. In many cases, they appeared in numerous and very different editions during the sixteenth and seventeenth centuries, and modern editions simply choose the version they believe to be the "best," on grounds of priority, amplitude, or aesthetic integrity.

The old storytelling cycle treating the breakup of the Han emerged as *The Romance of the Three Kingdoms (San-guo zhi yan-yi)*, traditionally attributed to one Luo Guan-zhong, the earliest edition of which is dated to 1522, followed by many subsequent editions. Many scholars believe that this was originally a Yuan work. The second of these novels is *Water Margin (Shui-hu zhuan)*, attributed to one Shi Nai-an; its earliest extant edition also comes from the early sixteenth century, and it too was reprinted in many differing commercial editions. This tells of a group of righteous bandits at the end of the Northern Song. The third novel is *The Journey to the West* (or *Monkey; Xi-you ji)*, attributed to Wu Cheng-en, the earliest extant edition dating to 1592. This tells the story of the Tang monk Xuan-zang (also called Tripitaka) and his journey to India to fetch Buddhist scriptures, aided by three supernatural disciples, the most important of whom was the ever resourceful "Monkey" (Sun Wu-kong). Branching off from *Water Margin* came the first original novelistic composition: this was *The Golden Lotus (Jin Ping Mei)*, probably completed in the late sixteenth century and first published in 1617. Linked tangentially to one of the major figures in *Water Margin*, it treats the sexual escapades of a powerful member of a local elite, Xi-men Qing, his excesses, and ultimate demise.

The Ming also saw the increasing popularity of the long Southern drama, spurred on by the vogue for *The Lute (Pi-pa ji)*, by Gao Ming (1305–ca. 1370), a melodramatic work about a poor but loyal wife who goes in search of her politically successful husband, who has been compelled to remarry. Southern drama had numerous regional styles, and among these a form known as *Kun-qu* emerged dominant in the sixteenth century. The immense popularity of these plays contributed to their transformation into a literary drama for reading as well as performance.

Ming culture became perhaps more memorable in the stylish individualism of its last sixty years than in all the two preceding centuries of the dynasty. Many scholars believe that the foundation of late Ming individualism can be traced back to the influential Neo-Confucian philosopher Wang Yang-ming (1472–1529). Wang Yang-ming's thought is too complex to permit easy characterization, but perhaps its best-known and most influential aspect was the claim that moral categories exist within the mind alone and do not depend on study and the outer forms of Confucianism. Wang Yang-ming's focus on individual self-cultivation gave some support to the remarkable turn against social norms that occurred toward the end of the sixteenth century. The eccentric philosopher Li Zhi (1527–1602) entitled his works *Fen-shu, Books to Be Burned;* in them, he offered a sharp critique of conventional moral judgments. His most influential essay, "On the Child Mind," argues that everything genuine follows from an immediacy that is inherently corrupted by learning and society; the argument is framed in a passionate defense of vernacular literature.

Li Zhi was greatly admired by the three Yuan brothers, the most famous of whom was Yuan Hong-dao (1568–1610). Yuan Hong-dao advocated a poetry of complete spontaneity, by which a person could give free expression to whatever was natural within him. Yuan Hong-dao even wrote a preface for his brother's poetry which declared that his brother's formal errors and stylistic lapses were more valuable than the passages in his works that were beautiful in a conventional sense: ordinary grace was a function of norms, while lapses came from the individual alone.

Yuan Hong-dao also singled out the crude popular songs of the villages as being the most perfect of the dynasty's literature. This led to a vogue in collecting popular song, most notably by Feng Meng-long (1574–1646). Feng published two collections of such songs, the most famous of which, the "Mountain Songs" *(Shan-ge)*, was composed in Wu dialect. The frankness of their eroticism was felt to be an expression of "natural" feeling. Feng Meng-long was widely involved in editing and publishing vernacular literature, of which three collections of vernacular stories are best known.

The age was fascinated with *qing,* a term that ranges from the more delicate "sentiment" to "passion." *Qing* was often paired with the motif of "dream," bridging the world of the senses and that of the mind; dream sometimes cast a haze of illusion around the experience of *qing* and sometimes became the means by which it could be realized in the world. Both *qing* and dream were strongly associated with the plays of Tang Xian-zu (1550–1617). Tang's *Peony Pavilion (Mu-dan ting)* was the most popular literary work of his day, and its celebration of love gave it a near-cult status. In *Peony Pavilion,* a young woman falls in love in a dream, then dies of longing, only to return to life when her dream lover appears in the flesh and takes up lodging near her grave.

The cult of *Peony Pavilion* was shared as much by women as by men. Literacy among elite women made great advances in the Ming. The number of female writers increased, and these writers looked back to the meager survivals in earlier literature to establish a tradition of women's literature. The heroines of the day were the great courtesans of Nanjing; poets and connoisseurs, they participated fully in the artistic life of the city and received the adulation of literati throughout the empire.

The fortunes of the Ming were, however, coming to an end. Famine and widespread corruption weakened the fabric of the state, and in the 1630s there were a number of uprisings that the government had difficulty controlling. Beyond the Great Wall in the Northeast, a non-Chinese people—the Manchus—had formed a highly disciplined state and military machine, and had gained the allegiance of the large population of Chinese frontiersmen living in the region. In 1644, the most powerful of the Chinese rebel armies, commanded by Li Zi-cheng, entered Beijing, and the Ming emperor committed suicide. The story goes that one of Li Zi-cheng's generals took the beautiful Yuan-yuan, promised as a concubine to Wu San-gui, the Ming general holding the fortifications in the Northeast against the armies of the Manchus. In rage, Wu San-gui opened the passes and invited in the Manchus, who quickly defeated Li Zi-cheng before turning to slowly conquer the rest of the country. They proclaimed their new dynasty the Qing.

元 Yuan Vernacular Song
明

In 1127, the Song Dynasty lost the North to the non-Chinese Jin Dynasty, a division that intensified the cultural gap between North and South China that had been growing over centuries. The Mongols, who replaced the Jin Dynasty in the North, established Da-du (modern Beijing) as their Chinese capital in 1264, and a few years later proclaimed themselves as a new dynasty, the Yuan. During the Yuan, Da-du developed a flourishing urban culture, one that seems to have prided itself on its vigor and roughness in contrast to Southern refinement, which its inhabitants often saw as effete. The former tunes of song lyrics from the Northern Song capital of Kai-feng were carried south and became an ossified literary form in the Southern Song. Some of those same Northern Song melodies and new ones went farther north and reappeared in Yuan Da-du transformed. These Yuan popular song lyrics are characterized by new themes, a new tone, and a striking use of Northern vernacular Chinese.

Since the same melodies were used in the aria suites of Yuan variety plays, the vernacular lyrics were called "independent songs" (san-qu). Some of these songs appear as single short lyrics; others appear in sets to the same tune, making variations on a single theme; still others occur in suites of different melodies, working together just like the song suites that formed the core of an act in a Yuan variety play. These song suites could be long lyrics, but many were narrative or dramatic monologues.

Guan Han-qing, who flourished in the last part of the thirteenth century and into the fourteenth, was both a dramatist and a lyricist of vernacular song; he was also the greatest master of the rough city slang of Da-du. He also obviously loved Da-du's urban culture. His most famous song suite, on the theme of "not giving in to old age," assumes the voice of an old rake celebrating life in the entertainment quarters of the city—drinking, gambling, and above all enjoying its courtesans, the "flowers" and "willows" described below. Such a suite should not be taken as a "realistic" portrait of Guan Han-qing or of anyone else, but as representing a new set of values in song, an anti-hero who is admired not for the qualities he claims to possess, but for the way in which he boldly claims those qualities of which society disapproves. He portrays himself as defiant, canny, and a survivor. The conventional values at which he snubs his nose are not simply proper Confucian social mores; he also mocks the conventional values of the pleasure quarters and its love affairs. Guan Han-qing is not the Song lyricist who stands with hesitant longing before the house of the beloved: he tells us at the outset that he has enjoyed them all.

Guan Han-qing (late 13th–early 14 century), to "A Spray of Flowers" (Not Giving In to Old Age)

I've plucked every bud hanging over the wall,
and picked every roadside branch of the willow.
The flowers I plucked had the softest red petals,
the willows I picked were the tenderest green.
A rogue and a lover, I'll rely
on my picking and plucking dexterity
'til flowers are ruined and willows wrecked.
I've picked and plucked half the years of my life,
a generation entirely spent
  lying with willows, sleeping with flowers.

to "Liang-zhou"

I'm champion rake of all the world,
the cosmic chieftain of rogues.
May those rosy cheeks never change,
  let them stay as they are forever.
For among the flowers I spend my time,
I forget my cares in wine;
I can:
  swirl the tealeaves,
  shoot craps,
  play checkers,
  do a shell game.
And I know whatever there is to know
  about music in every key—
nothing sad ever touches me.
I go with girls with silver harps
  on terraces of silver,
  who play upon their silver harps,
  and smiling, lean on silver screens.
I go with jade white goddesses
  and take them by their jade white hands,
  then shoulder to jade white shoulder,
  we go upstairs in mansions of jade.
I go with girls with pins of gold
  who sing their songs of golden threads,
  who raise their golden drinking cups
  and golden flagons brimming full.
You think I'm too old!
Forget it!
I'm the best known lover anywhere,
  I'm center stage,
I'm smooth,

sharp, too!
I'm commander in chief
   of the brocade legions
      and garrisons of flowers.
And I've played every district and province.

to Ge-wei

You boys are baby bunnies
   from sandy little rabbitholes
   on grassy hills,
   caught in the hunt
   for the very first time;
I'm an ol' pheasant cock plumed with gray;
   I've been caged,
   I've been snared,
a tried and true stud
   who's run the course.
I've been through ambushes, pot-shots,
   dummy spears,
and I never came out second-best.
So what if they say:
   "A man is finished at middle age"—
you think I'm going to let
   the years just slip away?

Coda

I'm a tough old bronze bean
   that can still go *boing,*
   steamed but not softened,
   stewed but not mush,
   whacked but not flattened,
   baked but not popped.
Who let you boys worm your way into the brocade noose
   of a thousand coils
   that you can't chop off
   and you can't cut down
   and you can't wriggle out
   and you can't untie?
The moon of Liang's park is what I enjoy,
Kaifeng wine is what I drink,
Luo-yang's flowers are what I like,
Zhang-tai's willows are what I pick.
Me, I can:
   recite poems,
   write ancient script,

    play all stringed instruments—
    woodwinds too;
and I can:
      sing "The Partridge,"
      dance "Dangling Hands,"
      I can hunt
      play soccer,
      play chess,
      shoot craps.
You can
      knock out my teeth,
      scrunch up my mouth,
      lame my legs,
      break both my hands;
but Heaven bestowed on me this gift
      for vice in each assorted kind,
so still I'll never quit.
Not till Yama the King of Hell
      himself gives me the call,
and demons come and nab me,
my three souls sink to Earth below,
my seven spirits float away
      into the murky dark,
then, Heaven, that's the time
I'll walk the lanes of misty flowers
      no more.

Although we find the practice earlier, in the Yuan, Ming, and Qing it became common for writers and anyone with cultural pretensions to take pseudonyms. Since writers often gave names to the libraries or "studios" where they worked, one of the most popular kinds of pseudonyms was the "studio name." Zhong Si-cheng, the fourteenth-century connoisseur of theater and vernacular song, named his studio for what he felt was his most outstanding trait.

Zhong Si-cheng (14th century), from a song sequence to "A Spray of Flowers" (A Word About Ugly Studio)

I. to "A Spray of Flowers"

    Born to dwell between Earth and Sky,
    endowed with humors of Dark and Light,
    and given a man-child's body, I
    was sure to make my way in the world.
    Whatever I did would have gone all right,
    and each particular suited me.

But comments provoked one point of contention:
friends old and new,
    no matter who,
snicker when they catch sight of me.

II. to "Liang-zhou"

Because my looks don't meet wide commendation,
my inner merits can't appear as they please;
half a life's writing brings no compensation—
for nothing my breast holds rich tapestries,
and my lips drip pearls of poetry.
I can't help this ashen complexion,
the missing teeth, the double jowls,
added to which are eyes like slits,
    the narrow brow,
a too short space 'twixt nose and lips,
and scraggly wisps of thinning hair.
If only I could have gotten
    Chen Ping's pure and jadelike glow,
    He Yan's handsome, gallant features;
if only I could have gotten
    Pan Yue's splendid looks and figure.
And I know
the real reason why!
I'm sick of facing my mirror each morning,
and furious at Mom and Dad
    for not having tried their very best!
Should the day ever come when a royal decree
    summons the homely to serve the state,
I guarantee
    I'll top the list.

III. to Ge-wei

There are times
at those idle moments as evening draws nigh
    at the back door I stand
with a winged black hat of gauze on hair
    piled sky-high,
and jet black boots sticking out from my gown
    that brushes the ground—
then all of a sudden I start to laugh.
I look like what?—
a modern-day
    queller of demons, Zhong Kui,
        who could not frighten a ghost away.

IV. to "Sheep-Herding Pass"

> If the hat is askew,
>   friends can blame you;
> but a face unappealing
>   is nobody's failing;
> it's true,
>   as they say,
>   men honor appearance,
> and a dignity of face
>   invites a certain deference.
> I think about this lying in bed
> and rage rises in my heart:
> I've lived these thirty years in vain,
> nine thousand times it's been on my mind—
> just like knots in lumber
>   you can't plane smooth,
> a congenital illness
>   no remedy can soothe.

V. to "Congratulating the Groom"

> Whatever can run in this world can't fly,
> no matter how much goes your way,
> no matter how gifted and clever you be—
> in quiet times I understand
>   the meaning of this for me,
> and secretly comfort myself this way.
> I have no urge to see the frontier
>   or by a pool to stroll:
> the fish in the pool would dive in fear,
> and frontier geese would fly off in alarm,
> and if I went to park and grove
>   even the commonest birds would flee.
> They'll paint me no portrait while I live,
> and dead, they'll write no poems for me.

. . .

IX. Coda

> I'll always recall one night in the rain
>   when the lamp had just gone out,
> the autumn wind blew over my bed,
>   and I was still far off in dream.
> There I met someone,
> he asked me join him,

and he said that I
was meant rise high.
"Having been a Confucian scholar,
you were to hold office as well;
a man who could take it easy,
with a fine eye for detail too.
But there was a certain moment
when best-laid plans went awry;
and since your body was formed thus,
regret can remedy naught.
I can only bring it about that you
receive an ample salary,
have many children and grandchildren,
a good marriage,
plenty of property,
a well-stocked granary,
good fortune added,
and great longevity.
I came here on purpose
just to let you know.
Soon I'm going to leave you,
and beg your forgiveness."
At last he heaved a few sighs
in a moment of remorse.
On waking I remembered him,
remembered who he was—
he was that very demon
    who shaped me in the womb back then
        and made me:
            unhandsome.

Vernacular song lyrics started out in the songs of the entertainment quarters, and many of the extant *san-qu* treat the world of romance and the courtesans. Sometimes bawdy, sometimes comic, sometimes merely coy, such lyrics are light and often delightful pieces.

Xu Zai-si (14th century), to "Dead Drunk in the East Wind" (*Chen-zui dong-feng*)

My sweetheart and I had long been apart,
I didn't know when we'd meet again.
Then all of a sudden I saw him today
passing right in front of my door.
I was going to shout,
    then worried that people around would stare.

So I sang out
   right then and there
      the popular "River Melody,"
  to let him know by the voice it was me.

Although the qualities of such songs often evaporate on reflection (and usually in translation), many depend on the surprising pleasure of vernacular usage, especially when a conventional languidly "poetic" situation is suddenly naturalized, both in language and sentiment.

Bo Pu (1226–after 1306), to "Victory Music" *(De sheng yue)*

I walk here all alone,
I've walked a trail into the ground,
and back and forth a thousand times
   I've walked in vain.
Won't you hurry up and let me know.
Come on,
   don't make me hang around till dawn!

Many of the Northern vernacular songs were sentimental love songs, churned out for the commerce of the entertainment quarters; others were song settings of commonplace poetic material. There was also a wit and irony that was relatively rare in classical poetry and the older song lyric.

Qiao Ji (d. 1345), to *Lü-yao-bian*, Of Myself

I didn't graduate in the top ten,
I'm not in "The Lives of Famous Men."
Now and then I'm Sage of Beer,
I find zen of poetry everywhere.
A cloud and mist valedictorian,
the drunken immortal of lakes and the river.
In conversation, witty and clever—
   my own kind of Royal Historian.
After forty years I still endure,
of life's finer pleasures,
   connoisseur.

In the early 1260s, a butterfly of remarkable size was sighted in Da-du. This was the stuff of vernacular song. Not only did it call to mind the conventional association of the butterfly as the gallant young rake tasting "flowers" (courtesans), but the memory of Zhuang Zhou's famous "butterfly dream" was irresistible (see p. 122).

Wang He-qing (late 13th century), to "Heaven Drunk" *(Zui-zhong Tian)*, Big Butterfly

It came crashing out of Zhuang Zhou's dream,
its two mighty pinions mounted east wind.
Three hundred famous gardens
    were every one picked clean—
who would ever have thought
    it was such a man about town?
It terrorized the honeybees
    chasing blossoms' scent,
and when it gently flapped its wings,
it fanned a gale of flowersellers
    east across the bridge.

Vernacular song did not, like most classical poetry and the older song lyric, avoid the body and physical love. Sometimes it was merely titillating, sometimes obscene, and often comic, as in Wang He-qing's literally "reversed" version of spending the night in bed with his girlfriend.

to "Helped Home Drunk" *(Zui fu gui)*

My lips were squeezed against her
    glossy coils of hair,
her back lay pressed against my breast—
hardly what they call
    "sweet cheeks nuzzled everywhere."
I had to heave my plaintive sighs
    into the nape of her neck.
I never saw her face all night,
my view:
    her ivory comb's backside.

Lan Chu-fang (14th century?), to "Four Pieces of Jade" *(Si-kuai yu)*, Passion

I am utterly bumbling,[1]
she is as homely as can be;
but no matter how bumbling and homely
    we've fallen deep in love.
Because she's homely, her heart is true,
which makes a bumbling fellow like me
    care for her all the more.

---

[1] In the context of Yuan urban culture, "bumbling," literally, "rustic," could perhaps best be translated by the American slang term "nerd."

Such a homely lover
and such a bumbling mate
make a match found only in Heaven.

One of the favorite songs was *Yi-ban-er*, literally, "A Half." Lyrics to this song usually concluded with the lines: "half one thing, half another." Although apparently
trivial, the significance of this song's popularity lies in its interest in conditions that
were intermediate or made up of contradictions; especially when applied to human
feeling, it marked, like Yuan irony, a growing interest in the complexity of human
behavior and feeling.

Guan Han-qing, to "A Half" *(Yi-ban-er)*

Cloudy coils of hair and hazy tresses,
    blacker than piled crows,
with a rustling of crimson satin
    a golden lotus foot shows.
No common flower over the wall
    is quite so pleasing:
you tell off your good-for-nothing lover
and half of you is furious,
    and half of you is teasing.

Xu Zai-si, to "Moon Palace" *(Chan-gong qu)*, Spring Passion

I had never felt longing all my life,
no sooner do I feel it now
than longing brings me injury.
My body, like a cloud adrift;
the heart, like willow catkins flying,
my force, like spider's floss
    drifting in air.
Only a thread of incense smoke remains
    still here,
And I, wondering where
    my high-class lover has gone.
Precisely when
    did the symptoms first appear?—
when the lamp had half dimmed its light
and the moon had grown
    half bright.

Although vernacular song had its beginnings in urban entertainment quarters, literary men soon used it to evoke idyllic rural scenes.

Zhang Ke-jiu (ca. 1280–after 1348), to "Someone Leaning on the Balustrade" *(Ping-lan ren)*, By the Lake

Far-off waters, sunlit skies
    bright with colored wisps of cloud
        sinking away.
Ancient shore, a fishing village
    where fishing rafts are spread.
The azure curtains of a tavern keeper's home.
A painted bridge where willow catkins blow.

Guan Yun-shi (1286–1324), to "Clear River" *(Qing-jiang yin)*

I gave up what little status I had
    and went away—
        it makes the heart feel good!
Beyond white clouds laughter's heard.
And if a few true friends and I
drink ourselves sick, who cares at all!
Our drunken sleeves go dancing
and we loathe
    a universe that seems too small.

Vernacular song took over and "translated" into its own idiom many of the standard themes and types of classical poetry and earlier literary song. The following is a standard occasion, writing a poem on a famous ancient site; in this case, Tong Pass, which guarded the approach to Chang-an.

Zhang Yang-hao (1270–1329), to "Sheep on the Hillside" *(Shan-po yang)*, Thoughts on the Past at Tong Pass

Here peaks and ridges seem to mass,
waves of the river seem enraged,
into river and hills and out again
    goes the road through Tong Pass.
I gaze toward the Western Capital,
it gives pause to thought.
This spot
    that Qin and Han marched past
        breaks the heart,
towers and chambered galleries
    turned to dirt all.
The common folk suffered
    when kingdoms rose;

the common folk suffered
    when kingdoms fell.

The Yuan Dynasty began in brutality and ended with a sense of corruption and ineptitude that went beyond even the infamously failed last reigns of earlier dynasties. Classical poetry may have directed barbed ironies against those in power, but the unsubtle sarcasm of the following anonymous vernacular song was almost unique. The "River Project" was a massive public works enterprise of 1351 to build a transport canal to Da-du. The introduction of paper money caused runaway inflation and combined with other factors to wreck the economy.

Anon., to "Drunk in an Age of Peace" *(Zui tai-ping)*

Glorious is our Mighty Yuan!—
all power is held by vile men.
The River Project and paper cash
    were root cause of our doom,
driving millions to insurrection.
Laws that govern slacken,
laws that punish, stern,
the common folk burn
    in rage:
men eat men,
cash buys cash,
things never before seen.
Thieves hold public office,
officials turn to thieves,
good men are confused with fools,
a sad state indeed.

Ma Zhi-yuan (1260–1325)

Writers of lyrics for vernacular song rarely show the kind of salient personalities that we find in classical poetry and even in Song literary song lyric. Rather than individuality, their preferences appear in the range of themes and styles that vernacular song offered. These lyricists often assumed the voices of conventional roles, not unlike the roles provided in drama. Guan Han-qing may be distinctive for his love of city slang and the culture of the demimonde, a love witnessed in both his plays and in his lyrics. Ma Zhi-yuan appears from his plays and songs as someone with rather more "literary" preferences, though little more of his life is known than of Guan Han-qing's.

One particularly popular form of *san-qu* was the short lyric describing a scene, perhaps related to the poetic vignettes of rural life found in the Southern Song and contemporary Yuan quatrains on paintings. The most famous short song lyric of the

Yuan is just such a simple description. It is often praised in traditional critical terms for its handling of stasis *(jing)* and motion *(dong).*

to "Heaven Pure Sand" *(Tian jing sha)*, Autumn Thoughts

Withered vines, old trees, twilight crows.
Small bridge, flowing water, people's homes.
Ancient road, the west wind, gaunt horse.
The evening sun sinks westward.
A man, broken-hearted, on a far horizon.

to "Shou-yang Melody" *(Shou-yang qu)*, Clearing Haze at a Market in the Hills

Past the village filled with flowers,
west of the thatched tavern.
Wisps of cloud brighten in late afternoon,
    the rain stops, the heavens clear.
Hills all around
    within the fading light
        of the sun hanging low in the sky.
To this brocade screen
    is added another swathe of azure green.

to "Shou-yang Melody" *(Shou-yang qu)*, A Sail Returns to the Distant Shore

The evening sun goes down,
tavern streamers calm.
Two or three boats have still
    not yet touched the shore.
Waters smell sweet from fallen blooms,
    a thatched cottage late in day.
Beside the broken bridge,
    each fishseller goes his way.

to "Shou-yang Melody" *(Shou-yang qu)*, Evening Bells in a Misty Temple

Chilly mist hangs thin,
the ancient temple pure.
Nearing dusk the sounds grow still
    from people praying to Buddha.
Borne with the western wind, a bell
    late in the day
        rung three or four times.

It will not let the aging monk remain
    deep in his meditation.

to "Shou-yang Melody" *(Shou-yang qu)*, Evening Sunshine in a Fishing Village

The rapping of mallets ends,[2]
in twilight sunbeams flash.
By a levee with green willows
    come sounds of fishermen's songs.
At several homes, from scrapwood gates,
    hang idle nets drying in sun.
All are snatched up within
    this picture of catching fish.

to "Shou-yang Melody" *(Shou-yang qu)*, Autumn Moonlight on Lake Dong-ting

Clouds veil the moon,
breeze plays the chimes:
two different kinds
of enhancement for my gloom.
I trim the silver lamp wick
    to write what's in the heart,
then give a long moan—
the sound
    blows out the flame.

The following suite of seven songs, one of Ma Zhi-yuan's most famous, begins with the call to seize pleasure while you can, and ends with the praise of the simple life.

A Suite on Autumn Thoughts

I. to "A Boat Going by Night" (Ye xing chuan)

The time passed in life's century,
    a dream of a butterfly.
Looking back, all
    that happened brings a sigh.
Spring comes today,
tomorrow flowers fall.
Hurry to offer another toast—
    night ends,
        the lamplight burns away.

---

[2]The mallets are used to frighten the fish into the nets.

II. to "Tall Trees Far Away" (Qiao-mu yao)

I imagine Qin's palaces,
　　the towers of the Han,
all have turned to meadows now
　　where sheep and cattle graze.
How else would woodsmen and fishermen
　　have their tales to tell?
Although great stone inscriptions lie
　　broken on their grassy tombs,
I can't make out the serpentine words.

III. to "Celebrating the Xuan-he Reign" (Qing Xuan-he)

They have come to fox tracks and rabbitholes,
so many proud and daring men.
The Three Kingdoms then,
　　a tripod's legs however strong,
　　　　cracked midway.
Was it Jin?
Was it Wei?

IV. to "The Wind That Brings Down Plum Blossoms" (Luo-mei-feng)

If Heaven makes you rich—
be not too intemperate.
Yet
　　fine days, fair nights last not long.
Then, rich man, let us say
　　your heart is stingy, hard as steel—
how could you just throw away
　　pleasures of moonlight and breeze
　　　　in your brocade hall?

V. to "Wind Enters Pines" (Feng ru song)

Before my eyes the crimson sun
　　sinks again to the west,
fast as a wagon rolls downhill.
Just look in your mirror tomorrow at dawn,
　　a further increase of snow white hair.
You'll get in bed and say farewell
　　forever to shoes left on the floor.
Mock not the dove's incompetence
　　because it borrows another's nest.
I bumble along and always play the fool.

VI. to "Keep Stirring Things Up" (Bo-bu-duan)

Fame and profit are done,
should's and shouldn't's are gone.

The world's red dust can never lure
    me out my door.
Green trees are the perfect cover
    for roof's corner,
and green hills fit the broken ledge
    in my garden wall.
And so much more!—
    my thatched cottage and bamboo hedge.

VII. to "Feast at the Pavilion of Parting" (Li-ting yan sha)

The crickets' chirping stops, I wake
    comfortable and snug;
but when the rooster crows come cares
    in thousands never ceasing.
When will it be through?
I view
    ants parade in packed maneuvers,
    chaotic swarms of bees that brew
    honey, and the furious din
    of horseflies seeking blood.
The Green Meadow Hall of Lord Pei Du,
Magistrate Tao at White Lotus Club.[3]
These things I love when autumn comes:
to pick chrysanthemums mixed with dew,
to split purple crabs with frost within,
to burn red leaves to warm my wine.
I think in our lives the cups will pass
    a limited number of rounds,
and how many times in all
    comes the autumn festival?
I charge my servant to keep in mind:
if Kong Rong comes seeking me,[4]
tell him he'll find
    me utterly drunk by the eastern hedge.

---

[3]Pei Du, one of the great ministers of the early ninth century, eventually retired to his estate called Green Meadow Hall, where he held famous parties for literary men. Magistrate Tao is Tao Qian, who, according to one erroneous legend, was associated with the monk Hui-yuan's famous "White Lotus Club."

[4]Kong Rong, an intellectual and literary man of the Three Kingdoms period, was supposed to have said that he had no worries as long as he had ample guests and the winecups were never empty.

元明 Variety Plays: Guan Han-qing, *Rescuing One of the Girls (Jiu feng-chen)*

Written drama in China appeared in the context of an established theatrical practice that was much older. In the urban culture Song and Jin dynasties, the skits and popular musical entertainments of earlier periods gradually assumed more complex and extended forms, with stories developed in suites of songs and improvised dialogue. In North China during the Yuan Dynasty there developed a kind of play called a "variety play," *za-ju*, consisting of four acts, usually with an additional short act known as the "wedge." The core of each act was a single suite of songs in the same musical mode, all sung by one of the leading characters. Between the songs, and often interrupting them, was spoken dialogue. The material of such plays was much the same as that of urban storytelling: great historical sagas, virtuous bandits, love stories from Tang tales, detective stories featuring the canny and virtuous Judge Bao, along with some lively stories of urban life, of which *Rescuing One of the Girls* is an example.

The relation between surviving printed editions of variety plays and the reality of theatrical practice is a complicated question. Though the songs, composed by the "dramatists," provided a degree of stability, such plays were almost certainly not performed from scripts. Rather, they were continually changed in reperformance by the professional actors, building on the strengths of a particular troupe and responding to the needs and inspiration of the performance. The earliest printed versions of such plays, dating from the thirteenth century, contain only the songs, with minimal stage direction and hints of dialogue. The fuller editions of Yuan variety plays, including the present text of *Rescuing One of the Girls,* are Ming recreations in writing of a complete variety play performance.

By its very nature, theater is a highly artificial medium. Readers and theatergoers of different traditions become used to the conventions of their own drama, and its artificiality seems less striking; but when a reader encounters a play from another culture, conventional dramatic devices can disrupt the illusion. Variety plays have many such intrusive devices. First and foremost are the songs that form the core of each act (in the translation below, the melody titles that make up the song suite have been omitted). When characters make their entrance they introduce themselves, often reciting a verse that identifies their type. Situations are explained rather than gradually revealed, as in most Western drama. Characters come and go on the stage with little regard for the unity of place, and when they are going to undertake some action, they often declare what they are doing to the audience, as was necessary in a theatrical tradition that used few stage props. For example, when a character is about to enter a house, he or she will declare, "I've come to so-and-so's house; I'll go in now." Finally, characters repeatedly summarize the situation before adding some new comment.

Very little is known about Guan Han-qing's life. He worked in the last part of the thirteenth and first two decades of the fourteenth century. More than any of his contemporary dramatists, Guan Han-qing seems the voice of the city culture of Da-du (now Beijing), a militant "counterculture" in both its language and values. A play like *Rescuing One of the Girls* represents something genuinely new in the Chinese literary tradition. There is a touching moment in Zhao Pan-er's first aria when she sings of the life of a courtesan; she says (see p. 749) that if she married,

> I'd pretend to act like an honest woman,
> to work at submission and be a good wife;
> but I can't help being what I am,
>   just a no-good dancehall girl,
> fickle in heart and always
>   meaning other than what I say.
> And how would the last act end?

The public values of Neo-Confucianism demanded absolute sincerity. The courtesan, however, is profoundly corrupted by always knowing better, seeing hypocrisy, conceiving of stratagems and alternatives. She is worldly and she knows too much, but this curse of lost innocence turns out, in a corrupt world, to be Zhao Pan-er's virtue. She is, perhaps, the first true "anti-hero" in the Chinese tradition. Good ends are achieved by lies. Zhao Pan-er's lies to the villain Zhou She might be justified, but she also bends the truth badly before the virtuous magistrate. Confucian social values are not the only targets in the play: the conventional values of Chinese romance are attacked, too, though they win out in the end.

Guan Han-qing's plays are crude, and except for the patriotic sentiment of critics that would make him "the Chinese Shakespeare," the obvious coarseness of his work can be too easily dismissed. Guan Han-qing is no Shakespeare, who could stand between court and commons, speak in both worlds, and transcend both. In *Rescuing One of the Girls,* Guan Han-qing revels in the common. There is nothing pretty about his world, and good is relative, measured against caricatures of evil. The courtesan's wiles are set against a relatively honest beastliness, and we applaud her victory. This was the horror of late imperial civilization, with its obsession with genuineness—that the lie may be humanly better than an odious truth.

The customs of sexual commerce in late imperial China differed in significant ways from those in the West. None of the available English words quite fits the situation, being either too rough or too sanitized. The borrowed French term *"demi-mondaine"* is closest to the status of the women in *Rescuing One of the Girls.* The women of the Chinese entertainment quarters were performers, singers, and dancers; however, there is very little reference to artistic accomplishments here (except perhaps in Song Yin-zhang's talent for nude somersaults). These women were also courtesans, who made their living by selling romance as much as sex, and they often looked to being bought out of the business and installed as mistresses or secondary wives. The language of marriage is always used in these transactions, but because such relationships were not sanctioned by the man's parents, they differed from the family alliances of "regular" marriages. The woman was entirely subject to the man's goodwill: he could either throw her out (as Zhao Pan-er anticipates Zhou She will do with Song Yin-zhang) or keep her against her will (as Zhou She in fact does).

ACT I

Enter ZHOU SHE.

ZHOU SHE [*recites*]:
> Thirty years gorging and guzzling,
> two decades lucky with girls;
> all my life I've never bothered
>   with costs of room and board,
> on booze and women I spend my cash.

The name's Zhou She. My family's from Zheng-zhou and I'm the son of a lieutenant governor. I've hung out in the dancehalls ever since I was a youngster. Here in Kaifeng there's a singer named Song Yin-zhang. She's got her heart set on marrying me, and I've got my heart set on marrying her. The only thing is that her mother won't go along with it. I've just gotten back from a business trip, and I guess I'll go to her place now to see her mother and bring up this question of our getting married. [*Exit*]

Enter MRS. SONG *and* SONG YIN-ZHANG.

MRS. SONG: I'm from Kaifeng. I was born a Li, but I'm a Song by marriage. My husband passed away some time ago. My daughter here, Yin-zhang, is all I've got left in the world. This girl of mine knows all there is to know about fast-talking and playing on words. Zhou She from Zheng-zhou has been her man friend for some time now. The two of them want to get married. I've tried every trick in the book to put a stop to it. [*to* SONG YIN-ZHANG] Listen Yin-zhang, it's not that I'm just trying raise difficulties in this marriage to Zhou She—I'm just afraid you're going to have a bad time of it later on.
SONG YIN-ZHANG: Don't worry, Momma. I've really got my heart set on marrying him.
MRS. SONG: All right, all right, go ahead and do what you want.

Enter ZHOU SHE.

ZHOU SHE: Here I am at their door. I'll go right in. [*Greets them*]
SONG YIN-ZHANG: Zhou She, you're here!
ZHOU SHE: I came right over to find out about us getting married. What's your mother say?
SONG YIN-ZHANG: My mother says it's okay.
ZHOU SHE: Well then, I'll go see her. [MRS. SONG *comes in and greets him.*]
    I came right away to find out about getting married to Yin-zhang.

MRS. SONG: It's a lucky day today—I'll go along with this, but don't go treating my daughter badly!

ZHOU SHE: I would never treat my girl badly. Come on, Momma, you go invite all the other girls and their friends while I go get things arranged.

MRS. SONG [*to* YIN-ZHANG]: Honey, you stay and take care of things here while I go invite all the girls.

ZHOU SHE [*recites*]:
> I've spent all my energy for years,
> today at last our wedding nears.

SONG YIN-ZHANG: It was all destined to work out this way.

MRS. SONG: But you can't always tell what will happen in love. [*Exeunt omnes*]

Enter AN XIU-SHI.

AN [*recites*]:
> I failed my exams like Liu Fen,
>   a thousand years of rue;
> yet like Fan Dan I keep my goals,
>   poor my whole life through.
> I figure that if Heaven
>   ever has its way,
> a man of books and learning
>   it surely won't betray.

The name's An Xiu-shi, from Luo-yang. I've studied Confucian texts since I was little, and I'm full of learning. My trouble is that all my life I've never been able to take my mind off drinking and girls. When I came to Kaifeng there was a singer, Song Yin-zhang, who became my girlfriend. She originally wanted to marry me, but now she's going to marry Zhou She instead. Her best friend is Zhao Pan-er. Why don't I go see her now to try to get her to talk Song Yin-zhang out of this. Is Zhao Pan-er home?

Enter ZHAO PAN-ER.

ZHAO: Zhao Pan-er's the name. I heard someone calling for me at the door. I'll go open it and see who it is. [*Greets* AN] I wondered who it was— it's you! Why are you here?

AN: I came all the way here because I want you to do me a favor. Yin-zhang was originally going to marry me, but now she's going to marry Zhou She instead. And I want to see if I can get you to talk her out of it.

ZHAO: Didn't she promise to marry you first? How can she want to marry someone else now? This marriage spells trouble for sure!

[*Sings*]

> Dancehall girls keep men company,
> we chase after money all our lives

for our "retirement plan"—
we can't waste time with winning ways
just to show how much we care
for some man that has our heart.

I think when it comes to marriage,
your timing can't be off,
    not a moment,
        not an instant.
How did he catch her fancy?
How did they get to meet?
Even if she's headstrong,
    and headlong
        to get it done as soon as she can,
she may well regret it later
    and hit herself on the head.
We seek happily-ever-after's,
to quit and settle down,
but it's just like the blackest ocean
    where it's hard to find your way.
In my view
    you'll never know another's mind,
    you'll never outsmart Heaven's design.

If "marriages made in Heaven"
    depended on just a "you" and "me,"
who wouldn't want to pick a person
    just to suit her fancy?
She may pick her way through millions—
but if she wants an honest man,
she'll probably search a lifetime
    and never find a mate;
but if she wants to marry
    a handsome, clever man,
she'll probably end up dumped,
    quite casually,
        halfway along the way.
Then whether she's dunked in dog-piss
or left on a piles of cowpies,
she'll find herself suddenly flat on her face—
and then when she finally opens her eyes,
    just who will she have to blame?

I can think of some married just a few days—
their looks were wrecked,
    they were gaunt as ghosts.
But they couldn't explain
and couldn't complain,

> they just cried in vain.
> I've seen some good-looking girls,
>   hot for marriage,
> who met some hard-hearted men
> and spent their lives sleeping alone—
> I think the whole thing sucks.

I can tell you what it would be like if I were to get married to one of my clients.

AN: What would it be like?

ZHAO [*sings*]:

> I'd pretend to act like an honest woman,
> to work at submission and be a good wife;
> but I can't help being what I am,
>   just a no-good dancehall girl,
> fickle in heart and always
>   meaning other than what I say.
> And how would the last act end?
> I may live in the lanes of the demimonde,
>   in the streets of willows and flowers,
> but nothing comes cheap to me.
>
> I don't fleece clients with phony wares,
> but they are out to gain
>   whatever little edge they can;
> corrupt of morals, every one,
> false in action, rash in deed.

If a guy has visited me a few times, and then I don't ask him for money, he'll think, "This girl's a golddigger."

> He'll just think I'm not coming clean,
> he'll say:
>   the girl means to bamboozle me.
>
> Some women love to be dancehall girls,
> and some love to be mistresses.
> Ladies who run a household
>   throw tantrums for nothing at all;
> we are merchants of illusion, with an eye
>   to earn interest on our capital—
> but if one of us gets married,
>   soon she comes to feel
>   the jab behind the feint.
> And that's a girl who cannot learn
>   from another girl's blunder.

You sit here a while, and I'll go try to talk her out of this marriage. Just don't be too overjoyed if I succeed, and don't be too disappointed if I don't.

AN: I won't stay. I'd rather go home and wait there to find out how it goes. Do the best you can for me. [*Exit*]

ZHAO PAN-ER *walks over and greets* SONG YIN-ZHANG.

ZHAO: Are you going out to pay a call, Yin-zhang?

SONG YIN-ZHANG: No, I'm not going out—I'm going to get married.

ZHAO: Well now, I've come just this moment to put in a good word for a man you can marry.

SONG YIN-ZHANG: Who's that?

ZHAO: An Xiu-shi, the scholar.

SONG YIN-ZHANG: Marry An Xiu-shi—me? We'd end up playing beggarman and beggar's wife!

ZHAO: Then who do you want to marry?

SONG YIN-ZHANG: I'm marrying Zhou She.

ZHAO: Listen, isn't it a bit soon for you to be getting married?

SONG YIN-ZHANG: What's too soon about it? It's "Hey, baby!" today and "Hey, baby!" tomorrow—a big pimple to squeeze all the pus out of.[1] But when I'm married, I'll be a "Mr. Zhang's wife" or a "Mr. Li's spouse." If I could have the title of a proper wife, I think it would be great, even if I had to die and become a ghost.

ZHAO [*sings*]:
> Before you act you'd better think,
> then think it through again.
> Right now you're young and green,
> I'll find you another man,
> and take my time.
> For your part it's easy—
> just keep snug as a bug at home;
> from your very best friend
> this sincere admonition:
> I don't think you could stand
> the man's disposition.

A man who's a husband can't act like a lover, and a man who's a lover can't act like a husband.

SONG YIN-ZHANG: Explain that to me.

ZHAO [*sings*]:
> "A man who's a husband
> can't act like a lover"—
> she doesn't know what that means.
> A lover can be just a hollow facade,
> a man who's a husband is honest inside.

SONG YIN-ZHANG: But Pan-er, Zhou She dresses so nicely, and he's really cute.

---

[1]This metaphor is based on a pun: *da-jie* ("Hey, baby," literally, "big sister"), the way one addresses a singing girl, and the homophone "big pimple."

ZHAO [*sings*]:
> Even if that fellow wore
>> a dung beetle's shining shell,
>
> what does he understand
>> of relationships in families?
>
> Why do you want to marry him?

SONG YIN-ZHANG: I want to marry him because he treats me well.

ZHAO: And just how does he treat you well?

SONG YIN-ZHANG: There's something for every season of the year. During those little naps I love to take in summertime, he fans me; and in winter he warms the covers for me and helps me rest comfortably. When I go off somewhere to pay a call, he fixes the collar ties on the clothes I wear and straightens my hairpins. And it's because he treats me well in things like this that I want to marry him with all my heart.

ZHAO: So that's why?

[*Sings*]

> Now I've heard how you really feel,
> the reason you do what you do,
> and I can't stop a bit of a smile.
> So he fans you to sleep in those hot summer months
> and in winter he warms things up—
> do you think he's worried you'll catch a chill
>> through your thick clothes?

> And when you're eating he takes a spoon
> to get out the gristle and skin;
> when you go out, he ties your collar
> and straightens up your clothes
> and in your hair arranges the pin.
> But all of this is just false show
> that girls never see through,
>> but fall more deeply in love.

> You think your love's sweet as honey,
> but once you're married and in his house,
> he'll probably dump you in less than a year.
> He'll soon bare his teeth and curl his lip,
> whack with fists,
>> kick with feet,
> and beat you till you're left in tears.

> Your boat will be in midriver then,
>> too late to fix the leaks,
> and who will you have to blame?
> First think things through,
>> or you'll be sorry.

> I can't talk you out of this now,
> but a day will come
> I'll have to figure out how
>   to save you from helpless pining.

Yin-zhang, if things go bad for you later on, just don't come complaining to me.

SONG YIN-ZHANG: Even if I were condemned to die, I wouldn't come complaining to you.

Enter ZHOU SHE.

ZHOU SHE: Spread out the wedding gifts, boys, so we can admire them a bit.

ZHAO: Is this guy that just came in Zhou She? If he doesn't say anything to me, I'll let it be; but if he says just one word, I'll give him a piece of my mind.

ZHOU SHE: So this is Zhao Pan-er?

ZHAO: That's right.

ZHOU SHE: Please, have something to eat and drink.

ZHAO: You—inviting me to eat something! I'm so hungry at home my cheeks are gaunt—oh no, there's nothing in any of *my* cooking pots. You think it's an autumn moon shining in the cellar, that I've never seen food like this!

ZHOU SHE: Look, I have something I'd like you to do for me, Miss. Would you vouch for the person I'm going to marry?

ZHAO: Vouch for whom?

ZHOU SHE: For Song Yin-zhang.

ZHAO: What do you want me to vouch for? Her needlework? Her cooking? Her embroidery? Her ability to furnish the bridal chamber? Her sewing? Her ability to raise children?

ZHOU SHE: [*Aside*] This bitch has got a mean tongue on her. [*to* ZHAO PAN-ER] Everything's all set anyway, so I don't need you.

ZHAO: Then I'm leaving. [*Goes out door*]

Enter AN XIU-SHI.

AN: How did your talk with Yin-zhang go?

ZHAO: I got nowhere.

AN: In that case I'll be off to the capital to take the examinations.

ZHAO: Don't go just yet. There's something in which I'm going to need you.

AN: I'll go along with you. I'll stay here in the inn to see what you come up with. [*Exit*]

ZHAO [*sings*]:

> That girl's a monster, a demon,
> a temptress who trips men up—
> don't be too sure those are legs in her pants;
> and when we spit out our blood for her,
> she thinks it's just red dye.
> Don't believe all the sweet-talk you hear.

752

She hates you so
> she would easily gouge out your eyes—
she's only happy
> if you stick close to her all the time.

[*Aside*] I hope she comes to her senses quickly.
> Our poor Shuang-lang, scholar lover,
had a golden tiara ready for her
> and cloudlike cape.

[*Aside*] He had the great lady in his hands,
> But instead, because of a tea seller's fortune,
she married the merchant Feng Kui.[2] [*Exit*]

ZHOU SHE: Now that we've said goodbye to your mother, get in the sedan chair, and we'll be off to Zheng-zhou.

[*Recites*]

No sooner out of the courtesan's gate
than you are the wife of a decent man.

SONG YIN-ZHANG [*continuing*]:
> What's got me worried is:
when I bear the abuse of this "decent man,"
> I'll think of becoming a whore again. [*Exeunt*]

ACT II

Enter ZHOU SHE *and* SONG YIN-ZHANG.

ZHOU SHE: I've ridden horses all my life, and now I've fallen off trying to ride an ass. I just about wore out my tongue trying to get this woman to marry me. I had her get into the sedan chair, I got on a horse, and we left Kaifeng on our way to Zheng-zhou. I let the sedan chair go on ahead because I was afraid that the better class of people would make me the butt of their jokes and say, "Zhou She has married Song Yin-zhang." Then I see the sedan chair bouncing up and down. So I go up ahead, give the guys who are carrying it a flick of my whip, and say, "Are you trying to put something over on me?" And I ask them, "Why are you making it bounce? Just carry it!" And they say, "It's not our doing—we don't know what the young lady is up to in there." When I lift the sedan chair curtain and take a look, I see her stripped down to the buff, turning somersaults. Then, when we get to my house, I tell her, "Sew up the quilting so that I can sleep under it." I come into the room and I see a quilt standing on end, as tall as the bed. So I shout, "Where are you, woman?" And I hear an answer from inside the quilt, "I'm here, Zhou She, inside the quilt." So I say, "What are you doing inside the quilt?" And she says,

---

[2]Zhao Pan-er here is alluding to a popular love story in which Su Xiao-qing was in love with the scholar Shuang-jian (or Shuang-lang), but was forced to marry the tea merchant Feng Kui. Shuang-jian, after getting office, finds a poem she has left, and eventually rescues her.

"I was sewing in the cotton stuffing, and I got myself stuck inside somehow." I pick up a stick and am just about to hit her when she says, "It's no big deal if you hit me, Zhou She, but don't hit old Mrs. Wang next door." And I say, "Great! You've got the neighbor in there too!"

SONG YIN-ZHANG: I never did any such thing!

ZHOU SHE: I haven't told the half of it. I may beat you to death with my own hands, you bitch, but I'm never going to sell you off or let you buy your way out. I'm going off to get something to drink now, and when I come back I'm going take my time beating you up. [*Exit*]

SONG YIN-ZHANG: You always get in big trouble if you don't believe what a good person says. Zhao Pan-er tried to talk me out of this, but I wouldn't listen, and no sooner did we get inside his house than he hit me fifty times just to teach me a lesson. He beats me and yells at me morning and night, and I'm sure I'm going to die at his hands. There's a peddler next door named Wang who's going to do some business in Kaifeng, and I've written a letter for him to take to my mother and Zhao Pan-er to have them come get me out of this. If they take too long, I'm not going to be among the living. Heaven! You're letting me get beaten to death! [*Exit*]

Enter MRS. SONG, *crying.*

MRS. SONG: I'm Song Yin-zhang's mother. My daughter went and married Zhou She, but yesterday Wang the peddler brought me a letter, and in it she writes, "No sooner did we get inside his house than he hit me fifty times just to teach me a lesson. Now he beats me and yells at me morning and night, and pretty soon I'm going to die. Please beg Pan-er to come get me out of this as quickly as she can." I'll take the letter to Zhao Pan-er to let her know and to see how we can get Ying-zhang away from there. Poor little Ying-zhang, you're going to be the death of me. [*Exit*]

Enter ZHAO PAN-ER.

ZHAO PAN-ER: The name's Zhao Pan-er. I keep wondering when I'm going to be able to get out of this way of making a living.

[*Sings*]

Getting married has been on my mind
    these past few years, and I've heard
how some girls paid their indenture
and some girls were bought free.
They made themselves suck up to rich men
and never realized
that rich men will break a dancehall girl
    and lightly toss her aside.
Every one of them,
    eyes bulging wide,
        is like fish dumped from a net;
every one of them,
    lips in a pout,

is like pigeon shot from the air.
No planting them in the Royal Park,
    those common roadside willows,
and no respectable household
    will ever put up with a whore.
At first men always mean it a little,
but in the long run
    it never works out well.

Who has not wedded impetuously?
or leapt at the chance of married life?
and then who hasn't been carelessly dumped?
We are bubbles all, adrift on the waters,
    each one after another.
We make our own folks into enemies,
    so mad they won't see us again,
like sun and moon or opposing stars,
    each rising as the other sets,
when we get caught in men's snares.
They show every form of ardent passion,
thousands of kinds of love and care—
until, in the end,
    the slate is wiped bare.

Enter Mrs. Song.

Mrs. Song: This is her house. I'll go in and find her. [*Greets her*] Pan-er,
    I'm terribly upset!
Zhao: Mrs. Song, why are you crying like this?
Mrs. Song: Let me tell you. Yin-zhang didn't listen to your advice and mar-
    ried Zhou She anyway. No sooner did she get inside his house than he
    hit her fifty times just to teach her a lesson. Now he's beating her within
    an inch of her life, and she can't last much longer. What are we going to
    do?
Zhao: So, Yin-zhang's being beaten.

[*Sings*]

I think back when she secretly married,[3]
I feared they would never get along.
The things I said then that needled her
now have all come true.
It was only last autumn you left.
He was the most shiftless
    of all shiftless men,
but you thought he really loved you
and that you both would be joined fast.

---

[3]The "secrecy" probably refers to Zhou She's parents.

So you spread out the lovebird covers
    and hung up the phoenix drapes,
hoping it would last like Heaven,
    endure as long as Earth;
but once you step past the threshold
    and know what he's like, you're through.
I've watched this sort of thing many a time,
and now it's no business of mine,
the whole thing's out of my hands.

[*Aside*] But Zhao Pan-er . . .

You're in a situation where
    if you let her die and don't save her,
you'll be shamed forever for failing
    the oath of sisterhood we swore.

So that's how it's turned out. Who let you marry him?
MRS. SONG: But Pan-er, Zhou She promised . . .
ZHAO [*sings*]:
    Doesn't each of them put on a woeful face
        and claim he's going to die?
    But when it comes right down to it,
        doesn't each of them change his mind halfway?
    You're the courtesan's all-too-honest mother—
    what young men say when they want a girl
        is the same the whole world over—

Zhou She is not the only liar.

    Doesn't each of them point to Heaven,
        all kinds of vows he swears—
    vows soon done, like autumn winds
        blowing past the ears.
MRS. SONG: But Pan-er, how are we going to save my daughter?
ZHAO: I've got a couple of bars of silver stashed away. We'll take those and
    go buy her away from him.
MRS. SONG: But he said he'll beat her to death rather than sell her off or let
    her buy her way out.

ZHAO PAN-ER *thinks a while, then says something in* MRS. SONG's *ear.*

ZHAO: . . . It's the only way.
MRS. SONG: But can you bring it off?
ZHAO: Don't worry. Let me have a look at the letter. [MRS. SONG *hands*
    her the letter and she reads]: "Dear Momma and Pan-er. I didn't
    believe your good advice and now I've ended up in big trouble. As soon
    as I got inside his house he hit me fifty times just to teach me a lesson.
    Now he beats me and yells at me morning and night, and I can't t
    ake the abuse any more. If you come soon, you may see me again,

but if you delay, you'll never see my face in this world again. Yin-zhang." Oh Yin-zhang, what got into you to do this in the first place?

[*Sings*]

> I think on how it used to be,
> when one of us worried,
>   we worried together,
> when one was in sorrow,
>   our sorrows were shared.
> Now she tells me she'll soon be gone,
>   buried on some grassy hill,
> a ghost who roams back alleys
>   begging for gifts of village wine—
> you told me that after you're gone . . .

Well, dear sister, didn't you yourself say, "It's Hey, baby! this and Hey, baby! that—a big pimple to squeeze all the pus out of." Better to get married and be a Mr. Zhang's wife or a Mr. Li's spouse.

[*Sings*]

> If I could be known as a proper wife.
> it would be great,
>   even if I had to die and turn a ghost.

Mrs. Song, has the man who brought the letter gone yet?

MRS. SONG: Not yet.

ZHAO: I'll write a letter and send it to Yin-zhang. [*Writes and sings*]

> I'll compose this letter myself
>   to send her all my love,
> and tell her not to let
>   a word of my scheme leak out.
> I'll send it to that once reckless
>   and now repentant girl,
> give greetings to the sufferer
>   whose body aches all over.

Didn't I try to talk you out of it, Yin-zhang?

> But there really was no reason
> you should find such a brute,
> thrashing you heartlessly with his stick
> till your fresh red blood oozes down,
> spending each morning in your home
>   like a criminal on death row—
> I'm sure you're not long for this world.
> What's more, you're living so far away
>   in Zheng-zhou
> that no one can watch over you,

757

> so it couldn't be helped that these awful things
> came about.

MRS. SONG [*weeping*]: How can my poor daughter stand it? How are you
going to get her out of this, Pan-er?

ZHAO: Don't worry, Mrs. Song.

[*Sings*]

> Just to make you bear it better
> I'll come up with another plan—
> I'll fix up these cloudy coils of hair
> and wispy tresses,

[*Aside*] and then on again with my gown of brocade,

> with its coral hooks
> and lotus buttons,
> I'll go wiggle my hips
> and be oh so sexy.

> I'll make these powdered cheeks of mine
> rescue your daughter-cadaver,
> I'll risk myself, in spite of all,
> so let him curse me and curse some more.
> I'm not just talking big now—
> he'll never escape the hands of this whore!

MRS. SONG: Keep a sharp eye out and be careful when you get there, Pan-
er. [*Weeps*] Oh daughter, you're going to be the death of me!

ZHAO [*sings*]:

> Just stop your heart from fretting,
> relax those worried brows,
> I'll pull it off and bring her back
> without a hitch.
> That bastard's girl-chasing heart
> will come like a puppy to me,
> trying to show how clever he is.

When I get there, I'll talk to him a little, and if he'll sign the divorce papers, that'll be it. But if he won't sign them, then I'll give him a few
pinches here and a little fondling there and a few hugs and a few squeezes
till his whole body melts like butter and goes completely numb. It will
be like rubbing a little sugar under his nose, and the guy will try to lick
it but he won't be able to get to it, and he'll try to bite it, but he won't
be able to reach it. I'll trick him into signing the divorce papers, and once
Yin-zhang gets hold of the divorce papers, she'll be out of there in a flash.
And at that point I'll make my own exit. [*Sings*]

> And won't it be a sensational scene
> when I make this man give her up! [*Exit*]

ACT III

Enter ZHOU SHE *and* INNKEEPER.

ZHOU SHE [*recites*]:
>   Everything's set by destiny,
>   no point in working—life drifts by.
>   Nothing but pretty women and wine
>   can ever fluster this heart of mine.

Listen, boy, when I had you open this establishment, it wasn't because I had an eye to get money for rent to take care of my family. If a good-looking woman comes to the inn, just call me—no matter whether she's on the government payroll or in business for herself.

INNKEEPER: Got it. But since you're always on the move, where am I going to find you at any particular time?

ZHOU SHE: You can find me in the whorehouse.

INNKEEPER: And if you're not in the whorehouse?

ZHOU SHE: You can find me in a gambling den.

INNKEEPER: And if you're not in a gambling den?

ZHOU SHE: Then you can find me in jail. [*Exit*]

Enter the errand boy ZHANG XIAO-XIAN *with suitcases.*

ZHANG XIAO-XIAN [*recites*]:
>   I make my living with cleated boots
>   and umbrella to keep off the rain,
>   my living is made passing love notes
>   that tell of secret passion.
>   I'm not an idle person, so
>   I never get to be idle,
>   and even when I have idle time, I'm
>   incapable of idling.

Zhang Xiao-xian's my name, which means "Just Slightly Idle." I've never been involved in regular business, but whenever a singer or one of the girls needs someone to pass messages back and forth between lovers, I'm always the one they call. This time Zhao Pan-er had me pack two suitcases of clothes and things to go to Zheng-zhou. Everything's set, and it's time to mount up, Miss.

Enter ZHAO PAN-ER.

ZHAO: Xiao-xian, do you think I can make that guy hot for me dressed up like this? [XIAO-XIAN *falls down*] What are you doing?

ZHANG XIAO-XIAN: You don't need to worry about making him hot for you—this time even I've melted down!

ZHAO [*sings*]:
>   I really feel bad for her,
>   worries fill my breast;

she's gotten herself in a mess
    with no way out.
That woman was hot-headed,
she didn't think it through,
and now I've got to make myself play
    one of that troupe who lead souls astray.

I'll puff my breath ever so slightly,
and set his heart aflame,
I'll make him kick the traces,
    go bolting out of the stall.
And I'll make out that he's a lover
    like no one else in the world.
Thinking this up is easy enough,
but no small thing to bring off,
and many's the time I would have preferred
    not to interfere;
it's the old lady I'm sorry for first,
    having no one to support her;
and second, being so used to the road,
    I've a special pity for travelers;
and third—well, craving a drink myself,
    I take pity on a drunkard.
So once we get there,
I'll give it my heart and soul.

And here as I've been talking we're already in Zheng-zhou. Xiao-xian,
take the horses while I stop here a while in the shade of this willow.

ZHANG XIAO-XIAN: Sure.

ZHAO: Just making idle conversation, Xiao-xian, but you know that people
from good families behave well, while people from the wrong sort of families have bad habits.

ZHANG XIAO-XIAN: Tell me what you mean.

ZHAO [*sings*]:

A high-class lady's a high-class lady;
a dancehall girl's a dancehall girl.
So what if she struts 'cross the threshold
    wiggling her hips,
she can't stop him bossing her around
    and making her into a slave—
and she has to put up with it silently.

Good families powder their faces
    lightly and with good taste,
unlike us, who gob it on;
good families comb out their tresses,
    with a slow and gracious ease,
unlike us, who just untie hairbands

leaving deep marks on the chin.
Good families well understand degrees
    of intimacy and reserve,
and know how to observe
    when to be distant, when to comply—
it's a sort of breeding that's quite distinct.
It's nothing like us at all—
monkeys locked in empty rooms,
with a thousand deceitful wiles,
with a million sham persuasions—
you can never get rid of the ways of a whore.

ZHANG XIAO-XIAN: Here's an inn. Let's stop here.

ZHAO: Call the innkeeper. [INNKEEPER *greets them*] Get a nice clean room ready for me and put my bags in it, then go ask Zhou She to come see me—tell him I've been waiting here a long time.

INNKEEPER: All right.

        INNKEEPER *walks away, calling out:*

Zhou She, where are you?

        Enter ZHOU SHE.

ZHOU SHE: What's going on?

INNKEEPER: There's a good-looking woman at the inn asking for you.

ZHOU SHE: Well, let's get going, then!

        Greets ZHAO PAN-ER. [*Aside*]:

Now here's a good-looking girlie.

ZHAO: Good to see you, Zhou She.

        [*Sings*]

My friend's got a good eye for men,
and she must have good luck too—
she's spruced up her splendid husband
    even more splendidly,
right in the prime of his youth.

ZHOU SHE: Now where have I met you? It was at a bar. You were playing the zither. And didn't I give you a strip of brown silk?

ZHAO [*to* ZHANG XIAO-XIAN]: Did you ever see that happen?

ZHANG XIAO-XIAN: I've never seen you with a strip of brown silk.

ZHOU SHE: Ah! Didn't I share a meal with you once when I was drinking at a bar, having come to Shen-xi after clearing out of Hang-zhou?[4]

ZHAO [*to* ZHANG XIAO-XIAN]: Did you ever see that happen?

ZHANG XIAO-XIAN: I never saw it.

---

[4]This may refer to Zhou She's travels, the business trips he mentioned in the first act, but some commentators suggest that these are streets in the entertainment quarters.

ZHAO [*sings*]:
>   You're always hot for new girls,
>   you grow forgetful and mix up the old,
>   what's more your eyesight is failing.
>   It's just like those lines in the ballad:
>   I, um, . . .
>   "knew you once beside that creek
>   of peach blooms in Wu-ling,
>   but now you feign conjectures
>   and recognize me not."
>   And here my own dreams have been fitful,
>   tormented because of you!

ZHOU SHE: Now I've got it. You're Zhao Pan-er, aren't you?

ZHAO: That's right.

ZHOU SHE: You're Zhao Pan-er! Well great, just great! You were the one trying to stop my marriage. Innkeeper, lock the door and beat up Xiao-xian here!

ZHANG XIAO-XIAN: Hey! Don't beat me up! Here the lady comes with a trousseau of embroideries and brocade, with toilette and bedding to marry you, and you want to beat me up?

ZHAO: Sit down, Zhou She, and listen to what I have to say. When you were in Kaifeng, people were always bringing up your name until my ears were all abuzz with you. But I never met you. By the time I got to meet you I was already a wreck—I couldn't eat or drink from thinking of you. When I heard you were going to marry Song Yin-zhang, how could I help getting upset? Here I wanted to marry you, Zhou She, and you were going to have me vouch for Yin-zhang instead.

[*Sings*]

>   And then since I was the older,
>   I put a good face on it,
>   supported the wedding—
>   don't you realize I was jealous,
>   and tried on purpose to break the match?
>   You may seem sharp on the outside,
>   but inside you're just a little slow.
>   But marry me now
>   and I'll let the whole thing go.

Look, I came here looking for you with the best intentions, bringing my carriage and horses and my whole trousseau, and now you want to beat me up and yell at me for no good reason. Turn the carriage around, Xiao-xian, we're going home.

ZHOU SHE: If I had known you came to marry me, I would never have wanted to have the little fellow beaten up!

ZHAO: You really didn't know? Well, since you didn't know, don't leave; just sit here and keep me company.

ZHOU SHE: I wouldn't mind sitting here with you for days—no, even for a year or two.

Enter SONG YIN-ZHANG.

SONG YIN-ZHANG: Since you haven't been home for a couple of days, I followed you here to the inn to see what you were up to. And here I find Zhao Pan-er sitting with you! That old whore is so shameless that she's even come after you here. Zhou She, you'd better not come home ever again, because when you do come, I'm going to take myself a knife and you can take yourself a knife, and we'll fight it out between us. [*Exit*]

ZHOU SHE [*taking his stick*]: I'm as ready as you are, and if the lady weren't present, I'd kill you in a moment.

ZHAO [*Aside, sings*]:
> I won't forgive him either,
> but why won't I dare be open about it?—
> I'll grit my teeth and bear the pain,
> but how can I watch you beat her up?

> Don't they say,
> "One night together as man and wife
> means a hundred nights of gentleness,"
> so calm yourself, man, stop fuming—

> if he's going to be rough,
> he ought to be rough in secret,
> he ought to think twice
> before acting this way in front of me—
> what genteel lover would ever
> beat a bargirl to death?

> But here I see him raging,
> patting that cruel stick,
> even the most hot-tempered men
> are not as bad as you.

[*To* ZHOU SHE]:

Suppose you beat her to death with that rough stick you're holding—what then?

ZHOU SHE: When a man beats his woman to death, he doesn't have to pay with his own life.

ZHAO: Now who would be willing to marry you if you go around saying things like that! [*Aside, sings*]:
> I'll pull the wool over his eyes,
> trick him to do what I want,

I'll leave this jerk nowhere to run.
Just watch me, little sister, see
one sweet-talking whore
    save a girl of the streets.

[*to* ZHOU SHE]: You almost made me fall for that one. While you were
sitting here, you sent for your wife to come make a scene and insult me.
Xiao-xian, turn the carriage around. We're going back.

ZHOU SHE: Come on, honey, sit down. I didn't know she was going to come
here. Strike me dead if I knew she was coming.

ZHAO: You really didn't have her come? The girl's no good. Here's the quick-
est way out—you get rid of Yin-zhang and I'll marry you right away.

ZHOU SHE: I'll divorce her as soon as I get home. [*Aside*] Whoa! Slow down
a moment! I've been beating that woman regularly, and she's so scared
of me that if I give her divorce papers, she'll be gone in a trail of smoke.
Then if this one won't marry me, I'll lose out on both sides. Don't go
rushing into things! I had better make sure of this woman. [*To* ZHAO
PAN-ER] Look, baby, I may have the wits of a donkey, but let's just say
I go home and divorce my wife, but then you just shut your eyes tight
and won't marry me. Then I'll be losing out on both sides. So you've got
to swear an oath.

ZHAO: You really want me to take an oath, Zhou She? All right, if you divorce your wife and I don't marry you . . . may horses trample me to
death in my own living room, may a candlewick crush my pelvic bone!
There now, you've forced me to take a really serious oath.

ZHOU SHE: Innkeeper, bring us some wine.

ZHAO: Don't buy any wine. I've got ten bottles of wine in my carriage.

ZHOU SHE: Then I'll go buy us some lamb.

ZHAO: No need to buy lamb. I've got a cooked lamb in my carriage.

ZHOU SHE: Fine. Well then, let me go buy some red silk.

ZHAO: Don't buy any red silk. In my luggage I have a matched pair of strips
of red gauze. Don't let it bother you, Zhou She. What's yours is mine,
and what's mine is yours.

[*Sings*]

One who is dear will be so ever,
as kin are always kin.
I, with my flowerlike body,
with my youth like a tender
    shoot of bamboo,
for a splendid marriage
will bring you in dower
    fine silver ingots.
I don't care
    if our life brings
        more chaff than wheat,
no matter if you take other women,

I'll bear with the worst you do—
you won't regret being my husband
    for all the rest of your life.
If you're broke, I'll be glad
    to share your poverty,
But if you're rich, well,
    don't mock me if my comfort
        breeds wantonness
        and makes people talk.
If that suits your wishes well,
    divorce the woman with you now.
I don't want you to spend a penny on me—
    it was I who came to you all on my own.
All I've saved, all that I have
    I put to your family's service;
sleek horses and light furs
    I bestow on you yourself;
I'll pay myself for the bridal suite
    where we become man and wife.

If I marry you, I won't be like Song Yin-zhang, who knew nothing of needlework, cooking, embroidery, how to furnish the bridal chamber, all kinds of household tasks.

[*Sings*]

Just write out the divorce papers
    and all you're owed will be squared away. [*Exeunt omnes*]

ACT IV

Enter SONG YIN-ZHANG.

SONG YIN-ZHANG: Zhou She ought to be back soon. [*Enter* ZHOU SHE. *She greets him*] What would you like to eat?

ZHOU SHE [*enraged*]: All right. Bring me a pen and a piece of paper. I'm going to write you divorce papers and I want you out of here right away!

SONG YIN-ZHANG [*takes the divorce papers but doesn't leave*]: What have I done to make you divorce me?

ZHOU SHE: Are you still here? Get out right now!

SONG YIN-ZHANG: So you're really divorcing me! Was this what you said back then when you wanted me? You treacherous man, you monster! You may want to get rid of me, but I won't go! [ZHOU SHE *pushes her out the door*] I'm out of his house! You're such a dimwit, Zhou She. And you, Pan-er, you were brilliant! I'm going to take these divorce papers straight to the inn to find her. [*Exit*]

ZHOU SHE: Now that this bitch is gone, I'll be off to the inn to marry Pan-er. [*Goes to inn, shouts*] Innkeeper, where's the woman who was just here?

INNKEEPER: She got in her carriage and left as soon as you were out the door.

ZHOU SHE: I've been had! Bring me my horse. I'm going to catch up with her.

INNKEEPER: The horse is foaling.

ZHOU SHE: Then harness the donkey.

INNKEEPER: The donkey's lame.

ZHOU SHE: All right, I'll catch up with her on foot.

INNKEEPER: I'll go after her with you. [*Exeunt*]

Enter ZHAO PAN-ER *and* SONG YIN-ZHANG.

SONG YIN-ZHANG: I would never have gotten out of there if it hadn't been for you.

ZHAO: Hurry up!

[*Sings*]

> I have to chuckle: so dependably
>   he wrote out the writ of divorce!
> and now where's our conniving friend?
> So sure of his way with women,
> so sure of the tricks of power,
> but he couldn't outwit my clever tongue
>   with its thousands and thousands of lines.

Let me have a look at the divorce papers, Yin-zhang. [SONG YIN-ZHANG *hands over the papers and* ZHAO PAN-ER *switches them*] If you ever want to get married again, Yin-zhang, everything depends on this piece of paper as proof, so take good care of it!

SONG YIN-ZHANG *takes the paper. Enter* ZHOU SHE, *catching up with them.*

ZHOU SHE [*shouting*]: Where do you think you're going, you bitch? You're my wife, Yin-zhang, so how do you think you're going to get away from me?

SONG YIN-ZHANG: You gave me divorce papers and kicked me out!

ZHOU SHE: Divorce papers have to have five fingerprints. How can one with only four fingerprints be the real thing?

SONG YIN-ZHANG *opens the paper to look at it.* ZHOU SHE *snatches it away from her and rips it to pieces with his teeth.*

SONG YIN-ZHANG: Pan-er! Zhou She has chewed up my divorce papers! [ZHAO PAN-ER *goes over to protect her*]

ZHOU SHE: You're also my wife.

ZHAO: How could I possibly be your wife?

ZHOU SHE: You drank my wine.

ZHAO: I had ten bottles of good wine in my carriage—you can't claim they were yours!

ZHOU SHE: You accepted my lamb.

ZHAO: I brought the cooked lamb myself—you can't claim it was yours!

ZHOU SHE: You accepted my pledge of red silk.

ZHAO: I brought my own piece of red gauze—you can't claim that was yours!

[*Sings*]

> The lamb and wine
> were from my own carriage,
> I brought the red gauze myself.
> You're corrupt through and through
>   and never true,
> laying false claim to another's goods.

ZHOU SHE: But you swore that you would marry me.

ZHAO [*sings*]:

> I was just stringing you along,
> I make my living
>   by taking such oaths and vows.
>
> And if you don't believe me,
> ask dancehall girls anywhere
>   who live in streets of flowers:
> is there one who would not swear
>   before a bright and scented candle?
> Is there one who would not call
>   on Heaven high and Earth so deep?
> Is there one who would not hazard
>   retribution from the gods
>   if she proved false?
> If all such pledges and vows had been valid,
> they and their kin would have all
>   long been dead.

You go along with him, Yin-zhang.

SONG YIN-ZHANG [*terrified*]: If I go with him I'll be a dead woman.

ZHAO [*sings*]:

> You never think ahead,
> so giddy and confused.

ZHOU SHE: The divorce papers have been destroyed, so what else can you do but go with me?

[SONG YIN-ZHANG *looks terrified*]

ZHAO: Don't be scared. The papers he tore to pieces in his teeth were a fake writ of divorce. [*Sings*]

> I had the standard form copied on purpose
>   and gave it to you,
> here's the original from before.

ZHOU SHE *snatches at it.*

Even nine oxen couldn't drag it away from me!

ZHOU SHE [*seizing* ZHAO PAN-ER *and* SONG YIN-ZHANG]: There are laws against this sort of thing. You and I are going before the magistrate. [*Exeunt*]

Enter Magistrate LI GONG-BI, *with* ZHANG QIAN, *the bailiff.*

LI GONG-BI [*recites*]:
>My fame and virtue in governing
>>are known to our emperor,
>on fine nights each household
>>need not lock the door.
>When rain stops folk go out
>>to plow in green wilds,
>no dogs bark under moonlight
>>in villages of flowers.

I am the governor of Zheng-zhou, Li Gong-bi. I'm holding morning court today to hear a few cases. Zhang Qian, prepare the docket.
ZHANG QIAN: Yes, sir!

Enter ZHOU SHE, ZHAO PAN-ER, SONG YIN-ZHANG, *and* MRS. SONG.

ZHOU SHE [*shouting*]: Justice, Your Honor!
LI GONG-BI: What's the accusation?
ZHOU SHE: Have mercy, Your Honor! I've been defrauded of my wife!
LI GONG-BI: And just who defrauded you of your wife?
ZHOU SHE: It was Zhao Pan-er who devised a scheme to defraud me of my wife, Song Yin-zhang.
LI GONG-BI: And what does the woman have to say?
ZHAO: Song Yin-zhang already has a husband, but she was forcibly taken by Zhou She to be his wife. What's more, he gave her divorce papers yesterday. So how could I have defrauded him?

[*Sings*]

>This guy is a vicious brute,
>his family, high-handed and rich,
>thoroughly false and conniving,
>he has never set foot on the path of truth.

>Song Yin-zhang has her own man,
>but he forced her into his home.
>Evil-tempered debaucher of girls,
>all too arrogant, ruthless and cruel,
>a villain,
>doing wrongs wherever he goes.
>Here are the divorce papers,
>I beg Your Honor to examine them.

Enter AN XIU-SHI *at back of stage.*

AN XIU-SHI: Pan-er just sent a message to me, saying, "Yin-zhang has her divorce papers. If you come quickly and make an accusation to the magistrate, you can get her as your wife." Here's the courtroom door. I'll yell, "Justice!"

LI GONG-BI: Who's that making noise outside the court? Bring him in.

ZHANG QIAN [*bringing* AN XIU-SHI *forward*]: The man making the complaint is here before Your Honor.

LI GONG-BI: Who are you accusing?

AN XIU-SHI: My name's An Xiu-shi, the fiancé of Song Yin-zhang, who was forcibly carried away by Zhou She to be his wife. I beg Your Honor to judge the matter.

LI GONG-BI: Who will stand as your guarantor?

AN XIU-SHI: Zhao Pan-er.

LI GONG-BI: Zhao Pan-er, you said that Song Yin-zhang already had a man who was to be her husband. Who is it?

ZHAO: It's this man, the student An Xiu-shi.

[*Sings*]

> In his youth he studied Confucian wisdom;
> he has learned the Nine Classics by heart;
> we are also from the same hometown,
> and since she accepted his pins and rings
>   and engagement gifts,
> she is clearly a good man's wife.

LI GONG-BI: Now I ask you, Zhao Pan-er: are you really the one who will stand as his guarantor?

ZHAO [*sings*]:

> The guarantees I put before you can be trusted—
> but how could he stand up to
>   that wife-stealer's schemes?
> That was no honorable marriage
> that so openly violated customs!
> I pray Your Honor give a decision today
> and unite them as man and wife.

LI GONG-BI: Zhou She, it's obvious to me that Song Yin-zhang already has a husband, so how can you still maintain that she is your wife? Were it not to spare your father the humiliation, I would turn you over to the authorities for punishment. So all present heed the judgment that I render now: Zhou She shall be flogged sixty times and reduced to the status of a commoner. Song Yin-zhang will go back to An Xiu-shi as his wife. Zhao Pan-er and the rest are all to return to their homes.

[*Recites verses*]

> It was all because of a bawd's greed,
> as Zhao Pan-er has in detail explained;
> Zhou She did not keep to his proper role,

and An the scholar will be joined with a wife.

All bow to the court and thank the Magistrate.

ZHAO [*sings*]:
>I've explained each detail to Your Worship
>to split greedy man from suffering girl.
>If Miss Noodlebrain stops making lifelong vows,
>in the quarter for lovers
>>our lovebirds will join once again,
>>>man and wife.

Thus:

>Scholar An among "flowers and willows"
>>accomplished his nuptials,
>And Zhao Pan-er, the prostitute,
>>rescued one of the girls.

from *The Romance of the Gods* 元
(Feng-shen yan-yi): 明
Ne-zha and His Father 引

The long Chinese prose romances of the Ming Dynasty, written in vernacular Chinese or in a mixed classical and vernacular style, grew out of story cycles that had evolved over the course of centuries. Such story cycles also were material for professional storytellers, and incidents from these cycles provided a rich source of plots for variety plays. The most famous of the prose romances were *The Romance of the Three Kingdoms (San-guo zhi yan-yi),* on the wars that followed the dissolution of the Han Dynasty; *Water Margin (Shui-hu zhuan),* on a band of righteous outlaws in the Song Dynasty; and *Monkey* or *The Journey to the West (Xi-you ji),* on how the ever resourceful Sun Wu-kong ("Monkey") and his companions guarded the Tang monk Tripitaka on his pilgrimage to India to fetch the Buddhist scriptures.

The sixteenth-century *Romance of the Gods (Feng-shen yan-yi)* is a fantastic elaboration of ancient history in one hundred chapters. It recounts the rise of the house of Zhou and the overthrow of the wicked last ruler of the Shang Dynasty and his infamous consort Da-ji, in the novel presented as an evil spirit in human guise. Past that broad statement of narrative theme, all resemblance to ancient history ceases. Both the Shang and the rising Zhou are aided by wizards, Daoist immortals, boddhisattvas, and spirits of various animals and inanimate objects in more or less human form. All have magical powers and engage in titanic battles using magical weapons. The souls of those killed in this combat are kept in reserve in the Jade Void Palace in Heaven, and at the end of the romance, these souls are appointed as gods by Jiang Zi-ya, the architect of the Zhou victory. It is from this "investiture of the gods" that the romance takes its name.

Incorporated into the romance is a version of the very old story of Ne-zha (or Nata in his Indian form), son of the demon-king *(devaraja)* Vaisravana (here known as one Li Jing, a failed Daoist acolyte turned general). When Jiang Zi-ya comes down the mountain and begins to assemble the forces to support the Zhou cause, Ne-zha becomes an important champion on the Zhou side. But before this occurs, early in *The Romance of the Gods,* three episodes are devoted to the story of Ne-zha's birth, his disastrous childhood exploits, and his subsequent conflict with his father.

Ne-zha has the terrifying charm of a deity's power in the mind of a seven-year-old. In contrast to the polite, reserved, and sometimes timorous male figures in elite literature, Ne-zha, like many other heroes of prose romance, tends to act on impulse—and his impulses are frequently violent. The only thing that can control such violence is a hierarchy of power, within which Ne-zha eventually finds his place. Like his close kin Sun Wu-kong ("Monkey"), Ne-zha eventually learns to "be" good by being forced to act good.

In Ne-zha's struggle with his father, an economy of moral exchange—whether of obligation or revenge—comes into conflict with the more absolute Confucian demand for filial piety. A child owes his corporeal existence, his "flesh and bones," to his parents. To Ne-zha's mind, once he has repaid that debt by an act of filial self-sacrifice and been reincarnated, there is no further bond between him and his father. To underscore that point, he consistently refers to his father as "Li Jing." It requires considerable coercion on the part of his Daoist master and his immortal associates to bring Ne-zha to his knees and say "Father" again.

The Romance of the Gods, attributed to one Xu Zhong-lin (died ca. 1566), draws everywhere on the occult lore of popular Daoism. This is a world where the high immortals dwell in caverns on magic mountains with fantastic names, surrounded by disciples who are gifted with a measure of the powers of their masters. Each of the high immortals is a master of magic arts and possesses magic treasures that serve as weapons. Despite their occasional claims of pacifism and serenity, they can be a hot-tempered and violent lot, ready to take offense and test their skills against others. The wisest of these high immortals (those who will be in the service of the Zhou) already know the future in some detail; they direct the course of the novel whose plot is predestined.

Episode XII: Ne-zha Is Born into the World at Chen-tang Pass

> Within the cavern Goldenray
>   there was a treasure rare
> who went down to the mortal realm
>   to aid a gentle liege.
> Already the glow of good fortune
>   shone from the line of Zhou;
> in turn the essential spirit
>   was lost in the House of Shang.
> The Great Cycle ever has needed
>   many to prop and brace;
> always in times of ascendant glory
>   was the shimmer of kalpa fires.
> In the moment of one cycle's ending
>   a new beginning is met,
> if court and commons both hide from sight
>   it is pointless to sigh with care.[1]

There was a commander at Chen-tang Pass whose name was Li Jing. At a young age he had studied the Way and practiced its discipline, honoring the

---

[1]Popular prose romances commonly punctuate the prose narrative with verse and rhymed descriptive passages. Unlike later novels, where the verse often is put to useful purposes, here the verse is often doggerel.

high immortal of Western Kun-lun, Antidote-to-Adversity, as his master. There he learned the magic technique of Elemental Vanishing. But because he could not perfect the Way of the Immortals, he was sent down the mountain to help King Zhow of the Shang. He came to hold the office of Commander and enjoyed the wealth and honor of the mortal world.

His principal wife, whose maiden name was Yin, had borne him two children: the eldest was named Jin-zha, and the next was named Mu-zha. Afterward Madam Yin again became with child, but after three years and six months she still hadn't given birth. This curious circumstance constantly troubled Li Jing. One day he pointed to his wife's belly and said, "To carry a child more than three years and still not give birth means that it must be some monster or demon." His wife, who was also upset, replied, "This pregnancy certainly doesn't bode well—I worry about it day and night." And hearing what she said, Li Jing felt quite unhappy.

At midnight that very night Madam Yin was sleeping soundly when she dreamed that a Daoist, his hair bound up in a double coil and dressed in Daoist robes, came right into her bedroom. The lady began to scold him, "You have absolutely no sense of how to behave! This is my bedroom. How did you get in here? This is terrible!" The Daoist only said, "Quick, take this child, foal of the unicorn." Before she could answer him, the Daoist took something in his hand and put it into her bosom. At this she woke up with a start, her whole body drenched in cold sweat. She hurriedly woke Commander Li and told him the whole thing: "I just dreamed thus and so. . . ." As she was speaking, Madam Yin could already feel the pains in her womb. Li Jing hastily got up and went to sit in the front hall, thinking to himself, "After carrying the baby for three years and six months, and now after what happened tonight, it's finally going to be born—but it remains to be seen whether it will be lucky or unlucky."

As he was pondering this, two maids came in a panic: "Sir, the madam has just given birth to a demon!" Hearing this, Li Jing hurried to her bedroom as quickly as he could and grabbed his precious sword; but what he saw was a globe of reddish vapor in the chamber, and an unearthly fragrance filled the whole room. There was a ball of flesh, dripping wet and perfectly round, like a wheel. Amazed, Li Jing hacked at it with his sword, and there came a sound as if it were ripping apart. Opening up the ball of flesh, out jumped a young child, filling the whole place with reddish light. His face was as white as powder, and there was a golden bracelet around his right hand; around his belly was a piece of fine red silk, and golden rays shot from his eyes.

The divine sage who had been incarnated into the mortal world and appeared at Chen-tang Pass was the officer who would go in the forefront of Jiang Zi-ya's army. He was the avatar of Numinous Pearl. That golden bracelet was the Cosmic Ring, and the name of that piece of fine red silk was the Celestial Confusion Cloth. These were the magic treasures that guarded Goldenray Cavern on Primordial Mountain.

When Li Jing hacked open the ball of flesh, he saw a young child emerge and begin running about everywhere. Astounded at this marvel, Li Jing went over and took the child up in his arms. It was so obviously a fine young boy that he couldn't harden himself to treat it as a demon and take its life. He then passed him to his wife so that she could have a look. Neither of them could help feeling affection for the boy, and each was delighted.

On the following day a number of Li Jing's subordinates came to offer him their congratulations. Li Jing had just finished sending them on their way when his adjutant came in and announced, "Sir, there's a Daoist outside who wants to see you." Since Li Jing had originally been a Daoist himself, he couldn't ignore his own kind and immediately replied, "Ask him to come in." The adjutant rushed out to invite the Daoist in. The latter strode straight into the great hall and, directly facing Li Jing, said, "A humble Daoist at your service, General." After quickly exchanging courtesies, Li Jing offered the Daoist the seat of honor. Without any show of polite reluctance, the Daoist sat right down. Li Jing then asked, "From which of the fabled mountains do you come, master, and from which cavern? And what do you have to tell me, that you visit this pass?" To this the Daoist replied, "I am the high immortal Unity from Goldenray Cavern on Primordial Mountain. I heard that you just had a son, and I came especially to congratulate you. I wonder if you would be so good as to let me have a look at the child?"

Hearing what the Daoist said, Li Jing told a servant to bring the child in. The servant brought out the child in her arms. Taking the child by the hand and looking him over, the Daoist asked, "What time of day was the child born?" "In the early morning before dawn," replied Li Jing. "Not good," said the Daoist. Li Jing asked, "Should we then not keep him?" "No, you should keep him," replied the Daoist, "but since he was born in the early morning hours, he will break the one thousand seven hundred injunctions against killing." The Daoist went on to ask, "Have you given him a name yet?" Li Jing replied that he had not, and the Daoist said, "Would it be all right if I gave him a name and made him my disciple?" To this Li Jing replied, "I would be glad for you to be his master." "How many sons do you have?" asked the Daoist. "Three now," replied Li Jing, "The eldest is called Jin-zha, and his master is the Exalted Celestial 'Extensive Dharma of Remarkable Culture' from Nimbus Cavern on Five Dragons Mountain. The next oldest is called Mu-zha, and his master is the high immortal 'Universal Goodness' from White Crane Cavern on Nine Lords Mountain. Since you want this child among your disciples, just give him a name in keeping with the others, and you will be his master." "For your third son I'll choose the name 'Ne-zha,' " said the Daoist. Li Jing thanked him, saying, "My gratitude is boundless for your generosity in bestowing this name on him." He then ordered his servants to prepare a vegetarian meal, but the Daoist declined. "This is unnecessary. I have things to attend to and must get back to my mountain right away." Since he was adamant in his refusal, all Li Jing could do was see the Daoist on his way out of the official compound. There the Daoist said goodbye and went off straightway.

Li Jing had been having no problems at the pass. Then suddenly the news came that four hundred counts of the empire had rebelled. He immediately issued orders to guard the pass fortifications closely, to drill the army and give his troops further training, and to defend the positions on Wild Horse Ridge.

Time sped by, and seasons changed. Before he knew it, seven years had passed. Ne-zha was seven years old and six feet tall. It was midsummer and the weather was blazing hot. Jiang Wen-huan, the Earl of the East, had rebelled and fought a great battle with Dou Rong at Spirit Roaming Pass, and therefore Li Jing was drilling and training his soldiers daily.

Ne-zha was growing restless and irritable from the heat. He went to pay his respects to his mother, and then, standing over to one side, said, "I want to go out to the other side of the pass fortifications to have some fun, but I thought I should ask you first, Mother." Madam Yin, who doted on her son, replied, "If you want to go out beyond the walls and have some fun, you should have a household guard take you. Don't try to have everything your own way, and come back quickly. I'm afraid you father will return from drilling the troops." "Yes, Mother," answered Ne-zha.

When Ne-zha went with the guard outside the walls of the pass, it was typical July weather and terribly hot.

> The true fires of the Daystar
>   were smelting the dust and dirt,
> the green willows and lovely grains
>   had almost turned to ash.
> The man on travels dreads its might,
>   too spent to lift his foot;
> the lady fair stands in fear of the heat,
>   too tired to climb the terrace.
> In the cool kiosk it's scorching and dry
>   like smoke from a blazing brand;
> in the river tower there is no breeze
>   as if buried in a fire.
> Speak not of the fragrance of lotuses
>   reaching the nooks of the park—
> Only with thunder and gentle rain
>   can a person's mood relax.

Ne-zha went out beyond the walls of the pass with his guard. After proceeding for a bit more than a mile, it became difficult to continue on because of the heat. His face streaming with sweat from the hike, Ne-zha told the guard, "Why don't we take a rest in the cool shade of those trees up ahead?" When the guard reached the shade of the green willows, he felt a sweet-smelling breeze brush over him and all his discomforts melted away. He rushed back to tell Ne-zha, "The shade of the willows is very pleasant and cool. We can get out of the heat there."

Hearing this, Ne-zha was immediately filled with delight and entered the grove. He undid the sash of his robe and relaxed, feeling completely happy. All at once over to one side he noticed clear waves rolling past and spilling green waters. Willows hung down along both shores, and there were gentle gusts of breeze; you could hear the waters splashing over jumbled stones along the banks.

Ne-zha got up at once and went over to the riverside, calling out to the guard, "I've gotten all hot since we left the pass, and my whole body is sweaty. I'm going to bathe myself on the rocks here for a while." To this the guard replied, "Be careful. We had better be getting back pretty soon, because your father will probably be returning." "It doesn't matter," said Ne-zha.

He then took off his clothes, sat on the rocks, and put his seven-foot-long Celestial Confusion Cloth in the water to wash it off. He didn't realize that this was Nine Bend River, which emptied into the Eastern Sea. When Ne-zha put his magic treasure into the water, it made all the water turn red. He swished it about, and the rivers heaved and shook; he shook it a bit, and the very universe shuddered. There was Ne-zha washing his cloth, not realizing that the great Crystal Palace of Waters was being deafened by the roar.

We turn now from Ne-zha washing his cloth to Ao-guang, dragon king of the Eastern Sea, who was sitting in his Crystal Palace when he heard a thundering din all around. He quickly called his attendants and asked, "There's no earthquake due—why are my palace halls shaking like this?" Then he deputed Li Gen, the yaksha of the Ocean Patrol,[2] to go the ocean-feeding rivers to find out what was causing this bizarre disturbance. When the yaksha got to Nine Bend River and looked around, he noticed that the water was all red and shimmering with light. But all he could see was one small boy washing a red kerchief in the water. The yaksha rose from the water and called out in a loud voice, "Boy, what kind demonic object is that you're holding, turning the water red and making our palace shake?"

When Ne-zha turned to look, he saw something in the water with a face blue as indigo, hair red as cinnabar, a huge mouth with fangs, and a large ax in his hand. Ne-zha said, "You there, creature, what sort of thing are you that you can talk?" At this the yaksha flew into a rage. "I am the yaksha assigned to the Ocean Patrol by my lord—how dare you insult me by calling me 'creature'?" And he leapt out of the water onto the shore, ready to swing his ax down on Ne-zha's head. Ne-zha was standing there stark naked; and when he saw the yaksha coming toward him with violent intent, he dodged, took the Cosmic Ring from around his right hand, and tossed it into the sky. This magic treasure was among the things that the Jade Void Palace on Mount Kun-lun had bestowed on the high immortal Unity to guard Gold-enray Cavern. No mere yaksha could survive that, and it came down right

---

[2] A demon. Originally Indian, the yaksha entered Chinese mythology and folklore through Buddhism.

on his head, dashing his brains out. The yaksha died immediately there on the shore.

"He's gotten my Cosmic Ring all messy," laughed Ne-zha, and he went back to sit on the rock and wash the ring. And how could the Crystal Palace survive this second magic treasure—the great halls of the palace were all in danger of being shaken down. "My yaksha hasn't come back from going to investigate," said Ao-guang. "This is a disaster!" As he was speaking, one of his dragon soldiers came in and reported, "Our dragon lord is hereby informed that the yaksha Li Gen has been killed on dry land by a young boy." Shocked, Ao-guang said, "Li Gen was commissioned by His Sacred Majesty himself in the Gallery of Numinous Aether. Who would dare kill him?" Then he gave the command, "Summon my dragon soldiers. I am going personally to see who this is."

At that moment the dragon king's Third Prince, Ao-bing, arrived and said, "Why are you so angry, Royal Father?" Ao-guang then told him the story of how Li Gen had been killed. "Don't trouble yourself, Royal Father," said Ao-bing, "your son will take care of it." Ao-bing quickly assembled his dragon troops, mounted his Waterproof Beast, raised his painted trident, and marched straight out of the Crystal Palace. As he cut through the waters, the breakers fell like mountains, raising waves and billows in every direction until the water had risen several feet on dry land. Ne-zha stood up and looked at the water, exclaiming, "What a flood!" Then he saw a water creature appearing amid the waves, on which was seated a man, all decked out in colorful clothes and brandishing his trident in a menacing way. "Who was it that killed our yaksha of the Ocean Patrol, Li Gen?" he shouted in a loud voice.

"It was me," replied Ne-zha. Once Ao-bing saw him, he asked, "Who are you?" "I am Ne-zha, the third son of Li Jing of Chen-tang Pass. My father is personally in charge of the defense of this region and master of the fortifications. I was washing myself here because of the heat and minding my own business. He came and insulted me, so I killed him—it doesn't really matter."

The Third Prince Ao-bing was shocked. "You vicious little tough! The yaksha Li Gen was given his post by his Sacred Majesty in Heaven. You have the gall to kill him and then dare to speak to me so rudely!" The Third Prince took his painted trident and aimed a blow at Ne-zha. Having no weapon with which to defend himself, Ne-zha dodged out of the way: "Hold on a moment! Who are you? I have the right to know who you are." "I am Ao-bing, the Third Prince of the Dragon King of the Eastern Sea." At this Ne-zha laughed. "So you're Ao-guang's son! You have no business acting so high and mighty. If you get me irritated, I'll catch you all, right down to that old sardine your father, and skin the lot of you." At this the Third Prince yelled, "My temper's going to explode! What a vicious little tough! Such a way to behave!" And he aimed another blow of his trident at Ne-zha.

Ne-zha was desperate and threw open his Celestial Confusion Cloth into the sky. Looking like a thousand burning embers, it came down and wrapped itself around the Third Prince, knocking him off of his Waterproof Beast. Ne-zha stepped forward and put his foot on Ao-bing's neck, then lifted his Cosmic Ring and brought it down on his head. This brought out the Third Prince's true form, a dragon stretched out straight on the ground. "I've revealed the little dragon's original appearance," said Ne-zha. "Fine, I'll pull out his tendons and make a dragon-tendon thong for my father's armor-pack."

Ne-zha pulled out the tendons of the Third Prince and took them straight back to the pass. His guard had been so frightened that his whole body was weak; as they drew near to the commander's gate, his legs were shaking so badly that he could barely walk. When Ne-zha went in to greet his mother, she said, "Where have you been, young man? You've been gone half the day!" "I've just been playing around outside the walls," answered Ne-zha, "and I hadn't realized it was getting so late." Then he went off to the garden behind the house.

When Li Jing returned from drilling his troops, he dismissed his attendants, took off his armor, and sat in the rear hall. There he worried about the misrule of King Zhow of the Shang, how he had driven the four hundred Peers of the Empire into rebellion, and how the plight of the people grew more dire with each passing day.

Back in the Crystal Palace, Ao-guang listened to the report of his dragon troops: "Ne-zha, the son of Li Jing of Chen-tang Pass, has killed the Third Prince and pulled out his tendons." Hearing this report, Ao-guang was shocked. "My son was a full-fledged deity, in charge of raising clouds, bringing rain, and nurturing the life of all things. What do you mean, he was killed? Li Jing—when you studied the Way on Western Kun-lun Mountain, you and I were on very good terms. You have let your son do this evil deed and kill my son—this is already an injury whose memory will last to the hundredth generation! But how dare he, on top of everything else, pull out my son's tendons! Even to speak of it pierces me to the very quick!"

Ao-guang flew into a great rage, rankled because he could not avenge his son right then and there. Accordingly, he transformed himself into a scholar and went directly to Chen-tang Pass. Reaching the commander's quarters, he addressed the gatekeeper, "Please inform your master that his old friend Ao-guang has come to pay a visit." The adjutant went into the inner apartments and announced, "There's an old friend of yours outside, Ao-guang, who has come to see you." "It's been many years since we last saw each other," said Li Jing, "I'm really lucky to meet him again today." And hastily neatening his clothes, he went out to welcome him.

Ao-guang entered the great hall, paid his respects, and sat down. Seeing the look of rage on Ao-guang's face, Li Jing was on the point of asking him what the matter was, when Ao-guang said, "Li Jing, my worthy brother, a fine son you've got there!" Li Jing laughed and answered him, "We haven't had a chance to get together for many years, brother, and we're really lucky to have this unexpected chance to meet today—why do you burst out with something like that? I have only three sons: the eldest is Jin-zha, the second oldest is Mu-zha, and my third son is Ne-zha. All are disciples of Daoist masters from the fabled mountains. They're far from perfect, but they're still not good-for-nothings. Don't misjudge them, brother."

"Brother," replied Ao-guang, "it is you who misjudge them, not I! Your son was washing himself in Nine Bend River; and I don't know what kind of magic arts he used, but he almost shook down my Crystal Palace. I sent my yaksha to see what was going on, and he killed my yaksha. My third son went to find out what was going on, and he also killed my third son—and he even pulled out all his tendons!" By this point Ao-guang felt such swelling bitterness in his heart that he burst out in rage: "Are you still going to pretend ignorance and defend him?"

Li Jing hurriedly answered, laughing even harder, "It's not my family. You're making a mistake in blaming me. My eldest son is on Nine Dragon Mountain studying the magic arts; my second son is studying the magic arts on Nine Lords Mountain. My third son is only seven years old and never goes outside the main gate. How could *he* have been able to do anything of that magnitude!" "But it *was* your third son, Ne-zha, who killed them," replied Ao-guang. At this Li Jing said, "This whole thing is truly bizarre. Don't be so hasty, brother. I'll have him come out and we can see what happened."

Li Jing then went back into the rear apartments, and Madam Yin asked him, "Who is that in the great hall?" "It's my old friend, Ao-guang," replied Li Jing. "Someone killed his Third Prince, and he claims that Ne-zha did it. I'm going to have Ne-zha come out now and introduce himself. Where is Ne-zha now?" Madam Yin thought to herself, "He did go outside of the walls today, but how could he have done something like this?" But she didn't dare tell this to her husband and simply said, "He's in the garden out back."

Li Jing went straight back into the garden and shouted, "Where are you, Ne-zha?" He called for quite a while without getting any reply, so Li Jing then went straight to Crabapple Terrace and noticed that the gate was locked. He stood there and shouted for Ne-zha in a loud voice. Ne-zha, who was inside, heard him and quickly opened the gate. "What have you been doing in there, son?" asked Li Jing. Ne-zha replied, "I went outside the pass fortifications today for no particular purpose and went to play at Nine Bend River. It was so hot I got down in the water to wash myself. There was this horrible old yaksha named Li Gen—I didn't do anything to provoke him, but he called me all kinds of names and then took his ax and tried to cut me in half. So I hit him with my ring and killed him. And there was some Third Prince or other called Ao-bing who tried to stick me with his trident. I wrapped him up in my Celestial Confusion Cloth on the shore, then stepped on his neck with my foot, and got him with my ring too! And to my surprise he turned out to be a dragon! Well, I thought to myself how dragon-tendons are so valuable, so I pulled all his tendons out and was just making a dragon-tendon thong for your armorpack, father."

Li Jing was so badly shaken that his mouth hung open as if he were a simpleton. He was tongue-tied and couldn't say a word. After a moment he screamed, "What a disaster you are! You've brought a catastrophe down on us! Quickly now, go see your uncle and explain it to him!" "Don't worry, Father," said Ne-zha. "If someone doesn't know, he can't be held responsible. And on top of that, I haven't done anything to the tendons yet—if he wants them, they're right here, in perfect shape. I'll go see him."

Ne-zha rushed to the great hall and paid his respects to Ao-guang, saying, "Uncle, I didn't know what I was doing and made a big mistake—I hope you'll forgive what I did. The tendons are still in their original condition—I haven't done a thing to them."

Seeing the tendons caused Ao-guang great pain, and he said to Li Jing, "Here you've begotten such an evil child, and you just told me that I was mistaken. Now he admits it himself, and you're still willing to let it pass. And on top of everything else my son was a full-fledged deity, while the yaksha Li Gen was given his commission by Heaven! How can you two, father and son, just do as you please and kill people for no good reason? Tomorrow I'm going to petition the Jade Emperor and ask that your spiritual masters deal with you!" At this Ao-guang departed in a towering rage.

Li Jing stamped his foot and, weeping loudly, cried out, "We are in serious trouble!" When his wife heard him weeping so piteously in the front courtyard, she immediately asked a servant to find out what was wrong. The servant reported back, "Today when the third young master went out to play, he killed the Third Prince of the dragon king. Just now the dragon king was arguing the matter with the master, and tomorrow he is going to petition the Heavenly Court for a judgment. I don't know why the master is weeping so."

Madam Yin quickly rushed to the front courtyard to see her husband. When Li Jing saw his wife coming, he immediately stopped crying and said with great bitterness, "I tried to become an immortal and didn't succeed. But no one would have expected that you would bear me such a fine son as this—someone who is going to bring disaster down on the entire family! That dragon prince was a full-fledged deity who brings rain, and Ne-zha wantonly murdered him. Tomorrow the Jade Emperor will act on the petition, and you and I have two days at the most before we both become ghosts under the executioner's blade!" Then he began crying again in utter despair. His wife was also streaming with tears, and she pointed to Ne-zha and said, "I had you in my womb for three years and six months before you were born, and I suffered I don't know how much misery. Little did I know that you would become the cause of the destruction of the whole family!"

Seeing his parents crying like this, Ne-zha felt very upset, and he got down on his knees before them. "Father, Mother—let me explain things. I'm not an ordinary mortal. I am the disciple of the high immortal Unity from Goldenray Cavern on Primordial Mountain. Both of my magic treasures were given me by my master, and I doubt that Ao-guang is any match for me. I'm going to go now to Primordial Mountain and ask my master what to do—he'll surely have an idea. People always say, 'When one person does something, that person is responsible.' I would never get my parents involved."

Ne-zha went out of the gate of the compound, picked up a handful of dirt and scattered it in the air, then vanished without a trace. Disappearing into a cloud of dust, he went to Primordial Mountain. There's a verse that supports this:

> Our lad paid a visit
> to Primordial Mountain;
> he gave account of the situation
> with Eastern Sea's Ao-guang.
> Before the Precious Virtue Gate
> he worked his dharma power—
> know now that immortals' magic arts
> are not for nothing famed.

Ne-zha disappeared in a cloud of dust and came to Goldenray Cavern on Primordial Mountain, where he awaited his master's bidding. The lad Golden Wisp quickly informed the master, "Ne-zha awaits your bidding." "Have him come in," replied the high immortal Unity. Golden Wisp went back to the door of the cavern and said to Ne-zha, "The master commands you to enter."

When Ne-zha came to the Sapphire-roaming Bench, he fell to the ground and paid his respects. "Since you're not at Chen-tang Pass, what's the story that brings you here?" asked the high immortal. "By your grace, master," said Ne-zha, "I was born as a mortal at Chen-tang Pass, and I am now seven years old. The other day I happened to be washing myself in Nine Bend River when Ao-guang's son, Ao-bing, unexpectedly did me injury by his vile words. On the spur of the moment I got mad and ended his life. Now Ao-guang is going to petition the Heavenly Court, and my parents are in a state of panic. I am very upset about this and have no way to save them. I had no alternative but to come to the mountain and earnestly entreat my master to pardon this crime I committed in my ignorance, in hopes that you will be so kind as to save them."

The high immortal thought to himself, "If Ne-zha in his ignorance made the mistake of killing Ao-bing, it was ordained by fate. Although Ao-guang is a king among the dragons, raising clouds and bringing rain, how can he pretend not to understand a sign sent down by Heaven? And bothering Heaven with such a small matter as this shows that he really doesn't know much about the shape of events." Quickly he called out, "Ne-zha, come over here! Open your gown!" The high immortal drew a Daoist talisman with his finger on Ne-zha's chest, and then instructed him, "When you reach Precious Virtue Gate, do thus and so. When you're done, go back to Chen-tang Pass and explain to your parents. I'm here to help you if there's a problem. This doesn't involve your parents in any way. Get going now!"

Ne-zha left Primordial Mountain and went straight to the Precious Virtue Gate of Heaven. It was, as they say: Rare scenes of Heaven's palaces, no semblance of the mortal world; lavender fog and reddish cloud webbed the Sapphire Void. Yes, the Upper Heavens were like nothing else at all:

> When first he mounted the Upper Realm, at once he caught sight of Heaven's halls; myriad streams of golden light spurting reddish rainbows, a thousand trails of magic vapors puffing lavender fog.
> And he saw Heaven's South Gate: Fashioned of dusky sapphire glass, adorned with glistening tripods.
> On both sides were four huge columns, and winding around each column was a red-whiskered dragon that raises clouds and drives the fog.
> Directly in the middle were two bridges of jade, and standing on those bridges were cinnabar-crested phoenixes, with their brightly colored feathers spread into the sky.
> Luminous wisps flashed with glints of celestial light; a sapphire fog cast its veil, covering Dipper and Sun.

> In Heaven there were thirty-three Palaces of the Immortals, among them:
>> The Palace of Dispatching Clouds,
>> The Kun-sha Palace,
>> The Palace of Lavender Aether,
>> The Palace of Supreme Yang,
>> The Palace of Supreme Yin,
>> The Palace of Transforming Joy;
> and on the golden roof-ridge of every palace was the Golden Griffin that can tell right from wrong.

> There were also seventy-two precious halls, among them:
>> The Hall of Dawn Audience,
>> The Hall of Rising through Emptiness,
>> The Hall of Precious Light,
>> The Hall Where Immortals Gather,
>> The Hall of Petitions;
> and on every hall there were jade unicorns lined as pillars.

> There were:
>> The Terrace of the Star of Long Life,
>> The Terrace of the Star of Rewards,
>> The Terrace of the Star of Wealth;
> and beneath those terraces were rare flowers that did not fade for millennium upon millennium.

There were:
   The Furnace for Refining Cinnabar,
   The Furnace of the Eight Trigrams,
   The Furnace of Liquid Fire;
and around these furnaces were brocade plants green ever through
   eons upon eons.

Gowns of ruby satin in the Hall of Sagely Audience shimmered with
   wisps of gold; lotus crowns at the foot of the Stairs to the Vermilion
   Plaza blazed with the glow of sapphire and gold.
In the Treasure Hall of Numinous Aether golden studs clustered upon
   the doors; before Galleries of the Sages assembled phoenixes danced
   on the crimson gates.
Covered passageways, winding porches stood out everywhere with
   intricate grillwork patterns; three-tiered eaves clustered all around,
   with dragons and phoenixes soaring at every level.
On top were gourd-shaped cupolas, lavender-looming, brightly
   glistening, smoothly rounded, freshly shining, clearly dazzling; all
   round were sounds of jade pendants, thickly clustering, densely
   layered, resonantly tinkling, *plink-a-plink* dribbling, brightly clear.
For as they say:
In Heaven's palaces strange things
   are present in all kinds;
in the world below things like these
   are every item rare.
Silver simurghs on golden towers
   join Precincts Lavender;
unusual blooms and wondrous plants
   reach Heavens of Alabaster.
The Jade Hare on his way to court
   passes beside the altar;
the Golden Crow, consorting with Sages,
   flies on down below.
Should ever a man have the lucky fate
   to come to Heaven's realm,
he will never fall back to the mortal world
   and escape its corrupting filth.

Ne-zha reached Precious Virtue Gate early and caught no sight of Ao-
guang. Seeing that the various gates of Heaven's palaces had not yet been
opened, Ne-zha stood below the Gate Where Immortals Gather. After a short
while he heard the jingling of Ao-guang's formal court attire coming directly
toward Heaven's South Gate.
   Seeing that Heaven's South Gate was not yet open, Ao-guang said, "I'm
early—the Yellow Turban warriors of the guard are still not here, so I'll have
to wait." Now Ne-zha could see Ao-guang, but Ao-guang could not see Ne-

zha—for the magic talisman that the high immortal Unity had drawn on Ne-zha's chest was called "The Seal of Invisibility," which, of course, was the reason that Ao-guang could not see Ne-zha.

Seeing Ao-guang waiting there, Ne-zha's heart flew into a rage. Striding over to Ao-guang, Ne-zha lifted his Cosmic Ring and bashed Ao-guang on the back, in the region behind the heart, with the blow known as "the hungry tiger paws its prey." Ao-guang fell to the ground, and Ne-zha went up and set his foot on Ao-guang's back. And if you want to know what happened to Ao-guang, just read the next episode.

Episode XIII: The High Immortal Unity Catches Rock-in-the-Stream

> What was, by nature, mere rock learned
>   to seize initiative,
> a womb of consciousness formed therein
>   for ten thousand years.
> It sucked in moonlight, fed on stars,
>   searched the pits in Earth,
> it added Fire, got hold of Water,
>   hid Heaven's Active Force.
> It rashly vaunted magic arts
>   of bringing fog and clouds,
> and listened to the immortals,
>   humming dragon, howling tiger.
> Caught in fires of eon's end
>   no recourse did it have—
> and thus we know that right and wrong
>   are finally brought full circle.

Ne-zha had put his foot on Ao-guang's back at Precious Virtue Gate; and when Ao-guang twisted his head around and recognized that it was Ne-zha, he was overcome with a burst of rage. But having been knocked down and held in place by Ne-zha's foot, he couldn't force himself up, so he heaped insults on him: "You brazen little bully! You haven't lost your baby teeth yet, and you're not even dry behind the ears, but you brutally killed an imperially commissioned yaksha, and on top of that you killed my Third Prince! What hostility did you bear him that you dared pull out his tendons? Such viciousness is a crime not to be pardoned. And now, on top of everything else, you have struck down the divinity in charge of raising clouds and bringing rain right outside of Precious Virtue Gate! There is no worse abuse of Heaven's generosity—even cutting your corpse up into mincemeat wouldn't settle the score!"

These insults threw Ne-zha into a fury, and he chafed that he couldn't kill Ao-guang then and there with his ring. But he had to follow Unity's instructions, so he held him down and said, "You just keep on shouting, but it wouldn't be a big deal if I killed you, you old sardine! You don't know who I am—I am none other than Numinous Pearl, the disciple of the high immortal Unity from Goldenray Cavern on Primordial Mountain. I'm under orders from the Jade Void Palace to take an avatar as the son in the house of Li Jing of Chen-tang Pass. Because the lineage of King Tang, the House of Shang, is to perish and the House of Zhou is to rise, Jiang Zi-ya will soon come down from his mountain. And I am to be the officer in the vanguard, helping Zhou crush the Shang king. I just happened to be washing myself in Nine Bend River when your people tried to push me around. I lost my temper and killed two of them—but that's nothing very important. But you go and present a complaint to Heaven. According to what my master says, it wouldn't matter even if I killed all you old lizards!"

Hearing this, Ao-guang kept at Ne-zha, "What a sweet child! Go ahead, hit me, hit me!" "You want me to hit you," said Ne-zha, "then I'll hit you." And he yanked up his fist and socked him on both sides a dozen or so times at one go, until Ao-guang was yelling. "You're a thick-skinned old lizard," Ne-zha declared. "I'm not going to hit you any more because it doesn't scare you. But there's an old saying, 'A dragon is scared of having its scales torn off; a tiger is scared of having its tendons pulled out.' " Ne-zha grabbed Ao-guang's court robes and pulled them half open, exposing the scales on his left side. Ne-zha then tore off several handfuls with his bare hands. After tearing off forty or fifty scales, fresh blood was streaming from the wound and it hurt right down to Ao-guang's bones. Unable to bear the pain, Ao-guang shouted, "Spare me!" "If you want me to spare your life," responded Ne-zha, "I'm not going to let you present your complaint to Heaven. I'll spare your life if you go with me to Chen-tang Pass. And if you don't do what I say, I'll kill you with my Cosmic Ring. If I do, the high immortal Unity will take charge, so I'm not scared of you."

Finding himself dealing with such a dreadful person, Ao-guang had no choice but to accept: "I would prefer to go with you." "Then I'll let you up," Ne-zha said. Ao-guang got up and was about to go with him when Ne-zha said, "I've heard how dragons can do transformations. If they want to be big, they can stretch all the way from Heaven to Earth; and if they want to be small, they can hide themselves in a mustard seed. I'm afraid that if you escaped, I wouldn't know where to find you. Change into a little tiny snake, and I'll carry you."

Unable to get away, Ao-guang had no choice but to change himself into a little green garden snake. Picking Ao-guang up and putting him in his sleeve, Ne-zha left Precious Virtue Gate and set off for Chen-tang Pass. In just an instant he arrived at the commander's compound. The household guard immediately reported to Li Jing, "The third young master is back." On hearing this, Li Jing was quite unhappy. Then he saw Ne-zha entering the compound and coming to greet his father.

Seeing the furrows in Li Jing's brow and the look of distress on his face, Ne-zha came forward to accept his punishment. "Where have you been!?" Li Jing asked him. "I went to the South Gate of Heaven," replied Ne-zha, "to ask Uncle Ao-guang not to present his complaint." At this Li Jing yelled in a loud voice, "Don't lie to me, you little monster! Who do you think you are that you would dare go to the region of Heaven! This is all a pack of wild stories to deceive your parents! It's driving me mad!"

"You don't have to get so angry, Father," said Ne-zha. "Uncle Ao-guang will bear me out in this." To this reply Li Jing said, "More nonsense! And just where is Uncle Ao-guang now?" "Right here," replied Ne-zha. And he pulled a green garden snake out of his sleeve and dropped it on the ground. In a puff of air Ao-guang changed himself back into human form. Li Jing gasped in amazement and quickly asked, "Why were you in that shape, brother?" Ao-guang was in a rage and told him the whole story of how he had been assaulted at the South Gate of Heaven, then gave Li Jing a look at the scales on his side: "You have begotten an evil child! I am going to get the dragon kings of all the four seas to go with me to the Hall of Numinous Aether and present a full account of the injuries I have suffered! Then we'll see how you're going to explain it away!" At this he turned into a gust of wind and left.

Li Jing stamped his foot and said, "This thing's going from bad to worse! What are we going to do?" Ne-zha came up to him, got down on his knees, and said, "Father, Mother, try not to worry. When I went to get help from my master, he told me that I wasn't reincarnated here merely on account of my own personal merit. I am under commission from the Jade Void Palace to protect a virtuous ruler. It wouldn't matter a bit even if I destroyed all the dragon kings of the four seas. If there's something too big for me to handle, my master will naturally take responsibility. So, Father, you shouldn't let it occupy your mind."

Being a Daoist, Li Jing was aware of the divine mysteries. What's more, he had seen that Ne-zha had the techniques to beat up Ao-guang at the South Gate of Heaven. Since he had been given some higher office by Heaven, there had to be some reason for it. Madam Yin, on the other hand, simply felt love for her son. Seeing Ne-zha standing off to the side and Li Jing fuming, bitterly angry at his son, she said to Ne-zha, "What are you still doing here? Get off to the back!"

Ne-zha did what his mother told him and went straight to the back garden. He sat there a while feeling glum, then left the garden and went straight up to the wall tower on the fortifications of Chen-tang Pass to catch some cool breeze. At this time the weather was terribly hot and he had never been to this spot before. Here he saw beautiful scenery: a vast, hazy expanse, where green willows hung gracefully, and gazing into the broad sky, it seemed like a round canopy of fire. As they say: All over the faces of travelers flowing beads drip down; an idle man escaping the heat waves the fan he holds.

Ne-zha took a look and said, "I never knew what fun this spot was!" Then, over on the weapons rack, he caught sight of a bow, which bore the name "Cosmic Bow," and three arrows, which bore the name "Heaven-Shakers." Ne-zha thought to himself, "The master told me I would be the officer in the vanguard when we destroy the empire of the Shang and the royal line of King Tang. When am I going to have a chance to practice my military skills if I don't do it now? And what's more, I have a bow and arrows right here ready for me. Why don't I practice a bit?"

Ne-zha's heart filled with delight. He took the bow in his hand, notched an arrow on the bowstring, and shot it to the southwest. The arrow went whizzing off, surrounded by a red light and swirling flashes of color. Ne-zha never should have shot this arrow. As they say: Along the river he made a cast of fishing line and hook; and from that moment made a catch of trials and tribulation.

Ne-zha didn't realize that this bow and these arrows were the magic treasures guarding Chen-tang Pass. The Cosmic Bow and the Heaven-Shakers had been handed down since the time the Yellow Emperor routed the rebel Chi-you. And during all that time no one had been able to use them. On this particular day, Ne-zha picked them up and shot an arrow; and he shot that arrow all the way to White Bone Cavern on Skeleton Mountain. A member of Lady Rock-in-the-Stream's household named the Sapphire Cloud lad had gone to the foot of the cliff, flower basket in hand, to pick herbs. The arrow hit him right in the throat, and he fell to the ground and died. When the lad Colored Cloud saw that Sapphire Cloud had been killed by an arrow, he rushed in to tell Lady Rock: "I don't know what's going on, but my brother has been shot in the throat by an arrow and killed."

Hearing this, Lady Rock went out of her cavern to the cliffside and saw that Sapphire Cloud had indeed been killed by an arrow. Then she noticed that there was a name inscribed on the arrow, just under the fletches: "Li Jing, Commanding Officer of Chen-tang Pass." In a rage, Lady Rock said, "Li Jing! When you couldn't be successful in achieving the Way, I had your master send you down the mountain to find wealth and honor in the mortal world. Now that you have become a great lord, not only do you not think to repay my goodness to you, you shoot my disciple with an arrow instead! Kindness has been answered by hostility." Then she shouted, "Colored Cloud, watch over the cavern. I'm going to get my hands on Li Jing and pay him back for this outrage."

Lady Rock mounted her blue simurgh and went off in a vast sweep of golden wisps and shimmering scarlet haze. As was said: The marvelous tricks of immortals never can run out; a foot away the blue simurgh arrived at Chen-tang Pass. There, in the middle of the sky, the Lady shouted in a loud voice, "Li Jing, come out here to me!"

Li Jing had no idea who was shouting for him; and when he rushed out to see, it looked like Lady Rock-in-the-Stream. Li Jing fell to his knees and bowed: "Your disciple Li Jing humbly greets you. I hope you will forgive me for failing to come out and welcome you properly." "A fine thing you've done," replied Lady Rock, "and here you're still making pretty speeches to me!" Then she took her Cloud-Ray Scarf, on which were the Eight Trigrams (with magic markings of four trigrams on the outer surface and able to enclose the treasures of all phenomena within), and threw it down, commanding her Yellow Turban warriors, "Take Li Jing to my cavern!" Out of nowhere the Yellow Turban warriors seized Li Jing and carried him away. When they got to White Bone Cavern, they let him go. Lady Rock left her blue simurgh and took a seat on her rush mat. The warriors brought Li Jing before her, and he got down on his knees. "Li Jing," said Lady Rock, "when you failed to achieve the Way of Immortals, you found wealth and honor in the mortal world. Who did you have to thank for this? Now I find that instead of thinking how to repay me, you have conceived malice against me. What explanation do you have for shooting my disciple Sapphire Cloud?"

This all came as a total surprise to Li Jing, who had no idea what was going on. "What have I done wrong, Lady?" said Li Jing. The Lady replied, "You answer my kindness with hostility, shoot and kill a member of my household, and you still pretend to know nothing!" "Where is the arrow?" asked Li Jing. "Bring the arrow for him to see!" commanded Lady Rock. When Li Jing looked at it, it was, in fact, one of the Heaven-Shakers. Li Jing was amazed and said, "The Cosmic Bow and the Heaven-Shaker arrows have been handed down since the time of the Yellow Emperor. They are now the magic treasure guarding Chen-tang Pass. But who was able to use them? All this comes from your disciple's bad luck lately, in which bizarre things have been happening. I hope that Your Ladyship will keep in mind that I am guiltless in this and wronged, and that it is hard to clear myself. Set me free to return to the pass and discover who shot the arrow, then I'll bring him back so that guilt and innocence may be assessed—I hope you will not punish someone who is guiltless. If I don't find who shot the arrow, then I will accept my death." To this Lady Rock said, "In this case I'll set you free to go back. But if you don't find out who did it, I'll ask your master to deal with you. Go now!"

Li Jing took the arrow back with him and reached the pass hidden in a cloud of dust. Making himself visible again, he entered the commander's compound. Madam Yin had not known what was going on when she saw Li Jing snatched away out of nowhere; and when Li Jing returned, she was in a state of panic. "Why were you just hauled off like that out of nowhere?" she asked. "I was frightened out of my wits!"

Li Jing stamped his foot and said with a sigh, "Wife, I've been at this post for twenty-five years now, and who could have expected the run of bad luck that I've been having recently? Up in the watchtower on the walls there is the Cosmic Bow and the Heaven-Shaker arrows, which are the magic treasures that protect this pass. Somebody or other shot one of those arrows and killed a disciple of Lady Rock-in-the-Stream. But my official title was on the arrow, so she had me taken away to pay for it with my life. I pleaded with her to let me come back here and find out who really did it. I won't be quits with her until I take that person back to her." Then Li Jing went on to say, "About that bow—nobody has ever been able to pull it. Could this possibly be Ne-zha's doing again?" "No, that's not possible," replied his wife. "Do you mean to suggest that with the whole Ao-guang affair not yet settled, he would stir up even more trouble? Besides, Ne-zha couldn't draw the bow."

Li Jing thought about it for a moment and had an idea. He called to his attendant, "Ask Ne-zha to come see me." In no time at all Ne-zha came in and stood over to one side. "You tell me that your master accepts responsibility for your actions," said Li Jing, "and that he told you to assist a virtuous ruler. Why don't you go practice your military skills a little so that you'll be more effective when the time comes." "I made up my mind to do just that," replied Ne-zha. "I was just in the watchtower on the wall, and I saw a bow and arrows there. I shot off one of the arrows, and it was surrounded by a reddish light and a cloud of lavender haze. I shot one good arrow clear out of sight!"

This drove Li Jing's temper to a point where he shouted, "You little troublemaker! First you kill the Third Prince, and the whole thing is still not settled. Now you provoke this other catastrophe!" His wife just held her tongue and said nothing. Not understanding the situation, Ne-zha asked, "Why? What else happened?" "That single arrow," replied Li Jing, "killed the disciple of Lady Rock-in-the-Stream. The Lady had me taken away, but I persuaded her to let me come back and find the person who shot the arrow. And now it turns out to be you! You go see the Lady and explain yourself to her!"

"Don't get so angry, Father," laughed Ne-zha. "Where does Lady Rock live? And where was her disciple? How could I have possibly killed him? I'm not going to take the blame if I'm being accused for nothing." Then Li Jing told him, "Lady Rock lives in White Bone Cavern on Skeleton Mountain. Since you've killed her disciple, you go see her." "What you say is reasonable, Father," replied Ne-zha. "Let's both go to the White Bone Cavern or whatever. But if it wasn't me who did it, I'm not coming back until I give her one hell of a whack! You go first; I'll follow along right behind you." And thus father and son went off to Skeleton Mountain hidden in a cloud of dust.

> Golden light rose from the arrow's flight,
> and in the Great Void red clouds shone.
> The high immortal is in our world now,
> the royal child may bide in peace.
> Boast not rashly of magic arts—
> you must learn to recite the Book of Jade.
> The millions of evils are hard to set right:
> the imperial army must be smashed.

On reaching Skeleton Mountain, Li Jing instructed Ne-zha, "You stay right here. I'm going to go in and report back to the Lady." At this Ne-zha smiled coldly. "And where will I be when she makes her groundless accusations against me and decides how she is going to deal with me?"

Li Jing went into the cavern and was received by Lady Rock. "Who shot my lad Sapphire Cloud?" Li Jing declared to the Lady, "It was my own wicked son, Ne-zha. I wouldn't dare disobey you in this, and I've brought him here to your cavern—he is outside awaiting your orders." The Lady then ordered Colored Cloud, "Have him brought in."

Seeing someone coming out of the cavern, Ne-zha thought to himself, "When you're going to strike a blow, be sure you're the first to strike. This is her lair, and I won't have the advantage in there." He lifted the Cosmic Ring and delivered a blow. Unprepared to protect himself, Colored Cloud took the blow on the neck and fell to the ground with a shriek, gravely wounded and in peril of his life. Hearing the sound of someone falling outside her cavern, the Lady rushed out. Colored Cloud was already on the ground, struggling for life. "You monster!" said Lady Rock. "You continue to do evil and have wounded another of my disciples!"

Ne-zha saw Lady Rock dressed in her golden crown with fishtail patterns, a huge red grown marked with the Eight Trigrams, and hemp shoes with silken ties; she was coming after him with the sword Tai-e in her hand. Ne-zha took back his ring and sent it spinning at her. Seeing that this was Unity's Cosmic Ring, the Lady said, "Aha! So it's you!" Then the Lady caught the Cosmic Ring in her hand. Ne-zha was shocked. Quickly he took out the seven-foot Celestial Confusion Cloth and threw it to wrap the Lady up in it. The Lady laughed aloud and raised her open sleeve to receive it. They watched as the Celestial Confusion Cloth fluttered down ever so lightly into the Lady's sleeve. "Come on, Ne-zha," shouted Lady Rock, "try using a few more of your master's magic weapons and see what my own magic arts are like!"

Having no weapons left with which to defend himself, Ne-zha had no choice but to turn and run away. Then the Lady shouted, "Li Jing, this has nothing to do with you—you had better go back." As Li Jing was returning to his pass, Lady Rock went chasing after Ne-zha. In flying clouds and lightning bolts and driving rain and gales, she stayed hard on his heels for a long time until he reached Primordial Mountain. When he got to Goldenray Cavern, he went into the gate in a panic and bowed down before his master.

"Why are you in such haste, Ne-zha?" asked the high immortal. To this Ne-zha replied, "Lady Rock has falsely accused me of shooting her disciple, and she took her magic sword to kill me. She's captured your Cosmic Ring and your Celestial Confusion Cloth. She's chasing after me, and she won't give up—she's right outside the cavern now. I didn't know what to do so I came to find you and beg you to save my life!"

The high immortal Unity said, "You little monster! Go back into the peach garden for a while, and let me go out and see what can be done." The high immortal went out and leaned against the gate to his cavern. There he saw Lady Rock coming along in furious pursuit, sword in hand and her face suffused with rage. Seeing the high immortal Unity, she bowed her head respectfully. "Greetings, brother." After Unity returned the courtesy, Lady Rock said, "Using your magic arts, brother, a disciple of yours has killed my lad Sapphire Cloud, seriously wounded my lad Colored Cloud, and then used the Cosmic Ring and the Celestial Confusion Cloth to try to harm me. So, brother, if you're willing to tell Ne-zha to come out to me, then we're still on good terms and the whole matter can be put to rest. But if you try to protect him, you'll be wasting your good efforts for someone who isn't worth it, and it won't be pretty."

"Ne-zha is inside my cavern," replied the high immortal, "and it's not hard to get him to come out—just go to Jade Void Palace and see the Elder of our sect. If he wants him delivered to you, I'll deliver him to you. But Ne-zha was sent into the world on the orders of the Heavenly Emperor, and he is to assist a virtuous ruler. I'm not protecting him for my own personal reasons."

At this the Lady laughed. "You've made a big mistake, brother—using your Elder to intimidate me. Do you really mean say that you're going to let your disciple run wild and do evil, killing my disciple, and then try to intimidate me with this high and mighty talk! Do you really think I'm no match for you? Should I just give up? Hear this:

Mysterious are the Way and its Power,
    coming from Primal Fusion;
whosoever perfects the vigor of Qian
    will attain life everlasting.
"Essence, Breath, and Spirit refined"—
    this is no idle theory;
"The Five Vapors honor the Primal as lord"—
    far from reckless words!
Sitting peacefully on the Gray Dragon
    I go to the Lavender Pole-Star
and joyously ride on the white crane
    descending to Mount Kun-lun.
Do not try then to dupe my sect
    with the Elder of your teaching—
the cycle of kalpas turns in a ring
    from sources in the thousands.

The high immortal Unity said, "Rock-in-the-Stream, I take this to mean that your mastery of the Way is pure and lofty. You belong to the Jie sect, the Teaching of Severing; I belong to the Chan sect, the Teaching of Open Access. Because, for the past fifteen hundred years, we have never managed to cut away the Three Corpse-spirits that curse the body, and because we have violated the injunctions against killing, we have been sent down to be born in the mortal world, where there will be campaigns and executions and killing and battles, by which the fated span of the eon will be brought to a close. The lineage of Shang, descended from King Tang, is to be destroyed, and the House of Zhou rise. In the Jade Void Palace, gods will be invested with powers, and they will enjoy wealth and power in the mortal world. The Three Teachings—Daoism, Buddhism, and Confucianism—have all subscribed to a 'List of the Gods,' and my own teacher has commanded that our sect send down our numerous disciples to be born into the world below to assist the virtuous ruler. Ne-zha is the incarnation of Numinous Pearl, who will assist Jiang Zi-ya destroy the royal line of Shang. He bears the command of the Elder of our sect, Primal Origin. If he harmed your disciples, it was destined by Heaven to be so. How can you claim to comprehend all that is or that you will eventually ascend to the heights? Those such as you should not worry or be filled with cares; you should feel neither humiliation nor elation. It would be best to practice self-control. Why be so easily stirred by a mere trifle and do harm to the grace of your Way?"

Lady Rock could not endure the fires that burned in her heart, and she shouted, "The Way is one—how can there be levels in it?" "Although the Way is one," replied the high immortal, "it comes out differently in each person. Let me explain it to you:

> Convergent rays of sun and moon
>   refined a bloom of gold:
> a single kernel of numinous pearl
>   shed light throughout the chamber.
> When he shakes Earth and Heaven,
>   the might of his Way is known;
> he will escape from life and death
>   when his deeds of merit are done.
> He will roam free through the universe,
>   leaving the trace of passage,
> then return to the Three Pure Realms
>   where his name will be established.
> Straight up through the rainbow clouds,
>   steady his path through sky,
> the lavender simurgh, the scarlet crane
>   will come on their own to greet him."

Flying into a great rage, Lady Rock took her magic sword in hand and swung it at the high immortal. Unity dodged the blow, then slipped back into his cavern. He there took his own sword, and dangling it from his hand, he secretly put something in his pouch. Then, facing eastern Kun-lun, he bowed down: "On this mountain today your disciple will set aside the injunction against killing." When he finished, he went out of the cavern and pointed at Lady Rock. "Your grounding is shallow, and your practice of the Way is weak—how dare you be so insolent as to commit mayhem on my mountain!" Lady Rock swung her sword at him again, and Unity blocked the blow with his own sword, saying, "Nicely done!"

Rock-in-the-Stream was actually the refined essence of a stone that had drawn on the numinous vapors of Heaven and Earth and had received the luminous essences of sun and moon. She had attained the Way for several thousand years but had still not achieved the fruit of true immortality. Now a Great Eon was coming to its close, and her original appearance could not survive—it was because of this that she had come to the mountain. The first reason was that Rock's own time had run out; and the second reason was that this was the place where Ne-zha would have his incarnation. Destiny is fixed, and it cannot be evaded.

Lady Rock and the high immortal Unity attacked one another back and forth, whirling up and down several times around and blocking each other's blows, and before long one could see only the glow of sparkling clouds. Then Lady Rock took out her dragon-whisker scarf with the Eight Trigrams and threw it into the air to wound the high immortal. But Unity only laughed and said, "Can thousands of evils ever even touch the right?" At this the high immortal recited several phrases and pointed to the scarf: "Fall now— what are you waiting for?" And the scarf with the Eight Trigrams came falling down. Lady Rock flew into a greater rage; her cheeks flushed as pink as peach blossoms, and her sword seemed like a snowflake. "When things reach this stage, we have to go on with it," commented Unity. He leapt out of the circle of the fight and tossed his Nine Dragons Net of Spiritual Fire into the sky. Rock was caught within the net and couldn't get out.

Seeing his master use the net to catch Rock, Ne-zha sighed, "If he'd only given this to me earlier, we wouldn't have had to waste so much energy!" Ne-zha then went out of the cavern to his master. When the high immortal Unity turned his head and saw his disciple coming, he thought, "Oh no! When the little devil sees my net, he's going to want it. But he can't use it yet. I can only hand it over to him when Jiang Zi-ya becomes the general." And the high immortal quickly shouted, "Ne-zha! Get going! The dragon rulers of the four seas have presented their petition to the Jade Emperor, and they've gone to seize your father and mother!"

Hearing this, Ne-zha's eyes welled with tears and he entreated the high immortal, "Master, have mercy on my parents! No son's heart can ever be at peace if he gets his parent implicated in troubles he himself has caused." Then he began to cry in a loud voice. Seeing Ne-zha in such a state, the high immortal whispered in his ear, "Do thus and so, and you can save your parents from harm." Ne-zha bowed in gratitude and went off to Chen-tang Pass hidden in a cloud of dust.

When the high immortal Unity caught her in his net, Lady Rock became completely disoriented. The high immortal clapped his hands together, and flames began to lick up from within the net, giving off a blazing light. Nine fire dragons spiraled upward around her—these were the spiritual fires of Concentrated Meditation that were burning Lady Rock. Then with a crash of thunder the Lady's true form emerged from the smelting: a large piece of rock. This rock had come into being out beyond the Purple and Brown of Heaven and Earth. It had passed through earth and water and fire and wind. And it had been refined into an Essence endowed with spiritual consciousness. But this day its destiny was settled, and in this place it was to die. Thus was its true form revealed. Herein the high immortal Unity had to relax the injunctions against killing. He retrieved his Net of Spiritual Fire, his Celestial Confusion Cloth, and his Universal Ring, and went back into his cavern.

Meanwhile Ne-zha was flying with all possible speed back to Chen-tang Pass. There he heard an uproar of voices in front of the commander's compound. When the crowd of guards saw that he had arrived, they hurriedly reported to Li Jing, "Your son is back." Standing before the dragon kings of the four seas—Ao-guang, Ao-shun, Ao-ming, and Ao-ji—Ne-zha shouted in a shrill voice, "When one person does something, that one person is responsible. I killed Ao-bing and Li Gen, and I must pay with my life. But it is not right that a son implicate his parents in what he himself has done." Then facing Ao-guang, he said, "I am not a person of small account. I am Numinous Pearl. I bear the commands of the Jade Void Palace, and it was my destiny to be born into the mortal world. This day I will cut open my belly, gouge out my intestines, and scrape the bones, returning this body of flesh to my parents so that they will not be implicated in my misdeeds. Will this satisfy you? For if it does not satisfy you, we will all go together to the Hall of Numinous Aether to see the Ruler of Heaven, and there I will tell my own story."

When Ao-guang heard this, he said, "All right, in this case your parents are spared, and you will be known for your filial devotion to your parents." Then the four dragon kings set Li Jing and his wife free. Ne-zha took a sword in his right hand. First he hacked off his other arm at the shoulder, then cut open his own belly, gouged out his intestines, and scraped the bone, scattering his seven earthly souls and his three heavenly souls, and his life was over. As they had agreed, the four dragon kings then returned.

Madam Yin, his mother, put Ne-zha's corpse in a wooden coffin and had it buried.

Ne-zha's souls had lost their physical lodging—he was the incarnation of a jewel that had borrowed the essences of physical life, and thus he had souls. Ne-zha was tossed wildly and whirled along with the wind straight to Primordial Mountain. And if you don't know what happened afterwards, read the next episode.

Episode XIV: The Reincarnation of Ne-zha from a Lotus Blossom

The mystery of immortals' power
    cannot be estimated:
to raise the dead and bring back life
    they have their strange techniques.
A grain of magic cinnabar
    restores the jewel of life,
in several stalks of lotus leaves
    the drifting soul returns.
To pass beyond the common world
    one needs not unclean bones,
to be a Sage one must seek out
    the soul-recalling scent.

From this point on the Ruler-Sage
  extended his domain,
the founding of the House of Zhou
  made use of helpers.

The lad Golden Wisp went into the cavern and informed the high immortal Unity, "I don't know what's going on. My fellow disciple Ne-zha was lost far in the darkness, then tossed wildly and whirled along; the wind brought him to rest here." When he heard this, the high immortal already understood what it meant, and he hurried out of the cavern. There he gave his instructions to Ne-zha: "This is not the place where you will rest secure. Go back to Chen-tang Pass and appear to your mother in a dream. Forty leagues from the pass is Azure Screen Mountain, and on the mountain there is a bare spot. Command your mother to have a Ne-zha Shrine constructed there. When you have received offerings of incense there for three years, you can again take your place in the mortal world and assist the true ruler. Get going quickly now! You can't hang around here!"

Hearing this, Ne-zha left Primordial Mountain for Chen-tang Pass. At exactly the hour of midnight, Ne-zha went to his mother's bedroom and called out, "Mother, I am your child Ne-zha. My soul has no resting place now, and I hope you will consider what pain I suffered in dying. Forty leagues from here there is a mountain named Azure Screen. Set up a shrine for me there and let me receive a little incense so that I can go live in Heaven. My gratitude for your kindness is greater than anyone can imagine."

Madam Yin woke up and realized that it had been a dream. Then she wept out loud. "Why are you crying?" asked Li Jing. Then his wife told him all about the dream.

Li Jing flew into a rage: "How can you still be crying for him? He caused us no small amount of harm! People always say that dreams come from the dreamer's own mind—the only reason your having such crazy dreams is because you're thinking about him. Don't be fooled." To this his wife said nothing.

The next night Ne-zha came to her again in a dream, and again the night after that. No sooner did Madam Yin close her eyes than there was Ne-zha standing before her. After a week or so, Ne-zha, whose soul was as hot-tempered in death as his personality had been belligerent in life, addressed his mother. "I've been here asking you to do this for a number of days now, and you don't care anything at all about how much I suffered when I died. If you won't make a shrine for me, I'm going to make so much trouble around here that you'll wish you had!"

This time when Madam Yin woke up, she didn't dare tell Li Jing. She secretly gave some taels of silver to a trusted servant, who broke ground for the construction on Azure Screen Mountain, erected the shrine, and had an image of Ne-zha fashioned. In ten months the work was done.

Here on Azure Screen Mountain Ne-zha made manifest his divine na-

ture and stirred the hearts of all the populace. Each one of their thousands
of prayers was answered. The buildings in the temple complex rose stately
and high, and all was perfectly regular.

> Through the shrine's arched gateway
>   stucco walls appeared,
> crimson doors and rings of bronze
>   arrayed on every side.
> Sapphire tiles and carved eaves,
>   three feet of water,
> several cypress and juniper trees,
>   a terrace in two layers.
> His jeweled place on the pedestal
>   was decorated with gold,
> dragon and phoenix banners all
>   with holy colors decked.
> The hooks that hung from the curtains
>   swallowed the half moon,
> ferocious demon judges
>   stood in the dirt and dust.
> The smoke of aloes and sandalwood
>   coiled into phoenixes,
> and day by day in droves
>   worshippers came to pray.

When Ne-zha made manifest his divine nature on Azure Screen Mountain, the common people who dwelled near and far on every side all came
to worship him with incense. They came in droves, like ants in an unceasing line, each day more numerous than the last. And he answered every one,
whether they prayed for blessings or to avert some evil. Time flew by, and
before he knew it, half a year had passed.

As we said earlier, the Earl of the East, Jiang Wen-huan, was avenging
his father; he mustered an army of four hundred thousand men and horse,
and at Spirit Roaming Pass he fought a great battle with Dou Rong, in which
Dou Rong was unable to achieve victory. As a result, Li Jing had been
drilling his army on Wild Horse Ridge and kept his own pass secure.

One day, while bringing his troops back past Azure Screen Mountain,
Li Jing saw the throngs going back and forth. The men and women going
to the temple to worship ranged from doddering old folks to babes in arms;
they went in droves like ants, and the smoke from their fires gathered above
them.

Still on horseback, Li Jing asked, "This is Azure Screen Mountain—why
this unbroken line of men and women in such numbers?" The adjutant
replied, "Half a year ago a god made manifest his divinity here. He answers
each one of thousands of prayers. If someone prays for blessings, blessings
come; if another wants to avert calamity, the calamity is gone. This is the

reason that men and women from all around have been stirred to offer him incense." On hearing this a thought rose in Li Jing's mind, and he asked the adjutant, "What's the name of this god?" "This is the Shrine of Ne-zha," replied the adjutant.

Li Jing flew into a rage and gave the order, "Make camp! I'm going up the mountain to worship and offer incense." His men stood there, and Li Jing let his horse race up the mountain toward the temple, while the men and women worshippers quickly opened a path for him. He let his horse race on right to the front of the main temple hall, where he saw an inscription hanging high above the gate, and on it was written: "The Temple of Ne-zha." When he went inside, he saw the image of Ne-zha, looking just as he had when alive. On either side stood the demon judges. Li Jing pointed to the statue and began to hurl insults at it. "You little beast! You caused all sorts of trouble for your parents when you were alive, and now that you're dead, you're making fools of the common people!" When he finished, he lifted his whip and with one blow shattered Ne-zha's gilded image into pieces. Li Jing's rage grew, and with one kick he knocked over each of the demon judges. He then issued the command, "Light fires! Burn the temple down!" Next, he instructed the people who had come to worship, "This is no god! You shouldn't worship him." The crowds were so frightened that they went running down the mountain as fast as they could go. By the time Li Jing got back on his horse, his rage had still not subsided. This is shown in the following verse:

> The moment that the valiant troops
> > reached Azure Screen Mountain,
> at once they saw the common folk
> > daily coming to worship.
> He whipped the gilded image,
> > shattered it to bits;
> he kicked the demon judges down,
> > and they too were destroyed.
> A fire burned the temple,
> > its flames then mounted high,
> the smoke passed through the air,
> > the light was blazing bright.
> And all because that vapor
> > reached Dipper and the Ox,
> strife between son and father
> > became a battlefield.

When Li Jing's troops entered Chen-tang Pass, he dismounted at the commander's compound and gave the order, "Dismiss the men." Li Jing went into the rear hall; and when his wife came to greet him, he berated her, "A fine son you bore! After all the harm he brought on me, you went ahead and had a shrine built for him to stir up delusions among the common folk! You won't give up until I've had to resign my badge of office! The government is run by ruthless and domineering ministers, on top of which I have no personal connections with Fei Zhong and You Hun. If anyone gets word of this to the capital at Zhao-ge, corrupt officials will impeach me for falsely calling on evil spirits, and everything that I have accomplished over the past years will be sacrificed for nothing. And all this would be because of what you have done, woman! Well, I burned his temple down today. And if you build it back up for him, I'll never forgive you!"

Turning now from Li Jing to Ne-zha, on that day Ne-zha had been away from his shrine working his divine powers; when he came back, he saw that nothing remained of his temple. The mountain was scorched bare, and the flames and smoke had not completely died out. His two demon judges came to meet him with tears in their eyes.

"What happened!?" asked Ne-zha. The demon judges replied, "Commander Li of Chen-tang Pass burst up the mountainside, smashed your gilded image, and burned down your shrine. We have no idea why." "Li Jing, there is nothing between you and me any more," said Ne-zha. "I gave my flesh and bones back to my parents, so how could you break my gilded image and burn my shrine, leaving me no place to rest?" Ne-zha felt extremely dispirited and brooded over the whole thing for a long time. "I had better go back to Primordial Mountain."

Having received the smoke from incense for half a year, Ne-zha already possessed a little form and voice. In a short while he reached the high mountain and went into the cavern. There the lad Golden Wisp led Ne-zha to see the high immortal Unity, who said, "How come you're here and not in your shrine receiving incense?" Ne-zha got down on his knees and explained the situation. "My father smashed my clay image and burned down my shrine. Since I had no place to stay, all I could do was come here. I beg you to have pity on me and save me."

Hearing this, the high immortal said, "Li Jing did wrong in this. Since you returned your flesh and bones to your parents, your presence on Azure Screen Mountain had nothing to do with him. Now that he has prevented you from receiving the smoke of offerings, how can you get a body? What's more, Jiang Zi-ya is due to come down from his mountain very soon. All right then, since it's for you, Ne-zha, I'll do you a good turn." He then told Golden Wisp, "Go pick two lotus blossoms and three lotus leaves from Five Lotus Pool and bring them to me." The lad rushed out and got the lotus blossoms and lotus leaves, then put them down. The high immortal first took the flowers and picked off the petals, spreading them into three separate groups, representing Heaven, Earth, and Man. He then snapped the ribs of the lotus leaves into the three hundred bones. The three leaves themselves were arranged in the positions of high, middle, and low, representing Heaven, Earth, and Man. Next the high immortal took a kernel of metallic mercury and placed it in the middle. Using the technique of Anticipating Nature, he set the vital energies operating through the ninefold turns. He divided the dragon of Li, which is the Sign of Fire, from the Tiger of Kan, which is the Sign of Water, thus separating the Female and Male Essences. Then he grabbed firm hold of Ne-zha's souls and heaped them into a pile on the lotus, shouting, "Hurry up, Ne-zha, take human form!" There was an echoing sound, and a man leapt forth. His face was white as powder, his lips were crimson, beams of light flashed from his eyes, and his body was fifteen feet tall. This was Ne-zha's reincarnation from a lotus blossom.

When he saw his master, Ne-zha fell to the ground and bowed. The high immortal then said, "It's really upsetting that Li Jing destroyed your clay image." "Honored Master," replied Ne-zha, "I cannot give up this desire to be revenged on him." "Come with me into the Peach Garden," said the high immortal. There the high immortal gave him the Fire-Point Spear, and in no time at all Ne-zha was familiar with its use. Ne-zha wanted to go down the mountain right then to take his revenge, and the high immortal said, "Your technique with the spear is fine. I'm giving you my pair of Wind-and-Fire Wheels to stand on, along with the talismans and spells to use them." The high immortal also entrusted him with a leopard-skin pouch in which he put the Cosmic Ring, the Celestial Confusion Cloth, and a brick of gold. "Be off with you now to Chen-tang Pass." Ne-zha bowed his head to the ground to thank his master, then mounted the Wind-and-Fire Wheels, planting his feet firmly upon them; he took the Fire-Point Spear in hand and went straight off to Chen-tang Pass. As the verse says:

> A pair of lotus blooms revealed
>   a body reincarnated,
> Numinous Pearl's second life
>   transcended common dust.
> His hand held a magic treasure,
>   a snake-pike lavender flamed;
> his feet on Wind-and-Fire Wheels,
>   in golden wisps of cloud.
> Within his pouch of leopard skin
>   was peace for all the world;
> inside his cloth of red brocade
>   were blessings for the folk.
> Of sages from every age
>   he was foremost of all,
> the tale from the chronicler's pen
>   is fresh for ten thousand years.

When Ne-zha reached Chen-tang Pass, he went straight through the walls and up to the commander's compound, where he called out in a loud voice, "Come out to me at once, Li Jing!" An adjutant went in and reported, "The third young master is outside. He's standing on Wind-and-Fire Wheels, holding the Fire-Point Spear in his hand, and calling for you by name. I don't know what's going on, but you had better go out and settle things with him."

"Nonsense," shouted Li Jing. "When a person is dead, he can't come back to life!" As he was saying this, another person came in and said, "If you don't get out there fast, he is going to fight his way into the compound."

Li Jing flew into a rage. "We'll see about that!" He quickly picked up his painted halberd, mounted his gray steed, and went out of the compound. There he saw Ne-zha standing on his Wind-and-Fire Wheels, holding the Fire-Point Spear, and of a size very different from what he had been before.

Li Jing was shocked and said, "You little beast! You did monstrous things while you were alive; and now that your soul has returned, you've come here to get us in trouble again!" "Li Jing!" replied Ne-zha, "I gave you back my flesh and bones, and there is no connection between us any more. Why did you go to Azure Screen Mountain, shatter my gilded image, and set fire to my shrine? Now I've got you, and I'm going to pay you back for the bitter hate you caused by that one blow!" Then he flourished his spear and thrust it, aiming a blow at Li Jing's head. Li Jing met the blow with his painted halberd. Around and around they spun, spear and halberd both raised.

Ne-zha's strength was boundless, and after only a few rounds Li Jing was quite overwhelmed: the strength of his sinews was spent and the sweat ran down his spine. All Li Jing could do was flee away to the Southeast. Ne-zha shouted after him in a loud voice, "Don't think I'll spare your life this time. Li Jing! I won't turn around until I've killed you!" And with this he went off after him.

In no time at all Ne-zha was just about to catch up—for his Wing-and-Fire Wheels were as fast as Li Jing's horse was slow. In his desperation Li Jing had no choice but to get off his horse and disappear in a cloud of dust. "Any old Daoist can do these magic tricks with the elements," laughed Ne-zha. "Do you really think that I'll let you go simply because you disappear in a cloud of dust?" He then stepped up onto his pair of Wind-and-Fire Wheels and set off chasing him in the sounds of a wind-driven fire, like flying clouds and a lightning bolt.

Li Jing was thinking to himself, "What am I going to do? This time when he catches up to me, I'll be killed by one thrust of his spear!" As Li Jing saw Ne-zha just about to close in on him, he suddenly heard someone singing a song:

> Beside a pool of clear water, bright moon;
> by a bank of green willows, peach blooms.
> A chaste savor distinct from all else:
> a few cloudy wisps flying up through the sky.

When Li Jing looked, he saw a Daoist lad, wearing a turban, a Daoist robe with wide sleeves, and hemp shoes with silken ties. This was Mu-zha, disciple of the high immortal Universal Goodness from White Crane Cavern on Nine Lords Mountain. "I'm here, Father," said Mu-zha. When Li Jing looked and saw that it was indeed his second son Mu-zha, he felt calmer. At that moment Ne-zha, riding his wheels, caught up and saw Li Jing conversing with a Daoist lad. When Ne-zha leapt down from his wheels, Mu-zha came toward him, shouting in a loud voice, "Slow down, there! You have a lot of nerve, you monster! For a son to kill his father violates every principle of ethical conduct. If you turn around and get out of here as quickly as you can, I'll spare you."

"Who are you to talk so high and mighty?" replied Ne-zha. To this, Mu-zha said, "You don't even recognize me! I am Mu-zha!" Realizing that this was his older brother, Ne-zha quickly shouted, "You don't understand the whole situation, brother." And then Ne-zha told him the story of what happened on Azure Screen Mountain in all its details. ". . . who is in the right, Li Jing or me?" "This is nonsense!" shouted Mu-zha, "Parents are always in the right—never the other way around!" But Ne-zha continued, "I hacked open my belly, gouged out my entrails, and gave him back my flesh and bone. There's nothing between us any more, so why should I still have any feelings for him as a parent?"

Mu-zha flew into a rage, "You unnatural son!" And he struck at Ne-zha with his sword. Ne-zha blocked the blow with his spear, saying, "There is no enmity between us, Mu-zha. Stand back and let me take my revenge on Li Jing." But Mu-zha only shouted, "What a monster! How can you possibly be so evil!" As Mu-zha again came at him with his sword, Ne-zha said, "This is the work of fate—choosing death rather than life." Then he returned the blow, striking toward Mu-zha's face. Circling around one another exchanging blows, the two brothers engaged in a great battle.

Noticing Li Jing standing over to one side, Ne-zha was afraid he would get away and grew impatient. Knocking aside Mu-zha's sword with his spear, Ne-zha took his golden brick and tossed it into the air. Catching Mu-zha off guard, the brick hit him on the back, in the region right behind the heart, and he fell to the ground. Then Ne-zha mounted his wheels to get Li Jing, who turned and ran off. "Even if you run to some island in the sea," shouted Ne-zha, "my hatred will not be appeased until I bring back your head!"

Li Jing flew off just like a bird that had lost its grove or a fish that had slipped through the net, without any sense of where he was going. After fleeing for quite some time, Li Jing saw that the situation was not good and sighed to himself, "Enough! I don't know what terrible things I must have done in a former life that first kept me from attaining the Way and then made me beget such a vindictive creature. But if it has to be this way, the best thing to do would be to die by my own hand so that I won't have to endure humiliation by this boy."

Just as he was about to kill himself, he heard someone shouting, "Don't do it, General Li!" The person then composed an extempore song that went:

Clear breeze brushing willows beyond the wilds,
blossoms bob in the water upon the pool.
If you ask of the place where I dwell in peace—
in the depths of white clouds I make my home.

The singer was the Exalted Celestial named "Extensive Dharma of Remarkable Culture" from Nimbus Cavern on Five Dragons Mountain, and
he approached with his dust-whisk in hand. Seeing him, Li Jing spoke.
"Venerable master, save my miserable life!" "Go into my cavern," replied
the Exalted Celestial, "and I will wait for him here."

In a moment Ne-zha came chasing up in pursuit, his spear in hand. He
was in a belligerent and violent temper, his feet planted on his Wind-and-
Fire Wheels. There he saw a Daoist, who may be described as follows:

> Hair drawn into double tufts, spreading into hazy cloud; a water-
> compound gown, tightly bound with silken ties.
> Immortal's air, a Daoist's bones, he wanders as he pleases; hidden in
> his breast are found countless mysteries.
> By the Gate of First Beginning in the Palace of Jade Void, the Chief of
> All Immortals goes to Coiling Peach Tree.
> Relying on the Five-fold Breaths, the Domineering was refined; the
> Immortal-fost'ring Way achieved by one of Heaven's Sovereign's
> line.

Ne-zha saw an immortal standing on the mountainside, but he didn't see
Li Jing. "Daoist," he asked, "have you seen a general pass by?" The Exalted
Celestial replied, "Just now a General Li went inside my Nimbus Cavern.
What do you want with him?" "He is my enemy, Daoist," said Ne-zha. "You
had better send him out of your cavern because this doesn't concern you. If
Li Jing gets away, I'll have a go at you with my spear instead of him."

To this the Exalted Celestial said, "Who are you? Such bloodthirstiness—
wanting to skewer even me with your spear!" Not realizing the sort of person this Daoist was, Ne-zha shouted, "I am Ne-zha, disciple of the high immortal Unity of Goldenray Cavern on Primordial Mountain! You can't go
treating me lightly!" The Exalted Celestial replied, "I've never heard of any
disciple of the high immortal Unity called Ne-zha. You can go act rudely
somewhere else, but not here at my place. If you keep on behaving this rudely
here, I'll take you off into my peach garden and let you languish there three
years after giving you two hundred strokes of the cane!"

Having no idea what was good for him, Ne-zha twirled his spear and
aimed a blow at the Exalted Celestial. The Exalted Celestial dodged and ran
back to his cavern. Ne-zha got on his wheels and chased after him. Turning
his head and seeing that Ne-zha had gotten close, the Exalted Celestial took
something out of his sleeve. This was named the Vanishing Dragon Stake,
also known as the Golden Lotus of the Seven Treasures. When he tossed it
into the air, winds rose up from all four directions and clouds came rolling
over the sky. Dust and dirt were lifted in the wind and struck with a sound.
Lost in the gloomy and murky darkness, Ne-zha couldn't tell where he was
going. Then all of a sudden his neck and two legs were clamped by metal
bands, and he found himself standing upright against a gleaming golden pillar. When Ne-zha opened his eyes wide to look, he found himself completely
unable to move.

"What a monster!" said the Exalted Celestial. "You've behaved very rudely indeed." Then he called to Jin-zha, "Fetch me my cane!" Jin-zha quick got the cane and brought it to the Exalted Celestial, who then said, "Beat him for me!" Jin-zha did as his master ordered; he took the cane and gave Ne-zha a beating until the true fires of Concentrated Meditation came pouring out from all Ne-zha's seven apertures. Then the Exalted Celestial said, "Stop now," and went off into the cavern with Jin-zha.

Ne-zha stood there thinking to himself, "Instead of catching up to Li Jing, I've been given a beating myself and can't even get away!" In the depths of his fury Ne-zha ground his teeth together, but there was nothing he could do but stand there burning with rage.

Reader, the high immortal Unity had knowingly sent Ne-zha here in order to subdue his murderous nature. Thus the high immortal already knew the situation he was in. As Ne-zha stood there seething, over to one side he caught sight of a broad gown with wide sleeves and hemp shoes with silken ties. It was the high immortal Unity.

Seeing him, Ne-zha shouted, "Master, save me!" He shouted this several times, but the high immortal ignored him and went directly into the cavern. There the lad White Cloud announced, "The high immortal Unity is here." The Exalted Celestial went out to welcome him, and, taking him by the hand, laughed, "Your disciple has asked me to give him some instruction." The two immortals then sat down. "Ne-zha's violation of the injunctions against killing had grown so serious," said the high immortal Unity, "that I sent him here to subdue the violence of his nature—but I had no idea he would end up committing a transgression against the Exalted Celestial himself!" Then the Exalted Celestial ordered Jin-zha, "Let Ne-zha come." Going to Ne-zha, Jin-zha said, "Your master is calling for you."

"Since you obviously didn't know what to do with me," replied Ne-zha, "you worked some kind of eye-blinding spell and then made me unable to move—and still you came and play around with me!" Jin-zha just laughed and said, "Close your eyes." And Ne-zha had no choice but to close his eyes. When Jin-zha had finished drawing the magic talisman, he took back the Vanishing Dragon Stake. When Ne-zha quickly looked around, neither the stake nor the metal bands were anywhere to be seen. Then, nodding his head, Ne-zha said, "All right, all right. I've really gotten the worst of it today. I'll go into the cavern now and meet my master, then I'll decide what to do."

The two of them went into the cave, where Ne-zha saw the Daoist who had beaten him sitting on the left side and his master sitting on the right. The high immortal Unity said, "Come over here and bow to your uncle!" Not daring to disobey his master's orders, he had to bow down, saying, "Thank you for the beating!" Then he turned and bowed to his own master.

At this the high immortal called out, "Li Jing, come over here." Li Jing fell to the ground and bowed his head. "As for what happened on Azure Screen Mountain, you really shouldn't have been so narrow-minded—that's the cause of this strife between son and father." Standing over to the side,

Ne-zha's temper was rising until his face seemed like it would catch on fire, and he felt that his hatred would not be appeased until he had devoured Li Jing. Both the immortals already understood what was on his mind. "From now on," said the high immortal, "neither of you, neither father nor son, may offend the other." Then he instructed Li Jing to leave first.

Li Jing thanked the high immortal and went straight out. This drove Ne-zha into a frenzy of rage, but he dared not say a word. He simply stood over to the side pinching his ears, rubbing his cheeks, and giving long sighs. Laughing secretly to himself, the high immortal said, "Ne-zha, go back now. Keep a close watch over my cavern. I'm going to play a game of chess with your uncle and I'll be back in a while."

Hearing this, Ne-zha was overjoyed and said, "Yes, sir!" He left the cavern as fast as he could, got on his Wind-and-Fire Wheels, and went off in pursuit of Li Jing. After chasing him for a long time, Ne-zha caught sight of Li Jing ahead of him riding in a cloud of dust. In a loud voice he shouted, "Don't try to run, Li Jing—I'm on my way!"

Seeing him, Li Jing cried out bitterly, "That Daoist didn't mean what he said. Since he sent me away first, he should not have let Ne-zha leave the mountain, and now he's after me. That was really a traitorous thing to do, to let him come chasing me after such a short time! What am I going to do!" And he fled on ahead.

With Ne-zha following hot on his heels, Li Jing saw no route of escape. Just as the situation was getting desperate, there appeared a Daoist up on a hilltop, leaning against a pine among the rocks. "Could that be Li Jing down there at the foot of the mountain?" said the Daoist. Li Jing lifted his head, saw a Daoist, and said, "Master, I am Li Jing." Then the Daoist said, "Why are you in such a hurry?" Li Jing replied, "Ne-zha is hot on my trail, master. Please save me!" "Quickly, come up the hill," said the Daoist, "and stand behind me. I'll save you." Li Jing climbed the hill and, still out of breath, took a position behind the Daoist. Then the sound of Ne-zha's Wind-and-Fire Wheels could be heard, and he was about to reach the foot of the hill. When Ne-zha saw the two of them standing there, he gave a frosty smile. "I don't think I'm going to get the worst of it this time!" And he rode his wheels up the hill.

"Are you, by chance, Ne-zha?" asked the Daoist. "That I am," replied Ne-zha. "Why do you have Li Jing standing there behind you?" "Why are you chasing him?" asked the Daoist. Ne-zha then told him the whole story of what had happened on Azure Screen Mountain. To this the Daoist said, "Since this was all cleared up at Five Dragon Mountain, you are breaking faith by chasing him again." "Stay out of this business between us," replied Ne-zha. "I am determined to get him today and assuage this bitter hatred that I feel."

To this, the Daoist said, "Well, since you won't have it any other way . . . " Then he turned to Li Jing and said, "Go fight him, and I'll watch." "Venerable master," said Li Jing, "this beast has boundless strength. I can't beat him." Then the Daoist straightened up, spit on Li Jing, and gave him a slap on the back, saying, "You beat him, and I'll watch. I'll be here so there's no problem." Li Jing had no choice but to take his halberd and thrust it at Ne-zha, who met the blow with his Fire-Point Spear.

There on the hilltop father and son battled for fifty or sixty rounds. But this time Ne-zha was hardpressed, until the sweat ran all over his face and his whole body was giving way with fatigue. Unable to fend off the painted halberd any longer, Ne-zha brooded to himself, "Li Jing could never beat me on his own. The reason has to be because the Daoist just spat on him and gave him a slap. I know what to do—I'll pretend to slip up, then strike. I'll run the Daoist through with my spear first, and then I'll get Li Jing."

Ne-zha leapt out of the circle of battle and aimed a thrust at the Daoist. The Daoist spread his mouth wide open, and a white lotus blossom emerged, blocking the Fire-Point Spear. "Stop now, Li Jing," said the Daoist. Hearing this, Li Jing hastily parried the Fire-Point Spear. Then the Daoist asked Ne-zha, "Listen, you monster! Your father and you may be trying to kill each other, but there's no enmity between us. Why did you just strike at me with your spear? My white lotus caught the blow—otherwise you would have gotten me by a sneak attack. What's going on?" "Li Jing couldn't beat me before," replied Ne-zha. "When you told him to fight with me, why did you spit on him and slap him on the back? This was obviously some trick of yours to keep me from winning in the fight. That's why I tried to stab you with my spear, to assuage my anger!"

"So you dare to try to stab me, monster!" said the Daoist. Ne-zha flew into a rage, twirled his spear, and aimed another blow at the Daoist's head. The Daoist jumped over to one side and raised his sleeves upward. There appeared winding wreaths of magic cloud and a vortex of lavender fog, from which an object fell; and Ne-zha found himself trapped inside a pagoda of intricate grillwork. Then the Daoist hit the pagoda with both hands, and a fire broke out inside. It burned Ne-zha until he shouted, "Spare my life!" From outside the pagoda, the Daoist asked, "Do you acknowledge your father, Ne-zha?" Ne-zha had no choice but to answer repeatedly, "I acknowledge him as my father, master!" "Since you have acknowledged him as your father," said the Daoist, "I will spare you." Thereupon the Daoist quickly took back the magic pagoda. When Ne-zha opened his eyes to look, there was not the least burn anywhere on his body. Ne-zha thought to himself, "How weird! This Daoist really is playing tricks on me!" "Ne-zha," said the Daoist, "since you have acknowledged Li Jing as your father, get down on the ground and bow to him." When Ne-zha seemed reluctant to do so, the Daoist was about to invoke the pagoda again, so Ne-zha had no alternative but to subdue his temper, keep his mouth shut, lower his head, and bow down. But still he looked unrepentant. So the Daoist said, "I want to hear you say 'Father' from your own lips." Ne-zha refused, and the Daoist said, "Ne-zha, since you won't say 'Father,' you still haven't given in. I'm getting my golden pagoda to burn you again." Desperate, Ne-zha repeatedly shouted in a loud voice, "Father! Your son admits he was in the wrong!"

Even though he had spoken these words with his lips, in his heart he had not given in. Secretly he ground his teeth, thinking to himself, "Li Jing, you're going to have to be taking this Daoist around with you for a long time!"

The Daoist then called to Li Jing: "Kneel down and I will tell you the secret of the golden pagoda. If Ne-zha refuses to obey, you can invoke this pagoda and burn him." Standing off to the side, Ne-zha silently cried out in anguish. Then the Daoist said, "Ne-zha, from now on you and your father are to be on good terms. At some time in the future you will both serve as officials in the same court, and there you will assist a virtuous ruler bring his work to fruition. Never again speak of what happened before. Ne-zha, go now." Seeing how the situation stood, Ne-zha had no choice but to return to Primordial Mountain.

Li Jing then knelt down and said, "Venerable Master, you have exercised the Way generously and have redeemed me from great peril. May I ask your name and the name of this mountain of the immortals?"

The Daoist replied, "I am the Daoist Burning Lamp of Primal Awareness Cavern on Magic Vulture Mountain. When you failed to perfect yourself in the Way, you were given riches and honor in the mortal world. Now Zhow, King of the Shang, has lost his virtue, and great turmoil is unleashed upon the world. You should not serve in office now; go hide yourself in a mountain valley and forget advantage and fame for while. Wait until Wu of the House of Zhou raises an army, and then come forth again to do great deeds." Li Jing bowed his head to the ground, then returned to his pass and subsequently disappeared.

The Daoist had been asked by the high immortal Unity to subdue Ne-zha's nature here to make him acknowledge his father. Later, the father and his three sons were to become sages in the flesh. Li Jing is the devaraja Vais-ravana, who bears the pagoda in his palm. A later poet wrote:

> Of yellow gold was fashioned
>   a grillwork pagoda,
> ten thousand threads of shining light
>   pierce the ninefold sky.
> It was not Burning Lamp alone
>   who used his dharma power—
> Heaven made son and father
>   to join again.

This was the second time that Ne-zha appeared at Chen-tang Pass. Afterwards Jiang Zi-ya came down from his mountain, at the same time King Wen finished his seven-year sentence in You-li Prison. And if you want to know what happened, read the following episode. . . .

Late Ming Informal Prose

Classical literature of the second half of the fifteenth and most of the sixteenth century was dominated by the influential literary group known as the "Archaists." The Archaists advocated strict adherence to formal models established by earlier writers. "Old style" verse was supposed to be modeled on the poetry of the Han and Wei, regulated poetry was supposed to be modeled on the High Tang, and prose was supposed to be modeled on pre-Qin writing. The theories of the Archaists were wonderfully teachable and well suited to the demands of an educational system growing rapidly in the new prosperity of the sixteenth century. Anthologies of model essays and poems served the schoolteacher and autodidact alike. Moreover, the insistence on strict imitation of models proved a useful way to prevent solecisms and awkwardness in student writers, for whom literary Chinese had become increasingly remote from the language they spoke.

At the same time, such a formalistic view of writing inspired a sense of falseness and artificiality that went against the most ancient values of Chinese literature, where poetry was supposed to give direct expression to feeling and whose prose was supposed to be an independent expression of the writer's values. It is not surprising, therefore, that Archaism provoked a strong reaction among certain groups of intellectuals during the second half of the sixteenth century (though Archaism retained its hold on the early stages of literary education). When the Archaists championed formal correctness, these new intellectuals of the late Ming championed informality, even awkwardness. When the Archaists championed discipline, these new intellectuals championed freedom and following one's natural inclinations. When the Archaists championed "moral seriousness," these new intellectuals championed trivial things and the unplanned surprises of the ordinary.

A major inspiration in this literary movement was the eccentric and heterodox intellectual Li Zhi. His discourse "On the Child-Mind" touched a whole younger generation. One consequence for literature was a new sense of the value of drama and prose fiction, of which Li Zhi spoke with approval. This was virtually the first time in the Chinese tradition that prose fiction and drama were not justified defensively, but rather treated as "literature" on a par with poetry and the essay. Another consequence was a renewed interest in informal prose. Anthologies of the period often refer to such works as "minor pieces" *(xiao-pin),* treating the experiences of daily life with humor and delight.

Although "On the Child-Mind" had literature as its primary topic and was immensely influential in subsequent literature, the essay itself is certainly not "literary," nor does it practice the values it preaches. Li Zhi's adoption of the ponderous style of Chinese philosophical writing may make the first part of his argument seem more difficult than it actually is. The "beginning of mind" (or with the ambiguity of literary Chinese, "beginnings in the mind") is both the presumed innocence of the child's response and immediate or impulsive thoughts and responses in anyone—something like the implicit "first thoughts" that must have been there in order to say we had "second thoughts" about something.

The "Way" *(Dao)* and "Inherent Pattern" *(li)* were key concepts in Neo-Confucianism, which had become state philosophical orthodoxy. Although the great Neo-Confucian philosophers argued that these were inherent both in the self and in the external world, Li Zhi was intensely aware of the social and psychological truth that these concepts and their application were learned and supported by social pressure. Thus, from Li Zhi's perspective, these most revered principles in Neo-Confucian thought were learned things that came from the outside and governed response, corrupting all that was spontaneous, natural, and innocent. The word translated as "inauthentic" *(jia),* which Li Zhi repeats again and again, means both "false" and "borrowed," in the sense of coming from elsewhere, not being one's own. Li's argument hinges on that range of meaning: what comes from the outside is "borrowed," not essentially one's own, and to represent oneself through such a borrowed medium is to be "false."

If this attack on the fundamental principles of Neo-Confucianism and the glorification of drama and fiction were not shocking enough to conservative sensibilities, Li Zhi went on in the final section to assault the integrity of the Confucian Classics themselves.

Li Zhi (1527–1602), "On the Child-Mind"

When I (using the pseudonym "Mountain Farmer of Dragon Cave") wrote on the play *Western Parlor,* I commented at the end: "Those who judge such matters may not think it is all right that I still have a child-mind."[1] The child-mind is the genuine mind; and if having the child-mind is taken as not being all right, then having a genuine mind is also taken as not being all right. Free of all falseness and entirely genuine, the child-mind is the original mind of one's very first thought. Loss of the child-mind means loss of the genuine mind, and a loss of the genuine mind means loss of the genuine person. One who is a person and not genuine will never again have beginnings.

As the child is the beginning of the person, so the child-mind is beginning of mind. How could mind's beginnings ever be lost—but then how does it happen that the child-mind is indeed lost so abruptly? Initially, things seen and heard come in through eyes and ears. And when we take these as a governing factor from without, the child-mind is lost. As we grow older, the Way and Inherent Pattern come in through what we see and hear. And when we take these as the governing factor from within, the child-mind is lost.[2]

---

[1] *The Western Parlor, Xi-xiang ji,* was a Yuan variety play by Wang Shi-fu, building on Yuan Zhen's "Ying-ying's Story."

[2] Note that Li Zhi very much includes what we hear from others and what we read among sense impressions; the Chinese term is "seeing and hearing," reading associated with the former and oral

After a long time, as what we see and hear of the Way and Inherent Pattern steadily increases, what we know and what we are aware of also steadily broadens. At that point we further learn that to be praised is desirable; we endeavor to enhance opinion of ourselves, and the child-mind is lost. We learn that to be criticized by others is undesirable; we endeavor to avoid that, and the child-mind is lost.

Everything we see and hear of the Way and Inherent Pattern comes from extensive reading and judgments about what is morally right. Of course the ancient Sages read and studied; however, even if they hadn't read and studied, the child-mind would have remained secure within them all by itself. Even though they read and studied extensively, they also guarded their child-mind and kept it from being lost. They were not like scholars of our time, who repress the child-mind by extensive reading and moral judgments. And since scholars have indeed repressed their child-minds by extensive reading and moral judgments, what use was there in the Sages writing so extensively and instituting their words if it only served to make scholars repress their child-minds?

Once the child-mind is repressed, when words are uttered, those words do not come from what lies deep within; when they reveal themselves in questions of governing, what they do lacks any core; and when they write, their writing cannot reach others and accomplish its ends. In such people there is none of the inner reserve that reveals itself as beauty; there is none of the frankness and real substance that gives off its own aura. And if such people try to write even one line with moral force in the words, they ultimately fail. What is the reason for this? Their child-minds have been repressed, and their minds are constituted of things external to themselves; that is, what they have seen and heard, questions of the Way and Innate Pattern.

Since their minds are constituted of things they have seen and heard, the Way and Innate Pattern, then their words come from those external things and are not the words that the child-mind would say on its own. However artful such words may be, what do they have to do with the self? Can an inauthentic person do otherwise than to speak inauthentic words, to act inauthentically, and to write inauthentically? In fact, once a person becomes inauthentic, then he is inauthentic in every way. It follows from this that if you speak inauthentically to an inauthentic person, the inauthentic person will be pleased; if you tell an inauthentic person about inauthentic action, the inauthentic person will be pleased; and if you talk over inauthentic writing with an inauthentic person, the inauthentic person will be pleased. Being inauthentic in every way, it becomes pleasing in every way. When the whole stage is filled with inauthenticity, how can the short person standing in the audience tell the difference? In this case, even if we have the most perfect

---

opinion with the latter. Primary sensory experience and these more linguistic forms of "seeing and hearing" are alike in being external. Awareness of the Way and Inherent Pattern can come either from direct observation or Neo-Confucian instruction, but Li Zhi is thinking very much of instruction here.

works of writing in the whole world, it is not uncommon that they are destroyed by inauthentic people and do not survive to be seen by later generations. The reason for this is that the most perfect works of writing in the whole world always come from the child-mind. If the child-mind were permanently preserved, then the Way and Inherent Pattern would not be practiced and external things seen and heard would not take over. If the child-mind were preserved, then literary quality would never be missing from writing and no person would lack literary ability. It wouldn't be at all like the kind of writing constructed to fit formal models, writing that is not literature!

Why should poems have to be like those in the ancient *Anthology*? Why should prose have to be like that of the pre-Qin period? Writing continued to change after those periods, turning into the Six Dynasties style and then turning into regulated poetry. It changed again and turned into classical tales; it changed and turned into the early play-scripts and variety plays.[3] It turned into *The Western Parlor*; it turned into the novel *Water Margin*; it turned into the formal essays that people practice today for the examination. Every time a person of great virtue speaks of the Way of the Sages, it is perfect writing, in times gone by as well as now—it cannot be judged in its historical relation to the tendencies of the age. This is the reason I feel moved by the inherent literary quality of anyone who has the child-mind—who cares about the Six Classics or the *Analects* or the *Mencius!*

But let's consider what we find in the Six Classics, the *Analects,* and the *Mencius*—if they're not passages of excessive adoration by some official historian, then they're inordinate praise by some official. If neither of the above, then it was inexperienced followers and dimwitted disciples writing down from memory what their teacher had said. They gave the first part without the last, or got the conclusion but left out the beginning. They wrote it in books according to what they had personally witnessed. Later scholars did not reflect critically, so they claimed that these had come from the Sages' own mouths and decided to view them as "Classics." Who realizes that for the most part these are not the words of the Sages? Even if they did come from the Sages, they were uttered for some particular purpose, nothing more than matching the treatment to the disease, applying a remedy at the proper moment to save this very same dimwitted disciple or inexperienced follower. If the medicine worked for the disease in question, that doesn't mean we should cling fast to it—we certainly shouldn't right away make it the perfect doctrine for thousands of generations!

Be that as it may, the Six Classics, the *Analects,* and the *Mencius* have in fact become the stock excuses for Neo-Confucians and an abundant resource for inauthentic people. It is perfectly obvious that they cannot speak in words that come from the child-mind. This is a sorry state of things in-

---

[3]"Play-scripts" *(yuan-ben)* were a Northern form of drama, no longer extant, that preceded the variety play.

deed! If only I could find someone who had never lost the child-mind of an authentic Sage and have a word with him about writing![4]

Yuan Hong-dao was a great admirer of Li Zhi's iconoclasm. Yuan Hong-dao and his two brothers formed one of the most influential literary groups of the turn of the seventeenth century. Although the Yuan brothers themselves wrote in literary Chinese, they were, like Li Zhi himself, champions of vernacular literature and folksong. In an age when classical literature seemed to possess a weary sameness and hollow formality, they desperately sought qualities of freshness, spontaneity, and some elusive attractiveness that could not be reduced to formula. The term *qu,* translated as "liveliness" below, was just such a quality; it appears in things by chance and can be appreciated only by those with "intuitive grasp." Because such intuitive grasp is a sign of distinction, other people "try" to attain it, but such self-conscious attempts immediately become false.

Yuan Hong-dao (1568–1610), On Chen Zheng-fu's Collected Works, *Intuitive Grasp*

What people of our time find the hardest to achieve is liveliness. Liveliness is like the colors of a mountain, or the taste in water, or the light on flowers, or the way a beautiful woman looks. Even the master of discourse cannot put down a single word about it; only those with intuitive grasp can understand it. People these days admire what is known for liveliness and seek the semblance of liveliness. For this reason, discriminating discussions of calligraphy and painting or delving deeply into antiques are thought to be pure and disinterested activities; involving oneself in the occult or removing oneself from the world's dirt and confusion is thought to evince detachment. On a lower level still, we have those like the connoisseurs of incense and tea in Su-zhou. These sorts of things are all the mere surfaces of liveliness—what do they have to do with spiritual feeling?

Liveliness, when it is achieved from what is natural, is deep; when achieved from study, it is shallow. When one is a child, one knows nothing of the existence of liveliness, but liveliness is present everywhere. The face is never grave; the eyes are never still; the mouth prattles trying to talk; the feet leap up and down and are never still. Life's most perfect happiness is truly never greater than at this time. This is, in fact, what Mencius meant by "not losing the heart of an infant" and what Lao-zi meant by "able to be the baby." This is the highest grade of liveliness, its correct enlightenment, its highest doctrine.

---

[4]In the closing line, Lu Zhi playfully echoes a famous passage on language in the "Outer Things" chapter of *Zhuang-zi:* "The reason for the net is the fish; when you get the fish, you forget the net. The reason for the snare is the rabbit; when you get the rabbit, you forget the snare. The reason for words is the idea; when you get the idea, you forget the words. If only I could find someone who has forgotten words and have a word with him!"

People of the forests and hills are not caught up and entangled in things; they are content to just pass their days; thus, though they do not seek for liveliness, liveliness is close at hand. The reason simpletons and ne'er-do-wells are close to liveliness is because they lack status. The lower one's status, the lower the things one wants. They go where their hearts take them, some for food and drink, others for women and entertainment, despising nothing and shrinking from nothing; feeling themselves cut off from all worldly expectations, they pay no attention to the world except to laugh at it. This also is a kind of liveliness.

But as the years gradually go by, as one's official position gradually gets higher, and as one's status gradually increases, one's body is as if in fetters and one's heart is as if stuck by thorns. One's hair, the body's apertures, one's bones and joints are all entangled by knowledge and experience; and though one becomes ever more deeply aware of the pattern of things, still one grows farther and farther away from liveliness.

My friend, Chen Zheng-fu, is deep in liveliness; and thus liveliness is the most prominent quality in his collected works, *Intuitive Grasp*, done in several chapters. If this were not so, I would not have written these comments for him, even if he had the principles of the martyr-recluse Bo Yi or were as noble as the hermit Yan Guang. Who would have thought that someone of your status, of your official rank, and someone in the prime of his years like yourself would have such a comprehension of liveliness?

Writing often celebrated refined pastimes and amusements of the intellectual elite: the connoisseurship of art, books, tea, flowers—along with some more unusual sports. There was a fascination with the special knowledge associated with each activity, even when that knowledge was invented on the spot. Writers often describe techniques, hierarchies of qualities, or different types of the activity, as in Yuan Hong-dao's account of spider-fighting.

Spider-Fighting

To my knowledge the technique of fighting spiders never existed in earlier times. My friend Gong San-mu invented the sport. San-mu was staying in the same lodgings as myself, and whenever the weather grew mild in spring, each of us would catch several small spiders, ones with rather long legs, raise them in a window, and, to amuse ourselves, make them fight for victory. Spiders are usually found in the shadowy spots on walls or under tables. Catch them when they have just formed a few long strands of their webs without cross-strands, taking care not to move too quickly, because if you move too quickly, they'll become frightened; and once frightened, they'll never be able to fight. You should take the females and not the males, because the male flees when he encounters an adversary. The male's legs are shorter and his belly thinner—it's quite easy to tell them apart.

The way to train them is this: take the offspring of another spider that has not yet hatched and stick it on a piece of paper in the window; when the female spider sees it, she will take it as her own offspring and protect it fiercely. When she sees the other spider coming, she will think it has come to take her own young and will do everything she can to fight the other off. You shouldn't use spiders who still have their eggs in their belly or whose young have already hatched. When they come on the field, they first grab one another with their legs; then after a few preliminary skirmishes, their ferocity intensifies, and they go at it tooth and nail until you can't see their bodies. The victor wraps her enemy up in threads and doesn't give up until the other is dead. There are also those who get frightened and run off in defeat in the middle of the battle; and there are some cases when the strengths are so equally matched that they quit after several rounds.

San-mu is always able to determine ahead of time which ones will win and which will lose. When he catches them, he'll say that this one will be a good fighter and that one won't be a good fighter and that these two are well matched—and it always works out just like he says. The jet black ones are the best; the ash gray ones second best; and the ones with mottled colors are the worst. We also have many special names for the types: "purple-black tiger," "hawk-talons," "tortoise-shell belly," "black Zhang Jing," "night prong," "cheery lass," "little iron lips," in each case named for what they resembled. You feed them flies and large black ants. We both knew how they looked when they were hungry or well fed, happy or enraged—but this gets into a lot of little details that I'm not going to include here. San-mu was very clever and good at poetry; as soon as he saw some skill or technique practiced deftly, he understood it—but also on this account he neglected his studies.

Since the Song Dynasty, informal letters to friends and family had been treated as a form separate from the stylized literary letters that an author would preserve in his collected works. Like letter collections in the West, these letters were often published separately. In their casualness and roughness of style, they perfectly suited the late Ming ideals of spontaneity and easy informality, and they were often included in anthologies of "minor pieces." Characteristic of late Ming self-consciousness, such letters frequently took as their topic the very values they sought to embody. Two letters by Yuan Hong-dao and one by Tu Long follow.

Letter to Li Zi-ran

Have you been writing any poems recently? If you're not writing poetry, how are you getting through these dreary days? A person can only be happy when he finds something to put his heart into. Some people put their hearts into chess, some into beautiful women, some into a particular skill or craft, some into writing. The reason that the most self-realized people of olden times were a level better than others was their unwillingness to simply pass their lives drifting along.

Every time I see people with nothing to put their hearts into—so busy all day long, as if they had lost something, worrying even though they have nothing to worry about, getting no joy out of a scene before them—I personally can't understand why. This is being in hell while alive—who needs the iron beds, the bronze pillars, knife mountains, and sword trees! It's too bad! There's probably nothing really hard to do in the whole world; and as long as you just get it over and done with haphazardly, your day will go along like water forming its own channel. With a talent like yours, Zi-ran, there's nothing in the whole world you couldn't do. I'm just afraid that you're too cautious and serious and not willing just to throw yourself into it and do it. Go ahead and try it. It's all right not to disappoint a true friend's intention to help you succeed.

Letter to Qiu Chang-ru

I've been very concerned since I heard how sick you've been. If you should die, all the grace and culture of the Southeast will be gone. Can I help being concerned? As a county magistrate, I've had to play the most hateful roles—they are indescribable. To give you a general idea: when I chance to meet a superior official, I'm a slave; when I entertain a guest who has dropped by, I'm a courtesan; when I manage money or grain, I'm a warehouse supervisor; when I explain things to the peasantry, I'm an old lady matchmaker. In the course of a single day, things blow hot and cold a hundred times, now bright and active, now dark and passive—the county magistrate experiences all the worst qualities of the everyday world. It's painful and it's like poison to me.

My brother was going to pass through Wu this autumn, and though he did pass through, he just wanted to sit around in the county office library reading books and poems, and we didn't get to go climb Tiger Hill as we had before with Mr. Hou.

Have you felt much of an inclination to travel lately? Even though, as chief officer of Mao-yuan here on the outskirts of Su-zhou, I don't have any money to give to visitors, still I have wine to get drunk on, tea to drink, the Great Lake as my spoonful of water on which to go boating, and Dong-ting Mountain as my lump of rock to climb—so I'm not too gloomy. What do you think?

Tu Long (1542–1605), From the Capital, to a Friend

In Beijing I cover my face and ride a brown horse; the wind rises and the dust flies, filling the streets and avenues. When I get home and dismount, both of my nostrils are as black as chimney-holes. The piss of men and horses mixes with the sandy dirt; and after it rains, you sink into the muck up to your knee or saddle. Peasants push ahead, whipping their half-lame donkeys, their shoulders rubbing against those of officials. When the cry comes to clear the way for a high official, when you can't get to duck quickly into a winding sidelane, you run wildly until you're breathless and the sweat flows down to your heels. That gives you a sense of what it's like here.

And I imagine the evening sunlight in some Yangzi River village far away, the fishing boats putting into shore, the last rays of the sun shooting back into the forest, and the sand bright as snow. Under flowering trees fishing nets dry in the sun, and the white planks and blue awnings of a tavern are half-hidden behind hanging willows. An old man comes out of a ramshackle gate, holding a fish and carrying a jug. To go strolling on the sands with a few good friends at this time would be far better than riding a horse into the mud in the capital.

Chen Ji-ru (1558–1639), A Colophon for "The History of Flowers"

Those who have a taste for the wilderness but experience no delight in it are woodsmen and herdsmen; those who let fruit rot without ever getting to taste it are hired gardeners and grocers; those who have flowering trees but cannot enjoy them are the nobility. Of the famous men of olden days, only Tao Qian found his interest held everywhere by mulberry and hemp, by pines and chrysanthemums, by fields and villages. Su Dong-po loved gardening and was able to touch flowers and trees with his own hands. This comes from a person's nature and cannot be forced. Force it, and even if you give someone the "History of Flowers," he will become irritable and throw it away. But if such things are close to your nature and you also love them, then I urge you to take this book with you to lie in the sun among the trees and watch carefully as the flowers blossom and fall. What difference is there between this and the course of the rise and fall of men and dynasties over the past thousand years? What we refer to as the "Twenty-one Dynastic Histories" may well all be in this one unorthodox history.

Zhang Dai belonged to the generation of Ming writers who, in their maturity, witnessed the fall of the Ming and the establishment of the Qing Dynasty. Like other writers of "minor pieces," Zhang Dai's best-known works, "The Dream Recollections of Tao-an" *(Tao-an meng-yi)* and "Tracing West Lake in Dream" *(Xi-hu meng-xun)*, treated special moments and small occasions; but Zhang Dai, writing after the fall of the Ming, recasts such moments through the haze of memory.

Zhang Dai (1597–1679), Night Theater on Gold Mountain ("The Dream Recollections of Tao-an")

One day after mid-autumn in 1629, en route from Zheng-jiang to Yan-zhou, we reached Bei-gu in the late afternoon and moored the boat at the mouth of the river. Moonbeams had been poured from an upturned bag into the water, and their light played flickering on the waves; misty vapors swallowed in the light, then spat it back out, whitening the sky. I was amazed and delighted; and when we moved the boat past Gold Mountain Temple, it was already about ten o'clock. As we went through the Dragon-King Chamber and into the main hall, everything was silent and black as pitch. Moonbeams leaked through the forest and lay widely scattered like patches of snow.

I told my servant boy to bring the props and costumes for a play, and we hung up lanterns throughout the main hall. And we performed two plays—*Han Shi-zhong, Prince of Qi, at Gold Mountain* and *The Great Battle on the Yangzi*. The drums and gongs resounded everywhere, and everyone in the whole temple got up to look. There were old monks rubbing the sleep out of their eyes with the backs of their hands, their mouths all hanging open in one accord. There was yawning and stretching and laughing and sneezing, until gradually their attention was fixed; and where these people were from, what they were doing, and when they had come—none of these things did they dare ask.

When the plays were over, the daylight was soon to arrive. We undid the moorings and crossed the river. The monks of the mountain followed us down to the foot of the mountain and for a long time followed us with their eyes, not knowing whether we were people or apparitions or ghosts.

Zhang Dai seems to have had a particular fondness for events that appear suddenly, full of light and noise, then disappear just as suddenly. The following piece is an example of Zhang's breathless, impressionistic prose at its most characteristic.

Mid-September on West Lake ("The Dream Recollections of Tao-an")

There is nothing at all to look at on West Lake in mid-September but people looking at the mid-September moon. There are five types of looking among people looking at the mid-September moon. One type looks at it thus: in great pleasure barges with cabins, flutes and drums playing, banquets teeming with tall-capped officials with lanterns, actors and servants in a tumult of voices and light, and though they call it "looking at the moon," they don't actually see the moon. Another type looks at it thus: they are also in pleasure barges, and these barges also have cabins, with famous courtesans and the flower of the fair sex, and those whose hands are held include handsome young catamites; laughter and cries are mixed together as they sit in circles on open-air platforms, with seductive glances cast right and left; they are right under the moon but they don't actually look at the moon. Yet another type looks at it thus: they are also in pleasure barges and there are also voices in song, with well-known singing girls and relaxed monks pouring small cups of wine and caroling softly, with gentle piping and strings played softly, throat and woodwind each coming forth in turn; they are also right under the moon, and they do look at the moon, but want others to look at them looking at the moon. Yet another type looks at it thus: neither in boat nor carriage and wearing neither cloak nor turban, but drunk from wine and having eaten their fill, they shout in small groups and make their way into the crowds. At Zhao-qing Temple and Broken Bridge they make a racket, and pretending to be drunk, they carol out of key; the moon they do indeed look at, and those looking at the moon they look at, and those not looking at the moon they also look at, and actually don't look at anything. Yet another type looks at it thus: in small boats with light awnings, clean tables and warm stoves, teapots soon to boil, and the pale white porcelain quietly passed round; good friends and fair ladies invite the moon to sit with them, sometimes concealing their reflections under trees, sometimes fleeing the din to the interior of the lake; they look at the moon, but no one sees how they look when looking at the moon, and they don't look at the moon self-consciously.

When the people of Hang-zhou go sailing on the lake, they go out mid-morning and come back in the early evening, avoiding the moon as if it were their enemy. But on this evening of such fair repute they all go out in throngs, usually giving their household guards some wine money as a bonus, and sedan-chair bearers, torches in hand, wait for them in lines along the shore. Once they get in their boats, they hurry the boatmen to push off as soon as possible from Broken Bridge, and catching up, they enter the swarm of other boats. Thus, before ten o'clock people's voices, the drums and piping, seem to boil up and crash, seem like nightmares or talking in one's sleep, seeming to deafen and drown out speech, until all together the large boats and small boats make for the shore, and one sees nothing but boat-pole knocking against boat-pole, boat bumping boat, shoulder rubbing shoulder, face looking at face. In a brief moment the excitement is over; the parties of officials break up, with black-robed government servants yelling to clear the road; sedan-chair bearers shout, and people in the boats become distressed that the city gates will be locked, and, with lanterns in hand like constellations of stars, they go off, everyone squeezed into groups. People on the shore also follow the crowds to make it to the city gates, gradually growing fewer and more scattered, until a moment later they're all gone.

Only then did we moor our boat near the shore. And as the stone stairs to Broken Bridge grew cool, we spread out mats on them and called to those still out to come drink with us. At this time the moon was like a newly polished mirror; the hills were again freshly adorned, and the face of the lake was again bathed clean. Those who had poured small cups of wine and caroled softly came forth; those who had concealed their reflections under the trees also came forth; we exchanged friendly words with them and urged them to sit with us. Companions in verse came by; well-known singing girls showed up; winecups and chopsticks lay still; throats and woodwinds sang out. The moonlight was gray and cool, and the guests didn't go their ways until the east was growing light. Then we pushed off in the boat again and slept off the wine in the midst of ten leagues of lotus blossoms, whose fragrance brushed over us, and our clear dreams were quite contented.

Viewing the Snow from "Heart of the Lake Pavilion" ("The Dream Recollections of Tao-an")

In February 1632, I was living at West Lake. There was a blizzard that lasted three days, and the sounds of birds and people on the lake ceased entirely. On the day in question, just as the night was drawing to a close, I took a small boat, and wrapped in a fur coat and huddled close to a portable stove, we went off by ourselves to look at the snow from Heart of the Lake Pavilion. There was a white haze of lake mist around the trees; the sky and the clouds and the mountains and the water were all white above and below. The only reflections on the lake were the single streak of the Long Embankment, the single dot of Heart of the Lake Pavilion, the single mustard seed of our boat, and the few specks of the people in the boat.

When I reached the pavilion, there were two people sitting on a rug and a servant boy who was tending a stove on which the water for heating wine had just come to a boil. When they saw me, they were delighted and said, "Who would have thought there would be anyone else on the lake!" They dragged me over to drink with them, and I took my leave after forcing myself to drink three mugs. When I asked who they were, I found out that they were from Jin-ling and were visiting. When I got in the boat, one of the boatmen mumbled, "I guess the gentleman here isn't all that foolish because there are others even more foolish than he is."

"Foolish" *(chi)* was a double-edged quality, sometime pejorative and sometimes positive. It was applied to those who were "besotted" by love but was also the term used to describe the innocence of children. To the boatman, going out in the freezing cold at the break of dawn is "foolishness" in one sense; Zhang Dai reports the story positively, because to him such "foolishness" is a quality in which he takes pride.

The Performance of Peng Tian-xi ("The Dream Recollections of Tao-an")

The performances of Peng Tian-xi were the finest in all the world, yet in every scene he stayed with the script and never altered a single word to suit his own taste. When he wanted a scene performed, he would invite the actors to his house and spend twenty or so pieces of silver; and in no time at all his family fortune of one hundred thousand was used up. Throughout the months of spring he was usually at West Lake and visited Shao-xing perhaps half a dozen times. He came to my house and played fifty or sixty scenes without ever exhausting the range of his art.

Tian-xi usually played villains and clowns. The most vicious and violent men of all time and the worst flatterers became even more cruel in passing through Tian-xi's heart, on Tian-xi's face they became still more wicked, and coming from Tian-xi's mouth they became even more malevolent. When he put himself in their positions, it seemed that even the evil of King Zhow of

Shang was not as bad as this. He would knit his brows and peer around, and there was really a sword in his heart and a dagger behind his smile; he had a demonic air and a deadliness so sinister that the audience felt dread. We may well say that all the book learning in Tian-xi's breast, all the mountains and streams in his breast, all the schemes and stratagems in his breast, and all his extraordinary and restless energy had nowhere to express itself, so that he expressed it in this singular way.

When I see a good play, I regret that I cannot wrap it up in fine brocade and pass it on forever without perishing. I have compared it to a whole night of fine moonlight in the heavens and to a cup of tea brewed just for the right amount of time—all of these provide only a moment's use, and yet we treasure them endlessly. When Huan Yin saw a fine spot in the landscape, he abruptly shouted, "It's just too much, too much!"[5] There truly are such things that are just too much, things the mouth cannot express.

Preface to "Tracing West Lake in a Dream"

I was born in the wrong time and have been far apart from West Lake for twenty-eight years. Nevertheless not a day has gone by when West Lake was not in my dreams, and the West Lake of my dreams has, in fact, never left me for a single day. Earlier, in 1654 and 1657, I twice went to West Lake; and of places like the mansions beyond mansions of the Shangs at the Yong-jin Gate, or the Qis' temporary lodgings, or the estates of the Qians and Yus, along with my own family's gardens—of a whole shore of lake villas there survived only shards of the tiles. Thus what still existed in my dreams was, in fact, not there at West Lake itself. And as for the view from Broken Bridge, all the lithe willows and tender peaches of bygone days, the mansions and pavilions for singing and dance, were as if swallowed up by a vast flood, and not one in a hundred survived.

I then fled the place as quickly as I could, telling myself that I had come here because of West Lake and that from what I now saw, it would be better to guard the West Lake of my dreams, where I could still keep it complete and unharmed. At that point I fancied how different my own dreams were from the dream of Li Bo. When Li Bo dreamed of Tian-mu, it was like a goddess or a renowned beauty; he dreamed of what he had never seen, and such a dream was illusion. But when I dream of West Lake, it is like my home garden and my family; I dream of what used to be, and such dreams are genuine.

I have now lived in lodgings rented from someone else for twenty-three years, but in my dreams I am still where I used to live. The young servant who served me then now has white hair, but in my dreams his hair is still done up like a young boy's. I cannot rid myself of these long-standing habits and cannot escape an old disposition; and both now and hereafter I can only

---

[5]In fact, the famous Eastern Jin aristocrat gave this response to hearing a song.

be melancholy in my Butterfly Cottage and walk slowly from my Bed of
Rude Awakening. My dreams are all that I have to hold to, a stream of scenes
of West Lake, still perfectly arranged and unmoving.

   When the children want to know about it, I may happen to tell them;
and it may be all speaking a dream from within a dream, but it is not speaking out of this present nightmare. Thus I came to write the seventy-two entries of "Tracing West Lake in a Dream" and leave them for generations to
come as a reflection of West Lake. I am like that man of the hills who returned from the seaside, praising the pleasures of seafood in glowing terms;
and everyone in his hometown crowded around him to lick his eyes. But,
unfortunately, once those precious relishes and sweet morsels of shellfish
pass the tongue, they are gone—and then how can licking the eyes ever satisfy the craving?

—The sixteenth of the seventh month, 1671.
By Zhang Dai, the old man of Butterfly Cottage in Gu-jian

Belatedness

Although the Ming and Qing was a theater-loving culture, the arguments made by
some late Ming intellectuals for the legitimacy of drama and prose fiction as "high"
literature were intended to shock common opinion. Poetry was still generally considered the most important literary form, and the High Tang was considered the
height of poetry and the immutable norm of poetic excellence. The more extreme
versions of such an opinion, held by the influential Archaists, declared that one
should not even read the classical poetry of the Song and Yuan dynasties, so far had
it diverged from the High Tang standard. That common opinion had serious consequences for contemporary poetic practice: new poems could either be like the Tang,
in which case they would be imitative, or unlike the Tang, in which case they would
be bad poems, swerving from the very qualities that seemed to define poetic excellence. The Archaists favored imitation; but a century of "Archaist" domination of
classical literature produced so much uninspired verse that new solutions had to be
found.

   This dilemma in classical poetry was only one aspect of a much larger problem
in elite culture during the Ming and Qing: how a contemporary writer or intellectual could establish his own worth in a culture where past achievements set the standards against which contemporary works were judged. A very similar dilemma can
be found in European culture from the Renaissance through the eighteenth century,
and the Chinese solutions parallel those of Europe in interesting ways. Both cultures
eventually produced a modern notion of "historicism," in which each period had
distinct qualities that defined what was "good" only for that period.

   To argue, as Li Zhi and others did, for the importance of vernacular literature
was one solution to the dilemma; that solution emerged victorious only in the twentieth century. Another solution was to go back and take a fresh look at classical poetry from periods other than the Tang, to develop a broader sense of what was "good"
in poetry, and to begin to develop a sense of relative historical value in which each

age had its own distinct strengths. The classical poetry of the Song, so maligned by the Archaists, was the ideal place to begin. Thus the late Ming saw a revival of interest in Song poetry and a cultivated admiration for precisely those ways in which it differed from Tang poetry. The following preface to a new edition of Song and Yuan poetry compiled by Yuan Zhong-dao catches the flavor of the times. It was an uneasy defense of the Song, and, as always, the image of the Tang loomed large in the background.

Yuan Zhong-dao was the younger brother of Yuan Hong-dao and a well-known literary figure in his own right.

Yuan Zhong-dao (1570–1623), A Preface to "Poetry of the Song and Yuan"

Poetry never reached a greater height than in the Tang. If a poem comes from the hand of someone in the Tang, it possesses color when you look at it, it possesses tone when you test it with a knock, and it seems to possess a bouquet when you sniff it. Even from as much as a thousand years ago, those poems are like blades just off the whetstone or the petals of flowers newly spread. The Song and Yuan masters who followed them found in song lyric and vernacular song the unique achievements of their own talents and feelings; and even if Tang writers had condescended to write in such forms, they would not necessarily have been able to surpass the Song and Yuan. But when it came to classical poetry, the Song and Yuan masters could only yield place to the Tang. Take a couplet like Chang Jian's on "Broken Mountain Temple":

> A bamboo trail leads through to hidden places,
> a meditation chamber deep in flowering trees.

Ou-yang Xiu claimed that he could never come up to that, even if he spent his whole life trying. Su Dong-po said that Ou-yang Xiu had, in fact, become sick of the rich flavors of meat and fine rice and developed a taste for conch—but this is not the case. Literature is bound up with the temper of the times. Comments like these do not mean that their talents were inferior to those of the Tang or that their learning was inferior—it was merely a limitation imposed by the temper of the times and an inability to force themselves to be the same. It is not a matter of want of effort that the Han and Wei was not like the *Classic of Poetry,* or that the Tang was not like the Han and Wei, or that the Song and Yuan were not like the Tang. Nevertheless, it is indeed an error to seize upon this and subsequently claim that the Song and Yuan had no poetry worthy of the name.

Past critics maintained that excellence in poetry was like the taste of salt in water or the pure pigment in colors, that the meaning was not exhausted when the words stopped. This is, in fact, true of countless individuals during each generation of the Tang and of countless poems by each of those individuals. In expressing their emotions and drawing scenes, they made what was far seem close at hand, and they made what was separate merge; their excellence lay in a sense of something held in reserve and in not expressing everything openly. Their style was elevated, their energy had an organic unity, and they observed the rules strictly. Yet they were extremely conservative in their choice of material for poems, and the path they took was a very narrow one. There is no question that the course of development they set in motion had no choice but to change, becoming the Mid-Tang and the Late Tang. Given the fact that Li Bo and Du Fu already could not help extending poetry's range in new directions in order to say everything they wanted to say, why blame the Song and Yuan masters for doing the same?

The Song and Yuan were the successors of the three phases of Tang poetry, and they spent all their efforts and skill in poetry, until the splendors of the universe were virtually all divulged with nothing left over. Those who made poems found themselves at an impasse where change was necessary. And they preferred to let each person bring out his own innate capacities, to let each person come up with his own devices and strategies in order to adequately convey what he wanted to say; they were never willing simply to repeat or imitate, to gather up the drops of spit left by others to die in the words of their predecessors.

Thus the full gamut of feeling was exhausted, and there was nothing they left undescribed; the full range of scenes was exhausted, and there was nothing they left unused in their poems. They left nothing undescribed, yet reached the point of describing what did not need to be described; they used everything, yet reached the point of using what did not need to be used. At their worst what they wrote could be preposterous, clumsy, crude, or slick and frivolous, as if they simply brought out poems like turning over a barrel or emptying a sack, without taking time to pick and choose. In general they took their sense of measure from their own sensibilities and learned rules only from their native wit; when a thought stirred them, they gave voice to it; and when the thought was done, they were silent. Even though they cannot compete with the Tang for the heights, still those points where their flashes of brilliance cannot be expunged should be preserved in this world together with the Tang. It is for this that Song and Yuan poems are being printed here.

When I read the Song and Yuan masters, I find that the talents of the most outstanding are high, their grace is also deep, and they read everything there was to read. Thus when they conceived poetic ideas and fashioned phrases, they tended to go far off on tangents; even if this was a different mode from any other period in history, they still made something worth handing on to posterity. I find it outrageous that later scholars, short on talent and with pedestrian sensibilities, didn't read over the books gathered together and just picked out the most superficial phrases of Tang poets on wind, clouds, moonlight, and dew, while at the same time looking on Song and Yuan writers as if they didn't exist. In fact, rhetoricians of recent times came up with the unprecedented claim that one should not read the writings of the Song and Yuan.

Any reader should draw from a wide range and garner what is best; each of those talented and ingenious men over the course of five or six centuries achieved something unique. When you take what's the best in them, it can always bring something out in one's spirit and wisdom. Is it not a great injustice to wipe them generally from consideration in one fell swoop? Ever since this theory that one should not read Song and Yuan poetry appeared, it has been the jungle in which closed-minded and lazy men have found refuge. Since one need not read their books, they don't need to be preserved either. In this case should we then just let the literary collections of the Song and Yuan be scattered to the winds and lost, and not be concerned with them any more?

Early in the Song, there were the collected works of the "Nine Monks"; it was said that if you put them together with Tang works, you couldn't tell them apart. By the middle of the Song, their collected works no longer survived. Lu You praised the poems of Pan Bin-lao as having an unequaled excellence. And yet today we have no way to get a glimpse of Pan's collected works. Huang Ting-jian had the highest words for Gao He's achievements in emulating Du Fu, but even the local gazetteer of his native Jiang-ling omits his name. Everywhere I see lines from the Song and Yuan written on a painting or on some set topic, and there are some extremely fine poems; but either we know of the person yet don't have his collected works, or we have his works yet these don't include that poem. From this we know that a great many Song and Yuan poems have not survived. If we look for them now, we will find one in a hundred or ten in a thousand that we ought to treasure, make our secret acquisitions, and extol publicly to keep this part of our culture from being lost forever; how then can they say that we need not read this and need not preserve it!

The calligraphy and paintings of the Song and Yuan are still preserved in the households of erudite connoisseurs and collectors and have become immortal now. Yet the fact that their poems alone are so rarely exhibited makes them truly lost classics. Pan Shi-heng of Xin-an has spent much effort seeking out and purchasing various collected works by Song and Yuan masters. He has had plates carved to print them in order to ensure that the writings of these two dynasties last forever, together with those of the Tang. This is a most welcome event in the past several centuries and one that is very much in accord with my own feelings on the matter. Thus I have not demurred and have written this introduction for him.

Diary

Although extensive travel diaries had been written since the Song, the great age of the diary in China began in the late Ming. One of the best diaries of the period is the long "Account of My Travels in Fei" by Yuan Zhong-dao. He begins by persuading himself that he needs to get out of the house and take a vacation: that a trip by boat would really be much better for his studies than staying at home trying to read.

Yuan Zhong-dao, from "Account of My Travels in Fei"

1.   December 1, 1608, in the Wan-li Reign. I've been staying in Yun-dang Valley. After I failed the examination last year in 1607, I lodged with Commander in Chief Qian of Yu-yang and came home this May. My brother Hong-dao had previously held an office in the Ministry of Rites and was on his way south in the winter of 1607–08 when he got news from the Ministry of Personnel. He went back to the capital this spring, while I stayed on at home. The bamboo in Yun-dang Valley grew leafier from each day to the next, and the flowers grew more splendid. At several spots among them I added pavilions and terraces, and I felt a strong determination to live a life of retirement.

2.   After living quietly for a few months, I suddenly longed to go traveling. In fact, while I was in Yun-dang Valley I had had a really good experience of the secluded life and was able to shut my door and study. But as things were, it couldn't go on that way very long. I was oppressed by family responsibilities and got caught up in social obligations to outsiders, such as writing responses and paying social calls; and habitual guests were intruding on me and disturbing me until finally I didn't have a moment to breathe. These are the reasons I wanted to go traveling: First, famous mountains and splendid rivers could flush clean the everyday concerns that filled me. Second, there are quite a few chapels in Wu and Yue where I could sit quietly and study. Third, even though my learning has reached the level of reliable interpretation, my intuitive powers are still not deep enough; beholding a scene gives rise to feelings, but there are still many points where I get bogged down on precipitous paths. On a trip I might meet famous monks and superior companions and be imbued with their improving influence, molding and quickening the sense of everyday routine that I have in my bones and making me susceptible to transformation. This is the reason I didn't dare cling to my peace and quiet.

3.   I happened to be with my uncle Gong Jing-ting when the talk turned to the question of traveling. I said, "Traveling shouldn't be pressured by questions of fame and profit; it's better just to go along with the river. However, when you go by river, it's also best to buy one's own boat and carry one's own provisions in it. Then, no matter whether you go quickly or slowly, no matter whether it's near or far, you can hope to come upon fine scenery and fine friends, and then you can linger there a long time and follow all your impulses to climb mountains, go sailing, or just hang around; and you won't be hurried along by your elders. Also there are a lot of storms on the rivers and lakes, and only when you have your own boat can you travel when you should travel and stop when you should stop—there is nothing more convenient than this." My uncle said, "I have a boat that I had made myself, as strong and solid as possible. Moreover, I've used it over the course of many

years, and now, nephew, I'll turn it over to you." At the time the boat was right in Sha-shi, the district capital.

4.   From town I crossed the river and went to the district capital to see to preparations for the trip. At night the sky looked quite bad, with dense clouds spread out on all sides. By daybreak the sky had cleared, and there were small ripples on the surface of the river. The atmosphere was clear and lovely. I took a short rest when I reached Yellow Rapids. In Wang Shi-peng's collected works this is written "Yellow Altar"—there must have been a reason.

5.   I went to the river to get a look at the boat that Uncle Jing-ting had given me, and it was quite sturdy. I got in the boat and made tea using river water—it was excellent. Then I took a stroll in the marketplace, recalling when I came here twenty years before, with the "girls like clouds." Too bad that it's so dreary and deserted now. . . .

[Yuan Zhong-dao sets off on the river. Any expectation of escaping the circle of friends and their demands would prove illusory—but one suspects that Zhong-dao never really wanted privacy in the first place. Letters also reach him.]

12.   I received a letter from my brother Hong-dao in which he said, "Now I really understand that I cannot be an active, enthusiastic official—my only fear is that I can't get away from this quickly." You can tell what was on his mind. I got a letter from Li Ben-ning that said, "I recently read the *Yu-yang Collection* and didn't know about the poems 'On the Words "Wild Goose." ' When it's convenient, I would be grateful if you would copy them out and send them to me." I had actually written that poem in the spring of 1606. Subsequently the monk Wu-ji wrote two more poems on the topic. Next Hong-dao and I locked horns in competition in front of Ju-luo Pavilion and together did ten more poems on the topic. Long Zhu-ling later saw them and admired them, and he too did ten matching poems. Long Jun-zhao also did ten matching poems, while the two official astrologers Zeng and Lei did two poems apiece. I had my poem printed in my *Yun-dang Collection.* . . .

29.   I embarked to go back to Gong-an and spent the night at He Cave. There was nothing else to do in the boat, so I read, revised poems, burned incense, made tea, and did calligraphy on fans. Thus I passed a day in ease.

30.   I got in the boat with my uncles Gong San-mu, Gong Jing-ting, and Gong Fang-ping. We moved the boat to the sandy beach on the northern shore, where we sat on mats and drew characters in the sand to amuse ourselves. I got some intuition of the excellence of the ancients in making seal impressions in clay and drawing in sand. The wind grew a little stronger, and we moved closer to the water's edge and listened to the waters churn-

ing. We boiled a fish and heated wine, then lay back drunk and sang boisterously. We saw the evening sun turn blood red and decorate the isles and sandbars. . . .

32. Night, there was a great blizzard. I had wanted to get in the boat and go to Sha-shi, but was finally prevented by the snowfall. Nevertheless, the bits of snow struck against the thousands of stalks of bamboo and made a tinkling sound. With the window dark and the fire red, I read a few chapters as my whim took me, but found little interest in them. And I thought it was too bad that whenever I wanted to go somewhere, something would come up that would keep me from it; still, I go when the course of things indicates, and when thwarted, I stop—I just go with the flow. This is what Huang Ting-jian meant by: "There is no spot I cannot find lodging for a dream."

These are just a few incidents from the early pages of Yuan Zhong-dao's diary, which goes on in this vein, detailing the small pleasures, pains, and incidents of that period of his life, for 310 pages in a modern edition (it would be about two to three times as long in English translation). Less than forty years later, we have a diary of a very different sort—short, and covering only ten days. But they were ten memorable days. The subtlety and cultivated ease of the late Ming has quite gone.

In 1645, Shi Ke-fa, commander of the Southern Ming forces, decided to make his stand against the advancing Qing armies in the city of Yang-zhou. After a siege of only seven days, the city fell, and what followed was the bloodiest chapter in the Qing conquest of the Ming.

Qing critics, perhaps unfairly, sometimes blamed late Ming aesthetic and intellectual culture for the fall of the dynasty. The late Ming sensibility, with its focus on private life and inner experience at the expense of concern for the polity, was afterward seen as decadence. The citizenry of Yang-zhou certainly paid a terrible price for their passivity and inability to act in their own defense, but they possessed the ability to tell the story with an intensity of detail that makes it still memorable, and that ability derived in no small part from an art of diary and "minor pieces" fostered in an age of heedless peace.

Wang Xiu-chu, from "Ten Days of Yang-zhou"

On the fourteenth of the fourth month in 1645, the High Commander Shi Ke-fa couldn't hold his position on the Bai-yang River and fled to Yang-zhou in disarray, closing the city walls tight to withstand the enemy. Up to the twenty-fourth, the walls had not yet been breached.

There were soldiers defending each of the gates that controlled access to the city. My own house was in the western part of the city, whose defense was under the command of someone named Yang. Soldiers and staff were distributed everywhere. I had two billeted in my house, as did each of the houses around me. These soldiers acted in a shamelessly overbearing way, and more than a thousand cash a day was spent to provide for them. Eventually we had no choice but to make plans as a group to entertain their commanding officer, and I even went to such lengths as to treat him with great deference, so that our relations gradually became cordial. The commanding officer was delighted and warned his troops to keep away from us.

This commanding officer liked music and was good mandolin player. He wanted to get some well-known courtesan to entertain him in his time off from his military duties. That evening he had invited us to drink with him. Everyone present was ready to indulge himself freely when all of a sudden a note came from the high commander; the officer looked it over and the color drained from his face. Immediately he went atop the walls, and all of us dispersed to our homes.

The next morning the high commander's proclamation was read out; and when it came to the words, "So long as there is one man in the city to withstand them, they will not oppress the common folk," all who heard it were stirred to tears. We also got news that a patrol had achieved a minor victory, and everyone touched their foreheads in celebration.

After midday, one of my wife's relations came from Gua-zhou to get away from the fleeing troops of the Earl of Xing-ping (Gao Jie was the Earl of Xing-ping, and the high commander had dispatched him out of the city to hold himself at a distance). Since my wife had not seen her in a long time, they were sobbing when they met; but I had already been told by several people that enemy troops had entered the walls. I quickly went out to see what I could find out, and someone said, "The relief column of Huang De-gong, the Count of Jing-nan, has arrived." Then I observed that the troops defending the wall were maintaining strict discipline. Next I went to the market, where there was an uproar of people talking. Men with their hair hanging loose and in bare feet appeared right afterward. I asked them what was happening, but they were in such a state of panic and so out of breath that they weren't able to answer me. All of a sudden a few dozen horsemen went galloping from the north toward the south in a disorderly mass like a surging wave; they were closely gathered around a single man—it was the high commander. It turned out that they had fled out to the east of the walls, but couldn't get through the soldiers assaulting the city, then had decided to flee through the south gates and thus had passed through here.[6] At this point I realized that there was no doubt the enemy had entered the city.

Abruptly a single horseman appeared going from north to south. He had let the reins drop and was going slowly, looking upward and crying out in despair; in front of him two foot soldiers led the horse by the bit and, out of affection, wouldn't abandon him—to this day I can see the picture clearly in my eyes, and I regret never having learned his name. When that horseman had gotten some distance away, the men who had been defending the wall began to come down in droves to hide, throwing away all their helmets

---

[6]When the Manchu troops had broken through Yang-zhou's defenses, Shi Ke-fa tried to commit suicide, but was saved by his escort and taken out of the city, where the Manchus eventually captured him and killed him.

and weapons. Together with them were those with head wounds and broken legs; and when I turned and looked at the wall towers, they were already completely empty.

Seeing that the city walls were too narrow to set up his cannons, the high commander had earlier ordered plank scaffolding to be erected on the parapets; room was left in the front for passage along the wall, while the back part reached to the roofs of people's houses, allowing extra space so that it could rest secure. Before this work was completed, the first of the enemy over the wall clasped their bows and descended with naked blades. The soldiers defending the wall were jammed against one another; and since the way was blocked off in front of them, they all escaped on the wooden planking. Crawling along, some managed to reach the roofs; but the new planking wasn't firmly fixed, and all at once the footing gave way; men were falling like leaves, and ninety percent died. Those who reached the roofs broke tiles wherever they stepped, all making sounds like swords and pikes striking one another, or like a rain of hailstones or shot; the clanking and crashing echoed all around without letup, and the people in the houses were in utter terror and frantic, not knowing what to do. Inside and outside main halls and deep into the women's apartments, everywhere the soldiers who had been defending the wall were climbing down from roofs and in their fear looking for some cubbyhole in which to hide themselves. The owners of the houses yelled at them but couldn't stop them. Doors to corridors and between adjoining rooms were shut, and all evidence of human habitation was hidden from sight.

The back of my main hall faced the wall, and from a crack in my window I peered out and saw soldiers moving along the wall south and then west. They were marching in strict order and even in the heavy rain they showed not the least suggestion of disarray, so I guessed they were a force sent to bring the situation under control, and at that my heart calmed down a little. Suddenly there was an urgent knocking at my door. This turned out to be one of my neighbors, who wanted me agree to go out as a group to welcome the Qing troops and set up a table with burning incense to show that we were not resisting. Even though I knew this wouldn't work, I still wouldn't go against the consensus of the group and at the moment answered, "All right." Then I changed into clothes of a different color and kept a lookout, but for a long time no one showed up.

When I went back to the rear window to get a look at what was happening on the wall, the companies of soldiers had somewhat thinned out; some were on the move and some were standing still. All at once I saw that there were some walking with women clustered among them, and I noticed that the colors of the women's clothes were all in the Yang-zhou fashion. Then I became very alarmed. I went back and said to my wife, "The soldiers are in the city. If something unforeseen should happen, you will have to commit suicide." My wife agreed and said, "I have a certain amount of silver that I want to turn over to you to take care of. We women no longer can envision staying alive in this world." And with tears streaming down her face, she got out her silver and gave it to me.

At this point a domestic came in, shouting urgently, "They're here! They're here!" I rushed out, and looking north I saw several horsemen coming, holding the reins and moving slowly. At once the man who had gone out to welcome the Qing troops bowed his head as though something had been said. At the time everyone was watching out for himself, and there was no normal interchange—even people a few feet away made no comment. When they got somewhat closer, I realized that they were going from house to house looking for money. Still their intentions seemed rather moderate: as soon as they got a little something, they would let people go and demand no more. Some people wouldn't give them what they wanted, but even though they would hold them at sword point, they still didn't hurt anyone. When I later learned that someone had been killed even though he made an offering of ten thousand taels, it was, in fact, because people from Yangzhou itself had led the enemy soldiers to do it.

Next they reached my threshold. One horseman singled me out, pointing to me and shouting to the horseman behind him, "Get something from the one with the indigo blue gown." At that the horseman behind dismounted, but I had already fled and hidden myself. Thereupon the rear horseman let me go, mounted up again, and left. I tried to figure it out to myself. "I'm dressed in rough clothing like a servant—why did they single me out?" After that my younger brother showed up, and one of my older brothers also came. I discussed with them what should be done: "The residences all around me belong to rich merchants. What am I going to do if they take me for a rich merchant as well?" I then entrusted my wife and the others to my eldest brother; he was to go out in the rain and take them as quickly as possible by back lanes to the house of my next oldest brother. His house lay behind the He family tombs, a stinkhole inhabited entirely by poor people.

I stayed on at the house by myself to see what would happen. All at once my oldest brother showed up and said, "The main roads are splattered with blood. What are you waiting for staying here? If we brothers can stay together dead or alive, we should have no regrets." So I reverently took the family's ancestral tablets in my hands and went with my eldest brother to the house of my other older brother. At that time one older and one younger brother, his wife and her child, along with my wife and one child, my two sisters-in-law, and one brother-in-law all took refuge in my brother's house.

Dusk was gradually falling, and the sounds of enemy soldiers killing people came from outside the gate, so we climbed up on the roof to hide for the time being. The rain was very heavy, and a dozen of us were huddled together in one rug, everyone's hair drenched. Outside the gate the voices crying out in pain kept ear and soul in a state of terror on into the night, when all gradually grew still. Only then did we dare get down from the roof, climbing down from the eaves, and lit a fire to cook our meal. Inside the city fires

829

had started up on every side—a dozen or so places nearby and more than we could count farther away. Red beams of light glinted like bolts of lightning, and the crackling sounds roared endlessly in our ears. We also heard the muffled sounds of blows being struck, and now and again we would look around in anguish—the misery was beyond description. When the food was ready, we looked at one another in such a state of shock that no one could use their chopsticks and no one could suggest a plan as to what to do. My wife took out the silver and broke it into four equal parts. My three brothers and I each hid one part. It was everywhere—in our hair, in our shoes, in our clothes, in our sashes. My wife also found a worn-out robe and some battered shoes for me so that I could be comfortable, and then I lay with my eyes wide open all the way to dawn. A bird was singing in the sky that night, its voice like the notes of a reed mouth organ, and there were also sounds like a baby crying, all not far from our heads. Later I asked the others about it, and they had all heard it too.

The twenty-sixth: After a while the force of the fires died down a bit. As the sky gradually grew brighter, we once again climbed up on the roof to keep out of sight, and there were already a dozen people hiding in the roof drains. All of a sudden by the eastern porch a man climbed up over the wall; a soldier was following him sword in hand, bounding along in pursuit as if flying. He looked and saw us, and the group of pursuers gave up on the man they had been chasing and ran in my direction. I was shaking with fear and immediately fled down from the roof; my elder brothers came next, and then my younger brother. After we had run over a hundred paces, we stopped. And from this point on I lost track of my wife and child, not knowing whether they lived or died.

The cunning soldiers were afraid that too many people would hide themselves, so they deceived people by claiming there were orders to bring calm to the populace and that there would be no executions. People in hiding scrambled to come out and follow them, and they had gathered a group of fifty or sixty, with women making up half. My elder brother said, "The four of us are helpless, and if we run into rampaging soldiers who ignore the orders, we won't escape. It would be better to join this large group where it will be easier to hide. And if it doesn't go well, I won't regret it as long as we can die together." At that time our minds were in turmoil, and we didn't know what the best stratagem would be to save our lives. So we all agreed and together went to join the group.

There were three Manchu soldiers in charge of the group. They searched everyone for silver and money, and my brothers were cleaned out of everything they carried, leaving only me unsearched. All of a sudden some people called out to me from the group of women. I looked closely and saw that they were the two concubines of my friend Zhu Shu. I hurriedly stopped them. Both women had disheveled hair and their flesh was showing; their feet were mired deep in the mud up to their calves. One of the women was still carrying her baby daughter. A soldier hit them with his whip and threw the baby into the mud, then drove everyone on. One soldier led the way, holding a sword; a second soldier brought up the rear hefting a long spear; the third soldier sometimes stayed in the group and sometimes went to either side of it to keep anyone from escaping. The several dozen men were driven along like dogs and sheep; if there was the least holding back, the soldiers would immediately beat the person and sometimes kill him on the spot. All the women were tied at the neck by a long rope, like pearls on a string; they would stumble at every other step, and their bodies were covered in mud.[7] Babies lay everywhere on the ground, some in between the hooves of horses and some under people's feet; brains and internal organs were smeared on the ground, and the sound of wailing filled the wilderness.

We walked across ditches and pools stuffed with piles of corpses, hands and feet layered on one another. The blood, flowing into the water, reddened its sapphire blue and made it multicolored. The canal was filled in until it was level with the ground. We came to the compound that had belonged to Judge Yao Yong-yan of the Court of Judicial Review and entered directly through the rear gate. The building held a deep maze of rooms, and everywhere there were piles of corpses. I thought for sure that this would be the place I was to die. But we wound our way through the rooms until we reached the front door, then went out into the street and came to another compound, which was the house of the western merchant Qiao Cheng-wang. This was the lair of the three soldiers.

We entered the gate, and one soldier was already there holding several beautiful women captive inside. Baskets and hampers had been sorted through, and brightly colored silks were heaped like mountains. When this soldier saw that the three others had arrived, he gave a loud laugh and immediately drove our group, the several dozen men, to the rear banquet hall, while keeping the women in a side chamber. In that chamber two square tables were set up, with three seamstresses and a middle-aged woman making clothes. That woman was from Yang-zhou; she was heavily made up in an elegant style and was dressed in splendid clothes with an elaborate hairdo. She was smiling and chattering as she gave orders. She appeared cheerful and quite content, and whenever she found something nice, she would immediately turn to the soldiers and beg to have it with wheedling, ingratiating airs. I regretted that I couldn't snatch one of those soldier's swords and cut the vile creature down. At one point a soldier said to the men, "When we were on the Korean campaign, we captured tens of thousands of women, and not one of them failed to keep her honor. How is it that glorious China has reached this level of shamelessness?" And this, alas, is how China came to these troubles.

The three soldiers then ordered the women to take off all their wet clothes, outer garments and underclothes from tip to toe. At the same time they ordered the women making clothes to measure them for length and girth to furnish them a change of fresh clothing. Under duress the women had no

---

[7]The women's difficulty in walking is no doubt due to their bound feet, making it impossible to keep pace in the muddy streets.

choice and were compelled to face them naked, with their private parts all exposed, and they looked like they would die of shame—the scene was beyond description. When the women had finished changing, they herded them over to drink wine, while keeping up an endless stream of joking and chatter. All of a sudden one of the soldiers hefted his sword and leapt up, shouting sharply to those in the rear banquet hall, "Come on, Southerners, come on!" Several men who approached had already been tied up, and my eldest brother was among them. My next oldest brother said, "Since the situation has come to this, what more can I say?" He then quickly took hold of my hand and pulled me forward; my younger brother also followed him.

At that time there were over fifty males who had been captured; with the mere lifting of a sword and a single shout, their souls took flight, and not a single man failed to go forward. As I followed my older brother out of the rear banquet hall, I saw that outside they were killing the men, and the group just stood in line, each awaiting his fate. At first I had thought that I too would willingly go to be tied up, but all at once, as if by divine aid, my heart balked, and I fled back into the rear banquet hall to hide. And none of those more than fifty men realized it.

The rooms on the west side at the back of the banquet hall still held all the old women, so I couldn't hide there. I went through the central hall to a back room, and it was filled with camels and horses feeding so that I couldn't get through. I felt an increasing sense of desperation, so I crouched down and went under the animals' bellies and came out on the other side after crawling under several bellies. If I had startled one of those camels or horses and one had lifted its hoof just a little, I would have immediately been smashed into mush. I passed through several more levels of rooms, but none offered a route of escape. Only at the side was there a rear gate that led to an alley, but the soldiers had already shut this gate tight with a long spike.

I went from the rear alley back toward the front of the compound and heard the sounds of killing in the front hall; at this my terror increased and I saw no recourse. I looked around and the kitchen was over to the left. The four men in it had been taken to serve as cooks. I asked if they would let me join them, thinking that if they used me to perform menial tasks such as tending the fire or drawing water, I might have a chance. But the four men adamantly refused, saying, "The four of us were selected for this task. If we pick someone else and add to out number, they will surely suspect us of trying to put something over on them, and ruin will come to us." When I wouldn't stop pleading, they got even more furious and wanted to seize me and take me outside.

Then I left and felt even more panic. I looked and saw that in front of the stairs there was a wooden frame, on which there was a jug. It wasn't very far from the room, so I climbed up on the frame; but as soon as my hand reached the jug, I lost my balance and fell, because the jug was empty inside and I had been exerting too much force.

Nothing could be done about it, so I ran quickly to the side alley gate and hit the spike with both my hands and shook it a hundred times. But I couldn't budge it. I then used a stone to hit it, and the sound reached the outer courtyard—I was terrified they would be alerted. I had no choice but to again use all my strength to move it. My fingers were cut and blood flowed, trickling in a stream down to both elbows. Suddenly the spike moved; and using all my strength, I pulled on it. When the spike was in my hand, I hastily worked at the bolt of the gate. The bolt was made of hibiscus wood, and swollen from having been soaked by the rain, so that it was twice as tight as the spike. I was desperate in the extreme, and the only thing I could do was to force the bolt. I couldn't pull the bolt, but the hinges suddenly snapped, and the door of the gate collapsed with a sound like thunder. I quickly leapt up and flew through the opening, and I still don't know where my strength came from. I ran quickly out the back gate and was right at the foot of the city wall.

At the time soldiers and horsemen were everywhere one went. Unable to go on, I ducked into the rear gate of the neighbor to the left of the Qiao compound. Every place a person could hide had someone in it, and they would never let anyone else in. Going from the rear to the front of the compound, I tried five times to get into a hiding place, and in each case it turned out the same way. When I reached the main gate overlooking the street, there were soldiers going back and forth in an unbroken stream. Everyone else had deserted the street as being too dangerous a place to stay. I hurried back in and found a bed. At the head of the bed was a canopy frame. After climbing up the post and curling up inside it, my panting subsided. All of a sudden I heard my younger brother crying out on the other side of the wall; then I heard the sound of a sword chopping; after three chopping sounds, all was silent. After a short interval I again heard my second oldest brother say with desperate earnestness, "I have silver in the cellar of my house; let me go and I'll give it to you." There was a blow and again it was silent. . . .

The narrator's troubles were far from over. When he finally found his wife and what was left of the family, the nightmare was just beginning.

元 Vernacular Stories:
明 Feng Meng-long and Lang-xian

Although the Song Dynasty is the age in which the origins of printed vernacular fiction and the setting for many stories emerged, the earliest actual printed vernacular stories date from the Yuan and early Ming in the fourteenth and fifteenth centuries. Early vernacular stories drew on the plots of stories in the classical language and covered the same range of themes, from tales of the supernatural to romance. To this, however, were added new topics in an urban setting, such as stories of crime and court cases.

Beyond the core of plot, vernacular fiction's resemblance to classical fiction ceases. Early vernacular stories also evoke the ethos of storytelling—addressing the reader, digressing, offering frequent judgments, citing verses, and giving descriptive passages in rhythmic prose. Characterization is more developed and the settings are described in more detail. Vernacular dialogue opened possibilities of nuance in expression that were impossible in the classical language.

Vernacular stories continued to be published throughout the Ming, but the form saw a major resurgence toward the end of the dynasty, in the early seventeenth century. In that remarkable era of fascination with all that was unconventional, serious intellectuals for the first time turned their attention to collecting popular literature and writing in the vernacular. Feng Meng-long (1574–1646) is now recognized as the central figure in this interest in vernacular literature. Feng collected folksongs and jokes, wrote plays and lyrics for popular songs, and elaborated old novels. In addition, he published three large collections of stories, some from his own hand.

"Du Tenth Sinks the Jewel Box in Anger," from Feng's collection *Common Words to Warn the World (Jing-shi tong-yan),* is based on a classical tale and serves as a good example of the conventions of vernacular stories. There is a long, chatty introduction setting the historical background, and, like a storyteller, the narrator breaks into the action with poems, wise sayings, and judgments.

Sixteenth-century China enjoyed a commercial boom comparable to that of contemporary Europe. The Song Dynasty may have seen the beginning of an urban mercantile culture, but the Ming of the sixteenth and seventeenth centuries witnessed its maturity. In Tang tales of romance, economic questions were sometimes present, but they were usually kept just beneath the surface; "Du Tenth Sinks the Jewel Box in Anger" belongs to a long tradition of courtesan romances, but here the exact costs, debts, and the balancing of accounts become central to the story. This is a world of commerce, in which objects are commodities with prices—prices that are sometimes set on things that should not belong in a world of commercial exchange.

Feng Meng-long (1574–1646), "Du Tenth Sinks the Jewel Box in Anger" (from *Common Words to Warn the World*)
Translated by Robert Ashmore

> The last barbarians swept away, the imperial seat is established;
>   soaring dragons and dancing phoenixes—a majestic scene!
> To the left, encircled in a sash of east-sea sky;
>   to the right, hugged by Tai-hang's ten-thousand-mountain walls.[1]
> Halberd and spear: the nine frontiers held in sway to the utmost passes;
>   gown and cap: the myriad fiefdoms look up in reverence to the
>   serene robes of state.
> In a peaceful age, the people rejoice in the realm of Hua-xu;[2]
>   for ever and ever, a golden jar gleaming in the sun.[3]

This poem is devoted to the praise of our dynasty's founding of the capital at Yan.[4] As for the situation of the Yan capital, it is guarded to the north by towering passes, and commands the region of central China to the south. It is truly a golden citadel, a heavenly mansion, a foundation not to be toppled in ten thousand years! In the beginning, Granddad Hong-wu swept away the barbarian dust and established his reign at Jin-ling.[5] This is the capital known as Nanjing. When Granddad Yong-le led his troops out of Bei-ping to pacify the turmoil,[6] the capital was removed to Yan. This is the capital known as Beijing. And all as a result of this removal, what had been a region of bleak chill was transformed into a realm of flowered brocade. From Granddad Yong-le the throne passed down through nine generations to Granddad Wan-li,[7] the eleventh Son of Heaven of our dynasty. He was wise and strong, perfect in both virtue and good fortune. He succeeded to the kingdom at the age of ten and ruled for forty-eight years, during which time he put down three armed uprisings. Which three were they?

The Prime Minister Toyotomi Hideyoshi of Japan, Bei Cheng-en of the Xi-xia, and Yang Ying-long of Bo-zhou.[8]

---

[1]The Bohai Gulf and the Tai-hang Mountain Range formed parts, respectively, of the eastern and southwestern borders of the Northern capital zone in the Ming. The directions "left" and "right" here, as in old Chinese maps, assume a viewer facing south.

[2]Hua-xu: a legendary state characterized by natural and social tranquility.

[3]"Golden jar:" a poetic figure for the solidity and permanence of a nation's borders.

[4]Yan is the ancient name for the region of Beijing.

[5]The Hong-wu emperor Zhu Yuan-zhang (1328–1398) founded the Ming Dynasty in 1368 after defeating the Mongol Yuan Dynasty.

[6]The Yong-le emperor Zhu Di (1360–1424), believed to have been Zhu Yuan-zhang's son by a lesser consort, successfully usurped the throne from his nephew, the Jian-wen emperor Zhu Yun-wen (1377–1402?), in a civil war lasting from 1399 to 1402. Zhu Di subsequently went to great lengths to justify his right of succession, and to depict his own victory in the civil war as the "pacification of turmoil."

[7]Zhu Yi-jun (1563–1620), emperor from 1573 to 1620.

[8]Toyotomi Hideyoshi (1536–1598) gained the title *kanpaku,* or "prime minister," in 1587. At this point, he was effectively military ruler of Japan. He orchestrated invasions of the Korean peninsula in 1592 and 1597.

Toyotomi Hideyoshi invaded Korea, and Bei Cheng-en and Yang Ying-long were native officials[9] who plotted revolt; they were put down one after the other. There were none among the distant tribes who were not frightened into submission, and they strove with one another to pay homage and tribute. Truly,

> One man's blessed fortune brings content to all;
> No trouble within the four seas mars the nation's peace.

Our story picks up during the twentieth year of the Wan-li period,[1] when the Japanese Prime Minister created discord by invading Korea. The King of Korea submitted a missive requesting assistance, and our celestial court dispatched troops to traverse the sea and go to the rescue. Around this time, a proposal by a Bureau of Households official was granted approval, to this effect:

In view of the present armed strife, our logistical supplies are insufficient. Let us provisionally adopt the precedent of accepting payment in exchange for positions in the imperial academy. . . .

Now it turns out that there were several types of advantage for those who bought academy scholar status in this way: it made it easier to study, easier to participate in the civil service exams, and easier to pass. All in all, it added up to a nice little prospect for career advancement. For this reason, the young masters of official families and the scions of wealthy houses became unwilling to take the ordinary licentiates' exam, preferring to take advantage of the quota and become academy scholars. Following the implementation of this practice, the number of scholars at the academies at each of the two capitals rose to over a thousand.

Among this number there was a young man surnamed Li, named Jia, with the cognomen Gan-xian, a native of Shao-xing Prefecture in Zhejiang. He was the eldest of the three sons of his father, Provincial Commissioner Li. From childhood he had been studying in the local school, but had not yet passed the district licentiates' examination. At this time he entered the academy at the Northern capital under the new provision. When he had been enrolled as an academy scholar, he would pass the time in the compound of the Ministry of Music[2] along with his townsman the academy scholar Liu

---

[9]Bo Cheng-en (d. 1592), along with his father, Bo Bai, led a military uprising on the northwestern frontier of the Ming in 1591; they were both killed when the uprising was put down by Ming troops. Yang Ying-long (d. 1600) was a hereditary leader under the Ming of the Miao ethnic minority in the Southwest. He led sporadic raids in the border region between Sichuan and Gui-zhou, sometimes escalating into full-scale revolt, from 1587 until his defeat and suicide in 1600. Ethnic enclaves in remote regions were administered on behalf of the Ming by dominant members of the local ethnic group; once granted, the posts became hereditary.

[1]1592 in the Western calendar.

[2]Originally a kind of imperial conservatory for the training and maintenance of musicians and dancers for the court, by the Ming, the term "Ministry of Music" could also be loosely applied to privately run brothels.

Yu-chun. There he encountered a famous courtesan. She was surnamed Du, named Mei, and was tenth-born of her generation, so in the quarters everyone called her Du Tenth.

She was

> High-toned allure from head to toe;
>   every inch coy scent.
> Two arcs of eyebrow traced with green of distant hills;
>   a pair of eyes bright with welling autumn floods.
> Face like a lotus bud—just like Wen-jun of the Zhuo clan;[3]
>   lips like cherries—not a jot inferior to Fan-su of the Bai
>   household.[4]
> Pity this slip of flawless jade
>   that fell by mistake amid whoredom's flowers and willows!

Du Tenth had lost her maidenhead at the age of thirteen, and was at this time nineteen. During those seven years there is no telling how many lordlings and ducal heirs she had gone through, leaving each of them wanton and besotted with passion—they wrecked households and squandered fortunes without the least regret. A jingle circulated around the quarters that went:

> When Tenth attends a drinking bout
> abstainers quaff till the wine runs out.
> When dandies meet Mei on their rounds,
> They swear the rest all look like hounds.

Now our young master Li was a dashing fellow who had never before encountered real womanly charms. When he ran into Du Tenth, his happiness exceeded all expectation. He took the whole burden of his youthful passion and loaded it on her alone. Our young master had a handsome face and a tender disposition, besides being a big spender and quick to say the right thing. So he and Du Tenth became an inseparable couple who got along in everything. Tenth, knowing how greedy and unjust her madam was, had long been meaning to go straight. Furthermore, when she noticed how sincere and earnest young master Li was toward her, she was very much inclined to throw in her lot with him. The thing was that master Li was deathly afraid of his old man, and did not dare take her up on her proposal. Nonetheless, the two grew ever more devoted to one another, and happily spent both day and night in each other's company, just like a married couple. They swore by seas and vowed by mountains that they would never have thoughts of another. Truly,

---

[3]Zhuo Wen-jun was the wife of the Han Dynasty writer Si-ma Xiang-ru.
[4]Fan-su was a singing-girl in the household of the Tang poet Bai Ju-yi.

Affection as deep as an unfathomed sea;
Loyalty as heavy as mountains, but higher.

Now as for Tenth's madam, what she saw was her girl being monopolized by Master Li—none of those other worthy heirs and lordlings who were drawn by Tenth's reputation could get so much as a peek. In the beginning, when Master Li was spending in grand style, the madam would hunch up her shoulders and laugh ingratiatingly, playing up to him for all she was worth. But days and months went by, and before they knew it, it had been over a year. Master Li's coffers gradually grew empty, and he was unable to spend according to his heart's desires. Then the madam began to snub him. And when old Commissioner Li back home heard that his son was passing his time whoring in the pleasure district, he repeatedly sent letters calling him back home. But Master Li was befuddled with Tenth's charms, and was forever putting off his departure. Later on he heard that his old man was in a towering rage at home, and he became more unwilling than ever to go back. The ancients said, "friendship based on profit grows cold when profit runs dry." But that Du Tenth had a real affection for Master Li, and the more she saw the hard financial straits he was in, the warmer she grew toward him. Her madam told her repeatedly to send Li Jia away from the premises, and when the madam saw that her girl was paying her no mind, she began herself making verbal attacks on Master Li, in hopes of angering him and thus provoking him to take his leave. But the young master was mannerly and subdued by nature, and only became ever more accommodating in his tone.

The madam had nothing for it, and could only browbeat Tenth day in and day out, saying, "In our profession we rely on our guests for both food and clothing. We 'see off the old at the back gate and welcome the new at the front.' Our forecourt stays as lively as a house on fire, and money piles up in a heap. That Li Jia has been hanging around here for over a year now. Forget about new guests, even our old patrons have been cut out of the picture. It's clear as clear can be that it's a ghost-catcher you've brought in here—not even a little ghost would dare set foot in this door! It's to the point where your old lady's household is running on nothing but wind. What way is this to do business?"

Du Tenth could not remain silent in the face of this dressing-down, and answered, "Master Li didn't show up here empty-handed. He's spent big money." The madam said, "That was then; this is now. You just tell him to go and spend some little money to keep your old lady and you in rice and firewood, and that'll do. Those girls in the other houses are all money trees—it's just like magic. Why does it have to be my place that's got all the bad luck? I've raised a money-losing white tiger. Every one of the seven necessities has to be seen to by my poor old self.[5] And it's to the point where

---

[5]The "seven necessities" were firewood, rice, cooking oil, salt, soybean paste, vinegar, and tea, referring generally to day-to-day household expenses.

I have to see to the upkeep of this bum of yours, you lousy slut! Where are my clothes and food supposed to come from? You go and tell that bum: if he's worth anything let him give me a few ounces of silver and buy you out so you can go off with him. Then I can find another girl to support me. How about that?"

Tenth said, "Mama, do you mean that or are you just kidding?" The madam knew that Li Jia had not a penny to his name, and had even pawned all his clothes. She figured he'd never be able to bring it off. So she replied, "When has your old lady ever told a lie? Of course I mean it." Tenth said, "Ma, how much money do you want from him?" The madam said, "If it were anyone else, I'd ask for a thousand or so. But I know that bum can't afford it, so I'll just ask for three hundred. Then I can go find another tart to take your place. But there's just one thing: he's got to give me the money within three days. I'll hand you over to him as soon as he hands me the cash. But if he hasn't got it within three days, then I'm not going to trouble my old self about any 'Master' this or 'Master' that—I'll cudgel his footsoles, and drive that vagrant right out the door. And when that day comes, don't you go finding fault with poor old me!"

Tenth said, "Though the young master may be a little strapped for cash here this far from home, I'm sure he can raise three hundred. But three days is such a short time. Give him ten, and you've got a deal." The madam thought to herself, "This bum has got nothing but a pair of empty hands. Even if I gave him a hundred days, where would he ever get the money? And if he can't raise the money, then no matter how shameless he may be, I'll bet he won't have the nerve to show his face at this door again. Then I can put this house back in style, and Mei won't have a thing to say about it." She answered, "For your sake, then, I'll give him ten days. But if the tenth day comes and he hasn't got the money, don't go trying to blame it on me."

Tenth said, "If he hasn't raised the money inside of ten days, then I'll bet he won't have the gall to come back here. I'm just afraid that if he gets the three hundred taels of silver, Mama may have second thoughts." The madam said, "My poor old self is now fifty-one years old, and I carefully keep the ten fast-days.[6] How should I dare to tell a lie? If you don't believe me, we can slap hands and swear on it. If I go back on my word, let me be reborn as a pig or a dog."

> The ocean's water can't be guessed in cups;
> that farcical old bawd has no goodwill.
> She's sure the struggling scholar's purse is dry,
> and speaks of marriage gifts to trick the girl.

That night, Tenth and the young master discussed their future as they lay in bed. The young master said, "It's not that I don't want this to work out. But getting a girl's name off the courtesans' register is extremely ex-

---

[6]The ten days in each month on which Buddhist lay believers were forbidden to eat meat or slaughter animals.

839

pensive. Nothing less than a thousand taels will do the trick. My purse is empty, down to the last speck. What can I do about it?" Tenth said, "I've already got Ma to agree to only three hundred, but it's got to be raised within ten days. I know you've used up all your traveling funds, but don't you have any friends or relatives in the capital who might lend you some? If you can raise the set amount, then I shall be yours alone, and we can be spared the overbearing behavior of that evil woman." The young master said, "My relations and friends have had nothing to do with me since I began spending all my time in the pleasure quarters. Tomorrow I'll pack up my things and set out, going to each house as if to take my leave. Then I'll bring up the topic of borrowing some money for traveling expenses. If I pool it all together, perhaps I could reach that figure."

He got up and dressed, said goodbye to Tenth, and set out. Tenth said, "Be sure to be quick about it. I will be waiting here for good news." The young master said, "I need no reminding about that." He set out from the gate of the quarters and went in turn to the places of his various relatives and friends, pretending that he was setting off for home and had come to take his leave. When they heard he was headed home, they were in fact glad to hear it. But then he came to the part about lacking traveling money and hoping to borrow some. The adage has it that "the mention of money dissolves predestined ties." His friends and relatives did not respond to his pitch, and, to tell the truth, they had good reason. They thought to themselves, "Here is this Master Li, a big-spending wastrel, enchanted with high living. He's been dallying here a year or so, and his father at home is sick with fury. And today he suddenly wants to set off on his return? There is no telling if this is real or an act. And what if it should turn out that the money he collects as 'traveling expenses' ends up being paid out on whoring debts? If his father should get wind of it, he'd take our good intentions as bad ones . . . One way or another we're sure to end up on somebody's bad side, so when all is said and done, it's cleaner just to turn him down." And so they answered, "It just happens we're a little short at the moment, and unfortunately can't help you out. It's really most embarrassing. . . ." And it was the same with each and every one of them; there was not a single man of noble sentiment to agree to spot him ten or twenty.

Master Li rushed about for three days in a row without a thing to show for it. He did not dare go back to tell Tenth it was no good, so he just made equivocal replies to buy time. When the fourth day came and he still hadn't come up with a plan, he felt too embarrassed to return to the quarters. And since he'd been staying at Du Mei's place lately, he did not even have lodgings of his own. So at this point he found himself with no place to spend the night. All he could do was go to the lodgings of his townsman, the academy scholar Liu, to stay over. When Liu Yu-chun saw the worry clouding the young master's face, he asked him what he had been up to. The young master told him all about how Du Tenth wanted to marry him. Yu-chun shook his head, saying, "I wouldn't be so sure about that. That Du Mei is the number-one courtesan in the pleasure district. If she wanted to go straight, wouldn't there have to be a marriage gift of ten measures of pearls and a good thousand in silver? How could that madam just ask for three hundred? I bet the madam is just down on you for having no money to spend, and taking up her girl's time for nothing. She's made up a plan to get you out of her house. As for the girl herself, she's been with you for a long time, and feels too much compunction to say it outright. She knows good and well you're empty-handed. But by setting this price of three hundred taels, and giving you ten days, she makes it seem like she's doing you a favor. And if you don't have the money in ten days, you won't very well be able to show your face at their door. Even if you did, she'd make fun of you and put you down. You'd end up with a good dose of humiliation, and would naturally find it impossible to settle down there again. This is an old brothel trick for getting rid of unwanted guests. My good friend, I hope you'll consider carefully—don't be taken in! If you want my advice, I'd say your best plan is to make a clean break right away."

On hearing this, the young master sat a long while in silence, not knowing what to think. Yu-chun continued, "My friend, make no mistake. If you really return home, the travel expenses won't come to that much, and there will still be people to help you out. But if it's three hundred you want, well then, forget ten days, in even ten months you could scarcely raise that amount. In this day and age, who do you expect will show understanding for your situation? That mist-and-flowers woman knows you've got nowhere to go to raise that kind of money, and is only telling you all this to put you in an impossible position."

The young master said, "Worthy brother, what you say is quite true." But though he said this, he was unable to fully resign himself to it in his heart. He continued as before to run about here and there looking for help—but at night he did not return to the quarters. The young master lodged for three days running in the rooms of academy scholar Liu, which made six all together. When Du Tenth saw that the master had gone several days without returning, she grew quite anxious, and sent her little servant boy Number Four to go out on the streets looking for him. When Number Four went out, it just happened that he ran into Master Li. Number Four called out to him, "Brother-in-law Li, the mistress is looking for you at home." The young master felt too ashamed to go, and answered, "I haven't got time today. I'll go tomorrow." But Number Four had received strict orders from Tenth, and grabbed hold of the young master and would not let go for anything. He said, "The mistress told me to find you. You've got to come along."

Now the young master was secretly missing that whore, so there was nothing for it but to give in and follow Number Four to the quarters. When he saw Tenth, he just stood there dumbly. Tenth asked him, "How is our plan progressing?" The young master began to shed tears. Tenth said, "Can it be that people have grown so unfeeling that you cannot raise the three hundred?" The young master, with tears in his eyes, said,

"Catching tigers cannot be considered easy,
but begging favors is what's truly hard."

I've been rushing about for six days in a row, and haven't a penny to show for it. With this pair of empty hands I've been ashamed to see you, so these few days I have not dared come here. Today I received your command, and come bearing up under shame. It is not that I haven't tried. But human feelings have in fact come to this pass." Tenth said, "Don't let that wicked crone hear any of this. Stay here tonight, my love—I have another idea." Tenth prepared food and drink, and shared a happy banquet with the young master.

When they'd slept half the night, Tenth said, "My love, can you really not come up with even a single coin? What is to become of the plan for my future?" The young master just wept, unable to answer a single word. Around the fifth watch, it gradually grew light. Tenth said, "The padded quilt I sleep on contains a hundred fifty taels in odd change. This is my private savings. My love, you may take it. I will take care of half of the three hundred, and you can take care of the other half. That should make things easier. But there are only four days left before our time is up. Be sure not to be late."

Tenth got up and gave the quilt to the young master, who was pleased beyond his wildest expectations. He called the servant boy to take the quilt away and took his leave. He went straight to Liu Yu-chun's place, and told him all that had happened the night before. When they opened up the quilt and looked inside, there were odd coins wrapped inside the stuffing. When they took them to exchange, the amount really did come out to one hundred and fifty taels. Yu-chun said, astounded, "This is truly a woman with sincere intentions. Since she has real feeling, she should not be let down. I will see to this on your behalf." The young master said, "If our dream is fulfilled, I promise not to forget you."

Then Liu Yu-chun, leaving Master Li at his place, set out himself to borrow money. Within two days, he had put together the one hundred and fifty taels, and handed them over the master, saying, "It was not for your sake that I borrowed this money, but rather because I am moved by the sincere feeling of Du Tenth."

When Li Jia had the three hundred in hand, it was like a gift dropped from Heaven, and he went off, beaming with joy, to see Tenth. It was only the ninth day, so he had not even used all ten of the allotted days. Tenth asked him, "A few days ago you had a hard time borrowing even the least bit. How is it that now you have suddenly got a hundred fifty taels?" The young master related to her the business with academy scholar Liu. Tenth raised her hands to her forehead, saying, "It is all thanks to the efforts of Mr. Liu that our desires have been fulfilled." The two of them were overcome with happiness, and spent another evening in the quarters.

The next day, Tenth rose early and said to Li Jia, "Once I've handed over this silver, I will be able to follow you. We should prepare the necessary carriages and boats. I have recently borrowed twenty taels of white silver, which you may take to cover our traveling expenses." The young master had just then been worrying that he had no source of traveling money, but had not dared speak of it. When he received this money, he was extremely happy. Before they'd done speaking, the madam came knocking at the door, saying, "Mei, today is the tenth day." When the master heard her call, he opened the door and asked her in, saying, "We have benefited from your kindness, and were just going to invite you here." With this he put the three hundred taels on the table.

The madam had not expected the young master to have money, and stood silently, her expression suddenly changing. She seemed to have it in mind to go back on her promise. Tenth said, "I have been in Mama's house for eight years, and the gold and treasures I have brought in are nothing short of a thousand talents. The happy occasion of my reformation today was granted from Mama's own lips. There is not one jot lacking of the three hundred taels, nor have we passed the time limit. If Mama should go back on her word and prevent us, my husband will take the silver away, and I will make an end of myself this very instant. I fear that then you will have lost both person and profit, and it will be too late for regrets." The madam had no reply to make to this, and pondered it over for a while to herself. In the end, all she could do was bring out a scale to weigh out the silver. She said, "Since it has come to this, I guess I won't be able to stop you. But if you mean to go then go at once. Don't imagine you'll take one bit of your clothes and jewelry along with you."

When she'd done saying this, she pushed the young master and Tenth out the chamber door, found a lock, and locked it right up. It was around November at this time, and Tenth, who had just got out of bed, had not even had time to dress. Wearing the old robe she happened to have on at the time, she bowed twice to her "Mama." Master Li also made a bow. With this they departed, husband and wife, from the door of that old crone.

The carp slips off the iron hook
and glides off without looking back.

The young master asked Tenth to wait up a moment. "I will go and call a sedan chair to carry you. For the time being we can go to Liu Rong-qing's lodgings, and make further plans from there." Tenth said, "All my sisters in the quarters have stood by me through thick and thin. By rights I should go and take my leave of them. What's more it was from them that I got the loan of that traveling money. It would not do to go without thanking them." Thereupon she went with the young master to the homes of all her sisters to thank them and to take leave of them. Of the sisters it was Xie Yue-lang and Xu Su-su who lived closest by, and they were also on especially good terms with Tenth. Tenth went first to Xie Yue-lang's house. When Yue-lang saw Tenth going about in a bare hairknot and old worn robe, she asked in bewilderment what had happened. Tenth told her the whole story, and led Li Jia in to see her. Tenth pointed to Yue-lang, saying, "The travel money I received the other day was the loan of this elder sister. My lord ought to thank her." Li Jia bowed again and again. Then Yue-lang asked Tenth to dress, going in the meanwhile to invite over Xu Su-su.

When Tenth had done making herself up, the two beauties Xie and Xu brought out their whole store—emerald brooches and gold bracelets, jade hairpins and precious earrings, patterned skirts and brocade-sleeved blouses, phoenix sashes and embroidered slippers, and they did up Tenth all over again, so that she looked like a completely different person. They also prepared wine for a celebratory banquet. Yue-lang gave up her own chamber to Li Jia and Du Mei to spend the night.

The next day, they had another big banquet and invited all the sisters from the quarters. None of those who were good friends with Tenth failed to appear, and they all drank to the health and happiness of bride and groom. With pipes and strings, song and dance, each made the most of her talents, intent on making it a joyful gathering. They kept at it right up until midnight. Then Tenth thanked each of the sisters in turn. The assembled sisters said, "Tenth is commander in the legion of glamour. She is now setting out with her man, and we will have no more chance of seeing her. On the day you choose to leave for good, we sisters should once more come to see you off." Yue-lang said to them, "When the time is fixed, I will come and notify you. Our sister will be journeying hundreds of miles over hill and dale along with her husband. Yet her savings are scanty, and she is not in the least prepared. This is a matter that should concern all of us. We should work together to ensure that our sister does not have to worry about being left without resources." All the sisters voiced their assent to this and went their separate ways.

That evening, the master and Tenth lodged once more at the Xie house. At the fifth watch, Tenth said to the young master, "After this departure of ours, where will we settle? Have you come up with some solid plan?" The master said, "My aged father is in the height of rage. If he learns that I've returned home along with a prostitute as my wife, he is sure to make trouble, and I may end up more trouble than help to you. I've thought over this again and again, and I still have no perfect plan." Tenth said, "How could the Heaven-ordained relation of father and son be permanently cut off? But since it is not a good idea to provoke him by a sudden confrontation, it would be better to take up temporary residence in the scenic region of Su-zhou and Hang-zhou. You can return first, and ask friends and relatives to intercede on your behalf before your reverend father and convince him to relent. Then you can come and take me home with you. In this way all will be well on both sides." The young master said, "This is well said."

The next day the two set out, taking leave of Xie Yue-lang, and went for a time to the lodgings of academy scholar Liu to get their luggage ready. When Du Tenth saw Liu Yu-chun, she prostrated herself before him and thanked him for the kind service which had allowed things to work out. "On some future day I swear that we will worthily repay your kindness." Yu-chun hurriedly returned her bow, saying, "You were stirred to true love for your favorite, and did not change your feelings on account of poverty. This makes you a hero among women. All your servant has done amounts to 'blowing a flame along with the wind'—really, what need is there to mention my insignificant efforts!"

The three of them spent another day drinking. The next morning, they selected an auspicious day for their departure and hired the necessary sedan chairs and horses. Tenth once more dispatched her servant boy to take a message to say goodbye to Xie Yue-lang. When it came time to leave, bearers and palanquins began arriving in great numbers. It was Xie Yue-lang and Xu Su-su, who had brought along all the sisters to say goodbye. Yue-lang said, "Tenth sister is following her husband into distant parts, yet their traveling purse is barren. We are by no means able to put aside our sisterly concern, and have raised a meager sum among ourselves. Tenth sister, you may take it under your care. It may be that in your long journey you fall short, and even this may be of some small use." When she had done speaking, she commanded the others to bring forward a gold-inlaid stationery box, which was locked up most securely so that there was no guessing what it might contain. Tenth neither refused it nor opened it to look inside. All she did was to thank them earnestly. In a short while carriage and horses were in readiness, and the attendant urged them to set out at once. Academy scholar Liu poured out three cups of parting wine, and saw them off as far as the outside of Chong-wen Gate, along with the troop of beauties. One by one they tearfully took their leave. Truly,

> None can predict a future meeting date
> This moment of parting is most hard to bear.

Now when Master Li and Du Tenth had traveled as far as the Lu Canal,[7] they left the land and took to boats. By good luck they were able to take advantage of the envoy boat from Gua-zhou,[8] which was about to set out on its return journey. They agreed on a price and reserved a cabin. When it came time to board, Master Li's purse had not the least bit of cash left in it. Now you may be asking, if Du Tenth gave the young master twenty taels of silver, how came it that he suddenly had nothing left? Well, the young master had been whoring in the quarters till his clothes were all bedraggled. When he got his hands on some money, he couldn't help but go to the pawnbroker's to redeem some clothes, and have a set of quilts and bedding made. What was left over was just enough to cover the carriage and horses.

Just as the young master was growing worried, Tenth said, "My husband, don't be troubled. The collection made by all my sisters will surely

[7]Lu Canal: a name for the northern section of the Grand Canal which linked the northern and mid-southern regions of China. The major embarkation point for traffic in and out of Beijing was at Tong-zhou, approximately twenty kilometers east of the city.
[8]Gua-zhou was a transport post at the mouth of the Grand Canal, on the northern bank of the Yangzi River.

help us out." With this, she took out the key and opened up the case. The young master, who was standing to one side, felt ashamed, and did not venture to peek at what was inside the box. Tenth pulled out a red silk pouch and tossed it onto the table, saying, "Why don't you open that up and take a look?" The young master lifted it up in his hand and felt that it was quite heavy. When he opened it up and took a look, he saw it was all white silver, together all of fifty taels. Tenth locked up the box once more without saying what else might be inside. She merely told the young master, "Thanks to the noble feelings of all my sisters, we will not only lack nothing on our journey, but there should be a little something to help with our household expenses while we pass the time in the South." The young master, startled and pleased all at once, said, "If I had not encountered you, my dear benefactress, I, Li Jia, would have been left without even a place to be buried. I will never dare forget this debt of gratitude as long as I live." From this time on, whenever their talk turned to events of the past, the young master would always be moved to tears, and Tenth would try gently to console him. And so they traveled on.

Before they knew it, they had reached Gua-zhou, and the big boat moored at the bank. The young master hired another boat, loaded their luggage onto it, and arranged that they should set out across the river at dawn. It was now around the beginning of January, and the moon was as bright as water as the young master and Tenth sat at the bow of the boat. The young master said, "Ever since we left the capital gate we've been penned up in one little cabin with people all around us, and have been unable to speak freely. Now we've got this whole boat to ourselves, and have no further cause for restraint. Furthermore, we've left the North behind us and are just now drawing near Jiang-nan. It is fitting that we should set ourselves at ease and drink as much as we please, so as to relieve our cooped-up feelings. Dear benefactress, what do you say to that?" Tenth said, "I have grown long unused to conversation and laughter, and I share this feeling of yours. That you should speak of it now is proof of our fellow nature."

Then the young master brought out drinking vessels and arrayed them on the deck, and spread out a felt mat for the two of them to sit on. The cups passed back and forth between them. When they were half-giddy with the wine, the young master, clutching his cup, said to Tenth, "Dear benefactress, your wondrous voice was counted finest among the quarters at the time when my unworthy self first made your acquaintance. Each time I heard one of your incomparable songs, I was unable to restrain the flight of my soul. Much has gone awry since then, and both of us have long been anxious and ill at ease. The simurgh's cry and the phoenix's song have long been silent. Now on this clear river under the bright moon, in the still of the night with no one else to hear, will you deign to sing me a song?"

Tenth as well felt a sudden stirring, and she unleashed her voice and varied her tone, tapping out the time with a fan. Crooning and murmuring, she sang from the scene "The Exam Champion Holds the Cup to Chan-juan" from the opera *Bowing to Moon Pavilion* by the Yuan writer Shi Jun-mei, to the tune of "Little Red Peach." Truly,

> The tone flies up to the Milky Way—clouds stop in their tracks;
> the echo sinks into the deep pool—fish come up to play.

Now on a neighboring boat there was a young man surnamed Sun, named Fu, with the cognomen Shan-lai, who was a native of Xin-an County in Hui-zhou. His family had been in the salt trade at Yang-zhou for generations and had amassed an immense fortune. Sun Fu was just twenty years old at this time, and was also a fellow of the Nanjing Imperial Academy. He was glamorous by nature, accustomed to buying smiles in the "blue houses," seeking happiness in rouge and powder just as if on a jaunt to enjoy breeze and moonlight. He was a commander in the legion of loverboys. Well, co-incidences will happen, and it came about that on that evening he was also moored at the ferry dock at Gua-zhou, drinking alone in boredom. Suddenly he heard the bright sound of a singing voice—chanting phoenix and piping simurgh could not compare to it in beauty. He rose and stood at the prow, listening raptly for a while.

Soon he divined that the sound was coming from the neighboring boat. Just as he was making ready to inquire, the resounding tones grew suddenly still. Thereupon he dispatched a servant to ask the boatmen what it was. All they knew was that the boat had been hired by his excellency Li, but they did not know the background of the singer. Sun Fu thought to himself, "This singer is certainly not of respectable background. Now, how can I get a look at her?" He mused over this, staying awake all night. When he'd stuck it out to the fifth watch, he suddenly heard the wind on the river kicking up fiercely. By dawn the sky was packed with dusky clouds, and snow swirled wildly about. How can we know about this scene? There is a poem bearing witness:

> A thousand hills wiped clean of clouds and trees;
>   the tracks on countless human paths swept clear.
> In poncho and rainhat, an old man on a skiff
>   fishes alone in the snow of the cold river.[9]

With this snowstorm enveloping the ford, the boats were unable to set out. Sun Fu commanded his helmsman to move the boat, mooring it by the side of Li Jia's boat. Sun Fu, in ermine cap and foxfur coat, opened the window and looked out, pretending to be enjoying the snowy scene. Du Tenth had just then finished washing. With her slender jade white hands, she lifted up the short curtain at the side of the boat and emptied the washbasin into the river. Her powdered face shone out for a moment, and Sun Fu got a peek. Sure enough, she was a heavenly beauty, and his soul was shaken and his

---

[9]This is the poem "River Snow," by the Tang poet Liu Zong-yuan (773–819), with minor alterations.

heart went wild. He stared intently at the spot, waiting for another chance to see her, but he had no such luck. He sat long in a funk, and then loudly chanted these two lines of Scholar Gao's "Poem of Plum Blossoms":[1]

> Snow fills the mountain slopes, the recluse lies at ease;
> moonlight shines beneath the forest's eaves—the lovely one approaches.

When Li Jia heard someone chanting poetry in the neighboring boat, he stretched his head out of the cabin to see who it was. And with this he fell right into Sun Fu's trap. Sun Fu was chanting that poem precisely in order to entice Master Li to poke his head out, so there would be a chance to start up a conversation. Right away Sun raised his hand in greeting and asked, "Respected friend, what is your surname and given name?" Master Li told him his name and native place, and of course it would not do not to ask Sun Fu in turn. Sun Fu introduced himself as well. Then they exchanged some idle talk of the academy, gradually growing more cordial as they chatted. Then Sun Fu said, "This snowstorm which has delayed our boats was Heaven's way of granting me the chance to meet you—this is truly a stroke of good fortune for me! Lodging on board a boat is tiresome and monotonous. It is my sincere wish to go ashore with you for a drink in the wineshop, so as to receive some small portion of your wise instruction. I earnestly beg that you not refuse me!" The young master said, "We have met like drifting duckweed on the water. What right have I to put you to such trouble?" Sun Fu said, "What can you possibly mean? 'Within the four seas all are brothers.'"[2]

He barked out an order to the boatmen to leap over and to the servant boy to hold open an umbrella and receive the young master on board his boat. Sun Fu came right up to the bow of his boat to greet him. Then, making room for the young master to lead the way, Sun followed up as they went ashore. Before they'd walked more than a few steps, they came upon a wineshop. The two walked upstairs and sought out a clean spot beside the window. The steward laid out wine and snacks before them. Sun Fu raised his cup and urged Master Li not to stand on ceremony, and the two of them sat drinking and enjoying the snowy scene. First they exchanged a few polite commonplaces, but soon the conversation turned toward affairs of the heart. The two of them were both men of the world, and found in each other sympathetic listeners.

As their talk became relaxed and unrestrained, they grew ever more confidential. Sun Fu sent away all the attendants and asked in a low voice, "Who was the clear-voiced singer on your boat last night?" Li Jia was just then anxious to play the man of the world, and he blurted out, "That was Du Tenth, the famous courtesan from Beijing." Sun Fu said, "If she is a sister from the quarters, how is it she has become part of your household?" Then

---

[1] Scholar Gao is the Ming Dynasty poet Gao Qi (1336–1374).
[2] A familiar quotation from the *Analects,* XII.5.

the young master told all about how he first met Du Tenth, how they became lovers, and how later she wanted to marry him and how he borrowed money to win her, from beginning to end in full detail.

Sun Fu said, "My dear friend, your return home with this beauty is certainly a happy event. What I wonder is, will your family be able to accept her?" The young master said, "My humble mate is no cause for concern. What worries me is my old father, who is by nature strict and unyielding. This is still causing me some hesitation." Sun Fu, adapting his strategy to the circumstances, asked, "If you fear your reverend father may not accept her, where do you plan to settle this lovely whom you are escorting? Have you spoken to her of this and made plans together?" The young master wrinkled up his brows and answered, "I have in fact discussed this matter with my unworthy consort." Sun Fu asked with a smile, "Surely your esteemed pet has a splendid strategem." The young master said, "It is her intention to take up temporary residence in Su-zhou or Hang-zhou, to linger for a while among the hills and lakes. She would have me return first and ask relations and friends to put things delicately before the head of my family. At such time as he shall change his ire to pleasure, we will consider how we may best return. But what do you make of this?"

Sun Fu sat murmuring to himself for a while, and put on an anxious expression. He said, "I made your acquaintance only a short time ago. If I presume on such a brief friendship to speak frankly to you, I truly fear that you will be offended." The young master said, "I find myself just now in need of your wise instruction. Why need you stand on ceremony like this?" Sun Fu said, "Your esteemed parent holds the keys of the provincial government, and is sure to be strict about maintaining propriety in the affairs of his household. From the beginning, he has been displeased that you frequented houses of ill fame. How then can he be expected to accept your marriage to an unchaste woman? Furthermore, which of your noble friends and relations will not be solicitous of the wishes of your esteemed parent? If you vainly ask them for favors, they are sure to refuse. And even supposing that some tactless one among them puts in a word on your behalf, once he sees that your esteemed parent does not mean to give in, he will surely change his tune. You will find yourself unable either to restore harmony to your family or to answer to your esteemed pet. Even whiling away the time amid the scenery of hills and lakes is no long-term solution. If some day your savings should run out, will you not be left with nowhere to turn?"

The young master knew that all he had left was the fifty taels of silver, and by now even that had largely been spent. When he heard this part about being left with no place to turn, he unconsciously began nodding his assent. Sun Fu continued, "I have one thing further to say. Will you indulge me by listening?" The young master said, "You are too kind. I beg you say everything that is on your mind." Sun Fu said, " 'Distant relations should not come between close ones.' On second thought, I think it is better not to say it." The young master said, "Just say it, what harm can there be in that?" Sun Fu said, "Of old it has been said, 'woman's nature is water, devoid of constancy.' How much more so of the league of mist and flowers, who lack truth and abound in artifice? Given that she is a famed courtesan of the pleasure districts, she must have acquaintances everywhere under the sun. It may just be that she has a previous engagement in the South, and is making use of you to bring her there, to run off with someone else." The young master said, "As for that, I really don't think that that is the case." Sun Fu said, "Even if it isn't, the young men of Jiang-nan are champion womanizers. If you keep such a lovely alone there, it is hard to be sure there won't be some 'fence-climbing and wall-tunneling.' And if you take her along home with you, it is certain you will further inflame your esteemed parent's anger against you. There really seems to be no good way out of your present situation. Moreover, the relation of father and son is sanctioned by Heaven, and is by no means to be abrogated. If you offend your father on account of a concubine, if you abandon your family due to a prostitute, everyone in the world will surely agree that you are a reckless and outlandish person. In the future your wife will not treat you as a husband, your brother will not treat you as brother, and your colleagues will not treat you as a colleague. How will you find a place to stand between Heaven and Earth? My friend, you really cannot but consider this carefully."

When the young master heard all this, he was dazed and at a loss for words. He edged his seat closer and asked, "As you see it, what advice would you give me?" Sun Fu said, "Your servant has one plan which could be most advantageous. I only fear that you, enamored as you are of the joys of pillow and mat, will not necessarily be able to carry it out, in which case it would be a mere waste of words to tell you." The young master said, "If you have a plan that can allow me once more to know the joy of a harmonious family, you are truly my benefactor. What need have you to be fearful of telling me?" Sun Fu said, "You have been roaming away from home for over a year, and your stern parent has become enraged. Chamber and tower are set at odds. Imagining myself in your position, it seems this must be a time when there can be no peace of mind in sleep or at table. However, the cause of your esteemed parent's anger with you is nothing more than your fondness for the land of 'flowers and willows,' for which you spend money like dirt. You must seem sure to turn out a homeless wastrel, and thus not suited to inherit the family fortune. To go home empty-handed at such a time would be just the thing to set him off. But if you are willing to set aside the affections of quilt and mattress, and act decisively when opportunity presents itself, I would be willing to present you with a thousand taels. With these thousand taels to placate your esteemed parent, you can claim that you kept to your chambers at the capital and have not wasted the least bit. Your esteemed parent is sure to believe this. From then on your family will be at peace, and there should be no further grumbling. In no time at all you could change disaster into good fortune. Please think this over carefully. It is not that I am covetous of the charms of the lovely one. The truth is that I am eager to give some small expression of my devotion to your welfare."

Now Li Jia had always been a man with no backbone who, when all was said and done, was terrified of his dad. Sun Fu's little talk went right to the heart of his fears. He rose and bowed, saying, "On hearing this instruction from you, the scales have fallen from my eyes. But my little consort has stood by me through a journey of hundreds of miles; I cannot in justice cut her off all at once. Allow me to return and discuss it with her. When I have received her earnest assent, I will come back and present my reply." Sun Fu said, "When you talk to her, you ought to put it delicately. But if she is really motivated by sincere loyalty to you, she's sure to be unwilling to cause father and son to split. She'll certainly do her part to bring about your successful return home."

The two of them drank a while longer, and when the wind settled and the snow stopped, it was already quite late. Sun Fu told his servant boy to settle the bill, and he led the young master by the hand down toward the boats. Truly,

> With strangers, say a third of what you think;
> don't throw out all your heart's designs at once.

Now we turn to Du Tenth in the boat. She set out wine and dainties, meaning to share a small banquet with the young master. When he failed to return all day, she trimmed a lamp and sat up waiting for him. When the young master came aboard, Tenth rose to greet him. He had a flustered expression and seemed to have something unhappy on his mind, so she poured out a full cup of warm wine and tried to console him. But the young master shook his head and refused to drink. Without uttering a single word, he went right to bed alone and lay down. Tenth was worried by this, and, after gathering up the cups and trays, she came and helped Master Li undress and make ready to sleep. She asked him, "What has happened that has put you in such a gloomy mood?" The young master just sighed, still not opening his mouth to speak. She asked him the same thing three or four times, but in the end she noticed he had already nodded off. Tenth could not resolve it in her mind, and sat at the side of the bed, unable to sleep.

In the middle of the night, the young master woke up and sighed once more. Tenth said, "My lord, what difficult matter do you have in your mind, that you sigh so?" The young master sat up, clutching the blankets about him, and made as if to speak, but stopped short several times. And then streams of tears began running down his cheeks. Tenth clasped the young master in her bosom and spoke softly to comfort him, saying, "You and I have been lovers for two years now, and we have held out to this day through innumerable trials and reversals, and every manner of difficulty. But through all the hundreds of miles of our journey together I have never seen you grieve like this. Now we are preparing to cross the river, on the verge of a new lifetime of happiness. How is it that you instead grow sad and troubled? There must surely be some reason. Husband and wife share all equally between them, in life and death. If any problem arises it can surely be talked over. Do not be afraid to say whatever is on your mind."

The young master, thus repeatedly egged on, could not hold out, and at last said tearfully, "I was left destitute and without recourse at the ends of the earth. I undeservingly received your forbearing indulgence, and you consented to follow me to this place. It is truly an incomparable favor that you have done me. But I have pondered it over and over; my father, in his position of local prominence, is subject to strict standards of propriety. Furthermore, he himself is stern and inflexible by nature. I fear that if I add to his ire, he is sure to run me out of the house. If you and I are forced to wander rootlessly, where shall we come to rest? The joys of husband and wife will be hard to preserve intact, while the relation of father and son will be broken. During the day, I received an invitation to drink from my new friend Mr. Sun of Xin-an. He considered this problem on my behalf . . . yet my poor heart feels as if it is being cut!"

Tenth said in great alarm, "What is it you mean to do?" The young master said, "Being as I was personally involved in the situation, I was unable to grasp it clearly. Now my friend Sun has devised a plan for me which seems quite good. My only fear is that you, my love, will not give your assent to it." Tenth said, "Who is this friend Sun? If the plan is a good one, what can there be against following it?" The young master said, "My friend Sun is named Fu, a salt merchant from Xin-an. He is a stylish young fellow. During the night he heard the clear tones of your voice, and thus inquired about you. I told him your background, as well as the reasons making my return home difficult. He has it in mind to take you in for one thousand taels. With that thousand taels I will have a pretext on which to call on my parents, and you, my dear benefactress, will also have someone to rely on. But I cannot bear to give up the affection I feel for you. It is for this reason that I am grieved and weep." When he had said this his tears fell like rain.

Tenth removed her hands from him and laughed coldly, saying, "The man who devised this plan for you is truly a great hero. The fortune of the thousand taels will enable you to restore your position in your family, and I will go to another man so as not to be a burden to you. 'Originating in feeling and stopping in accordance with propriety'[3]—truly this can be called a strategy with advantage on all sides. Where are the thousand taels?" The young master dried his tears and said, "Since I had not received your approval, the money has not yet been exchanged. It is still over at his boat." Tenth said, "Go first thing in the morning to settle it with him. You mustn't let this opportunity slip by. But a thousand taels of silver is a serious matter. You must be sure to have it counted out in full and securely in your hands before I go over to his boat—do not fall victim to an unscrupulous trader." By this time it was nearly the fourth watch, and Tenth got up and lit a lamp and made herself up, saying, "Today's dressing is for the purpose of 'welcoming the new and seeing off the old.' It's no ordinary occasion."

---

[3]"Originating in feeling and stopping in accordance with propriety"—a quote from the "Great Preface" to the *Classic of Poetry*.

Having said this, she attentively made herself up with powder and perfume. In her ornate bracelets and embroidered jacket, she looked splendid. A fragrant breeze seemed to play about her, and she radiated a brilliance that dazzled all who saw her. By the time she was done dressing, it was just beginning to grow light outside. Sun Fu's servant boy came to the bow of their boat to await news. Tenth looked in at the young master, smiling as though pleased with how things were going, and urged him to go and give his reply, and to quickly count out the silver in full. The young master went in person to Sun Fu's boat, and replied that he agreed to everything. Sun Fu said, "Counting out the silver is not a problem. But I would like to have the lovely's make-up stand as security." The young master went back once more to pass this reply on to Tenth. She pointed to the gold-inlaid stationery box, saying, "Go on and take it."

Sun Fu was greatly pleased. He then took one thousand taels of white silver, and sent it off to the young master's boat. Tenth counted it out herself and found to that it was sufficient in both purity and amount, without the least error. Thereupon she grasped the gunwale and waved to Sun Fu, and as soon as Sun Fu saw her, his soul flew out of him. Tenth opened her crimson lips, exposing gleaming teeth, saying, "Please send back that box I sent over just now. In it are some travel documents of Master Li's which should be picked out and returned to him." Sun Fu already regarded Tenth as a turtle in his trap, and without hesitation ordered his servant to carry that gold-inlaid stationery box right over and place it at the prow of Li Jia's boat. Tenth took out the key and opened the lock. Inside the box were many small drawers. Tenth asked the young master to pull out the first drawer to look, and there was all kingfisher feathers and bright pendants, jade hairpins and jeweled earrings filling it up inside, probably worth several hundred taels.

Tenth threw it all right into the river. Li Jia and Sun Fu and the rest of the people on the boats were all astonished. She then told the young master to open another drawer. It was filled with jade whistles and golden pipes. He opened another drawer full of antique knicknacks of ancient jade and purple gold, probably worth several thousand. Tenth threw all this into the great river. People began gathering on the bank, until they packed the entire shoreline. They said with one voice, "What a shame!" and were left standing there, wondering what it was all about.

Finally Li Jia opened one more drawer. Inside this drawer there was another box. When he opened the box and looked, there were handfuls of priceless pearls, and all sorts of sapphires, cat's-eyes, and rare treasures such as they had never seen before. There was no guessing at their worth. The crowd of people all cheered lustily, and the noise of their commotion was like thunder. Tenth made as if to throw these things as well into the river. In that instant Li Jia was overcome with remorse. He clasped Tenth and wailed aloud. Then Sun Fu came over as well and tried to reason with her. Tenth pushed the young master to one side and cursed Sun Fu, saying, "Mr. Li and I have endured every kind of hardship. It was no easy thing for us to come this far. But you with your lecherous intentions hatched a cunning plot that has dissolved all our destined life together in a single day, and destroyed the love and affection between us. You are my sworn enemy. If I have consciousness after death, I swear I will take my grievance against you to the clear-eyed gods. And you dream of sharing the joy of pillow and mat with me!"

Then she said to Li Jia, "I languished in a fallen life for several years, during which time I amassed some private savings. This was meant as a provision against old age. I did not intend for those mountain vows and ocean oaths that we exchanged to be broken even in our declining years. That day as we were leaving the capital, I used the pretext of my sisters' parting gifts to store these hundred treasures in this box. There is no less than ten thousand taels here. I meant to use this to set you up in such style that you could return to see your parents without shame. Perhaps they might have taken pity on me for my sincerity and allowed me to assist your wife in the duties of the household, so that I could live out my life relying on you, with no regrets to my dying day. How could I have guessed that your trust in me was so shallow that you could be confused by groundless counsel? You have abandoned me at midjourney and betrayed my earnest heart. Today, before these many eyes, I open this box to reveal its contents, so that you may learn that a thousand taels is no great thing. In my jewel case there is true jade; I regret that you lack eyes in your head to see it. Born in an ill-fated hour, I fell into the bonds of a shameful life. And just as I made good my escape, I have been cast aside once more. Today every person who has ears and eyes can witness that it is not I who have betrayed you, but rather you who have betrayed me!"

At this the crowd that had gathered to watch all shed tears, every last one of them, and they all cursed Master Li for a heartless deceiver. The young master was both ashamed and grieved. He wept with remorse, and was just beginning to beg for her forgiveness when, clutching the treasure box, she plunged right into the heart of the river. The crowd cried out in alarm for someone to save her. But all that could be seen were dark clouds over the river, and the restless waves—there was no trace of her. Alas, a famed courtesan, beautiful as flowers or jade, left all at once to be entombed in fishes' bellies!

> The three souls settle to the water-kingdom's trackless depths;
> the seven spirits set off on the distant road of darkness.

At the time, the people who were watching gnashed their teeth in fury, climbing over one another in their desire to thrash Li Jia and Sun Fu, which startled these two so badly they didn't know what to do. They hurriedly called out to the boatmen to set out, and went off in separate directions. Li Jia sat in his boat looking at the thousand taels and thinking back on Tenth, brooding day in and day out on his shame. These oppressive feelings eventually drove him crazy, and he never recovered as long as he lived. As for Sun Fu, after the shock of that day he fell ill and was bedridden for over a month. All day he would see Du Tenth beside him, cursing him. In time, he died. People said it was revenge exacted from the depths of the river.

And now we speak of that Liu Yu-chun. When his stint in the academy at the capital was up, he packed up his things to return home, and moored at Gua-bu.[4] He happened to drop a bronze washbasin in the river as he was washing his face over the water, and he sought out a fisherman to fish it up with his net. When the net came out, what was inside was a little case. Yu-chun opened the case to look, and in it were bright pearls and rare treasures, precious things of inestimable price. Yu-chun richly rewarded the fisherman, and kept the things by his bedside to play with them. That night in a dream he saw a woman out in the river, striding toward him over the waves. When he looked closely, it was Du Tenth. She approached him and greeted him, and complained to him of Mr. Li's unfeeling behavior. She also said, "I was the recipient of your gracious assistance, when you helped us out with that hundred and fifty taels. I originally meant to seek out a way to repay you when we came to the end of our journey. Little did I know that there was to be no constancy from beginning to end. Yet I often bear your noble favor in mind, unable to forget it. This morning I presented you a small case by way of the fisherman as a small token of my heartfelt thanks. From this time on, we shall never meet." When she had done speaking, he awoke all at once in alarm. Only then did he realize that Tenth had died, and he sighed with pity for several days.

Those who later assessed the merits of this case felt that Sun Fu, who thought nothing of throwing away a thousand taels in a plot to steal away a lovely woman, was certainly no gentleman, while Li Jia, who failed to recognize Du Tenth's sincere devotion, was a vulgar person not even worth talking about. But most of all they wondered why a rare hero among women like Tenth could not find a mate worthy of her, to ride away together on a Qin Terrace phoenix.[5] Yet she mistakenly took up with Master Li, casting bright pearls and lovely jade before a blind man. The result was that gratitude was made enmity, and their ten thousand feelings of affection were changed to flowing water. This is most pitiful! A poem lamenting this event says:

> Do not talk idly of romance if you don't know the game;
> a world is hidden there within love's name.
> If one knew all of love that was in love to know,
> the epithet "romantic" should be thought no cause for shame.

---

[4]Gua-bu is on the north bank of the Yangzi, about sixty kilometers upstream of Gua-zhou. It seems possible that the two places are conflated here.

[5]A reference to the story of Xiao Shi and Nong Yu, daughter of Duke Mu of the state of Qin. Xiao Shi was an expert player of the *xiao,* a whistlelike instrument, and could imitate the call of the phoenix. At last, a phoenix descended to the couple at the terrace built for them by Duke Mu and carried them off to Heaven together.

In Feng Meng-long's final collection of stories, *Constant Words to Awaken the World (Xing-shi heng-yan)*, there appears a group of stories by another hand, a writer known only by his pseudonym Lang-xian, the "Wild Immortal," also tentatively identified as the author of another collection of vernacular stories entitled *The Rocks Nod Their Heads (Shi dian tou)*. "Censor Xue Finds Immortality in the Guise of a Fish," based on a Tang tale, is one of the Lang-xian stories in Feng's collection.

The tale of heaven-sent suffering that leads to enlightenment and the renunciation of public life had a long history in the literary tradition, but rarely did it take on the comic dimensions it has here. Trapped in the body of a fish, Censor Xue rails helplessly against his friends and colleagues as they debate whether to dine on him. The mode of filleting and preparation, in which Censor Xue had himself instructed his cook, is described in loving culinary detail, with the good censor himself as the main course under consideration.

Lang-xian, "Censor Xue Finds Immortality in the Guise of a Fish" (from *Constant Words to Awaken the World*) Translated by Robert Ashmore

Pray, how did that white dragon come to be?
—all through a puny fish's sincerity.
Though now the dragon sport in the broad stream,
    if rain and cloud's force failed him,
    wouldn't he be bogged in mire?

To learn the transformations of the airy soul,
    rest rudderless, always empty.
It's not sudden joy that dulls the senses:
    Zhuang Zhou was once a butterfly,
    and Xue Wei became a fish.

The story has it that in the Qian-yuan era [A.D. 758–760] of the Tang emperor Su-zong there was an official by the name of Xue Wei. This Xue Wei was a native of the Wu district, who had passed the *jin-shi* examination at the end of the Tian-bao era [A.D. 742–756]. He started out as a district prefect in Fu-feng, where he built up quite a reputation. Later he was transferred to the post of Censor in Qing-cheng district in Sichuan. His wife, a certain Madam Gu, from the leading family of Wu County, was a lovely woman with a kind and gentle temperament. The two of them were a perfect match, and lived together in mutual love and respect. Before they knew it three years had gone by at the new post, and the district magistrate left town on a promotion. Censor Xue's superiors, knowing well his character and ability, appointed him to take over the seal of the district administration.

Now this Qing-cheng district was made up of remote mountains and deep valleys with rocky and infertile soil. Years of poor harvests had left the people destitute, and from time to time there were outbreaks of banditry. As soon as Censor Xue took over the district administration, he instituted a system of local accountability, and enlisted the cooperation of the citizenry in apprehending bandits wherever they cropped up. He also set up a public academy to foster young talent, and opened the relief granaries to assist the helpless and destitute. Every spring he would go personally into each village to supervise the plowing and planting, and would exhort the people with well-meaning words to do their best to play their allotted roles in the community. As a result of all this, crops flourished throughout the county and the very bandits were transformed into upright citizens. Truly, public order reached the point that "doors were left open at night, and lost valuables remained where they fell by the roadside." The common folk, out of gratitude for the benefit which had been bestowed on them, composed a ditty in praise of the Censor's achievements.

Which went,

In autumn there's harvest,
and plowing in spring.
no overseer extorts rent;
our doors lie unlatched at night.

The people set happily to their tasks,
schools bring culture's blessings:
moral and material benefit,
all through Father Xue's goodness.

From this day on in our children's line,
we vow to preserve his name.
what will we call them?
"Xue's son" and "Little Xue."

That Censor Xue was not only an upright and compassionate official who loved the people like his own children; in his dealings with his colleagues, too, he was respectful and modest, treating them well in every way. As it happens, in that district seat there were a deputy magistrate, a censor, and two prefects. The district magistrate was called Zou Pang. He was also a *jin-shi* graduate—in fact, it happened that he was a good friend of Xue's from the same class. The two prefects were named Lei Ji and Pei Kuan, and they also performed their duties in a scrupulous and ethical manner. The four of them had so much in common in character and interest that whenever they had a spare moment, they could be found together discussing poetry, playing chess, or sitting beside flowers or in the shade of a bamboo grove, sharing a drink together. They were constant companions who got on splendidly.

One evening, just when the Seventh Night festival had come around, Censor Xue and his wife were together in their official quarters to "pray for skill" and hold their own private celebration . . . (Now as it happens, on the evening of the Seventh Night festival, every family of whatever social station would be sure to set out some wine and a few dainties for the banquet of "praying for skill and threading the needle." Now why do you imagine that was? It all came about because of a certain daughter of the Emperor of

Heaven, named the Weaver Woman, who worked away at her loom day and night. The Emperor of Heaven was fond of her for her industry, and married her to Oxherd to be his wife. But—who'd have guessed it!—once the Weaver Woman had married Oxherd, she was carried away with the joys of love, and spent the days combing her hair and making herself up; she never tended to loom and shuttle any more. The Emperor of Heaven was enraged, and banished the Weaver Woman to live on the east side of the Milky Way, and Oxherd to live on the west. In the whole year they were permitted to meet just once, on this seventh day of the seventh month. On this day, magpies were sent to fill in the Milky Way for them so that they could cross over. Because of this, the people of this world would keep track of the time when they were to cross, and, standing out beneath the stars and moon, would thread colored threads through needles' eyes—if one could thread it through, that meant "receiving skill," and if one couldn't that meant "missing skill." In this way they would predict their skill in handiwork during the year to come. Now just stop and think for a moment: Oxherd and Weaver Woman had been longing all year for this one night when they could finally meet. What's more, they were only given three or four hours to pour out their sincere longing all at once, still fearing there might not be time enough to tell it all. How could they possibly have enough spare time to come to the human world delivering skill? Is this not an absurd tale?)

Now on that evening, Censor Xue was in his courtyard, exchanging toasts with his wife. Losing track of the time, they sat up until deep in the night. Unexpectedly, Censor Xue took a little chill from the dewy night breezes, and this chill soon grew into a serious illness. His whole body felt as hot as if it were being roasted over coals and sweat poured from him like rain. Gradually he stopped eating altogether, and lost track of what was going on around him. He mumbled, "I can't hold out another instant! Why must you force me to stay here? Why don't you just let me go. . . ." Now you may well imagine that when a sick person begins speaking like this, it is not good news. It so frightened Madam Gu that her wits and courage both flew from her in an instant. But could she just sit there and watch him die? Of course she had to call in doctors and consult diviners, summoning spirits and offering up vows to the gods. As it happens, in that district there was a certain Qing-cheng Mountain—the fifth immortal grotto of the Daoist sect. On that mountain stood a temple in which there was an image of Lao-zi which had been proven to be of marvelous efficacy. Truly, if one prayed to it for clear skies one got clear skies, if for rain then it rained; if one prayed for a son one got a son, if for a daughter, a daughter. Pilgrims flocked there from far and wide. So Madam Gu wrote out a spirit-petition, and sent people to that Lao-zi temple to pray. She'd also heard that the fortune-slips of that temple were most accurate, so she had them on one hand pray for the protection of the Censor, to extend his lifespan and avert the calamity besetting him, and on the other to ask for a fortune-slip, to try to get some idea how the thing was likely to come out. And as for those three colleagues, who had long admired Censor Xue for his virtue, when they heard what had happened, they went on foot to the mountain to present offerings of incense, and to express their willingness to forfeit part of their own allotted lifespans in order to release the Censor from his peril. And just when the three colleagues had turned back homeward, there came the elders of the entire county, leading the common folk, who came in a body to prostrate themselves and pray. It was proof of the good effect of the Censor's accustomed way of governing that he could win over the hearts of the people like this.

Now the slip they drew was number thirty-two. The rhyme on that slip said:

> A hundred streams flow down to the river,
> Peer down in the deep and hold back a shiver.
> Why wander to Longmen to seek what you wish?
> Three foot two, the enchanted fish.

A servant was sent to take a copy of this riddle back to the lady at the district seat, yet she could make no more of it than they. She thought to herself, "I have heard that the slips people have received in the past have always suited the person in question in every detail. How is it the one we've drawn speaks of some condition not the least like my husband's? Is this a good omen, or an evil one? It's really beyond me." Her hopes and fears grew more tangled and confused than ever, and her anxiety increased. But then she thought, "It's plain that this slip may have no bearing on the situation at all. Let me find a doctor to treat the disease—that at least is a sound approach." And she commissioned people to search about. Well, they found out about a certain Daoist adept named "Eight Hundred" Li, who lived in the prefectural capital of Cheng-du. He was said to have been the leading disciple of the great Master Sun;[6] and, since he'd received eight hundred secret cures from his teacher, people called him "Eight Hundred" Li. And truly, when he was called in to treat someone, the sickness would be gone as soon as he'd set his hand to it; he was uncannily effective. He'd hung a New Year's couplet over his door which read,

> Like Druggist Kang, I never change my price;[7]
> Like Doctor Feng, I have apricots in groves.[8]

The thing was, when you called him in, you could never be quite sure he'd come. If he did agree to come, then you could bet there was some hope for that patient. The fees he required were also different from the common run of doctors: Sometimes he'd demand several hundred taels before he'd

---

[6]Master Sun: Sun Si-miao (581–682), a hermit-scholar famed during the early Tang Dynasty for his medical expertise. The dates given here are based on Sun's own report, but popular tradition suggested he had lived several hundred years.

[7]"Druggist Kang": Han Kang (mid-2nd c.), a hermit-sage who, hoping to avoid the public eye, supported himself selling herbal medicines in the Eastern Han capital of Chang-an. He became famous in spite of himself for never changing a price in thirty years.

[8]Doctor Feng was a legendary doctor said to have been active around the turn of the third century. He is supposed to have asked the patients he cured to plant apricot trees in lieu of monetary payment.

so much as opened up his medicine case; at other times even after curing the patient he would not ask for a single penny in compensation—he'd just want someone to treat him to one roaring drunk. Sometimes he'd set out as soon as he got the summons; at other times there was no budging him no matter how one begged. He was a hard one to fathom. As a general rule, though, if one were sincere about it he'd be willing to come.

When Madam Gu learned of this medical man, she immediately dispatched a servant bearing tokens of earnest to set out in the middle of the night and invite that "Eight Hundred" Li. As luck would have it, he was in the prefectural capital, and came as soon as he was called. With this the lady's mind was eased somewhat. Who'd have known that as soon as he set foot in the door, before even taking a pulse, he said, "Though this illness looks mortal, it is nonetheless not mortal. What do you mean by asking me here?" Right away the lady related the whole story of the onset of the sickness, as well as the rhyme they'd drawn at the Lao-zi temple, for the doctor's consideration, begging him to prescribe a cure. That "Eight Hundred" Li just snorted sarcastically, saying, "This disease doesn't make it into the medical books. I've got no medicine to prescribe for it. All you can do is to keep feeling about his chest after he's dead—as long as he's not cold, you must not lay him in his coffin! After two weeks or three weeks or so, when he gets the hankering to eat something, he'll come around of his own. That slip from the Lao-zi temple, though accurate, will only become clear after the fact; it is not something we can make a guess about just now." He absolutely refused to administer any medicine, and set off again without further delay. There was no telling what to make of this. Would this disease of the Censor's really clear up of its own with no need for medicine? Or had the doctor simply made up an excuse to leave because the disease was already too advanced for a cure to be attempted?

Truly,

Green dragon and white tiger walk together;
no way of knowing what your lot might be.

When the lady saw that "Eight Hundred" Li had gone, she sighed, "When a doctor with a reputation like his is unwilling to give treatment, could there be any other who would dare to try? It's sure the disease has progressed past cure! All that we can do is wait helplessly for death to come." She sat by the Censor as his fever raged for seven days and seven nights, growing steadily more severe. Then all at once he lost consciousness, and no amount of calling could bring him around again. The lady gave way to sobbing, and meanwhile sent word to the three colleagues, so they could set about preparations for the funeral. These three were just on their way to see how things stood, and when they heard the evil news they all shed tears. They hurried to the official residence to weep before the body, and then spoke with the lady, consoling her for a while. As it was early autumn and the weather was still hot, they set out separately to see to the coffin and burial garments right away. By the third day all had been put in readiness, and it should have been time to close up the coffin.

But just then as the lady was weeping bitterly, slumped down over the body, she felt that, sure enough, there was a slight hint of warmth about the chest. For this she began to think there might be something to the words of "Eight Hundred" Li, and wanted to leave the body lying in the bed. But the domestics all said, "That's always been the way of it. Dead people can keep warm about the chest for as long as three or four days; they don't really turn cold right after they die. So what does that prove? It's now early September, and the heat has not yet abated. If there is so much as a thunderclap, that body will swell up in a second—then how will you ever get it into that coffin?" The lady said, "Master Li said that as long as his chest wasn't cold, he was not to be put in the coffin. Well, he's warm now, and even if I didn't believe what Master Li said, I'd keep watch over him for half a month or twenty days—how could I bear to shut him up after just three days, and still warm? Anyway, the coffin is all ready; just leave me to keep watch day and night. As soon as his chest grows cold I'll put him in—that won't be too late. O Heaven! Only let Master Li's words come true. If I can tend my man back to health, it won't be saving just one life, but, counting me, two lives."

They all tried again and again to dissuade her, but she just wouldn't listen. And since they couldn't outstubborn her, they had no choice but to go along with her: they left the Censor lying in his bed, with his wife keeping constant watch. Enough on that account for now.

Now when the Censor's illness entered the seventh day, his body grew extremely hot, so that he could not bear it for so much as another moment. His mind was completely taken up with the idea of finding a cool spot to relax a spell—perhaps then, he thought, there might be some hope of the sickness abating. So he slipped off quietly, evading the notice of his wife and colleagues, and, picking up a bamboo staff, quietly left the official quarters without calling anyone to wait on him. In a twinkling he'd reached the outside of the town walls. He felt like a bird leaving its cage, or a fish slipping free from a net. Filled with delight, he put all thought of sickness behind him.

Now you may be wondering how the Censor, being an official, was able to leave his quarters without a single person taking note of it. As it turns out, the depth of his longing had given rise to a dream, and it was his dreaming soul which felt all this was happening. His body remained behind as before on the bed—how could *it* have gone anywhere? Of course, this left the one watching over the body to weep and wail without cease day and night, hoping against hope to pull life back from the maw of death. How could she have known that the dreamer was drifting and floating without the least hindrance, himself in fact drawing joy from the heart of suffering?

Censor Xue went out the South Gate and then headed off into the mountains. He came to a certain mountain called Dragonsease. On that mountain there was a pavilion that had been built by the Sui emperor Wen on the occasion of the investiture of his son Yang Xiu as Duke of Shu. It was named

"Refuge from Heat." Around it on all four sides was lush forest and long bamboos. Breezes came from all directions, and there was not the least ray of sunlight. So that King of Shu, whenever the sultry days came, would marshal his court guests off to this pavilion to escape the heat. It was truly a fine cool spot! Just then when the Censor caught sight of it, he felt his spirits set at ease. "If I hadn't come out from the town, how should I ever have known that there was a setting like this in the mountains? I've been assigned to Qingcheng for a long while, yet I have never come to this place. And those colleagues of mine, how could they find out about it? I ought to tell them, so that we could bring wine goblets to this spot and hold a Heat-shunning Banquet. It's a shame that, in this worthy setting, I lack my worthy friends to share it—when all is said and done there's something missing."

The scene which lay before him was lovely, and he composed a poem then and there. It went:

A half-day's leisure snatched from drifting life,
on ruin's brink, I've scaled this slope alone.
Though here I draw breath close to Heaven's gates,
don't let me float away without return!

Censor Xue sat a while in the pavilion, and then set off once again into the mountains. There were no trees shading that mountain path, so it could not compare to the cool comfort of the pavilion and he felt more and more stifled as he went along. When bit by bit he'd covered three or four miles, off in the distance he made out a large river.

Now what river do you suppose that was? Back when Great Yu was taming the floods,[9] he channeled the Min River out of the Min Mountains. When he'd passed through the lands of Mao-zhou and Sheng-zhou, he further carved out this river, which is called the Tuo. To this very day, from the bank of this river hangs a great iron chain—there's no telling just how long it is, since it's sunk down in the riverbottom. This is the spot where Great Yu chained up Ying Dragon—it turns out that when Yu was taming the floods, whenever he came to a place where the watercourse was blocked, he'd send that Ying Dragon on ahead. Let those peaks and crags be never so tall, just one flip of Ying Dragon's tail, and in an instant they'd be split in two. That's why Great Yu is also referred to as "Wondrous Yu": if he did not know how to command such creatures, how could he have set the floods to rest within just eight years? To this day on the Si River there is another iron chain, which holds down Water Mother (the form of this creature is like a macaque). Now at this Tuo River, it was the Ying dragon. Both of these creatures were chained up after the work of taming the floods had been accomplished, in order to prevent any future trouble. Is that not a miraculous feat?

---

[9]Great Yu was the legendary founder of the Xia Dynasty, credited with saving the people from rampant flooding by digging China's system of rivers.

Just then the Censor was feeling oppressed by the heat as he walked along. Besides, he was suffering from a fever. When he suddenly caught sight of this stretch of the Tuo River, broad and rolling, extending without break to the horizon, he naturally felt a fresh coolness penetrating to his very marrow. He wished he could make every step into three and fly off at once like a sail-cart. He didn't realize, however, that though it looked very close from up on the mountain, once he'd come down, his path was cut off by East Pool before he could reach the Tuo. This pool was quite large. The water was clear as a mirror, and one could see right to the bottom even in the deepest parts. And the bamboos along the banks shone with a fresh greenness you could touch. The Censor took off his clothes and went into the pool to bathe.

It happens that the Censor was from the Wu region—he had grown up in the land of ponds and lakes. He had learned to dive from childhood. Since he'd become a grown man, this skill of his had fallen into long disuse. Unexpectedly coming here today, he felt the old joy come back to him with doubled force. As he splashed about, he happened to sigh to himself, "This swimming of humans can't compare with that of the fishes, after all! I wish I could borrow a suit of scales to grow onto my body, so I could swim about freely where I pleased—now that would be more like it!" Just then there appeared a little fish by his side who, eyeing the Censor, said to him, "If you want to be a fish, there's no problem to it. Why speak of 'borrowing'? Wait here while I go to He Bo to work on it for you." And almost before he'd finished saying this, the little fish was gone. This gave the Censor quite a scare, and he thought, "How was I to know there were magical creatures in this water? This is no place for swimming alone. I'd best get out of here with no delay!"

Little did the Censor know that, having once felt such a desire, he could not but be subjected to such a course of karmic retribution.

It led to:

Robe and cap:
doffed for a time along with human cares.
Scaly armor:
soon seen springing forth upon the water.

Censor Xue paused, sunk in thought, and was about to put his clothes back on and make his way home, when the little fish suddenly reappeared with news, saying, "Congratulations! He Bo has made his will known." And there came a fish-headed person, astride a large fish, with innumerable little fishes in attendance before and behind, who read out He Bo's decree.

Which said,

Town dwellers, water-wanderers: floaters and sinkers go by separate paths. If not through some special penchant, who could pass freely along both?

Yon Qing-cheng Censor Xue Wei, native of Wu, member of the lesser orders of officialdom, joys in the watery vastness of the clear river, and swims with happy abandon; wearied by the commotion of the dusty world, he shakes off his robes and departs. Let him undergo for a time the scaly transfiguration, yet not for life. Let him assume the duties of Crimson Carp of East Pond.

Pay heed! Those who indulge in far-roving pleasures with no thought of return will surely be punished by the clear-eyed spirits; those who ignore the thin hook and gulp the sweet bait will find it hard to escape the calamity of block and blade. See that you do not, by some error, bring shame on our kind. Heed these words!

When the Censor had done listening to the reading of this decree, he glanced down at his body to find that it had already grown scales—from head to toe, he'd been transformed into a golden carp. Though he was shocked and amazed, still he thought to himself, "Since it's come to this, let me at least go and swim to my heart's content, to learn the pleasures of the watery life." And from that time on, there was no spot among the three rivers and five lakes which he did not visit in his travels as he wandered about according to his whim.

It turns out that as He Bo's decree had appointed him Crimson Carp of East Pool, that East Pool was like a fixed address to him; and no matter how far afield he traveled, he'd at least have to come back there to rest. Now being tied down to that one little place began in time to make him feel a bit restless. After a few days, that little fish came again and said to the Censor, "Have you not heard that in Ping-yang Prefecture in Shan-xi there is a mountain called Long-men, or Dragongate? It was drilled through by Great Yu when he was taming the floods. Beneath the mountain is the Yellow River. Now since there is a stream at the top of the mountain that joins up with the waters of the Milky Way, rushing down to become the headwaters of the Yellow River, that spot is named Riverford. As we speak, the eighth month is coming around, and the autumn floods will soon rush down, heralded by thunder. All the carp under Heaven will go there to jump Dragongate. Why don't you request a leave of absence from He Bo, and go yourself to jump? If you make it across you will become a dragon—wouldn't that beat being a carp?"

Now it just happened that right then the Censor was beginning to grow a bit fed up with living in East Pool; when he heard about this, he was overjoyed. Right away, he took leave of the little fish, and headed straight for He Bo's place. Now He Bo's palatial halls all have coral columns and tortoise-shell rafters—a real dragon castle, a sea treasury, different in its own way in every detail from the ones of this world. At this time, carp from all the regions under He Bo's jurisdiction—the Min, Tuo, Ba, Yu, Fu, Qian, Ping-jiang, She-hong, Zhuo-jin, Jia-ling, and Qing-yi rivers, along with the Five Streams, the Lu Waters, the Sevengate Shallows, and the Three Straits of Qu-tang—had come to request leaves of absence to go and jump Dragongate. The Censor, as the only golden carp present, was appointed their representative, to lead them in to their audience with He Bo. In keeping with ancient custom, a general banquet was held, just like those held in this world to see off the candidates for the civil service exams. The Censor and the carp of the various regions partook of the banquet, gave thanks for imperial bounty, and set off together for Dragongate to jump. Who'd have guessed, they couldn't make it over, and returned with dotted foreheads. Now you may ask, "What's this about 'dotted foreheads'?" That is because when the carp try to jump through Dragongate they have to fight their way against the current, concentrating all their blood and vital spirits in the center of their foreheads, so that it looks as if they've been dotted there with a red brush. That's why people of this world refer to unsuccessful exam candidates as having "dotted foreheads"—it all stems from this. Truly,

> Hardpressed to pass through Dragongate's fierce flood,
> in shame they bear the forehead's splotch of blood.

Now in Qing-jiang County there lived a fisherman named Zhao Gan, who made his living, along with his wife, netting fish out on the Tuo River. All unexpectedly he'd netted a great snapping turtle that had dragged the net along with it—even Zhao Gan himself was nearly pulled into the river. His wife berated him, saying, "We depended on that net as our sole capital, to keep the two of us alive. Now that you've gone and lost our only fixed asset, how do you expect to come by any liquid assets to buy a new one? What's more, those people from the district government come by every so often to pick up a fish. What will you come up with to satisfy them now?" The two of them argued over this the whole night. Zhao Gan could not stand up to her browbeating, and had nothing for it but to rig up a fishing pole and make ready to come fish at East Pool. Now why do you suppose that Zhao Gan left that great river behind, and came instead to this pool to fish? As it happens, the current of the Tuo River is of the fastest, and thus perfect for netting, but unsuited to pole-fishing. So he thought of coming to East Pool to try his luck at this new line of work. He stuck a fragrant lump of oily dough on the end of that pole and tossed it into the water.

Now Censor Xue, ever since his return from getting his forehead dotted at Dragongate, had been out of sorts, and had hidden himself away in East Pool for several days without venturing out to look for something to eat. His belly was just then aching with hunger. When Zhao Gan's fishing boat came paddling up, he couldn't resist following after it, just to see what was afoot. As soon as he smelled the fragrance of that bait, he felt a great longing to eat it. He already had it up to his lips when he thought to himself, "I know good and well that there's a hook in this bait. If I swallow it, won't he have then caught me? Though I've turned for a time into a fish, is there really no other place for me to look for food, that I must eat only what's on his hook?" And he returned to play about in the shadows of the boat's hull. But how could he resist the overpowering fragrance of that bait, which seemed to bore its way right into his nostrils? What's more, he was very hungry—he really couldn't hold out any longer. He thought, "I am a human being, and who knows how much I weigh. And this little hook is going to drag me away? And what if he does pull me out? I'm a third-grade magistrate in the district government, and he is the fisherman Zhao Gan. He cannot fail to know me, and will naturally send me on my way home to the district seat. So won't I still end up eating his bait for free?" He'd barely closed his mouth around the bait, and hadn't even had time to swallow when Zhao Gan have a tug, and pulled him out. This is what is known as:

the eyes see through the trick,
but the belly can't hold back.

When that Zhao Gan saw he'd hooked a golden carp about three feet long, he clapped both hands to his head and cried out, "Heavenly day! If only I can catch a few more like this, I'll have enough money to tie a new net in no time!" The Censor called out to him repeatedly, "Zhao Gan! You are a fisherman under my jurisdiction. Hurry up and send me back to my office." But that Zhao Gan paid him no attention, and went right ahead and strung a straw rope through the Censor's gills and threw him into the hold. Then his wife said to him, "The district government is always sending people at odd intervals to pick up fish. Now as I see it, with a fish as big as this one, if some ministry errand-runner catches sight of it and takes it away, just how much government compensation do you think you'll get for it? We'd do better to hide it away among the reeds along the bank and wait for a peddler to come along, so we can sell it on the free market. And we'll have that much more to spend ourselves." Zhao Gan said, "Good idea," and took the fish off to hide in the reeds, covering it with an old straw poncho. He came back and said to his wife, "If we can get a good price for this one, I'll take some of the money and buy some beer for the two of us to get good and drunk. If our luck holds through the night, who's to say tomorrow I won't catch two?"

Now not too long after that Zhao Gan had hidden the fish and brought the boat back, sure enough there came an errand-runner from the district administration, named Zhang Bi, who called out to Zhao Gan, saying, "Fifth-Granddad Pei wants an extra large carp to poach. I came out to the Tuo this morning to find you, but now you've moved over here, making me search high and low for you, till I'm all sweaty and out of breath. Hurry up now and pick me out a big one, and come along with me to deliver it." Zhao Gan said, "I'm much to blame for making you go out of your way, sir. It's not that I wanted to move to this spot. But the other day I lost my net, and have no money to buy a new one, so I had no choice. I have to hook a few here until I can make up the money. But no big fish will take my hook—all I've got is three or four pounds of small ones. If you want those, take them." Zhang Bi said, "Fifth-Granddad Pei's orders were to get a big one. How can I report back with small ones?"

With a lunge he jumped down onto the boat and lifted up the well cover to look. Sure enough, they were all small ones. He was about to take those and try and make do. But then he thought to himself, "In a big wide stretch like this, how could there really be no big fish? It's certain this guy is up to something. He must have the big ones hidden away somewhere." With that he went ashore and searched all around, but couldn't find anything. Next, he went over to look among the reeds. There was an old straw poncho flapping wildly up and down. Zhang Bi guessed there must be a fish under there. When he strode up and lifted the poncho to look, it was a golden carp about three feet long. When Zhao Gan and his wife saw what had happened they could only curse their luck. Zhang Bi paid them no mind, but simply picked up that fish and stalked off. He looked back over his shoulder and said, "A fine job of deception! You just wait till I've reported this to Fifth-Granddad Pei—you'll get a sound beating, you rascal!"

The Censor cried out in a loud voice, "Zhang Bi! Zhang Bi! You too must certainly know me. I've come by chance to East Pool, and am amusing myself as a fish. How is it that seeing me you do not kowtow, but just sweep me up and rush off?" Zhang Bi paid not the slightest attention. He made straight for the district seat, with that fish dangling by his side. Zhao Gan followed at a distance. And all the while Zhang Bi was walking, the Censor was cursing him.

Zhang Bi carried the fish up to the town gate, where there was a soldier named Hu Jian on guard. Hu Jian said to Zhang Bi, "What a huge fish! Fifth-Granddad Pei has called all the granddads to a banquet, and they're all waiting just for that fish, so they can make poached carp. They say you've been gone a long time with no word, and they just sent out an express message to summon you. You'd sure enough better make it quick." When the Censor lifted his head to look, it was that same south gate, called the "Greeting Fragrance Gate," through which he'd gone out the other day. He called out to the gatekeeper, saying, "Hu Jian! Hu Jian! The other day when I left town, I instructed you that I was leaving on my own and that you needn't notify the other granddads, or send anyone along to attend on me. Can it be that before I've been gone even one month, you've already forgotten? Now you should go and notify the other granddads, and assign someone to attend on me. How is it that you pay me no heed—such impudence!" Yet oddly the gatekeeper seemed not to hear, just like Zhang Bi. That Zhang Bi went straight on with the fish into the town gate, Censor Xue all the while yelling and cursing without break.

There inside the gate were a clerk of the Households Bureau and a clerk of the Penal Bureau, sitting opposite each other over a chessboard. That Households Bureau clerk said, "Yugh! A fish that size must weigh over ten pounds!" The Penal Bureau clerk said, "What a lovely golden carp! He should be put in the 'Emerald Ripples' Pool of rear hall in the ministry compound just for the pleasure of looking at him—what a shame to waste him just to make poached carp!" The Censor bellowed, "You two clerks wait on me all day in the ministry. Though I may have turned into a fish, you should recognize me. How is it that on seeing me you don't stand up, or run to make report to the other granddads?" Those two clerks just sat there as before playing chess, as if they hadn't heard a thing. The Censor thought, "The saying has it that 'a dog's obeyed in office.' Can it be that now that I've no control over you, you've lost all fear of me whatsoever? Do you think that since I've been away these few days, my office has been taken away? And even if it had been taken away, I have still not left my post; when it comes down to it I do have power over you. Just wait till I meet my colleagues. We'll write up reprimands against the lot of you slaves, and have you flogged till skin splits and flesh bursts. . . ."

Dear Audience: take careful note of this situation, for in the next installment the outcome will be made clear.

Now Madam Gu kept careful watch over Censor Xue's corpse, and before she knew it, more than twenty days had gone by. Yet the flesh remained as firm as ever, showing no signs of deterioration. When she stretched out her hand to feel the region of his heart, it seemed as if it had grown if anything warmer than before. Bit by bit, the warmth extended, till up as far as the throat and down as far as the navel the body was not very cold at all. When she thought back on the words of Master "Eight Hundred" Li, it seemed as if they really were coming at least partly true. Thereupon she pricked out some blood from her forehead and wrote out a spirit-petition. She asked a few advanced Daoist adepts to hold a service to pray for a magical cure, and protection for the Censor in his return to life. She made vows to rebuild the Lao-zi temple, and to erect a golden image if her prayers were answered. On the day when her petition was to be submitted, the three colleagues and the civil functionaries and common people of the entire district all burned incense and prayed on the Censor's behalf, as they had on that former day.

I'm reminded of that old saying, "The blessed person bears the stamp of Heaven": now with an official as virtuous as Censor Xue, and with all the civil servants and commoners of the county praying on his behalf, could there be any fear that it would all come to nothing? It was just that this was a person who'd been dead over twenty days whom they were trying to restore to life. Though no one who ever made a petition at that Lao-zi temple ever had it go unanswered, still, of those souls that report before the hall of King Yama, not a single one can ever return.

Truly,

Trust that good will ever come of good,
doubt not the power of the unseen gods.

Now on that night the adepts laid out seven bright lamps on the altar, in the form of the seven stars of the Big Dipper. As it happens, the seventh star of the Big Dipper is called the "dipper handle." In spring it points to the east, in summer to the south, in autumn to the west, and in winter to the north, spinning about up there in Heaven. Only the fourth star, called "Heaven's Hinge," never moves. For this reason, the lamp in the position corresponding to "Heaven's Hinge" is specially designated as the "Life-lamp." If this lamp is bright, then the person concerned will have no trouble; if it is dark, then that person will be beleaguered by illness; and if that lamp goes out, then one can be sure that person has little chance of recovery.

Now on that evening the presiding adept raised the ritual implements in his hands and chanted incantations, praying fervently for the dispersal of the evil influences. He entered into a trance, and personally submitted the petition to the star-official, requesting that Censor Xue's soul be permitted to return to the world of light. When the others went to look at the seven lamps, they were all burning brightly, and one felt that the Life-lamp was especially brilliant—manifesting the truth of the saying that he was not yet meant to die. The adept congratulated the lady on her good fortune, saying, "The Censor's Life-lamp is glowing with doubled brilliance. His return to life will be at any time now. Above all you must remember not to give way to excessive grieving, for fear that you may disturb the peace of his spirit and make his return more difficult." The lady thanked him with tears in her eyes, saying, "If it comes out in this way, then I will not have gone through this ceremony and the bitterness of these long days and nights of watching in vain." When she'd heard this news, she felt her spirits lighten somewhat. Without knowing it she grew groggy and fell asleep, and dreamed a dream:

As clear as day she saw the Censor all in a panic, rushing in at the gate as naked as a newborn infant, his entire body stained with fresh blood. Covering his neck with both hands, he said, "Confounded luck! I was sailing out on the river in high spirits, when all at once a wild wind rose up and great waves stirred. My boat was overturned, throwing me into the water. By good fortune the river god took compassion on me, seeing as my allotted span was not yet up, and sent me out of the river and on my way, bestowing on me a suit of golden chainmail. Just as I made to seek out the road into town, I unexpectedly encountered a gang of robbers blocking the way. With designs on my golden armor, they killed me with a single stroke. If you have a thought for our marital bond, take care to keep watch over my soul and bring me back."

When the lady heard this in her dream, she unwittingly let out a great cry, and with this awoke. She thought, "Just now that Daoist priest said that he would not die; how comes it that I've had such a horrible dream? Yet I remember that phrase from the book of dream interpretation: 'Those dreamed dead will live.' For all I can tell it may be that he has just now escaped calamity through penitence, and for this reason appeared without a stitch of clothing. All I can do is keep close watch over the body every moment."

The next day the lady divided up the offerings from the votive altar and sent them over to the three colleagues—this is known as "scattering fortune." Prefect Pei, acting as host, invited the others to his home for a ceremonial banquet. This is known as "drinking fortune." It was for this reason that Prefect Pei had sent Zhang Bi to the fisherman's home to fetch a big fish to poach, to go along with the wine.

In the end it was Second-grade Zou whose feelings for his old classmate proved the stronger, as he sighed before the laden board, "This is no ordinary drinking party, but has been called for the purpose of summoning Censor Xue back to life—half of the very dishes on this table come from the vo-tive altar. Not knowing whether Censor Xue is to live or die, how can we call up any appetite for food?" Fifth-grade Pei then said, "The ancients did not sigh over their food. Do you think that you are alone in your worry for your classmate? Do we not also worry for our colleague? I hear the priests said that his return to life would occur either last night or today. Let's wait until that fish comes so we have something to chase our drink, drink our-selves silly, and wait here for news of him. Won't that fulfill both our pub-lic and our private obligations?"

That day it was not until the early afternoon that Zhang Bi came into the courtyard with the fish dangling at his side. As it came out, Fifth-grade Pei had been made to wait just for that fish, and he was sitting there eating peaches as he watched Second-grade Zou and Fourth-grade Lei play backgammon. When he glanced up and saw Zhang Bi sitting there, he flew off the handle and yelled out, "I sent you to get fish and bring it here—how is it you've been gone so long? You mean to tell me that if I hadn't sent out that express message to summon you, you wouldn't have come at all?" Zhang Bi kowtowed and told in detail the story of how Zhao Gan had hid-den the big fish away. Then Fifth-grade Pei ordered the attendant on duty to drag Zhao Gan down and give him fifty good lashes with a whip. Zhao Gan was left with skin in tatters and broken flesh, fresh blood streaming down his legs. Now why do you think that Zhao Gan didn't go away ear-lier, but instead had to follow Zhang Bi all the way back to the county seat, as if just to come looking for this beating? It was those few pennies of gov-ernment compensation he was thinking of! Yet in the end he got fifty lashes and never saw any payment. Wasn't he just like that golden carp that had taken his hook? Truly,

> In this world life and death are all for gain,
> no thought of pause until our final day.

Fifth-grade Pei ran Zhao Gan off. When he lifted that fish to look, he saw it was a golden carp, over three feet long. He happily exclaimed, "This fish is excellent! Send it at once to the kitchen to poach." Censor Xue cried out, "What do you mean 'fish'? I am your colleague. How can you fail to recognize me? Now I have endured a great number of insults and have been waiting just to complain to you gentlemen, so that you can help me to exact revenge. How is it that you too take me for a fish, and send me off to the kitchen to poach? If I am poached, will that not be a case of wrongful death? For nothing I've worked side by side with you all these years—you don't show the least sympathy!" But while he said all this, those colleagues of his paid no attention whatsoever. The Censor was then worked up in the extreme and burst out, "Classmate Zou, we were *jin-shi* graduates together back in the Tong-bao era. We used to be the best of friends back at the cap-ital and have now been made colleagues here. You're not like the rest of them—how can you sit there and see me taken off to death without a word?" Then Second-grade Zou said to Fifth-grade Pei, "In my humble opinion, this fish should not be poached. There is a big pond for releasing life up at the Lao-zi temple on Qing-cheng Mountain, and a lot of the people who go up there to hold services buy fish, turtles, and shellfish to release in the pond. Since today's feast is made up partly of the 'scattered fortune' from Censor Xue's service, we would do better to release this fish there as well, to plant this karmic seed."

Fourth-grade Lei interjected, "Releasing the fish is a noble idea! The teaching of karmic retribution does not permit of doubt. Furthermore, we have plenty of delicacies for our banquet as it is; what need have we to eat poached carp as well?" At this, Censor Xue, who was still lying out in the courtyard, said, "Classmate Zou, you really are a scatterbrain! If you've a mind to save me, why not just send me back to my quarters? What is the point of sending me back up into the mountains—won't I perish of thirst? Still, that would beat dying at the hands of the cook. Just wait till I've got to the pool for releasing life and have returned to my true form, and put on my robes and trappings to be an official again. Forget about Zhao Gan and that lot of curs—let's just see which of you will have the nerve to come and look me in the eye!"

As he was blustering to this effect, Fifth-grade Pei replied again, saying, "Old man, if you want to release this fish, that is a manifestation of the sacred call to cherish life—how should I presume to interfere? But that ceremony of intercession was performed according to the tenets of Daoism, bearing no relation to Buddhist teachings. If you wish to establish good karma, this is not the proper occasion. Just think: Heaven brings all things to fruition expressly for the sustenance of humankind. Take fish, for example: if they were not caught and eaten by people, then all would be fish beneath the sky, and even the riverways would be blocked up. Everyone does what they can to make themselves good, but this is a matter of the heart and not of the mouth. Thus the old saw has it: 'The Buddha sits within the heart; meat and liquor pass by through the gullet.' And: "If you would abide by Buddhist law, then abandon the desire of even a sip of cool water.' Do you really believe that just eating this fish will do harm to the sincerity of our feelings for our departed colleague? A perfectly good fish, and you won't poach it, but want to release it to no good purpose? How are we to know just because we don't eat it that it will not be eaten by an otter instead? It will die just the same. So when all is said and done, it is better that we eat it." When the Censor heard this, he yelled out, "Look, your two guests both want to release me. You really are muleheaded! Not only is your feeling for a colleague most tepid, it turns out that you also utterly lack any understanding of the deference due of a host to his guests!"

Now it turns out that Fourth-grade Lei was diffident by nature. Seeing how Fifth-grade Pei really had his heart set on making poached carp, he said to Second-grade Zou, "Mr. Pei does not go in for karmic retribution, so it looks as if there is no saving this fish. Yet today as he is acting as our host, and wants to take this fish to offer us, how can we be adamant in refusing him? As I see it, it is not that we really mean to kill this fish; let's just say that its allotted span has run out today and there is thus no saving it." Immediately the Censor burst out, "Mr. Lei, you really are spineless! How do you come to be arguing on both sides at once? If you want him to release me and he proves unwilling, you should continue to reason with him. How can you turn around and persuade Classmate Zou to give up the thought of rescuing me? Is it that you've been living on a tight budget and haven't had any fish to eat in a long time, so that you're hoping for a chance to eat your fill when the poached carp is ready?"

All the Censor could do was to turn again to Second-grade Zou, saying, "Classmate! Classmate! Don't tell me you're just putting on a show of friendship! A few insincere high-sounding words, and that's that? Will you not let out so much as another peep on my behalf? Of old it's been truly said, 'When one is to die and the other to live, the true depth of feeling comes clear.' If it were not that today I come to die and you to live, how should I ever have known that your feelings for your classmate are as shallow as this? If one day the term of my release comes, you just wait till I've returned to my old form—can I not do as that Secretary Zhai did and hang those words of spite up at my door for you to see? Classmate, classmate, I only fear that when you come to regret this, it will be too late!" Though the Censor was shouting and making quite a racket, host and guests all behaved exactly as if they had not heard a thing.

Then Fifth-grade Pei called in the kitchen servant Wang Shi-liang, since he was a skilled cook and made the best poached carp. Pei handed the fish over to him, saying, "We want it to be both good and fast. Otherwise we'll take you out just like that Zhao Gan and serve you up fifty lashes of the whip." Wang Shi-liang answered that he understood and reached over to pick up the fish. The Censor was so terrified that the three souls flew out the top of his head and the seven spirits sank through the floor. He wept piteously, and said, "In the old days, we colleagues were as inseparable as brothers. Why is it that today no matter how I beg you, you think only of killing me? Ah, I have it: you surely envy me the administrative seal—that's why you have brewed up this villainy. I'll have you know, this seal was bestowed on me by the authorities; I did not come by it through plotting! But if you'll only agree to let me go home, I'll resign this instant. What is so hard about that?" When he'd said this, he once more burst into tears. Yet, who'd have imagined, his colleagues acted as if they had not heard! And the Censor was rushed straight off to the kitchen.

In no time at all a chopping block had been brought over and the Censor laid on top of it. When he looked up, he saw it was the very man who had always served him as cook. He yelled out, "Wang Shi-liang! Can you not see that I am Third-Granddad Xue? If I hadn't passed all those Wu regional recipes on to you, what dishes would you have been able to come up with on your own, that all your masters should play up to you so? Now you should consider the debt of gratitude you owe to me for bringing you up in the world. Hurry now, and report who I am to all the granddads, and have me sent along home! What do you mean by putting me up on the chopping board like this?"

Yet strangely Wang Shi-liang paid not the least attention. Picking up the knife in his right hand, he pushed down with his left on the fish's head. This so discomfited the Censor that he flew into a rage. He snarled, "You cur! So you save all your fawning for Fifth-grade Pei and have no fear of me! Do you imagine I have no means of getting back at you?" He began to thrash about, and flipped his tail right up in Wang Shi-liang's face, catching him just like the slap of an open palm to the side of the head, leaving him with eyes dimmed and ears ringing. The cook brought both hands up to cover his face and let the knife fall clattering to the floor. As he stooped back down to pick up the knife, he sneered, "All right, fish! If you're so sassy, let's just wait and see how you like swimming around in my pot!"

It turns out that making poached carp calls for the sharpest knife possible—the fish must be sliced as thin as snowflakes, to be dipped into boiling water for just a moment and then scooped out. With the addition of a little pepper and some sesame oil, it comes out naturally tender and fresh-tasting. So Wang Shi-liang went once more to whet his knife. The Censor, when his repeated calls still brought no response, let out a mournful sigh, and thought, "When that knife is sharpened, my life is at an end. Thinking back now on the time I lay sick at home, that seems bearable compared to this. Why did I ever steal out alone, to undergo this torment? If only I'd never seen East Pool, or, even if I'd seen it, if only I'd never thought to go in bathing. Or having gone in, if only I'd never wished to turn into a fish! If I hadn't wished for that, I'd never have received He Bo's summons, and all this would never have happened. Still, before I'd become a fish there was the little fish egging me on; after I'd become a fish, that Zhao Gan came along to trick me. It is all the workings of fate, and I've brought it on myself. How can I blame anyone else? I only pity my poor wife, left alone in our residence, without son or daughter—on whom can she rely? If only I could somehow get a message to her, so that I could die without regrets!" As he was moaning and weeping like this, Wang Shi-liang took the freshly honed blade and chopped off his head with a single stroke. Truly,

> While three inches of breath remain,
> who's willing to give up the least advantage?
> When the six-foot body passes,
> it all fades like a dream on a spring day.

Alas, poor Censor!

Now while over here Wang Shi-liang had just chopped off the fish's head, back in the official residence in the district administration compound, Censor Xue suddenly sprang upright on his bier. Forget about Madam Gu, who, being a woman, was nearly frightened to death—even all those household servants watching over the body wagged their heads and let their tongues loll out, saying, "Strange! We've been keeping close watch all along, and no cat has jumped over the body. How is it then that the corpse has been drawn upright?" Then the Censor gave a sigh and said, "How many days is it that I've been unconscious?" His wife replied, "Don't try to scare me! You've been dead for over twenty days, and we wondered whether you could ever live again." The Censor said, "When did I ever die? I just had a dream. I never guessed I'd been dreaming that long." Then he called out to the servants, "Go over to look in on my three colleagues. Right now they're sitting in the hall, getting ready to eat poached carp. You tell them to put down their chopsticks and not to eat it. Have them come over right away to my residence to have a word with me."

Sure enough, the colleagues were in the hall drinking, and the poached carp had just been brought in. They were just making ready to pick up their chopsticks, when suddenly Censor Xue's messenger announced, "The Censor has come around. He requests that you three gentlemen not eat the fish, but come at once to the ministry to have a word." Those three were so shocked they all leapt to their feet, saying, "To think that Doctor 'Eight Hundred' Li's diagnosis and the lamps in the Lao-zi temple were so uncannily accurate!" They rushed over to the Xue residence, calling out, "Congratulations, congratulations!" The Censor said, "Gentlemen, do you know what has happened? That golden carp you poached just now was yours truly. If it had not been for that knife stroke of Wang Shi-liang's, it's more than likely there would have been no waking from that dream."

The three of them stared vacantly, not taking in what he was saying. They said, "How could such a thing be possible? If it please Your Excellency, try telling it to us from the beginning, so that we may give you our undivided attention." Censor Xue said, "Just now when Zhang Bi arrived with the fish, Classmate Zou and Mr. Lei were playing backgammon, while you, Mr. Pei, were sitting to one side eating peaches, were you not? Zhang Bi reported that the fisherman Zhao Gan had hidden away the big fish and tried to pass off some little ones. Mr. Pei was furious, and had Zhao Gan given fifty lashes. Did this happen?" The three of them said, "Sure enough, it is as you say. But how is it that Your Excellency knows this in such detail?" The Censor said, "Now go and summon Zhao Gan, Zhang Bi, that soldier Hu Jian who watches the Greeting Fragrance Gate, and those two clerks of the Households and Penal Bureaus, along with the cook Wang Shi-liang, and let me ask them a few questions."

The three colleagues sent off servants to call the lot of them in. When they had all been assembled there, the Censor said, "Zhao Gan, you were fishing in East Pool and caught a golden carp about three feet long; on your wife's instructions, you hid it among the reeds, covered with an old straw poncho. When Zhang Bi came for fish you claimed not to have any large ones. But the fish was discovered by Zhang Bi, who carried it up to the Welcoming Fragrance Gate. There the gatekeeper Hu Jian said that Fifth-Grand-dad Pei had sent an express note to summon him and he'd better make it quick. He then went inside the gate, where these two clerks were sitting facing each other, playing chess. One said, 'That fish is frightfully large! It will certainly make good poached carp!' The other said, 'Such a lovely fish! It should be kept in the pond of the rear hall, not wasted on poaching.' When Wang Shi-liang held the fish down on the chopping board, the fish flipped its tail up and hit him in the face. He went again to sharpen his knife before letting the blade fall. Now, did all those things happen?"

Zhao Gan and the others all said in amazement, "Every one of them. But how did Granddad Xue come to know all this?" The Censor said, "I was that fish. Ever since being caught, I've been yelling without pause, demanding to be sent home, yet none of you paid me any heed. What was the meaning of that?"

Zhao Gan and the rest of them all kowtowed, saying, "Your servants truly heard nothing. If we had heard, how should we have dared not to send your eminence back to the ministry?" The Censor also asked Prefect Pei, "When you, sir, wanted to make poached carp, Classmate Zou repeatedly urged you to release the fish, and Mr. Lei chimed in to the same effect. Yet you would not listen, instead calling Wang Shi-liang and urging him to set about his business. Thereupon I burst out crying, saying, 'In vain have I been your colleague all this while, that today you are hell-bent on killing me!' Was this the action of a man of humane sentiments? Now forget for the time being Mr. Pei's lack of courtesy; Classmate Zou, and you too, Mr. Lei, did not intercede with a single word on my behalf. What am I to make of this?"

The three of them simply looked at one another, saying, "When did we ever hear the least sound?" And they rose together to beg forgiveness. The Censor laughed, saying, "As long as this fish did not die, I could not live. What's past is past; there is no need to mention the matter further." With this he dismissed Zhao Gan and the others. The three colleagues also took their leave and returned to their homes. They threw the fish into the water and swore that from that moment on they would never eat fish again.

It turns out that when the Censor had been crying out and weeping, there had never been any sound at all; all that happened was that the fish's mouth opened and closed. So there was good reason for the three colleagues and Zhao Gan and the rest to have heard nothing.

Now when Madam Gu reflected back on the wording of the slip from the Lao-zi temple, there was not one thing which had not been fulfilled. So she told the Censor in full detail of the matter of the fortune-slip and the votive offering she'd made; she hoped to see to the fulfilling of the vows she'd made. The Censor said in amazement, "After all the time I've been here, I'd only heard that there was a Lao-zi temple on Qing-cheng Mountain, which drew quite a number of pilgrims. How could I have known that it possessed magical efficacy like this?"

Right away he began seven days of fasting and prayer, and then, setting lamps and incense in readiness, prepared to go in person to the temple to fulfill the vows. At the same time he sent people to make cost estimates for lumber, for the setting up of the golden image, and for all the necessary labor. Drawing on his personal fortune and on his government salary, he made the necessary purchases, and awaited an auspicious day to begin the work. On the morning of the seventh day, he dismissed his servants, and, accompanied only by a pageboy of twelve or thirteen, set out alone from his residence, prostrating himself at every step, toward Qing-cheng Mountain. Just when he'd got halfway up the mountain slope, as he was making his obeisance, he suddenly heard someone calling out to him, saying, "Censor Xue. You know what?" The Censor gave a start, and when he looked up, there was a herdboy in a broad straw hat, holding a small flute in his hand, seated sideways on the back of a blue cow, who had just rounded a bend in the mountain slope. Censor Xue said, "And what is it that you'd have me know?" That herdboy said, "Did you know that among the immortals there was a certain Qin Gao, who first ascended to Heaven astride a scarlet carp? One night at the table of the Queen Mother of the West, he stole a glance at that Tian Si-fei who plays the Cloud-glockenspiel, and succumbed to worldly thoughts. For this the two of them were banished into the mortal world. Now, your former self was just this Qin Gao; and that wife of yours was Tian Si-fei. Since your arrival at your post here, you've been enamored of the realm of the senses, unable to leave it behind. So you were sent to act temporarily as Crimson Carp of East Pool and to undergo all manner of sufferings, so that you might change your ways. Why do you still not come to your senses? Can it be that you still have not awakened from your dream?"

The Censor said, "According to what you say, I was once an immortal. Yet now I've fallen into delusion. What I need, then, is a teacher to prompt my memory." The herdboy said, "If it's prompting you want, the person is closer than a thousand leagues; in fact, as close as the end of your nose. That master 'Eight Hundred' Li of Cheng-du Prefecture—is he not an immortal? Back in Han times, he was called Han Kang, and was there in Chang-an all along, selling medicines and never changing his price. Later on a woman saw through his disguise, and he changed his name to 'Eight Hundred' Li. People all say it's because he received eight hundred secret cures from Sun Si-miao. What they don't know is that his skills are far superior to those of Sage Sun; in fact, he's been alive for over eight hundred years. Now the term of your banishment and that of your wife will soon be at an end, and you are both due to be restored to the register of immortals. Why don't you ask that 'Eight Hundred' Li, and have him clear away your worldly delusion?"

Now it just happened that Madam Gu had only told him about the matter of the votive offering, and hadn't told him yet about "Eight Hundred" Li and his diagnosis. Thus when the herdboy mentioned the name "Eight Hundred," the Censor had not the least idea who that was. He thought to himself, "What does a herdboy in the mountain wilds know? He's just making up this whole outlandish tale; it's not worth taking seriously. Let me just stick to fulfilling these vows, prostrating myself at every step—that is the important thing." He'd hardly expected that as soon as his head was turned, that herdboy and ox would both change into a wisp of purple mist, which floated up into the sky. Truly,

Face to face with immortals, you still don't know them;
how can you hope to know your former lives?

The Censor, already somewhat mystified by the uncanny nature of his transformation into a fish, on seeing this herdboy float away on a breeze, was even more at a loss. He tried to settle his doubts, thinking, "Was even that herdboy part of a dream?" Yet in the end he couldn't make up his mind just what to think.

In time he'd made his way all the way to the Lao-zi shrine at the top of the mountain, and kowtowed in thanks for the protection of the spirits which had allowed him to return to life. All that remained was to fix an auspicious day to fulfill the vow to rebuild the temple. When he'd paid his respects and rose to leave, he noticed that the spirit-image of Lao-zi had exactly the appearance of that herdboy. And there by the dais was an image of a blue cow just like the one the herdboy had been riding. Only then did the realization come to him who it was who had appeared to him, and he exclaimed, "It's clear as can be that that herdboy just now was the supreme Lao-zi, guiding me to return to the ranks of immortals. Yet I've got eyes in my head to no good purpose, and let this chance slip by me!" With that he threw himself down again and begged forgiveness.

When he'd returned home, he told his wife in full detail all that the herdboy had said. Only then did she say, "When you were dangerously ill, we invited in the master 'Eight Hundred' Li from Cheng-du Prefecture to come examine you. He said the case was 'mortal yet not mortal,' and that we must wait after your death for half a month to twenty-odd days, and you'd gradually come back around of your own accord; there was no need to administer medicines. When he was about to leave, he said again, 'That fortune-slip is true as true can be. Only after you've seen the fish will it become clear.' As I see it, if he can tell the past and future like that, he really must be an immortal. Never mind about Lord Lao-zi appearing to you and directing you to go to him; even if he were not an immortal, just for his trouble in coming to diagnose you, and so accurately at that, you ought to go and thank him."

When the Censor had heard all this, he said, "So there was this layer of circumstance as well! Indeed, how should I fail to go and thank him?" He performed seven more days of ritual purification, and set off on foot for Cheng-du to seek out Master "Eight Hundred" Li. Just by luck, on the day he arrived, "Eight Hundred" Li was sitting in his medicine shop. As soon as he saw the Censor, he asked him, "So have you woken from your dream yet?" The Censor threw himself down on the ground and said, "Your disciple has now awakened. I only request, Master, that you instruct me, so that I may free myself of this world and quickly hear of the great way." "Eight Hundred" Li laughed and said, "Now you're not some novice with no spiritual root who needs to learn about alchemical philters and all that. In your former existence you were a banished immortal—the supreme Lord Lao-zi has already explicitly revealed as much to you. You don't recognize yourself, and come asking another to recognize you? Can it be that you know only a certain Censor of Qing-cheng County?"

On hearing these words, realization came to the Censor in a flood, and he prostrated himself in thanks, saying, "Now your disciple has well and truly awakened! Yet there remains the matter of the vow at the Lao-zi temple. When I have fulfilled this vow, I'll quit my post and bring my wife along, so that together with Master we may make good our return to the immortal rolls!" With that he took leave of "Eight Hundred" Li and hurried back to Qing-cheng County, where he told his wife all that "Eight Hundred" Li had said. She also realized the truth upon hearing these words, that she had been that Tian Si-fei who played the Cloud-glockenspiel before the Western Queen Mother, who had fallen from that state as a result of worldly stirring. That night she and the Censor settled down in separate chambers, burning incense and meditating, striving to realize their karmic destiny. The next day, the Censor sent his seal of office over to Second-grade Zou, asking him to take over the post, and submitted a report to his superiors. In the meanwhile, he was urging on the workers in the construction of the great halls and courts, and of the golden image. It was all most impressive and orderly.

At last the day came when the work was completed, and Second-grade Zou, in order to fulfill a vow of his own, wanted to pitch in part of his salary to help with the costs. He arranged to meet with the two county prefects, whereupon they all went over to the Censor's quarters to inform him of their wishes. The servants thought he was in his room meditating, and went in to announce the visitors. But all they saw was a poem left lying on the writing desk. There was no telling where the Censor and the lady had gone. The servants handed that poem to Second-grade Zou to read. It was composed by the Censor as a farewell to his colleagues and to the clerks and people of the county. The poem read:

> Through dreamed fish-body, happily unscathed;
> if I'd been truly fish, then death too would be true.
> Wherever life is death must be as well;
> I long to part from life and death, free from this world's red dust.

When Second-grade Zou had done reading, he could not contain his sighs, and said, "If my classmate meant to take orders and cultivate his soul, he ought to have left us with at least a word of farewell. As it is, I cannot help feeling a deep regret. Still, I'll wager he's not gone far." And he sent people to search all around, yet there was no further trace of him. Just as Zou was standing there dumbfounded, Fifth-grade Pei laughed, saying, "You two gentlemen are really dense! I'll bet he's still unable to shake off his love of the aquatic life; more than likely he's gone to play carp again. Just go down to East Pool and catch him, and there'll be an end of it. . . ."

Enough of these wild speculations of the three colleagues. To return to Censor Xue and his wife, they were headed to nowhere else but to call on "Eight

Hundred" Li. That "Eight Hundred" Li laughed and said to the Censor, "Your former self was Qin Gao. Since you've not too far to go in your rise to immortality, you should have a red carp waiting for you at East Pool. Today, we'll return your red carp to you as before. What say you to that?" And to the lady, "Since your banishment, Dong Shuang-cheng has temporarily filled in for you playing the Cloud-glockenspiel before the Queen Mother of the West. Now it is time for you to play again."

Naturally the race of immortals are in on all the secrets, and there's no need for any incantations or spiritual techniques—with a laugh they understand all. At that time, the Censor and his wife said in turn to "Eight Hundred" Li, "Through all these years of selling cures and practicing medicine, saving and enlightening the multitudes, your accumulated merit is quite considerable. What need have you to linger in the world of mortals?" "Eight Hundred" Li said, "It is my destiny to make the ascent along with you. I have been waiting for you here." In a moment, auspicious clouds twined about them and prodigious mists appeared in profusion. The music of immortals rang out in the heavens, and phoenixes and cranes soared about. Immortal boys and girls clasping banners and canopies came forward to lead them on their way: The Censor on his red carp, the lady riding a lavender haze, and "Eight Hundred" Li astride a white crane, they ascended into Heaven together. Young and old throughout the city of Cheng-du all saw it and made obeisance toward the skies, with no end of sighing at the marvel. To this day, the wondrous "Bridge of Immortal Ascent" marks the spot where they ascended.

The poem says,

Confused and churning, this plot is novel:
    a man turned fish, and fish made man again.
Once recognized, dream form can't hinder nature;
    through form to perfect nature is the way of the immortal.

元明 Tang Xian-zu, *Peony Pavilion:* Selected Acts

While the Northern "variety play" *(za-ju)* was flourishing in the Yuan capital at Da-du in the thirteenth century, a very different kind of drama was also taking shape in the South. Although "variety plays" continued as a genre of purely literary drama through the Qing, the form had largely disappeared from the popular theater by the late fifteenth century. Throughout the Ming, Southern drama continued to grow in prominence, both as popular theater and as an elite literary form. These Southern-style plays (so named for their musical style and its provenance—they were written by northerners and southerners alike) continued to be the dominant form of literary drama through the nineteenth century.

Southern-style drama came to be known as *chuan-qi,* "accounts of remarkable things," the same generic term applied to Tang tales (which provided many of the plots for the plays). For the sake of convenience, we will refer to *chuan-qi* plays as "dramatic romances." Dramatic romances were often vast, sprawling works, usually with twenty to fifty scenes. Unlike the Northern variety play's restriction to one singer per scene, dramatic romances allowed the free alternation of singing parts, including duets and choruses. The plots of dramatic romances were often intricate, with numerous subplots, usually weaving together one or more love stories with political intrigue and/or warfare.

As classical poetry and song lyric had dominated the middle period of Chinese literature through the Song, so drama was arguably the most popular literary form of the Ming and the first half century of the Qing. Plays were widely read and performed, with performances both of entire works and individual acts. By the late sixteenth century, dramatists were already writing with a strong sense of the history of earlier plays, and like modern film directors, they could assume that a significant part of their audience would enjoy echoes of earlier works. Famous arias were circulated in songbooks and became as much a part of a standard repertoire of memorized texts as classical poetry; and as in the Renaissance West, the use of theatrical metaphors to describe social and political life became common. One famous passage translates quite literally, "All the world's a stage."

It is difficult to draw the line between drama as theater and drama as literature. Not all great theater is good literature, and certainly not all great dramatic literature is good theater. There is, however, a significant body of plays that provides ample but different pleasures in both reading and performance. Many variety plays and dramatic romances are like the libretti of some famous Western operas: they were probably a delight as theatrical spectacle but seem vapid as literary texts. By the fifteenth century, however, plays were being published to be read—some primarily intended to be read. Famous plays were often published in fine, illustrated editions, sometimes with elaborate literary commentary.

Although certain earlier dramatic romances were intended for reading as well as performance, the most important figure in literary *chuan-qi* was Tang Xian-zu (1550–1617). His four main plays are known as "Lin-chuan's Four Dreams" (Linchuan being Tang Xian-zu's toponym). Dream serves an essential role in each of these works, not only as a plot device but also as a thematic concern that touches both the Buddhist idea of the emptiness of experience and an illusionist notion of theater itself. The most famous of the four plays is *Peony Pavilion (Mu-dan ting)*, written in 1598, and consisting of 55 scenes (340 pages in Cyril Birch's complete translation).

An Aristotelian economy of plot is not characteristic of Chinese dramatic romances. As the play opens, a young scholar named Liu recounts a dream of a beautiful young woman standing beneath a plum tree and takes Meng-mei (Dreamed of Plum) as his name. Unbeknownst to Liu Meng-mei, the young woman in the dream is Du Li-niang, the daughter of the prefect of Nan-an. Forced by her father to study the *Classic of Poetry*, she reads the first poem, "Fishhawk," celebrating the perfect marriage, and is so aroused by it that she arranges to go for a long walk in the flower garden behind the residence.

Her passions stirred by spring, she returns to her rooms, falls asleep, and is visited by Liu Meng-mei in a dream. Liu Meng-mei carries her out into the garden and they make love by the peony pavilion; when Du Li-niang wakes up, she is so overwhelmed by a sense of loss that she pines away and dies. But before expiring, she paints her own portrait, and as her dying wish the portrait is buried by the peony pavilion, while she herself is buried beneath the plum tree in the garden.

After Du Li-niang's death, the family moves away; later, Liu Meng-mei, having become sick on his way to the capital, takes up lodging in the garden to recuperate and discovers Du Li-niang's portrait. Meanwhile Du Li-niang has received permission in the underworld to return to Earth, and she visits Liu, instructing him to disinter her body. Liu Meng-mei digs up her corpse, which has suffered no decay. Du Li-niang revives; the couple marries and goes on to the capital, where Liu Meng-mei passes the examination with the highest honors.

In one of the other plot strands, Du Li-niang's father is playing a major role in defending the dynasty from invasion. After numerous complications, including Liu Meng-mei's being charged with grave-robbing, the final fourteen scenes manage to get the couple together with her parents, until at last, in a scene at court, Du Li-niang's father accepts the marriage.

First comes Tang Xian-zu's own "Introductory Comment" on the play.

An Introductory Comment on *Peony Pavilion*

The young women of the world experience the feelings of love, but can any of them compare with Du Li-niang? No sooner did she dream of her man than she grew sick; the sickness became protracted; at last she reached the point of painting her likeness with her own hand in order to preserve it for others; then she died. Three years she lay dead; and then, from the dark world below, once again she sought the man of whom she had dreamed; then she came to life. Someone like Du Li-niang may well be called a person with the feelings of love.

No one knows where love comes from, but once it comes, it goes deep. The living can die from it; the dead can be brought to life. And if the living cannot die from it or if the dead cannot be brought back to life, then it is not the ultimate love.

Why should the feelings of love experienced in dream not necessarily be genuine? Are there not quite a few people in this world who are living in a dream? When the relationship between lovers depends on bedding together or intimacy awaits the renunciation of public office, we are on the level of mere flesh.

The story of her father, Governor Du, resembles that of Li Zhong-wen, the governor of the capital of Wu in the Jin, and the love story involving Feng Xiao-jiang, the governor of Guang-zhou. I changed them a bit and elaborated them. As for Governor Du's torture of Liu Meng-mei to make him confess to grave-robbing, this resembles the Han Prince of Sui-yang's interrogation of Mr. Dan.[1]

The things that may happen in a human life cannot all happen in a single lifetime. I am not someone of comprehensive knowledge, and I must always investigate matters to consider whether they are rational. But when we say that something cannot happen rationally, how do we know that it might not be inevitable through the feeling of love?

The steamy, perfervid, and sometimes precious poetry of "Waking Suddenly from Dream" (below) made it one of the most popular scenes in the play and a standard piece in the performing repertoire of *Kun-qu,* the most influential performance tradition of dramatic romance (though the scene was bowdlerized and revised for singing). In the late seventeenth-century-play *Peach Blossom Fan,* the heroine Xiang-jun is shown learning to sing one of the suites from this scene as part of her training as a courtesan. As Du Li-niang learns of passion from reading the *Classic of Poetry,* so Xiang-jun learns to be the romantic heroine who gives all for love from reading *Peony Pavilion.* In both cases, the lessons learned were not at all what was intended by those in charge of the girls' education.

WAKING SUDDENLY FROM DREAM (X)

Enter Du Li-niang *and her maid,* Spring Scent.

Du Li-niang [*sings*]:
> Back from dreams in orioles' warbling,
> a tumult of bright spring weather
>   everywhere, and here I stand
> in the heart of this small garden.

---

[1]These are all earlier tales whose plot elements served as sources for *Peony Pavilion.*

SPRING SCENT [*sings*]:
> The stick of aloes burns away, its smoke is gone,
> thrown down,
>> the last embroidery threads—
> why does this spring touch my feelings
>> so much more than springtimes past?

DU LI-NIANG [*recites*]:
> I gazed down toward Plum Pass
>> at dawn,
> last night's make-up traces fading.

SPRING SCENT [*continuing*]:
> Hair done in tumbling coils
>> with swallow cut-outs to welcome spring
> as you lean upon the railing.

DU LI-NIANG:
> "Cut but never severed,
> put in order,
>> then tangled again—"
> a melancholy without cause.

SPRING SCENT:
> I have issued instructions to orioles
> and have given direction to swallows
>> that hurry along the flowers,
> to take advantage of the spring
> and come see, come see.

DU LI-NIANG: Did you have someone sweep up the path through the flowers?

SPRING SCENT: I did.

DU LI-NIANG: Then get out my clothes and vanity mirror and bring them to me.

SPRING SCENT *leaves and returns with clothes and vanity mirror.*

SPRING SCENT [*recites*]:
> Done combing her cloudlike tresses,
>> she looks into the mirror,
> ready to change her lacy gown
>> she adds another sachet.

Here's what you asked for.

DU LI-NIANG [*sings*]:
> Sunlit floss comes windborne coiling
>> into my quiet yard,
> swaying and bobbing, spring is like thread.
> I stop a moment to straighten
> the flowered pins in my hair
> to suddenly find that the mirror plunders

half my face, prodding
　　my sparkling tresses to one side. [*Walks away*]
Though I pace my chambers, do I dare
let my body be seen entire?

SPRING SCENT:
　　You're nicely dressed up today.

DU LI-NIANG [*sings*]:
　　Note the skirt's madder red,
　　　　set off by vivid azure,
　　the opulent glitter of flowered pins
　　　　richly inlaid with gems—
　　you can tell
　　　　my lifelong love of such,
　　　　comes from my nature—
　　spring's finest touch
　　　　is seen by no man ever.
　　No matter if, at the sight,
　　　　the fish dive deep
　　　　or wild geese come down
　　　　　　or birds squawk out in alarm,
　　I only fear to shame the flowers,
　　　　to make the moon hide away,
　　　　　　and blossoms will quiver from sorrow.

SPRING SCENT: It's time for breakfast. Let's go. [*They walk*] Just look!

[*Recites*]

Gold dust on painted walkways,
　　half is scattering of stars,
the moss at the lodge by the pool,
　　a single swathe of green.
Walking through grass, afraid to stain
　　new stockings of brocade,
feeling sorry that flowers ache
　　from the tiny golden bells.[2]

DU LI-NIANG: If I hadn't come to the garden, how could I have ever known
how beautiful spring was. [*Sings*]
　　Coy lavenders, fetching reds
　　　　bloom everywhere, here
　　　　all left to this broken well
　　and tumbled wall. Fair season,
　　　　fine scene—overwhelming
　　　　weather. Where

---

[2]A reference to a story about the Tang Prince of Ning early in the 740s. He had bells hung by red threads from flowers' branches, to scare away birds that might harm the blooms. Here, hyperbolically, even the smallest bells might themselves hurt the flowers when rung.

and in whose garden shall we find
pleasure and the heart's delight?

My father and mother have never mentioned such scenery.
TOGETHER:
> Drifting in at dawn, at twilight
>> roll away
> clouds and colored wisps
>> through azure balustrades,
> streaming rain, petals in wind,
> a painted boat in misty waves,
> the girl behind her brocade screen
>> has long ignored
>> such splendor of spring.

SPRING SCENT: All the flowers have bloomed, but it's still early for the peony.
DU LI-NIANG:
> Throughout green hills the nightjar cries
>> red tears of blood; and out beyond
> the blackberry, the threads
>> of mist coil drunkenly.

Oh, Spring Scent!
> And though the peony be fair,
> how can it maintain its sway
>> when spring is leaving?

SPRING SCENT: The orioles and swallows are mating!
TOGETHER:
> Idly I stare
> where twittering swallows crisply speak
>> words cut clear,
> and from the warbling orioles comes
>> a bright and liquid melody.

DU LI-NIANG: Let's go.
SPRING SCENT: I really can't get enough of this garden.
DU LI-NIANG: Let it go! [*They walk on; she sings*]
> When you cannot get enough, you are ensnared,
> then to enjoy each
>> of the twelve pavilions is wasted.
> When the first impulse wears away,
>> it is better by far
>>> to turn back home and idly pass the day.

They arrive.

SPRING SCENT [*recites*]:
> Open the gate to my western parlor,
> in the eastern parlor make my bed.
> The vase has purples-that-shine-in-hills,

to the brazier aloeswood incense add.

You rest here a bit while I go check with your mother. [*Exit*]

DU LI-NIANG [*sighs and recites*]:

In silence back from a springtime stroll,
I'll do my face in the fashion of spring.

Oh, spring, now that I have become attached to you, what am I going to do with myself when you go? Ai! Weather like this really wears a person out. Where is Spring Scent? [*She looks around, then lays her head down, mumbling*] My goodness! Is it really true that spring's beauty can upset a person so? I've always read poems and lyrics, and in olden days young women's passions were stirred by spring, then when autumn came that passion turned to pain. That was really no lie. Now is my sixteenth year and I have not yet encountered a man who has "snapped the cassia twig."[3] Now that I feel this sudden yearning for springtime passion, how will I get a visitor to my lunar palace?[4] Once upon a time Lady Han got to meet young Yu You, and Zhang chanced on Cui Ying-ying; and lovers got together in *The Account of the Poem on a Red Leaf* and "Cui Hui's Story."[5] These fair ladies and talented young men first got together in secret, and they all formed marriage alliances later. [*Sighs*] I was born into a family of officials and I have grown up in an illustrious household. Yet I have already reached fifteen, the age to have one's hair pinned up, without having found a worthy mate. I'm wasting the spring of my life, whose years flash past me. [*Weeps*] What a pity that this complexion so like a flower is destined to end up like a leaf. [*Sings*]

I cannot purge this riot of passion,
I am suddenly plunged into secret despair.
Young and winsome, for me must be chosen
a match from a house of equal station,
equal station, kin to the very gods.
Yet what blessed union would squander
the green spring of my youthful years?
Who sees my slumbering passion?
So must I remain retiring and demure.
But secret dreams will lead me where?—
rolled on unseen with the light of spring.

---

[3]I.e., had success in the examinations.

[4]Du Li-niang is comparing her loneliness to that of the moon goddess Chang E.

[5]Lady Han, in the Tang palace, once composed a poem of her loneliness and longing on a red leaf; she let it float out on the palace moat, where it was found by Yu You. His consequent passion for her and their love story was elaborated in a play by Tang Xian-zu's contemporary Wang Ji-de, *The Account of the Poem on a Red Leaf*. The love story of Zhang and Cui Ying-ying given in "Ying-ying's Story" (see p. 540) was elaborated and given a happy ending in the Yuan play *The Account of the Western Parlor*, which is the version Du Li-niang has in mind. The story of the courtesan Cui Hui and her lover Pei Jing-zhong involves Cui sending Pei a painting of herself, as Du Li-niang will leave a painting for Liu Meng-mei.

As I waver here
to whom can I tell heart's secret care?
I burn away,
my life is cursed, unless
I demand that Heaven tell me why.

I'm completely worn out. I'll put my head down and sleep a while.

She goes to sleep and a dream comes. Enter LIU MENG-MEI, *holding a willow*
(liu) *branch.*

LIU MENG-MEI [*recites*]:

As orioles meet the sunlight's warmth
    their singing voices mellow,
so when a man finds love and passion,
    he laughs out loud from joy.
A whole pathful of fallen flowers
    go off down to the waters,
this is the morning young Ruan Zhao
    reaches Mount Tian-tai.[6]

I followed Du Li-niang back along the path, but where has she gone now?
[*Turns and looks at her*] Ah, there you are! [Du LI-NIANG *startles awake
and they see one another*] Here you are—I was looking for you everywhere. [Du LI-NIANG *gives him a sidelong glance but says nothing*] I just
snapped off half a branch of a weeping willow in the flower garden. Since
you are so well versed in literature, would you write a poem for this willow branch? [Du LI-NIANG *is at first delighted and is about to speak but
stops*]
Du LI-NIANG [*Aside*]: I've never met this man—how did he get in here?
LIU MENG-MEI [*laughing*]: I'm madly in love with you.

[*Sings*]

Because of your flowerlike beauty,
and your youth flowing past like water,
I've looked for you everywhere.
And you were here,
    self-pitying in your lonely chamber.

Let's go somewhere and talk.

Du LI-NIANG *smiles but won't go.* LIU MENG-MEI *pulls her by her clothes.*

Du LI-NIANG [*softly*]: Where are we going?
LIU MENG-MEI [*sings*]:
Pass round by the railing
    where peonies stand,

---

[6]This alludes to a story of Ruan Zhao and a companion who encountered two goddesses in the Tian-
tai Mountains and stayed with them half a year. It became a standard figure for a love affair.

close by the great Tai-hu rock.

Du Li-niang [*softly*]: But what are we going there for?

Liu Meng-mei [*sings*]:

> To unfasten your collar's buttons
> and loosen the sash of your gown.
> You will hold your sleeves pressed
>   tight against teeth,
> then after you bear
>   my tender attentions,
>   enjoy a moment's sleep.

Du Li-niang *is embarrassed.* Liu Meng-mei *puts his arms around her and she pushes him away.*

Together [*sing*]:

> Where have we met before
> that we look at each other unsure?
> How at a wonderful moment like this
> could we come together without a word?

Liu Meng-mei *forces his arms around* Du Li-niang *and exeunt. Enter* Flower God, *with cap under bound-up hair, a red gown, and flowers stuck in cap and gown.*

Flower God [*recites*]:

> As supervisor who expedites flowers
>   I cherish the flower-days,
> inspecting spring's endeavors
>   another year goes its way.
> The visitor suffers heartbreak, drenched
>   under a rain of reds,
> and mortals are lured to be hung in dream
>   beside these colored clouds.

I am the flower god who manages the rear flower garden of the Nan-an district residence. Du Li-niang and Liu Meng-mei are fated to marry in the future. Since Miss Du was so upset after her little spring excursion, she had Mr. Liu come into her dream. We flower gods have a special tender spot for fair young maidens, so I came to watch over her, wanting her to enjoy perfect bliss in her lovemaking. [*Sings*]

> Now the turbid Yang force simmers up
>   transforming,
> and see how he, squirming like worm,
>   fans her passion.
> Likewise her soul quivers at the crack
>   in charming azure foliage.
> This is but shadows' conjunction,
> fancies brought to fullness within,

things appearing inside Karmic Cause.
But, ah, these lewd doings have stained
    my galleries of flowers.

I'll pinch off a blossom and let it fall to wake her. [*He goes toward the stage entrance dropping flowers*]
    How can she linger in her dream,
        woozy with spring?—
    in red flecks of tattered flowers falling.

Young man, your dream is now half-done. When the dream is over, be so good as to escort Miss Du back to her chambers. I go now. [*Exit*]

    Enter DU LI-NIANG *and* LIU MENG-MEI, *holding hands.*

LIU MENG-MEI [*sings*]:
    For this one moment
        Heaven gives ease,
    sprawled in grass,
        asleep on flowers.

How are you? [DU LI-NIANG *lowers her head*]
    She nods her cloudlike coils of hair,
    with tousled red and azure skewed.

Don't forget this!
    how I clasped you tight
    and languidly lingered—
    I wish only our flesh
        could fuse in a ball,
    we drew forth red droplets
        that shimmered in the sun.
DU LI-NIANG: You had better go now.
TOGETHER [*sing*]:
    Where have we met before
    that we look at each other unsure?
    How at a wonderful moment like this
    could we come together without a word?
LIU MENG-MEI: Your body is worn out. Take care of yourself. [*He goes with her back to where she was and she resumes her position asleep; he pats her lightly*] I'm going now. [*He starts off, then turns back*] You've got to take care of yourself now. I'll be back to see you.

    [*Recites*]

    She brought along a third of the rain
        that comes with springtime's glory,
    she slept away a whole cloudburst
        on Wu Mountain. [*Exit*]
DU LI-NIANG [*suddenly waking and softly calling out*]: You've gone, you've gone! [*She sinks back into sleep*]

Enter MRS. DU.

MRS. DU [*recites*]:
>   My husband sits in a yellow hall,
>   my sweet daughter stands by her window.
>   Even on her embroidered dress
>   the birds and flowers are all in pairs.

Daughter, how come you have dozed off here?

DU LI-NIANG [*waking and opening her mouth as if calling* LIU]: Aiya!

MRS. DU: Child, what's going on?

DU LI-NIANG [*getting up, startled*]: Momma, you're here!

MRS. DU: Child, why don't you do some needlework or read something for pleasure to ease your mind? Why are you sleeping here in broad daylight?

DU LI-NIANG: I happened to go out to enjoy myself in the flower garden, but I suddenly felt upset by the excitement of springtime and returned to my rooms. There was nothing else to do, and without knowing it, I was worn out and took a little nap. I hope you'll excuse me for not being awake to greet you.

MRS. DU: The flower garden is too isolated—don't go there to take walks.

DU LI-NIANG: Yes, Mother.

MRS. DU: Now go off to your classroom and study.

DU LI-NIANG: The teacher's not here so we have a little time off.

MRS. DU [*sighing*]: When a daughter grows up, it's natural that she gets moody, so I'll just let her be for a while. As they say,

[*Recites*]

>   She's pulled one way and another by her children,
>   a mother's lot is hard toil. [*Exit*]

DU LI-NIANG [*giving a long sigh as she watches her mother leave*]: Heavens! Today was certainly full of pleasant surprises for me! I chanced to go into the flower garden, and with all the flowers blossoming around me, the scene stirred me. My spirits sagged and I went back and took a nap in my room. Suddenly I saw a young man, about twenty years old, handsome and so very attractive. He had broken a strand of willow branch in the garden, and laughing, he said to me, "Since you are so well versed in literature, would you write a poem for this willow branch?" At that moment I was going to give him an answer, but I thought it over, and since I'd never met him before and didn't know his name, how could I casually hold a conversation with him just like that?

As I was thinking about this, he came out with some lines about how heartsick he was, then he threw his arms around me and we went off to beside the peony pavilion, right by the railing, and we made love together. Both of our hearts were in perfect accord, with a thousand shows of love and a million tendernesses. When our pleasure was finished, he escorted me back to where I was sleeping and said "Take care of yourself" a few times. I was just about to see him out the door when my mother suddenly came in and woke me up.

My whole body is in a cold sweat. This was really one of those "life-times lived in a dream." I was all flustered when I greeted my mother, and she rambled on at me. I had nothing to say back to her because my mind was still on what happened in the dream and I hadn't calmed down. I feel a constant restlessness, as if I had lost something. Oh Mother, you told me to go to the classroom and study—I don't know any book I can read that will get rid of this depression. [*Wipes away tears and sings*]

> Rain's sweet scent, a puff of cloud
> just came to my side in dream.
> But, alas, the lady of the house
> called me awake from my fitful sleep
>   by the gauze-screened window.
> A burst of fresh cold sweat
>   sticks to me and stings.
> It drives my heart to distraction,
>   my footsteps freeze,
>   my thoughts waver,
>   my hair hangs askew.
> All spirit is almost spent,
> and since neither sitting nor standing pleases me,
> let me go off back to sleep!

Enter Spring Scent.

SPRING SCENT [*recites*]:

> Her evening toilette melts powder's streaks,
> spring dampness makes scenting clothes a waste.

The covers have been scented, so let's go to sleep.

DU LI-NIANG [*sings*]:

> This spring-troubled heart is weary
>   from roaming; it seeks
> no scented broidered quilts to sleep.
> Heaven!—if you care,
>   let not that dream be gone too far.

[*Recites*]

> To idly roam and gaze on spring
>   I left the painted hall, [Zhang Yue]
> screening willows and open plums
>   give overpowering scent. [Luo Ye]
> I wonder where young Liu and Ruan
>   met the two fairy maids?— [Xu Hun]
> with a turn of the head spring's east wind
>   breaks the heart for good. [Wei Zhuang]

In many cultures, one of the most durable and revealing conventions in early tradi-tions of romantic love is falling in love upon seeing a portrait of the beloved or hearing a description of him or her; and in the Chinese tradition, sometimes upon reading a person's writings. Liu Meng-mei, strolling in the garden where, unknown to him, Du Li-niang lies buried, finds the self-portrait Du Li-niang made before she died. The portrait shows her holding a plum branch, and the poem he discovers makes reference to willows and plums. He finds this portentous, in that his surname Liu means "willow," and the name he has taken, Meng-mei, means "Dreamed of Plum."

LOOKING OVER THE PORTRAIT (XXVI)

Enter Liu Meng-mei.

Liu Meng-mei [*recites*]:
> On leaves of the plantain tree
>   raindrops do not stay,
> on branches of the peony
>   soon the breeze will draw away.
> Unclear, the portrait's meaning,
>   let eyes focus there
> where barely to announce itself
>   spring light makes its way.

Feeling lonely and somewhat downhearted during my travels, I took a stroll in the garden at the rear of the compound. At the foot of the Great Lake rock, I picked up a small painting on a scroll. I think it must be of the Boddhisattva Guan-yin. It was well protected in a precious case. The past ten days have been stormy, so I couldn't unroll it and take a close look; but happily the weather today is pleasant and bright, so I can examine it and offer my devotions. [*Opens the box and unrolls scroll*]

[*Sings*]
> As in the Silver River of stars
>   the autumn moonlight hangs,
> her body divine unrolls,
> free from attachments, self-contained.
> Here confirmed
>   are all her sacred signs.
> She is really in holy Potala, yet
> we chance to meet
>   here by the southern sea.
> But [*reflectively*]
>   why is her radiant majesty
>   not set upon her lotus seat?
> And wait a moment more!—
> why, beneath her Xiang silk skirt,
>   is there a pair
>   of wave-traversing, dainty feet?

If this is Guan-yin, why does she have bound feet? I'd better look this over more closely.

> I'll think a little bit about
> the image in the picture.

That's it!

> I'll bet
>> it's probably a small Chang E
>>> that hung in someone's studio,
>> painted with such charm and grace.

Well, if this is Chang E, I really ought to make some gesture of my respect.

> Tell me true, Chang E, will I
> snap the spray of cassia.[7]

But wait!—how come this Chang E

> beside her image has no trace
>> of lucky cloud?
> And this cracked bark
>> does not seem like
> the tiny blooms of her cassia grove.

It may not be Guan-yin and it may not be Chang E, but there couldn't possibly be a mortal girl like this.

> Amazed am I
>> and overwhelmed:
> I think I've met her once before,
> and I grope for it in memory.

Let me have a good look. What this drawn by a professional painter or by the beauty's own hand?

> I wonder from where
> came this painting's maiden fair,
> beams of moonglow
>> that appear
> beneath the brush.
> Someone like her
> would have made all the flower-kind bow low.
> Her grace entirely innate,
> a hard thing to delineate;
> pale tresses, springtime wisps,
> who could even approximate?

When I think about it, no professional painter could have done this.

> Most likely only she herself
> could have made this likeness.

---

[7]That is, pass the examination, playing on the image of the cassia tree that grows in the moon.

Just a minute—if you look very closely at the top of the scroll, there are a few lines of tiny characters. [*Looks*] Hmm. It's a quatrain. [*Reads it out loud*]

> Viewed up close it's obvious,
>> and very much like me,
> seen afar, immortal flying
>> self-contained and free.
> If someday I could join the man
>> in the palace of the moon,
> it will be by the flowering plum,
>> or by the willow tree.

So this really is a picture of a mortal girl amusing herself. But what did she mean by: "It will be by the flowering plum, /or by the willow tree"? This is very strange!

[Sings]

> Mountain passes and Plum Ridge,
>> a single swathe of sky—
> I look and wonder how she knew
> that I,
>> Liu Meng-mei
> would be coming through.
> I wonder what she meant to say
> by "join the palace of the moon"?
> I'll be glad—but take it slow,
> think it over carefully:
> for I am Liu, the "Willow,"
> and Meng-mei, "Dreamed of Plum"—
> why should Chang E bother
> here to fix my name?
> Lost in thought, I ponder:
> could my dream be true?

> But O how she turns her gaze on me!
> From light in empty air descends
> beauty's slender grace,
> stirring spring plantain,
> billowing silk and lace.
> Springtime passions there remain
> confined between her brows
> that trace
>> two azure hills of spring,
> and balmy tresses of spring haze.
> Who could lightly disregard
>> two pairs of eyes
> meeting in such mutual gaze?

And I am awash in the flash
    of the turning glance
and the unflinching sidelong stare.

But why she is holding a piece of a leafy plum sprig in her hand, just as
if she were holding me?
    A leafy plum sprig in her hand,
    a whispered poem, entice
    heart's passions to a fall.
    For me, a painted feast
        sates hunger; and for her,
    plum-gazing to slake thirst.[8]
    You, my dear,
        never open mouth's lotus-bud
            even a bit,
    but smiles suppressed,
        behind the pale brushstroke
            of her crimson lips,
    give strong intimation of her passion.
    It seems she want to sadly speak—
    all she needs is a puff of breath.

Her painting is like that of Cui Hui; her poem is like Su Hui; and her
calligraphy is exactly like that of Lady Wei. I may have some classical
dignity in my own work, but I'll never be this girl's match. Having met
her unexpectedly like this, I'll write a poem to match hers.
    Her painting's excellence is due
        to nature and not art—
    if not an immortal of Heaven,
        then an immortal of Earth.
    Is he near or far—that man
        she'd join in the moon?—
    still there is some springtime here
        by plum and willow tree.

[Sings]

Plying the brush she shows her skill,
    good at writing poems,
their splendor enters stream and hill,
    and others sing along.

I'm going to call out to her as loud as I can. My beauty! My love!
Do you know

---

[8]That is, the painting is all he has to satisfy his desire, while the woman in the painting has the plum
in her hand to take the place of him. This alludes to a story in which Cao Cao's soldiers were suffering from thirst, and Cao Cao told them there was a grove of plum trees up ahead where they could
satisfy their thirst.

I am shouting my throat raw,
crying to my Zhen-zhen,
   the painting that came alive.
I call to you to sneeze
   a spray of heavenly petals.[9]
The feet that skim the waves
would splendidly descend—
I do not see her image stir.

So, I'm all alone here. But I'll keep looking over her portrait and examining it, bowing to it, calling out to it, and praising it.
For laying hands on such as her
   I deserve congratulation—
surely Willow and the Plum
   have some deep connection.
And yet, my love, your eyes do slay me,
   image without body.

One should not too single-mindedly
   make the painting bear reproach, [Bo Ju-yi]
but can one let it always hang
   here at the courtyard door? [Wu Qiao]
In despair I write a poem,
   hidden among willows, [Si-kong Tu]
it adds to drunkenness of spring,
   sobering grows still harder. [Zhang Jie]

In the scene before "Secret Union," the Daoist nun who lives in the compound holds a ceremony for Du Li-niang, who roams in ghostly form about the place. Du Li-niang eventually hears Liu Meng-mei calling out to her. As scene XXVIII, "Secret Union," opens, Liu Meng-mei continues his lover's discourse, then falls asleep, to be visited by Du Li-niang.

SECRET UNION (XXVIII)

Enter LIU MENG-MEI.

LIU MENG-MEI [*sings*]:
   Where is the goddess I glimpsed?—
   her image blurs into empty air
      like moonlight veiling sand.
   Bereft, I linger here,
   lost in a wordless reverie.

---

[9]A sneeze was supposed to be a sign that someone, especially one's beloved, was speaking of or thinking of a person.

And now already the evening sun
    sinks down into the west.

[*Recites*]

A single puff of rose red cloud
    came down from Heaven on high,
her coy smile, like a blossom,
    jade's beguiling grace.
Who can picture forth for me
    that sweet and living face,
facing me and holding back
    a passion she cannot speak?

Ever since I encountered her features, in the passionate bloom of their spring, she has been on my mind day and night. Now as the hours of night grow late, I'll spend a little time reciting those pearls of verse and mulling over her spirit. And if, by chance, she should come to me in dream, it would be for me a spring breeze passing. [*He unrolls the painting and looks it over*] Just look at this beauty, her spirit restrained but wanting so much to speak, her eyes pouring forth gentle waves. It makes me think of those lines by Wang Bo: "Sinking wisps of rose red cloud fly level with the solitary heron; and autumn waters share the same color with broad expanse of sky."

[*Sings*]

The evening breeze blows down
one threadlike wisp of cloud
    from Wu-ling stream,[1]
descending and emerging, she
    of overwhelming grace.
Chaste and without flaw,
bright against the crimson lace
fresh in the window screen.
And once again
    I take this little painting
and hang it in my heart.

Dear girl, thinking of you will be the death of me.
    So delicate, so reticent, sweet maid,
    tender and refined, she seems
        of noble family.
I envisage her,
        swept away by a passionate heart,
            looking in the mirror,

---

[1]"Wu-ling stream" refers to "Peach Blossom Spring," which by the late imperial period had become, in the popular imagination, the dwelling place of immortals.

and painting springlike features here,
    her feelings locked within—
could she envisage then the man
    who, finding this, would rouse her?

She comes in flight like moonbeams,
leaving me to find
    a magnitude of melancholy sky.

Usually I can sleep any night facing the moon. These past few nights, though—
    Its secret beauty sends
    darkling flashes of lunar loveliness,
        a brilliance overwhelming.
    They raise a clamor in my besotted heart,
    and whether night or light of day
        my troubled yearnings fix on her.
    If I did not fear to stain
        your painting by taking it in hand,
    I would lie in bed,
        arms wrapped around your image.

I think that we are surely destined to be lovers. Let me read out those
lines of her poem one more time.

[*Reads out poem*]

    She chose to speak in the poem
    for one who would understand—
    of destiny shared by "willow" and "plum."
    Her passionate feelings gush
        from the crack
            in poolside rock,
    and E-lü-hua, the goddess, flew
        into this painting's silken mesh.

I should bow down before her.
    I am in torment,
    before cheeks' glow
        and streak of brow
            scratched into my heart,
    and the one I love
        is not off beyond the horizon.

As I stay here on my journey, how can I get her to meet me for just one
brief moment of love?
    I hate how this narrow strip resists
        our double metamorphosis—
    put us on a painted screen,
        I but a straw,
            leaning against her jade white bough.

Love, can your ears, moon crescents crossed
    by cloud-wisp tresses, hear
anything at all I say
    from this broken heart?

I'm ridiculous—
flirting with her as I speak.
She is the autumn moon that hangs
    by clouds' edge over the seas,
or azure shadow in misty skies,
    brushed over distant hills.
She should be my companion
    in pure, unruffled ease—
how can one even try
    to tease her into passion?

I speak as if reciting spells
or reading out the scriptures.
The very stones may nod their heads,
    and flowers rain from Heaven.
Yet why does such devotion not
    bring the immortal maiden down?
It is that she
    will not go strolling casually.

        Wind rises within, and LIU *takes the scroll.*

To make the goddess stay,
fearing the wind's cruel caress,
I hold fast
    to the ivory roller
        on scroll's brocade.
I'm afraid she's going to be damaged. I'd better find some master to copy
the scroll.
    I waste my breath!—
how could such glorious majesty,
    Guan-yin who views the moon in water,
come as mortal to my bed?
Perhaps I'll meet her somewhere in the flesh,
then I'll ask her how much love she feels,
and it will be no less
    than the sense conveyed
        by this portrait of spring's passionate mood.
I'll trim the lamp wick again to look closely just one more time.
    Such presence divine
        would surely be feigned
            if found in the world of mortal men.

[*From within, a wind blows the lamp's flame*]

Such a gust of cold wind I feel!
   Take care lest sparks fall
      on the painting's image.
   Enough now—I'll try to sleep,
      closing the gauze window screen,
         and of her dream.

Goes to sleep. Enter the soul of Du Li-niang.

Du Li-niang [*recites*]:
   Long lying in the world below,
      but no dream ever comes,
   from my life there still remain
      so many passions.
   My moonlit soul goes following
      the painting's pull,
   I find him in the sound of sighs
      borne upon the wind.

I am the soul of Du Li-niang, who had a dream of a garden in full flower and then died of longing. It was then that I painted my own features in the bloom of youth and buried it beneath the Great Lake rock. On it I wrote:
   If someday I could join the man
      in palace of the moon,
   it will be by the flowering plum,
      or by the willow tree.

After wandering here several evenings, little did I expect to hear from inside the eastern chambers a student cry out with a restrained voice, "My beloved, my beauty!" There was misery in the sound of his voice, and it stirred my very soul. I softly flitted into his chambers, where I saw a small painting hung high on the wall. When I examined it more carefully, it was the painting of my own youthful features that I had left behind. On the back there was a companion piece to my poem. When I looked at the signature, it was by Liu Meng-mei of Ling-nan. "By the flowering plum—*mei*—or by the willow tree—*liu*"—there must be some destiny at work here! And now with the leave of the authorities in the dark world below, I have taken this fine night to finish out that dream begun before. And I feel such bitter pain when I think of it.

[*Sings*]

I fear
   how fragrance fades and powder chills
      from tears
  shed on the sheer vermilion gauze,
  to Gao-tang's lodge again I come
      to enjoy the glow of the moon.

Then all at once I turn and gasp in shame
    at these disheveled coils of hair,
I pat them straight.

Ah, and here is his room right before me!

    I fear being duped by the too straight way
        that leads to Peach Blossom Spring,
    let me swiftly be sure that it is him.

LIU MENG-MEI [*reciting her poem in his sleep*]:
    If someday I could join the man
        in palace of the moon,
    it will be by the flowering plum,
        or by the willow tree.

Dearest!

DU LI-NIANG [*listening with emotion*]:
    His cries break
        the heart and make
            tears flow—
    these lines from my lost poem
    he has without mistake.

I wonder if he's already asleep. [*Peeks*]

LIU MENG-MEI *cries out again.*

From within the screen where he sleeps
    he recites with fierce sighs.
Keeping the noise low
I'll rap at his window frame of azure bamboo.

LIU MENG-MEI [*waking up suddenly*]: Dearest!
DU LI-NIANG (*moved*):
    I'll send the sweet soul off
        to draw near.
LIU MENG-MEI: Hmmm. That sound of tapping on the bamboo outside my
    door—was it the wind or a person?
DU LI-NIANG: A person.
LIU MENG-MEI: At this time of night you must be the Sister bringing tea.[2]
    You really shouldn't have.
DU LI-NIANG: No, not her.
LIU MENG-MEI: Then are you the itinerant nun staying here?
DU LI-NIANG: No.
LIU MENG-MEI: Now that's really strange. And it's not the good Sister either.

---

[2]The Sister is the Daoist nun, "Sister Stone," who had established a small convent of the grounds of Governor Du's former residence.

I wonder who it could be. Let me open the door and take a look. [*Opens the door and looks around*]

[*Sings*]

Out of nowhere a lovely maid,
whose charms bedazzle
with uncommon wonder.

Du Li-niang *smiles and slips inside.* Liu Meng-mei *quickly closes the door.*

Du Li-niang: Hello, young gentleman.

Liu Meng-mei: May I ask you, miss, where you come from and why have you come here so deep in the night?

Du Li-niang: Guess.

Liu Meng-mei [*sings*]:

I'll bet it's because of that lout
Zhang Qian, whose raft
has invaded your River of Stars,[3]
or it must be little Liang Yu-qing
fleeing the punishment by night
of Heaven's officers?[4]

Du Li-niang: Those are both immortals of Heaven. How could they be here?

Liu Meng-mei:

Are you the phoenix of bright colors
wrongly mated to a crow?

Du Li-niang *shakes her head.*

Liu Meng-mei:

Did I somewhere for your sake
to the green poplar tie my horse?

Du Li-niang: We never met.

Liu Meng-mei:

It must be your vision is blurred,
mistaking me for Tao Qian;[5]
if not, then perhaps you strayed,

---

[3]This is a common mixing of two allusions: first, of the Han explorer Zhang Qian, sent to find the source of the Yellow River; and second, of the old man who rode a raft up into the River of Stars, where he saw the Weaver Star. Liu Meng-mei is here comparing himself to the intruder on the raft and Du Li-niang to the Weaver Star.

[4]Liang Yu-qing was supposed to have been the immortal handmaiden of the Weaver. She ran off with the star Tai-bo to Earth.

[5]Tao Qian's "Peach Blossom Spring," the refuge in the mountain cut off from history, became mixed up with another story about peach blossoms, in which two young men, Liu Zhen and Ruan Zhao, met two goddesses. In this confusion Tao Qian sometimes became, incongruously, the figure of the handsome young man that caught the goddess's roving eye. Liu Meng-mei suggests that Du Li-niang is such a goddess, but a dim-sighted one.

eloping down the Lin-qiong Road.[6]

DU LI-NIANG: There is no mistake.

LIU MENG-MEI: Are you looking for a lamp?

> And yet you go about by night
> without a lamp?[7]
> And thus you wish to share my lamp,
> red sleeves by my window of sapphire gauze.

DU LI-NIANG [*sings*]:

> I am not that heavenly maid
> who scattered the blossoms of sacred scent
> in vain;[8]
> nor am I the scholar's lamp
> idly moist with waxen tears.
> I am not like Zhao Swallow-in-Flight,
> who came with reputation stained;[9]
> yet neither am I Zhuo Wen-jun
> who would hold fast
> to newly widowed chastity.
> You, young sir, once strayed in flowers,
> the dreaming butterfly.

LIU MENG-MEI [*thinking*]: Yes, I did have such a dream before.

DU LI-NIANG:

> Thus did I, to oriole fifes,
> go to the willow array.
> And if you wonder where my rooms are—
> not so far—
> just some doors down from Song Yu's neighbor.[1]

LIU MENG-MEI [*thinking*]: Yes! Turning west from the flower garden at sundown I saw a young woman walking.

DU LI-NIANG: That was I.

LIU MENG-MEI: Who is your family?

DU LI-NIANG [*sings*]:

> Off beyond the setting sun,

---

[6]This refers to the story of Zhuo Wen-jun, who, after hearing the Han writer Si-ma Xiang-ru play his harp, ran off with him to Lin-qiong. Again, Liu Meng-mei suggests that Du Li-niang has the wrong man.

[7]Liu Meng-mei is alluding to the "Domestic Regulations" of the *Classic of Rites,* in which it says that a woman must have a lamp when she travels by night, and when she has no lamp, she should stay put.

[8]This refers to a story in the *Vimalakirti sutra,* in which a heavenly maiden scattered divine blossoms on the body of the sick Vimalakirti—blossoms that did not cling to his body because of his spiritual attainments.

[9]The Han consort Zhao Swallow-in-Flight was said to have had an affair before entering the imperial harem.

[1]"Song Yu's neighbor" is a literary allusion to a poetic exposition that became proverbial for the beautiful "girl next door."

on the horizon
  of fragrant prairies,
mother and father are all alone,
  none other there.
My age is sixteen years, a bloom
sheltered by leaves from wind,
  chaste beyond reproach.
Spring left,
  I was stirred to sighs,
when suddenly I glimpsed
  your manly grace.
For no other purpose have I come
but to trim the lamp wick in the breeze
and chat at ease
  by the western window.

LIU MENG-MEI [*aside*]: Remarkable that such sensual beauty exists in this mortal world! Out of nowhere in the middle of the night I have met a bright-moon pearl. What can I say?

[*Sings to* DU LI-NIANG]

Wonder-struck by beauty,
her loveliness beyond compare,
a smile flashes, passion's
  silver taper.
The full moon seems to retire,
and I wonder
  what night this could be
    for the raft drifting through stars.
A woman with hairpins of gold
  comes in night's cold,
a spirit of the upper air
  to the bed of mortal man.

[*Aside*]

Yet I wonder of what sort of household
is she the child,
to welcome me in this fashion?

I'll ask more about her. [*Turning back to* DU LI-NIANG] Is this perhaps a dream that you come to visit me so deep in the night?

DU LI-NIANG [*smiling*]: It is no dream; it is real. But I'm afraid you won't have me.

LIU MENG-MEI: And I'm afraid it's not real. But if I am really beloved by such a beauty, then I am happy beyond all expectation. How could I dare refuse?

DU LI-NIANG: Don't worry—I have truly set my hopes on you.

[*Sings*]

On cold slopes of a secret valley,
you make me blossom flowers by night.[2]
In no way was I ever wed,
as here you will discover
one by good family closely kept.
At the peony pavilion
loving heart's affection;
by the lake rock's side,
shy and blushing bride;
window of the scholar's room,
in rattling of wind.
Let this fine night not be lost,
the cool breeze, bright moon
    costs us nothing.[3]

LIU MENG-MEI:

In amazement melts the soul
and wakes from sleep in moonlit chill.
A burst of sudden splendor,
    and I wonder
if this might be
    Wu Mountain in a dream.[4]
I am humbled by the way you tread
    in flowers' shade
        without the least dread,
by the way you touch green moss
    not sliding on its slipperiness,
by the way you ignore
    a daughter's obligation,
        feeling no intimidation,
and, certain that there is no error,
    in the way you've chosen me.
Look how the Dipper's slanting low,
and how the flowers droop—
this late at night the flowers sleep.
Laugh merrily,
chant in bliss,
no breeze and moon will better this.

---

[2]This refers to a verse by Empress Wu, in which she commanded the flowers to blossom in the night and not wait until dawn.

[3]"Cool breeze, bright moon" was a phrase that had become, in contexts like the present one, a standard figure for a sexual encounter.

[4]Wu Mountain's goddess meeting the King of Chu was a standard figure for a sexual encounter, either illusory or a reality so bewildering that it seems like illusion.

> Lend me of your own free will
> 　your lovely softness,
> 　　and sweet charms,
> and bear as I humble it,
> 　humble it for but a moment.

DU LI-NIANG: Please forgive me, but let me first say one thing to you in all earnest.

LIU MENG-MEI: Don't hold back—say whatever you want.

DU LI-NIANG: In this moment I give this precious body of mine to you. Do not betray this love I feel. My lifelong wish would be fulfilled if every night I could share pillow and mat with you.

LIU MENG-MEI [*laughing*]: Since you love me, how could I ever put you out of my mind?

DU LI-NIANG: One more thing. Let me go back before the rooster crows. Don't try to see me off—so that you will stay out of the early morning wind.

LIU MENG-MEI: As you say. But let me ask your name.

DU LI-NIANG [*sighs and sings*]:

> Flower must have its root,
> 　the jade, its sprout,
> but were I to tell, it would call forth
> 　too great a sound of gale.

LIU MENG-MEI:

> I look forward to your coming nightly from now on.

DU LI-NIANG:

> And now with me
> let us annotate and compare
> 　this very first flower
> 　　in the spring breeze.

LIU MENG-MEI:

> Surging manner, wild scent,
> 　never encountered before, [Han Yu]

DU LI-NIANG:

> the moon slants past the high chamber,
> 　the bell before the dawn. [Li Shang-yin]

LIU MENG-MEI:

> Dawn clouds go in by night,
> 　no trace of their passage, [Li Bo]

DU LI-NIANG:

> I wonder from which of the peaks
> 　the goddess came. [Zhang Zi-rong]

The Qing Dynasty

THE QING DYNASTY: PERIOD INTRODUCTION   Early in the seventeenth century, the Manchus, a Tungusic people, consolidated a small regional state beyond the northeastern frontiers of the Ming. They built a powerful army, drawing on the large Chinese population of the region as well as their own ethnic group. In 1644, after the rebel Li Zi-cheng had taken Beijing and the Ming emperor committed suicide, the Ming general Wu San-gui  opened the passes to the Manchu army and joined with them to crush Li Zi-cheng's forces. The Manchus were poised for a conquest of China; but China was a very large country and not one to be easily swallowed by a small regional state, however professional its military machine. The conquest was aided by the incompetence, dissolution, or defection of numerous large Ming armies, and when Shi Ke-fa, one of the few Ming generals with any resolution, tried to hold the city of Yang-zhou with a small force, his quick defeat and the subsequent sack of that once prosperous city served well to intimidate others who contemplated resistance. Vigorous defenses were mounted in some regions, but the inability of Ming forces to coordinate resistance ensured their ineffectiveness, and all opposition was brutally suppressed. When the Qing armies descended on Nanjing, where a new Ming regime had been established under the Prince of Fu, the Ming "restoration" government simply dissolved.

The early decades of Qing rule required the elimination of a series of Ming pretenders and several resistance movements. The Qing showed a ruthlessness in establishing its authority that was comparable to that of the Ming in its own early years; and if the Manchu rulers never won the general love of their Chinese subjects, they eventually enforced a degree of intimidated docility. Male Chinese subjects were required to shave their heads except for a long pigtail or queue worn in the Manchu style. Although the queue appeared as one of the most striking characteristics of "Chinese" attire to early Western observers, it was to the Chinese an often-hated symbol of foreign domination.

Like other frontier peoples who had conquered China, the Manchus faced the problem of becoming absorbed into the general Chinese population. The Jurchen Jin of the twelfth and thirteenth centuries came from a people closely related to the Manchus, and they had disappeared into the population of North China leaving scarcely a trace. The Mongols, by contrast, had maintained their separateness, but had never been able to quite establish themselves as effective rulers. The Manchus found themselves as overlords of a multi-ethnic empire, including Mongols, Turks, and Tibetans as well as Chinese, and they sought to ensure a measure of ethnic separation. Manchus were supposed to marry only Manchus to preserve the integrity of the people. Blood was, however, a less powerful force than culture; within a few generations, the sinicization of the ruling Manchu elite was complete. Alarmed Qing emperors required the study of the Manchu language for Manchus in China, and encouraged young Manchus to spend time in Manchuria and experience the manly virtues of their forebears.

The Manchu state had never been entirely Manchu, even before the conquest of China proper. The Manchu military organization was composed of military units known as "banners," some of which were Manchu and some Chinese. The so-called bannermen and their descendants, Chinese and Manchu alike, were given preferential treatment in positions in the Qing government.

While trying desperately to protect their ethnic identity, the Manchu emperors, unlike their Mongol predecessors, set out to be exemplary Chinese rulers. They were, if anything, more puritanically Confucian than the Chinese, and they set a tone of pious propriety that had consequences in the civil service and in elite culture in general. Censors were ready to denounce not only any book that contained imagined ethnic slurs but also any book deemed "injurious to the public morals." The "literary inquisition" of the eighteenth century cast a pall of anxiety over writing, and the relative liberty of the late Ming, including the first decades of Qing rule, gave way to a general caution.

Although the Ming had been suffering from internal disturbances for decades, the overthrow of the dynasty and the establishment of the Qing within the course of a year profoundly shocked Chinese intellectuals. Many became monks or retired permanently to private life, either because they had previously served the Ming or out of a lingering sense of loyalty to the old dynasty. Coming to terms with the Ming's destruction remained a preoccupation of writers for decades after the conquest. The works of Zhang Dai (1597–1679) represent one form of homage to the fallen dynasty in dreamlike prose sketches of life in the Southern cities on the eve of the conquest.

Kong Shang-ren's play *Peach Blossom Fan* (1699) represents the culmination of attempts to represent the fate of the Ming. Written by a dramatist born in 1648, after the Qing conquest, *Peach Blossom Fan* tells the story of two lovers whose fate is intertwined with that of the "Southern Ming," the restoration regime in Nanjing that lasted only a year. The play generally avoids reference to the Qing and its armies, and when they are mentioned, it is usually in complimentary terms. The Southern Ming is depicted as destroying itself through incompetence, greed, and a preoccupation with domestic intrigue.

The early Qing saw a strong reaction against late Ming individualism and a fascination with the imagination on the part of some intellectuals. A new empiricism appeared in almost all branches of learning. Inspired interpretation was replaced by reasoning from evidence. One area of scholarly research with profound consequences was historical phonology—the study of the way in which the pronunciation of characters had changed over time. It was recognized that before the long process of standardizing the script in the Qin and Han, scribes had often chosen characters purely to represent sounds. Such characters are called "loan characters" and they occur throughout ancient texts. Armed with their new proto-science of historical phonology, scholars began making new guesses about loan characters in ancient texts and producing interpretations of the Confucian Classics that were very different from the received interpretations. Since the Confucian Classics had a scriptural authority in the constitution of the state and elite society, such excellent scholarship was inherently destabilizing and increased the gap between serious scholars and the still orthodox interpretations of the Southern Song Neo-Confucian Zhu Xi. A culture founded on ancient texts thus found itself no longer certain of the meaning of those texts.

"Literature" in the Qing was not conceived as a single category; rather, it was a large field of distinct genres, some coming down in an unbroken tradition from the Tang and Song, and others revived after a long period of relative neglect. Qing literature was, moreover, closely linked to scholarship on earlier literature and its re-publication. The Qing government sponsored numerous scholarly projects, such as the compilation of the *Complete Tang Poetry* (1705). Scholars, readers, and writers often specialized in one or more genres and styles. The "song lyric" of the Song, for example, was sometimes written as a purely literary form in the Ming—the old music had been long lost—but it was not popular. Yet the last decade of the Ming witnessed a major revival in the composition of song lyrics in the Song tradition, and this revival began a new and unbroken tradition of song lyric composition that continued well into the twentieth century. Some writers wrote in other forms, but many specialized only in the song lyric. It had its own history of contending schools in the Qing, with anthologies and an immense corpus of critical writing. Moreover, this history of Qing song lyric was inextricably linked to scholarship and criticism on the song lyric of the Song Dynasty. The Qing lyricist presumed that his or her readers would be thoroughly familiar with his Song predecessors and would recognize in his work how he positioned himself in relation to the history of song lyric. This is not to say that Qing lyrics were necessarily imitative—in fact, the Qing tradition of the genre is far richer in range and style than the Song—but Qing originality was founded upon a presumed body of learning and a familiarity with critical debate.

Similar specialties existed in the various periods of classical poetry, in "old style" prose and formal prose, in informal prose genres, in vernacular song lyric, in variety plays (which by this point had become a purely literary genre). The classical tale of the supernatural had a long history, stretching back to the period immediately following the Han. Despite the seventeenth-century vogue for vernacular short stories, the classical tale (ranging in scale from the anecdote to something approaching a novella) had been composed continuously. In the late seventeenth century, it reemerged to prominence in *Liao-zhai's Record of Wonders,* by Pu Song-ling (1640–1715). This large collection of supernatural tales was immensely popular, and it spawned renewed interest in the genre, taking the form of numerous versions of such tales in the eighteenth and nineteenth centuries.

Pu Song-ling's collection of supernatural stories—like the editions of Tang poets, the anthologies of "old style" prose, famous plays, and all the major vernacular novels—was printed with extensive critical commentaries. Such commentaries might be printed in the margins, in between the lines, or after passages. Earlier works, such as the Tang poets or "old style" prose writers, usually had scholarly commentaries as well. Critical commentary was not an academic addition to works usually read without commentary; rather, it was almost impossible to find an edition of Pu Song-ling or the famous novels without a commentary. For Tang and Song writers, editions and anthologies without commentaries were the less popular, more scholarly forms. Commentaries indicated literary techniques, brought out hidden implications in passages, and in longer works called attention to the overall structure. Not until the twentieth century, in part following the Western model and in part seeking to break free of the habits of traditional criticism, would such works be printed without the critical commentaries.

The two outstanding novels of the eighteenth century represent a major transformation of the genre from its predecessors in the sixteenth and seventeenth centuries. The eighteenth-century novels are by known authors, and the rough exuberance of vernacular Chinese in earlier long fiction has been supplanted by a much sharper and more refined vernacular. Both of these novels were not printed until decades after the deaths of their authors. The first is *The Scholars (Ru-lin wai-shi)*, by Wu Jing-zi (1701–1754), first published in 1803. A medley of interlocking episodes, *The Scholars* is a savagely satirical portrait of late imperial society, its hypocrisy and the failure of its values. But probably the defining work of Qing literature is *Story of the Stone* (or *Dream of the Red Chamber; Hong-lou meng*), by Cao Xue-qin (1715–1763). Cao worked on versions of his novel over the course of about two decades, leaving it incomplete after eighty chapters. The first printed edition of 1791 was completed by the addition of another forty chapters by Gao E (ca. 1740–ca. 1815).

Story of the Stone quickly became more than a success: like Shakespeare in English or *Don Quixote* in Spanish, it won the utter devotion of readers soon after its publication and that devotion has not diminished to the present day. On one level it is the story of a magic piece of jade, destined to be born into the world and achieve enlightenment by experiencing the disillusionment of love. The novel tells the story of an adolescent boy, Bao-yu ("Precious Jade"), born into a powerful Qing household just passing from the height of its powers into decline. Bao-yu lives surrounded by women—maidservants, sisters, cousins, and the older women of the household. But his passion is reserved for his hypersensitive cousin Dai-yu ("Black Jade"). *Story of the Stone* is an extraordinarily rich novel in the physical and cultural details of life in eighteenth-century China; it is no less rich in the complexity of its vision of the society, with moments of everyday pettiness and tenderness framed in a larger and dangerous world of men and political power.

Story of the Stone was perhaps particularly moving because it represented the very end of traditional Chinese civilization as a world unto itself. During the nineteenth century, the Western powers made their presence felt in ways that would change China forever. The Jesuit missionaries of the Ming and early Qing had sought to cultivate China's rulers and elite. Their technical knowledge and devices elicited the fascination of many Chinese intellectuals; but although the early missionaries won a select body of converts, their goal of the general conversion of China to a Christian country was not on the horizon. Church politics and other factors eventually led the Qing government to a general prohibition against Christianity in 1723.

In a little more than a century, Europe would return to China in full force. Opium, initially smoked with tabacco, increased in use in China through the course of the eighteenth century. By early in the nineteenth century, addiction had risen to a serious level and the subsequent drain on silver reserves led to an increase in commodity prices. By the 1830s, the problem had reached crisis proportions. A zealous reformer, Lin Ze-xu, was dispatched by the Qing government to Canton, the primary port of the Anglo-Chinese opium trade, where he destroyed all the existing opium stocks. This and other sources of friction between the English and the Chinese, including the understandable reluctance of the English to turn their nationals over to what they saw as the barbaric practices of the Chinese legal system, eventually led to the Opium War in 1840. After English fleets decisively defeated Qing naval forces and coastal defenses, the war was finally brought to an end by the Treaty of Nanjing in 1842, by which Hong Kong was annexed and the English were given extraterritorial rights at five major Chinese ports; by these rights the English could live in their own compounds and were subject to English rather than Chinese law. Once England had exposed the helplessness of China in face of Western military technology, in the decades that followed other Western powers competed to enforce upon China their own treaties, with their own ports and the same rights as the English.

In the middle of the century, the Qing faced an even more devastating challenge. The period from 1850 through the early 1860s saw the rebellion of the *Tai-ping tian-guo,* the "Heavenly Kingdom of Great Peace." The *Tai-ping tian-guo* was a theocratic movement based on a syncretism of Christianity and native Chinese millenarianism. The Tai-pings held Central China, including the great city of Nanjing, and they defeated Qing armies again and again until Zeng Guo-fan (1811–1872), the Qing intellectual and general, at last suppressed them. In 1864, after a prolonged siege, Nanjing was at last taken and the city was sacked by Qing troops. While the war with the Tai-pings was under way, the Western powers were demanding legations in Beijing on a status of diplomatic equality, the right to travel in the interior of China, opening the country to missionaries, and more territorial concessions for trade. Negotiations broke down, and in 1860 a joint Anglo-French army invaded Beijing, sending the Qing court into flight to their Manchurian capital at Jehol. The resulting Treaty of Beijing gave France and England everything they had demanded. In 1885, after hostilities, the French claimed Vietnam; Russia and Germany, in the meantime, were also winning concessions under threat of force. In 1894, the Sino-Japanese War broke out, leading to yet another humiliation for the Qing and treaty concessions to the Japanese.

A half century of repeated military and political humiliation left both the Qing government and much of the Chinese populace with a deep hatred for Japan and the Western powers. Within the foreign concessions, governed by the laws of the foreign powers, Chinese were treated as second-class citizens with few rights, and they experienced Western racism. Western gunboats patrolled the coast and the Yangzi River, ready to suppress any threat to foreign nationals. Eventually, in 1899, the festering rage broke out in the Boxer Rebellion, a secret society sworn to rid China of all foreigners. All foreigners were attacked, especially missionaries, and in 1900 the foreign legations in Beijing were besieged. A relief force made up of detachments from Japan and the Western powers marched from Tian-jin to Beijing, and predictably the Qing government was forced to pay large sums in reparations.

The encounter with the West brought other changes as well. Western novels began to be translated, first freely recast in classical Chinese, but later translated accurately. Toward the end of the nineteenth century newspapers made their appearance, containing serialized novels that already showed Western influence. Students went off to Europe and the United States, and primarily to Japan, bringing back not only technical expertise but also Western literature and thought. As an East Asian nation that had successfully adapted to the encounter with the West, Japan was seen as a model of what China could become. In 1905, the old imperial civil service examinations were abolished, and at last, in 1911, the Qing was overthrown with remarkable ease and the Republic was established. China's troubles were far from over, but the old imperial system was gone forever.

From the late Qing through the first decades of the Republic, classical literature continued to be written in the old forms; but a new literature was taking shape, a literature informed by Western and Japanese models. On May 4, 1919, a large student protest called for basic cultural reform, including the abandonment of classical Chinese in favor of the written vernacular. Literary and cultural traditions attenuate and transform slowly, but sometimes a single date can serve as a symbol of change. The May Fourth movement is generally understood as the beginning of modern Chinese literature.

Li Yu, *Silent Operas* 清
(Wu-sheng xi)

Prior to the seventeenth century, Chinese fiction and drama usually embellished older stories rather than inventing new ones. Even when an author invented a story, literary convention demanded that it be presented as if it came from some outside source, either a contemporary or an earlier text. The dramatist and storywriter Li Yu (1611–1680) took great pride in telling readers that his stories were the products of his own fertile wit, and he rarely lets his readers forget his authorial presence.

Like many Qing writers, Li Yu failed the civil service examination and had to rely on his literary reputation to make a living. To support himself, he took the unusual course of organizing a theatrical company and taking it on tour. As in the English theatrical companies of the Elizabethan and Jacobean eras, Li Yu also wrote the material. Writing and publishing his plays was no less a business venture, and was as much to attract patronage as for direct income. Part of what Li Yu sold was an image of Epicurean pleasures and pastimes embodied in the essays entitled "Random Ventures in Idleness" *(Xian-qing ou-ji)*. These include sections on gardening, eating and drinking, architecture, and health, as well as several on drama.

Li Yu wrote voluminously, turning out ten comedies of romantic intrigue, a pornographic novel, and several collections of stories. "An Actress Scorns Wealth and Honor . . ." is drawn from the first of the story collections, entitled *Silent Operas (Wu-sheng xi)*. The story shows a preoccupation with theater that characterized both Li Yu and his age. The interplay of truth and feigned appearances moves back and forth across the boundaries of the stage, with Li Yu's voice ever present in the background to draw conclusions for us. The intrusive narrator had long been a feature of Chinese stories, but Li Yu plays the role with an ironic and self-congratulating gusto that is his trademark.

"An Actress Scorns Wealth and Honor to Preserve Her Chastity"
Translated by Patrick Hanan

Poem:

> Beauty's power to stir the heart
> Is heightened by her acting art.
> Though her singing make a thousand cry,
> No tear will come to Beauty's eye.

Lyric:

> A pretty bawd with a singing voice—
> Charms, she has them all.
> Her constant smile will banish care,
> Till all men think she favours them,
> Their hearts in thrall.
>
> They risk their lives to make her gifts,
> Not stopping till they die.
> They shower her with precious gems,
> And when they get no sweets in turn,[1]
> They think—she's shy.

Both poem and lyric make the point that when it comes to charm, actresses are in a different class altogether from the ordinary run of prostitutes. Men lose their hearts to actresses, the strait-laced turning into romantics and the tight-fisted into big spenders. Why should this be? Because in training to become actresses, these women have practised those warbling, dulcet tones and that delicate, willowy grace of theirs to perfection. There is no need for them to affect such things in company, for they come naturally. When actresses are placed beside girls of good family, their impurity outshines the latter's purity; when put beside prostitutes, their naturalness highlights the others' affectedness. In addition, that carpet on the stage is a most peculiar thing, for it hurts the ugly woman as it helps the beauty. When an ugly woman comes on stage, she appears even uglier, but when a beautiful woman does so, her beauty is enhanced. It is common for a woman of middling attractiveness off-stage to look like the reincarnation of Xishi or Yang Guifei[2] as soon as she sets foot on stage and begins her performance, at which point even a perfect beauty cannot compare with her. There are two reasons for this. Firstly, actors and actresses are predestined for their trade and have a god, Erlang, who watches over them. And secondly, the impression they make is the result of long training, not something that can be produced by a mere act of will.

However that may be, the four lowliest classes in society consist of prostitutes, entertainers, lictors and slaves.[3] Thus actresses, as both prostitutes and entertainers, combine two of the four classes. Why, then, should an actress be made the subject of a story? Because when a person from the lowliest class of all performs the noblest deed of all, it is fully as remarkable as a magic mushroom growing out of a dunghill, and it deserves to be publicized.

---

[1]The allusion is to the love song "Mugua" in the *Poetry Classic:* "She threw a tree-peach to me; / As requital I gave her a bright greenstone," etc. See Arthur Waley, trans., *The Book of Songs* (New York: Grove Press, 1987), p. 31.
[2]Of the Zhou and Tang dynasties, respectively, they came to personify ideals of beauty.
[3]Sons born to people in any of these occupations were excluded from the civil service examinations.

Whereas other stories relate an anecdote as a prologue to the story proper, this one will follow a different course. It has no need to play the host ushering in the guest, for it will generate the child from the mother. To begin with the dunghill and go on from there to tell of the magic mushroom—that is something entirely new in literary composition.

Let me tell how in Xi'an county of Quzhou prefecture in Zhejiang there was a township of moderate size named Yang Village in which all of the inhabitants, men as well as women, took up acting as a career. Now, actors are produced in every part of the country, not just this one, but actresses were the specialty of this area, because the singing and acting here were remarkably authentic. If geomancy was one factor, genetic inheritance was certainly another. Because an actress's parents were actor and actress themselves, they brought into play during the sexual act, before the seed was sown, the very same voices and movements that they employed on stage. Thus the essential ingredients of an acting career were already present in the father's semen and the mother's blood. Moreover, during the mother's pregnancy, she would continue to act full time. The ancients held the theory that a child's education begins *in utero;*[4] thus the mother's dulcet tones and willowy grace would have been instilled in the child before birth. And once she was born, everything she saw or heard had to do with the theatre. Custom eventually turned into instinct, and she proved a natural performer. How could anyone who took up acting at a later stage even begin to compare with her? Which explains why this locality produced several outstanding actresses in every generation.

Actresses in other parts of the country, who began as prostitutes, would act during the day and entertain their clients by night, using their acting merely to attract custom. But these actresses, with their "three do's and three don't's," were quite different.

What were these do's and don't's of theirs?

Do let them look, but don't let them taste.
Do let them have the name, but don't let them have the reality.
Do let them plan, but don't let them succeed.

While they were on stage, the whole of their persons was visible to the audience, and even off-stage they were still playful and flirtatious. However, when it came to that goblet of aromatic wine they possessed, they would let men water at the mouth but not wet their lips. This was what was meant by "letting them look but not taste."

When young noblemen or rich merchants tried to use their power or money to get them into bed, the actresses never refused outright, but their consent was merely verbal. They would plead illness, claiming they could not make love at the moment, or else pretend that their husbands objected

---

[4]I.e., *taijiao,* by which the embryo is held to be morally influenced by the mother's behaviour.

and suggest that their admirers await some other opportunity. But the days would go by, and they would remain as unattainable as ever. This was what was meant by "letting them have the name but not the reality."

Even if they went to bed with their admirers and behaved so passionately that you would think them genuinely in love, in their eyes it was just a performance, as if they were playing a romantic scene or two with their leading men. While the play was on, they were utterly serious, but when they left the stage, they left their seriousness behind. Lovestruck young men would frequently offer large sums of money to buy them out, but although they consented, and let their admirers scheme away from dawn to dusk heedless of the costs of courtship, the plans would all end up as a spring dream, for the actresses could never bring themselves to marry. This was what was meant by "letting them plan but not succeed."

What was their motive for being so difficult? You must understand that their hearts were not set on preserving their chastity for their husbands' sake, but on making money for those husbands, and not small sums of money either, but large amounts. A man's true feeling for a woman does not arise from the bodily contact, but from the eye contact that precedes it. A gourmand at a feast will smell the aroma of the food before he sits down to dinner and start watering at the mouth, feeling he has never in all his life met with such delicacies; but after he gets the food into his mouth and has wolfed down a meal of it, if a second gourmet dinner is brought out, he will feel disgust rather than desire. Now, at the sight of a woman, a man is like the gourmand at the sight of food; you can allow him to smell the aroma but not to start eating, for once he does so, he will lose interest, and it will be impossible to set his mouth watering again. Therefore the actresses from this locality, who were well aware of the principle involved, did not enter lightly into liaisons, but made this tripartite formula of theirs a family heirloom. Mothers passed it down to daughters, and mothers-in-law to daughters-in-law, through scores of generations, until one day an unfilial daughter came along who rejected the formula outright and would let men do *anything*—taste as well as look, have the reality as well as the name, succeed as well as plan. As the proverb so aptly puts it: "Every case is a law unto itself." After years of this accommodating attitude, she had cooperated with her husband to earn a large sum of money—as well as a reputation for unconventional behaviour.

Her surname was Liu and her personal name Jiangxian, and she lived at the end of the Jiajing era.[5] She was as pretty as a flower and as fair as jade, she had an excellent voice and a beautiful figure, and she was blessed with a sharp intelligence. Other actresses could play only one role, but she had an exceptional versatility and would play the heroine or the hero, a man or

---

[5]1522–66.

a woman, as the manager wished. And she had another talent too, of a free, unfettered kind; after the main play was over, she would quickly put on a painted face and play the *jing* or *chou*.[6] Her byplay was sparklingly original, and every word of it impressed her audience. They lost their hearts to her, and there was no man who did not wish to take her to bed. And she was exceptionally accommodating by nature, too. It was not absolutely necessary that you be endowed with Pan An's looks and Cao Zhi's talent;[7] in fact, even if you could neither read nor write, and were as ugly as sin, she would go to bed with you just so long as you could put up a large enough sum of money.

From accepting the ugly as well as the handsome, she came to be patronised by the stupid as well as the intelligent, and before she was thirty she had amassed a large fortune and established her husband as a local worthy of some note. But although her business expanded, she never gave up her profession, and would entrust her property to others while she and her husband went on tour. Their hope was to have a child who would one day take over their responsibilities and allow them to retire.

But "when things reach one extreme, they turn back toward the other." After years of trying, this couple produced a daughter, another unfilial daughter, who scorned not only the traditional family code but her own mother's rules as well. In the end she created a true play out of a false play, one that would be performed for thousands of years to come.

Her childhood name was Miaogu, and she was as pretty as a flower and as fair as jade, a truly outstanding beauty whose charms were too numerous to mention. An old jingle sums her up:

One trace of powder—she'd be too pale;
One touch of rouge—she'd be too red;
One inch more—she'd be too tall;
One inch less—she'd be too short.

As for her voice, which "stopped the passing clouds and lingered among the roof-beams,"[8] it was her forte and there is no need to speak of it. Not only did she cause thousands to applaud her extraordinary art, she was capable of suddenly driving the whole world crazy and leaving her audience hanging between life and death. How did this happen? Because when she came to a moving love scene, the audience's eyes would suddenly glaze over and their mouths drop open, as if the sight had driven them to their deaths. Then, just as suddenly, they would begin dancing with joy, as if the sight

---

[6]Conventional role-types of the traditional Chinese theatre that are distinguished by costume, make-up, and acting style. *Jing* generally portrayed warriors or villains; *chou* generally portrayed comic characters.

[7]Pan Yue or Pan An (247–300) and Cao Zhi (192–232), personifications of male beauty and intelligence respectively.

[8]A cliché for beautiful song derived from the *Lie Zi* ("Tang wen").

had restored them to life. As a result, they raved over her, saying: "What kind of woman is this, to hold the power of life and death over us?" Her troupe became famous simply because she was its lead actress.

But Heaven never makes one creature without making another to match it. It so happened that there was also a male lead of unprecedented quality, and when he came to be paired with Miaogu, theirs could truly be called a match made in Heaven. And there was another remarkable thing about this actor too; he did not start out as a male lead, but was promoted from the ranks of the *jing* and the *chou*. But in order to tell the story of this romance of theirs, it is necessary to begin at the beginning.

When Miaogu was eleven or twelve, before she was capable of acting in a full-length play, she would often join her mother in doing isolated scenes. There was a young student there at the time whose surname was Tan and whose personal name was Chuyu, and who came from Xiangyang prefecture in Huguang. His was an established family, but he had lost his mother as a child, and when his father went away to study, the little boy had been taken along. His father died while away from home, and the son was left with no one to depend on. He had drifted about from place to place in eastern Jiangsu and in Zhejiang, and was now sixteen years old. One glance at Miaogu was enough to convince him that she was a ravishing beauty, and he determined to get to know her now, while she was still a virgin. Using an interest in drama as a pretext, he made constant visits to the green-room. He hoped to declare his passion with his eyes and arouse thoughts of love in her; he would begin with the *apertura* and gradually work his way through to the *continuatio* and *exordium*.[9] Alas for his hopes! Her parents exercised such strict control over her that, except in acting class, she was not allowed to talk to anyone outside the family. Although Tan spent months covertly watching her, he found no opening for his advances.

One day he heard that Miaogu's troupe was fully staffed except for a *jing* and that they were looking for some bright young man to study alongside her. Since Tan was at a loose end anyway, how could he pass up such an opportunity? He went at once to see Jiangxian and her husband and told them of his desire to join the troupe. They were delighted, and invited him to stay behind, make his bows to the teacher, and begin practising with Miaogu that very day. Needless to say, as an intelligent youth, he picked up the art very quickly. For her part, Miaogu, although still a child, was better educated than many an adult. Even before Tan joined the troupe, she had admired his looks and, noting how assiduously he attended the theatre, had realized that "the Old Tippler's mind was definitely on something other than his wine."[1] When he joined the troupe, she realized that he had been driven by his passion for her into disregarding the lowly status of actors; he was using the drama class as a means of offering her his allegiance, even at the

---

[9] Names for the first three parts of the eight-part ("eight-legged") examination essay.
[1] Ouyang Xiu (1007–1072) styled himself *Zuiweng*, "Old Tippler." The quotation is from his essay "Zuiweng ting ji."

cost of playing a "painted face."[2] He was obviously a romantic spirit, and she wished to entrust her heart to him.

Unfortunately their drama teacher proved even stricter than her father. He forbade all whispering when his pupils were reciting plays, and his main concern, when they were practising their movements, was that they should not touch. In effect, Tan was playing Liang Shanbo to Miaogu's Zhu Ying-tai,[3] for although they studied side by side, they never managed to exchange a single word of love. Their only hope was to wait until their next lives and then, like Liang and Zhu, turn into butterflies and go off together.

After some time, Tan began to regret his decision. "In acting," he thought, "the male lead is the only role to study, if you want to preserve a shred of gentility. Even if our love is not predestined and can never be ful-filled, on stage we'd at least have a 'pretext to expound the faith,' and could open our hearts to each other. If I called her wife, she would have to call me husband. Although it could never be a real marriage, why not seize those fleeting moments of love to consummate our desire and give meaning to my joining the troupe? This painted face role is beneath my dignity as a man! In any case, I'm depressed beyond words by the parts I have to play, which are all either bumpkins or menials. And how can I stand the bile that rises in me as I watch with starving eyes while she plays wife to another man?"

One day, when the teacher was out of the classroom and the pupils were all in their places reciting, Tan, who was sitting close to Miaogu, was tempted to take this chance to declare his love but feared that the others might overhear. Fortunately, apart from Miaogu and himself,[4] no one else in the troupe knew any classical Chinese. If he spoke in the vernacular, they would understand, but if he sprinkled in a few classical expressions, they would be left in the dark. So while everyone was reciting, Tan kept his eyes on Miaogu and spoke to her, as if practising his part:

"O Mistress, Mistress, most intelligent creature as thou art, how canst thou not be aware of my purpose in coming?"

Miaogu replied, also as if reciting: "Man is not made of wood or stone, so how can he be unaware? It grieveth me that I cannot speak my love!"

Tan continued: "Madam watcheth closely, and the pedagogue is strict. How long must I wait ere I fulfill the desire of three lifetimes?"

"We can but give each other our hearts and await another day. Here, before the gaze of all, there is, i'faith, no chance of a tryst. Pray cease thy too, too sanguine hopes."

Tan continued in a low voice: "I am ashamed to go on playing painted faces, and I beseech thee to intercede with thy parents and have me promoted

---

[2]This refers to the *jing* role-type, in which the actors' faces are heavily made up, and sometimes also to the *chou*.

[3]A famous romantic legend. Dressed as a boy, Zhu Yingtai studies alongside Liang Shanbo. When he discovers her sex, he tries to marry her, but she is already betrothed. After his death, she is passing by his grave when it suddenly opens up for her. Their souls fly away together as butterflies.

[4]The text says "male and female leads," but Tan has not yet become the male lead.

to male lead, so that we can join in wedlock on the stage as an auspicious omen of future love. What sayest thou, milady?"

"Well said, forsooth, but if the suggestion issue from your humble servant, it will but arouse parental suspicion and close the very door we wish to open. Thou must needs use a stratagem."

"And what stratagem would that be, pray?"

"The troupe setteth great value upon thy services, and if thou wishest to leave, disdaining to play the painted face, nought will be denied thee. With Xiao He at the ruler's side, thou canst count on Han Xin's being summoned back to court."[5]

"I shall respectfully do thy bidding," said Tan, with a nod.

A few days later, following her suggestion, he went and took leave of his teacher and also of Jiangxian and her husband, saying that he wished to return home and resume his studies. Jiangxian and her husband were aghast.

"But you've just finished your training and are about to go on tour! Why give it all up so suddenly?" Together with the drama teacher, they probed the reason for his change of heart.

" 'Even in poverty one must not give up one's aspirations,' " said Tan. "I did receive an education, but because of the decline in my family's fortunes, I had no choice but to enter this lowly profession. My intention, in donning an actor's garb, was to express the frustration I felt. I assumed that, as principal *jing*, I would be playing either Guan Yunchang or the Hegemon of Chu,[6] and that although I would have to apply some greasepaint, at least in the more stirring scenes I could be true to my nobler self. It never occurred to me that, in nine plays out of ten, I would be playing petty rogues, and that I would hardly ever have a chance to play a superior man. No true gentleman would put up with such a dishonourable role, and I am unwilling to do so any more."

"Since you regard a painted face as beneath you, by all means choose a role more to your liking. There's no need to be *inflexible!*"

Tan then offered his assessment of the various roles. "As for the secondary female roles, I'm afraid a man would be sacrificing his manhood if he stooped to play them. And in the case of the secondary male roles, I'm afraid a young man would be losing his youthful vigour if he played an old fellow. The only possibility would be the junior male lead, but he so often works through others, helping them make their names, that he fails to establish an identity of his own and present us with a nobler self, and that is why I wouldn't consider the role."

At this point the drama teacher remarked to Jiangxian and her husband: "From what he's saying, it's quite clear that he has set his heart on being the male lead. In my opinion, his looks and voice are of the right calibre. The only problem is that the male lead's part is longer than anyone else's, and we've

---

[5]Early in his career, the famous general Han Xin, feeling unappreciated, deserted. Xiao He, the prime minister, who believed strongly in Han, raced after him, brought him back, and persuaded the ruler to appoint him commander-in-chief.

[6]The warrior figures Guan Yu and Xiang Yu, of the Three Kingdoms and Qin dynasties, respectively.

already finished rehearsing and are about to go on tour. Even if we make him the male lead, how is he going to memorize all those scripts at once?"

Tan gave a laugh. "The only question is whether I'd *accept* the male lead. If I did, my memory would be more than a match for those few dozen old plays. At the rate of one a day, I'd be learning ten every ten days. If we delay the tour by a month, surely the thirty plays I'll have memorized by then will be enough for any repertoire!"

The drama teacher had been with Tan long enough to know his powers of memory, so he urged Jiangxian and her husband to appoint him male lead and make the present male lead a painted face. In fact Tan's memory was so good that he was able to recall his lines after a single reading. In less than a month, he had learned the thirty scripts, and he and Miaogu set off.

During his period of training, Tan had had to contend with her parents' protectiveness inside the house and the drama teacher's surveillance outside it, as well as with their classmates' constant presence, and he had failed to come up with any effective way of expressing his love. But he had assumed that, once they went on tour and the whole troupe was away from home, they would, as colleagues, have to start behaving like members of the same family—that is to say, there would be no segregation among them and no suspicion. While rubbing shoulders with Miaogu, he should not find it too difficult to inhale her warm fragrance and stroke her soft, translucent flesh.

To his dismay, he found that the rules of conduct in the green-room were twice as strict again as in the women's quarters. Every man in the world could make a play for the female lead—except her fellow actors! The rule was not of Jiangxian's or her husband's devising; there was a founding father of the acting profession, the god Erlang, and he it was who had established it. Byplay among the actors and actresses offended against morality as much as incest between brother and sister. On stage you might jest and banter to your heart's content, but as soon as you stepped off it, you had to treat the actresses with perfect decorum and refrain from the slightest jest. The merest hint of an affair was enough to offend against the god's taboo, and not only would business go into a decline, the whole troupe would fall ill. Thus after Miaogu went on tour, she had to endure not only her parents' protectiveness and her teacher's surveillance but also her fellow actors' scrutiny. When they saw her sitting beside Tan, they would sidle over to spy on them, fearing they might start an affair that would affect not only themselves but the entire troupe.

Pity these poor lovers, whose mouths were officially sealed, as it were, and who could no longer employ even the classical language to communicate! Their only recourse was to "use the past to express the present" on stage, and to try to guess each other's hidden meanings. Whereas other actors and actresses preferred being off-stage, because on stage they had to exert themselves and off-stage they could relax, Tan and Miaogu preferred the stage, because there they could play husband and wife, while off-stage they had to hold themselves above suspicion.

On stage, as male and female leads, they formed a dazzling couple, and every man in the audience fell in love with her and every woman with him. Inevitably, because they took such delight in their acting, they threw themselves into every scene, and the same old plays, as performed by them, took on an entirely new guise. In the romantic parts, the passion of their courtship and lovemaking seemed to spring from the very marrow of their bones. None of this was present in the play, but it never failed to captivate the audience. In the tragic parts, their tirades against Heaven and Earth, their piteous lamentations, seemed to issue from the very depths of their being. None of this was in the printed text either, but it never failed to move the audience to tears. What was the reason? Because what other actors performed was the play, whereas they performed the truth. When a play is performed as a play, no matter how well it is done, the male lead remains the male lead and the female lead the female lead, and their spirits never join. Thus tragedy does not seem tragic, nor joy joyous. When a play is performed as a play, the audience looks on it as a play. But if it is performed as the truth, the female lead's spirit is fixed on the male lead while his soul is held in her hands, and they fuse into a single person who feels the joys and woes of each. Thus tragedy seems tragic and joy joyous. Tan and Miaogu acted their plays as if they were the truth, and the audiences looked upon them in the same light.

Their very presence in the troupe helped raise the position of their mediocre fellow actors. Other troupes earned no more than three to six taels per play, but this troupe charged twelve taels, exclusive of the female lead's gratuities. For a hundred miles around, whenever the rich and eminent were planning theatricals, they tried to engage the troupe. Those who succeeded were proud of the fact, while those who failed took it as a personal disgrace.

Because of the new troupe's success, Jiangxian handed over control of the old troupe to her husband so that she could accompany Miaogu. Her aim was to instruct her daughter in the feminine wiles needed to make a fortune. But Miaogu had given her heart irrevocably to Tan and refused to associate with other men. Whereas they thought her the apple of their eye, she thought them a thorn in her flesh. Get her to a party to accompany the guests in their drinking, and she would declare that she never drank and refuse to let the wine cup touch her lips. Say something personal to her, and her face would drop and she would find an excuse to leave. Rich young men squandered large sums of money to make her acquaintance, but they received not a smile nor a frown in return, let alone any other favours. If jewellery was created for her, she would wear it only once or twice, and then melt it down and use the silver. If any clothes were made for her, she would put them in the props trunk for the supporting actresses and not wear them herself. In her heart she was determined "not to take a second husband" and to remain chaste for Tan Chuyu, but she could tell no one of her resolve.

One day the troupe brought its plays to a place named Port X, in which there was an old temple called Lord Yan's Temple.[7] Lord Yan was a deity

---

[7]Temples were built to Lord Yan during the Ming Dynasty. According to legend, he was a Song or

in charge of wind and wave who, enfeoffed as the Marquis Pacifier-of-Waves, had demonstrated striking magical powers. The temple was built beside a stream, where the god's birthday was celebrated on the third day of the tenth month with theatricals arranged by the temple's benefactors. In past years they had invited Jiangxian's troupe, but when they heard that the junior troupe was even better, they sealed up the booking fee and sent it off well in advance, which is how Jiangxian and her daughter came to be present.

In the past, the whole troupe, men as well as women, had arrived together, but this time there had been a misunderstanding, and Tan and Miaogu arrived before the others. They had been waiting years for this fleeting chance and were not about to let it slip. But the temple was hardly the place to make love, and they contented themselves with expressing their true feelings for each other, after which they knelt down before Lord Yan's image and swore an oath together: "Neither I, Tan Chuyu, nor I, Liu Miaogu, will ever accept another in marriage. If our parents deny our plea, we will join each other in death. We will never betray our love or reject our commitment. If either of us breaks this vow, let him or her be destroyed."

Just as they finished, they saw the other members of the troupe arriving. Fortunately they escaped in time, and their secret was safe. Otherwise, "suspicion would have seen ghosts in the dark,"[8] and many ill-fated things might have happened. After that day's performance, they returned to their rented quarters for the night, and there I shall leave them.

Let me now tell of one of the temple's benefactors, a very rich man who had bought himself an official post and served a term in the capital. He was worth a good hundred thousand, and by now, approaching the age of fifty, he had eleven concubines to his name. When Jiangxian was younger, she, too, had come under his tutelage, but he now observed that Miaogu was ten times as beautiful as her mother, and he was prepared to put up a large sum to marry her and fill up his complement of "Twelve Golden Hairpins."[9]

Inviting both mother and daughter to stay, he treated them royally. Needless to say, he renewed his friendship with Jiangxian, offering her his tutelage once more. Then, at their moment of greatest intimacy, he expressed his earnest desire to marry her daughter. Jiangxian would have agreed, but for one consideration: that her daughter was a money-tree who, if she could only be straightened out, was capable of making many large sums far surpassing this one betrothal gift. On the other hand, Jiangxian would have declined, but for a second consideration: that her daughter was of a very stubborn nature and had refused to make money for her parents; rather than have her offend people with her sulking fits, it might be better to marry her off in exchange for ready money.

Yuan official who, after death, was deified and put in charge of calming storms. He is said to have received the title Marquis Pacifier-of-Waves at the beginning of the Ming Dynasty.

[8]A cliché derived from the *Lie Zi* ("Kouyi").

[9]A reference to one man's having twelve concubines.

Unable to decide the issue, Jiangxian was forced to hedge. "It's a most generous offer, which I dare not refuse. But my daughter is still very young, not yet fifteen. Moreover, we've hired a drama teacher to give her lessons. There'll be time enough for marriage after she's been working for a few years and has made some money for us. I really wouldn't presume to give my consent at this point."

"I see," said the rich man. "Well, this time next year we'll be holding our theatricals again, and I'll invite you over and ask you for an answer."

"Very well," said Jiangxian.

A few days later the performances came to an end and she took her leave.

Her motive, in replying like this, was to observe her daughter closely over the course of the next year. If the girl were prepared to change her mind and make some money for her parents, she would be kept at home to work, but if she should prove incorrigible, Jiangxian would have this offer to fall back on. Therefore, after leaving the rich man, she took an entirely different attitude toward her daughter and opposed her at every turn. If the girl failed to obey, she would be screamed at, and if screaming produced no effect, she would be beaten. Miaogu's will, however, was as firm as iron or stone, and she yielded not an inch. When bullied beyond endurance, she would refuse to perform and even threaten suicide.

Next year, towards the end of the ninth month, the rich man sent a servant with an invitation for Jiangxian. On greeting her, he asked for her answer, and she, since her daughter was clearly not the stuff of which great fortunes are made, accepted with alacrity. He then weighed out a betrothal gift of a thousand taels and handed it over. The wedding was set for the evening of the third, just after the last performance.

All this while, Jiangxian, reluctant to bring the subject up, had been keeping Miaogu in the dark. Not until the evening of the second did she inform her.

"When I brought you into the world, I went to great trouble to give you a training, in the hope that you would cooperate with us and work hard to improve the family's position. But you've been wilful from the very start, and have actually turned against money. You don't know your place in society, you pout when you meet people, and one day you're going to find yourself in real trouble. This business is simply not for you, and you'd better pack up your costumes and get married as soon as you can. I know a gentleman who's very rich and who has served in office. If you became his wife, you'd be a lady of sorts, and what's more, you'd never want for anything the rest of your life. I've already accepted his betrothal gift and promised you to him as a concubine, and the wedding is set for tomorrow. Now don't start acting up, or you'll make your mother *very* cross."

At first Miaogu was shocked out of her wits. She stared wide-eyed at her mother.

"Mother, you've made a mistake," she said at last. "I'm already married, and a virtuous woman does not take a second husband. Remarriage is out of the question."

Jiangxian had no idea what her daughter was talking about. Her face hardened.

"Where is this husband of yours? Your father and I have had nothing to say about it. Surely you haven't taken it upon yourself to arrange a marriage?"

"Of course not! You can't arrange your own marriage! You and Daddy matched me with him when I was just a child. You know perfectly well the one I mean, you're just pretending not to understand."

"What an *extraordinary* thing to say! Well, won't you tell me who he is?"

"Tan Chuyu, the male lead, of course. Before he joined the troupe, he used to pay us constant visits, always on my account. Even when he joined, it was just an excuse to get a foot in the door and be closer to me. Then later on, when he refused to play the *jing* and insisted on changing to the male lead so that he could be paired with me, he did it because he wanted you to guess his intentions, since he couldn't declare them openly. You and Daddy have played the male and female leads, you've been in romantic plays together, so you *must* have guessed his intentions. If you didn't want me to marry him, you shouldn't have taken him on for training in the first place, but even if you did take him on, you certainly shouldn't have switched him to male lead. By letting him do both things, you made it quite clear that you guessed his intentions and approved of the marriage. Every day since we began our performances, he's been the husband and I the wife, as tens of thousands in our audiences can attest. Everyone says that ours is a match made in heaven. Yet now, after we've been husband and wife for years, you suddenly tell me to betray him! Impossible! You're so used to making such compromises in your own life, Mother, that they don't shock you any more. I may be an unfilial child, but my virtue is unsullied, and I'm not going to sully it now. I would *never* do anything so outrageous!"

Jiangxian gave an involuntary hoot of laughter, then spat out a reply, "You must be dreaming! Playing husband and wife on stage isn't to be taken seriously. Tell me: what do you think the word 'play' means? It's called a 'play,' so it's 'playful.' How can you take it as real? How many actresses have you noticed marrying their leading men?"

"Everything else in the world can be taken playfully except marriage. When I began acting with him, I was ignorant of moral principle and thought we were just acting in a play, so I readily called him husband. By now I'm in the habit and cannot correct myself. All I can do is make the best of my situation and recognize him as my husband. Other actresses, who are ignorant of moral principle or who have lost their chastity, are free not to marry their leading men. But I do understand moral principle, and I *have* preserved my chastity, and so *my* only course is to marry Tan Chuyu."

Jiangxian realized that no matter what was said, she and her daughter would still be at cross purposes, so she stopped trying to persuade her and, after a brief, angry outburst, took herself off to bed.

Next morning, when breakfast and lunch had passed and the time for the performance had almost arrived, the rich man appeared in the theatre dressed in his finest clothes and began parading up and down in front of the stage, hoping to catch the audience's eye and make them sigh with envy: "He's going to get this unattainable beauty into his seraglio, where he'll enjoy himself at will." He would dearly have loved to emblazon the words "I've Won the Queen of the Flowers"[1] across his forehead and bask in the audience's applause.

Tan was furious at the sight. He expected that Miaogu would make a violent scene, refuse to go on, and eventually do so only after a beating from her mother. But the world is full of surprises. Although Miaogu had protested violently the night before, after a night's sleep, she seemed reconciled to her future. She looked perfectly happy, sitting there in the green-room without the trace of a pout. She even made an appeal to her fellow actors: "I shall soon be saying goodbye to you all. We've been together for years, but the play we do today will be the first real one we've ever done. The others were all make-believe. I'm asking all of you to back me up and do your level best."

Then she turned to Tan. "So far you've always played a make-believe hero, but this time you're going to play a real one. So do your very best to work with me."

"I don't know what you mean by doing my best. I wish you'd explain."

"Just watch me and do as I do. So long as we act in concert, you'll be doing your best."

Tan was deeply hurt, for what she was saying ran counter to everything he had come to expect. When the rich man came swaggering into the green-room to ask for the repertoire, Tan, in a bitter mood, watched closely for Miaogu's reaction, thinking that with her nemesis there before her, she would surely flush with anger. But she not only showed no anger, she seemed to beam with delight.

"Mother tells me," she said, standing up to address him, "that after the performance today I shall be going to your house."

"Just so."

"In that case, out of all the plays I've learned, today's is the only one I still have a chance to perform. After today the audience will never have another chance to see me. So you must let me put on my finest performance, both to demonstrate my abilities and also to take my leave of the audience. Would that be agreeable?"

"Of course it's agreeable."

"In that case, I shan't let you choose the play, I'll choose it myself. I'll

---

[1]"Queen of Flowers" was a name given to Wang Meiniang, heroine of a Ming romantic story. The most famous courtesan of her time, she is won over by the devoted attentions of a humble oil seller. His winning of her is referred to, in the titles of both the Ming story and the Ming play based on it, as *Zhan huakui,* "Possessing (or Winning) the Queen of the Flowers."

do a play I'm familiar with, one that will let me do full justice to my talents."

"Quite right. You choose, by all means. But I wonder which one you'll pick?"

Miaogu took the repertoire, hesitated, then pointed to a title. "Let's do *The Thorn Hairpin*,"[2] she said.

The rich man thought for a moment, then began laughing. "You're not comparing me with Sun Ruquan, by doing *The Thorn Hairpin*? Oh, very well. So long as you're willing to marry me, it's no great hardship to be Sun Ruquan for a little while. And now that that's settled, let's have everybody on stage!"

Once the play was chosen, the cast dressed and took the stage, where they all put forth their best efforts, as Miaogu had asked. No words were dropped from the songs, no passages from the speech. Only Tan, sick at heart, failed to give of his best. Fortunately, Miaogu was there to cover for him; after he had sung the first word or two of a song, she would quickly join him in a duet, saving him from utter disgrace.

As for her performance, it was divine, superb throughout. In the first few scenes, however fine the acting, she failed to captivate the audience, but when she came to "Sending the Bride Away to Her Wedding,"[3] the scene touched her own anguish and her performance became spellbinding, as she unconsciously bared her heart and soul. Each syllable was worth a piece of gold, each word produced a tear, until, in the most harrowing passage of all, not only was her face streaming with tears, there was not a dry eye in the audience of over a thousand. Then when she came to "Clasping a Rock and Plunging into the River,"[4] her rendering seemed even more tragic. Not only did the audience shed tears, the very elements seemed to grieve; the sun went in and dark clouds covered the sky as with primeval gloom. Normally Qian Yulian expresses only her private anguish and does not denounce anyone. But the way Miaogu played the role was different; she inserted a new passage at the point where Yulian intends to throw herself into the river but has not yet clasped the rock to her bosom, and now Yulian cursed Sun Ruquan by name. The rich man happened to be sitting beside the stage. Miaogu stood facing him, and every time she spoke the words "False-hearted rogue" she pointed at him, and every time she said "Damned villain" she stared him in the eye.

He knew that her curses were meant for him, but he couldn't help feel-

---

[2]A Southern play of disputed authorship, written probably in the fourteenth century. Wang Shipeng marries Qian Yulian, then leaves for the capital to take the examination. A rival suitor, Sun Ruquan, forges a letter of divorce from him. Yulian throws herself into the river, from which she is rescued by an official's boat. Eventually, she and Wang rediscover each other when sacrificing at the same temple. The thorn hairpin, the humble engagement gift which was all his family could afford, serves to prove her identity.
[3]Scene 10 ("Bi jia").
[4]Scene 26 ("Tou jiang").

ing a twinge of conscience and tried hard to be fair-minded. Far from getting angry, he nodded his head and exclaimed in admiration: "Quite right!"

After a volley of curses, Miaogu clasped the rock to her bosom and went to throw herself into the river. Other actresses, in doing this scene, would jump from the back of the stage into the green-room, pretending to jump into the river but actually jumping on to dry land. But Miaogu's way of throwing herself into the river differed again. Here, too, she wrote a new script that was even more remarkable than the first.

The temple lay opposite a broad stream, and the stage had been erected outside the temple gate, with its back resting on the bank and its front extending out over the water. Clasping the rock, Miaogu went straight to the front of the stage, from which, as she concluded her song, she gave a mighty leap—right into the river. She had acted out a real play, just as she had promised.

Shocked almost to death, the audience clamoured for someone to rescue her. But before anyone could try, a second person had jumped in to join her. How did that come about? As Miaogu was about to jump, she had suddenly turned around and shouted in the direction of the green-room: "Husband, Wang Shipeng! Your wife can stand this persecution no longer and is going to throw herself into the river. How can you go on living without me?" Tan, who was sitting on the props trunk at the time, rushed on stage. When he saw Miaogu's leap, his one fear was that he might be too late to catch her up, so he flung himself like an arrow into the water. He hoped they would die in each other's arms, but he was far from sure that he would ever be able to find her.

By this time the whole audience knew that Miaogu had chosen *The Thorn Hairpin* with this outcome in mind. Her cursing of the rich man had been an incidental thing, to raise her spirits, not an attempt to get some verbal satisfaction before resigning herself to marriage. She had pleaded her case fully the night before and her mother had not relented, so she knew she would not be able to preserve her chastity after the day's performance. Rather than stab herself in her room and turn into a mute ghost, she preferred to die openly and forthrightly in front of others, providing people with a tale to tell for centuries to come.

That whole night she lay awake planning what to do, and composed this remarkable script. Her first stroke of brilliance was in keeping a smile on her face and betraying no resentment, which lulled people into complacency and allowed her to pursue her aim. Otherwise, she would never have been allowed to perform such a highly sensitive play. Her second stroke was in not leaving the choice of play to someone else, but choosing it herself, which gave her a pretext for expressing her feelings and venting her grievances. Had she chosen some other play, even if she had inserted a few clever remarks here and there, she could not have expressed her grievances as directly or as satisfyingly. The third stroke of brilliance was that she did not try to arrange the double suicide in secret, but publicly invited her lover to be her ghostly companion, a move worthy of the maxim "An upright person does not do underhand things." If she had tried to arrange the suicide behind people's backs, she would probably have failed to kill herself on this occasion and been forced to wait until after her marriage to Sun Ruquan before emulating Qian Yulian.

Afterwards the poets all wrote elegies, one of which ran:

They swore to die before they'd break their vow.
Why call them mad? They'd promises to keep.
As one they leapt into the raging flood,
And turned to sole (soul) mates in the wat'ry deep.[5]

Let me now tell of the lovers after they leapt into the water. The skies had just cleared after heavy rain, and the mountain streams were raging torrents. This broad stream, with its steep banks, was different from others—"a mighty river spilling down for hundreds of miles."[6] Within minutes after the lovers had leapt into the water, it had swept them away to another district altogether, far beyond any hope of rescue, which is why the audience, for all their shouting, did nothing to save them.

From the stage Jiangxian saw her daughter drown and began beating her breast and stamping her feet, weeping without pause. Two thoughts distressed her: firstly, she had lost her money-tree and had no one left to make her fortune, and secondly, now that her daughter was dead, she might have to return the betrothal gift, a case of "losing both the person and the purse in one fell swoop." But then, after weeping for a while, she made a sudden volte-face. Ignoring the relationship of mistress to patron, she charged the rich man with using his money to drive her daughter to her death and declared that she was going straight to the authorities to file a complaint.

The audience already envied the rich man because of the way he had flaunted himself. Now, on hearing that he had driven the girl to her death, they were positively gleeful and rose up in arms, ready to go before the prefect and lodge a petition. Fortunately for him, the rich man knew the ropes well enough to settle the case privately through an intermediary. He arranged a peaceful solution by letting Jiangxian keep the thousand-tael betrothal gift and distributing another thousand or more to buy the audience's silence. He had failed in his attempt to marry Qian Yulian, merely spending a couple of wasted hours as Sun Ruquan. His only consolation was the thought that a girl "flirts by cursing the one she fancies." He told himself that he had been personally cursed by the most beautiful girl in the world.

In Tonglu county of Yanzhou prefecture, there was a riverside hamlet by the name of Port Newtown which had very few inhabitants, all of whom were engaged in fishing. Among them was a man surnamed Mo, known as

---

[5] *Bimuyu* are sole or flatfish. The male and female are said to be inseparable; hence, like butterflies and mandarin ducks, they symbolize devoted lovers. "Sole mates" is a pun on "soulmates."
[6] A cliché, derived from the Song writer Chen Liang, which is most often applied to a forceful, majestic style.

Fisherman Mo, who lived with his wife in a tiny thatched hut that they had built beside the bank. On this particular day, expecting some large fish to be swept down by the flood waters, they set out their big net and took turns pulling it up.[7] Then, a long way off, they made out amid the waves something that was heading downstream. Taking it to be a large fish, Mo waited until it came near and netted it at his first attempt. But, strangely enough, although it had been clearly visible on the surface, no sooner was it in the net than it suddenly fell back and tried to submerge. Mo pulled as hard as he could, but he was unable to budge the net. He had to get his wife to help him, and together, with the last ounce of their strength, they managed to pull it out of the water.

A shock awaited them when they raised their heads and looked into the net. It was no fish they had caught, but two bodies, face pressed against face, breast against breast, as if trussed up together. Filled with compassion for the dead, Mo wanted to give them a decent burial. He tied the rope to a tree, and he and his wife, with a great deal of effort, managed to lift them out of the net. On examining them closely, they found they were a man and a woman locked together in a tight embrace, as if they had been cast into the river in the act of love. Mo and his wife were puzzled. Then they looked closely at the faces and saw that the bodies were not quite dead. While the faces and feet were ice-cold, the nostrils retained a little warmth, even though all breathing seemed to have stopped.

"They can obviously be revived," said Mo. "We'd better give them mouth-to-mouth. Wouldn't it be wonderful if we could save both lives—like building a fourteen-storey pagoda!"[8]

"Yes, indeed!" said his wife.

He put his mouth against the man's, and she put her mouth against the woman's, and they blew their warm breath down into the two bodies. Within minutes the pair had revived. They were helped into the hut and asked how they had come so close to drowning.

They poured out their hearts to their rescuers. The man proved to be Tan Chuyu and the woman Liu Miaogu. They had leapt into the water in turn, fearing they might never find each other. But it seemed as if someone amidst the waves were leading them together and preventing them from drifting apart. It seemed, too, as if a gigantic fish were carrying them on its back along the surface of the water, so that they didn't drown in the course of travelling a hundred miles. When the fish came near the net, it seemed to sense that there were rescuers at hand and, as if wishing to deliver its charges and return, it shook them off its back and swam away. That was why they were on the surface one moment and submerged the next. Fortunately the net was there to stop them from sinking to the bottom, and the mighty heave that

---

[7]The illustration in the *Silent Operas, Combined Collection (Wusheng xi heji)*, an earlier anthology than *Priceless Jade*, shows a large basket-shaped net suspended from a stout wooden pole that can be raised or lowered with a rope.
[8]Pagodas are built with an odd number of storeys, to a maximum of thirteen.

Mo and his wife gave on the rope brought them up. Tan and Miaogu knew that they owed their lives to Lord Yan's miraculous powers, and they kowtowed to the heavens before bowing in gratitude to their rescuers. When Mo and his wife learned they were a virtuous couple, they offered them their hospitality, insisting the pair stay in the hut and treating them generously. Then, as soon as Tan and Miaogu had recovered, they urged them to go further afield, because if the news of their rescue ever reached her parents, someone would be sent for them, and they would not be able to continue as husband and wife.

Tan discussed the problem with Miaogu. "Since I come from Huguang, why don't we go back there? My family doesn't own much land, but if we work it, we should be able to grow a little food for ourselves. Let me get back to my studies and put in a few years' hard work, and I'm sure I'll succeed."

"You're absolutely right, but it's such a long way to go. We have nothing to our name, so where is the money coming from?"

Mo could tell from Tan's face that the man was no loser, and he decided to offer him an examination loan. "How much will you need for the journey?" he asked.

"Anything would do. If we are very careful, ten taels should get us by."

"That's no problem. I've collected several purses from my fishing. I'll get the money together and lend it to you—on one condition. If you fail, I don't want a penny of it back. But if you study and succeed in the examinations, I must be repaid tenfold. Nothing less will do."

"Han Xin received a single meal from the washerwoman and repaid her with a thousand taels.[9] You've saved our lives—much more than a meal! I'd want to reward you handsomely anyway, even if you weren't offering us a loan, and all the more now that you're being so generous. If I should fail, never mind, but if I succeed, I assure you I shan't limit myself to a thousand taels, let alone a mere hundred."

Mo and his wife saw that he was eager to set off, and so they prepared a farewell feast. As might be expected, they provided delicacies from the seas and rivers rather than from the mountains, dishes such as shrimp, fish, crab, and turtle. There is no segregation of the sexes among poor folk, and the two couples sat down together and drank until they were merry. Then, after a night's sleep, they arose and Fisherman Mo gathered together ten taels in loose silver and gave it to the young couple, after which they took their leave. From hardship itself, of course, they did not take their leave, but suffered all the rigours of a hurried and difficult journey.

In less than a month they arrived. They fixed up a tumbledown house on the property, moved into it, and set about bringing the abandoned fields under cultivation in order to provide for themselves. Since Miaogu had been busy studying acting from childhood on, she was utterly ignorant of women's

---

[9]In Han Xin's *Shi ji* biography, the washerwoman feeds him for twenty or thirty days and he later rewards her with a thousand catties of gold.

skills. Even her slippers and leggings had been made for her by others. Now, as Tan's wife, she was studying these skills for the first time, but her quick intelligence proved equal to the task, and she learned at the first attempt. She spent her days weaving hemp and straw, and making shoes and stockings, all to bring in a little money and support her husband's studies. At first Tan would labour in the fields during the day and study by night, but Miaogu was so afraid the farmwork would distract him from his studies that she persuaded him to give it up and depend on her handiwork alone for their needs. Lest his studies be affected, she would not even let him go and buy provisions, but entrusted those chores to a neighbour.

After three years of study, Tan began taking the examinations. He hit the mark every time, no matter what the level of the examination. After entering the prefectural school, he passed the provincial and metropolitan examinations. Then, following the palace examination, he was appointed judge[1] of Dingzhou prefecture in Fujian. Since Fujian is adjacent to Huguang, he ought by rights to have travelled down the Yangzi and revisited his home en route, enacting a splendid "Returning Home in Triumph" scene.[2] But his desire to repay his benefactor was far stronger than any thought of basking in hometown glory, so he sent a servant to fetch his wife and bring her to Jingkou to join him. From there they travelled through Zhejiang to Quzhou and Yanzhou prefectures in order to worship Lord Yan and to repay and thank Fisherman Mo and his wife. Tan felt it would be embarrassing if his subordinates learned that he had begun life as an actor, so he sent the welcoming party back to wait for him at Pucheng, while he and his wife enjoyed the mountains and lakes alone.

Arriving in Port Newtown, they found Mo and his wife fishing and sent a servant over with a card to say that "the man they had rescued was now an official and on the way to his post. He was passing through and desired to wait on them." Overcome with joy, Mo and his wife hastily took off their bamboo hats and hemp coats, and without waiting for their visitors to come ashore, went on board to congratulate them. Tan and Miaogu begged them to take the place of honour while they bowed before them four times.

Tan appealed to Mo: "Fishing is such a hard life, and it brings in so little money. Why not throw your nets away and come with me to my post, where you'll be able to enjoy a little wealth and prestige?" While her husband was issuing his invitation, Miaogu, without waiting for their consent, told her servants to start packing up their belongings. But Mo stopped the servants from going ashore.

"Your Honour, My Lady," he began, shaking his head, "please forgive me, but my wife and I are incapable of enjoying that sort of wealth and prestige; in fact we're not even *willing* to accept it. Fishing may be a hard life

---

[1] *Jietui* meant a prefectural judge in Song times.
[2] The title of a common scene in which the hero returns home after his triumph in the metropolitan and palace examinations.

and the earnings small, but it has its pleasures too. We fishermen are lucky enough to live among blue hills and green waters, and to enjoy the clear moonlight and the cool breeze. We need pay no money for good wine and meat, just catch a few fish and use them for barter. We send no cards to invite our friends, just eat with them whenever they come by. It's no idle boast to say that we're the only people in the world who enjoy such pleasures. There *is* some hardship, true, and the earnings are small, but at least they're reliable. If you lead an idle life, you'll constantly be dreaming of big sums of money. If fate is against you, you won't succeed anyway, but even if you should make money, you're bound to suffer trouble and anxiety before parting with it. You're proposing that I accompany you to your post, where all my needs will be met, a case of 'one man's windfall, shared with all,' which is fine. But I would never feel at ease there and I cannot accept your offer, I'm ashamed to say. Moreover, my wife and I are accustomed to our freedom. If we found ourselves penned up in an official residence, unable to move, our frustration would surely bring on an illness. You'd be over there in the courtroom trying cases and punishing tax evaders, but the sounds of the lash and the cries of the punished would drift into the residence, and how could we, tender-hearted as we are, bear the pain we'd feel on their account? For that reason I prefer to go on living in poverty and must decline to share in your wealth and prestige. Let me say, however, how much I appreciate the generous offer."

Tan's enthusiasm was distinctly chilled by this rendering of "Fisherman's Pride."[3] "If that's the way you feel, I would never dream of trying to press you," he said. "The trouble is that I've only just passed the examinations and have not held office, so I still cannot repay that generous loan you gave me. However, as soon as I'm in office, I'll send for you and throw a few opportunities your way. When you've made some money, you can come back here, buy some land, and have enough over to live on for the rest of your days. At least you'll get *some* recompense for saving our lives. Now, don't turn this offer down, whatever you do."

Again Mo shook his head. "I'm still unwilling," he said. "Gratuities and commissions are not for unworldly folk like us. We leave that sort of thing to those medicine men who pass themselves off as recluses.[4] I'm not smooth-tongued or thick-skinned enough for all the self-promotion and chicanery involved. The only thing I ask is that when you've been in office a year or so, you set aside a few taels you've honestly come by, either from your salary or your savings, and send them along to me so that my wife and I can pro-

---

[3]The title of a well-known aria type in the drama ("Yujia ao").
[4]The word *shanren*, recluses, came to refer also to self-styled recluses, especially writers and artists who made a living from itinerant patronage seeking, an increasingly common phenomenon from the mid-Ming on. As such, the term generally carried a derisory tone. Later in his life, Li Yu himself came to depend on this very activity.

vide for our funeral things. You'd be doing us a great favour. But I will never, ever go about asking for patronage, so don't send for me, whatever you do."

Tan's respect for Mo was all the greater because of this refusal. He now ordered a farewell feast prepared on board, but this time only mountain delicacies were served, not seafood, because the latter was local produce for Mo and his wife and Tan would not have dreamed of giving them ordinary fare. And although he was now a distinguished man himself, he chose to ignore the segregation of the sexes and had both couples sit and eat together. Because their friendship had been formed while he was still poor and unknown, he did not dare behave toward them as an official. Hosts and guests ate and drank the whole night through, until finally, at the fifth watch, they took leave of each other.

By the time Tan and Miaogu reached the scene of their suffering, it was the beginning of the eleventh month, a full month after Lord Yan's birthday. "What a pity we couldn't have been here a month earlier!" said Tan. "There'd still have been some actors in the temple, and we could have had a play performed. What a fine thing that would have been, to celebrate the god's birthday and express our thanks to him at the same time!"

"Just what I was thinking," said Miaogu, "but the birthday is long past, and I doubt that there are any actors to be found in such a rural area. We'll simply have to prepare the offerings and sacrifice in silence."

As they approached, however, they could see from a long way off that the stage was still standing in front of Lord Yan's Temple, and that the table and chairs were still on it, as if the performances were not over. Tan sent one of his servants off to inquire. It appeared that there had been several days of heavy rain at the beginning of the tenth month, and that there was no shelter for the audience. Now, people who put on ritual plays claim to be doing it for the god's benefit, but actually they do it for the audience. If the conditions don't suit the audience, the god will scarcely be allowed to enjoy the play on his own! So the benefactors cancelled the performances and arranged a make-up celebration for the third day of the following month. Tan and Miaogu had happened to arrive just as the performances concluded and the actors were about to be dismissed. Coincidence though this was, the power of the god may also have had something to do with it. Perhaps he wanted this romance, which began in the theatre, to end in the theatre, and so delayed the festival until their arrival, thus setting up a "Happy Reunion" finale.[5]

Tan sent a second servant off to find out which troupe was performing. The answer came back that it was the same troupe as before, except that the male and female leads were new. Jiangxian now played the male lead, and her daughter-in-law, Miaogu's sister-in-law, a girl of sixteen or seventeen, played the female lead. After Miaogu's death, there had been no one to take her place, and the daughter-in-law had been brought in as a substitute. Although neither could compare with Tan or Miaogu, they were so much bet-

---

[5]The last scene of a Southern play ("Tuanyuan") is traditionally a reunion after all conflicts have been resolved.

ter than their competition that the temple's benefactors had continued to invite them.

When she heard that her mother was present, Miaogu was eager to summon her at once, but her husband resisted. "If we see her now, the finale will be very dull indeed. To create a little excitement, we'll have to do thus-and-thus."[6]

"You're perfectly right," said Miaogu.

Tan told one of his stewards to draw twelve taels and write out a calling card, then give the following message to the temple benefactors: "My master is passing through here on the way to his post. He met with a typhoon on the river and made a pledge to the god that he would like to redeem at this temple. He also wishes to engage the actors for one play, in consideration of which he remits the normal booking fee in full."

The benefactors, presented with this opportunity both to do someone a favour as well as to see another play, were only too glad to accept. Tan told his servants to prepare a pig and a sheep in sacrifice and place them before the god's image. They were to explain that their master had caught a cold and could not go ashore, but that he would moor his boat alongside the temple, with the cabin door opposite the god's image, and that he and his wife would bow and give thanks from behind the curtain. Afterwards they would sit and enjoy a little wine as they watched the play.

Jiangxian now approached to show them the repertoire. "Your Honour, which play would you like us to perform?" she asked from outside the cabin.

Tan told a servant to reply for him: "The Mistress had a dream last night in which Lord Yan wanted to have *The Thorn Hairpin* performed, so please do that play." Jiangxian took back the repertoire and returned to the greenroom, where she dressed as Wang Shipeng.

Gentle reader, why do you suppose Tan and his wife chose this play again? Were there no other good plays besides *The Thorn Hairpin*? You must understand that they were less interested in seeing the play than in testing Jiangxian's love for her daughter. It was *The Thorn Hairpin* that Miaogu had been performing when she leapt into the water, and their reason for choosing the same play was to force Jiangxian to relive the experience. If she wept a few genuine tears during the tragic scene, it would mean that she had repented, and they would invite her on board to meet them. But if she played the scenes routinely, without any sign of distress, there would be no need to meet with her, and they could slip quietly away. That was why they chose this play, of all plays. The choice was another example of Tan's shrewdness.

Jiangxian now appeared on stage as Wang Shipeng. During the first few scenes, she showed no distress. Only when she came to the scene in which her daughter-in-law, like Miaogu, played Yulian throwing herself into the river, did her conscience begin to trouble her. Despite herself, "the cruel cat

[6]The author wishes to hide the plan from the reader.

suddenly began crying over the dead mouse." But it was clear from the way she cried that she was trying to keep the fact from the audience, because she fought back her sobs and kept dabbing at her eyes with her sleeve. However, when she came to "Sacrificing to the River,"[7] she could control herself no longer and burst into unrestrained sobbing. Whereas before she had cried out "Qian Yulian, wife, where are you?", she now, as she continued sobbing, forgot where she was and substituted the word "child" for "wife." The audience knew she was weeping for Miaogu, but not even Master Zhou[8] would have had the heart to criticize her mistake.

When Miaogu noticed how heartbrokenly her mother was weeping, her own tears streamed down too, streaking her make-up. She told a maid to pull the curtain aside and cried out: "Mother! Don't cry! Your daughter didn't die! I'm here!"

Jiangxian stared wide-eyed at the boat and saw Tan Chuyu and her daughter sitting there side by side, wine cups in front of them, like a couple of wronged ghosts who had learned of the sacrifice being held on stage and had come to partake of it. Panic-stricken, she screamed at the actors in the green-room: "My daughter's ghost! Come quick!"

The troupe dashed on stage, and, looking intently at the boat, declared: "It's her ghost, all right. There's no doubt about it."

Hearing talk of ghosts, the audience panicked and turned to flee, at which point one of Tan's stewards, a resourceful fellow, stood up in the bow and shouted to them: "There's no cause for alarm. Those aren't ghosts you see in the boat, they're the real Master Tan and his lady. They were rescued after they leapt into the water, and then the master passed the examinations, and now he's been appointed prefect of Dingzhou. He's passing through here on the way to his post. He and his lady owe their lives to one of Lord Yan's miracles, and that's why they're giving thanks here today."

At this, the audience turned back again and, instead of fleeing, pressed forward to get a good look at this couple who had been saved from suicide, hoping to have an item of news to take home. The theatre became a heaving mass of humanity, and the very old and the very young were forced into the water or trampled underfoot. Tan saw the danger and hurriedly consulted with his wife: "We've already shown ourselves and can't hide any more. I suggest we go on stage together and let everyone take a good look at us. Otherwise someone will be crushed to death."

"Very well," she said.

They changed into their formal clothes, Tan putting on his crimson collar and Miaogu her phoenix hood and cloud mantilla. Under new bright-blue parasols they stepped ashore surrounded by servants and maids. First they went to the image of Lord Yan and bowed low four more times. Then

---

[7] Scene 30 ("Ji jiang"). Actually it is not Wang but his mother who sacrifices, and the words quoted do not appear in the play.
[8] Zhou Yu (175–210), who came to represent the expert critic of music.

they went on stage and paid their respects to Jiangxian. Finally, they called all their fellow actors and actresses over and greeted them one by one.

Jiangxian and the rest of the troupe asked how they had come to be rescued. Tan told of someone leading them through the water, of a great fish carrying them on its back, of the fish's sudden disappearance when it reached the net, and of their fortunate rescue by the fisherman and his wife. He told his story in a loud, ringing voice so that all those on and off the stage could hear it and learn to venerate the god all the more by knowing of his spiritual power.

Everyone was astounded. The benefactors came forward to offer their congratulations. The rich benefactor who had tried to marry Miaogu was afraid that Tan's and Miaogu's hatred would turn to thoughts of revenge, so he hastily prepared some lavish presents and begged the others to intercede for him.

But Tan would accept none of the presents. "Without the stimulus this gentleman provided, not only would our romance not have succeeded, I would still be an actor; I could never have risen to the position I hold. He is not an enemy of ours, quite the contrary. How could I even *think* of revenge?" The benefactors marvelled at him and praised his generosity.

Miaogu turned to her mother. "Now that your son-in-law is a national graduate and your daughter a lady, surely you won't want to go on with your acting? Pack up your things as quickly as you can and come and live with us, so that you won't have to make a spectacle of yourself any more."

Jiangxian was delighted that her daughter and son-in-law bore her no grudge. Handing the troupe's management over to her daughter-in-law, she went off with Miaogu to enjoy a life of wealth and prestige. But within a month of her arrival she came down with an illness that defied every attempt at cure, and in the end she had to get her daughter to send her back again. Once she was home, the illness vanished of its own accord, without further treatment. As soon as she recovered, she went on tour again, enjoyed excellent health, and suffered no further misfortune.

Why? In the first place, she had been destined for an actress's career by the eight characters of her birth[9] and could not be away from the theatre for a day without incurring some mishap. Clearly, if someone has a lowly fate, not even her own child will be able to raise her to a higher status, let alone anyone else. Hence poor men should resign themselves to their lot, not hate the rich and eminent for failing to raise them up. Secondly, Jiangxian had grown accustomed to a frivolous life and could not suddenly switch to a serious one. Compare the case of a maidservant promoted to a wife, or a servant-boy adopted as a son; not only will their lowly destinies show in their faces, they will get no pleasure from their new status but instead will feel strain, which in turn will give rise to illness. Therefore prostitutes who reform and get married, like priests who leave the priesthood—unless they do

---

[9]The eight characters represent the year, month, day, and hour of birth.

so of their own volition and are not pressured into it—will not be able to persevere and will ultimately revert to their old professions.

Let me turn now to Tan, who, after serving six months in his new post, sent Mo five hundred taels with the promise of more to come, to a total of over a thousand. But Mo, a scrupulously honest man, kept only one hundred, as the tenfold repayment of his loan, and sent the rest back.

When his term of office was over, Tan set off for the capital and again passed through Quzhou, Yanzhou, and other towns. He renovated Lord Yan's Temple and also bought several acres of sacrificial land, which he handed over to the benefactors to fund future sacrifices and theatricals with. From there he went on to Port Newtown to visit Fisherman Mo.

Mo opened with a few disdainful remarks designed to chip away at Tan's evident vanity and love of luxury, then went on to speak of matters of gain and loss to attack his cupidity. Now, Tan already possessed a certain spiritual capacity. In his days as an actor, he had noted how high the excitement was as long as the play lasted—"one thousand in tears, ten thousand in love"—but that once it was over and the gongs and drums were silent, the audience would stream out of the theatre without a single backward glance, as if they were cutting him dead. Clearly, there was no play in the world that did not come to an end and no excitement that would last forever. Therefore he had never felt any very strong desire for wealth and prestige. Now, as he listened to Mo's enlightening talk, he felt as if he had been subjected to "a blow and a shout"[1] just at the moment he awakened from a dream, and he would never let himself be deluded again.

No longer did he have the slightest desire to seek promotion in the capital or enjoy his hometown glory. Instead, by the side of Two Mile Stream in Tonglu county, he bought an acre or two of hilly ground and built a thatched hut on it. He spent his days fishing, partly to follow the lofty example of Yan Ziling[2] and partly to receive Fisherman Mo's guidance. By Mo he was introduced to a circle of friends, ploughmen and woodcutters, men of noble character who possessed the talent, if not the desire, to succeed in public life. By spending his days with them, Tan learned something of fishing, woodcutting, and farming. Miaogu, too, had her circle of friends, introduced to her by Mo's wife, wise women who could have helped their husbands succeed in public life but chose not to press them. By spending her days with these women, she learned something of raising silkworms and spinning silk.

Both Tan and Miaogu lived on into their nineties. The only pity was that they had no son. This was partly because Miaogu's beauty was of the delicate type that is not conducive to bearing sons, and partly because Tan was so deeply devoted to his wife that he could not contemplate taking a concubine.

---

[1] A Buddhist notion, it refers to a salutary shock administered by a religious mentor.
[2] Yan Guang, whose style was Ziling, of the Han Dynasty. Li Yu often used him as a symbol of the high-minded recluse who refused office.

Critique

This romance has seven peculiar features, all of which fly in the face of common sense. One: an exceptionally wanton mother gives birth to a perfectly chaste daughter. Two: someone from the lowliest social level performs the noblest action. Three: whereas playwrights have always developed plays from real events, this story develops real events from a play. Four: whereas the *jing* and *chou* roles have always been something for the male lead to fall back on, here they serve as stepping-stones to his position. Five: since cults are established by the gods, Erlang, as the patron of the acting profession, ought to have been called upon to play the celestial matchmaker; instead he is left out, and it is Lord Yan, with no connection to acting, who takes his place. Six: in fiction it is the main character who, without exception, takes the subordinate characters away with him; when Tan Chuyu meets with sudden success, the normal thing would have been for him to take Fisherman Mo off to become wealthy and eminent, instead of which it is the peripheral Mo who takes Tan off to become a high-minded recluse. Seven: plays and stories have to end in an exciting finale to suit contemporary taste—without such an ending, they would be rejected by their audiences—and yet this story ends in rustic solitude.

One might well consider himself lucky if all of these unnatural and unreasonable things did not provoke the reader's irritation. How then, can one explain the fact that they cause the reader to start praising the story's novelty as soon as he opens the book and leave him dancing on air as he closes it? Impossible! All we can do is curse the author as a peculiar romancer who deals in peculiarities.

清 Kong Shang-ren, *Peach Blossom Fan:* Selected Acts

Kong Shang-ren's (1648–1718) *Peach Blossom Fan* is an historical drama that treats the brief Southern Ming regime set up in Nanjing in 1644 after the capture of Beijing by the rebel Li Zi-cheng and the suicide of the legitimate Chong-zhen Emperor of the Ming. This was the period of the Manchu invasion, which put an end to the "Southern Ming" in the process of establishing the Qing Dynasty. Strong sentiment for the Ming still lingered in the late seventeenth century when *Peach Blossom Fan* was written (1699), and the Qing government was proportionally sensitive to any hint of criticism. Luckily for Kong Shang-ren, the "Southern Ming" was so incompetent and corrupt that an historically accurate portrayal would not offend Qing imperial sensibilities. At the same time a passionate loyalty to the Ming could be represented, not directed against the Qing but against the self-destructive folly of the Southern Ming court.

In the play, Kong Shang-ren argued with some justification that the historical events portrayed were themselves theater: the "Southern Ming" was show rather than substance. Each of the two sections into which the forty acts are divided is introduced by an old man, once a minor participant in the events represented, speaking from the fictitious present of the play's performance in 1684. He concludes the introduction to the second half with a verse that underscores the point:

> In those days reality was a play,
> this play today seems reality.
> From sidelines I watch a second time—
> Heaven preserves the man with cold eyes.

The characters in the play all are based on individuals who took part in the actual historical events, and Kong Shang-ren drew extensively on historical documents. At the center of the action is the love story of Hou Fang-yu, one of the most famous writers of the day, and the courtesan Li Xiang-jun. The historical Hou Fang-yu was acquainted with Li Xiang-jun and even wrote a brief biography of her; but as with other characters, the more everyday facts and events of history are transformed under the imperatives of dramatic romance.

Performances of songs, plays, and popular storytelling, along with ceremonies staged like performances, occur throughout *Peach Blossom Fan*. The arch villain, Ruan Da-cheng, was not only a part of the corrupt Southern Ming government, he was also the preeminent playwright of his own day. References to Ruan's most famous play, *The Swallow Letter,* recur often as an example of a flawed, hollow art (it is also the favorite play of Prince Fu, who becomes the theater-loving Southern Ming emperor). Again and again, *Peach Blossom Fan* comes back to questions of role playing, feigning, and the way the genuine can appear within a role. The finest example is the young heroine Li Xiang-jun, who is first taught to sing the role of a romantic heroine and finally becomes the kind of character she plays.

One of the most remarkable figures in the first half of the play is the painter Yang Wen-cong. It is he who gives Li Xiang-jun her name and he who eventually paints the bloodstains on Xiang-jun's fan into peach blossoms, from which the play takes its title. Moving easily between the camps of the good characters and the villains, Yang Wen-cong is the cause of the lovers coming together, the cause of their separation, and the one who initiates the events that lead to their eventual reunion. The scenes translated here are the Prologue and the three central scenes that involve Yang and the fan. Finally, part of the last reunion scene tells the ultimate fate of the fan.

The Prologue opens with a fictive first performance of the play in 1684, the beginning of a new grand cycle in the Chinese dating system. The old man, once an officiant at the Ming ancestral temple, praises the good government of the reigning Kang-xi emperor to help allay any hint of disloyalty.

PROLOGUE (I), OCTOBER 1684

Enter an OLD MAN *with a white beard, a felt hat, and Daoist robes.*

OLD MAN:
> Is there such an antique as I?—
> antique of neither bronze nor jade,
> but my face gives off an antique gloss.
> The last soul surviving, companions gone—
> why flinch from young men's scorn?
> The outrage that once filled my breast
>   has all been swept away,
> and now I may well linger on, wherever
>   I find drink and song.
> Now children revere their parents,
>   state officers are true,
>   all things rest secure,
> so yearn no more for the ginseng root
>   that makes a man live long.

The sun shines gloriously on this age of sage-kings, and flowers bloom in the onset of a new cycle of years. There are no bandits in the hills, while gods and immortals fill the earth. I was once an Officiant at the Court of Imperial Sacrifices in Nanjing, a post of no great prestige or pay, so my name may be withheld here. It has been my great good fortune to have escaped disaster, and I have been alive these ninety-seven years, during which I have witnessed much of splendor and ruin. And now I have reached the first year of a new hundred-and-eighty-year cycle. A ruler comparable to Yao and Shun is on the throne, and ministers like Yu and Gao have been installed to aid him. Everywhere the populace is happy, and the harvests have been abundant year after year. This is the twenty-third year of the Kang-xi Reign, and twenty-one signs of good luck have appeared.

VOICE [*offstage*]: What are these signs of good luck?

OLD MAN [*counting them off on his fingers*]:

    The Yellow River Diagram appeared.
    The Luo River Inscription appeared.
    The Star of Virtue brightened.
    Auspicious clouds manifested themselves.
    A sweet dew fell.
    An oily rain came down.
    A phoenix roosted.
    A unicorn roamed.
    The ming plant came out.
    The sacred mushroom grew.
    There were no waves on the sea.
    The Yellow River cleared.

Every single one of these occurred—doesn't that deserve celebration? I'm delighted to have lived to see such glorious times, and I roam about everywhere. In the Tai-ping Gardens yesterday I saw a new play being put on, entitled *Peach Blossom Fan*, which concerned what happened around Nanjing in the last years of the Ming. It treated the emotions of separation and reunion, and it described how people felt about the splendor and ruin of men and kingdoms. The events really happened and the people were real ones; it was all accurate. I not only heard of these things, I saw them all with my own eyes. Even more amusing, I, now a frail old man, was actually put on the stage as one of the minor characters. This inspired tears, laughter, rage, and condemnation in me. And no one in the whole audience realized that I, just an old man to them, was really one of the persons in the play.

VOICE [*offstage*]: Who wrote this fine play?

OLD MAN: Don't you gentlemen know that the most famous playwrights don't reveal their names. But when you observe how he apportions praise and criticism, it must come from someone with a family tradition in the study of *The Springs and Autumns;* and its suitability for singing shows that the author clearly had family instruction in the *Classic of Poetry.*

VOICE [*offstage*]: In that case it's obviously the Hermit of Yun-ting Mountain.

OLD MAN: To whom are you referring?

VOICE [*offstage*]: There's going to be a gathering of the upper crust of officialdom, and they're going to have this very play performed. Since you're one of the characters in it and since you've also heard this new version, why don't you give us an outline of the plot beforehand, and we'll all listen carefully.

OLD MAN: It's all in the lyrics to "Fragrance Fills the Yard," sung by the Daoist Zhang Wei.

[*Sings*]

A young gentleman, Hou Fang-yu,
sometime resident in Nanjing,
was matched with the Southland's fairest;
Harm worked unseen by vicious lies
in one night split this loving pair.
They saw the world turned upside down,
the Jiang-Huai garrisons amok.
Next a blind prince took the throne,
choosing performers, his only concern,
while faction's ills raised wicked ministers.

Their bond of love could not continue:
she in her tower with martyr's ardor,
he in his dungeon, in deep despair.
They owed thanks to Liu and old Su
whose earnest endeavors set them free.
At midnight ruler and minister fled,
who laments a loyal soul in misty waves?
And the peach blossom fan
shredded on the altar lay,
and I shall show you how they strayed.

VOICE [*offstage*]: Excellent! Excellent! But sometimes we couldn't quite understand you because of the ringing quality of the melody. Summarize it again in a few lines.

OLD MAN: Let me try.

[*Recites*]

The traitors Ma and Ruan lurked with swords
　　both inside the court and out;
deft Liu and Su went back and forth
　　seeking to tie the secret threads.
Young Hou Fang-yu found true love's course
　　broken beyond recall,
Zhang Wei the Daoist gave judgment
　　on glory and the fall.

But here as I'm talking, Hou Fang-yu has already come on stage. Let's all watch.

Inherent in *Peach Blossom Fan* is a fascination with acting roles, both the kind that occur on stage and the kind that occur in the political and social world. In scene II, "Teaching the Song," we meet the heroine, Li Xiang-jun, at first the pure type of the nubile virgin, literally nameless. From the painter Yang Wen-cong she receives both a name and a marriage "plot," in which she is supposed to play her appointed role. Between her naming and the suggestion of a match, she practices singing the role of Du Li-niang in *Peony Pavilion,* the romantic heroine's role for which she is destined both on stage and off. At her side, however, is the music teacher Su Kun-sheng, whose insistent corrections constantly remind us of the artifice of role.

The stage is set in the pleasure quarters of Nanjing, by the Qin-Huai River.

TEACHING THE SONG (II), APRIL 1643

Enter MADAM LI ZHEN-LI, *elegantly made up.*

LI [*sings*]:

> With dark-drawn brows, I do not close
> the doors of this red mansion.
> On Long Plank Bridge thin willow strands
> flirt and draw the passing riders.
> I tighten up the harp strings
> and deftly work the mouth organ's pouch.

[*Recites*]

> Blooms of pear are like the snow,
>   the grasses like a mist,
> springtime comes to the Qin-Huai,
>   here on both its shores.
> Courtesans' parlors in a row
>   look out on the waters,
> and from each house reflections cast
>   the fetching images of girls.

I am Li Zhen-li, and I belong to the finest troupe of singers, to the most famous band of "misty flowers" and "moonlit breeze." I was born and bred in the pleasure quarters, where I have welcomed clients and sent them on their way across Long Bridge. This face, with its powder and paint, has not yet lost its bloom, and ample charms remain to me. I have raised one adopted daughter, a tender and gentle little thing, just now beginning to take part in our elegant soirées; but in her shy grace, she has not yet gone behind the lotus bed curtains. There is hereabouts a re-tired county magistrate called Yang Wen-cong, who is the brother-in-law of Ma Shi-ying, the governor-general of Feng-yang, and a sworn friend of Ruan Da-zheng, the former head of the Court of Imperial En-tertainments. On his frequent visits to my establishment, Yang has often praised my daughter and wants to arrange for a client to "do up her hair."[1] The spring weather is so bright and inviting today, I suspect he'll be here for a visit. [*Calls out*] Maid, open the curtains and sweep up, and keep your eye out to see if any visitors are coming.

VOICE [*offstage*]: Yes, ma'am.

---

[1]Having one's hair done up marked the passage into womanhood; here it is a euphemism for tak-ing her virginity.

Enter YANG WEN-CONG.

YANG [*recites*]:
>   Triple Mountain's scenery is
>   a resource for my paintings,
>   the flair of Southern Dynasties
>   courses through my poems.

I am Yang Wen-cong, a licentiate and former county magistrate who has retired from my post to live a quiet life. Li Zhen-li, the famous courtesan of the Qin-Huai, is an old friend of mine, and I'm taking advantage of the spring weather to pay her a visit and have a chat. Here I am now. I'll be going in. [*Enters*] Where's the lady? [*Greets her*] Splendid! See how the petals of the plum have fallen and the fronds of the willows are turning yellow. Soft and rich in color, spring's beauty is everywhere in the yard, which makes me wonder how we may best spend these moments.

LI: It is lovely indeed. Come to the little room upstairs. I'll burn some incense and put on some tea, and we can read over some poems.

YANG: Even better! [*They climb stairs. He recites*]
>   Curtain stripes seem to cage the bird on its perch,
>   flowers' shadows seem to guard the fish in its bowl.

These are your daughter's apartments. Where is she?

LI: She hasn't yet finished dressing; she's still in the bedroom.

YANG: Ask her to come out.

LI [*calling out*]: Come out, child. Mr. Yang is here.

YANG [*reading the poems on her walls*]: How remarkable! These are all poems inscribed to her by well-known figures! [*He clasps his hands behind his back and recites them*]

Enter HEROINE, *splendidly made up.*

HEROINE [*sings*]:
>   Just now called back from sweetest dreams,
>   I threw off red coverlets
>   broidered with mated ducks.
>   I put on lipstick and glossy rouge
>   and hastily did my hair
>   in a ponytail with straying tresses.
>   What relief is there for spring's moodiness?—
>   just learning new lyrics for songs.

[*Greets* YANG] Good-day, sir!

YANG: You have grown even more stunning in these past few days since I saw you last. These poems are not at all wrong in their praise of you. [*Reads on and registers surprise*] Well, look at this! Such prominent figures as Zhang Pu and Xia Yun-yi have both written poems to you. I really must write you a poem of my own, using their rhymes. [LI ZHEN-LI brings him a brush and inkstone. YANG *takes the brush in hand and mulls over it a long time, as if ready to recite*] I can't do as well as them; I might as well hide my weaknesses by decorating your white wall here with a few black-ink drawings of orchids.

LI: That's even better!

YANG [*looking at the wall*]: Here's a rock like a fist painted by Lan Ying. I can use his painting as a background and draw my orchids over at the side of the rock. [*Paints and sings*]

> The white wall glows
> > like rippling silk,
> Here I sketch the *Li Sao*'s
> > poetic temper.[2]
> Tender leaves and scented sheaths,
> rain-burdened, drunk in streaks of mist.
> This rock of Xuan-zhou, ink-flowers shattered,
> with several spots of gray moss,
> > tingeing the pavements randomly.

[*Goes back and looks at it*] Not bad!

> No match, of course, for black-ink orchids
> > done by masters of the Yuan,
> > > that mood of nonchalance,
> but our own famous beauties should wear
> > Xiang orchids at their waists.

LI: This is truly the brushwork of a master. You have added much beauty to our apartments.

YANG: You're making fun of me. [*To* HEROINE] Tell me your professional name so that I can write it here in the dedication.

HEROINE: I'm still young and don't have a professional name yet.

LI: Why don't you do her the honor of giving her a name?

YANG: There is a passage in *The Zuo Tradition*: "And because [the] orchid has the sweetest smell in all the land, people will wear it in their sashes and be fond of it."[3] Why don't we call her Xiang-jun, "Queen of Sweet Fragrance"?

LI: Excellent! Xiang-jun, come over and thank Mr. Yang.

XIANG-JUN [*bowing*]: Thank you very much, sir.

YANG [*laughing*]: We even have a name for these chambers. [*Writes the dedication*] "In mid-spring, this sixteenth year of the Chong-zhen Reign, 1643, I chanced to draw these orchids in ink in the Chambers of Beguiling Fragrance to win a smile from Xiang-jun, who is Queen of Sweet Fragrance. Yang Wen-cong of Gui-yang."

---

[2]By the emblematic associations within the *Li Sao* itself, the orchid was, in its solitary purity, associated with Qu Yuan.
[3]See p. 81.

Lɪ: Both the paintings and the calligraphy are superb, worthy of acclaim as a double perfection. Thank you so much! [*All sit*]

Yᴀɴɢ: As I see it, Xiang-jun here may be the most beautiful woman in the land, but I don't know her level of skill in the arts.

Lɪ: She has always been spoiled and allowed to have her own way, so she didn't study anything. But just recently I've asked one of the habitués of the pleasure quarters to give her lessons in singing.

Yᴀɴɢ: Who is it?

Lɪ: Someone called Su Kun-sheng.

Yᴀɴɢ: Yes, Su Kun-sheng. His real name is Zhou Ru-song, originally from He-nan and now a resident of Wu-xi. I have known him well for some time—he is a true master. What suites of songs has he taught her?

Lɪ: The "Four Dream Plays" of Tang Xian-zu.

Yᴀɴɢ: How much of them has she learned?

Lɪ: She's just now learned half of *Peony Pavilion*. [*Calls to* Xɪᴀɴɢ-ᴊᴜɴ] Child, Mr. Yang here is no stranger to us. Get out your score and practice some of the songs you know. After your teacher quizzes you, you can try some new tunes.

Xɪᴀɴɢ-ᴊᴜɴ: How can I practice my singing with a guest present?

Lɪ: Don't be silly! For those of us in the quarter the costume for singing and dancing is the endowment that provides us our food. How are you going to get by if you won't practice singing? [Xɪᴀɴɢ-ᴊᴜɴ *looks at her score*]

Lɪ [*sings*]:

> When born among bevies of powder and paint,
> and entering blossom and oriole troupes,
> a throat that can carry an aria
> is the place where we find our wealth.
> Don't lightly throw your heart away,
> but study "The early morning wind
>   and dying moonlight sinking";[4]
> then with red clapper's slow beat,
> from Yi-chun performers you'll steal the glow,[5]
> and tied before you gate will be seen
>   horses of princes.

Enter Su Kᴜɴ-sʜᴇɴɢ, *wearing a headband and in informal dress.*

Su [*recites*]:

> Idly I come to azure lodges
>   to train my parakeet,
> lazily leaving vermilion gates
>   to see the peonies.

---

[4]This phrase is adapted from a famous lyric by the Northern Sung lyricist Liu Yong.
[5]Yi-chun Palace was the site of the famous "Pear Garden Academy" of imperial musicians and singers during the reign of Xuan-zong in the Tang.

I am Su Kun-sheng. I've left Ruan Da-cheng's levee to come here to the plea-sure quarters. Taking this beautiful girl through her lessons is certainly a lot better than toadying to that foster child of a eunuch. [*Goes in and greets them*] Well, Yang Wen-cong, fancy meeting you here. It's been some time.

YANG: My compliments, Kun-sheng, on taking such a stunning beauty as a pupil.

LI: Your teacher, Mr. Su, is here. Go pay him the proper welcome, child.

XIANG-JUN *bows.*

SU: No need for that. Have you memorized thoroughly the song I taught you yesterday?

XIANG-JUN: I have.

SU: We'll take advantage of Mr. Yang's presence as our audience to ask him for pointers as you go over it with me.

YANG: I just want you to show me how it should be performed.

XIANG-JUN [*seated opposite* SU, *sings*]:[6]

> Coy lavenders, fetching reds
> > bloom everywhere, here
> > all given to this broken well
> and tumbled wall. Fair season,
> > fine scene, overwhelming
> > weather . . .

SU: Wrong! Wrong! "Fair" gets a beat and "overwhelming" gets a beat; don't run the two clauses together. Let's try it again.

XIANG-JUN:

> > > Fair season,
> > fine scene—overwhelming
> > weather. Where
> and in whose garden shall we find
> pleasure and the heart's delight?
> Drifting in at dawn, at twilight
> > roll away
> clouds and colored wisps
> > through azure balustrades
> streaming rain, petals in wind . . .

SU: No, that's not right again. "Streaming" carries a special weight in the melody; it should be sung from the diaphragm.

XIANG-JUN:

> streaming rain, petals in wind,
> a painted boat in misty waves,
> the girl behind her brocade screen
> > has seen but dimly
> > such splendor of spring.

---

[6]The aria she sings is from "Waking from Dream" in *Peony Pavilion.*

SU: Excellent! Excellent! Exactly right! Let's go on.

XIANG-JUN:

> Throughout green hills the nightjar cries
> > its tears of blood; and out beyond
> the blackberry the threads
> > of mist coil drunkenly.
> And though the peony be fair,
> > how can it maintain its sway
> > > when spring is leaving?

SU: These lines are a bit rough. Try them again.

XIANG-JUN:

> And though the peony be fair,
> > how can it maintain its sway
> > > when spring is leaving?
> Idly I stare
> where twittering swallows crisply speak
> > words cut clear,
> and from the warbling orioles comes
> > a bright and liquid melody.

SU: Fine! Now you've completed another suite of songs.

YANG [*to* LI ZHEN-LI]: I'm pleased to see that your daughter is so quick. I have no doubt she will become a famous courtesan. [*To* SU] I met young Hou Fang-yu the other day, the son of Hou, the executive in the Ministry of Revenue. He is well provided for, and he also is known for his talent. At present he is looking for a woman of distinguished beauty. Do you know him, Kong-sheng?

SU: Our families are from the same region. He is, indeed, a young man of great talent.

YANG: We'd be making no mistake if we arranged a union between these two.

[*Sings*]

> Fair match for our Sapphire, now sixteen:[7]
> she sings charming songs,
> he rides a sleek horse.
> He will lavish her with turban brocades,[8]
> and hand in hand they will drain their cups.
> Wedding poems will speed them to bed,
> a lacquered coach to greet the bride.
> With a rare young noble as her mate,

---

[7]Sapphire, Bi-yu, was the legendary concubine of the Prince of Ru-nan in the Southern Dynasties.

[8]Brocade used for turbans was the standard figure for gifts (i.e., payment) to a courtesan.

> year after year she will never let
>> her Ruan Zhao go away,[9]
> by the spring waters of Peach Leaf Ford
>> he will buy a cottage and stay.[1]

LI: It would be just wonderful if such a young gentleman were willing to come "do up her hair." I hope you will do what you can to help in bringing this match about.

YANG: It is on my mind.

LI [*sings*]:

> No pearl can compare to this girl of mine,
> who mimics the new oriole's sweet cries,
> in springtime closed behind many gates,
>> never known by man.

We can't waste such a glorious spring day. Let's go have a little wine downstairs.

YANG: Sounds good to me. [*Recites*]

> In front of Little Su's curtain,
>> flowers fill the meadow,[2]

LI:

> orioles tipsy, swallows languid
>> across the springtime banks.

XIANG-JUN:

> In my red silk handkerchief
>> are fruits of cherry,

SU:

> waiting for Pan Yue's carriage
>> to pass west of the lane.[3]

Having arranged the sale of Xiang-jun's virginity, Yang Wen-cong anticipates a conventional union of "talented youth and fair maid." Xiang-jun has studied the role she is to play. After all, as her mother Li Zhen-li reminds her, it is by playing roles (singing in musical drama and making customers fall in love with her) that she must make her living. But instead of becoming the actress-courtesan who merely plays roles, Xiang-jun learns her role too well and actually becomes the romantic heroine.

In the acts that follow, factional politics creep into the conventional love match. The villain Ruan Da-cheng, rudely scorned by the politically progressive young men of Nanjing, is looking for someone to support his cause and win acceptance for him among the local elite. Yang Wen-cong tells Ruan of the match he has proposed between Li Xiang-jun and Hou Fang-yu, and he suggests that if Ruan were to provide

---

[9]The story of Ruan Zhao and Liu Zhen's encounter with two immortal maidens in the mountains and their staying with them for more than half a year became a standard figure for losing oneself in a love affair. "Young Ruan Goes Away," *Ruan-lang gui*, was a famous melody.

[1]Peach Leaf was another famous concubine of the Southern Dynasties. Peach Leaf Ford, where Wang Xian-zhi of the Jin supposedly wrote a quatrain to the young lady in question, was on the Qin-Huai River, in the area of the pleasure quarters of Nanjing.

[2]Little Su was another famous courtesan of the Southern Dynasties.

[3]The Jin writer Pan Yue was known for his good looks. One story has it that when he traveled in his carriage, the women would gather around him and throw fruit to him as a sign of their attraction.

the "wedding gifts" (the price for Li Xiang-jun's virginity), Hou Fang-yu would be obligated to return the favor and use his influence with his friends on Ruan's behalf. Ruan Da-cheng agrees to the plan eagerly.

Yang Wen-cong then makes the proposal to Hou Fang-yu, intimating that Yang himself will cover the cost of the wedding gifts. He arranges for Hou Fang-yu and Li Xiang-jun to meet, and Hou is properly smitten by her beauty and shy charm. There is a "wedding" banquet and the couple go off happily to bed. In the sobriety of the morning after, Li Xiang-jun, hitherto docile and usually silent, begins to speak for herself, insisting on learning the truth of where the wedding gifts came from. When she knows the truth, she acts on it, causing the complications that will drive the play's love story. Hou Fang-yu, on the other hand, is initially more willing to participate in a world of compromises.

REFUSING THE TROUSSEAU (VII), MAY 1643

Enter SERVANT, *picking up the nightstools.*

SERVANT:

> Tortoise piss, tortoise piss
> spews out little tortoises,
> blood of turtle, blood of turtle
> turns to little turtles fertile.
> Tortoise piss and turtle blood,
> whose is whose I cannot guess;
> turtle blood and tortoise piss,
> can't say if it's that or this.
> Whose is whose I cannot guess,
> can't say who the father is;
> who can tell one from another?—
> can't say who's the father's brother.

[*Laughing*] Tsk, tsk, tsk. Last night Miss Xiang-jun lost her virginity, and the hoopla went on half the night. I got up early today and have to scrub out the nightstools and empty the chamberpots. There's so much to get done. I wonder how much longer the client and our girl are going to spend in each other's arms. [*Scrubs the nightstools*]

Enter YANG WEN-CONG.

YANG [*sings*]:

> They spend nights deep in willow lanes
>   of Ping-kang Ward,[4]
> and outside the gate a flower peddler
>   wakes them suddenly from dreams.
> The finely wrought door still unopened,
> and the curtain hooks are tinkling,

---

[4]The Ping-kang Ward was the pleasure quarter of the Tang capital Chang-an.

953

with spring blocked off by ten layers
    of hanging lace.

I've come early to offer Hou Fang-yu my congratulations, but as you can see, the door to the establishment is closed tight and there's not a sound from the servants. I suppose they haven't gotten up yet. [*Calls out*] You, boy, go over to the newlyweds' window and tell them that I've come to offer my congratulations.

SERVANT: They got to sleep rather late last night, and they may not have gotten up yet. Why don't you come again tomorrow, sir.

YANG [*laughing*]: Don't be silly. Quick, now, go find out!

LI [*from within*]: Boy, who's that who just came?

SERVANT: It's Yang Wen-cong, who's come to offer his congratulations.

LI [*enters hurriedly, recites*]:
    Head rests on pillow, spring nights too brief,
      but good often comes from a knock at the gate.

[*Greets* YANG] Thank you so much for bringing about this lifelong union for my daughter.

YANG: Think nothing of it. Have the newlyweds risen yet?

LI: They went to sleep late last night and still haven't gotten up yet. [*Gestures to* YANG *to sit*] Please have a seat while I go hurry them up.

YANG: There's no need for that.

Exit LI ZHEN-LI.

YANG [*sings*]:
    Young passion is heady like flower wine,
    so fine that they think of nothing else
    but to share that sweet black land of sleep.

Which would have been impossible, of course, failing my help.
    Pearls and kingfisher feathers gleam,
    silks and satins ripple and rustle,
    each and every item of new attire
    is proclamation of love's desire.

Enter LI ZHEN-LI.

LI: It's so charming. They're both in there buttoning each other up and looking in the mirror to see how they look as a pair. They've finished combing and washing up, but they're not through with getting dressed. Let's go into their rooms together and call them out to drink a cup of wine to help their hangover.

YANG: It was unforgivable of me to have woken them. [*Exeunt*]

Enter HOU FANG-YU *and* XIANG-JUN, *fully made up.*

HOU and XIANG-JUN [*sing*]:
    Passion's cloud joining
      to cloudburst and rain

scratches a wondrous itch in the heart—
who now disturbs the sleeping pair
    of mated ducks?
Blankets heaved in waves of red,
as we joyously took full measure
    of all love's pleasure.
A lingering scent on the pillow,
a lingering scent on the handkerchief,
sensations that melt the rapturous soul
tasted now as we rise from dream.

      Enter YANG WEN-CONG *and* LI ZHEN-LI.

YANG: Well, you've gotten up at last. Congratulations. [*He bows, then sits*]
    Did you like the wedding night verse I wrote for you yesterday evening?
HOU [*bowing*]: Thank you very much. [*Laughs*] It was the height of excel-
    lence—except for one little point . . .
YANG: What little point?
HOU: However tiny Xiang-jun may be, she deserves be kept in a chamber
    of gold, but [*looks in his sleeves*] how would I get her in my sleeves?[5]

      All laugh.

YANG: I'm sure you also must have written something fine last night when
    you two declared your love.
HOU: I just scribbled out something hastily—I wouldn't dare show you.
YANG: And where is the poem?
XIANG-JUN: The poem is on the fan.

  XIANG-JUN *takes the fan out of her sleeve and gives it to* YANG WEN-CONG,
        who looks it over.

YANG: It's a white satin palace fan. [*Sniffs it*] And it has a subtle aroma. [*Re-
    cites the poem*]
    "Blue mansions line the road,
        a single path slants through,
    here the prince first drives
        the Count of Fu-ping's coach.
    Everywhere upon Blue Creek
        there are magnolia trees—
    no match for blooms of peach and plum
        in the east wind of spring."[6]

---

[5]The Han emperor Wu-di said that if he could get A-jiao as his consort, he would keep her in a
chamber of gold. Hou Fang-yu is referring to a line in Yang's poem in which she would be "hidden
in his sleeves," suggesting an embrace rather than Hou Fang-yu's joking interpretation.
[6]The poem is not repeated in this act, but I have included it from scene VI. The poem is, in fact, a
variation on one by the historical Hou Fang-yu. The praise of "peach and plum" over the magno-

Excellent! Only Xiang-jun would not be put to shame by this poem. [*Hands it back to* XIANG-JUN] Take care of it. [XIANG-JUN *puts away the fan.* YANG *sings*]

> Scent of peach and scent of plum,
>> fragrance at its sweetest,
> all written on a satin fan.
> Lest they meet the tossing gusts
>> of wild winds,
> hide it close within your sleeve,
> hide it close within your sleeve.

[*Looks at* XIANG-JUN] After her wedding night, Xiang-jun seems to have an even more sensual beauty. [*To* HOU FANG-YU] You're a lucky man to enjoy this splendid creature.

HOU: Xiang-jun's natural beauty makes her the fairest in the land, but the pearl and kingfisher ornaments that she wears in her hair today and all her silken finery add something extra to her utterly flowerlike beauty. She is entirely lovable.

LI: This is all thanks to Mr. Yang's assistance.

[*Sings*]

> He sent the turbans of brocade,
> the chests of varied gems,
> fringed curtains wound with pearls
>> and kingfisher feathers, silver
> candlesticks, shades of gauze
>> shining through the night,
> golden cups for offering wine
>> to go along with song at feasts.

> And now he has come to see you so early today.
>> As though you were his very own
>>> children he raised himself,
>> first providing the needed trousseau,
>> now also paying this early call.

XIANG-JUN: It seems to me, Mr. Yang, that even though you're a close relative of the governor-general, Ma Shi-ying, you are in rather difficult financial circumstances yourself and live on the goodwill of others; why should you so casually throw away your money into the bottomless pit of the pleasure quarters? For my own part, I am embarrassed to receive it; and on your side, it was given anonymously. Please make things clear to us so that we can plan how to repay such generosity.

HOU: Xiang-jun is quite right to ask this. You and I have met like duckweeds drifting on the water; your show of kindness the other day was so generous that I feel uncomfortable.

---

lia plays on Xiang-jun's surname Li, which is the word for "plum." Peach blossoms will play an even larger role in the play.

YANG: Since I have been asked, I can only tell you the truth. The trousseau and the party cost somewhat over two hundred pieces of silver, and all of it came from a gentleman from Huai-ning.

HOU: Who from Huai-ning?

YANG: Ruan Yuan-hai, who was the head of the Court of Imperial Entertainments.

HOU: Do you mean Ruan Da-cheng from An-hui?

YANG: That's right.

HOU: Why has he been so lavish?

YANG: He simply wants to become acquainted with you.

[*Sings*]

> He admires your prospects and panache,
> your name for talent like Luo-yang's Zuo Si,
> your writings like those of Si-ma Xiang-ru.
> Wherever you go, you find welcome;
> all crowd around the young man in the coach.[7]
> In the finest spots of the Qin-Huai
> you sought a fair maiden for your side,
> but you lacked the spread for the marriage bed
>> and lotus make-up.

You wonder who did this—
> the senior Ruan of the southern branch[8]
> put himself out for your wedding apparel.

HOU: Ruan Da-cheng was an acquaintance of my father's, but I despise him and have had nothing to do with him for a long time. I can't understand this unexpected show of generosity to me now.

YANG: Ruan Da-cheng has a problem that troubles him and he would like to put it before you.

HOU: Please explain.

YANG: Ruan Da-cheng used to be associated with Zhao Nan-xing and was one of our own.[9] When he later became associated with the faction of Wei Zhong-xian, the eunuch, it was only to protect the East Grove faction.[1] He had no idea that once the Wei Zhong-xian faction was defeated, the East Grove faction would treat him like an arch enemy. Members of the Restoration Society have recently advocated attacking him, and they viciously beat up and humiliated him. This is a fight within the same household. Even though Ruan Da-cheng has many former associates, no one will try to explain his side of the story because his actions were so

---

[7]The reference again is to Pan Yue.

[8]This refers specifically to the Wei poet and eccentric Ruan Ji, to whom Ruan Da-cheng is, somewhat outrageously, compared.

[9]Zhao Nan-xing had been a senior Ming official who was unjustly denounced and sent into exile by the Wei Zhong-xian faction.

[1]The East Grove Society was a group of late Ming intellectuals dedicated to reforming the Ming government. After they were purged, a successor group, the Restoration Society, was formed.

dubious. Every day he weeps toward Heaven, saying, "It is painful to be so savaged by one's own group. No one but Hou Fang-yu of He-nan can save me." This is the reason that he now seeks so earnestly to make your acquaintance.

HOU: Well, in this case I can see why he feels such anguish, and it seems to me that he deserves some pity. Even if he had really been a member of Wei Zhong-xian's faction, he's come around again and is sorry for his mistakes. One shouldn't ostracize him so absolutely, and even less if there's an explanation for what he did. Ding-sheng and Ci-wei are both close friends of mine. I'll go see them tomorrow and try to resolve this.

YANG: It would be a great blessing for us if you would do this.

XIANG-JUN [*angrily*]: What are you saying! Ruan Da-cheng rushed to join the corrupt men in power and lost all sense of shame. There is not a grown woman or young girl who would not spit on him and curse him. If you try to save him when others attack him, what camp will you be putting yourself in?

[*Sings*]

> You aren't thinking
> when you speak like this so frivolously.
> You want to rescue him from ruin,
> you want to rescue him from ruin,
> but beware lest the judgment fall on you.

The only reason you're going to speak for him is because he provided my trousseau; that is disregarding the common good and selling oneself for private benefit. Don't you realize that I find all these bangles and hairpins and skirts and gowns beneath contempt. [*She pulls out hairpins and takes off gown*]

> I take off these skirts,
> accepting poverty;
> in homespun and simple adornments
> a person's name smells sweet.[2]

YANG: You're being far too hot-tempered, Xiang-jun.

LI: What a pity to throw away such fine things on the floor! [*She picks them up*]

HOU: Splendid! Her judgment in this matter is better than mine. I truly stand in awe of her. [*To* YANG] Please don't think ill of me in this. It's not that I wouldn't accept your suggestion, but I fear the scorn of women.

[*Sings*]

> In the pleasure quarters' lanes
> they can lecture on principle and good name;
> while school and court,
> while school and court

---

[2]In this line, Xiang-jun is playing on her name, "Queen of Sweet Fragrance."

confuse virtue and vice,
and cannot tell black from white.

My friends in the Restoration Society have always held me in esteem because of my sense of right. But if I associate myself with someone who is corrupt, they will all rise and attack me; and I won't have a chance to save myself, not to mention someone else.

Principles and good name
are no common things;
one must consider carefully
what is serious and what is negligible.

YANG: Considering Ruan Da-cheng's goodwill, you shouldn't act so drastically.

HOU: I may be foolish, but I'm not going to throw myself in a well to save someone else.

YANG: In that case, I will take my leave.

HOU: All these things in the chests belong to Ruan Da-cheng. Since Xiang-jun has no use for them, there's no point in keeping them, so would you have them taken away?

YANG: As the couplet goes:
One full of feeling finds himself
upset by lack of feeling,
I came here following my whim;
the whim done, I return.[3] [*Exit*]

XIANG-JUN *shows herself upset.*

HOU [*looking at* XIANG-JUN]: When I look at your natural beauty, pulling out a few pearls and feathers and taking off your fine silken gown, your perfect beauty is doubled in its perfection, and I think you are even more lovable.

LI: Whatever you say, it's still too bad to give up so many fine things.

[*Sings*]

Gold and pearls come to you,
you carelessly throw them away;
these spoiled and childish poses betray
all my hard efforts to sponsor you.

HOU: These things aren't worth brooding over. I'll make the loss good in kind.

LI: Then it will be all right.

[*Recites*]

The money spent on powder and paint
costs some consideration,

---

[3]This couplet, quoted as proverbial, is constructed of a line from a lyric by Su Shi and a metrical rephrasing of a passage in *New Stories and Tales of the Times.*

XIANG-JUN:
> homespun skirts and hairpins of twig
> > do not bother me.

HOU:
> What matters is our Xiang Princess
> > could take off her pendants,[4]

XIANG-JUN:
> the standard of taste does not follow
> > the fashions of the times.

Ruan Da-cheng, infuriated by Hou Fang-yu's refusal of his wedding gifts, uses the opportunity of unrest in the army to accuse Hou of plotting rebellion. Yang Wen-cong hurries to warn Hou Fang-yu to escape before he is arrested. After parting from Xiang-jun, who swears to remain faithful to him, Hou puts himself under the protection of the great general Shi Ke-fa, a friend of Hou's father. Meanwhile the Ming armies are collapsing everywhere, the rebel Li Zi-cheng takes Beijing, and the Ming emperor commits suicide. The Manchu armies of the Qing come down from the Northeast and take North China (an event treated in the play only with the utmost discretion). A new Ming regime is established in the South, with its capital in Nan-jing. The new emperor is a figurehead, the drama-loving former Prince Fu, with the villains Ma Shi-ying and Ruan Da-cheng as the powers behind the throne.

With Hou Fang-yu out of the picture, Yang Wen-cong suggests to Ma Shi-ying a new match for Xiang-jun. When she refuses, officers are sent to compel her to remarry. Yang goes along to try to prevent trouble. Xiang-jun persists in her refusal and tries to commit suicide by banging her head on the floor—staining the fan, her wedding gift from Hou Fang-yu, with spots of her blood. Seeing that Xiang-jun will harm herself if they persist, Li Zhen-li offers to go in Xiang-jun's place. Li Zhen-li is taken off, and as the next scene opens, Xiang-jun is left alone in the house, lamenting her fate.

SENDING THE FAN (XXIII), JANUARY 1645

Enter XIANG-JUN, *looking ill, her head wrapped with a kerchief as bandage.*

XIANG-JUN [*sings*]:
> These icy silks pierced through
> > by wind's harsh chill,
> the heart too dull
> > to light the scented brazier.
> The single thread of blood, here
> > at the tip of brow,
> is a more becoming red than red of rouge.
> My lonely shadow stands in fear,

---

[4]When goddesses such as the Xiang Princess (*Xiang-jun,* punning on Xiang-jun's name) take off their pendants, it is usually the sign of plighting troth with a man; here it seems to refer to Xiang-jun's stripping away her ornaments in rejecting the trousseau.

a weak soul tossed about, my life
suspended as by a spring floss strand.
A frosty moonlight fills the upper rooms,
    the nighttime stretches on and on,
and daylight will not melt this pain.

[*Sits*] In a moment when I had no other choice, I inflicted wounds on my
own flesh as the only way to save myself. By doing so I managed to keep
my honor intact. But now I lie here, sick and alone in these empty rooms,
under cold blankets within chilly bed curtains, with no companion. It's
so cold and lonely here.

    Freezing clouds and patchy snow
        block Long Bridge,
    the red mansions are closed up tight,
        and men seeking pleasure, few.
    Low beyond the balcony the lines of geese
        write signs in the skies,
    and from the curtained windows
        icicles hang;
    the charcoal chills, the incense burns away,
    and I grow gaunt
        in the sharp evening wind.

Though I live here in the blue mansions of the pleasure quarters, all scenes
of love and passion are finished for me from now on.

    Past patterned doors winds wail,
    the parrot calls for tea, its skill
        displayed for its pleasure alone;
    the chambers are still,
    the snow white cat hugs the pillow
        sound asleep.
    My skirt, pomegranate red,
        ripped to shreds,
           waist dancing in wind,
    and phoenix-decorated boots,
        slit to pieces
        the wave-pacing soles;
    with sorrow's increase sickness grows,
    never again will these chambers allow
        the turmoil of passion.

I think back on when Hou Fang-yu had to flee for his life in such haste,
and now I don't know where he's gone. How can he know that I am living here alone in this empty house, protecting my honor for his sake?

            [*Rises and sings*]

    I recall how in an instant
        all thrill of charming song was swept away,

at midnight passion's flood forsaken;
I look for him at Peach Leaf Ford,
I seek him out by Swallow Jetty—
just hills with roiling clouds
    where winds blow high,
        and wild geese faint and far.
Who would have thought
    that though the plums will bloom again
        reliably,
the man would be still farther away?
I lean on the balcony
    and concentrate my gaze,
but autumn floods from lovely eyes
are frozen hard by sour wind.

It enrages me how the servants of that evil man crowded into my gate and insisted that I get married. How could I ever betray Hou Fang-yu?

    They took advantage of a courtesan
        whose fate is fragile, not her own;
    their awful arrogance depended on
        the Minister's authority.
    To keep this alabaster body pure
    I could not help rending
        these features like flower.

The saddest thing of all is how my mother sacrificed herself for my sake and was whisked away. [*Points*] See her bed there as it always was, but when will she come back?

    Just like a petal of peach,
        borne on snow-capped billows,
    or floss of willow, tossed in wind;
    her sleeves hid a face like the breeze of spring,
    as she left the court of Han at dusk.[5]
    Such loneliness—the dust
        that covers her quilt
            not brushed away;
    a silence where a flower bloomed,
        which I admire alone.

A rush of sourness catches me unawares when I consider this.

    It seems to goad me in the heart,
    so many teardrops spilled.
    No girlfriends call me away
        to idle pastimes,

---

[5]Li Zhen-li's forced marriage (in Xiang-jun's place) is here compared to Wang Zhao-jun being sent from the Han court to marry the Xiong-nu Khan.

I listen to the clack of hooks
    hanging from the curtain.

Sitting here with nothing to do, I'll take out the fan with Hou Fang-yu's poem and look at it. [*She takes out fan*] Oh no! It's ruined, stained all over with drops of my blood. What am I going to do?
    Look at them—some far apart,
        some thick together,
    dark spots and pale,
    with fresh blood haphazardly stained.
    Not sprinkled from the nightjar's tears,
    these are the peach blooms of my cheeks
        turned to a red rain,
    falling speck after speck, splattering
        the icy silk.

Oh Hou Fang-yu! This was all for you.
    You caused me to dishevel
        hair's cloudy coils
    and mar my slender waist;
    Senseless I lay like the Consort
        on Ma-wei's slope interred;[6]
    my blood streamed like the concubine
        who leapt from tower's heights.[7]
    I feared the shouts of those below
    and left my too frail soul uncalled.
    In silver mirror, afterglow
        of scarlet cloud,
    and on the lovers' pillow,
        red tears in spring flood.
    In the heart a rancor sprouts,
    and melancholy sits upon the brows,
    I washed away the rouge,
    that stained the seafolk gauze.

I feel a weariness coming over me. I'll doze here a moment at my dressing table. [*Falls asleep on the fan*]

        Enter YANG WEN-CONG *in everyday clothes.*

YANG [*recites*]:
    I recognize this red mansion
        that slants on the water's face,
    a row of dying willows
        bearing the last of the crows.

---

[6]The reference here is to Yang the Prized Consort, whose death was demanded by the imperial guard when Xuan-zong fled Chang-an.

[7]Green Pearl, the concubine of Shi Chong, threw herself from a tower rather than be taken from him by a powerful enemy.

Enter Su Kun-sheng.

Su [*recites*]:
>   The silver harp and castanets,
>   a lovely maiden's yard,
>   now with wind-blown snow the same
>   as the home of a recluse.

Yang [*turning his head and greeting him*]: Ah! Good to see you, Mr. Su.

Su: After Li Zhen-li got married, Xiang-jun has been living alone. I can't stop worrying about her, so I always come by to visit.

Yang: The day that Li Zhen-li had to go, I stayed with Xiang-jun the entire night, but I've been so busy at the office these past few days that I haven't been able to get away. Just now I was going to the eastern part of the city to pay a visit, and I thought I'd look in on her.

They enter her apartments.

Su: Xiang-jun won't come downstairs, so why don't we go upstairs to talk to her.

Yang: Fine. [*They climb stairs.* Yang *points*] Look how depressed and sickly Xiang-jun seems, all worn out dozing there at her dressing table. Let's not wake her up for a while.

Su: Her fan is spread out here by her face. Why does it have so many splotches of red?

Yang: This was Hou Fang-yu's wedding gift to her. She has always kept it hidden and wasn't willing to show it. I imagine she's left it out here to dry because it got stained with blood from her face. [*Pulls away fan and looks at it*] These spots of blood are a gorgeous red! I'll add some branches and leaves and decorate it for her. [*Thinks*] But I don't have any green paint.

Su: I'll pick some of these plants in the flowerpots and squeeze fresh sap from them—that can serve in place of paint.

Yang: An excellent idea. [Su Kun-sheng *squeezes plants and* Yang *paints and recites*]
>   The leaves share the green of aromatic plants,
>   the blooms draw their red from a lady fair.

The painting is finished. Su Kun-sheng *looks at it with delight.*

Su: Superb! It's some broken sprays of peach blossoms.

Yang [*laughing*]: It's a true peach blossom fan.

Xiang-jun [*waking startled*]: Mr. Yang, Mr. Su, I'm glad to see you both. Please forgive me. [*She invites them to sit down*]

Yang: During these past few days when I haven't come to look in on you, the wound on your forehead has gotten better. [*Laughs*] I have a painted fan here that I would like to present to you. [*Hands fan to* Xiang-jun]

Xiang-jun [*looking at it*]: This is my old fan that was ruined by bloodstains! I can't even look at it. [*Puts it in her sleeve*]

SU: But there's some marvelous painting on it—how can you not take a look and admire it?

XIANG-JUN: When was this painting done?

YANG: It's my fault. I've just ruined it.

XIANG-JUN [*looks at the fan and sighs*]: Ah! The unhappy fate of peach blossoms, tossed and fallen on this fan. Thank you, Mr. Yang, for painting my own portrait in this.

[*Sings*]

Every blossom breaks the heart,
lazily smiling in springtime breeze;
every petal melts the soul,
sadly swirled in the current.
Fetching colors freshly picked,
drawn from nature;
even old masters like Xu Xi
could hardly have painted these.[8]
Vermilion's tint is mixed on cherry lips,
first sketch made on lotus cheeks,
then in a few strokes, red peach blooms,
    depicting the truth within.
You added some azure twigs and leaves,
remarkably fresh and fair,
and of an unfortunate woman
    drew the portrait in blooms of peach.

YANG: Now that you have this peach blossom fan, you need a companion like Zhou Yu to notice you and appreciate you.[9] Do you really mean to live here as a widow in the spring of your life like Chang E in the moon?

XIANG-JUN: Don't go on like this. Guan Pan-pan was also a courtesan, and didn't she stay locked up in Swallow Tower until old age?[1]

SU: If Hou Fang-yu were to come back tomorrow, wouldn't you come down from your tower then?

XIANG-JUN: In that case I'd have a glorious married life ahead and would enjoy everything. I wouldn't just come down from my tower, I'd want to go roaming everywhere.

YANG: We don't often see such a long-suffering sense of honor these days. [*To* SU KUN-SHENG] Mr. Su, I would feel a lot less worried if you would go find Hou Fang-yu and bring him back here, out of the affection of a teacher for his student.

---

[8]Xu Xi was a famous painter of flowers and vegetation of the tenth century.

[9]Literally, "a young master Zhou to pay attention to the tune," referring to Zhou Yu, the admiral of the Wu fleet in the Three Kingdoms, who was said to have had a particularly fine ear for music. Yang Wen-cong is, of course, continuing his campaign to have her remarry.

[1]Pan-pan, the concubine of the powerful Tang military governor Zhang Jian-feng, refused to remarry after his death. Although such behavior was considered proper for first wives, it was an unusual sign of devotion on the part of a concubine.

SU: Yes, I've had it in mind to go visit him for some time now, and I've found out that he served on the Huai for half a year with Shi Ke-fa, then from the Huai he came to Nanjing, and from Nanjing he went to Yang-zhou. Now he's gone off again with the army of General Gao Jie to defend the Yellow River. I was going to go back to my home-town soon, and on the way I can go look for him when I have the chance. [*To* XIANG-JUN] It would be a good idea if I had a letter from you.

XIANG-JUN [*to* YANG WEN-CONG]: My words come out without literary pol-ish. Would you write for me Mr. Yang?

YANG: Just tell me how to write what is in your heart.

XIANG-JUN: Just let me think a moment . . . [*Thinks*] No, no! All my griefs and sufferings are on the fan, so take the fan with you.

SU [*delighted*]: Well, this is a whole new style in personal letters.

XIANG-JUN: Wait while I wrap it up. [*Wraps up fan, then sings*]:
He plied the brush's silvery hairs
and will know these lines he wrote before.
Specks stain the red marks of the dice—
newly painted, hold it fast.
For though the fan be small,
it has heart's blood, ten thousand streaks;
wrapped up in my handkerchief,
with hairribbon wound about,
saying much more than palindrome brocade.[2]

SU [*taking the fan*]: I'll take good care of it and deliver it for you.

XIANG-JUN: When are you going to leave?

SU: I'll get my things ready in the next few days.

XIANG-JUN: I just hope that you'll set out soon.

SU: All right.

YANG: Let's go downstairs now. [*To* XIANG-JUN] Take good care of your-self. When we tell Hou Fang-yu of the hardships you have endured to stay true to him, he will naturally come to get you.

SU: I won't be back before I leave. As they say, [*recites*]
A new letter sent afar:
the peach blossom fan,

YANG [*capping couplet*]:
a yard forever shut up tight:
the Tower of the Swallows.[3] [*Exeunt*]

XIANG-JUN [*wiping away tears*]: Mama hasn't returned and now my teacher is going away too. It's going to be even more lonely closed up here in my room.

---

[2]This refers to the famous palindrome woven into brocade by Su Hui and sent to her husband, both to express her love and to call him home.
[3]The Tower of the Swallows is where Guan Pan-pan, the beloved concubine of Zhang Jian-feng, shut herself up after his death.

[*Sings*]

The warbler's throat has done with
    melodies of North and South,
the icy strings have given up
    tunes of Sui and Chen,
my lips will no more play the pipes,
the flute is thrown aside,
the mouth organ is broken,
and castanets are cast away.
I wish only the fan's swift delivery,
that my teacher be ready to set off soon;
Let my young Liu come on the third of May,[4]
then hand in hand we'll come down from the tower,
and eat our fill of peach blossom gruel.[5]

[*Recites*]

The letter will reach the garden of Liang
    ere the snow has melted,
when the path along Blue Creek
    will be blocked by springtime floods.
Peach Root and Peach Leaf
    are visited by none,[6]
by Ding-zi Curtain
    there is a broken bridge.[7]

Hou Fang-yu finally receives the fan and makes his way back to Nanjing, only to discover that, through the machinations of Ruan Da-cheng, Xiang-jun has been taken away into the imperial harem to perform for the drama-loving emperor. Along with a group of his friends, Hou Fang-yu is arrested for his ties to the Restoration Society and thrown into prison. Meanwhile, the Southern Ming is crumbling before the Qing armies advancing on Nanjing. As the city is about to fall, Xiang-jun and Hou Fang-yu escape separately, and they make their way to refuge in the mountains.

    Around the central love story are numerous subplots that tell the grand story of the destruction of the Ming Dynasty. The threads of all these interwoven stories come together in scene XL, "Accepting the Way," presided over by Zhang Wei, originally an officer in the imperial guard in Beijing who had buried the Chong-zhen emperor after his suicide. Zhang Wei had made his way to the Southern Ming court in Nanjing. There he was given a high post but eventually grew disillusioned by the corruption and theatrical falseness of the regime. His decision to withdraw from public life was inspired by another painting of peach blossoms—this one of the idyllic

---

[4]The reference is to Liu Zhen.
[5]This was evidently a custom of Luo-yang for the Cold Food Festival.
[6]For Peach Leaf, see note on p. 952; Peach Root was her sister.
[7]Ding-zi Curtain was a spot in the Nanjing pleasure quarters.

retreat of Peach Blossom Spring. The painting was done by Lan Ying, who had taken up residence in Xiang-jun's quarters after she was carried off to the imperial palace; and it was Lan Ying, working on this painting, whom Hou Fang-yu had discovered on coming back to Nanjing and going in search of Xiang-jun. Indeed, Hou Fang-yu himself writes the inscription on the painting that helps convince Zhang Wei to withdraw. When Zhang Wei leaves public life, he becomes the abbot of a Daoist monastery in the mountains, the very monastery in which gather the various figures in the play after fleeing Nanjing.

In the first part of "Accepting the Way," Zhang Wei laments the Chong-zhen emperor (the Ming emperor who had taken his own life when Beijing fell); then Zhang has visions of the loyalists who died defending the dynasty. We pick up the scene as Xiang-jun and Hou Fang-yu come from separate directions to listen to Zhang Wei's sermon. Xiang-jun is accompanied by Bian Yu-jing, a former courtesan who has become a Daoist nun, while Hou Fang-yu is accompanied by a Daoist priest, Ding Ji-zhi, a former balladeer.

FROM "ACCEPTING THE WAY" (XL), SEPTEMBER 1645

Enter BIAN YU-JING, *leading* XIANG-JUN.

BIAN YU-JING: The greatest joy in Heaven and among mortal men comes from doing good. We and a group of Daoist nuns have just strung up votive banners before the altar to Empress Zhou, and now we come to the lecture hall to listen to the abbot's sermon.

XIANG-JUN: May I just come along?

BIAN YU-JING [*pointing*]: See all the Daoists and laypersons in the two side porches; there are too many to count, so there shouldn't be any problem with you watching. [BIAN *bows before the altar*] Your disciple Bian Yu-jing prostrates herself. [*Together with* XIANG-JUN, *she stands back to one side*]

Enter DING JI-ZHI.

DING JI-ZHI: Hard to be born in human form, hard to learn of the Way. [*He bows before the altar*] Your disciple Ding Ji-zhi prostrates himself. [*Calls out*] Hou Fang-yu! This is the lecture hall. To come here will bring you joy.

Enter HOU FANG-YU *hurriedly.*

HOU: Here I am. Long weary of the sufferings of the secular world, I now see the path that can lead to immortality. [*Stands back to one side with* DING JI-ZHI]

ZHANG WEI [*hitting his lectern*]: You good folk listening in the wings, you should abandon your worldly hearts utterly, for only then can you seek the path that will lead you upward. If you still have even a grain of base passion, you will have to endure a thousand more revolutions of the karmic cycle.

HOU [*looks at* XIANG-JUN *from behind the fan and is startled*]: That's Xiang-jun standing over there. How did she come to be here? [*He pushes forward urgently*]

XIANG-JUN [*sees him and is startled*]: Hou Fang-yu, I almost died of longing for you.

[*Sings*]

I think back on how you abruptly left me,
faint and far
    across the silvery River of Stars
        no bridge could span,
a barrier higher than
    the very edge of sky.
No way to convey a letter,
I struggled in vain to reach you in dream,
and yet the passion did not end;
and when I escaped, the road to you
    seemed even further away.

HOU [*pointing to the fan*]: When I looked at these peach blossoms on the fan, I wondered how I would ever repay your love.

[*Sings*]

See how fresh blood covered the fan
    and bloomed into red blossoms of peach,
    as they say flowers fell from Dharma Heaven.[8]

XIANG-JUN *and* HOU FANG-YU *examine the fan together.* DING JI-ZHI *pulls away* HOU FANG-YU, *while* BIAN YU-JING *pulls away* XIANG-JUN.

BIAN YU-JING: The abbot is at the altar. You can't go discussing how you feel about one another now!

HOU FANG-YU *and* XIANG-JUN *cannot be restrained.* ZHANG WEI *slams his hand on the lectern in fury.*

ZHANG WEI: What sort of young people are you, making love talk in a place like this? [*He comes quickly down from the altar, snatches the fan out of* HOU FANG-YU'S *and* XIANG-JUN'S *hands, tears it up, and throws it on the ground*] These pure and unsullied precincts of the Way have no room for lecherous young men and loose girls to get together and flirt with one another.

---

[8]When Abbot Guang-cheng reached the best part in his lectures on the sutras, flowers were supposed to have fallen from Heaven.

CAI YI-SO [*recognizing them*]: Aiya! This is Hou Fang-yu of He-nan. Your Reverence knew him once.

ZHANG WEI: Who's the girl?

LAN YING: I know her. She's Xiang-jun. I used to live in her apartments. She is Hou Fang-yu's concubine.

ZHANG WEI: And where have the two of them come from?

DING JI-ZHI: Hou is staying at my Lodge of Finding the Genuine.

BIAN YU-JING: Li Xiang-jun is staying at my Retreat of the Genuine Accumulated.

HOU [*bowing to* ZHANG WEI]: This is Master Zhang Wei, who was so merciful to me in the past.

ZHANG WEI: So you're Hou Fang-yu. I'm glad you were able to escape from prison. Did you know that it was on account of you that I renounced the world?

HOU: How could I have known?

CAI YI-SO: I am Cai Yi-so. I also renounced the world on account of you. I'll tell you at leisure how all this came to pass.

LAN YING: I am Lan Ying. I brought Xiang-jun here looking for you, but I didn't think we would finally meet you.

HOU: Xiang-jun and I will need lifetimes to repay your kindness in taking us in, Ding Ji-zhi and Bian Yu-jing, and to repay the feeling you two showed in guiding us, Cai Yi-so and Lan Ying.

XIANG-JUN: And don't forget Su Kun-sheng, who accompanied me here.

HOU: And Liu Jing-ting, who came with me.

XIANG-JUN: The way in which Su and Liu stayed with us through everything, without flinching in desperate situations, is even more moving.

HOU: When my wife and I get home, we hope to repay you all for everything.

ZHANG WEI: In all this babbling and jabbering, what do you think you are talking about? Great upheavals have turned Heaven and Earth upside down, and you're still clinging to the love and passion that has taken root within you. Isn't this ludicrous!

HOU: You are wrong in this! A man and a woman founding a household has always been the primary human relationship, a focus for love through separation and reunion, through grief and joy. How can you be concerned about this?

ZHANG WEI [*furiously*]: Aaah! Two besotted worms. Just where is your nation, where is your family, where is your prince, where is your father? Is it only this little bit of romantic love you can't cut away?

[*Sings*]

Pathetic trifling of man and maid—
the world turned upside down
    and you don't care;
you babble on
    with wanton phrases, lurid words,

tugging clothes and holding hands, declare
a happily-ever-after to the gods.
Don't you realize that long ago
    your fated wedlock was erased
        from registries in Heaven?
With thudding wingbeats mated ducks
    wake from dream
        and fly apart,
the precious mirror of reunion
    lies in fragments on the ground,
        happy endings proved unsound.
Blush at this bad performance of your scene,
    inspiring bystanders' laughter—
the great path lies before you clear,
    flee on it immediately!

HOU [*bowing*]: What you have just said makes a cold sweat run down me, as if suddenly waking up from a dream.

ZHANG WEI: Did you understand?

HOU: I understood.

ZHANG WEI: Since you understood, go accept Ding Ji-zhi as your teacher right here and now.

    HOU FANG-YU *goes and bows to* DING JI-ZHI.

XIANG-JUN: I also understood.

ZHANG WEI: Since you understood, right here and now go accept Bian Yu-jing as your teacher.

    XIANG-JUN *goes and bows to* BIAN YU-JING.

ZHANG WEI [*instructing* DING *and* BIAN]: Dress them for the parts of Daoists.

    HOU FANG-YU *and* XIANG-JUN *change clothes.*

DING and BIAN: Would Your Reverence please take the seat at the altar so that we can present our disciples to you.

ZHANG WEI *climbs back to the altar and seats himself.* DING JI-ZHI *leads* HOU FANG-YU *and* BIAN YU-JING *leads* XIANG-JUN *before him; they bow.*

ZHANG WEI [*sings*]:
    Weed out the sprouts of passion,
    weed out the sprouts of passion
    and behold
        jade leaves and boughs of gold
            wither up and die;
    cut out the embryo of love,
    cut out the embryo of love
    and hear
        phoenix chick and dragon spawn cry out.

Bubble swirling in the water,
bubble swirling in the water,
a spark struck from flint,
a spark struck from flint;
half this life adrift remains
and now you will learn the Teaching.

[*Pointing*] The male has his proper domain, which lies to the south and corresponds to the trigram Li; go then at once south of the southern mountains, where you will learn the Genuine and study the Way.

HOU: Yes. Now I understand the rightness of the great Way, and feel regret recognizing the strength of my passion. [*Exit* DING JI-ZHI *to the left, leading* HOU FANG-YU]

ZHANG WEI [*pointing*]: The female has her proper domain, which lies to the north and matches the trigram Kan; go then at once north of the northern mountains, where you will learn the Genuine and study the Way.

XIANG-JUN: Yes. In the turn of a head everything all proved to be illusion. Who was that man facing me? [*Exit* BIAN YU-JING *to the right, leading* XIANG-JUN]

ZHANG WEI [*descending from the altar with a loud laugh; sings*]:
Note that when those two parted
no lovelorn glances passed.
Thanks to my having ripped
    shred by shred
        the peach blossom fan,
no more may besotted worms
    spin their soft cocoons of thread
        enwrapping themselves a thousand times.

[*Recites*]

White bones and blue ashes lie
    forever in the weeds,
the peach blossom fan bids goodbye
    to a southern dynasty.
Never again will come those dreams
    of glory and the fall,
but when will love of man and maid
    melt away once and for all?

Hong Sheng (1605–1704), 清
The Palace of Lasting Life:
Selected Acts

The long tradition of versions of the love story between the Tang emperor Xuan-zong and Yang the Prized Consort culminated in *The Palace of Lasting Life (Chang-sheng dian),* a dramatic romance in fifty scenes by Hong Sheng. The first draft of the play was done in 1679, with a more or less complete version appearing around 1684, and the final version in 1688. It was immediately successful and remains, together with *Peach Blossom Fan,* the high point of Qing drama.

There are few dramatic surprises in *The Palace of Lasting Life.* The scenes mostly elaborate well-known incidents in a familiar story. Perhaps Hong Sheng's most significant addition was the elaborate world of gods, goddesses, and minor deities, who weave their way through the story and at last bring the Emperor and Lady Yang together in the moon to the strains of "Skirts of Rainbow." The play's considerable appeal lies in its poetry and the sense of spectacle created through that poetry.

If dramatic romance has a claim to be great literature, it is not by plot or characterization, but by shifting perspectives that lend depth and complexity to the significance of events and things. We can see this in famous scenes such as "Stocking-Viewing," in which the sentimental musician Li Mo, a Daoist abbess, and Guo Cong-jin, a peasant, view the relic of Lady Yang's stocking used by the innkeeper "Granny" Wang to attract business to her establishment. Each reads the object's significance in a different way. On a larger, deeper level, each scene in the play is set in a web of relationships to parallel scenes that constantly redefine perspective. In one scene, we see couriers trampling down a peasant's grain field in their hurry to bring fresh lychee fruit in time for Lady Yang's birthday. In the next, we see the Emperor offering the fruit to Lady Yang as a birthday surprise. As she eats the fresh fruit with delight, blind as the Emperor is blind to the suffering that lies behind the moment's pleasure, we can view the fruit both as a thoughtful gift of love and as the occasion of larger human suffering. Both scenes return to mind when the Emperor, desperate and hungry in his flight from the rebel armies of An Lu-shan, is offered a dish of plain barley by a peasant.

Motifs appear and disappear in continual variations, giving the play a complex unity of a very different sort from the unity of plot expected in Western drama. A central motif of the play is the music "Rainbow Skirts," which first appears in the eleventh scene as performed for Lady Yang during a dream visit to the moon. Taken back to Earth and transcribed by Lady Yang from memory, the music passes through a wide variety of situations and characters. In the end, when Lady Yang and the Emperor are to be reunited in Heaven, that mortal version of "Skirts of Rainbow" is preferred by Chang E, the goddess of the moon, to the original version.

Dramatis Personae

Xuan-zong, Li Long-ji, Emperor of the Tang, whose reign is the Tian-bao, avatar of the immortal Kong-sheng

Lady Yang, Yang Yu-huan, the Prized Consort, Tai-zhen, beloved of Xuan-zong and avatar of the immortal Jade Consort

Gao Li-shi, Chief Eunuch

An Lu-shan, frontier general who rebels against the dynasty

Zhang Qian, administrator for Yang Guo-zhong, Chief Minister, uncle of Lady Yang

Yang Guo-zhong, Chief Minister, uncle of Lady Yang

Lady Han, Lady Yang's sister

Lady Guo, Lady Yang's sister

Lady Qin, Lady Yang's sister

Guo Zi-yi, Tang general responsible for recapturing the capital

Peasant Woman

Homely Girl

Flowerseller

Young Squire

Tavern Waiter

Chang E, goddess of the moon

Han-huang, attendant of Chang E

Yong-xin, maid of Lady Yang

Nian-nu, maid of Lady Yang

Li Gui-nian, head of the imperial music ensemble

Ma Xian-qi, chime player in imperial ensemble

Lei Hai-qing, mandolin player in imperial ensemble

He Huai-zhi, mandolin player in imperial ensemble

Huang Fan-chuo, player of the clappers in imperial ensemble

Li Mo, scholar and amateur flute player

First and Second Couriers

Farmer

Blind Fortuneteller and His Wife

Station Attendant

Weaver Woman, "Heaven's Daughter," goddess and star, permitted to meet her beloved Oxherd once a year, on the Seventh Eve of the seventh month

Two Immortal Handmaidens

Oxherd, god and star, consort of the Weaver

Chen Yuan-li, officer in charge of the imperial guard

Guo Cong-jin, an old peasant

Granny Wang, tavern keeper

First, Second, and Third Travelers, from Shan-xi

Dancehall Girl

Nun, abbess of the Lodge of Maidenly Purity

Two Guardian Deities

Local God

Yang Tong-you, a wizard

974

PROLOGUE AND ARGUMENT (I)

Enter PROLOGUE.

PROLOGUE:

On passion's stage, in olden times as now,
whose hearts stayed true until the end?
If only lovers keep their faith
    and never fail,
at last they will be joined again.
No separation troubles them,
        though miles in thousands lie between
        from north to south;
and life or death for two such hearts
    is no concern.
I scorn those men
    and women of this world
    who complain
        of harshness in their fate—
this is lack of love.

Love stirs even stone,
and can turn
    the Earth and Heaven.
It stands revealed in light of sun,
it lasts in histories.
Think of the loyal subject,
    think of the filial child—
all come to this because of love.
As Confucius did not cut away
    the love songs of Zheng and Wei,
we set this law to melody.
And we have taken Tai-zhen's Story,
    new lyrics, new score,
which is love, and nothing more.

Bright Sovereign of the Tian-bao Reign,
his Consort Yang Yu-huan,
to meet were fated long before.
He let her bathe in Hua-qing Pool,
she then first felt his favor's flood.
She prayed for skill on the Seventh Eve
    in the Palace of Lasting Life,
where they swore the sweet vow
    to be forever man and wife.
Her wondrous dance was just completed,
but ere the clear song was done,
from Fan-yang war drums boomed.

Then came the post station at Ma-wei;
the royal army would not go on:
for the rouged beauty, a last farewell.
His journey west was filled with pain:
he could not bear the space between
    the world below and this of mortal men.
The fortunate repentance of her errant soul
restored her to the gods' immortal roll.
And when the royal coach returned,
    he meant to have her reinterred,
but only her perfume bag remained.
Heaven's daughter pledged their reunion,
through a winged adept her love was conveyed
by inlaid box and golden hairpin sent.
Their story lasts on—
    of meeting in the palace of the moon
    and of the dance called "Rainbow Skirts"—
now shown upon the lyric stage.

The Tang's Bright Sovereign finds pleasure
    in the feast where "Rainbow Skirts" is played;
the soul of Prized Consort Yang is severed
    when the Yu-yang army rebels.
A wizard who went to the god's great city
    for a lunar meeting serves as guide;
The Weaver Star fulfills the vow
    made in the Palace of Lasting Life.

DECLARATION OF LOVE (II)

Enter the Tang EMPEROR XUAN-ZONG, *followed by* TWO EUNUCHS.

EMPEROR [*sings*]:
    This mitered crown scrapes the sky, while I
    sit on my southward-facing throne,
    ruling by royal presence alone,
    with hills and rivers joined as one
    by sovereign Tang.
    From cloudy heights the rain
    restores the spring, and deep in palace grounds
    the plants and trees breathe scent in unison.
    An early morning levee in an age of peace
    while spring is in such finery!—
    why should this hold me back from pleasure?
    May I spend my life's remaining days
        in passion's soft delights,
    and I will not yearn for lands of gods
        in white clouds.

[*Recites*][1]

A blooming splendor enters harem gates,
and palace trees give off a springtime glow.

Heaven takes joy in seasonal accord,
men are in harmony, nothing goes amiss.

The Nine Songs extol polity's priorities,
with Six Dances disperse the robes of court.

Now other amusements, Yang Terrace's delight,
where last week the rain flew at twilight.

I, who am now the Great Tang's Tian-bao Emperor, once rose up from my princely estate, where I had waited biding my time, and took my own place in the imperial succession. I have consistently chosen good men to employ in my government, placing the likes of Yao Chong and Song Jing in charge in the Hall of Audience. I have followed good advice as water flows downhill, setting the likes of Zhang Jiu-ling and Han Xiu in my ministries. I further am pleased that the atmosphere remains undisturbed for thousands of miles along our frontiers, while among the common folk rice is so cheap it costs three coppers a measure. It is truly the government of an age of peace, almost equal to the Zhen-guan Reign of my ancestor Tai-zong. It has become customary to dispense with corporal punishments, which makes my reign in no way inferior to the times of Emperor Wen of the Han.

Recently, in leisure from my responsibilities, my feelings have found an outlet in music and the attraction of women. Just yesterday I saw a palace lady, one Yang Yu-huan, of a virtuous nature, soft and gentle, of full-fleshed charms and striking beauty. Then I divined this lucky day to enroll her in the harem as my Prized Consort. I have sent orders that she be granted a bath in Hua-qing Pool and have commanded the palace ladies Yong-xin and Nian-nu to wait on her and help her change. And soon Gao Li-shi will bring her into my presence—that must be them coming now.

Enter GAO LI-SHI *and the* TWO PALACE LADIES *holding fans,
leading the Consort* YANG YU-HUAN.

LADY YANG [*sings*]:
    I rejoice how favor's flood descends
        from Heaven upon me.
    My bathing done and fully groomed,
    I make haste to the bright regalia.

---

[1]The last three couplets of this poem are rearranged from an actual poem in five couplets by Xuan-zong. Xuan-zong's original poem is set in summer and involves a banquet of officials. By rewriting an opening couplet, Hong Sheng makes it spring and locates the scene in the harem.

PALACE LADIES:

> "In all Six Harems none have seen her,
>> and now at once they worry,"
> they stand in lines on Golden Stairs
>> to steal a distant glimpse.

They arrive, and GAO LI-SHI *advances and kneels before the* EMPEROR.

GAO: Your humble servant Gao Li-shi salutes Your Majesty and begs to inform you that Lady Yang, now formally registered as the Prized Consort, has arrived at the palace gates and awaits your instructions.

EMPEROR: Have her come forward.

GAO: His Imperial Majesty instructs the Prized Consort Yang to approach the throne.

LADY YANG [*coming forward and bowing*]: Your Majesty's Prized Consort Yang Yu-huan salutes Your Majesty and wishes you everlasting life.

EUNUCH ATTENDANT: Rise now.

LADY YANG: Though of humble origin and plain appearance, I have been selected for the harem. I was surprised to hear that I had been granted such favor, and I'm so nervous I'm afraid I'm going fall to pieces.

EMPEROR: You are descended from an eminent family and blessed with both beauty and virtue. My heart is well content to receive you for service in the bedchamber.

LADY YANG: Long live Your Majesty!

GAO: Rise now. [LADY YANG *rises*]

EMPEROR: Have them set out the banquet.

GAO LI-SHI passes on the imperial instructions. Music is played within.
LADY YANG gives wine to the EMPEROR, *and a* PALACE LADY *gives*
wine to LADY YANG. *The* EMPEROR *is seated in the center, with*
LADY YANG *seated beside him.*

EMPEROR [*sings*]:

> Throughout this great realm everywhere
> I sought a "maiden pure and fair"
> to lead all ladies of the court.
> This very morning Heaven granted me
> such loveliness—she truly has no peer
> in all the Earth.
> I do surmise
> no other woman will share
> my favor in Alabaster Palace,
> and tablets of jade will bear
> the titles of her praise;
> three thousand beauties in powder and paint
>> must willingly yield to her.

ALL:

> And may this love stay full and fair
>> as Heaven lasts and Earth endures.

LADY YANG [*sings*]:
> Although I bask in commendation,
> I brood a while in fear
> that one so plain and lowly never dare
> to join him in Peppered Chamber.
> Receiving here such love and favor
> parts me at once from mortal men.
> I shall emulate:
> Handmaiden Feng, who faced a bear,
>   protecting Han's Emperor Yuan,
> and Lady Ban's prudence refusing to share
>   a coach with Emperor Cheng;
> forever with scarlet stylus in hand,
>   a woman chronicler,
>   at my ruler's side I will attend.

ALL:
> And may this love stay full and fair
>   as Heaven lasts and Earth endures.

PALACE LADIES [*sing*]:
> In enjoying pleasure
> I wonder who from this moment on
> will be first in all the harem?
> As with Flying Swallow, the Lady Zhao,
>   in the Palace of Shining Light,
> whenever love and favor come,
> they always fall on one alone.
> So modestly decline no more
> to dress yourself in a golden room,
> or in jade mansions sing songs through,
> or pass on flagons of cloudy brew
>   for thousands of years forever more.

ALL:
> And may this love stay full and fair
>   as Heaven lasts and Earth endures.

EUNUCHS [*sing*]:
> We look up and behold
> "sunlight circling dragon scales,"
> "pheasant tails shifting in clouds";
> delight shows on His Majesty's face
>   before his new beauty freshly groomed.
> So keep the wine coming apace,
> whose scent blends with breeze of spring
>   through the palaces swirling.
> Enjoy these things:
>   the round moon's swaying gold,
>   "tatters of cloud scattering lace,"

> and dusk that draws on quickly where
>> clouds of many hues crowd
>>> the imperial palace.

ALL:
> And may this love stay full and fair
>> as Heaven lasts and Earth endures.

GAO: The moon has risen. It is time for Your Majesty to have the banquet cleared.

EMPEROR: Lady Yang and I will stroll before the stairs and enjoy the moon-light for a while.

Music within. The EMPEROR *leads* LADY YANG *forward by the hand while the others step back. They stand there together.*

EMPEROR [*sings*]:
> Down I come from the golden hall
> more closely to study her features
>> by the lamplight of the moon,
> no courtyard flower can compare
>> to her sweet countenance
>> as against me she gently presses.
> The shadows of her tresses,
>> the rays upon her gown,
> contrasts of dark and light display
>> her thousand full-fleshed charms.

> [*Laughs softly and faces* LADY YANG]

> The pleasures of this evening,
> its cool breeze and shining moon,
> bring laughter at the dream-rain
>> once darkening Gao-tang.

LADY YANG [*sings*]:
> Companion of your revels,
> from now on I am blessed to wait
>> attending on my Lord.
> Standing a while on marble stairs,
> Heaven speaks and comes the spring
> whose scent enwinds the royal guard,
> and jade dew coldly soaks our garb.
> Now I look around and peer
>> at golden palaces in tiers
>>> where ducks joined in mated pairs
>>> have settled for the night.

EMPEROR: Take the lanterns off to the Western Palace.

EUNUCHS and PALACE LADIES, *each holding a lantern, go off, leading the* EM-PEROR *and* LADY YANG.

ALL [*singing*]:
>Flashing flames,
>a thousand rows,
>>the crowding light of silver candles goes;
>And when we turn to look
>>through beaded curtains drawn aslant,
>a silver river of stars out there
>>faintly glows.
>Through tiered walkways and winding halls
>everywhere
>>the scented powder of petals
>>wafts upon the air.
>How seems the night? The moon
>stands high above the palms
>>of the statue Immortals of Bronze.
>This is the night that reigns supreme
>>in beauty of spring weather,
>red covers the azure screen,
>and inside brocade clouds will be
>>a matched phoenix pair.
>"Bloom of Jasper," "Trees of Jade,"
>>"Night Moon and Spring River"—
>each note sung in unison,
>as moonbeams pass the palace walls.
>We lift the hanging arras of lace
>and help the lovers, tipsy still,
>>into the orchid chamber.

GAO: We have reached the West Palace, Your Majesty.

EMPEROR: Let my attendants withdraw.

GAO: A spring breeze blows through lavender halls,

EUNUCHS: And Heaven's music from pearled mansions falls. [*Exeunt attendants*]

EMPEROR [*sings*]:
>Flame-plumes on the candle sway,
>into the window moonlight shines,
>let me now speak each particular
>>of love on this wonderful night.

TOGETHER:
>Think not how this night drags on
>>in the harem's other wings and halls.

PALACE LADIES *help the* EMPEROR *and* LADY YANG *change clothes, then exit.*
The EMPEROR *and* LADY YANG *seat themselves.*

EMPEROR:
>The silver candles' turning beams
>>scatter across your gauze and lace;

LADY YANG:
>   where the royal scent is strongest
>   is the depth of love I bear.

EMPEROR:
>   This night throughout the harem
>   brooding brows will stare,

BOTH:
>   tomorrow's rivals in singing
>   our "Song of a Jewel Found."

EMPEROR: Our vow to stay together through old age will begin from this very night. [*Takes a hairpin and box out of his sleeve*] I brought this golden hairpin and inlaid box as special tokens of our love.

[*Sings*]

>   This golden hairpin and inlaid box
>   with clustered jewels and medallions
>   of kingfisher plumes
>   have I guarded next to my heart
>   and have taken care to keep them
>   no matter what.

>   Tonight I give you this hair-pick:
>   to adorn your cloudlike coils of hair
>   with a phoenix pair
>   stuck in aslant.

>   And forever may this box:
>   stay hidden in your brocade sleeve,
>   tightly wrapped in scented silk.
>   May we be like those phoenixes,
>   in flight together, wing to wing;
>   may we be linked like the box pattern,
>   an interlocked love-knot of rings.

He gives these to LADY YANG *and she receives them with thanks.*

LADY YANG [*sings*]:
>   For the golden hairpin take my thanks,
>   and for the inlaid box,
>   and for the grace of your desire.
>   But I worry my plainness cannot repay
>   the drops of rain and dew that fall
>   from him who is Heaven's Son. [*Looks around*]
>   But as I observe
>   phoenixes soaring and dragons that coil,
>   I do so love those heads
>   paired in infatuation,
>   and these twinned panels interlocked.

May our love be as firm as this metal:
    may the hairpin be never divided,
        may the box be always whole.

EMPEROR:

The pale light of the spring moon
    shines on sprays of flowers, [Yuan Zhen]

LADY YANG:

this was the moment when first she received
    the flood of royal favor. [Bo Ju-yi]

EMPEROR:

Ever leaning against this woman like jade,
    the heart is intoxicated, [Yong Tao]

BOTH:

year after year and on forever
    may we find joy here. [Zhao Yan-zhao]

BRIBE (III)

Enter AN LU-SHAN *dressed like an archer, wearing a felt hat.*

AN [*sings*]:

Hopes dashed, I helplessly mourn
    the promise my youth;
heartsick as well to fall,
    trapped in the toils of law.
Yet ambitions beyond the common run
    are hard to overawe,
and how can anyone quell
    such surging savage energy
        rising a thousand yards?
Yet I had best endure the while.

[*Recites*]

My belly hangs down across my lap,
    my strength can lift a thousand pounds;
shrewd enough and filled with schemes,
    daring beyond all bounds.
Who would have thought such dragon-spawn
    would willingly shrink from harm?—
when rivers and seas seethe in my turmoil,
    then men will shake in alarm.

Know me as An Lu-shan, from Liu-cheng in Ying-zhou. After my mother Ah-shi-de prayed for a son on Ya-luo Mountain, she went home and gave birth to me. Because of this she gave me the name Lu-shan, which signifies "Mountain of Fortune." At that moment rays of light filled her tent; and the birds and beasts, chirping and yelping, all cowered and fled. I later went with my mother when she was remarried to An Yan-yan, and

983

I took his surname, An. Know me then as An Lu-shan, native of Liu-cheng in Ying-zhou. I enlisted in the army of the regional commander, Zhang Shou-gui, who thought I showed signs of remarkable things and treated me as his foster son. He put me in charge of a strike force and sent me off to assail the Xi Tribes and the Khitan. But on one occasion I grew overconfident and advanced carelessly, and my troops were slaughtered and routed. Thanks to Commander Zhang's leniency and his affection for me, I was not executed; but I have been sent under guard to the capital to ask for imperial instructions in the case.

I reached the capital just yesterday, and it is not yet decided whether things will go well or ill for me. But I am delighted that I have a sworn brother here called Zhang Qian, who is an administrator in the office of Chief Minister Yang Guo-zhong. Yesterday I paid off the officers escorting me, to set me free for a while. I asked Zhang Qian to take a bribe to the Chief Minister, and he accepted my gifts. He told me to wait for his answer, so I had better hurry ahead to see what will happen. [*Walks on*] Come on, I'm not such a bad fellow—who would have thought I would end up like this? It makes me really mad to think about it!

[*Sings*]

A wild dragon-serpent was I,
just waiting to cleave the sea
    and spill great rivers over their shore;
but now I've turned to a turtle,
    out of the water, stuck in a jar—
and this is what enrages me,
    a trap that was sprung so suddenly
        on a man of such daring and mettle.
Had I known that reverses in battle
    would mean the headsman's ax,
I would rather have died in the desert
    and escaped being bound in chains—
        both feet falling from under me.
Now I depend entirely
    on gold changing hands in the dark,
to get me out of this pit.
And yet I reckon that Heaven
    had purpose in making me
and would not, halfway along my course,
    let me be broken for naught.

Now I've reached the Minister's gate. I'll wait for Zhang Qian to come out.

Enter ZHANG QIAN.

ZHANG [*recites*]:
    The brother-in-law of our ruler
        is ranked with the Three High Lords,

and I, of the Minister's household,
>   hold an office of seventh degree. [*Greets* AN]

Welcome, brother An! The Minister has accepted all your gifts and will
have you meet with him in the Ministry office.

AN [*bowing*]: Thank you for taking care of things for me.

ZHANG: Since the Minister hasn't come out yet, let's go wait a while in my
office. Everything lies in the hands of him who in the Secretariat shapes
destiny . . .

AN: . . . to rescue a man who suffered reversals out in the frontier passes.
[*Exeunt*]

>   *Enter* YANG GUO-ZHONG *with attendants.*

YANG GUO-ZHONG [*sings*]:
>   Her rise to glory is vaunted
>   within the palace grounds,
>   and royal favor extends
>   to homes of his marriage kin;
>   brothers, sisters, and cousins all
>   receive His fond regard.
>   In the Secretariat I alone
>   hold power in the court:
>   the hands of men will be burned
>   by the blazing wind
>   of my authority.

>   [*Recites*]

>   Rule of the kingdom comes to me,
>   it lies within my grasp,
>   eight Council seats, three Ministries
>   hold me in highest awe.
>   I leave the court in late afternoon
>   returning to my mansion,
>   then countless officials and underlings
>   bow in servility.

As uncle of the Prized Consort of the Western Palace, I, Yang Guo-zhong,
occupy the post of Minister of the Right and hold the rank of Minister
of Works. I share that imperial splendor which shines like the sun and
moon, and in my hands are commands that have the force of a thun-
derstorm. [*Chuckles*] If I do engage in every excess and take whatever I
happen to desire, it is merely enjoying myself while I have the chance.
By taking bribes and amassing power I have the might to turn Heaven.
[*To attendants*] Leave me now. [*Exeunt attendants*]

Zhang Qian has just given me a report on a frontier general, one An
Lu-shan, who has been brought to the capital for punishment because
he lost a battle. He sent gifts to my office to get me to spare his life. It

seems to me that victories and defeats are quite normal for military men; and if he happened to suffer a setback, the situation is forgivable. [*Laughs*] So I'll spare his life—it's only because our court treasures its human talents. But I've ordered that he be brought to meet me to see for myself.

Enter ZHANG *from behind.*

ZHANG: Zhang Qian reporting. An Lu-shan is waiting outside to meet you.
YANG GUO-ZHONG: Have him come in.
ZHANG: Yes, sir. [*Exit*]

Enter ZHANG QIAN, *leading* AN LU-SHAN *in a blue robe and small felt hat.*

ZHANG: Come this way.
AN [*coming forward on his knees*]: An Lu-shan, in disgrace, greets Your Excellency with all humility.
YANG GUO-ZHONG: You may rise.
AN: It is fitting that a condemned prisoner report to you on his knees.
YANG GUO-ZHONG: Zhang Qian has already explained your purpose in coming. Now tell me the particular circumstances of your offense.
AN: Well, Your Excellency, here's what happened. I was carrying out orders to attack the Xi and the Khitan . . .
YANG GUO-ZHONG: Stand while you explain.
AN [*rises and sings*]:
>   Confident in our courage,
>   we charged into the fray,
>   no foe could stand in our way.
>   But their warriors caught us unaware,
>   surrounded us that night.
>   And then we faced the naked blade,
>   our quivers bare.
YANG GUO-ZHONG: How did you get away?
AN [*replying*]: I cut a bloody path through the encirclement and fled.

> [*Sings*]

>   A single horse, a single spear,
>   I was lucky to escape,
>   and now my only hope—
>   that of past deeds consideration
>   and my small record might redeem
>   this grave transgression.
>   Yet never did I think today
>   I'd face my execution! [*Kowtows*]
>   Show mercy, Your Excellency!
>   take pity on me!
YANG GUO-ZHONG [*rising, sings*]:
>   Breach of rules, loss of troops
>   touch statutes of the gravest kind;

and though I hold the reins of power,
  I dare not act as I please.
The punishment prescribed is clear
  and hard to change. I fear
I have not the might to turn Heaven.

AN [*kneeling and weeping*]: If only Your Excellency would help me, I will live.

YANG GUO-ZHONG [*smiling*]:
  I may have some slight
    power to persuade,
  but herein lie devices
    I cannot now explain.

AN [*kowtowing*]: Everything depends on Your Excellency taking personal charge of the case!

YANG GUO-ZHONG: All right. Wait until I go to court tomorrow, and I'll do what seems best under the circumstances.

[*Sings*]

  When the chance comes,
  I'll open the net
  and spare your life.

AN [*kowtowing*]: I am indebted to Your Excellency's great kindness. Permit me to repay you by being your horse, your spaniel. I'll take my leave now.

YANG GUO-ZHONG: Zhang Qian, show him out.

ZHANG [*exiting with* AN LU-SHAN]:
  Eyes now gaze for the victory pennant,
  ears listen for welcome news. [*Exeunt*]

YANG GUO-ZHONG [*thinking*]: It seems to me that this An Lu-shan is really nothing but a minor frontier officer who has never been noted for any particular accomplishments. If I make an exception in his case by circumventing a death sentence and saving him, it will inevitably arouse His Majesty's suspicions. [*Laughs*] I've got it! In his letter to the throne the other day, Commander Zhang spoke of An Lu-shan's knowledge of the languages of the nomad tribes and his fine grasp of various military skills, which made him suitable for employment as a frontier general. I'll drop a hint in the Ministry of War to take this line, and then present a request to His Majesty to have him summoned before the throne and examined. In this process I'll take the opportunity to get an imperial decision in his favor. That's the best way.

  The mettle to make all power one's own
    is daring to the core, [Lu Zhao-lin]
  one puts on a thousand faces
    all in the blink of an eye. [Wu Rong]
  To build a pile of yellow gold
    may buy one's execution, [Li Xian-yong]

who knows but that selfish purposes
        might even serve the common weal. [Du Xun-he]

In the intervening scene, the Emperor observes Lady Yang as she takes a daytime nap. After she wakes, they go together to a pavilion. Yang Guo-zhong enters and arranges an audience with the Emperor for An Lu-shan. Then the Emperor suggests to Lady Yang that they go to the Bending River Park to view the peonies.

OUTING ON A SPRING HOLIDAY (V)

Enter the chief eunuch Gao Li-shi.

Gao [*sings*]:
        In the harem's exalted ranks
                I hold the highest place,
        I serve His Majesty personally
                from dawn till the sun goes down.
        Newly decked in formal gown
                of gold, sable, and jade,
        in all my goings I enjoy
                his special grace.

    I, Gao Li-shi, the eunuch Commander of the Palace Horse Guard, am charged with managing everything within the harem; and my power looms over that of all other court officers. I take every opportunity to suck out the very marrow of His Majesty's wishes and to probe his mind. By prudence and an ingratiating manner I have come to enjoy imperial favor. Today is the holiday of the Third Day of the Third Month, and His Majesty, in the company of the Prized Consort, is going to pay a visit to the Bending River Park. He has commanded me to summon the Minister Yang Guo-zhong, as well as the Ladies of Qin, Han, and Guo, to join the imperial retinue. I have to give them His Majesty's instructions.

[*Recites*]

    To the Ward of the Marriage kin make known the word
        that today He will grace Chang-yang Palace. [*Exit*]

Enter An Lu-shan *in an official's cap and sash, followed by attendants.*

An [*sings*]:
        Since I sought protection
                from a mighty clan,
        the rain and dew of royal grace
                have been renewed.
        The one-time officer in chains delights to be
                in service near the throne—

here someday
    may daring purposes unfold.

Since I was restored to my post by His Majesty's generosity, I have been held in the highest favor. What most amuses him is my huge belly that hangs down over my waist. One day I had an audience with the Emperor, and he jokingly asked me what I had in there. And I answered, "Only a sincere and loyal heart." His Majesty's face showed his great pleasure in my answer, and from that time on he has placed increasing confidence in me, promising that someday soon he will make me a prince. It has been quite an extraordinary turn of events. All of you, leave me now. [*Exeunt entourage*]

Today is the Third Day of the Third Month. The Emperor and Lady Yang are going to visit the Bending River Park, with the Three Ladies accompanying them. Every girl and gentleman of the city has gone to see them. I'm going to change into more comfortable clothes and ride off there myself to have some fun.

    Changes clothes, mounts horse, and sets off.

No sooner am I through the gate than, look, how the scented dust fills the road, with horses and carriages like clouds. What a commotion! It is as they say:
    Drifting floss upon the road
        entwines the drunken traveler,
    singing birds behind the flowers
        call to passers-by. [*Exit*]

Enter Two Princes, *a* Young Nobleman, *and a* Student,
    all splendidly attired.

ALL [*sing*]:
    People are roused by spring's beauty,
    and we adore
        flower-filled breezes as if fanned,
        squadrons formed by willow mist.
    Where'er we pass
        we see no trace
            of the red dust
    of the capital's lavender lanes. [*They greet one another*]
Good-day to you.
PRINCES: Today is the Purification Ceremony and we're going to the Bending River to enjoy ourselves.
YOUNG NOBLEMAN and STUDENT: I wonder if that group of carriages over there is the Three Ladies coming. We had better hurry. [*They walk on, singing*]
    A tumultuous cavalcade
    of broidered curtains, coaches fine,

wound with kingfisher feathers and pearls.
Rival attractions, each
      trying to catch preeminence.
Billowing tendrils of musky scent
and orchid borne on the wind,
you can tell them even far away
      by their colorful gowns and pendants' glint. [*Exeunt*]

Enter the LADY OF HAN *in an embroidered gown, the* LADY OF GUO *in a*
      white gown, and the LADY OF QIN *in a scarlet gown, each riding*
            in a coach followed by servants and maids-in-waiting.

ALL [*sing*]:
      Here is our array:
      clouds of figured gauze
      a contest of enchantment,
      each making brave display
            of wispy tresses and jet black brows.
      Graced with royal favor, we
      have come together to survey
            springtime at the river
                  by particular decree.
HAN: I, the Lady Han . . .
GUO: . . . and I, the Lady Guo . . .
QIN: . . . and I, the Lady Qin
TOGETHER: . . . have received a summons to visit the Bending River. So let's
      be quickly on our way.
SERVANTS: Yes ma'am.
LADIES [*sing*]:
      Crimson wheels
      crush scented sward,
      where earrings lost and hairpins dropped
      lie mingled with the fallen flowers.
      Such is our glorious lot,
      the kin-by-marriage now will join
            the royal retinue,
      advancing bevies of palace finery. [*Exeunt*]

      Enter AN LU-SHAN *on horseback; catches sight of the*
                  THREE LADIES *leaving.*

AN [*sings*]:
      Such marvels!
      With a turning glimpse I see
      unparalleled divinity,
      that in an instant holds the soul in thrall.
      They go in coaches so remote
      it maddens me I can't approach.

I was on my way to the Bending River, when I had the good fortune to run into the Three Ladies. Each single one of them has a divine beauty. They can claim to be the fairest of the land. Emperor of Tang—you already have Lady Yang, and now on top of that you have these three sisters of hers. Now, that's the life!

This, my critical observation:
when all the fairest flowers belong to one,
we understand
    the majesty of Heaven's Son.

I'll just gallop forward and get a full view once.
Gazing into the dust before me
these hungry eyes see but a blur—
I'll have to keep urging my horse ahead.

Gallops ahead. Enter ATTENDANT, *who blocks his way.*

ATTENDANT: Hey! His Excellency the Minister is here! Who dares push his way through so brazenly?

Enter YANG GUO-ZHONG *on horseback.*

YANG GUO-ZHONG: What's causing all the fuss?

YANG GUO-ZHONG *and* AN LU-SHAN *look at one another.*
AN LU-SHAN *turns his horse and hastily exits.*

ATTENDANT: I just met this man who was brazenly pushing his way through here on horseback, so I blocked his way.
YANG GUO-ZHONG [*laughing*]: That was An Lu-shan who just rode off. But why did he get out of here so quickly when he caught sight of me? [*Thinks it over*] Where are the carriages of the Three Ladies?
ATTENDANT: Just ahead.
YANG GUO-ZHONG: I see! How dare that scum An Lu-shan behave with such rudeness!

[*Sings*]

An outrage!—
insolence to royal kin,
rudely pushing above his station
to join the scented carriages.
Sudden fury swells within,
I scarcely can contain it.

Tell the entourage to form a tight circle around those carriages and to drive off all idle onlookers. [*They do as he says*]
Hurry now, do not delay—
use golden whips to clear the way
and pursue with well-wrought saddles
    their painted wheels.

ATTENDANT:
> Ye who pass, take care!—
> come not too close, and fear
> lest you provoke the Minister's ire. [*Exeunt omnes*]

Enter PEASANT WOMAN, HOMELY GIRL, FLOWERSELLER, *and* YOUNG SQUIRE.

WOMEN [*sing*]:
> Our fresh finery
> gives us some glamour,
> yokels are we,
> peculiar our manner,
> yet we can love
>> how sweet-smelling grasses
>> stick to skirts,
> how the wildflowers
>> pile in our tresses.

> *They meet.*

PEASANT WOMAN: Are you all on your way to visit the Bending River?

OTHERS: That's right. Both the Emperor and his lady are there today, and we're all going to have a look.

HOMELY GIRL: They say that the Emperor dotes on his lady just as if she were a jewel. I wonder which of the two of us is prettier. [FLOWERSELLER *laughs;* YOUNG SQUIRE *eyes the* HOMELY GIRL] And why are you looking at me so boldly?

YOUNG SQUIRE: I was just noticing that your face has some jewels of its own.

HOMELY GIRL: What jewels?

YOUNG SQUIRE: Well, your eyes are an inlay of cats-eye; your forehead is decorated with streaks like the banded agate; the beeswax yellow of amber adorns your teeth; and of coral are your lips carved.

> *The* PEASANT WOMAN *laughs; the* HOMELY GIRL *hits the* YOUNG SQUIRE
> *with her fan.*

HOMELY GIRL: You can just babble on, but you've got no "jewels" at all.

YOUNG SQUIRE: Who says?

HOMELY GIRL: But your "backdoor" *is* like a silver mine—so many people have been working to open up a pit in it!

PEASANT WOMAN: Quit joking around. I've heard that when the carriages of the Three Ladies pass by, they drop things all along the way. Let's hurry up and see if we can find something.

HOMELY GIRL: Let's get going.

> *They walk on, the* HOMELY GIRL *flirtatiously teasing the* YOUNG SQUIRE.

TOGETHER [*sing*]:
> Slowly rises the gentle breeze
>> and sweeps the clouds through sunlit skies,

once carriages so plush pass by,
springtime comes to plants and trees.
YOUNG SQUIRE: Maybe we'll find something if we look around in the grass
here.
FLOWERSELLER: Well, I've got to go now.
By crimson gates and fancy kiosks to cry
with all my heart:
"Flowers for sale! Come buy! Come buy!"

Exit FLOWERSELLER, *crying, "Flowers for sale"; others continue looking and
each finds something.*

HOMELY GIRL [*to* PEASANT WOMAN]: What did you find?
PEASANT WOMAN: A hairpin.
HOMELY GIRL [*inspecting it*]: It's gold! And it's got a tiny scarlet gemstone
on top. What luck!
PEASANT WOMAN [*to* HOMELY GIRL]: What about you?
HOMELY GIRL: A single phoenix slipper.
PEASANT WOMAN: That's nice. Why don't you try it on?
HOMELY GIRL [*stretching out her foot to compare the size*]: Phooey! I could-
n't even get a toe in it! But I will take this pearl off the tip. [*Picks off the
pearl and throws the slipper away*]
YOUNG SQUIRE: Let me keep that.
HOMELY GIRL: You're really going to keep that thing? Let me take a look at
what you picked up.
YOUNG SQUIRE: It's a golden box wrapped in a scarf of merman lace.
HOMELY GIRL [*taking it and looking inside*]: Hey, there are thin wafers, all
black and yellow, with a slightly sweet smell—I'll bet they're aphrodisi-
acs!
YOUNG SQUIRE [*laughing*]: It's aromatic tea.
HOMELY GIRL: Let me give it a taste. [*She and* PEASANT WOMAN *chew some,
then each spits it out*]
PEASANT WOMAN: Yech, it's bitter! How can anyone eat that?
YOUNG SQUIRE [*taking it back*]: Cut it out. Let's all go on ahead. [*They walk
on*]
TOGETHER [*sing*]:
It's the time for idle butterflies and bees,
willow-welcomed, lured by flowers;
gazing where waters downward spill
from Dragon Tower—
Bending River is drawing near.

Exeunt YOUNG SQUIRE *and* PEASANT WOMAN;
the HOMELY GIRL *is left behind alone.*

HOMELY GIRL [*shouting*]: Wait a minute! I've got to pee bad. I'll just piss a
little hole in the sand over here. [*Exit*]

Enter the THREE LADIES *with* ATTENDANTS *and* MAIDS.

LADIES [*sing*]:

> Scent in clothes, scent of flowers,
> > odors mingle wantonly;
> oriole voices, voices laughing
> > heard faintly mixed together.
> See willow catkins shed their snow,
> > covering white duckweed,
> pair by pair the bluebirds go,
> bearing garlands of fallen red.
> Of spring's bright weather
> two parts in three are gone,
> in the slowing light of the lovely sun
> > our carriages hurry ahead.

ATTENDANT: My Ladies, we have come to the Bending River.

HAN: Where is His Excellency the Minister?

ATTENDANT: His Imperial Majesty is in Spring Prospect Palace, and His Excellency the Minister has gone ahead there.

LADIES HAN, QIN, *and* GUO *get down from their carriages.*

LADIES: Isn't this a lovely scene, after all!

[*Sing*]

> Around the Bending River's shores,
> around the Bending River's shores,
> red petals tipsy, evenly spreading green.
> By the Bending River's waters,
> by the Bending River's waters,
> new reeds grow and willow leaves are fine.

Enter GAO LI-SHI *with a young eunuch; he reins in his horse.*

GAO [*recites*]:

> Royal decree brings a peach-spotted horse
> > chomping its bit of jade,
> as mount on which to seat a skirt
> > with gilded butterflies. [*Greets them*]

A decree given orally by His Imperial Majesty: The Ladies Han and Qin are to be granted a feast in one of the detached villas. Lady Guo is ordered to ride this horse to the palace, where she will join Madam Yang for a feast.

LADIES [*kneeling*]: Long live His Majesty! [*They rise*]

GAO [*to* LADY GUO]: Please mount up.

GUO [*sings*]:

> Inner Household officer
> pressing me so urgently.
> Sisters, I leave you alone now
> > and approach the royal breeze of spring.

QIN and HAN [*sing*]:
> Not for nothing did you paint
> > pale moth-wing brows
> to meet His Exalted Majesty.

> *Exit* LADY GUO *on horseback, led by* GAO LI-SHI.

QIN: Look how our sister, as favored as Empress Pei, rides off with a snap of her whip.

HAN: Let her do as she will.

MAID: Will their Ladyships please come now to the villa to dine.
> Pink peaches and sapphire willows,
> > spring in the festival hall, [Shen Quan-qi]

HAN:

> spring excursions are of a piece,
> > their experience shared by all. [Zhang E]

QIN:

> Yet I would enjoy an Emperor's love
> > and pleasure beyond all bounds, [Wu Ping-yi]

TOGETHER:

> and facing breeze I laugh apart
> > at those of springtime's splendid light. [Du Mu]

In the intervening scenes, the Emperor's interest in the Lady Yang's sister, the Lady Guo, leads to a rift between him and Lady Yang, and between the sisters. In a pique, the Emperor sends Lady Yang back to her home, but then is overcome with remorse. When Lady Yang sends him a token of her love, the Emperor has her recalled.

OMEN (X)

> *Enter* GUO ZI-YI, *in turban, wearing a sword.*

GUO [*recites*]:
> No one understands my mind,
> > my purpose fair and bold,
> this sword my sole protection
> > and my whole livelihood.
> When all the world is set aright
> > and troubled times repaired,
> that is the moment all will see
> > that I am a real man.

I am Guo Zi-yi from Zheng County in Hua-zhou. I have mastered the lore of warfare, and I am equally well versed in questions of policy. My aims are to bestride the whole earth and leave a legacy of peace and stability in the kingdom. Now, with the military examinations behind me, I have come to the capital to await selection for a post. But I find myself here at a time when Yang Guo-zhong is secretly abusing his power and An Lu-shan is enjoying an excess of imperial favor. The authority of the court will soon have been abused beyond all repair. Still, without even a minor post, I don't know when I will be able to exert all my efforts on behalf of the court.

[*Sings*]

> A man's bold thoughts must find expression;
> I am not one who looks up and cries,
>   afraid that the sky will fall.
> Yet I despise
>   that swallow-kind
>   nesting complacently in the hall—
> not one among them spies
>   the ravens on the roof.
> They take no care
>   of the tiger penned or caged bear,
> in temples they let the rats run wild,
>   let foxes make lairs in the wall.
> I, like Zu Di long ago,
> when I hear the roosters crow,
>   often rise to dance at night,
>   resolved to save the state from peril.
> I think of frequent rise and fall
>   of dynasties since time began;
> I'll make my deeds of glory known
>   to last within the world
> and never let my name grow old
>   among woodsmen and fishermen.

And now that I've reached the Chang-an market, I'm going to get drunk.
[*Walks on*]

> I slowly pace the royal streets
> for brief respite from brooding cares
> and from my travels to find ease.
> Jostling crowds go to and fro,
> reeling like drunks that can't stand straight—
> Not here we find that lord of Chu,
>   singing as he walks his way,
>   the only sober man?[2]

---

[2]The reference here is to Qu Yuan, who wrote in "The Fisherman":
> The whole of this age is filthy,
> and I alone am clean.
> The crowds of men are all drunk,
> and I alone am sober.

I look for a like-hearted companion,
but I am discouraged now to find
    the fisherman Tai-gong is gone,
    tiger-shooting Li Guang is far,
    dog-butcher Fan Kuai is no more.[3] [*Exit*]

Enter TAVERN WAITER.

WAITER [*recites*]:
    This tavern that I run
        is of the highest class:
    no credit for oaths and forfeits,
        you've got to pay your bill.
    As long as you have cash enough,
        be my guest and drink,
    but if you're broke, I will not waste
        even a drop of water.

I'm a waiter in the great Xin-feng Tavern in the Chang-an market. Our tavern lies right between the east and west market districts, where crowds of people are always passing in both directions. Everyone comes to our tavern to have a few drinks—people from the city and outsiders, princes and lords, officials and market folk, military men and commoners. Some just buy a drink; some order food with their drinks; some buy wine and take it off with them; some bring their wine and drink it inside. I'm always taking orders. But here comes another customer.

Enter GUO ZI-YI.

GUO [*sings*]:
    I gaze afar on green willows
        swept aslant at the corners
            of painted mansions,
    blue tavern banners rattling,
        they dance away from the breeze—
    I wish I could find some Jing Ke,
        who drank in the market of Yan,
        to come share my wine with me.[4]

---

[3]This is a rather heterogeneous assortment of exemplary figures of antiquity to whose company Guo Zi-yi feels suited. Tai-gong or Lü Shang was an aging fisherman when discovered by King Wen and made an important minister in the rise of Zhou. Li Guang was one of the greatest of the Western Han generals against the Xiong-nu. Fan Kuai, originally a dog butcher, was an important early Western Han minister.

[4]Jing Ke was the retainer-assassin of Prince Dan of Yan and serves as the type of hero that Guo Zi-yi would like to know.

[*Calls out*] Waiter!

WAITER [*welcoming him*]: Do come in, sir, and have a seat upstairs.
GUO [*climbing stairs*]: This is really a nice tavern.

[*Sings*]

> Spacious windows and balconies,
>> the sunlight clear, refreshing breeze,
> and on stucco walls all around
>> are frescoes of the drunken gods.

WAITER: Do you want something to drink now or are you waiting for someone?
GUO: I'll have a few drinks by myself. Do you have some good wine for me?
WAITER: Indeed we do. [*Brings wine*] Here it is.
VOICE [*calling from within*]: Waiter! Come here! [WAITER *exits in a hurry*]
GUO [*drinking, sings*]:

> No magistrate Tao Qian am I,
>> idle and fond of wine,
> nor do I ape the rude Guan Fu,
>> mastered by his cups,
> headlong drinking made him
>> overbearing, rough.
> My sober eyes stay open wide—
>> does anyone take note?
> I wonder if the Land of Drink
>> is deep enough to let me in?
> I listen to the hubbub here
>> of streets and shops,
> and one of Gao-yang's drinkers
>> is lonely and quite lost. [*Gets up to look*]

Enter eunuchs and officials, all sumptuously attired, followed by servants carrying golden coins and wine, and leading sheep. They circle the stage and exeunt. Enter WAITER *with wine.*

WAITER: Here's warm wine, sir.
GUO: I have a question for you, waiter. Where were those officials outside going?
WAITER: Drink up while I tell you. His Imperial Majesty has made a gift of newly built mansions to the Minister Yang Guo-zhong, and to the three Ladies of Han, Guo, and Qin. These four compounds were built adjoining one another in the Xuan-yang Quarter, and all are modeled on the building style of the imperial palace. These days if one of those families builds something, they want it to be better than their neighbor's. And when the neighbor builds, he wants it to be still better than the first family's building. If someone sees that his neighbor has built something splendid, he will tear down his own house and build anew. And he won't rest until he's sure that he has something as good as his

neighbor. A single hall can cost upward of ten million strings of copper cash. Today the work has been completed on the Yangs' mansions, and all the great and small officials of the court are taking presents of sheep and wine. Everyone was passing by here on their way to offer congratulations.

GUO [*shocked*]: Can this be true?

WAITER: Let me go see to warming some more wine for you.

GUO [*sighing*]: This is what happens when the favor that the Emperor shows his in-laws reaches such degree!

[*Sings*]

No common clan should arrogate
    the privilege of the throne
in contests of extravagance,
    vain show of earth and wood.
Here grandees gladly scamper off
    to bend their servile waists,
rivals to reach the gates of power
    like thronging to a fair.
Will no one stand before the throne
    and tell the way the people feel?—
Their sapphire and vermilion tiles
    are all smeared with blood.

[*Rises*]

I suddenly find my heart is filled with fury—the wine has gone to my head without my realizing it. Let me steady myself by taking a look at the walls. [*Looks*] On this wall here someone has written some lines of poetry in small characters. Let me have a look. [*Reads them out*]

"Yan's market stands deserted,
from Han Pass no horse returns.
Should you meet a ghost beneath the hill,
tie her gauze robes on a ring."

This is really quite strange!

[*Sings*]

Here my eyes came to rest,
and line by line I read it out
    from the first.
Considered carefully, this poem
    hardly foretells a happy lot.

Let me see who wrote it. [*Reads on*] "Written by Li Xia-zhou." That name is quite familiar—yes, that's it—I've heard of a soothsayer named Li Xia-zhou, who knows all that has passed and all things to come. He must be the one.

[*Sings*]

Herein are things best left unsaid,
  hidden in enigmatic words,
but now we have no Master Du
  to solve the riddle of the verse.[5]
Perhaps this was some drunken scrawl,
  the hand's whim, a tangled flight
    of crows across the wall.

[*Noise offstage.* GUO *calls*] Waiter!

Enter WAITER.

WAITER: What do you want, sir?
GUO: Why is there so much noise below?
WAITER: If you just look down from the window, you can see for yourself.

GUO *looks out. Enter* AN LU-SHAN, *mounted, dressed as an imperial prince, with attendants clear the way before him. He circles the stage and exits.*

GUO: Who was that?
WAITER [*laughing*]: Didn't you see his huge belly? That was An Lu-shan. He is a particular favorite of His Majesty and once was even permitted into the imperial section of the Golden Rooster Tent. Today His Majesty enfeoffed him as the Prince of Dong-ping. He has just now left court after thanking the Emperor for his kindness, and now he is headed back to his new mansion outside Dong-hua Gate, which brings him past our establishment.
GUO [*shaken with anger*]: So this is An Lu-shan! What did he ever accomplish that he should so suddenly be made a prince? I can read the signs of treachery on this dog's face. This will surely be the person who will bring war upon the whole world.

[*Sings*]

I see what he is:
  a savage-hearted, half-breed, sheep-herding slave,
the bee's eyes and jackal's voice show
  a crafty schemer for sure.
How could they bring such a wild wolf
  into the house to dwell?—
don't they see how this fulfills
  the prophecy on the wall?
He and the Emperor's marriage kin—
  the whole lot show signs of witchery.
WAITER: What has gotten you so upset, sir?

---

[5]Du Da-bo was the proverbial figure in vernacular literature of someone who could solve poetic riddles.

GUO [*sings*]:
> I can't help
>> this spreading, prickling chill
>> that makes my hairs to stand on end
>>> against my cap,
> and this searing rage that heaves
>> swelling in my breast,
> again and again I turn my eyes
>> to the rare sword that clinks at my waist.

WAITER: Please calm down, sir. Let me bring you another jug.

GUO:
> Even if I emptied a thousand cups
> and drank down a hundred jugs,
> it would still not free me
>> from this engulfing weight of care.

I'll drink no more. Here, take the money for the wine.

WAITER [*taking money*]:
> For others it is:
>> "A few cups can calm a host of ills."
> but in your case:
>> "One outburst stirs a thousand cares." [*Exit*]

GUO ZI-YI *descends the stairs and walks along.*

GUO: I'll go back to my lodgings for a while.

[*Sings*]

> I see the tangled situation of the times,
>> it strikes me to the heart with pain.
> I came on cryptic lines
>> of prophecy within a poem;
> two things I cannot grasp—
>> Heaven's will and minds of men—
> which sets me to futile brooding,
> and knits my brows in furrows.
> I see now the sunlight sink to dusk
>> as I reach my dreary inn,
>>> lost and bewildered.

Goes into lodgings and sits. Enter BODYGUARD. *Greets him.*

BODYGUARD: An announcement has come from court, master.

GUO [*reading it*]:
> "Ministry of Military Affairs:
> Regarding: official appointment
> His Imperial Majesty instructs that Guo Zi-yi be posted to the
>> Tian-de Army."

My orders have come through. I'll have to get my things packed right away and set off for my post immediately. [BODYGUARD *sets to work*] Though the post is low and the duties minor, from now on I can at least do my best for the court.

[Sings]

> Like the fish in a foot of water
> > I still can stretch my fins,
> like the bird caught among hawthorns
> > I still can spread my wings.
> I rejoice that it is my lot
> > to spurn the clouds and rise
> > > to Heaven's avenues,
> at last I will set the universe aright,
> and I intend
> > a legacy of glorious deeds
> > > to last a million years.
> And though foul witchery's abroad,
> I can do no less than on these shoulders bear
> > the sun and moon,
> and with my own hand
> > prop up the Great Tang.

> My horse's hooves have trod the dust
> > several years for naught, [Hu Su]
> but always a man of daring
> > will seize the crucial spot. [Si-kong Tu]
> A low official, on his own,
> > blocked from the starry heights, [Wang Jian]
> yet I wonder who else there is
> > to worry for our land. [Lü Wen]

THE MUSIC (XI)

Enter CHANG E with attendant HAN HUANG.

CHANG E [*sings*]:
> The finest nights lie under the sway
> > of my clear beams alone,
> unsullied by the dust's least mote
> > since time began.
> Windborne dews are strewn
> > through crystal air
> and splash the moon's silver rays, in a stream
> of faintly tossing notes
> > of music of the gods.

[*Recites*]

> I pound the herbs of lasting life
> > far from the changing eons' dust,
> a clear and alluring countenance,
> > by nature pure, by nature true.
> Look carefully among the clouds
> > where Heaven's scented blossoms fall—
> there I rest in this single orb
> > by the gray-green Cassia Tree.

I, Chang E, have always been mistress of the Supreme Yin. The legend that I was once the wife of Hou Yi is a baseless rumor. This many-jeweled orb has lasted for thirty-six thousand years, a radiantly glowing wheel of one thousand and two hundred miles. Here the Hare of Jade and the Silver Toad produce a perfect jewel of everlasting brightness. And here too the White Elm and the Cinnabar Cassia have been planted to bring forth wondrous blooms forever. We have a piece of the music of the gods, "Coats of Feathers, Rainbow Skirts," long kept secret in the moon-palace and never passed down to the world of mortal men. But now in that realm below there is a Tang Son of Heaven who loves music and can truly understand it. His consort, Yang Yu-huan, was, in her former life, the Jade Consort of Peng-lai, the Isle of the Gods, and she used to come visit the moon. I am planning to summon her soul here in dream and let her listen to this melody once again; then when she wakes, I'll make sure she remembers it and puts it down in notation for string and wind instruments. In the end the music of the gods in Heaven will linger as a lovely tale among mortal men. Wonderful! Come here, Han-huang!

HAN-HUANG: Here I am.

CHANG E: I want you to go to the harem of the Tang palace and bring the soul of Yang Yu-huan here in dream to listen to a melody. When the melody is done, take her back to where she was before.

HAN-HUANG: Yes, madam.

CHANG E [*recites*]:

> As she peacefully rests on her pillow
> > let her dream that she visits the gods
> and secretly be taught the notes
> > of millennial melody.

HAN-HUANG: By your orders, Lady, I will now leave the moon-palace and go off to the palace of Tang. [*Goes off, singing*]

> Glowing, the River of Light arcs down,
> stars flash faintly, thickly strewn.
> I peer to the world of dust below
> and see but scented fog and haze.
> I have left our Jade Precincts,
> > orderly and clear; I let

my pendants toss their windborne rays
and robes on colored wisps throw light,
as I tread with tiny pace
    stepping stones of reddish cloud.
I will take the music of Heaven
    to give to the harem's queen
and secretly summon her sweet soul
    into the sparkling Moon.

    Here I am in the women's quarters of the Tang palace.
See the fish-form locks shut fast
and the dragon-arras drawn—
there Yang the Consort lies asleep,
    like a cherry-apple bloom,
    heightening her charm.
Softly now I'll wake her
clinging to her icy bed. [*Calling*]

    Get up, my Lady.

        Enter LADY YANG *as a dreaming soul.*

LADY YANG [*sings*]:
    I was just enjoying the cool of night,
        fatigued from bouts of "clouds and rain";
    I was drifting into tipsy sleep,
        still wearing my powder and paint.
HAN-HUANG: Come, my Lady.
LADY YANG: Who is that calling to me from under the eaves so deep in the harem?

            [*Sings*]

    This surely is no palace maid with news
    who comes so lightly to these painted eaves.
HAN-HUANG: Quickly, madam!
LADY YANG [*stretching wearily, sings*]:
    Charmingly hesitant, groggy I stretch
    and ever so slowly open the drapes.

    [*Coming out, she meets* HAN-HUANG] Oh, it's a palace lady!
HAN-HUANG [*sings*]:
    I am not from Chang-men Palace,
        in service there because I was spurned.
LADY YANG: If you are not a palace lady, then perhaps you are some beauty from separate apartments.
HAN-HUANG [*sings*]:
    No, I am not ranked among
        those Concubines called "Fair-of-Face,"
    who once did catch the eye of the throne.

LADY YANG: Then who are you?

HAN-HUANG: I am the handmaiden in the moon, and my name is Han-huang,

[*Sings*]

> so my name is on the registers
>> of the Alabaster Palace
>>> and the moon's great galleries.

LADY YANG: You're an immortal from the moon! Why have you come here?

HAN-HUANG [*sings*]:

> I've just now come on instructions
>> of the goddess Chang E herself
> to ask you to come and dispel the heat
>> under Cassia Palace's flowers.

LADY YANG: Amazing!

HAN-HUANG: No need to hang back, my Lady. Come with me now and I'll take you there.

TOGETHER [*sing*]:

> We head off into sapphire space,
> and gradually beneath our feet
>> the clouds appear;
> we pace
>> upon blue wisps, the winds
> play gently in the listening ear.
> Now eyes first fix
> on dangling stars
>> that seem within the fingers' grasp,
> and soon we see the shimmering glow,
>> the images of a palace
>>> sunk within a mirror.

LADY YANG: Strange! It's midsummer. Why is it so chilly here?

HAN-HUANG: These are the lunar precincts of the Supreme Yin, known in the world of mortal men as the Palace of Spreading Cold. Please come in.

LADY YANG [*delighted*]: Just imagine—here I am, a person of gross corporeal substance and ordinary looks, who this evening gets to visit the lunar precincts. I'm really lucky.

[*Moves ahead, looking around, sings*]

> To visit such a splendid site
> brings me such satisfied delight!

[*Thinking it over*] And yet it seems I have seen all these sights sometime before.

[*Sings*]

Circling these pavements of jade,
winding under the sapphire eaves,
vistas vaguely familiar
    leave me wondering.

    Isn't that cassia over there blooming too early?

HAN-HUANG: This is the Cinnabar Cassia of the moon, ever in flower all the
year long, scented in leaf and bloom.

LADY YANG [*examining it*]: Such lovely flowers!

[*Sings*]

Insatiate observer,
pleasures multiply.
Golden blooms unfurl,
joined with azure leaves.
Swelling fragrance in the air
    penetrates the gown
of someone hidden here away
    in the Cassia's shade.

[*Music is played offstage*] Look at the troupe of immortal maidens in pale
jackets and red skirts coming out from under the cassia playing music.
So beautiful to the ear!

HAN-HUANG: This is the melody "Coats of Feathers, Rainbow Skirts."

Enter between four and eight IMMORTAL MAIDENS, *wearing white jackets, red
skirts, cloud-brocade capes, necklaces, and trailing sashes, each playing music
and singing as they circle the stage.* LADY YANG *and* HAN-HUANG *stand off to
the side, watching.*

IMMORTAL MAIDENS [*sing*]:
    Bringing Heaven's music,
        clustered flowers compete
            each to be the choice,
    swishing skirts of rainbow
        soaking in the dew.
    Far cut off from time's slow passage
        in the world's red dust,
    here expressed is pure enchantment
        of alabaster terraces.
    But though the agile tongue may trill the pipes
    and slender marble fingers pluck the strings
        with harmonies increasing,
    we waken not the nightmare dream
        in the world of mortal men,
    nor do we halt
        the motion of the water-clock
            in palaces of Heaven.

On her pillow she visits gods,
and hearing the coda the melodies end,
gift to one who can understand ·
    music, to transcribe again. [*Exeunt*]

LADY YANG: This music is so wonderful! Its purity and tenderness touch my
very soul. This is really something not to be found in the mortal world.

[*Sings*]

I seem to have seen beauteous forms,
    a company of fairy maids,
        in a blur, in a haze;
I heard their clear notes to the end,
    they linger still in mind.
I count each ringing of the chime,
I count each ringing of the chime,
and plunder every syllable
    with light tap of my phoenix shoe,
and following the shifts in key,
    I catch the melody,
        marking it by fingertip.
My cheeks, embarrassed, glow—
how foolishly I thought well
    of charm I had in song
        and dancing skill,
now humbled by comparison
    to dignified performance here
        of Heaven's tune.

Would it be possible to meet the Moon Queen?

HAN-HUANG: It is still too soon for you to meet the Moon Queen. And now
the sky is gradually growing bright. It is time for you to go back to your
palace.

[*Sings*]

But you should keep in mind
    that you found your way to the moon.

LADY YANG:
Without a flaw will I recall
    new notes of melody.

HAN-HUANG:
It's just too bad that half the night
    you had to leave the king to sleep alone. [*Exit* LADY YANG]

Yang the Prized Consort has gone back to the Tang palace. I had better
go find my Lady the Moon Queen and report to her on my mission.
Sapphire tiles, beech balustrades,
    halls of the moon drew open, [Cao Tang]

and take then the bright moonlight
    to send you on your way. [Ding Xian-zhi]
Though permitted that Heaven's music
    be heard by mortal man, [Li Shang-yin]
now mortal man is hurried along
    by drops of the water-clock. [Huang Tao]

In the following scene, Lady Yang appears writing out the score of the music she heard in the moon. While Lady Yang goes to change her clothes, the Emperor comes in and catches sight of the score. Lady Yang returns, and in the ensuing discussion the Emperor tells her that Guo Zi-yi ("Omen") has been given a frontier command. The Emperor then suggests that her composition be rehearsed by the musicians of the imperial music academy for performance.

In the next scene, Yang Guo-zhong and An Lu-shan have a violent quarrel, after which each denounces the other to the Emperor. To prevent further conflict between his two favorites, the Emperor appoints An Lu-shan to take over the northeastern military command at Fan-yang.

MELODY-THEFT (XIV)

Enter YONG-XIN *and* NIAN-NU *with the score in hand.*

YONG-XIN [*sings*]:
    The score of "Rainbow Skirts" is done,
NIAN-NU [*joining in*]:
    deep behind the latticed windows
    she copied out the secret text; and then,
    with perfumed throat and mouth like jade,
    she had us learn this perfect tune.
YONG-XIN: After my Lady produced a new score of "Rainbow Skirts," she taught it to the two of us.[6] Soon His Majesty will visit Hua-qing Palace; and when he does, "Rainbow Skirts" will be performed. We have been commanded to give the score to Li Gui-nian in Chao-yuan Tower and show him the particulars of how it is to be performed. He then will have the members of the Pear Garden Ensemble rehearse it every night.
NIAN-NU: We have already taught them the whole prelude, and they have that down. Today we should teach them the central movement.
YONG-XIN: Just look at the moonlight tonight, like water—perfect for performing music! It's time to take the score off to the tower.
TOGETHER [*walking on*]:
    Just now the cool moon rises
    over the high tower,

---

[6]Chinese musical notation was less precise than Western notation. A score was accompanied by instruction in its performance.

drapes are furled in sweet south wind,
    shining upon crystal.
Such clear heights suit perfectly
notes of fairy music
    from halls of Spreading Cold. [*Exeunt*]

Enter LI GUI-NIAN, *a gray-whiskered old man, head of the imperial music ensemble.*

LI GUI-NIAN [*sings*]:
    My name long known as court musician,
    now in old age with new promotion,
        Conductor of the Ensemble.
    On call from dawn to dusk
    I serve my shift in the Inner Court.

Previously but a common musician, I, Li Gui-nian, received His Majesty's appointment to head the Music Academy of the Pear Garden. Lady Yang has recently composed a new melody called "Rainbow Skirts," and Yong-xin and Nian-nu have been instructed to teach me how to execute the score. We are learning to play it in Chao-yuan Tower, for it is to be performed very soon. We have to do a rush rehearsal every night. I had better call my fellow musicians to get going. Where are you?

Enter MA XIAN-QI, *chime player.*

MA XIAN-QI [*recites*]:
    When chimes are played by Xian-qi,
        amazement strikes the very gods,

Enter LEI HAI-QING, *mandolin player.*[7]

LEI HAI-QING:
    the iron pick strives to commend
        Lei Hai-qing.

Enter HE HUAI-ZHI, *an elderly mandolin player with a white beard.*

HE HUAI-ZHI:
    The mandolin of aging He
        dominates the stage,

Enter HUANG FAN-CHUO, *clapper player.*

HUANG FAN-CHUO:
    I, Fan-chuo, born a Huang,
        am master of the clappers.

---

[7]Lei Hai-qing played an unusual mandolin with a stone bridge, crane-tendon strings, and an iron pick.

All greet LI GUI-NIAN.

TOGETHER: Here we are, sir.
LI GUI-NIAN: Welcome. Now, gentlemen,

[*Sings*]

>Our Ruler has given us commands
>to rehearse "Rainbow Skirts" with speed
>>and take no break.
>Yong-xin and Nian-nu, lovely maids,
>have brought the short, corrected score,
>>marked for the red ivory clapper,
>and how they wait in the moonlight
>>in Chao-yuan Tower.

ENSEMBLE: In that case we had best get going.
LI GUI-NIAN [*sings*]:

>Together then, gentlemen. [*They walk on*]
>With the water-clock's slow dripping
>>the cool of night comes on,
>we will work through this new music
>>until we get it right,
>we will work through this new music
>>until we get it right. [*Exeunt omnes*]

Enter LI MO, *in scholar's garb.*

LI MO [*sings*]:

>I indulge youth's uncurbed stirrings,
>>the imp of romance prods me on
>to shape my heart through the wondrous truth
>>that lives in melody.
>I've heard tell this very night
>>in the precincts of Peng-lai Palace
>a new song will be played
>from a wondrous score transcribed.

Though originally from the Southland, I've been staying here in the capital. Ever since youth I've been expert in the rules of music and am particularly well known for my mastery of the iron flute. I recently heard that in the palace a new melody was composed, called "Coats of Feathers, Rainbow Skirts." The Master Musician Li Gui-nian and others are rehearsing it every night in Chao-yuan Tower. I long to hear this new piece, but I have no way to get hold of the score, kept secret. I've made inquiries about that tower, and it turns out to be right beside the wall, outside which sounds can be heard. So I've put my iron flute in my sleeve and come here to Mount Li, taking advantage of this moonlight as bright as day, to listen to it unseen. And what wonderful scenery I've seen all along the way!

Walking on, sings:

The woodlands gather twilight haze,
    the weather is cool and clear,
into cold skies the mountains rise,
    crossed by the moon's glittering rays.
What a lovely scene!—
Just as if I
    were strolling through a painting.

*A red curtain is hung across the stage to serve as the wall,
behind which is a tower.*

I've made it to the palace wall in no time at all.
    Among the colored clouds I see
outlines of great watchtowers—
sequestered traceries of light
    set off in moon's brightness.
These shimmering beams confound my sight,
these shimmering beams confound my sight.
And I fancy the royal aura there
    courses unseen,
while everywhere
    in mansions of gods
women like jade idly lean
    upon the balustrades.

I've heard that Chao-yuan Tower lies at the west end of the imperial park,
so I'll go following the red wall to make my way there.

Walking on, sings:

Under the shadows of flowers
the royal road runs smooth,
I walk on ever so slowly
    hugging the red wall. [*Gazes*]

I see a tall mansion appearing over the top of the wall in the shadows of
the weeping willows—I bet that's it.

[*Sings*]

When I fix my gaze and look closely,
when I fix my gaze and look closely,
I see billowing blurs of painted curtains
half concealing patterned windows. [*Points*]
Isn't that a red lantern up there!

Yong-xin *and* Nian-nu *climb the tower on the other side of the wall.*
Li Gui-nian *and the musicians speak from within.*

LI GUI-NIAN: Today we should rehearse the central movement. Let's all play it through once, starting with the prelude.

LI MO: There seem to be voices coming from up there, hidden behind the light of the lantern. This is obviously the place. I'll keep out of sight here and listen.

Stands out of sight of the tower and listens, singing:

Softly, now, softly,
    hidden in blackness,
I secretly listen in the shadow of the wall.

Music is played within. LI MO *takes his flute out of his sleeve.*

I'll take out my flute and repeat each passage, carefully memorizing all the fine points of the notes and rhythm.

[*Sings*]

I have listened until the moon is high,
    after the first watch,
now at last strings sound together.
And deep in the night with everyone still
I delight how palace walls resound
with ringing sounds equally answering.
And the mind, in a flash, has learned the notes,
and the mind, in a flash, has learned the notes.

As the music of the full orchestra is heard faintly offstage, LI MO *repeats the passage on his flute. The music then stops.* YONG-XIN *and* NIAN-NU *sing the after-song within the tower.* LI MO *accompanies them on the flute.*

YONG-XIN and NIAN-NU [*sing*]:
    Black-dragon pearls are strewn,
    a sudden shock when we come to the prelude.
    Rolling clouds are shadows of sleeves,
    wind-tossed snow whirling,
        light dancing breeze.
    Wind-tossed snow whirling,
        light dancing breeze,
    in the pale outline of misty brows,
        a charm beyond measure.

LI MO [*continuing the song*]:
    And the mind, in a flash, has learned the notes,
    and the mind, in a flash, has learned the notes.

Full orchestra plays softly within as before. YONG-XIN *and* NIAN-NU *sing within,* LI MO *accompanying them on the flute.*

YONG-XIN and NIAN-NU [*sing*]:
    Pearls glow shining on azure,

the phoenix soars upward, the simurgh stays.
On Mount of Jade, on Peng-lai Peak
the Primal Goddess waves her sleeve
    to lead along Shuang-cheng.
The Primal Goddess waves her sleeve
    to lead along Shuang-cheng,
E-lü-hua turns her shoulder,
    to summon Xu Fei-qiong.[8]

LI MO [*continuing the song*]:
And the mind, in a flash, has learned the notes,
and the mind, in a flash, has learned the notes.

Full orchestra plays softly within as before. YONG-XIN *and* NIAN-NU *sing within,* LI MO *still accompanying them on the flute.*

YONG-XIN and NIAN-NU [*sing*]:
Notes come fast, headlong the tune,
strings and woodwinds in frenzy.
Soaring clouds stop suddenly,
dancing sleeves draw slowly back,
    and sport a lighter grace.
Dancing sleeves draw slowly back,
    and sport a lighter grace,
a single note of singing flies
    up to alabaster skies.

LI MO [*continuing the song*]:
And the mind, in a flash, has learned the notes,
and the mind, in a flash, has learned the notes.

The full orchestra goes through it offstage. YONG-XIN *and* NIAN-NU *exit.*

LI MO: What a wondrous melody—like bamboo tapping together in the autumn wind or the clinking of springtime ice, a clear stream of note of the god's music and truly not something from the world of mortal men! It was a real stroke of luck to steal it all in my flute.

[*Sings*]

"Rainbow Skirts," music of Heaven,
heard by a traveler over the wall.
Notes and rhythm clear,
keys rightly used,
as in the breeze sounds soft and loud
    each respond to the other.
I stole it in my flute
and when I let it out,
    nothing will be missing.

---

[8]The figures mentioned in this stanza are various goddesses and immortals.

It is quiet now, and no sound is heard from the tower. I imagine they will play no more.

[*Sings*]

Musicians scatter, the song is done,
    the red mansions grow still,
in fading moonlight on half the wall
    shadows of flowers sway.

Look how the River of Stars sinks down and the moon sets, the Dipper turns and Orion lies across the sky. Time to go back.

Puts his flute in his sleeve and walks on, singing:

Turning back
to follow the homeward path.
I hear on the Jade River's flowing stream,
    its echoes clear and remote,
like a trailing note
    of "Rainbow Skirts."

Hall and mansion rest in sky,
    clear in the light of the moon, [Du Mu]
around high clouds the song revolves
    and night is still more cool. [Zhao Gu]
I stole for myself several melodies
    recently composed, [Yuan Zhen]
when I play my flute in the tavern now
    it will be the newest tune. [Zhang Hu]

BRINGING HER FRUIT (XV)

Enter First Courier, *carrying a basket of lychees hung from a pole, whipping on his horse.*

First Courier [*sings*]:
Alone I've sat astride the saddle
    and traveled thousands of miles,
great were the hardships I endured
    to bring these lychees to her.
An agent sent by royal command
    cannot act on his own,
now I account all fortune and fame
    less than a life of ease.
If only, when I reach Chang-an,
    the Consort will be pleased.

I am a courier on the Western Circuit. Since the Consort Yang adores fresh lychees, His Majesty has decreed that Fu-zhou is to send them as tribute every year. The weather has been hot and journey long. But I cannot shrink from this task and now must make my horse fly on. [*Exit galloping, singing reprise, "If only, when I reach Chang-an . . ."*]

Enter Second Courier, *carrying a basket of lychees, whipping on his horse.*

Second Courier [*sings*]:
>Hai-nan's lychees, of all most sweet,
>will please the palate of Lady Yang.
>When picked they are wrapped within their leaves
>and in small bamboo baskets sealed.
>My steed stops not by night or day
>   to make this delivery,
>and all along the way
>   I fear delay—
>whenever a post station comes in sight,
>   I rush for it straightway.

I am a courier on the Hai-nan Circuit. Since Madam Yang adores fresh lychees, the ones produced in Hai-nan—which are far better than those from Fu-zhou—must be brought as tribute by imperial decree, together with those of Fu-zhou. But the journey from Hai-nan is even longer than from Fu-zhou. After seven days pass, the lychees' flavor and aroma will be lost. I must gallop on swiftly. [*Exit galloping, singing reprise "All along the way I fear delay . . ."*]

Enter old Farmer.

Farmer [*sings*]:
>A farmer's plowing and sowing
>   is a lot of effort and pain,
>we worry about dry weather,
>we worry about the rain.
>These few sprouts are all we have
>   the whole year through,
>and with the harvest half of that
>   is taken as revenue—
>I wonder sadly how much grain
>   will ever reach our bellies.
>Every day I hope it will ripen,
>I pray to the gods
>   and seek help from Heaven.

I come from the eastern village of Jin-cheng County. I have a family of eight, and we depend entirely on these few acres of poor fields for our livelihood. I heard this morning that couriers delivering fresh lychees are following the most direct route all along the way, and no one knows how much of the growing grain of framers they have trampled. This is why

I've come out specially to watch over my own fields. [*Gazes off*] There are a pair of fortunetellers coming this way.

Enter a blind FORTUNETELLER, *holding a clapper in his hand, and his* WIFE, *a blind woman, plucking a single-string guitar.*

FORTUNETELLER [*sings*]:
> I live in Bao-cheng
> and go now to Chang-an,
> keen observer of the turning year
>   and of its ruling stars.
> Of life as well as death
> my judgments are made clear;
> this mouth of ironclad prophecy
>   everywhere is famed.
> A gentleman, though blind,
> possessed of insight divine—
> I give a cry:
> To the gods come pray
> and learn your fate.

FORTUNETELLER'S WIFE: Old man, we've been traveling for many days now and my feet have gotten so sore that I really can't go on any further. At this point I'm not making prophecies about lives, just struggling to stay alive.

FORTUNETELLER: Well, mother, I just heard someone talking hereabouts. Let me go ask him where we are. [*Calls out*] Sir, what place is this?

FARMER: This is the eastern village of Jin-cheng County, bordering on the western part of Wei-cheng.

FORTUNETELLER [*bowing*]: Thank you.

Horsebells are heard within. FARMER *looks off in that direction.*

FARMER: Oh no! A group of riders is coming! [*Shouts*] Sirs, you there on the horses! Keep to the main road! Don't trample the grain growing in the fields!

FORTUNETELLER [*addressing his* WIFE]: Good news, mother—the capital isn't far now. I'll go on ahead to hire a young donkey for you to ride.

FORTUNETELLER *walks on, singing reprise, "A gentleman, though blind . . ."* Enter FIRST COURIER, *whipping on his horse and singing again, "If only, when I reach Chang-an . . ."* He hits the FORTUNETELLER *and his* WIFE *and knocks them down, then exits.* Enter SECOND COURIER, *whipping on his horse and singing reprise, "All along the way I fear delay . . ."* He tramples the FORTUNETELLER *to death under his horse, then exits. The* FARMER, *weeping, stamps his feet, facing the place where the* COURIERS *exited.*

FARMER: Heaven! See how this entire field has been trampled by those bastards! I have nothing left! It's going to be hard enough for the family to survive, and now they're going to be after us for the tax grain. What am I going to do? This is terrible!

FORTUNETELLER'S WIFE [*crawling*]: They trampled us down! Old man, where are you? [*Feels the body*] Here's my old man. Why don't you say something? Have you been knocked out? [*Feels further*] There's something dripping wet on your head! [*Feels him again, then smells her hand*] This is awful—they've crushed out his brains! [*Shouts, weeping*] Heaven! Call the authorities!

FARMER [*turning around to look*]: One of the fortunetellers has been trampled to death here!

FORTUNETELLER'S WIFE [*getting up and bowing her head*]: I've got to find the local authorities to bring back those horsemen to pay for my husband's life.

FARMER: Those horsemen were delivering fresh lychees to Lady Yang. Who knows how many people they've trampled to death along the way. No one can make them pay for those lives—and a blind person like yourself has even less chance.

FORTUNETELLER'S WIFE: What am I going to do then? [*Weeping*] Oh, old man, I saw that your fate was to die on the road, but now how am I going to take care of your body?

FARMER: All right. You'll never find the local authorities on your own. I'll help you pick him up and bury him.

FORTUNETELLER'S WIFE: Well, thank you then. It would be just fine if I go with you.

They pick up the FORTUNETELLER *together and go off, alternately weeping and flirting.*

Enter ATTENDANT *of government way station.*

ATTENDANT [*sings*]:
> The stationmaster ran away,
> the stationmaster ran away,
> the horses died and all that's left
>   is a single horse's prick.
> Of attendants there is one;
> of grain and cash,
>   almost none.
> Beaten and bawled out,
> I have to hold them off alone,
> I have to hold them off alone.

I'm just an attendant in the Wei-cheng Station. Because Lady Yang adores fresh lychees and because her birthday is on August 1, both Fu-zhou and Hai-nan have sent couriers bringing offerings, and they all want to get there as quickly as possible. Their route passes through this way station. I can't help it that there isn't any grain or cash remaining in the station and that all we have left for them is one scrawny nag. The official in charge was afraid of getting beaten, and he ran off to no one knows where, leaving me, an underling, in charge of the whole station. How am I going to deal with the couriers when they come? Let them do as they will.

Enter First Courier, *galloping.*

First Courier [*sings*]:
> In rays through brown dust the sun
> > bites into the mountain peak,
>
> faster, faster, faster,
> closer to Chang-an. [*Dismounts*]

Attendant! Get me a fresh horse, and be quick about it!

Attendant takes the horse. First Courier *sets down his fruit basket and straightens his clothing. Enter* Second Courier, *galloping.*

Second Courier [*sings*]:
> Sweat pours from all my body,
> > my every limb is stiff,
>
> hurry, hurry, hurry,
> quickly change my mount. [*Dismounts*]

Attendant! Get me a fresh horse, and be quick about it!

Attendant *takes his horse.* Second Courier *puts down fruit basket and sees* First Courier.

Second Courier: Good-day, sir. Are you bringing lychees?

First Courier: I am.

Second Courier: Attendant! Where is the wine and food for the next stage of the journey?

Attendant: There is none prepared.

First Courier: All right. We won't eat. Bring the horses quickly.

Attendant: There are two of you gentlemen, but the station has only one horse left—who will ride it depends on the two of you.

Second Courier: What! A major way station like Wei-cheng and only one horse? Quick—call that dog of a stationmaster of yours so I can ask him where all the station's horses have gone.

Attendant: If you are wondering about the station horses, over the course of the past few years they have all been ridden to death by gentlemen bringing lychees. The official in charge of the station saw there was nothing he could do about it, so now he's run away.

Second Courier: Since the official in charge of the station has run away, we will hold you responsible.

Attendant [*pointing*]: Isn't that just one horse over there in the stable?

First Courier: Attendant, since I got here first, give it to me to ride.

Second Courier: I have had a longer journey, coming from Hai-nan, so let me take it.

FIRST COURIER [*heading within, sings*]:
> I will be first for a fresh horse,
> and I'm not going to argue with you.

SECOND COURIER [*dragging him back, singing*]:
> Don't try to throw your weight around,
> you'll provoke me to use my fists.

FIRST COURIER [*taking his lychees in hand, singing*]: Don't you dare spill my lychees!

SECOND COURIER [*taking his lychees and facing* FIRST COURIER]: Don't you
dare break my bamboo basket.

ATTENDANT [*trying to appease them, singing*]:
> Stop it now!—
> calm your rage.
> The best thing would be for both of you
> > to ride the horse together.

SECOND COURIER [*puts down his lychees and hits* ATTENDANT]:
> What blather!
> I'm going to beat *you* to death,
> > you putrid piece of muck.

FIRST COURIER [*puts down lychees and beats* ATTENDANT]:
> I'm going to beat you too,
> > you shameless crook.

SECOND COURIER [*sings*]:
> Smooth-talking pilferer
> > of government mounts.

FIRST COURIER [*sings*]:
> Misuse of imperial property,
> > a gallon of gall.

BOTH [*sing*]:
> A flurry of lashes, fists
> pummel painfully,
> we will thrash until
> > you can't bear it,
> and then we'll have our horses.

ATTENDANT [*kowtowing, sings*]:
> I kowtow again and again to the ground,
> hoping Your Excellencies
> > will lay off a bit.

COURIERS: If you want us to be done with you, get us fresh horses quickly.

ATTENDANT [*sings*]:
> There in front of behold
> > the only horse in the station . . .

COURIERS [*sing*]:
> We need one more!

ATTENDANT [*sings*]:
> That second horse may prove to be
> > rather hard to provide.

COURIERS: If you don't have it, then we'll beat you.

ATTENDANT [*sings*]:

> Just loosen your hold a while
>   and hear what I have to say—
> I'll have to take off my clothes
>   to give you to pawn for beer.

FIRST COURIER: Who wants your old clothes!

SECOND COURIER [*looks at coat, puts it on*]: All right. I'm really in a hurry.
I'll ride the horse I had and get a fresh one at the next stop.

> SECOND COURIER *takes fruit and mounts, singing reprise,*
>   *"All along the way I fear delay." Exits.*

FIRST COURIER: Quick! Get me the fresh horse!

ATTENDANT: Here it is.

> FIRST COURIER *takes fruit and mounts, singing reprise,*
>   *"If only, when I reach Chang-an." Exits.*

ATTENDANT: Lady Yang, Lady Yang—all this because of a few lychees!

> The golden chains of iron gates
>   open at break of day, [Cui Ye]
> a royal parchment flies its way,
>   words of decree return. [Yuan Zhen]
> The sounds of whips of post riders
>   swift as a lightning bolt, [Li Ying]
> and no one realizes that these
>   are her lychees coming. [Du Mu]

THE CIRCLE FOR DANCE (XVI)

Enter EMPEROR, *leading two palace attendants and* GAO LI-SHI.

EMPEROR [*sings*]:

> The hills are peaceful, breeze is light,
>   the daylight hours last long,
> horn lamps shine in palace halls,
>   a thousand yards of cloud.
> Purple vapors come from the east
> and, gazing west to Onyx Pool,
> the bluebird makes its fluttering descent
>   into the courtyard.[9]

---

[9]The phrase "Purple vapors come from the east," used in Du Fu's "Autumn Stirrings" *(Qiu-xing ba-shou)*, refers to Lao-zi, the putative ancestor of the Tang royal house, going westward through the passes to become an immortal. Onyx Pool was in the Kun-lun Mountains, where Zhou King Mu feasted with the Queen Mother of the West. From her home in the Kun-lun Mountains, the Queen Mother of the West once went to visit the Han emperor Wu in Chang-an, sending her attendant bluebird ahead as a herald of her visit. These lines seem to prefigure the anticipated meeting between the Emperor (a Li like Lao-zi) and Lady Yang.

Lady Yang and I have come to Mount Li to escape the summer heat. Today is the first of August and the Lady's birthday, so I have arranged a special banquet in the Palace of Lasting Life to celebrate it. Then we will also have the new song "Rainbow Skirts" performed. Gao Li-shi, go to the harem and tell the Lady to come to the hall.

GAO: As you command.

GAO LI-SHI *faces within and passes on the message. From within comes the answer, "As you command." Enter* LADY YANG, *elaborately dressed, with* YONG-XIN *and* NIAN-NU.

LADY YANG [*sings*]:

> In pepper-scented chambers sunbeams glow,
> blooming branches play on window grills.
> From the gate is hung a small flap
>   of imperial yellow,
> embroidered with a phoenix pair
> soaring on high beside the rainbow clouds.

[*Greeting the* EMPEROR] Your servant Yang greets Your Majesty. Long live Your Majesty!

EMPEROR: And may such long life be shared with you, my Consort.

LADY YANG *is seated.*

EMPEROR [*recites*]:

> In deep recesses of purple cloud
>   the Maiden Star shines bright,

LADY YANG:

> the Magic Peach, drenched in dew,
>   flourishes in sun's light,

YONG-XIN and NIAN-NU:

> facing the flowers year after year
>   may this couple never grow old,

GAO LI-SHI [*joining in*]:

> and in this Palace of Lasting Life
>   we wish you life everlasting.

EMPEROR: Since today is your birthday, I have arranged a special banquet for lasting life so that we can enjoy ourselves together all day long.

LADY YANG: I am overwhelmed by this kindness shown to me on my birthday, and I would like to offer a toast to long life.

GAO LI-SHI: The wine is ready.

LADY YANG *bows and presents the wine to the* EMPEROR, *who offers her a cup in return.* LADY YANG *drinks, kneeling, then bows her head to the floor and cries, "Long live Your Majesty!" Then she resumes her seat.*

EMPEROR [*sings*]:

> There's a scent in the breeze, the sun is bright,
> see blazing light shake on the single leaf

of the ming plant.[1]
Now the magnificent feast begins
with South Mountain reflected from afar
in goblets filled with wisps of cloud.

TOGETHER:
Fruit formed of pods embracing,
the peach tree lives a thousand years;
paired flowers on a single stalk,
the lotuses bloom for ten yards.
Suited for pleasures,
this palace, well-named "Lasting Life,"
is a realm to match immortal lands.

Enter a palace EUNUCH, *bearing a document.*

EUNUCH [*recites*]:
I hold in my hands a red placard
with golden flourish adorned,
we have all come to the precious halls
to wish you a thousand years.

[*Greets them*] Your Majesty, my Lady—the Minister Yang Guo-zhong
and the Ladies of Han, Guo, and Qin offer you this card with felicita-
tions, and send their good wishes from outside the court.

GAO LI-SHI *takes the card and hands it over to the* EMPEROR, *who reads it.*

EMPEROR: Our thanks to them. Let the Minister not feel he has to observe
all the courtesies, but let him go back to court and take care of business.
The Three Ladies should come join us when Lady Yang and I go back
to the palace for the banquet.

EUNUCH: As you command. [*Exit*]

Enter SECOND EUNUCH, *carrying the lychees covered with a yellow cloth.*

SECOND EUNUCH [*recites*]:
For this feast of longevity
in the gods' Onyx Park,
from the fiery South are offered
the lychees known as "youngest maid."

[*Greets them*] Your Majesty, here are fresh lychees presented from Fu-
zhou and Hai-nan.

EMPEROR: Bring them here.

GAO LI-SHI *takes the lychees and removes the cloth covering them,*
then presents them to the EMPEROR.

My Lady, since you love this fruit, I sent a special edict to these places

---

[1] The fabulous ming plant was supposed to grow a new leaf every day through the first half of the
month, then lose a leaf daily during the second half of the month. Since the present day is the first
of the month, there is only one leaf.

to have them brought to you with all possible haste. And today these fine fruits have arrived just in time for your birthday banquet. Let us drink another cup together.

LADY YANG: Long live Your Majesty!

EMPEROR: Maids, bring wine.

NIAN-NU *and* YONG-XIN *bring wine.*

LADY YANG [*sings*]:
> A basketful,
> fair fruits' aroma,
> wrapped in yellow, brought from afar,
>> from west and south by royal command.
> I love their rich and ripe
>> red velvety skin
> with crystalline balls of white within,
> a pure fragrance in the hand,
> on teeth a moisture sweet and cool.

TOGETHER:
> Now must the fiery date give way
>> and the pear of immortality,
> for on these eternal terraces
> at a banquet of longevity
> these join the Goddess of Onyx Pool
>> in offering alabaster sap.

EMPEROR: Gao Li-shi, give my command to Li Gui-nian to bring the musicians of the Pear Garden Academy into the hall to attend on us.

GAO LI-SHI: As you command.

GAO LI-SHI *passes command within. Enter* LI GUI-NIAN *with musicians* LEI HAI-QING, HE HUAI-ZHI, MA XIAN-QI, *and* HUANG FAN-CHUO, *all in brocade gowns and splendid caps, responding, "As you command."*

LI GUI-NIAN [*recites*]:
> Red clappers are ready,
>> the zither pegs tuned,
> urging on one dressed in lace
>> to mount the stage for dance.
> We've changed into new headgear,
>> the saffron-colored caps,
> and in our troop have come here
>> before the royal throne.

[*Greets* EMPEROR] The musician Li Gui-nian brings the Pear Garden Troupe to greet Your Majesty and the Lady.

EMPEROR: Li Gui-nian, the other day you performed the overture of "Rainbow Skirts." Have you thoroughly rehearsed the second movement, "Coats of Feathers"?

LI GUI-NIAN: We have.

EMPEROR: Well, put your heart into the performance.

LI GUI-NIAN: As you command. [*Rises and exits*]

LADY YANG: Your Majesty, in the six sections of the overture the only tempo is largo with no andante, while in the six sections of the middle movement the tempo is andante but with no allegro, and for this there is no choreography yet.

[*Sings*]

It lifts as with a breeze,
in the mood of notes, a vibrancy,
stopping the brightly colored clouds in flight
and whirling around the rainbow beams.

The third movement of "Coats of Feathers" is called the "Ornamented Section."
There every word and every note
contains the motion of a dance.

There are the slow notes, the tremolos, the rubatos,
echoing bell-like and clear,
a string of black-dragon pearls.

There is the statement of the theme, the exposition, and the finale,
each matching a thousand lithe positions
on the dance rug.

And then there is the *hua-fan,* the *dao-he,* the side beat, the fast beat, and the stolen beat,
so many tones of melody,
all rising together with slow dance,
unfolding in the interplay
with leisurely song.

EMPEROR: You have described all the fine points of the song and dance.

LADY YANG: I have had a circular surface of azure constructed. Let me dance thereon to give Your Majesty some pleasure of entertainment.

EMPEROR: I have never had a chance to see your finesse in dance, Lady. Yong-xin, Nian-nu, along with Zheng Guan-yin and Xie Ah-man, are to attend upon Lady Yang and bring in the azure circle.

YONG-XIN and NIAN-NU: As you command.

LADY YANG [*rising*]: May I withdraw to change clothes, sire?

[*Recites*]

I'll put my costume in order
dress up once again,
then this body will fly upon
the circular surface of azure.

Exit LADY YANG *with* YONG-XIN *and* NIAN-NU.

EMPEROR: Gao Li-shi, instruct Li Gui-nian to have the Pear Garden Ensemble play
the music according to the score. I will keep the rhythm myself on a Jie drum.
GAO LI-SHI: As you command.

GAO *conveys the instructions within. The* EMPEROR *rises to change.* LI GUI-
NIAN *and the other musicians play music offstage. A circle of azure is placed
on the stage. Enter* LADY YANG, *wearing a splendid cap, a white embroidered
gown, a necklace, a brocade cloud-mantle, kingfisher-decorated sleeves, and
a great red dancing skirt.* YONG-XIN *and* NIAN-NU, *along with* ZHENG GUAN-
YIN *and* XIE AH-MAN, *are all wearing white gowns for dancing, and holding
multicolored rainbow streamers and peacock cloud fans. They step upon the
azure circle, crowding around* LADY YANG *and completely hiding her. The
music stops and the pennons and fans slowly draw back, to show* LADY YANG
dancing on the circle with YONG-XIN, NIAN-NU, ZHENG GUAN-YIN, *and* XIE
AH-MAN *singing.* GAO LI-SHI *kneels, holding the drum, while the* EMPEROR *assumes his seat and beats on it. Offstage, the musicians join in.*

ALL [*sing*]:
Figured lace joins blossoms' light,
a bud of red cloud ripples in the sky.
Behold the rainbow streamers circling round,
as scent from Heaven tumultuously falls.
With steady grace
fan shadows slowly draw apart and show
    her bright array.
In every way
    like those spirits of the air
that fall through moonbeams in their flight.
Now lightly tossing in the breeze,
she spreads her colored sleeves,
and on the azure circle shows her skill.
In windborne undulations
    she forward comes, then draws away,
as bloom of lotus meets the wind
upon its bobbing leafy pad.
With cuffs upraised toward sky
    as though about to fly,
her body bends in sudden turns
    passing through measures unforeseen.

[*Dancing more swiftly*]

Now lost in whirling ecstasy,
spray of flowers catching gusts,
    twig of willow rising,
phoenix outline mounting high,
    shape of simurgh soaring.

Words cannot tell such charm of form,
upward blown by Heaven's wind
amid the players' frenzied tones.
From icy strings and stops of jade
    the notes are piercing clear,
from phoenix reeds and ivory pipes
    come floods of melody.
Now blending with the beat of drum,
    swelling and diminishing,
new modes of music compassed and performed.
Her trailing skirts of gold recall
how Lady Zhao was held by all
    when dancing she took flight.

EMPEROR *stops drumming;* GAO LI-SHI *carries drum away.*

The dancing halts,
her wispy skirts draw in.

    LADY YANG *bows to* EMPEROR.

And once again her forehead bows,
and she shouts, "Long live His Majesty!"

YONG-XIN, NIAN-NU, ZHENG GUAN-YIN, *and* XIE AH-MAN *help* LADY YANG *off the dancing circle.* ZHENG GUAN-YIN *and* XIE AH-MAN *withdraw.* EMPEROR *rises, comes forward, and takes* LADY YANG'*s hand.*

EMPEROR: That was splendid! That was a dance! It gave a powerful impression of unearthliness, with intoxicating beauties appearing everywhere. Just like the eddying wind or whirling snow or a swallow in flight or the swimming dragon. You are unsurpassed in a millennium. Maids, see to some wine! I am going to toast Lady Yang.

YONG-XIN *and* NIAN-NU *bring wine;* EMPEROR *raises his cup and sings:*

I lift this flagon of gold
and face you with a gentle smile,
bidding those cherry lips to lightly taste
    drop by drop. [*Hands it to Lady Yang*]
Now drain it to the dregs,
my gift of gratitude to you for having strained
    limbs and waist in dance.
LADY YANG [*taking the cup and thanking* EMPEROR]:
Long live Your Majesty! [*sings*]
This jadelike brew bestowed by his own hand
    are favor's broad waves,
I feel only shame that this exceeds
    the merits of my paltry skills.

EMPEROR [*looking at Lady Yang*]:
>When I gaze closely on her face,
>how she holds the cup,
>every kind of lover's grace
>>strikes a man to the heart.

Let your payment be ten bolts of golden brocade figured with mated ducks and a hairpin of purple-rubbed gold from the river Li. [*Takes out a sachet*] Here also is a sachet of eight precious brocade pouches filled with ambergris to hang from your waist, to add to your dance costume.

LADY YANG [*taking sachet and thanking* EMPEROR]: Long live Your Majesty!

EMPEROR [*taking* LADY YANG *by the hand and walking*]:
>This fair dance of "Rainbow Skirts"
>>can be enjoyed forever,
>fit complement to my prayer
>>for your long life.

LADY YANG:
>My body is redolent throughout
>>with the unforeseen flood of favor.

EMPEROR [*recites*]:
>the secret galleries of Lasting Life
>>rest against gray sky, [Wu Rong]

LADY YANG:
>the jadelike sweet wines are portioned
>>in flagons for the toast. [Zhang Yue]

EMPEROR:
>Done with drinking, I cherish still more
>>the paired sleeves of the dance, [Han Hong]

LADY YANG:
>all over my body I newly bear
>>scents of rainbow-cloud. [Cao Tang]

Meanwhile, at his command in Fan-yang in the Northeast, An Lu-shan has been quietly removing his Chinese generals and replacing them with Central Asians like himself. He watches a great hunt in which he reviews his army's prowess, secretly plotting rebellion.

At the same time, Lady Yang is suffering the torments of jealousy because the Emperor has developed an interest in a new favorite known as the Plum Consort. The Emperor is dallying with the Plum Consort in a pavilion when Lady Yang comes to the door and demands admission. The Emperor, flustered, hides the Plum Consort, and in a comic scene that bears witness to the Emperor's infatuated weakness before Lady Yang, she accuses him of deceiving her. The Emperor at first beats a hasty retreat, then returns to console her and reassure her of his love.

Returning to the frontier, Guo Zi-yi's scouts inform him of An Lu-shan's preparations for rebellion and how imperial investigators have been deceived into reporting his loyalty. Meanwhile, back near the capital, the steamy pleasures of female voyeurism innocently echo the more destructive envy that fuels An Lu-shan's ambitions.

PEEKING AT THE BATHERS (XXI)

Enter FIRST PALACE MAID.

FIRST MAID [*sings*]:
>Since youth my face was nature's gift
>of pocking;
>foremost in bevies of palace demoiselles
>in sweeping.
>I met a young eunuch by the stairs,
>adawdling,
>I stuck out my hand and stroked his pants—
>but nothing.

[*Recites in doggerel*]

>I'm number one of the palace maids,
>my standard is top-notch:
>my cheeks are smeared with powder,
>my mouth, a lipstick splotch.
>My twinkling eyes are bells of bronze,
>I flatten my brows to a line,
>My dainty digits, ten pestles,
>my willowy waist, great pine.
>My naked body is lacquer coarse
>and my footsies are bigger
>   than an outrigger
>   built to run a rapids' course.
>Lady Yang dotes on my cleverness,
>and picked me for "Rainbow Skirts" chorus;
>but my vocal cords were a sonorous wonder,
>from singing lips rose peals of thunder.
>And my body proved a bit too bumbling
>for I danced the royal table tumbling.
>This did the royal dander inflame:
>from the roll of dancers he struck my name.
>I forthwith departed for Mount Li
>to serve in Warmsprings Gallery.
>The royal coach set off yesterday
>to Hua-qing with Lady Yang to stay.
>They will jointly bathe in warm pools here
>   by imperial writ,
>so I must sweep and clean and get everything set.

But here as I'm rambling on, another palace lady is coming.

Enter Second Palace Maid.

Second Maid [*sings*]:
>We have frittered away the spring of youth,
>the harem's bitter women,
>we stamp our feet and beat our breasts in vain,
>none knows our pain.
>We have wasted our lives without a man,
>the dance of the wild goose
>>flying alone.

They greet one another.

First Maid: What's this "wild goose dance" you're talking about? Now that His Majesty has Lady Yang's "Skirts of Rainbow," he doesn't even care for the Plum Consort's "Startled Swan" dance any more.

Second Maid: How true! I used to be a maid of the Plum Consort. But since my Lady took sick and died after returning from the Azure Tower in humiliation, I got sent off to this place.

First Maid: That's how it is. Lady Yang is so jealous that we should give up even dreaming of a day when we will enjoy the Emperor's attentions.

Second Maid: Let's drop it.

First Maid: His Majesty is just about to arrive. Let's you and I go to the outer corridor to wait for him.

They move to the edge of the stage. Enter Eunuchs, *leading the* Emperor,
Lady Yang, Nian-nu, *and* Yong-xin.

Emperor [*sings*]:
>Around this pleasure palace the scenes
>>are private and rare:
>see how beside the carved beams,
>and beyond the pearl screens
>the rain rolls off and clouds fly.
>There, winding away,
>several turns of vermilion rails
>>ring painted streams,
>and long walkways in rising tiers
>>touch the azure haze.
>A red wall encircles all
>with passage opened through marble doors.

Eunuchs: Your Majesty, we have come to Warmsprings Palace.

Emperor: Leave us now. [*Exeunt* Eunuchs] My Lady,
>Behold clear channels gushing under,
>the turning wavelets and furrowed ripples,
>whose soft luster of fragrant fountains
>>well suits your pale flesh.

Let us bathe here, my Lady. [NIAN-NU *and* YONG-XIN *remove the outer robes from* EMPEROR *and* LADY YANG]
> Now softly undo your cloudlike gown,
> pearl-glow already showing through
>> and jade's white sheen,
> I cannot but stand facing you,
>> cannot but love you,
>> cannot but care for you,
>> cannot but gaze on you,
>> cannot but cherish you.

EMPEROR *gives* LADY YANG *a hand down into the baths.*

YONG-XIN: Seeing the love that His Majesty and Lady Yang share, Nian-nu, is enough to make a person die of envy.

NIAN-NU: Indeed it is.

YONG-XIN [*sings*]:
> On flowered dawns in one another's arms,
> embracing on moonlit nights,
> they taste that soft and warm pleasure,
>> the body's savor.

NIAN-NU:
> Like shadow and form, linked always together,
> indivisible as when a knife cuts water.
> A thousand small accommodations,
>> and hundred compliances,
> two people joined
>> in flesh and in heart.
> The tongue has no words for love's secret,
> nor can the written word convey
>> that bed with lovebird curtains
> where they lie together forever twined.

YONG-XIN: You and I have waited on Lady Yang for many years now, and though we have seen her charming face, we have never had a glimpse of her naked body. Why don't we steal a peek through this gap in the hangings.

NIAN-NU: A good idea.

Both peer through the curtains within.

TOGETHER [*sing*]:
> As we steal a glimpse
> of her naked body before us spread
> like a lotus riding upon the waves,
> its charming glow besprent with dew.
> The fragrant unguents melt away
>> from delicate wrists and arms,
> a lithe torso rolling with sapphire ripples.

YONG-XIN:
>Her frame, bright wisp of cloud,
>her flesh is steeped in snow.

NIAN-NU:
>A swathe of creamy skin,
>>paired buds poking through,

YONG-XIN:
>a half speck of spring conceals
>>the small and musky navel.

NIAN-NU:
>And I love the spot her red wraps gape
>just barely revealing her private parts.

>Yong-xin, look at His Majesty,
>how he fixes his gaze on her!
>And he smiles steadily
>like someone who's lost his wits.

TOGETHER:
>Not just we her palace maids
>>almost take leave of our senses,
>even the ruler, used to the sight,
>>can't control himself.

YONG-XIN:
>Would that the springtime waters run dry!

NIAN-NU:
>Or that her marble mass be bathed
>>until it senseless swoons!

YONG-XIN:
>Kisses unceasing upon her sweet shoulders,

NIAN-NU:
>his arm ever circles her slender waist;

YONG-XIN:
>our lady says nothing,
>>and discreetly smiles,
>>>withholding her passion.

NIAN-NU:
>And they are content,
>as magic liquids and springtime breeze
>sweep across them drunkenly.

YONG-XIN:
>The light on the waves is warm,
>rays of the sun cast their glow,
>as this pair of dragons frolic,
>>rising out of the level pool.

TOGETHER:
>Almost like King Xiang of Chu
>>falling from thirst by Yang Terrace,

and she, just like the goddess,
   brings back the twilight rain.

Enter FIRST *and* SECOND MAIDS, *unnoticed, laughing.*

MAIDS: You two seem to be having a good time. Let us get to see too.

YONG-XIN and NIAN-NU: We're just waiting on Lady Yang while she is bathing. What's the "good time" about that?

MAIDS: I'll bet you weren't just waiting on Lady Yang, but stealing a peek at His Majesty in there.

YONG-XIN and NIAN-NU: Shame on you! Don't talk nonsense. His Majesty and Lady Yang are coming out now.

Exeunt MAIDS. *Enter* EMPEROR *and* LADY YANG.

EMPEROR [*sings*]:
   Rising from the warm pool
     fresh cool runs through flesh,
   I observe the increase
     of radiant loveliness
      within your face.
   Most charming—the scattered flecks
     of make-up left
   and in azure streaks a gloss appears
     in drying clouds of hair.

YONG-XIN *and* NIAN-NU *help* EMPEROR *and* LADY YANG *to change.* LADY YANG *has a look of lassitude, and* YONG-XIN *and* NIAN-NU *hold her up.*

EMPEROR:
   You look like a willow in wind
   or a bloom affrighted by dew.
   So languid you can't hold yourself up,
   charming in your frailty,
   needing others to help you along.

Enter two EUNUCHS *with attendants pulling a small carriage.*

EUNUCHS: If Your Majesty and our Lady would please get in the carriage, we will go back to Hua-qing Palace.

EMPEROR: Let the carriage follow behind.

EUNUCHS: As you command, sire.

EMPEROR [*taking* LADY YANG *by the hand, sings*]:
   Let you and I go shoulder to shoulder
   and hand in hand,
   who needs a carriage to rush beneath the flowers?—
   let us go back with a fine breeze on our faces.

TOGETHER:
   The one who's always on my mind
   turns the mind to thoughts of love,

even those unfeeling flowers and birds
    are fools of feeling,
all alike know to pair
    and seek a common roost.

EMPEROR [*recites*]:
    The breath of flowers, exactly like
        incense of compound scent, [Du Fu]

LADY YANG:
    avoiding breeze, having just emerged
        from a tub's warm waters. [Wang Jian]

EMPEROR:
    Attendants, hold her up,
        charming in her frailty, [Bo Ju-yi]

LADY YANG:
    laughing, I lean by the east window
        on a bench of white jade. [Li Bo]

SECRET PLEDGE (XXII)

Enter the goddess WEAVER WOMAN, *with two*
IMMORTAL HANDMAIDENS.

WEAVER [*sings*]:
    Clouds shelter my jade shuttle
    as with skill I weave the threads on the loom.
    Pangs of longing never come
        to palaces of Heaven—yet
    hearing this night is the Seventh Eve,
    I think back abruptly on times gone by.

        [*Recites Qin Guan's lyrics*]

Fine wisps of cloud sport their craft,
shooting stars bear the news,
and now far off in the River of Stars
    we will make the crossing unseen.
To meet just once in fall's metal wind
    and in the jade white dews
turns out to be better by far
    than the countless meetings of mortals.

Our tender feelings seem like water,
this sweet moment is as in a dream—
how can we bear to turn their heads
    to the path leading back across Magpie Bridge?
But so long as both of us love
    and so long as our love lasts on,
it does not need to be done
    every night and every morning at dawn.

I am that Weaver Woman who, according to the decree of the High God, wedded the Oxherd to become a heavenly husband and wife. Every year on the Seventh Eve we cross the River of Stars and meet. In the world below, this day is the Seventh Eve of the seventh month in the tenth year of the Tian-bao Reign. See how there are no waves on the River of Light, which will soon be filled with magpies. I had best set aside my weaving for a while and get myself dressed up.

Music is played faintly within. Enter magpies, which fly around stage. A bridge is set up and the magpies fly to either end.

IMMORTAL HANDMAIDENS: The Magpie Bridge is erected. You may cross the River of Stars now, my Lady.

WEAVER WOMAN *rises and walks toward it.*

WEAVER [*sings*]:
    I set aside my woven words
    and briefly ride a scented coach.
ALL [*sing*]:
    For no clouds stain the sapphire sky,
    and fresh cool comes with evening's breeze. [*They step upon the bridge*]
    We tread the bridge through shadows strewn
    as down below us shines
        Star-River's resplendent clarity.
    By these new joys overwhelmed:
        the new moon's slender sliver,
        the moistness of the sparkling dew,
    as magpies ply their wings below
        in circling pairs;
    we note at once how the Silver Stream
        takes on new aspects in the fall.
IMMORTAL HANDMAIDENS: My Lady, we have crossed the Milky Way.
WEAVER: Down there underneath the Star-River, I can just barely make out a puff of incense smoke, coiling as it rises into the sky. Where is it coming from?
IMMORTAL HANDMAIDENS: That is Yang Yu-huan, the Prized Consort of the Tang Emperor, praying for skill in the palace.[2]
WEAVER: It's good that she has such a true heart. The Oxherd and I will go down to watch her.

---

[2]"Praying for skill" was one of the various customs of the Seventh Eve. The "skill" referred to is primarily skill in weaving, a gift that the Weaver Woman star might well grant—though in the case of the Prized Consort, "skill" is meant in a broader sense of "artful charm." When a woman "prayed for skill," she would capture a spider and put it in a box. Then she would see how much of a web it spun by the next day, and that would tell her the degree to which her wish had been granted.

ALL [*sing*]:
> Heavenly meetings of lovers last on
>   year after year right here,
> and we smile at love's fate in the mortal world
>   that is in an instant gone. [*Exeunt omnes*]

Enter two attendant EUNUCHS, *holding lanterns, followed by* EMPEROR.

EMPEROR [*sings*]:
> Tranquil autumn light
> engulfed in wisps of sapphire smoke
>   bringing on the dark of night.
> Showers pass the beech trees
>   leaving a faint chill;
> the Silver River arcs around
> with frail wisps of cloud
>   adorning the Paired Stars. [*Laughter within; the* EMPEROR *listens*]
> I listen closely—borne on the breeze
> is happy laughter past the flowers
>   in shadows of the trees.

    Eunuch! What's all that laughter for?

EUNUCH [*asking within*]: His Majesty asks: what's all that laughter for?

VOICE [*from within*]: My Lady Yang has come to the Palace of Lasting Life
to pray for skill.

EUNUCH [*replying to* EMPEROR's *question*]: My Lady Yang has come to the
Palace of Lasting Life to pray for skill.

EMPEROR: Attendants, don't announce my arrival. Let me sneak in quietly.

[*Sings*]

> Put the red lanterns away,
> let me softly slip within
>   to the dragon-court
>   to get a better view.

EMPEROR *moves off to the edge of the stage. Enter* LADY YANG, *with* YONG-
XIN *and* NIAN-NU, *accompanied by two palace girls carrying a box of incense,
a silk fan, a vase of flowers, a wax doll, and a golden basin.*[3]

LADY YANG [*sings*]:
> The palace yard
> is sunk in haze
>   from incense of golden braziers,
> half concealing the candles' rays.
> A spider the size of a grain of rice,
>   here securely enclosed

---

[3]Floating a wax doll in a basin of water was a ceremony associated with praying for fertility.

> beans set to sprout in a pan of gold,
> and sprays
> of blossoms unfurl in a silver vase.

YONG-XIN and NIAN-NU: We have reached the Palace of Lasting Life, and all the preparations have been readied for you to make the prayer for skill. Would you now take a stick of incense, my Lady?

They take flower vase, doll, and basin, and set them on a table. YONG-XIN *holds out the box of incense and* LADY YANG *takes a stick.*

LADY YANG: I, Yang Yu-huan, with a reverent and earnest heart hereby respectfully address the Paired Stars. I humbly entreat your divine aid.

[*Sings*]

> I pray that the love shown
> by hairpin and box
> long stay firm,
> let the fan be not abandoned
> when winds of autumn come.[4]

EMPEROR [*secretly observing her, sings*]:
> She is so lovely to my sight,
> bowing low on alabaster stairs,
> and I can hear
> her muffled sounds of prayers.

YONG-XIN and NIAN-NU [*seeing* EMPEROR]: His Majesty is here!

LADY YANG *quickly turns and bows down before the* EMPEROR. EMPEROR *lifts her up.*

EMPEROR: And what's this mischief you are up to?

LADY YANG: Tonight is the Seventh Eve, and I've set out fruit to pray for skill from the Weaver Woman, Heaven's Daughter.

EMPEROR [*laughing*]: You've already plundered Heaven of all its skill. Why would you have to pray for more?

LADY YANG: You make me tremble with shame at such excessive praise.

LADY YANG *and* EMPEROR *are seated. Exeunt* YONG-XIN, NIAN-NU, *and the two palace girls.*

EMPEROR: My Lady, I think on how the Weaver and the Oxherd are separated by the Silver River and get to meet only once a year. Such longing is no easy thing to bear.

[*Sings*]

> Night stretches on in autumn sky,
> the sapphire river of stars is clear,

---

[4]This refers to a poem attributed to the rejected favorite Pan Jie-yu, in which the court lady compares herself to a fan, cast away once the cool of autumn comes.

the holy wayfarers have barely a chance
    each to greet the other,
helpless that Heaven grants them a meeting
    that lasts but an instant,
and all too soon the rooster's crow
    reaches their ears.
Then in the cold of clouds
    and chill of dew
they hurry back
    to yearlong solitudes.

LADY YANG: It makes me sad when Your Majesty speaks of the pain that the Paired Stars feel when they part. It's too bad that mortal men don't know how things are in Heaven.

[*Sings*]

If we asked, we would find
they suffer terribly the pangs of longing. [*Wipes away tears*]

EMPEROR: Why are you crying?

LADY YANG: I realize that even though the Weaver and the Oxherd get to meet only once a year, their love will continue as long as Heaven lasts and Earth endures. I'm afraid that the love Your Majesty and I share cannot possibly last as long as theirs.

EMPEROR: What's this, now!

[*Sings*]

Though mated gods have everlasting life,
compared to worldly bonds like ours
    they're not much better off.
In mortal lifespans we may seize
    all the excitement of romance,
we have our moments and our scenes
that heighten passion and pleasure—
why then sob with sorrow so? [*Moves closer to Lady Yang and
    speaks softly*]
How can the Paired Stars compare
    to you and I who share
        every night and every dawn?

LADY YANG: The love you have shown me is deep, but tonight there are a few things I want to say . . . [*Stops herself*]

EMPEROR: You can say whatever you want to.

LADY YANG [*facing* EMPEROR, *choked with sobbing*]: I have had your favor and kind regard more than any woman in the harem. I am just afraid that as time passes, I will gradually lose that love and that I will end up as Zhuo Wen-jun did with Si-ma Xiang-ru, lamenting promises betrayed.

[*Sings*]

My heart aches whenever this thought comes,
and I brood how, lowly and poor,
    I've served in the royal chambers,
and have been raised so high
    to wait on your wardrobe, share your coach.
But I fear that in the blink of an eye
flowers grow old
    and nothing remains of spring—
on lasting favor can none rely. [*Weeping, grasps his clothes*]
If I could get this love to stay
and last on long,
I would even die.
If I could get this love to run
its full course to the end,
in death I would close my eyes.
Then I would be far better than she
    who once danced and sang
        for Princess Ping-yang,
then the ruler's love changed
and lonely in Chang-men Palace
her spirit crushed, teardrops fell
and her heart broke in helpless weeping
    for the fate of fair faces.

EMPEROR [*taking his sleeve and wiping away* LADY YANG'S *tears*]: Cease such
    sad thoughts, my dear. The love that I feel for you cannot be compared
    to such casual attractions.

[*Sings*]

Cease heart's cares,
no more shed tears
fearing time passing
will bring about change. [*Takes* LADY YANG'S *hand*]
Honeycake, honeycake,
    stuck together fast,
never an instant apart.

TOGETHER [*sing*]:
Or consider the long and trailing vine
lost among flowers, in dark of the moon,
then none can tell
    its shadow from form.

LADY YANG: Since you love me so much, I ask you to take an oath with me
    here under the Paired Stars to keep our love steadfast to the end.

EMPEROR: Then let's both go burn incense and make our vow.

TOGETHER [*sing*]:
>   Leaning shoulder to shoulder,
>   we descend the stairs hand in hand.
>   Above the halls stretches the River of Light,

LADY YANG [*sings*]:
>   and suddenly I feel a chill
>   creep into my gown of mesh.

EMPEROR [*sings*]:
>   Let us now, speaking softly,
>   swear by the mountains and seas.

EMPEROR *offers incense, bows, and swears with* LADY YANG.

>   By the paired stars above, I, Li Long-ji . . .

LADY YANG: and I, Yang Yu-huan . . .

TOGETHER: . . . because of the depth of our love, wish to remain together as
man and wife in every one of our future lives and never to be parted.
May the Paired Stars stand as witnesses if this vow is ever betrayed.

EMPEROR [*bowing, sings*]:
>   If in Heaven, may we become
>   those birds that fly on shared wing,

LADY YANG [*clasping hands and bowing head, sings*]:
>   if on Earth, then may we become
>   branches that twine together.

TOGETHER [*sing*]:
>   Heaven lasts, the Earth endures,
>   yet a time will come when they're gone,
>   yet this oath of ours will continue
>   and never finally end.

LADY YANG [*thanking* EMPEROR *with head bowed*]: I am deeply moved by
your love and will keep this vow made tonight to the death.

EMPEROR [*taking* LADY YANG *by the hand, sings*]:
>   Here in the Palace of Lasting Life
>   private vows were said,

LADY YANG [*sings*]:
>   but who is there tonight
>   to be our witness?

EMPEROR [*pointing, sings*]:
>   There by the bridge across the Silvery River
>   that pair of stars,
>   Oxherd and the Weaver. [*Exeunt*]

Enter OXHERD *wearing cloud-figured turban and robes of an immortal, accompanied by the* WEAVER WOMAN *with her two* IMMORTAL HANDMAIDENS.

WEAVER [*sings*]:
>   They made their vows, their secret troth,

and prayed with heartfelt reverence,
an undivided love in two,
whose mouths shared the same words.

OXHERD: Goddess, see what love the Tang Emperor and Yang Yu-huan share!

[*Sings*]

Silently embracing,
leaning shoulder to shoulder,
no breach between them.

You and I have had the good fortune to be united in Heaven, and we should direct what is played out on the stage of love below. Not only that—they made their vows before us, so we should watch over them.

[*Sings*]

They yearn to be birds that fly on paired wing,
aspire to be branches joined,
wish to share future lifetimes—
    this is true love indeed—
and we should have them ever be
    guardians of romance
        in the world of mortal men.

WEAVER: Yet a disaster will befall them both, and death will part them. But if at last they do not forswear the vows they took tonight, then we will arrange their reunion.

OXHERD: What you say, goddess, is true. But look how the colors of night draw to their close. Let us make our way back to our palace in the stars.

Takes WEAVER WOMAN'S *hand and they walk.*

TOGETHER [*sing*]:
        Heavenly meetings of lovers last on
            year after year right here,
        and we smile at love's fate in the mortal world
            that is in an instant gone.

        No need that years and months speed on
            in the world of mortal men— [Luo Ye]
        the star-bridge stretches across the sky,
            magpies turn back in flight. [Li Shang-yin]
        Say not that meetings
            in Heaven are too few, [Li Ying]
        we simply do not have the heart
            to send the asked-for skill. [Luo Yin]

In the next scenes, An Lu-shan appears in rebellion, defeating the imperial army under Ge-shu Han and breaking through the passes that defend the capital. The Emperor is feasting with Lady Yang when the news arrives that An Lu-shan has defeated the imperial army and is threatening Chang-an. As the scene closes, the Emperor plans to flee the capital the next morning.

JADE BURIAL (XXV)

Enter CHEN YUAN-LI, *officer in charge of the imperial guard, with attendant soldiers.*

CHEN [*sings*]:
> On we speed, throngs
>> of pikes and pennons, on
> we speed,
> Plumed Guards ward the royal coach,
> the royal coach.
> In panic fleeing the mutineers,
>> we set off on the march.
> The road is rough,
> the men trudge through,
> when at last
> will we make Cheng-du?

Because An Lu-shan has rebelled and taken Tong Pass, His Majesty is making a journey to Shu to escape the fighting. He has ordered me, Chen Yuan-li, the Long-wu general, to take charge of the palace troops that will serve as his escort. We have just completed one stage of the journey and reached Ma-wei Station. [*Uproar within*] You soldiers, what's the reason for all the noise?

SOLDIERS [*within*]: The rebellion of An Lu-shan and the fact that the Emperor has been forced to flee is all Yang Guo-zhong's fault—he abused his power and stirred up the revolt. Unless this traitor is executed, we will rather die than escort the Emperor any further.

CHEN: There is no need for such rowdiness. Stay quietly in camp for a while, and I will state the case to His Majesty, who will make the decision.

Offstage, soldiers agree. Exit CHEN, *leading his guards, singing the reprise,* "The road is rough, the men trudge through," *etc. Enter* EMPEROR *and* LADY YANG *on horseback, followed by* YONG-XIN *and* NIAN-NU.

EMPEROR [*sings*]:
> Drops of tears are shed
>> for my palace in panic forsaken,
> and I sigh
>> at this rag-tag retinue
> heading to Cheng-du
>> off beyond the edge of sky.
> On and on, ever farther
>> from the capital,

through half a dozen isolated
    rivers and hills,
interspersed with a few
    deserted shacks and fallen tiles.

GAO: We have reached Ma-wei Station. May it please Your Majesty to rest here a while.

> EMPEROR *and* LADY YANG *dismount, go in, and are seated.*

EMPEROR: How wrong I was! What a mistake I made in showering favor on someone who turned out to be a rebel! It's I who has brought us to this flight—I cannot tell you how much I regret it. My dear, if only I had not involved you in these adversities!

LADY YANG: Of course I should be with you. I could never refuse to go through these hardships. I only hope that the rebels will be crushed soon so that Your Majesty can return to the capital. [*More shouting within*]

SOLDIERS [*within*]: Yang Guo-zhong took all power to himself and betrayed the state. Now he is even aligning himself with Tibet. Either he dies or we die, this we swear! Whoever wants to kill Yang Guo-zhong, come with us quickly!

> *Enter* SOLDIERS *carrying swords, chasing* YANG GUO-ZHONG *around the stage. They kill* YANG GUO-ZHONG, *then exit, shouting.*

EMPEROR [*alarmed*]: Gao Li-shi, what's all that noise outside? Tell Chen Yuan-li that he is to report to me at once.

GAO: As Your Majesty instructs. [*Passes command to* CHEN YUAN-LI *outside, who enters and greets* EMPEROR]

CHEN: Chen Yuan-li reporting.

EMPEROR: Why are the soldiers in such an uproar?

CHEN: Your Majesty, Yang Guo-zhong instigated this rebellion by taking all power upon himself. He also had private contacts with Tibet. This aroused the rage of the Grand Army, and as a result they killed Yang Guo-zhong.

EMPEROR [*alarmed*]: Can it be? [LADY YANG *turns away and wipes tears from her eyes.* EMPEROR *ponders*] All right then, give the orders to set out.

CHEN [*going out and giving orders*]: These are His Majesty's instructions: He pardons you for taking it on yourselves to kill Yang Guo-zhong. Now let us be on our way quickly.

SOLDIERS [*again shouting from within*]: Yang Guo-zhong may have been executed, but there is still Lady Yang. We won't accompany the Emperor unless Lady Yang is killed.

CHEN [*to* EMPEROR]: The soldiers say that even though Yang Guo-zhong has been executed, they won't set off as long as Lady Yang is alive. I hope Your Majesty can overcome your private feelings and do what is right.

EMPEROR [*greatly alarmed*]: How can they even suggest such a thing! [LADY YANG *clutches* EMPEROR'S *gown in terror*] General,

[*Sings*]

Even if Yang Guo-zhong owed
    atonement for his crimes,
already he has been seized and killed.
But the Consort spent her time with me
    deep within the palace—
why should she
    stir the army's mistrust?

CHEN: Your Majesty is clearly right, but the soldiers are in a fury, and I don't
see what we can do about it.

EMPEROR [*sings*]:

Come, sir,
make sure at once they understand
such a wild demand
    is not their place! [*More shouting within*]

CHEN [*sings*]:

Your Majesty,
    hear the uproar in the ranks!—
how can I restrain their rage?

LADY YANG [*weeping, sings*]:

Your Majesty,
I am shocked and stunned
    by outcomes unforeseen;
already distressed that my uncle was slain,
I too find my fortunes turned.
Former lifetimes fix our fate;
forfeit is my own life now.
I pray my Lord surrender me up at once—
though to say so breaks my heart . . .

EMPEROR: No more such talk, my Lady! [*More shouting within*]

SOLDIERS [*within*]: Unless Lady Yang is killed, we absolutely refuse to escort
the Emperor!

CHEN: Your Majesty, even though Lady Yang has done nothing wrong, Yang
Guo-zhong was her blood uncle. The soldiers around Your Majesty are
not going to feel safe while she lives. If the soldiers feel safe, then Your
Majesty is safe. I beg you to give it some thought.

EMPEROR [*pondering, sings*]:

I ponder in silence,
my thoughts in confusion.

LADY YANG [*weeps; clutching* EMPEROR'*s robes, sings*]:

It hurts so—
    how can I let you go!

TOGETHER [*sing*]:

Poor ducks, mated pair,
tossed by winds and waves of storm,
caught in its cruel tyranny. [*More shouting within*]

LADY YANG [*weeping, sings*]: The soldiers make my heart leap in alarm,
EMPEROR [*lost in thought, suddenly embraces* LADY YANG *weeping, sings*]:
My Lady,
I simply cannot bear this.

Enter SOLDIERS *shouting. They circle stage and surround the station.*

GAO: Your Majesty, soldiers outside have surrounded the station pavilion.
If we hesitate further, they may get even more violent. What will we do?
EMPEROR: Chen Yuan-li, go out there immediately and calm the army. I will
find a way.
CHEN: As you command. [*Exit*]

EMPEROR *and* LADY YANG *embrace, weeping.*

LADY YANG [*sings*]:
The trembling soul takes flight,
tears in crossing tracks are shed.
EMPEROR [*sings*]:
In all my sovereign might,
less joy have I than he who wed
Mourn-No-More.[5]
TOGETHER [*weeping, sings*]:
How can love conjoined with right
be instantly cast aside?
LADY YANG [*kneeling*]: I have enjoyed so much love from Your Majesty that
even my death cannot repay it. In this present crisis I hope you will per-
mit me to end my life in order to pacify the army. If Your Majesty can
make it safely to Shu, then I am content to die.

[*Sings*]

I see no other way to quell the army's fury,
so gladly will I end my life,
gladly will I end my life. [*Weeping, she buries her head in his
bosom*]
EMPEROR: How can you say such a thing? If you sacrifice your life, what
would I care about the honors of my great palaces or the wealth of all
the world? Let the empire be destroyed and my family die, I refuse to
abandon you.

[*Sings*]

Let them howl,
I will feign to be deaf and blind—
the wrong was entirely mine.

---

[5]That is, the Emperor is less fortunate than commoners who get to live to old age with their spouses.
The lines allude to the last couplet of a poem by Li Shang-yin on "Ma-wei": "How is it that having
been for four decades Son of Heaven/is less than the Lu's home, which has Mourn-No-More."

> Here blooms a flower of such grace
> I cannot bear to see it felled
> by tempests and to say
>   our last farewell
> at the very edge of sky.
> And if still they thwart my will,
> to the brown sand let me fall
>   in your place.

LADY YANG: However deep Your Majesty's love may be, when things have reached this point, there is no way to save my life. If you persist in trying to hold on to me, then the good will be destroyed with the bad, and the wrongs for which I am responsible will be multiplied. I beg Your Majesty to give me up in order to preserve the imperial house.

GAO [*kneeling, wiping away tears*]: Since my Lady has shown herself so heroic in her willingness to sacrifice her life, I hope Your Majesty will accept your responsibility to the state and try to set aside your love. [*More shouting within*]

EMPEROR [*weeping, stamps his foot*]: All right then. Since Lady Yang is so determined, I cannot compel her. Gao Li-shi, just . . . just let my Lady do as she will. [*Covers his face and exit, sobbing*]

LADY YANG [*making ceremonial bow*]: Long live the Emperor! [*Collapses in tears*]

GAO [*addressing* SOLDIERS *within*]: Soldiers, listen! His Imperial Majesty has given instructions that Lady Yang is to end her life.

SOLDIERS [*shouting within*]: Long live the Emperor! Long live the Emperor! Long live the Emperor!

GAO [*helping* LADY YANG *to her feet*]: My Lady, please come back here with me. [*Helps her along*]

LADY YANG [*weeping, sings*]:
> A lifetime of separation
>   can happen in a moment,
> the fairest face of all the age
>   is dying for her lord. [*They reach a chapel*]

GAO: Here is the Buddhist chapel.

LADY YANG [*going in*]: Stop a while and let me say a prayer to the Buddha. [*Bows*] Lord Buddha, think on Yang Yu-huan, [*sings*]
> deep in sin,
> deep in sin,
> yet I hope that Buddha will redeem me.

GAO: My Lady, may you be reborn in Heaven.

LADY YANG *rises, weeping;* GAO LI-SHI *kneels, weeping.*

My Lady, are there any words you want to charge me with?

LADY YANG: Gao Li-shi, the Emperor is getting on in years, and after I die, you will be the only old friend he has left who can divine what is on his mind, and you must take care to serve him. And expostulate with him on my behalf not to think of me any more.

GAO [*weeping*]: I understand.

LADY YANG: Gao Li-shi, there's one more thing. [*Takes out hairpin and box*] This two-branched hairpin and inlaid box were given me by the Emperor as tokens of his love. Bring them with you and bury them with me—make sure you don't forget!

GAO [*receiving hairpin and box*]: I understand.

LADY YANG [*weeping, sings*]:
> The heartbreak and the pain
> and bitterness beyond all words!

Enter CHEN YUAN-LI, *pushing his way in at the head of his troops.*

CHEN: Since you have, Lady, been instructed to die, what are you waiting for, delaying His Majesty's journey?

SOLDIERS *advance, shouting.*

GAO [*blocking their advance*]: You soldiers can't come in here. My Lady Yang is this very moment going to return to Heaven.

LADY YANG: Chen Yuan-li, Chen Yuan-li . . . [*sings*]
> You did not use the weight of command
>   against the mutineers—
> instead you force me to take my life.

GAO: Oh no! The soldiers are pushing their way in!

LADY YANG [*looks around*]: All right! All right! This pear tree will be the spot where Yang Yu-huan meets her end. [*Takes a white silk sash from around her waist and bows*] I, Yang Yu-huan, reverently thank His Majesty for his love, and I will never see him again from this time forward.

GAO LI-SHI *sheds tears, and* LADY YANG, *weeping,*
puts the noose around her neck.

LADY YANG: My Lord!
> Death now ends my fated span,
>   to Yellow Springs I descend,
> yet beside the king's yellow banners
>   my soul will remain.

She hangs herself.

CHEN: The Consort Yang is dead. Soldiers, withdraw at once!
[*Exeunt* SOLDIERS]

GAO [*weeping*]: Oh, my Lady! [*Exit*]

Enter EMPEROR.

EMPEROR [*recites*]:
> "The six-fold army would not set forth,
>   nothing could be done,

and the fragile arch of her lovely brows
    died there before the horses."
GAO [*entering with white silk sash*]: Your Majesty, I am here to inform you
    that Lady Yang has returned to Heaven. [EMPEROR *has a numb expression and doesn't answer;* GAO LI-SHI *repeats*] Lady Yang has returned to Heaven, and this is the white silk sash with which she hung herself.
EMPEROR [*looking at sash, beside himself with weeping*]: My Consort, my
    Consort! Grief will drive me to my death!

        Falls down; GAO LI-SHI *lifts him up.*

EMPEROR [*sings*]:
    Her features were once like the peach in bloom,
    like the peach in bloom,
GAO [*sings*]:
    her life ends this morning with pear flowers,
    with pear flowers.

[*Takes out hairpin and box*] My Lady charged me to have this golden hairpin
    and inlaid box buried with her.

EMPEROR [*weeping, looks at the hairpin and box, sings*]:
    This hairpin and this box,
    were the seeds of our ruin.
    In the Palace of Lasting Life
    we shared mutual joy;
    at Ma-wei Station
    all joys are gone.
GAO: How are we going to prepare her for burial properly in all this con-
    fusion?
EMPEROR: Never mind. Wrap her body in a brocade for the time being. Make
    careful note where you bury her so that we can rebury her later with
    proper ceremony. Attach the hairpin and the box to my Lady's clothes.
GAO: As you command. [*Exit*]
EMPEROR [*weeping, sings*]:
    Warm fragrance, voluptuous jade,
        pass away in an instant,
    in this life I will see her no more

        Enter CHEN YUAN-LI *and kneels.*

CHEN: Would Your Majesty make ready to set out?
EMPEROR [*stamping his foot in anger, sings*]:
    What does it matter whether I go west or not?

Shouting within. Orders are given. Enter troops. Enter GAO LI-SHI, *who leads*
    EMPEROR *to horse and helps him mount.*

TOGETHER [*sing*]:
    A long stretch of sky, patches of fog,

cold winds rattle the pennons and banners.
Slowly we make the long journey,
the troops of guards are foul with dust.
Who would have guessed that ruler and ruled
would share such peril?
Everywhere hated rebels pillage,
and beacon fires continue—
when will we get to slay
    those tigers and jackals?
We gaze toward the sharp tips
    of Shu's mountains afar,
then peer back toward the palace towers,
through several spots of drifting clouds,
though close by, Chang-an
    is hidden,
Chang-an is hidden.

In the west the royal regalia brushed
    Shu's clouds in their flight, [Zhang He]
Heaven and Earth were thick with dust,
    the vessels of state, in peril. [Wu Rong]
Her cicada wing tresses did not follow
    the royal carriage away, [Gao Bing]
only ducks and egrets, startled to flight,
    go instantly, one with another. [Qian Qi]

GIFT OF A MEAL (XXVI)

Enter EMPEROR *with* GAO LI-SHI.

EMPEROR [*sings*]:
    Troubled lovely brows too lightly lost,
    my nightlong grief assumes a thousand shapes.
    Too listless to crack my golden whip
        in early morn,
    now, past noon, I have not tasted
        a single precious grain.

I journeyed westward in headlong flight, and yesterday at Ma-wei Station the army refused to go on. I had no choice but to let Lady Yang die. [*Weeps*] I have reigned as Son of Heaven for nothing and now at last have become one of the most hard-hearted men of all time. I've forced myself to journey on another stage and now have come into the territory of Fu-feng. I am having the retinue stop at Feng-yi Palace because I have to rest a moment.

Enter GUO CONG-JIN, *an old peasant, bringing a dish of cooked barley.*

GUO [*recites*]:
>Sunning my back, I may
>>meet the Son of Heaven,
>from this gift of garden vegetables
>>know a man from the countryside.[6]

I am Guo Cong-jin, an old fellow who lives in the countryside around Fu-feng. I heard that the Emperor was on his way west and had stopped a while at Feng-yi Palace, so I cooked him up a bowl of barley and have brought it to give to him as a mark of my respect. [*Greets* GAO LI-SHI] Your Honor, would you be so good as to announce that Guo Cong-jin from the countryside has brought a meal.

GAO LI-SHI *announces him.*

EMPEROR: Have him come forward.

GUO [*coming closer and greeting* EMPEROR]: Guo Cong-jin, a commoner, greets Your Majesty.

EMPEROR: Where are you from?

GUO [*sings*]:
>In Fu-feng born and bred,
>I worked the land till hair grew white,
>feeling blessed that times were good.
>I heard of a sudden rebellion
>from which the royal cortege roamed,
>and I felt infinite alarm.
>I brought this bowl of barley
>and came, bowed with humility,
>>to bannered gates
>>>to set it before Your Majesty.
>I pray, my Lord, do not despise
>>fare so coarse—
>sustenance from a peasant.

EMPEROR: I am grateful to you. Gao Li-shi, bring it here.

GAO *takes the food and brings it to the* EMPEROR, *who looks at it.*

EMPEROR: I have dwelled retired, deep in the palace, and have never once tasted this.

[*Sings*]

>It was my wont
>to be served at table by royal cooks;
>dainty confections like gold and jade
>filled a square yard before my plate,
>the rarest morsels of every taste—
>yet I would dismiss them as flavored ineptly.

---

[6]This alludes to the proverbial story of the common man who felt so comfortable sunning his back that he went to tell the emperor, so that he could enjoy it as well.

Never would I have dreamed that today I would be satisfying my hunger with something like this.

[*Sings*]

So drab,
barley mixed with bran—
how can I get it down my throat?

Eats a little, then sets it aside.

How like it was for the Prince of Xiao
lost by the Hu-tuo River!⁷

GUO: Do you know who is responsible for our present troubles?

EMPEROR: Who would you say is responsible?

GUO: If you will pardon any offense it might give, I'll risk telling you straight out.

EMPEROR: Speak freely.

GUO: Yang Guo-zhong is responsible.

[*Sings*]

The man ran rampant,
taking advantage of kinship's ties,
hungry for power, receiving bribes,
his poison spread throughout the world.
He feuded a decade with An Lu-shan,
till finally armed troops
    rose up in Yu-yang.

EMPEROR: I had no idea that Yang Guo-zhong had started a feud or that An Lu-shan was plotting rebellion.

GUO [*sings*]:

Many a day had An Lu-shan
hidden treason in his heart,
and all in the whole world knew
    the shape of his treachery.

Last year someone sent a letter to the throne giving Your Majesty evidence of An Lu-shan's treachery, but Your Majesty had the man put to death.

[*Sings*]

Thereafter who would willingly face
    the headsman's ax
to state the case to the throne?

---

⁷The "Prince of Xiao" was the emperor Guang-wu, who restored the Han Dynasty in A.D. 25. Earlier he had once been in desperate straits by the Hu-tuo River and had been sent food by a sympathetic officer.

EMPEROR [*with a bitter expression*]: Then it was my own blindness that brought us to this.

[*Sings*]

Thinking it over
with clear sight and sharp mind
a prince must always watch closely.

I recall when Yao Chong and Song Jing were my ministers.

[*Sings*]

They would always come with honest words,
and the mood of the folk, though far away,
seemed right there in the hall with me.

But somehow after Yao Chong and Song Jing died, the officials that filled the court all tended to be greedy for position and trying to win my favor. Guo Cong-jin:

[*Sings*]

It turns out none could compare to you,
loyal here in the countryside,
pointing out to me
     the treacherous frontier soldier,
     the unscrupulous minister.

GUO: But then if Your Majesty had not been brought to come here, how could someone like myself have ever gotten to meet you face to face?

EMPEROR [*sings*]:

And now you have made me eat
     repentance's bitter fruit—
        though too late—
and anger fills a hungry stomach.

GUO: Your Majesty should rest now a while. I will take my leave now. [*Sighs and recites*]

Even if a thousand stalks of snow
     fill my head with white,
none can burn a loyal heart
     into an inch of ash. [*Exit*]

Enter COURIER, *with two attendants carrying multicolored silks.*

COURIER [*sings*]:

Over paths for birds and twisting sheepgut trails
I bring spring silks on the long post road.
Often did chains of hills resound
     with the riders' bells
that drew us daily nearer
     the Emperor's city.

I am a courier on the Cheng-du Circuit, and acting under the command of the military governor, I am bringing one hundred thousand bolts of bright spring silk to the capital. When I heard that His Majesty had come to Fu-feng, I came here to present them. [*to* GAO LI-SHI] Would you be so good as to announce to His Majesty that the Cheng-du courier has arrived with the annual tribute of spring silks.

GAO LI-SHI *approaches* EMPEROR *and informs him.*

EMPEROR: Count the silk and accept the shipment, then send the courier back.

The two attendants come forward with silks, then exeunt with COURIER.

EMPEROR: Assemble my officers and troops. I have something to say to them directly.

GAO: His Majesty summons the officers and troops of the Long-wu Guard to hear his instructions.

Enter GUARDS.

GUARDS [*recite*]:
> We rise at dawn to the sound of kettledrums
> and sleep at night clinging to saddles.

The officers and troops of the Long-wu Guard humbly greet Your Majesty.

EMPEROR: Heed what I have to say.

[Sings]

> Upheaval has brought things unforeseen—
> we flee from the fighting afar
>   and fare through unfamiliar lands.
> In our frantic exodus you toiled
>   to come with my retinue,
> But today
>   I've pondered a better course for you.

GUARDS: What are Your Majesty's instructions?

EMPEROR [*sings*]:
> Men on campaign think back on home,
> men on campaign think back on home,
> and the roads to Shu are like climbing sky.
> I cannot bear to embroil you
> and make you too lightly forsake
>   fathers and mothers, children and wives.

Therefore I will make my own way very slowly to Cheng-du, accompanied by the court officers and the young princes of the blood. Today each of you may return to your own home.

[*Sings*]

You may cease to venture further on this course,
   toiling on in hunger and cold.

Gao Li-shi, take the spring silks that the courier brought me and divide them among the officers and troops as payment for the costs they have incurred on the journey.

[*Sings*]

Unable to give the army its wages,
   I portion out this silk
   to serve as your pay.

GUARDS: Your Majesty's instructions cut us to the very quick. Armies have always been fed for a thousand days so that they may be used for a single morning.

[*Sing*]

Unable to wipe out those tigers and jackals,
   unable to wipe out those tigers and jackals,
   your fierce commanders feel helpless shame.
   We want to go with you, even to death,
   our battle cries for vigor depend
      on imperial majesty.

We dare not accept these spring silks. [*Sing*]
   Keep them until some future time
      when rewards are due for deeds,
   and may High Heaven look closely to see
   any heart's perfidy—
   we will never fail you.

EMPEROR: However deep your sense of loyalty may be, something in my heart cannot bear having you accompany me, so you must go back.

GUARDS: Is it that you distrust us on account of Lady Yang's death?

EMPEROR: No, [*sings*]
   But old folks in Chang-an
      are left in suspense—
   go back now,
   and tell them their Emperor
      has come to no harm.

GUARDS: Don't say such things, Your Majesty. We want to go with you. We swear our undivided loyalty.

EMPEROR and GUARDS [*sing*]:
   When the pall of evil is swept away,
   we will turn back together
      to the royal domain.

EMPEROR: It's grown dark. We'll make camp here for tonight and set out early tomorrow.

GUARDS: Yes, sir!

> Sandstorms fly for thousands of miles,
> war drums moan, [Qian Qi]

GAO:

> and the setting sun sinks under,
> lower into the hills. [Luo Bin-wang]

EMPEROR:

> The pain and remorse I feel today
> does no good at all, [Wei Zhuang]

GAO:

> yet they cannot bear that his carriage wheels
> head westward all alone. [Zhou Xian]

In the intervening scene, Lady Yang appears as a ghost trying to catch up with the Emperor, but she is tossed about by the wind. There she witnesses demons from the underworld dragging away Lady Guo and Yang Guo-zhong. Returning to Ma-wei Station, Lady Yang is given the protection of the local god, who informs her that she is an immortal banished to Earth and will not be carried off to the underworld.

DENOUNCING THE REBEL (XXVIII)

Enter LEI HAI-QING, *carrying his mandolin.*

LEI [*recites*]:

> Civil servants and generals, all
> former officers of the crown—
> I hate their two-faced treachery,
> serving this upstart court.
> In the Pear Garden Academy
> some constancy remains:
> musicians will not shamelessly cling
> to that slender thread of life.

I am Lei Hai-qing, and I enjoyed the kindness of our Tian-bao Emperor, waiting at his service in the Pear Garden Academy. Then An Lu-shan unexpectedly rebelled, taking Chang-an; the Emperor went west to Sichuan. The civil and military officials who filled his court used to enjoy high positions and rich salaries, passing privilege on to their children and gaining fiefs for their wives; they enjoyed that splendor and became rich and noble—and each item of that came from the kindness of the court. But now every single one of them is hungry to stay alive and fears death. They turn their backs on what is right and forget what kindnesses they received, rushing in an unbroken stream to submit to their new ruler. They think only of their security and pleasures in the present moment and pay

no heed to the disgrace of their names for all time. It makes one feel
ashamed and angry! Even though I am only a musician, I could never do
anything so shamefully self-serving.

Today, An Lu-shan and all his renegades are holding a great banquet
by the Pool of Frozen Sapphire, and the Pear Garden Academy has been
given instructions to perform for him. I'll take this opportunity to get
close to him, and then I'll denounce him roundly and show this fury I
feel. Then I won't care if they tear me to pieces. So I'll be going now with
my mandolin in arm.

[*Sings*]

Even though we
are but musicians of low degree,
rough-hewn, ignorant, and naïve,
though we never studied or advised,
never passed the examinations
never stood high in the courtiers' ranks,
still in the temper of our blood
and in our breast
there is some conviction of the right
    and a sense of loyalty.
Beholding now the ruin wreaked,
and living through hardship and peril,
meeting sad alterations in these times,
I cannot help grinding my teeth in pain,
my voice stifled, my hate restrained.

And how I hate!—
that putrid backwoods general,
    reeking slime, an ooze
        upon the dragon throne,
a warty toad with wild fancies
    to dine upon the goose,[8]
he actually forced our prince to flee
    southward across the horizon.
Are such outrages to be borne?
Even if
I ate his flesh and slept on his skin,
    this hate wouldn't be scraped away.
And who would have thought that those witless,
    crooked-hearted, treacherous,
        renegade dogs
whose used to flap their mouths
    prating Devotion and Loyalty,

---

[8]This was a proverb for reaching above one's station.

would at peril's point sell out
    from lust for wealth and honor?—
They soon came wagging their tails as one,
    receiving new positions,
and show their ruler's worst enemy
    deep gratitude for favor shown.
Are your false faces capable of shame?

I haven't seen a single person dare
act as faithful subject of the throne.
Now, Lei Hai-qing,
if I don't take this weight upon me,
for nothing am I flesh and blood.
If I hold unfailingly to right
and keep from dishonor's stain,
I would willingly die and die again. [*Exit*]

Enter AN LU-SHAN *with* TWO SOLDIERS.

AN [*sings*]:
    I have seized control of these rivers and hills
        and named my dynasty the Yan,
    my gown is dyed royal yellow,
    on my head is the sky-touching crown.
    And now in cool fall at Frozen Sapphire
    my little troupes of the Pear Garden
    for a splendid feast will dance and sing.

Once I raised the standards of rebellion at Fan-yang, no one stood in my way, and I made a long drive to the west, all the way to Chang-an. The Tang Emperor fled to Shu, and all his splendid mountains and rivers have fallen into my hands. [*Laughs*] It's wonderful! Today I'm bringing together all my officials at Frozen Sapphire Pool to hold a feast in celebration of an age of peace and have a good time. Attendants—have all my officials arrived on time?

SOLDIER: They are all awaiting your pleasure in the outer gallery.

AN: Let them know that they may come in.

SOLDIER: As Your Majesty commands. [*Makes announcement*] His Highness announces that all the officials may enter.

Enter four turncoat OFFICIALS.

OFFICIALS [*recite*]:
    Today we have a new Emperor,
    who used to be a minister back then.
    We simply see that times have changed—
    it's not that we're ingrates and traitors. [*They greet* AN]

May Your Majesty live ten thousand years! Long live Your Majesty!

AN: Be at ease. I am taking the day off today from my official duties and holding a special feast at Frozen Sapphire Pool to celebrate an age of peace with you.

OFFICIALS: Long live Your Majesty!

SOLDIER: The feast is ready. If Your Majesty pleases, we may go now.

Music is played within. The four turncoat OFFICIALS *kneel and offer wine.*

AN [*sings*]:

> Beside this sapphire pool the dragon sports,
> and colored clouds draw back to show
> the fresh and lucent autumn weather.
> Roaming through these purple halls,
> I rest my riding crop a while.
> I hold a feast
> and scarlet-gowned minions scurry,
> phoenix blades slice fine,
> rolling up brocade sleeves,
> streak-patterned plates are proffered full.

OFFICIALS *offer wine and bow.*

> By this jasper pool
> warrior generals like bears,
>   civil officers like herons
> bow as they pass fountains of wine.

Attendants, call in the Pear Garden musicians to perform.

SOLDIER: As Your Majesty commands. [*Facing within*] His Highness commands the Pear Garden musicians to perform for him. [*Music from within*]

AN [*sings*]:

> At my feast
> the musicians play "Balance of Heaven."
> And "Rainbow Skirts" of days gone by
> again is sung,
> half rising into clouds,
> half blowing down along the wind.
> Sounds rarely heard—
> apart from pure precincts of the moon,
> only in the garden of Aloes Pavilion.
> Today this music, tones of the gods,
> is played no longer during the Tang.

A fine performance!

OFFICIALS: We feel that Your Majesty truly enjoys good fortune equal to Heaven, for the Tian-bao Emperor of Tang spent no one knows how much energy in having them learn this piece of music perfectly, and now he has left it to Your Majesty to enjoy.

AN [*laughing*]: There is something in what you say. More wine!

SOLDIERS *bring wine.* LEI HAI-QING *weeps within and sings.*

LEI:

Kettledrums crashed in You-zhou,
thousands of households lie in weeds,
with smoke of beacon fires in wilds
    on every side.
Leaves fall in deserted palaces,
when suddenly one shocked to hear
    this song played!
The strangest of transformations,
truly Heaven and Earth are overturned,
truly men grieve and spirits rage.

[*Weeps loudly*] O my Emperor!

when again will you hold your court
with golden bells and officials all
    bowing amid the dance?

AN: Who's that weeping? How strange!

SOLDIER: It's the musician Lei Hai-qing.

AN: Bring him in here. [SOLDIERS *drag* LEI HAI-QING *before* AN] Lei Hai-qing, this is terrible—I'm holding a feast to celebrate an age of peace, and for some reason you dare to weep.

LEI [*denouncing him*]: An Lu-shan, you are only a failed frontier general whose losses made you deserve beheading. Spared by imperial mercy, you were made general and prince. But instead of doing your best to repay the throne, you dared to raise your troops and start a rebellion, polluting this holy city and driving our Emperor into flight. By this crime your evil has reached its full measure, and in no time at all imperial troops will come to destroy you—so what's this about a "banquet for an age of peace"!

AN [*in a rage*]: How dare you! Now that I have ascended the throne, all the officials have sworn obedience to me. How can a musician of such little account as yourself dare act so insolently! Soldiers, draw your swords and watch him.

SOLDIERS *draw their swords.* LEI *points at* AN LU-SHAN *and denounces him.*

LEI [*sings*]:

I curse such utter treachery,
heart of beast, false face of man,
body's hairs bristle in rage.
Though I am a musician, of low degree,
I am not like these shameless officials.

An Lu-shan,

you have stolen the sacred throne,
and disobeyed Heaven above;
soon your corpse will be streaked with blood.

Throws his mandolin at AN.

I throw my mandolin
to crush a renegade's head
    and avenge the Emperor of the Kai-yuan.

SOLDIERS *seize the mandolin.*

AN: Take this man away immediately and kill him. [*Exit soldiers, carrying*
LEI HAI-QING *away to execution*] This is infuriating!
OFFICIALS: Calm your anger, Your Majesty. Why care about an ignorant musician?
AN: I'm not in a good mood any more. You may leave me now.
OFFICIALS: As you command. We will see Your Majesty off back to the
    palace. [*They kneel*]
AN [*recites*]:
    When with wine one meets good friends,
        a thousand cups are too few;
    when talking at cross-purposes,
        a half a line is too much. [*Exit in fury*]
OFFICIALS [*rising*]: He deserved to die. Imagine, a musician thinking to act the part
    of a loyal official! Could it be that we here at the feast have been humiliated?

[*Sing*]

Everyone dresses himself for his role,
and what is a "loyal official" worth?
And, Lei Hai-qing,
    since you never wore an official's black cap,
        you were short on savvy.

[*Recite*]

The blood that has flowed in the land of Qin
    has become a river, [Luo Yin]
whether a slave or whether a king
    is the outcome of chance. [Li Shan-fu]
What person in this world will pity
    those who suffer for principle?— [Lu Xi-sheng]
all one should do is make merry
    and never turn back. [Xue Ji]

BELLS (XXIX)

GAO LI-SHI [*shouting from within*]: Hurry forward, soldiers. Wait for us up
    ahead. [*Gongs ring within*] Please mount up, Your Majesty.

Enter EMPEROR *on horseback, with* GAO LI-SHI *following.*

EMPEROR [*sings*]:
    I journey on these thousands of miles,

my heart grown heavy on the road.
See where the clouds and hills form tiers
in tangled twists like the grief I feel.
A limitless expanse of leafless trees
 echoes with autumn sounds,
and in long skies a lone wild goose
  joins with these its melancholy cries.

Since leaving Ma-wei Station I have tasted my fill of bitterness. The other day I sent a courier with the imperial seal and an investiture tablet, by which I abdicate in favor of the Crown Prince. We have traveled a month, and now draw close to Shu. And I can take some joy in gradually getting farther from the rebel armies so that we can go forward at a more leisurely pace. But whenever I come upon the birds singing and falling flowers or blue waters and green hills, they never fail to encourage sad thoughts, so lovely are they!

GAO: Your Majesty, you are already thoroughly worn out by the rigors of the journey. I beg you to banish such thoughts and not bring upon yourself such excess of pain.

EMPEROR: Oh Gao Li-shi, Lady Yang and I sat side by side at table and walked shoulder to shoulder. And now in the panic of my flight westward, I sent her to such a terrible end—how am I going to get her out of my mind? [*Weeps and sings*]

This brings up things that pain the heart,
tears seem to pour from my eyes.
When I look back to Ma-wei slope,
a bitterness unbidden swells my breast.

GAO: There is a plank walkway on the mountains ahead. Would Your Majesty please take a firm grip on the reins and proceed very slowly?

EMPEROR [*sings*]:

Flags and banners fluttering,
the dying sunlight at their backs
their shadows waving in the wind.
The horses on these rugged roads
 never stop a moment.
Only somber clouds and darkening skies,
the gibbons' sad cries
 that tear at the heart,
the nightjar shrieking bloody tears,
terrible to hear—
so utterly disheartening,
so utterly disheartening.
Behold a desolation:
the foot of E-mei Mountain
 where few men pass,
cold rains, wind-driven, greet me,
 and strike me in the face.

GAO: It's raining. Would Your Majesty be so good as to come up to Sword Tower to get out of the rain?

> EMPEROR *dismounts, climbs the tower, and seats himself.*

GAO [*addressing* SOLDIERS *within*]: We're going to stop here a while, men. We'll set off again as soon as the rain stops. [SOLDIERS *respond from within*]

EMPEROR [*recites*]:

> I climbed a high place all alone,
>   my mood grew still more pained,
> hills of Shu, Shu's waters,
>   I hate such magnitudes.
> I know not whence or why the wind
>   comes blowing on the rain
> whose every drop is one more note
>   splashing on the heart.

[*Sound of bells within*] Listen to those sounds from way over there, never ceasing. They can drive a person mad with their din. Gao Li-shi, see what they are.

GAO: It's just the sound of the rain in the forest joined with the bell chimes hanging from the eaves that echo in the wind.

EMPEROR: Ay! These bells make such a lovely sound!

> [*Sings*]

> Clinking, tinkling,
> they fill the air with tingling chill,
>   the heart leaps in alarm.
> I listen to them far away,
>   beyond the trees, beyond the hill,
> their sounds at war within the storm,
> echoing high, ringing low.
> Each drop that falls is one more note,
> each drop that falls is one more note,
> splattering the blood-streaked tears
>   of a melancholy man.
> This wounding scene before me brings
> recollection of her leaf-strewn grave.
> White poplars whistle in the wind,
>   the rain gusts violently—
> these moments when her lonely soul
>   feels solitude and chill.
> Cold is the light from ghost-fires,
> a riot of fireflies in soggy grass.
> I repent betraying you in panic,
>   betraying you.

I am left alone in this mortal world
and truly lack desire to live.
And this I say to that woman most fair:
I will join you later or sooner,
    companion in that dark world below.
I am stricken by stillness of empty hills,
where bell sounds answer each other,
the plankway up is steep and rough,
like these writhing coils within,
    and a pain that never levels out.

GAO: Don't torture yourself, Your Majesty. The rain has stopped now. Please come down and we'll be off. [EMPEROR *descends from the tower and mounts his horse.* GAO LI-SHI *goes within*] Forward, men! [GAO LI-SHI *follows* EMPEROR]

EMPEROR [*sings*]:
The road ahead goes on and on,
    my sorrow undepleted,
calling her soul to return,
    leaving my capital,
        both of these haunt the heart.

TOGETHER:
After the rain the mountain spires
    are thousands of specks of green
        beyond which I cannot see.

EMPEROR:
Unbroken ranges at Sword Tower
    color a thousand miles, [Luo Bin-wang]
here someone cut from one he loves
    doubles the grief he feels. [Luo Ye]
The royal carriage fruitlessly struggles
    against the rain and mire, [Qin Tao-yu]
bells in the downpour, a melody,
    several lines of tears. [Du Mu]

In the scene that follows, Lady Yang's ghost appears, reflecting on her past life and expressing remorse for the wrongs she has done. The local god overhears her and gives her a permit allowing her to wander in the vicinity of Ma-wei Station.

In the next scene, we see Guo Zi-yi defeating An Lu-shan's generals. The scene then shifts back to Cheng-du, where the Emperor, having abdicated in favor of the Crown Prince, has learned of the defeat of An Lu-shan's army. The Emperor has ordered that a statue of Lady Yang be made; when the statue is brought in, he laments before it. The local god of Ma-wei Station reports to the Weaver Star that Lady Yang has repented of the wrongs she had committed while alive, and the Weaver Star says that she can now be forgiven. The local god goes on to say that Lady Yang still clings fast to her love for the Emperor. The scenes that follow treat the assassination of An Lu-shan by one of his adopted sons and Guo Zi-yi's recapture of the capital.

STOCKING-VIEWING (XXXVI)

Enter GRANNY WANG, *an old tavern keeper.*

GRANNY WANG [*sings*]:
>This spot on the slope
>>at Ma-wei Station,
>was an unfrequented location—
>but then I found Lady Yang's
>>stocking of brocade.
>When I opened shop and resumed my trade
>>selling beer,
>travelers going both ways
>>all stop here.
>Now free from worries
>I spend my days.

For a long time I've made my living keeping a rundown tavern here on Ma-wei Slope. When An Lu-shan rose in rebellion, the whole populace fled. At the time I went into the Buddhist chapel within the precincts of the station and saw a single brocade stocking beneath a pear tree, something left by Lady Yang. I kept it, and to my great surprise it has turned out to be a treasure. Now that Marshal Guo Zi-yi has smashed the rebels and retaken the capital, peace has returned; and I run my tavern here as I used to. But, hearing that I have this brocade stocking, people near and far come to drink in my tavern and ask to see the stocking. In addition to the cost of the wine I charge extra for looking at the stocking, so that my life has grown quite prosperous. [*Laughs*] This has been a real stroke of luck. This morning I am going to set up the tavern, for I expect customers will be on their way. [*Exit*]

Enter LI MO, *dressed as a scholar.*

LI MO [*sings*]:
>The royal carriage headed west,
>and left a depth of bitterness
>>forever in this ancient station.
>I am touched by his last farewell
>>to a face so fair,
>like Green Barrow's desolation
>>where Zhao-jun lies buried on the steppes,[9]
>or Purple Jade, Fu-cha's hapless daughter,
>>dying untimely, then melting away.[1]

---

[9]Wang Zhao-jun, a beautiful court lady, unrecognized by the Han emperor because she was misrepresented by a spiteful court painter, was sent off to Central Asia to cement a marriage alliance with the Khan. Her tomb, a spot of greenery in the steppes, was known as Green Barrow.
[1]Purple Jade was the daughter of Fu-cha, the King of Wu. She died of her hopeless passion for Han Zhong, who later saw her beside her tomb, at which she melted away like mist.

I couldn't get out of the capital before because troops were blocking the roads; but now I am glad to see that peace is returning. I've heard that in Granny Wang's tavern by Ma-wei Slope there is one of Lady Yang's brocade stockings, and I'm going there to ask her to let me look at it. Hey, there's a Daoist nun coming along.

Enter NUN.

NUN [*recites*]:
> Epochal changes fill my eyes,
>   for all I wipe back tears,
> only a brocade stocking remains
>   offered for people to see. [*Greets* LI MO]

LI MO: Where are you from, sister?

NUN: I am the abbess of the Lodge of Maidenly Purity in Jin-ling. I had gone to the capital to seek scriptures, but because of the war I couldn't return. I recently learned that Granny Wang has one of Lady Yang's brocade stockings in her tavern, and I've come here to see it.

LI MO: So you've come to see the stocking, too. Why don't we go there together? [*They continue on*]

TOGETHER [*sing*]:
> Fair as jade, she is gone,
>   too far to find,
> yet the heart feels pain for a brocade rag
>   that remains in a rustic inn.
> Here we'll buy wine and slowly drink
> a while to closely study
>   what so draws curiosity.

LI MO: This is the place. Let's go right in. [*Both go in*]

GRANNY WANG [*greeting them*]: Please take a seat inside. [LI MO *and* NUN *are seated*]

Enter GUO CONG-JIN, *the old peasant.*

GUO: I'm so happy the fighting has stopped that I'm on my way to Mount Hua to make an offering. Passing by Ma-wei Slope just now, I feel worn out from walking. There's a tavern hereabouts, and I think I'll go drink a few cups. [*Enters*] Tavern keeper, bring me some beer.

GRANNY WANG: Here you are.

GUO [*greeting* LI MO *and* NUN]: Nice to meet you.

LI MO [*addressing* GRANNY WANG]: The first reason we came here was to have a drink, but the second was that we heard you have a brocade stocking that belonged to Lady Yang, and we wanted you to let us look at it.

GRANNY WANG [*laughing*]: Indeed, I do have such a brocade stocking, but . . .

[*Sings*]

> I guard this treasure most closely
> and keep it always well wrapped
>> and hidden away.
> I want its traces of scent not to fade,
> I want its powders and oils to stay
> and let no dirt stain it.
> A fascinating thing it is,
>> a thing to amaze;
> travelers wanting to see it
>> are eager to come here to drink.
> So if you don't mind spending a bit,
> I would gladly let you closely study
>> what so draws curiosity.

LI MO: This is as it should be. It's quite all right to be charged extra, apart from the cost of the wine.

GRANNY WANG: In that case let me go get it. [*She exits, then returns with stocking; recites*]

> Her jadelike toes are through wearing it,
>> it still bears traces of oils,
> even closely wrapped in scarf of gauze
>> you still can smell the scent.

Here is the brocade stocking, sir. Have a look.

LI MO [*taking it and unwrapping it, he looks at it with the* NUN]: Just look at the intricate workmanship of the pattern in the brocade! It's the highest quality. It still has its gloss, and its rare scent has not dissipated. This is truly something not of this mortal world.

NUN: What a wonderful scent! [GUO CONG-JING *keeps drinking and pays no attention*]

LI MO [*getting up with the stocking in hand, looking at it, sings*]:

> See the thin lining of scented cotton,
> supple and light as a cloud of the gods.
> In golden palaces long ago
> its tiny paces were seen by none.
> How sad that today at a bar
> it is displayed so casually
>> to the common eye.
> Traces of thread, needlemarks,
> each layer wounds the heart.
> Too bad that this loveliest lady ever,
>> who suffered the greatest wrong ever,
> left nothing but this relic, eternally fragrant,
>> to be passed on eternally.

GUO [*irritated*]: Damnit, sir, how come you are gawking at that? As I see it, the Tian-bao Emperor made a wreck of the dynasty because he so favored the Prized Consort, spending day and night with her in pleasure. The result was that war rose on all sides and the common folk were reduced to misery. Now as the years of my life are drawing to a close, to meet with such turmoil and upheaval! Seeing this brocade stocking today only makes me feel bitter.

[*Sings*]

I imagine back then when newly made
and with red lotuses tightly sewn
   it showed, touching the ground,
then hidden
   by six-paneled Xiang silk skirts,
and our Lord
   doted upon her every motion.
These heights of joy provoke
   the working of our ruin
and great harm wreaked on all the folk.
Today the matter's done, the person's gone,
this survives alone.
But no sooner do I glimpse the scented stocking toe
   than misery returns,
and recalling our calamity
   again I wipe back tears.

GRANNY WANG: Why does seeing this brocade stocking upset him so much? I'll bet he's not willing to pay the extra charge.

GUO: What extra charge?

GRANNY WANG: You're obviously an old peasant, understanding nothing about "viewing charges."

LI MO: You shouldn't argue about such trivial things. [*to* NUN] Sister, take a close look. [*to* GRANNY WANG] I'll pay the charges for everyone. [*Hands it on*]

NUN [*takes it, getting up to look at it*]: I think on Lady Yang, the loveliest face of the age, a life of love ended so abruptly. Even though the stocking survives today, such a beauty will not come again. Such a sad thing!

[*Sings*]

See these specks of azure, hooks of red,
leaves and flowers well wrought still.
That pair of gleaming feet is gone,
one stocking remains, one phoenix alone.
Emptiness all—
and in her fall and her abandonment,
   unending bitterness,
a dream that faded at Ma-wei.
Such beauty for which a kingdom fell

is but a mirage, no use at all.
Look not on these fraying threads
    and recall where once she walked,
but rather believe that all splendor
    is swept off with the winds of dawn.

[*Passes stocking back to* GRANNY WANG] I think that Lady Yang was actually a goddess who was reborn in the mortal world. I am going to ask you to donate this stocking to the Lodge of Maidenly Purity in Jin-ling, where we will revere it as a sacred relic of the gods. What do you say to that?

GRANNY WANG [*laughing*]: I'm old and have neither sons nor daughters. My livelihood for the rest of my life is entirely in this stocking. I really can't do as you suggest.

LI MO: What would you say if I offered you a good price for it?

GUO: Why would you want something that still stinks?

GRANNY WANG: I'm not going to sell it.

GUO [*paying his bill*]: Here, take the price for the beer.

LI MO [*paying his bill*]: Here is the charge for all of us looking at the stocking.

GRANNY WANG [*taking the money*]: Thank you very much.

[*Recites*]

Never tire of getting drunk
    in splendor of spring weather, [Bao Rong]

NUN:

how many kingfisher feathers and pearls
    have fallen to scented dust? [Lu Lun]

LI MO:

All that's left, half up the slope,
    this moon bending round, [Li Yi]

GUO:

the hubbub out in these meadows
    draws people who want to look. [Song Zhi-wen]

THE CORPSE RELEASED (XXXVII)

Enter LADY YANG *as a spirit.*

LADY YANG [*sings*]:
Swept along rippling in wind,
    a shadow that never stays,
but sighs, wondering
    where I will lodge on the road ahead?
The living are parted from the dead,
    endless space lies in between—

the man is not seen,
passion does not cease,
nor does bitterness pass.

[*Recites a lyric*]

Life's ultimate romance is done,
and pointless to repine
    at cruel destiny.
Yet how can I now grind away
    "love's" firm inscription,
that is the heart's inlay?
But now enjoy this moment's ease
this moment's ease—
none question the gift of the fading moon
    and early morning breeze.

I am the spirit of Yang Yu-huan. Since receiving a travel permit from the local god, I have let myself be carried by the wind from one place to another. And I'm glad that neither will Heaven take me in nor Earth take charge of me. Nothing ties me down, and I drift along in utter abandon. The only thing is that I can't find my way to the Emperor and meet him again. [*Looks sad*] I feel so miserable. I'll go along with the wind now and see where it takes me. [*She moves on and sings*]

My soul goes riding on the wind,
    as if I roamed in dream,
the road is sunk in shadow,
    I cannot tell apart
        daylight and dark.
Through wild woods I pass and briefly pause,
suddenly hearing the mournful cries
    of birds in the chilly haze—
they frighten me away,
    I cannot stay.
Blue phosphorescence drifts through tangled grass,
and I use it to light my way
    as I go on ahead in the dark.
What place is this,
where the corner of a great hall lies
    in shadowing layers of cloud?

[*She looks*] This is the main gate of the West Palace! Why don't I go in and take a look?

She starts to go in. Enter two Guardian Deities, *with faces painted black and white, metal armor, each holding tablet and whip. They take their positions on a spot above her.*

GUARDIAN DEITIES [*recite*]:
> While living, we were heroes,
>> we kept the world at peace,
> dead, we are the dread spirits
>> who guard the palace gate.

> [*They lift whips and tablets to block* LADY YANG]

Wherever you come from, ghost-woman, you cannot break your way in here!

LADY YANG [*taking out travel permit*]: I am Yang Yu-huan. Here is my travel permit.

GUARDIAN DEITIES: It's Lady Yang herself! Now that An Lu-shan has been assassinated and his son Qing-xu has fled, Guo Zi-yi has purged the palace precincts of their filth. The old Emperor is far away in Shu, and the new Emperor is still staying at Ling-wu. Therefore the great compound is silent and deserted, and the palace gates are all locked and barred. You are welcome to go in, my Lady. We deities will withdraw and leave you. [*Exeunt*]

LADY YANG [*entering*]: Look! [*recites*]
> The palace flowers are one and all
>> branches that break the heart,
> there is no one behind the curtains
>> that hang and touch the ground.
> I walk to where a painted screen
>> encloses a special spot—
> clearly I see the hairpin and box
>> at the moment he gave me his love.

She weeps. On the stage have been set her old bed and curtains, along with various objects.

> *Sings.*
> I linger here bewildered—
>> romance of bygone days. [*Sits on bed*]
> I recall when first he gave
>> the hairpin and the box,
> firmly planting this affection.
> We both to foolish love held fast. [*Rises*]
> But who would have guessed
>> with what haste
>>> grim fate would tear us apart?

Look there how desolate and deserted are Aloeswood Pavilion and Calyx Mansion! [*Climbs stairs*]
> No one climbs the painted tower,
> no flowers bloom in pairs,
> and no new ballads are performed—
> now all is bleakness everywhere,
>> engendering sorrow.

At such a melancholy scene
I can't help shedding tears.

This is the Palace of Lasting Life! It all comes back to me now . . . [*She weeps. On stage has been set the table with incense she used in praying for skill in the Palace of Lasting Life*] Over here was where I was that day . . .
 setting out incense, fruit, and melons to pray
  for skill that night,

 and over there is where
 we bowed toward Oxherd and Weaver,
  shoulder to shoulder, in secret prayer.

Oh, my Emperor! If only I could see you for a little while! But the guardian deities have just now told me that the Emperor is still in Shu. I'll slip back out of the palace gates and go to the Wei River Bridge to look west toward Sichuan. [*Walks and sings*]
 Into the clear fall scene I stare. [*Steps on bridge*]
 I gaze but cannot see
  E-Mei Mountain rising high
   in cold clouds and distant trees.
 Thoughts turn to the royal exile there,
 his body weary, his shadow alone.
 In sharp frosts his sickly horse
 stands on Cheng-du's Thousand-Mile Bridge—
 I wonder if he's well.
 But even if his health is good,
 I'm sure he's gaunt because of me.

I'll fly off to him! [*She begins to fly but is whirled around by the wind*] Oh Heaven!
 I thought this light and frail soul
  could fly away;
 but the journey grew farther and farther still,
  with a thousand streams and a million hills.

[*Looks around. A Buddhist shrine and pear tree are placed on stage*] There's a deserted Buddhist shrine all locked up, with a slanting pear tree. It seems that a gust of wind has blown me all the way back to Ma-wei Station!

[Sings]

 The night is cold by the station wall,
 a single lamp's faint light leaks through.
 And all around the Buddha's hall,
 shadowy winds are rising.
 I see the empty stables' moon-framed dark—
 a sudden lance of pain brings tears.

Before me stands that pear tree,
    hidden back and resting on the eaves—
sweet scent severed, white flesh fell,
    this is the spot where I am interred.
The love scene here was played to the end,
and of my doomed life's destiny
    all that remains
        is the story.
Once rosy-cheeked and ravishing,
    fortunes were spent for my smile;
now bleached bones lie forsaken
    in a half-formed mound of soil.

Yet when I call to mind the depth of affection that I received when alive, I die without regrets. Only love's destined ties that I could not see through to the end leave this heart of mine restless and unable to forget, even for thousands of eons.

[Sings]

I look back in vain—
destined love in dream;
the waters flowed away,
    the flowers fell,
and what remains
    is just this speck of old passion.
Like spring's silkworm dying,
still spinning out its thread.
Whether grieving in the royal lodge
    by Sword-Gate Pass
or keeping close to Ma-wei Slope
    in the land of death,
I think at least we share this pain
    that keeps going on.
When will golden pin and inlaid box
    again be fair and whole,
and the incense wisp that bore our vows
    made on the Seventh Eve,
        now broken, be rejoined?

Enter LOCAL GOD.

LOCAL GOD [*recites*]:
    From Heaven a courier brings a decree
    for the secret soul in the underworld.

[*Greets her*] Consort, the Lady, Heaven's Daughter, comes bearing the High God's command, and you should make yourself ready to receive her. I'll be gone now.

LADY YANG: Thank you. [*Exeunt separately*]

Enter four immortal maidens carrying water basin, banners, and standards. They lead the WEAVER WOMAN, *who holds the decree in her hands.*

WEAVER [*sings*]:
>From Heaven's precincts comes the jade decree,
>attending in front and behind
>>crane and phoenix fly.
>Because her love is genuine,
>she is recalled
>>to peaks of Peng-lai.

Enter LOCAL GOD, *who kneels and greets her.*

LOCAL GOD: As the local god of Ma-wei Slope, I bid your ladyship welcome.

WEAVER: Spirit, where is the soul of Lady Yang? Summon her here immediately so that she can hear the reading of the jade decree.

LOCAL GOD: As you command. [*Exit*]

Reenters with LADY YANG, *no longer costumed as ghost. They kneel.*

WEAVER [*reading out decree*]: The jade decree has come; kneel then and listen as I read. Thus sayeth the Jade Emperor: You, Yu-huan of the House of Yang, were originally Tai-zhen, the Jade Consort, who, through a minor misdeed, was exiled for a short span in the mortal world. Your affections strayed, as they should not have, into a worldly love, which caused you to fall upon great affliction. Now, according to the report of Our Daughter, you appeal to Heaven and repent your errors; the burden of your transgression has been expiated and your genuine love deserves mercy. I hereby authorize the use of the body-refining techniques of the Supreme Yin, that you may again be listed in the registers of immortals, and be given lodging in the dwellings of the immortal spirits on Peng-lai. Give ye thanks now for this kindness.

LADY YANG [*touching her head to the ground*]: All hail, his Holy Highness! [*to* WEAVER] I also bow to Heaven's Daughter.

WEAVER: Rise, Tai-zhen. On the Seventh Eve of the tenth year of the Tian-bao Reign, just as I was crossing the River of Stars, I saw you and the Tang Emperor in the Palace of Lasting Life secretly vowing the depth of your love. Then, more recently, I heard from the local god of Ma-wei that you were sincere in your repentance, and I made a report to the high god, from whom we now have his own sacred words.

LADY YANG: Thank you, your ladyship, for all your help.

WEAVER [*taking the basin of water and giving it to the* LOCAL GOD]: This is fluid jade and liquid gold. Take it and go with the Jade Consort to her grave. There wet her original body. Once you have refined the physical body and etherealized it, the body will be released from the dross physical corpse and rise up to the sky. When the process is completed, escort her with music and banners to the precincts of the immortals on Peng-lai. I will go now and turn in the jade decree.

LOCAL GOD: As you command.

WEAVER [*recites*]:
>My coach returns to the paired phoenix gates,
>clouds crowding around my seven-phase gown.[2] [*Exit with immortal handmaidens*]

LOCAL GOD: Congratulations, my Lady. Let's go to the grave now. [*He takes the water basin and leads Lady Yang, singing*]
>East of the meadow the road goes north,
>east of the meadow the road goes north,
>and there I see a small mound.

We're there.

LADY YANG [*looking sad, sings*]:
>So this is the bog where beauty rests,
>   where the scent lies sequestered
>   from life gone by.

LOCAL GOD: By command of the Deity of the Western Peak, I have preserved this immortal's body here. Let me lift it out.

Goes to stage door and drags in LADY YANG's *corpse, wrapped in a brocade coverlet.* LOCAL GOD *removes the brocade coverlet and holds corpse up in standing position.*

LADY YANG [*startled, sings*]:
>My body looks like it used to be,
>my body looks like it used to be,
>but the eyes are tightly closed,
>and red lips are shut and say nothing.

LOCAL GOD [*wetting the corpse with the water*]:
>I sprinkle it through with liquid gold,
>I sprinkle it through with liquid gold,
>and holy radiance floats on the face,

Corpse opens eyes.

LADY YANG:
>and suddenly glances like fall floods flow.

The corpse's hands and feet move. All at once it takes a few steps toward
LADY YANG.

LADY YANG [*alarmed*]:
>In an instant it lives again,
>in an instant it lives again,
>and moves forward,
>in appearance no different from me. [*She pauses, worried*]

---

[2]The "seven phases" are the seven nightly positions in the sky occupied by the Weaver Star, associated with her weaving.

But wait! If this Yang Yu-huan is alive, where will I, the other Yang Yu-huan, go?

The corpse suddenly begins to move toward LADY YANG, *who looks stupefied as she faces it.*

LOCAL GOD [*clapping his hands and shouting*]:
  My Lady, don't be misled,
  she is in fact you,
  and you are in fact she.

  Addressing LADY YANG *and pointing to corpse.*

  This husk of a body is her,

  Addressing corpse and pointing to LADY YANG.

  this soul is her.
  Let the true nature use the frame,
  that ere now was cut in twain.

The corpse chases LADY YANG *swiftly around the stage. Then* LADY YANG *runs into the corpse and they fall down together. Corpse makes a hidden exit.*

  The original spirit enters its shell,
  the original spirit enters its shell,
  like a second quickening in the womb,
  or twin rings fused as one.
LADY YANG [*rising, stands steadily and slowly sings*]:
  Suddenly waking from fogs of dream,
  suddenly waking from fogs of dream,
  long I had lost the "I" that used to be,
  now spirit and body are whole again.
  I think back in a daze,
  I think back in a daze,
  now Zhuang Zhou am I indeed,
  but of the butterfly what remains?

  I never expected that these cold bones would live again, and that the soul, separated from the body, would fuse with it again. Truly, I thank Heaven.
    Like a traveler who lost his home,
    like a traveler who lost his home,
    I come back to the very spot,
    and the dwelling is there as it used to be.
  Deity, let me thank you for all your trouble.
LOCAL GOD: It was nothing. [*They bow to one another*]
LADY YANG [*sings*]:
    Thank you for guarding me through the year,
    thank you for guarding me through the year,

from rot and decay keeping me whole,
and sheltering the lost and sundered soul.

LOCAL GOD: The music and banners are all ready and wait to escort you to the dwellings of the immortal spirits.

LADY YANG [*about to set off, then stopping*]: Wait a moment. Now I have been transformed and the corpse is gone. Someday His Majesty will return and eventually he will want to come and rebury me. I have to leave something here for him to recognize. Deity, would you take the brocade coverlet in which I was wrapped and rebury it in the grave? And don't let it disintegrate.

LOCAL GOD: As you command. [*He takes the brocade coverlet, but it flies off*] How strange! How very strange! The brocade coverlet turned into a many-colored cloud and flew off into the sky.

LADY YANG [*gazing after it*]: Ah, I see! When you were refining the physical body, some of the liquid gold got on the brocade coverlet, and thus it has acquired some immortal life force.

[*Sings*]

Colored cloud transformed and flying through air,
colored cloud transformed and flying through air,
seems to mimic the roaming immortals,
but what now will I leave behind?

The golden hairpin and inlaid box are things I must keep close with me. I don't have anything else besides these. [*She ponders*] Ah, I've got it! I wear a brocade sachet at my breast, which the Emperor gave me when I danced on the azure disk. I'll leave that behind. [*She takes off sachet and sings*]

I hold the brocade sachet in hand,
I hold the brocade sachet in hand, [*sadly*]
someday my Lord will recover this—
better by far
than seeing no trace of me again.

[*Hands brocade sachet to* LOCAL GOD] Deity, take this sachet and put it in the grave.

LOCAL GOD [*accepting it*]: As you command. [*Exits, then reenters*] I have placed the sachet as you required.

Enter four IMMORTAL MAIDENS *with music and banners.*

IMMORTAL MAIDENS [*greeting* LADY YANG]: We handmaidens of Tai-zhen's compound in Peng-lai greet you. Would your ladyship please change your clothes and come with us?

Music within. LADY YANG *changes her clothes.*

LOCAL GOD: Goodbye, my Lady.

LADY YANG: Goodbye, Deity. [*Exit* LOCAL GOD; IMMORTAL MAIDENS *and* LADY YANG *set out*]

[*Sings*]

Off toward Ying-zhou
where cloudy vapors shroud the air,
a cluster of gold and sapphire spires appears.
For immortals there the months and years
last on and on, as long as love.
When love is genuine and true,
through thousands of eons it will not wane.
To the golden hairpin and inlaid box I hold tight
right to the summit of Mount Peng-lai.

Ascends to a high place, then exits.

Melted away is the scent that once
    hung tied upon my breast, [Zhang Hu]
many feelings and filled with love,
    of course I can't forget. [Lu Gui-meng]
From this spot to Mount Peng-lai
    the journey is not far, [Li Shang-yin]
the worlds of Heaven and mortal men
    are both in distance faint. [Cao Tang]

BALLAD (XXXVIII)

Enter LI GUI-NIAN, *looking even older, in worn-out clothes and hat, carrying mandolin.*

LI GUI-NIAN [*recites*]:
    No sooner did the drums of war
        come rising from Yu-yang
    than suddenly we saw the vines
        grow over palace walls.
    All that's left is this old man,
        survivor with white hair,
    who sets his lasting pain to song
        that tells of glory and the fall.

I am that Li Gui-nian who used to be a musician in the court ensemble and served in the Pear Garden Academy, blessed by great favor from His Imperial Majesty. After I directed the rehearsal of "Rainbow Skirts" in Chao-yuan Tower, the song was performed for the Emperor, and the dragon countenance was greatly pleased. His Majesty and Lady Yang rewarded me with over twenty thousand cash. No one imagined that An Lu-shan would rise in rebellion and take Chang-an, driving His Majesty into flight to the West and making the common folk flee for their lives. We too, the musicians of the Pear Garden Academy, were driven thither and yon, each escaping as best he could. I came to the Southland and used up the last of my money here. I have had to take this mandolin and sing songs just to provide myself with a meager living.

Today there's a big fair at Vulture Peak Temple by Blue Creek. There will be a crowd, so I'm going there to perform. [*Sighs*] When I think how I used to sing before the Son of Heaven, and now must beat my clapper from door to door, it really makes me lose heart. [*Walks on, singing*]

> In life's last years, caught unawares,
>   I met with chaos, refugee
> harried at every crossroad, finding
>   ruin and poverty.
> My face, made black by storms of war,
> while thinning hair and frosty beard
>   are turned a melancholy white.
> Today adrift on far horizons,
> all I have is my mandolin.
> Hiding my face in shame, I go
>   up the long avenue,
> down the short lane.
> No Gao Jian-li am I, who strummed
>   his cithern, sang sad songs—[3]
> more like Wu Zi-xu, who blew
>   his flute and begged.[4]

> I think on how it used to be:
> I played clear song and rushed to serve
>   in golden galleries,
> and there composed new melodies
>   at the call
>   of the alabaster throne.
> From Heaven's heights, the royal grace
>   came flooding like the sea,
>   more than words can express:
> snows cleared from the sky when he
>   went to Warm Springs on Mount Li,
> in Xing-qing Pool the lotus bloomed,
>   and skiffs of the immortals sailed,
> and in the halls of Hua-qing Palace

---

[3]Gao Jian-li was the friend of Jing Ke, the retainer of the Prince of Yan, who attempted to assassinate the First Emperor of Qin. When he set out, Gao Jian-li played his zither and sang a song of a few lines.

[4]One legend of Wu Zi-xu was that when he escaped to Wu after the murder of his father and brother, he survived by playing the flute and begging.

he enjoyed the moonlight's charm
or on Calyx Tower took pleasure
    in the scent of flowers.

At the moment when I bathed
    in streams of royal admiration,
all at once there came about
    a strange and tragic alteration.
His phoenix carriage fled in dust,
    exiled prince at Sword-Gate Pass;
the fairest lady in the land
    lay stained with blood on Ma-wei Slope.
While I, through the Southland, weep away
    these lean bones and gaunt frame.
Destitute and wretched, I
    can only go from door to door
        hawking "Rainbow Skirts," the royal score—
and no one thirsts
    for such brilliant melody.
I merely stand before these plants and trees
    that bury parks and tombs
        of the Six Dynasties,
my eyes are filled with glory and fall. [*Moves over to edge of stage*]

                    Enter LI MO *in scholar's garb.*

LI MO [*recites*]:
    Flowers stir the traveler's eyes,
    springtime wounds the homesick heart.
    Since she of Rainbow Skirts is gone,
    none remain who know true music's tone.

I am Li Mo. Earlier I stayed a time in the Western Capital, but after the
rebellion I came back here. Outside the palace wall I surreptitiously
transcribed several sections of "Rainbow Skirts," but since that time I
have not been able to get my hands on the complete score. Recently I
heard that there is an old man who makes his living with the mandolin.
Everyone says that his technique is exceptional, like that of the former
performers of the Pear Garden Academy. Today is the great fair at Vulture Peak Temple, and I am sure he'll be there, so I'm going to go try to
find him. Look at the throngs of visitors coming along the road!

Enter three TRAVELERS *from Shan-xi, variously attired, with a* DANCEHALL
                                GIRL.

FIRST TRAVELER [*recites*]:
    We peacefully stroll seeking sweetness,
        unwilling to waste a fine spring,

SECOND TRAVELER [*recites*]:
>   for the while to view this splendid fair
>   we follow the travelers.

THIRD TRAVELER: Hey, honey, you and I should [*recites*]:
>   have our fun while the time is right,
>   not let it pass us by,

DANCEHALL GIRL [*recites*]:
>   let's listen to the mandolin
>   play a recent song.

LI MO [*to* SECOND TRAVELER]: Excuse me, sir. May I ask the young lady what "recent song on the mandolin" she was referring to?

SECOND TRAVELER: Don't you know about the old man who came here just recently and plays the mandolin with such great skill? Since there's a fair today at Vulture Peak Temple, we're all going together to listen to him.

LI MO: I was just on my way to look for this person. Would it be all right if I joined you?

ALL: That would be just fine. [*They walk on*] On we go, and here we have come to the Vulture Peak Temple. Let's go in. [*They go in*]

SECOND TRAVELER: I think that circle over there with plank benches all around must be it. Let's make our way in together and have a seat to listen. [*They all sit*]

Enter LI GUI-NIAN.

LI GUI-NIAN [*greeting them*]: Welcome. I imagine you all are here to hear my songs, so please make yourselves comfortable. I welcome your comments.

ALL: Go on.

LI GUI-NIAN [*strumming his mandolin and singing*]:
>   Dream's illusions,
>   glory and fall—
>   so many I can't sing them all—
>   and a grief that stirs your sighs
>   is too great for me to play;
>   only desolation fills my eyes
>   facing these rivers and hills.
>   Let me in swift strings convey
>   the bitterness repressed,
>   and in altering melody trace
>   the troubles and the pain,
>   thus slowly will I play for you
>   what happened years ago
>   in the Tian-bao Reign.

FIRST TRAVELER: "The Story of the Tian-bao"—now that's a good topic.

THIRD TRAVELER: Hey, honey—what song is he going to sing? Is it going to be one of our Western songs?

DANCEHALL GIRL: Something like that.

LI MO: Sir, you can't sing the whole story of the Tian-bao Reign in one performance. Sing for us how Lady Yang first came to the palace back then.

LI GUI-NIAN [*sings*]:

> At first peace reigned throughout the world
> > under our royal Tang,
> when he sought the beauty of woman,
> > and chose the fairest brows.
> There was a lovely girl,
> > grown up in the house of Yang,
> deep in the women's chamber
> > a jewel without flaws.
> Once our ruler saw her,
> > he was overcome with joy,
> he gave her the golden hairpin,
> > he gave her the inlaid box,
> in Zhao-yang Palace she was judged
> > the foremost flower.

DANCEHALL GIRL: What did the lady look like?

THIRD TRAVELER: Was she as cute as my little honey here?

SECOND TRAVELER: Just let him sing.

LI GUI-NIAN [*sings*]:

> That lady had an inborn grace,
> > like a goddess, features fair,
> modest and retiring past compare.
> The very flowers concede defeat
> > to her twin cheeks, and to her waist
> > > would willows yield,
> more ravishing than Wang Zhao-jun,
> of Xi Shi, double the allure,
> as if Guan-yin came flying there
> > from summits in the sea,
> or like Chang E, who stole away
> > from the sapphire heights of sky.
> Her spring mood was all winsomeness,
> her spring tipsiness had a pleasing air,
> in spring sleep her dreams were still.
> Even the finest painter
> > could never draw her various charms.

SECOND TRAVELER [*laughing*]: When I listen to this old man telling of Lady Yang's stunning beauty in such a lively way, it's as if he had seen her with his own eyes. He's obviously not telling the truth.

THIRD TRAVELER: As long as he sings the story well, who cares whether he's telling the truth or not. Now hurry up and sing for us how the Emperor treated her in those days.

LI GUI-NIAN [*sings*]:
> Our Lord and ruler looked on her
>> like a pearl without a peer,
>
> he lifted her high in his palm
>> all the day long.
>
> Surpassing Zhao Swallow-in-Flight newly groomed
>> in palaces of Han, they were
>
> kingfishers nesting in mansions of jade,
> mated ducks enclosed in golden galleries,
> embracing by night, in day side by side.
> It made the clever man of state
>> befuddled and besotted,
>
> of his own heart no longer master.
> In the court his sway grew lax,
> he stood in the center of passion's stage,
> a hundred details can't describe
>> their settings for romance.
>
> When walking, they walked together,
> when seated, they were face to face.
> As a pair
> they actually lay on the royal throne,
> and gained in trade shared pleasure
>> in moonlit nights and dawns of flowers.

THIRD TRAVELER [*falling over*]: Aiya! It's so real! When I hear this, I feel like a snowman by a fire.

DANCEHALL GIRL [*helping him up*]: What do you mean by that?

THIRD TRAVELER: I'm melted. [*All laugh*]

LI MO: Back then in the palace there was a song call "Coats of Feathers, Rainbow Skirts," which I've heard some say was composed by the Emperor himself, while others say that it was done by Lady Yang. Perhaps you know the facts of the matter? Please sing about this for me.

LI GUI-NIAN [*sings*]:
> Back then
> in Lotus Courts
>> the Lady Yang arranged those notes with care,
>
> she wrote the score,
>> new version of the "Rainbow Skirts."
>
> In person, when the days grew long,
>> she taught it to her maids.
>
> With pale hands spread,
> she beat the clappers of sandalwood,
> as every note and every word
>> emerged between
>>> those gleaming teeth and ruby lips.

Like the sound of a string
>of black-dragon pearls
>>easily echoing the tones,
like swallows and orioles
>trilling their melodies,
like fountains gurgling under blooms
>flowing into mountain streams,
like sutra-chanting crisp and clear
>under the bright moon,
like shrilling in the lofty cold, the cranes
>on Mount Hou's crest,
like pendants of some spirit of the air,
>tinkling in the night,
>>striding through the empty sky.
She passed it on
>to the Pear Garden ensemble,
to the Academy's companies,
and the Lady pirouetting on the azure disk
>drew our ruler's pleased regard.

LI MO: This stream of divine notes in my ears depicts her well indeed.

FIRST TRAVELER [*sighing*]: And yet it's too bad that the Emperor's infatuation with Lady Yang, spending his days from dawn to dusk in pleasures, brought about the uprising of the army in Yu-yang. It's painful even to mention it.

LI MO: But sir, don't hold a grudge against Lady Yang for this. What happened then was due to mistakes in giving responsibility to a frontier general and leaving the government to a power-hungry minister. This is what brought about the overthrow of the royal government and caused the upheavals all over the world. If the old ministers Yao and Song had still been alive, this would never have happened.

FIRST TRAVELER: What you say is true.

LI GUI-NIAN: If the rebellion of the Yu-yang armies is mentioned, that really was a cataclysm that was sad to behold and painful to hear of. But if you all wouldn't mind, let me sing about it more fully.

ALL: Certainly.

LI GUI-NIAN [*sings*]:

As the music throbbed and droned
>to dancing of the "Rainbow Skirts,"
all at once there came the boom
>and rumble of the battle drum
>>rising from Yu-yang.
Then a fruitless gibbering hum,
>droves of letters to the throne
>>discussing the frontier,
startling both high and low,
>and nothing was done.

Soon there was a roaring din,
in frightened alarm, stunned
in panic and terror, they pressed
squeezing through gates to the road leading west,
with the royal carriage bringing along
    the Consort, charming in her tears.
Then all one could see were soldiers
    dense around them in a mob,
hear their savage, cruel words,
brawling, bellowing, yelling,
all around in thunderous strife.
They drove apart
    the loving, the adoring,
    the doting and the caring
        Emperor and wife.
In those brief moments there was drawn
    a most melancholy picture:
    "the loveliest of women ends her life."

        FIRST *and* SECOND TRAVELERS *both sigh.*

LI MO [*weeping*]: It is really terrible that such a Heaven-sent beauty should
    come to such a sad and violent end.
THIRD TRAVELER [*laughing*]: It's only a ballad. Why are you shedding tears
    in earnest?
DANCEHALL GIRL: Where was Lady Yang buried after she died?
LI GUI-NIAN [*sings*]:
    By the ramshackle building of Ma-wei Station,
    off at an angle from a forlorn
        chapel to the Buddha.
    The fairest face of a generation
        died there for her lord,
    and grief to last a thousand years
        dripped in blood on her scarf of gauze.
    Her tombstone is a blasted tree,
        marking her sad fate,
    her grave, a bit of earth scooped out—
        it breaks the heart.
    Never again will men pass by
        that desolate moor,
    and on the trackless edge of sky who mourns
        for the pear blossoms' fall?
    Pity her solitary soul
        harboring her sense of wrong,
    kept company alone
        by the wailing cry
            of Emperor Wang,

     turned into the nightjar
       weeping to the moon.

FIRST TRAVELER: What did Chang-an look like after the devastation of the rebellion?

LI GUI-NIAN: Ladies and gentlemen, Chang-an, once a splendid place of embroidered brocade, was an utterly unbearable sight after it was sacked by An Lu-shan. Listen as I play some more.

[*Sings*]

    Once the royal coach went west
      along the road to Shu,
    in Chang-an soldiers ran amok.
    In the Purple Residence no more
      did the thousand officers
        come to morning audience,
    all its splendor
      instantly was swept away,
    instantly was swept away.
    From the harem's crimson doors
      long-legged spiders hang,
    and in daylight foxes howl
      right beside the royal couch.
    Owls shriek,
    weeds grow tall.
    Wild deer run everywhere,
    willows of the royal park and palace flowers
      half withered and fallen.
    Who is there to sweep them up,
    sweep them up?
    Bare beams set with tortoise shell
      are fouled by swallows' spatterings,
    and all that remains is the crescent moon
      shining in the dusk.
    I sigh at such desolation,
    a stench pervading everywhere,
    a stench pervading everywhere,
    the jade pavements bare
      but for piles of horse dung.

THIRD TRAVELER: My god, we've been listening half the day, and I'm going wild with hunger. Hey, honey, why don't you and I go have a drink and get some garlic dumplings to eat? [*Takes some coins from his pocket and gives them to* LI GUI-NIAN, *then exits, bantering with the* DANCEHALL GIRL]

FIRST TRAVELER: It's getting late, let's get going. [*Gives* LI GUI-NIAN *silver*] Here's something for you to buy a drink with.

LI GUI-NIAN: Thank you very much.

FIRST TRAVELER: There was an immense pain of glory and fall in what you
    sang.

SECOND TRAVELER: And you brought the audience to tears. [*Exeunt two*
    TRAVELERS]

LI MO: Old man, it's obvious from your mandolin playing that you are no
    ordinary musician. From whom did you learn? Please tell me everything.

LI GUI-NIAN [*sings*]:
> This mandolin once served
>   the Kai-yuan Emperor
> and again brings forth
>   heart's pain and falling tears.

LI MO: Someone who says this was obviously one of the court musicians of
    the Pear Garden Academy.

LI GUI-NIAN [*sings*]:
> My name indeed was on the list
>   in the Pear Garden Academy,
> I stood in attendance among the flowers
>   of Aloes Pavilion,
> and accompanied Hua-qing Palace feasts.

LI MO: Are you old He?

LI GUI-NIAN [*sings*]:
> No, I'm not He Huai-zhi.

LI MO: Perhaps then you are Huang Fan-chuo?

LI GUI-NIAN [*sings*]:
> Huang and I were the seniors.

LI MO: So then you must be Lei Hai-qing!

LI GUI-NIAN [*sings*]:
> Though I play the mandolin,
>   my name is not Lei:
> he died long ago cursing treason,
>   his name lives on.

LI MO: Then you must be Ma Xian-qi.

LI GUI-NIAN [*sings*]:
> Nor am I the master of stone chime,
>   the famous Ma Xian-qi—
> speak no more of those old friends of mine.

LI MO: How did you come to be here?

LI GUI-NIAN [*sings*]:
> With ruin of the royal house,
>   destruction of the state,
>   fighting broke out everywhere,
> and I was left to roam alone
>   in the Southland.

LI MO: But then who are you?

LI GUI-NIAN [*sings*]:
> Since you keep on pressing me on who I am,

know then
    that my name among the musicians
      was Li Gui-nian.

LI MO [*bowing*]: Ah! So you are Li Gui-nian, the leader of the troupe! I am honored to make your acquaintance.

LI GUI-NIAN: What is your name, sir? And how do you come to know who I am?

LI MO: I am Li Mo.

LI GUI-NIAN: Are you perhaps the Li who plays the iron flute?

LI MO: That's right.

LI GUI-NIAN: I'm very pleased to meet you. [*Bows*]

LI MO: Can I ask you if you remember the entire score of "Rainbow Skirts"?

LI GUI-NIAN: I still remember it. Why do you ask?

LI MO: To tell you the truth, sir, I've always loved music and was staying in Chang-an before. When you were rehearsing "Rainbow Skirts" at Chao-yuan Tower, I was secretly listening very carefully outside the palace walls, and managed to get down several sections on my iron flute. But I didn't get the entire score. I've been searching everywhere to find it, but no one knows it. But I have been fortunate enough to meet you here today, and I wonder if you might be willing to teach it to me.

LI GUI-NIAN: Since I've met someone who truly understands music, why should I hesitate to teach him my poor skills?

LI MO: I would be very grateful if you would do so. Let me ask where you are staying?

LI GUI-NIAN: I am down on my luck now and just wander about. I'm not staying anywhere.

LI MO: How would you like to stay at my lodgings so that I can learn it with care?

LI GUI-NIAN: That would be just fine.

[*Sings*]

Like a frightened crow circling a tree,
    I keep away from the empty boughs,
And now, beyond hope, I find myself
    a swallow seeking familiar nest
      among the painted beams.
Today one connoisseur delights
    to find another of his kind;
this meeting was remarkable,
exhilarating match of minds.
I will slowly teach you "Rainbow Skirts"
    to pass on for a thousand years.

[*Recites*]

A welcome thing to pass along
    the lanes of peach and willow, [Zhang Ji]

Li Mo:
> now I turn my coach aside
>> to seek the recluse ivy-clad. [Bo Ju-yi]

Li Gui-nian:
> If today the music lover
>> will linger on to listen, [Liu Yu-xi]

Li Mo:
> no place in all the Southland
>> will fail to hear the song. [Gu Kuang]

In the scene that follows, Li Gui-nian appears again, visiting a nunnery, where he finds a shrine dedicated to Lady Yang. Here he meets Lady Yang's two maids, Yong-xin and Nian-nu.

THE IMMORTAL'S RECOLLECTIONS (XL)

Enter Lady Yang *as an immortal, followed by an attendant spirit.*

Lady Yang [*sings*]:
> Borne aloft by phoenix and crane,
>> I left to never return,
> and now look back in vain
>> to the distance between
>>> Heaven and mortal men.
> Yet what happened before at Upright Hall
> and in the Palace of Lasting Life
> pulls without measure on the heart.

> [*Recites lyric*]

> Blurred by distance, depths of cloud
>> enclose those marble rooms,
> now back on the lists of immortals,
>> my thoughts are in a daze.
> I look back
>> and cannot help
>>> expense of recollection.

> By alabaster stairs
>> within the agate trees
>>> all at once I see
> outlines of bright phoenixes
>> roosting in their pairs—
> thoughts so often put from mind
>> again lay claim to me.

I have had the good fortune to receive a decree from the Heavenly Emperor restoring me to my place among the immortals, and I have again taken up my residence in Tai-zhen's compound. Yet those tokens by which we pledged our love have never left me for a moment. And the heart finds it impossible to forsake those vows we made on the Seventh Eve. It's such a long tale.

[*Sings*]

Driven apart in an instant,
    nothing could be done,
yet between us remains such mutual care.
Life and death could not rend love's bond,
but all that's left is bitter pain
    massing like hills.
There he, in sorrow unceasing, his thoughts
    captive of love's old history;
here I, with tears that never dry,
    shed bloody by a remnant soul—
we both waste sighs.
Before we formed those fabled fish
    that share a single eye,
troubles were upon us; and when drake
from duck is split, what matters
immortality?

She takes out the hairpin and box and looks at them.

See those feelings present still
    in golden hairpin, paneled box—
who would have thought while Heaven lasts
    and Earth endures
        our vows would be forsaken?
When will the blue phoenix come
    to do my will,
to reunite our destinies,
to let us meet again
to give bitter account of our miseries?

Enter HAN HUANG.

HAN HUANG [*recites*]:
    I make the climb up Peng-lai,
        gaze from the mountain's height,
    where ocean waves are shallow and clear,
        there comes a crane in flight.

On orders from my Lady, the Mistress of the Moon, I've come to get the new score of "Rainbow Skirts" from Tai-zhen, the Jade Consort. Now that I'm here, I might as well go in. [*Approaches and greets her*] Madam.
LADY YANG: Why have you come, spirit?

HAN HUANG [*laughing*]: Do you still recognize me? I'm Han Huang.

LADY YANG [*thinking it over*]: Aren't you the immortal spirit from the moon?

HAN HUANG: That's right.

LADY YANG: Please have a seat. [HAN HUANG *sits*] It's hard to believe that it's been several years since I took leave of you in that dream. You have come a long way to pay me a visit, so tell me what your purpose is.

HAN HUANG: Listen while I explain it to you.

[*Sings*]

> Because the music "Rainbow Skirts"
>   played in the Palace of Spreading Cold
> caught your genius's fancy
> and you scored anew with precision,

> I've been ordered by my Lady, the Mistress of the Moon,
>   to visit the true musician
>   to pay a far call on Mount Peng-lai,
>   and borrow that score of days gone by
>   for my Lady herself to read.

LADY YANG: I see. Back then I had the good fortune to hear the music of immortals in my dream. But even though I copied it down in an arrangement for strings and woodwinds, I'm still embarrassed at its imperfections and mistakes.

[*Sings*]

> Why should royalty of the moon
> so blindly choose this remnant tune?—
> for here my recollections turn
> round and round in weeping. [*Weeps*]

HAN HUANG: Lady, why are you spilling these tears?

LADY YANG:

> Having lived through Armageddon,
> and having myself been crushed,
> I am pained how these notes
>   grow cold and fade.
> The crimson strings are broken,
> and I am ashamed
>   to let this tune again be played.

Please explain to the Lady of the Moon that I do not dare answer her bidding with that old score from the foul and common world. I beg her forgiveness.

HAN HUANG: Lady, don't refuse so stubbornly. My Lady, the Mistress of the Moon,

[*Sings*]

> holds your fine wit in esteem,
>   a rare thing ever,
> framing these new melodies,
>   matchless among mortals.
> Though sadly late she seeks it,
> do not disappoint, please,
> her respectful attention.

LADY YANG: Since the Lady of the Moon has been so gracious as to send you to me, I have a copy here that I wrote out on first coming to this mountain and chancing to recall the past.

HAN HUANG: That would be wonderful.

LADY YANG: Maid, go get it for me. [MAID *exits and brings back the score*]

MAID: Here it is.

LADY YANG: Spirit, though the score has been fetched, maybe it would be best if it could be recopied.

HAN HUANG: Why?

LADY YANG [*sings*]:

> See how the notes blur into ruin,
> lines smudged and broken,
> all stained by tracks of tears.

HAN HUANG: It doesn't matter.

LADY YANG [*giving her back the score*]: All right, but please explain this to the Lady of the Moon—and tell her that since I copied it from dream, there are many mistakes in the notes and tempo, so that I would be glad to have her correct it.

HAN HUANG: I'll do that. And now I must take my leave. [*Recites*]:

> From the very first until
>   the music was complete, [Wang Jian]

LADY YANG:

> how could it happen that Chang E
>   knew in such detail? [Tang Yan-qian]

HAN HUANG:

> Marvel not with what feeling
>   she felt sorrow at this song, [Liu Yu-xi]

LADY YANG:

> such beauty adrift in the moonlight
>   is set to meet with whom? [Li Shang-yin]

Exit HAN HUANG *with score.*

LADY YANG: Maid, lock the gate to my grotto and follow me in.

Exit, followed by MAID.

In the scenes that follow, women are conscripted to disinter Lady Yang's corpse. Since Lady Yang has undergone a bodily metamorphosis into an immortal, they find only the sachet that Lady Yang had purposefully left behind. The Emperor has the sachet ceremonially buried, and Guo Zi-yi appears to escort him back to the capital.

At their annual meeting on the Seventh Eve, the Oxherd and Weaver stars discuss the love shared by Lady Yang and the Emperor. They debate whether the Emperor, having surrendered Lady Yang to his mutinous guards, has failed in his vows of undying love. Before reaching a decision about helping the lovers be reunited, they will look for signs of remorse.

The next scene opens with the Emperor staying awake on a rainy night, grief-stricken over the loss of Lady Yang. Urged to sleep by Gao Li-shi, the Emperor is awakened by two heavenly messengers who tell him that Lady Yang awaits him. The Emperor rises and follows them out into the city, where his way is barred by Chen Yuan-li, the officer who had demanded Lady Yang's death at Ma-wei Station. The Emperor, enraged, orders the messengers to kill Chen. After Chen Yuan-li's execution, the messengers bring the Emperor to Ma-wei Station and v anish. The Emperor is looking in vain for Lady Yang when the station itself vanishes, and he finds himself by a river. A demon rises out of the water to attack him and a god enters swiftly to fight the demon off. At the end of the scene, Gao Li-shi hurries in and the Emperor wakes up to find that it had all been a dream. Even so, the Emperor decides that it must have been Lady Yang's spirit that inspired the dream, and he determines to summon a wizard to go search for her in the world beyond.

In the scene that follows, the wizard goes to look for Lady Yang in the underworld. Unable to locate her there, he sets off for Heaven, where he meets the Weaver Star. Assured by the wizard of the Emperor's unswerving love, the Weaver directs the wizard to Peng-lai, the isle of the immortals. The Weaver next summons Lady Yang to test the firmness of her love, and convinced at last of the lovers' devotion, she promises Lady Yang that she and the Emperor will be reunited. Eventually, the wizard reaches Peng-lai and conveys the Emperor's love to Lady Yang, who gives him half the hairpin and half the paneled box as a proof that she has been contacted. She sends word to the Emperor that they are to meet again soon in the moon. The Emperor, aged and sick, receives the tokens and the message through Gao Li-shi, and anxiously awaits his reunion with Lady Yang.

REUNION (L)

Enter YANG TONG-YOU, *a* WIZARD.

WIZARD [*sings*]:
>A single love has conjured forth
>this wedding between Heaven and man.
>And if the love they bear
>>knows no alteration ever,
>the wish they made so long before
>>can truly be attained.

I am the wizard Yang Tong-you, who previously discovered Lady Yang's soul living on the isle of Peng-lai. I received her personal instructions to bring the Emperor to the Moon Palace to meet her on Mid-autumn Eve. The Emperor is really the high immortal Kong-sheng, and this night of the full moon in October is the proper time for him to fly up to Heaven. Just after dusk now, you can see the sapphire sky like water and the silvery River of Stars without a speck of dust. It's time now to lead the Emperor on his way. But as I stand here speaking, here comes the Emperor himself out of the palace.

Enter EMPEROR.

EMPEROR [*sings*]:
> Clouds open in the distant sky,
>>   translucent sapphire,
> and shimmering moonbeams brighten
>>   alabaster halls.

WIZARD [*greets him*]: Your Majesty, I am your humble subject, the wizard.
EMPEROR: Don't stand on ceremony. Tonight . . .

[*Sings*]

> Since you brought her engagement
>>   to meet in the palace of moon,
> I have kept impatient watch
>>   for twilight's passage.
> To the high reaches of blue clouds
> I trust to you to guide my feet.

WIZARD: Night's colors have darkened. Let's be on our way. [*They proceed, as* WIZARD *recites a song lyric*]
> Where is the bright moon found?—
> I wave my hand, we climb blue sky.

EMPEROR [*continuing the* WIZARD's *lines with lines by Su Shi*]:
> I wonder—for those in sky palaces
> it is "this evening" of what year?

WIZARD [*continuing Su Shi's lyric*]:
> I'd go there riding winds, but fear
> those onyx halls and domes of jade
> are up so high
>>   I could not bear the cold.

TOGETHER [*continuing*]:
> Then rise and dance,
>>   cool shadows capering—
> how can anything compare
>>   to the world of mortal men?

EMPEROR: Master, the road to Heaven is so far, how can we fly the full distance?
WIZARD: Don't worry, Your Majesty. I'll toss this magic whisk that I have

in my hand, and it will turn into a bridge for immortal spirits of the air, and it will take you right to the Moon Palace. [WIZARD *tosses his whisk, which turns into a bridge, then exits*]

EMPEROR: Just look, a bridge has materialized out of nowhere and the wizard has suddenly disappeared. I'll just have to make my way over the bridge by myself.

[*Sings*]

> Below my every footstep see
>   a rainbow-colored path appear,
> all the way to the stars' Silver River
>   and wisps of the upper air—
> there nothing is clear, all
>   is shrouded in scented haze. [*Music within*]
> Somewhere I hear played
>   "Heaven's Balance" melody;
> and I must be drawing near
>   the lunar groves of cassia. [*Withdraws*]

Enter CHANG E, *followed by* IMMORTAL MAIDENS *holding fans.*

CHANG E [*sings*]:
> Our jade disk, full circle now,
>   adds its autumn light,
> and with "Rainbow Skirts" playing,
> our chaste revels
>   are appointed to begin.

I am Chang E, the Lady of the Moon. Here in the moon we use to have a suite of Heaven's music called "Rainbow Skirts." Long ago Yang Tai-zhen, the Prized Consort of the Tang Emperor, heard it in her dream, then wrote down a score that appeared in the world of mortal men. It turned out that her version of the melody was even better than the one here in Heaven. Recently Lady Yang has been confirmed among the ranks of the immortals. I had someone go to Peng-lai to find a copy of her score and worked it into the "Heaven's Balance" suite, planning to have it performed this evening. Heaven's Daughter unexpectedly took pity on their deep love and wanted their destiny together to continue. She has asked me to lend my lunar precincts as a place where the two might meet. And now Yang Tai-zhen has sent the wizard Yang Tong-you to bring the Tang Emperor here tonight. This is a story that will last forever.

[*Sings*]

> His love endured,
> his faith was firm,
> so fitting it is that goddess and man
>   meet again.

Thus was Heaven's Daughter moved
and made things come out well for them.

All you, my immortal handmaidens, keep a lookout for Tai-zhen's arrival, and have her wait the while in the shade of the cassia tree. After she has seen the Emperor, I will meet with them.

IMMORTAL MAIDENS: As you wish.

TOGETHER [*sing*]:
Now at its finest is cassia's splendor,
now the sparkling dew is fresh.
We bring the loving pair together,
in Heaven's chaste, inviolate zones.

Exit CHANG E. *The Moon Palace is set up on stage, and the* IMMORTAL MAIDENS *stand waiting at the palace gate. Enter* LADY YANG *with her* IMMORTAL HANDMAIDENS.

LADY YANG [*sings*]:
I left Jade Hill's immortal bowers
and reached these glittering galleries
to catch sight of the face of mortal man,
    one purple-born.
The wish of past and future lives
    is here fulfilled,
this evening's meeting will excel
    encounters in years gone by. [*Arrives*]

IMMORTAL MAIDENS: Please come in.

LADY YANG [*going in*]: Where is her ladyship of the Moon?

IMMORTAL MAIDENS: The Lady instructed us to invite you to wait here a short while until the Emperor sees you. She will meet you after that. Please sit a while.

LADY YANG *sits as the* IMMORTAL MAIDENS *stand beside the moon palace watching out for the* EMPEROR. *Enter* EMPEROR.

EMPEROR [*sings*]:
On and on I cross this bridge
whose end somehow eludes me,
And I, as moving in a dream,
whirl around astride the wind.
The clear glow is conspicuous,
but once inside its light,
    vision fails me and I see
only dim shapes of terrace and hall,
as Heaven's sweet odors invisibly
    brush across my face. [*Reads*]

"The Precincts of Extensive Cold and Pure Space." This must mean the precincts of the moon.

[*Sings*]

> I made a date to meet her here,
> so why do I not see
>> that spirit of the air
>>> from Peng-lai's bowers?

IMMORTAL MAIDENS [*welcoming him*]: Are you the Emperor?

EMPEROR: That I am.

IMMORTAL MAIDENS: The Jade Consort has already been here for some time. Please come.

EMPEROR: Where is Lady Yang?

LADY YANG: Where is the Emperor?

EMPEROR [*seeing* LADY YANG *and weeping*]: My Consort!

LADY YANG: My Emperor! [*They embrace*]

EMPEROR [*sings*]:

> Meeting at once we join hands,
> choked with pain, words hard to find.
> It seems to me that day
>> when jade was broken, sweet scent crushed,
> was all because my strength was weak,
> entangling you in grievous wrong,
> the fault was mine entirely.
> Even now shame fills my heart,
> which keeps me from saying how much
>> I've longed for you.

LADY YANG: Your Highness, come now!

[*Sings*]

> The roots of my own misdeeds went deep,
>> my fate adverse,
> these led to my undoing, and involved you
> so that you almost could not escape.
> The jade flesh perished in blooms of pear,
> the soul, cut loose, with the nightjar flew.
> But due to our vow
>> still unfulfilled,
> with pain I recalled our shattered union,
> and with foolish stubbornness clung
>> to old promises made.
> I am grateful you did not forsake me,
> but yearned with a single intensity,
> and sought me throughout
>> sky's Sapphire Web and Yellow Springs.

EMPEROR: When I passed back by Ma-wei, I was going to have your body reburied. To my surprise there was no trace of your bones, and all that was left was a single sachet. After that I thought of you day and night, and I had a wizard look everywhere for your soul.

1095

[Sings]

As soon as he reached the spirits' hill,
    he sought you out
and passed on the message of the heart.

Takes out hairpin and box.

Of the hairpin this single branch,
    of the box this single panel,
and also you mentioned the words of our vow
    made on that night of praying for skill.

LADY YANG [*taking out her pieces of the hairpin and box*]: Here are the pieces
of hairpin and box that I have.

TOGETHER [*sing*]:
Now is the inlaid box rejoined,
and, paired in flight, upon the pin
    once more are swallows matched.
We helplessly recall
    unbearable despondency,
and seeing each other again
    we cannot help
        streaming tears.

LADY YANG: We have the Weaver Woman, Heaven's Daughter, to thank for
taking pity on us and allowing our divided fates to be reunited. Our meeting this evening is truly not by chance.

[Sings]

By that immortal spirit's grace
the intertwined boughs
    and birds that flew wing to wing
are joined again as they were before.
Heaven has mended parting's pain,
and filled in sorrow's sea.

TOGETHER [*sing*]:
Thank Gray Heaven for its pity,
so restoring loving hearts.
Newly inscribed as immortal spouse,
high in the lavender wisps of cloud
eternity will attest our wondrous fate.

IMMORTAL MAIDEN: The Lady of the Moon is here.

Enter CHANG E.

CHANG E [*recites*]:
The shadow of the white elm
    shows clearly in the moon,
red cassia fragrance whirls
    in breeze beyond the clouds.

EMPEROR [*greeting her*]: Your Ladyship.

CHANG E: Sire.

LADY YANG: Mistress.

CHANG E: Don't stand on ceremony. Please be seated. [*All sit*] Your Majesty, Madam, I want to congratulate you on your restoration to the immortals and that your love can now continue forever. Put all that happened before out of your minds.

[*Sings*]

The only threat is lack of love—
why fret if shared lives are broken?
You two were tempered by separation
and by death, smashed
through love's barriers to display
    love's true face,
showing thus the thread
of karmic connection, contingency
    and consequent grace.
All common meetings will seem pale
encountering each other here
in the round moon's palace, where
    all things come to circle full.

IMMORTAL MAIDEN: The ruling comes from the Most High.

Enter WEAVER STAR, *carrying the ruling.*

WEAVER [*recites*]:
A thousand strands of artful weave
    done in Heaven,
a hundred lifespans' destiny
    binding mortal men.

EMPEROR *and* LADY YANG *kneel.*

"This is the Jade Emperor's decree for Li Long-ji, Emperor of the Tang, and for his Consort, Yang Yu-huan: Verily ye two were once the high immortal Kong-sheng and an immortal of Peng-lai who, on account of a small infraction, had to dwell a while in the mortal world. Now, the term of your exile having expired, I have approved what Heaven's Daughter has recommended. I have examined the depth of your love for one another and command that you be lodged in the palace of the Dao-li Heaven of Heart's Desire, to be man and wife forever. Let it be so."

EMPEROR *and* LADY YANG [*bowing*]: Hail the High God! [*They rise.* WEAVER WOMAN *greets them and all are seated*]

WEAVER: Your Majesty, Tai-zhen—your two hearts have been steadfast and your love has been proven. Now you have become man and wife in Heaven, which cannot be compared with mortal marriage.

[*Sings*]

From Dao-li, Heaven of Heart's Desire,
watch Earth's red dust and sapphire sea
   change their places instantly.
Eternal couple, free
of each and every tangling care.
Ranging at will,
passing moments everywhere
enjoying the moon and breeze,
without the lingering desire
for body's pleasure, childish folly.
Gather now that bygone love,
   the hairpin and the box,
for endless ages live out now
   the wish you made before.

CHANG E: The spirits are all assembled, and the moon banquet is suitably
laid. Let us now lift our cups in a toast to congratulate the Emperor and
the Jade Consort. Have the wine served. [*Enter* IMMORTAL MAIDENS *with
wine*] Here it is now. [*Raises a toast and sings*]

In this pure immaculate hall
see the spirits gathered all,
lined upon the silken mats.
Here among the cassia blooms
   a holy pair,
in cassia blooms a holy pair
will rule love forever more.

ALL [*continuing*]:
They meet upon this splendid night,
two divided, now made whole;
Shining on this splendid night,
the moon is also full and whole.

WEAVER [*facing* LADY YANG]:
Blind love steadfast unto death,
   feeling all too firm,
      this I esteem,

[*facing* EMPEROR]:

while you win scorn
   for sometimes shifting in your vow.
All you saw were phantom flowers,
   conjured shadows all,
conjured shadows, phantom flowers—
sweep that worldly dust away, and now
   jointly rise to Heaven.

ALL [*continuing*]:
>They meet upon this splendid night,
>two divided, now made whole;
>Shining on this splendid night,
>the moon is also full and whole.

EMPEROR and LADY YANG:
>We thank Chang E for empathy
>>with love's subtle inflections;
>and thanks to Heaven's Daughter too
>>for mending our afflictions.
>We went through walls of misery
>>and seas of sorrow without bounds,
>through walls of misery
>>and seas of sorrow without bounds,
>And now at once
>>we do renounce
>>>passion's folly with a smile.

ALL [*continuing*]:
>They meet upon this splendid night,
>two divided, now made whole;
>Shining on this splendid night,
>the moon is also full and whole.
>Life, death, the realm of ghosts
>>and immortality—
>>>they've seen them all,
>and soon in Heaven's palaces,
>>two lotuses will bloom
>>>upon one stem,
>and then will be fulfilled the vow
>>made in the Palace of Lasting Life.

WEAVER: For our gathering this evening we will have the Jade Consort's newly scored version of "Rainbow Skirts." Where are my Heavenly Maids? [*Enter* HEAVENLY MAIDS *with instruments*]

HEAVENLY MAIDS [*recite*]:
>By night in moonlight sing away
>>the "Calling Phoenix" melody,
>and Heaven's winds blow down below
>>notes of "Walking in the Sky."

>At your service.

WEAVER: Dance for us now "Rainbow Skirts."

HEAVENLY MAIDS [*dancing*]:
>Fragrant is the cassia orb
>as we perform new melody,
>into dancing rows divided.
>Pendants of the spirits spring,

rushing past in alternation,
carried on the Heavens' breeze
bearing ringing sounds afar.
Winding like the dragon's motion
    rising through a thousand forms,
wingbeats like the phoenix turning
    rainbow colors manifest.
Wispy skirts go sweeping past,
face to face with sleeves widespread,
    sewn with alabaster thread.
Puffs of azure cloud disperse,
piling streams of autumn light.
Beside the oboes cranesdown capes
    swirl and undulate
        showing forth on Gou-shi's crest;
rainbow streamers scintillate
    gathering beside the cushions
        for the Jasper Pool feast;
fragrance wafting, groups of damsels
    send jade petals scattering
        in Galleries of Unblown Buds.
One stands forth singly,
mounts with swan-steps,
then hides the phoenix form
and slips past down below.
Gowns are gathered, fans deployed,
    precisely to the beat,
each syllable, one soaring turn.
They match the manner of the pace
of the Goddess of the Luo
    crossing waves,
stir visions of Wu Mountain's goddess
    moving clouds.
Round and round the tones and poses
    sweep along.
And with slow and sensual pace they tread
    the stratosphere in song,
as to the notes of melody
    the tinkling beats respond.
Glinting buds of red
open in the wind;
chasing silver stars,
rippling streams of cloud.
Unlike delights of mortal men
let lotuses be spread
    and on these slowly tread

paired swallows lightly tossing.
Treading Air,
Treading Air upon the onyx terraces
Fei-qiong stirs a frenzy;
Nong-yu,
Nong-yu on Qin's terraces
plays her panpipes urgently.
Earthly passions, godlike thoughts
    both deliberating.
Now the style of "Heaven's Balance"
    melody is changed,
artfully composed the final strains
    spinning without ending.
The silver moon is gleaming,
the water-clock of jade drips on,
to last a thousand years one sung,
    dancing "Skirts of Rainbow."

WEAVER: What a wonderful piece of music! It truly will reign supreme for a millennium. Play this music to accompany the high immortal Kong-sheng and the Jade Consort to the palace in the Dao-li Heaven of Heart's Desire.

CHANG E: My heavenly maidens, let this music be played as you lead them on their way. [HEAVENLY MAIDENS *lead* EMPEROR *and* LADY YANG *away, playing music*]

Gods and spirits are lovers all;
and though Peng-lai Isle lies far,
you can get there through love.
From its first roots love works its way
through eons and through life and death,
until at last the lovers join.
Unions in this world of dust
    pass with anxious haste,
But there's a Heaven of Heart's Desire
    where love goes on forever.
This differs from that common dream,
beguiled by grief and joy alike,
where gentle care and passion come
    at last to emptiness.
Leap from that cave of wandering folly,
cut free the reins of fantasy—
golden shackles fall away,
chains of jade grow loose.
Laugh as you ride your phoenix pair
to Heaven's palaces,
    insouciant and free.

Thus is the former "Rainbow Skirts"

here composed anew.
When sung to those who understand,
    their hearts will know,
and this will make love stay
    for all eternity.

Who made the drunken dancer brush
    against the seat of the guest? [Zhang Yue]
Spirits of the upper realms
    await those banished down below. [Fang Gan]
Before they heard the "Rainbow Skirts"
    played the whole way through, [Wu Rong]
the fragrant wind had carried them
    to Da-luo Heaven. [Wei Xuan]
See a palace built by waters,
    named for "Lasting Life," [Wang Jian]
Heaven's roads stretch on and on
    to touch the sky's pure heights. [Cao Tang]
And from this must the Jade Emperor
    break the common rule, [Si-kong Tu]
that gods and spirits have their fates
    which are not bound to love. [Li Shang-yin]

Pu Song-ling (1640–1715), 清
Liao-zhai's Record of Wonders

Stories of marvels and encounters with supernatural beings had been popular in China at least since the Han Dynasty, but the favorite compendium of all such stories was *Liao-zhai's Record of Wonders (Liao-zhai zhi-yi),* by Pu Song-ling. By the Qing, the number of educated men who sought public office far exceeded the number of available positions. Pu Song-ling failed the provincial examinations and spent his life in the employ of officials and local gentry in his native Shan-dong. A preliminary version of *Liao-zhai's Record of Wonders* was completed in 1679, though he continued to add to it in the decades that followed. Numerous versions of the collection circulated in manuscript, but the work was not published until 1766. Held up as a model of classical prose style and exposition, *Liao-zhai's Record of Wonders* transformed the venerable genre of the supernatural tale into high art.

The supernatural tale seems to have answered some hunger for the strange that is a component of societies that are relatively stable and ordinary. In the Chinese version, strangeness often took the form of an abrupt intrusion of a sexual relationship into ordinary life. In *Liao-zhai's Record of Wonders,* the strange and the ordinary are often in competition; ghosts, were-beasts, and immortal beings may be domesticated, but their powers eventually reveal themselves in the common world. This constant play on appearance and a truth that lies behind appearance is worked out through the social roles and obligations that shape human relationships, especially between men and women.

One striking difference between many of Pu Song-ling's literary ghost stories and their Western counterparts is the frequent undercurrent of whimsy and humor, found precisely in the conjunction of the ordinary and the supernatural, the domestic and demonic. In "Lian-xiang," the protagonist, young Sang, lies on his deathbed listening to his two rival girlfriends debate the relative destructive powers of ghosts and foxes, suddenly realizing the each was, in fact, the supernatural creature that the other had claimed. The narrator's comment: "Fortunately he was so used to them that he wasn't alarmed by them at all." At the very moment that the supernatural reveals itself in the ordinary world, he finds that the strange has become ordinary.

One further aspect of the domestication of the strange is the intrusion of the narrator at the end of each story, offering a judgment as the "Chronicler of Wonders," in the manner of a Chinese official historian.

Lian-xiang

A native of Yi-zhou, one Sang Xiao, also known as Sang Zi-ming, had been orphaned in his youth and taken up lodging in Red Blossom Port. Sang was the sort of person who enjoyed the quiet, sedate life. Every day he would go out to take his meals with a neighbor to his east, but he would spend the rest of his time just sitting at home. His neighbor once jokingly asked him, "Aren't you afraid of ghosts and foxes, living all by yourself?" Sang laughed and replied, "Why should a grown man be afraid of ghosts and foxes? Should a male of either type come, I have a sharp sword. If it's a female, I should open the gate and welcome her in."

Sang's neighbor then went home and hatched a scheme with some friends. They used a ladder to boost a courtesan over the way, and in no time she was there knocking at his gate. When Sang peeked out and asked who she was, the courtesan said she was a ghost. Sang was utterly terrified, and she could hear the sound of his teeth chattering. The courtesan then backed away and left. Early the next day, Sang's neighbor came to see Sang in his study; Sang related what he had seen and announced that he was going back to his native district. At this the neighbor clapped his hands together and asked, "Why didn't you open the door and welcome her in?" Immediately Sang realized he had been hoodwinked and went back to the quiet life he had led before.

A half a year went by, and then one night a young woman came knocking at his study. Sang thought that this was another joke being played on him by his friend, so he opened the door and asked her in. She turned out to be a beauty worth dying for. Sang was surprised and asked her where she had come from. She replied, "My name is Lian-xiang, and I am a courtesan who lives west of here." Since there were many establishments in the red light district of the port, Sang believed her. When he put out the candle and got in bed with her, their lovemaking was perfect. From that time on, she would suddenly show up every fifteenth night.

One evening as he was sitting alone, lost in thought, a young woman came flitting in. Thinking it was Xiang-lian, Sang greeted her and was talking to her; but when he caught sight of her face, it was someone else altogether. She was just fifteen or sixteen, with billowing sleeves and her hair in bangs, a winsome and charming creature, who seemed uncertain whether to come any closer or to withdraw. Sang was aghast, suspecting she was a fox. The young woman said, "My name is Li, and I come from a good family. I am an admirer of your noble disposition and cultivation, and now I have the good fortune to be able to come and make your acquaintance."

Sang was delighted; but when he took her hand, it was cold as ice. And he asked her, "Why are you so chilly?" She replied, "How could it be otherwise, being so young and tender, yet left alone in the cold each night, in the frost and dew?" And when he had untied the folds of her dress, she was indeed a true virgin. She said to him, "Because of the love I feel for you, I have now, in a short span, failed to preserve my innocence. If you do not look on me as unworthy, I would like to share your bed always. But do you, perhaps, have another woman for your bedroom?" Sang told her that there was no one else but a nearby prostitute and that she didn't come to visit him often. At this the young woman said, "I'll be careful to avoid her. I don't belong to the same class as those women of the entertainment quarters, so you have to keep this completely secret. When she comes, I'll leave; and then when she leaves, I'll come back."

As the roosters were crowing and she was about to go, she gave him an embroidered slipper and said, "By fondling this thing I have worn on my body, you can let me know that you are longing for me. But take care not to fondle it when anyone else is around." When Sang took it and examined it, he saw that it was as sharply pointed as a knitting needle. And his heart was filled with love and desire. There was no one with him the following evening, so he took it out and examined it. In a flash the young woman was suddenly there, and they then shared tender intimacies. From then on whenever he took out the slipper, the young woman would respond to his thoughts and come to him. He thought this unusual and questioned her about it, but she only laughed and said, "It's just coincidence."

One night when Lian-xiang came, she said with alarm, "How is it that you look so pallid and drained of vitality?" Sang said, "I hadn't been aware of it." Lian-xiang later took her leave and promised to come again in ten days. After Lian-xiang left, Miss Li came regularly, leaving no evening free. She asked him, "Why hasn't your lover come in such a long time?" Sang then told her about the interval she had stipulated. Li laughed and asked, "In your eyes, how do I compare to Lian-xiang in beauty?" Sang replied, "Both of you are extraordinary, but Lian-xiang's skin is pleasantly warm." At this, Li colored and said, "If you are telling me to my face that she and I are matched in beauty, then she must be a veritable goddess of the moon-palace, and I am obviously not her equal." After that she grew sulky. Then, as she reckoned it, the ten days were already up; and forbidding Sang to say a word, she intended to get a glimpse of Lian-xiang.

On the following night Lian-xiang finally came, and they laughed and talked quite cheerfully. But when they went to bed, she was shocked and said, "This is terrible! It's been only ten days since I saw you last—how could you have deteriorated so badly? Can you assure me that you haven't been meeting with someone else?" Sang asked her to explain, and Lian-xiang said, "I can see the evidence in your vital signs. Your pulse is fluctuating wildly, like tangled threads. This is the symptom of the presence of a ghost."

The next night Li came, and Sang asked, "Did you get a glimpse of Lian-xiang?" Li answered, "She *is* beautiful. As a matter of fact, I would even say that in the whole *human* world there's no woman so lovely. That's because she's a fox. When she left, I tailed her—her lair is in the hill to the south."

Sang suspected Li was simply jealous and gave her a flippant reply. But the next evening, he teased Lian-xiang: "I really don't believe it, but someone claimed you were a fox." Lian-xiang pressed him to tell her who had said this, but Sang laughed and answered, "I was just teasing you." Then Lian-xiang asked, "Just how are foxes different from human beings?" Sang replied, "Those who are bewitched by them grow sick, and in the worst cases they die. This is the reason people are terrified of them." Lian-xiang said, "It's not so. When someone your age sleeps with a fox, their vitality is restored after only three days. So even if one were a fox, what harm would it do? But suppose there were a creature that sapped a person's energy every day—there are people far worse than foxes. With all the corpses and ghosts of people who died of consumption and other diseases, it's hardly just foxes that cause people to die. In any case, someone has obviously been talking about me." Sang did his best to persuade her that this wasn't so, but Lian-xiang questioned him ever more vigorously. At last Sang had no choice but to tell her the whole story. Then Lian-xiang said, "I was really astounded at how sickly you had grown. But how else could you have reached this condition so suddenly? The creature must not be human. Don't say anything about this, but tomorrow night, I have to spy on her as she did on me."

That night, Li came. She hadn't exchanged more than a few words with Sang when she heard a cough outside the window and disappeared immediately. Then Lian-xiang came in and said, "You're in serious danger. She really is a ghost. If you keep on being intimate with her and don't break it off quickly, the dark path is close at hand!" Sang thought she was jealous and said nothing. Lian-xiang then said, "I realize that you can't just put aside your love for her, but still I can't bear to watch you die. Tomorrow, I'm going to bring you some medicine to get rid of this malady brought on by an excess of the feminine principle. Fortunately the disease hasn't taken deep root in you, and it should be gone in ten days. I ask you to share a bed with me so that I can keep an eye on the cure."

The next night she brought out some finely chopped herbs and made Sang take them. In a little while he had a few bouts of diarrhea, after which he felt that his entrails had been purged clear and his energy invigorated. Although he felt grateful to Lian-xiang, he still didn't believe that his sickness had been due to a ghost. Every night Lian-xiang pressed close to him under the covers; but when Sang wanted to make love, she stopped him immediately. After several days, his flesh was back to its former fullness. When she was about to leave, Lian-xiang urged him with all her might to break off with Li, and Sang pretended to agree. But as soon as he closed the door and trimmed the lamp wick, he immediately took hold of the slipper and turned his thoughts to Li. Suddenly there she was. Having been kept away from him for several days, she looked rather resentful; but Sang explained, "These past few nights I've been having shamanistic therapy. Please don't be annoyed with me. I still care about you." At this Li grew somewhat more cheerful. But later in bed Sang whispered to her, "I love you very much, but there are those that claim you're really a ghost." Li was tongue-tied for a long time, then rebuked him, "That wanton fox must have bewitched you into believing her. If you don't break off with her, I won't come here any more!" Then she burst into tears. Sang said all sorts of things to make her feel better, then gave up.

The following night when Lian-xiang appeared, she knew that Li had come again, and she said angrily, "You must want to die." Sang laughed, saying, "Why are you so jealous of her?" At this Lian-xiang grew even angrier: "The seeds of death had been planted in you, and I got rid of them for you. What would have happened if I hadn't been jealous?" Then Sang attributed words to Li to tease Lian-xiang: "She says that my sickness the other day was the evil eye brought on by a fox." At this, Lian-xiang said with a sigh, "It really does happen as you say, but you have been duped and don't know it. The whole thing is bound to turn out badly; and then even if I spoke with a hundred tongues, how could I explain myself. I'll leave you now. When I see you again in a hundred days, you will be bedridden." Sang couldn't get her to stay, and she departed at once in indignation.

From then on, Li was always with him morning and night. After a little more than two months, he began to feel very weak. At first he still tried to shake it off by himself, but he grew steadily more gaunt and emaciated until all he could eat was a bowl of thick porridge. He was ready to go back to where his family lived, but he still was too attached to Li to bear to leave her so abruptly. After a few more days, the sickness became debilitating, and he couldn't get up any more. When Sang's neighbor saw how feeble he had become, he sent his servant every day to see to Sang's meals. It was only at this point that Sang began to suspect Li and said to her, "I regret not having listened to Lian-xiang's advice. It has brought me to this." After saying that, he lost consciousness. A while later he came to; and when he opened his eyes and looked around, Li was gone, obviously having decided to have nothing more to do with him. Sang lay there emaciated, alone in his study, longing for Lian-xiang as one might hope for a great bounty.

One day as he was lost in reverie, someone suddenly lifted the curtain and came in. It was Lian-xiang. Standing by his bed, she said with a sad smile, "Well, my naïve friend, was I wrong?" Sang was choked up for a long time, then admitted how wrong he had been and asked her to rescue him. Lian-xiang said, "The disease has entered the vital regions below the heart, and there's no way to save you. I came to say my last farewell to you, and to show you that it was not jealousy." Sang was terribly upset and said, "There's something I have beneath my pillow—please destroy it for me." Lian-xiang reached under and found the slipper, then took it over in the lamp to examine it, turning it over in her hand. In a flash Li entered the room, but then suddenly caught sight of Lian-xiang and turned to make her escape. Lian-xiang blocked the doorway with her body, and Li found herself hemmed in with no way out.

When Sang took her to task for everything she had done to him, Li had no way to answer. Lian-xiang laughed. "Now I have a chance to confront you face to face. Some time ago you told our young friend that his previous illness could only have been brought on by me. How about now?" Li bowed her head and admitted she had been in the wrong. Then Lian-xiang said, "You're so beautiful, and yet you used love against him as if he were your enemy."

At that, Li fell to the floor and burst into tears, begging for mercy. Lian-xiang then helped her up and questioned her in detail about her life. Li said, "I was the daughter of the Assistant Li. I died young and was buried here just outside the walls. Li Shang-yin wrote how when the spring silkworm dies, its threads of longing end. In my case the spring silkworm may have died, but those threads remained and did not end. I just wanted to live with him happily; it was never my intention to bring about his death." Then Lian-xiang said, "I have heard that ghosts gain advantage by someone's death, because after that person dies they can be with him forever. Is that true?" Li answered, "No, it's not true. When two ghosts meet, there's no way they can enjoy themselves together. If they could, there are more than enough young men in the underworld!" Lian-xiang said, "Foolish girl! A man can't take doing it every night even with a human being—much less with a ghost!" Then Li asked, "But foxes bring about people's deaths. What technique do you have that this is not true for you?" Lian-xiang answered, "Those are the vampire foxes that suck the vital essences out of a person—I'm not that sort. There really are foxes that don't do people any harm, but there are absolutely no ghosts that don't do people harm—the Yin humors are too strong in them."

As Sang heard them talking, he realized for the first time that they really were a fox and a ghost. Fortunately he was so used to them that he wasn't alarmed by them at all. The only thing on his mind was his sinking breath, now as thin as a thread; and without realizing it, he groaned in misery. Lian-xiang consulted with Li. "What are we going to do about him?" Li blushed crimson and demurred. Lian-xiang laughed and said, "I'm afraid that if he gets strong and healthy again, you'll be so jealous you'll be eating sour grapes." Li straightened her sleeves in a demure attitude: "If there were some doctor of national standing who could undo my betrayal of our friend, then I would bury my head in the earth and never be so shameless as to show my face in the world again."

Lian-xiang then opened a pouch and took out some medicine. "I knew long ago it would reach this stage, so after leaving Sang I gathered these herbs on the Three Mountains of the immortals; and now that they have been curing for three months, the ingredients are at last ready. If he takes these, they will restore him to health, even if the malignancy has brought him to the edge of death. Nevertheless, the medicine must be helped along by the very same means by which he contracted the disease. That means that it is you who must do your best to save him." Li asked, "What is required?" Lian-xiang answered, "A drop of spit from your mouth. I will put in the pill, and then you put your mouth on his and spit into it." A glow of embarrassment rose on Li's cheeks; she lowered her head and fidgeted, looking at the slipper. Then Lian-xiang teased her, "I guess the slipper is the only thing that satisfies you." At this Li became even more ashamed and seemed as though she couldn't endure it. Lian-xiang then said, "This is an ordinary remedy for fevers—why are you holding back in this case?" Then she put the pill between Sang's lips and put increasing pressure on Li. Li had no choice but to spit on it. Lian-xiang said, "Again!" And she spit on it again. After spitting on it a few more times, the pill finally went down his throat. After a short while, there was a rumbling in his belly like the sound of thunder. She gave him another pill and this time touched her own lips to his and dissolved it with her breath. Sang felt a fire in his abdomen, and his vitality flared forth. Lian-xiang said, "He's better!"

When Li heard the rooster crow, she grew anxious and departed. Since Sang was still an invalid, Lian-xiang had to stay and nurse him, since he had no way to get his own meals. She locked up the door to give the false impression that he had gone back to his home region so that no one would come to visit him. She kept by his side day and night, and every evening Li too would come and give her wholehearted help. She treated Xiang-lian like a sister, and Xiang-lian too came to feel a deep affection for her.

After three months, Sang was as healthy as ever. After that Li would stay away for several evenings at a time, and when she did come, she would take a quick look and leave. When she faced them, she seemed troubled and unhappy. Lian-xiang would always try to get her to spend the night with them, but she was never willing. Once Sang went after her and picked her up to bring her back; her body was as light as one of the straw dolls used in burials. When she found that she couldn't get away, she lay down in her clothes and curled her body into a ball that wasn't even two feet wide. Lian-xiang increasingly felt sorry for her and secretly had Sang put his arms around her and try to be intimate with her, but he couldn't wake her up even by shaking her. Sang fell off to sleep; and when he woke up and looked for her, she was long gone.

For more than ten days after that, she didn't come again. She was very much on Sang's mind, and he would often take out the slipper and fondle it together with Lian-xiang. Lian-xiang said, "It's so lonely now. I still care for her, and as a man you must feel it even more." Then Sang said, "It used to be that she would come whenever I fondled the slipper; I did always wonder about that, but I never suspected she was a ghost. Now looking at this slipper and thinking of her face really makes me miserable." Then he began to weep.

The wealthy Zhang household had a fifteen-year-old daughter, Yan-er, who died suddenly without showing any signs of sickness. After a night had passed, she returned to consciousness. She got up, looked around, and started to run away. The Zhangs barred the door, and she couldn't get out. At this the young woman said, "I'm the spirit of the daughter of Assistant Li. I have been deeply touched by the kind attentions of Mr. Sang, and there's a piece of footwear of mine that still remains at his house. I really am a ghost, so it's not going to do any good to lock me up." Since there was a certain coherence in what she was saying, they questioned her about how she came to her present state. But she simply looked around in bewilderment, confused and unable to explain herself. Someone said that Mr. Sang was sick and had gone back to his native region, but the young woman insisted that this was erroneous.

The people in the household were quite perplexed. Sang's neighbor to the east heard about this, so he climbed over the wall to peek in Sang's house; there he saw Sang talking together with a beautiful woman. He burst in to catch them by surprise, but in a moment of confusion he lost track of her. Alarmed, the neighbor asked Sang for an explanation; and Sang laughed. "As I said to you quite clearly before, if it was a female I'd invite her in."

Then Sang's neighbor told him what Yan-er had said. Sang unlocked the door and wanted to go find out what was going on, but there was no way he could.

When Mrs. Zhang heard that Sang had not, after all, gone back to his native place, she thought the whole matter was even stranger. She sent an old serving woman to get the slipper, which Sang produced and handed over to her. Yan-er was delighted when she got it; but when she tried to put it on, it was smaller than her foot by a full inch, and she was greatly alarmed. When she then took a mirror to look at herself, she was in a daze, suddenly realizing that she had come to life in this other body. At she explained the full course of events, and at last her mother believed her. When the young woman looked at her face in the mirror, she wept loudly, saying, "I had some self-confidence in my looks back then, yet whenever I saw Lian-xiang, I still felt embarrassment by comparison. But as it is now, I'm even less attractive as a human being than as a ghost." She would just hold the slipper and wail inconsolably. She covered herself up with a quilt and lay stiff. They would try to feed her, but she wouldn't eat, and her flesh and skin became all swollen. For a full seven days she didn't eat; but she did not die and the swelling gradually subsided. At that point, she felt so hungry she couldn't bear it and began to eat again. After several days itching covered her whole body, and the skin all fell away. When she got up in the morning, her bed slippers fell from her feet, and when she went to put them on again, they were too large and didn't fit. Then she tried on her old slipper, and now it fit perfectly. She was delighted. Then she looked at herself in the mirror again and found that her brows, her eyes, her cheeks, and chin were all just as they had been originally—and at this she was even more delighted. She then bathed, combed her hair, and went to see her mother, and all who saw her were pleased.

When Lian-xiang heard about this marvel, she urged Sang to send a matchmaker with an offer of marriage; but because of the discrepancy in the fortunes of the two households, Sang didn't dare proceed with rash haste. On the old lady's birthday, he went along with her sons-in-law to congratulate her. The old lady saw his name and had Yan-er look through the curtain to see if she recognized him. Sang was the last to arrive, and the young woman burst out, grabbed his sleeve, and wanted to go home with him. Only after her mother scolded her did she grow embarrassed and go back in. Sang had gotten a clear look at her, and without knowing it, tears began to fall from his eyes. At this, he prostrated himself on the floor in front of the old lady and didn't get up. She in turn helped him up and didn't take it as bad manners. As Sang left, he asked one of the young woman's uncles to represent him in negotiations for the marriage. The old woman deliberated and chose a lucky day for to take him as her son-in-law.

When Sang went back, he told Lian-xiang about this, and they discussed how to handle matters; but then Lian-xiang grew depressed for a long time and finally wanted to take her leave of him. Sang grew quite alarmed and wept. Then Lian-xiang said, "You are going to be married with all the proper ceremonies, and if I go along with you, I'll lose all respect." Sang planned with Lian-xiang to first take her back to her own home, and then to go get Yan-er and bring her back as his bride. Lian-xiang agreed. Sang then explained the situation to Mrs. Zhang, who, on hearing that he had a concubine, became furious and reproached him bitterly. But Yan-er did her best to explain matters, and Mrs. Zhang did as she asked. When the day came, Sang went to get his bride and bring her home. The furnishings of his house had been extremely messy and ill kept; but when he got back, there were woolen rugs laid down on the ground from the gate into the main hall, and thousands of lanterns in sparkling rows like brocade. Lian-xiang helped the new bride under the green wedding awning, and when the bridal veil was lifted, they were as happy to see one another as ever.

Lian-xiang joined them in the ritual exchange of winecups and questioned Yan-er in detail on the marvel of her recent spirit wandering. Yan-er then said, "That day, I was depressed and upset. I just felt that I was no longer human and that my body had become something unclean. After I left you, I was so distraught that I didn't go back to my grave but let myself drift along with the wind. Whenever I saw a living person, I felt envious of them. In the daytime I stayed among the plants and trees, and by night I let my feet drift along. Then I happened to come to the Zhang household and saw a young girl lying on a bed. I approached her and then came right up next to her, not knowing that I could come to life."

When Lian-xiang heard this, she remained quiet, as if something were on her mind. Several months later, Lian-xiang gave birth to a child. After the delivery she became gravely ill, and her condition steadily deteriorated. She clutched Yan-er's arm and said, "If I can burden you with my bastard, let my son be your son." Yan-er wept and reassured her. They called in a shaman doctor, but Lian-xiang immediately sent him away. As she lay on her deathbed, her breath grew ragged, while Sang and Yan-er were both weeping. Suddenly she opened her eyes and said, "Don't be like that. You find joy in life; I find joy in death. If destiny permits, ten years from now we may get to meet again." After uttering these words, she was gone. When they drew back the covers to gather her up, the corpse had changed into a fox. Sang couldn't bear to treat her as something unhuman and gave her a lavish funeral.

They named her son Kit, and Yan-er treated him if he were her own issue. Every year at the Qing-ming Festival she would take Kit in her arms and go weep at Lian-xiang's tomb. After several years Sang won a provincial degree from his native region, and the household gradually became more affluent. Yan-er had unfortunately not had a child of her own, and while Kit was very clever, he was frail and sickly. Yan-er always wanted Sang to take a concubine. One day a servant announced, "There's an old lady outside the gate with a girl she wants to sell." Yan-er called out to have them brought in. When she saw her, she said amazed, "Lian-xiang has reappeared!" When Sang looked at her and saw that she did indeed resemble Lian-xiang, he too was shocked. They asked how old she was, and woman answered that she was fourteen. "How much do you want for her?" And the old woman said, "This little piece of flesh is all I have. It's enough for me that I find a place, that I am able to get enough eat and that in the future my old bones not just be thrown in some ditch."

Sang paid her well and let her stay. Yan-er took the girl by the hand and took her into a room where they could be private; then she pinched the girl's chin and said with a laugh, "Do you recognize me?" The girl replied that she did not, and Yan-er questioned her about her background. The girl said, "My name is Wei, and my father was a bean-paste merchant in Xu-cheng. He's been dead three years." When Yan-er thought about it and counted, Lian-xiang had been dead for exactly fourteen years. She looked the girl over carefully again, and all her features and the way she moved bore an uncanny resemblance. Then she patted the girl on the top of the head, shouting, "Lian-xiang! Lian-xiang! Don't fool us in your promise to see us again in ten years!"

All of a sudden the young girl seemed as if waking from a dream and said, "Huh?" Then she looked Yan-er over carefully. Sang laughed and said, "It's like that line of verse:

As if they were old acquaintances,
    the swallows come back again."

Tears streaming down her face, the girl said, "It's true! I heard my mother say that when I was born, I could already speak. They thought it was unlucky, so they gave me dog's blood to drink in order to forget my previous existence. Today it's like just waking up from a dream. Aren't you my friend Li, who was ashamed to be a ghost?" Then they all talked about their earlier lives together, with grief and joy mingling.

One day on the festival for visiting the graves, Yan-er said, "This is the day that Sang and I go to weep at your tomb every year." Then the girl joined them on the visit to the tomb; the wild grasses were growing everywhere, while the trees planted by the tomb had already reached a double handspan in girth. The girl too sighed, and Yan-er said to Sang, "Lian-xiang and I have been close to one another in two lifetimes now, and we can't bear to be apart. Our bones should be buried in the same grave." Sang did as she asked; he opened Li's tomb to get her remains, then took them back to bury with Lian-xiang's. Friends and relatives heard about this marvel and stood by the graveside in formal attire. Unexpectedly there were hundreds gathered there.

In 1670, I visited Yi-zhou during my travels south; unable to go on because of a storm, I stopped at an inn there. A certain Liu Zi-jing was there, a relative of Sang's, and he showed me a work entitled "Mr. Sang's Story" by Wang Zi-zhang, a member of his set. This was a long work of more than ten thousand characters. I finished reading it, and the above is an abbreviated version.

Here follows the judgment of the Chronicler of Wonders: A dead person sought to live, and a living person sought to die. Is not a human body the hardest thing to attain in this world? Yet it seems to happen that those who have such a human body always use it in such a way that they come to shamefulness that makes them in life inferior to the fox, and in simply vanishing away their death is inferior to the ghost.

Xiao-cui

Wang, the Grand Chamberlain of Ceremonials, was a native of Yue. When he was still a boy, he was napping, when all of a sudden the sky grew dark and there was a mighty clap of thunder. An animal larger than a cat came and hid under his body, squirming and refusing to go. After a while the sky cleared up, and the animal immediately went straight out. When Wang looked closely and saw that it was not a cat, he grew frightened and called to his big brother in the other room. His brother heard him and said cheerfully, "Well, brother, you're going to reach a very exalted position—this was a fox that came to you to escape being destroyed by thunder and lightning."

Afterward the young man did indeed pass the metropolitan examination at a young age, and he rose from the post of county magistrate to become a Censor. He had one son whose name was Yuan-feng, a simpleton who at the age of sixteen didn't know the difference between male and female. As a result, no one of his own class was willing to marry their daughters to him. Wang was worried about him.

It happened that a woman brought a girl to his gate and requested that she be made Yuan-feng's wife. When Wang looked the girl over, she smiled in the most fetching manner—she was a beauty of the highest order. Delighted, he asked the name, and the woman said, "Our family is named Yu, and my daughter is Xiao-cui. She's sixteen." He then discussed the question of price with her, and she said, "With me she has eaten rough fare and has never been able to eat her fill. Now in a single day she will find herself living in spacious apartments, waited on by servants, and having all the meat and fine rice she can eat. If she is content, then my own wishes are satisfied. I'm not going to haggle over a price for her as if I were selling vegetables!"

Wang's wife was very pleased and rewarded the woman generously. Then the woman bade her daughter bow to Wang and his wife and instructed her: "These are to be your parents. You should serve them conscientiously. I'm very busy and am going away for a while. I'll be back in a few days." Wang ordered his servant to hitch up the carriage to see her home, but the woman said, "I don't live far from here, and I don't want to be a bother." Then she went out the gate. Xiao-cui didn't seem to miss her at all, but at once went to the dressing table and began to play around with various ways of making herself up. Wang's wife doted on her.

After several days, the mother did not return. They asked Xiao-cui where she lived, but she seemed befuddled and couldn't tell them the way. Consequently they set up separate apartments, and had her formally married to Yuan-feng. When the relatives heard that the Wangs had picked up a poor girl as Yuan-feng's bride, they all made fun of them; but when they saw the girl, everyone was amazed, and the gossip quieted down.

Xiao-cui was also very clever and could see what pleased and angered her in-laws. For their part, Wang and his wife were fond of the girl far beyond an ordinary affection, and they were apprehensive lest she dislike their son for his simple-mindedness. But Xiao-cui was very good-natured, and didn't despise him for it at all. Instead she enjoyed having a good time; she sewed a piece of cloth into a round ball and then kicked it about for fun. Wearing leather shoes, she could kick it twenty or thirty paces, then inveigle Yuan-feng to run after it and pick it up for her. Yuan-feng and the maids were always going one after another, running with sweat.

One day Wang Senior happened to be passing by. With a *thunk* the ball came flying and hit him square in the face. Xiao-cui and the maids all made themselves scarce, but Yuan-feng continued to leap up and down as he ran to get it. Wang Senior was angry and threw a rock at him, whereupon the boy collapsed to the ground, crying. Wang Senior informed his wife about this, and she went to reprimand the girl. Xiao-cui lowered her head with a faint smile, while digging her hands into the bed. Once Mrs. Wang had left, she went back to her old pranks. Using powder and paint, she made up Yuan-feng's face to look like a ghost. When Mrs. Wang saw this, she grew furious and shouted insults at the girl. Xiao-cui just leaned against a table and fiddled with her sash, not frightened but also not saying anything. Mrs. Wang couldn't stand it any more and took a cane to her son. When Yuan-feng started yelling, the girl's expression changed and she bent her knees to beg Mrs. Wang to show mercy. Mrs. Wang's rage abruptly left her; she let go of the cane and left.

Smiling, Xiao-cui then pulled Yuan-feng into a room, where she brushed the dust off his clothes, wiped the tears from his eyes, rubbed the welts where he had been beaten, and fed him dates and chestnuts. Yuan-feng stopped crying and cheered up. Xiao-cui then shut the gate of the courtyard and again dressed Yuan-feng up, this time as the Overlord Xiang Yu and then as the Khan of the desert.[1] She for her own part put on fine clothes, tied her waist tight, and did the swaying dance of Yu in the commander's tent.[2] Then she would stick the tail feather of a pheasant in her piled hair, and strum the mandolin in a continuous flood of notes.[3] They did this every day, laughing and making an uproar in the room. Since Wang Senior thought his son was a simpleton, he couldn't bring himself to scold his son's wife too harshly. When he heard a bit of what was going on, he seemed to dismiss the matter.

On the same street about a dozen doors down there was another Mr. Wang, a Supervisory Censor, and the two Wangs couldn't stand one another.

---

[1]Here and with the ghost make-up, Xiao-cui is probably imitating conventional theatrical costume.
[2]This refers to the famous scene in the *Historical Records* and in later theater in which Xiang Yu, the great competitor of Liu Bang for the empire after the fall of the Qin, finds himself at last surrounded by Han troops and holds a small feast in which he laments his fate and bids farewell to his lady Yu.
[3]Here Yuan-feng is playing the Khan to whom the Han court lady Wang Zhao-jun was married against her will. Xiao-cui plays Wang Zhao-jun, lamenting her fate on the mandolin.

The triennial review of officials for promotion had just taken place, and Censor Wang resented that our Mr. Wang had been given charge of the seal of the Investigator for the He-nan Circuit. Censor Wang was looking for a way to harm him. Wang Senior knew about his machinations and was very worried, having no way to protect himself. One evening when he retired early, Xiao-cui put on a cap and sash and dressed herself up as the Chief Minister. She cut threads of white silk to make herself a full beard and also dressed up two of the serving girls in blue gowns to act as her bodyguards. Then she secretly mounted herself astride one of the horses in the stable and went out, saying in play, "I am going to pay a call on Mr. Wang."

She galloped to the gate of Supervisory Censor Wang and struck her attendants with her riding whip, declaring loudly, "I was going to pay a call on *Investigator* Wang! Why should I bother to pay a call on *Supervisory Censor* Wang?" Then she turned the horse around and went back home. But when she had almost reached the gate, the gatekeeper mistakenly took her for the real thing and rushed in to inform Wang Senior. Wang Senior hurriedly got up to go out to welcome him. When he realized that this was a prank of his son's wife, he was furious and said to Mrs. Wang, "Others have chastised me for my shortcomings, but now this clown character from the women of my own household pays me a visit to announce them publicly. My downfall must not be far off!" Mrs. Wang grew angry, rushed into Xiao-cui's room, and yelled at her. But Xiao-cui only smiled foolishly and didn't offer a word in her defense. Mrs. Wang would have whipped her, but she couldn't bring himself to; she would have put her out of the house, but then she would have had no home. Both husband and wife were so upset and annoyed that they couldn't go to sleep all night long.

The Chief Minister at the time was a flamboyant figure; his behavior, his attire, and his entourage were little different from Xiao-cui's costume; and Supervisory Censor Wang also made the mistake of taking her for the real thing. He went to keep watch at Wang Senior's gate that night, and when the guest had not left by midnight, he suspected that the Chief Minister and Wang Senior were hatching some secret plot. The next day when he saw Wang Senior at dawn court, he asked him, "Did His Excellency go to your house last night?" Suspecting that the Supervisory Censor was making fun of him, Wang Senior hemmed and hawed in embarrassment and didn't really answer him. At this, Censor Wang's suspicions were confirmed even more strongly; he laid his plots against Wang Senior to rest and from that point on tried to get into Wang Senior's good graces. Wang Senior figured out what had been going through Censor Wang's mind and was privately delighted; yet he secretly directed his wife to urge Xiao-cui to mend her ways. Xiao-cui answered her with a smile.

After another year the Chief Minister was dismissed from office, and it happened that a private letter sent to Wang Senior was mistakenly delivered to Supervisory Censor Wang. Censor Wang was delighted and first used good friends of Wang Senior to go borrow ten thousand cash. Wang Senior refused. Then the Censor himself went to Wang Senior's house. Wang Senior was looking for his official cap and gown but could find neither; the Censor waited for him for a long time and then became angry at Wang Senior's cavalier treatment of him and was about to leave in a huff. Suddenly he saw Yuan-feng dressed in imperial dragon robes and a crown of jade; there was a young woman pushing him out from behind the door. The Censor was quite shocked, but then he smiled and was nice to the lad. Making him take off the imperial robes and crown, the Censor took them and left.

When Wang Senior came out hurriedly, his visitor was already long gone. When he heard what had happened, his face turned white, and weeping loudly, he said, "This young woman is our nemesis. On this very day our entire family and all our relations will be executed." And together with Mrs. Wang he took a stick and went off to find Xiao-cui. Xiao-cui already knew this and closed her door, bearing their curses and insults. Wang Senior was furious and took an ax to her door. From within, Xiao-cui smiled and told him, "Don't work yourself up into such a rage, sir. As long as I am here, I will bear the rack and tongs and headsman's ax myself and I won't let any harm come to you, my in-laws. If you go on like this, do you want to kill me to shut me up?" And then Wang Senior stopped.

When Censor Wang got home, he wrote out a denunciation to the throne indicting Wang Senior for lèse-majesté, using the imperial robes and crown for evidence. His Majesty was surprised and examined the evidence: the "crown" was plaited from sorghum stalks, while the "robes" were a tattered piece of yellow bundling cloth. The Emperor was furious at such false charges. He also had Yuan-feng summoned to his presence; and when he saw from his manner that Yuan-feng was obviously simple-minded, he said with a laugh, "So this would be our Son of Heaven." Then he had Censor Wang sent down to the Judiciary for trial. Censor Wang had also charged that there was a witch girl in Wang Senior's house. The judiciary thoroughly questioned the family servants, and they all said that it was just a simple-minded boy and his touched wife who spent their days playing games. The neighbors also offered nothing to contradict this. The case was then closed and ex-Censor Wang was sent off to serve in the army in Yun-nan.

From this point on, Wang Senior considered Xiao-cui something extraordinary. And since her mother had not returned in such a long time, he considered that she might not be a human being. He sent his wife to question her, but Xiao-cui just laughed and said nothing. When she was pressed even harder, she covered her mouth and said, "Don't you realize that I'm the daughter of the Jade Emperor in Heaven?"

Soon afterward Wang was promoted to one of the senior positions in the capital. He was over fifty and always felt troubled at not having any grandchildren. Xiao-cui had lived with them three years, and every night she slept apart from Yuan-feng, so it seemed that they had never had intimate relations. Mrs. Wang moved the bed and directed Yuan-feng to sleep together with his wife. After several days, Yuan-feng came and told his mother, "Take my bed away—I absolutely won't come back. Every night Xiao-cui puts her feet and thighs on my belly, and I can hardly breathe. She's also got the habit of poking around a person's thighs." Every one of the maids was smirking. Mrs. Wang shouted at them, whacked them, and made them leave.

One day Xiao-cui was bathing in her chamber. Yuan-feng saw her and wanted to join her. Xiao-cui laughed and stopped him, ordering him to wait a while. When she got out, she poured more scalding hot water into the tub, took off his robe and pants, and then with a maid helped him to get in. Yuan-feng felt like he was suffocating from the steam and shouted that he wanted to get out. Xiao-cui wouldn't listen to him and covered him over with a blanket. After a while he ceased to make any more sounds, and when they opened it to look, he had expired. Xiao-cui smiled contentedly and was not alarmed. She dragged him out and lay him on the bed. She wiped his body until it was dry and clean, and then put a double quilt over him. Mrs. Wang had heard about this and came into the room weeping: "You crazy girl! Why did you kill my son?"

Xiao-cui beamed her most charming smile and said, "With a son as simple-minded as this, you're better off with none at all." Mrs. Wang grew even more enraged and charged Xiao-cui with her head lowered. All the maids tried to pull her back and calm her down. Amid all this commotion, one maid declared, "Yuan-feng just groaned!" When Mrs. Wang stopped weeping and felt him, she found he was breathing, and a great sweat was pouring from his body, soaking the mat and bedding. After a little while longer the sweat stopped, and he suddenly opened his eyes and looked all around, scrutinizing each member of the household as if he didn't recognize them. Then he said, "When I think back on the past, it all seems like a dream—why is that?" Since his speech no longer seemed simple-minded, Mrs. Wang was amazed. She took him by the hand to go consult with his father, and on being questioned repeatedly, he was in fact no longer simple-minded. They were delighted as if they had just obtained a rare treasure.

When evening came, they moved his bed back to where it had been, and again made it up with covers and a blanket to watch what he would do. When Yuan-feng entered the room, he sent all the maidservants away. When they looked in the next morning, the bed had not been slept in. From that point on there was no more simple-mindedness on his part or craziness on her part; all was rosy between husband and wife, and the two were inseparable.

After more than a year, Wang Senior was impeached by the faction of Censor Wang and dismissed from office for a minor offense. The family had a jade vase long ago presented to them by the Vice-Censor of Guang-xi, its value a thousand pieces of cash. They had taken it out to offer as a bribe to a powerful official. Xiao-cui liked it and was holding it when it slipped from her hands and shattered. She was so ashamed that she threw herself down. Wang Senior and his wife, being on edge because of his dismissal from office, flew into a rage when they heard about it. In turn they yelled at her and cursed her. Then Xiao-cui roused herself and went out, saying to Yuan-feng, "During the time I've been in your family, the things I've protected and preserved have not been limited to just a single vase, so why am I not left with some respect! I'll tell you the truth: I am not a human being. When my mother was going to be struck by lightning, she was very generously protected by your father. Moreover, you and I have a predestined span of five years together, so she brought me to repay that kindness he once did and to fulfill an abiding wish. I have been spat upon, I have borne curses, and more hairs have been pulled from my head than I can count. The reason I didn't go off immediately was because our five years together were not up. But now, how can I stay here one moment longer!" With that she went off in a temper, and by the time he went after her, she was long gone.

Wang Senior was despondent and felt lost, but his regrets did no good. When Yuan-feng entered her chamber and cast eyes on the powders and slippers she had left behind, he broke into tears and wanted to die. He was unwilling to eat or sleep and every day grew more wasted and emaciated. Wang Senior was quite worried and quickly set about to arrange a second marriage to console him, but Yuan-feng was not pleased with the idea. He only sought out a skilled painter to portray Xiao-cui's likeness, and day and night for almost two years he would pour libations and pray before it.

It happened once that for one reason or another he was coming back from another village as the bright moon was already casting its glow. Outside the village there was a garden of a gentry household, and as Yuan-feng rode his horse past outside the wall, he heard someone laughing and talking. He pulled up on the reins and had his groom hold the bridle. When he stood on the saddle and looked over, there were two girls playing on the other side. Clouds were passing over the moon and it was so dusky he couldn't make them out clearly. He heard one who was wearing azure clothes say, "You should be kicked out of here!" Then one wearing red clothes said, "You're in my garden. Who's going to get kicked out?" Then the one in azure replied, "You're shameless. You couldn't be a wife and got yourself driven away, and you still presume to claim this as your property?" The one wearing red said, "Well, it's better than being an old maid without ever having been betrothed."

When Yuan-feng listened to the sound of her voice, it sounded very much like Xiao-cui's, and he quickly called to her. The one in azure went off, saying, "I'm not going to quarrel with you any more. Your young man has come." Then the one in red came over, and it was indeed Xiao-cui. He was beside himself with delight. She had him climb over the wall and helped him down, saying, "I haven't seen you for years. You're all skin and bones!" Yuan-feng took hold of her hands and wept, telling her everything and how much he had missed her. Xiao-cui said, "I knew it, but I couldn't bring myself to face your family again. Now as I was playing with my big sister in the garden, we've met again unexpectedly—this shows that what is predestined can't be avoided."

He asked her to come home with him, but she refused. Then he asked to stay in her garden, and to this she agreed. Yuan-feng sent a servant to hurry off and tell his mother. His mother got up in surprise and went off in a sedan chair. The lock was opened, and she came into the pavilion in the garden. Xiao-cui immediately rushed over to welcome her politely. Mrs. Wang clutched her arm and shed tears, earnestly declaring her previous faults, and virtually overwhelmed, she said, "If you are willing to overlook those painful memories, come home with me and comfort me in my old age." But Xiao-cui adamantly refused. Mrs. Wang was then concerned that this pavilion out in the wilds was too solitary and dreary, and she made plans to have many people work there. But Xiao-cui said, "We don't want to have anyone else around but the two serving girls who formerly were with us day and night, for we can't entirely do without someone to take care of us; beyond that, I would have only an old servant to act as the gatekeeper. We don't need any others at all." Mrs. Wang agreed to everything she said. She left Yuan-feng to convalesce in the garden, providing him only his food and other daily needs. Xiao-cui urged Yuan-feng to marry again, but he wouldn't go along with her.

After more than a year, Xiao-cui's features and her voice gradually became different from what they had been previously. When Yuan-feng took out her portrait and compared it with her present state, they were as far apart as two different people. He thought this very strange. Xiao-cui said, "When you look at me today, how can my beauty compare to what it used to be?" Yuan-feng said, "You're beautiful as you are now, but not quite as much so as you used to be." Xiao-cui said, "You mean, I've gotten old!" Yuan-feng replied, "How could you get old so quickly, only in your early twenties?" Xiao-cui laughed and burned the portrait, and when Yuan-feng tried to rescue it, it was already ashes. One day she said to Yuan-feng, "Before, when I lived at your house, your father said that I would die without bearing any children. Your parents are old, and I truly cannot bear a child; I'm afraid that this will ruin the succession of your family line. Please marry someone and set her up in your home. She could wait on your parents all the time and you could go back and forth between here and there—that would work out well in every way."

Yuan-feng agreed and sent the bride-price to the home of the Han-lin Compiler Zhong. When the blessed day drew near, Xiao-cui prepared clothes and slippers for the new bride and had them sent to her mother's home. And when the bride entered Wang's gate her speech, her appearance, and her movements were not the slightest bit different from those of Xiao-cui. Yuan-feng thought this extremely strange. When he went to the pavilion in her garden, he didn't know where Xiao-cui was. He asked a servant girl, and she took out a red cloth kerchief, saying, "Madam has gone to her mother's home for a time, and she left this for you." He unrolled the kerchief, and a ring was knotted to it, and in his heart he knew that she was not coming back. Then he took the serving girls and went home with them.

Even though he never forgot Xiao-cui for a moment, Yuan-feng was fortunate that every time he looked at his new bride, it was like seeing his old love. Then he realized that Xiao-cui had foreseen his marriage to Miss Zhong and had first changed her own appearance in order to comfort him when he would miss her in days to come.

Here follows the judgment of the Chronicler of Wonders: A fox still thought to repay a kindness done, even one done through unconscious virtue. Were they not contemptible who, having received the blessing of a second lease on life, yet were still aghast at a broken pot? As the moon wanes and is full again, so in the mortal world division came to fullness and reunion. And then, at her ease she departed. Now we can see that the loves of immortals are deeper still than those in the common world.

Blue Maid

Huo Huan, also known as Huo Kuang-jiu, was a native of Jin. His father, a county sheriff, had died before his time, leaving Huo Huan at a very tender age. Huo Huan was an exceptionally clever boy, and at the age of eleven he was enrolled among students for a civil service position as a "gifted lad."[4] But his mother, who doted on him to excess, forbade him to leave the family compound, and by the age of thirteen he still couldn't tell all his uncles and cousins apart.

In the same ward of the city there was a review judge, a Mr. Wu, who became a devotee of the Way and went off into the mountains, never to return. He had a daughter, Blue Maid, fourteen years of age and beautiful beyond the common measure. When younger, she had surreptitiously read her father's books and come to idolize the Maiden Goddess He. When her father disappeared, she made up her mind not to marry, and her mother could do nothing about it.

One day Huo Huan caught a glimpse of her outside the gate. Although the boy knew nothing about such things, he felt an intense love for her, but he couldn't explain it in words. He straightway told his mother to send someone to arrange an engagement. His mother knew that it would not be possible and raised objections. Huo Huan grew depressed and dissatisfied; and his mother, fearing to thwart her son's will, engaged a go-between to convey the proposal to the Wu family. As expected, they did not agree. Huo Huan was constantly brooding and trying to devise schemes, but he could see no way.

It happened once that a Daoist came to their gate, carrying in his hand a small hand-spade about a foot in length. Huo Huan took it to look it over and asked, "What's it used for?" The Daoist answered, "It's a tool for digging out herbs. Although it's small, it can penetrate hard stone." Huo Huan didn't really believe him, so the Daoist immediately cut into the stone of the garden wall, which, at every motion of his hand, fell away as if it were decomposed. Huo Huan was amazed; he kept on examining it and didn't put it down. The Daoist then laughed and said, "Since you like it so much, let me give it to you as a gift." Huo Huan was delighted and tried to give him money for it, but the Daoist refused to accept it and left.

When Huo Huan took it back and tried it on a range of rock and brick,

---

[4]"Gifted lad" was the term used for those who passed the preliminary qualifying examination at a young age.

there was hardly any resistance. All of a sudden it came to his mind that if he made a hole in the wall, he could see that beautiful girl, not realizing that it was wrongful behavior. After the bell of the watch had rung, he cut his way right through the wall and went directly to the Wu mansion. There, after digging holes through several more layers of walls, he reached the inner courtyard. He saw a lamp fire still burning in a small chamber; and when he hid himself and spied in, it was Blue Maid taking off her evening attire. In a little while, the candle went out and all was silent. When he made a hole in the next wall and went inside, the girl was already sound asleep. Then he took off his shoes and quietly got on her bed. He was afraid that if she woke, startled, he would be yelled at and forced to leave; so he nestled down by the side of her embroidered gown, smelling her sweet breath, and his heart's desire was secretly satisfied. After his endeavors through half the night, he was utterly exhausted; and closing his eyes just a little, he went off to sleep without realizing it.

The girl woke up and heard the sound of breathing. Then she opened her eyes and saw light coming in through the hole. Terrified, she hurriedly got up and in the darkness unbolted the door and got out of the room. Then she knocked on the windows and called to the women of the household, who lit lanterns, grabbed canes, and went to her room. When they got there they saw a young adolescent, dressed as a student, sleeping oblivious on her embroidered bed. Examining him carefully, they recognized him as young Huo. Only after they prodded him did he wake up, and then he got up at once, his eyes sparkling like shooting stars. He didn't even seem to be very frightened, just too embarrassed to say a word. Since everyone was treating him like a burglar, he was afraid they were going to yell at him.

At that point, Huo began to cry and said, "I'm not a burglar—it was really only because I was in love with Blue Maid and wanted to be close to her sweetness." But everyone then doubted that a child could have dug holes in several walls. At this, Huo Huan took out his spade and told them about its remarkable powers. They each put it to the test and were utterly astounded, exclaiming that it was a gift from the gods. They were all going to tell Mrs. Wu, but Blue Maid hung her head in brooding and seemed to think this would not be a good thing to do. The other women divined what was on her mind, so they said, "This boy is from an eminent and respectable household, and he hasn't violated your honor in the least. The best thing to do would be to let him loose and make him leave, then to have him once again seek a betrothal. In the morning we'll make up an excuse to your mother about a burglar. How would that be?" Blue Maid didn't answer, and the women then hurried Huo Huan to get going. Huo Huan wanted his spade back, and they all laughed and said, "You foolish boy! You still can't forget this tool of ruin!"

Huo Huan spied a phoenix hairpin beside the pillow and furtively put it in his sleeve, but a maid saw him do it and instantly told everybody. Blue Maid said nothing, nor did she get angry. One old woman slapped him on the neck and said, "Don't think he's so innocent—he's extremely tricky";

and she dragged him along to the hole he had dug, from which he then made his way out.

When Huo Huan got home, he didn't dare tell his mother the truth. He simply urged her to send the matchmaker to the Wus again. But Huo Huan's mother couldn't bear an open rejection and instructed all the matchmakers to arrange a marriage with someone else as quickly as possible. Blue Maid found out about this and her heart was in a panic. She secretly conveyed her innermost feelings to her mother. The mother was pleased and let the matchmaker know. It happened, however, that a young servant girl let out the secret of what had gone on previously, and Mrs. Wu felt so humiliated that she couldn't contain her rage. When the matchmaker arrived, she met an even greater outburst of anger, as Mrs. Wu struck the ground with her cane and railed against Huo Huan and his mother as well. The matchmaker was frightened and snuck back, giving Mrs. Huo a full account of how things stood. Then Huo Huan's mother also flew into a rage, saying, "I was totally ignorant of what that wicked boy did. Why should I bear the brunt of such rudeness! Why didn't they kill that wild boy and that wanton girl both while they were twining their legs together!"

From that point on, whenever she met her relations she would immediately tell the whole story. When Blue Maid heard about this, she could have died from shame. And Mrs. Wu too greatly regretted the whole thing, but there was nothing she could do to stop Mrs. Huo from talking. Blue Maid secretly sent someone to tactfully approach Huo Huan's mother, swearing to her that she would not marry anyone else. Her words were very moving; and Mrs. Huo, touched by them, spoke of it no further. And negotiations to arrange another marriage for Huo Huan were subsequently halted.

It happened that a Mr. Ou-yang of Shensi was magistrate of the town, and when he saw Huo Huan's writing, he developed a high opinion of his capacities. Sometimes he had Huo summoned to the county office, where he treated him with the greatest kindness and generosity. One day he asked Huo Huan, "Are you married?" To which Huo Huan replied that he was not yet. When Ou-yang questioned him in some detail, Huo Huan responded, "Long ago I became pledged to the young daughter of the former review judge Mr. Wu, but later, because of a minor feud, the matter has been left hanging." Ou-yang asked him, "Do you still want to go through with it or not?" At this Huo Huan grew embarrassed and said nothing. Ou-yang laughed and said, "I'll get it done for you." At once he sent the sheriff and the local schoolteacher with the proper bride gifts to the Wus. Mrs. Wu was delighted, and the betrothal was settled.

When the year of engagement passed, Huo Huan brought Blue Maid home as his bride. As soon as Blue Maid entered the gate, she threw the spade on the ground, saying, "This is a thing for burglars. Get rid of it." But Huo Huan laughed. "Don't snub our go-between!" Then he hung it as a treasure from his sash, and it never left his person. Blue Maid was of a gentle, kindly, yet reticent disposition. Every day she would pay her respects to her mother-in-law three times, but for the remainder of the day she would just close her door and sit quietly, not concerning herself very much with household duties. Yet if Huo's mother were gone elsewhere to offer condolences or congratulations, the management of household affairs was always in good order.

After more than a year, she gave birth to a son, Meng-xian. She left everything to the charge of a wet nurse and seemed not to be particularly concerned for the child. After another five years, she abruptly said to Huo Huan, "By now the course of our love has lasted eight years. Our time left together is short and the separation will be long. Nothing can be done about it!" Huo Huan was startled and asked her to explain, but she kept silent, and in full attire went to pay her respects to her mother-in-law, then returned to her own room. When he went after Blue Maid to question her, she was lying on her bed, face up, and not breathing. Both mother and son mourned for her deeply. They purchased a fine coffin for her and had her buried. Huo's mother was already frail and aging. Whenever she took the child in her arms, she would think of his mother, and it was as if her heart would break. After this she grew sick and became so exhausted that she could not get up. She felt a revulsion against taking any nourishment. The only thing she wanted was a certain fish dish that could not be obtained anywhere close by, but could be purchased only at a place a hundred miles away.

At the time the hired couriers had all been sent on various errands; and Huo, who was genuinely devoted to his mother, was in a hurry and couldn't wait. Taking money for his expenses, he set off by himself, and didn't stop traveling day and night. But then he found himself in the mountains, with the sunlight already sinking to darkness; he was hobbling on both feet and couldn't go an inch further. An old man came up behind him and said, "You must have gotten blisters on your feet." Huo Huan answered that he had. Then the old man led him over to sit by the side of the road and struck some flint to make a fire. Using some herbs he had in a paper packet, he steamed both of Huo Huan's feet. When Huo tried to walk again, not only had the pain stopped but he also felt stronger and more energetic. Deeply touched, Huo Huan expressed his gratitude, and the old man asked, "Why are you in such a hurry?" Huo explained that his mother was sick, and from there proceeded to tell the events that led up to it. The old man then asked, "Why don't you marry someone else?" Huo Huan answered that he had not found a good-looking woman. The old man then pointed to a mountain village in the distance and said, "There's a good-looking woman there. If only you could go off with me there, I would arrange something for you." But Huo declined on the grounds that his mother was sick and required a certain fish. At this the old man folded his hands and said that if he should come to the village someday, he should just ask for Old Wang. Then he went his way. When Huo got home, he cooked the fish and offered it to his mother. Huo's mother improved somewhat, and in several days she quickly got better.

Huo Huan then had a servant and horse readied to go look for the old man. When he reached the spot he had been before, he could no longer tell where the village was. He wandered around for some time as the evening glow of the sun gradually sank away. The hills and valleys were very confusing; unable to get a clear view to orient himself, Huo climbed a hilltop with his servant to look for a village. The mountain path was rough and steep, too difficult to continue to ride, so he went up on foot, engulfed in the darkening colors of mist. There he paced about, looking in all directions, but there was still no sign of a village. He started down the mountain but couldn't find the path back. Anxiety seemed to burn in his heart like a fire. As he sought some refuge in the wilderness, night's blackness descended the sheer cliff. Fortunately, several feet below him there was a swathe of wild moss; and when he lowered himself and lay on it, its width was just enough for his body. When he looked down, all was blackness and he couldn't see the bottom. Huo was terrified and didn't dare make the least movement. He was also fortunate that there were small trees growing all along the side of the slope that held his body back like a railing.

After a while he noticed that near his feet there was a small cave opening. Huo felt overjoyed, and keeping his back against the rock, he wriggled into it. There he felt safer and hoped to wait until daybreak to call for help. Shortly thereafter, there was a beam of light like a star in the deeper part of the cave. He started to go toward it, and after a couple of miles he suddenly caught sight of a cottage with a porch; there were no lamps or candles, yet the light there was bright as day. A beautiful woman came out from a room; he looked at her carefully, and it was Blue Maid. When she saw Huo, she was startled. "How could you get in here?" Without taking the time to explain, Huo took her hands and sobbed pitiably. Blue Maid tried to comfort him. When she asked about his mother and their son, Huo gave an account of all their troubles, and Blue Maid also grew melancholy. Then Huo said, "You've been dead for more than a year now—this must be the underworld." Blue Maid replied, "No, this is a precinct of the immortals. I didn't die back then, and what you buried was only a bamboo cane. Since you have come here, you have the destiny to become an immortal."

Thereupon she took him in to pay his respects to her father, a man with a long beard seated at the head of the hall. Huo hastened to bow to him, and Blue Maid said, "Mr. Huo has come." The old man rose in surprise, took his hand, and politely asked after him. Then he said, "It's a wonderful thing that you've come here—it's your fate to stay here." But Huo politely declined, saying that he could not stay long because of his mother. The old man said, "I understand that, but there won't be any harm if you linger on here a few days." Then they fed him fine foods and wine, and in the west hall they had a serving girl set up a bed, which she covered with brocade bedding.

As Huo was withdrawing for the night, he tried to get Blue Maid to share the bed with him. She refused him, saying, "This is not the sort of place to permit such improper intimacies." But Huo clutched her arm and wouldn't let her go. Outside the window could be heard the derisive laughter of the serving girl, and Blue Maid became even more embarrassed. As they were struggling, the old man came in and screamed at Huo, "Be gone at once! Your commonness defiles my cave!" Huo had always been obstinate, and unable to endure the embarrassment, he colored and said, "The feelings that occur between and man and a woman can't be helped—why must you spy on me? I don't mind getting out of here right now; just have your daughter go along with me."

The old man didn't object and ordered Blue Maid to go with him, opening the back door to see them off. Once he had tricked Huo into going out the gate, the father shut the door and disappeared. When Huo looked around, there wasn't the slightest seam or crack in the sheer cliff that loomed before him. He was utterly alone and had no place to go. He looked up into the sky where the sinking moon was hanging on high and the stars had already grown sparse.

He remained there in despair for quite some time, and then his grief turned to resentment. He faced the cliff and shouted, but there was no reply. His fury mounted; he took the spade from his waist and set to digging his way in through the rock, hacking away and cursing. In the twinkling of an eye he had burrowed in three or four feet, and he heard the muffled sound of someone saying, "Damn him!" Huo then put all his strength into it and dug even more quickly. Suddenly the end of his cave opened wide into a double door. He pushed Blue Maid out through the tunnel, saying, "Let's go, let's go!" At once the wall closed up again behind them. Then she said angrily, "Since you loved me as your wife, how can you treat my father like this? What kind of old Daoist was it gave you that disastrous tool that can aggravate and persecute a person to death!"

Having found Blue Maid, Huo's mood was somewhat calmer. He didn't argue any more but simply worried about the danger of the road and how hard it would be to get back. Blue Maid broke off two branches and had each of them put the branches between their legs. At once these transformed into horses and in no time they arrived at his house. By that point, Huo had been missing for seven days.

Huo had previously become separated from his servant. The servant looked for Huo but couldn't find him, then went back and informed Huo's mother. His mother sent people to search everywhere in the mountain valleys for him, but no trace was found. Huo's mother had been beside herself with worry, and when she heard that her son had returned, she went out overjoyed to welcome him back. When she looked up and saw Blue Maid, she almost collapsed from the shock. Huo told her the general story, and his mother became calmer and more cheerful. Because of the bizarre nature of what had happened to her, Blue Maid was worried about provoking general gossip and wanted to have the family move at once. Huo's mother agreed with her. They had an estate in another district, and after a fixed period they set off to go there, and no one knew anything about it.

They lived together there for eighteen years. Blue Maid had a daughter who married into the Li family of the same town. Afterward, Huo's mother passed away at a ripe old age. Blue Maid told Huo, "In the field of tall grasses of my home there is a pheasant nesting on eight eggs. That's where she should be buried. You and our son Meng-xian should take the coffin there and see to the funeral service. Our son is already grown, and it is fitting that he should remain in the mourning hut by the grave. There's no need to have him return with you." Huo did as she said, and came back alone after the funeral. After more than a month, Meng-xian went to visit them, and his father and mother were both long gone. He asked an old servant about them, and she said, "They went to a funeral and never came back." He knew that a marvel had transpired, but all he could do was heave a great sigh.

Meng-xian's reputation as a writer was much bruited about, but he had difficulties in the examination and in forty days he did not pass. Later, as part of the local quota of candidates, he participated in the Shun-tian examination, where he met a young man in the same dormitory as himself. This young man was seventeen or eighteen, a splendid and nonchalant young man with a certain spiritual manner. Meng-xian was quite drawn to him. When he looked at his paper, Meng-xian saw that he was Huo Zhong-xian, on stipend from Shun-tian district.[5] Shocked, he stared in disbelief and told his own name. Zhong-xian also thought it remarkable and asked where he was from and his relatives.

Meng-xian told him in detail, at which Zhong-xian was delighted and said, "When I set off for the capital, my father advised me that among the examinees if I met someone named Huo from Shansi, he was of my family, and that I should welcome the acquaintance. Now it's happened. But how is it that our names are so similar?" Meng-xian then questioned him about the names of his parents and grandparents, and when Zhong-xian finished, Meng-xian said in surprise, "But these my own father and mother!" Zhong-xian was still uncertain because of the disparity in age, but Meng-xian said, "My father and mother are both immortals—how can one judge their age by their appearance?" When he told the story of all that had transpired, Zhong-xian believed him.

After the examination, they didn't take time off to rest but made travel preparations and returned to Zhong-xian's home together. As soon as they reached the gate, one of the family servants came out to welcome them and told them that the night before their father and mother had disappeared. Both men were very surprised. Zhong-xian went in and asked his wife to tell him about it. His wife said, "Last night we were drinking wine together, and your mother said to me, 'You and your husband are still young and inexperienced. But tomorrow his elder brother will come, and I won't worry any more.' When I went into their rooms in the morning, they were de-

[5]It is common practice to vary the names of brothers and sisters in a set, distinguishing them by changing one character of a two-character given name. Often, as in this case, the variation indicates the degree of seniority. Meng-xian is thus the "Senior Immortal," and Zhong-xian is the "Middle-Brother Immortal." For someone named Huo Meng-xian, who thought he was an only son, to meet someone named Huo Zhong-xian might be startling because this would be the proper name to give to his younger brother.

serted." When the brothers heard this, they stamped their feet and were stricken with grief. Zhong-xian still wanted to go after them, but gave up when Meng-xian expressed the opinion that it would do no good. Zhong-xian had passed the district examination. But since the family tombs were located in Jin, he went back there with his brother. They still hoped that their father and mother were still in the mortal world somewhere and asked for information about them wherever they went. But no trace of them was ever found.

Here follows the judgment of the Chronicler of Wonders: In making a hole in the wall and going to sleep on her bed, he showed naïveté in thought; in digging through the cliff and abusing the old man, he showed rash wildness in action; the reason why the immortal brought the couple together was purely a desire to reward his devotion to his mother with a gift of eternal life. Nevertheless, having mingled with the mortal world and begotten children, why couldn't they have stayed to the end? What brought her to abandon her sons several times in thirty years? Strange indeed!

清 Qing Classical Poetry and Song Lyric

Like the Elizabethan period in the English-speaking world, the Tang Dynasty held for later readers an aura of unattainable perfection in poetry, an age when great poems seemed to come with ease, even to undistinguished writers.

The classical poetry and song lyric of the Qing Dynasty was, in many ways, far richer than the Tang, but the genius of Qing poetry has been obscured by several factors. First, the immense volume of poetry written during the dynasty and the huge collections of its most prominent poets make it difficult for individual poems to stand out and claim the degree of attention they deserve. Second, Qing poets drew on a great depth of learning and familiarity with earlier poetry that they took for granted in their audience. They could not foresee an age when their allusions would require learned footnotes and their fine turns of phrase would go unobserved by most readers. (Still less could they have imagined being translated into a language in which all their literature and culture was largely unknown.) Finally, the classical language they used had changed much since the Tang, whose poems can often be translated almost literally, leaving the beauty of their images still apparent. The literary language of the Qing was filled with set phrases, often figurative, that sound ludicrously artificial in English. Fortunately, there are poems and poets that can be understood with a minimum of annotation, and these will form the greater part of our selection below.

One of the most striking characteristics of Qing classical poetry is the degree to which it spread through all levels of elite society. The Ming and Qing saw a dramatic rise in literacy, and by the Qing, the size of the reading and writing public was very large in absolute numbers, if not as a percentage of the population as a whole. Poetry increasingly became the means to participate in subgroups within literate society. There was an interest in regional and local traditions as never before, with immense pride in earlier poets associated with a particular locale. Women poets formed groups, exchanging verses and defining a tradition of women's poetry in their prefaces. Family traditions were important, and families often bore the cost of publishing works by their members. Indeed, poetry became one of the many means to establish social prestige.

The history of Qing poetry is of such complexity that it cannot easily be represented in a short section such as this. The fall of the Ming and its aftermath was a profound shock to the culture, and it inspired some of the finest classical poetry since the Tang. Du Fu, the "poet-historian," was a powerful model, and numerous poems bear moving witness both to particular incidents in the Qing conquest and to the spirit of resistance. As the dynasty consolidated its rule late in the seventeenth century, the Manchu rulers were understandably disturbed by such poetry, and it was censored. Many remarkable poets were lost in obscurity and their works recovered and republished only in the twentieth century.

The turbulence of the conquest was followed by a long period of peace and prosperity, lasting from the late eighteenth into the early nineteenth century. With the Qing authorities ever vigilant against potential slights, poets tended to avoid political topics. The old disputes of Ming poetics resurfaced in new guises: a school of Formalists *(ge-diao pai)* reworked the old values of the Archaists into something less wooden; the school of Natural Wit *(xing-ling pai),* represented in the present selection by Zhao Yi (1727–1814), carried on the late Ming interest in immediacy and genuine expression; and the school of Spiritual Resonance *(shen-yun pai),* led by Wang Shi-zhen (1634–1711), argued for the centrality of elusive poetic images that transcended both form and self-expression. And there were others, such as the Manchu lyricist Nara Singde (1655–1685) and the classical poet Huang Jing-yen (1749–1783), who belonged to no school, discovering their own distinctive poetic voices apart from contemporary literary debates. Although there was no shortage of poetic talent, the weight of the poetic tradition and the limitations it imposed made themselves felt. Poets had been writing on the same topics in the same poetic language for a millennium, and while there was a degree of innovation, in a large sense poetry had become a comfortably restricted mode of expression in a world that had changed profoundly since the Tang.

In the political and cultural crises of the nineteenth and early twentieth centuries, classical poetry was tested for its ability to account for a world that was being transformed with violent swiftness. Although it had some successes in adapting to the changes in the culture, classical poetry treating "modern" themes often calls attention to the disparity between the modern reality and the language of poetic representation. When a lyricist treated the Japanese Rape of Nanjing in the 1930s in the old poetic language, the unprecedented violence of modern warfare was recast in the guise of a tragedy that had befallen the city over and over again for fifteen hundred years.

It is artificial to declare the end of classical literature with the May Fourth movement of 1919, which advocated the exclusive use of vernacular Chinese and the replacement of traditional literary genres with the new genres from Japan and the West. Western influence had been slowly transforming Chinese literature for many decades prior to 1919; and although the young elite enthusiastically took up the vernacular literature movement, its goals were not fully realized until its gradual institution in the school system closer to the middle of the twentieth century. There is no question that classical poetry and, to a lesser degree, literary song lyric were weary forms, weighted down by their history, and unable to match the liberty of the new vernacular poetry *(xin-shi)* inspired by Western models. Nevertheless, valuable classical poetry continued to be written through the 1930s, and the form is still practiced today, primarily by older scholars.

Gu Yan-wu (1613–1682)

Gu Yan-wu was one of the leading scholars of the early Qing: an historian, classical philologist, antiquarian, and poet. Though still a relatively young man at the time of the conquest, he remained passionately loyal to the Ming. "Autumn Hills" is one of his earlier poems, on the Qing conquest.

Autumn Hills (first of two)

Autumn hills, more autumn hills,
and through those hills swell autumn rains.

They fought by the rivermouth yesterday,
today they fight beside those hills.

I've heard that our right flank crumbled,
I now see the left's resistance fade.

Our banners and pennons lie buried in earth,
by walls dance ladders and battering rams.

In but a morning, defeat at Chang-ping,[1]
the corpses lie covering ridges and slopes.

Three hundred barges set off for the north,
and on every barge are fair-faced girls.

Camels crowd river ports of Wu,
fifes playing, they enter the passes to Yan.[2]

Men of Yan and Ying of olden days
are still found south of the city.[3]

Wu Wei-ye (1609–1671)

Wu Wei-ye (or Wu Mei-cun, as he is often known) was one of the two best-known poets of the period around the Qing conquest. A member of the Restoration Society, Wu belonged to the late Ming social world described in the play *Peach Blossom Fan,* and his poetry on the Qing conquest of the South and its aftermath is among the finest work in a period whose hardships inspired much memorable poetry. Reluctantly persuaded to serve in the Qing government briefly in the 1650s, Wu suffered a deep sense of having betrayed the Ming, and he gave up his post willingly on the death of his mother.

The following poem of 1645 is from a set in which Wu is fleeing with his family from the invading Qing army. Wu moves back and forth from the peaceful scene around him to the crumbling Southern Ming state beyond his vision. "Nature's Moat" was a kenning for the Yangzi River, supposed to protect the Southland against invasion from the North.

---

[1]Chang-ping was the site of a famous battle in the Qin unification when Qin armies were supposed to have massacred four hundred thousand soldiers of the state of Zhao.
[2]Yan, into whose passes the victorious Qing armies enter, represents the region around Beijing.
[3]Yan and Ying were two of the great cities of the ancient state of Chu. After the Qin conquest of those cities, Chu grandees, unwilling to serve Qin, settled south of the Qi capital at Lin-ze. Here, of course, the allusion expresses the determined resistance of southerners to the Qing conquest.

Escaping the Fighting (fifth of six)

The moon came out, the village ahead turned white,
on the creek its rays shone like washed silk.

We lifted oars and drifted midstream,
sang bravely to winds that broke up sound.

Not that Nature's Moat could not hold,
but constant depravities worked this grief.

Woe to you who made plans for our state—
you have lost us half our rivers and hills!

The boatman prances, placing the punt,
and our small boat runs swift as an arrow.

Too bad that troops of the Yangzi and Huai,
our "dread berserkers," put up no fight.

To this lone cabin sounds of an iron flute come,
hearing its notes, my tears fall like sleet.

What have I done in this life
to live in such times of anguish and ruin?

In bygone days I roamed all the land,
I come at last to the Five Lakes' shores.

Wearing hemp sandals and used to flight,
on hard times fallen, a simple common man.

Du Fu's poems during the An Lu-shan Rebellion provided a powerful model for poets writing on the Qing conquest of the Ming. These could be simple narratives of small incidents that revealed the larger conditions of the times. In the following poem, a roving band of Ming soldiers, having fled the advancing Qing armies, plunder a village where Wu Wei-ye is staying. Wu cannot help think of the expenses lavished on the army, which now seeks only to get out of harm's way.

Escaping the Fighting (last of six)

Marauders came when I rose at dawn,
a warship was moored by the market bridge.

A disorderly band of a dozen or so
came on shore to buy local beer.

Their gear was not a civilian's,
but swords and bows had been lost.

They bullied and beat an old shopkeeper,
men of no account, with raging looks.

And I wondered who their commander was,
coming here from an urge to roam carefree.

Our army used to press hard for taxes,
its orders were strict, no leeway at all.

They spoke ever of hardships for men on campaign—
unpitied, the plowman's grueling toil.

The Southland now is defeated,
desolation spreads a thousand miles.

In this place only villagers dwell,
there's no room for your banners and pennons.

Go show the enemy your daring—
don't use it to frighten folk like us.

The relation between the details of a poet's experiences and the poetic past is complicated in Qing poetry. Old poems echo in the background of Qing poems, but this may be something more than literary allusion: familiar old poems were probably a part of making sense of experience itself, and they provided models for response.

The following poem, in which Wu Wei-ye laments the death of his infant daughter, is no less moving and no less heartfelt for being in the style of Du Fu. The poet's real fear that his newborn daughter's cries would reveal the family's hiding place also recalls Du Fu fleeing the "death and destruction" of the An Lu-shan Rebellion with *his* family in a passage from "Song of Peng-ya."

My baby girl gnawed at me in her hunger,
and I feared wild beasts would hear her cries:
I held her to my chest, covered her mouth,
but she twisted and turned, crying louder in rage.

A Lament for My Daughter (first of three)

You were born amid death and destruction,
the whole family lay hidden by roadside.

I feared your cries, thought of leaving you there,
we got away, and I loved you much more.

Children caught in catastrophe's course.
pike and shield harassed your brief years.

State's rise and fall affects all the world,
but when I think back, my distress is doubled.

"West Fields" is an idyllic poem on visiting the estate of Wu's friend Wang Yan-ke after the Qing conquest. Behind this and other poems in the set is a long tradition of lyrics, from Tao Qian to such works as Du Fu's "Autumn Wilds" and Su Dong-po's "East Slope," about withdrawing to farming in face of adversity.

West Fields (first of four)

You dig and build, of world's troubles weary,
in wilderness fields you find nature's way.

Here north of the city you came by chance,
beside the west creek studied Halting.[4]

Your greatness makes practice of privacy hard,
region's remoteness stirs report by the crowd.

Then I, all at once, come to visit you,
oars enter this reed and cattail sky.

The setting sun floats over distant trees,
in mulberries rises a faint hint of smoke.

The path turns, I lose my way on the creek,
but the ducks precede me, leading the boat.

A fragrance close by, I smell lotuses,
recumbent, I enter blooms fresh and lovely.

Men's voices emerge from weeping willows,
a fishing raft slants by the bending shore.

You take my hand, look at me, smile:
"These are indeed my 'Western Fields.'

If always I could get a guest like you,
we'd enjoy the delights of the wilds together.

We'll sit on the grass, drain a jug of beer,
and find some joy in the years that remain."

Mooring in the Evening

Winter hoes go in line along the shore,
light oars yaw, swept by the tide.

---

[4]"Halting" is the Buddhist cessation of desire and activity.

The trees shed the last of tattered leaves,
winds blow a tangle of evening crows.

Where sand is deep, it holds the tracks of pigs,
the stream grows still and echoes with a fish spear.

We ask for fire, the village beer comes,
our cooking smoke rises through reed flowers.

Some of Wu Wei-ye's finest poems are long narratives filled with allusions and historical references, which unfortunately do not fare well in translation. In the following poem, of which only the opening is translated, Wu Wei-ye returns to Nanjing (formerly Jin-ling) after the Qing conquest. From the ruins of the Ming Imperial Academy, where Wu had served, he turns to the other Ming sites in this city that had been both the first and final Ming capital.

from Thoughts Stirred on Meeting the Gardener of the Royal Academy in Nanjing

Cold tides dashed on the ruined fort,
fiery clouds set Red Hill ablaze;
it was June when I reached Jin-ling,
on the tenth I crossed Great Pontoon Bridge.
The spots I had visited serving here
have all of them slipped from memory.
I met an old gardener on the road,
who asked me from where I had come.
Then I vaguely recognized a former employee,
and the circumstances caused heart's pain.
He opened the gate and invited me in,
broken buildings, a low surrounding wall.
Then he pointed into a clump of weeds,
saying this was the Royal Academy.
The office buildings were rubble piles,
which he gardened on lease to pay his tax.
He had changed the means of his livelihood,
but had made this his garden from nostalgia.
In troubled times he had kept to this land,
unwilling to go to another place.
I took the chance to walk over the site,
and at every step my brooding increased.
On the gray slopes backed against the water
had been the hall where I used to stay.
From all the world students gathered here,
compositions turned in at the Six Lodges.

Pines and junipers, all ten spans in girth,
and the ringing sounds of pipes and bells.
A hundred-acre clear and rippling pond,
with drooping willows all around the shore,
splendid porches overhanging pools,
where fragrant scent of lotus blew.
Chatting and laughing, all noble companions,
in flowers and moonlight we drained our cups.
There was a pavilion to the south
where beech and bamboo gave off a light cool. . . .

Wang Shi-zhen (1634–1711)

If the poetry of the mid-seventeenth century wears well, it is because the dissolution and fall of the Ming provided an immediately engaging topic that went beyond the arid literary disputes of the preceding era. Wang Shi-zhen was the most influential poet of the first post-conquest generation. Wang and his poetry are known for a principle, *shen-yun,* roughly translated as "spiritual resonance." This is a vague, evocative term for a vague evocative quality that was associated with certain High Tang poets and especially with their quatrains.

Wang Shi-zhen represents both some of the best and the worst sides of Qing poetry. Much of his poetry was about either social exchange or capturing moments on his travels; the engagement of poetry around the Qing conquest was gone. Wang was a craftsman, who could turn the situation or the beauty of the momentary scene into polished poetry.

Crossing the Ancient Barrier Pass in the Rain (1672)

Perilous walkways, flying cascades,
    the mountain a thousand yards high,
I point afar to a fortress tower
    there among twilight clouds.
And suddenly the west wind brings
    whooshing gusts of rain—
ash tree flowers will fill the road
    as I cross the ancient pass.

On the Ba River Bridge: Sent Home to My Wife (second of two)

Mount Tai-hua and Mount Zhong-nan
    are here thousands of miles away,
not a place in this westward journey
    that doesn't break my heart.
Should my lady happen to toss a coin
    to find out of my fate—

in autumn rain and autumn wind
    I cross the Ba River Bridge.

If Wang Shi-zhen sometimes sounds like Wang Wei, it was because the perfection of Wang Wei's poetic art (rather than Wang Wei's values) captured Wang Shi-zhen's affection.

Farm Home by Cu-lai Mountain

On I go through empty azure mist,
appearing, fading, still more lovely shapes.

Road to the village through sapphire trees,
the green hill faces a shrine on the peak.

In deep woods chickens and dogs grow still,
after much rain, sprouts on the slope are rich.

Someday I'll plant the north slope of Gui—
nor will I be slow to plow on my own.

On the Qing-yang Road

Tall bamboo blanket a sunlit stream,
whose rippling glints by an empty bend.
As the sun goes down, snow melts away,
and homes are right there in the cold green.

What I Saw on the Northern Outskirts of Zhen-zhou

The cloud cover pressed on the city walls
as I left Zhen-zhou's outskirts at dawn.
Past the outskirts, a striped bamboo grove
and the wind blew down the last of the snow.

At Daybreak I Crossed the Ping-jiang River and Climbed on Foot to the Summit of Crossing-Above-Clouds Mountain

I really did "cross above clouds,"
    roaming wine in hand,
the utter wonder of Han-jia
    crowns all this western land.

Its nine peaks face to the sun
    and chant the river leaves,
three watercourses flood on through,
    embracing the district hall.

From the old man of Fu's pavilion
    the mountains grow more fair,
and springs gush from the coiled hair
    of an ancient statue of Buddha.

As Su Dong-po grew older,
    his home in Shu was on his mind,
he wanted no fief of ten thousand homes
    in the world of mortal men.

Nara Singde (1655–1685)

Nara Singde (or, in the sinified version, Na-lan Xing-de) was a Manchu bannerman (a member of the Qing military caste) and an officer in the imperial guard. He often accompanied the Kang-xi emperor on his various journeys of state.

The early seventeenth century had seen a major revival of the song lyric as a purely literary form. Song Dynasty tune patterns were still used, even though the original music had been long lost. The song lyric took on a very different tone from classical poetry: it was often dreamy and evocative, the preferred form for love poetry. Nara Singde's lyrics, particularly a number of pieces on the death of his wife, are considered among the finest in the dynasty.

to "Like a Dream" *(Ru meng ling)*

It was the moment when the pulley creaked
    on the golden well, and fallen petals
filled the pavements, cold and red.
All at once I met her—
no telling for sure
    what lay in her heart
or the look in her eyes.
Who can think it through and know? But now
it begins:
    striped marks on body from bamboo mat,
    a shadow in candlelight.

to "Clear and Even Music" *(Qing-ping yue)*

Tresses in stormy tangles and coils,
she comes and I never know just when.
Weary we lean
    on marble railings of balconies
watching the halo around the moon,
Easily then
    talk turns to whispers,
    her fragrance draws near.

A soft breeze blows past the window screen,
meeting her now is a world away.
And from this moment on:
    all the pain of spring and being apart,
in growing dusk facing the blossoms of pear.

to "Seeking Fragrant Plants" *(Xun fang-cao)*, Account of a Dream in Xiao Temple

How can I pass these nights far from home?
I dreamed I was with her,
    reciting poems together,
by the latticed window. And annoyed,
she feigned a smile and said,
"If you weren't so lonely there,
would you still have wanted to come?"

I had to leave all too quickly;
I had planned to stay
    until temple bells were struck at dawn.
She suddenly pressed close to me—
then a spark flashed from lamp wick falling,
and I was here facing
    fire in a globe of glass.

to "Golden Threads" *(Jin-lü qu)*, Thoughts on the Anniversary of My Wife's Death

When will this misery end?
Dripping on empty stairs, the rain
    of night's coldest hours is done,
a weather for funerals of flowers.
These past three years went on and on,
    her soul, too far to come in dreams,
and may I wake from this dream soon!
I guess by now I've grown aware
    this mortal world holds no appeal.
Better to be
    below the soil
        in those halls of endless night,
cool there and clear,
    a plot of earth to bury care.
The pact of love, hairpin and box,
is forsaken in the end.

If I could get a letter
    from streams in the world below,

I'd like to know
    her joys and sorrows this past year,
who she's staying with. For me
it's restless tossing all night long;
I cannot bear to hear
    strings of marriage played again.
I hope we'll be
    true lovers in a life to come, then fear
we both have luckless destinies,
and future fate will be unkind
    in last moonlight and failing wind.
My tears are gone,
ashes of paper rise.[5]

to "Like a Dream" *(Ru meng ling)*

In thousands of tents the men are drunk.
Starlight shimmers, about to sink.
My homeward dreams are blocked
    by Wolf River
and poked to pieces by river sounds.
Then I go back to sleep,
go back to sleep understanding
that waking has no appeal.

to "Butterflies Love Flowers" *(Die lian hua)*, On the Frontier

The rivers and hills have no single master
    in ancient times and now,
and in the notes of the bugles
herdsmen's horses constantly come and go.
Of this bleak wilderness filling my eyes
    Whom can I tell?—
west winds blow red maples
    and make them old.

Where could pains suffered silently here
    ever find expression?
Lances and armored horses,
the road to Green Tomb in twilight.[6]
Carried away, my feelings deepen,
    how deep do they go?—

---

[5]The "ashes" are from the paper money burned in commemoration of the dead.
[6]Green Tomb was the legendary burial place of Wang Zhao-jun, a beautiful Han court lady who was married against her will to the Khan of the Xiong-nu.

evening sunshine deep in the mountains,
    deep in autumn, the rain.

Zhao yi (1727–1814)

Zhao Yi was one of a group of poets associated with the "school of Natural Wit" *(xing-ling pai),* whose most prominent advocate was Yuan Mei (1716–1798) and which played an influential role in the literary world of the eighteenth century. The school of Natural Wit advocated a spontaneous ease in composition and lightness of touch in poetry that was opposed to the elevated "spiritual resonance" of Wang Shi-zhen and his followers. Zhao Yi was an historian, literary critic, and eminent intellectual, who for a period in his life served in the Qing government with distinction.

Poems on My Dwelling in the Rear Park (second of nine)

I've suffered poverty years on end,
but this year's been especially hard.
My wife and children came in and declared
there will be no breakfast tomorrow.
I laughed and told them to go away,
that I couldn't be bothered just now.
I'm presently writing a little poem
and there's still a word not quite right.
Just wait until I finish the poem
and I'll take care of the groceries.
Look on the streets of the capital—
no civil servants lie there starving to death!

Poems on My Dwelling in the Rear Park (third of nine)

A visitor suddenly knocked at my door
with an offer of cash for some writing.
He asked me to do a tomb inscription
and insisted I make it flattering:
in political life, a Gong Sui or Huang Ba;
in learning, a Zheng or Zhu Xi.
I thought it would be amusing,
so I did just as he required.
I patched a piece of fine phrases together,
and, lo and behold, a true gentleman!
I checked this against what he really did,
it was hardly an ounce to my ten pounds.
Suppose what I wrote is handed down—
who could tell if the man was a fool or wise?
And perhaps they will cite it as evidence,

to be copied at last in historical tomes.
Now I see that in histories of old
the most part belongs to pure puffery.

Returning on Yang Lake

My canvas sail billows lightly,
    the evening breeze is soft,
I turn to look at Yang Mountain,
    set right in the sunset glow.

Egrets dot the sapphire sky,
    a flying word writ in white,
the trees dress up in red leaves,
    presented with scarlet gowns.

The poet's mood, the limpid waters
    empty without a speck,
the heart's concerns, a peaceful cloud
    distracted, not flying away.

I most enjoy the fishermen's songs,
    their sounds in the creaking of oars,
and rapping the rhythm on boatsides,
    going with me all the way home.

Zhao Yi served a period as a magistrate of a district in Guang-xi, which was populated primarily by non-Chinese. These indigenous peoples of southwestern China evoked many of the same responses in eighteenth-century Chinese intellectuals that the native peoples of the Americas evoked in Europeans. Sometimes they were described as murderous and thieving savages; at other times they were the "noble savage," whose natural behavior put to shame those with the artificial trappings of civilization. In the following verse, Zhao Yi describes their courtship customs involving song exchanges between young men and women. Zhao Yi associates the freedom to choose one's own mate (not to mention unbound feet) with primal antiquity and an innocence lost in China.

Local Song

In months of spring, April and May,
    the fairgrounds are in flower,
girls of the tribes, primped and rouged,
    go to the fairgrounds to court.
Long skirts and wide sleeves,
    all in fresh finery,
one sees no bow-bent slippers
    and dainty feet three inches wide.
A young man of unknown family
    comes to sing her songs,

it's not necessary that he be
    kin by marriage or blood.
She only looks at his young face
    fresh as a blossom of peach,
and as he sings, so she sings back
    in verses never-ending.
In every single note is borne
    currents of tender passion,
light as the drifting floss
    that curls through the sky.
There are times when suddenly
    it is blown apart by the breeze,
notes carried over the hills ahead,
    in quavering afterechoes.
And touching, when the song concludes
    fervent glances are cast,
and she promises to meet him
    by night in the glow of the moon.
These melodies speak mostly
    of the red berries of passion,
folkways that rarely write
    of green plums as they fall.[7]
Here in our age we truly find
    unimpeded succession,
it is as if entering the hazy space
    of the Hua-xu dream.[8]
I see now that our ritual laws
    arose in later times,
folk of No-Care's and Ge-tian's day
    knew nothing of them at all.[9]
Have you not seen how two by two
    the butterflies form pairs,
and without need of a go-between
    they settle the marriage bond?

In Bed

Lying in bed I thought of a poem
    and worried that I would forget,
I threw on my clothes and got up to write
    in the dying light of the lamp.

---

[7]"Green plums as they fall" refers to a poem in the *Classic of Poetry,* traditionally interpreted as referring to marriage in the appropriate season (these young women seem to be rushing it).
[8]The "Hua-xu dream," described in the Daoist Classic *Lie-zi,* was the Yellow Emperor's dream of a primordial world of innocence.

My wife broke out in laughter:
    why take such pains, old man—
when the youngsters are at their studies
    they're not so caught up as this?

Livelihood

Our subsistence grows steadily bleaker,
the harvest was bad; just stony fields remain.

For fuel, we burn trees that stood leaf to leaf,
for meals, count on cash from writing inscriptions.

The servant is young, I send my son on errands,
the house so bare the watchdog sleeps freely.

And faintly I hear the maids telling stories
of our days of feasting and me in official robes.

On Poetry (two of five)

I
The life I see all around me turns
    on the Potter's Wheel of Change:
Heaven's skill and human craft
    always compete for the new.
The poet provides a new idea
    that lasts five hundred years,
but when it's reached a thousand years,
    it seems like a cliché.

II
Poems of Li Bo and Du Fu
    have passed through thousands of mouths,
and by now they've come to seem
    not vivid or new at all.
In every age our hills and our rivers
    bring forth men of talent
and each holds sway over poetry
    for a span of five hundred years.

---

[9]No-Cares and Ge-tian were mythical rulers of earliest antiquity.

Huang Jing-ren (1749–1783)

Huang Jing-ren perfectly fulfilled the expectations for a certain type of Chinese poet: talented, unsuccessful, impoverished, and doomed to die at a relatively young age. It was a role Huang Jing-ren accepted completely, and though there was an element of posing, it sometimes made possible a poetic daring that is lacking in more socially successful writers. Many critics believed, with some reason, that Huang Jing-ren was the outstanding poet of the dynasty.

Written at Night at an Inn in the Hills (second and third of three)

The city people are different
    in their troubling fantasies;
to my eyes this world and I
    are a wisp in autumn sky.
Just now those thousands of homes must all
    be sharing the very same dream:
above them, a white haze,
    hangs low, then rises high.

All night long these mountain windows
    stand open on every side,
with rivers and lakes before and behind,
    where my thoughts go on and on.
So stand at the window, set torch ablaze,
    hold it high,
and watch the fish and dragons come,
    to drink in the light.

[title lost]

My home lies east of the eastern sea:
sea-castle mirages, familiar sights
    for a mind that is the same.

I shed ten years of tears for my shadow
    in the deepest parts of hills,
but when I glimpsed a mountain ape,
    my heart knew also delight.

Is this life perhaps? Or death? Neither
    are worth my shouting in rage;
brows knit in a frown, then form a smile—
    which of those moments is real?

Magnificent is the Shaper of Things—
    how will he use me now?

Not of mist and cloud does he conjure shapes,
    he conjures his shapes in me.[1]

Visiting Ju-fa-yuan Temple with Wang Qiu-cheng and Zhang He-chai

I left the ancient temple in twilight mist,
    afraid on my return to find
my study in its autumn
    as empty as these waters.
As night's black colors grew on my clothes,
    I could not brush them away,
and wondered where to find other hills
    still red in the evening sun.

A Companion Piece to a Poem by Qian Bai-quan

Here where the master, his whisk in hand,
    once discoursed on the sutras,
we feel now the autumn chill
    in August already upon us.
So much noise from crowds,
    travelers outside these gates—
yet after the great bell's single sound
    there is sound no more.

Dreaming of a Friend One Night

I am in halves: half here far from home,
    and half in a dream of home,
as the west wind rolls the leaves along
    and rain beats on corridors.

I am a shadow, companioned by clouds
    threading through the passes;
now the moonlight joins me as always
    under this roof and rafters.

You speak to me with such kindness and care,
    but somehow I don't comprehend,

---

[1]The last couplet refers to a passage in the *Zhuang-zi,* in which one zany Daoist visits another, wracked by disease and dying: "Then Zi-li leaned against the doorway and spoke to Zi-lai, 'Magnificent indeed is the Shaper of Things. I wonder what it's going to make you into; I wonder where it's going to have you go. Will you be a rat's liver? A bug's arm, perhaps?' "

and cannot see what would stop me
    from taking your hand right now:

Then I wake up: on my pillow
    there's not a spot left dry;
through the open curtains the hazy blur
    of the long road to be traveled.

Offhand Compositions: New Year's Eve 1774

I

Laughter and talk in a thousand homes,
    the water-clock drips on,
yet I feel a misery coming unseen
    from beyond the world of things.
Silent, I stand on the market bridge,
    recognized by none,
watching a single star like the moon
    such a long, long time.

II

Year after year I waste this eve
    reciting poems,
beside the lamp my children
    often secretly laugh at me.
Yet how could the likes of you understand
    how much I regret
wastefully spending the heart's strength
    to be a poet.

Although classical poetry continued to be written using the old circumscribed range of topics throughout the nineteenth century, some voices were trying to express the new cultural realities that China was confronting with the slow dissolution of Qing rule and the intrusion of the West. The corruption and sporadic violence of nineteenth-century China again and again were met with a desire to bring about reform. Classical literature and classical writing in general can be taken as an emblem of the cultural problem. Historical depth was the virtue of classical writing, but by figuring everything in terms of precedents and prior usage, critics and writers alike had difficulty accounting for what was truly new.

Gong Zi-zhen (1792–1841)

Gong Zi-zhen's most famous poems are the 315 quatrains written in the cyclical year *ji-hai,* 1839, on a journey from Beijing to his home in Hang-zhou. Poets and lyricists like Huang Jing-ren or Nara Singde complicated the clichés of the poetic language to the point where they created something unique and fresh. Gong Zizhen's quatrains are often epigrammatic: he addresses poetic clichés and the commonplaces of cultural response directly. At other times, the quatrains suggest an almost melancholy resignation. Many are extremely allusive; given below are just a few of the most famous that can be done in English without extensive annotation.

Poems of the Year *Ji-hai*, 1839

V

The sorrow of leaving sweeps over me,
    the bright sun sinks in sky,
a poet on horseback heads eastward
    and at once is past the horizon.
The fallen red petals are not
    things without a heart—
they change into the mud of spring
    to nurture still more flowers.

The following piece is on opium addicts, who filled the levels of officialdom during the opium scourge of the nineteenth century. The first couplet seems to describe an opium den. In the second couplet, Gong suggests that the addict go take a provincial post in the poppy-growing counties of West and Southwest China, where even during the Cold Food Festival, when cooking fires (and by implication, the burning of opium) are supposed to be extinguished, he could stay high (perhaps fancifully under the influence of the poppies?).

LXXXVI

The addicts' lamps are ranged in groups,
    scattered autumn fireflies,
a registrar, fallen on hard times,
    his tear-filled eyes aglow.
Why not go govern a city
    in some county of poppy flowers,
and sleep through spring never waking
    in the Cold Food Festival?

CXXV

All life in China's nine regions
    depends on the thundering storm,
thousands of horses all struck dumb
    is deplorable indeed.
I urge the Lord of Heaven
    to shake us up again
and grant us human talent
    not bound to a single kind.

When I was passing Zhen-jiang, I saw a service for the Jade Emperor, the Wind God, and the Thunder God, with thousands and thousand of worshippers. The Daoist priest begged me to write a supplicant verse.

CLXX
The sorrows and joys of my youthful years
    surpass those of others,
I wept and sang without cause
    and every word was true.
A grown man now, I get around,
    naïveté mixed with guile,
but the "child-mind" returns again
    to this body in its dreams.

Another Repentance

Buddhists tell of kalpa fires
    dissolving all when they come—
what is it endures a thousand years,
    raging like tidal bore?

I have ground away the light of day
    in writings to save the state,
dark insights and mad ingenuities
    recur in midnight hours.

They surge in me like a boiling flood,
    needing a sword's blow to sever;
once gone, they are tangled still in thought,
    consigned to the flute of poetry.

Heart's medicine, heart's native wit
    are both the heart's disease:
I am resolved to burn in the lamp
    these words of parable.

"From Spring to Autumn . . ." makes use of one of the favorite figures for representations, and for poetic representations in particular: the dragon flying in the sky with the clouds that accompany it. In order to catch its animate changes, the best representations of the dragon were supposed to show only fragments of the creature behind the cloud, from which the whole could be inferred.

From Spring to Autumn of 1827 Some Things Came to Me Which I Wrote Down Haphazardly (last of fifteen)

I once wrote a poem swearing off poems;
it was 1820, the poem was wordy.

The most pressing things you want to say
have always been hard to say clearly.

So I'll try to say them with cunning words,
but before I can say them, my voice fails.

I seek no forgiveness from the gods,
and would even less speak it to living men.

To the east of a cloud, one scale exposed,
one claw is exposed on the other side.

But better than showing scale and claw
is to show no claw and scale at all.

More true still of the things I've said—
of scale and claw the lingering trace.

I repent my writings from the very first,
in heart's silence I will strive for Void.

This year I truly swear off poems—
the problem is not that my talent is gone.

Huang Zun-xian (1848–1905)

Not only did Huang Zun-xian represent the most important attempt to reform classical poetry in the nineteenth century, he was also a Qing diplomat and political figure of some note, serving in Chinese embassies and consulates in Tokyo, San Francisco, London, and Singapore. He tried to strip away the allusions, the clichés, and the commonplaces of response in classical poetry and to open up the poetry to the objects and experiences of the new world China was entering. The Chinese poetic language was, however, a stubborn thing. The poems written in the West, such as a long, rather horrified verse narrative on witnessing the turbulent party politics of the 1884 American election, offer rare and frequently surprising perspectives. The following political epigram, written in 1885, protests the British occupation of Hong Kong.

On Reaching Hong Kong

The waters are those of Yao's time,
　　the sun is the same as Xia's,
also the cap and gown I wear
　　are the uniform of Han.
Climbing the tower, I look all around—
　　this truly is my land,
yet on the great flags I do not see
　　our yellow dragon.

The greater part of Huang Zun-xian's collected poems are on the standard topics of classical poetry; though good, these poems do not stand out strongly. More interesting are those works where the sensibility cultivated by practicing classical poetry accounts for a new experience. In the following quatrain, Huang crosses the international dateline on the second day of the second month, known as the "dawn of flowers." Not only are there no flowers here to enjoy on the two "dawns of flowers." An additional day seems a gratuitous gift for someone worried about wasting the time of his life. It produces a particular problem in arranging the diary—the repetition of a day, but one that is little different from the adjoining day of the same name.

Various Responses on an Ocean Voyage (one of fourteen)

On the eighteenth day of the first month I set off from Yokohama by paddle-wheeled steamer to America, and arrived on the twelfth of the second month. I had nothing to do in the boat, so I wrote these lines haphazardly.

> In the years and months of my middle age
>   I endure being tossed by winds,
> more than half of the time of my life
>   has been thrown away in travels.
> Today to break my melancholy
>   I edit my diary:
> in only one year I have received
>   twice the "dawn of flowers."

Qiu Jin (1879–1907)

Qiu Jin was a member of the revolutionary generation and a martyr of the Revolution. Married and with two children, she left her family in 1904 and went to Japan to study. There she joined the movement to overthrow the Qing government. After returning to China, she founded a newspaper for women and continued her revolutionary activities. Involved in an abortive uprising in An-hui and Zhe-jiang in 1907, she was captured by Qing authorities, and executed.

This poem was written in 1904, after China's various humiliations at the hands of Japan and the Western powers. Qiu Jin was then on her way to Japan. The "bronze camels" were originally in Luo-yang; Suo Jing in the Jin prophesied that he would see them growing with scrub and thorns, and the demise of the Western Jin fulfilled his prophecy. Later the bronze camels came to stand for dynastic ruin.

Mr. Ishii of Japan Seeks a Matching Verse (using his rhymes)

> It is rash to say that a woman
>   can never be a hero,
> I ride the wind thousands of miles
>   heading eastward alone.

The poet's mood: a single sail
    on the vast expanse of sea;
soul in dream: the sparkle of moonlight
    on three isles of Japan.

The bronze camels have fallen,
    in sorrow I turn to look;
the sweating horse at last is shamed
    that the deed is left undone.

Such as this is heart's pain
    and anger for my own land—
how could I dare in my travels
    just pass through the breeze of spring!

On the Yellow Sea: A Man from Japan Sought Some Verses and Also Showed Me a Map of the Russo-Japanese War

Riding the wind for thousands of miles
    I left and now return,
a lone body on the eastern sea,
    spring thunder in her breast.

Can I bear to look at this map and see
    how the colors change;
am I willing to let our rivers and hills
    be left to the kalpa fires?

Strong wine can't melt away
    tears of care for our land;
to save these times we must depend
    on talent beyond the common.

We will spend the blood that flows
    from a hundred thousand skulls,
but we must exert our strength to turn
    Heaven and Earth aright.

Wang Guo-wei (1877–1927)

Wang Guo-wei was one of the most remarkable late Qing and early Republican intellectuals. He was a scholar of Western philosophy and lover of Schopenhauer; a critic who wrote studies (still used) on the novel *Story of the Stone,* on early drama, and on song lyrics; a scholar of ancient epigraphy; and an historian of the Yuan Dynasty. He was also an ardent Qing loyalist, which is one of the reasons offered to explain his suicide in 1927.

    Not only was Wang Guo-wei probably the single most influential critic and theorist of the song lyric, his own works are some of the finest examples of the genre in the early twentieth century. During an age when momentous political concerns often dominated literature, Wang Guo-wei's song lyrics kept to the old motifs and perfected them according to his own theories of *jing-jie*, the visionary "world" created in a poem.

to "Putting on Lipstick" *(Dian jiang chun)*

Waves follow the currents of cloud,
and the oarsmen's song goes slowly
    over the waves away.
Several sounds of the oarlocks
go far into shores of cattails and rushes.

Where setting sunlight strikes current
are several specks of idle egrets and gulls.
At the spot where they fly off low
are countless reeds
that speak in the rustling wind.

As a student of Western thought and literature as well as of Chinese literature, Wang Guo-wei well understood the artificiality of the form in which he worked. More than many of his best-known Chinese contemporaries, Wang gloried in that special poetic world, like many of his Western counterparts. Perhaps such aesthetic radicalism (confined to his work in song lyric) permitted him the whimsical insight of the lyric that follows.

to "Washing Creek Sands" *(Huan xi sha)*

Does something real lie behind
    the words in your new songs?
Fancy phrases such as these
    can make you want to laugh.
"Broken-hearted in lamplight"—
    now who did you write that for?

I lean on the desk and peer around
    at recent compositions,
then turn off the light and reckon up
    joys known in the past—
trivial passions of the heart,
    and nothing corresponds.

This lyric is a fitting coda for classical Chinese literature. Wang Guo-wei is the modern poet, familiar with Western thought and literature, who chooses to work in the old forms. From ancient times, poetry in its various forms was supposed to give outer expression to what lies in the heart. But there is a moment when Wang looks back at his lyrics and realizes they are just words, old clichés, that no longer match what he really felt. If the old poetry is no longer adequate for the consciousness of the modern Chinese writer, however, it is adequate—in this lyric—to declare its own failure.

Selected Further Readings

The first section is devoted to translations of Chinese literature. The second list (at p. 1159) is a brief introduction to critical studies of Chinese literature. Note that the critical studies often contain extensive translations of material not found elsewhere. Both lists are primarily limited to works in English, though works in French and German have been included in cases where they fill gaps or have reference value.

Translations

GENERAL ANTHOLOGIES

Birch, Cyril, ed. *Anthology of Chinese Literature*. 2 vols. New York, 1965.

Chang Hsin-chang. *Chinese Literature: Nature Poetry*. New York, 1977.

———. *Chinese Literature: Popular Fiction and Drama*. Edinburgh, 1973.

Davis, A. R., ed. *The Penguin Book of Chinese Verse*. Baltimore, 1962.

de Bary, William T., W. T. Chan, and Burton Watson, eds. *Sources of Chinese Tradition*. New York, 1960.

Ebrey, Patricia Buckley. *Chinese Civilization and Society: A Sourcebook*. New York, 1981.

Lin, Yutang. *The Importance of Understanding*. Cleveland, 1960 (paperback ed. entitled *Translations from the Chinese*).

———. *The Wisdom of China and India*. New York, 1942; reprinted Taipei, 1968.

Liu Wu-chi. *K'uei Hsing: A Repository of Asian Literature in Translation*. Bloomington, Ind., 1974.

———, and Irving Lo, eds. *Sunflower Splendor: Three Thousand Years of Chinese Poetry*. Garden City, N.Y., 1975.

Mair, Victor, ed. *The Columbia Anthology of Traditional Chinese Literature*. New York, 1994.

Payne, Robert, ed. *The White Pony: An Anthology of Chinese Poetry from the Earliest Times to the Present Day, Newly Translated*. New York, 1947.

Rexroth, Kenneth. *One Hundred Poems from the Chinese*. New York, 1959.

———. *Love and the Turning Year: One Hundred More Poems from the Chinese*. New York, 1970.

———, and Ling Chung. *The Orchid Boat: Women Poets of China*. New York, 1972.

Strassberg, Richard E. *Inscribed Landscapes: Travel Writing from Imperial China*. Berkeley, 1994.

Waley, Arthur. *Chinese Poems*. London, 1946.

———. *The Temple and Other Poems*. New York, 1926.

Watson, Burton. *Columbia Book of Chinese Poetry*. New York, 1984.

Yip, Wai-lim. *Chinese Poetry: Major Modes and Genres*. Berkeley, Los Angeles, and London, 1972.

EARLY LITERATURE (TO THE END OF THE EASTERN HAN)

The *Classic of Poetry (Shi-jing)*

Hightower, James R. *Han Shih Wai-chuan: Han Ying's Illustrations of the Didactic Applications of the Classic of Songs*. Cambridge, Mass., 1952.

Karlgren, Bernhardt. *The Book of Odes.* Stockholm, 1950.

Legge, James. *The Chinese Classics.* 5 vols., reprinted Hong Kong, 1960 (English translations of the Confucian canon, including the *Classic of Poetry*).

Pound, Ezra. *The Classic Anthology Defined by Confucius.* Cambridge, Mass., 1954.

Waley, Arthur. *The Book of Songs.* 1937, 1960; new ed. New York, 1987.

Early Prose

Birrel, Anne. *Chinese Mythology: An Introduction.* Baltimore, 1993.

Crump, J. I. *Chan-kuo Ts'e.* Oxford, 1970; revised ed. San Francisco, 1979.

Graham, Angus. *The Book of Lieh-tzu.* 1960; New York, 1990.

———. *Chuang Tzu: The Inner Chapters.* London, 1981.

Knoblock, John. *Xunzi.* 3 vols. Stanford, Calif., 1988, 1990, 1994.

Lau, D. C. *The Analects.* Harmondsworth, Middlesex, 1979.

———. *Lao Tzu: Tao Te Ching.* Harmondsworth, Middlesex, 1963.

———. *Mencius.* Harmondsworth, Middlesex, 1970.

Waley, Arthur. *The Analects of Confucius.* London, 1938.

Watson, Burton. *Courtier and Commoner in Ancient China: Selections from the History of the Former Han.* New York, 1974.

———. *Han Fei Tzu, Basic Writings.* New York, 1964.

———. *Hsun-tsu, Basic Writings.* New York, 1963.

———. *Records of the Grand Historian: Chapters from the Shih Chi of Ssu-ma Ch'ien.* New York, 1958.

———. *Records of the Grand Historian: Translated from the Shih chi of Ssu-ma Ch'ien.* 2 vols. New York, 1961.

———. *The Tso Chuan: Selections from China's Oldest Narrative History.* New York, 1989.

———. *The Writings of Chuang Tzu.* New York, 1968.

Chu-ci* and *Fu

Hawkes, David. *Ch'u T'zu: Songs of the South.* Oxford, 1959; much revised ed. *(The Songs of the South)* London, 1985.

Hervouet, Yves. *Le Chapitre 117 de Che ki: Biographie de Sseu-ma Hsiang-jou.* Paris, 1972.

Knechtges, David. *The Han-shu Biography of Yang Xiong.* Tempe, Ariz., 1982.

———. "Ssu-ma Hsiang-ju's 'Tall Gate Rhapsody.' " *Harvard Journal of Asiatic Studies,* 41.1 (1981).

———. *Wen Xuan or Selections of Refined Literature.* 2 vols. Princeton, N.J., 1982, 1987.

———, and Jerry Swanson. "Seven Stimuli for the Prince: The Ch'i-fa of Mei Ch'eng." *Monumenta Serica,* 29 (1970–71).

Waley, Arthur. *The Nine Songs: A Study of Shamanism in Ancient China.* London, 1955.

———. *The Temple and Other Poems.* London, 1925.

Watson, Burton. *Chinese Rhyme-Prose: Poems in the Fu Form from the Han and Six Dynasties Period.* New York, 1971.

———. *Records of the Grand Historian: Translated from the Shih chi of Ssu-ma Ch'ien.* 2 vols. New York, 1961.

LITERATURE OF THE LATE HAN TO THE SUI

Birrel, Anne. *New Songs from a Jade Terrace.* New York, 1982.

———. *Popular Songs and Ballads of Han China.* London, 1988.

Davis, A. R. *T'ao Yüan-ming.* 2 vols. Cambridge, 1984.

Diény, Jean-Pierre. *Les dix-neuf poèmes anciens.* Paris, 1963.

Frodsham, J. D. *The Murmuring Stream: The Life and Works of the Chinese Nature Poet Hsieh Ling-yün (385–433).* Kuala Lumpur, 1967.

———, and Ch'eng Hsi. *An Anthology of Chinese Verse: Han Wei Chin and the Northern and Southern Dynasties.* Oxford, 1967.

Graham, William T., Jr. *"The Lament for the South": Yü Hsin's "Ai Chiang-nan fu."* Cambridge, 1980.

———. "Mi Heng's 'Rhapsody on a Parrot.' " *Harvard Journal of Asiatic Studies,* 39 (1979).

Henricks, Robert G. *Philosophy and Argumentation in Third Century China.* Princeton, N.J., 1983.

Hightower, James Robert. *The Poetry of T'ao Ch'ien.* Oxford, 1970.

Holzman, Donald. *Poetry and Politics: The Life and Works of Juan Chi.* Cambridge, 1976.

Kent, George. *Worlds of Dust and Jade: 47 Poems and Ballads of the Third Century Chinese Poet Ts'ao Chih.* New York, 1960.

Marney, John. *Beyond the Mulberries: An Anthology of Palace-Style Poetry by Emperor Chien-wen of the Liang Dynasty (503–551).* Taipei, 1982.

Mather, Richard. "The Mystical Ascent of the T'ien-t'ai Mountains: Sun Ch'o's *Yu T'ien-t'ai-shan Fu.*" *Monumenta Serica,* 20 (1961).

———. *Shih-shuo hsin-yü: A New Account of Tales of the World.* Minneapolis, 1976.

Miao, Ronald C. *Early Medieval Chinese Poetry: The Life and Verse of Wang Ts'an (A.D. 177–217).* Wiesbaden, 1982.

van Gulik, R. H. *Hsi K'ang and His Poetical Essay on the Lute.* Tokyo, 1941.

von den Steinen, D. "Poems of Ts'ao Ts'ao." *Monumenta Serica,* 4 (1939–40).

TANG POETRY: GENERAL

Bynner, Witter. *The Jade Mountain: A Chinese Anthology.* New York, 1929, 1957, 1964.

Graham, Angus. *Poems of the Late T'ang.* Baltimore, 1965.

Lattimore, David. *The Harmony of the World: Chinese Poems.* Providence, R.I., 1976.

Stimson, Hugh M. *Fifty-five T'ang Poems: A Text in the Reading and Understanding of T'ang Poetry.* New Haven, Conn., 1976.

TANG POETRY: INDIVIDUAL POETS

Eide, Elling. *Poems by Li Po.* Privately printed, 1984.

Frodsham, J. D. *The Poems of Li Ho.* Oxford, 1970.

Hawkes, David. *A Little Primer of Tu Fu.* Oxford, 1967.

Henricks, Robert G. *The Poetry of Han-shan: A Complete Annotated Translation of Cold Mountain.* Albany, N.Y., 1990.

Hung, William. *Tu Fu, China's Greatest Poet.* Cambridge, 1952.

Kubin, Wolfgang. *Das lyrische Werk des Tu Mu.* Wiesbaden, 1976.

Larsen, Jeanne. *Brocade River Poems: Selected Works of the T'ang Dynasty Courtesan Xue Tao.* Princeton, N.J., 1987.

Levi, Howard S., et al. *Translations from Po Chü-i's Collected Works.* 4 vols. New York, 1971–75.

Liu, James J. Y. *The Poetry of Li Shang-yin.* Chicago, 1969.

Obata, Shigeyoshi. *The Works of Li Po.* New York, 1922.

Red Pine. *The Collected Songs of Cold Mountain.* Port Townsend, Wash., 1983.

Robinson, G. W. *Poems of Wang Wei.* Baltimore, 1973.

Snyder, Gary. *Riprap, & Cold Mountain Poems.* San Francisco, 1958, 1990.

von Zach, Erwin. *Han Yü's poetische Werke.* James R. Hightower, ed. Cambridge, 1952.

———. *Tu Fu's Gedichte.* James R. Hightower, ed. Cambridge, 1952.

Waley, Arthur. *The Life and Times of Po Chu-i, 772–846* A.D. London, 1949.

———. *The Poetry and Career of Li Po.* London, 1950.

Watson, Burton. *Cold Mountain: 100 Poems by the T'ang Poet Han-shan.* New York, 1962.

Yates, Robin D. S. *Washing Silk: The Life and Selected Poetry of Wei Chuang (834?–910).* Cambridge, Mass., 1988.

Yip, Wai-lim. *Hiding the Universe: Poems by Wang Wei.* New York, 1972.

Yu, Pauline. *The Poetry of Wang Wei.* Bloomington, Ind., 1980.

EARLY FICTION, *CHUAN-QI,* PROSE ESSAYS, AND OTHER GENRES

Birch, Cyril. *Chinese Myths and Fantasies.* Oxford/New York, 1961.

Chang, H. C. *Chinese Literature 3: Tales of the Supernatural.* Edinburgh, 1983.

Cohen, Alvin P. *Tales of Vengeful Ghosts: A Sixth-Century Collection of Chinese Avenging Ghost Stories.* Taipei, 1982.

Dudbridge, Glen. *The Tale of Li Wa.* London, 1983.

Eberhard, Wolfram. *Chinese Fairy Tales and Folk Tales* (translated from the German by Desmond Parsons). London, 1937; New York, 1938.

Kao, Karl S. Y., ed. *Classical Chinese Tales of the Supernatural and the Fantastic.* Bloomington, Ind., 1985.

Levy, Howard S. *China's First Novellette: The Dwelling of the Playful Goddesses, by Chang Wen-ch'eng (ca. 657–730).* Tokyo, 1965.

Liu Shih Shun. *Chinese Classical Prose: The Eight Masters of the T'ang-Sung Period.* Hong Kong, 1979.

Ma, Y. W., and Joseph Lau, eds. *Traditional Chinese Stories: Themes and Variations.* New York, 1978.

Mair, Victor. *Tun-huang Popular Narratives.* Cambridge/New York, 1983.

Waley, Arthur. *Ballads and Stories from Tunhuang: An Anthology.* London, 1960.

Yang Hsien-yi, and Gladys Yang. *The Dragon King's Daughter: Ten T'ang Dynasty Stories.* Beijing, 1954.

———. *The Man Who Sold a Ghost: Chinese Tales of the 3rd–6th Century.* Beijing, 1958.

———. *Stories About Being Afraid of Ghosts.* Beijing, 1961.

SHI POETRY OF THE SONG DYNASTY AND LATER

Bullett, Gerald. *Five Seasons of a Golden Year: A Chinese Pastoral.* Hong Kong, 1980 (translations from Fan Cheng-da).

Chaves, Jonathan. *The Columbia Book of Later Chinese Poetry: Yuan, Ming, and Ch'ing Dynasties.* New York, 1986.

———. *Heaven My Blanket, Earth My Pillow: Poems by Yang Wan-li.* New York, 1975.

Lo, Irving Yucheng, and William Schultz, eds. *Waiting for the Unicorn: Poems and Lyrics of China's Last Dynasty, 1644–1911.* Bloomington, Ind., 1986.

Schmidt, J. D. *Stone Lake: The Poetry of Fan Chengda (1126–1193).* Cambridge, 1992.

Waley, Arthur. *Yüan Mei: Eighteenth Century Chinese Poet.* London, 1957; reprinted Stanford, Calif., 1970.

Watson, Burton. *The Old Man Who Does As He Pleases: Selections from the Poetry and Prose of Lu Yu.* New York, 1973.

———. *Su Tung-p'o: Selections from a Sung Dynasty Poet.* New York, 1965.

SONG LYRIC *(CI)*

Bryant, Daniel. *Lyric Poets of the Southern T'ang: Feng Yen-ssu (903–960) and Li Yü (937–978)*. Vancouver, 1982.

Fusek, Lois. *Among the Flowers: English Translation*. New York, 1982.

Hightower, James R. "The Songwriter Liu Yung." *Harvard Journal of Asiatic Studies,* 41.2 (1981), pp. 323–76; 42.1 (1982), pp. 5–66.

———. "The Songs of Chou Pang-yen." *Harvard Journal of Asiatic Studies,* 37.2 (1977).

Landau, Julie. *Beyond Spring: Tz'u Poems of the Sung Dynasty*. New York, 1994.

Liu, James J. Y. *Major Lyricists of the Northern Sung: A.D. 960–1126*. Princeton, N.J., 1974.

Lo, Irving. *Hsin Ch'i-chi*. New York, 1971.

Rexroth, Kenneth, and Ling Chung. *Li Ch'ing-chao: Complete Poems*. New York, 1979.

Wixted, John Timothy. *The Song Poetry of Wei Chuang (836–910)*. Tempe, Ariz., 1978.

Yates, Robin D. S. *Washing Silk: The Life and Selected Poetry of Wei Chuang (834?–910)*. Cambridge, Mass., 1988.

VERNACULAR SONG AND DRAMA

Arlington, L. C., and Harold Acton. *Famous Chinese Plays*. New York, 1963.

Birch, Cyril. *The Peony Pavilion (Mudan Ting)*. Bloomington, Ind., 1980.

Ch'en, Li-li. *Master Tung's Western Chamber Romance (Tung Hsi-hsiang Chu-kung-tiao): A Chinese Chantfable*. Cambridge/New York, 1976.

Ch'en Shih-hsiang, and Harold Acton, with Cyril Birch. *The Peach Blossom Fan*. Berkeley, Los Angeles, and London, 1976.

Dolby, William. *Eight Chinese Plays: From the 13th Century to the Present*. London, 1978.

Dolezelova-Velingerova, M., and J. I. Crump. *Ballad of the Hidden Dragon (Liu Chih-yuan chu-kung tiao)*. Oxford, 1971.

Hayden, George A. *Crime and Punishment in Medieval Chinese Drama: Three Judge Pao Plays*. Cambridge, Mass., 1978.

Idema, Wilt, and Stephen West. *Chinese Theater 1100–1450; A Source Book*. Wiesbaden, 1982.

———. *The Moon and the Zither: The Story of the Western Wing*. Berkeley, 1991.

Liu Jung-en. *Six Yüan Plays*. Baltimore, 1972.

Mulligan, Jean. *The Lute: Kao Ming's "P'i-p'a Chi."* New York, 1980.

Radtke, Kurt W. *Poetry of the Yuan Dynasty*. Canberra, Australia, 1984.

Seaton, Jerome B. *The Wine of Eternal Life: Taoist Drinking Songs from the Yuan Dynasty*. Ann Arbor, Mich., 1978.

Shih Chung-wen. *Injustice to Tou O (Tou O Yuan): A Study and Translation*. Cambridge, 1972.

Yang Hsien-yi, and Gladys Yang. *The Palace of Eternal Youth*. Beijing, 1955.

———. *Selected Plays of Kuan Han-ch'ing*. Beijing, 1958.

MING AND QING CLASSICAL PROSE AND FICTION

Chaves, Jonathan. *Pilgrim of the Clouds: Poems and Essays by Yuan Hung-tao and His Brothers*. New York, 1978.

Giles, H. *Strange Stories from a Chinese Studio*. Shanghai, 1916.

Li Chi. *The Travel Diaries of Hsu Hsia-k'o*. Hong Kong, 1974.

Lu Yunzhong. *Pu Songling: Strange Tales of Liaozhai*. Hong Kong, 1982.

Mair, Denis C., and Victor H. Mair. *Strange Stories from Make-do Studio*. Beijing, 1989.

Mowry Li, Hua-yüan. *Chinese Love Stories from the "Ch'ing-shih."* Hamden, Conn., 1983.

Pratt, Leonard, and Chiang Su-hui. *Shen Fu: Six Records of a Floating Life.* Harmondsworth, Middlesex, 1983.
Yang Hsien-yi, and Gladys Yang. *Pu Songling: Selected Tales of Liaozhai.* Beijing, 1981.

VERNACULAR FICTION: *HUABEN* AND VERNACULAR STORIES

Acton, Harold, and Lu Yihsieh. *Four Cautionary Tales.* London, 1947 (translations from Feng Menglong's *Xing-shi heng-yan* collection).
Bauer, Wolfgang, and Herbert Franke, eds. *The Golden Casket* (trans. Christopher Levenson). Baltimore, 1967.
Birch, Cyril. *Stories from a Ming Collection.* London, 1958 (translations from the *Gu-jin xiao-shuo* collection).
Dolby, William. *The Perfect Lady by Mistake.* London, 1976 (translations from Feng Meng-long's collections).
Hanan, Patrick. *A Tower for the Summer Heat.* New York, 1992 (translations from Li Yu).
———, ed. *Silent Opera (Wusheng xi) by Li Yu.* Hong Kong, 1990.
Ma, Y. W., and Joseph Lau, eds. *Traditional Chinese Stories: Themes and Variations.* New York, 1978.
Scott, John. *The Lecherous Academician.* London, 1973 (translations from Ling Meng-chu's collections).
van Gulik, R. H. *Dee Goong An: Three Murder Cases Solved by Judge Dee.* Tokyo, 1949.
Yang Hsien-yi, and Gladys Yang. *The Courtesan's Jewel Box: Chinese Stories of the 10th–17th Centuries.* Beijing, 1957 (translations from the collections of Feng Meng-long and Ling Meng-chu).

VERNACULAR FICTION: THE CHINESE NOVEL

Brewitt-Taylor, C. H. *San Kuo, or Romance of the Three Kingdoms.* 2 vols. Shanghai, 1925.
Egerton, Clement. *The Golden Lotus.* 4 vols. London, 1939 (translation of *Jin Ping Mei*).
Gu Zhizhong. *The Creation of the Gods.* 2 vols. Beijing, 1992 (translation of *Feng-shen yan-yi*).
Hanan, Patrick. *The Carnal Prayer Mat (Rou putuan) by Li Yu.* New York, 1990.
Hawkes, David, and John Minford. *The Story of the Stone: A Chinese Novel in Five Volumes.* Harmondsworth, Middlesex/New York, 1973–86.
Lin Shuen-fu, and Larry Schulz. *Tower of Myriad Mirrors: A Supplement to the Journey to the West, by Tung Yueh (1620–1686).* Berkeley, 1978.
Lin, Tai-yi. *Flowers in the Mirror.* Berkeley, 1965 (translation of *Jing hua yuan*).
Martin, Richard. *Jou Pu Tuan (The Prayer Mat of Flesh).* New York, 1963.
Roberts, Moss. *Three Kingdoms: A Historical Novel.* Berkeley/Beijing, 1991.
Shadick, Harold. *The Travels of Lao Ts'an.* Ithaca, N.Y., 1952.
Shapiro, Sidney. *Outlaws of the Marsh.* 3 vols. Beijing, 1980 (translation of *Shuihu zhuan*).
Waley, Arthur. *Monkey.* London, 1942 (abridged translation of *Xiyou ji*).
Yang Hsien-yi, and Gladys Yang. *Wu Ching-tzu: The Scholars.* Beijing, 1957.
Yu, Anthony. *The Journey to the West.* 4 vols. Chicago, 1977–83.

THEORIES OF LITERATURE

Bodman, Richard W. "Poetics and Prosody in Early Medieval China: A Study and Translation of Kûkai's Bunkyô hifuron." Unpublished Ph.D. dissertation, Cornell University, 1978.

Ch'en Shih-hsiang. *Essay on Literature.* Portland, Me., 1953 (translation of the "Poetic Exposition on Literature"). Reprinted in Cyril Birch, ed. *Anthology of Chinese Literature, From Earliest Times to the Fourteenth Century.* New York, 1965.

Owen, Stephen. *Readings in Chinese Literary Thought.* Cambridge, Mass., 1992.

Shi, Vincent Y. C. *The Literary Mind and the Carving of Dragons.* New York, 1959; bilingual reprint Taipei, 1970.

Wong, Siu-kit. *Early Chinese Literary Criticism.* Hong Kong, 1983.

Selected Critical Studies

GENERAL

Birch, Cyril, ed. *Studies in Chinese Literary Genres.* Berkeley, 1974.

Bishop, John L., ed. *Studies in Chinese Literature.* Cambridge, 1966.

Cheng, François. *Chinese Poetic Writing* (trans. Donald A. Riggs and Jerome Seaton). Bloomington, Ind., 1982.

Chow Tse-tsung, ed. *Wen-lin: Studies in the Chinese Humanities.* Madison, Wis., 1968.

Frankel, Hans. *The Flowering Plum and the Palace Lady.* New Haven, Conn., 1976.

Giles, Herbert. *A History of Chinese Literature.* London, 1901.

Hightower, James Robert. *Topics in Chinese Literature.* Cambridge, 1950.

Lee, Peter H. *Celebration of Continuity: Themes in East Asian Poetry.* New Haven, Conn., 1976.

Levy, Dore J. *Chinese Narrative Poetry: The Late Han Through T'ang Dynasties.* Durham, N.C., 1988.

Li, Wai-yee. *Enchantment and Disenchantment: Love and Illusion in Chinese Literature.* Princeton, N.J., 1993.

Lin Shuen-fu, and Stephen Owen, eds. *The Vitality of the Lyric Voice.* Princeton, N.J., 1986.

Liu, James J. Y. *The Art of Chinese Poetry.* Chicago, 1962.

———. *Essentials of Chinese Literary Art.* North Scituate, R.I., 1979.

———. *Language Paradox Poetics: A Chinese Perspective.* Princeton, N.J., 1988.

Liu Wu-chi. *An Introduction to Chinese Literature.* Bloomington, Ind., 1968.

Lynn, Richard John. *Guide to Chinese Poetry and Drama.* Boston, 1984.

Nienhauser, William H., ed. *Critical Essays on Chinese Literature.* Hong Kong, 1976.

———. *The Indiana Companion to Traditional Chinese Literature.* Bloomington, Ind., 1986.

Owen, Stephen. *Mi-lou: Poetry and the Labyrinth of Desire.* Cambridge, Mass, 1989.

———. *Remembrances: The Experience of the Past in Classical Chinese Literature.* Cambridge, Mass., 1986.

———. *Traditional Chinese Poetry and Poetics: Omen of the World.* Madison, Wis., 1985.

Yang, Winston L. Y., Peter Li, and Nathan Mao. *Classical Chinese Fiction: A Guide to Its Study and Appreciation.* Boston, 1978.

EARLY LITERATURE (TO THE END OF THE HAN)

Crump, J. I. *Intrigues: Studies of the Chan-kuo Ts'e.* Ann Arbor, Mich., 1964.

Egan, Ronald C. "Narratives in *Tso chuan.*" *Harvard Journal of Asiatic Studies,* 37.2 (1977).

Hawkes, David. "The Quest of the Goddess." *Asia Major,* 13, 1–2 (1967); reprinted in Cyril Birch, ed., *Studies in Chinese Literary Genres.* Berkeley, 1974.

Knechtges, David. *The Han Rhapsody: A Study of the Fu of Yang Hsiung.* London, 1975.

Rigel, Jeffrey K. "Poetry and the Legend of Confucius' Exile." *Journal of the American Oriental Society,* vol. 106, no. 1 (January–March 1986), pp. 13–22.

Wang Ching-hsien. *The Bell and the Drum: Shih Ching as Formulaic Poetry in the Oral Tradition.* Berkeley, 1974.

————. *From Ritual to Allegory: Seven Essays in Early Chinese Poetry.* Hong Kong, 1988.

Waters, Geoffrey. *Three Elegies of Ch'u. An Introduction to the Traditional Interpretation of the Ch'u-tz'u.* Madison, Wis., 1985.

Watson, Burton. *Early Chinese Literature.* New York, 1962.

Yu, Pauline. *The Reading of Imagery in the Chinese Tradition.* Princeton, N.J., 1987.

LITERATURE FROM THE END OF THE HAN TO THE SUI

Allen, Joseph R. *In the Voice of Others: Chinese Music Bureau Poetry.* Ann Arbor, Mich., 1992.

Birrel, Anne. *Popular Songs and Ballads of Han China.* London, 1988.

Chang, Kang-i Sun. *Six Dynasties Poetry.* Princeton, N.J., 1986.

Diény, Jean-Pierre. *Les dix-neuf poèmes anciens.* Paris, 1963.

Frankel, Hans H. "Yüeh-fu Poetry." In Cyril Birch, ed., *Chinese Literary Genres.* Berkeley, 1974.

————. "Fifteen Poems by Ts'ao Chih: An Attempt at a New Approach." *Journal of the American Oriental Society,* 84 (1964).

Frodsham, J. D. "The Origins of Chinese Nature Poetry." *Asia Major,* 7.1 (1960).

Graham, William T., and James Robert Hightower. "Yü Hsin's 'Songs of Sorrow.' " *Harvard Journal of Asiatic Studies,* 43.1 (1983).

Hightower, James Robert. "Allusion in the Poetry of T'ao Ch'ien." *Harvard Journal of Asiatic Studies,* 31 (1971).

————. "The *Fu* of T'ao Ch'ien." *Harvard Journal of Asiatic Studies,* 17 (1954).

Holzman, Donald, *La vie et la pensée de Hsi K'ang.* Leiden, 1957.

Marney, John. *Chiang Yen.* Boston, 1981.

————. *Liang Chien-wen ti.* Boston, 1978.

Mather, Richard B. *The Poet Shen Yüeh (441–513): The Reticent Marquis.* Princeton, N.J., 1988.

Miao, Ronald C. "Palace-Style Poetry: The Courtly Treatment of Glamor and Love." In Ronald Miao, ed., *Studies in Chinese Poetry and Poetics.* Vol. 1. San Francisco, 1978.

Owen, Stephen. "Deadwood: The Barren Tree from Yü Hsin to Han Yü." *CLEAR,* 1.2 (1979).

Rushton, Peter. "An Interpretation of Hsi K'ang's Eighteen Poems Presented to Hsi Hsi on His Entry into the Army." *Journal of the Americal Oriental Society,* 99.2 (1979).

Watson, Burton, *Chinese Lyricism.* New York, 1971.

TANG POETRY: GENERAL

Kao Yu-kung, and Mei Tsu-lin. "Syntax, Diction, and Imagery in T'ang Poetry." *Harvard Journal of Asiatic Studies,* 31 (1971), pp. 49–136.

————. "Tu Fu's 'Autumn Meditations': An Exercise in Linguistic Criticism." *Harvard Journal of Asiatic Studies,* 28 (1968).

Nienhauser, William H. *Bibliography of Selected Western Works on T'ang Dynasty Literature.* Taipei, 1988.

Owen, Stephen. *The Great Age of Chinese Poetry: The High T'ang.* New Haven, Conn., 1980.

————. *The Poetry of the Early T'ang.* New Haven, Conn., 1977.

Schafer, Edward. *The Divine Woman: Dragon Ladies and Rain Maidens in T'ang Literature.* Berkeley, 1973.

TANG POETRY: INDIVIDUAL POETS

Chan Marie. "The Frontier Poems of Ts'en Shen." *Journal of the American Oriental Society,* 98.4 (October–December 1978), pp. 420–37.

————. *Kao Shih.* Boston, 1978.

Cheng Chi-hsien. *Analyse formelle de l'oeuvre poetique d'un auteur des Tang: Zhang Ruo-xu.* Paris, 1970.

Chou Shan. "Beginning with Images in the Nature Poetry of Wang Wei." *Harvard Journal of Asiatic Studies,* 42.1 (1982), pp. 117–37.

Davis, A. R. *Tu Fu.* New York, 1971.

Demiéville, Paul. *L'oeuvre de Wang le Zélateur (Wang Fan-tche). Poèmes populaires des t'ang, VIII–IX siècle.* Paris, 1982.

Hartman, Charles. *Han Yü and the T'ang Search for Unity.* Princeton, N.J., 1985.

Hung, William. *Tu Fu, China's Greatest Poet.* Cambridge, 1952.

Kroll, Paul. *Meng Hao-jan.* Boston, 1981.

Lee, Joseph J. *Wang Ch'ang-ling.* Boston, 1982.

Liu, James J. Y. *The Poetry of Li Shang-yin.* Chicago, 1969.

Nienhauser, William, et al. *Liu Tsung-yüan.* New York, 1973.

————. *P'i Jih-hsiu.* Boston, 1979.

Owen, Stephen. *The Poetry of Meng Chiao and Han Yü.* New Haven, Conn., 1975.

Palandri, Angela. *Yüan Chen.* New York, 1977.

Rouzer, Paul. *Writing Another's Dream: The Poetry of Wen Tingyun.* Stanford, Calif., 1993.

Schafer, Edward H. *Mirages on the Sea of Time: The Taoist Poetry of Ts'ao T'ang.* Berkeley, 1985.

Tu Kuo-ch'ing. *Li Ho.* Boston, 1979.

Wagner, Marsha. *Wang Wei.* Boston, 1981.

Waley, Arthur. *The Life and Times of Po Chü-yi.* London, 1949.

————. *The Poetry and Career of Li Po.* London, 1950.

Wong Siu-kit. *The Genius of Li Po.* Hong Kong, 1974.

CLASSICAL FICTION, PROSE ESSAYS, AND MISCELLANEA

Edwards, E. D. *Chinese Prose Literature of the T'ang Period.* London, 1938.

Lu Xun, *A Brief History of Classical Chinese Fiction* (trans. Yang Hsien-yi and Gladys Yang). Beijing, 1959.

Ma, Y. W. "Fact and Fantasy in T'ang Tales." *CLEAR,* 2.2 (July 1980).

Schafer, Edward H. *The Golden Peaches of Samarkand: A Study of T'ang Exotics.* Berkeley, 1963.

————. *Pacing the Void: T'ang Approaches to the Stars.* Berkeley, 1977.

————. *Shore of Pearls.* Berkeley, 1970.

————. *The Vermilion Bird: T'ang Images of the South.* Berkeley, 1967.

Wong, Timothy C. "Self and Society in T'ang Dynasty Love Tales." *Journal of the American Oriental Society,* 99.1 (1979).

SONG DYNASTY AND LATER POETRY

Chang, Kang-i Sun. *The Late Ming Poet Ch'en Tzu-lung: Crises of Love and Loyalism.* New Haven, Conn., 1991.

Chaves, Jonathan. *Mei Yao-ch'en and the Development of Early Sung Poetry.* New York, 1976.

Duke, Michael S. *Lu Yu.* Boston, 1977.

Egan, Ronald C. *The Literary Works of Ou-yang-hsiu (1007–1072).* Cambridge, 1984.

————. *Word, Image, and Deed in the Life of Su Shih.* Cambridge, 1994.

Fuller, Michael. *The Road to East Slope: The Development of Su Shih's Poetic Voice.* Stanford, Calif., 1990.

Lai, T. C. *T'ang Yin, Poet/Painter (1470–1524).* Hong Kong, 1971.

Mote, F. W. *The Poet Kao Ch'i*. Princeton, N.J., 1962.

Palumbo-Liu, David. *The Poetics of Appropriation: The Literary Theory and Practice of Huang Tingjian*. Stanford, Calif., 1993.

Schmidt, J. D. *Stone Lake: The Poetry of Fan Chengda (1126–1193)*. Cambridge, 1992.

———. *Yang Wan-li*. Boston, 1976.

Waley, Arthur. *Yüan Mei: Eighteenth Century Chinese Poet*. London, 1957; reprinted Stanford, Calif., 1970.

Wong, Shirleen. *Kung Tzu-chen*. Boston, 1975.

Yoshikawa Kojiro, *Five Hundred Years of Chinese Poetry, 1150–1650* (trans. John Timothy Wixted). Princeton, N.J., 1989.

———. *An Introduction to Sung Poetry* (trans. Burton Watson). Cambridge, Mass., 1967.

SONG LYRIC *(CI)*: GENERAL STUDIES

Chang Kang-i (Sun). *The Evolution of Chinese Tz'u Poetry: From Late T'ang to Northern Sung*. Princeton, N.J., 1980.

———. "Symbolic and Allegorical Meanings in the *Yueh-fu pu-t'i* Poem Series." *Harvard Journal of Asiatic Studies*, 46.2 (1986), pp. 353–85.

Ch'en Shih-ch'uan, "The Rise of *Tz'u* Reconsidered." *Journal of the Americal Oriental Society*, 90.2 (1970).

Fong, Grace. "Persona and Mask in the Song Lyric *(Ci)*." *Harvard Journal of Asiatic Studies*, 50.2 (1990), pp. 459–84.

Liu, James J. Y. *Major Lyricists of the Northern Sung:* A.D. 960–1126. Princeton, N.J., 1974.

———. "Some Literary Qualities of the Lyric *(Tz'u)*." In Cyril Birch, ed., *Studies in Chinese Literary Genres*. Berkeley, 1974.

Pien, Rulan Chao. *Song Dynasty Musical Sources and Their Interpretation*. Cambridge, 1967.

Soong, Stephen C., ed. *Song Without Music: Chinese Tz'u Poetry*. Hong Kong, 1980.

Yu, Pauline, ed. *Voices of the Song Lyric in China*. Berkeley, 1994.

SONG LYRIC: INDIVIDUAL AUTHORS

Fong, Grace. *Wu Wenying and the Art of Southern Song Ci Poetry*. Princeton, N.J., 1987.

Lin Shuen-fu. *The Transformation of the Chinese Lyrical Tradition: Chiang K'uei and Southern Sung Tz'u Poetry*. Princeton, N.J., 1978.

Lo, Irving. *Hsin Ch'i-chi*. New York, 1971.

VERNACULAR SONG AND DRAMA

Crump, James I. *Chinese Theater in the Days of Khubilai Khan*. Tucson, Ariz., 1980.

———. *Songs from Xanadu*. Ann Arbor, Mich., 1983.

Dolby, William. *A History of Chinese Drama*. London, 1976.

Henry, Eric P. *Chinese Amusement: The Lively Plays of Li Yu*. Hamden, Conn., 1980.

Hsia, C. T. "Time and the Human Condition in the Plays of T'ang Hsien-tsu." In Theodore de Bary, ed., *Self and Society in Ming Thought*. New York, 1970.

Hung, Josephine. *Ming Drama*. Taipei, 1966.

Idema, Wilt, and Stephen West. *Chinese Theater 1100–1450; A Source Book*. Wiesbaden, 1982.

Lopez, Manuel D. *Chinese Drama: An Annotated Bibliography of Commentary, Criticism, and Plays in English Translation*. Methuden, N.J., 1991.

Lynn, Richard. *Kuan Yün-shih*. Boston, 1980.

Mackerras, Colin, ed. *Chinese Theater from Its Origins to the Present Day*. Honolulu, 1983.

Perng Ching-hsi. *Double Jeopardy: A Critique of Seven Yüan Courtroom Dramas*. Ann Arbor, Mich., 1978.

Schlepp, Wayne. *San-ch'ü: Its Technique and Imagery*. Madison, Wis., 1970.

Scott, A. C. *The Classical Theatre of China*. New York, 1957.

Shih, Chung-wen. *The Golden Age of Chinese Drama: Yuan Tsa-chü*. Princeton, N.J., 1976.

Strassberg, Richard E. *The World of K'ung Shang-jen: A Man of Letters in Early Ch'ing China*. New York, 1983.

West, Stephen. *Vaudeville and Narrative: Aspects of Chin Theater*. Wiesbaden, 1977.

MING AND QING FICTION

Bishop, John L. *The Colloquial Short Story in China: A Study of the San-yen Collection*. Cambridge, Mass., 1956.

Dudbridge, Glen. *The Hsi-yu Chi: A Study of the Antecedents to the Sixteenth-Century Chinese Novel*. Cambridge, Mass., 1970.

Hanan, Patrick. *The Chinese Short Story: Studies in Dating, Authorship, and Composition*. Cambridge, Mass., 1973.

———. *The Chinese Vernacular Story*. Cambridge, Mass., 1981.

———. *The Invention of Li Yü*. Cambridge, Mass., 1989.

Hegel, Robert. *The Novel in Seventeenth-Century China*. New York, 1981.

Hsia, C. T. *The Classic Chinese Novel: A Critical Introduction*. New York, 1968.

Idema, W. L. *Chinese Vernacular Fiction: The Formative Period*. Leiden, 1974.

Li, Peter. *Ts'eng P'u*. Boston, 1980.

Lu, Sheldon Hsiao-peng. *From Historicity to Fictionality: The Chinese Poetics of Fictionality*. Stanford, Calif., 1994.

Mao, Nathan, and Liu, Ts'un-yan. *Li Yu*. Boston, 1977.

Plaks, Andrew. *Archetype and Allegory in the Dream of the Red Chamber*. Princeton, N.J., 1976.

———. *Four Masterworks of the Ming Novel*. Princeton, N.J., 1987.

———, ed. *Chinese Narrative: Critical and Theoretical Essays*. Princeton, N.J., 1977.

Roylston, David L, ed. *How to Read the Chinese Novel*. Princeton, N.J., 1990.

Wong, Timothy C. *Wu Ching-tzu*. Boston, 1978.

Yang, Winston L. Y., and Curtis Adkins, eds. *Critical Essays on Chinese Fiction*. Hong Kong, 1980.

Yu, Anthony C. "The Quest of Brother Amor: Buddhist Intimations in *The Story of the Stone*." *Harvard Journal of Asiatic Studies*, 49.1 (1989), pp. 55–92.

Zeitlin, Judith. *Historian of the Strange: Pu Songling and the Chinese Classical Tale*. Stanford, Calif., 1993.

THEORIES OF LITERATURE

Bush, Susan, and Christian Murck, . *Theories of the Arts in China*. Princeton, N.J., 1983.

Hightower, James Robert. "The Wen hsüan and Genre Theory." *Harvard Journal of Asiatic Studies,* 18 (1955). Reprinted in J. L. Bishop, ed., *Studies in Chinese Literature* (Harvard-Yenching Institute Series XXI).

Liu, James J. Y. *Chinese Theories of Literature*. Chicago, 1975.

Owen, Stephen. *Readings in Chinese Literary Thought*. Cambridge, 1992.

Rickett, Adele. *Wang Kuo-wei's Jen-chien tz'u-hua: A Study in Chinese Literary Criticism.* Hong Kong, 1977.

———, ed. *Chinese Approaches to Literature from Confucius to Liang Ch'i-ch'ao.* Princeton, N.J., 1978.

Saussy, Haun. *The Problem of a Chinese Aesthetic.* Stanford, Calif., 1993.

Tu, Ching-i, trans. *Poetic Remarks in the Human World: Jen Chien Tz'u Hua.* Taipei, 1970.

Van Zoeren, Steven. *Poetry and Personality: Reading, Exegesis, and Hermeneutics in Traditional China.* Stanford, Calif., 1991.

Wixted, John Timothy. *Poems on Poetry: Literary Criticism by Yuan Hao-wen (1190–1257).* Wiesbaden, 1982.

Yeh Chia-ying, and Jan Walls. "Theory, Standards, and Practice of Criticizing Poetry in Chung Jung's Shih-p'in." In Ronald Miao, ed., *Studies in Chinese Poetry and Poetics.* Vol. 1. San Francisco, 1978.

Yu, Pauline. *The Reading of Imagery in the Chinese Tradition.* Princeton, N.J., 1987.

———. "Ssu-k'ung T'u's Shih-p'in: Poetic Theory in Poetic Form." In Ronald Miao, ed., *Studies in Chinese Poetry and Poetics.* Vol. 1. San Francisco, 1978.

COMPARATIVE LITERATURE

Eoyang, Eugene. *The Transparent Eye: Reflections on Translation, Chinese Literature, and Comparative Poetics.* Bloomington, Ind., 1993.

Miner, Earl. *Comparative Poetics: An Intercultural Essay on Theories of Literature.* Princeton, N.J., 1990.

Yip, Wai-lim. *Diffusion of Distances: Dialogues Between Chinese and Western Poetics.* Berkeley, 1993.

Zlang Longxi. *The Tao and the Logos: Literary Hermeneutics, East and West.* Durham, N.C., 1992.

Acknowledgments

Many of the translations here had gathered over the years, long before I developed the intention to do this book. Most, however, were done over the past four years, especially during summers, when I enjoyed the benefits of a translation grant from the Bureau of Cultural Planning and Development of the Republic of China.

This book owes a deep debt to my students, who have taken much time editing, correcting, and responding. The students in my Chinese literature in translation class have caught countless typos and have been forthright with their disapproval. What they did not like, I generally left out or changed. There is no critic so innocently ruthless as a roomful of thirty faces.

Over the years I have had numerous graduate students help me in preparing versions of the growing manuscript: Jeanette Ryan, Sophie Volpp, Pauline Lin, and Robert Ashmore. I have especially benefited from the help of Shang Wei, Chang Shu-hsiang, and Pauline Lin in the translations from drama. Pauline Lin in particular went above and beyond the call of duty in transporting chunks of the manuscript around over the years to the far corners of the globe and sending back criticisms. In the final stages, special thanks are due to David Schaberg, whose careful reading brought innumerable lapses in sense and omitted lines to my attention. It is humbling to discover how, after living with a manuscript such a long time, one comes to look but not see.

I would also like to thank Anna Karvellas and the staff at Norton for their unfailing energy, care, and good humor in putting an author through his paces.

Finally I must thank my wife Phyllis, who has always known which of a set of choices "sounds best," and who has steadfastly helped me over the years in the preparation of yet another "big book."

A few of the selections have been previously published, sometimes in modified versions, in the following works:

Robert Ashmore, translator, "Du Tenth Sinks the Jewel Box in Anger" and "Censor Xue Finds Immortality in the Guise of a Fish." Reprinted with the permission of the translator.

Patrick Hanan, translator, "An Actress Scorns Wealth and Honor . . ." from *Silent Operas* by Li Yu (Hong Kong: Renditions Paperbacks, 1990). Copyright © 1990 by Research Centre for Translation, Chinese University of Hong Kong. Reprinted with the permission of the publishers.

Pauline Yu, editor, *Voices of the Song Lyric in China*. Copyright © 1994 by The Regents of the University of California. Used with the permission of University of California Press.

Maynard Mack, General Editor, *The Norton Anthology of World Masterpieces, Sixth Edition*. Copyright © 1995 by W. W. Norton & Company, Inc. Reprinted with the permission of the publisher.

Stephen Owen, *The Great Age of Chinese Poetry: The High T'ang*. Copyright © 1981 by Yale University. Used with the permission of Yale University Press.

Stephen Owen, *Mi-Lou: Poetry and the Labyrinth of Desire*. Copyright © 1989 by the President and Fellows of Harvard College. Used with the permission of Harvard University Press.

Stephen Owen, *Readings in Chinese Literary Thought*. Copyright © 1992 by the President and Fellows of Harvard College. Used with the permission of the Council of East Asian Studies, Harvard University.

Stephen Owen, *Remembrances: The Experience of the Past in Chinese Literature*. Copyright © 1986 by the President and Fellows of Harvard College. Used with the permission of Harvard University Press.

Stephen Owen, *Traditional Chinese Poetry and Poetics: An Omen of the World*. Copyright © 1985 by the Board of Regents of the University of Wisconsin System. Reprinted with the permission of the University of Wisconsin Press.

Bo Ju-yi, "Letter to Yuan Zhen" from "Bai Juyi: Letter to Yuan Zhen," *Renditions: A Chinese English Translation Magazine,* 41 & 42 (1994): 51–55. Used with the permission of *Renditions,* Research Centre for Translation, The Chinese University of Hong Kong.

Author, First Line, and Title Index

General Index

"Account of My Travels in Fei" (Yuan Zhong-dao), 823
"Account of Peach Blossom Spring, An" (Tao Qian), 309
Account of the Compass, The (Wen Tian-xiang), 704–20
Account of the Poem on a Red Leaf, The (Wang Ji-de), 886*n*
Account of the Western Parlor, The, 886*n*
Account of the Western Verandah (Xi-xiang Ji) (*The Moon and the Zither*), 557
accounts of visits (*you-ji*), 610–14
  landscape, 622–25
  of Su Shi, 622–24
Aeneid (Virgil), 441
aesthetics of omission, 69
Afghanistan, 244*n*
"Airs" (*Feng*) section of Classic of Poetry, 11, 30–57
  correspondences in, 34–44
  lovers in, 53–57
  misunderstanding in, 44, 50
  organization of, 30
  purpose of, 65, 66
  satire in, 52
A-jiao, 955*n*
alchemy, 176, 224
alcoholic beverages, translation and, xlvi
Analects (*Lun-yu*) (Confucius), 5, 31, 350*n*, 397, 436*n*, 500, 848*n*
  Tao Qian influenced by, 312–14
anecdotes, parables and profound jokes, 295–310, 320
  chuan-qi, 518–49
  collections of, 305–9
  from *Han Fei-zi*, 299–300
  of High Tang, 410
  from *Lie-zi*, 302–5
  from *Zhuang-zi*, 295–99
An-hui, 1150
An Lu-shan, 367, 425, 455

An Lu-shan Rebellion, 367, 368, 385, 397, 442, 1131
  poetry of, 420–25
Anthology, The (*Wen Xuan*) (Prince Zhao-ming), 343
Archaist movement, 244, 725, 807, 1129
aristocracy:
  of Southern Dynasties, 225
  meritocracy vs., 553–54
"Autumn Stirrings" (Du Fu), 1020*n*
"Autumn Wilds" (Du Fu), 1133

Ba (overlord), 4
ba-gu wen (eight-legged essay), 725
bamboo, as writing material, 9
Ban Gu, 135, 215
Bao Jiao, 495*n*
Bao Zhao, 323–24, 630
beech trees, 482*n*
Bei-gong Wen-zi, 60
Beijing (Da-du), 704, 723, 724, 727, 728, 835*n*, 909
Beijing, Treaty of, 913
Bi, Battle of, 77
bi (disk), 84
bi (comparison), 34, 66
bi (that), 116*n*
Bin, 12, 18
biography, 215
  by Si-ma Quian, 142–44
Bi-yu (Sapphire), 951
Black Tortoise (Xuan-wu), 180*n*
blow fish, 650–51
Bo Bai, 836*n*
Bo Cheng-en, 836*n*
Bo Ju-yi, 496–502, 837*n*
  feast poem of, 289
  occasional poetry of, 496–97
  private persona of, 497–99
  on Yang Yu-huan, 442–47, 496
bone, as writing material, 3

1195